D1189502

Hist 1851

A Gift From
The Friends of The Library
William P. Faust
Public Library of Westland

THE UNITED STATES

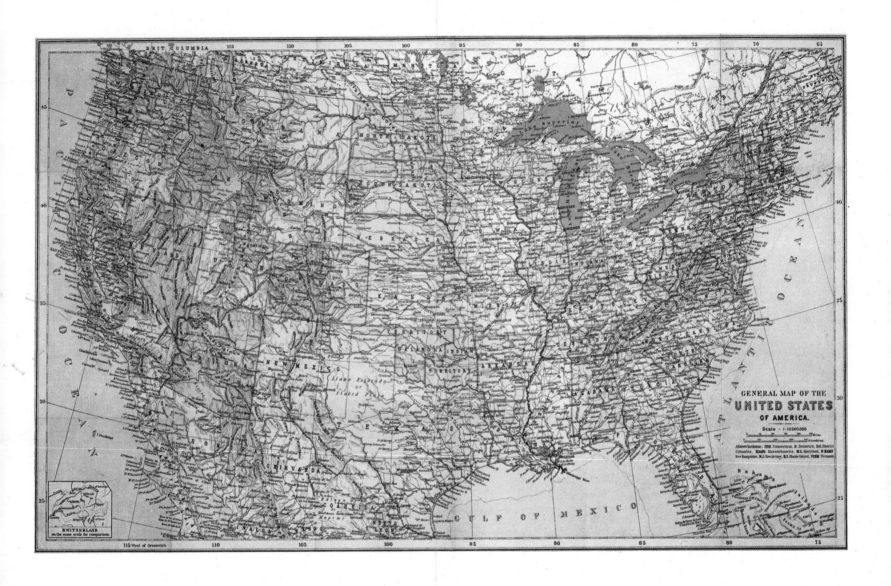

GENERAL MAP OF THE
UNITED STATES
OF AMERICA.

Scale = 1:10000000

THE UNITED STATES

With an Excursion into Mexico

A Handbook for Travellers
—1893—

Edited by Karl Baedeker

New Introduction by Henry Steele Commager

DA CAPO PRESS • NEW YORK • 1971

An unabridged republication of the first
American *Baedeker* published in Leipzig
and New York in 1893.

Library of Congress Catalog Card Number 76-77703
ISBN 0-306-71341-1

Copyright © 1971 by Da Capo Press, Inc.
A Subsidiary of Plenum Publishing Corporation
227 West 17th Street, New York, New York 10011

All Rights Reserved

Manufactured in the United States of America

INTRODUCTION

Baedeker is a generic name, so familiar now that it has lost any connection with the originator of the guidebooks and instead come to represent an institution. In this respect, Karl Baedeker, who started the business so modestly back in 1824, shares the fate of other men whose success has condemned them to a kind of frozen institutionality —Roget and Webster, for example, or Michelin, the French equivalent of Baedeker, and Bradshaw, the railroad guide. A *Baedeker* is in short one of those *vade mecums* without which, we are tempted to believe, society cannot function, and one which also helps to define our kind of society, for society is known by the things it takes for granted. And that remarkable pioneer in guidebooks, Karl Baedeker of Coblenz, did indeed set a pattern for travel in the nineteenth century and impose it upon the millions of his own countrymen and of Englishmen and Americans who would no more travel on the Continent without their *Baedeker* than without their *Tauchnitz*.

In 1893, the firm of Baedeker, having all but exhausted the possibilities of Western Europe—they had been at it for seventy years, after all—decided to extend their coverage to the United States. Quite a bold decision, that. For while of all the countries in the world the United States was incontrovertibly the greatest magnet, the five million or so Europeans who had landed on American shores during the previous decade had not come as tourists. Decidedly not. They were immigrants and *Baedekers* were for travelers, not immigrants: for those who came to see and buy and enjoy—those who needed to know what trains to take (imagine having a choice!), what cities to visit, what hotels to patronize, what luxuries to carry home, what historic monuments to contemplate (and probably sneer at), what scenic wonders to compare with the Alps and with the Lake Country. By the decade of the nineties—so the House of Baedeker had concluded— the United States had reached a degree of finish, of sophistication, and perhaps of interest, which would make it attractive to the kind of visitors who had for so long swarmed over the ancient lands of Europe.

In a sense, of course, the United States had always tempted visitors who were neither immigrants nor tourists, and who were indeed curious about this strange new world. No other nation had inspired so large a literature of analysis and interpretation, none so elaborate a commentary. But these visitors, who cluttered up the newspapers and the journals and the libraries with their observations, were a very different breed from those who studied the cathedrals of France or the antiquities of Italy. They were officials like Tocqueville or Grattan, they were literary men and women like Mrs. Trollope and her son Anthony, or Dickens or Oscar Wilde, they were journalists like "Bull Run" Russell or George Steevens, they were scholars—and inevitably lecturers—like Matthew Arnold or E.A. Freeman, they were even explorers like Prince Maximilian of Wied or Paul Frenzeny. They were, in short, men who had no need of guidebooks; they were themselves guidebooks. Moreover, in most cases their every need was anticipated and provided for—everything was "laid on."

The new *Baedeker* was, as the subtitle made clear, a "Handbook for Travellers." To edit this guide, the House of Baedeker made a happy choice—James Fullarton Muirhead. A Scotsman, trained at Edinburgh, Muirhead was an old lag with encyclopedias and such, and had done time, as it were, at the Baedeker factory in Leipzig. For over a decade, he had been English editor of the Baedeker series in London. More to the point, he was at home in the United States. He had married an American woman, he had traveled in America, he was even then contemplating a book which, when finally published in 1898, would turn out to be among the best of many British works on the United States. This book, *America the Land of Contrasts*, was thorough, penetrating, lively, amiable; it displayed, that is, all the right qualities, and revealed that the author was indeed at home in this land of contrasts.

The House of Baedeker had never been content (as most modern guides are) with information about trains, food, and hotels, alone. It aimed higher, for its audience (so at least the Baedekers and the audience believed) was sophisticated, literate, and curious, eager to know much more about the country they visited than the mechanics of tourism. The Baedeker guidebooks therefore provided authoritative essays on the geography, history, government, art, and culture of those countries fortunate enough to belong to the Club.

To provide these for the United States, Mr. Muirhead had the good judgment and good fortune to enlist a distinguished group of contributors. To explain the mysteries of American government and politics, there was none other than James Bryce (not yet Lord Bryce), Regius Professor of Civil Law at the University of Oxford and author, in three volumes no less, of the most comprehensive and perspicacious book on the United States ever written, *The American Commonwealth*. Muirhead's choices for the other essays were no less fortunate. For history he enlisted John Bach McMaster of the University of Pennsylvania, already under way with his magisterial survey of American social history, a survey still unsurpassed in scope and sweep. For ethnology he found O.T. Mason, curator of ethnology at the Smithsonian Institution and leading expert on the American Indian; for physical geography the remarkable Nathaniel Shaler, Professor of Geology at Harvard University, geologist of the state of Kentucky, and author of one of the earliest studies of ecology, *Man and the Earth*. For art there was William Coffin, himself a landscape painter, and the distinguished art critic for the New York *Evening Post* and the *Nation*; for architecture the incomparable Montgomery Schuyler, whose critical writings on contemporary architecture remain the best of their kind in our literature.

A Baedeker specialty had always been maps—large maps of provinces and regions, detailed maps of cities. Though the prospect of providing maps for a country the size of the United States was daunting, the Baedekers boldly undertook to meet the challenge. Responsibility for preparing the maps was assigned to Henry Gannett, chief geographer of the United States Geological Survey, geographer of the United States Census, author of a volume of topographic maps of the United States and of a masterly survey of American geography. The maps which resulted were fully up to the standards of the European *Baedekers* and far ahead of those of today.

It was, all in all, such a galaxy of talent and expertise as could not be found—and has not since been found—for any guidebook.

*****

In a sense, this *Baedeker* came at precisely the right moment. It caught the United States in transition from the old to the modern, from the rural to the urban, the agricultural to the industrial, the sectional to the national, and, one is tempted to add, from the primitive to the wasted. In the mountain vastness of the Far West Indians still followed their ancient ways, and it was only a few years since Custer had made his Last Stand and Geronimo had waged his desperate war in the mountains of New Mexico. Railroad builders had just completed the last of the transcontinentals, great herds of cattle still followed the Goodnight and Chisholm Trails to the grasslands of the north, and miners panned for gold in the swift streams of the Rockies.

But already a new America was coming up over the horizon. A New South was emerging uncertainly from the Old. The Great Plains were being taken over by farmers, and cattle were grazing behind barbed wire fences. Great mining companies, controlled in the East, were supplanting the individual miner celebrated by Bret Harte, and in 1890 the Census Bureau had announced the inexorable passing of the frontier. New immigration was replacing the old—
    wild motley throngs,
    Men from the Volga and the Tartar steppes,
as the proper Thomas Bailey Aldrich wrote, and soon Jacob Riis, himself an immigrant from Denmark, could describe in mordant terms "How the Other Half Lives."

Giant corporations organized American industry, giant unions welded together American workingmen, giant banks created a Wall Street that was as much symbol as reality, and, with the beginnings of federal regulation of interstate commerce and of trusts, giant government was on the way. Social changes reflected the economic. As the poor huddled in the slums of the great cities and the rich withdrew to suburbs or to retreats like Newport or Tuxedo, the disparity between rich and poor grew more and more glaring. Farm boys, black as well as white, found their way to the cities or, equally decisive, urbanized their country towns. Girls moved out of the kitchen and the schoolroom and the nursery into business and industry, foreshadowing the time when women would claim and achieve emancipation, and not only emancipation but political power. Americans had never had classes in the Old World sense of the term, but now such class distinctions as had lingered in Boston or Philadelphia or Charleston gave way to forces of social dispersion and to the redistribution of wealth, and economic classes took the place of social ones.

Literature and the arts responded to the new currents. William Dean Howells, Stephen Crane, Frank Norris, Hamlin Garland, and Theodore Dreiser depicted the American scene with a realism closer to Zola than to earlier masters like Nathaniel Hawthorne. Even as the dazzling Columbia Exposition celebrating the three hundredth anniversary of the discovery of America rose along Chicago's lakefront, boasting once again the imperishable glories of Greek and Roman art, Frank Lloyd Wright began to challenge the old artistic certainties with a new functionalism and the first skyscrapers rose from the prairie cities of the West, while the mordant Henry Adams saw in the Exposition not the persistence of a classical age, but the beginning of an age that would be dominated by the dynamo.

This was the United States which Baedeker spread before the fascinated eyes of Old World visitors in 1893. It is as fascinating to us today as it was to contemporaries—and almost as strange.

Amherst, Massachusetts   HENRY STEELE COMMAGER
May, 1971

THE UNITED STATES

PREFACE.

The *Handbook to the United States*, undertaken in response to repeated requests from British and American tourists, is intended to help the traveller in planning his tour and disposing of his time to the best advantage and thus to enable him the more thoroughly to enjoy and appreciate the objects of interest he meets with. The writer is *Mr. J. F. Muirhead, M. A.*, who has for several years taken part in the English editions of Baedeker's Handbooks, and has personally visited the greater part of the districts described.

No one is better aware than the Editor himself of the imperfections almost inseparable from the first edition of a guide-book; and the vast extent and rapidly changing conditions of the United States have made the preparation of the present volume a peculiarly difficult task. For its improvement, however, he confidently and gratefully looks forward to a continuance of those valuable corrections and suggestions with which travellers have long been in the habit of favouring him. Hotel-bills, with annotations showing the traveller's opinion as to his treatment and accommodation, are particularly useful.

In the preparation of the Handbook the Editor has received most material aid from friends in all parts of the United States, so many in number as to preclude an enumeration of their names. In particular he wishes to express his obligations to the superior officials of the leading Railway Companies, who have been, almost without exception, uniformly courteous and helpful; to many officials of the Federal and State Governments; to the keepers of the most important libraries, museums, and galleries of art; to the officials of the Appalachian Mountain Club; and to the professors of numerous universities and colleges.

It is hoped that the various monographs of the Introduction, though sometimes going beyond the recognized functions of a guide-book, will be found of material value to the tourist. Each has been written by an undoubted authority on the subject of which it treats; and their general aim is to enable the traveller who studies them to give an intelligent appreciation to the political, social, industrial, and physical aspects of a great country that is much less accurately known by the average European than its importance warrants.

On the MAPS and PLANS the Editor has bestowed especial care; and it is believed that in this respect the Handbook is more completely equipped than any other publication of the kind relating to the United States. Such merit as they possess is largely due to the kind and efficient coöperation of *Mr. Henry Gannett*, Chief Topographer of the United States Geological Survey.

The POPULATIONS are those of the census of 1890; but it should be borne in mind that, in so progressive a country as the United States, these are often very much below the figures of 1893.

HOTELS. The Editor has endeavoured to enumerate, not only the first-class hotels, but also the more deserving of the cheaper houses. The comfort of an American hotel is, however, much more likely to be in the direct ratio of charges than is the case in Europe (comp. p. xxvi). Although changes frequently take place, and prices generally have an upward tendency, the average charges stated in the Handbook will enable the traveller to form a fair estimate of his expenditure. The value of the asterisks, which are used as marks of commendation, is relative only, signifying that the houses are good of their kind.

To hotel-proprietors, tradesmen, and others the Editor begs to intimate that a character for fair dealing and courtesy towards travellers forms the sole passport to his commendation, and that advertisements of every kind are strictly excluded from his Handbooks. Hotelkeepers are also warned against persons representing themselves as agents for Baedeker's Handbooks.

A Handbook to *Canada* is now being prepared and will appear during the present year.

CONTENTS.

		Page
I.	Money. Expenses. Passports. Custom House. Time	xvii
II.	Voyage from Europe to the United States.	xviii
III.	Railways. Steamers. Coaches	xix
IV.	Plan of Tour	xxiii
V.	Hotels and Restaurants	xxv
VI.	Post and Telegraph System.	xxviii
VII.	Glossary	xxix
VIII.	General Hints	xxx
IX.	A Short History of American Politics, by *John Bach McMaster*	xxxii
X.	Constitution and Political Institutions of the United States, by *James Bryce*	xlvi
XI.	Aborigines and Aboriginal Remains, by *O. T. Mason*	lxii
XII.	Physiography of North America, by *N. S. Shaler*	lxvii
XIII.	Climate and Climatic Resorts of the United States, by *E. C. Wendt*	lxxvi
XIV.	The Fine Arts in America	lxxxii
	a. Painting and Sculpture, by *William A. Coffin*.	lxxxii
	b. Architecture, by *Montgomery Schuyler*	lxxxvii
XV.	Sports, by *Henry Harmon Neill*	xciii
XVI.	Educational, Charitable, Penal, and Industrial Institutions	xcvi
XVII.	Bibliography.	xcix

Route		Page
1.	From Europe to New York	1
	a. From Liverpool to New York	1
	b. From Southampton to New York	3
	c. From Hamburg to New York	4
	d. From Bremen to New York	4
	e. From Havre to New York.	5
	f. From Antwerp to New York.	5
	g. From Glasgow to New York.	5
2.	New York	6
	Environs of New York 50. — From New York to Chatham 51.	
3.	Brooklyn and Long Island	52
	Coney Island. Rockaway Beach. Long Beach 55, 56.	
4.	From New York to Boston.	57
	a. Viâ New Haven, Hartford, and Springfield	57

Route   Page

b. Viâ New York and New England Railway 62

c. Viâ Providence and the Shore Line 62
From New London to Brattleboro 63. — Watch Hill and Block Island 63. — Narragansett Pier 64.

d. Viâ Long Island and Eastern States Line 65

e. By Steamboat 66
From New London to Boston 67. — Newport 68. — From Fall River to Boston 72.

5. Boston 72
Cambridge 83. — Charlestown 85. — Environs of Boston 85, 86.

6. From Boston to Plymouth. 86
a. Viâ Abington. 86
b. Viâ South Shore 86

7. From Boston to Martha's Vineyard and Nantucket 87

8. Fom Boston to Provincetown. Cape Cod. 88

9. From Boston to Portland 89
a. By the Eastern Division of the Boston and Maine Railroad 89
Nahant 90. — Marblehead 90. — From Beverly to Gloucester and Rockport ('North Shore') 92. — Salisbury Beach and Plum Island 93. — Isles of Shoals 94. — York Beach 94.

b. By the Western Division of the Boston and Maine Railroad 94
Casco Bay and Environs of Portland 97.

10. From Portland to Mount Desert. Moosehead Lake. . . . 97
a. Viâ Bangor 97
From Bangor to St. John and to Greenville 98. — Moosehead Lake 99.

b. Viâ Rockland 99
Popham Beach. Boothbay. Squirrel Island 99. — Camden 100.

11. Mount Desert. 101

12. From Portland to Lewiston, Farmington, and the Rangeley Lakes. 105

13. From Boston to Campobello. Grand Manan 107

14. From Portland to Montreal and Quebec 108
a. Viâ the Grand Trunk Railway 108
Poland Springs 107. — Routes to Rangeley Lakes 108, 109.

b. Viâ the Maine Central Railway 110
From Quebec Junction to Quebec 111.

15. From Boston to Montreal 112
a. Viâ Rutland and Burlington 112
From Concord to Lexington 113. — Dublin 113. — From St. Albans to Richford 115.

b. Viâ Lowell and Concord 115
From Concord to Claremont Junction 115. — Woodstock 117. — Stowe and Mt. Mansfield 117.

c. Viâ Concord, Plymouth, Wells River, and Newport . . 117
Lake Winnepesaukee 118. — From Plymouth to North Woodstock 119. — From Wells River Junction to Groveton Junction and to Montpelier 119. — Lake Memphremagog 120.

d. Viâ Portsmouth and North Conway. 120

Route   Page
16. The White Mountains 121
    a. North Conway 123. — b. Jackson and the Glen House
    124. — c. Gorham 125. — d. Crawford House and the Notch
    126. — e. Fabyan House 127. — f. Bethlehem and Maple-
    wood. — g. The Franconia Mts. Profile House 128. — h. Jef-
    ferson Hill 130. — i. Mt. Washington 131.

17. From Boston to Albany. 133
    a. By Boston & Albany Railroad. 133
    From Pittsfield to North Adams 134.
    b. Viâ the Hoosac Tunnel. 134

18. From New York to Pittsfield (Berkshire Hills) 135
    Litchfield 135.

19. The Berkshire Hills 136

20. From New York to Montreal. 141
    a. Viâ Connecticut Valley. 141
    Mt. Holyoke. Hadley 142.

    b. Viâ Albany (or Troy), Saratoga, and Lake Champlain . 143
    From Fort Edward to Caldwell 144.

    c. Viâ Troy, Rutland, and Burlington 145
    d. Viâ Herkimer and Malone 145

21. From New York to Albany 146
    a. By Steamer 146
    b. Viâ Railway on the East Bank. 150
    c. Viâ Railway on the West Bank 152
    Delaware and Hudson Canal 153.

22. Albany 154

23. From Albany to Binghamton 158
    Howe's Cave 158. — Sharon Springs 158. — Cooperstown
    and Otsego Lake 158.

24. The Catskill Mountains. 159
    a. From Catskill to the Catskill Mountain House and the Hotel
    Kaaterskill 160. — b. From Kingston (Rondout) to the Hotel
    Kaaterskill 163. — c. From Rondout (Kingston) to Bloom-
    ville 164.

25. The Adirondack Mountains 165
    a. From Plattsburg to St. Regis, Tupper, and Saranac Lakes
    167. — b. From Port Kent to Ausable Chasm and Lake Placid
    170. — c. From Westport to Elizabethtown, Keene Valley,
    and Lake Placid 170. — d. From Saratoga to North Creek
    176. — e. From Herkimer to Malone viâ the Tupper and
    Saranac Lakes 178.

26. Saratoga. 179
    Environs of Saratoga. Mt. McGregor 182.

27. Lake George and Lake Champlain 182

28. From New York to Buffalo and Niagara Falls 186
    a. Viâ New York Central and Hudson River Railway. . . 186
    Johnstown. The Six Nations 187. — From Utica to Ogdens-
    burg. Trenton Falls 188. — From Utica to Binghamton.
    Richfield Springs 188. — Cayuga Lake. Ithaca 190. — Seneca
    Lake. Watkins Glen. Havana Glen 191.

Route   Page

   b. Viâ West Shore Railway 195

   c. Viâ Delaware, Lackawanna, & Western Railway . . . 195
      Delaware Water Gap 196.

   d. Viâ Erie Railway 198

29. Niagara Falls 199

30. The St. Lawrence River and the Thousand Islands. . . . 206

31. From New York to Philadelphia 208
   a. Viâ Pennsylvania Railroad 208
      Princeton College 208. — Bordentown 209.
   b. Viâ Royal Blue Line. 209

32. Philadelphia 210
      Camden 221. — Germantown and Chestnut Hill 221. — From
      Philadelphia to West Chester 209.

33. Summer and Winter Resorts of New Jersey. 221
      a. From New York to Long Branch and Point Pleasant by
      Rail 221. — b. From New York to Long Branch viâ Atlantic
      Highlands and Sandy Hook 222. — c. From Philadelphia to
      Long Branch 223. — d. Barnegat Bay 224. — e. From New
      York to Lakewood and Atlantic City 224. — f. From Philadel-
      phia to Atlantic City 225. — g. From Philadelphia to Cape
      May City 226.

34. From Philadelphia to Buffalo 226
      Easton 227. — Valley of Wyoming 228.

35. From Philadelphia to Reading and Williamsport. 229
      From Port Clinton to Pottsville 230.

36. From Philadelphia to Erie 230
      From Williamsport to Nordmont 230. — From Emporium to
      Buffalo 231.

37. From Philadelphia to Harrisburg and Pittsburg 231
      From Harrisburg to Gettysburg, to Winchester, to Reading,
      and to Williamsport 232, 233.

38. Gettysburg 235

39. Pittsburg 240
      From Pittsburg to Connellsville, to Buffalo, to Erie, to
      Cleveland, and to Wheeling 243.

40. From Philadelphia to Baltimore 244
      From Wilmington to Cape Charles 244.

41. Baltimore 244
      Chesapeake Bay 249. — From Baltimore to Williamsport, to
      Harrisburg, to Martinsburg, and to Annapolis 250.

42. From Baltimore to Washington. 251

43. Washington 251
      Excursions from Washington: Georgetown, Arlington, Mt.
      Vernon, etc. 262, 263.

44. From Pittsburg to Chicago 263
   a. Viâ Crestline and Fort Wayne. 263
   b. Viâ Columbus and Logansport 264

45. From Baltimore to Chicago 265
      Frederick 265. — Wheeling 266.

Route   Page

46. From Buffalo to Chicago 267
  a. Viâ Lake Shore & Michigan Southern Railroad. . . . 267
  b. Viâ New York, Chicago, & St. Louis Railroad 270
  c. Viâ Michigan Central Railroad 270
    From Detroit to Lansing and Grand Rapids, to Port Huron,
    and to Mackinac Island 273.
  d. Viâ Grand Trunk Railway 274
  e. By Steamer 275
47. From New York to Chicago 276
  a. Viâ Philadelphia and Pittsburg 276
  b. Viâ Buffalo and Detroit 277
  c. Viâ Buffalo and Hamilton 277
  d. Viâ Buffalo and Cleveland 277
  e. Viâ Salamanca and Marion (Chautauqua) 278
  f. Viâ Baltimore and Washington 279
48. Chicago 279
    Pullman. Excursions from Chicago 286.
49. From Chicago to Milwaukee. 287
    Waukesha 288.
50. From Chicago to St. Paul and Minneapolis 288
  a. Viâ Chicago, Milwaukee, and St. Paul Railroad . . . 288
  b. Viâ Chicago & North-Western Railway 289
  c. Viâ Albert Lea Route · 290
  d. Viâ Chicago Great Western Railway 290
  e. Viâ Chicago, Burlington, & Quincy Railroad. 290
  f. Viâ Wisconsin Central Railroad 291
51. St. Paul and Minneapolis. 291
    Minnehaha Falls. Lake Minnetonka 295. — From Minneapolis
    to Sault Ste. Marie 295.
52. From St. Paul to Duluth 295
53. From Duluth to Sault Ste. Marie. 296
  a. By Railway 296
  b. By Steamer 297
54. From St. Paul to Winnipeg. 299
55. From St. Paul to Everett and Seattle 299
    From Pacific Junction to Helena and Butte 300.
56. From Chicago to St. Louis 301
  a. Viâ Illinois Central Railroad 301
  b. Viâ Chicago & Alton Railroad. 302
57. From Chicago to Cincinnati 302
  a. Viâ Indianapolis 302
  b. Viâ Logansport. 303
58. From New York to Cincinnati 303
  a. Viâ Pennsylvania Railroad 303
  b. Viâ Chesapeake & Ohio Railroad. 304
  c. Viâ Cleveland 306

Route   Page
  d. Viâ Baltimore & Ohio Railroad 306
  e. Viâ Erie Railway 306
59. Cincinnati 307
    Covington. Newport. Serpent Mound 309.
60. From New York to St. Louis 310
  a. Viâ Cleveland and Indianapolis 310
  b. Viâ Philadelphia and Pittsburg 310
  c. Viâ Wabash Railroad 310
  d. Viâ Cincinnati 311
61. St. Louis 311
62. From St. Louis to Louisville 315
    Wyandotte Cave 315. — From Louisville to Lexington 316.
63. From Cincinnati to New Orleans 316
  a. Viâ Chattanooga (Queen & Crescent Route) 316
    Blue Grass Region 317.
  b. Viâ Louisville and Nashville 318
    Mammoth Cave of Kentucky 318.
64. From Chicago and St. Louis to New Orleans 319
65. From Louisville to Memphis and New Orleans 320
66. From St. Paul to New Orleans by the Mississippi River . 322
67. From Washington to Richmond 326
    Battlefields round Richmond 329. — From Richmond to West
    Point and Yorktown 330.
68. From Richmond to Norfolk and Old Point Comfort . . . 330
  a. By Steamer 330
    Portsmouth. Virginia Beach. Currituck Sound 331.
  b. Viâ Chesapeake & Ohio Railroad 331
69. From Norfolk to Roanoke 333
    Dismal Swamp. Battlefields round Petersburg 333.
70. From Washington to New Orleans 334
  a. Viâ Richmond & Danville Railroad 334
    From Greensborough to Raleigh and Goldsborough 335. —
    Clarksville, Tallulah Falls, etc. 335, 336. — Environs of
    Mobile 337.
  b. Viâ the Shenandoah Valley 338
    From Radford to Columbus 340. — Roan Mt. and Cloudland
    Hotel 340. — Cumberland Gap 341. — From Cleveland to
    Mobile 341. — From Chattanooga to Brunswick and to
    Memphis 342.
71. From Salisbury to Asheville and Paint Rock 343
    Blowing Rock 343. — Excursions from Asheville 345. — From
    Asheville to Spartanburg and to Murphy 345.
72. From Richmond to Charleston 346
  a. Viâ Weldon (Wilmington) 346
  b. Viâ Charlotte and Columbia 347
73. Charleston 347
    Magnolia Cemetery, Magnolia Gardens, etc. 349, 350.
74. From Richmond to Savannah 350

Route   Page

   a. Viâ Charleston 350
      Beaufort. Port Royal 350.

   b. Viâ Columbia and Augusta 350
      Aiken 350. — Summerville 351. — Environs of Savannah
      352, 353.

75. From New York to Florida 353
   a. Viâ Atlantic Coast Line 353
      From Waycross to Bainbridge. Thomasville 354.
   b. Viâ Richmond & Danville Railroad 354
   c. By Steamer 355
      From Jacksonville to Fernandina 355. — Pablo Beach 356.

76. From Jacksonville to St. Augustine 356
77. The St. John's River 359
      From Palatka to Ormond, Titusville, and Rockledge 359.

78. The Ocklawaha River 360
79. From Jacksonville to Tampa 361
   a. Viâ Sanford 361
      From Enterprise Junction to Titusville 361. — From Sanford
      to Tarpon Springs and St. Petersburg 362. — Key West 363.
   b. Viâ Waldo and Ocala 363
      From Waldo to Cedar Keys 363.

80. The Indian River 364
      Lake Worth 365.

81. From Jacksonville to Tallahassee, Pensacola, and New
   Orleans 365
82. New Orleans 366
      Excursions from New Orleans 370.

83. From St. Paul to Tacoma and Portland 370
      Butte City 373. — Broadwater 374. — Cascade Mts. 376. —
      Mt. Rainier 377. — Olympia 377.

84. The Yellowstone National Park 378
      a. From Livingston to Mammoth Hot Springs 380. — b. From
      Mammoth Hot Springs to the Lower Geyser Basin 381. —
      c. From the Lower Geyser Basin to the Upper Geyser Basin
      383. — d. From the Lower Geyser Basin to Yellowstone
      Lake 385. — e. From Yellowstone Lake to Yellowstone
      Cañon 386. — f. From Yellowstone Cañon to Mammoth Hot
      Springs 388.

85. From Chicago to Council Bluffs and Omaha 388
   a. Viâ Chicago, Milwaukee, & St. Paul Railway 388
   b. Viâ Chicago & North-Western Railway 389
   c. Viâ Chicago, Rock Island, & Pacific Railway 390
   d. Viâ Chicago, Burlington, & Quincy Railroad 390
86. From Council Bluffs and Omaha to Portland 391
      North Park 392. — From Beaver Cañon to the Yellowstone
      Park 392. — Shoshone Falls 393. — Mt. Hood 394.

87. From Council Bluffs and Omaha to San Francisco 395
      From Ogden to Pocatello 396. — From Reno to Virginia City
      397. — Sierra Nevada 397. — From Sacramento to Lathrop.
      Calaveras Grove 398.

Route   Page
88. From Chicago to Kansas City 399
    a. Viâ Atchison, Topeka, & Santa Fé Railroad 399
        From Kansas City to Dallas, Fort Worth, and Houston 400.
    b. Viâ Chicago & Alton Railroad. 400
    c. Viâ Wabash Railroad 401
    d. Viâ Chicago & Rock Island Railway 401
    e. Viâ Chicago Great Western Railway 401
    f. Viâ Burlington Route 402
    g. Viâ Chicago, Milwaukee, & St. Paul Railway. 402
89. From St. Louis to Kansas City aud Denver 402
90. From St. Louis to Texarkana 403
    Hot Springs, Arkansas 404.

91. From Kansas City to San Francisco. 405
    a. Viâ Union Pacific Railway System 405
        Leavenworth 405. — From Denver to Golden, Central City,
        and Graymont 407. — From Denver to Boulder and Forth
        Collins, and to Leadville 408. — From Denver to Gunnison
        (South Park), Around the Circle, and to La Junta 409.
    b. Viâ Atchison, Topeka, & Santa Fé Railroad 410
        From Newton to Galveston. Oklahoma 410. — Las Vegas
        Hot Springs 411. — Santa Fé 412. — From Albuquerque to
        El Paso 412. — Grand Cañon of the Colorado 413.

92. From Denver to Salt Lake City and Ogden 414
    a. Viâ Denver & Rio Grande Railroad. 414
        Excursions from Colorado Springs (Garden of the Gods, Pike's
        Peak, Manitou, etc.) 416, 417. — From Pueblo to Alamosa
        (San Luis Park), Durango (Mancos Cliff Dwellings), Silverton,
        and Ouray, 418-420. — From Salida to Grand Junction viâ
        Leadville 421. — Sangre de Cristo Range 421. — Crested
        Butte 421.
    b. Viâ Colorado Midland Railway 423
        Salt Lake City 424. — Great Salt Lake 427.

93. San Francisco. 428
        Excursions from San Francisco: Cliff House, Mt. San Bruno,
        Mare Island, San Francisco Bay, Sausalito, Mt. Tamalpais,
        San Rafael, Geyser Springs, Alameda, Calistoga, Mt. Diablo,
        Sonoma, etc. 432-434.

94. From San Francisco to San José, Santa Cruz, and Monterey 436
    a. Viâ Standard-Gauge Railway 436
        Pescadero 437. — Stanford University 437. — Lick Observatory
        438. — El Paso de Robles. San Luis Obispo 438. — Excur-
        sions from Monterey 440.
    b. Viâ Narrow-Gauge Railway. 440
        Big Trees of Santa Cruz 440.

95. From San Francisco to Los Angeles and Santa Barbara . . 441
        Sequoia National Park 442. — Ojai Valley 443. — Excursions
        from Santa Barbara 444.

96. Los Angeles 445
        Santa Monica. Redondo Beach. San Pedro. Santa Catalina 446.

Route   Page

97. From Los Angeles to Pasadena, San Bernardino, and Barstow 446
Excursions from Pasadena 447. — From San Bernardino to
San Diego, to Redlands, to Bear Valley, etc. 448.

98. From Los Angeles to San Diego and National City . . . 448
Coronado Beach 449.

99. The Yosemite Valley 450
Mariposa Grove of Big Trees 452. — Excursions in the High
Sierra 458.

100. From San Francisco to Portland. 458
Mt. Shasta 459. — Crater Lake 460. — Excursions from
Portland 461.

101. From San Francisco to New Orleans 462
From San Antonio to Rockport or Aransas Pass, to Austin,
and to Laredo 466. — From Houston to Galveston 467.

102. From New Orleans to Dallas, Fort Worth, and El Paso . 468
Great Staked Plain 469.

103. From Tacoma to Puget Sound, Victoria, and Alaska. . . 469
From Seattle to Vancouver 471. — Vancouver Island 472. —
Silver Bow and Treadwell Mines 477.

Mexico.

Introductory Notes 481
104. From Laredo to the City of Mexico. 482
Nevado de Toluca 483.

105. From Eagle Pass to the City of Mexico 484
106. From El Paso to the City of Mexico 485
From Zacatecas to Guadalupe 486. — From Aguascalientes to
Tampico 486. — Guanajuato. From Irapuato to Guadalajara 487.

107. The City of Mexico 488
Excursions from the City of Mexico. Chapultepec. Guada-
lupe Hidalgo. Floating Gardens. Arbol de la Noche Triste.
Ascent of Popocatepetl 491, 492.

108. From the City of Mexico to Vera Cruz 492
From Apizaco to Puebla. Cholula 492. — Jalapa 494.

Index. 495

Maps.

1. The FARTHER ENVIRONS OF NEW YORK; p. 4.
2. The NEARER ENVIRONS OF NEW YORK; p. 20
3. RAILWAY MAP OF THE NEW ENGLAND STATES; p. 68
4. The ENVIRONS OF BOSTON; p. 68
5. MOUNT DESERT ISLAND; p. 100
6. The WHITE MOUNTAINS; p. 132
7. The CATSKILL MOUNTAINS; p. 164
8. The ADIRONDACK MOUNTAINS; p. 164
9. RAILWAY MAP OF THE MIDDLE STATES; p. 228
10. The ENVIRONS OF GETTYSBURG; p. 236

11. The BATTLEFIELD OF GETTYSBURG; p. 237
12. The ENVIRONS OF CHARLESTON; p. 347
13. NORTHERN FLORIDA; p. 356
14. The YELLOWSTONE NATIONAL PARK; p. 388
15. The ENVIRONS OF SAN FRANCISCO; p. 436
16. THE YOSEMITE VALLEY; p. 452
17. GENERAL MAP OF THE UNITED STATES, frontispiece

Plans.

1. ALBANY (p. 148).—2. BALTIMORE (p. 244).—3. BOSTON (p. 84).
— 4. BUFFALO (p. 196). — 5. CHICAGO, central part (p. 276). — 6.
CHICAGO, general plan (p. 276). — 7. CINCINNATI (p. 308). — 8.
CLEVELAND (p. 260). — 9. METROPOLITAN MUSEUM OF ART (p. 42). —
10. MINNEAPOLIS (p. 292). — 11. NEW ORLEANS (p. 366). — 12. NEW
YORK (p. 20). — 13. NIAGARA FALLS (p. 196). — 14. PHILADELPHIA
(p. 212). — 15. PITTSBURG (p. 244). — 16. RICHMOND (p. 324). — 17.
ST. AUGUSTINE (p. 356). — 18. ST. LOUIS (p. 308). — 19. ST. PAUL
(p. 292). — 20. SALT LAKE CITY (p. 424).— 21. SAN FRANCISCO (p.
436). — 22. SAVANNAH (p. 350). — 23. WASHINGTON (p. 260).

Abbreviations.

R. = Room; B. = Breakfast; D. = Dinner; L. = Luncheon.
— N. = North, Northern, etc.; S. = South, etc.; E. = East, etc.;
W. = West, etc. — M. = English (or American) Mile; ft. = Engl.
foot; min. = minute; hr. = hour. — Ho. = House; Ave. =
Avenue; St. = Street; R.R. = railroad; Mt. = Mountain. — U.S.
= United States.

The letter *d* with a date, after the name of a person, indicates
the year of his death. The number of feet given after the name of
a place shows its height above the sea-level. The number of miles
placed before the principal places on railway-routes indicates their
distance from the starting-point of the route.

ASTERISKS are used as marks of commendation.

INTRODUCTION.

I. Money. Expenses. Passports. Custom House. Time.

Money. The currency of the United States is arranged on a decimal system, of which the dollar ($), divided into 100 cents (c.), is the unit. The *Gold* coins are the pieces of $1, $2¹/₂, $5, $10, and $20. The *Silver* coins are the dollar, half-dollar, quarter dollar (= 1 s.), and 'dime' (10 c.). The 5 c. piece or 'nickel' is made of *Nickel*, and there are *Bronze* pieces of 1 c. (¹/₂ d.) and 2 c. (1 d.). The U. S. *Paper Currency* consists of Gold Notes (of the denomination of $20, $50, $100, $500, $1000, $5000, and $10,000), United States Notes ('greenbacks'), U. S. Treasury Notes, and Silver Certificates. The last three are issued for $1, $2, $5, $10, $20, $50, $100, $500, and $1000. All are redeemable at par. The *National Bank Bills*, for the same amounts, are also universally current. Throughout nearly the whole of the country notes are much more common than coins for all sums of $1 and upwards; but in California gold and silver are in almost exclusive use. For practical purposes the dollar may be reckoned as 4 s. and $5 as 1 l.; but the actual rate of exchange for 1 l. is generally between $4.80 and $4.90 (or $1 = about 4 s. 2 d.).

The European visitor to the United States will find it convenient to carry his money in the form of letters of credit, or circular notes, which are readily procurable at the principal banks. Foreign money does not circulate in the United States, even the Canadian coins of exactly the same form and value as American coins being generally refused; but Bank of England notes are usually taken at their full value at the hotels of all the larger cities. — Post Office Orders (see p. xxviii) are not convenient for strangers, as evidence of identity is generally required before payment; but most of the large Express Companies (see pp. xxviii, 15) issue Money Orders that are cashed at sight in the same way as Post Office Orders in Great Britain.

Expenses. The expenses of a visit to the United States depend, of course, on the habits and tastes of the traveller, but are almost inevitably from one-fourth to one-third higher than those of European travel. The distances to be traversed are so great that railway fares are sure to be absolutely, even when not relatively, higher (comp. p. xxi); and comfortable hotels of the second or third class are comparatively rare. Persons of moderate requirements, however, by frequenting boarding-houses instead of hotels and avoiding carriage hire as much as possible, may travel comfortably (exclusive of long continuous journeys) for $5-7¹/₂ (20-30 s.)

a day; but it would be safer to reckon on a daily expenditure of at least $10 (2*l*.). An entire day (24 hrs.) spent on the train (*i.e.* a journey of 500-800 M.) costs, with Pullman car accommodation and meals, about $20 (4*l*.). The cost of living varies considerably in different parts of the country; and New York, where most visitors land, is, perhaps, the most expensive city in America. Comp. pp. xxvi, 9.

Passports are not necessary in the United States, though occasionally useful in procuring delivery of registered and poste restante letters.

Custom House. The custom-house examination of the luggage of travellers entering the United States is generally conducted courteously but often with considerable minuteness. Nothing is admitted free of duty except the personal effects of the traveller, and unusually liberal supplies of unworn clothing are apt to be regarded with considerable suspicion. The traveller should be careful to 'declare' everything he has of a dutiable nature, as otherwise it is liable to summary confiscation (comp. p. xix).

Time. For the convenience of railways and others a *Standard of Time* for the United States was agreed upon in 1883, and a system adopted by which the country was divided into four sections, each of 15° of longitude (1 hr.). *Eastern Time*, or that of the 75th Meridian, prevails from the Atlantic Coast to a line running through Detroit and Charleston. *Central Time* (of Meridian 90), 1 hr. slower, extends thence to a line running from Bismarck (N.D.) to the mouth of the Rio Grande. *Mountain Time* (105° lon.) extends to the W. borders of Idaho, Utah, and Arizona. *Pacific Time* (120°) covers the rest of the country. Thus noon at New York is 11 a.m. at Chicago, 10 a.m. at Denver, and 9 a.m. at San Francisco. True local or mean solar time may be anywhere from 1 min. to 30 min. ahead or behind the standard time; and in some cases, where the local clocks keep true time and the railway clocks keep standard time, the results are confusing.

II. Voyage from Europe to the United States.

The chief routes from Europe to the United States are indicated in R. 1. (comp. also p. 6); and the steamers of any of the companies there mentioned afford comfortable accommodation and speedy transit. The fares vary considerably according to season and the character of the vessel; but the extremes for a saloon-passage may be placed at $50 (10*l*.) and $500 (100*l*.) the latter sum securing a suite of deck-rooms on the largest, finest, and quickest boats in the service. The average rate for a good stateroom in a good steamer may be reckoned at $75-125 (15-25*l*.). The intermediate or second cabin costs $30-65 (6-13*l*.), the steerage $20-30 (4-6*l*.). The slowest steamers, as a general rule, have the lowest fares; and for those who do not object to a prolongation of the voyage they often offer as much comfort as the 'ocean greyhounds.'

The average duration of the passage across the Atlantic is 7-10 days. The best time for crossing is in summer. Passengers should pack clothing and other necessaries for the voyage in small flat boxes (*not* portmanteaus), such as can lie easily in the cabin, as all bulky luggage is stowed away in the hold. Stateroom trunks should not exceed 3 ft. in length, 1½-2 ft. in breadth, and 15 inches in height. Trunks not wanted on board should be marked 'Hold' or 'Not Wanted', the others 'Cabin' or 'Wanted'. The steamship companies generally provide labels for this purpose. Dress for the voyage should be of a plain and serviceable description, and it is advisable, even in midsummer, to be provided with warm clothing. A deck-chair, which may be purchased at the dock or on the steamer before sailing (from 7s. upwards), is a luxury that may almost be called a necessary. This should be distinctly marked with the owner's name or initials, and may be left in charge of the Steamship Co.'s agents until the return-journey. On going on board, the traveller should apply to the purser or chief steward for a seat at table, as the same seats are retained throughout the voyage. It is usual to give a fee of 10s. (2½ dollars) to the table-steward and to the stateroom steward, and small gratuities are also expected by the boot-cleaner, the bath-steward, etc. The stateroom steward should not be 'tipped' until he has brought all the passenger's small baggage safely on to the landing-stage. — Landing at New York, see pp. 3, 6.

The custom-house officer usually boards vessels at the Quarantine Station (see p. 2) and furnishes blank forms on which the passengers 'declare' any dutiable articles they may have in their trunks. The luggage is examined in the covered hall adjoining the wharf, where it is arranged as far as possible in alphabetical order by the initials of the owners' names (comp. p. 6). After the examination the traveller may hire a carriage to take himself and his baggage to his destination, or he may send his trunks by a transfer-agent or express man (see p. xxii) and go himself on foot or by tramway. Telegraph messengers and representatives of hotels also meet the steamers.

III. Railways. Steamers. Coaches.

Railways. The United States now contain about 170,000 M. of railway, or nearly as much as all the rest of the world put together. The lines are all in private hands, and the capital invested in them amounts to about $10,000,000,000 (2,000,000,000*l*.). Between 20 and 30 corporations report over 1000 M. of track each, while the Union Pacific Railroad alone operates nearly 11,000 M. The total number of employees is not far short of 900,000. The railway mileage per 1 sq.M. of surface varies in the different states from about ¼ M. in New Jersey and Massachusetts to about 1/119 M. in Nevada. Illinois has about 10,500 M. of railway, Rhode Island about 225 M. In 1890 the number of passengers carried was 520,439,820 and the average distance travelled by each was 20-25 M.

The equipments of American railways are, as is well known, very different from those of European railways. Instead of comparatively small coaches, divided into compartments holding 6-8 people each, the American railways have long cars (like an enlarged tramway-car), holding 60-70 pers., entered by doors at each end, and having a longitudinal passage down the middle, with the seats on each side of it. Each seat has room for two passengers. Local and short-distance trains, especially in the East, generally have one class of carriage only, but all long-distance trains are also furnished with drawing-room (parlor) cars by day and sleeping-cars

b*

at night, which accommodate about 24-30 people in the same space as the ordinary cars and are in every way much more comfortable. Second class and emigrant carriages are also found on some long-distance trains and in parts of the South and West, but scarcely concern the tourist. Smoking is not permitted except in the cars ('Smokers') specially provided for the purpose and generally found at the forward end of the train. Smoking compartments are also usually found in the parlor-cars. The parlor and sleeping-cars are generally the property of special corporations, of which the Pullman Palace Car Co. (p. 286) is the chief; but on a few railways they belong to the railway company itself. The vexed question of whether the American or the European railway-carriage is the more comfortable is hard to decide. It may be said generally, however, that the small compartment system would never have done for the long journeys of America, while the parlor cars certainly offer greater comfort in proportion to their expense than the European first-class carriages do. A *Limited Vestibuled Train*, such as that described at p. 276, comes measurably near the ideal of comfortable railway travelling, and reduces to a minimum the bodily discomfort and tedium of long railway journeys. In comparing the ordinary American car with the second-class or the best third-class carriages of Europe, some travellers may be inclined to give the preference for short journeys to the latter. The seats in the American cars offer very limited room for two persons, and their backs are too low to afford any support to the head; a single crying infant or spoiled child annoys 60-70 persons instead of the few in one compartment; the passenger has little control over his window, as someone in the car is sure to object if he opens it; the continual opening and shutting of the doors, with the consequent draughts, are annoying; the incessant visitation of the train-boy, with his books, candy, and other articles for sale, renders a quiet nap almost impossible; while, in the event of an accident, there are only two exits for 60 people instead of six or eight. On the other hand the liberty of moving about the car, or, in fact, from end to end of the train, the toilette accommodation, and the amusement of watching one's fellow-passengers greatly mitigate the tedium of a long journey; while the publicity prevents any risk of the railway crimes sometimes perpetrated in the separate compartments of the European system. Rugs as a rule are not necessary, as the cars are apt to be over, rather than under, heated. Little accommodation is provided in the way of luggage racks, so that travellers should reduce their hand-baggage to the smallest possible dimensions. — In the sleeping-car, the passenger engages a *Half-Section*, consisting of a so-called 'double berth', which, however, is rarely used by more than one person. If desirous of more air and space, he may engage a whole *Section* (at double the rate of a half-section), but in many cases a passenger is not allowed to monopolize a whole section to the exclusion of those not otherwise able to find accommodation. Parties of 2-4 may secure *Drawing Rooms*, or private compartments. A lower berth is generally considered preferable to an upper berth, as it is easier to get into and commands the window; but, by what seems a somewhat illiberal regulation of the sleeping-car companies, the upper berth is always let down, whether occupied or not, unless the whole section is paid for. So far nothing has been done towards reserving a special part of the car for ladies, except in the shape of a small toilette and dressing room. — *Dining Cars* are often attached to long-distance trains, and the meals and service upon them are generally better than those of the railway restaurants. — Tickets are collected on the train by the *Conductor* (guard), who sometimes gives numbered checks in exchange for them. Separate tickets are issued for the seats in parlor-cars and the berths in sleeping-cars; and such cars generally have special conductors. Fees are never given except to the coloured *Porters* of the parlor-cars, who brush the traveller's clothes and (on overnight journey) boots and expect about 25 c. a day. In America the traveller is left to rely upon his own common sense still more freely than in England, and no attempt is made to take care of him in the patriarchal fashion of Continental railways. He should therefore be careful, to see that he is in his proper car, etc. The conductor calls 'all aboard', when the train is about to start, but on many lines no warning bell is rung. The names of the places passed are not shown distinctly (sometimes not at all) at the stations, and the brake-man, whose duty it is to announce each station as the train reaches it, is apt to be entirely unintelligible. A special word of caution may be given as to the frequent necessity for crossing the tracks, as the rails are frequently flush with the floor of the station and foot-bridges or tunnels are rarely provided. Each locomotive carries a large bell, which is tolled as it approaches stations or level ('grade') crossings. — With the excep-tion of the main line trains in the Eastern States, the speed of American trains is generally lower than that of English trains; and over a large portion of the South and West it does not exceed 20-25 M. per hour even for through-trains.

Fares vary so much in different parts of the country that it is difficult to state an average. Perhaps 3-4 c. (1½-2 d.) per mile will be found nearly correct on the whole, though in E. states the rate is frequently lower, especially for season, 'commutation' (good for so many trips), or mileage tickets, while in the S. and W. 4 c. is often exceeded. The extra rate for the palace cars (½-1 c. per mile) is low as compared with the difference between the first and third class fares in England, and the extra comfort afforded is very great. Return tickets ('excursion' or 'round trip' tickets) are usually issued at considerable reductions (comp. also p. xxv). The 1000 M. Tickets, from which the conductor collects coupons representing the number of miles travelled, is a convenient arrangement which European railways might do well to introduce. A distinction is frequently made between 'Limited' and 'Unlimited' tickets, the former and cheaper ad-mitting of continuous passage only, without 'stopovers'; and the latter being available until used and admitting of 'stopovers' at any place on the route. Tickets may sometimes be obtained at lower than the regula-tion rates at the offices of the so-called 'Scalpers', found in all large towns; but the stranger should hardly attempt to deal with them unless aided by a friendly expert. Railway-fares change more frequently in the United States than in Europe, so that the continued accuracy of those given throughout the Handbook cannot be guaranteed. — At the railway stations, the place of the first, second, and third class waiting-rooms of Europe is taken by a *Ladies' Room*, in which men are also generally admit-ted if not smoking, and a *Men's Room*, in which smoking is usually permitted.

Among the American *Railway Terms* with which the traveller should be familiar (in addition to those already incidentally mentioned) are ꜩhe following. *Railroad* is generally used instead of railway (the latter term being more often applied to street railways, *i.e.* tramways), while the word 'Road' alone is often used to mean railroad. The carriages are called *Cars*. The *Conductor* (generally addressed as 'Captain' in the South and West) is aided by *Brakemen*, whose duties include attention to the heating and lighting of the cars. A slow train is called an *Accommoda-tion* or *Way Train*. The *Ticket Office* is never called booking-office. Lug-gage is *Baggage*, and is expedited through the *Baggage Master* (see below). *Depot* is very commonly used instead of station, and in many places the latter word, when used alone, means police station. Other terms in com-mon use are: *turn-out* = siding; *bumper* = buffer; *box-car* = closed goods car; *caboose* = guard's van; *freight-train* = goods train; *cars* = train; *to pull out* = to start; *way station* = small, wayside station; *cow-catcher* = fender in front of engine; *switch* = shunt; *switches* = points.

The railway system of the United States is so vast that it is imprac-ticable to produce such complete *Railway Guides* as those of European countries. The fullest is the *Travellers' Official Guide*, a bulky volume of 8-900 pp., published monthly at New York (50 c.). Other general monthly guides are *Rand-McNally's* (40 c.) and *Appleton's* (25 c.). Local collections of time-tables are everywhere procurable, and those of each railway com-pany may be obtained gratis at the ticket-office and in hotels. All the more important railway companies publish a mass of 'folders' and descriptive pamphlets, which are distributed gratis and give a great deal of informa-tion about the country traversed. These are often very skilfully prepared and well illustrated.

Luggage. Each passenger on an American railway is generally entitled to 150 lbs. of luggage ('baggage') free; but overweight, unless exorbitant, is seldom charged for. The so-called *Check System* makes the management of luggage very simple. On arrival at the station, the traveller shows his railway ticket and hands over his impedimenta to the Baggage Master, who fastens a small brass tag to each article and gives the passenger brass 'checks' with corresponding numbers. The railway company then becomes responsible for the luggage and holds it until reclaimed at the passenger's destination by the presentation of the duplicate check. As the train approaches the larger cities a *Transfer Agent* usually walks through the cars, undertaking the delivery of luggage and giving receipts in exchange for the checks. The charge for this is usually 25 c. per package, and it is thus more economical (though a composition may sometimes be effected for a number of articles) to have one large trunk instead of two or three smaller ones. The hotel porters who meet the train will also take the traveller's checks and see that his baggage is delivered at the hotel. In starting, the trunks may be sent to the railway station in the same way, either through a transfer agent or the hotel porter; and if the traveller already has his railway ticket they may be checked through from the house or hotel to his destination. Baggage, unaccompanied by its owner, may be sent to any part of the country by the *Express Companies* (comp. p. 15), which charge in proportion to weight and distance. The drawbacks to the transfer system are that the baggage must usually be ready to be called for before the traveller himself requires to start, and that sometimes (especially in New York) a little delay may take place in its delivery; but this may, of course, be avoided by the more expensive plan of using a carriage between the house and railway-station.

Steamers. Some of the American steamers, such as the Fall River and Hudson boats (pp. 66, 146), offer comforts and luxuries such as are scarcely known in Europe, and their fares are usually moderate. Where the fare does not include a separate stateroom, the traveller by night will find the extra expenditure for one ($1-2) more than compensated for. Meals are sometimes included in the fare and are sometimes served either à la carte or at a fixed price. Throughout the Handbook the traveller will find indicated the routes on which he may advantageously prefer the steamer to the railway.

Coaches, usually called *Stages*, and in some country places *Barges*, have now been replaced by railways throughout nearly the whole of the United States, but in places like the Yosemite (p. 450), the Yellowstone (p. 378), and some of the other mountainous and rural districts the traveller is still dependent on this mode of conveyance. The roads are generally so bad, that the delights of coaching as known in England are for the most part conspicuously absent. The speed seldom exceeds 6 M. an hour and is sometimes less than this. The fares are relatively high.

Carriages. Carriage-hire is very high in the United States in spite of the fact that both the price of horses and their keep are usually lower than in England. Fares vary so much that it is impossible to give any general approximation, but they are rarely less than twice as high as in Europe. When the traveller drives himself in a 'buggy' or other small carriage, the rates are relatively much lower.

IV. Plan of Tour.

The plan of tour must depend entirely on the traveller's taste and the time he has at his disposal. It is manifestly impossible to cover more than a limited section of so vast a territory in an ordinary travelling season; but the enormous distances are practically much diminished by the comfortable arrangements for travelling at night (comp. p. xx). Among the grandest natural features of the country, one or other of which should certainly be visited if in any wise practicable, are Niagara Falls (R. 29), the Yellowstone Park (R. 84), the Yosemite Valley (R. 99), Alaska (R. 103), and the Grand Cañon of the Colorado (p. 413). Along with these may be mentioned the cañons, mountains, and fantastic rocks of Colorado (RR. 91, 92), the grand isolated snow-covered volcanic cones of the Pacific coast (pp. 377, 394, 459, etc.), the Mammoth Cave of Kentucky (p. 318), the Cavern of Luray (p. 339), the Natural Bridge of Virginia (p. 339), and the Shoshone Falls (p. 393). Among the most easily accessible regions of fine scenery are the Adirondacks (R. 25), including the Ausable Chasm (p. 170), the White Mts. (R. 16), the Catskills (R. 24), Mt. Desert (R. 11), the Hudson (R. 21), and the Delaware Water Gap (p. 196). Visitors to the S., besides the climate and vegetation, will find much to repay them, especially in such quaint old cities as New Orleans (R. 82). California (RR. 93-101) abounds in objects of interest and beauty. The trip into Mexico (RR. 104-108) is well worth the making. Travellers who make the trip to the Pacific Coast and back will do well so to plan their journey as to include the wonderful scenery of the Denver & Rio Grande Railroad (R. 92), as well as a trip into the Yellowstone Park, while the W. part of the Canadian Pacific Railway, between Vancouver and Banff (about 600 M.; see *Baedeker's Canada*), offers the grandest railway scenery in North America. Most of the larger cities have their own special points of interest, and a visit to the national capital (p. 251) should by all means be made. Chicago (p. 279) will, of course, be the objective point of most visitors to the United States in 1893, and should be approached either viâ the Pennsylvania Railroad (R. 47a), by the B. & O. route (R. 47f), or by one of the Buffalo routes (RR. 47b, c, & d).

Where the territory included is so vast and the possible combinations of tours so endless, it may seem almost useless to attempt to draw up any specimen tours. The following, however, though not intrinsically better than hundreds of others, may serve to give the traveller some idea of the distances to be traversed and of the average expenses of locomotion. It is, perhaps, needless to say that the traveller will enjoy himself better if he content himself with a less rapid rate of progress than that here indicated. A daily outlay of $10-12 will probably cover all the regular travelling expenses on the under-noted tours; and this rate may be much diminished by longer halts.

a. A Week from New York.
(Railway Expenses about $ 40.)   Days

New York to *Albany* by steamer (R. 21a)   1
Albany to *Buffalo* and *Niagara* (RR. 28, 29) 1¹/₂
Niagara to *Toronto* (see *Baedeker's Canada*) . . . .   ¹/₂
Toronto to *Montreal* by Lake Ontario and the St. Lawrence (R. 30)   1¹/₂
Montreal to *Boston* (RR. 15, 5)   2
Boston to *New York* (R. 4) . . . .   ¹/₂
                                                                    ———
                                                                     7

Visits to the *Catskills* (R. 24), *Adirondacks* (R. 25), and *White Mts.* (R. 16)
may easily be combined with the above tour. Or we may go from Montreal to *Quebec* (see *Baedeker's Canada;* ¹/₂ day) and thence to *Portland* (RR. 14, 9)
or to Boston direct (R. 15).

b. A Fortnight from New York.
(Railway Fares about $ 60.)

New York to *Niagara* as above (RR. 21, 28, 29) 2¹/₂
Niagara to *Chicago* (R. 46)   1
Chicago (R. 48)   3
Chicago to *Washington* and at Washington (RR. 45, 43)   3
Washington to *Baltimore* (RR. 42, 41)   1
Baltimore to *Philadelphia* (R. 40) . . . .   ¹/₂
Philadelphia and back to *New York* (RR. 32, 31)   2
                                                                    ———
                                                                     13

c. Three Weeks from New York.
(Railway Fares about $ 120.)

New York to *Chicago* as above (RR. 21, 28, 29, 46) 6¹/₂
Chigaco to *St. Louis* (RR. 56, 61) 1¹/₂
St. Louis to *New Orleans* (RR. 64, 82)   2
New Orleans to *Jacksonville* (RR. 81, 75)   2
Jacksonville to *St. Augustine* (R. 76)   1
St. Augustine to *Richmond* (RR. 75a, 67) 1¹/₂
Richmond to *Washington* (R. 67) . . . .   ¹/₂
Washington and back to *New York* as above (RR. 43, 42, 41, 32, 31)   5
                                                                    ———
                                                                     19

d. Six Weeks from New York.
(Railway Fares $ 300-350.)

New York to *Chicago* as above (RR. 21, 28, 29, 46) 6¹/₂
Chicago to *St. Paul* and *Minneapolis* (RR. 50, 51) . . . . : . . .   2
St. Paul to *Livingston* (R. 83) 1¹/₂
Yellowstone Park (R. 84)   6
Livingston to *Portland* (R. 83, 100)   2
Portland to *San Francisco* (R. 100) 1¹/₂
San Francisco, with excursions to *Monterey,* etc. (RR. 93, 94) . . .   5
San Francisco to the *Yosemite* and back (RR. 95, 99)   4
San Francisco to *Salt Lake City* (RR. 87, 92)   3
Salt Lake City to *Denver* viâ the *Marshall Pass* (RR. 92, 91) 1¹/₂
Denver to *Colorado Springs* and back, with excursions to *Manitou* etc.
  (R. 92)   4
Denver to *St. Louis* (RR. 89, 61) 2¹/₂
St. Louis to *New York* (R. 60) 1¹/₂
                                                                    ———
                                                                     41

e. Two Months from New York.
(Railway Fares $ 350-400.)

To *San Francisco* as above (RR. 21, 28, 29, 46, 50, 51, 83, 84, 100,
  93, 94) 24¹/₂
San Francisco to the *Yosemite* (RR. 95, 99) 3¹/₂
Yosemite to *Los Angeles* (*Pasadena,* etc.; RR. 95, 96, 97) 3¹/₂

IV. PLAN OF TOUR. xxxiii

Days

Los Angeles viâ *Barstow* and *Flagstaff* to the *Grand Cañon of the Colorado* (RR. 97, 91b) 3
Flagstaff to *Colorado Springs* (*Manitou*, etc.; RR. 91b, 92) 4
Colorado Springs to *Denver* (RR. 92, 91a) 1
Excursions from Denver, incl. *Marshall Pass* (RR. 91a, 92a) 4
Denver to *Kansas City* and *St. Louis* (R. 89) 2¹/₂
St. Louis to *Cincinnati* (R. 60d) 1¹/₂
Cincinnati to *Washington* (R. 58d) 1
Washington, and thence to *New York* as in R. b. (RR. 43, 42, 41, 40, 32, 31) 6¹/₂

——
54

The following table of the distances from New York of a few important points, together with the present railway fares and approximate length of the journey, may not be without interest. The fares are for first-class, 'unlimited' tickets, but do not include sleeping-car rates.

San Francisco: distance 3500 M; fare $ 95-100; time of transit 5¹/₂ days. — *Chicago:* 912-1048 M.; $ 21¹/₄-26¹/₂; 24-32 hrs. — *New Orleans:* 1370 M.; $ 34; 40 hrs. — *Jacksonville* (Florida): 1030 M.; $ 30; 40 hrs. — *Cincinnati:* 760 M.; $ 21¹/₂; 24 hrs. — *St. Louis:* 1060 M.; $ 31; 32 hrs. — *St. Paul:* 1330 M.; $ 35; 37 hrs. — *Denver:* 2100 M.; $ 50-55; 2¹/₂ days. — *Kansas City:* 1400 M.; $ 35-40; 38 hrs. — *Montreal:* 400 M.; $ 10; 14 hrs. — *Philadelphia:* 90 M.; $ 2¹/₂; 2-2¹/₂ hrs. — *Washington:* 228 M.; $ 6¹/₂; 5 hrs. — *Boston:* 215-230 M.; $ 5; 6 hrs. — *Richmond:* 345 M.; $ 11; 10 hrs. — *Salt Lake City:* 2800 M.; $ 75-80; 3¹/₂ days. — *Los Angeles:* 3400 M.; $ 95-100; 5-5¹/₂ days.

Excursion Agents. Travellers may sometimes find it advantageous to avail themselves of the facilities for tours in the United States offered by Messrs. *Raymond & Whitcomb* (296 Washington St., Boston), *Thomas Cook & Son* (1225 Broadway, New York), and *H. Gaze & Son* (113 Broadway, New York). These firms have agencies in all the most frequented resorts throughout the country, and have made special arrangements for visitors to the World's Columbian Exhibition (p. 282, 285). Raymond & Whitcomb arrange for a large series of excursions in special vestibuled trains, under the care of one of their representatives, which relieve the inexperienced traveller of almost all the inconveniences of a journey in a strange land. The arrangements are made so as to afford the widest possible freedom of movement in every way, and the charges are reasonable. For the Raymond trip into Mexico, see p. 481. — Most of the railway companies issue tickets for circular tours on favourable conditions, and some of them (such as the Pennsylvania R.R.) also arrange personally conducted excursions in special trains.

The **Pedestrian** is unquestionably the most independent of travellers, but, except in a few districts such as the Adirondacks (p. 165) and the White Mts. (p. 121), walking tours are not much in vogue in the United States, where, indeed, the extremes of temperature and the scarcity of well-marked foot-paths often offer considerable obstacles. For a short tour a couple of flannel shirts, a pair of worsted stockings, slippers, the articles of the toilet, a light waterproof, and a stout umbrella will generally be found a sufficient equipment. Strong and well-tried boots are essential to comfort. Heavy and complicated knapsacks should be avoided; a light pouch or game-bag is far less irksome, and its position may be shifted at pleasure. A more extensive reserve of clothing should not exceed the limits of a small portmanteau, which may be forwarded from town to town by express. The pedestrian should bear in mind that darkness sets in suddenly in the United States, without the long twilight of European summers.

V. Hotels and Restaurants.

Hotels. The quality of the hotels of the United States varies very greatly in different localities; but it is, perhaps, safe to say that the best American houses will be found fully as comfortable as the first-class hotels of Europe by all who can accommodate themselves to the manners of the country and do not demand everything precisely as they have been used to at home. The luxury of some of the leading American hotels is, indeed, seldom paralleled in Europe. The charges are little, if at all, higher than those of the best European houses; but the comforts often afforded by the smaller and less pretentious inns of the old country can seldom be looked for from American houses of the second or third class, and the traveller who wishes to economize will find boarding-houses (see p. xxvii) preferable. When ladies are of the party, it is advisable to frequent the best hotels only. The hotels of the South, except where built and managed by Northern enterprize, are apt to be poor and (in proportion to their accommodation) dear; many of the hotels in the West, on the other hand, even in the newest cities, are astonishingly good, and California contains some of the best and cheapest hotels in the United States. The food is generally abundant and of good quality, though the cuisine is unequal (comp. p. xxvii). Beds are almost uniformly excellent. The quality of the service varies and may be considered, though with many exceptions, as one of the weak points of American hotels.

A distinction is made between *Hotels on the American Plan*, in which a fixed charge is made per day for board and lodging, and *Hotels on the European Plan*, in which a fixed charge is made for rooms only, while meals are taken *à la carte* either in the hotel or elsewhere. No separate charge is made for service. The European system is becoming more and more common in the larger cities, especially in the East; but the American plan is universal in the smaller towns and country districts. Many hotels in the large cities offer a choice of systems. The rate of hotels on the American plan varies from about $5 per day in the best houses down to $2 per day or even less in the smaller towns; and $3-4 a day will probably be found about the average rate on an ordinary tour. The charge for a room at a good hotel on the European plan is from $1 upwards. Many of the American hotels vary their rate according to the room, and where two prices are mentioned in the Handbook the traveller should indicate the rate he wishes to pay. Most of the objections to rooms on the upper floor are obviated by the excellent service of 'elevators' (lifts). Very large reductions are made by the week or for two persons occupying the same room; and very much higher prices may be paid for extra accommodation. Throughout the Handbook the insertion of a price behind the name of a hotel ($5) means its rate on the American plan; where the hotel is on the European plan (exclusively or alternatively) the price of the room is indicated (R. from $1). The above rates include all the ordinary requirements of hotel life, and no 'extras' appear in the bill. The custom of giving fees to the servants is by no means so general as in Europe, though it is becoming more common in the Eastern States. Even there, however, it is practically confined to a small gratuity to the porter and, if the stay is prolonged, an occasional 'refresher' to the regular waiter. In hotels on the American system the meals are usually served at regular hours (a latitude of about 2 hrs. being allowed for each). The daily charge is considered as made up of four items (room, breakfast, dinner, and supper), and the visitor should see that his bill begins with the first meal he takes. Thus, at a $4 a day house, if the traveller arrives before supper and leaves after breakfast the next day, his bill will be $3; if he arrives after supper and leaves at the same time, $2; and so on. No allowance is made for absence from meals. Dinner is usually served in the middle of the day, except in large cities.

On reaching the hotel, the traveller enters the *Office*, a large and often comfortably fitted up apartment, used as a general rendezvous and smoking-room, not only by the hotel-guests, but often also by local residents. On one side of it is the desk of the *Hotel Clerk*, who keeps the keys of the bedrooms, supplies unlimited letter-paper gratis, and is supposed to be more or less omniscient on all points on which the traveller is likely to require information. Here the visitor enters his name in the 'register' kept for the purpose, and has his room assigned to him by the clerk, who details a 'bell-boy' to show him the way to his room and carry up his hand-baggage. If he has not already disposed of his 'baggage-checks' in the way described at p. xxii, he should now give them to the clerk and ask to have his trunks fetched from the station and sent up to his room. If he has already parted with his checks, he identifies his baggage in the hall when it arrives and tells the head-porter what room he wishes it sent to. On entering the dining-room the visitor is shown to his seat by the head-waiter, instead of selecting the first vacant seat that suits his fancy. The table-waiter then hands the guest the menu of the day, from which (in hotels on the American plan) he orders what he chooses. Many Americans order the whole of their meals at once, but this is by no means necessary except in primitive localities or inferior hotels. The key of the bedroom should always be left at the office when the visitor goes out. Guests do not leave their boots at the bedroom door to be blacked as in Europe, but will find a 'boot-black' in the toilette-room (fee 10 c.; elsewhere 5 c.). Large American hotels also generally contain a barber's shop (shave 20-25 c.; elsewhere 15 c.), railway ticket, express, and livery offices, book-stalls, etc.

The following hints may be useful to hotel keepers who wish to meet the tastes of European visitors. The wash-basins in the bedrooms should be much larger than is generally the case. Two or three large towels are preferable to the half-dozen small ones usually provided. A carafe or jug of fresh drinking water (not necessarily iced) and a tumbler should always be kept in each bedroom. If it were possible to give baths more easily and cheaply, it would be a great boon to English visitors. At present a bath attached to a bedroom costs $1 (4*s.*) a day extra, while the charge for using the public bathroom is usually 35-75 c. (1*s.* 6*d.*-3*s.*). No hotel can be considered first-class or receive an asterisk of commendation which refuses to supply food to travellers who are prevented from appearing at the regular meal hours.

Boarding Houses. For a stay of more than a day or two the visitor will sometimes find it convenient and more economical to live at a *Boarding House*. These abound everywhere and can easily be found on enquiry. Their rates vary from about $8 a week upwards. At many places the keepers of such houses also receive transient guests, and they are generally preferable to inferior hotels. — *Furnished Apartments* are easily procured in the larger cities, from $4-5 a week upwards (comp. p. 9). Soap, curiously enough, though provided in hotels, is not provided in boarding-houses or lodgings.

Restaurants. In New York and other large cities the traveller will find many excellent restaurants, but in other places he will do well to take his meals at his hotel or boarding-house. Restaurants are attached to all hotels on the European plan (p. xxvi). A single traveller will generally find the *à la carte* restaurants rather expensive, but one portion will usually be found enough for two guests and two portions ample for three. The *table d'hôte* restaurants, on the other hand, often give excellent value for their charges (comp. p. 9).

Soup, fish, poultry, game, and sweet dishes are generally good; but the

beef and mutton are often inferior to those of England. Oysters, served
in a great variety of styles, are large, plentiful, and comparatively cheap.
In America wine or beer is much less frequently drunk at meals than
in Europe, and the visitor is not expected to order liquor 'for the good
of the house'. Iced water is the universal beverage, and a cup of tea or
coffee is included in all meals at a fixed price. Wine is generally poor
or dear, and often both. It is much to be regretted that, outside of California, the native vintages, which are often superior to the cheap imported
wines, seldom appear on the wine-list; and travellers will do good service
by making a point of demanding Californian wines and expressing surprise
when they cannot be furnished. Liquors of all kinds are sold at *Saloons*
(public houses) and *Hotel Bars* (comp. p. 10). Restaurants which solicit
the patronage of 'gents' should be avoided. The meals on dining-cars
and 'buffet cars' are generally preferable to those at railway restaurants.
Tipping the waiter is not as a rule necessary or even (outside of the
large Eastern cities) expected, but it may be found serviceable where
several meals are taken at the same place. The custom, however, is by no
means so firmly rooted as in Europe and should not be encouraged.
Cafés, in the European sense, are seldom found in the United States
except in New Orleans (p. 366) and a few other cities with a large French
or German element in the population. The name, however, is constantly
used as the equivalent of restaurant.

VI. Post and Telegraph Offices.

Post Office. The regulations of the American postal service are
essentially similar to those of Great Britain, though the practice of
delivering letters at the houses of the addressees has not been extended to the rural districts. The service is, perhaps, not quite so
prompt and accurate. The supply of letter-boxes is generally abundant, but the number of fully equipped post-offices is much lower
(proportionately) than in England. Stamps are sold at all drug-stores,
and hotels, and often by letter carriers.

All 'mailable' matter for transmission within the United States and to
Canada and Mexico is divided into four classes: 1st. Letters and all
Sealed Packets (rate of postage 2 c. per oz. or fraction thereof); 2nd. Newspapers and Periodicals (1 c. per 4 oz.); 3rd. Books, etc. (1 c. per 2 oz.);
4th. Merchandise and Samples (1 c. per oz.). Postal cards 1 c.; reply postal
cards 2 c. A 'special delivery stamp' (10 c.) affixed to a letter, in addition
to the ordinary postage, entitles it to immediate delivery by special messenger. Letters to countries in the Postal Union cost 5 c., postal cards 2 c.,
books and newspapers 2 c. per oz. The *Registration Fee* is 8 c.; the stamp
must be affixed to the letter before presentation for registration, and the
name and address of the sender must be written on the back of the envelope. Undeliverable letters will be returned free to the sender, if a request
to that effect be written or printed on the envelope.

Domestic Money Orders are issued by money-order post-offices for any
amount up to $100, at the following rates: for sums not exceeding $5,
5 c.; $5-10, 8 c.; $10-15, 10 c.; $15-30, 15 c.; $30-40, 20 c.; $40-50, 25 c.;
$60-70, 30 c.; $60-70, 35 c.; $70-80, 40 c.; $80-100, 45 c. For strangers
these are not so convenient as the money-orders of the *Express Companies*
(comp. p. xvii), as identification of the payee is demanded. *Postal Notes,*
for sums less than $5, are issued for a fee of 3 c., and may pass from
hand to hand like ordinary currency within a period of three months.
Foreign Money Orders cost 10 c. for each $10, the limit being $50.

Telegraph Offices. The telegraphs of the United States are
mainly in the hands of the *Western Union Telegraph Co.,* with its
headquarters in New York (p. 14), and the service is neither so

cheap nor so prompt and trustworthy as that of Great Britain. In 1891 there were in the United States 187,981 M. of line and 715,591 M. of wire, while the number of despatches was 59,148,343. The rates from New York are given at p. 15, and from them may be roughly estimated the probable rates from other parts of the country. — In 1891 the United States contained 240,412 M. of *Telephone Wires*, used by 202,931 regular subscribers (comp. p. 15). Telephones are in operation in all large, and many of the small, towns throughout the country.

VII. Glossary.

The following short list of words in frequent use in the United States in a sense not commonly known in England may be found of service. The speech of the cultivated American, of course, varies little from the speech of the cultivated Englishman, and no misunderstanding is likely to arise in their verbal intercourse; but it will not unfrequently be found that railway officials, cabmen, waiters, and the like do not know what is meant by the British equivalents of the following expressions. It must not be understood that the under-noted words are all in use throughout the whole of the United States. A New Englander, for instance, may tell you that 'he never heard such a word', when you use a term in regular use by all classes in the West or South. The list, which might be extended indefinitely, does not attempt to enumerate the local names for different kinds of food, implements, etc.; nor does it mean to include words that are solely and avowedly 'slang'. Purely technical terms are also, for the most part, avoided. Comp. p. xxi (railway terms), p. xxvii, etc.

Bed-spread, coverlet, counterpane.
Biscuit, hot tea-rolls.
Bit (California), 12½ c. (two bits 25 c., eight bits $ 1).
Blank, Telegraph, Telegraph form.
Blind, shutter.
Block, square mass of building bounded by four streets.
Boots, used only of boots coming up wholly or partly to the knee. Comp. *Shoes* and *Ties*.
Boss, master, head, person in authority.
Bowl, basin.
Bright, clever.
Broncho, native (Californian) horse.
Bug, beetle, coleopterous insect of any kind.
Bureau, chest of drawers.
Calico, printed cotton cloth.
Carom, cannon (at billiards).
Chicken, fowl of any age.
Chowder, a kind of thick soup.
City, corporate town or municipal borough.

Clerk, shopman.
Clever, good-natured.
Corn, Maize or Indian corn.
Cracker, biscuit; also, in the Southern States, a poor white man.
Creek (pron. crick), a small stream.
Cunning, neat, pretty, tiny. *Cute* is often used in much the same sense.
Cuspidor, spittoon.
Cutter, light, one-horse sleigh.
Deck, pack of cards.
Dirt, earth, soil (*e.g.*, a 'dirt tennis-court').
Drummer, commercial traveller.
Dry Goods, dress materials, drapery, etc.
Dumb, (often) stupid (Ger. *dumm*).
Elevator, lift.
Fall, autumn.
Fix, to arrange, make, put in order, settle, see to, etc.
Fleshy, stout.
Grip-sack, hand-bag.
Gums, overshoes (see *Rubbers*).
Gun, to go shooting.

Hack, cab; *hackman*, cabman.
Help, servant.
Hitch, harness; *hitching-post*, post to tie horses to.
Horse-Car, tramway.
Hunt, to go shooting.
Lines, reins.
Lot, a piece or division of land.
Lumber, timber.
Lunch, a slight meal at any hour of the day.
Mad, vexed, cross.
Mail, to post; postal matter; postal service.
Mucilage, liquid gum.
Muslin, cotton cloth.
Nasty, disgusting (not used before 'ears polite').
Notions, small wares.
Observatory, (often) belvedere or view-tower (Ger. *Aussichtsthurm*).
Parlor, drawing-room.
Piazza, veranda.
Pie, tart or pie.
Pitcher, jug.
Prince Albert (Coat), frock-coat.
Rapid Transit, a general name for tramways, elevated railroads, and similar means of city and suburban locomotion.
Recitation, lesson, college lecture.
Ride, applied to any mode of conveyance (horse, carriage, boat, etc.).
Right away, directly.
Rock, stone of any size; to throw stones.

Rooster, cock.
Rubbers, galoshes, overshoes.
Run, to manage, carry on (a business, etc.).
Sack, *Sacque*, jacket.
Safe, larder (meat-safe, etc.).
Ship, to send goods by train as well by sea.
Shoes, boots not coming above the ancle.
Shortage, deficiency.
Sick, ill.
Smart, stylish, fashionable.
Sophomore, student in his second year at college. Students of the first, third, and fourth years are named *Freshmen*, *Juniors*, and *Seniors*.
Span, pair of horses.
Spool (of cotton), reel (of thread).
Stage, coach, omnibus.
Store, shop.
Street-car, tramway.
Take out. An American takes a lady 'out' to dinner, while an Englishman takes her 'in'.
Ties, low shoes; railway sleepers.
Town, township or parish (thus one hears of the highest mountain or the best crop in the town).
Ugly, ill-tempered.
Under-waist, bodice.
Wagon, carriage.
Waist, body (of a dress).
Wilt, fade, wither.
Window-shade, blind.

In the United States *First Floor* is synonymous with *Ground Floor*, while *Second Floor* corresponds to the English *First Floor*, and so on. Throughout the Handbook these terms are used in conformity with the English custom.

VIII. General Hints.

The first requisites for the enjoyment of a tour in the United States are an absence of prejudice and a willingness to accommodate oneself to the customs of the country. If the traveller exercise a little patience, he will often find that ways which strike him as unreasonable or even disagreeable are more suitable to the environment than those of his own home would be. He should from the outset reconcile himself to the absence of deference or servility on the part of those he considers his social inferiors; but if ready himself to be courteous on a footing of equality he will seldom meet any real impoliteness. In a great many ways travelling in the United States is, to one who understands it, more comfortable than in Europe. The average Englishman will probably find the chief physical discomforts in the dirt of the city streets, the roughness of the country roads, the winter overheating of hotels and railway cars (70-75° Fahr. being by no means unusual), and (in many places) the habit of spitting on the floor; but the Americans themselves are now keenly alive to these weak points and are doing their best to remove them.

Throughout almost the whole country travelling is now as safe as in the most civilized parts of Europe, and the carrying of arms, which indeed is forbidden in many states, is as unnecessary here as there. Those who contemplate excursions into districts remote from the highways of travel should take local advice as to their equipment. — The social forms of America are, in their essentials, similar to those of England; and the visitor will do well to disabuse himself of the idea that laxity in their observance will be less objectionable in the one country than in the other. He will, of course, find various minor differences in different parts of the country, but good manners will nowhere be at a discount. — No limit is placed on the number of passengers admitted to public conveyances, and straps are provided in the cars of tramways and elevated railways to enable those who cannot obtain seats to maintain their equilibrium. — The prices of almost all manufactured goods are much higher in the United States than in Europe; and the traveller should therefore come provided with an ample supply of all the articles of personal use he or she is likely to require, down to such small items as pins and needles, tapes and ribbons, dress ties and gloves, toilette requisites, buttons, and matches (generally very poor in America). An important exception to the above rule is boots and shoes, which are excellently made in the United States and cost, if anything, rather less than in England. Cotton goods are also as cheap as in Europe. — Indoor clothing for American use should be rather thinner in texture than is usual in England, but winter wraps for outdoor use require to be much thicker. The thick woollen gowns that English ladies wear in winter would be uncomfortably warm in the ordinary winter temperature of American hotels and railway carriages; and a thin soft silk will, perhaps, be found the most comfortable travelling dress on account of its non-absorption of dust. Overshoes ('arctics' and 'rubbers') are quite necessary in winter and are worn almost as much by men as by women. — Weddings frequently take place in the evening, and are managed by a set of 'ushers' chosen from the bridegroom's friends. — The rule of the road in America follows the Continental, not the English system, vehicles passing each other to the right.

The art of the *Barber and Hair-Dresser* has been developed to a high point in the United States, where the 'tonsorial saloons' are often very luxurious. The prices, however, are high (15-25 c. for a shave, including hair-brushing and the application of essences; hair-cutting 25-35 c., shampooing 15-25 c., 'sea foam' or 'dry shampoo' 10-20 c., etc.).

Public Conveniences are not usually provided in American cities, but their place is practically supplied by the lavatories of hotels, to which passers-by resort freely. Accommodation is also furnished at railway-stations. Such public conveniences as do exist in New York and other large cities are disgracefully inadequate in number, size, and equipment.

Public Holidays. The only holidays observed in all the states are Independence Day (July 4th) and Christmas Day (Dec. 25th). New Year's Day (Jan. 1st) and Washington's Birthday (Feb. 22nd) are celebrated in nearly all the states. Decoration Day (May 30th) is set apart in the N. and W. states for decorating with flowers the graves of those who fell in the Civil War; and some of the S. states have a Memorial Day for the same purpose. Thanksgiving Day (last Thurs. in Nov.) is observed with practical unanimity; and General Election Day and Labor Day (Sept. 5th) are each celebrated by a large number of states. In addition to the above, each state has its own special holidays.

IX. A Short History of American Politics
by
John Bach McMaster.

What is now the territory of the United States has been derived from six European nations. Resting on the discovery by Columbus, and the Bulls of the Popes, Spain claimed the whole Continent, but has been in actual possession only of the Gulf coast from Florida to Texas, and of the interior from the Mississippi to the Pacific. The Swedes once had settlements on the Delaware. The Dutch, following up the voyage of Hudson to the river bearing his name, claimed and held the country from the Delaware to the Connecticut. The French discovered the St. Lawrence and explored and held military possession of the valleys of the Mississippi and Ohio and the Great Lakes. The English by virtue of the voyages of the Cabots claimed the Atlantic coast and there founded the colonies which grew into the thirteen United States. Alaska was purchased from Russia.

In the course of the struggle, sometimes peaceful, often bloody, by which the rule of these nations has been thrown off, the Dutch conquered the Swedes; the English conquered the Dutch and the French; the United States expelled the English and in time by purchase or conquest drove out the Spaniards and the Mexicans.

The first serious struggle for possession occurred in the middle of the 18th cent., when the English moving westward met the French moving eastward at the sources of the river Ohio. In that struggle which has come down to us as the 'French and Indian War' France was worsted and, retiring from this continent, divided her possessions between England and Spain. To England she gave Canada and the islands and shores of the Gulf of St. Lawrence and, entering what is now the United States, drew a line down the middle of the Mississippi River and gave all to the E. of that line (save the island on which is the city of New Orleans) to Great Britain, and all to the W. of it to Spain; Spain at the same time gave Florida to England as the price of Cuba.

Having thus come into possession of all the country to the E. of the Great River, King George determined to send out an army of 10,000 men to defend the colonies, and have the latter bear a part of the expense. This part he attempted to collect by duties on goods imported and by a Stamp Tax (1765) on legal documents and printed matter. No tax for revenue had before been laid on America by act of Parliament. The colonists therefore resisted this first attempt and raising the cry 'no taxation without representation' they forced Parliament to repeal the Stamp Tax in 1766. The right to tax was at the same time distinctly asserted, and in 1767 was again used, and duties laid on paints, oils, lead, glass, and tea. Once more the colonists resisted and, by refusing to import any goods, wares, or merchandise of English make, so distressed the manufacturers of England that Parliament repealed every tax save that on tea. All the tea needed in America was now smuggled in from Holland. The East India Company, deprived of the American market, became embarrassed, and, calling on Parliament for aid, was suffered to export tea, a privilege never before enjoyed. Selecting commissioners in Boston, New York, Philadelphia, and Charleston, cargoes of tea were duly consigned to them; but the people would not allow a pound of it to be sold. At Boston men disguised as Indians boarded the tea ships and threw the boxes into the harbour (comp. p. 78).

As a punishment for this, Parliament shut the port of Boston and deprived the people of Massachusetts of many functions of local government. The Assembly of Massachusetts thereupon called for a General Congress to meet at Philadelphia on Sept. 5th, 1774. The colonies gladly responded and this Congress, having issued a Declaration of Rights and addresses to the King, to Parliament, and to the People of England, adjourned to await the result. The day for the reassembling of Congress was May 10th, 1775; but before that day came, the attempt of *Gage* to seize military stores brought on a fight at Lexington (April 19th, 1775; p. 113). The fight at Lexington was followed by the siege of the British in Boston, by the formation of the 'Continental Army', by the appointment of *George Washington* to command it, by the battle of Bunker Hill (June 17th, 1775; p. 85), and by an expedition against Quebec, which came to naught, on the last day of the year.

Lord Howe meantime had succeeded Gage in command of the British at Boston, and, finding himself hard pressed by Washington, evacuated the city and sailed for Halifax. Believing New York was to be attacked, Washington now hurried to Long Island, where (August 27th, 1776; p. 52) Howe defeated him, took possession of New York, and drove him first up the Hudson and then southward across New Jersey.

Congress, which (July 4th, 1776) had declared the colonies to be free and independent states, now fled from Philadelphia to Baltimore. But Washington, turning in his retreat, surprised and captured the British outpost at Trenton (p. 209). Cornwallis instantly hurried toward that town, but Washington, passing around the British rear, attacked and captured (at Princeton, Jan. 3rd, 1777; p. 208) a detachment on its march to Trenton, and then went into winter quarters at Morristown.

With the return of spring Howe, finding that he could not reach Philadelphia by land without passing in front of the Continental Army stretched out on a strongly intrenched line across New Jersey, went by sea. Washington met him at Chadd's Ford on the Brandywine (p. 244), was defeated, and on Sept. 25th, 1777, Howe entered Philadelphia. In the attempt to dislodge him Wash-

ington fought and lost the battle of Germantown (Oct. 4th, 1777;
p. 221). The loss of Philadelphia was more than made good by the
capture of *Burgoyne* and his army at Saratoga (Oct. 17th, 1777;
p. 180), while on his way from Canada to New York City.
The fruits of this victory were the recognition of the Independence
of the United States by France, the treaty of alliance with France
(Feb. 8th, 1778), and the evacuation of Philadelphia by *Clinton*,
who had succeeded Howe. Washington, who had spent the winter
at Valley Forge (p. 229), instantly followed, and overtaking Clinton
at Monmouth fought and won the battle at that place (June 29th,
1778). Clinton escaped to New York, and Washington, drawing his
army in a circle about the city from Morristown on the S. to West
Point on the N., awaited further movements.
    Turning towards the Southern States, the British commander now
despatched an expedition which took Savannah and overran the State
of Georgia. The year which followed (1779) is memorable for the
capture of Stony Point by *Anthony Wayne* (p. 148), for the treason
of *Benedict Arnold* (pp. 148, 152), for the execution of *Major John
André* (p. 150), for the capture of the Serapis by *Paul Jones* after
one of the most desperate naval battles on record, and by the failure
of an attempt by the Americans to retake Savannah (p. 351). In
1780 Clinton led an expedition from New York to Charleston, took
the city, swept over South Carolina, and, leaving Cornwallis in command, hurried back to New York. *Gates*, who now attempted to
dislodge the British, was beaten. *Greene*, who succeeded Gates, won
the battle of the Cowpens (Jan. 17th, 1781; p. 335). This victory
brought up *Cornwallis*, who chased Greene across the State of North
Carolina to Guilford Court House (p. 335), where Greene was
beaten and Cornwallis forced to retreat to Wilmington. Moving
southward, Greene was again beaten in two pitched battles, but
forced the British to withdraw within their lines at Charleston
and Savannah.
    Cornwallis meantime moved from Wilmington into Virginia and
took possession of Yorktown. And now Washington, who had long
been watching New York, again took the offensive, hurried across
New Jersey and Pennsylvania, and, while a French fleet closed the
Chesapeake Bay, he besieged Cornwallis by land, till (Oct. 19th,
1781) the British General surrendered (p. 330). This practically
ended the war.
    The Treaty of Peace, in 1783, actually ended it, secured the
independence of the United States and fixed her boundaries, roughly
speaking, as the Atlantic Ocean on the E., the Mississippi on the
W., New Brunswick, the St. Lawrence, and the Great Lakes on the
N., and the parallel of 31° on the S.
    While the war was still raging Congress had framed an instrument
of government, which the States ratified and put in force on Mar. 1st,
1781. This instrument of government which bound the thirteen States

in perpetual union was known as the Articles of Confederation, and established a government as bad as any yet devised by man. There was no executive, no judiciary, and only the semblance of a legislature. The Congress consisted of not more than seven nor less than two delegates from each State; sat in secret session; was presided over by a President elected from its own members; and could not pass any law unless the delegates of nine states assented. It could wage war, make treaties, and borrow money; but it could not lay a tax of any kind whatsoever; nor regulate commerce between the States, or with foreign powers; and was dependent entirely on the liberality of the States for revenue. This defect proved fatal. Inability to regulate foreign commerce by duties stripped the country of its specie. Lack of specie forced the States to issue paper money. Paper money was followed by tender acts and force acts and, in some places, by a violent stoppage of justice by the debtor class. A commercial and financial crisis followed and the people of the States, reduced to desperation, gladly acceded to a call for a national trade convention which met in Philadelphia in May, 1787. The instructions of the delegates bade them suggest amendments to the Articles of Confederation. But the convention, considering the Articles too bad to be mended, framed the Constitution which the people, acting through conventions in the various states, ratified during 1787 and 1788.

On Mar. 4th, 1789, the Constitution became the 'supreme law of the land.' In the first congress no trace of party lines is visible. But the work of establishing government had not gone far when differences of opinion sprang up; when the cry of partial legislation was raised, and the people all over the country began to divide into two great parties, — those who favoured and those who opposed a liberal construction of the language of the Constitution and the establishment of a strong national government. The friends of national government took the name of Federalists, and under the lead of *Alexander Hamilton* who, as Secretary of the Treasury, marked out the financial policy of the administration, they funded the foreign and domestic debt occasioned by the war for independence, assumed the debts incurred by the States in that struggle, set up a national bank with branches, and laid a tax on distilled liquors. Each one of these acts was met with violent opposition as designed to benefit a class, as unconstitutional, and as highly detrimental to the interests of the South. Against the Federalists were now brought charges of a leaning towards monarchy and aristocracy. Great Britain it was said has a funded debt, a bank, and an excise. These things are, therefore, monarchical institutions. But the Federalists have introduced them into the Unitet States. The Federalists, therefore, are aristocrats, monarchists, and monopolists.

Of all who believed these charges, none believed them more sincerely than *Thomas Jefferson*, Secretary of Stade. Seeing in these

c *

acts a wide departure from the true principles of democracy, he set himself to work to organize a party of opposition, and was soon looked up to as the recognized leader of the Federal Republicans. Hardly had the two parties thus been called into existence by difference of opinion on questions of home affairs, when they were parted yet more widely, and the dispute between them intensely embittered by questions of foreign affairs. In 1793 the French Republic declared war against England, and sent a minister to the United States. As the United States was bound to France by the Treaty of Alliance and by a Treaty of Amity and Commerce, and was not bound to Great Britain by any commercial treaty whatever, it seemed not unlikely that she would be dragged unwillingly into the war. But Washington with the advice of his secretaries proclaimed neutrality, and from that time every Republican was the firm friend of France and every Federalist the ally of England. Then began a seven years' struggle for neutrality. France threw open her colonial ports to neutral commerce. Great Britain asserting the 'Rule of the War of 1756', a rule prescribing that no neutral should have, in time of war, a trade it did not have in peace, declared this trade was contraband and seized the ships of the United States engaged in it. The Republicans denounced neutrality and attempted to force a war. The Federalists in alarm dispatched *John Jay*, the Chief Justice, to London with offers of a commercial treaty. England responded and on Feb. 29th, 1796, the first treaty of Amity and Commerce between her and the United States became law. At this France took offence, rejected the new minister (C. C. Pinckney) from the United States, and drove him from her soil; suspended the treaties, insulted a special commission (sent out in the interest of peace), with demands for bribes and tribute, and brought on a quasi-war. Never since the days of Bunker Hill had the country been so stirred as this act of the French Directory stirred it in the summer of 1798. Then was written our national song 'Hail Columbia'. Then was established the department of the Navy. Then, under the cry, 'Millions for defence; not a cent for tribute', went forth that gallant little fleet which humbled the tricolour in the West Indies and brought France to her senses.

With the elevation of Napoleon to the First Consulship came peace in 1800. In that same year the Federalists fell from power never to return. Once in power the Republicans began to carry out the principles they had so long preached. They reduced the National debt; they repealed the internal taxes. They sold the Navy; boldly assaulted the Supreme Court; and in 1811, when the Charter of the National Bank expired, refused to renew it. Their doctrine of strict construction, however, was ruined, when, in 1803, they bought the Province of Louisiana from France and added to the public domain that splendid region which lies between the Mississippi and the Rocky Mountains. At that moment it seemed as if the people were about to enter on a career of unwonted prosperity. But Napoleon suddenly made war on England, and by 1806 the United States was involved in a desperate struggle of nine years both with France and England for commercial independence. Great Britain searched our ships, impressed our sailors, violated the neutrality of our ports, and by the decisions of her admiralty courts and by orders in council sought to ruin our neutral commerce with Europe, unless carried on through her ports and under her license. Napoleon attacked us with his decrees of Berlin and Milan, and sought to ruin our neutral commerce with England. The United States retaliated by means of the Embargo and Nonintercourse, and, in 1812, by declared war.

With the cessation of hostilities, another epoch in our history begins. From the day when Washington proclaimed neutrality in 1793, to the day when the people celebrated, with bonfires and with fireworks, and with public dinners, the return of peace in 1815, the political and industrial history of the United States is deeply affected by the political history of Europe. It was questions of foreign policy, not of domestic policy that divided the two parties, that took up the time of Congress, that raised up and pulled down politicians. But after 1815 foreign affairs sank into insignificance, and for the next thirty years the history of the United States is the history of the political and economic development of the country to the E. of the Mississippi River.

The opposition which the Federalists made to the War completed their ruin. In 1816 for the last time they put forward a presidential candidate, carried three states out of nineteen, and expired in the effort. During the eight years of *Monroe's* administration (1817-1825) but one great and harmonious party ruled the political destinies of the country. This remarkable period has come down to us in history as the 'Era of good feelings'. It was indeed such an era, and so good were the feelings that in 1820 when Monroe was re-elected no competitor was named to run against him. Every State, every electoral vote save one was his. Even that one was his. But the elector who controlled it, threw it away on John Quincy Adams lest Monroe should have the unanimous vote of the Presidential electors, an honour which has been bestowed on no man save Washington.

In the midst of this harmony, however, events were fast ripening for a great schism. Under the protection offered by the commercial restrictions which began with the Embargo and ended with the peace, manufactures had sprung up and flourished. If they were to continue to flourish they must continue to be protected, and the question of free trade and protection rose for the first time into really national importance. The rush of population into the West led to the admission of Indiana (1816), Mississippi (1817), Illinois (1818), Alabama (1819), and Missouri (1820) into the Union, and brought up for serious discussion the uses to be made of public lands lying within them. The steamboat, which had been adopted far and wide, had produced a demand for some improved means of communication by land to join the great water highways of the country and opened the era of internal improvements. The application of Missouri for admission into the Union brought up the question of the admission of slavery to the W. of the Mississippi. A series of decisions of the Supreme Court, setting aside acts of the State legislatures, gave new prominence to the question of State rights.

The Missouri question was settled by the famous Compromise of 1820 (the first great political compromise) which drew the line 36° 30′ from the Mississippi to the 100th Meridian, and pledged all to the N. of it, save Missouri, to freedom. But the others were not to be settled by compromise, and in the campaign of 1824 the once harmonious Republican party was rent in pieces. Each of the four quarters of the Republic put a candidate in the field and 'the scrub-race for the presidency' began. The new manufacturing interests of the East put forward *John Quincy Adams.* The West, demanding internal improvements at public expense, had for its candidate *Henry Clay. William H. Crawford* of Georgia (nominated by a caucus of congressmen) represented the old Republican party of the South. *Andrew Jackson* of Tennessee stood for the new Democracy, for the people, with all their hatred of monopolies and class control, their prejudices, their half-formed notions, their violent outbursts of feeling. Behind none of them was there an organized party. But taking the name of 'Adams men' and 'Clay men', 'Crawford men' and 'Jackson men', the friends of each entered the campaign and lost it. No candidate secured a majority of the electoral college, and the House of Representatives chose John Quincy Adams.

Under the administration of Adams (1825-1829) the men who wished for protection and the men who wished for internal improvements at Government expense united, took the name first of National Republicans and then of Whigs, and, led on by Henry Clay and *Daniel Webster,* carried through the high protection tariffs of 1828 and 1832. The friends of Jackson and Crawford took the name of Democrats, won the election of 1829, and, during twelve years, governed the country. In the course of these years the population of the United States rose to 17,000,000, and the number of states to twenty-six. Steam navigation began on the Ocean; two thousand miles of railroad were built in the land; new inventions came into use; and the social and industrial life of the people was completely revolutionized. The National debt was paid; a surplus accumulated in the Treasury; the sale of public lands rose from $3,000,000 in 1831 to $25,000,000 in 1836; and the rage for internal improvements burned more fiercely than ever. A great financial panic spread over the country; the Charter of the National Bank expired; a hundred 'wild-cat banks' sprang up to take its place; and the question of the abolition of slavery became troublesome.

On the great questions which grew out of this condition of affairs the position of the two parties was well defined. The Democrats demanded a strict construction of the Constitution; no internal improvements at public expense; a surrender of the public lands to the state in which they lay; no tariff for protection; no National Bank; no agitation of the question of abolition of slavery; the establishment of sub-treasuries for the safe keeping of the public funds, and the distribution of the surplus revenue. The Whigs demanded a re-charter of the National Bank; a tariff for protection; the expenditure of the surplus on internal improvements; the distribution of the money derived from the sale of public lands; a limitation of the veto power of the President; and no removals from office for political reasons.

The Democrats, true to their principles, and having the power, carried them out. They destroyed the Bank; they defeated bill after bill for the construction of roads and canals; they distributed $ 38,000,000 of the surplus revenue among the states, and, by the cartage of immense sums of money from the East to the far distant West, hastened that inevitable financial crisis known as the 'panic of 1837'. Andrew Jackson had just been succeeded in the Presidency by *Martin Van Buren* (1837-1841) and on him the storm burst in all its fury. But he stood it bravely, held to a strict construction of the Constitution, insisted that the panic would right itself without interference by the Government, and stoutly refused to meddle. Since the refusal of Congress to re-charter the Bank of the United States, whose charter expired in 1836, the revenue of the Government had been deposited in certain 'pet banks' designated by the Secretary of the Treasury. Every one of them failed in the panic of 1837. Van Buren therefore recommended 'the divorce of Bank and State', and after a struggle of three years his friends carried the 'sub-treasury' scheme in 1840. This law cast off all connection between the State Banks and the Government, put the collectors of the revenue under heavy bonds to keep the money safely till called for by the Secretary of the Treasury, and limited payments to or by the United States to specie.

The year 1840 was presidential year and is memorable for the introduction of new political methods; for the rise of a new and vigorous party; and for the appearance of a new political issue. The new machinery consisted in the permanent introduction of the National Convention for the nomination of a president, now used by the Democrats for the second time, and by the Whigs for the first; in the promulgation of a party platform by the convention, now used by the Democrats for the first time; and in the use of mass meetings, processions, songs, and all the paraphernalia of a modern campaign by the Whigs. The new party was the Liberty Party and

the new issue the 'absolute and unqualified divorce of the General
Government from slavery, and the restoration of equality of rights
among men'. The principles of that party were: slavery is against
natural right, is strictly local, is a state institution, and derives no
support from the authority of Congress, which has no power to set
up or continue slavery anywhere; every treaty, every act, establishing, favouring, or continuing slavery in the District of Columbia,
in the territories, on the high seas is, therefore, unconstitutional.

The candidate of this party was *James Gillespie Birney*. The
Democrats nominated Martin Van Buren. The Whigs put forward
William Henry Harrison and elected him. Harrison died one month
after his inauguration, and *John Tyler*, the Vice-President, and a
Democrat of the Calhoun wing became president. The Whig policy
as sketched by Clay was the repeal of the sub-treasury act; the
charter of a National Bank; a tariff for protection; and the distribution of the sales of public lands. To the repeal of the sub-
treasury act Tyler gladly assented. To the establishment of a bank
even when called 'Fiscal Corporation', he would not assent, and,
having twice vetoed such bills, was read out of the party by a
formal manifesto issued by Whig Congressmen. It mattered little
however, for the question of the hour was not the bank, nor the
tariff, nor the distribution of the sales of lands, but the annexation
of the Republic of Texas. Joined to the demand for the re-occupation
of Oregon, it became the chief plank in the Democratic platform
of 1844. The Whig platform said not a word on the subject, and
the Liberty Party, turning with loathing from the cowardice of
Clay, voted again for Birney, gave the State of New York to the
Democrats, and with it the presidency. Accepting the result of the
election as an 'instruction from the people', Congress passed the
needed act and Tyler in the last hours of his administration declared
Texas annexed.

The boundary of the new State was ill-defined. Texas claimed
to the Rio Grande. Mexico would probably have acknowledged the
Nueces River. The United States attempted to enforce the claim of
Texas, sent troops to the Rio Grande, and so brought on the Mexican War. At its close the boundary of the United States was carried
to the S. from 42° to the Gila River, and what is now California,
Nevada, Arizona, New Mexico, Utah, and more than half of Wyoming and Colorado were added to the public domain. While the
war was still raging, *Polk*, who had succeeded Tyler, asked for
$ 2,000,000 to aid him in negotiating peace. Well knowing that
the money was to be used to buy land from Mexico, *David Wilmot*
moved in the House of Representatives that from all territory bought
with the money slavery should be excluded. This was the famous
Wilmot proviso. It failed of adoption and the territory was acquired in
1848, with its character as to slavery or freedom wholly undetermined.

And now the old parties began to break up. Democrats who

believed in the Wilmot proviso, and Whigs who detested the annexation of Texas, the war with Mexico, and the extension of slavery went over in a body to the Liberty Party, formed with it the 'Freesoil Party', nominated Martin Van Buren, and gave him 300,000 votes. In their platform they declared that Congress had no more power .to make a slave than to make a king; that they accepted the issue thrust on them by the South; that to the demand for more slave states and more slave territories they answered, no more slave states, no more slave territories; and that on their banner was inscribed 'Free Soil, Free Speech, Free Labor, and Free Men'. As the defection of Whigs to the Liberty Party in 1844 gave New York State to the Democrats and elected Polk, so the defection of Democrats to the Free Soilers in 1848 gave New York to the Whigs and elected *Taylor*. As Harrison, the first Whig President, died one month after taking office, so Taylor, the second Whig President, died suddenly when a little over one year in office, just as the great Whig Compromise of 1850 was closing. The imperative need of civil government in the new territory, the discovery of gold in California, the rush of men from all parts of the earth to the Pacific Coast forced Congress to establish organized territories. The question was shall they be opened or closed to slavery? But, as the soil had been free when acquired from Mexico, the question really was shall the United States establish slavery? The Democrats, holding that slaves were property, claimed the right to take them into any territory, and asserting the principle of squatter sovereignty', claimed the right of the people living in any territory to settle for themselves whether it should be slave or free. The Free Soilers demanded that the soil having been free when a part of Mexico should be free as a part of the United States. Between these two Clay now stepped in to act as pacificator. Taking up the grievances of each side, he framed and carried through the measure known as the Compromise of 1850, the third great political Compromise in our history. The fruit of this was the admission of California, as a free state; the passage of a more stringent law for the recovery of fugitive slaves; the abolition of the slave tradein the District of Columbia; and the organization of Utah and New Mexico on the basis of 'squatter sovereignty'. This done, Senators and Representatives of all parties joined in a manifesto, declaring that the issues resting on slavery were dead issues, and that they would neither vote for, nor work for any man who thought otherwise. But thousands did think otherwise. The action of Clay pleased none. Anti-slavery men deserted him in the North; pro-slavery men deserted him in the South; and in 1852 the Whig party carried but four states out of thirty-one and perished. Even its two great leaders Clay and Webster were, by that time, in their graves.

Excited by such success the Democrats, led on by *Stephen A. Douglass*, now broke through the compromise of 1820 and in

1854 applied 'squatter sovereignty' to the organization of the territories of Kansas and Nebraska. Against this violation State legislatures, the people, the pulpit, and the press protested vigorously, for every acre of Kansas and Nebraska lay to the N. of 36° 30′ and was solemnly pledged to freedom. But the Democratic leaders would not listen and drove from their ranks another detachment of voters. The effect was soon manifest. The little parties began to unite and when, in 1856, the time came to elect another President, the Republican party of to-day was fully organized and ready. Once more and for the last time for 28 years the Democrats won. The administration of *James Buchanan* (1567-1861) marks an epoch. The question before the country was that of the extension of slavery into the new territories. Hardly had he been inaugurated when the Supreme Court handed down a decision on the case of Dred Scott, which denied the right of Congress to legislate on slavery, set aside the compromises of 1820 and 1850 as unconstitutional, and opened all the territories to slavery. From that moment the Whig and Democratic parties began to break up rapidly till, when 1860 came, four parties and four presidential candidates were in the field. The Democratic party, having finally split at the National Convention for nominating a president and vice-president, the southern wing put forward *Breckenridge* and *Lane* and demanded that Congress should protect slavery in the territories. The northern wing nominated *Stephen A. Douglass* and declared for squatter sovereignty and the Compromise of 1850. A third party, taking the name of 'Constitutional Union', declared for the Constitution and the Union at any price and no agitation of slavery, nominated *Bell* and *Everett*, and drew the support of the old Whigs of the Clay and Webster school. The Republicans, declaring that Congress should prohibit slavery in the territories, nominated *Abraham Lincoln* and *Hannibal Hamlin* and won the election.

The State of South Carolina immediately seceded and before the end of Feb. 1861, was followed by Georgia, Florida, Alabama, Mississippi, Louisiana, and Texas. Taking the name of the Confederate States of America they formed first a temporary and then a permanent government, elected *Jefferson Davis* President, raised an army, and besieged Fort Sumter in Charleston Harbour. The attempt to relieve the fort brought on the bombardment and surrender (April 19th, 1861). The Confederate States were now joined by Virginia, North Carolina, Arkansas, and Tennessee. Richmond was made the capital, and the Civil War opened in earnest.

The line of separation between the States then became the Potomac River, the Ohio River, and a line across S. Missouri and Indian Territory to New Mexico. Along this line the troops of the Union were drawn up in many places under many commanders. Yet there were in the main but three great armies. That of the E. or Potomac under *Gen. McClellan*; that of the centre or the Ohio under *Gen. Buell*; that of the W. or Missouri under *Gen. Halleck*.

In command of all as Lieutenant-General was *Winfield Scott*. Confronting them were the troops of the Confederacy, drawn up in three corresponding armies: that of N. Virginia under *Johnston* and *Lee*, that of the Cumberland under *Albert Sidney Johnston*, and that of the trans-Mississippi under *McCulloch* and *Price*.

Yielding to the demand of the North for the capture of Richmond before the Confederate congress could meet there (July 20, 1861), *McDowell* went forth with thirty-eight thousand three-months volunteers to the ever memorable field of Bull Run (p. 334). But the serious campaigning did not begin until Jan., 1862. Then the whole line west of the Alleghenies (made up of the armies of Ohio and the Missouri), turning on Pittsburg as a centre, swept southward, captured Forts Henry and Donelson, defeated the Confederates at Shiloh (p. 343), captured Corinth (p. 343), took Island No. 10 (p. 324), and drove them from Fort Pillow. Meantime *Farragut* entered the Mississippi from the Gulf (see p. 368), passed Forts Jackson and St. Phillip, captured New Orleans, and sent Commodore Davis up the river to take Memphis. Memphis fell June 6th, 1862, and, save for Vicksburg, the Mississippi was open to navigation. When the year closed the Confederates had been driven to the E. into the mountains of Tennessee, where (Dec. 31st, 1862-Jan. 2nd, 1863) was fought the desperate and bloody battle of Murfreesboro'. The Union troops won, and the Confederate army fell back to Chattanooga (p. 342).

With the Army of the Potomac meantime all had gone ill. The affair at Bull Run in July, 1861, had been followed by the transfer of the army to McClellan. But McClellan wasted time, wore out the patience of the North, and forced Lincoln to issue General Order No. 1 for a forward movement of all the armies on Feb. 22nd, 1862. Obedient to this McClellan began his 'Peninsula Campaign' against Richmond, was out-generaled by Lee, and in the second battle of Bull Run (p. 334) suffered so crushing a defeat that Lee ventured to cross the Potomac, enter Maryland, and encounter McClellan on the field of Antietam (p. 338). In that battle Lee was beaten and fled across the Potomac. But McClellan failed to follow up the victory and was removed, the command of the Army of the Potomac passing to *Burnside*. Burnside led it across the Potomac and the Rappahannock and on Dec. 13th, 1862, lost the battle of Fredericksburg (p. 326). For this he was replaced by *Hooker*, who May 1st-4th, 1863, fought and lost the battle of Chancellorsville (p. 326). Lee now again took the offensive, crossed the Potomac, entered Pennsylvania, and at Gettysburg met the Army of the Potomac under *Meade* (p. 326). On that field was fought the decisive battle of the war. Then (July 1st-4th, 1863) the backbone of the Confederacy was broken, and the two armies returned to their old positions in Virginia.

While Meade was beating Lee at Gettysburg, *Grant* captured

Vicksburg (July 1st-3rd, 1863; see p. 321). For this he was sent to command the army of *Rosecrans*, then besieged by *Bragg* at Chattanooga (p. 342). Again success attended him and, in Nov., he stormed Lookout Mountain, defeated Bragg in the famous 'Battle above the Clouds' (p. 342), and drove him in disorder through the mountains. For these signal victories he was raised to the rank of Lieutenant-General (in 1864) and placed in command of the Armies of the United States.

That year is memorable for the great march of *Sherman* to the E. from Chattanooga to the sea (p. 351), for the victories of *Sheridan* in the Valley of the Shenandoah (p. 338), for the Wilderness Campaign of Grant (p. 326), the shutting up of Lee in Richmond, and by the re-election of Lincoln. His competitor was *General McClellan*, whom the northern Democrats put foward on the platform that the war was a failure and that peace should be made with the South. In the spring of 1865 came the retreat of Lee from Richmond, and on April 9th, his surrender at Appomattox Court House (p. 333). On April 15th, 1865, Lincoln was assassinated (p. 261), and *Andrew Johnson* became President.

With the succession of Johnson the era of Reconstruction, political and social, begins. The outcome of political reconstruction was the 13th, 14th, and 15th amendments to the Constitution of the United States, the impeachment of Andrew Johnson, and a long list of acts to protect and assist the Freedmen of the South. The outcome of social reconstruction was the rise of the Ku Klux Klan, the passage and use of the Force Act, and the dreadful condition of affairs which ruined the South for a decade.

In the North the effect of such measures was to split the Republican party and put seven Presidential candidates in the field in 1872. One represented the Temperance party; another the Labour party, denouncing Chinese labour and the non-taxation of Government land; a third was the Liberal Republican, demanding union, amnesty, and civil rights, accusing Grant of packing the Supreme Court in the interests of corporations, and calling for a repeal of the Ku Klux Laws. The Liberal Republicans having chosen *Horace Greeley* as their candidate, the Democrats accepted and endorsed him. But he pleased neither party and the discontented Liberals and the discontented Democrats each chose a candidate of their own. The Republicans nominated Grant and elected him. His second term (1873-1877) was the nadir of our politics, both State and National, and ended with the disputed election and the rise of the Independent or 'Greenback Party', demanding the repeal of the Act for the resumption of specie payments and the issue of United States 'greenback' notes, convertible into bonds, as the currency of the country. Double returns and doubtful returns from the S. States put the votes of thirteen electors in dispute. As the House was Democratic and the Senate Republican, the joint rule under which the Electoral votes had been counted since 1865 could not be adopted. A compromise was necessary and on Jan. 29th, 1877, the Electoral Commission of five Senators, five Representatives, and five Judges of the Supreme Court was created to decide on the doubtful returns. Of the fifteen eight were Republicans and seven Democrats, and by a strict party vote the thirteen Electoral votes were given to the Republicans and *Rutherford B. Hayes* declared elected.

The memorable events of his term (1877-1881) were the resumption of specie payments on Jan. 1st, 1879; the passage of the Bland Silver Bill, restoring the silver dollar to the list of coins, making it legal tender, and providing for the coinage of not less than 2,000,000 nor more than 4,000,000 each month; and the rapid growth of the National or Greenback-Labour party. Hayes was followed in 1881 by *James A. Garfield*, whose contest with the Senators from New York over the distribution of patronage led to his assassination by the hand of a crazy applicant for office. *Chester A. Arthur* then became President, was followed in 1885 by *Grover Cleveland*, who was succeeded in 1889 by *Benjamin Harrison*, who was in turn succeeded in 1893 by Grover Cleveland. Thus for the first time in thirty-six years the Democratic party is again in control of the House, the Senate, and the Presidency.

States and Territories of the United States.

States.	Area in sq. M.	Pop. in 1890	States.	Area in sq. M.	Pop. in 1890
1. Alabama	51,540	1,513,017	28. New York	47,620	5,997,853
2. Arkansas	53,045	1,128,179	29. North Carolina	48,580	1,617,947
3. California	155,980	1,208,130	30. North Dakota	70,195	182,719
4. Colorado	103,645	412,198	31. Ohio	40,760	3,672,316
5. Connecticut	4,845	746,258	32. Oregon	94,560	313,767
6. Delaware	1,960	168,493	33. Pennsylvania	44,985	5,258,014
7. Florida	54,240	391,422	34. Rhode Island	1,085	345,506
8. Georgia	58,980	1,837,353	35. South Carolina	30,170	1,151,149
9. Idaho	84,290	84,385	36. South Dakota	76,850	328,808
10. Illinois	56,000	3,826,351	37. Tennessee	41,750	1,767,518
11. Indiana	35,910	2,192,404	38. Texas	262,290	2,235,523
12. Iowa	55,475	1,911,896	39. Vermont	9,135	332,422
13. Kansas	81,700	1,427,096	40. Virginia	40,125	1,655,980
14. Kentucky	40,000	1,858,635	41. Washington	66,880	349,390
15. Louisiana	45,420	1,118,587	42. West Virginia	24,645	762,794
16. Maine	29,895	661,086	43. Wisconsin	54,450	1,686,880
17. Maryland	9,860	1,042,390	44. Wyoming	97,575	60,705
18. Massachusetts	8,040	2,238,943			
19. Michigan	57,430	2,093,889	**TERRITORIES.**		
20. Minnesota	79,205	1,301,826			
21. Mississippi	46,340	1,289,600	Arizona	112,920	59,620
22. Missouri	68,735	2,679,184	New Mexico	122,460	153,593
23. Montana	145,310	132,159	Oklahoma	38,830	61,834
24. Nebraska	76,840	1,058,910	Utah	82,190	207,905
25. Nevada	109,740	45,761			
26. New Hampshire	9,005	376,530	District of Columbia	60	230,392
27. New Jersey	7,455	1,444,933	Alaska	531,410	31,795

Total: 3,501,410 62,654,045

Presidents of the United States.

1. George Washington 1789-97.	13. Millard Fillmore 1850-53.
2. John Adams 1797-1801.	14. Franklin Pierce 1853-57.
3. Thomas Jefferson 1801-1809.	15. James Buchanan 1857-61.
4. James Madison 1809-17.	16. Abraham Lincoln 1861-65.
5. James Monroe 1817-25.	17. Andrew Johnson 1865-69.
6. John Quincy Adams 1825-29.	18. Ulysses S. Grant 1869-77.
7. Andrew Jackson 1829-37.	19. Rutherford B. Hayes 1877-81.
8. Martin Van Buren 1837-41.	20. James A. Garfield 1881.
9. William H. Harrison 1841.	21. Chester A. Arthur 1881-85.
10. John Tyler 1841-45.	22. Grover Cleveland 1885-89.
11. James K. Polk 1845-49.	23. Benjamin Harrison 1889-93.
12. Zachary Taylor 1849-50.	24. Grover Cleveland 1893-97.

X. Constitution and Government of the United States
by James Bryce,
Author of 'The American Commonwealth'.

The United States form a Federal Republic — that is to say, a Republic created by the union of a number of separate commonwealths, each of which retains some powers of government though it has yielded others to the Federation as a whole. The circumstances under which this Union took place have been already described in the historical sketch. It was established by the adoption of an instrument called the Constitution drafted by a Convention which met at Philadelphia in 1787, accepted and ratified by the (then 13) States in the years 1788-91. The Constitution prescribes (1) the structure of the Federal Government and the respective functions of its several parts, (2) the powers of the Federal Government and restrictions imposed upon it, (3) the relations of the Federal Government to the States and of the States to one another, (4) certain restrictions imposed upon the States. It does not specify the powers of the States, because these are assumed as pre-existing; the States when they created the Federal Government having retained for themselves most of the powers which they previously enjoyed.

The Constitution is the supreme law of the land, binding everywhere upon all authorities and persons. It can be altered in either of two ways: (a) The Federal Legislature may by a two-thirds vote in each of the two Houses prepare amendments and send them to the States. If ratified by the State Legislatures or by Conventions (*i.e.* assemblies elected by the people for the purpose) in three-fourths of the States, they take effect and become part of the Constitution. (b) The legislatures of two-thirds of the States may require the Federal Legislature to call a Constitutional Convention to prepare amendments to the Constitution. These amendments when ratified by three-fourths of the State Legislatures or State Conventions (as the case may be), take effect as parts of the Constitution. Fifteen amendments have been actually made, all drafted by the Federal Legislature and ratified by the State Legislatures. As the States created the Federation and as they still exercise most of the ordinary functions of government, it is convenient to describe them first.

The States and their Government. There are now 44 States in the Union. Although differing very greatly in size, population, and character, they have all of them the same frame of government. In all of them this frame is regulated by a constitution which each State has enacted for itself and which, being the direct expression of the popular will, is the supreme law of the State, binding all authorities and persons therein. Such a constitution always contains a so-called Bill of Rights, declaring the general principles of the government and the primordial rights of the citizen, and usually contains also a great number of administrative and financial regulations belonging to the sphere of ordinary law. The habit has grown up of late years of dealing, by means of these instruments, with most of the current questions on which public opinion calls for legislation. These constitutions are frequently changed by amendments which (in most States) are passed by the Legislature by certain prescribed majorities and then submitted to the vote of the people. When it is desired to make an entirely new constitution a special body called a Convention is elected for the purpose, and the instrument drafted by it is almost invariably submitted to the people to be voted upon.

State Governments. The Legislature. In every State the Legislature consists of two bodies, both alike elected by the people, though in districts of different sizes. The smaller body (whose members are elected in the larger districts) is called the Senate and varies in number from 9 to 51. The larger body is usually called the Assembly or House of Representatives and varies in number from 21 to 321. The suffrage has now everywhere been extended to all adult males who have resided in a certain (usually a short) period within the State. In one State (Wyoming) it is enjoyed by women also and in several women vote at municipal or school committee elections. The Senate is usually elected for four years — sometimes, however, for three, two, or even one. The House is usually elected for two years. Both Houses have similar powers, save that in most States Money Bills must originate in the House of Representatives. The powers of these Legislatures are limited, and in the case of the newer constitutions very strictly limited, by the State Constitution. If they pass any statute contravening its provisions, or infringing any of the restrictions it has imposed, such a statute is void. All members of State Legislatures are paid, usually at the rate of about $5 a day. They are generally required by law and almost invariably required by custom to be resident in the district from which they are chosen.

These legislative bodies are not greatly respected, nor is a seat in them greatly desired by the better class of citizens. In a few States, such as New York, Pennsylvania, and Louisiana, there is a pretty large proportion of corrupt members.

The State Executive. In every State the head of the Executive is the Governor, elected by popular vote for a term of (rarely one) usually two, three, or even four years. He receives a salary of from $1000 to $10,000. He is responsible for the execution of the laws and the maintenance of order in the State, whose militia he commands. He has, except in four States, the right to veto any bill passed by the Legislature, but the bill may be re-passed over his veto by a majority (usually two-thirds) in both Houses. He is assisted by a Secretary of State and several other officials, who, however, are not named by him but elected directly by the people.

The State Judiciary. In eight States the Judges are appointed by the governor; in all the rest they are elected either by the people or (in five States) by the State Legislature for terms varying, for the Superior judges, from two to twenty-one years, eight to ten years being the average. In four, however, they hold for life. Their salaries range from $2000 to $10,000 per annum, but in most states do not exceed $5000. Such salaries, coupled with the uncertainty of re-election, have been found too small to attract the best legal talent, and complaints are often made that the Bench is not as strong as the Bar which practises before it. Corruption, however, is rare, especially among the judges of the higher courts. There have not been more than three or four States in which it has been proved to exist, and in some of these it does not exist now. It is, of course, the function of the Courts to determine, when a case comes before them, the validity or invalidity of a State Statute which is alleged to transgress any provision of the State Constitution. Very frequently they are obliged to declare such statutes to be unconstitutional; and in this way the Legislature is effectively restrained from destroying the securities which the Constitution provides.

Local Government, Rural and Urban. The organization of local government is within the province of State Legislation and there are many differences between the systems in force in different States. As regards the cities (the term applied in America to any municipality) the scheme of government is usually as follows.

There is always a Mayor, the head of the executive, elected for one, two, or three years, receiving a substantial salary, and charged with the maintenance of order and general oversight of municipal affairs. There is always a legislature, consisting either of one or of two representative bodies elected for short terms, generally in wards, and (in most cases) receiving salaries. The other officials, including the police justices and local civil judges, are either elected by the people or appointed by the Mayor, with or without the concurrence of the Legislature. The tendency of late years has been to vest larger and larger powers in the Mayor. In some cities there is a distinct board of Police Commissioners (sometimes appointed by the State), and in most the management of the Public Schools is kept distinct from the rest of the municipal government and given to a separately elected School Committee.

As regards Rural Government two systems may be distinguished, in the one of which the township, in the other the county, is the administrative unit.

The township, called in the New England States the Town, is a small district corresponding roughly to the Commune of France, or the Gemeinde of Germany. Its area is in the Western States usually 6 sq. M. and its average population from 500 to 2000. Its inhabitants choose annually a small number (usually six or seven) officials, who manage all local affairs, roads, police, poor relief, and (in some States) sanitary matters, collect local taxes for these purposes, and also choose one or more local justices. In the New England States and in most parts of the West the inhabitants are accustomed to meet at least once in spring, in some places several times a year, to receive the reports of their officers, vote the taxes, and pass resolutions upon any other business that may be brought before them. This gathering is called the Town Meeting. Schools are usually managed by a separate School Committee, but sometimes by the township officers.

Above the township stands the county, whose area averages (in the Western States) 5-600 sq. M. In the older States it is usually smaller. Its business is administered by a board of (usually) three to five persons, elected annually and receiving small salaries. The county has charge of prisons, lunatic asylums, main roads, and in some States of the alms-houses provided for relief of the poor. In other States this function is left to the townships, which administer a little out-door relief. Pauperism is not a serious evil except in the large cities; in most rural districts it scarcely exists.

This Township and County System prevails over all the Northern and Middle States and is on the whole purely and efficiently administered.

In the other parts of the Union, i.e. in all or nearly all of the former Slave States, there are no townships; the unit of government is the county, to whose yearly elected officers all local business whatever is intrusted. The Southern counties are generally somewhat larger but not more populous than those of the Northern States. Local government is altogether less developed and less perfectly vitalised in this part of the country, but within the last twenty years sensible progress has been made — least, of course, in the districts where the coloured population is largest, such as Louisiana, Mississippi, and South Carolina. Townships are beginning to appear in some States and the growth of education makes the School Districts and Committees an important factor in giving the people interest in local affairs.

The Americans are as a rule well satisfied with their system of rural local government, which in many respects might serve as a model to Europe, being more free and popular than that of Germany or France or Italy, more complete than that of England. With their municipal government on the other hand the liveliest discontent exists. The larger cities especially have in most cases fallen into the hands of unscrupulous gangs of adventurers, commonly known as Rings, who monopolise the offices and emoluments, job the contracts for public works, incur large debts for the city, and in some few cases enrich themselves by plundering the public funds, while occasionally securing impunity by placing their creatures and dependents in judicial posts.

Many attempts have been made to bring about reforms by changing the frame of municipal government, but so far no great success has been attained. The root of the evil seems to lie partly in the presence in these great cities of a vast multitude of ignorant voters — mostly recent immigrants from Europe — who, since they pay little or no direct taxation, have no interest in economy; and partly in the indifference of the better class of citizens, who are apt to neglect the duty of voting at municipal elections, or when they do vote condone the faults of a Ring which professes to belong to their own political party. The smaller cities, down to those with a population of from 8000 to 10,000, present similar though less glaring faults; and on the whole it may be said that municipal government is the one conspicuous failure of American democracy.

Distribution of Powers between the States and the Federal Government. When the people of the United States created the Federal Government by the adoption of the Constitution, the States retained in their own hands all power, authority, and jurisdiction which was not delegated to the Federal Government. Accordingly the field of State action remains not only wide but undefined. It includes the maintenance of law and order within the State, control of the State militia and police, the organization of local government both urban and rural. The whole field of ordinary law as well civil as criminal, comprising the law of marriage and other family relations, of property and inheritance, of contracts and torts, of offences at common law or otherwise, is within the scope of State legislation. So also is the law relating to trade within the State, including the law of corporations and the regulation of railways and canals, as well as the control of education, charities, the care of the poor, and matters pertaining to religion. The State courts have of course a jurisdiction commensurate with the sphere of State legislation; *i.e.* they try all causes arising under State law and punish all offences against it. The State has also an unlimited power of taxing all persons and property (except as hereinafter mentioned) within its area, of borrowing money, and of applying its funds as it pleases.

The powers and jurisdiction of the Federal Government on the other hand are restricted, being those, and no others, which have been either expressly or by implication conferred upon it by the Federal Constitution. They therefore admit of being specified and are the following.

Control of the Conduct of War.   Post Offices and Post Roads.
Relations with Foreign States.   Patents and Copyright.
Offences against International Law.   Duties of Custom and Excise.
Army and Navy.   Coinage and Currency; Weights and
Commerce with other Countries and   Measures.
    between the States.   Naturalization;
with the power of imposing and inflicting penalties for offences connected
with the matters foregoing.

On all these subjects the Federal Legislature has the exclusive
right of legislating, and the Federal Executive and Judiciary have,
of course, the right and duty of enforcing such legislation. There are
also a few subjects, including bankruptcy, which the Federal Legislature may deal with, but which, if left untouched by Federal
Statutes, State legislation may regulate. There was at one time a
uniform Federal bankrupt law; at present there is none, and the
matter is regulated by each State in its own way.

Besides this allotment and division of power, the Constitution
imposes certain restrictions both on the Federal Government and
on the State Governments. The former is disabled from suspending
the writ of *habeas corpus* or passing an *ex post facto* law, from
abridging the freedom of speech or of the press, or the right of
bearing arms, from making certain changes in legal procedure, from
giving any commercial preference to any particular State, from establishing or prohibiting any religion. Each State, on the other hand,
is restrained from making any treaty or taking other international
action; from coining money or making anything but gold or silver
coin legal tender; passing any *ex post facto* law or law impairing the
obligation of contracts; setting up any but a republican form of Government; maintaining slavery; denying the right of voting in respect
of race, colour, or previous condition of servitude; abridging the privileges of a U. S. citizen or denying to any person within its jurisdiction the equal protection of the laws; depriving any person of life,
liberty, or property without due process of law. Neither can any
State, except with the consent of the Federal Legislature, impose any
duty on exports or imports, or keep ships of war or troops (except
its own militia) in time of peace.

Where there is a doubt as to whether a particular power is
possessed by one or other authority, the legal presumption is in
favour of its being possessed by a State, because the original States
were all of them self-governing commonwealths with a general power
over their citizens; while the legal presumption is against the Federal
Government, because the powers it has received have been enumerated in the Federal Constitution. However it is not deemed necessary
that these powers should have been all expressly mentioned. It is
sufficient if they arise by necessary inference.

Structure of the Federal Government. The Federal Government
consists of three departments or organs, which the Constitution has
endeavored to keep distinct: *viz.*, the Legislature, the Executive, and
the Judiciary. The powers of these three extend over every part of

d *

the country alike, but of course touch those matters only which lie
within the purview and competence of the Federal Government.
The Legislature. The Federal Legislature, called Congress, consists
of two chambers — the Senate and the House of Representatives. The
Senate is composed of two persons from each State : *i.e.*, at present
of 88 persons, and is presided over by the Vice-President of the
United States. Senators are chosen in each State by the legislature
thereof, a circumstance which has largely contributed to cause those
bodies themselves to be elected on the lines of the great national
parties. Each senator sits for six years, and one-third of the body go
out of office every two years, being of course re-eligible. The Senate,
besides its legislative powers, which are equal to those of the House
(except in one point, *viz.* : that Money Bills must originate in the
House), has also two important executive powers. One of these is
the right of approving or rejecting nominations to office made by the
President, a right which is freely exercised except as regards Cabinet
offices, which custom leaves entirely within the President's discretion. The other is the power of approving treaties, which must be
submitted by the President to the Senate and are not valid until
ratified by a majority of two-thirds of the Senators present. The Senate
has also the judicial power of sitting as a High Court to try impeach-
ments preferred by the House of Representatives against the President
or any other of the great officials, including the Federal Judges. When
the Senate sits in this capacity the Chief Justice of the United States
presides. A majority of two-thirds is required for conviction. Andrew
Johnson is the only President who has ever been impeached (1867),
and in his case the requisite majority was not obtained.

The post of Senator, being dignified, powerful, and comparatively
permanent, is much sought after and is indeed the chief object of
ambition to successful members of Congress or pushing State politicians. It is these attractions rather than the method of indirect election by the State legislatures, which have drawn so much political
ability into the Senate. At present many of the Senators are men of
great wealth and some of them are accused of having made their way
into it chiefly by their wealth, the State legislatures being not infre-
quently open to this kind of influence. It has often been proposed
to vest the election directly in the people of each State, and probably
this would be a better method than the present. Although the States
differ vastly in size and importance, the Senators from the small States
exert as much influence as those from the greatest, being indeed
often superior in ability to the latter.

The House of Representatives consists at present of 356 persons
elected by districts of nearly equal size, the boundaries of the districts being in each State determined by State legislation. The members are elected for two years, elections being always held in the
November of a year bearing an even number; *e.g.* 1892, 1894, 1896.
Members are almost invariably chosen from the district in which

they reside. Like the Senators, they receive a salary of $ 5000 a year, besides mileage (travelling expenses). They are (especially in the North and West) less frequently re-elected than is the case with Senators; and it generally happens that about one-half of the members of each House have not sat in the preceding House. Usually more than half of the members belong to the legal profession, though many of these do not practise law. Although elected in November, a new House does not come into existence till the 4th March following and is seldom summoned by the President to meet until the December of the same year. The first function of a House is to choose its Speaker, who always belongs to the majority and is permitted to use all the functions of the Chair in the interests of his party. Having a large control over the conduct of business and the function of nominating all the committees of the House and assigning to each its chairman, his power is very great. All bills are referred after second reading, which is given as a matter of course, to one of the standing committees, of which there are usually at least fifty, each of from 3 to 16 members, and if reported back by the committee is considered in committee of the whole House when time can be found for the purpose. As the number of bills brought into each Congress now reaches or exceeds twenty thousand, many are not reported back, and a great many more are never taken up, or if taken up are not com pleted, by the House. The chairmanships of the chief committees such as those on Ways and Means, Appropriations, Rivers and Harbours, Foreign Relations, and Judiciary, are important posts which carry great influence and are much desired by leading men. There are also a considerable number of select committees appointed from time to time to deal with special questions. (A similar system of Committees prevails in the Senate, where, however, the Committees are appointed not by the presiding officer but by the Senate itself.) The House has a power of closing its debates and coming to a division by voting the 'previous question', and uses this power freely. In the Senate no similar power exists. In each body the presence of one-half of the total number is required to make a quorum.

Both the Senate and the House have the power of holding secret sessions; and this power is frequently exercised by the former, especially when the confirmation of appointments is under consideration.

Although Congress attempts much, it accomplishes comparatively little. The opportunities for delaying business are manifold; there is little recognized leadership, and therefore many cross-currents; the two Houses often differ, throwing out or amending in material points one another's bills. In these conflicts the Senate more often prevails than the House does, because it is a smaller and on the whole a better organized body. There is little direct corruption in either House, but a good deal of demagogism and of what is called 'log-rolling', this form of evil being extended by the enormous number of bills relating to particular persons, places, or undertakings, which are promoted in the interests of private individuals and are pushed by the miscellaneous crowd of unrecognized agents called the 'Lobby'. In each House each of the great parties is in the habit of holding from time to time party meetings to determine its policy in the House, and the decisions of the majority at such meetings are deemed binding on the members and usually obeyed. This is called 'going into caucus'.

The Executive. The President of the United States is chosen by persons who are elected in each State for that purpose and that purpose only. In every State the voters (*i.e.* the same voters as those who elect members of Congress) elect on the first Tuesday in November every fourth year a number of Presidential electors equal to the total representation of the State in Congress (*i.e.* two Senators *plus* so many members of the House of Representatives). Thus New York has 36 Presidential Electors, Pennsylvania 32, Delaware and five other small States only three each. These Electors meet subsequently and vote for the President. Should no person voted for receive a majority of the votes of all the electors appointed, the choice of a President goes over to the House of Representatives, which elects by States, each State having one vote only, and an absolute majority being required. Although it was originally intended that the Presidential electors should be free to choose whatever person they thought best, it has long since become the rule that they shall vote for the candidate nominated by the party which has chosen them as electors; and they are in fact nothing more than a contrivance by which the people, that is, the party which commands a majority of votes, chooses the President. However, as the election takes place by States, and as even a very small popular majority in a particular state can throw the whole electtoral vote of that State for one candidate, while in one or more other States a very large popular majority can do no more than throw the electoral vote of the State for the other candidate, it sometimes happens that the candidate who gets the majority of the electors' votes, and is therefore chosen, has not obtained a majority of the total popular votes cast. Another consequence of this device is that whereas the contest is always very keen in States where parties are equally balanced, it is quite languid where one party is known to have a majority, because the greater or smaller size of that majority makes no difference in the general result over the whole Union. The Presidential electors are now usually chosen by a popular vote all over each State, but they were at one time chosen by the State Legislatures, and also for a time, in many States, by districts. Michigan has recently reintroduced the district plan.

The President must be thirty-five years of age and a native citizen of the United States. He is legally re-eligible any number of times, but custom (dating from George Washington) has established the rule that he must not be re-elected more than once. He receives a salary of $ 50,000 (10,000*l.*).

The President's executive duties are of five kinds:

(a). He is commander-in-chief of the Army and Navy (and of State militia when in Federal service) and commissions all officers.

(b). He appoints all the chief and many minor officials, but the consent of the Senate is required, and is sometimes withheld, except to what are called Cabinet offices.

(c). He has a general supervision over the whole Federal administration and the duty of seeing that the (Federal) laws are duly executed. Should disorder arise anywhere which the State authorities are unable to suppress, they may invoke his aid to restore tranquillity.

(d). He conducts the foreign policy of the nation, and negotiates treaties, which, however, require the approval of the Senate. The power of declaring war rests with Congress.

(e). He may recommend measures to Congress, and has the right, when a bill passed by Congress is sent to him, of returning it with his objections. If in both Houses of Congress it is again passed by a majority of two-thirds in each House, it becomes law notwithstanding his objections; if not, it is lost. This so-called Veto power has been largely exercised, especially by recent Presidents. Between 1884 and 1888 no fewer than 304 bills, most of them private or personal bills, were vetoed, and very few were repassed over the veto.

The Administration or Cabinet consists at present of eight ministers, *viz.*: Secretary of State (who has the conduct of foreign affairs), Secretary of the Treasury (Finance Minister), Secretary of War, Attorney General (Minister of Federal justice as well as legal adviser), Secretary of the Navy, Postmaster General, Secretary of the Interior (with charge of Indian Affairs, of the management of the public lands, and of pensions), Secretary of Agriculture. None of these, nor any other officer of the Government, can sit in Congress. They are appointed and dismissible by the President, and are primarily responsible to him rather than to Congress, which can get rid of them only by impeachment, a process applicable rather to specific offences than to incompetence, and not applicable at all to mere divergence of policy from that which the majority of Congress desires. The Cabinet is therefore something quite different from what is called a cabinet in European countries. It does not relieve the President of responsibility; he may consult it as much or as little as he pleases, and he need not be guided by its advice.

The Federal Judiciary. There are four sets of Federal Courts:

(a). The District Courts, 55 in number, in which the District Judges sit, receiving salaries of $ 5000.

(b). The Circuit Courts, held in the nine judicial circuits, and served by the Circuit judges, now 18 in number (salary $ 6000), together with a judge of the Supreme Court, one such judge being allotted to each circuit.

(c). The Circuit Courts of Appeal, entertaining appeals from the District or Circuit Courts.

(d). The Supreme Court, consisting of a Chief Justice and

eight puisne justices who sit at Washington and have original jurisdiction in cases affecting ambassadors, or where a State is a party to
the suit. In other cases they are a Court of Appeal from inferior
Federal Courts. The salary is $8000 ($8500 for the Chief Justice).
All these judges are appointed by the President with the consent
of the Senate, and hold office for life, unless removed by impeachment. Only four have ever been impeached, and two of these were
acquitted. A place on the Supreme Bench is much desired and
prized; and the permanence of tenure secures a pretty high average
of knowledge and capacity, considering the smallness of the salaries
paid also in the inferior Federal courts.

The jurisdiction of the Federal Courts extends over the whole
Union, but is limited to certain classes of cases, civil and criminal,
the most important whereof are the following.

Cases affecting ambassadors and other foreign ministers, cases of
admiralty and maritime jurisdiction, controversies to which the
United States shall be a party, controversies between States, or
between citizens of different States, or between a State, or any of
its citizens, and any foreign State or its subjects or citizens, cases
arising under the Federal Constitution, or some law or treaty duly
made by the Federal government. If, as frequently happens in the
three last-mentioned sets of cases, the action has begun in a State
Court, there is a full right to have it removed into a Federal Court,
and this may be done even in an action which was supposed to in-
volve questions of State Law only, if in the course of the proceedings
some point of Federal Law arises. The result of these arrangements
is to secure to the Federal Courts the cognizance not only of all international and inter-State questions, but also of all those which in any
way depend upon Federal Legislation. Thus the arm of the National
Government is extended over the whole Union, each Federal Court
having an officer called the U.S. Marshal to execute its judgments,
and being entitled to demand the aid of the local authorities in case
of resistance.

There is nothing special or peculiar in the powers of the Supreme
Court, or of the American Federal Courts generally; nor have they,
as is sometimes supposed, a right to review and annul the acts either
of Congress or of the State Legislatures. The importance of their
functions arises from the fact that in the United States the Constitution is the supreme law of the land everywhere, so that if any
Statute passed by Congress, or any Constitution enacted by a State,
or any Statute passed by a State Legislature, conflicts with the
Federal Constitution, such Statute or State Constitution is as a
matter of law invalid and null, and must be treated as such by all
persons concerned. The authorities whose function it is to ascertain
and determine whether it does or does not conflict with the Federal
Constitution are the Courts of Law; and as the Supreme Federal
Court is the highest court of appeal in all questions involving the

Federal Constitution,' all important and difficult cases are carried
to it and its decision is final. The Courts, and especially the Supreme
Court, of each State exercise a similar function in cases where a
State Statute is alleged to be in conflict with a State Constitution, the
latter, of course, as being a law of higher degree, prevailing against
the former. No court, however, pronounces upon the validity of a
law unless in an action or other regular legal proceeding between
parties, for the decision of which it becomes necessary to settle
whether or no the law is valid. (In a few States, the Governor or
the Legislature may consult the Supreme Court on constitutional
points, but the opinions so given by a Court are not deemed to be
binding like a judgment in an action.) As in all questions of Federal
Law the State Courts are bound to follow and apply the decisions
of the Federal Courts, so also in all questions of State Law, when
these come before a Federal Court, such Court ought to follow and
apply the decisions of the highest court of the particular State in
question. That is to say, the Federal Courts are not higher than the
State Courts, but have a different sphere of action, nor are they,
except as regards questions arising under the Federal Constitution,
called to overrule decisions of the State Courts.

General Working of the Federal Government. The salient feature
of the Federal or national Government is that it consists of three departments, each designed to work independently of the other two.
Thus the Federal Executive, the President and his Ministers, are
independent of Congress. The President is elected (indirectly) by
the people, and cannot be displaced by Congress (except by impeachment). The Ministers are appointed by the President, and cannot
be dismissed by Congress nor even restrained in their action, except
in so far as legislation may operate to restrain them; and as Congress
is debarred from intruding into certain administrative details, its
legislation cannot reach these. The President cannot dissolve Congress, which is elected for a fixed period, and cannot check its
legislation, if there is a majority of two-thirds against him in both
Houses. The conduct of foreign affairs, however, and the making
of appointments belong partly to him and partly to the Senate, so
that in this sphere he and one branch of Congress are closely associated. The third department, the Judiciary, is independent of the
other two, for though its members are appointed by the President
with the consent of the Senate, they cannot be ejected from office
except by impeachment. All these departments are deemed to derive
their respective powers directly from the people, Congress and the
President by election, the Judges from the Constitution which the
people enacted and which it is their duty to interpret. Thus the
principle of Popular Sovereignty is consistently carried out. That
principle is, however, even more conspicuous in the State Governments, because in them not only are all the leading officials directly
elected by the people, and (in the great majority of the States) the

judges also, but also because the people constantly legislate directly (without the intervention of the State Legislatures) by enacting State constitutions or constitutional amendments. Although, however, in this aspect the Federal Government (and still more the State Governments) may appear to be very democratic, the following important restrictions have been provided to prevent sudden or violent change. (a) The Legislature, which is the strongest power, is divided into two coördinate and jealous houses. (b) The Legislature is further restrained by the veto of the President. (c) The Legislature is limited to certain subjects and disabled from certain kinds of action. (d) The President is held in check by Congress, which can refuse money, and by the Senate in foreign affairs and appointments. (e) He has, moreover, only a very small standing army at his disposal.

Conjoint Working of the Federal and State Governments. Although the Federal Government is in constant action by its laws, its oflicials, and its judges over the territory included in the States, comparatively little friction arises between the two sets of authorities. As respects elections, all State elections are conducted under State laws, Federal elections to some extent under Federal laws, so far as these have prescribed certain rules, but chiefly under State laws, because Congress has left many points untouched. As regards finance, all direct taxation is imposed by the State Legislatures, while the Federal Government raises its revenue by duties of customs and excise. The chief difficulties which have been felt of late years are connected with the divergences of law between the different States, especially as regards marriage and divorce, and with the control of commerce and the organs of transportation, especially railroads. The Federal Government can legislate only with regard to trade between the States and to navigable waters within more than one State and railroads so far as they carry traffic between States. Many intricate problems have arisen as to the respective scope of Federal and State action on such matters; but these have, since the Civil War, been peaceably adjusted by the Courts as interpreters of the Constitution.

Extra-State Dominions of the United States. Washington, the capital of the Union, stands in a piece of ground comprising 70 sq. M. which has been set apart as the seat of Federal Government, and is governed by three Commissioners appointed by the President. It is called the Federal District of Columbia. Alaska (purchased from Russia in 1867) is also directly governed by Federal oflicials (named by the President) and by statutes of Congress. As its population consists almost entirely of semi-civilized or savage Indians, it has no share in the government of the Union. The same remark applies to the Indian Territory lying to the W. of the State of Arkansas, where, however, the principal Indian tribes have made great progress in education and settled habits.

There are also four *Territories* (Utah, Arizona, New Mexico, and Oklahoma). The Union is a union of States only, and these districts, still thinly peopled, have not yet been admitted to the dignity of Statehood. Each Territory however enjoys local self-government, having a legislature of two Houses which can pass Statutes, subject, however, to the unrestricted authority of Congress to annul them and legislate directly. In each of these there is a Governor appointed by the President; and part of the law in force has been directly enacted by Congress. Each Territory sends a delegate to the Federal House of Representatives who is allowed to speak but not to vote.

Practical Working of the Government. The Party System. The character of the political institutions of the country has been so largely affected by the political parties that a few words regarding their organization and methods are needed in order to understand the actual working of the Government.

Since the adoption of the Federal Constitution in 1788-9, the people of the United States have been, except for a few years (from about 1818 till 1826), pretty sharply divided into two parties. Occasionally, three or even four parties have appeared; these however have been short-lived. From 1789 till 1818 the two great parties were the Federalists and (Democratic) Republicans; the Federalists then disappeared, while from about 1830 till 1854 the Republicans, now called simply Democrats, were opposed by a party called Whigs. In 1856 a new party who took the name of Republicans came into being, carried the Presidential Election of 1860 and have continued until now contending with the Democrats. Minor present parties are the Prohibitionists and the so-called 'Populists' or People's Party (comp. Section IX of Introd.). Both the two great parties have created and maintain themselves by exceedingly strong and well ordered organizations, existing over the whole country as a body of political machinery far more effective than has ever been seen elsewhere. The causes which have made such machinery necessary are chiefly these three.

Elections are very numerous, because all the chief State and City officials and all members of representative assemblies are chosen by the people and chosen for short terms. Even those official posts which are not directly conferred by popular vote, such as all the Federal offices, are usually held at the pleasure of the President or some other high official, who has for the last sixty years been accustomed to appoint members of his own party to them, dismissing those whom he finds on coming into power, if they belong to the opposite party. The desire to have or to retain these posts furnishes a strong personal motive for exertion on behalf of a party, because one's livelihood may depend upon it. Moreover the social equality which prevails generally in America prevents the masses from being disposed to follow men conspicuous by rank, wealth, or intelligence, and makes it necessary to have organizations in order to supply the absence of that spontaneous allegiance and natural grouping which do much to hold parties together socially in the free countries of the Old World. As there are in the United States comparatively few persons with sufficient leisure to devote themselves to political work from purely public motives, it has been thought necessary that this work should be done by those who have a pecuniary interest in the success of their party; and these persons, making such work their profession, have been able to carry this political machine to an unprecedented point of effectiveness.

In every local area which elects an official or a representative (such as a City Ward or a Rural Township) each of the two great parties has a local association which selects from the resident members of the party a candidate to be run for every elective post or office at the next election. The meeting of the local members of the party which makes this selection is called a Primary Meeting. Where an election is to take place for a wider area (such as a Congressional district or a State Assembly district, or a City) the candidate is selected by a party meeting called a Convention, consisting of delegates from all of the primaries within that area. Where the election is that of the President of the United States, the party candidate is selected by a very large body called the National Nominating Convention, consisting of delegates chosen by Conventions held in the several States. The number of delegates to this greatest of all Conventions is double that of the number of Presidential electors plus two delegates from each Territory, that is to say, it is at present 896.

Very rarely does any candidate offer himself for election to any post unless he has been selected by a Primary or a Convention as the party candidate. Sometimes, however, in local elections (especially in cities) a third organization is created in view of a particular election or group of elections, which nominates what is called an 'Independent' or 'Citizens' candidate, outside the regular organizations of the two great parties. And when a third or fourth party (such as the Prohibitionists or the so-called People's Party) exists, it establishes in that part of the country where it has substantial strength, an organization like that of the Democrats or the Republicans; and nominates its candidates in the same way. Great importance is attached to 'getting the nomination', because a large number of voters in each party are disposed (especially in great cities) to adhere to the candidate whom the organization has chosen, with comparatively little regard either to the precise shade of his opinions or to his intellectual capacity. Great pains are therefore bestowed on securing the nomination, and where there are two local factions within a party, the strife between them over the nomination is often more bitter than that between the hostile parties. Bribery, personation, and even physical violence are sometimes resorted to in order to carry a nomination of delegates in a Primary or of candidates in a Nominating Convention; so that in many States it has been deemed needful to pass laws for regulating these party meetings and preventing corruption or unfairness in connection with them. So, also, when the control of the nomination for the Presidency lies between two prominent and popular party leaders, the Convention is a scene not only of active and pro-tracted intrigue behind the scenes, but of passionate excitement dur-ing the voting.

This system of party machinery, and the habit which the voters have of supporting those candidates only whom the official machine nominates, have become one of the main causes of misgovernment in the largest cities. In those cities there is a large poor and com-paratively ignorant multitude which, since it pays an exceedingly small part of the local taxation, has a very slight interest in econo-mical and prudent administration. It falls easily under the dominion of leaders belonging to its own class who care little for real political issues, but make their living out of the city offices and the op-portunities of enrichment which such offices supply, and it votes blindly for the candidates whom those leaders, through their con-trol of the organization, put forward as the 'regular party candi-dates'. These candidates are, of course, in league with the men who 'run the machine'; and when they obtain office, they reward their supporters by posts in their gift, sometimes also by securing for them impunity from punishment, for in the lower parts of some cities the nominating machinery has fallen into the grasp of cliques which, if not actually criminal, occasionally use criminals as their tools. An-other source of the strength of these dangerous elements in politics has lain in the profuse use of money. Bribery has been not uncommon, both in City, State, Congressional, and Presidential elections. Efforts, however, which seem likely to be successful, have lately been made to repress it by the adoption in nearly all the States of laws creat-ing a really secret ballot. Some States have also sought to limit election expenditure; and it may be said generally that the spirit of reform is actively at work upon all that relates to the election system. Intimidation is rare, except in the Southern States, where it is still occasionally, though much more rarely than twenty years ago, prac-tised upon the negroes. Seeing that the great majority of the negro voters are illiterate and possessed of little political knowledge, white men otherwise friendly to the coloured people justify both this and the more frequent use of various tricks and devices as the only remedies against the evils which might follow the predom nanceof the coloured vote in those States, where the whites are in a minority.

As visitors from Europe, who usually spend most of their time in the great cities, are apt to overestimate these blemishes in the dem-ocratic institutions of the U. S., it is well to observe that they are far from prevailing over the whole country, that they are not a nec-essary incident to democratic institutions but largely due to causes which may prove transitory, and that they do not prevent the govern-ment both of the Nation and of the States from being, on the whole, efficient and popular, conformable to the wishes of the people and sufficient for their needs. — There is no *Established Church* in the United States, nor is any preference given by the law of any State to any one religious body over any other body, although such was formerly the case in the older States, and might be now enacted, so far as the Federal Constitution is concerned, in any State. However all the States have, each for itself, pronounced in favour of absolute religious equality and embodied such a provision in their respective constitutions. When questions relating to the temporalities of any ecclesiastical body or person come before the courts of law, they are dealt with by the ordinary law like other questions of contract and property. Religious feeling seldom enters into political strife, and there is a general desire to prevent its intrusion either in Federal or in State matters.

XI. Aborigines and Aboriginal Remains,

By
Professor O. T. Mason,
of the Smithsonian Institution.

The aboriginal history of the United States divides itself into two chapters, the *Archaeologic* and the *Ethnographic*. The former relates to a period about whose beginning there is much dispute and whose close shades into the latter imperceptibly. The ethnographic chapter opens with the romantic adventures of Ponce de Leon (p. 356) in Florida with the Timucua Indians and is not yet closed.

I. Archæology. The archæologist from abroad will find in the United States no such imposing ruins as meet his eyes everywhere in the Old World. Not even with Mexico or Central America or Peru can the ruins scattered over the Federal Republic enter into competition. The same is true of the age of these relics. It has been both alleged and disputed with vehemence, and that by eminent authorities on both sides, that at Trenton (p. 209), Madisonville and Comerstown in Ohio, Little Falls in Minnesota, Table Mountain in California, and elsewhere, palæolithic man, away back in glacial times, left traces of his existence. But the true remains of antiquity within the borders of the United States are the shell-heaps, bone-heaps, and refuse-heaps; the ancient quarries, workshops, and mines; evidences of primitive agriculture; graves and cemeteries; mounds and earthworks; pueblos, cliff-dwellings, and cave-dwellings; trails, reservoirs, and aqueducts; pictographs and sculptures; relics of ancient arts and industries; crania and skeletons belonging to vanished peoples. And these relate to a grade of culture upon which all advanced races once stood. These remains and relics are quite unevenly distributed over the States, just as populations and industrial centres are scattered to-day.

Shell - Heaps, Bone - Heaps, Refuse - Heaps. Along the Atlantic Coast, up and down the great affluents of the Mississippi, on the shores of the Gulf of Mexico and of the Pacific Ocean, are vast accumulations of shells, left by former savage tribes. Mingled with the

shells are bones of the dead and the apparatus which they used in
their lifetimes. In each locality the mollusks whose remains are
discovered were of those species which still abound in the region. The
most celebrated shell-heaps are found along the New England shores,
in the Chesapeake Bay, throughout Florida, in Mobile Harbour, on
the Tennessee River, at Santa Barbara and San Francisco in California, and about the shallows in Washington State. Bone-heaps are
found on the plains of Dakota and are the remains of ancient buffalo
feasts. The refuse-heaps are all that is left on ancient Indian camp-
sites, and there is scarcely a town in the Union that is not near one
or more of these old habitations of the past.

Quarries, Workshops, and Mines.† The aborigines of the United
States had no other industrial life than that which belongs to the
stone age. They quarried quartz, quartzite, novaculite, jasper, argil-
lite, steatite, catlinite, slate, mica, volcanic rocks, always from the
best sources of the material. The quarrying was, of course, simply
the opening of shallow pits and drifts, by means of the rudests tools
of wood, antler, and bone; and in the exercise of the most rudimentary
engineering. They blocked out the art product at the quarry, leaving millions of spalls and rejected pieces, which resemble somewhat
the so-called palæolithic implements. They manufactured these substances by flaking, chipping, pecking, boring, sawing, and grinding,
using as tools hammers, saws, drills, polishers, etc., of stone and
other materials at hand. Copper abounded in the W. central states,
the raw material coming from Keweenaw and Ontonagon counties,
Michigan. This copper was not smelted, but treated as a stone. It
was cold-hammered on stone anvils with stone hammers, ground
into shape on sandstone, and finished after the manner of a stone
implement.†† All the relics of the ancient Americans of this region
are of the neolithic type, though the tourist will doubtless be told
that this is not true and will be shown all sorts of marvellous things.

Primitive Agriculture.††† Not only are finished implements recovered that must have been used in rude tillage; but, in S. Michigan
especially, the whites found that they had been anticipated. Garden
beds or rows were discovered, where maize, pumpkins, beans, and
other indigenous plants had been cultivated.

Graves and Cemeteries.†††† The best-known antiquities of the

† *Holmes,* Am. Anthropologist, Wash., iii, p. 24, and elsewhere.
 Moorehead, Prim. Man in Ohio, N.Y. 1892, Chap. IV.
†† *Whittlesey,* Smithsonian Contributions, Vol. xiii.
††† American Antiquarian, Vols. 1 and 7.
†††† *Yarrow,* Mortuary Customs. I. Am. Rep. Bur. Ethnol., Wash.,
 pp. 87-204, fig. 1-47.
 Moorehead, Prim. Man in Ohio, N.Y., 1892, Chap. V. See also *Short,*
 N. Americans of Antiquity (Harpers).
 Archaeol. Explor. Lit. & Sc. Soc. of Madisonville, 1879, p. ii; appendix.
 J. Cincin. Soc. Nat. Hist., iii; 1 and 3.
 Thruston, Antiq. of Tennessee.
 Yarrow, in Wheeler, 'Survey W. of 100th Merid.' VII.

United States are the ancient cemeteries, the mounds, and the earth-works. It is very difficult to discover an Indian grave to the E. of the Alleghenies or to the W. of the 100th meridian. Within those limits they occur everywhere. The disposal of the dead was different in all the families of tribes. Inhumation, embalmment, in-urning, surface disposal, aërial sepulture, aquatic burial, cremation, all had their advocates and practitioners. The most celebrated ceme-teries are at Madisonville (Ohio), near Nashville (p. 319), and near Santa Barbara (p. 443).

Mounds and Earthworks. The mound and earthwork region in-cludes W. New York, N. W. Pennsylvania, W. Virginia, N. Carolina, S. Carolina, Georgia, Florida, Alabama, Mississippi, Arkansas, Tennessee, Kentucky, Ohio, Indiana, Illinois, Iowa, E. Missouri, S. Michigan, Wisconsin, and Dakota.

'Within this territory are the copper mines of Lake Superior, the salt-mines of Illinois and Kentucky, the garden beds of Michigan, the pipe-stone quarry of Minnesota, the extensive potteries of Missouri, the stone-graves of Illinois and Tennessee, the workshops, the stone cairns, the stone walls, the ancient roadways, and the old walled towns of Georgia, the hut rings of Arkansas, the shelter caves of Tennessee and Ohio, the mica mines in South Carolina, the quarries in Flint Ridge (Ohio); the ancient hearths of Ohio, the bone beds and alabaster caves in Indiana, the shell-heaps of Florida, oil wells, and ancient mines and rock inscriptions'. [*Peet,* 'The Mound-Builders: their works and their relics' (Chicago; p. 35).]

Both mounds and earthworks are, however, to be seen sparingly everywhere. The largest mounds in the United States are in Illinois, opposite St. Louis (p. 311), and no one should spend a day in that city without taking a trip across the great steel bridge and visiting the *Cahokia Mound* near E. St. Louis. In the neighbourhood are over fifty others of enormous size. In the cemetery at Marietta (p. 269), and at Grave Creek, on the Ohio river, 12 M. below Wheel-ing (p. 266), may be seen mounds of great size.† The most famous tumulus in the United States is the *Great Serpent Mound* (p. 309), which, with the land adjacent, is the property of the Peabody Museum, in Cambridge (p. 84).††

To the E. of the Rocky Mountains, the most interesting remains are the earthworks. And of these there are two sorts, those designed for defence and those erected for ceremonial purposes. The former are found on bluffs and tongues of land with precipitous sides. These natural forts are strengthened by ditch banks and stone heaps and gateways covered within and without by mounds. The latter, on the contrary, are in exposed plains. Their ditch banks are in circles and polygonal figures and the parts are arranged as for religious and social occasions.

Besides those already mentioned the following defensive and ceremo-nial works may be mentioned (all in Ohio): — the Great Mound, at Miamis-burg; Fort Ancient, Warren Co.; the Newark Works; the *Alligator* Mound,

---

† *Putnam*, An. Rep. Peabody Mus., Cambridge, Mass., xii and xiii, pp. ii & 470.

†† *Putnam*, Century Magazin. March and April, 1890.

near Granville; the Stone Fort, near Bourneville; the Fortified Hill in Butler Co.; the Liberty Township Works; and the Hopeton Works.

Consult *Thomas's Catalogue* for full list (Bulletin of the Bureau of Ethnology, Washington); also Smithsonian Contributions, Vol. I.

Pueblos, Cliff-dwellings, and Cave-dwellings. In the drainage of the Colorado and the Rio Grande, within the boundaries of Colorado, Utah, New Mexico, Arizona, and the N. tier of Mexican states are the pueblos and the cliff-dwellings. Twenty-one pueblos along the Rio Grande, between $34^{\circ}\ 45' - 36^{\circ}\ 30'$ N. lat., are still inhabited by two different stocks of Indians, the Tañoan and the Keresan. The Zuñi, residing near the W. border of New Mexico, on the 30th parallel, speak an independent language; and the Moki, on the reservation of the same name, N.E. Arizona (see p. 413), dwelling in seven towns or pueblos, belong to the Shoshonean linguistic stock. Besides these inhabited villages of stone and adobe, there are many hundreds in the territory just named that have long been tenantless, and most of them are in ruins. The largest of them and by far the most imposing ruin within the United States is the *Casa Grande* (see p. 463), or *Casa de Montezuma*, which, Bancroft says, [†] has been mentioned by every writer on American antiquity. The material is adobe made into large blocks. Three buildings are standing, one of them sufficiently preserved to show the original form. The largest collection of ruined pueblos in this region yet examined was surveyed by the Hemenway S.W. Expedition in 1888. The group lies on the Salado river, near the town of Phœnix (p. 463). [††] In the cañon regions bordering and opening into the Colorado river channel, especially upon the San Juan and the Dolores and their tributaries, are to be found cliff and cave dwellings innumerable. These are easily explained by the nature of the geologic formations. In the precipitous walls there are strata of soft stone sandwiched between layers of hard material. The action of the elements has carved out these soft layers, leaving a roof above and a floor below upon which the ancient cliff-dweller built his home. Indeed, he did not wait for the frost and the rain to do the work, but with his pick-axe of hard basalt dug out a cave for himself by making a tiny doorway in the face of the cliff and excavating behind this as many chambers as he pleased. Many of these cliff and cavate habitations are high up and difficult of access, but they overlook long valleys of arable land. [†††] The relics found in this region are the envy of collectors, and the natives still manufacture excellent pottery, to imitate the old. The ancient is far superior in quality to the new, and hundreds of dollars are paid for a single piece, though fragments of the finest ware may be had for the picking up.

Trails, Reservoirs, and Aqueducts. For the purposes of war and

[†] *Bancroft*, Native Races, N. Y., 1875, IV, 621-635.
[††] *Cushing*, in the Compte Rendu of the Berlin meeting of the Society of Americanists.
[†††] *Bancroft*, Native Races, N. Y., 1875, IV. 650-664.

trade the savages traversed the United States from end to end. They had no beasts of burden save the dog, consequently they made portages from stream to stream, carried their canoes and loads across on their backs, and then pursued their journey. The traces of these ancient paths of primitive commerce may yet be seen. In the same rude manner these savages had learned to store up and conduct water for home use and for irrigation. Especially in the South West are the works of this class to be studied.

Pictographs and Sculptures. The very ancient people and their modern representatives had attained to that form of writing called pictographic. The traveller will see in museums all sorts of figures scratched on bark, painted on skin or wood, etched on bone or ivory, engraved on pieces of stone, and he will often come upon the same designs sketched on cliffs and boulders. These constitute the written language of the aborigines. In true sculpture they were not at all adept and they had no alphabetic writing.. Once in a while mysterious bits of stone turn up with Cypriote or other characters thereon, but they never belonged to the civilization of this continent.

Relics of Ancient Art. As before mentioned the native tribes were in the neolithic stone age. Therefore, it is not exaggerating to say that the whole surface of the United States was strewn with relics. In every ancient grave, mound, or ruin they abound. The tourist will have no trouble to find in every town a museum containing these objects and in every hamlet some one whose house is packed with them. So desirable are they that thousands are fraudulently made and palmed off upon the unwary. These spurious objects find their way into foreign collections and very much embarrass the problems of archæology.

Crania and Skeletons. Much difficulty has been encountered by archæologists in distinguishing the crania of the truly prehistoric American from those of the Indians encountered by the early explorers. The problem is further embarrassed by artificial deformations and by changes produced by the pressure of the soil. Excellent collections exist in Cambridge, Philadelphia, Washington, Cincinnati, and St. Louis.[†]

Ethnography. The native tribes that once covered the entire domain of the Union belonged to fifty independent linguistic stocks. Some of these were spread over vast areas, for example, the Algonkian, Athapascan, Iroquoian, Muskhogean, Shoshonean, and Siouan. But the majority of stocks occupied small areas, chiefly along the Pacific coast. [††]

But a wonderful change has come over the surface of the United States in two centuries. Excepting a few small settlements of In-

---

[†] For the best résumé of the literature on the Archæologic Chapter, see *Winsor*, Narr. & Crit. Hist. of Am., I., pp. 329-412 (Boston, 1889).
[††] See exhaustive account in vii. An. Rep. Bur. Ethnol., Wash., 1891, pp. 1-142, with map.

dians here and there, they are gone from the Atlantic States. Only the Cherokees in North Carolina, the Seminoles in Florida, the Iroquois in New York, and the Chippewa tribes about Lake Superior remain to the E. of the Mississippi river. The aboriginal title gave way to the title of discovery, and the feeble Indian title of occupancy has been swept away by the tide of European imigration. There are at present, as regards title and legal status, several kinds of Indians in the Union.

1. Citizen Indians. The State of Massachusetts and the United States in certain cases have conferred upon Indians the full rights of citizenship.

2. In a few states, notably New York, reservations are granted to Indians and they are protected in their tribal rights therein.

3. Roving Indians are still at large in greater or smaller bands, especially in the Rocky Mountain region.

4. In acquiring its S.W. territory from Mexico the United States inherited three kinds of Indians: the Pueblo Indians, the Mission Indians, and the wild tribes. The status of these is most confusing.

5. But the great mass of Indians in the Union are in some sort of relation to the United States and hold their lands by (1) Executive Order, (2) by Treaty or by Act of Congress, (3) by Patent to the tribe, (4) by Patent to individuals.

For the relinquishment of their ancient homes the United States has also entered into agreements to pay to the tribes certain annuities in money and goods. Under these circumstances there are some of them who are the richest communities in the world. In the Osage tribe every man, woman, and child is worth $1500. The five civilized tribes in the Indian Territory and the New York Iroquois preserve their autonomy and make their own laws, but also have a government agent. Many thousand Indians have their lands 'alloted' and thus have lately become citizens, the title to the land being inalienable for 25 year.†

XII. Physiography of North America.

By

N. S. Shaler,

Professor of Geology in Harvard University.

Although the traveller in North America may be most interested in the people or their social and material accomplishments, he will find it desirable at the outset of his journey to consider the physical conditions of the land, the nature of the climate, soil, and under earth: — circumstances which have gone far to determine the history and development of the people who have come to the country from the old world.

The continent of North America is in many ways sharply contrasted with that of Europe. The last-named land consists mainly of great peninsulas and islands, which are geographic dependencies of the great Asiatic field. It is, indeed, a mere fringe of the great Eurasian continent. North America, on the other hand, is a mass of land distinctly separated from other areas, with a relatively undiversified shore, and with an interior country which is but slightly divided into

---

† See Rep. Commn. Ind. Aff. (Wash., 1891) and Thayer in *Atlantic Monthly*, Oct., 1891.

isolated areas by distinct geographic features such as seas or mountain chains. This geographic unity of the N. part of the New World is due, as is the case with all its other conspicuous features, to the geological history of the country; it will therefore be well to preface the account of its detailed features by a very brief description of the steps by which its development was brought about.

In the Laurentian age, the earliest epoch which geologists can trace in the history of the earth, the continent of North America appears to have consisted of certain islands, probably lying in the neighbouring seas beyond the present limits of the land, the positions of which are as yet unknown. In the Cambrian period we find the Laurentian rocks, which were formed on the older sea floors, raised above the ocean level, and constituting considerable islands, the larger of which were grouped about Hudson's Bay, there being smaller isles in the field now occupied by the Appalachian Mountains and in that of the Cordilleras, as we should term those elevations which lie between the E. face of the Rocky Mountains and the ranges which border the Pacific Coast.

From the debris of the ancient islands which prefigured the continent, together with the deposits of organic remains accumulated in the seas, the strata of the Silurian and Devonian ages were formed. These in turn were partly uplifted in dry land, thus adding to the area of the imperfect continent by the growth of its constantly enlarging island nucleus. Yet other marine accumulations, formed in the now shallowed seas, afforded the beginning of the carboniferous strata. The accumulation of these beds and the slow uprising of the land soon brought the continent to a state where there were very extensive low-lying plains forming a large part of what is now the Mississippi Valley, as well as the field now occupied by the Allegheny Mts., which then had not been elevated, and forming a fringe along the E. coast of the continent. On these plains there developed extensive bogs, which from time to time were depressed beneath the level of the sea and buried beneath accumulations of mud and sand, thus affording the beginning of the coal beds which constitute so important a feature in the economic resources of the country.

After the close of the great coal-making time the Allegheny Mountains were uplifted, and the ranges of the Cordilleras begun in earlier times were much increased in extent. From this period of the new red sandstone or Trias, we may fairly date the probable union of the original scattered islands of the continent, which had now taken much the shape it has at present. The great interior sea, the remnant of which now forms the Gulf of Mexico and which in the earlier ages had divided the Cordillerean from the Appalachian lands, still extended as a narrower water far to the N., but in the Jurassic and Cretaceous time, this Mexican Sea shrank away with the uplifting of the land, and its place was occupied by a vast system of fresh water lakes stretching along the E. front of the Rocky Mountains.

These basins endured for many geological periods; they were, however, gradually filled with the detritus from the mountains of the West.

In the Tertiary period, the last great section of geologic time, North America gradually assumed its existing aspect. The Great Lakes before mentioned were gradually filled, the lowlands of the S. states and of the Atlantic coast to the S. of New York rose above the sea, and the mountains of the Cordilleras gained a yet greater measure of elevation. In the closing stages of this Tertiary time there came the glacial epoch, during which the ice sheets, now practically limited to Greenland and Alaska, were extended so as to cover nearly one-half of the continent, the margin of the snowy field being for a time carried as far S. as the Potomac and the borders of the Ohio River at Cincinnati, mantling the region to the N. with an icy covering having a depth of several thousand feet. At this stage of the geological history the N. portion of the land was deeply depressed, while the S. portion was much elevated. When the ice went off, the continent, at least in its E. part, remained for a time at a lower level than at present. Only in what we may term the present geologic day has the continent quite recovered from the singular disturbance of its physical and vital conditions which the ice time brought about.

One of the most important results of the geological history of North America has been the development of this continent to a point where its surface is characterized by certain broad and simple topographic features. It is, indeed, on many accounts, the most typical of the greater land-masses. The eastern and western shores are bordered by tolerably continuous mountain ranges: those facing the Atlantic extend though with various interruptions from Greenland to Alabama; those next the Pacific from the peninsula of Alaska to Central America. South of the Rio Grande these Cordilleras form the attenuated mass of the continent in which lie Mexico and the states of Central America. Between these mountain ranges and the neighbouring oceans there is a relatively narrow belt of plains or low-lying valleys. The principal portion of the continental area, however, lies between these mountain systems in the form of a great shallow trough. The southern half of this basin constitutes the great valley of the Mississippi. Its northern portion is possessed by various river systems draining into the Arctic and Atlantic Oceans, of which the Mackenzie and the St. Lawrence are the most important. The last named river system is peculiar in the fact that it is the greatest stream in the world which is fed mainly from lakes.

If we could contrast this over-brief story of the geological development of North America with a similar account of the leading events which have taken place in Europe, we should readily note the fact that the former land has had a relatively simple history. Fewer mountain systems have been developed upon it, and consequently its shores lack the great peninsulas and islands which are so characteristic a feature in the old world. To this same architectural simplicity we may attribute the generally uniform character exhibited by the interior portions of the continent.

The conditions of the ancient history of North America have served to provide its fields with an abundant and precious store of the materials which fit its lands to be the seats of a varied and complicated economic life. Of these underground resources we can only note the more important. First among them we may reckon the stores of burnable material: — coals, petroleum, and rock or natural gas, substances which in our modern conditions have come to be of the greatest consequence to mankind. The *Coal Deposits* of North America are on the whole more extensive, afford a greater variety of fuel, and are better placed for economic use than are the similar deposits of any other continent. They range in quality from the soft, rather woody, imperfectly formed coals known as lignites, to beds which afford the hardest anthracites, coals so far changed from their original condition that they burn without flame much in the manner of charcoal. The greater part of the good coals lie in the region to the E. of the Mississippi, while the lignites and other poorer fuels are found in the country between that great river and the Pacific Ocean. The excellent coals both of the E. and W. were generally formed during the carboniferous age; the lignites and other poorer materials of this nature were almost altogether accumulated in the Cretaceous and Tertiary periods.

The *Petroleum* of North America occupies a larger portion of the country and affords a more ample supply of the material than those of any other land save the region about the shores of the Caspian Sea, known as the Baiku district. The best of the American wells lie in the basin of the Ohio River. Traces of similar deposits occur at various points in the Cordilleras and on the coast of California. All the more valuable petroleum deposits of America lie in rocks below the lowest coals in strata of the Devonian and Silurian ages, where they were formed by slow chemical change of the fossil remnants of ancient marine life. The abundance of these accumulations of petroleum in North America is due to the fact that the beds in which the fluid has been formed lie in horizontal attitudes, in a position where the fluid has been retained by the unbroken strata notwithstanding the great pressure of the rock gases which tend to drive it forth to the surface.

The *Natural* or *Rock Gases* which of late years have played an important part in the industries of this country, serving for fuel and for illuminating purposes alike, owe their origin and preservation to the same conditions which have brought about the accumulation of petroleum. These substances, though the one is fluid and the other gaseous in form, are chemically akin, and are indeed only varied results of the same natural actions. They are both alike often formed in rocks where the strata abound in fossils. The reason why these materials do not often occur in Europe is probably due to the fact that the strata of that country have been so much ruptured and tilted by the mountain-building forces, which have affected almost every part of that country, that oil and gas have alike escaped to the surface of the earth by passages which these dislocating actions have provided for them. In North America on the other hand, where vast areas of strata still lie in substantially the same position in which they were formed, the substances have been to a great extent retained in the rocks where they were produced.

The store of rock gases known to exist in this country will probably be exhausted within twenty years of the present time. The resources in the way of petroleum are also likely to be used before the middle of the next century. The fuel in the form of coal exists in such quantity that there is no reason to apprehend a serious diminution of the store for many centuries or perhaps even thousands of years to come.

Next in importance after the fuels of North America, we may rank the ores from which *Iron* can be manufactured. These exist in great quantity in almost every important district of the continent, and at many points they are very advantageously placed in relation to supplies of fuel and to the transportation routes. The largest, though not the richest, store of iron ores in North America lies in the district of the Appalachian Mountains between the Potomac River and S. Alabama. In this field the ores have the general character of those which have afforded the basis of the great industry in Great Britain. As in that country, these Appalachian deposits are very favourably placed in relation to coke-making coals with which they are to be smelted. The other conditions for the development of the great industry are in this district also very favourable, so that experts in the matter look to this field as likely to be the principal seat of iron production in North America.

Next after the Appalachian field, the most important deposits of iron ore in North America lie in the region about the head of Lake Superior. In this field the deposits are of a very high grade, but they are much more costly to mine than those before referred to and they are unfortunately far removed from the coking coals of Pennsylvania and Kentucky, which are the nearest good fuels to the Lake Superior mines. It is now the custom to convey these ores mainly to the coal district about the headwaters of the Ohio River. The Cordillerean district abounds in iron ores, but as these Western iron ores are rarely near coals fit for use in furnaces, they cannot be regarded as of great economic importance. The ores from the region to the E. of the Mississippi afford the basis for an iron manufacturing industry which has already equalled that of Great Britain, and at its present rapid rate of growth gives promise of exceeding that of all European countries before the end of the present century.

The *Copper Deposits* of North America are to be ranked as next in importance to those which afford iron. Ores of this nature are extensively diffused in the older rocks of this country, but it is only in N. Michigan and in the Cordilleras that they have been proved to have great economic value. In the Michigan district the material occurs in a metallic form, and in such abundance that, notwithstanding the very high price of labour in that region, the product of the mine goes to the world's markets under conditions which enable the establishments to compete with the production of any other country. In the Cordilleras of North America the metal occurs, as is usual in other lands, in the form of ordinary ores, but the deposits are of such great extent and richness that they have proved very profitable.

The mines producing *Zinc* and *Lead* are now practically limited to Missouri and the Cordilleras, though a portion of the former metal is still obtained from New Jersey. A large part of the lead which now enters the markets of this country is obtained from the silver ores of the Rocky Mountain district, and as it is won as a bi-product, it is produced at a low cost.

The *Gold* and *Silver Fields* of North America, which have considerable economic value, are altogether limited to the mountainous district in the W. part of the continent. The S. portion of the Appalachian system afforded in the early part of this century, with the cheap slave-labour of that country, profitable mines of gold, but efforts to work the deposits since the close of the Civil War have proved universally unprofitable. There are a few successful gold mines in Nova Scotia, but they are commercially unimportant. The evidence goes to show that the Cordillerean region alone is to be looked to for large supplies of the precious metals.

Various other metalliferous ores exist in North America and play a subordinate part in its mining industry. *Tin* occurs at many points, but it has so far proved unprofitable to work the deposits, the main reason for the failure being the cost of labour involved in the work of production. Doubtless the most important of these less valued elements of mineral resources which the continent of North America affords is the group of fertilizing materials which of late years have come to play so important a part in the agriculture of this and other countries. The *Phosphate Deposits* of the S.E. part of the United States, particularly those of South Carolina and Florida, are now the basis of a large industry.

The soils of North America have, as the agricultural history of the country shows, a prevailingly fertile nature. In the region to the E. of the Mississippi within the limits of the United States over 95 per cent of the area affords conditions favourable for tillage. This region of maximum fertility extends over a portion of the area to the W. of the great river, but from about the 100th meridian to near the shores of the Pacific the rainfall is prevailingly insufficient for the needs of the farm. Crops can in general only be assured by a process of artificial watering, and the whole of the great Cordillerean field within the limits of the United States, and a large portion of that area in the republic of Mexico, a district amounting to near one-third of the continent, which would otherwise be fit for agriculture, is rendered sterile by the scanty rainfall. On this account the continent has as a whole less arable land in proportion to its size than Europe; moreover, more than one-fifth of its fields lie so far to the N. that they are not suited for agriculture; thus not more than three-fifths of the continent is naturally suited for husbandry. It should be noted, however, that the fields richest in metals lie in the arid districts, and that in this part of the realm there are areas aggregating more than 50,000 sq. M. which can by irrigation be made exceedingly productive and will afford a wide range of crops.

The climate of North America is prevailingly much more variable than that of Europe. Between the arctic regions and the warm district of the tropics, there are no mountain barriers, and the land is so unbroken by true seas that the winter winds are not tempered or obstructed in their movement. The result is that the summer heat, even as far N. as the northernmost cultivated districts of Canada, is great and commonly enduring, while the winter's cold occasionally penetrates to the borders of the Gulf of Mexico, even S. Florida being liable to frosts of sufficient severity to destroy the more sensitive tropical plants. The only portion of the United States which has tolerably equable atmospheric conditions, is the coast belt of the Pacific from San Francisco to the S. This region has a climate in many ways resembling that of N. Africa.

The peculiarities of surface and of climate which result therefrom give rise in North America to certain classes of storms which are little known in any other land. In the region of the Cordilleras great whirling movements of the air arise in places where the barometer is low, which move with considerable speed to the E. across the country. Passing beyond the Atlantic coast-line, these great circular storms, which generally have a diameter of several hundred miles, continue their way over the ocean, and often after a due time appear on the coast of Europe. In the landward part of their journey these storms rarely have such severity as to damage property. It often happens, however, especially during the spring season, that on the S.E. face of these advancing cyclones, small but very intense whirlings of the air are produced, which are known as tornadoes. These accidents often give rise to winds of singular intensity, movements of the air so energetic that they may disrupt the stoutest buildings, throw railway trains from the track, and by the upward rush of the atmosphere in their centres lift the bodies of men and animals to the height of hundreds of feet above the earth. Fortunately the paths of these tornadoes, or hurricanes, as they are locally called, are relatively very narrow, and the distance to which they course in their N.E. movement is short. The breadth of their destructive path rarely exceeds half-a-mile, and the distance to which the destruction is carried is generally less than twenty miles. Although occasional

visitations of this nature have been experienced throughout all the
United States to the E. of the Rocky Mountains, the district in
which they are really to be apprehended and where they are likely
to prove in a considerable measure destructive to life and property,
appears to be limited to the N. and central parts of the Mississippi
Valley, and the basin of the Ohio River north of Central Kentucky.

The waters of the Gulf of Mexico and of the neighbouring Carrib-
bean Sea, as well as the shores of the main land and islands of that
realm, constitute a field where another class of air-whirlings, the
marine cyclones, also termed hurricanes, are frequently developed.
These storms are much more enduring and more powerful than those
formed upon the land ; they often march from the regions where they
are developed slowly up the Atlantic coast of the United States until they gradually penetrate to a realm of the sea where the air next
the surface is so cool that they no longer receive the impulse which
led to their development. These marine cyclones find their parallel
in similar atmospheric convulsions which affect the Indian Ocean and
the China Seas. In both realms the disturbance of the atmosphere
is due to the heated condition of the air next the surface of the
ocean, and its consequent upward movement into the upper parts of
the aerial realm. The whirling movement is the simple consequent
of this ascent of the air through a narrow channel. It finds its like-
ness in the whirling imparted to the water in a wash - basin when it
flows through the opening in the bottom of the vessel.

Another class of atmospheric actions in a measure peculiar to
North America is found in the 'Cloud Bursts', or sudden torrential
rains, which occasionally though rarely occur in the E. portion of the
Cordilleras. In these accidents, though the region is on the whole
arid, the rain occasionally falls over an area of limited extent with such
rapidity that the air becomes almost unbreathable, and dry stream-
beds are in a few minutes converted into raging torrents. Although in
their characteristic intensity these cloud bursts are limited to certain
parts of the W. mountain district, a conspicuously rapid precipitation
occasionally occurs in the more E. portion of the United States.

In its original state, that in which it was found by the first Europeans who landed on its shores, the E. part of North America was
seat of the greatest forest of broad-leaved trees,intermingled with
pines and firs, which the world afforded. Although this noble Appalachian forest has suffered much from axe and fire, it still in part
remains in its primæval state, forming a broad fringe of arboreal vegetation from the Gulf of St. Lawrence to Central Texas, extending
inland to the central portion of the Ohio Valley and up the Mississippi to near its confluence with the Ohio and Missouri Rivers. To
the N. and W. of this great woodland lay a region of generally treeless plains. The district of the Cordilleras was scantily forested, and
along the Pacific Coast and on the W. slope of the Sierra Nevada from
Central California to the N., extended noble forests of narrow-leaf

trees. Across the N. part of the continent the heavy growth of timber, somewhat stunted by the severity of the climate, extended from the Pacific to the Atlantic shores. As a whole the continent bore an ampler mantle of forest growth than any part of the old world beyond the limits of the tropics.

The traveller who for the first time visits North America should take care not to hamper his vision by pre-conceptions as to the beauty of natural scenery based upon the physiography of the old world. As a whole the aspect of the N. continent of the new world differs greatly from that of the old. In the former land there are none of those admirable combinations of snow-clad mountains and fertile valleys which lend such a charm to the scenery of Switzerland. In general the surface lacks those elements of detail which contribute so much to the picturesque aspect of a landscape. The scenery of North America is generally characterized by a largeness of mould and simplicity of outline dependent on the relatively uncomplicated nature of its geological history. The plains are vast and but little varied by elevations. The mountains of the Appalachian district have a singular continuity in their ridges, which, though it gives them a certain architectural beauty, deprives them of detail. The grander elevations of the Cordilleras, though attaining to about the altitude of the Alps, rise from a much more elevated base than the Swiss mountains, and therefore make a less striking impression upon the eye. At few points on the continent do mountains or even considerable hills come near to the coast, and the result is that the shore line has a monotony of aspect which is much contrasted with the sea margin of Europe.

The lovers of picturesque beauty in nature may well seek in North America the charm of its primæval forests, the beauty of its great plains when they bear their spring-time flowers, and the attractions which are presented by the greater rivers with their noble valleys and often marvellous gorges. Of these cañons or defiles cut by the streams, those of the Cordilleras are by far the greatest in the world. That of the Colorado and that of the Yosemite, each in its way eminently peculiar, and differing one from the other in origin and in aspect, are doubtless the most striking features of the continent, for they are unequalled in any other land.

The hystory of the aborigines in North America shows that this continent was only moderately well fitted for the nurture of races in their steps of passage from the primitive condition of man towards the ways of civilization. Though a remarkably fertile region, and abounding in game, the land contains none of those fortunate peninsulas, or districts walled about by mountains or the sea, which in the old world have afforded such admirable cradle-places for infant states. Thus it came to pass that in this country any tribe which attained some advance in civilization and became worth plundering was subjected to unending incursions from the neighbouring more savage folk. Only in Mexico and Central America did any of the primitive tribes advance beyond the stages of barbarism. The better fortune of those countries was probably due in the main to their more secluded positions. Moreover in North America the primitive people found no animals which were well suited for domestication or could render much help to man. The only beast which gave much promise of such aid, the bison, though a domesticable animal, has proved on the whole intractable and unfit for the uses of man.

The united conditions of the continent which made it on the whole unsuited for the nurture of peoples in the first stages of their advance has been an advantage to the European folk who have been transplanted to this part of the new world. The simple geographic character of the country has made access to its different parts relatively easy, and brought about its subjugation to the uses of man with marvellous rapidity. Some have feared that owing to the lack of diversities in the conditions of the continent, the people developed upon it would have an excessive uniformity in character and quality. The history of the populations, however, seems to show that the variety in climate, in soil or under-earth products,

and in the occupations which these features require of people, are sufficient to ensure considerable difference in the folk developed in different
sections of the land. Under the mask of a common language, which,
though varied by provincial peculiarities, is a perfect means of communication among the greater part of the folk to the N. of Mexico, the acute
observer will detect varieties in essential quality quite as great as those
which separate the people who dwell in different parts of Great Britain,
France, or Germany. Though in some part these peculiarities may have
been due to the diverse origin of the folk, they are in the main to be
attributed to the effects of the local conditions of climate and occupations.

It is evident that the climate of North America, except those parts
which have a subtropical character and the regions of the Far North which
are too cold for tillage, are admirably suited to the uses of the European
peoples from the states in the N. part of that continent. The descendants
of the colonies from England, France, and Germany planted on this soil
more than two centures ago between Florida and Labrador have all greatly
prospered. They have increased in numbers at a more rapid rate than
their kindred of the old world, their average life is as great if not greater,
and their endurance of labour of all kinds is in no wise diminished. The
history of the Civil War shows that in the essential qualities these men
of the new world have lost nothing of their primitive strength.

Fortunately for the transplanted population of America, the conditions
of soil, climate, and earth-resources permit the people to continue on the
ways of advancement in the occupations of life which were trodden by their
forefathers in the old world. The agriculture and the mechanic arts required
no change whatever on the part of the immigrants; the nature of the country seemed to welcome them to the new-found shores.

XIII. Climate and Climatic Resorts of the United States.

By

Edmund Charles Wendt, M. D., of New York.

Without some knowledge of the physical geography and topography of a country, an intelligent appreciation of its climatic peculiarities is not possible. This is particularly well seen in relation
to the climatology of the United States. Extending from well-nigh
arctic to almost subtropical regions, and from the level of the sea
to elevations of nearly 15,000 ft.; covering a vast expanse of partly
arid inland territory, and showing an enormous coast-line laved by
two great oceans, it should not be surprising that every conceivable
variety of climate may be found within its borders.

As compared with Europe, perhaps the most noteworthy feature
of the American climate consists in its greater range of temperature
and comparative dryness. The E. is also strikingly colder than the
W. coast as well as the European countries of corresponding latitudes. This circumstance has led to much confusion, and has given
the United States an undeserved reputation of being everywhere
colder than Europe. It is quite true that, if New York, for example, be compared to cities of the same latitude, like Naples, Madrid,
and Constantinople, or if Boston be contrasted with Rome, the
American towns will be found decidedly colder. On the other hand
if cities on the W. coast, like San Francisco or Portland, be selected
for comparison, only trifling differences will appear.

Variations of Temperature. The mean annual temperature varies to

XIII. CLIMATE. lxxxv

the extent of over 40° Fahr. in different parts of the Union. Extremes of actually recorded temperatures extend from -56° Fahr. to 121° Fahr. in the shade, a range of 177°. Taking the mean temperature of July as representing the hot season, we find in different sections of the country variations of more than 30° — *viz.* from 60° to over 90° Fahr. Again taking Jan. as a representative cold month, we find a range of over 50° — *viz.* from 10° Fahr. to above 60°. Now it must not be forgotten that in the United States, perhaps more than elsewhere, temperature and climate are not merely questions of so many degrees of latitude. The lines for similar annual means (isothermal lines) are considerably modified by ocean currents and winds, besides being deflected by the interposition of lofty mountain chains.

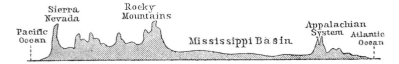

The Mountain Ranges. The two main ranges are the *Appalachian System* in the E. and the *Cordillerean System* (Rocky Mts. and Sierra Nevada) in the W. As will be seen later on, the W. highlands have a climate peculiar to themselves. They run from N.W. to S.E. for nearly 5000 M., *i.e.* from Alaska to Mexico, and gradually slope to the E., so as to fill in from one-third to one-half of the N. American continent. The E. or Appalachian system extends in a S.W. direction from Nova Scotia to Alabama, a distance of over 1500 M. Its width averages hardly one-fifth, and the elevation of its peaks and plateaus not one-half that of the W. highlands. Hence its effect on local climate is much less pronounced (Guyot). Between these great mountain ranges the vast *Mississippi Basin* stretches out for thousands of miles, from truly arctic regions to the warm waters of the Gulf of Mexico. This basin also includes the Great Lake district, one of the prominent features of the N. states. The climate of this region is controlled by the vast expanse of these veritable 'inland oceans'.

Three Main Climatic Divisions. In accordance with the brief description just given, we recognize three main climatic divisions in the United States.

1. An *Eastern Region,* extending from the foot of the Rocky Mts. to the Atlantic seaboard, and including the entire Appalachian system.

2. The *Plateau and Mountain Region of the Western Highlands.*

3. The *Pacific Slope,* to the W. of the Sierra Nevada range.

The peculiarities of each region may be briefly stated as follows:

1. The Atlantic seaboard is moderately moist, and, in general, rather equable. It is, however, subject to summer 'hot spells', and winter 'cold snaps' of a very trying kind. The altitude of the Appalachian system is not sufficient to very materially affect the distribution of heat, winds, and rainfall, so that the change is a gradual one, as we approach the dry interior zone of the Great Mississippi Basin.

The latter region, about 1,245,000 sq. M. in extent, is in general warm and moderately equable. Extensive forests supply adequate moisture to the air, but where trees are sparse, the atmosphere becomes excessively dry. The Great Lakes temper this region on the N. and the Gulf of Mexico warms it on the S. Nevertheless Europeans often complain both of great summer heat and extreme winter cold; sensations which the thermometer rarely fails to justify. The numerous local departures from this general condition cannot be considered here.

2. The Plateau and Mountain Region is dry and cold. The higher peaks are Alpine in character. The great plateaus, situated between the border chain of the Sierra Nevada and the Rocky Mts., are on an average 5000 ft. above sea-level. Some of them are fully 6000 ft. high. The climate there is harsh, cold, and very dry. It is a common mistake, however, to suppose that these elevated plateaus are merely barren wastes. Especially at the lower levels richly fertile valleys are everywhere found to alternate with sandy treeless tracts, salt lakes, and marshy wastes. That there are corresponding differences in local climates can only be alluded to in this place. During the height of summer the days are hot, but as soon as the sun sets, the air grows chilly, and the nights are always cold.

3. The mountain slope of the Pacific is characterized by abruptness and great irregularity. Its climate is varied. The narrow strip bordering on the ocean is much warmer, more humid, and very decidedly more equable than corresponding interior latitudes and the Atlantic coast. This Pacific section is farther distinguished by a well-marked wet season, corresponding to the E. winter, and an equally well-defined dry season, corresponding to the E. summer. Moreover, cool summers and mild winters, as well as the complete absence of those extreme variations, which elsewhere mar the climate of the States, render the Pacific coast pleasantly conspicuous. It is here that some of the most popular winter and summer health-resorts have been established.

Some Special Features. In regard to temperature, it is significant that, in spite of the wide range of the thermometer, something like 98 per cent of the entire population inhabit those regions in which the annual means extend from 40° to 70° Fahr. only. Roughly calculated, therefore, the average annual temperature of the whole United States is 55° Fahr. But foreigners are of course more interested in the extremes of heat and cold, which are disagreeably perceptible in almost all the states. The most delightful season of the year is unquestionably the so-called 'Indian summer', *i.e.* the few Autumn weeks which precede the actual onset of winter. It would be difficult to imagine anything more exhilarating than the crisp air, brilliant sunshine, clear blue skies, and grateful temperature characterizing the closing days of an 'Indian summer' at its best.

The summer temperature is everywhere higher than in Europe, with the exception of certain districts on the Pacific slopes already alluded to. The hottest regions of the country are naturally the southernmost parts of the southernmost states (Florida, Alabama, Louisiana, etc.). Here the annual mean rises to 75° Fahr., which is almost that of tropical climes. In the valley of the Lower Colorado, in California and Arizona, the summer mean rises to 90° Fahr. In Texas temperatures of 110°, and in Arizona and parts of California of 115°, are no great rarity, and yet here the great dryness of the atmosphere makes the heat seem less oppressive than in humid regions at a much lower range of temperature. In almost all the states of the Union several extremely hot days are to be looked for every summer. And in the more prolonged 'hot spells' the mortality from heat-stroke and diarrhœal diseases becomes alarming to a degree quite unknown in Europe. The severity of the winter is most felt in the elevated parts of New England, the higher plains of N. Minnesota and Dakota, and the lofty mountain plateaus of the Rockies. There the usual mean may descend below 40° Fahr. In upper Minnesota the winter mean is only 10° Fahr. On the whole, it may be said that American winters are more severe than those of Europe, always excepting, of course, the S. states. In the Atlantic and Middle states the winter is generally steady. Ice and snow may be counted on during one-half of the three coldest winter months. But to the W. of the Mississippi great irregularities are experienced. Mild and open periods there alternate with intense cold and violent storms. As we approach the Pacific increased mildness is observed. Continuous snow and ice are unknown along the whole W. coast from Vancouver to San Diego. Moreover, the temperature is so equable there that the winter mean is only 5-15° below that of summer. In the S. occasional cold storms are experienced, although the thermometer at New Orleans, for example, rarely descends below the freezing point. Yet the S. winter is fitful and at times trying. It begins and ends early, lasting from about Nov. until February. But there is absolutely no periodicity in the various irregularities observed, so that elaborate calculations based on averages may be rudely upset by the eccentricity of certain seasons. It is always well to be prepared for 'any kind of weather' in the United States.

Rainfall. The rainfall is quite unevenly distributed through the United States. In the E. section it is abundant, while the great W. plains and prairies are often parched with prolonged drought This has led to the general employment there of irrigation, without which agriculture could not flourish. In the strip along the Pacific coast a very plentiful precipitation occurs. The heaviest deposit of rain takes place in the borderlands of the Gulf, namely the S. parts of Louisiana, Mississippi, and Alabama, the E. part of Texas, and the W. coast of Florida. The annual quantity of water amounts to about 65 inches there. But at Philadelphia it is 45 inches, and at

Chicago only about 30. All over the E. the rainfall is abundant in spring and summer. It usually occurs in heavy showers, often accompanied by violent electrical discharges. On the Pacific coast, apart from the regularly recurring winter rains, little or no precipitation of water takes place. But at a short distance inland profuse summer rains are again observed. In the mountainous highlands heavy winter snows augment the annual volume of watery precipitation. The most arid tracts of the United States are in W. Arizona, S. Nevada, and S.E. California. The annual rainfall there descends from 15 to 8 inches and less. Broadly speaking the United States may be said to be favoured by an abundance of rain, with a relatively small proportion of rainy days. Fogs occur in the seaboard states, but they are neither as frequent nor as heavy as those known in many European countries.

Winds. The prevailing winds of the United States are westerly, like those of other countries situated in middle latitudes. Around the Gulf of Mexico the main current of the atmosphere moves in an E. or S.E. direction. Along the Atlantic coast region the predominating winds are S.W. in summer, and N.W. in winter. In a large S.W. district, including Nebraska, Kansas, Colorado, Arkansas, Texas, New Mexico, Utah, and Arizona, the summer winds come from the S., and the winter winds have a N. direction. In the region of the Rocky Mountains the winds are so irregular that none of them can be said to be 'prevalent'. In the tract between the Mississippi and the Appalachian ranges, both summer and winter winds are S.W. and W. It may be borne in mind that in the United States the S.W. winds blow over an expanse of warm water, while the N.E. winds hail from a frigid ocean, and the N.W. from frozen deserts.

Storms and Blizzards. The regularly recurring winter storms are most violent on the E. seaboard. The term 'blizzard' is employed to denote the blinding snow-storms with intense cold and high winds, which have their true home only in the W. but which are sometimes observed in the Atlantic States. †

Climatic Resorts.

The custom of spending the winter in the South and the summer at the seaside has nowhere assumed more formidable proportions than in the United States, and a few of the more important climatic resorts are named and characterised below. Comp. also the notices throughout the Handbook.

WINTER RESORTS. The best known winter-stations are in Florida, California, the Carolinas, Georgia, and Virginia. A large proportion of the invalids visiting these regions are the victims of consumption, but sufferers from gout, rheumatism, neurasthenia,

---

† A violent blizzard occurred, in New York on March 12th, 1888. The snow was piled up in drifts of 10-30 ft., stopping all communication.

chlorosis, anæmia, diseases of the kidneys, affections of the heart, insomnia, chronic bronchitis, asthma, and over-work are often signally benefited by a stay at one or other of the resorts named below. In making one's choice of a winter's residence, the factor of accommodation should not be lost sight of; and it may be stated generally that the sanitary arrangements of American health-resorts are far superior to most places of the kind in Europe. In some of the hotels every conceivable modern comfort and luxury are provided (comp. pp. 357, 440, 450).

In *Florida* (RR. 75-81) the themperature is equable, the atmosphere is neither too dry nor too moist, the sunshine abundant, and the soil sandy. Consumptives do well there, especially in the early stages of the disease. The only drawback is the possibility of malaria; but the dangers arising from this source have been grossly exaggerated. — *Southern California* has, perhaps, the most delightful climate in the world (comp. p. 445). The air is genially warm and dry, yet not enervating as in more tropical climates, and more salubrious general conditions can nowhere be found. *Santa Barbara* (p. 443), *Los Angeles* (p. 445), and *San Diego* (*Coronado Beach;* p. 449) are among the chief resorts, the first named showing the least variation between the day and night temperatures, while the other two enjoy an almost total immunity from fog. At San Diego the coast-winds are sometimes inconvenient for invalids with throat-troubles. *San Bernardino* (p. 448) is more inland and has a rather bracing, but not irritating, climate, which some consumptives find more beneficial than that of other Californian resorts. *Monterey* (p. 439), *Santa Cruz* (p. 441), *Pasadena* (p. 446), *Redondo Beach* (p. 446), and *San Rafael* (p. 433), have all their special advantages. — *Thomasville* (p. 354), in Georgia, and *Aiken* (p. 350), in South Carolina, are much frequented by weak-chested persons, who find benefit in the balsamic fragrance of their pine forests. The advantages of *Asheville*, North Carolina, have been sufficiently indicated at p. 344. *Old Point Comfort* (p. 322), *Virginia Beach* (p. 331), and *Newport News* (p. 331), in Virginia, are fashionable intermediate stations for invalids on their way back to the North. — *Lakewood* (p. 225), in New Jersey, and *Cumberland Gap Park*, in Tennessee (comp. p. 341), are also favourably known. — *Colorado Springs* (p. 415), *Manitou* (p. 417), and *Saranac Lake* (p. 166) are the chief resorts for the high-altitude treatment of consumption.

SUMMER RESORTS. *Newport* (p. 68), *Nahant* (p. 90), *New London* (p. 63), *Narragansett Pier* (p. 64), *Bar Harbor* (p. 102), *Long Branch* (p. 56), *Atlantic City* (p. 225), *Cape May* (p. 224), and parts of *Long Island* (p. 55) are the most fashionable SEA-SIDE RESORTS. Sea-bathing in the United States differs somewhat from British and Continental practices. Permanent bath-houses on the beach take the place of bathing-coaches, and the institution of bathing-

masters is almost unknown. Men and women bathe together. The
temperature of the water of the Atlantic Ocean in summer is so
warm (often exceeding 70° Fahr.), that bathers frequently remain
in it an hour or more, apparently without harm.

The chief MOUNTAIN RESORTS are in the *Catskills* (p. 195), the
Adirondacks (p. 165), the *White Mts.* (p. 121), the *Green Mts.*
(p. 117), the *Berkshires* (p. 136), and the *Alleghenies* (pp. 341,
343, etc.).

The United States contains nearly 9000 MINERAL SPRINGS. While,
however, these waters are chemically equal to any in the world, it
must be admitted that their scientific employment for the cure of
disease has not hitherto been developed as at the famous European
spas. *Saratoga Springs* (p. 179) has, perhaps, the best claim to
ranking with the latter in its mode of life and methods of treatment.
The celebrated *Hot. Springs*, *Arkansas*, are described at p. 404.
Among the most popular SULPHUR SPRINGS are *Blount Springs* (Ala.),
Blue Lick Springs (Ky.), *White Sulphur Springs* (p. 305), *Sharon*
(p. 158), and *Richfield Springs* (p. 188). — Good IRON WATERS are
found at *Sharon* (p. 158), *Cresson Springs* (p. 234), *Schoole's Mt.*
(p. 196), and *Milford* (N. H.). — *Crab Orchard* (Ky.), *Bedford*
(p. 234), and *Saratoga* (p. 179) have good PURGATIVE SPRINGS. —
Among well-known THERMAL WATERS are those of the *Hot. Springs,
Arkansas* (see above), *San Bernardino* (p. 448), *Calistoga* (p. 434),
and *Salt Lake* (p. 437).

XIV. The Fine Arts in America.

a. PAINTING AND SCULPTURE

by

William A. Coffin.

Marvellous progress in the fine arts has been made in the United States since the Centennial Exhibition at Philadelphia in 1876,
when popular interest in Art received a decided impulse; and for
something more than a decade the influx of American artists returning in large numbers from study in the European art centres, prin-
cipally from Paris, has had a strongly marked influence on the
tendencies of the American school. Before proceeding, however, to
the consideration of the conditions in which American art stands
before the public at the present day, it is pertinent to give briefly
some account of its earlier history.

Previous to the Revolutionary period we find a Scottish artist
named *John Watson* painting portraits in Philadelphia about 1715,
and another Scotsman, *John Symbert*, similarly occupied in Boston
from 1725 to 1751. *John Singleton Copley*, born in Boston in 1737,
began to paint portraits there about 1751. He went to London subsequently, became a Royal Academician in 1779, and died in London

in 1815. He painted many celebrities of his time in the Colonies, and his works are among those most highly valued in early American art. *Benjamin West*, born at Springfield, Pennsylvania, in 1738, painted portraits in Philadelphia in 1756, went to Italy in 1760, and thence to London in 1763. He was elected president of the Royal Academy on the death of Sir Joshua Reynolds in 1792. He died in London in 1820, and his works, both portraits and compositions, are to be found in collections in the United States and England. At the Pennsylvania Academy of Fine Arts in Philadelphia one of his most celebrated pictures, 'Death on the Pale Horse', is in the permanent collection, and the Boston Museum possesses his 'King Lear', another notable work. *Charles Wilson Peale*, who was a colonel in the Continental army, painted portraits of Washington and other men of the time that are of historical and artistic interest. *John Trumbull*, son of Jonathan Trumbull, Colonial Governor of Connecticut, a graduate of Harvard and (like Peale) a colonel in the army who had previously given his attention to the art of painting, gave up his commission and went to London to study under West. He is best known as a painter of military pictures representing the battles of the Revolution and the French and English war in Canada, and also painted numerous portraits and miniatures. An interesting collection which includes the most important of his works belongs to the Yale University and is on exhibition in the galleries of the art school connected with the institution at New Haven (see p. 58).

Gilbert Stuart, born at Narragansett, Rhode Island, in 1755, is the most famous of all the portrait-painters of the Revolutionary period, and his work compares very favourably with that of his contemporaries in Europe. He was a pupil of West in London and returned to America in 1792. He settled in Boston, after painting portraits two years in New York, Philadelphia, and Washington, and died there in 1828. The best portraits of Washington are those from his hand, and the list of his other portraits is a long one, including many of the best known men in the first Congresses of the United States and military and civic dignitaries. Portraits by Stuart are in the collections at the Museum of Fine Arts, Boston (p. 80); at the Metropolitan Museum (p. 42), the Lenox Library (p. 36), and the New York Historical Society (p. 40), New York; and at the Pennsylvania Academy of Fine Arts, Philadelphia (p. 216). *John Vanderlyn* and *Thomas Sully* (an Englishman who came to America at an early age) were portrait-painters of note contemporary with Stuart and Trumbull. *Washington Allston*, born in South Carolina in 1779 and a graduate of Harvard in the class of 1800, went to London to study in the schools of the Royal Academy in 1801. He settled in Boston in 1818, and painted historical and religious subjects as well as portraits, and is considered one of the most talented of American artists. One of the best of his works is the 'Jeremiah' in the Yale University collection at New Haven (p. 58), and there are others at the Boston Museum of Fine Arts and elsewhere. *Samuel F. B. Morse* (1791-1872), the inventor of the telegraph, who graduated at Yale in 1810 and was a pupil of Allston, devoted himself to historical painting in the beginning of his career in the first quarter of the present century.

On the 8th of November, 1825, a number of young artists and students in New York established the New York Drawing Association. On the 16th of January, 1826, they chose from their number fifteen artists who were directed to choose fifteen others, and the thirty thus selected constituted a new society which was called the National Academy of Design. Among the first fifteen of these founders of the Academy were *Thomas S. Cummings, William Dunlap, Asher B. Durand, John Frazee,* and *Henry Inman.* Among the second fifteen were *Thomas Cole, William Jewett, Rembrandt Peale, John Vanderlyn,* and *Samuel Waldo. Thomas Cole* was the first American landscape-painter, and *Durand* and *Thomas Doughty* were prominent among those who followed his lead in taking up this branch of painting. *Inman* was a noted portrait-painter, as were *Waldo* and *Jewett, Vanderlyn* (who has already been mentioned), and *Rembrandt Peale.* In the years following the founding of the Academy *G. P. A. Healey* (who went to Paris to study under Baron Gros and Couture), *Thomas Rossiter* and *William Hunt* of Boston (pupils of Couture), *William Page, Daniel Huntington, Charles L. Elliott,* and *Robert W. Weir* among others gained wide reputations as portrait and figure painters, and in landscape *John F. Kensett* and *Sanford R. Gifford* became especially famous. Some of the contemporaries and the immediate successors in point of historical sequence of these men, elected to membership in the Academy or chosen as Associates, from about the middle of the forties to the beginning of the seventies, form what is sometimes referred to as the 'Older School' of American painters. The Academy held its sixty-seventh annual exhibition in the spring of 1892, and its eleventh autumn exhibition the same year.

In sculpture the first American artists to be noted are *John Frazee, Hiram Powers,* and *Horatio Greenough,* one of whose representative works is the equestrian statue of Washington in the Capitol grounds at Washington (p. 253). Frazee was born in 1790 and Powers and Greenough in 1805. *Thomas Crawford, Randolph Rogers, Thomas Ball, W. W. Story,* and *Henry K. Brown,* whose equestrian statues of Washington in Union Square, New York (p. 32), and of General Scott at Washington (p. 262) are especially worthy of mention among the achievements of the earlier American sculptors, should be grouped with Frazee, Powers, and Greenough, though they are chronologically later. This summary brings us to the period uniting the old and new, the time when American art, having made for itself a dignified place in the national civilization, was conservative in its processes and faithful to time-honored traditions and had not yet felt to any appreciable degree the influences of the great revival that followed the appearance of Delacroix and Géricault, the famous men of 1830, and the Fontainebleau group in France. We find *Huntington, Baker, Le Clear, Eastman Johnson, J. B. Flagg, Hicks,* and others prominent as portrait-painters; *Guy, J. G. Brown, Henry, Loop, Mayer,* and *Wilmarth,* noted painters of figure subjects; *F. E. Church, Bierstadt, Cropsey, Bellows, Whittredge, Thos. Moran, De Haas, David Johnson, James M. Hart, Wm. Hart,* and *McEntee* the chief painters of landscapes, marines, and cattle-pieces, and *J. Q. A. Ward* and *Launt Thompson,* the sculptors of the day. We find in their work sincerity of purpose, much artistic feeling, and individuality. Except in a few cases, however, there is little to show that their art had developed under other than indigenous influences.

American art at the present time, broadly speaking, means art in New York, for though there is much that is of value produced in Boston and Philadelphia and something worth noting here and there in some other cities, the best work of the artists in these places is usually seen in New York. In considering the modern 'Movement' in New York it is fair to say that we cover the whole country, and the condition of the fine arts in the United States may be measured by applying the gauge to what is to be seen in New York. If a few individual factors be thus omitted, it does not affect the test as a whole. This is nearly as true of New York in the United States as it is of Paris in France and much more so than of London in Great Britain. It was in 1877 and 1878 that the first of a little band of artists that has now grown into an army almost, and is sometimes styled the 'New School' and sometimes the 'Younger Men', made their appearance in New York and excited public interest by their work at the Academy exhibitions. They came from their studies in Paris and Munich and with characteristic American promptitude founded a society of their own. Some of the home artists who were in sympathy with their aims joined with them, and the new Society called the American Art Association was formed at a meeting held in New York on June 1st, 1877, at which *Augustus St. Gaudens, Wyatt Eaton, Walter Shirlaw,* and *Mrs. R. W. Gilder* were present; and before the first exhibition was held in the spring of 1878 the names of the following artists, among others, were placed on the roll of the Society: *Olin L. Warner, R. Swain Gifford, Louis C. Tiffany, J. Alden Weir, Homer D. Martin, John La Farge, William Sartain, W. H. Low, A. H. Wyant, R. C. Minor,* and *George Inness.* The name of the organization was changed in February, 1878, to the Society of American Artists, and it was incorporated under that title in 1882. It has held exhibitions in New York every spring since 1878 with the exception of 1885. Its discarded title, the American Art Association, has meanwhile been assumed by a business company, which conducts sales of collections and deals in works of art. The Society of American Artists has now 125 members, about twenty of whom reside in Europe, and is a progressive, vigorous body, whose yearly exhibition is one of the most important events in the American art world. Whatever feeling of antagonism to the Academy may have existed at the outset of the new movement has now disappeared, and the Academy and the Society are friendly rivals. But young artists have been coming from Europe and establishing themselves in New York for the past fifteen years, and their number increases steadily and rapidly. These younger men are very good painters as a rule; the space at the Academy is too limited to give room for their work and that of the Academicians and associates and other men who, though they do not belong to the Academy, hold a position in American art by reason of long residence and recognized ability; and the Society has been expected to offer the vigorous young school a fitting place to exhibit. It has done this, especially in the past six years, since 1886, most successfully. It has recently, in connection with the Architectural League of New York and the Art Students' League, secured a permanent home and spacious galleries in the new building of the American Fine Arts Society (the executive society of the alliance) in West 57th St.

The highest standard of excellence is maintained at the exhibitions of the Society of American Artists, where the visitor will obtain an impression of what motives and purposes inspire the younger men and will see a collection of works of art that for individuality in conception and cleverness of treatment may justly be ranked with the best displays offered in the European capitals. The exhibitions at the Academy are somewhat larger, but uneven in quality, though the younger men are usually pretty well represented and the best work of the older school is there shown. Comparison between the two exhibitions will be found to be instructive and interesting. The number of American artists who are well trained is now very large. This is due to study abroad, the strong influence of the French school on the younger men, and the methods now followed in the instruction of pupils in the art schools. The number of those who do thoroughly good work and are individual in the presentation of their motives is altogether too great to give more than the names of a few or them. Perhaps it will not be invidious to mention those of *Homer, Chase, Dewing, Mowbray, Brush, Weir, Cox, Thayer, Blashfield, Inness, La Farge, Low, Millet, Wyatt Eaton, Tarbell, Vinton, Blum, Maynard, H. O. Walker, H. B. Jones, Tryon, Donoho, Platt, Horatio Walker,* and *Robinson* among the most prominent painters, and *St. Gaudens, French, Warner, MacMonnies, Hartley, Adams,* and *Elwell* among the sculptors. The American artists who reside abroad are frequently represented in the New York exhibitions, and *Sargent, Abbey, Harrison, Dannat, Gay, Bridgman, Melchers, Pearce, Hitchcock, Vail, McEwen,* and others are as well known at home as in Paris. When at the Universal Exhibition at Paris in 1889 the American section in the fine arts department included the works of the artists at home and abroad, it was conceded by many that in interest, in technical excellence, and in individuality the American exhibition ranked second to none but that of France itself. The intelligent observer who comes to the United States and takes the opportunity to study American art as it is to-day cannot but be impressed with the value of its present achievement. The high place it is destined to occupy in the future is plainly indicated in the startling rapidity of its progress and the earnestness of purpose of the artists who are each day adding to its renown.

The visitor to New York will find in the autumn an exhibition of current American art a the Academy in November and December; an exhibition of the New York Water Color Club, a young society organized in 1890, whose purpose it is to hold annual exhibitions in the art season before the holidays and which has had three very interesting ones at that time; in February and March the regular annual exhibition of the American Water Color Society, with the New York Etching Club, at the Academy (one of the best and most interesting of all the exhibitions); and in April and May the regular annual exhibitions of the Academy and the Society of American Artists. In addition to these there are usually, throughout the season, numerous special exhibitions in the galleries of the dealers of the works of individual artists, and at the American Art Association and the Fifth Avenue Art Galleries there is a constant succession of exhibitions — some of them often of great importance, as when notable private collections are shown before being sold at auction. The *Metropolitan Museum* (p. 42), with the valuable additions made recently, compares very favourably with the great galleries of Europe. The exhibitions of the Architectural League, held annually in Dec., are interesting to the non-professional visitor, as the scope of the exhibition includes decorative art, and the architectural portion of the display has many popular as well as technical features. For those who wish to be informed as to the facilities for instruction in the fine arts in New York it may be mentioned that the schools of the Art Students' League, where there are over a thousand pupils on the rolls, rank with the schools of Paris in the quality of the work produced by the students, and that excellent schools are maintained also by the National Academy of Design, the Metropolitan Museum, and the Cooper Union. Through the provisions of a fund raised by Mr. J. A. Chanler, an art student is chosen in a general competition to be sent abroad to study for five years, and one of these prizemen was sent from New York and one from Boston for the first time in 1891.

In Philadelphia annual exhibitions of American art are held at the Pennsylvania Academy of the Fine Arts (founded in 1805), and the permanent collections are valuable and interesting. Exhibitions are also held by the Art Club of Philadelphia and by the Philadelphia Society of Artists. In Boston the collections of the Museum of Fine Arts are of great value both from the artistic and the historical standpoint, and exhibitions of the work of American artists are given each season by the Boston Art Club and other societies. In most of the larger cities, such as Chicago, St. Louis, and Cincinnati, and in many towns in the East and West there are art institutions and schools, and exhibitions to which New York artists are among the contributors are held with considerable regularity.

b. ARCHITECTURE

by

Montgomery Schuyler.

The sources of the settlement of the United States were so many and so various that we should expect to find a corresponding variety in the building of the colonies. As a matter of fact, however, by the time the settlements upon the Atlantic seaboard had become sufficiently established to project durable or pretentious buildings, the English influence had become predominant, and the colonists took their fashions from England in architecture as in other things. The Spanish settlements within the present limits of the United States were unimportant compared with those farther to the South. The trifling remains of Spanish building in Florida and Louisiana are not to be compared with the monuments erected by the Spaniards in Mexico, where some of the churches in size and costliness and elaboration of detail are by no means unworthy examples of the Spanish Renaissance of the 17th century. The only considerable town on the Atlantic coast that is not of English origin is New York, which was already a place of some importance when the New Netherlands were ceded to Great Britain by the treaty of Breda in 1667. It was built in the then prevailing fashion of Holland. The 'Flemish Renaissance', which has lately appealed to English architects as containing valuable suggestions for modern building, did not impress the new masters of New Amsterdam. The crow-stepped gables and steep tiled roofs of the Dutch settlers were displaced by dwellings and warehouses of English architecture executed by English mechanics. It is unlikely that any specimen of Dutch architecture was erected, either in New York or in Albany (which retained its Dutch characteristics longer), after the beginning of the 18th century. There are now no Dutch buildings left in New York, and it is believed that there is but one in Albany. There are, however, here and there Dutch farmhouses left on Long Island and in New Jersey; a manor-house of the Van Rensselaers, patroons of Rensselaerswyck, is still standing near Albany (p. 157); there is an occasional Dutch church in the oldest parts of New York State and New Jersey; and part of the Philipse manor house, now the City Hall of Yonkers (p. 150), is of Dutch architecture. These relics are all of the 17th century and are interesting rather historically than architecturally. They do not invalidate the rule that by the time the colonists were able and disposed to erect buildings of any architectural pretensions, their models were the contemporary buildings of England.

The public buildings of the colonial period were mainly churches, and these, where they were more than mere 'meeting-houses', were imitated from the churches of Sir Christopher Wren and his successors. Of these St. Michael's (p. 348), built in 1752 in Charleston, is the most conspicuous and perhaps the most successful. Burke, in his 'Account of the European Settlements in America' (1757), says of it: 'the church is spacious and executed in very handsome taste, exceeding everything of that kind which we have in America'. The design is attributed, on the strength of a contemporaneous newspaper paragraph, to 'Mr. Gibson', but this is probably a mistake for Mr. Gibbs, the architect of St. Martin's-in-the-Fields in London and the Radcliffe Library at Oxford, being at the time one of the most successful of English architects and perhaps the most distinguished

of the immediate followers of Wren. The resemblances between
St. Michael's and St. Martin's tend to strengthen this conjecture.
St. Paul's (p. 28) in New York (1767) was the most important of
the colonial churches of the city and in style resembles St. Michael's,
being ultimately inspired by Wren's city churches in London.

A local tradition refers the design of the College of William and
Mary (p. 332), at Williamsburg, Va., to Sir Christopher Wren himself, but the architecture scarcely bears out the legend. It is, however,
in Virginia and in Maryland that the colonial architecture is seen at
its best. The great tobacco-planters of those colonies formed a real
landed gentry, such as could scarcely be said to exist in any other of
the colonies, excepting the holders of manorial grants on the Hudson
River, who were much fewer in numbers. The farmers of New England and Pennsylvania were a yeomanry and there were very few
landed proprietors in New England who could rival the scale of living
of the tobacco-planters, whose estates and agricultural operations were
extensive, whose habits were hospitable and commonly extravagant,
and who lived up to their easily acquired incomes. They possessed
real 'seats', and these are the most pretentious and the most interesting examples of colonial domestic architecture. Such mansions as
Brandon, Shirley, and Westover in Virginia (see p. 330), and Home-
wood and Whitehall in Maryland, testify to a high degree not only
of social refinement on the part of their owners but of skill on the
part of the artisans who built them, for the profession of architecture
was almost if not quite unknown to the colonies. The architecture
of these mansions consisted in a simple, almost invariably symmetrical
composition, often a centre with wings connected with it by a curtain-
wall, in a careful and generally successful proportioning of these
parts and of the stories, which were usually two and very rarely more
than three, and in the refined though conventional design and skilful
execution of the detail, especially of the detail in woodwork. The
porch was the feature of the front, and in houses of much pretension
generally exhibited an order, consisting of a pair of columns sustain-
ing an entablature and a pediment. The bricks were imported from
England, or often, in the northern colonies, from Holland, and stone
was sparingly employed. Many of the country seats of the landed
gentry have been piously preserved, but in towns the colonial houses
have been for the most part destroyed. Annapolis (p. 250), in Maryland, named after Princess Anne, has been left on one side by the
march of improvement and remains to show many specimens of the
Georgian architecture, which still give it a strong resemblance to an
English town that has remained inactive for a century.

The colonial architecture continued to prevail after the close of
the politically colonial period. The first Capitol of the United States
at Washington was a very good specimen of it, although the design
of it has been obscured by the later additions in a different taste.
Although the plan which was accepted was the work of an amateur,

the work of construction was assigned to a trained architect, to whom the design of the building was really due. At the instigation of Jefferson, then President and himself a dabbler in architecture, the architect attempted to compose an 'American order' by conventionalising the foliage of plants peculiar to this continent. Some of the capitals engendered by this essay are to be seen in the interior of the Capitol (p. 88), but it is upon the whole fortunate that no attempt was made to employ them in the exterior decoration. The building was burned by the British in 1814, but was rebuilt with additions and variations during the next decade. To the same period belong the State House of Massachusetts at Boston, the City Hall of New York, and the Merchants' Exchange of Philadelphia, all specimens of educated and discreet architecture, as it was at that time understood in Europe.

The inspiration of these works and of others like them was distinctly Roman. The Greek revival that was stimulated in Europe by the publication of Stuart's work on Athens was somewhat belated in reaching the United States, where the Roman Renaissance of Wren and his successors was in full possession. The Grecian temple was adopted at the national capital as the model of a modern public building about 1835, with such modifications as were compelled by practical requirements. The Treasury, of the Ionic order, the Doric building of the Interior Department, commonly called the Patent Office, and the Corinthian General Post Office were among the first fruits of this cult. From Washington it gradually spread over the United States, Girard College (p. 217) at Philadelphia and the Sub-Treasury and the Custom House at New York being among the finest and most monumental of the American reproductions. For the next 15 years the Grecian temple in stone or brick was commonly adopted for churches as well as for public buildings, while it was reproduced in wood for dwellings of architectural pretensions, either in town or country. In 1851 the extension of the Capitol at Washington was begun. It consists of two wings, fronted with Corinthian colonnades, making the extreme length of the building 750 feet, and the addition of a central dome of cast iron, which attains the disproportionate height of over 300 feet and is, in other respects, not very successfully adjusted to the building which it crowns. The Capitol thus completed became the model for American public buildings. Nearly all the State Houses have followed its general disposition and have included a lofty dome.

Although there are some earlier churches in a style which the designers of them believed to be Gothic, the Gothic revival in the United States may be said to have begun with the erection of Trinity Church (p. 27) in New York in 1846, which remains, perhaps, the most admirable piece of ecclesiastical architecture in that city. Within a few years thereafter Gothic had almost entirely superseded classic architecture as a style for churches, although in commercial buildings

the models of the Renaissance were preferred, and these were imitated
in fronts of cast-iron to an extent quite unknown elsewhere. The
Gothic designers, however, insisted upon the applicability of their
style to all uses and made many essays of more or less interest, in
public, commercial, and domestic building, of which there are
examples in all the Atlantic cities.

Up to this time, although among the leading American architects
were Germans and Frenchmen as well as Englishmen, and an increasing proportion of native designers who had made their studies
at the Ecole des Beaux Arts, or in the office of Continental architects,
the architecture of the country had upon the whole been a faint and
belated reflection of the current architecture of England. This continued to be the case during a brief season of experiments with
'Queen Anne'. But at this time there arose an American architect
whose personal force, manifested for the most part in his own free
version of the Southern French Romanesque, very deeply impressed
his contemporaries and his successors and greatly affected the building of the whole country. This was *Mr. H. H. Richardson* (1838-86),
who came into a national celebrity with the completion of Trinity
Church, Boston, in 1877, when the author was thirty-nine years old.
In the nine years of life that remained to him, he made such an impression upon his profession that almost every American town bears
traces of his influence. His own most noteworthy works, besides
Trinity, are the county-buildings at Pittsburg (p. 241), the Senate
Chamber, the Court of Appeals, and the Western Staircase of the
Capitol of New York at Albany (p. 155), the Albany City Hall (p. 156),
the Cincinnati Board of Trade (p. 308), Sever Hall and Austin Hall
at Cambridge (p. 83), and a warehouse in Chicago (p. 284). As
might have been expected, he has had many imitators, but the extent
and the value of his services to American architecture are best seen
in the work of architects who have recognized the force that lay in
his simple and large treatment, and have recognized also that the
force of this treatment was independent of the detail he employed
and of the style in which he worked. This lesson has been learned
and applied by the architects of many of the towering 'elevator buildings' erected for commercial purposes, which are so marked features
of the American cities, and are the unique contribution of American
architects to their art. The introduction of the elevator made possible
a great increase in the number of stories of a commercial building,
which before that introduction were usually limited to five, whereas
quite three times that number have been proved to be practicable
and profitable. The earliest of the elevator buildings were the Western
Union building (p. 28; since partly destroyed and rebuilt) and the
Tribune building (p. 29) in New York, and these are but twenty
years old. The architectural problem presented by these structures
was entirely new, and no precedents could be invoked for their
treatment. Many of the different solutions of it offered by American

architects are of high ingenuity and interest. Boston, New York, Philadelphia, and Chicago offer numerous commercial buildings that are impressive and admirable pieces of architecture, although the conditions of their erection have compelled the designers to disregard many accepted canons of their art, and they seem voluntarily to have disregarded many others. Some of these structures are unmistakable and tolerably consistent examples of historic styles, but others, equally successful, are impossible to classify.

While American architects have been compelled to contribute to architecture a new type in the elevator building, they have won successes not less genuine, though of course less startling, in domestic architecture. Here also they are almost equally independent of convention, and this, as is often apparent in their successful essays, not from ignorance but from deliberate choice. The discipline of the schools has enabled a designer to produce work that is clearly scholarly and as clearly not scholastic. Dwellings of recent erection are to be found in the suburbs of Boston, in the new 'West Side' of New York, on all three 'sides' of Chicago, and indeed in all the chief towns of the North and North-West that are so far from being examples of styles that they betray a complete freedom of eclecticism and that are yet evidently the work of accomplished and artistic designers. The massiveness of the Romanesque in which Mr. Richardson worked sometimes even in his hands degenerated into a coarseness and clumsiness that are especially repugnant to the spirit of domestic architecture. His imitators have exaggerated these defects and omitted the qualities which in his work atoned for them, and the most successful of recent American dwellings that can be classified as Romanesque are of a lighter and more enriched Romanesque than that which he employed. The French Renaissance of Francis I. has appealed to many of the architects as a style at once free and picturesque and at the same time refined, and some interesting houses have been done in it, especially in New York (comp. p. 35) and Philadelphia. In country-houses, also, American architects have had their successes, and a fairly comprehensive view of their achievements in this kind can be had from a sojourn at any of the watering-places on the coast of New England or New Jersey. Architecturally as well as otherwise Newport is the most interesting of these.

The European historians and critics of architecture who have so long been insisting that 'Art is not archæology' may find in the current building of the United States that precept reduced to practice. An absolute freedom is the rule alike among competent and incompetent architects, subject with the former class to the artistic unity of the resulting work. In commercial and domestic architecture, along with much wildness and crudity, this freedom has produced much that is interesting and suggestive to the European student of architecture, and that gives good hope for the progress of architecture in the United States.

XV. Sports
by
Henry Harmon Neill.

Only within thirty years have outdoor sports become a popular form of amusement in the United States; previous to that time base-ball and trotting alone claimed attention. To-day, however, nearly every game familiar to Englishmen is played in the Eastern half of the country, and many are known throughout all the states. The growth has been so rapid that its postponement until the present generation now seems surprising. Perhaps the explanation is that in a new country outdoor labour is so general as to forbid outdoor play; or that Americans have until recently been too busy to amuse themselves except after sundown.

To enter into the spirit of American pastimes, an Englishman need only learn to admire the gait of the trotting horse and to admit the merits of base-ball as a substitute for cricket. All other sports are conducted substantially upon English models. The *Running Horses* (*i.e.*, race-horses) are all of English blood, and the tracks are becoming annually more like those of Great Britain, straight and hilly courses replacing the level oval mile once universal; the *Yachts* are growing more substantial in build and more English in model; *Foot-ball* as played in the States is a modification of the Rugby game; *Lawn Tennis, Cricket, Lacrosse,* and *Polo* are played in the same way in both countries; while *Rowing* and *Canoeing* are equally popular on each side of the Atlantic.

Though the theory that **Base-ball** is a development of '*Rounders*' is vehemently disputed, the 'National Game' is easily understood by anyone familiar with the old English pastime. It is played in every village, town, and city, and by every school, college, university, and athletic club in the country; but the games most worth seeing are those of the (professional) *National League*, in New York, Boston, Brooklyn, Cincinnati, Chicago, Washington, Philadelphia, Pittsburg, St. Louis, Baltimore, and Louisville. The club 'representing' each of these cities plays a series of home and home games with every other; the winner of the greatest number is the champion of the year. Minor 'Leagues' are the *Eastern, Southern,* and *Western,* with clubs in the smaller cities. The best amateur games are those of the colleges (especially *Harvard*, *Yale*, *Pennsylvania*, *Princeton*, and *Cornell*) and of the *Amateur Atlantic Union* and the *Amateur League*. The season begins in May and ends in October. A base-ball team consists of nine men, including the pitcher, catcher, and seven fielders. Enormous salaries (sometimes $15,000 a year) are paid to the best professional players, and the game is the vehicle of a huge amount of betting.

Horse Races. See p. 17 under New York. Other meetings are held during the season in or near Chicago, St. Louis, Cincinnati, Louisville, New Orleans, Washington, Saratoga, and elsewhere; but the racing there is not very good.

Trotting Races take place during the season, from May to Sept., on 1500 tracks in the United States owned by as many associations, and at all county and state fairs as well as on many private tracks at brood-farms and elsewhere. Stakes, purses, and added moneys amount to more than $3,000,000 annually; and the capital invested in horses, tracks, stables, farms, etc., is enormous. The tracks are level, with start and finish directly in front of the grand stand, and are either 1 M. or ¹/₂ M. in length. They are always of earth, and are usually elliptical in shape, though the recently divised 'kite-shaped track' is becoming popular for its increased speed. In this there is one straight stretch of ¹/₃ M., then a wide turn of ¹/₃ M., and then a straight run of ¹/₃ M. back to the start and finish. The horses are driven in two-wheeled 'sulkies' of little weight, and the handicaping is exclusively by time-classes. Records of every race are kept by two national associations. Horses that have never trotted a mile in less than 2 min. 40 secs. are in one class; those that have never beaten 2.35 in another; those that have never beaten 2.30 in a third; and so on down to 2.10, which has been beaten but a dozen times. Races are always run in heats, and the winner must win three heats. With a dozen entries (or even six or eight, the more usual number) a race may thus occupy an entire afternoon, and require many heats before a decision is reached. Betting is common at every meeting, but is not so prominent as at running tracks. The best trotting races are to be seen at the tracks of the 'Grand Circuit' and the 'Western Southern Circuit'. These give meetings, of from four to eight days each, in or near Philadelphia, Pittsburg, Cleveland, Buffalo, Rochester, Springfield, and Hartford in the Eastern States, and at Sturgis (Mich.), Grand Rapids (Mich.), Chicago (Ill.), Independence (Iowa), Fort Wayne (Ind.), Richmond (Ind.), Cambridge City (Ind.), Terre Haute (Ind.), St. Louis (Mo.), Nashville (Tenn.), and Columbia (Tenn.). — The best brood-farms for the development of trotting horses are in Kentucky and California. Each farm has an annual auction-sale of its produce, either at home or in New York City. At the stables of Mr. Robert Bonner in New York City are the fastest trotters in the world; they may be seen upon application to the owner by letter.

Hunting is much in vogue in the neighbourhood of New York, though the place of a fox is generally taken by a 'drag'. There is a meet every other day with one of the packs of *Meadow Brook*, *Rockaway*, *Orange*, or *White Plains*. Boston, Philadelphia, and Washington also support packs. The wild fox is hunted in the *Geneseo Valley* (N. Y.) and at *Media* (Pa.). Near the cities the sport is indulged in mainly by active business men who cannot spare more than an afternoon for it.

Shooting and Fishing are generally free to all-comers during the legal season, though the number of game and fish-preserves is increasing. The *Game Laws* are different in each of the States and Territories, and cannot be condensed. The periodical 'Fur, Fin, and Feather' (114 Warren St., New York City), contains them all, with the latest amendments.

Of the 33,000 sq. M. in the state of *Maine* more than one-half is an almost uninhabited wilderness of forest. Here are 1500 lakes, thousands of streams and rivulets, and miles upon miles of hunting-grounds, where the sportsman may find large game and small and fishing and shooting of almost all kinds. His visit should be made not earlier than the middle of July, when the black fly has passed, and should continue until after the first of October, when the open season for deer, caribou, and moose begins. By law he may fish in fresh water from May to Sept. inclusive, and hunt from Oct. to Dec. inclusive, the greater sport being permitted from the day the quieter ceases. Bears, foxes, wild-cats, and wolves he may kill at any time, and opportunities for doing so are not unlikely to occur. Ducks, geese, loons, and herons abound; and small game of every kind is common. The region may be entered at *Greenville*, on *Moosehead Lake* (p. 99), the largest sheet of water in the State. Here guides may be obtained at $3 per day, who furnish canoes, cooking utensils, and tents. It is best, of course, to camp out. For this, one guide is required for each visitor; food will cost about $1 per day, and other equipment may be purchased beforehand, or hired at Greenville or any other point selected for entering the woods. A good rifle, a pole (fishing-rod), lines, flies, reels, stout boots, and plenty of blankets — these are the necessities, and beyond these one may take an outfit as complete or as modest as desired. Care should be taken in the selection of guides. In July and Aug. it is not easy to get good ones. A party of four, with four or five guides, is as large as is desirable.

The *Rangeley Lakes* (p. 106) are more accessible than Greenville, but the sport there is not so good; the wilderness, however, may be penetrated in canoes from either point for hundreds of miles, with increasing chances of game.

The *Adirondack Region* (p. 165) has a smaller area than the Maine wilderness, and the shooting is not so good. Deer may be met with, however, the open season lasting from Aug. 15th to Nov. 1st. But although large hotels, steam-launches, and even railroads are now found throughout the Adirondacks, the trout-fishing is still excellent. The season lasts from May 1st to Sept. 15th. A large part of the region is owned by the State and reserved as a public park. August is the best month for a visit; and the sportsman may go directly to one of the hotels in the region, relying upon the guides, provisions, and equipments there to be found.

There is also good hunting in the mountains of Pennsylvania, the Virginias, Tennessee, and North Carolina; and in the Far West the biggest game is found. Deer are abundant, too, in Louisiana, Mississippi, Florida, and Alabama, and venison has within recent years been cheaper than beef in the markets of New Orleans. But the limits of this article forbid more than a mention of these facts.

Wild Fowl abound on the coast from Maine to Florida; the season for duck, &c., usually opens about Sept. 1st and continues to April.

Tarpon Fishing in the deep-sea water off Florida, best from Feb. to May, is a superb sport (comp. p. 353).

Buffaloes are nearly extinct. There are not over 1000 on the continent; of these 500 are in Yellowstone Park, where the sound of a gun is never heard.

The *Mountain Sheep* and *Rocky Mountain Goat*, in the Far West, are generally protected by law from Jan. to Sept.; in some states they cannot be legally killed at all.

Bicycling. The roads in the United States are as a rule bad, and in the days of the old 'ordinary' (high-wheeled) bicycle touring could not be recommended except in the immediate neighbourhood of the larger cities, or upon a few main highways connecting these with each other. Since the advent of the pneumatic-tired 'safety' bicycle this obstacle is much less serious, and long tours, even across the continent, are now often made. The *League of American Wheelmen*, which has divisions in every State, is doing what it can to improve the country roads, and its great influence gives hope of success. Already by political action, it has secured for the wheelman many rights formerly denied him, including the freedom of public parks, in almost all cities, on an equality with other vehicles. Clubs exist in every city. Annual race-meetings are held in each State during the riding season; and other meetings are not infrequent. Chief among the latter is the annual 'Wheel about the Hub' (third Frid., Sat., & Sun. in Sept.) of the *Boston Bicycle Club* (the oldest in America, dating from 1878). The *Cyclists' Touring Club* of England is represented in the United States by a Chief Consul at Boston (Mr. Frank W. Weston, Savin Hill, Dorchester) and Consuls in many towns and cities; and manufacturers or dealers, from whom information may be sought and wheels hired, are to be found in almost every town.

Lawn Tennis. The annual *All-comers Tournament* is held at Newport in August; the winner plays the champion of the year before for the championship at singles. A *Western Championship Tournament* at doubles occurs in Chicago in July, and an *Eastern* in New York, Saratoga, or Philadelphia; the winners of these meet at Newport. The *Ladies Championships* are decided in Philadelphia. All these are open to members of recognized clubs, American or foreign. There are many minor tournaments during the season (May to Oct.), usually open to strangers. A *Tropical Championship Tournament* is held in St. Augustine, Florida, during the winter. The *National Association* is the governing body, and there are clubs and courts in every city.

Cricket. The best clubs are in Philadelphia; in New York and Chicago a few Englishmen play, and some of the colleges have elevens. The game, however, has never secured a good foothold, being generally considered too Alexandrine as compared with base-ball.

Polo and **Court Tennis** have their headquarters at Newport. — **Lacrosse** is mainly a Canadian game, but there is a Lacrosse League in the cities of the Atlantic coast.

Rowing. The *National Association of Amateur Oarsmen* is the governing body, and holds an annual regatta, over a different course each year. Other associations are the *New England*, the *Middle States*, the *Harlem*, and the *Southern*. The best eight-oared crews are those of *Harvard*, *Yale*, *Columbia*, *Cornell*, and *Pennsylvania Universities*. Harvard and Yale race at New London (p. 63) in June; the others either there or on the Hudson River or Cayuga Lake, New York State.

Canoeing. The *American Canoe Association* holds an annual meeting in Aug., usually in Northern New York. There are canoeists on almost every stream in the country, and clubs innumerable. Sailing is developed at the expense of paddling ; in other respects the customs are similar to those in England.

Foot-ball. The game played is a development of the Rugby game, but is played with teams of eleven a side instead of fifteen. *Yale*, *Harvard*, and *Princeton* have the best elevens. They play in Nov. in New York and Springfield (p. 60), having previously met minor teams from other colleges and from the athletic clubs. The *Collegiate League* includes Yale, Princeton, Pennsylvania, and Wesleyan; the *Athletic League* includes the Crescents of Brooklyn, the Orange A. C. of New Jersey, and the 'New York A. C. and Manhattan A. C. of New York. Chicago has an eleven of college graduates, and the game is making rapid headway elsewhere. Its season is very short, however, beginning in Sept. and closing with November.

Bowling ('Ten-Pins') is a favourite amusement of both sexes, throughout the United States, and alleys are attached to most gymnasia and athletic club buildings.

Athletics. The track events are the same as those contested in England, though long-distance and cross-country running has far fewer lovers, and the short races (100 yards to $^1/_2$ M.) are more generally contested. In hurdling and jumping the standards are very high; walking is not much practised. The owner of the first pair of 'spiked shoes' ever used in the United States, and the winner of the first amateur foot-race ever run here, are still comparatively young men. In weight-throwing the rules differ radically from the English. The chief athletic clubs (outside of New York) are the *Boston A. A.*, the *Columbia A. C.* (Washington), the *Southern A. C.* (New Orleans), the *Crescent A. C.* (Brooklyn), the *Olympic A. C.* (San Francisco), the *Buffalo A. C.*, the *Detroit A. C.*, and the *A. C. of the Schuylkill Navy* (Philadelphia). All these hold spring and autumn meetings; and indoor games are held in armouries and other large halls, so that the season practically lasts throughout the year. It is at its height, however, in June and Sept. Many of the colleges send representatives to the *Intercollegiate Athletic Association's* meeting in New York in May; Harvard, Yale, Columbia, and Princeton lead the others. These and many others hold annual meetings in May.

XVI. Educational, Charitable, Penal, and Industrial Institutions.

The object of many visitors to the United States is to study its systems of schools, prisons, or charities, or to inspect the working of its leading industrial establishments. For such visitors the subjoined brief index-lists may be serviceable.

a. Educational Institutions,

by *Professor N. M. Butler* of Columbia College.

Public Education is regulated by the several States. The United States Bureau of Education, established in 1867 (Dr. William T. Harris, present Commissioner of Education), maintains a library and educational museum at Washington and issues an annual report. It has, however, no direct authority over education in the States.

Each State maintains an elaborate system of public schools; those of the N. and W. States (*e. g.*, New York, Massachusetts, New Jersey, Michigan, Minnesota, Iowa, etc.) are especially well organized and administered. In addition to providing free elementary and secondary education, many of the W. States maintain free universities, the original funds for the endowment of the same having been derived from the sale or rental of public lands given by Congress for the purpose. The largest of these is the University of Michigan at Ann Arbor (p. 274), with nearly 3000 students. The University of Wisconsin at Madison (p. 289) and the University of California at Berkeley (p. 399) are also worthy of special notice.

As a rule, however, the great colleges and universities are private foundations managed by a corporation or board of trustees. Of these the oldest and most influential is Harvard University (founded in 1636) at Cambridge (p. 83). In 1889-90 the gross annual expenditures of Harvard, including the cost of new buildings, rose to $ 995,437. Over 2900 students are now in attendance. The other great universities of this class are Johns Hopkins University at Baltimore (p. 248, founded in 1876), which has had a profound influence on higher education in America; Columbia College in New York (p. 39; founded as a college in 1754, reorganized as a university in 1890); Cornell University at Ithaca (p. 190; founded in 1865); Yale University (p. 58; founded in 1700); and the University of Virginia, Charlottesville (p. 304; founded in 1819). Among the newly founded institutions are the Catholic University of America at Washington (p. 262), and the University of Chicago (p. 285).

There are nearly 400 colleges in the United States in addition to the great universities. The best known colleges are Princeton (p. 208), Amherst (p. 36), Williams (p. 141), Hamilton (Clinton, N. Y.), Miami (Ohio), Lafayette (p. 227), Rutgers (p. 208), Pennsylvania (p. 219), and Stanford (p. 437).

The leading colleges for women are Wellesley (p. 61), Vassar (p. 151), Smith (p. 142) and Bryn Mawr (p. 231).

Of the great technical schools for the training of engineers, architects, etc., the most worthy of a visit are the Massachusetts Institute of Technology (p. 79), Stevens Institute of Technology (p. 51), Rennselaer Polytechnic Institute (Troy, p. 145), and Rose Polytechnic Institute (Terre Haute, p. 310).

Of city school systems the best are those of Minneapolis and St. Paul (pp. 291-293), Indianapolis (p. 302), Denver (p. 406), Boston and Brookline (R. 5), and Brooklyn (p. 52). Duluth (p. 295) and Denver have the finest high-school buildings and equipment. Kindergartens will be found in the public schools of Boston, Philadelphia (p. 210), Paterson (p. 196), San Francisco (p. 428), and elsewhere.

b. Correctional and Charitable Institutions,

by *Warren F. Spalding.*

Penal Institutions. New York State Penitentiaries at Sing Sing (p. 151) and Auburn (p. 190). — Institutions on Blackwell's Island (p. 50). — Eastern Penitentiary at Philadelphia (p. 217; the only prison in the country managed on the 'separate system'). — Western Penitentiary, at Allegheny (p. 243). — Massachusetts State Prison at Charlestown (p. 85). — Boston House of Industry, at Deer Island (p. 85). — Northern Illinois Penitentiary, at Joliet (p. 290). — Ohio Penitentiary, at Columbus (p. 264). — California State Prison, at San Quentin (Cal.).

Reformatories. New York State Reformatory, Elmira (p. 197). — Massachusetts Reformatory, Concord (p. 113). — Reformatory Prison for

Women, Sherborn, Mass. (near South Framingham; p. 61). — Pennsylvania Industrial Reformatory, Huntington (p. 233). — Michigan Reformatory, Ionia (Mich.).

Lunatic Hospitals and Asylums. Mount Hope Retreat for the Insane, Baltimore (p. 250). — McLean Asylum for the Insane, Somerville (p. 112). — Eastern Michigan Asylum for the Insane, Pontiac (Mich.). — State Lunatic Asylum, Utica (p. 187). — Willard Asylum for the Insane, Willard (N.Y.). — Massachusetts Lunatic Hospital and Asylums at Worcester (p. 61), Danvers (Mass.), Westborough (Mass.), and Tewksbury (Mass.). — Ohio Asylums for the Insane at Columbus (p. 264), Toledo (p. 269), and Cleveland (p. 267). — Hospital for the Insane in Philadelphia (p. 220). — Illinois Eastern Hospital for the Insane, at Kankakee (p. 302). — Hospital for Dipsomaniacs and Inebriates at Foxborough (Mass.), opened in 1893.

Institutions for the Blind. Perkins Institution for the Blind, Boston (p. 82). — Illinois Institution for the Education of the Blind, Jacksonville (p. 400). — New York Institutions for the Blind, at New York (p. 40) and Batavia (p. 192). — Pennsylvania Institution for the Instruction of the Blind, Philadelphia (p. 210). — Ohio Institution for the Education of the Blind, Columbus (p. 264).

Institutions for the Deaf. The most important of these are at Northampton (p. 142), Flint (Mich.), New York City (p. 38), Columbus (p. 264), Indianapolis (p. 303), Jacksonville (p. 400), Hartford (p. 59), Philadelphia (p. 218), Knoxville (p. 341), and Delavan (Wis.).

Reformatories for Youth. Among the largest of these are the institutions at West Meriden (Conn.), Plainfield (p. 209), Baltimore (p. 244), Carroll (Md.), Westborough (Mass.; for boys), Lancaster (Mass.; for girls), Lansing (p. 273), Jamesburg (N. J.), Randall's Island (p. 50), Rochester (p. 191), Westchester (N.Y.), Lancaster (Ohio), Cincinnati (p. 307), Philadelphia (p. 210), Morganza (Pa.), Providence (p. 64), and Waukesha (p. 283).

c. Industrial Establishments.

I. METALLIC INDUSTRIES AND MACHINERY. Homestead and Braddock Steel Works, near Pittsburg (see p. 242); Pennsylvania Steel Co., at Steelton (p. 232) and Sparrow's Point (p. 246); Cambria Steel Co., Johnstown (p. 234); Illinois Steel Co., Chicago (p. 282); iron and steel works at Cleveland (p. 267), Buffalo (p. 192), Wilmington (p. 244), Bethlehem (p. 226), and Birmingham (p. 343); agricultural machinery at Chicago (p. 282; McCormick), Louisville (p. 315, Avery), Columbus (p. 264), Akron (p. 278), Springfield (p. 306), Canton (p. 263), and Hoosick Falls (p. 135); sewing machines at Bridgeport (p. 57) and Elizabeth (p. 208); silver and plated goods at Providence (p. 64), New York (p. 6; Whiting Co.), Meriden (Conn.), Taunton (p. 72), and Attleborough (p. 65); bicycles at Hartford (p. 59); stoves at Troy (p. 145) and Buffalo (p. 192); wire at Worcester (p. 60); safes at Cincinnati (p. 307); smelting works at Denver (p. 406); locomotives at Philadelphia (Baldwin's; p. 217) and Altoona (p. 234). — II. TEXTILE INDUSTRIES. Cotton at Manchester (p. 116), Lawrence (p. 95), Fall River (p. 72), Chicopee (p. 142), Baltimore (p. 244; cotton-duck), Charleston (p. 347), and Augusta (p. 350); woollens at Lawrence (p. 95), Lowell (p. 116), and Providence (p. 64); linen at Willimantic (p. 62); carpets at Philadelphia (p. 210) and Lowell (p. 116); silk at South Manchester (Conn.) and Paterson (p. 196). — III. FOOD PRODUCTS. Flour at Minneapolis (p. 293) and St. Louis (p. 311); malt liquors at St. Louis (p. 312), Milwaukee (p. 276), and Rochester (p. 191); wine at St. Louis (p. 311), Charlottesville (p. 304), and in California (comp. p. 434); meat packing at Chicago (p. 286), Kansas City (p. 400), and Omaha (p. 388); sugar at Brooklyn (p. 52) and Philadelphia (p. 219). — IV. GLASS AND POTTERY. Trenton (p. 209); Elwood (Ind.); Findlay (Ohio); Pittsburg (see pp. 241, 242). — V. CARRIAGES. Columbus (p. 264); South Bend (p. 270; Studebaker); Concord (p. 116); Cincinnati (p. 307); New York (p. 6; Cunningham). — VI. RAILWAY ROLLING STOCK. Pullman (p. 286); Buffalo (p. 194; Wagner); Dayton (p. 306); Philadelphia (locomotives; p. 217); Altoona (p. 234). — VII. SHIPS. Philadelphia (p. 219); Chester (p. 244); Wilmington (p. 249); San Francisco (p. 228); Cleveland (p. 267);

Superior (p. 296; whalebacks); Bath (p. 99; sailing vessels). — VIII. PAPER.
Holyoke (p. 142); Springfield (p. 60; envelopes). — IX. OIL. Cleveland
(p. 267); Bayonne (N. J.); Memphis (p. 320; cotton seed oil); New Orleans
(p. 366; cotton seed oil). — X. TOBACCO. St. Louis (p. 311); Richmond
(p. 326); Durham (p. 335); Jersey City (p. 51). — XI. FIRE-ARMS. Springfield
(p. 60); Hartford (p. 59). — XII. BOOTS and SHOES. Lynn (p. 90). — XIII.
PIANOS. New York (Steinway); Boston (p. 72; Chickering). — XIV. WATCHES.
Waltham (p. 112); Waterbury (p. 62). — XV. ELECTRIC WORKS. Lynn (p. 90;
Thompson-Houston) and Newark (p. 208; Edison). — XVI. MARBLE QUAR-
RIES of Vermont (Rutland; p. 114) and Tennessee (Knoxville; p. 341).

XVII. Bibliography.

The following is a very small selection of the most recent, interesting, and easily accessible books on some of the main topics on
which visitors to the United States should be informed. A few of
the best records of the impressions of English travellers are included.
Numerous other works of local interest are referred to throughout
the text of the Handbook. The asterisks indicate publications of
special interest and importance.

**The American Commonwealth, by *James Bryce* (new ed., 1893; the
best and most comprehensive account of the political and social institutions
of the United States). — *De la Démocratie aux États-Unis, by *A. C. H.
de Tocqueville* (1835; trans. by *Henry Reeve*, with notes by *Francis Bowen*,
1882). — *The Federalist, a series of essays by *Hamilton, Madison*, and *Jay*
(1787-8; ed. by *H. C. Lodge*, 1888). — *Constitutional and Political History
of the United States, by *Prof. H. von Holst* (trans. by *J. J. Lalor*; 1876-85).
— History of American Politics, by *Alex. Johnson* (1882). — *American
Political Ideas, and *Civil Government in the United States, two lucid
little books by *John Fiske* (1885 and 1890). — *Our Government, by *Macy*
(1887). — See also the *John Hopkins University Studies in Historical and
Political Science, ed. by *Prof. Herbert B. Adams*.

Histories of the United States, by *George Bancroft, J. B. McMaster,
Justin Winsor, R. Hildreth, B. J. Lossing, Henry Adams* (1891), *J. C. Ridpath*
(a good popular manual), *T. W. Higginson* (for children), and *J. A. Doyle*
(best general short history). — The American Colonies previous to the
Declaration of Independence, and The English in America by *J. A. Doyle*
(1869 and 1882-7). — A Short History of the War of Secession, by *Rossiter
Johnson* (1888). — History of the Civil War in America, by the *Comte de
Paris* (1875-88). — History of American Industries, by *B. J. Lossing* (1879).

*The United States, by *Prof. J. D. Whitney*, is a mine of information
on the physical geography and material resources of the country (1889).
Comp. *Elisée Reclus*' Nouvelle Géographie Universelle (vol. XVI, 1892).

*A Visit to the States, by *Joel Cook* (letters reprinted from the 'Times',
recommended for reading on the voyage across the Atlantic; 1887-8; two
series, 1s. each). — *Some Impressions of the United States, by *E. A.
Freeman* (1883). — Discourses on America, by *Matthew Arnold* (1885). —
American Notes, by *Charles Dickens* (1842). — White and Black in America,
by *Sir George Campbell* (1889). — Three Visits to America, by *Emily Faithful* (1884). — To-day in America, by *Joseph Hatton* (1881). — Through the
Light Continent, by *William Saunders* (1879). — Jonathan and his Continent,
and A Frenchman in America, by *Max O'Rell* (1889 and 1891). — Our Kin
across the Sea, by *J. C. Firth* (1888).

Maps. The leading *General Maps* of the United States are those of the
General Land Office and the U. S. Geological Survey (Washington). The
former also publishes a series of maps (10-18 M. per inch) of those states
in which public lands have existed (*i.e.* all except those on the Atlantic
seaboard). — The only official *Detailed Maps* of any part of the United

g*

States are those of the Geological Survey, published on three scales (1 : 62,500 or about 1 M. per inch; 1 : 125,000 or 2 M. per inch; and 1 : 250,000 or 4 M. per inch). About 600,000 sq. M. have been surveyed, in various parts of the country. These maps can be obtained only on application to the Director of the Geol. Survey. The U. S. Coast Survey is producing charts of the coast, which may be obtained at Washington or from the agencies of the Survey in the large maritime cities. Charts of the Great Lakes, published by the U. S. Corps of Engineers, may be purchased from the Chief of Engineers (Washington). The maps of the Wheeler and Hayden Surveys, covering extensive regions in the West (4 M. per inch), can now be obtained only of second-hand booksellers. Maps of the whole or parts of their states have been published by the Geological Surveys of New Jersey, New Hampshire, Pennsylvania, Kentucky, Wisconsin, Missouri, Arkansas, Texas, Minnesota, California, etc.

1. From Europe to New York.

An overwhelming proportion of European visitors to the United States land at New York, and the following brief notes on the chief oceanic routes to that port may prove serviceable. Lines also run from European ports to Boston (see p. 73), Philadelphia (p. 210), Baltimore (p.244), etc. For general hints as to the voyage, see p.xxx.

a. From Liverpool to New York.

This is the route followed by the *White Star*, *Cunard*, *National*, *Guion*, and *Allan* (monthly) steamship companies. The fastest steamers take about 6½ days from port to port (comp. p. 3), the slowest 8-9 days. The distance varies from 3000 to 3100 nautical miles (ca. 3600-3750 Engl. M.) according to the course followed. New York time is about 5 hrs. behind that of Liverpool.

Liverpool, see *Baedeker's Handbook to Great Britain*. Passengers usually reach the Atlantic steamers by tenders starting from the N. end of the Landing Stage. As we pass down the wide estuary of the *Mersey* we see the crowded docks of Liverpool to the right, while to the left lies *New Brighton*, with its pier, fort, and lighthouse. The mouth of the river is marked by a lightship, which we reach in about 2 hrs. after starting. Farther on, in clear weather, we see the Welsh coast to the left (S.), where the *Little* and *Great Orme's Heads* are the most prominent points, backed by the distant *Snowdon Group*. A little later we skirt the N. coast of the *Isle of Anglesey*, then turn to the left, and steer to the S.W. through *St. George's Channel*, soon losing sight of land. The *Skerries*, with a lighthouse, lie off the N.W. point of Anglesey.

The first part of the Irish coast sighted is usually *Carnsore Point*, in *Wexford*, the S.W. corner of the island. In about 12-15 hrs. after leaving Liverpool we enter the beautiful inner harbour of *Queenstown* (about 230 knots from Liverpool), where a halt is made to take on board the mails and additional passengers arriving from England viâ the Holyhead route. Sometimes the halt is long enough to allow a visit to Queenstown, beautifully situated on *Great Island*, or even to (10 M.) *Cork*, which may be reached either by rail (½ hr.; seats to left) or by the river *Lea*.

On leaving Queenstown, we skirt the S. coast of Ireland for some distance, passing several bold rocky headlands. The last piece of European land seen is usually the *Fastnet Rock* (lighthouse), off *Cape Clear Island*, 60 M. to the S.W. of Queenstown.

In crossing the Atlantic Ocean from E. to W. the steamer descends through about 11 degrees of latitude (Queenstown 51° 50′ N. lat., New York 40° 42′ 43″). The course varies somewhat according to the season of the year and from other causes. The northerly route (followed from July to Jan.) takes the steamers over the *Grand Bank of Newfoundland* (30-80 fathoms), while the southerly route followed for the rest of the year passes to the S. of it. Among the few events which cause a break in the similarity of day to day are the occasional sight of an *Ice Berg* (an object of great beauty), usually seen above 42° N. lat. and between 45° and 50° E. long., and the passing of other vessels. Whales, dolphins, porpoises, etc., are also seen from time to time. The 'day's run' of the steamer, given in nautical miles (7 'knots' = about 8 Engl. M.), is usually posted up every day at noon in the companion-way. The traveller should remember that his watch will gain about $3/4$ hr. daily in going W. and lose the same amount in going E.

The following list of the colours of the funnels ('smokestacks') of the principal steamship lines will help the traveller to identify the steamers he meets. *Allan*, red, with black and white bands and black top; *Anchor*, black (English flag); *Compagnie Générale Transatlantique*, red, with black top (French flag); *Cunard*, red, with black top; *Guion*, black, with red band; *Hamburg*, buff or black (German flag); *International (Inman)*, black, with white band; *National*, white, with black top; *North German Lloyd*, buff; *Red Star*, cream, with red star; *White Star*, salmon, with black top.

The competition among the pilots of New York is so keen that the pilot-boat often meets the steamer hundreds of miles from land. The pilot dues vary with the tonnage of the vessel, but average about $230 (46 *l.*) for taking the vessel in and out. The first American land sighted is usually either *Fire Island* (p. 5) or the *Navesink Highlands* (p. 223), each with a lighthouse. About **3** hrs. after sighting land we approach *Sandy Hook Bar*, the Highlands standing out boldly to the left. The time of the voyage is reckoned to (or from) Sandy Hook. The chief passage across the bar is afforded by the *Gedney Channel*, which is marked by six buoys with red and white electric lights and is available for large vessels at all states of the tide. Smaller ships may use the *South Channel*. We leave the lighthouse of *Sandy Hook* (p. 223; white light) to the left, enter the *Lower Bay of New York* (p. 23), and steer to the N. toward the *Narrows*, or entrance to *New York Bay* proper (p. 23), between the wooded *Staten Island* (p. 50) on the left and *Long Island* (p. 55) to the right. On the former are *Fort Wadsworth, Fort Tompkins*, and a lighthouse; on the latter lies *Fort Hamilton*, while on a rocky island in the channel is *Fort Lafayette*, where many Southern prisoners were confined during the Civil War. About 3 M. farther up is the *Quarantine Station*, off which all vessels anchor until they have been cleared by the officer of the Board of Health. The custom-house officers also usually come on board here (see p. xix). About half-way between the Quarantine Station and New York, to the left, is *Robin's Reef*, with a white lighthouse.

As we advance up the beautiful *New York Harbour* (p. 23) the city of *Brooklyn* (p. 52) lies to the right and *Jersey City* (p. 51) to the left, while *New York* lies straight ahead. *Bedloe's Island*, with the colossal statue of *Liberty enlightening the World*, lies nearly in mid-channel, while *Governor's Island*, with its old fort, lies to the right, close inshore. To the left, beyond Bedloe's Island, is the small *Ellis Island*, where emigrants now land and are taken care of, in a large building provided for the purpose, until they can be forwarded to their final destinations (comp. p. 25). The wonderful **Brooklyn Bridge* (p. 30), spanning the *East River* (p. 23) and connecting New York with Brooklyn, is seen to the right.

The **Statue of Liberty*, on Bedloe's Island, presented to the United States by the French Republic, in commemoration of the 100th anniversary of the Declaration of Independence, was designed by *Auguste Bartholdi* and erected in 1886. It is 151 ft. high (to the top of the torch), is made of copper and iron, and weighs 225 tons. The granite pedestal on which it stands, designed by *R. M. Hunt*, is 155 ft. high and was contributed by citizens of the United States. A stairway ascends inside the figure to the head, which can accommodate 40 persons and commands a magnificent **View of New York and its vicinity (nearly as good from the first balcony). At night the torch is lit by electricity. Steamers run at frequent intervals to Bedloe's Island from the Battery (see p. 25; return-fare 25 c.).

As the steamer approaches her dock, in the *North (Hudson) River*, the conspicuous features in New York include the *Produce Exchange* (p. 25), with its square Florentine tower; the towers of the *Cotton Exchange* (p. 27); the *Washington Building* (p. 25); the spire of *Trinity Church* (p. 27), rising among the huge business blocks of *Broadway* (p. 26); the Mansard towers of the *Post Office* (p. 28); and the lofty dome of the *World Building* (p. 29). Passengers are landed directly on the wharf, attend to the custom-house examination of their baggage (comp. p. xix), and then drive to their destination, either taking their trunks with them or entrusting them to one of the numerous transfer-agents or express-agents who meet the steamer (comp. p. xxii).

New York, see R. 2.

b. From Southampton to New York.

In 1893 the *Inman Steamship Co.* was reconstituted as the *International Navigation Co.*, sailing under the American flag, and changed its starting-point from Liverpool to *Southampton* (3075 knots to New York; 6^1/$_2$-7^1/$_2$ days). Passengers are conveyed free of charge from London to Southampton (1^3/$_4$ hr.), where they embark at the new Empress Dock. The steamers 'New York' and 'Paris' of this company hold the record at present for the fastest passages across the Atlantic (from New York to Queenstown, 5 days, 19 hrs., 57 min. ; from Queenstown to New York, 5 days, 14 hrs., 24 min.). Southampton time is 4 hrs. 54 min. ahead of that of New York.

Southampton, see *Baedeker's Great Britain*. The steamer descends *Southampton Water* and passes through the *Solent*, affording a good view of *Hurst Castle* to the right and of the *Needles* to the left (lighthouse; red flashing light). The time of the voyage is reckoned from this point. To the right lie *St. Alban's Head*, the *Bill of Portland*, and *Start Point* (white flashing light). *Eddystone Lighthouse* (one fixed and one flashing light) is seen to the right, in *Plymouth Bay*. The last point seen of the English mainland is *Lizard Head*, in Cornwall, and the last European land sighted is the *Scilly Isles* (lighthouse), about 30 M. to the S.W. of the Land's End. — The rest of the voyage is similar to that described in R. 1a.

c. From Hamburg to New York.

The Express Steamers of the *Hamburg-American Packet Co.* ply to New York viâ Southampton (7¹/₂-8 days; from Southampton to New York, 3075 knots, in 6¹/₂-7 days), and the Regular Service Steamers run either viâ Havre or to New York direct (3505 knots, in 10-11 days).

The Express Steamers start from *Cuxhaven*, at the mouth of the Elbe, 58 M. from Hamburg, to which passengers are forwarded by special train, while the other boats start from Hamburg (see *Baedeker's Handbook to Northern Germany*) itself (wharf at the Grosse Grasbrook). At Cuxhaven and Southampton passengers embark by tenders. Passengers are carried between London and Southampton free of charge, generally by special trains. New York time is 4 hrs. 54 min. behind that of Southampton and 5 hrs. 35 min. behind that of Hamburg.

Leaving *Cuxhaven*, the steamer steers to the N.W., passing the three *Elbe Lightships* and affording a distant view of the red rocks of *Heligoland* to the right. Various other German, Dutch, and Belgian lights are visible. The first English lights are those of the *Galloper Lightship* and the *Goodwin Sands*, while the first part of the coast to come in sight is usually near *Dover*. Farther on we pass through the *Straits of Dover*, with the English and French coasts visible to the right and left. The steamer of the direct service either keeps on her way through mid-channel or diverges to the left to call at *Havre* (comp. below), while the express-steamer hugs the English coast, passing *Dungeness*, *Beachy Head*, and various lightships. *Hastings*, between Dungeness and Beachy Head, and *Brighton*, 15 M. to the W. of the latter, are sometimes visible. In front appears the picturesque *Isle of Wight*, with *Ryde*, *Cowes*, and the towers of *Osborne*, the marine home of Queen Victoria. The steamer passes through the sheltered *Spithead Roads*, between the Isle of Wight and the mainland (with *Portsmouth* to the right), and enters *Southampton Water* (430 knots), where it generally anchors off *Calshot Castle*, to receive the British mails and passengers from *Southampton* (see *Baedeker's Great Britain*). Thence to New York, see R. 1 b. The dock of the Hamburg Co. is at *Hoboken* (p. 51), on the W. side of the *North River*, whence passengers are conveyed to New York by large ferry-steamers.

d. From Bremen to New York.

The Express Steamers of the *North German Lloyd (Norddeutscher Lloyd)* run to *New York* (3560 knots, in 8 days) viâ *Southampton*, but others run to New York direct. The steamers start from (40 M.) *Bremerhaven*, at the mouth of the *Weser*, to which passengers are forwarded by special train. See *Baedeker's Northern Germany*. New York time is 5¹/₂ hrs. behind that of Bremen.

On issuing from the mouth of th *Weser*, the steamer steers to the N.W., with the *Jahdebusen* opening to the left. A little farther on it passes the *East Frisian Islands*. The rest of the voyage is similar to that described in R. 1c. *Southampton* is about 460 M. from Bremerhaven.

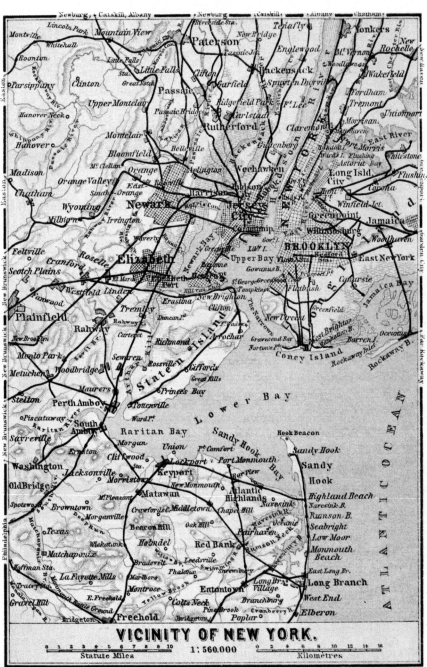

VICINITY OF NEW YORK.

1 : 560,000

Statute Miles

Kilomètres

Wagner & Debes' Geog. Establ. Leipzig.

e. From Havre to New York.

This route is followed by the French steamers of the *Compagnie Générale Transatlantique.* The distance is 3095 knots and the average time 7-8 days. Some of the Hamburg steamers (R. 1c) also call here. New York time is 5 hrs. behind that of Havre.

Havre, see *Baedeker's Handbook to Northern France.* The steamer steers out into the *English Channel*, affording distant views of *Cape La Hogue, Cape La Hague*, and the *Channel Islands* to the left, and of the *Scilly Islands* to the right. The farther course of the voyage resembles that of the steamers of the German and International lines, as above described. The first American land seen is usually *Cape Race* in Newfoundland.

f. From Antwerp to New York.

This is the route of the *Red Star Line* (3340-3410 knots, in 8 days). New York time is 5¹/₄ hrs. behind that of Antwerp.

Antwerp, see *Baedeker's Handbook to Holland and Belgium.* The steamer descends the *West Schelde*, with the Dutch province of *Zealand* on either side, passes (40 M.) *Flushing*, on the island of *Walcheren* (right), and enters the *North Sea.* In very clear weather the towers of *Bruges* and *Ostend* may sometimes be distinguished to the left farther on. Several light-ships are passed, and the first English land sighted is the *South Forelands*, high chalk cliffs, with two fixed electric lights. The steamers call at *Boulogne* and *Southampton.* Their subsequent course is similar to that of the German, French, and International Line steamers (see above).

g. From Glasgow to New York.

This is the regular route of the *Anchor Line*, and is also one of the routes of the *Allan Line* (2900 knots, in 9-10 days; *Moville*, 2780 knots, in 8-9 days). Passengers may join the steamer at Glasgow, *Greenock*, or *Moville.* The difference of time between Glasgow and New York is 4³/₄ hrs.

Glasgow and the beautiful voyage down the *Firth of Clyde* are described in *Baedeker's Handbook to Great Britain.* Among the chief points passed are *Dumbarton* (r.), *Greenock* (l.), *Gourock* (l.), *Toward Point* (l.), the *Isle of Bute* (r.), the *Cumbrae Islands* (l.), the *Isle of Arran* (r.), and *Ayr* (l.). On leaving the estuary of the river the steamer rounds the *Mull of Cantyre* (right) and proceeds to the W. along the N. coast of Ireland, passing the island of *Rathlin* and affording a distant view to the left of the *Giant's Causeway.* It then ascends *Lough Foyle* to *Moville*, the port of *Londonderry*, where mail and extra-passengers are taken on board. On issuing from Lough Foyle the steamer steers at first to the W. and then, after passing *Malin Head*, the northernmost point of Ireland, to the S.W. The last part of Ireland seen is usually *Tory Island* (lighthouse) or the island of *Arranmore*, off the coast of *Donegal.* The general course followed across the Atlantic by the Glasgow steamers is considerably to the N. of that of the Liverpool boats, not joining the latter till the *Banks of Newfoundland* (p. 2), with their fogs and ice-bergs.

2. New York.

Arrival. Railway Stations. Steamers.

Arrival. Strangers arriving in New York by sea will find an explanation of the custom-house formalities at p. xix. All the main steamship landings are near tramway-lines (p. 11), and numerous hacks and cabs are always in waiting (bargaining advisable; fare to hotel for 1-2 pers., luggage included, about $2). A few hotels send carriages to meet the European steamers. Transfer Agents (see pp. xxii, 15) are also on hand to receive trunks and forward them to any address (25-50 c.). Travellers landing on the New Jersey side cross to New York by ferry, and will generally find it convenient to do so in cabs. Those coming by railway from the S. and W. cross the river by ferries in connection with the railways, and claim their baggage at the ferry-house in New York (see below). Travellers from Canada and the North, or from the West by the N. Y. C. R. R. route, arrive at the Grand Central Depot (see p. 37), in the heart of the city, and may use the Elevated Railway (see p. 10) to reach their city destination. Cab-fares, see p. 13.

Railway Stations *(Depots).* The *Grand Central Depot*, E. 42nd St., between Lexington and Vanderbilt Avenues, is the only terminal station in New York proper. It is a large, handsome, and well-arranged building (restaurant in the basement), and is used by the trains of the New York Central & Hudson River Railroad (entr. from Vanderbilt Ave.; for Canada and the N., Chicago and the W., etc.), the New York & Harlem Railroad (entr. in Vanderbilt Ave.), and the New York, New Haven, & Hartford Railroad (entr. in 42nd St.; for Boston and New England, etc.). — Some local trains of the Hudson River Ry., for stations up to Spuyten Duyvil (p. 150), start from the station at Tenth Ave. and W. 30th St.

The other great railway systems have their depots on the New Jersey side of the North River and convey passengers to and from them by large ferry-boats. The ferry-houses, however, furnish the same opportunities for the purchase of tickets, checking baggage, etc., as the railway-stations, and the times of departure and arrival of trains by these lines are given with reference to the New York side of the river. — *Pennsylvania Railway Station*, Exchange Place, Jersey City, reached by ferries from Desbrosses St. (the main New York station of the company) and Cortlandt St., used by trains of the Pennsylvania Railroad (for all points in the West and South) and the Lehigh Valley, the N. Y., Susquehanna & Western, and the New Jersey Midland railways. — *Erie Railroad Station*, Pavonia Ave., Jersey City, reached by ferries from Chambers St. and W. 23rd St., used by the New York, Lake Erie & Western, the New Jersey & New York, the New York & Greenwood Lake, and the Northern New Jersey railroads. — *West Shore Station*, Weehawken, reached by ferries from Franklin St. and W. 42nd St., used by the West Shore Railroad (for the same districts as the N. Y. Central Railroad) and the New York, Ontario, & Western Railroad. — *Delaware, Lackawanna, and Western Station*, Hoboken, reached by ferries from Christopher St. and Barclay St., used by the Delaware, Lackawanna, & Western Railroad (for New Jersey, Pennsylvania, and Western New York) and the Morris & Essex Railroad. — *Central Railroad of New Jersey Depot*, Communipaw, reached by ferry from Liberty St., used also by the New Jersey Southern Railroad.

For *Brooklyn* stations, see p. 52. — The station of the *New York and Northern Railroad*, at 155th St., is reached by the Sixth and Ninth Avenue Elevated Railroads (comp. p. 11).

Steamers. 1. OCEAN STEAMSHIPS. The following is a list of the chief Passenger Steamship Companies between New York and Europe, with their docks, city-offices, and days of sailing (comp. also R. 1 and p. xviii). *White Star Line*, Dock 45, foot of W. 10th St. (office, 41 Broadway; Wed.); *International Navigation Co.* (formerly *Inman Line*), Pier 14, foot of Vesey St. (office, 6 Bowling Green; Wed. and Sat.); *Cunard Co.*, Dock 40, Clarkson St. (office, 4 Bowling Green; Sat. & Thurs.); *Guion*, Dock 38, King St. (office,

35 Broadway; Sat.); *Anchor Line*, Dock 41, Leroy St. (office, 7 Bowling Green; Sat.); *Allan Line*, pier at the foot of W. 21st St. (office, 53 Broadway); *Compagnie Générale Transatlantique*, Dock 42, Morton St. (office, 3 Bowling Green; Sat.); *North German Lloyd*, Hoboken (office, 2 Bowling Green; Tues. & Sat.; to Genoa fortnightly); *Hamburg American Packet Co.*, Hoboken (office, 37 Broadway; Sat., Thurs., & Tues.; to Genoa and the Orient in winter); *Red Star Line*, Jersey City, near the Penn. R. R. Depot (office, 6 Bowling Green; Wed.). — Other ocean-going steamships ply to the ports of S. and Central America, the West Indies, Mexico, Cuba, Florida, New Orleans, Richmond, and other ports of the Southern States, the Mediterranean ports, Boston, Philadelphia, Portland (Maine), Newfoundland, etc. — The times of departure and other information are advertised in the daily papers.

2. RIVER, SOUND, AND HARBOUR STEAMERS. The following are a few of the principal points on the Hudson, Long Island Sound, and N. Y. Harbour, reached by steamer from New York. For full information on these and other lines, reference must be made to current time-tables and daily pap ers. The larger American river steamboats are very finely fitted up, and the traveller should not omit an inspection of one of the Fall River or Hudson River boats, even if he does not travel by them. They are very unlike European boats, rising in house-like tiers high above the water, and propelled by paddle-wheels and 'walking-beam' engines, the long shafts of which protrude above the middle of the deck. The 'smoke-stacks' or funnels are also unlike the European pattern. There are good restaurants on board, and a comfortable private state-room may be obtained for a small addition to the regular fare (usually $ 1-2 per night). The Hudson River boats cease running in winter, but most of the Sound boats ply throughout the year. — To *Albany* (p. 154), either by the Day Line, the People's Line, or the Citizen's Line (fares, etc., see p. 146). — To *Catskill* (p. 151), and *Hudson* (p. 151), either by the Albany Day Line (see above; $ 1½; 6¾ hrs.) or from the foot of Jay St. ($ 1; night-boat, 11 hrs.). — To *Rondout* (p. 153), by the Albany Day Line (see above) or by the 'Mary Powell', Vestry St. — To *Troy* (p. 145), by Albany Day Line ($ 2; 10⅓ hrs.) or Citizen's Line ($ 1½, $ 2½; 12 hrs.; see above). — *West Point* (p. 152), by Albany Day Line (see above; 75 c., $ 1; 3¼ hrs.) or by the 'Mary Powell' (see above; same fares; 3 hrs.). — To *Boston* (p. 72), by the Fall River, Providence, Norwich, or Stonington line (fare $ 2-4 acc. to the season; 12½-14½ hrs.; for all details, see p. 66). — To *Coney Island* (p. 55), from Pier 1, hourly or oftener in summer (fare 35 c., return 50 c.; 50 min.). — To *Long Branch* (p. 223), about 8 times daily, from Rector St. ($ 1; 1¼ hr.). — To *Providence* (p. 64), from Warren St., North River, daily (fare $ 2¼; 12½ hrs.), or viâ Stonington (p. 63) from Spring St., N. R., daily in 10 hrs. ($ 1.35). — *Ferries*, see p. 14.

Hotels, Restaurants, etc.

Hotels (comp. p. xxv). The distinction between the fo urgeographical groups in which the hotels of New York are here distributed is a somewhat arbitrary one, but it will perhaps give the traveller some help in selecting his quarters. As a general rule those who wish to be near the business-districts should select a 'Down Town' hotel, or at any rate, one not higher up than 14th St., while the ordinary tourist will probably find himself best suited in or near Union or Madison Squares. For the difference between the 'American' and 'European' plans, see p. xxvi.

Down Town (from the Battery to Canal St.). 1. On the European Plan: *ASTOR HOUSE (Pl. a; B, 3), 221 Broadway, opposite the Post Office, an old and popular house, much frequented by business-men, R. from $ 1½; COSMOPOLITAN (Pl. b; B, 2), 129 Chambers St., R. from $ 1; SMITH & McNEIL'S (Pl. d; B, 2), 199 Washington St., R. from 50 c. — 2. American Plan: EARLE'S (Pl. e; C, 3), 241 Canal St., unpretending, $ 2 per day.

Between Canal St. and 14th St. 1. European Plan: *BREVOORT HOUSE (Pl. f; D, E, 3), at the corner of Fifth Ave. and 8th St., an aristocratic and quiet family hotel, patronised by English visitors, R. from $ 2; ST.

DENIS (Pl. g; E, 3), good cuisine, R. from $1; METROPOLITAN (Pl. h; D, 3),
R. from $1; SINCLAIR HOUSE (Pl. i; D, 3), R. from $1; these all in
Broadway (Nos. 797, 584, and 754); HÔTEL MARTIN (Pl. l; E, 3; French),
17 University Place, cor. 9th St., R. from $1; ST. STEPHEN (Pl. m; E, 3),
46 East 11th St., R. from $1; GRIFFOU (Pl. n; E, 3), 19 W. 9th St., a
small French house. — 2. American and European: *BROADWAY CENTRAL
(Pl. o; D,3), 671 Broadway (1000 beds), from $2½, R. $1; COLONNADE
(Pl. k; D, 3), 726 Broadway and 35-39 Lafayette Sq., $2, R. from $1, D.
75 c.; NEW YORK HOTEL (Pl. p; D, 3), 721 Broadway, R. from $1; HÔTEL
ESPANOL E HISPANO-AMERICANO (Pl. q; E, 2), 116 W. 14th St. (Spanish).
   From 14th St. to 26th St. (incl. *Union Sq.* and *Madison Sq.*). **1.** American Plan: FIFTH AVENUE HOTEL (Pl. r; F, 3), Madison Sq., at the corner
of 23rd St., long one of the most noted hotels in New York, with accommodation for 1000 guests, frequented by officials and politicians, from
$5 per day; *WESTMINSTER (Pl. s; E, 3), Irving Place, cor. 16th St., a
quiet house, patronised by diplomats, from $3. — **2.** European Plan:
HOFFMAN HOUSE (Pl. t; F, 3), Madison Sq., cor. of 24th St., much frequented by politicians, R. from $2; ALBEMARLE (Pl. v; F, 3), cor. Broad-
way. and 24th St., adjoining Madison Sq., R. $2; *EVERETT HO. (Pl. w;
E, 3), N. side of Union Sq., cor. 4th Ave. & 17th St., an old-established
and comfortable house, R. from $1½; GLENHAM (Pl. x; F, 3), 155 Fifth
Ave., R. from $1; ST. JAMES (Pl. y; F, 3), 1133 Broadway, R. $2, fre-
quented by sporting men; UNION SQUARE HOTEL (Pl. z; E, 3), 16 Union
Sq., R. $2; HOTEL DAM, 104 E. 15th St. — **3.** American and European
Plan: *BRUNSWICK (Pl. u; F, 3), 225 Fifth Ave., cor. of 26th St. and
Madison Sq., a fashionable house, R. from $2; VICTORIA (Pl. bb; F, 3),
at the intersection of Broadway, Fifth Ave., and 27th St., close to Madison
Sq., R. from $2½, Amer. plan from $4½; CLARENDON (Pl. cc; E, 3),
219 Fourth Ave., cor. 18th St., a favourite house with English visitors;
STURTEVANT (Pl. dd; F, 3), 1186 Broadway, frequented by army and navy
men, from $3½, R. from $1½; ASHLAND (Pl. ee; F, 3), Fourth Ave.,
cor. 24th St., commercial, $2-3, R. $1.
   Above Madison Square. **1.** American Plan: *WINDSOR (Pl. ff; H, 3),
Fifth Ave. and 46th St., one of the largest and handsomest hotels in New
York, a favourite resort of brokers and financiers, from $5-6; VENDOME
(Pl. D; G, 2), Broadway, cor. 41st St., $4; SAN REMO (Pl. hh; K, 2), Eighth
Ave., cor. 74th St., facing Central Park. — **2.** European Plan: *WALDORF
(Pl. aa; I, 3), Fifth Ave., cor. 33rd St., finely fitted up, R. from $2½; HOL-
LAND HOUSE (Pl. kk; F, G, 3), Fifth Ave., cor. 30th St., another magni-
ficent hotel, R. from $2; NEW NETHERLANDS HOUSE (Pl. ll; I, 3), a luxur-
ious new house, Fifth Ave., cor. 59th St.; IMPERIAL (Pl. mm; F, 3), a new
and handsome house, Broadway, cor. 32nd St., R. from $2; NORMANDIE
(Pl. nn; G, 2), GILSEY (Pl. oo; F, 3), and GRAND (Pl. pp; F, 3), all in
Broadway (38th St., 29th St., 31st St.), R. about $2; BUCKINGHAM (Pl. rr;
H, 3), LANGHAM (Pl. ss; H, 3), large family hotels in Fifth Ave. (50th and
52nd Sts.); ST. CLOUD (Pl. tt; G, 2), MÉTROPOLE (Pl. uu; G, 2), BARRETT
HOUSE (Pl. vv; G, 2), Broadway (42nd, 41st, 43rd Sts.), R. from $1;
GRAND UNION (Pl. xx; G, 3), 42nd St., opp. the Grand Central Depot, R.
from $1; COLEMAN HOUSE (Pl. yy; F, 3), 1169 Broadway, R. from $1;
RENAISSANCE, 43rd St.; MT. MORRIS HOTEL (Pl. zz; O, 4), Third Ave., cor.
130th St., R. from $1. — **3.** American and European Plan: *MURRAY HILL
(Pl. A; G, 3), Park Ave., cor. 41st St., near the Grand Central Depot,
R. from $1½, Amer. plan from $4½; *SAVOY HOTEL (Pl. B; H, I, 3), S.E.
cor. of Fifth Ave. and 59th St., R. & board from $4½, R. from $2; PLAZA
(Pl. C; I, 3), a new and sumptuously equipped house in Fifth Ave. (cor.
59th St.), adjoining Central Park; MADISON AVENUE HOTEL (Pl. ii; I, 3),
Madison Ave., cor. 58th St.; ORIENTAL (Pl. qq; G, 2), Broadway, cor. 39th
St.; PARK AVENUE HOTEL (Pl. E; F, 3), Fourth Ave., cor. 32nd St., from
$3½, R. from $1.
   Most of the hotels take in guests by the week or month at very considerable reductions of their daily rates (comp. p. xxvi); and when two
persons occupy one room the charge is often materially diminished. Many
of the uptown hotels are almost entirely occupied by permanent guests

and are little used by tourists. Fees to waiters and bell-boys are unfortunately becoming more and more customary in New York hotels.

Boarding Houses. Good board can be procured in New York from $8 a week upwards, varying according to the situation and locality of the house. For $15-25 one should obtain good accommodation in the best neighbourhood (*e.g.* near Madison Sq.). Above Washington Square and between 7th and Lexington Avenues boarding-houses may be found in every block. Many are in E. 21st St., Gramercy Park, Irving Place, and Madison Ave., while immense numbers can be found on the W. side by a little search or a carefully worded advertisement. A distinct understanding should be come to beforehand, and references should be asked for in houses not specially recommended. Light, heat, service (but not boot-cleaning), and the use of a bath should be included in the price for board.

Furnished Rooms may be obtained in convenient quarters from $4-5 per week upwards, and breakfast is sometimes provided in the same house. But the English custom of living in lodgings, ordering one's own meals, and having them cooked and served by the landlady is unknown in New York.

Restaurants. The distinction made below between *à la carte* and *table-d'hôte* restaurants is not necessarily mutually exclusive, but indicates the general custom at the different houses. At all the high-priced *à la carte* restaurants one portion is generally enough for two persons, and two portions are abundant for three. Many of the *table-d'hôte* dinners are wonderfully good for the prices charged, but the *à la carte* restaurants are usually dear for a person dining alone. The following list divides the restaurants into two groups, above and below 14th St. It is customary, but by no means necessary except in dining repeatedly at the same place, to give a small fee to the waiter, varying from 5 c. in the cheaper restaurants to 25 c. in the best. Wine (generally poor and dear, except at the foreign restaurants) and beer (5-10 c. per glass, 15-25 c. per pint) may be usually obtained, but are comparatively seldom used at meals.

Up-Town Restaurants (above 14th St.). 1. A la carte. *Delmonico's*, Madison Sq., cor. 5th Avenue and 26th St., a famous house, with high charges; public and private rooms, café, ball-rooms, etc.; crowded about 7-8 p.m. and after the theatres. *Café Brunswick*, at the Hotel Brunswick (see p. 8), similar accommodation and charges; restaurants at the *Holland Ho.*, *Waldorf*, *Hoffman House*, *Gilsey House*, *Plaza*, *Everett Ho.*, *Imperial*, and other hotels on the European plan, see above; *Sherry*, Fifth Ave., cor. of 37th St.; *Bancel & Pastorini*, 1140 Third Avenue, small; *Heim*, 29 W. 27th St.; *Clark*, 22 W. 23rd St., near Broadway, much frequented by ladies; *Dorlon*, 6 E. 23rd St. (Madison Sq.), famous for oysters and fish; *Coleman House* (see above; half-portions served); *Parker House*, cor. Broadway and 34th St., frequented by actors; *O'Neill*, 358 Sixth Avenue, cor. 22nd St., less fashionable and expensive; *Mouquin*, 438 Sixth Avenue; *Petit Vefour*, W. 28th St.; *Browne's Chop House*, 31 W. 27th St.; *Engel*, 73 W. 35th St.; *The Studio*, Sixth Ave., between 20th and 21st St., frequented for supper after the theatre (men only); *Metropolis*, 24 E. 14th St., near Union Sq., moderate prices, music in the afternoon and evening, much frequented at luncheon by ladies and others; *Columbia*, 48 E. 14th St., a similar establishment. — 2. Table-d'hôte Restaurants (D. usually from 5 to 8): *Brunswick*, see above, D. $1½; *Morello*, 4 W. 29th St., D. with wine $1¼; *Moretti*, 22 E. 21st St., D. with wine $1; *Murray Hill Hotel Restaurant* (see above), D. 75 c. (dearer in dining-room of hotel); *Plavano*, 28 E. 23rd St., D. with wine $1; *Purssell*, 910 Broadway, D. $1; *Drentel*, 9 W. 28th St., near Fifth Avenue, D. $1; *Riccadonna*, 42 Union Sq. E.; *Knickerbocker*, 456 Sixth Avenue, D. with wine 75 c., (men); *Columbia*, 48 E. 14th St., D. (5 to 8) 75 c.; *Hôtel Hungaria*, Union Sq. (E. side), D. with wine 75 c.

Down Town Restaurants. 1. A la carte. *Café Savarin*, in the Equitable Building (p. 27), 120 Broadway, finely fitted up, high charges; *St. Denis Hotel (Taylor's Restaurant)*, good cuisine and native wines, see p. 8; *Sinclair House* (see p. 8), charges moderate; *Fleischmann's Vienna Bakery*, Broadway, cor. 10th St., tea or coffee, with rolls, 25 c., restaurant upstairs (closes at 8.30 p.m.); *Delmonico*, 2 S. William St. and 22 Broad St.; *Astor House* (see above), a much-frequented restaurant (2000-2500 luncheons served daily), with luncheon-counters, etc.; *Hoffman Café*, 7 Beaver St. and 60 Broadway; *Metropolitan Hotel Restaurant*, with extensive lunch-counters, 584 Broadway; *Mouquin*, 149 Fulton St. and 20 Ann St.: *Fisk*, 76 Broad St.; *Nash & Brush*, 16 Park Place, moderate charges; *Sutherland*, 64 Liberty St.; *Solari*, 44 University Place, good cuisine; *Hôtel Martin*, 17 University Pl., cor. 9th St., French cuisine; *Gould*, 135 Nassau St., much frequented for berries and cream in the season; *Smith & McNeil*, 197 Washington St., moderate; *Close's Temperance Eating Rooms*, 100 Duane St., much frequented, moderate, good 'dairy' dishes; *Farrish's Chop House*, 64 John St.; *Old Tom's Chop House*, Thames St. — 2. Tables-d'hôte. *Café Martin*, see above, D. $1; *Tramasure*, 54 E. 11th St.; *Metropolitan Hotel*, see above; *Vianest*, 87 Fulton St., D. 40 c.; *Delisle*, 92 Fulton St., 113 Pearl St., and 66 Beaver St., D. 50, L. 35 c.; *Reicher*, 153 Sixth Avenue, D. 35 c., good Rhine wine at moderate prices, German cuisine, for gentlemen; *Colombo* (Neapolitan), 51 Third Ave., near 10th St., D. 75c.; *Vattel*, 4th St., D. 50 c.; *Griffou*, 19 W. 9th St., D. 50 c.

Among the places specially frequented by ladies may be mentioned *Purssell's*, see above; *St. Denis Hotel*, see above; the *Vienna Café*, see above; *Naething's*, 118 Fulton St.; the luncheon-room at *Macy's* (p. 32); the *Women's Exchange*, 329 Fifth Ave.; *Tenney's*, see below; *Simpson's*, 54 W. 23rd St.; *Clark's*, see p. 9..

Oyster Saloons. *Dorlon*, 6 W. 23rd St. (Madison Sq.), 96 & 187 Fulton Market; *Clark*, Sixth Ave., near 30th St.; *O'Neill*, see p. 9; *Burns*, 783 & 904 Sixth Ave.; *Stewart*, Third Ave., near 14th St.; *Silsbee*, Sixth Ave., near 14th St.; also at nearly all other restaurants and at the *Markets*.

The *Hotel Bars* are a characteristic American feature, which may be studied to perfection in New York. Probably that at the *Hoffman House* is the finest, with numerous pictures (incl. a good example of Bouguereau) and elaborate fitting up (no drink under 25 c.); other good bars at most of the leading hotels; *Stewart's*, 8 Warren St., with good pictures (shown to ladies, 9-11 a. m.); the *Fog Horn*, Ninth Ave., cor. 23rd St. The 'free lunches' given at the Hoffman House and many other bars are elaborate enough to suggest enormous profits on the beverages, which alone are paid for.

Confectioners. *Huyler*, 150 and 863 Broadway and 21 W. 42nd St., also famous for 'ice cream soda' and other refreshing summer-drinks; *Maillard*, 120, 178, and 1097 Broadway; *Brummell*, 831 Broadway, 2 W. 14th St., and 293 Sixth Avenue; *Weidman*, 1211 Broadway; *Purssell's*, see above; *Tenney*, 915 Broadway; *Macy*, 14th St., cor. Sixth Ave. — Soda-water flavoured with syrups of various kinds, 'ice-cream sodas', egg and other 'phosphates', and other non-alcoholic beverages are very popular in America and may be procured at all bars, confectioners, and cafés, and also at all drug-stores (prices from 5 c. upwards). The 'Soda Fountain' at the drug-store is, indeed, a prominent American institution.

City Railroads. Tramways. Post Office, etc.

Elevated Railroads (Manhattan Railway Co., 71 Broadway). The bulk of the passenger traffic in New York is carried on by the four *Elevated Railroads*, which now carry fully 200 million passengers annually. There are two lines on the E. side of the city (Second and Third Avenues), and two on the W. (Sixth and Ninth Avenues). The most frequented is the Third Avenue line, next to which comes the Sixth Avenue; but all are disagreeably crowded at business hours. Apart from this, the 'L', as it is popularly called, affords a very pleasant mode of conveyance, contrasting advantageously with the underground railway in London. The track may be described as a continuous viaduct or bridge, supported on iron columns. The general height is about on a level with the first-floor windows of the houses, but at places it is much higher than this, the Ninth Avenue line attaining an elevation of 65 ft. at 110th St., where it forms a bold curve in passing from Ninth to Eighth Avenue. The stations occur about every five blocks in the lower quarters, and are nowhere more than 1/2 M.

apart. Passengers ascend from the street by the staircases to the right
(looking in the direction in which they wish to travel), buy a ticket at
the ticket-office, and drop it into the 'chopper-box' at the entrance to the
platform. The uniform fare, for any distance, is 5 c.; children under five,
free. The trains run at intervals of a few minutes during the day, and
during the business-hours morning and evening follow each other with
hardly an intermission. The Ninth Avenue trains cease running about
8 p.m., and those of the Second Avenue at midnight, but the trains on
the Third and Sixth Avenues run all night, at intervals of 10 min. and
$^1/_4$ hr. respectively. The trains run on all lines on Sunday, at somewhat
less frequent intervals. All four lines start from South Ferry, adjoining
the Barge Office (p. 25). They vary in length from $8^1/_2$ M. to $10^3/_4$ M.
Short branches run from the Third Avenue Line to the City Hall, the 34th St.
Ferry (these two also from Second Ave.), and the Grand Central Depot.
Passengers should ascertain whether or not they change cars at the busy
Chatham Sq. station. The Sixth Avenue line proper ends at Central Park
(59th St.), but a branch diverges to Ninth Avenue at 53rd St., and at least
half of the trains ('Harlem trains'; red or green signals and lamps) follow
this route. The Second, Third, and Ninth Avenue Lines end at the Harlem
River (see Plan), the last connecting with the *N. Y. City and Northern Railroad* for High Bridge (p. 49) and points in Westchester County. The
Sixth Avenue Line has the cleanest cars and is used by the pleasantest
class of passengers, and should therefore be preferred when practicable.
The name of the station is announced by the conductor on arrival, and
the name of the 'next station' on leaving the station. The names are
always placarded at the stations, but are not always visible from the cars.
The following is a list of the stations.

2nd Ave. — South Ferry, Hanover Sq., Fulton St., Franklin Sq., Chatham Sq. (change cars for City Hall), Canal St., Grand St., Rivington St.,
1st, 8th, 14th, 19th, 23rd, 34th (change cars for Hunter's Point), 42nd, 50th,
57th, 65th, 70th, 80th, 86th, 92nd, 99th, 111th, 117th, 121st, 127th, 129th Sts.

3rd Ave. — South Ferry, Hanover Sq., Fulton St., Franklin Sq., Chatham Sq. (change cars for City Hall), Canal St., Grand St., Houston St.,
9th, 14th, 18th, 23rd, 28th, 34th (change cars for Hunter's Point), 42nd
(change cars for Grand Central Depot), 47th, 53rd, 59th, 67th, 76th, 84th,
89th, 100th, 116th, 125th, 129th Sts.

6th Ave. — South Ferry, Rector St., Cortlandt St., Park Pl., Chambers St.,
Franklin St., Grand St., Bleecker St., 8th, 14th, 18th, 23rd, 28th, 33rd,
42nd, 50th (change cars for 59th St. & Sixth Ave.), 8th Ave. & 53rd, 59th, 66th,
72nd, 81st, 93rd, 104th, 110th, 116th, 125th, 135th, 145th, 155th Sts. (stations
from 59th to 104th are on Ninth Ave., 116th to 155th on Eighth Ave.).

9th Ave. — South Ferry, Rector St., Cortlandt St., Barclay St., Warren
St., Franklin St., Desbrosses St., Houston St., Christopher St., 14th, 23rd,
30th, 34th, 42nd, 50th, 59th, 72nd, 81st, 93rd, 104th, 116th, 125th, 135th,
145th, 155th Sts.

There is also an elevated railroad, the *Suburban Rapid Transit*, in the
'Annexed District', beyond the Harlem River, connecting with the Second
and Third Avenue Lines at 128th and 129th St. Stations: 128th, 129th, 133rd,
138th, 143rd, 149th, 156th, 161st, 166th, 170th, 174th, and 177th Sts. (fare 5 c.).

Brooklyn Bridge Railway. Cable-cars, in trains of three, cross the
Brooklyn Bridge (see p. 30) in 6 min, running at intervals of about
1 minute (fare 3 c., 10 tickets 25 c.). At the New York end the platforms
communicate directly with the City Hall branch of the Third Avenue
Elevated, and the various Brooklyn Elevated Railroads begin on a level
with the other end of the bridge. Comp. p. 52.

Tramways. Nearly all the avenues running N. and S. and most of
the important cross-streets are traversed by *Tramways (Horse Cars, Street
Cars, Surface Cars, Cable Cars, Electric Cars)*. Uniform fare for any distance
5 c. Overcrowding is nearly as constant, especially on the Broadway
cars, as on the Elevated Railroad. Transfer tickets are often furnished
without extra charge for the cross-lines. The cars nominally stop only
at the upper crossings going up, and at the lower crossings going down

town. Most lines run every few minutes. The following is a list of the chief lines.

A. THE NORTH AND SOUTH LINES. — 1. BROADWAY LINE (cable-cars). From *South Ferry* (p. 14) through Whitehall St., Broadway, 44th St., and Seventh Avenue to *Central Park* (transfers for University Place and Seventh Avenue lines). Car light-brown, lamps red.

2. BROADWAY AND UNIVERSITY PLACE LINE. From Broadway through Barclay Street, Church, Canal, Greene Streets, Clinton Place, University Place, Union Square, Broadway, Seventh Avenue, 59th Street, to *Central Park.* C. cream-coloured, L. yellow.

3. FOURTH AVENUE LINE. From *Broadway*, opposite the Astor House, through Centre St., Grand St., the Bowery, and Fourth Avenue to Grand Central Depot, 42nd St. (p. 37); transfer at 32nd St. for 34th St. Ferry. C. yellow, L. red.

4. MADISON AVENUE LINE. From the *Astor House* (p. 7) as above to 42nd St., and thence through Vanderbilt Ave., 44th Ave., Madison Ave. to *86th St.* Some cars go on to *Mott Haven* (138th St.). A few of the cars on Lines 3 & 4 are propelled by the electric motor. C. yellow, L. red.

5. THIRD AVENUE LINE. From the *Astor House* through Park Row, Chatham St., the Bowery, and Third Avenue, to *Harlem* (p. 49). Cars run all night. To be converted into a cable line. Fare above 65th St. 6 c. C. red, L. green.

6. FIRST AND SECOND AVENUE LINES. From the foot of *Fulton St.* (p. 28) through Fulton, Water, South, Oliver, and Chatham St., the Bowery, and Grand, Forsyth, and Houston St., and along Second Ave. to 128th St., *Harlem*; returning through Second Ave., 23rd St., First Ave., Houston St., and Allen St., to Grand St. and thence as above. A branch of this line runs from 125th St. by 1st and 2nd Avenues to *Astor Place* (p. 31) and Broadway. C. yellow, L. red.

7. SIXTH AVENUE LINE. From corner of Broadway and Vesey St., through Church St., Chambers St., W. Broadway, Canal, Varick, and Carmine St., and 6th Ave. to *59th St.* and *Central Park* (p. 48). All night. C. yellow, L. green.

8. SEVENTH AVENUE LINE. From Whitehall St. (p. 25), through Broadway, Park Place, Church, Canal, and Sullivan St., Clinton Place, Greenwich Ave., and 7th Ave. to *59th St.* and *Central Park* (p. 48). C. red; L. green.

9. EIGHTH AVENUE LINE. From cor. of *Broadway* and *Vesey St.* to Canal St. as in No. 7, and thence by Hudson St. and Eighth Ave. to *59th St.* and *Central Park* (p. 48). Runs all night. C. red, L. red.

10. NINTH AVENUE LINE. From the corner of *Broadway* and *Fulton St.* (p. 28), through Fulton St., Greenwich St., and 9th Ave., to *55th St.* C. red, L. white.

11. TENTH AVENUE LINE (*West Side Belt Line*). From South Ferry, through Whitehall St., Bowling Green, Battery Place, West St., and 10th Ave., to *54th St.* The cars run all night and pass all the W. side ferries. C. and L. red.

12. EAST RIVER AND AVENUE A LINE (*East Side Belt Line*). From South Ferry, through Whitehall, South, Broad, Water, South, Grand, and Houston St., Ave. D, 14th St., Ave. A, 21st St., 1st Ave., 59th St. (Central Park), and 10th Ave., to *53rd St.*, where it connects with No. 11. This line passes all the E. side ferries. C. and L. red.

13. BLEECKER STREET AND FULTON FERRY LINE. From *Fulton Ferry* (p. 28) through Fulton, William, and Ann St., Park Row, Centre, Leonard, Elm, Howard, Crosby, Bleecker, Macdougal, W. 4th, W. 12th, Hudson, and 14th St., 9th Ave., and 23rd St., to *23rd St. Ferry.* L. green. A branch from Bleecker St. connects this line and No. 1 with *Brooklyn Bridge* (p. 30).

14. CITY HALL, AVENUE B, AND THIRTY FOURTH ST. LINE. From the *Post Office* (p. 28), through Park Row, Chatham St., E. Broadway, Avenue B, 14th St., 1st Ave., and 34th St. to *34th St. Ferry* (p. 14). C. and L. blue.

15. DRY DOCK AND EAST BROADWAY LINE. From the *Post Office* (p. 28) through Park Row, E. Broadway, Grand St., Ave. D., 14th St., and Ave. A., to *23rd St. Ferry* (p. 14). C. green, L. white.

Three lines also leave 130th St., to the S. of *Harlem Bridge* (p. 49), for points in the 'Annexed District' (p. 50) beyond the river.

B. Cross-town Lines (E. and W.). — 16. Grand and Cortlandt St. Line From *Grand St. Ferry* (p. 14), through Grand St., E. Broadway, Canal St., Walker St., W. Broadway, and Washington St., to *Cortlandt St. Ferry* (p. 14). C. and L. yellow.

17. Avenue C Line. From *Erie R. R. Ferry*, Chambers St. (p. 14), through West St., Charlton St., Prince St. (in returning Houston St.), the Bowery, Stanton St., Avenue C, 18th St., Ave. A, 23rd St., 1st Ave., 35th St., and Lexington Ave., to *42nd St.* L. yellow.

18. Forty-Second and Grand St. Line. From *Grand St. Ferry* (p. 14), through Goerck St., 2nd St., Ave. A, 14th St., 4th Ave., 23rd St., Broadway, 34th St., 10th Ave., and 42nd St., to *Weehawken Ferry* (p. 14). C. green.

19. Desbrosses, Vestry, and Grand St. Line. From *Grand St. Ferry* (p. 14), through Grand, Sullivan, Vestry, Greenwich, and Desbrosses St., to *Desbrosses St. Ferry* (p. 14). Cars run all night. C. blue, L. white.

20. Fourteenth St. Line. From *Christopher St. Ferry* (p. 14), through Greenwich St., 9th Ave., and 14th St. (passing Union Sq.), to *Fourth Avenue*. Branch to connect with ferry at foot of W. 14 St. C. green, L. yellow.

21. Christopher and Tenth St. Line. From *Christopher St. Ferry* (p. 14), through Christopher St., Greenwich Ave., 8th St., Ave. A, and E. 10th St. to *Ferry* at foot of E. 10th St. (p. 14). C. white, L. red.

22. Central Cross-Town Railroad. From *23rd St. East River Ferry* (p. 14), through Ave. A, 18th St., Broadway, 14th St., 7th Ave., and W. 11th St. to *Christopher St. Ferry* (p. 14). C. & L. blue.

23. Twenty-Third St. and Erie Ferry. From end to end of 23rd St. (C. light-brown, L. red), with a branch viâ 2nd Ave., 28th St., and 1st Ave. to *Erie Ferry*, 34th St. (p. 14; L. blue).

24. Harlem and Manhattanville Cable Line. From E. end of 125th St., through 125th St. and Manhattan St., to Manhattanville (p. 48; 130th St.), on the Hudson, with branch through 10th Ave. to 187th St. (Washington Heights), passing High Bridge (p. 49). C. yellow, L. red. It is intended to continue this line down Third Ave. to the City Hall.

25. South Ferry and Vesey St. Line. From *South Ferry* (p. 14), through Whitehall St., Battery Place, and New Church St. to *Vesey St.*, returning viâ State St. C. red, L. blue.

26. Forty-Second St. and Boulevard Line. From *34th St. Ferry* (East River; p. 23), through 1st Ave., 42nd St., 7th Ave., Broadway, 59th St., *Boulevard* (p. 33), 42nd St. and Manhattan St., to *Fort Lee Ferry* (p. 14), W. 129th St. This line runs near Riverside Park (p. 48). A branch-line runs along 42nd St. to *Weehawken Ferry*, and another runs viâ 1st Ave., 110th St., and St. Nicholas Avenue to *Fort Lee Ferry* (p. 14).

27. Chambers St. Line. From the *Erie R. R. Ferry*, Chambers St. (p. 14), through Chambers, Duane, Chatham, and New Chambers St., to *James Slip* (Pl. B, 4). C. red. Branch from foot of Grand St. to *Erie Ferry* (p. 14).

Omnibuses ('Stages') run from Bleecker St. through S. Fifth Avenue, Washington Sq., and Fifth Avenue to 82nd St.

Carriages. The cab system is in a very undeveloped condition in New York, owing partly to the high fares, partly to the abundance of tramway and railway accommodation, and partly to the bad paving of the streets, which makes driving, outside a few favoured localities, anything but a pleasure. *Hackney Carriages*, however, are in waiting at the railway stations, ferries, and principal steamboat docks, and are also found on stands at Madison Sq., Union Sq., City Hall Park, and many other points. The fares are as follows: *Hackney Carriages* or *Coaches*, to carry 1-4 pers., generally with two horses, $1 for the first mile, and 40 c. for each 1/2 M. addit.; per hr. $1 1/2, each addit. 1/2 hr. 75 c., waiting 38 c. per 1/4 hr. *Cabs* and *Hansoms* for 1-2 pers., 50, 25 c., $1 1/2, 50 c., 25 c. One trunk, not exceeding 50 lbs. in weight, free; extra luggage 25 c. per piece. Children under eight years of age, free. Carriages hired from hotels or livery-stables are somewhat dearer. The authorised table of fares should be hung in each carriage. In case of dispute the driver should be told to drive to the nearest police-office or to the City Hall, where a complaint may be made to the *Mayor's Marshal*, Room No. 1. In all cases a distinct bargain should be made beforehand, and it is often possible to make one on more favourable terms than the legal fares. The *City Improvement Society*, 126 E. 23rd St., issues cards bearing the legal tariff to all cabmen willing to exhibit them, and the public will do well to prefer these when possible.

Ferries (see Plan). To *Brooklyn*, from Catherine St., Fulton St., Wall St., and Whitehall St. (South Ferry). To *Williamsburgh* or *East Brooklyn*, from Grand St., Roosevelt St., E. Houston St., and E. 23rd St. To *Greenpoint*, from E. 10th St. and E. 23rd St. To *Hunter's Point, Long Island City*, from James Slip and E. 34th St. To *Astoria, Long Island City*, from E. 92nd St. and Beekman St. To *Jersey City:* from Desbrosses St. and from Cortlandt St. to Pennsylvania Railway Station; from Chambers St. and from W. 23rd St. to Pavonia Avenue and Erie Railroad; from Liberty St. to Communipaw (Central Railroad of New Jersey); from W. 34th St. to Montgomery St. To *Hoboken*, from Barclay, Christopher, and W. 14th Sts. To *Weehawken*, from W. 42nd St. and Jay St. To *Fort Lee*, from W. 130th St. (10 c.) and Canal St. (15 c.). To *Staten Island*, from South Ferry (10 c.). To *Randall's*, to *Blackwell's*, to *Hart's*, and to *Ward's Island* from E. 26th St. (fares 20-40 c.). To *Bedloe's Island* and to *Governor's Island* from the Battery. The 'Brooklyn Annex' is an important ferry connecting Brooklyn (Fulton St., near the Suspension Bridge) with the various railway termini in New Jersey and Weehawken (fare 10 c.). The ferries ply at frequent intervals, the more important running every few minutes in the business-hours. Fares generally 1-6 c. The ferry-boats are comfortable and very unlike European steamers. One side is devoted to a ladies' cabin, but men may also use this when not smoking. In 1891 these ferries carried about 180 million passengers.

Post Office. The *General Post Office* (see p. 28), City Hall Park, is open day and night; closed on Sun. except 9-11 a.m. The *Money Order Office*, on the second floor, Rooms 16-34, is open daily, except Sun. and holidays, 10-6. The General Delivery windows (for 'Poste Restante' letters) are on the ground-floor, Park Row side. The Registered Letter Office is on the mezzanine floor. Besides the G.P.O. district, the city is divided into nineteen postal districts, each served by a branch post-office or *Station*, designated by letters of the alphabet (Station A, etc.; open 7-8, Sun. 9-11 a.m.), and there are also 20 *Sub-Stations*, in druggists' shops, where all the ordinary postal services are rendered, including the issue of domestic or inland money orders. Letters within New York are delivered more expeditiously if the 'station letter' is affixed to the address. Letters are also expedited in delivery if posted on the same side of Fifth Ave. (E. or W.) as their destination. Stamps are also sold in about 100 shops (chiefly druggists') throughout the city; and letters may be posted in about 1600 *Letter-Boxes*, affixed to lamp-posts, or in any hotel. From 4 to 28 collections, and from 3 to 9 deliveries are made daily according to the district. Letters are collected on Sun. (at less frequent intervals), but not delivered; mail matter may, however, be obtained on Sun., 9-11 a.m., at Section 17, Park Row Lobby, G.P.O. The time of closing of foreign mails is advertised in the daily papers; the chief European mails are despatched on Wed. and Saturday. — Comp. p. xxviii and the *New York Post Office Guide* (free, on application at G.P.O.).

Telegraph Offices (comp. p. xxviii). *Western Union Telegraph Co.* (p. 28), 195 Broadway; chief branch-offices, 16, 599, 854, and 1227 Broadway, 821 Sixth Avenue, Fifth Ave. (cor. 23rd St.), and 134 E. 125th St. All these are open day and night. There are also about 115 other branch-offices throughout the city, including all the principal hotels and the Grand Central Depot, and Atlantic Cable messages are received at about 40 of these. The rate for local messages in New York and Brooklyn is 15 c. per 10 words, and 1 c. for each additional word; for other parts of the United States it varies from 25 c. to $1 per 10 words. — *Commercial Cable Co.* 8 Broad St. and several branch-offices; *Postal Telegraph and*

Cable Co., 187 Broadway and many branch-offices. The rate per word for cable messages to Great Britain, Ireland, France, and Germany is 25 c.; Belgium and Switzerland 31 c.; Holland, Italy 32 c.; Denmark and Norway 35 c.; Austro-Hungary 34 c.; Sweden 39 c.; Russia 43 c.

Telephone Offices. The telephonic communication of New York is mainly in the hands of the *Metropolitan Co.*, 18 Cortlandt St., and the *Southern Bell Telephone Co.*, 195 Broadway, which have numerous branch-offices throughout the city, at any of which persons may be put in com-munication with members of the Telephone Exchange at the rate of 15 c. per 5 minutes. These offices are generally located in hotels, drug-stores, telegraph-stations, ferry-houses, and so on. The 'Long Distance Tele-phone', at some of these stations, communicates with Chicago, Albany, Boston, Philadelphia, Washington, etc.

Messenger Service. This is carried on by the *American District Tele-graph Co.* (8 Dey St.) and the *Postal Telegraph Co.* (187 Broadway), which have numerous offices throughout New York, generally in the stations of the *Western Union Telegraph Co.* Message boys can be summoned by the 'automatic calls' found in hotels, banks, offices, and many private houses. Fees by tariff (about 30 c. per hour).

Express Service. Broadway below Trinity Church is the headquarters of the numerous companies of New York, by which baggage may be ex-pressed to all parts of the world. Among the chief, all in Broadway, are : *Adams Express Co.*, No. 59; *American Express Co.*, No. 65; *United States Express Co.*, No. 49; *Wells, Fargo, & Co.*, No. 63. For expressing baggage within the United States, the traveller will, however, seldom need to leave his hotel. Among the chief 'Transfer Companies' for transferring luggage within New York and Brooklyn are *Westcott* (12 Park Place) and *Dodd's New York Transfer Co.* (1 Astor House, Broadway); 25-50 c. per trunk, according to distance.

Theatres. Concerts. Sport. Clubs, etc.

Theatres. *Metropolitan Opera House*, Broadway (burned in 1892). — *Academy of Music*, cor. of Irving Pl. and 14th St., now used for specta-cular dramas, etc.; prices 25 c. to $1, balcony $1/2-1, family circle 25 c. — *Daly's Theatre*, corner of Broadway and 30th St., Shakespearian and modern comedy (Miss Ada Rehan); orchestra stalls $1½-2, balcony $1-2, 2nd balcony 50-75 c. — *Madison Square Theatre*, with a double stage, one part of which can be lifted and 'set' while the other is in use), 4 W. 24th St., domestic comedy; seats $½-2. — *Palmer's Theatre* (late *Wallack's*), Broadway, cor. 30th St., high-class comedy; $½-1½. — *Broadway Theatre*, Broadway, cor. 41st St.; comedies, light operas, etc.; 35 c.-$1½. — *Fifth Avenue Theatre*, Broadway, cor. 28th St.; a 'star theatre', with performances by good English and other visiting actors; $½-1½. — *Lyceum*, Fourth Avenue, between 23d and 24th Sts.; comedy; $½-1½. — *Star Theatre*, Broadway, cor. 13th St.; $¼-1½. — *Casino*, Broadway, cor. 39th St.; operettas; adm. $½-1½; in summer, concerts on the roof, see p. 16. — *Grand Opera House*, Eighth Ave., cor. 23rd St., a large house (2000 seats); popular and spectacular pieces; $¼-1. — *Niblo's Garden Theatre*, 580 Broadway; a large house (2000 seats), for spectacular pieces and melodrama; $¼-1. — *Garden Theatre*, in Madison Square Garden (p. 39); comic opera; $½-1½. — *Union Square Theatre*, S. side of Union Sq.; popular pieces; $¼-1½. — *New Park Theatre*, Broadway, cor. 35th St.; $¼-1. — *Standard Theatre*, Broadway, cor. 33rd St.; $¼-1½. — *Abbey's Theatre*, cor. of Broadway and 38th St. (in progress). — *Harrigan's Theatre*, W. 36th St., to the E. of Sixth Ave. (dramas of Irish and Coloured life in New York). — *Hammerstein's Manhattan Opera House*, 34th St., betw. Sixth and Seventh Avenues, for opera and drama; $½-2. — *Bijou Theatre*, Broadway, between 30th and 31st Sts.; $¼-1½. — *Fourteenth St. Theatre*, near Sixth Ave.; popular pieces; $¼-1. — *Amberg's*, cor. of Irving Place and E. 15th St.; performances in German. — *Thalia*, 48 Bowery; formerly, as the 'Bowery Theatre', the leading theatre of New York, but now relinquished to 'down town' performances in German; prices low. — *Berkeley Lyceum*, 44th St., leased by the American Academy of the Dramatic Arts. — *Proctor's Twenty-Third St. Theatre*, a little to the W. of Sixth Ave.; $ 1/4-1 1/2. — *Third Avenue Theatre* (Jacobs'), between 30th and 31st Sts.; melodrama and popular pieces; $ 1/4-1. — *Herrmann's*, Broadway, cor. 29th St. — *Harlem Opera House*, 125th St., near Seventh Ave.; $ 1/4-1 1/2. — *Columbus Theatre*, 125th St., near Fourth Ave.; $ 1/4-1. — *Tony Pastor's*, in Tammany Hall Building (p. 32), a theatre of varieties; adm. $ 1/4-1. — There are several other theatres in the Bowery, not always of the most reputable class. See advertisements in the daily papers. The performances at the New York theatres, unless otherwise stated in the advertisements, begin at 8 or 8.15 p.m. Tickets may be bought in advance at 111 Broadway and the chief hotels (small premium charged), but this is not often necessary. Full dress is nowhere compulsory, but is customary at the Opera. Ladies generally retain their hats, even when accompanied by gentle men in evening-dress.

Places of Amusement. *Madison Square Garden* (p. 39), a huge block bounded by Madison and Fourth Avenues and 26th and 27th Sts., containing an amphitheatre, accommodating 15,000 people and used for horse-shows, flower-shows, equestrian performances, and the like; a theatre (see p. 15); a large concert and ball-room (1500 people); a restaurant; and an open-air garden on the roof (4000 people). *View of New York, by day or night, from the Tower (300 ft. high; elevator; adm. 25 c.; open till 10 p.m.). — *Eden Musée*, 23rd St., between Fifth and Sixth Avenues; a wax-work show, with good musical performances, smoking-room, etc., open 11-11, Sun. 1-11; adm. 50 c. — *Koster & Bial*, W. 23rd St., a beer-garden, with variety performances at 8 p.m., and thrice weekly at 2 p.m.; adm. 25 c. and 50 c. — *Casino Garden*, on the top of the Casino Theatre (p. 14), a beer-garden, with musical performances (in summer); adm. free to visitors of the theatre. — The so-called '*Dime Museums*' can scarcely be recommended, and visitors should also steer clear of most of the '*Concert Saloons*'. — *Panorama of Niagara*, at the corner of Fourth Avenue and 19th St.; open 10-11; adm. 50 c. — *American Institute Fair*, held in Oct. and Nov. in the large building at the corner of Third Ave. and 63rd St.

Concerts. Whether owing to the large German element in its population or to other causes, it is undeniable that New York cultivates high class music with distinguished success and enjoys a series of concerts ranking with the best in Europe. The most fashionable are the concerts of the *Philharmonic Society* (founded 1842), given monthly during the season (Nov.-April) in the Carnegie Music Hall (p. 40; conductor Anton Seidl) on Saturdays at 8 p.m.; public rehearsals on the Fridays before the concert at 2 p.m., at reduced prices. Other good series of concerts are given at the Carnegie Music Hall (p. 40), in winter, by the *Symphony Society* and the *Oratorio Society* (both conducted by Damrosch), also with public rehearsals on the preceding afternoons. Excellent concerts are also given by the *Metropolitan* and *Rubinstein Societies* (Carnegie Music Hall), the *Arion Society* (in the club-house in Park Avenue, p. 38), the *Liederkranz* (58th St., between Park and Lexington Avenues), the *Beethoven Männerchor*, the *Sängerbund*, the *Mendelssohn Glee Club* (W. 40th St.), etc. The above concerts are mainly attended by members and subscribers, but a limited number of single tickets are generally obtainable. A good concert of classical music is given in the Lenox Lyceum (Madison Ave., cor. 59th St.), every Sun. at 8 p.m. ($ 1/2-1); and Sun. evening concerts are also given at *Amberg's Theatre* (see p. 15), the *Casino* (p. 15), *Madison Square Garden* (see above), and numerous other German resorts. In summer bands play at frequent intervals in *Central Park* (Sat. & Sun. afternoons), the *Battery*, *Tompkins Square*, and several other public gardens and parks. — For details, see the daily newspapers.

Exhibitions of Paintings. *Metropolitan Museum*, see p. 42; *Lenox Library*, see p. 36; *New York Historical Society*, see p. 40; *Annual Exhibition* at the National Academy of Design (p. 37) in spring and (less important) autumn; *Society of American Artists*, in the building of the

Society of Fine Arts, W. 57th St., betw. Seventh Ave. and Broadway (April); *Water Colour Society*, at the Academy of Design (Jan. or Feb.); *American Art Association*, 6 E. 23rd St. Other exhibitions, at irregular intervals are given by the *Art Students' League*, the *Art Guild*, the *Society of Decorative Art*, the *Salmagundi Club*, the *Tile Club*, the *Kit-Kat Club*, etc. Adm. to the above generally 25 c. There are usually fair collections of pictures for sale in the galleries of the Art Dealers. — Among the finest private collections are those of *Mrs. W. H. Vanderbilt*, *Mr. H. G. Marquand*, *Mrs. Wm. Astor*, *Mr. Wm. Rockefeller*, *Mr. Ed. D. Adams*, *Mr. August Belmont*, *Mr. H. O. Havemeyer*, *Mr. Wm. J. Evans*, *Mr. Ben. Altman*, *Mr. R. H. Halsted*, *Mr. Albert Spencer*, *Mr. James A. Garland*, *Mr. Cyrus J. Lawrence*, *Mr. Charles A. Dana*, and *Mr. T. B. Clarke*. Visitors specially interested will generally be admitted to these on previous application by letter, enclosing card. Visitors are also received at the *Studios* of the leading artists, many of whom have their regular reception days.

Sport. The chief HORSE RACES near New York are those of the *Monmouth Park Association* at Monmouth Park, N. J. (p. 224); the *New York Jockey Club* at Morris Park; the *Brooklyn Jockey Club* at Gravesend, between Brooklyn and Coney Island; and the *Coney Island Jockey Club* at Sheepshead Bay. Each holds two 15-day meetings between the middle of May and the end of September (see daily papers). Adm. to each racetrack $1; grand stand and paddock each 50c. extra. TROTTING RACES take place at Fleetwood Park (10 M.). The famous *Stables of Mr. Robt. Bonner*, owner of Maud S. and Sunol, may be seen on application to Mr· Bonner at 8 W. 56th St. or at the New York Ledger Office, 182 William St. — Fox HUNTING (with a 'drag' or carted fox) is carried on in Long Island, Staten Island, and New Jersey. — The chief YACHT CLUBS are the *New York* (260 yachts), *Seawanhaka*, *American* (steam-yachts), *Atlantic*, *Larchmont*, *Harlem*, etc.; and numerous regattas are held in the harbour and Long Island Sound. — ROWING is best on the Harlem River, where boats may be hired for about 50 c. an hour. There are many clubs here, and a few on the Hudson. — CANOEING is practised all round Manhattan Island. The *New York Canoe Club* has its headquarters at Tompkinsville, Staten Island (p. 51). — DRIVING. The fashionable drive is through Central Park, where all the best equipages in New York may be seen on fine afternoons. The chief resort of the owners of 'fast trotters' is Seventh Avenue, to the N. of Central Park, and its continuation beyond the Harlem River to Fleetwood Park, and all who are interested in horses should try to see the scene here. The *Coaching Club* and the *Tandem Club* (twice) parade on Saturdays in May in Central and Riverside Parks. — RIDING is best seen and enjoyed in Central and Riverside Parks. The New York Riding Club has a fine club-house and ring in 58th St., between Fifth and Madison Aves. — FISHING, for striped bass, blue fish, weak fish, etc., is practised at various points near New York on the coasts of Long Island and New Jersey. Steamers specially built for deep-sea fishing leave New York every morning in the season and lie out at sea all day (see daily papers). — BASEBALL is played from May to Nov. The chief professional contests take place in the grounds at Eighth Ave. and 157th St., at the end of the Sixth Ave. El. R. R. See daily papers. — CRICKET. The chief clubs are the *Staten Island*, at Tompkinsville (p. 51); the *St. George*, at Hoboken; the *Berkeley Athletic Club*, at Morris Dock; and the *Manhattan*, at Prospect Park. — LAWN TENNIS. The chief clubs are the *New York* at 147th St. and St. Nicholas Ave. and the *Staten Island*, *St. George*, and *Berkeley* mentioned above. Tennis courts are attached to the various athletic clubs, and there are hundreds of courts in Central Park. From May to Oct. strangers may play in the *Tennis Building*, 41st St., near Seventh Ave. — RACQUET CLUB, 43rd St., between Fifth and Sixth Aves. — CYCLING. Among the best-known of the innumerable cycling clubs are the *New York Bicycle Club*, the *Citizens' Club*, and the *Ixion*. Wheels may be hired of the dealers near Central Park. — SKATING is practised on the lakes in Central Park, Van Cortlandt Park (p. 50; best), and Prospect Park. — ATHLETICS. *University Athletic Club*, 26th St., cor. of Sixth Ave.; *New*

York Athletic Club, at the corner of Sixth Ave. and 55th St., with open-air grounds on Travers Island, Long Island Sound; *Manhattan Athletic Club* (best club-house), at the corner of Madison Ave. and 45th St., with grounds at 155th St.; *Central Turn-Verein* (German gymnastic society), with 2500 members, 68th St., near Third Ave.; *Staten Island Club*, see above; *Columbia College*, with grounds at Williamsbridge; *Young Men's Christian Association*, with grounds at Mott Haven and gymnasia at 23rd St. (p. 37) and at S.W. 125th St.; *Berkeley Ladies' Athletic Association*, 44th St., betw. Fifth and Sixth Aves. The *Amateur Athletic Union* has its office at the N. Y. Athletic Club. — FOOTBALL is played in autumn by the athletic clubs and colleges. The chief game is that between Yale and Princeton Universities, played at New York or Brooklyn on the last Thurs. of November. — SHOOTING. The famous rifle-ranges at Creedmoor, Long Island, 13½ M. from the City Hall, now belong to the New York State militia. There are several gun-clubs for 'trap' and pigeon-shooting in New Jersey.

Clubs. The chief clubs, to which strangers can obtain access only when introduced by a member, are the following: *Manhattan Club*, 96 Fifth Ave., see p. 34; *Union League*, Fifth Ave., cor. 39th St., see p. 34; *Union*, Fifth Ave., cor. 21st St. (1000 members; social); *University* Madison, Sq., cor. E. 26th St., for college graduates; *Century* (p. 34), 43rd St. (literary and artistic; celebrated meetings on the first Sat. of each month); *Metropolitan*, Fifth Ave., cor. 60th St. (in progress); *Lotos* (p. 34), 149 Fifth Ave., opposite the Union; *Knickerbocker*, Fifth Ave., cor. 32nd St. (300 members; sporting and fashionable); *Reform*, Fifth Ave., cor. 27th St. (for those interested in political reforms; 800 members); *New York*, Fifth Ave., cor. 35th St.; *St. Nicholas Club*, Fifth Ave., cor. 37th St. (300 members; confined to descendants of old New York families); *Aldine Club*, 20 Lafayette Place; *Authors' Club*, 19 W. 24th St.; *Press Club*, 120 Nassau St.; *Players' Club*, 16 Gramercy Park, with interesting pictures and relics; *Tenderloin Club*, 114 W. 32nd St., a unique Bohemian club (walls of one room decorated with knives, bottles, etc., embedded in the plastering); *Calumet Club*, Fifth Ave., cor. 29th St.; *German Club (Deutscher Verein*; p. 35), 59th St., facing Central Park; *Progress Club*, Fifth Ave., cor. 63rd St., Hebrew; *Harmonie*, 45 W. 42nd St., Hebrew; *Arion* (p. 38), Park Ave., cor. 59th St. (German and musical); *Freundschaft* (p. 38), Park Ave., cor. 72nd St. (German); *Cercle Français*, 26 W. 24th St.; *Sorosis*, a women's club, meeting monthly at Delmonico's; *Ladies' New York Club*, 28 E. 22nd St.; *Berkeley Club*, for women, see above; *Women's University Club*, Madison Ave. (receptions on Sat.); *Women's Press Club*, 126 E. 23rd St.

Shops. Libraries. Baths. Churches. Streets. Collections.

Shops (*'Stores'*). Many of the New York shops are very large and handsome, easily bearing comparison with those of Europe. The prices, however, are, as a rule, considerably higher. The chief shopping resorts are Broadway, from 8th to 34th St.; Fifth Ave., from 14th to 42nd St.; Twenty-Third St., between Fifth and Sixth Ave.; Fourteenth St., between Broadway and Sixth Ave.; and Sixth Avenue, from 12th to 23rd St. (the last two localities somewhat cheaper than the others). An evening visit to Grand St., E. of the Bowery (p. 29), will show the shopping of the tenement-districts in full swing. A characteristic feature is formed by the large 'Dry Goods' stores, huge establishments in the style of the Bon Marché in Paris, containing almost everything necessary for a complete outfit. Among these may be mentioned *Arnold & Constable*, Broadway, cor. 19th St.; *Lord & Taylor*, 895 Broadway; *Altman*, 301 Sixth Ave.; *Hilton, Hughes, & Co.*, Broadway, cor. 10th St.; *Macy*, cor. of 14th St. and 6th Ave.; *Stern*, 32 W. 23rd St.; *McCreery*, 801 Broadway, cor. 11th St.; *Daniell*, 761 Broadway; *O'Neill*, 321 Sixth Ave. *Ridley*, 301 Grand St.

Booksellers. *Charles Scribner's Sons*, 743-745 Broadway, one of the largest and handsomest book-shops in the world; *G. P. Putnam's Sons*, 27 W. 23rd St.; *Brentano*, 124 Fifth Ave.; *Dodd, Mead, & Co.*, 5 E. 19th St.; *Rand, McNally, & Co.*, 323 Broadway (maps, guidebooks, etc.);

Westermann, 812 Broadway (German books); *Dutton*, 31 W. 23rd St.; *Christern*, 254 Fifth Ave. (French and other foreign books); *Weatherley*, Fifth Ave; *Stechert*, 810 Broadway (German); *Methodist Book Concern*, 150 Fifth Ave. — SECOND-HAND BOOKSELLERS: *Leggatt*, Chambers St.; *Clark*, 34 Park Place; *Bouton*, 8 W. 28th St.

Bankers. *Brown Brothers & Co.*, 59 Wall St.; *J. Kennedy Tod & Co.*, 45 Wall St.; *Drexel, Morgan, & Co.*, 23 Wall St.: *Lazard Frères*, 10 Wall St.; *J. & W. Seligman & Co.*, 21 Broad St.; *A. Belmont & Co.*, 25 Nassau St.; *Bank of Montreal*, 59 Wall St.; *Bank of British North America*, 52 Wall St.; *Blair & Co.*, 33 Wall St.

Baths. Hot and cold baths may be obtained at all the hotels (25 c.-75 c.) and large barbers' shops (25 c.). Turkish and Russian baths ($1/2-11/2) may be obtained at the following: *Britlon's*, 130 W. 41st St., cor. Broadway; *Hoffman House* (p. 32); *Windsor*, at Windsor Hotel (p. 34), 57 E. 46th St.; *Capes & Ryan*, 18 Lafayette Place; *Ariston*, cor. Broadway and 55th St.; *Everard*, 28 W. 28th St.; *Produce Exchange*, 8 Broadway; *Smith*, 7 E. 46th St. — *Salt Water Swimming Baths*, at the Battery (25 c., warm 30 c.).

Libraries and Reading Rooms. *Astor Library*, see p. 31 (9 to 4 or 5); *Mercantile Library* (p. 31), on introduction by a member (8-9); *Lenox Library*, see p. 36 (11-4); *Cooper Institute Reading Room* (see p. 31), open free, 8 a.m. to 10 p.m.; *Apprentices' Library*, 18 E. 16th St. (8-9); *Y. M. C. A. Reading Rooms*, free, at 52 E. 23rd St.; 361 Madison Ave., 5 W. 125th St., etc. (8-10); *Young Women's Christian Association*, 7 E. 15th St.; *New York Free Circulating Library*, 49 Bond St., with several branches (9-9); *New York Society Library*, University Place, founded in 1754 (70,000 vols.; 8-6, reading-room 8-10; for members only); *Historical Society* (p. 40), for strangers on the introduction of a member (9-6); *Harlem Library*, cor. Third Avenue and 123rd St. (15,000 vols.; 9-9, free); *Aguilar Free Library*, 206 E. Broadway and 721 Lexington Ave.; *Mott Memorial Library* (medical), 64 Madison Ave. (11-9); *New York Hospital Library*, 8 W. 16th St. (medical); *Law Institute Library*, Post Office Rooms, 116-122, 4th floor (legal; 35,000 vols.; 9-5); *Bar Association Library*, 7 W. 29th St. (legal; 8-12; for members); *American Institute Library*, 115 W. 38th St. (agricultural and industrial; 9-6 or 9-9); *Geographical Society*, 32 W. 28th St. — There are also good libraries at Columbia College (p. 39), the *University of New York*, and some of the clubs. Among the finest **Private Libraries** are those of the late *S. J. Tilden*, 15 Gramercy Square; *Augustin Daly* (dramatic); *W. L. Andrews; L. N. Lawson; T. J. McKee* (dramatic); and *W. B. Isham*, 5 E. 61st St.

Newspapers. The periodical publications of New York embrace about 56 daily papers, 270 weekly papers and periodicals, and 350 monthly journals and magazines. Among the chief morning papers are the *Herald* (3 c.; Independent), the *Times* (3 c.; Independent), the *Tribune* (3 c.; Republican), the *World* (2 c.; Democratic), the *Sun* (2 c.; Independent), the *Star* (2 c.; Independent), the *Press* (1 c.; Repub. and Protectionist), the German *Staatszeitung* (3 c.; Dem.). The chief evening papers are the *Evening Post* (3 c.; an excellent Independent and Free Trade organ), the evening editions of the *Sun* and *World* (1 c. each), the *Telegram* (the evening edition of the Herald; 1 c.), and the *Mail and Express* (2 c.; Repub.). Most of the daily papers publish Sunday editions; price 5 c. Among the weeklies are the *Nation*, a high-class political and literary journal; the *Critic*, a literary journal; *Frank Leslie's, Harper's Weekly, Harper's Bazar* (for ladies), the *Illustrated American*, and other illustrated papers; *Life, Puck, Judge*, and other comic journals; the *Scottish American Journal* (7 c.); and numerous technical and professional journals. The leading monthly magazines include the *Century, Scribner's, Harper's*, the *Forum*, the *North American Review*, the *Popular Science Monthly*, and the *Cosmopolitan*.

Churches. There are in all about 600 churches in New York, of which one-seventh are Roman Catholic. The services in the Protestant churches usually begin at 10.30 or 11 a.m. and 8 p.m. The Sat. papers publish a list of the preachers for Sunday, and information is freely given at the hotels, at the City Mission, Fourth Ave., cor. 22nd St., or at the Y. M. C. A. The following list mentions a few of the chief congregations.

BAPTIST. *Calvary Church*, W. 57th St., between Sixth and Seventh Ave. (Rev. Dr. McArthur); *Fifth Avenue*, W. 46th St., near Fifth Ave. Rev. W. Faunce); *Judson Memorial*, Washington Sq. (Rev. Dr. Judson; see p. 33).

CONGREGATIONAL. *Broadway Tabernacle*, Sixth Ave.. cor. 34th St.; *Pilgrim*, Madison Ave., cor. 121st St. (Rev. Dr. Virgin).

DUTCH REFORMED. *Collegiate*, Fifth Ave., cor. 48th St. (Rev. Dr. Coe); *Madison Avenue*, Madison Ave.; cor. 57th St. (Rev. Dr. Kittredge).

FRIENDS or QUAKERS. *Meeting-houses*, E. 15th St., cor. Rutherford Place, and 144 E. 20th St. (Orthodox).

LUTHERAN. *Gustavus Adolphus Swedish Evangelical*, 150 E. 22nd St. (Rev. Dr. Lindberg); *St. James*, 870 Madison Ave. (Rev. Dr. Remensnyder); *St. Peter's German Evangelical*, Lexington Ave., cor. 46th St. (Rev. Dr. Moldehnke).

METHODIST EPISCOPAL. *Calvary*, Seventh Ave., cor. 29th St. (Rev. Dr. Day); *Cornell Memorial*, E. 76th St., near 2nd Ave. (Rev. Dr. Byrnes); *Madison Avenue*, 659 Madison Ave. (Rev. Dr. McChesney); *St. James*, Madison Ave., cor. E. 126th St. (Rev. Dr. Price).

PRESBYTERIAN. *Fifth Avenue*, cor. 55th St. (Rev. Dr. Hall); *Fourth Avenue*, 286 Fourth Ave. (Rev. I. R. Davies); *Harlem*, 43 E. 125th St. (Rev. Dr. Ramsay); *Madison Square*, 506 Madison Ave. (Rev. Dr. Parkhurst); *University Place*, cor. E. 10th St. (Rev. Dr. Alexander).

PROTESTANT EPISCOPAL. *All Souls*, Madison Ave., cor. 66th St. (Rev. Dr. Heber Newton); *Calvary*, 273 Fourth Ave. (Rev. Dr. Satterlee); *Grace Church*, 800 Broadway (Rev. Dr. Huntington; see p. 31); *Heavenly Rest*, 551 Fifth Ave. (Rev. Dr. Morgan; see p. 34); *St. Bartholomew*, 348 Fifth Ave. (Rev. Dr. Greer); *St. George's*, 7 Rutherford Place (Rev. Dr. Rainsford; see p. 40); *St. Michael*, Amsterdam Ave., near W. 99th St. (Rev. Dr. Peters); *Trinity*, Broadway, at the corner of Rector St. (Rev. Dr. Morgan Dix; comp. p. 27).

ROMAN CATHOLIC. *St. Patrick's Cathedral*, Fifth Ave. (see p. 35); *All Saints*, Madison Ave.; cor. 129th St.; *St. Francis Xavier*, 36 W. 16th St.; *St. Stephen's*, 149 E. 28th St.; *St. Paul the Apostle*, Ninth Ave., cor. 59th St.; *St. Gabriel*, 312 E. 37th St.; *St. Agnes*, 143 E. 43rd St.; *Sacred Heart*, 447 W. 51st St.; *St. Joseph*, 59 Sixth Ave. There are several German, French, Italian, and Polish R. C. Churches. Numerous services.

SWEDENBORGIAN or NEW JERUSALEM CHURCHES at 114 E. 35th St., and 20 Cooper Union (German).

SYNAGOGUES. *Bethel.* Lexington Ave., cor. 63rd St. (Rev. Dr. Kohler); *Shaaray Tefilla*, 127 W. 44th St. (Rev. Dr. de Mendes); *Temple Emanu-El*, Fifth Ave., cor. 43rd St. (Rev. Dr. Gottheil).

UNITARIAN. *All Souls*, Fourth Avenue, cor. 20th St. (Rev. T. C. Williams); *Messiah*, 64 E. 34th St. (Rev. Dr. Robert Collyer).

UNIVERSALIST. Church of the Divine Paternity, Fifth Ave., cor. 45th St. (Rev. Dr. Eaton).

Among the chief churches for *Coloured Persons* are *St. Benedict the Moor's* (R. C.), 210 Bleecker St., and the Methodist Episcopal Churches of *Zion* (351 Bleecker St.) and *Bethel* (214 Sullivan St.).

The New York Fire Department has its headquarters at 157 E. 67th St. The force, which consists of upwards of 1000 men, with 92 steam fire engines, is under the supervision of three Fire Commissioners. Its annual cost is about $ 2,300,000 (460,000 *l.*), and it has to deal yearly with 2500-3000 fires. The service and equipment are excellent, and a visit to an engine house is interesting. The *Insurance Patrol*, maintained by the Board of Fire Underwriters, co-operates with the firemen in extinguishing fire, besides devoting itself to the special work of rescuing and guarding property.

Streets. Above 13th St. the streets of New York are laid out very regularly and cross each other at right angles, the only exception being the old thoroughfare of Broadway, which crosses the island diagonally from S.S.E. to N.N.W. The streets in the lower part of the island are generally named after colonial worthies. Higher up those running across

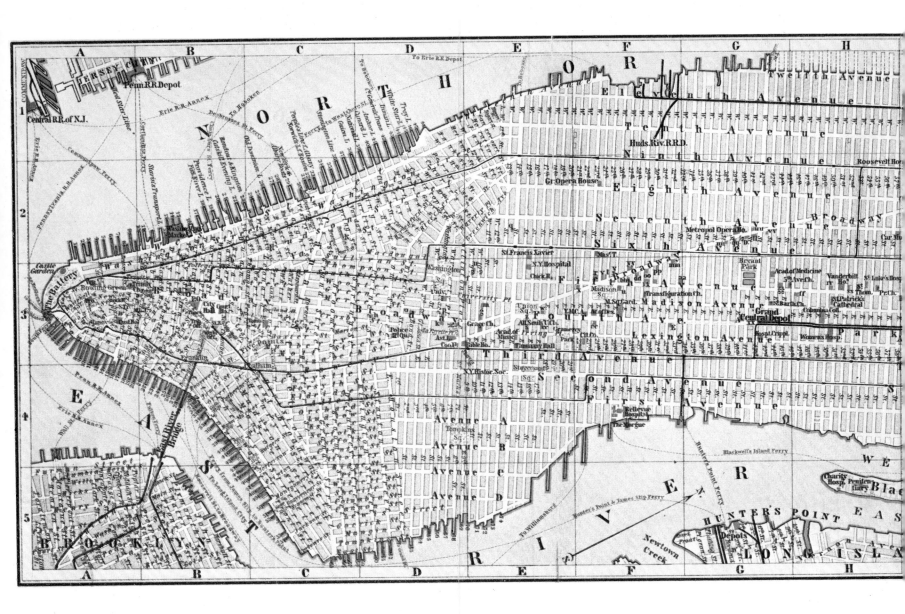

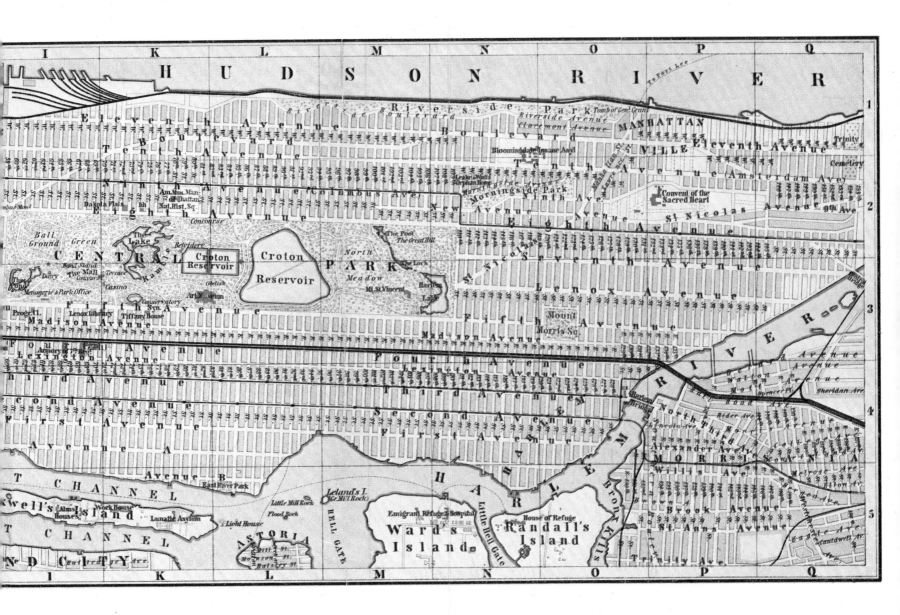

the island from E. to W. are numbered consecutively from 1 up to 225, while those running N. and S. are named Avenues and numbered from 1 to 12. In the widest part of the island, to the E. of First Avenue, are the additional short avenues A, B, C and D, while higher up, between Third and Fourth and between Fourth and Fifth Avenues respectively, are Lexington Avenue and Madison Avenue. The numbers in the avenues begin at the S. and run towards the N., the even on the W. side, the odd on the E. Twenty blocks average 1 M. Above 8th St. the cross-streets are known as E. and W. with reference to their position to Fifth Ave., and their numbers begin at this avenue and run E. and W. A new hundred is begun at each numbered or lettered avenue. The avenues are usually 100 ft. wide, and the cross-streets 60-100 ft. The names of the streets are generally given on the corner lamp-posts. Those of French or other foreign origin are usually anglicized in pronunciation (*e.g.* Desbrosses St., pron. Dess-bross-es St.). New Yorkers rarely add the word 'street' after the name of a street; thus one will give his address as 'corner of 5th Ave. and 57th'; while the conductor of the Elevated Railroad will announce a station as 'Grand' or '23rd.'

Books of Reference. Among the most recent guidebooks to New York are 'Manhattan: Historic and Artistic', by *C. F. Ober* and *C. M. Westover* (1892; 50 c.), the 'Sun's Guide to New York' (25c.), 'A Week in New York', by *Ernest Ingersoll* (50c.), and *Kobbe's* 'New York and its Environs' ($ 1.25). *Appletons'* 'Dictionary of New York' (30c.) is in the style of Dickens' 'Dictionary of London', and *Theodore Roosevelt's* 'New York', in the Historic Town Series (Longmans, 1891; $ 1.25), is an extremely interesting little volume. *King's* 'Handbook of New York' (1892; illus.; $ 1) contains a mass of miscellaneous information. Addresses can be found in *Trow's Directory*, which may be consulted at any drug-store or hotel-office.

Police Stations. The *Central Police Station* and *Office of the Commissioners of Police* is at 300 Mulberry St., and there are 36 Municipal Police Stations throughout the city. The police force consists of about 3650 patrolmen, 'roundsmen', and officers. The 'Broadway Squad' consists of specially fine-looking men.

British Consulate, 24 State St.; Consul-general, *Wm. Lane Booker.*

Collections. The following is a list of the principal Exhibitions Collections, etc., with the hours at which they are open.

Assay Office, United States (p. 26), open daily 10-2 (Sat. 10-12); free.
City Hall (p. 28), daily, 10-4, free.
Custom House, United States (p. 26), daily, 10-2; free.
Geological Museum at *Columbia College* (p. 39), daily, 10-4, free.
Libraries. Astor (p. 31), daily, free; *Mercantile* (p. 31), daily, free; *Lenox* (p. 36), daily, 10-5, free (closed in summer).
Madison Square Garden (pp. 16, 39). Visitors admitted to the tower (*View), daily, 10-10; 25c.
**Metropolitan Museum of Art* (p. 42), daily, 10 to dusk; on Mon. and Tues. 25c., at other times free; also on Tues. and Sat. 8-10, and on Sun. afternoon.
**Natural History Museum* (p. 41), daily, except Mon., 9-5, also on Wed. & Sat. 6-10 p.m., and on Sun. afternoon; free.
New York Historical Society (p. 40); daily, on introduction by a member.
Picture Galleries. See *Metropolitan Museum, Lenox Library*, and *New York Historical Society.*
Produce Exchange (p. 25); daily; visitors admitted to the balcony; business-hours, 9-4; free.
**St. Patrick's Cathedral* (p. 35); all day; frequent services.
*Stock Exchange (p. 27); business-hours, 10-3; visitors admitted to the gallery; free.
Sub-Treasury of the United States (p. 26); daily, 10-3; free (vaults shown to visitors introduced to the Assistant Treasurer).
*Trinity Church (p. 27); open all day; Sun. services at 7.30, 10.30, 3.30 (choral), and 8; week-day services at 9 and 3.

World Office (p. 29); visitors admitted to the Dome (*View), 9-1; free. *Zoological Garden* (p. 41), daily; free.

Principal Attractions. *Metropolitan Art Museum* (p. 42); *Natural History Museum* (p. 41); *St. Patrick's Cathedral* (p. 35); *Lenox Library* (p. 36); *Walk or drive in Broadway* (p. 26) and *Fifth Avenue* (p. 33); *View from the World Office* (p. 29), *Produce Exchange* (p. 25), *Equitable Building* (p. 27), *Statue of Liberty* (p. 3), or *Madison Square Garden* (p. 39); *Central Park* (p. 40); *Brooklyn Suspension Bridge* (p. 30); *Riverside Drive* (p. 48); *High Bridge* (p. 49); *Washington Bridge* (p. 49); *Stock Exchange* (p. 27); *Trinity Church* (p. 27); *Tiffany* and *Vanderbilt Houses* (pp. 39, 35); *Grace Church* (p. 31); *Harbour* (p. 23); *Ninth Avenue Elevated Railroad* at 110th St. (p. 10). — In summer the visitor should take a trip in one of the *Starin Excursion Steamers*, which start at the foot of Cortlandt St., almost hourly, and proceed round the Battery, up the E. River, and through Hell Gate and Long Island Sound to Glen Island (p. 67), affording a good idea of the configuration of Manhattan Island and of the traffic in the harbour and rivers (return-fare 40 c.).

New York, the largest and wealthiest city of the New World, and inferior in commercial and financial importance to London alone among the cities of the globe, is situated at the head of New York Bay, 18 M. from the ocean, in 40° 42′ 43″ N. lat. and 74° 0′3″ W. long. It lies mainly on *Manhattan Island*, a long and narrow tongue of land bounded by the *Hudson* or *North River* on the W. and the *East River* (part of *Long Island Sound*) on the E., and separated from the mainland on the N. and N.E. by the narrow *Harlem River* and *Spuyten Duyvil Creek;* but the municipal limits now also include a portion of the mainland beyond the Harlem River and several small islands in New York Bay and the E. River. Its total area is 42 sq. M., of which 22 sq. M. are on Manhattan Island; its greatest length (from the Battery to Yonkers) is 16 M., its greatest breadth (from the Hudson to the mouth of the Bronx) is 4¼ M. Manhattan Island is 13 M. long, and varies in width from about ¼-½ M. (at its extremities) to 2½ M., the general width being about 1¾-2 M. Manhattan Island is very rocky, the chief formations being gneiss and limestone; and except in the S. portion, which is covered with deep alluvial deposits, a great amount of blasting was necessary to prepare sites for houses and streets. For about half of its length from the S. it slopes on each side from a central ridge, and at the upper end the ground rises precipitously from the Hudson to a height of 240 ft. (Washington Heights), descending rapidly on the E. side to the Harlem Flats. The population in 1890, according to the government census, amounted to 1,515,301. In 1699 New York contained only about 6000 inhab. and in 1776 about 22,000 (comp. p. 24); and at the first United States census (1790) it had 33,131. In 1800 the population was 60,515; in 1820, 123,706; in 1840, 312,710; in 1860, 813,669; and in 1880, 1,206,299. If we include Brooklyn (p. 52), Jersey City (p. 51), and the less important suburbs, all forming practically one large city on New York Bay, we find a total population of about 2½ millions. The population is composed of very heterogeneous elements, including about 400,000 Irish, nearly as many Germans, 25,000 Italians, and 10,000 Chinese; and if we exclude the children of foreign parents born in New York, probably not more than one-fourth or one-fifth of the inhabitants can be described as native Americans. A large proportion are Roman Catholics. The death rate is about 25 per 1000.

The lower and older part of the town is irregularly laid out, and many of the streets are narrow and winding. The old buildings, however, have been almost entirely replaced by huge new piles of offices, banks, and warehouses. This part of the city is entirely given up to business and is the chief seat of its vast commercial enterprise and wealth. Above 13th St. New York is laid out with great regularity (arrangement of the streets, see p. 20), but the precipitous banks of the Hudson at the N. end of the island (comp. p. 49) have necessitated some deviation from chessboard regularity in that district. Nearly the whole of Manhattan Island, as far as 155th St., is now covered with streets and buildings, but much of the narrow part of the island beyond that point and a still larger proportion of the 'Annexed District' beyond the Harlem River (p. 50) have not yet been built over. The names of many of the villages absorbed by the growth of the city still cling to the districts here (Manhattanville, Harlem, Washington Heights, Morrisania, etc.). In proportion to its size New York is, perhaps, somewhat poorly furnished with open spaces, but Central Park (p. 40) is one of the finest parks in the world, and ample open spaces have been reserved beyond the Harlem River (comp. p. 50). The handsomest streets and residences are generally near the centre of the island, the most fashionable quarters being Fifth Avenue, Madison Avenue, and the portions of the cross-streets contiguous to these thoroughfares. The islands in the harbour belong to the U. S. Government, while those in the E. River are occupied by charitable and correctional institutions belonging to the city. New York is connected with Brooklyn by a fine suspension bridge (see p. 30); and various schemes for bridging or tunnelling the Hudson are now in progress or in contemplation. Several bridges cross the Harlem River.

*New York Harbour (comp. p. 2) is one of the finest in the world, affording ample accommodation and depth of water for the largest vessels. The *Upper Bay* or *New York Harbour Proper*, 8 M. long and 4-5 M. wide, is completely landlocked and contains several islands. It communicates through the *Narrows* (p. 2) with *Lower New York Bay*, which is protected from the ocean by a bar running N. from Sandy Hook in New Jersey (18 M. from the Battery) towards Long Island. The bar is crossed by two channels, admitting vessels of 25-30 ft. draught. At the Battery the harbour divides into two branches: the *Hudson* or *North River* to the left and the *East River* to the right. The latter is really a tidal channel connecting New York Bay with Long Island Sound. Manhattan Island, between the two rivers, has a water front of about 30 M. , all of which is available for sea-going vessels except about 5 M. on the Harlem River (comp., however, p. 50). On the other side of the North River, here about 1 M. wide, lies the *State of New Jersey*, with the cities of Jersey City, Hoboken, etc. (comp. p. 51; ferries, see p. 14). To the E. of East River is *Long Island*, with Brooklyn and Long Island City (comp. R. 3). The shipping is mainly confined to the North River below 23rd St. , and to the East River below Grand St. The former contains the docks of the Transatlantic lines, some of which are on the New Jersey side. A walk along South St. shows the shipping in the East River, representing a large proportion both of the foreign and domestic trade of New York. Both rivers are alive with ferry-boats. For the islands, Hell Gate, etc., see pp. 2, 50, 66.

History. Manhattan Island and the mouth of the Hudson are said to have been visited by the Florentine Verrazzani in 1524, but the authentic history of New York begins with the exploration of *Henry Hudson* in 1609 (see p. 146). The first permanent settlement on Manhattan Island was made by the Dutch West India Co. in 1624, and the first regular governor was *Peter Minuit*, a Westphalian, who bought the island from the Indians for 60 guilders (about § 25 or 5*l.*). The little town he founded was christened *New Amsterdam* and by 1650 had about 1000 inhabitants. The citizens established farms, traded for furs with the Indians, and entrenched themselves in fortifications, the N. limit of which coincided with the present line of Wall St. (p. 26). *Peter Stuyvesant*, the last of the four Dutch governors, arrived in 1647. In 1664 the town was seized, in time of peace, by the English under *Col. Nicholls*, and though retaken by the Dutch in 1673, it passed permanently into English possession by treaty in the following year. The first English governor was *Sir Edmund Andros*. The name of the town was changed to *New York* in honour of the Duke of York, to whom his brother, Charles II. , had granted the entire province. Among the chief incidents in the Anglo-Colonial period were the usurpation of *Leisler*, leader of the progressive party, in 1689-91, and the *Negro Insurrection* in 1741, the coloured slaves forming at this time not far short of half the population. In 1765 the delegates of nine of the thirteen colonies met in New York to protest against the Stamp Act and to assert the doctrine of no taxation without representation; and the first actual bloodshed of the Revolution took place here in 1770 (six weeks before the Boston Massacre, p. 77), in a scuffle with the soldiers who tried to remove the 'Liberty Pole' of the Sons of Liberty. At this time New York had about 20,000 inhab. (less than either Boston or Philadelphia); and the Ratzer Map of 1767 shows that the town extended to the neighourhood of the present City Hall Park (p. 28). The town was occupied by Washington in 1776, but after the battles of Long Island and Harlem Heights (see p. 48) the Americans retired, and New York became the British headquarters for seven years. The British troops evacuated the city on Nov. 25th, 1783. From 1785 to 1790 New York was the seat of the Federal Government, and it was the State capital down to 1797. *Hamilton, Jay*, and *Burr* were among the prominent men of this period. At the beginning of the present century the city had 60,000 inhab., and since then its growth has been very rapid, the tide of immigration setting in powerfully after the war of 1812, in which New York suffered considerably from the blockade. In 1807 the first steamboat was put on the Hudson (see p. 146), and in 1825 a great impulse to the city's commerce was given by the opening of the Erie Canal (p. 154). The Harlem Railway dates from 1831; the Elevated Railroad from 1878; gas-lighting from 1825; the use of electricity for illumination from about 1881. In the Civil War New York sent 116,000 men to the Federal armies, but in 1863 it was the scene of a riot in opposition to the draft, which cost 1000 lives. For several years the city suffered under the machinations of the so-called '*Tweed Ring*', which had gained control of the municipal government; but in 1872 'Boss' Tweed and several of his fellow-conspirators were convicted of embezzlement of public funds and imprisoned. In March, 1888, New York was visited by a terrible 'blizzard', or storm of wind and snow, which cut off all communication with the outside world for several days and caused many deaths and much suffering. — *Washington Irving* (1783-1839) was a native of New York.

Commerce and Industry. The importance of New York as a commercial centre is shown by the fact that about 60 per cent. of the entire foreign trade of the United States is carried on through its port. In 1891 the value of foreign imports and exports was $907,576,550 (188,970,985*l.*), while the harbour was entered by 5112 vessels, of 6,711,020 tons burden, and cleared by 4949, of 6,567,796 tons. The duties collected on imports amounted to $122,771,867. About three-fourths of the immigrants into the United States land at New York, the number in 1891 being 430,884. In 1890 the valuation of property was $1,785,857,338. The city debt at the beginning of 1892 was $150,333,460. The manufactures of New York, though relatively less important than its commerce, are very varied and extensive, producing in 1890 goods to the value of $783,941,023 (157,788,200*l.*) and employing 365,000 hands.

The S. extremity of the island on which New York stands is occupied by the BATTERY, a pleasant little park of about 20 acres in extent, commanding a good view of the harbour but now somewhat marred by the intrusion of the elevated railroad. It takes its name from the old fort erected here by the early Dutch settlers and was long the fashionable quarter for residences. The large circular erection on the W. side is *Castle Garden*, formerly the landing-place and temporary quarters of immigrants, which have now been transferred to Ellis Island (p. 3). It was at one time a concert-hall, where Jenny Lind made her first appearance in America (1850), is now temporarily in use as an armory for the Naval Reserve, and, it is said, is to be converted into an aquarium. The *United States Barge Office*, a tasteful building with a tower 90 ft. high, a little to the E., is an appendage of the custom-house. The steamers for Bedloe's Island (see p. 3) and Staten Island (p. 50) start from the Battery.

Looking to the N. from the Battery, we see in front of us two large red buildings: the *Washington Building* (p. 26) to the left and the PRODUCE EXCHANGE (Pl. i; A, 3) to the right. The latter, a huge brick and terracotta structure in the Italian Renaissance style, contains numerous offices and a large hall (1st floor), 220 ft. long, 144 ft. wide, and 60 ft. high (adm., see. p 21). The tower, 225 ft. high, commands a fine *View of the city and harbour (elevator). Upwards of 20,000 people daily use the elevators in this building.

Whitehall Street, containing the *U.S. Army Building*, leads hence to the S.E. to the South, Hamilton, and 39th St. ferries to Brooklyn (p. 14). A little to the E., at the S.E. corner of Broad St. and Pearl St., is what remains of the old *Fraunces Tavern*, where Washington took farewell of his officers in 1783. No. 73, Pearl St., was the first Dutch tavern, afterwards the Stadhuys or City Hall (tablet).

The small open space between the Produce Exchange and the Washington Building is the BOWLING GREEN, the cradle of New York, formerly surrounded by the houses of eminent citizens.

The buildings on the S. side, mainly steamboat-offices, occupy the site of Fort Amsterdam, from which the Battery took its name (see above), and which included the governor's house and a chapel. The fort was built in 1626 and demolished in 1787. Its site is indicated by a tablet placed by the Holland Society on No. 4, Bowling Green. A statue of George III., which formerly stood here, was pulled down on the day of the Declaration of Independence (July 4th, 1776) and melted into bullets. The Washington Building (see below) is on the site of the house erected in 1760 by Archibald Kennedy, Collector of the Port of New York, and afterwards occupied by the British generals Cornwallis, Howe, and Clinton. It was here that Benedict Arnold, also occupying a house on the Green, carried on his negotiations with the last-named. The railing round the Bowling Green circle dates from before the Revolution.

At the Bowling Green begins *Broadway, the chief street in New York, extending hence to the Central Park, a distance of 5 M., beyond which its continuation is known as the *Boulevard*. The whole of Broadway up to 59 th St. is the scene of a most busy and varied traffic, which reaches its culminating point in the lower part of the street during business-hours. This part of the street is almost entirely occupied by wholesale houses, insurance offices, banks, and the like; but farther up are numerous fine shops ('stores'). Broadway is no longer, as in the Dutch colonial days of its christening, the broadest street in New York, but it is still the most important. No. 1 Broadway, to the left, is the above-mentioned *Washington Building*, a lofty pile of offices erected by Mr. Cyrus W. Field, of ocean cable fame; the back and side windows afford splendid views of the harbour. Other conspicuous business premises in the lower part of Broadway are the large *Welles* and *Standard Oil Co. Buildings* (to the right, Nos. 18, 26) and *Aldrich Court* (Nos. 43-45; left), on the site of the first habitation of white men on Manhattan Island (tablet of the Holland Society). Opposite the last is the *Tower Building* (No. 50), 185 ft. high and only 25 ft. wide. A little higher up, at the corner of Exchange Place, is the handsome *Consolidated Stock and Petroleum Exchange* (visitors admitted to the gallery), where 2,500,000,000 barrels of petroleum are sold annually. Farther on are *Trinity Church* and *Wall St.* (see below).

Wall Street, diverging from Broadway to the right, is the Lombard Street of New York, 'the great nerve centre of all American business', and the financial barometer of the country', where 'finance and transportation, the two determining powers in business, have their headquarters'. The street, which follows the line of the walls of the Dutch city, consists mainly of a series of substantial and handsome banks and insurance offices. To the left, one block from Broadway, at the corner of Nassau St., is the **United States Sub Treasury** (Pl. A, 3; adm., see 21), a marble structure with a Doric portico, approached by a flight of steps bearing a large bronze statue of *George Washington*, by J. Q. A. Ward, erected in 1883. The building occupies the site of the old *Federal Hall*, in which the first U.S. Congress was held and Washington inaugurated as President. Next to the Sub-Treasury is the *U.S. Assay Office* (adm., p. 21), where strangers may see the processes of assaying and refining the crude bullion. Opposite, at the corner of Broad St. (see below), is the *Drexel Building*, a handsome white marble structure in the Renaissance style. Farther along Wall St., at the corner of William St., is the **U.S. Custom House**

(Pl. A, 3), a massive pile of dark-coloured granite, with an Ionic colon-nade (columns 38 ft. high). The interior (open 10-3) consists of a huge rotunda, covered by a dome supported by eight enormous columns of Italian marble, with elaborate Corinthian capitals. — Farther on, Wall St. crosses *Pearl Street* (with the *Cotton Exchange*), *Water St.*, and *Front St.*, and ends at *South St.* and the ferry to Montague St., Brooklyn.

BROAD ST., a busy street leaving Wall St. opposite the Sub-Treasury, contains the *Stock Exchange (Pl. 2; A, 3), a high marble building to the right, with other entrances in Wall St. and New St. Strangers, who are admitted to a gallery overlooking the hall (entr., 13 Wall St.), should not omit a visit to this strange scene of business, tumult, and excitement, a wilder scene probably than that presented in any European exchange (bus·iness-hours 10-3). The value of railway and other stocks dealt with here daily often amounts to $30,000,000 (6,000,000*l.*), besides of government bonds. As much as $36,000 (7200*l.*) has been paid for a seat in the New York Stock Exchange, and 4000*l.* is the regular fee. There are about 1200 members. — Opposite the Exchange, adjoining the Drexel Building (see above), is the *Mills Building*, an enormous pile in red brick, in which Mr. Grover Cleveland has his office. Broad St. ends at South St., a little to the N. of the Battery (p. 25).

NASSAU ST., running N. from Wall St., opposite Broad St., contains the office of the *Mutual Life Insurance Co.* (value of policies in 1893 $750,000,000), one of the largest and handsomest business structures in New York, but not seen to advantage in this narrow street. It harbours the *New York Chamber of Commerce.* A tablet commemorates the fact that this was the site of the Middle Dutch Church (1727). The business of the *New York Clearing House Association*, at the corner of Pine and Nassau St., averages $115,000,000 daily and amounts to $35,000,000,000 (7,000,000,000*l.*) per year.

On the W. side of Broadway, opposite the beginning of Wall St., rises *Trinity Church (Pl. A, 3; comp. p. xc), a handsome Gothic edifice of brown stone, by *R. M. Upjohn*, 192 ft. long, 80 ft. wide, and 60 ft. high, with a spire 2o5 ft. high (view; permit from rector necessary). The present building dates from 1839-46, but occupies the site of a church of 1696. The church owns property to the value of at least 1,000,000*l.*, producing an income of 100,000*l.*, used in the support of several subsidiary churches and numerous charities (comp. p. 155).

The INTERIOR (adm., see p. 24), dimly lighted by stained glass, affords a strange contrast to the bustling life of Broadway. The chancel is at the W. end. The altar and reredos, built as a memorial of William B. Astor, are handsomely adorned with marble and mosaics. The bronze are a memorial of John Jacob Astor. — In the N.E. corner of the doors CHURCHYARD is a Gothic *Monument* in memory of American patriots who died in British prisons during the Revolution. Adjacent is a bronze sta-tue of *Judge Watts*, Recorder of New York under the British, erected in 1892. By the S. railing of the churchyard is the grave of *Alexander Hamilton* (d. 1804; tomb with pyramidal top). *Robert Fulton* (d. 1815), the father of the steamboat, lies in the vault of the Livingston family, near the S. side of the chancel. Close to the S.E. corner of the church is the monument of *Capt. Lawrence*, slain in 1813 in his gallant defence of the 'Chesapeake' against the British frigate 'Shannon'. Among the other tombs are those of the ill-fated *Charlotte Temple*, *Albert Gallatin* (Secretary of the Treasury 1801-13), *Gen. Phil. Kearney* (d. 1862), and *Wm. Bradford* (d. 1752), printer of the first New York newspaper.

Nearly opposite Trinity Church is the building of the *Union Trust Co.* (No. 80), one of the most successful architectural efforts of its kind in the United States. On the same side, between Pine St. and Cedar St., is the office of the *Equitable Life Insurance Co.*, said to be the largest building in New York (1500 tenants). This company has issued upwards of 200,000 policies, of the value of $850,000,000 (170,000,000*l.*). Visitors should not fail to visit the interior of this huge edifice. The roof, on which is a signal-service station of the U.S. government (popularly known as 'Old Probability'), commands a magnificent *View of the city, the harbour, the N. and E. rivers, Brooklyn, etc. (elevator). — Several other huge buildings, among them that of the *Western Union Telegraph Co.* (No. 195) and the tall and narrow office of the *Mail & Express*, are passed on the left ere we reach Fulton St. (see below).

Fulton Street, one the busiest streets in New York, leads E. to *Fulton Market* (fish, oysters, etc.) and *Fulton Ferry* (for Brooklyn) and W. to *Washington Market*, which should be visited for the sake of its wonderful display of fruit, vegetables, and other provisions. In Dey St. (Pl. B, 3), at the corner of Church St., is the new 13-story *Havemeyer Building*.

At the S.E. corner of Fulton St. is the red brick building of the *Evening Post* (long edited by Wm. C. Bryant), and a little higher up on the same side are the *Park Bank* and the *New York Herald Office*. Opposite is **St. Paul's Church** (Pl. B, 3) the oldest church in New York (1756). It faces W. (entr. by gate in Vesey St.).

The graveyard contains some interesting monuments (*Emmet*, the Irish patriot, monument to the S.E. of the church; *G. F. Cooke*, the actor), and in the portico at the E. end of the church (next Broadway) there is a memorial of *General Montgomery*, who fell at the storming of Quebec in 1775. The square pews in which George Washington and Governor Clinton used to sit, in the N. and S. aisles, are shown, but the pews have been renewed since their day. Comp. p. xxx.

Broadway now reaches the S. end of the open space known as *City Hall Park* (Pl. B, 3), the site of the ancient 'Commons' or pasturage, in and around which stand several important buildings. In the apex between Broadway and *Park Row* (p. 29) is the **Post Office,** a large Renaissance building, with a mansard roof, completed in 1876. Its four façades are respectively 290, 340, 130, and 230 ft. long. On the fourth floor are the *United States Courts*. About 2500 men are employed here, and nearly 1,200,000,000 letters and other postal packets are annually dealt with (comp. p. 14). — Behind the Post Office, to the N., is the *City Hall (see p. 21), containing the headquarters of the Mayor and other municipal authorities. It is a well-proportioned building in the Italian style, with a central portico, two projecting wings, and a cupola clocktower. The architect was *John McComb*. The rear was built of freestone, as it was supposed at the time it was erected (1803-12) that no one of importance would ever live to the N. of the building.

The *Governor's Room* (open to visitors, 10-4), used for official receptions, contains the chairs used in the first U.S. Congress, the chair in which Washington was inaugurated as President, the desk on which he wrote his first message to Congress, Jefferson's desk, and other relics. Among the portraits are those of Hamilton, Lafayette, and several governors of New York. Jefferson is commemorated by a statue. The *Council Chamber* contains a large portrait of Washington by Trumbull.

To the N. of the City Hall is the **Court House** (Pl. B, 3; 1861-

67), a large building of white marble, with its principal entrance, garnished with lofty Corinthian columns, facing Chambers St. The interior, which contains the State Courts and several municipal offices, is well fitted up. The building, owing to the scandalous 'Ring frauds', cost 12 millions dollars (2,400,000*l.*). Opposite the Court House, in Chambers St., are various *City Offices*. To the E. of the City Hall is the *Register Office*.

Park Row (Pl. B, 1) bounding the S.W. side of the City Hall Park, contains the offices of many of the principal New York newspapers, which rank among the largest and most imposing buildings in the city. Perhaps the most solid and satisfactory is that of the *New *York Times*, by Geo. B. Post, in light-coloured stone, with circular windows; the entrance, however, is disproportionately small. Next to it (to the N.) is the *Tribune Building*, of red brick with white facings and a clock-tower 285ft. high. The *Pulitzer Building*, with the *World Office*, of brown stone, with a dome, is the tallest and largest of all, and a splendid *View of New York is obtained from the dome (310 ft.; elevator). Opposite these offices, in Printing House Square, is a bronze *Statue of Benjamin Franklin* (the tutelary deity of American journalism), by Plassman, and in front of the Tribune Building is a seated bronze figure, by J. Q. A. Ward, of its famous founder *Horace Greeley*, erected in 1872. The grey granite building of the *Staats-Zeitung* is at the corner of Tryon Place.

The part of Park Row beyond this point, and the adjacent *Chatham St.* and *Baxter St.* (the 'Bay'), are mainly occupied by Jewish dealers in old clothes and other articles. Park Row ends at Chatham Square, whence the ***Bowery**, originally named from the Dutch 'Baurreis' or farms in this part of the town, runs N. to the junction of Third and Fourth Avenues (see p. 40). The Bowery is now full of drinking-saloons, dime museums, small theatres, and hucksters' stalls, and presents one of the most crowded and characteristic scenes in New York, though it is much less 'rowdy' than when Dickens described it in his 'American Notes'. Its residents are mainly Germans and Poles. — **Five Points**, the district (roughly speaking) between Park Row (S.E.), Centre St. (W.), and Grand St. (N.), formerly bore, and to some extent still bears, the reputation of being the most evil district in New York, the home of rowdies, thieves, and drunkards. Like the Seven Dials in London, it has, however, of late been much improved by the construction of new streets, the removal of old rookeries, and the invasion of commerce. It took its name from the 'five points' formed by the intersection of Worth (then Anthony), Baxter, and Park Streets; and here now stand the *Five Points Mission* and the *Five Points House of Industry* (visitors courteously received). Perhaps the most interesting parts of the district now are the Italian quarter in *Mulberry St.*, with its famous 'Bend', and *Chinatown* in *Mott St.*, the squalor of which presents some elements of the picturesque. The swinging lanterns and banners of Chinatown give a curiously oriental air to this part of the city. Visits may be paid to the *Joss House* at No. 6. and the *Chinese Restaurant* at No. 18 Mott St. It is hardly prudent to visit the *Opium Joints* except in the company of a detective. — In *New Chambers St.*, leading to the right from Park Row, is the *Newsboys Lodging House*, erected by the Children's Aid Society (p. 31), which has given shelter in the last 40 years to about 250,000 boys, at a total expense of about $150,000 (90,000*l.*). — On the W. side of City Hall Park are the starting-point of the City Hall branch of the Third Avenue Elevated Railroad (see p. 11) and the approaches to *Brooklyn Bridge* (p. 30).

The great *East River Bridge (Pl. B, 4; p. 11), generally known as *Brooklyn Bridge*, connecting New York with the city of Brooklyn (p. 52), is the largest suspension-bridge in the world and is equally interesting as a marvel of engineering skill and as a model of grace and beauty. Its New York terminus is in Park Row, facing the City Hall Park, where it has direct connection with the Elevated Railway (comp. p. 11), while the Brooklyn end is at Sands St. The bridge affords accommodation for two railway-tracks (comp. p. 11), two carriage-roadways, and a wide raised footway in the centre. It was begun in 1870 and opened for traffic in 1883, at a total expense of nearly $ 15,000,000 (3,000,000*l*.). It was designed by *John A. Roebling*, who died in 1879 from an accident, and was completed by his son *Washington Roebling*. The bridge was taken over by the State in 1875. The toll for vehicles is 5 c.; carfare 3 c.; the toll for pedestrians was abolished in 1891.

The total length of the bridge, including the approaches, is 5990 ft. (1¹/₈ M.); and the distance between the piers is 1600 ft. (main spans of Forth Bridge 1700 ft.; Suspension Bridge over the Danube at Budapest 1250 ft.; Menai Suspension Bridge 580 ft.). The width is 85 ft., and the height above high-water 135 ft. The gigantic stone piers, rising 270 ft. above high-water, are built on caissons sunk upon the rocky bed of the stream, which is 45 ft. below the surface on the Brooklyn side and 80 ft. on the New York side. The bridge itself, which is entirely of iron and steel, is suspended from the towers by four 16-inch steel-wire cables, which are anchored' at each end by 35,000 cubic yards of solid masonry. The four cables contain 14,360 M. of wire, and their weight is about 3600 tons. The hanging cables attached to the large ones number 2172. — Upwards of 40,000,000 persons cross the bridge annually, nine-tenths of these in the cable-trains. The largest number of passengers ever carried by the trains in one day was 159,259 (April 30th, 1889). The *View from the raised promenade in the middle of the bridge is one which no visitor to New York should miss. To the N. is the E. River, with its busy shipping; to the S. is the Harbour, with the Statue of Liberty (p. 2) in the distance; to the W. is New York; to the right, Brooklyn. The view by night is very striking.

The section of Broadway above the City Hall Park contains numerous railway and scalpers' offices (see p. xxi) and wholesale warehouses of 'dry goods' (*i.e.* haberdashery, drapery, etc.). At the corner of Chambers St., to the right, is a large marble building erected for the mammoth firm of drapers, *A. T. Stewart & Co.*, but now occupied by offices. To the left is the *Chemical National Bank*, which, with a capital of but $ 300,000 (60,000*l*.), holds $ 25,000,000 (5,000,000*l*.) on deposit, while its shares sell for 45 or 46 times their par value. At No. 343 Broadway (corner of Leonard St.) rises the *New York Life Insurance Office*.

Two blocks to the right (W.) of this point, between Elm St. and Centre St., is the building known as the *Tombs (Pl. C, 3; shown by permit from the Commissioners of Public Charities, C6 Third Ave.), the city prison of New York, also containing a Police Court and Court of Special Sessions. It is a heavy granite building in an Egyptian style, with the main entrance in Centre St. The portico is supported by four columns. The first execution by electricity took place here in 1890. A large new building is being erected close by for the *Criminal Courts*.

Farther up Broadway the predominant warehouses are those of

clothiers and furriers. The principal cross-streets are *Canal Street* (once the bed of a stream crossing the Island), *Grand Street* (see p. 18), and *Houston Street*. The section of Broadway between Bond St. and Grace Church (see below) is the district *par excellence* of the booksellers, who also congregate in the adjoining streets.

To the right, opposite No. 345 Broadway, opens the wide **Astor Place**, with the handsome new building of the *Mercantile Library* (p. 31), completed in 1891. The library occupies the site of the old opera-house, in front of which, in 1849, took place the famous riot between the partizans of the actors Forest and Macready. It contains a large and handsome reading-room and possesses 220,000 volumes. — In *Lafayette Place*, which runs to the S. from Astor Place, are the ***Astor Library** (Pl. D, 3), a large red structure with wings, and *St. Joseph's Home*, for street-waifs. The Astor Library contains about 280,000 vols., and is the chief consulting library in New York. It was originally founded in 1848 by John Jacob Astor and has since been liberally endowed by his sons and grandsons, the united benefactions of the family amounting to about $1,700,000 (340,000 *l.*). The library possesses the first, second, and fourth folio editions of Shakespeare (1623, 1632, 1685) and numerous valuable autographs, incunabula, and MSS. The collection of paintings bequeathed to the Astor Library by J. J. Astor includes two Meissoniers and other good French works. About 70,000 readers use the library annually. — Astor Place also contains the *Aldine Club* (see p. 18) and the famous *De Vinne Press*, which produces, perhaps, the most artistic typography of America.

At the junction of Astor Place and Third Avenue stands the **Cooper Institute** or **Union** (Pl. D, 3), a large building of brown sandstone, founded and endowed in 1857 by Peter Cooper, a wealthy and philanthropic citizen, at a total cost of nearly $1,000,000 (200,000 *l.*). It contains a fine free library and reading-room, free schools of science and art (attended by 3500 students), and a large lecture-hall. The average daily number of readers is about 2000. The Sunday-evening lectures are attended by huge crowds. — Opposite to the Cooper Union is the *Bible House*, the headquarters of the *American Bible Society*, which has published and distributed 55,000,000 copies of the Bible or parts of it, in upwards of 80 different languages and dialects. The library contains some interesting MSS. and early printed volumes. — At No. 24 St. Mark's Place (Eighth St.), between Second and Third Avenues, is the **Children's Aid Society**, one of the most praiseworthy benevolent institutions in New York, founded in 1853 by its late secretary, *C. Loring Brace* (d. 1890). This society has established 21 industrial schools, 6 lodging-houses (comp. p. 29), 12 night-schools, and 2 free reading-rooms in different parts of the city, and has also four summer-homes for children. It has placed about 7500 orphan children in good homes in the South and West.

Beyond Astor Place Broadway passes (right) the large building occupied by *Hilton, Hughes, & Co.*, the successors of A. T. Stewart & Co. The street then inclines to the left. At the bend rises ***Grace Church** (Pl. E, 3; Epis.), which, with the adjoining rectory, chantry, and church-house, forms, perhaps, the most attractive ecclesiastical group in New York. The present church, which is of white limestone and has a lofty marble spire, was erected in 1843-46 from the designs of *James Renwick, Jun.* The interior is well-proportioned (open daily, 9-5; good musical services), and all the windows contain stained glass. — At 14th St. Broadway reaches ***Union Square**, which is embellished with pleasure-grounds, statues, and an ornamental fountain. On the W. side, at the corner of 15th St., is *Tiffany's*, one of the finest goldsmith's and jeweller's shops in the world (visitors welcomed even when not purchasers). Near the S.E. corner is a good *Equestrian Statue of Washington*, by H. K. Browne; in the centre of the S. side is a bronze *Statue of Lafayette*, by Bartholdi; and in the S.W. corner is a *Statue of Abraham Lincoln* (1865), by H.K. Browne. The pavement on the S. side of Union Sq., between Broadway and Fourth Avenue, is known as the 'Rialto' or 'Slave-Market', as the resort of actors in search of engagements.

FOURTEENTH STREET, which Broadway intersects at Union Sq., is one of the chief arteries of cross-town traffic (tramway), and the part to the W. of Broadway contains many of the busiest shops in the city and presents a scene of great animation and variety. Among the shops may be mentioned *Macy's*, at the corner of Sixth Avenue, a large establishment in the style of the Bon Marché in Paris or Whiteley's in London. To the E., between Union Sq. and Third Avenue, are *Steinway Hall* (no longer used for concerts), the *Academy of Music* (Pl. E, 3; p. 15), and **Tammany Hall** (Pl. E, 3; 1867), all on the N. side of the street. Tammany Hall is the seat of the *Tammany Society*, which was established in 1789 for benevolent purposes, but soon developed into a strong political (Democratic) institution and is now the centre of the party of local politicians named after the building. The name is a corruption of that of Tamenund, a famous Indian seer (see 'The Last of the Mohicans', by *Fenimore Cooper*, chap. 28), and the officers of the society bear the Indian titles of sachems and the like.

Broadway between Union Sq. and Madison Sq. (see below) is one of the chief shopping-resorts of New York, containing many fine stores for the sale of furniture, dry goods, etc. At 23rd St. it intersects Fifth Avenue (p. 33) and skirts the W. side of *Madison Square, another prettily laid out public garden, containing a bronze *Statue of Admiral Farragut* (1801-70), by St. Gaudens (N.W. corner), an obelisk to the memory of *General Worth* (1794-1849; W. side), and a *Statue of William H. Seward* (1801-72), by Randolph Rogers (S.W. angle). The statue of Farragut is the finest in New York, and the imaginative treatment of the pedestal is very beautiful. On the W. side of the square are the *Fifth Avenue Hotel* and the *Hoffman House* (p. 8), two of the foremost hotels in the city, and at the corner of 26th St. is *Delmonico's Restaurant* (p. 9), nearly opposite which is the *Brunswick Hotel* (p. 8).

At the S.E. corner of the square are the *Madison Sq. Presbyterian Church* (Rev. Dr. Parkhurst) and the *Metropolitan Insurance Building*, and at the N.E. corner is the huge *Madison Square Garden* (Pl. F, 3; see p. 39).

Like 14th St., TWENTY-THIRD STREET, to the W. of Broadway, is one of the chief shopping-resorts of New York, and its wide side-pavements are generally crowded with purchasers. Perhaps the most notable shop is the large and fashionable 'dry goods' store of *Stern* (No. 32). At the corner of Sixth Avenue (p. 40) is the imposing *Masonic Temple* (Pl. F, 2), surmounted by a dome 155 ft. high and containing a hall to seat 1200 persons. Between Seventh and Eighth Avenues is the lofty *Chelsea Apartment House*, and at the corner of the latter is the *Grand Opera House* (Pl. F, 2; pp. 15, 40). To the E. of Madison Sq. Twenty-Third St. passes between the *School of Design* and the *Y.M.C.A.* (see p. 37) and runs down to the E. river.

Between Madison Square and 42nd St. Broadway passes numerous theatres, which follow each other in rapid succession (see p. 15). In the same part of Broadway are numerous large and fine hotels.

At the corner of 32nd St. is the handsome *Union Dime Savings Bank.* At 33rd St. Broadway crosses Sixth Avenue, passing under the Elevated Railroad. To the right, at the corner of 34th St., is the *Congregational Tabernacle.* At the corner of 35th St. is the new concrete building of the *New York Herald.* The **Metropolitan Opera House** (Pl. G, 2; p. 15), burned out in 1892, stood between 39th St. and 40th St. Seventh Ave. is crossed at 43rd St. Beyond 42nd St. Broadway is uninteresting, but there are some lofty spec imens of apartment-houses or French flats near its head. At No. 1644 (r.) is the *American Horse Exchange*, the Tattersall's of New York. At 59th St. Broadway reaches the S.W. corner of Central Park (p. 40) and intersects Eighth Avenue, and beyond this point it runs to the N.W. under the name of the **Boulevard**, which it bears in right of its great width and its rows of trees. In the open space at the crossing of Eighth Avenue stands the **Columbus Monument** (Pl. I, 2), by *Gaetano Russo*, erected in 1892 (the 400th anniversary of the discovery of America) and consisting of a tall shaft surmounted by a marble statue (in all, 77 ft. high).

Fifth Avenue, the chief street in New York from the standpoint of wealth and fashion, begins at *Washington Square* (see below), to the N. of West 4th St. and a little to the W. of Broadway, and runs N. to the Harlem River (p. 49), a distance of 6 M. The lowest part of the avenue has now been largely invaded by shops, offices, and hotels, but above 42nd St. it consists of handsome private residences, forming, perhaps, a more imposing show of affluence and comfort than any other street in the world. The avenue has been kept sacred from the marring touch of the tramway or the elevated railroad, but it is traversed by a line of 'stages' or omnibuses (p. 13). The avenue is wide and well-paved; most of the buildings are of brown sandstone, which gives it a somewhat monotonous air. On a fine afternoon Fifth Avenue is alive with carriages and horsemen on their way to and from Central Park (comp. p. 41), and it is, perhaps, seen at its best on a fine Sunday, when the churches are emptying.

WASHINGTON SQUARE (Pl. D, 3), pleasantly laid out on the site of an old burial-ground, contains a bronze *Statue of Garibaldi* (1807-82), by Turini, erected in 1888. On the E. side is the *University of the City of New York* (Pl. D, 3), a good Gothic building erected in 1832-35, with a large chapel (800-1000 students). [The medical department of the University is in E. 26th St. and was erected in 1879-87.] Adjoining this on the S. is a *Baptist Church*, with two Perp. towers. On the S. side of the square are the *Judson Memorial Buildings*, including a church On the N. side is a row of substantial oldtime residences, which still retain an air of undeniable respectability. The *Washington Centennial Memorial Arch*, by Stanford White, spans the S. entrance of Fifth Ave. — *University Place*, skirting Washington Sq. on the E., runs to Union Sq. (p. 31).

Following Fifth Avenue to the N. from Washington Sq., we pass several substantial old residences and the *Brevoort House* (p. 7; cor. of 8th St.). At the corner of 10th St. is the Episcopal *Church of the Ascension* (with good stained-glass windows and a fine altar-piece by *La Farge*), and at 12th St. is the *First Presbyterian Church*, both of brown stone, with square towers. In crossing the busy 14th St. (p. 32) we see Union Sq. (p. 31) to the right. At 16th St. is the tall *Judge Building.*

In 15th St., a little to the W. of Fifth Avenue, is the large building of the *New York Hospital* (Pl. E, 3). In 16th St., but extending back to 15th St., are the ornate *Church* and *College of St. Francis Xavier* (Pl. E, 2), the American headquarters of the Jesuits (500 pupils).

At the left corner of 18th St. is *Chickering Hall* (Pl. E, 3), a concert-hall in which Dr. Felix Adler lectures before the Society of Ethical Culture on Sun. morning. At 20th St. (l.) is the *Methodist Book Concern*, one of the largest book-houses in the world; at 21st St. are the *Union Club* (l.), and the *Lotos Club* (r.). At 23rd St. (p. 32) the Avenue intersects Broadway and skirts Madison Sq. (see p. 32). At the corner of 29th St. are the *Dutch Reformed Collegiate Church* and the *Calumet Club* (No. 267), and in 29th St., a little to the E., is the odd-looking *Church of the Transfiguration* (Pl. F, 3), popularly known as the 'Little Church round the Corner'. The *Knickerbocker Club* (p. 18) stands at the corner of 32nd St. (r.). At the corner of 34th St. is the large white marble palace built by Mr. A. T. Stewart as his private residence, at a cost of $3,000,000 (600,000*l.*), and now occupied by the **Manhattan Club** (p. 18), the chief Democratic club of New York (1000 members). The new building of the *Lotos Club* (see above) is at 35th St. The **Union League Club,** the chief Republican club of New York, is a handsome and substantial building at the corner of 39th St., and the interior is very tastefully fitted up (1500 members). Between 40th St. and 42nd St., to the left, is the disused *Reservoir of the Croton Aqueduct*, in which the water is kept ready for use in case of fire. A little to the E., in 42nd St., is the *Grand Central Depot* (pp. 6, 37). At the S.E. corner of 42nd St. rises the tasteful *Columbia Bank.* The **Temple Emanu-El,** or chief synagogue of New York, at the corner of 43rd St., is a fine specimen of Moorish architecture, with a richly decorated interior.

In *W. 43rd St.*, between Fifth and Sixth Avenues, are three handsome new buildings, completed in 1890-91. To the right (N.) is the new *Century Club* (p. 18), a Renaissance structure, with a loggia in the second story and ornamental iron-work over some of the windows. Adjoining the Century Club is the *New York Academy of Medicine* (Pl. G, 3), a substantial and handsome edifice, with a front of reddish-brown stone, in a semi-Egyptian style. Beyond this are the extensive quarters of the *Racquet Club* (p. 17).

At the corner of 45th St. is the *Church of the Divine Paternity* (Universalist), and between 45th St. and 46th St. (r.) is the elaborately decorated *Church of the Heavenly Rest*. The large *Windsor Hotel* (p. 8) occupies the block between 46th St. and 47th St. (r.). The *Dutch Reformed Church*, at the corner of of 48th St., is one of the handsomest and most elaborately adorned ecclesiastical edifices in the city. It is in the 14th cent. or Dec. Gothic style and has a crocketed spire, 270 ft. high.

Between 50th and 51st St. (Pl. H, 3), to the right, stands *St. Patrick's Cathedral (R.C.), an extensive building of white marble, in the Dec. style, and the most important ecclesiastical edifice in the United States. It is 400 ft. long, 125 ft. wide, and 112 ft. high; the transept is 180 ft. across, and the two beautiful spires are 332 ft. high. The building, which was designed by *James Renwick*, was erected in 1850-79, at a cost of $2,000,000 (400,000*l.*), but $500,000 more are needed for its completion.

The INTERIOR, which seems a little short in proportion to its height, is dignified and imposing, and the fact that all the windows are filled with good modern stained glass adds to the effect. The *Transepts* are shallow. The massive white marble columns supporting the roof are 35 ft. high. The altars and church-furniture are very elaborate. There are seats for 2500 persons, and standing-room for as many more. — Adjoining the cathedral are the two large *Roman Catholic Orphan Asylums.*

Between 50th and 51st Sts. (Pl. H, 3), to the left, are the homes of *Mrs. W. H. Vanderbilt* and her daughters, two brown-stone mansions, closely resembling each other and united by a connecting passage. They are adorned with exquisite bands and plaques of carving, which, however, is scarcely seen well enough to be properly appreciated. The railings which surround them are a fine specimen of metal-work. The Indiana-stone house above these, at the corner of 52nd St., in a more varied and striking style, is the *Residence of Mr. W. K. Vanderbilt*, by R. M. Hunt. It resembles a French château of the transitional period (15-16th cent.). The carving on the doorway and window above it almost challenge comparison with the finest work of the kind in European churches. At the N.W. corner of 57th St. is the house of *Mr. Cornelius Vanderbilt*, by George B. Post, a red brick edifice with grey facings, in the French château style of the 16-17th cent., with a huge new ball-room.

St. Thomas's Church (Epis.; Pl. H, 3), at 53rd St., contains fine interior decorations by La Farge and an altar-piece by St. Gaudens (good choir). To the left, between 54th and 55th Sts., facing the former, is *St. Luke's Hospital*, a tasteful structure with two low campanile towers. The *Fifth Avenue Presbyterian Church* (Pl. H, 3; Dr. Hall's; cor. 55th St.) is probably the largest in the world of this denomination, and has one of the loftiest spires in the city. Its pastor is said to 'preach to 50,000,000*l.* every Sunday'.

Fifty-Seventh St., both to the E. and W. of Fifth Avenue, contains several very striking façades, which the student of modern domestic architecture should not fail to see. Other interesting windows, porches, and gables, may be seen in 34th, 36th, 37th, and other streets near Fifth Avenue.

At 59th St. (Pl. I, 3), where Fifth Avenue reaches Central Park (p. 40), are three huge new hotels: the *Plaza* (p. 8; l.), the *Savoy* (p. 8; r.), and the *New Netherlands* (p. 8; r.).

In *59th Street*, facing Central Park, are the *De la Salle Institute*, the new building of the *Deutscher Verein* (German Club), and the fine row of the *Navarro Apartment Houses*, named after the chief towns of Spain.

Between 59th St. and 110th St. Fifth Avenue skirts the E. side of Central Park, having buildings on one side only. Among these,

3 *

many of which are very handsome, may be mentioned the new *Metropolitan Club* (in progress), at the corner of 60th St., the *Progress Club*, at the corner of 63rd St., the *Havemeyer House*, at the corner of 66th St., the *Synagogue*, at the corner of 76th St., and the *Brokaw House*, at the corner of 79th St.

Between 70th and 71st Sts. is the ***Lenox Library** (Pl. I, K, 3), built and endowed by *Mr. James Lenox* (1800-80), who also presented the ground on which it stands and most of its contents. The building, erected in 1870-77, is of light-coloured limestone, with projecting wings and a frontage of nearly 200 ft. Adm., see p. 21. Guide to the Paintings and Sculptures 15 c.

The Library proper, consisting of about 65,000 vols., occupies the S. part of the ground-floor. It is rich in early American works, musical works (bequeathed by Mr. J. W. Drexel), and books relating to Shakespeare and the Bible. It is a free reference-library.

The *North Hall* (to the left on the ground-floor) contains a fine collection of **Rare Books** and **MSS.**, most of them exhibited under glass. Among the chief treasures are the *Mazarin Bible* (Gutenberg & Fust, ca. 1455; prob. the first book printed with movable types); a folio *Latin Bible*, with notes in the handwriting of Melanchthon; *Coverdale's Bible* (1535); *Tyndale's New Testament* (1536); *Eliot's Indian Bible*; the first editions of *The Pilgrim's Progress*, *The Complete Angler*, *Paradise Lost*, *Comus*, and *Lycidas;* two copies of the *First Folio Shakespeare*, and also copies of the *Second*, *Third*, and *Fourth Folios*; the *Biblia Pauperum* (ca. 1430) and other block-books; the *Recuyell of the Histories of Troye* (Caxton, ca. 1475; the first book printed in English); the *Bay Psalm Book*, the first book printed in the United States (Cambridge, 1640); the *Doctrina Christiana*, printed in Mexico about 1544; a magnificent vellum MS. of the Gospels, with illuminations and miniatures by *Giulio Clovio;* and various books, MSS., and maps relating to the discovery of America. An alcove in this hall contains *Paintings on Porcelain*, *Mosaics*, *Enamels*, etc.

The **Picture Gallery** (catalogue 15 c.), on the first floor, comprises works by *Andrea del Sarto*, *F. E. Church*, *A. Bierstadt*, *Sir David Wilkie*, *John Constable*, *Sir Henry Raeburn*, *Munkacsy*, *Sir Joshua Reynolds*, *Verboeckhoven*, *Gilbert Stuart*, *Sir E. Landseer*, *Horace Vernet*, *Copley*, *Gainsborough*, *Turner*, *E. Zamacois*, etc.

The **Sculptures** include works by *Hiram Powers* (No. 3), *Gibson* (2), *Sir John Steel* (7, 10), and *Barrias* (19). In the vestibule are four ancient Roman busts.

The ***Stuart Collections**, bequeathed by *Mrs. Robert Stuart* (d. 1892), along with a sum of $ 300,000, occupy a gallery erected for them over the N. wing. They include a library of 10,000 vols. and 240 modern paintings, comprising works by *Gérôme*, *Corot*, *Rosa Bonheur*, *Troyon*, *Meissonier*, *Detaille*, *Bouguereau*, *Vibert*, *Jimenez*, *Alvarez*, *Diaz*, *Munkacsy*, *Brozik*, *Clays*, *Koekkoek*, *Verboeckhoven*, *Knaus*, *Meyer von Bremen*, *Cropsey*, *Brighton*, *Kensett*, *Church*, *Cole*, *Inness*, *J. A. Walker*, etc.

In Central Park, close to Fifth Avenue at 82nd St., is the *Metropolitan Museum of Art* (p. 42).

At 120th St. Fifth Avenue reaches MOUNT MORRIS SQUARE (Pl. O, 3), the mound in the centre of which commands good views. Beyond Mt. Morris Sq. the avenue is lined with handsome villas, surrounded by gardens. It ends at the Harlem River (144th St.; Pl. P, 3).

Fourth Avenue diverges from Third Avenue at the W. end of E. 5th St. and at first runs N. towards Union Sq. (p. 31), passing the *Cooper Union* (p. 31) and the *Bible House* (p. 31). At Union Sq. it turns N.E. At the corner of 18th St. is the *Florence Apart-*

ment House, at 19th St. is a *Panorama* (p. 16), at 20th St. (r.)
is *All Souls Unitarian Church*, and at 21st St. is *Calvary Church*.

The *National Academy of Design (Pl. F, 3), at the N.E. corner
of 23rd St. , a tasteful building of grey and white marble faced
with blue stone (entr. on 23rd St.; p. 16), is a partial reproduction of the Doge's Palace at Venice.

The National Academy of Design is one of the chief art institutions of the
United States, corresponding to some extent with the 'Academy' in Lon-
don, and like it consisting of Academicians (N.A.) and Associates (A.N.A.).
Exhibitions of works of art are held in spring and autumn (adm. 25c.),
that in the former season being the more important and fashionable. The
Schools of Art held here attract numerous pupils and do excellent service.
— Other excellent art-schools are those of the *Art Students' League*, in the
building of the American Fine Art Society (p. 17), attended by 1000 pupils.

Opposite, at the S.W. corner of 23rd St., is the substantial building of the **Young Men's Christian Association.**

The Young Men's Christian Association of the City of New York, organized in 1852 and incorporated in 1866, aims at the spiritual, mental,
social, and physical improvement of young men by the support and
maintenance of lectures, libraries, reading-rooms, social and religious
meetings, evening-classes, gymnasiums, and athletic grounds, and by providing attractive places of safe evening resort. In 1869 the large Twenty-
third Street Association Building was completed at a cost of nearly
$ 500,000. Since then five other buildings have been built or purchased
by the Association at a cost of $ 470,000, exclusive of the Railroad Men's
Building, erected by Mr. Cornelius Vanderbilt at a cost of about $ 125,000.
The work is carried on at fourteen different points. The aggregate attendance at the rooms is about 1,250,000 a year, and strangers are always
welcome as visitors. The average membership is over 7000; the annual
expenses are about $ 100,000, less than one-third of which is met by mem-
bership fees, the balance being provided by gifts from friends, rentals,
and other sources. — The aggregate membership of the Y. M. C. A. in the
United States and Canada is about 250,000.

At 27th St., to the left, extending back to Madison Avenue
(p. 39), is *Madison Square Garden* (see p. 16). At 34th St.
Fourth Avenue assumes the name of *Park Avenue, and the portion of it between this point and 42nd St. forms one of the handsomest streets of the city. The Fourth Avenue tramway line is here
relegated to a subway below the street, and the ventilating openings are surrounded with small gardens which give a cheerful and
pleasant air to the thoroughfare, here 140 ft. wide. On the W.
side of the avenue stand the Unitarian *Church of the Messiah* (34th
St.), and the Presbyterian *Church of the Covenant* (35th St.). At
40th St. is the *Murray Hill Hotel* (p. 8).

This part of Park Avenue traverses the aristocratic quarter of **Murray
Hill,** bounded by Third and Sixth Avenues, 32nd St., and 45th St. The
Murray Mansion, which gave name to the district, has disappeared.

At 42nd St. Park Avenue is interrupted by the **Grand Central
Depot** (Pl. G, 3; see p. 6), the main building of which occupies
the whole block between the line of Park Avenue, Vanderbilt
Avenue, 42nd St., and 45th St.

This enormous railway-station, constructed of red brick with white
facings, is nearly 700 ft. long and 240 ft. wide, and is covered with an
iron and glass roof, 110 ft. high, with a span of 200 ft. The above dimen-

sions are exclusive of an addition to the E. of the line of Park Avenue, recently added for incoming trains. About 250 trains (800 cars) arrive at and leave the station daily. It contains 19 tracks, 12 for outgoing and 7 for incoming trains. Comp. p. 6.

For the next ten blocks or so Park Avenue, or what would otherwise be Park Avenue, is occupied by the various lines of railway issuing from the Grand Central Depot, but at 51st St., where the *Women's Hospital* rises to the right, the avenue begins to re-assert itself, and higher up the railway burrows underneath through a series of tunnels. Above 67th St., where the street is very wide, Park Avenue may again claim to be one of the finest thoroughfares of New York, and here, as lower down, the openings of the tunnels are pleasantly hidden by small gardens. At the corner of 59th St., to the right, rises the large yellow building of the *Arion*, a German club. Among the numerous lofty piles of flats is the *Yosemite*, at the S.W. corner of 62nd St. Between 66th and 67th St., to the right, is the large and conspicuous **Armoury of the Seventh Regiment** (Pl. I, 3) the fashionable regiment of New York, enrolled in 1804 and proud of its long period of distinguished service in the field. The armoury is very finely fitted up, the huge drill-hall is 300 ft. long and 200 ft. wide. At the adjacent corner is the *Hahnemann Hospital*. The **Normal College** (Pl. I, 3), between 68th and 69th St., is a spacious building in an ecclesiastical Gothic style, with a lofty square tower (1600 pupils). To the left are the *Union Theological Seminary* and (70th St.) the *Lenox* or *Presbyterian Hospital*, an effective building, extending back to Madison Ave. (p. 39). At the corner of 77th St. is the *German Hospital*. The *Freundschaft Club, at the S.E. corner of 72nd St., has an interior fitted up in a style worthy of its fine exterior. Another great *Armoury* crowns the hill at 94th St. The avenue reaches the Harlem River at 136th St., near the bridge of the Hudson River Railway.

Lexington Avenue, beginning at Gramercy Park and running N. to Harlem Bridge (130th St.) between Third and Fourth Avenues, also contains a number of large and important buildings. Among these may be mentioned the *College of the City of New York* (Pl. F, 3), at the corner of 23rd St. (900 students; library of 25,000 vols.); the *Hospital for Cripples*, 42nd St.; the *Women's Hospital*, 49th St. (extending to Park Ave., comp. above); the *Synagogues* at the corners of 55th, 63rd, and 72nd Sts.; the so-called *Lexington Avenue Opera House* ('Terrace Garden'); the *Mt. Sinai Hospital*, 66th St., opposite the back of the Seventh Regiment Armoury (see above); and the *Institution for Deaf Mutes*, 67th St.

Between Fourth and Fifth Avenues, and parallel with them, runs *Madison Avenue, beginning at Madison Sq. (p. 32) and ending at 140th St. on the Harlem River. Hitherto uninvaded by shops, it forms one of the finest streets of private houses in New York, rivalling even Fifth Avenue in the splendour of its residences. At the beginning of the avenue, at the N.E. corner of the square and occupying a whole block, is **Madison Square Garden** (Pl. F, 3), a huge erection 425 ft. long and 200 ft. wide (see p. 16). The building includes the *Garden Theatre* (p. 15). The figure of Diana, on the tower, is by St. Gaudens. — Madison Avenue crosses 42nd St. just above the Grand Central Depot (p. 37) and beyond this point is traversed by tramway-cars. At the N.E. corner of 42nd St. is *Holy Trinity Church*, of which the chromatic effects of the stones and tiles form a characteristic feature; at 44th St. is the *Church of St. Bartholomew*, in the Italian style; and at 45th St. are the *Manhattan Athletic Club* (p. 17; with gymnasium, swimming baths, etc.) and the *Railroad Branch of the Y. M. C. A.* — At 49th St. we reach *****Columbia College** (Pl. H, 3), the oldest, largest, and most important educational institution in New York. It has about 200 professors and teachers and nearly 1700 students, and ranks with the foremost colleges of America. Among its alumni are Gouverneur Morris, John Jay, Alex. Hamilton, and De Witt Clinton.

Columbia College received its first charter in 1754 as *King's College*, and the first college-building was erected a few years later near the lower end of the island. In 1776 the college was suspended owing to its 'Tory' proclivities, but in 1784 it was re-incorporated under its present title. In 1867 the college was removed to its present site, where several spacious buildings have been erected. The college includes the six departments of Arts, Law, Political Science, Philosophy, Mines, and Medicine, the first five of which have their rooms at the college buildings in Madison Avenue. The medical school of Columbia is the *College of Physicians and Surgeons*, in 60th St., between 9th and 10th Avenues, which, thanks to the endowments of the Vanderbilt family ($ 1,000,000), is one of the best equipped schools of the kind in the world. *Columbia College Library* contains upwards of 100,000 volumes (entr. from 49th St.). The *School of Mines* contains a well-arranged Geological Museum (open to the public). The *Barnard College for Women*, 343 Madison Avenue, is in connection with Columbia College. — A new site for Columbia College has recently been bought farther up town (see p. 48) and the college is to be removed thither.

At the N.E. corner of 50th St., forming three sides of a hollow square, is the huge *Villard Mansion*, now occupied by several families. Opposite, at the back of St. Patrick's Cathedral (p. 35), is the *House of the Archbishop of New York* (R. C.). The extensive buildings at the next corners are *Roman Catholic Orphanages* (see p. 35). At 70th St., behind the Lenox Library (p. 36), the avenue expands into a small square, to the right of which is the *Lenox Hospital* (p. 38). At the N.W. corner of 72nd St. rises the *****Tiffany House** (Pl. K, 3), by *McKim, Mead, & White*, one of the most picturesque and striking residences in America.

The lowest story is of stone, the upper stories of light-coloured brick. The entrance, facing 72nd St., is under a large archway, guarded by a portcullis. Above this is a recessed balcony, and at the S.E. corner is a round turret, reaching to the eaves of the high-pitched roof. Towards Madison Avenue rises a large and lofty gable. The space under the roof forms a spacious studio, containing an interesting collection of objects of art, and is very tastefully fitted up (adm. only by private introduction). The adjoining low house is part of the original Tiffany mansion.

Beyond this point Madison Avenue consists of rows of handsome and substantial dwelling-houses.

The remaining avenues which traverse Manhattan Island from S. to N. do not demand a detailed description. **First, Second,** and **Third Avenues** consist mainly of tenement houses and small retail shops, while the amenity of the last two is not enhanced by the elevated railroads which follow their course. In its lower part Second Avenue, which is not joined by the railway till 23rd St. (see p. 11), is, however, still a very respectable residential quarter, with the homes of several old New York families. At E. 15th St. it crosses STUYVESANT SQUARE, with the large *Church of St. George* (polychrome interior). — At the corner of 11th St. is the building of the New York Historical Society (Pl. E, 4), founded in 1804 (adm., see p. 21). In the basement is the *Lenox Collection of Assyrian Marbles*, from Nineveh. On the first floor are the *Hall, Committee Rooms*, etc. The second floor contains the *Library* of 75,000 vols., mainly relating to the history of America. On the third floor is the *Abbott Collection of Egyptian Antiquities* (incl. three mummies of the Sacred Bull). The *Gallery of Art*, on the fourth floor, contains about 900 works, many of which are ascribed to masters of the first rank. On the staircase and in the vestibule are numerous *Portraits.*

[*St. Mark's Church*, in Stuyvesant Place, leading from E. 10th St. to Astor Place, stands near the site of the 'Bowerie' or farm-house of Governor Stuyvesant (comp. p. 29) and contains his tombstone (E. wall; from an older chapel) and other old monuments. *Governor Stuyvesant's Pear Tree*, which he planted in 1644 as a memorial 'by which his name might still be remembered'. stood for 200 years at the N.E. corner of Third Ave. and 13th St. (memorial tablet).]

At the foot of E. 28th St., a little to the E. of First Avenue, is the extensive **Bellevue Hospital** (Pl. F, 4); and in the same street, to the W. of Third Avenue, is *St. Stephen's* (R.C.), containing some good paintings and an elaborate altar-piece. The new *Power House of the Cable Tramway*, at the corner of Third Ave. and 65th St., is interesting. — **Sixth Avenue,** the route of a W. side elevated railway, begins at Carmine St., to the S.W. of Washington Square, and ends at Central Park (59th St.). It is one of the chief seats of retail trade in New York, containing several of the largest 'dry goods' and other shops. Its prolongation beyond the park is known as *Lenox Avenue.* Among the chief buildings it passes are the *Jefferson Market Police Court* at 10th St., the *Masonic Temple*, cor. of 23rd St. (p. 32), and the *Standard Theatre* (p. 15). At 41st St. the avenue skirts the pretty little *Bryant Park* (Pl. G, 3). — **Seventh** and **Eighth Avenues** may almost be called W. side editions of Second and Third Avenues minus the elevated railroad. Among the few conspicuous buildings are the *State Arsenal*, at the corner of Seventh Avenue and 35th St.; the new *Carnegie Music Hall* (Pl. H, I, 2), at the corner of Seventh Ave. and 57th St.; and the *Grand Opera House* (Pl. F, 2; p. 15), in Eighth Avenue, at the corner of 23rd St. The part of Eighth Ave. skirting the W. side of Central Park, and known as *Central Park West*, is a fashionable residence-quarter. At the corner of 72nd St. are the huge *Dakota Flats* (Pl. K, 2), conspicuous in many views of the city. Above Central Park Eighth Ave is traversed by the elevated railroad, which follows **Ninth Avenue** to 110th St. In Ninth Ave., near 20th St. (Chelsea Sq), is the extensive building of the *Protestant Episcopal Theological Seminary;* at 34th St. is the *New York Institution for the Blind;* and at 59th St. is the large *Roosevelt Hospital* (Pl, I, 2). Between 77th St. and 81st St. Ninth Avenue skirts *Manhattan Square*, a bay of Central Park, with the Natural History Museum (p. 41).

The great promenade and open-air resort of New York is ***Central Park** (Pl. I-N, 2, 3), occupying the centre of Manhattan Island, between 59th and 110th St., covering 840 acres of ground, and measuring $2^1/_2$ M. long by $1/_2$ M. wide. It was designed in 1858 by *Messrs. Olmsted* and *Vaux*, and cost about $15,000,000 (3,000,000*l.*). The ground was originally a tract of swamp and rock, and its transformation into one of the most beautiful parks in the world is an important monument of American skill and perseverance.

Central Park differs from most English parks in substituting a multiplicity of small picturesque scenes for broad expanses of turf and simple groves of great trees. There are 400 acres of groves, shrubberies, and glades, and 43 acres of ponds. The park is practically divided into two distinct portions by the *Croton Reservoirs*, 143 acres in extent. There are about 10 M. of fine 'Telford' drives, 6 M. of bridle-paths, and 30 M. of foot-paths. Four concealed transverse-roads (65th, 79th, 85th, and 97th Sts.), passing under or over the park drives and walks by arches of masonry, enable ordinary traffic to cross the park without annoyance to visitors. The park is enclosed by a low cut-stone wall and has 20 entrances. The fashionable time for driving and riding is in the afternoon from 4 to 7, and the 'Corso' here almost challenges comparison with that in Hyde Park. The S. side of the park may be reached by the Sixth Avenue Elevated Railroad, by the Fifth Avenue omnibuses, and by several lines of tramway; and points higher up may be reached by the tramway lines on Fourth and Eighth Avenues, while the elevated railroads on Third and Ninth Avenues pass within a block or two. Park Carriages stand at the 5th and 8th Ave. entrances to the park and take visitors to the N. end of the park and back for 25 c. each, with the privilege of alighting at any point and completing the round in another carriage. Other hackney-carriages charge 50c. each. Meals may be had at the *Casino* (near the Mall) and at *M'Gowan's Pass Tavern* (N. end), and light refreshments at the *Dairy*.

The chief promenade is the **Mall**, near the Fifth Avenue entrance, which is lined with fine elms and contains several statues and groups of sculpture, including Shakespeare, Scott, Beethoven, and the Indian Hunter. Near its N. end is the music-stand, where a band plays on Wed., Sat., and Sun. afternoons. The *Terrace*, at the N. end of the Mall, is a fine pile of masonry, whence flights of steps descend to the *Bethesda Fountain* and to the *Lake*, used for boating in summer (boat 30 c. per ¹/₂ hr., short row 10 c.) and skating in winter. The most extensive *View in the Park is afforded by the *Belvedere*, which occupies the highest point of the *Ramble*, to the N. of the lake. The *N. Park*, beyond the Croton Reservoir, has fewer artificial features than the S. Park, but its natural beauties are greater and the *Harlem Meer* (12 acres) is very picturesque. Near the S.E. corner of the park (nearest entrance in 64th St.) are the *Old State Arsenal* and a small *Zoological Garden*, the collection in which is apt to be largest in winter, when various menageries temporarily deposit their animals here. On the W. side of the park, in Manhattan Sq. (see p. 40), is the *American Museum of Natural History* (see below), and on the E. side, opposite 82nd St., is the *Metropolitan Museum of Art* (see p. 42). To the W. of the latter museum rises *Cleopatra's Needle, an Egyptian obelisk from Alexandria, presented by Khedive Ismail Pasha to the City of New York in 1877. Like the companion obelisk in London, this monolith was originally brought from Heliopolis (On), where it was erected and inscribed by Thothmes III. about 1500 B.C. One of the faces also bears inscriptions added by Ramses II. three centuries later (about the time of Moses). The obelisk is of red syenite, is 69 ft. high, and weighs 200 tons. The bronze crabs at the base are modern reproductions (comp. p. 44). Among the other monuments in the park are statues of Daniel Webster, Bolivar, Alex. Hamilton, and Samuel Morse, allegorical figures of Commerce and the Pilgrim, and several busts and animal groups.

In Manhattan Sq. (see p. 40), on the W. side of Central Park, between 77th and 81st streets, stands the *American Museum of Natural History** (Pl. K, 2), which was incorporated in 1869. Of the two adjoining blocks of which it at present consists, that to the N., in red brick with granite trimmings, was erected from the designs of *Olmsted* and *Vaux* in 1874-77. The S. block, which possesses a very handsome and solid-looking Romanesque façade of red granite, was designed by *J. C. Cady & Co.* and finished in 1891. Large and imposing as these structures are, they form only about one-ninth of the complete scheme of the museum-buildings, which are intended eventually to occupy the entire area (about 18 acres) between 8th and 9th Avenues and 77th and 81st Streets. The present entrance is on the S. side of the building, where visitors may either enter the main floor from the top of the arch or the ground-floor from the carriage-drive below and behind it (adm., see p. 21; restaurant on the ground-floor, S. wing). The Museum received its charter from the State of New York, but the ground and building belong to the City of New York, while the current expenses are defrayed by the Trustees, the City, and private subscriptions. The growth of the Museum has been very rapid, and its collections are now valued at $ 3,000,000 (600,000*l.*). It owes large benefactions to private individuals, particularly to *Mr. Morris K. Jesup*, President of the Board of Trustees. The interior is admirably arranged and lighted.

GROUND FLOOR. The lowest floor of the S. building, which we enter first, contains the *Lecture Room*, conveniently fitted up and accommodating about 1000 persons. Free lectures, illustrated by stereopticon views, are delivered here by Prof. Bickmore to the school-teachers of New York State, the state giving a grant in aid of this laudable effort to bring the work of the museum into organic connection with the national system of schools. The passages leading round the lecture-room to the ground-floor of the N. wing contain the *Jesup Collection of the Building Stones* of America. — The ground-floor of the N. wing is occupied by the **Jesup Collection of North American Woods*, the finest collection of the kind in existence, including, besides the specimens of wood, photographs of the growing trees, maps of their habitats, and beautiful paintings of their leaves, etc.

MAIN FLOOR. In the S. wing this is devoted to *Mammalia*, in the N. wing to *Birds* (12,000 mounted specimens), each collection being continued in the gallery above. Among the skeletons is one of 'Jumbo', a huge African elephant brought by Barnum from England to America in 1882 (12 ft. high). The stuffed groups of buffaloes and moose deserve attention, while the collections of *Monkeys* and *Insects* (gallery) are unusually complete. One of the skeletons here is that of the chimpanzee 'Mr. Crowley'. The floor is devoted to the *General Collection of Birds*, the gallery to the *Birds of North America*.

SECOND FLOOR. In the S. wing of this floor are the collections of *Shells, Gems* (Tiffany Collection, etc.) and *Minerals* (W. wing). In the N. wing are the *Geological and Palaeontological Collections*.

THIRD FLOOR. The S. wing contains the *Anthropological* and *Ethnographical Collections*, among which may be mentioned the Alaska series, the models of cliff-dwellings from Arizona and Colorado, and the large war-canoe from Queen Charlotte Island (suspended from the roof). These are adjoined on the W. by the *Library* (30,000 vols.). The N. wing is devoted to students' rooms.

The **Metropolitan Museum of Art,* on the E. side of Central Park, opposite the 81st St. entrance (nearest Elev. Ry. station at 84th St., Third Ave.), is a somewhat unpretending building of red brick with granite facings, measuring 235 ft. in length by 224 ft. in breadth, and erected in 1879. Like the Natural History Museum (see above) this is only an insignificant fraction of the buildings destined eventually to occupy this site; and a new block is

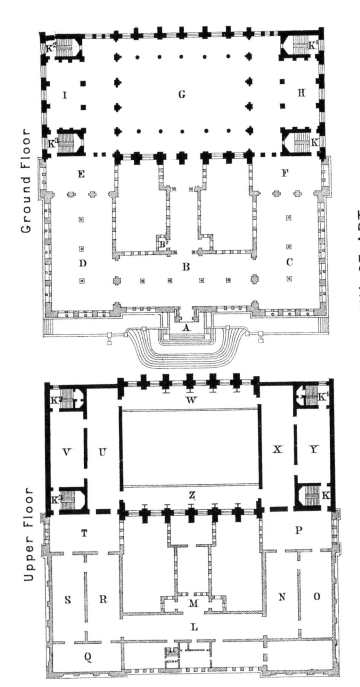

Ground Floor

Upper Floor

METROPOLITAN MUSEUM OF ART.

now in progress. The museum was incorporated in 1871 and has grown since then with marvellous rapidity. In 1879, when moved into the present building, the collections were valued at about $400,000; their present value is upwards of $7,000,000 (1,400,000*l.*). Among the chief features of the museum is the *Cesnola Collection of Cypriote Antiquities, the largest and most valuable collection of Phœnician and archaic Greek art in the world, illustrating the manner in which the arts of Egypt and Assyria were transmitted by the Phœnicians and adopted by the Greeks. These objects, which were found by Gen. Cesnola in 1865 et seq., while U.S. consul in the island of Cyprus, are now distributed throughout the various departments of the museum to which they individually belong. The historical collection of glass is unexcelled in its illustration of the art of glass-making from the earliest times to the present day, and that of Assyrian cylinders is second only to the series in the British Museum. Among the *Ancient Pictures* are good examples of Rembrandt, Van Dyck, Frans Hals, Velazquez, Rubens, Van der Meer, Jacob Ruysdael, and other masters. The *Modern Paintings* are extremely valuable, the French (Meissonier, Detaille, Rosa Bonheur, Corot, etc.), the German, the English, and the American schools being all represented by good examples. The *Musical Instruments* are also interesting. — The main entrance of the Museum is in the S. façade (adm., see **p. 21**). Director, *General L. P. di Cesnola.* General guide 10 c., special catalogues 10 c. each. Most of the objects are labelled.

The museum received its charter from the State of New York, but the building itself and [the ground on which it stands are loaned by the City of New York (comp. p. 42). The gifts of private donors, in money and in kind, have been of the most generous nature, and from two-thirds to three-fourths of the costs of maintenance are borne by members of the corporation. Lavatories for ladies and gentlemen are in the basement, on the W. side. The number of daily visitors to the Museum varies from 2000 to 8000.

Ground Floor. On entering by the principal door (Pl. A), we find ourselves in the HALL OF CASTS OF ANCIENT SCULPTURES (Pl. B), which includes reproductions of many of the most notable statues and friezes of Classical, Egyptian, and Assyrian art. In the pier at the end of the N. Extension of this hall (opposite the doorway) is a relief of the Assumption, by *Luca della Robbia* (1400-1480), an original from the mortuary chapel of the Princes of Piombino. The alcove to the left contains locks, keys, hinges, door-plates, and other Renaissance iron-work. — To the E. of Hall B (to the right on entering) is the HALL OF ANCIENT SCULPTURE AND EGYPTIAN ANTIQUITIES (Pl. C). The wall-cases to the W. contain statuettes, amulets, scarabæi, figurines, Græco-Egyptian tombstones, the sarcophagus of a child, and other Egyptian antiquities; in the floor-cases on the same side are mummies. In the centre are standards with swinging leaves, containing textile fabrics from the Fayûm (4th cent. B. C. to 11th cent. A.D.). Most of the other objects in this room belong to the *Cesnola Cypriote Collection*, including heads and other fragments of statues, statuettes (many with traces of colouring), alabaster vases (by the pier adjoining Hall B), inscribed lamps (N.E. piers), etc. All forms of ancient art, from Assyrian to Græco-Roman, are represented in the sculptures. On the N.W. pier are Assyrian tablets. — To the N. of Hall C is the ROOM OF ANCIENT TERRACOTTAS (Pl. F), chiefly containing objects of the

Cesnola Collection. In Case 1 (N. wall) are some interesting representations of Venus, from the earliest rude approximations to the human
form to works of the best Greek period. The floor-cases of Egyptian antiquities (p. 43) extend into this room. Four floor-cases contain Greek
funereal urns from Alexandria. In the N.E. corner is a staircase (Pl. K)
ascending to the upper floor (comp. p. 45).

The HALL OF ANCIENT STATUARY, INSCRIPTIONS, AND BRONZES (Pl. H),
to the N. of Hall F, also owes most of its contents to Gen. Cesnola's
discoveries. These include statues, funereal sculptures, bronzes, and inscriptions. At the N. end of the hall is a fine *Sarcophagus*, partly in
the Assyrian and partly in the Greek style, found at Amathus, a Phœnician city in Cyprus, and dating probably from the 6th cent. B.C. Adjacent, on the wall, are three slabs of Persian tiles. The sarcophagus from
Golgos (ca. B. C. 600) also illustrates the mingling of Assyrian and Greek
art. In the N.E. corner, near the Staircase (Pl. K 1), are the original
bronze *Crabs* placed under Cleopatra's Needle (see p. 41). At the S. end
of the room is a fine marble *Sarcophagus* from Rome (prob. 2nd cent.
A.D.). On the standards is the *Baker Collection* of textiles from the
Fayûm. — We next enter, to the W., the HALL OF ARCHITECTURAL CASTS
(Pl. G.), which is lighted from the roof and in general appearance recalls the Architectural Court at South Kensington Museum. Among the
chief objects reproduced here are the Pulpit of Siena Cathedral, by *Nic. Pi-
sano* (1288); the Parthenon; the Pantheon; the Monument of Lysicrates;
the Temple of Amen-Ra, at Karnak; the Portico of the Erechtheum; Notre
Dame; a bay of the cloisters of St. John in Laterano (12th cent.); the
Shrine of St. Sebaldus, Nuremberg, by *Peter Vischer* (1519); the façade of
the Guild-House of the Butchers, Hildesheim (1529). In the S.E. corner
is a quasi - reproduction of an angle of the Parthenon. On the E. wall
is a large painting of Justinian and his Councillors, by *Benjamin Constant.*
At the other end hangs Diana's Hunting Party, a huge picture by *Hans
Makart*, and figures of Victory, by *G. Richter*, and Peace, by *L. Knaus.*
On the N. gallery and part of the S. are casts of the frieze of the cella
of the Parthenon; and on the W. half of the S. gallery are representations
from the temple of Wingless Victory and the Mausoleum of Halicarnassus.
In the corners are four metopes from the Parthenon. — HALL I, in the
N.W. part of the building, corresponding to Hall H (see above), contains
the MODERN SCULPTURES, among which are examples of *Hiram Powers,
Gibson, W. W. Story, Rinehart, Millet, Albano, Bartlett, Schwanthaler,
Fischer, Thorvaldsen, Canova* (Napoleon), and *Barye* (cast). — Beyond
the staircase (K 3) we enter the ROOM OF CARVED WOOD AND MUSICAL
INSTRUMENTS (Pl. E), containing the fine collections of Musical Instruments (mainly antique) made by *Mr. J. W. Drexel* and *Mrs. Crosby
Brown*, and also numerous specimens of work in wood, carved and
inlaid. By the pier adjoining the Modern Sculpture Room is a chair
that belonged to *Rubens*, and among the other larger objects are a
Cabinet made of American woods, a carved *Clock* (English, 1640), and
a *Cabinet* inlaid with Oriental porcelain. — We finish our tour of the
ground - floor with the HALL OF GLASS AND ANCIENT POTTERY (Pl. D),
the contents of which are among the chief boasts of the Museum. By
the E. Wall are cases containing *Egyptian, Phoenician, Greek, and
Roman Glass* from the Cesnola Collection, dating from B.C. 800 down-
wards. It includes exquisite specimens of iridescent glass. The floor-
cases on the same side of the room contain the Marquand (Charvet) and
Jarves collections of *Ancient, Mediaeval, and Modern Glass.* The floor-cases
on the other side and the wall-cases to the W. and S. contain the Cesnola collection of *Phoenician, Greek, and Graeco-Roman Pottery.* Among the
finest specimens is the 'Great Vase of Curium' in floor-case 7. Above
the wall-cases hang several interesting *Rhodian Amphorae.* The Cesnola
collections in this room illustrate the history of the ceramic art from B.C.
1500 to the 4th or 5th cent. of our era. Idalium was probably destroyed
in the 9th, and Curium in the 6th cent. B.C. The standards in the middle
of this hall contain fine collections of *Lace, presented by Mrs. Astor (European) and Mrs. Stuart (Oriental), and bought from Mrs. McCallum.

STAIRCASES ascend to the Upper Floor from both ends of Halls H and I. On the walls of Stairway K (S.E.) are a fine painting-like mosaic of Pæstum by *Rinaldi*, a St. Christopher by *Pollajuolo* (fresco), the Seasons by *J. J. Horemans*, a Cherub by *Correggio*, an Apostle by *Dürer*, and other old paintings. Stairway K 1 (N.E.) has a hunting-scene by *Rubens* and other works. On Stairway K 2 (N.W.) are landscapes by *R. B. Browning, Kensett*, etc. Stairway K 3 (S.W.) is hung with the Muses by *Fagnani* (portraits of New York ladies), a good specimen of *Boucher*, a drawing by *Mutter* ('In Memoriam'), etc.

Upper Floor. We begin our tour of this floor with Room P, reached by Staircase K (S.E.).

ROOM P. *American Antiquities*, including ancient and modern idols and fetishes of New Mexico and relics of the Mound Builders, Mexicans, Peruvians, etc. — This room communicates with both Rooms N and O. We enter the former (door to the right or W.).

ROOM N. contains the **Moore Collection*, presented to the Museum in 1891 and including Chinese porcelain, Japanese textiles, bronze-work, and basket-work, European, Egyptian, Greek, and Roman glass, Oriental ornaments, and Arab c metal-work. — The S.E. door leads into —

ROOM O, containing a **Collection of Old Masters and Pictures of the English School*, presented to the Museum by Mr. Henry G. Marquand (valued at $500,000; catalogue 10 c.). To the left: 1. *Jan van Eyck* (?1390-1440), Virgin and Child; 2. *Gaspar Netscher* (1639-84), Card-party; 3. *Velazquez* (1599-1660), Olivarez; 4. *Old Crome* (1769-1821), Landscape; 6. *Teniers the Younger* (1610-94), Landscape; *10. *Frans Hals* (1584-1666), Portrait; *11. *Cuyp* (1606-72), Landscape with cattle; 12. *Juriaan Ovens* (1620-78), Portrait (dated 1650); *14. *Hals*, His wife; 16. *Metsu* (1615-58), Music-lesson; 17. *Velazquez*, Don Carlos, eldest son of Philip IV.; *18. *Velazquez*, Portrait of himself; 21. *J. van Eyck*, Deposition from the Cross; *22. *J. van der Meer* (1632-96), Young woman at a casement; 24. *Gainsborough* (1727-88), Landscape; 26. *Hogarth* (1697-1764), Miss Rich; *Hals*, *27. The smoker, 28. Two gentlemen; 29. *Moroni* (1510-78), Portrait; 30. *Holbein* (1496-1554), Abp. Cranmer; *31. *Van Dyck* (1599-1641), Lady with a ruff; *33. *Rembrandt* (1607-69), Portrait, of his latest period (1665); *32. *Leon. da Vinci* (1453-1519), Girl with cherries; *34. *Rubens* (1577-1640), Susannah and the Elders (Susannah a portrait of his second wife, Helena Fourment; painted after 1630); 36. *Ruysdael* (1625-81), Landscape; *Rembrandt*, 36. The Mills, *37. Man in broad-brim hat and wide collar (ca. 1640), *38. Adoration of the Shepherds; 39. *Gainsborough*, Girl with a cat; 40. *Turner* (1775-1851), Saltash; 41. *Reynolds*, Portrait; *Rubens*, 42. Portrait, 43. Pyramus and Thisbe; *46. *Van Dyck*, Duke of Richmond and Lennox; *47. *Constable* (1770-1837), Valley Farm; 48. *Velazquez*, Mariana, second wife of Philip IV.; 49. *Masaccio* (1402-29), Man and woman; 50. *Lucas van Leyden* (1494-1533), Christ before Pilate (distemper). — We now return through Room N to —

ROOM L (Gallery of Drawings, Etchings, and Photographs). The drawings include specimens by *Raphael, Michael Angelo, Leon. da Vinci, Correggio, Veronese, Tintoretto, Andrea del Sarto, Domenichino, Carracci, Guido Reni, Murillo, Velazquez, Dürer, Van Dyck, Rembrandt, Rubens, Teniers, Watteau, Greuze*, and *Claude Lorrain*. Among the etchings are works by *Seymour Haden, Turner, Whistler*, etc. On the S. wall is a large fresco by *Chavannes*, representing figures emblematical of the Sorbonne, with Science, Poetry, History, etc. At present, however, the walls of this room are covered by large *Tapestries*, partly on loan and partly belonging to the Museum. The other objects in this room include Capo di Monte ware, malachite and enamel vases, reproductions of Tanagra statuettes, illuminated MSS., etc. The alcove on the N. side (Pl. M) contains water-colours by *Wm. T. Richards* and others. To the left (W.) is a case of volumes containing photographs, with an ingenious arrangement for turning the leaves without exposing them to soiling. — We now pass through Room R into —

ROOM Q (Gallery of Gems, Miniatures, and Gold and Silver Ornaments). The wall-cases to the S. contain the **Cesnola Collection of Cypriote Ornaments* (mainly from Curium), containing beautiful specimens of gold jewellery, fibulæ, rings, votive ornaments, etc. Some are of gold plated

with silver. The sard with Boreas and Orithyia is a very fine example
of Greek art emerging from the archaic stage, and the chalcedony with
the Rape of Proserpine 'may safely be placed at the head of all that is
known in the archaic style'. To the W. is the *Johnston-King Collection
of Engraved Gems;* also *Watches* and *Snuff-boxes.* To the E. is the *Moses
Lazarus Collection of Miniatures and Snuff-boxes.* To the N. are *Coins,
Assyrian Cylinders, American Silver and Gold Ornaments,* etc. In the N.E.
corner-case are the *Bryant Vase*, by Tiffany, presented to the poet on
his 80th birthday, a *Gold Medal* struck by the King of Italy in honour of
Gen. Cesnola (1882), etc. The S.E. case has *Silver Objects* from the Cesnola
Collection; the N.W. case, *Silver Repoussé Work* from the Demidoff Collec-
tion; the S.W. case, two Sèvres Vases. The centre-cases contain *Fans.*
The *Tapestry* dates from 1778. — We next enter —

Room S (Catharine Lorillard Wolfe Collection). The collection of
modern paintings bequeathed to the Museum by *Miss C. L. Wolfe* (1823-87),
along with an endowment of $200,000, contains several fine French and
German paintings and also some English and American works (special
catalogue of modern pictures 10c.). To the right of the door by which
we enter hangs No. 1, a portrait of Miss Wolfe by *Cabanel.* To the left
(other side of door): 2. *Daniel Huntington*, John David Wolfe, father of
Miss C. L. Wolfe; 3. *Rosa Bonheur*, Hound; 10. *Dupré*, Hay-wagon; 11.
Decamps, Night patrol at Smyrna; 12. *Knaus*, Old woman and cats; *13.
Van Marcke*, Cattle; 15. *Bonnat*, Fellah woman and child; 18. *Munkacsy*,
Pawnbroker's shop; 19. *Vibert*, A reprimand; 20. *Bargue*, Bashi Bazouk;
21. *Berne-Bellecour*, The Intended; *22. *Troyon*, Dutch cattle; 25. *Merle*,
Falling leaves; 27. *Rosa Bonheur*, Weaning the calves; 28. *W. von Kaul-
bach*, Crusaders before Jerusalem (a large allegorical work); 30. *Le Fèbvre*,
Girl of Capri; 36. *Piloty*, The Wise and Foolish Virgins; 37. *Lambert*, Cat
and kittens; 38. *Desgoffe*, Still-life (original objects in the Louvre and
selected by Miss Wolfe for the artist); 44. *Schreyer*, Arabs on the march;
45. *Le Roux*, Roman ladies at the tomb of their ancestors; *48. *Gérôme*,
Prayer in a Cairene mosque; 49. *Hans Makart*, Dream after the ball; 50.
Wappers, Confidences; *52. *Cot*, The storm; 53. *Bonnat*, Roman girl; 56.
Pasini, Entrance to a mosque; 57. *Rousseau*, River-scene; *59. *Corot*, Ville
d'Avray; 60. *Troyon*, Cow; 65. *Meissonier*, Sign-painter; 69. *Boldini*, Gossip.

Room R (Wolfe Collection continued). — *70. *Meissonier*, Adrian and
Willem Van de Velde; 71. *Gérôme*, Arab boy; 72. *Kaulbach*, Girl's head;
75. *Jules Breton*, Peasant girl knitting: *76. *Couture*, Idle student; 77. *A.
Achenbach*, Sunset; *81. *Jules Breton*, Religious procession in Brittany;
82. *Marchal*, Evening in Alsace; 83. *Defregger*, German peasant girl; 86.
Bouguereau, Brother and sister; 90. *Louis Haghe*, A toast in the guard-
room; 91. *Meissonier*, General and adjutant; 92. *Narcisse Diaz*, Holy
Family; 100. *Detaille*, Skirmish between Cossacks and the Old Guard; 101.
Horace Vernet, Study for a picture of the Corso; 107. *Vibert*, The startled
confessor; 103. *Henner*, Bather; *112. *Gabriel Max*, The last token; 113.
Isabey, Banquet-hall; 115. *Schenck*, Lost (a scene in Auvergne); 117. *Cabanel*,
The Shulamite Woman (Song of Solomon, 8); *121. *Ludwig Knaus*, Holy
Family; 122. *Roybert*, Game of cards; 127. *Leloir*, Opportunity makes the
thief; 128. *Falero*, Twin stars; 129. *Doré*, Retreat from Moscow; 137. *Detaille*,
Cuirassier; 142. *Bida*, Massacre of the Mamelukes in 1811.

Room T contains *Memorials of George Washington, Benjamin Franklin,*
and *Lafayette,* including portraits (among others two by Chinese artists
and the earliest known portrait of Washington, a miniature), busts, medallions, etc.

We now pass across the landing of Staircase K 3 and enter Room V,
which, with Room U, contains *Modern Paintings,* including some French
masterpieces, several German, English, and Dutch paintings, and many
American works.

Room V. To the left: 22. *Kensett*, Lake George; 29. *Bonnat*, John T.
Johnston, first President of the Metropolitan Museum of Art; 30. *J. F.
Cropsey*, Landscape; 32. *Lerolle*, Organ rehearsal; 33. *Josef Israels*, Expec-
iation; 36. *Kensett*, Landscape; 37. *C. G. Helquist*, The 'Opprobrious Entry'
into Stockholm of Bishops Peder Sonnavater and Master Knut, who had

unsuccessfully rebelled against Charles I.; 40. *Pecht*, Richard Wagner; *41. *Francois Auguste Bonheur* (brother of Rosa; b. 1824), Woodland and cattle, with fine sunlight effect; 44. *Hoffer*, Copy of Couture's 'Decadence of Rome'; 47. *Clays*, Celebration of the freedom of the port of Antwerp (1863); 48. *Julien Dupré*, The balloon; 49-51. *Kensett*, Landscapes; 52. *Israels*, The bashful suitor; 58. *Bolton Jones*, Spring; 59. *George Fuller*, Nydia ('Last Days of Pompeii'); 60. *Glisenti*, The hunter's story; 61. *C. Piloty*, Thusnelda at the triumphal entry of Germanicus into Rome, a huge canvas (replica of the picture at Munich); 65. *J. W. Alexander*, Walt Whitman.

ROOM U. To the left (entering from S. door of V): 66. *Carl Marr*, Gossip; 67. *Julius Schrader*, Alex. von Humboldt, with Chimborazo in the background. — *71. *Meissonier*, Friedland, 1807 (one of the few large canvases of this painter, intended, in the master's own words, to represent 'Napoleon at the zenith of his glory, and the love and adoration of the soldiers for the great Captain for whom they were ready to die'). It was bought by Mr. Henry Hilton for $66,000 (13,200 *l.*) and presented by him to the Museum. — 72. *C. H. Davis*, Evening; *75. *Fortuny*, Spanish lady; 76. *Dannat*, A quartette.

*78. *Rosa Bonheur*, Horse Fair, the artist's masterpiece, familiar from Thomas Landseer's engraving. A quarter-size replica is in the London National Gallery, and there are other still smaller reproductions. This, the original picture, was purchased by Mr. Cornelius Vanderbilt, on the dispersal of the Stewart collection, for $53,000 (10,600 *l.*), and given by him to the Museum. — 84. *Gustave Brion*, Raft on the Rhine; 86. *Clairin*, Moorish Sentinel; 88. *Maignan*, 'L'attentat d'Anagni', an incident in the life of Pope Boniface VIII.; 92. *George Inness*, Evening; *93. *E. Detaille*, Defence of Champigny, a masterpiece, presented by Mr. Hilton; 96. *Mauve*, Spring; 99. *Meyer von Bremen*, Evening prayer (a small watercolour); 100. *Koller*, Hugo van der Goes painting the portrait of Mary of Burgundy; 101. *Robt. Wylie*, Death of a Vendean chief; 104. *C. F. Ulrich*, Glass-blowers of Murano; 105. *Baixeras*, Barcelona boatmen; 107-109, 114, 121. *Kensett*, Landscapes; 111. *Inness*, Autumn oaks; 118. *Bargue*, Footman asleep; 119. *Picknell*, Bleak December; 120. *J. Alden Weir*, Idle hours; 125. *Elihu Vedder*, Sentinel; 128. *L'Hermitte*, Vintage.

GALLERY W, which we enter from the N. door in Room U, contains *Chinese, Japanese, and other Oriental Porcelain* and a collection of *Japanese Swords*. This gallery overlooks the Architectural Court (p. 44). The parallel GALLERY Z (entered from the S.E. door of Room U) contains the *Collection of Oriental Art*, comprising good specimens of almost all styles and materials of Japanese art.

ROOM X, entered from gallery W or gallery Z, contains the *Loan Collection of Paintings*, which changes from time to time. The numbering begins to the S. of the N.E. door. Among the works now on exhibition here are the following: 1. *Boughton*, Luccombe Chine, Isle of Wight; 2. *Carl Marr*, The mystery of life; 9. *Bastien Le Page*, Joan of Arc (presented by Mr. Erwin Davis); 17. *Becker*, Emp. Maximilian receiving the Venetian embassy; 20. *Merle*, Spinner; 22. *Corot*, Pond; 26. *Meissonier*, Man reading; 33. *Dupré*, Landscape; 39. *Vaislav Brozik* (b. 1852), Columbus at the Court of Ferdinand and Isabella (a huge work, presented by Mr. M. K. Jesup); 40. *Bierstadt* (b. 1829), Donner Lake, California (p. 397); 45. *Gilbert Stuart*, John Jay; 50. *Delort*, Dutch fleet in the Texel captured by French hussars (1794); *53. *Alma Tadema*, Reading Homer; *56. *Gilbert Stuart*, George Washington; 58. *Trumbull*, Alex. Hamilton; 59. *Henner*, Magdalen at the Sepulchre; 60. *C. Y. Turner*, Bridal procession.

ROOM Y. Old Masters. The numbering begins at the door leading from Staircase K. To the left: 2. *Rachel Ruysch* (1664-1750), Flowers and fruit; 4. *Greuze*, Study for a head; 5. *Karel de Moor* (1656-1738), Burgomaster of Leyden and his wife; 7. *Teniers the Younger*, Marriage festival; 5. *Jan and Andries Both* (1610-50), Italian scene; 11. *B. van der Helst* (1613-70), Dutch burgomaster; 12. *Jan Steen* (1626-79), Dutch Kermesse; 13. *A. de Vries* (17th cent.), Portrait; 14. *Aart de Gelder* (1645-1727), Dutch admiral; *15. *Sir Peter Lely* (1618-80), Portrait; 21. *S. Ruysdael* (1605-70), Sea-piece; 20. *Lucas Cranach the Younger* (d. 1536), Portrait; *30. *Sir Joshua Reynolds*

(1723-92), Hon. Henry Fane and his guardians Inigo Jones and Charles Blair (a large group recalling the so-called 'Three Graces' in the London National Gallery); 38. *Gaspar Netscher*, Dutch lady; 46. *M. van Heemskerk* (1498-1574), His father; *49. *Rubens*, Return of the Holy Family from Egypt; *50. *Frans Hals*, Hille Bobbe of Haarlem, the Sailor's Venus; *58. *J. de Heem* (1603-50), Still-life; 59. *Cranach the Elder* (1472 1533), Elector Frederick of Saxony; °70. *Van Dyck*, St. Martha interceding for the cessation of the plague at Tarascon; 71. *Pannini* (1695 1768), Interior of St. Peter's; 72. *Jacob Jordaens* (1593-1678), The philosophers; 74. *Isaac van Ostade* (1601-58), Fiddler; °77. *Jordaens*, Visit of the young St. John the Baptist to the Holy Child; 79. *Fyt* (1609-61), Game; 80. *Hobbema* (1637-1709), Dutch scene; 81. *Jan Wouverman* (1629-66), The halt; 82. *A. van der Neer* (1619-83), Sunset; 86. *Carlo Maratta* (1625-1713), Clement IX; 90. *Teniers the Elder*, Dutch kitchen; 94. *Snyders* (1579-1651), Fruit.

The Basement Rooms, which are not open to the public, contain a large number of objects for which at present there is no room in the galleries.

A small and narrow new park, beginning in 110th St., near the N.W. corner of Central Park and extending thence to 123rd St., is now in course of formation. It is named *Morningside Park* (Pl. N, O, 2) and is overlooked by the Sixth Ave. El. Ry.

The stately *Riverside Drive or Park* (Pl. L-O, 1), skirting the hills fronting on the Hudson from 71st St. to 127th St. (ca. 3 M.), is one of the most striking roads that any city can boast of and affords beautiful views of the river. Handsome houses are springing up along it, and it bids fair to become the most attractive residential quarter of New York. At 88th St. is a copy of *Houdon's Statue of Washington* (p. 327). Near the N. end of the drive, on Claremont Heights (W. 122nd St.), is the *Tomb of General Ulysses S. Grant* (Pl. O, 1; 1822-85), where a magnificent monument, costing $500,000 (100,000*l.*), is now in course of erection. Adjacent is the *Claremont Tavern.*

The S. end of Riverside Drive may be reached by the tramway-cars on the Boulevard (p. 13) or by the Sixth Ave. 'El' to 72nd St. (1/2 M.); the N. end and Grant's Tomb by the cable-cars on 125th St. (p. 13).

To the E. of Riverside Park, in large grounds bounded by Amsterdam (10th) Ave., the Boulevard, 116th St., and 120th St., are the extensive buildings of the *Bloomingdale Insane Asylum* (Pl. N, O, 1, 2), to be replaced by the new buildings of Columbia College (p. 39). A little to the S.W. of this (111th St., between Tenth Ave. and Morningside Park) is the large *Leake & Watts Orphanage*, the site of which has been secured for the new Episcopal Cathedral of St. John the Divine, the corner-stone of which was laid on Dec. 27th, 1892. To the N. of Riverside Park lies the district of *Manhattanville*, containing many old residences and the *Convent of the Sacred Heart* (Pl. P, 2), with its fine grounds. The *Sheltering Arms*, at the corner of Amsterdam Ave. and 129th St., is a refuge for destitute children. In 143rd St., between Amsterdam Ave. and West End Ave., is the *Coloured Orphan Asylum*. Between 153rd and 155th St., adjoining the river, is *Trinity Church Cemetery* (Pl. Q, 1, 2), in two sections united by bridges over the Boulevard. This was the scene of the hardest fighting in the battle of Harlem Heights (Sept. 16th, 1776).

The picturesque district of ***Washington Heights,** extending
from about this point to Spuyten Duyvil Creek and from the
Hudson to the Harlem, repays a visit and affords fine views of the
Hudson and the Palisades (p. 147).

This district, which is now a favourite residence quarter, was the ground
of desperate conflicts during the Revolutionary period. A few remains still
exist, between 182nd and 186th St., of *Fort Washington* (on the highest point
of the island, 260 ft. above the river), which was heroically but unsuccessfully
defended against the British in Nov., 1776, after the battle of Harlem Heights.
Before and during the latter battle, Washington had his headquarters at
old *Jumel House* (161st St., overlooking the Harlem), then the home of
Col. Roger Morris and his wife (Washington's old love, Mary Phillipse).
The house was afterwards bought by Mme. Jumel, with whom Aaron
Burr lived here 'during the days of his octogenarian love'. The *Grange*,
the home of *Alex. Hamilton*, lies at the corner of Tenth Ave. and 141st St.
Near the house are 13 trees planted by Hamilton to symbolise the 13 Original States. The house originally occupied by *Audubon*, the naturalist,
is on the river, at the foot of 155th St.

At the corner of Eleventh Ave. and 162nd St. is the *Institution for the
Deaf and Dumb*, at 176th St. is the *Juvenile Asylum*, and at Amsterdam
(Tenth) Ave. and 191st St. is the *Isabella Home*, a handsome Renaissance
building for the aged. The rocky bluff on which the latter stands is
known as *Fort George*, from a redoubt built here during the Revolution.
Extensive improvements are taking place here in all directions, and a
fine new drive has been formed along the river.

Of the bridges crossing the Harlem River two only call for special
remark: High Bridge and Washington Bridge. ***High Bridge,** at
175th St., constructed to carry the Croton Aqueduct (see below)
across the Harlem, is 1460 feet long and consists of 13 arches,
the highest of which is 116 ft. The water is carried across in iron
pipes protected by brick-work, and above is the bridgeway, for
walkers only (*View). There are restaurants at both ends of the
bridge (Park Hotel, at the W. end). A good view is also obtained
from the embankment of the Reservoir, at the end of the bridge,
or the adjoining Water Tower. A little farther up, at 181st St., is the
new ***Washington Bridge,** constructed in 1886-90 at a cost of nearly
$ 2,700,000 (540,000*l.*). It is of steel, except the stone abutments
and small parts of iron, and has a total length of 2400 ft., with two
central arches, each of 510 ft. span. The roadway, which is asphalted,
is 150 ft., the lower centre of the arches 135 ft. above the river.

A convenient way to visit these two bridges is to take the Sixth Ave.
El. Ry. to 155th St. and go thence by the Northern Railway (without
descending to the street; fare 5c.) to the foot of High Bridge. We then
cross the bridge and walk along the W. bank of the Harlem to Washington
Bridge, whence we return by cable-car to 125th St. (El. Ry. on Eighth Ave.).

The new *McCombs' Dam Bridge* and the *Viaduct* connecting it with the
top of Washington Heights (155th St.) are other important engineering
works now in progress.

The **Water Supply** of New York is obtained from the watershed
of the *Croton*, a stream in Westchester Co., about 40 M. from New York.
The *Old Croton Aqueduct*, which crosses the High Bridge (see above), was
constructed in 1842 and has a capacity of about 100 million gallons a day.
The **New Croton Aqueduct*, a wonderful piece of engineering, constructed
in 1883-90, at a cost of about $25,000,000 (5,000,000*l.*), is in the form of
a tunnel, 14 ft. high, at an average depth of 150 ft. below the surface.
It is carried under the Harlem River at a depth of 300 ft. below the

river-bed. When the new storage reservoirs in the Croton district are finished, it will have a daily capacity of about 300 million gallons. Both aqueducts discharge their waters at Central Park, where the large reservoir (see p. 41) has a capacity of 1,000,000,000 gallons. The iron mains distributing the water through the city have an aggregate length of 660 M. The new dam of the Croton Water Works, at *Quaker Bridge*, is the largest in the world, being 1350 ft. long, 277 ft. high, and 216 ft. wide at the base.

An act was passed in 1876 for the improvement of the navigation of the Harlem River (which is simply a tidal channel) by the construction of a *Ship Canal*, but there is some chance of this work being relinquished in favour of a scheme for filling in the Harlem River.

The so-called **Annexed District** (see p. 23), to the N. and E. of the Harlem, calls for little notice. It includes *Morrisania* (perpetuating the name of Gouverneur Morris), *West Farms*, *Fordham*, *Mott Haven*, *Williamsbridge* (a favourite Sun. resort of French residents), and several other villages now incorporated with the city. Large new park-spaces have been reserved here, but are not yet fully laid out. Among these are *Van Cortlandt Park* (1070 acres), *Bronx Park* (655 acres), *Crotona Park* (135 acres), and *Pelham Bay Park* (1740 acres), adjoining Long Island Sound, 4 M. to the E. of Bronx Park and 15 M. from the City Hall. *Central Avenue*, beginning at M'Comb's Dam Bridge, is a favourite drive (comp. p. 17). The Annexed District is traversed by several lines of horse-cars, the Suburban Elevated Railway (to 172nd St.; p. 11), and by the Harlem, Hudson River, New Haven and Hartford, and Northern New York railways (p. 6).

The **Islands** in the East River contain various charitable and correctional institutions belonging to the city, permission to visit which may be obtained from the Commissioners of Public Charities, 66 Third Ave. (ferry from E. 26th St.). *Blackwell's Island*, 120 acres in extent, is a long narrow island, extending from about 50th St. to 86th St., and containing the Penitentiary, Female Lunatic Asylum, Workhouse, Alms Houses, and Charity Hospital. To be 'sent to the Island' is the New York euphemism for committal to the Penitentiary. *Ward's Island* (200 acres), opposite 110th St., has the Male Lunatic Asylum, Inebriate Asylum, and State Emigrant Hospital. Ward's Island is separated from Astoria and Blackwell's Island by *Hell Gate*, a sharp bend in the river, through which the water rushes at a great rate. The sunken reefs which formerly made it highly dangerous to navigation were removed by nitro-glycerine explosions in 1876 and 1885. On *Randall's Island*, to the N. of Ward's and opposite the Harlem River, are the Idiot Asylum, the House of Refuge, and the Nursery, Children's, and Infants' Hospitals. — The *Islands in the Harbour* have been described at p. 2.

Environs of New York.

(1). STATEN ISLAND (ferry from Whitehall St. to St. George in ½ hr.; fare to St. George or any other station between Erastina and Arrochar 10c.). — **Staten Island**, on the S. side of New York Harbour, separated from New Jersey by the *Staten Island Sound* and the *Kill van Kull* and from Long Island by the *Narrows* (p. 2), has an area of about 60 sq. M. and (1890) 51,693 inhabitants. The surface of the island is diversified and hilly, and it is dotted with small villages and the villas of New Yorkers. The hills afford good views of New York Harbour and the ocean. Among the best of its fine drives is the *Richmond Terrace*, skirting the N. shore. From *St. George* railways (Staten Island Rapid Transit) run to the W. along the N. shore, to the S.E. to *Fort Wadsworth* and *Arrochar*, and to the S. to *Tottenville*, diverging from the Arrochar line at Clifton. The first-mentioned line passes (1 M.) *New Brighton* (Castleton Hotel; Pavilion, $4, etc.), the largest village in the island, with numerous villas and hotels; 1¾ M. *Sailors' Snug Harbour*, with a large Seamen's Asylum (income $100,000), on the lawn of which is a fine statue of its founder R. R. Randall, by St. Gaudens; 2½ M. *Livingston*, with the Staten Island Cricket Club, the Staten Island Athletic Club, etc.; 4 M. *Port Richmond*, with the house (now St. James Hotel), in which Aaron Burr died in 1836;

5½ M. *Erastina*, with the pleasure-resort called the Erastina Grove. Beyond Erastina the railway crosses the Sound to New Jersey. — At (1 M.) *Tompkinsville* (Bay View Hotel), on the Arrochar line, are the head-quarters of the Seawanhaka Yacht Club (p. 17) and the New York Canoe Club (p. 17); 1¾ M *Stapleton*, the birthplace of Commodore Cornelius Vanderbilt (1794-1877), who took the first step towards amassing his huge fortune by starting a ferry to New York; 2½ M. *Clifton*, with a house once occupied by Garibaldi; 3½ M. *Fort Wadsworth* (p. 2); 4½ M. *Arrochar* or *South Beach*, a popular day-resort for New Yorkers (boating, bathing, etc.). — The longest line is that runnig S. to Tottenville. Beyond Clifton (see above) it passes (6 M.) *Grant City*, with the mausolea of the Vanderbilt family; 9½ M. *Giffords*, a fishing-resort; 11 M. *Woods of Arden*, with picnic grounds; 13 M. *Prince's Bay*, another fishing-place; 16 M. *Tottenville* (Union House), with the old Billop House (ca. 1670), where Gen. Howe met Franklin and John Adams after the battle of Long Island (p. 32). Tottenville is connected by ferry with *Perth Amboy* (p. 222). Many points in the interior of the islands are still very quiet and primitive, and the pedestrian will find numerous pleasant walks. For farther details, see *Kobbe's* 'Staten Island'.

(2). NEW JERSEY SHORE. The cities on the right bank of the Hudson or N. River, immediately opposite New York, though practically forming part of that city, are in a different state (New Jersey) and under independent government. They offer little of special interest for the tourist. Ferries, see p. 4. **Jersey City** *(Taylor's Hotel)*, the southernmost and largest, with a population of (1890) 163,000, contains many glass-works, sugar-refineries, machine-shops, foundries, and other industrial establishments, the stations of about half the railways centring at New York (comp. p. 6), and the docks of a few of the Transatlantic steamship companies. With the exception of a few churches and a new city hall (in progress), it has almost no handsome buildings. — To the N. of Jersey City lies **Hoboken**, with large silk-factories and (1890) 43,648 inhab., a large proportion of whom are Germans. It also contains the wharves of some European steamships. *Stevens Park*, on the river, contains the *Stevens Institute*, a polytechnic school of good reputation. *Castle Stevens*, the house of its founder, the late Commodore Stevens, is on the hill above. Farther to the N. are the *Elysian Fields*, an open common, affording good views of the river, but now much neglected. — Beyond the Elysian Fields lies *Weehawken*, with about 2000 inhabitants. It was the scene of the duel between Alex. Hamilton and Aaron Burr — *Guttenberg* (1917 inhab.), on the hill behind Weehawken, has a winter race-course and a large brewery, with a beer-garden on the roof. — Behind Hoboken lies *Hudson City*, with the Schützen Park, a favourite resort of the Germans of New York. — *Fort Lee*, on the site of the revolutionary fort of that name, at the point where the higher part of the *Palisades* (p. 147) begins, nearly opposite 170th St., is now the property of an Association, which has built a good hotel and pavilion and laid out the small Palisades Park. Boating and bathing are among the attractions. It is reached by ferry from Canal St. (15 c.) or 129th St. (10 c.). The *View from the Palisades farther up is very fine.

(3) *Brooklyn*, *Coney Island*, and other resorts on *Long Island*, see R. 3.

Among other points to which excursions are easily made from New York are *Long Branch* and the other seaside resorts of the New Jersey coast (see R. 33); *Yonkers*, *Dobbs Ferry*, *Tarrytown*, and other points on the Hudson (see R. 21); *Glen Island* (p. 67), *New Rochelle*. and other places on Long Island Sound (R. 4); and *Greenwood Lake* (p. 198).

FROM NEW YORK TO CHATHAM, 127 M., railway (Harlem Division of N. Y. C. & H. R. R. R.) in 3½-4¾ hrs. This line is much used by residents of the suburban districts to the N. of Manhattan Island. — From New York to (12 M.) *Woodlawn*, see p. 57. Our line follows the course of the *Bronx River* (to the left). 44 M. *Golden's Bridge* is the junction of a line to (7 M.) *Lake Mahopac*. 52 M. *Brewster's* (p. 62), junction of the N. Y. & N. E. R. R. to Boston. — From (127 M.) *Chatham* lines run to (38 M.) *Lebanon Springs* (p. 140) and (57 M.) *Bennington* and to (17 M.) *Hudson* (p. 151).

3. Brooklyn and Long Island.

Coney Island. Rockaway Beach.

Brooklyn. — **Hotels.** St. George, Pineapple St., $ 3-5, R. from $1; Pierrepoint House, Montague St., cor. Hicks St., $ 3-3¹/₂; Mansion House, Brooklyn Heights, opposite Wall St.. $ 3-3¹/₂, all near Brooklyn Bridge; Clarendon, Washington St., R. from $ 1.

Railway Stations. *Flatbush Avenue Station*, Flatbush Ave., cor. 4th Ave., for the trains of the Long Island Railroad (for all points on Long Island; also to Boston, see p. 65); *Union Depot*, Fifth Ave., cor. 36th St., for Coney Island, Unionville, West Brighton, etc.; *Brooklyn & Brighton Beach Station*, cor. Atlantic and Franklin Avenues, for Brighton Beach.

Elevated Railroads. Five lines of Elevated Railway, similar to those in New York (p. 10), traverse Brooklyn in various directions (fare 5c.). Four of these radiate from Brooklyn Bridge (or Fulton Ferry), and one starts at the foot of Broadway (opp. Grand St., New York). — There are also numerous *Horse-Car Lines*.

Ferries to New York, see p. 14. — **Bridge Cars**, see p. 14.

Brooklyn, with (1890) 806,343 inhab., is the fourth city of the United States in size and industrial interest, but it is so overshadowed by the proximity of New York as to bulk much less largely in the public eye than many smaller cities. It lies immediately opposite New York, at the W. end of Long Island, and covers an area of about 21 sq. M. It is popularly known as the 'City of Churches', and has also been called the 'Dormitory of New York' from the fact that so many of its residents are New York business men, returning to Brooklyn in the evening.

Brooklyn (Breuckelen) was founded by Walloons in 1623, the first settlement being near Wallabout Bay (p. 66). The most outstanding event in its history is the battle of Long Island (Aug. 26th, 1776), fought on the heights behind the town, in which the British defeated the Americans (see p. 54). — The value of Brooklyn's manufactures in 1890 was $ 253,000,000 (50,600,000*l.*). They include sugar and oil refining, ship-building, meat-packing, and the making of chemicals, coffee, cordage, carpets, and boilers. Its commerce is also very important.

Fulton Street, the Broadway of Brooklyn, begins at Fulton Ferry (p. 4), almost under the shadow of Brooklyn Bridge, and runs hence first to the S. and then to the E., with a total length of 6 M. It is traversed by the King's Co. Elevated Railroad and several tramways. Following it from the bridge or ferry we soon reach (10 min.) an open space in front of the **City Hall**, a large white marble building, with an Ionic portico and a tower. Opposite is a spirited statue of *Henry Ward Beecher* (see p. 52), by J. Q. A. Ward. To the E. of the City Hall is the **County Court House,** a handsome edifice in a Corinthian style. Behind the City Hall, adjoining the Court House, are the *Municipal Buildings* and the **Hall of Records*. — At the corner of Washington St. and Johnson St., a little to the N. of the City Hall Square, is the new ***Post Office,** a really fine building, much superior in style to the usual Mansard-roof structures which seem typical of U.S. Federal architecture throughout the country. Its situation, however, does not show it to advantage.

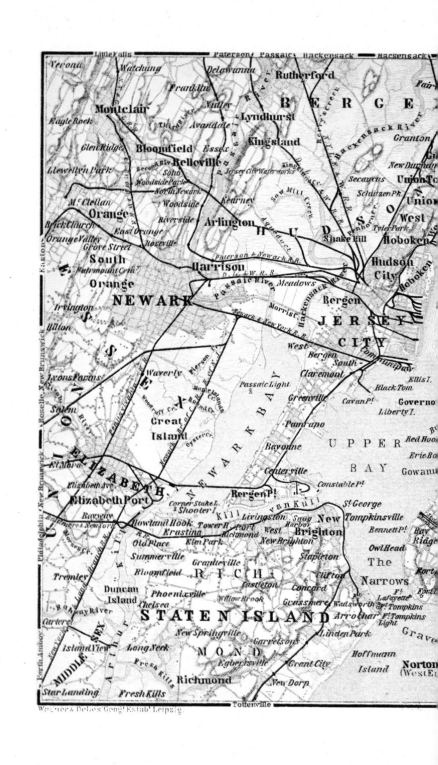

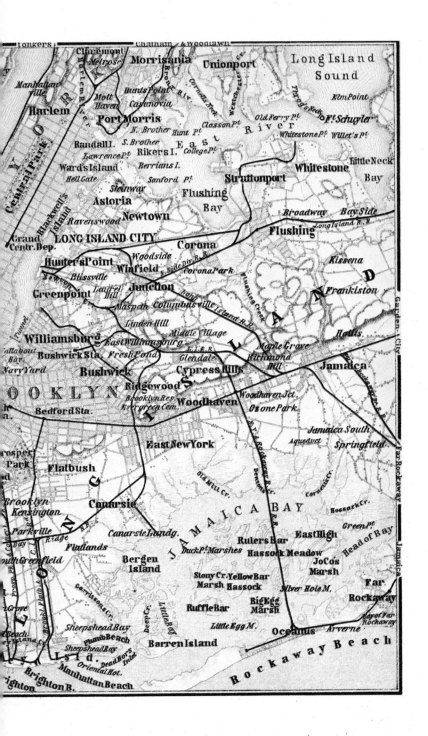

From the City Hall Square *Montague Street*, containing the *Academy of Music* (good concerts), the *Art Association Building* (exhibitions of pictures), and the *Brooklyn Library* (100,000 vols.), leads W. to the river, ending in a terrace which commands an excellent *View of New York and the harbour. The district in which we now find ourselves, known as *Brooklyn or Columbia Heights, is, perhaps, the pleasantest part of the city and contains many of the finest residences. In this quarter are the three hotels mentioned at p. 52, numerous large apartment-houses, and many of the leading clubs (Hamilton, Jefferson, Brooklyn, Excelsior). The 'Heights' rise abruptly from the river to an elevation of 70-100 ft., leaving at their base room for a single narrow street. The chief street of the 'Heights' and the most fashionable Sunday promenade in Brooklyn is CLINTON STREET, extending from Fulton St. (crossing Montague St.) to *Gowanus Bay*. In this street, at the corner of Pierrepoint St. (the street before Montague St.), is the handsome building of the **Long Island Historical Society,** which possesses a library of 60,000 vols. and a small museum. In Pierrepoint St. are the *Dutch Reformed Church* and the Unitarian *Church of the Saviour* (cor. of Monroe Place). At the corner of Montague St. is *Holy Trinity Church*, the leading Episcopal church of Brooklyn, with a spire 275 ft. high. In Remsen St., the next cross-street, at the corner of Henry St., is the Congregational *Church of the Pilgrims* (Rev. Dr. Storrs), with a piece of the original 'Plymouth Rock' (see p. 87) immured in its façade. A little farther on in Clinton St., at the corner of Livingston St. (left), is the handsome *Church of St. Ann* (Episcopal). Clinton St. then crosses ATLANTIC AVENUE, a wide and busy street descending on the right to the ferry for Whitehall St., New York (p. 14).

Plymouth Church, the most famous ecclesiastical edifice in Brooklyn, where the late *Henry Ward Beecher* (d. 1887) drew crowds for 40 years, stands at the N. end of the Heights, in Orange St., between Hicks St. and Henry St., 1/3 M. from Brooklyn Bridge. It is a large building without architectural pretensions. The present minister is *Dr. Lyman Abbot.*

Returning to the City Hall and continuing to follow Fulton St. towards the E., we soon reach, at the corner of Bond St. (right), the building of the *Young Men's Christian Association*, with a fine gymnasium. Fort Green St., 1/2 M. farther on, leads to the left to the small (3 min.) *Washington Park*, laid out on the site of the Revolutionary earthworks known as Fort Green. Fort Green Place, to the right, leads to the (5 min.) *Flatbush Station* (p. 52). Clinton Avenue, nine blocks farther, leads to the left to the (5 min.) **Tabernacle,** a huge new building at the corner of Greene Ave., in which Dr. Talmage preaches every Sunday to 3-4000 hearers.

In Ryerson St., between Willoughby and De Kalb Avenues, about 1/4 M. to the E. of Clinton Ave., are the extensive buildings of the *Pratt Institute, one of the best equipped technical institutions in the world, founded and endowed in 1884-87 by Mr. Charles Pratt, 'to promote manual and industrial education, and to inculcate habits of industry and thrift'. Its schools of technology, domestic science, art, music, mechanics, etc., are attended by 3300 students. Visitors are admitted on Mon., Wed., & Frid., 10-12 and 3-5 (in winter also 7.30-9.30 p.m.); the Technical Museum is open on Mon. and Frid., 7.30-9.30 p.m., and on Wed., 3-5. None interested in technical education should fail to visit this institution. The *Froebel Academy*, 686 Lafayette Ave., is under the direction of the Pratt Institute.

Clinton Avenue ends on the N. at the **U.S. Navy Yard** on *Wallabout Bay*, the chief naval station in the country, employing 2000 men (adm. on application at the gate on Tues. and Sat., strangers on other days also; entr. in Flushing Ave.). The yard proper covers about 45 acres, while 100 acres more belong to it. Among the most prominent features of the yard are two Dry Docks, 465 ft. and 307 ft. long respectively. The *United States Naval Lyceum*, in the yard, contains interesting collections. Some war-vessels are generally moored here, while others are on the stocks. To the E. is the *U. S. Naval Hospital*, with its pillared front.

The largest of the **Docks** of Brooklyn is the *Atlantic Basin*, about 1½ M. to the S. of the Bridge, with an area of 40 acres and 2 M. of wharfage. About ¾ M. farther S., on Gowanus Bay, are the *Erie Docks*.

Perhaps Brooklyn's chief attraction for strangers is the beautiful ***Prospect Park**, finely situated on an elevated ridge in the S.W. part of the city and commanding excellent views of Brooklyn, New York, the harbour, the ocean, and Long Island.

The principal entrance is at the end of Flatbush Ave. (tramway from Fulton Ferry), and the Plaza in front of it is adorned with a *Statue of Lincoln*, a *Memorial Arch* for soldiers and sailors of the Civil War, and a fine statue, by Fred. Macmonnies (b. at Brooklyn in 1864), of *James Stranahan* (b. 1808). Drive through the park in the park-carriages 25c. each.

Prospect Park, which has an area of 550 acres, is not so elaborately laid out as Central Park, but has, perhaps, more natural beauty. It contains many fine trees. The lake at the S. side is 60 acres in extent. *Look-Out Hill* is 185 ft. above the sea. Concerts are given here on Saturdays. In the park is a monument to *John Howard Payne* (1792-1852), author of 'Home, Sweet Home'. A tablet in *Battle Pass* commemorates the battle of Long Island (p. 52). — From the Plaza the *Eastern Parkway*, a fine boulevard, 200 ft. wide, runs E. to the (2½ M.) part of Brooklyn known as *East New York*. Near the S. entrance begins the **Ocean Parkway*, a similar boulevard, which runs all the way to (5 M.) *Coney Island* (p. 55) and forms one of the pleasantest approaches to that resort. The drive from Prospect Park along Bay Ridge to *Fort Hamilton* (1½ hr.) affords continuous views of New York Harbour.

Ninth Avenue and other streets adjoining Prospect Park contain some of the finest residences in Brooklyn. Among the largest and handsomest buildings bordering on the Park are the huge *Riding and Driving Club* (near the Plaza) and the **Montauk Club* (cor. 8th Ave.).

·Following Ninth Avenue towards the S. from the S.W. entrance of Prospect Park, we soon reach (½ M.) the N.E. entrance of ***Greenwood Cemetery**, one of the most beautiful cities of the dead in America, rivalling Prospect Park in the charms of its undulating surface and extensive views. It is 400 acres in extent.

The principal (N.) entrance is in Fifth Ave. (cor. 25th St.), the terminus of the Fifth Avenue Elevated Railroad from the Brooklyn Bridge. The entrance gateway is an elaborate structure of brown stone, 142 ft.

wide, with basreliefs and a tower 100 ft. high. Plans of the cemetery may be obtained here (10 c.), showing the positions of the graves. Among the monuments of special interest, either from their subject or treatment, are those to the *New York Volunteers* (Section H), *Roger Williams* (p. 64; Sec. 130), *De Witt Clinton* (p. 154; 108), *Elias P. Howe* (the inventor of the sewing machine; H), *S. F. B. Morse* (inventor of the electric telegraph; 25), *Horace Greeley* (p. 29; 35), *Henry Ward Beecher* (p. 53; 140), *Lola Montez*, *John Matthews* (64), the *Pilots* (111), the *Firemen* (2), *Peter Cooper* (p. 31, 101), *A. S. Scribner* (160), *James Gordon Bennett* (107). and the *Brooklyn Theatre Fire Victims* (N). The expensive monument of *Char-- lotte Canda* (92) scarcely justifies its reputation. One of the chief attractions of Greenwood is the beauty of the blossoming of the dog-wood (*Cornus Florida*) at the end of May or beginning of June.

Among other points of more or less interest not included in the above rapid survey are the *Roman Catholic Cathedral* (cor. Lafayette and Vanderbilt Ave.); the handsome Roman Catholic church of *St. Augustine* (cor. Sixth Ave. and Sterling Place); the *Polytechnic Institute*, Livingston St. ; the *Young Women's Christian Association*, cor. Flatbush Ave. and Schermerhorn St.; and the *Cemetery of the Evergreens*. — The BROOKLYN INSTITUTE, founded in 1824 and rechartered in 1890, is an academy of arts and sciences with about 2000 members. It contains 25 departments, each of which holds regular meetings and courses of lectures. A grant of $8^{1}/_{4}$ acres of Prospect Park land has been made to the Institute, which is about to erect on it a large Museum, 425 ft. square.

To the N. of Brooklyn, and separated from it by *Newton Creek*, lies **Long Island City**, a place of no particular interest, with (1890) 30,506 inhabitants. It is made up of *Hunter's Point*, *Astoria*, and *Ravenswood*, the last of which contains pleasant residences and extensive nurseries. In Hunter's Point (ferry to 34th St., New York) is the terminus of the *Long Island Railroad* (trains for all points in Long Island).

Long Island, a narrow, fish-shaped island, 120 M. long and 8-20 M. wide, extends along the coast of New York and Connecticut from the mouth of the Hudson to a point beyond the mouth of the Connecticut River, enclosing between itself and the mainland the comparatively sheltered waterway of *Long Island Sound* (p. 66). Its area is 1680 sq. M. and its population (1890) 1,029,097 (incl. Brooklyn). The surface is generally level. A sandy barrier, at some distance from the main shore, extends along nearly the whole S. coast of the island, broken at intervals by narrow inlets; and here are situated Coney Island and other popular seaside-resorts of the New Yorkers. A few of these are mentioned below, but the ordinary tourist may safely neglect Long Island, with the exception, perhaps, of a flying visit to the Margate-like attractions of Coney Island.

Coney Island, the name given to the westernmost section of the flat sand-bar above mentioned, is simply a barren strip of white sand, 5 M. long and $1/_{4}$-1 M. wide, separated from the mainland by a small creek and from the next section of the bar (Rockaway Beach) by a narrow inlet opening into Jamaica Bay. The island is divided into four distincts parts: *West End* or *Norton's Point*, *West Brighton*, *Brighton Beach*, and *Manhattan Beach*. Those who merely wish to see Coney Island for a few hours should go to West Brighton and return viâ Manhattan Beach. The hotels at the latter are the best places to pass the night. It is estimated that at least 10 million visitors resort to Coney Island every season (June-Sept.), and hundreds of thousands are sometimes there on the same day. The prices at the hotels and restaurants are highest at the E. end, and lowest at the W. end of the island; but at the dearer houses one portion is generally ample for two persons. A brightly written sketch of this 'American Brighton' is given by Mr. Cook in his 'Visit to the United States' (p. 72).

West End or *Norton's Point* (*Norton's Hotel*) is the old original Coney Island, but now scarcely repays a visit.

West Brighton (*West Brighton Hotel*), about the middle of the island, is the most crowded and characteristic, though not the most fashionable part of it; and the scene here on a fine Sunday in summer beggars description. The beach swarms with all the peripatetic shows of a popular seaside-resort; and among the permanent attractions are two iron *Piers* (1000-1300 ft. long), a colossal *Elephant*, 150 ft. high (with a restaurant, dancing-rooms, etc., in its interior), and a tall *Observatory* (*View). West Brighton may be reached from New York by steamer from Pier 1 (at the Battery) or from W. 23rd St. (return-fare 50c.), or by steamer from Whitehall St. to *Bay Ridge* and thence by the Sea Beach R. R. (same fare); from Brooklyn by the Prospect Park and Coney Island R. R. (return-fare 35 c.), by the Bath and Coney Island R. R. (same fare), or by the Ocean Parkway (p. 54). It is connected with (3/4 M.) Brighton Beach by a fine drive called the *Concourse* and by an elevated railroad (5 c.).

Brighton Beach (*Brighton Beach Hotel*) consists of a huge hotel, a refreshment pavilion, several bathing-houses, and a band-stand, in which an excellent orchestra performs in summer. It is specially frequented by the Brooklynites, who reach it either viâ West Brighton (see above) or by the Brighton Beach and Brooklyn Railway (20 c., return-fare 35 c.). It is connected with (1/2 M.) Manhattan Beach by the *Marine Railway* (5 c.).

Manhattan Beach (*Manhattan Beach Hotel*, on the European plan, a huge wooden structure, 660 ft. long; *Oriental*, Amer. plan, for more permanent guests) is the most fashionable part of Coney Island and the most comfortable for ordinary tastes. The hotels have large pleasure-grounds and bathing accommodations for many hundreds of visitors (adm. to amphitheatre overlooking the Manhattan bathing enclosure, 10 c.), and music is furnished afternoon and evening by a good band. The beach is illuminated by electricity, and a display of fireworks is given almost nightly. Manhattan Beach may be reached viâ West Brighton or Brighton Beach (see above); from New York by ferry to Hunter's Point (see p. 14) and thence by train; or from the Flatbush Ave. station at Brooklyn (return-fare 50 c.). Passengers holding return-tickets to West Brighton or Manhattan Beach can return by either route.

Rockaway Beach (*Carman House*), the next section of the sand-bar, is a less crowded and somewhat cheaper edition of Coney Island. The trip to it from New York by steamer (1½ hr.; return-fare 50 c.; see advts. in daily papers) affords an excellent survey of New York Harbour and Coney Island. It may also be reached by railway from Long Island City (34th St. ferry; comp. p. 55). *Far Rockaway*, at the E. end of the beach, contains several summer-hotels and is not invaded by the excursionists.

Long Beach (**Long Beach Hotel*, $ 4-5), the next sand-strip, is one of the best bathing-beaches on Long Island, and is frequented by summer residents rather than by excursionists. It is reached by railway viâ Long Island City (comp. p. 55; return-fare 50 c.). Farther to the N. is the *Great South Beach*, a curious strip of sand 40 M. long and 1/4-5 M. wide. *Fire Island* (Surf House), at its W. extremity, reached by ferry from (8 M.) *Babylon* (Argyle Hotel, $3½-4), on the main coast, attained a world-wide notoriety in 1892 by its purchase as a quarantine station and by the resistance of the natives to the landing of the unfortunate passengers of the 'Normannia'. The light of Fire Island Lighthouse is often the first object in America seen by the visitor from Europe, and the signal-station here announces the approach of the steamers 4 hrs. before they reach their docks (comp. p. 2). The *Great South Bay*, between the South Beach and the main coast, is a favourite shooting (wild-fowl) and fishing ground, and the villages along its shores (on the S. division of the Long Island R. R.) are much frequented in summer by New Yorkers.

Among other points on Long Island (all reached by the Long Island Railway) are *Garden City* (19 M. from New York), laid out by A. T. Stewart as a model suburban residence for New Yorkers and containing a handsome Episcopal cathedral built by him; *Shelter Island* (Prospect Ho., $ 3¹/₂-4; Manhanset Ho., $4), in *Gardiner's Bay*, a frequented summer-resort; *Sag Harbor*, a large village at the E. end of the island, with a coasting-trade; *Flushing*, 8 M. from Long Island, with 8436 inhab. and the homes of many New Yorkers; *Brentwood* (The Austral, $4), a pine-wood resort in the interior of the island; and *Creedmoor*, with its rifle-range (p. 18), 5 M. beyond Flushing. On the E. Long Island ends in the bold bluffs of *Montauk Point*, with its lighthouse.

4. From New York to Boston.
a. Viâ New Haven, Hartford, and Springfield.

234 M. RAILWAY (*New York, New Haven, and Hartford Railroad* to Springfield; *Boston and Albany Railroad* thence to Boston) in 5²/₃-6¹/₂ hrs. (fare $5, sleeping-berth $1¹/₂, seat in drawing-room car $1); five express trains daily, including one at night (11 p.m., arriving at 6.15 a.m.). Dining-car on the afternoon train (D. $1) and buffet-cars on all other trains.

The train starts from the *Grand Central Depot* (p. 6), runs through the long tunnels under Park Avenue (see p. 37), crosses the *Harlem River*, and traverses the somewhat unkempt environs of New York. To the right, at (9 M.) *Fordham*, are the large buildings of the Jesuit *St. John's College*. A little farther on, to the left, lies *Woodlawn Cemetery*, and beyond (12 M.) *Woodlawn* our line diverges to the right from the New York and Harlem R. R. and skirts *Long Island Sound* (p. 66). — 16¹/₂ M. *New Rochelle*, founded by Huguenot refugees in 1691. Thomas Paine (1737-1809) had a farm here, granted to him by New York State, and is commemorated by a monument. — 24 M. *Rye*, the station for (2 M.) *Rye Beach*, a summer-resort on the Sound. — Beyond (25¹/₂ M.) *Port Chester* we cross the *Byram River* and enter *New England*. — 28 M. **Greenwich** (*Belle Haven*, $3; Lenox House, $2; *Indian Harbor House*, at Indian Harbor, 1 M. to the S.E.), the first station in *Connecticut* (pron. Connéticut; the 'Nut-meg State'), is a small town with 10,131 inhab., pleasantly situated on heights overlooking Long Island Sound. It was settled in 1640 and contains the villas of many New Yorkers.

33¹/₂ M. **Stamford** (*Stamford House, Union*, $2; *Ocean House*, finely situated on Shippan Point, 1³/₄ M. to the S.), with 15,700 inhab., is a town of the same age as Greenwich and is also a favourite residence and summer-resort of New York merchants (steamer to New York 35c.). — 41¹/₂ M. *South Norwalk* (Mahackemo, $2-2¹/₂) is the station for (1¹/₂ M.; tramway) *Norwalk* (Norwalk House, $2; pop. 17,747), another summer-resort, and the junction of the Danbury and Norwalk branch of the Housatonic Railway (see p. 135). — 51 M. *Fairfield* (Merwin House, Manor House, $3) has, perhaps, the best bathing-beach on Long Island Sound.

56 M. **Bridgeport** (*Atlantic House*, $2¹/₂; *Wilson House*, $2), a flourishing city of (1890) 48,866 inhab., lies on an inlet of the

Sound, at the mouth of the *Pequonnock River*. It possesses important manufactures of sewing - machines (Wheeler & Wilson, Howe), small - arms, ammunition, carriages, and other articles (total value in 1890, $22,000,000). The winter-quarters of Barnum & Bailey's Circus are at Bridgeport. *Golden Hill*, above the town, with numerous villas, affords good views. Bridgeport is the junction of the Housatonic R. R. (R. 18). Steamers daily to New York (50c.). — Farther on the train crosses salt-marshes and enters the large Union Depot at —

73 M. **New Haven** (*New Haven House*, $4-5; *Elliott Ho.*, 3-3¹/₂; *Tontine, Tremont*, $2¹/₂-3; *Rail. Restaurant*; cab 50c. per drive, 2 pers. 35c. each), the largest city of Connecticut and seat of Yale College, is a well-built city, situated at the head of a bay of (4 M.) Long Island Sound and surrounded by hills. It is known as the 'City of Elms', from the fine trees which shade its streets, and carries on a considerable trade and numerous manufactures (value in 1890 $29,000,000). The town was founded in 1638. In 1800 it had about 5000 inhab., and in 1890 it had 81,298.

The *Union Depot* faces the *Harbour*. About ¹/₂ M. to the N. is the *Public Green, on which are the *City Hall*, three *Churches*, and the *State House*. At the back of *Centre Church* is a monument to *John Dixwell*, the regicide.

In College St., which skirts the W. side of the Green, are the substantial buildings of *Yale University, which is second in dignity and importance to Harvard alone among the universities of America. Besides the Academic Department, it has schools of Science, Theology, Medicine, Law, Fine Arts, and Philosophy. It has 180 instructors and over 1900 students.

Yale University was founded at Killingworth in 1700 and established at New Haven in 1717. It was named in honour of *Elihu Yale* (1648-1721), a native of New Haven, who became Governor of Madras and of the East India Co. He presented it with 400*l.* Perhaps the most eminent of its Presidents was *Timothy Dwight* (1795-1817), and the list of its alumni includes Eli Whitney (inventor of the cotton-gin), Samuel Morse, Jonathan Edwards, Noah Webster, Theodore Winthrop (author of 'Cecil Dreeme'), E. C. Stedman, J. Fenimore Cooper, N. P. Willis, etc.

Among the most prominent buildings of the University are the *Art School*, containing a good collection of Italian, American, and other paintings and sculptures (p. lxxxiii); the *Peabody Museum of Natural History*, in which the mineralogical collections are especially fine; the *Sheffield Scientific School* (four halls), munificently endowed and finely equipped; the *Osborn Hall; Battell Chapel*; the new *Gymnasium* (Elm St.); the *Alumni Hall; Dwight Hall;* the *Divinity School;* the *Observatory;* the *Physical Laboratory;* and the *Chemical Laboratory.* The *Library* contains over 200,000 volumes.

The *Old Burying Ground, in Grove St., at the head of High St., a little to the right of the Green, contains the graves of *Sam. Morse* (1791-1872), *Noah Webster* (1758-1843), *President Timothy Dwight* (1752-1817), *Theodore Winthrop* (1828-61), and *Eli Whitney* (1765-1825). — To the N. from Grove St. runs Hillhouse Avenue, the most beautiful of the elm-shaded streets of New Haven. It ends at *Sachem's Wood.*

ENVIRONS. **East** and **West Rocks** are two masses of trap-rock on the plain near the city. The *East Rock* (360 ft.), 2 M. from the Green (tramway viâ State St.) has been made a public park and is surmounted by a war-monument (Inn; *View). The *West Rock* (400 ft.), 2¹/₄ M. to the N.W. of the Green (tramway through Chapel St.), ascended with more difficulty, is also a good point of view. Goffe and Whalley, two of the regicides, lay concealed here in the *Judge's Cave.* — **Savin Rock** (*Sea-View Ho.*, $3) is a bold promontory, commanding a view of Long Island Sound (p. 66; tramway from the Green). — A STEAMER plies twice daily from New Haven to *New York* in 5 hrs. (75 c., return-fare $1.25, state-room $1).

Beyond New Haven the train turns to the left and runs inland (N.). To the left we obtain a good view of the *East* and *West Rocks* (see above). The line follows the *Quinnipiac* valley.

110 M. **Hartford** (*Allyn House,* near the rail. station, $4; *Capitol,* $3; *Heublein,* R. from $1; *City Hotel,* $2-3; *United States Hotel,* $2¹/₂-3; *Rail. Restaurant;* cab 50 c. for each pers. to any point in the city), the capital of *Connecticut,* is finely situated on the *Connecticut River,* at its confluence with the *Park River,* 50 M. from Long Island Sound. It contains extensive manufactories of steam-engines, small-arms (Colt's Factory), bicycles (Pope Manufacturing Co.), etc., and is noted for its powerful insurance companies (assets $150,000,000). A Dutch fort was established here in 1633, and the town was founded three years later. Its population is (1890) 53,230. — The *Union Depot* is near the centre of the town. To the S.W. of it, beyond the *Park River,* lies *Bushnell Park,* containing the handsome white marble *CAPITOL, a conspicuous object in most views of the town. The *Senate Chamber* contains a good portrait of Washington, by Stuart. Fine view from the *Dome* (250 ft.). — Following Capitol Avenue to the E. and then turning to the left, along *Main Street,* we reach (right) the WADSWORTH ATHENÆUM, containing a gallery of paintings and sculptures, a library, and the collections of the *Historical Society* (9-4). Adjacent is the *Etna Life Insurance Building*, and a little farther on is the *Post Office.* Opposite is the *Connecticut Mutual Life Insurance Co.* By continuing to follow Main St. in the same direction we reach (20 min.) the *State Arsenal.*

Near the State House are the *High School,* the *Hartford Orphan Asylum,* and the *Hartford Theological Institute.* — About 1 M. to the S. is *Trinity College,* an E. E. building by Burges of London. — The *Colt Firearms Factory* is in the S.E. part of the city, and near it is the handsome *Church of the Good Shepherd,* erected in memory of Col. Colt, inventor of the revolver, by his wife.

A tablet at the corner of *Charter Oak Place* marks the site of the 'Charter Oak', where in 1687 a colonial gentleman hid the charter of Connecticut (now in the Capitol), to save it from the clutches of Sir Edmund Andros (p. 24). — Among other large buildings are the *Retreat for the Insane,* the *Deaf and Dumb Asylum,* the *Old Folks Home,* and the *City Hospital.*

Mr. *S. L. Clemens* ('Mark Twain'; 351 Farmington Ave.), *Mr. Charles Dudley Warner,* and *Mrs. Harriet Beecher Stowe* (Nos. 37 and 49 Forest St.)

are residents of Hartford. — **Many** pleasant *Drives* may be taken in the vicinity (*Talcott Mt.*, *Tumbledown Brook*, etc.). — *Steamers* ply daily to *New York*, *Sag Harbor* (p. 57), etc.

Beyond Hartford (Capitol conspicuous to the right) the train continues to follow the same general direction (N.N.E.), crossing the Connecticut River. Between (127 M.) *Thompsonville* and (132 M.) *Longmeadow* we enter *Massachusetts* (the 'Bay State').

136 M. **Springfield** (*Massasoit House*, $ 3-5; *Cooley's*, $ 2¹/₂; *Warwick*, $ 2¹/₂-3; *Haynes' Hotel*, $ 2-3; *Railway Restaurant*), a pretty little city on the E. bank of the Connecticut, dating from 1636, carries on a great variety of industries, the most important of which is the manufacture of small-arms. Pop. (1890) 44, 179. The UNITED STATES ARMOURY, in a park to the E. of the station (reached viâ State St.), employs about 500 hands and turns out 30,000 Springfield rifles annually (apply at office for a pass; no adm. on Sun.). View from tower. The *Arsenal* contains 225,000 stand of arms. During the Civil War 800,000 guns were made here. Among the principal buildings are the *Church of the Unity*, *Christ Church*, the *Memorial Church* (N. end of city), the *Court House*, the *Railway Station* (those two designed by H. H. Richardson), the *City Hall*, and the *City Library* (75,000 vols.; also a museum). A visit may also be paid to *Forest Park* (S.; ponds covered with lotus-plants), *Stearns Park* (with the *Puritan*, a statue by St. Gaudens), and the two *Cemeteries*. The annual foot-ball match between Yale and Harvard is played at Springfield *(Hampden Park)*. Good views are obtained from *Crescent Hill Road* (S.) and from the bridges.

At Springfield our train joins the Boston and Albany R. R. and turns to the E. (right). Little of interest is passed before Worcester.

190 M. **Worcester** (*Bay State*, $ 2¹/₂-3¹/₂; *Lincoln*, *Waldo*, $ 2¹/₂-3; *Colonnade*, $ 2; *Brunswick*, $ 2¹/₂-3; *Rail. Restᶜ ant;* cab 50c. for each pers., tramways 5c.), the second city of Massachusetts and 'heart of the Commonwealth', with (1890) 84,655 inhab., occupies a pleasant hill-girt site near the *Blackstone River*. Its manufactures are of a most heterogeneous character, the staples being iron, copper, and steel wire, machinery, envelopes, boots and shoes, organs, and pianos (value of manufactured products in 1890, $ 39,860,000 or 7,972,000*l.*).

From the *Union Depot*, by H. H. Richardson, we proceed to the W. through Front St. to (5 min.) the COMMON, which contains a *War Monument* and a *Memorial of Col. Timothy Bigelow*.

Along the W. side of the Common runs MAIN STREET, which we at first follow towards the right, passing Pearl St. (l.), with the *Post Office*. The street ends at *Lincoln Square*, just on this side of which, to the left, stand two *Court Houses* and the building of the *AMERICAN ANTIQUARIAN SOCIETY (open 9-5, except Sat. afternoon).

This society, one of the leading learned bodies of America, was founded in 1812 and possesses a valuable library of 90,000 vols. (esp. rich on American subjects) and an interesting collection of relics. The collection of newspapers, comprising over 4000 vols., extends from the *Boston News Letter* of 1704 down to the present day.

In Lincoln Sq. stands the old *Salisbury House*, an interesting specimen of a Colonial mansion.

Highland Street leads to the W. from Lincoln Sq. to *Elm Park* and (1 M.) *Newton Hill* (670 ft.), which commands an extensive *View of the city and its surroundings. — *Salisbury Street* runs N.W. to (½ M.) *Salisbury Pond*, on which are the huge *Wire Works of Washburn & Moen* (interesting processes). The old *Bancroft House*, in which George Bancroft (1800-91), the historian, was born, is in this street, 1 M. from the square. — *Belmont St.* leads to the E., between *Millstone Hill* and *Bell Pond*, to (1½ M.) the enormous *State Lunatic Asylum (1000 patients; *View).

Following Main St. to the left (S.) from the Common, we pass several churches and reach (1½ M.; to the right) the large, though not handsome CLARK UNIVERSITY, opened in 1887 and intended rather for the endowment of research than for ordinary educational purposes. The *Chemical Department* is admirably equipped. — Main St. ends ½ M. farther on at WEBSTER SQUARE.

From this point an *Electric Tramway* runs through *Cherry Valley* to *Leicester* and (12 M.) *Spencer*. — A pleasant walk of 2 M. may be taken round **Coe's Pond*, to the W. of Webster Sq.

Among other buildings of interest are the *Free Public Library* (80,000 vols.), Elm St.; the *High School*, Walnut St.; the *Natural Historical Society's Museum*, Foster St. (9-5); *All Saints' Church*, Irving St.; the *Polytechnic Institute;* the *Oread Institute;* and the *College of the Holy Cross* (R. C.), commandingly situated on *Mt. St. James* (690 ft.), to the S. of the town.

Among the pleasantest excursions from Worcester is that to *Lake Quinsigamond, 2 M. to the E., reached by electric tramway.

Beyond Worcester the train makes an abrupt turn to the right (S.) and passes *Lake Quinsigamond* (left; comp. above). — 213 M. **South Framingham** (*Old Colony Ho.*, $ 2½; pop. 9239), a manufacturing place and junction of several railways.

The railway to (29 M.) Lowell passes (7 M.) *Sudbury*, near which is an old Colonial tavern, the original of Longfellow's 'Wayside Inn'.

Cochituate Lake, to the left, near (217 M.) *Natick* (9118 inhab.), is one of the sources of Boston's water-supply. To the left of (220 M.) *Wellesley* (Bon Air Hotel) are the buildings of **Wellesley College*, one of the best-known colleges for women in the United States, situated in a beautiful park (700 students). — 224 M. *Auburndale* (Woodlawn Park Hotel); 225 M. *West Newton;* 227 M. *Newtonville;* 228 M. *Newton*, all included in the wealthy suburban city of *Newton* (24,379 inhab.). 230 M. *Brighton*, with a large cattle-market and slaughter-houses. To the left is the *Charles River*. The train then skirts the N. end of *Brookline* (p. 85; stat. *Cottage Farm*), affording a good view (left) of the *Charles River*, *Cambridge* (p. 83), *Boston* (with the gilded dome of the State House), and *Charlestown Heights* (p. 85). In entering Boston we pass over the 'Back Bay' (p. 82), with *Back Bay Park* to the right.

234 M. *Boston* (Boston & Albany Depot), see R. 5.

b. Viâ New York and New England Railway.

This railway runs between New York and Boston in the three following combinations.

(1). By NEW YORK, NEW HAVEN, AND HARTFORD R.R. to (127 M.) *Willimantic* and thence by NEW YORK AND NEW ENGLAND R.R. to (86 M.) *Boston*. This, the so-called 'Air Line' route (referring to the 'Air Line Division' of the N.Y.N.H. & H.R.R. from New Haven to Willimantic), is the shortest route (213 M. in 5³/₄-7¹/₂ hrs.) between the two cities and is described below. Its best train is the 'White Train' at 3 p.m. (in each direction), with parlor and dining-cars (fares as above).

(2). By N.Y.N.H. & H.R.R. to (110 M.) *Hartford* and thence by N.Y. & N.E. R.R. to (32 M.) *Willimantic* and (86 M.) *Boston* (in all 228 M., in 6¹/₂ hrs.; fares, parlor-cars, and dining-cars as above). The first part of this route is described in R. 4a, the last part is described below. Between Hartford and Willimantic the chief stations are (8 M.) *Manchester* (a manufacturing town; 8222 inhab.) and (12 M.) *Vernon*.

(3). By N. Y. SIXTH AVENUE ELEVATED R. R. to 155th St. (see p. 11), thence by NEW YORK AND NORTHERN RAILROAD to (54 M.) *Brewsters*, and thence by N.Y. & N.E.R.R. to *Willimantic* and (191 M.) *Boston* (245 M. in all, in about 8 hrs.; fares as above). This route is not much used by passengers from New York to Boston, except at night, but affords direct connection with the country to the W. of the Hudson. The chief stations between Brewsters and Hartford are: 64 M. (from New York) *Danbury* (Turner Hotel, $3), a town of 16,552 inhab., with large hat-factories, and the junction of the Danbury and Norwalk R. R. (see p. 57); 70 M. *Hawleyville*, junction of the Housatonic R. R. (see p. 135); 94 M. **Waterbury** (*Scovill*, $2¹/₂; *Cooley, Franklin*, $2), a prosperous manufacturing town with 28,646 inhab. and the junction of the Naugatuck R. R., well known for the cheap 'Waterbury watches', of which about 300,000 are turned out here yearly; 118 M. *New Britain* (Ruswin, $2¹/₂-3), the birthplace of Elihu Burritt (1810-79), the 'Learned Blacksmith', a busy town with 19,007 inhab., engaged in making locks, jewellery, and hardware.

From New York to (73 M.) *New Haven*, see R. 4a. The 'Air Line Division' (see above) here diverges to the right from the line to Hartford. 97 M. **Middletown** (*McDonough*, $2¹/₂), the junction of the line from Saybrook to Hartford, is a busy town of 9013 inhab., on the *Connecticut River*. It is the seat of the *Wesleyan University* (200 students; *View from the chapel-tower; good library and collections of natural history), the *Berkley Divinity School* (Episcopal), and the *State Insane Asylum*. — 98 M. *Portland*, with fine quarries of red sandstone. — 127 M. **Willimantic** (*Hooker Ho.*, $2¹/₂), a manufacturing borough on the river of the same name, with 8648 inhab., is the point where we join the N.Y. & N.E. R.R. and is also the junction of the Central Vermont R.R. (see above). — 152 M. *Putnam;* 160 M. *East Thompson*, the junction of lines to *Southbridge*, Worcester (p. 61), and Norwich (p. 67). 178 M. *Woonsocket Junction;* 205 M. *Hyde Park;* 208 M. *Dorchester*, the last two suburban towns of Boston. The train crosses the *South Bay*, traverses *South Boston*, and enters the Summer Street terminus at—

213 M. *Boston* (see R. 5).

c. Viâ Providence and the Shore Line.

232 M. RAILWAY in 5²/₃-7 hrs. (fares, etc., as above). N. Y. N. H. & H.R.R. to (124 M.) *New London;* NEW YORK, PROVIDENCE, AND BOSTON R.R. thence to (186 M.) *Providence;* OLD COLONY R.R. thence to (231 M.) *Boston.*

— A vestibuled train with through-carriages runs on this route from Boston to Washington, the train being carried from Harlem River to Jersey City (see p. 51) by steamboat (day-service; D. on steamer $1).

From New York to (73 M.) *New Haven*, see p. 58. The 'Shore Line Division' of the N. Y. N. H. & H.R.R. crosses the *Quinnipiac* and continues to follow the shore of *Long Island Sound*, of which it affords fine views. 82 M. *Branford* (Branford Point House, Double Beach House, and several other summer-hotels) and (85 M.) *Stony Creek* (Island View Ho., etc.) are popular bathing-resorts. 89 M. *Guilford* (Guilford Point Ho., to the S. of the town) was the birth-place of the poet Fitz-Greene Halleck (1790-1867). At (105 M.) *Saybrook*, near the mouth of the *Connecticut River*, we intersect the Conn. Valley R.R., which begins at *Old Saybrook* or *Saybrook Point*, 2 M. to the S., and runs to Middletown, etc. (see p. 62). Beyond Saybrook we cross the wide Connecticut.

124 M. **New London** (*Crocker House*, $ 2½-3½; *Fort Griswold Ho.*, across the river, $ 3-4), a small city on the right bank of the *Thames*, with 13,757 inhab. and an excellent harbour, defended by *Fort Trumbull* (seen from the station) and *Fort Griswold* (on the other side of the river). Just above the town is a *U. S. Navy Yard*. Whaling and sealing are carried on, though by no means on the same scale as of old. The Yale and Harvard boat-race is decided here in June or July, and several other colleges have boat-houses on the Thames. The *Public Library* is handsome.

The *Obelisk* (134 ft. high), which stands out so prominently on the *Groton Heights*, on the E. bank of the river (ferry 4c.), was erected to commemorate the burning of the town by Arnold and the massacre of Fort Griswold on Sept. 6th, 1781 (*View from the top; adm. 10c.). — At the mouth of the Thames, 3 M. from New London, is the *Pequot House* ($ 3-4), a favourite resort (steamer from New London). — Steamers also ply from New London to *White Beach*, Newport (p. 68), Block Island (see below), Norwich (p. 67), Sag Harbor (p. 57), New York, etc. (see below).

FROM NEW LONDON TO BRATTLEBORO, 121 M., *New London & Northern R.R.* (a branch of the Central Vermont R.R.) in 5 hrs. — 13 M. *Norwich*, see p. 67; 30 M. *Willimantic* (p. 62); 65 M. *Palmer*. — 85 M. **Amherst** (*Amherst Ho.*, $ 2½), with 4000 inhab., is chiefly interesting as the site of AMHERST COLLEGE, one of the leading educational institutions of New England (founded in 1821; 3-400 students). Among the chief buildings of the college are the *Memorial Chapel*, the *Walker Hall*, and the *Gymnasium*. Its collections of Assyrian sculptures, minerals, casts, and ancient tracks in stone are of great importance. — 100 M. *Miller's Falls* (p. 134); 111 M. *South Vernon* (p. 143). — 121 M. *Brattleboro*, see p. 143.

We now follow the tracks of the New York, Providence, and Boston R.R., crossing the Thames by a huge swing-bridge (view), to (126 M.) *Groton* (see above). — 136 M. **Stonington** (*Hoxie Ho.*, $ 2), a quiet town with 7184 inhab., is the terminus of the 'Stonington Line' of steamers from New York (see p. 66).

Steamers ply daily from Stonington to (4 M.) *Watch Hill* and (20 M.) *Block Island*. — **Watch Hill** (*Watch Hill Ho.*, *Ocean*, *Larkin*, $4; *Plimpton*, *Narragansett*, $ 2½-4; *Atlantic*, $ 2-3) is a sea-bathing place at the S.W. extremity of Rhode Island (comp. p. 64), commanding fine views. — **Block Island** (*Ocean View*, $ 3-5; *Spring Ho.*, $ 3½; *Manisses*, $ 2½-3½; *Eureka*, $ 2-3), an island 8 M. long and 2-4 M. broad, situated 10 M. from the coast of Rhode Island, is a much-frequented summer-resort (mean summer temp. 73°). It is also reached by steamer from New York direct and from Providence and Newport (comp. p. 68).

Beyond Stonington the train turns inland and enters *Rhode Island*, the smallest state in the Union ('Little Rhody'; 50 M. by 40 M.), but first in the proportion of manufactures to population. We cross the *Pawcatuck* and reach (142 M.) *Westerly* (Dixon Ho.), whence steamers ply to *Watch Hill* (see above). Between (153 M.) *Carolina* and Kingston the train passes through the famous *Cedar Swamp (Narragansett Fort)*, where King Philip and his Indians were almost annihilated in Dec., 1675. — 159 M. *Kingston*, the junction of a line to (9 M.) *Narragansett Pier*.

Narragansett Pier (*Gladstone, Rockingham,* $4-6; *Matthewson, Continental,* $4-5; *Tower Hill,* on Narragansett Heights, $3; *Atlantic, Berwick, Massasoit,* $3-4; *Arlington,* $3, and many others; also *Lodging* and *Boarding Houses*), second only to Newport among the Rhode Island seaside-resorts, has a splendid beach and good opportunities for boating, fishing, and driving. Good views are obtained from *Narragansett Heights* (200 ft.) and the top of *Hazard's Castle* (165 ft.). Among the other attractions is a large *Casino*. The rocks are fine both in form and colour. *Point Judith* (p. 67) lies 5 M. to the S., and at *Hammond's Mills,* 7 M. to the N., is the house in which *Gilbert Stuart* (p. lxxxiii) was born in 1755. *Commodore Perry* (1785-1819; p. 268) was a native of Narragansett. Steamers ply daily to Newport (p. 68) and Providence (see below).

166 M. *Wickford Junction,* for (3 M.) *Wickford,* whence steamers ply daily to Newport (comp. p. 68).

186 M. **Providence.** — *Hotels:* NARRAGANSETT, cor. Broad St. and Dorrance St., $35; DORRANCE, Westminster St., R. from $1; CENTRAL, R. from 50 c. — *Tramways* through the chief streets. — *Steamers* to New York, Newport, Mount Hope, Block Island, etc.

Providence, one of the capitals of Rhode Island and the second city in New England, with (1890) 132,146 inhab., is pleasantly situated on *Providence River* (the N. arm of Narragansett Bay), at the influx of the *Seekonk River.*

Providence was founded by Roger Williams in 1636, after his expulsion from Massachusetts. It carries on important manufactures of cotton and woollen goods, steam-engine s(Corliss Co.), silver-plate (Gorham Co.), iron, etc. (total value, in 1890, $73,000,000 or 14,600,000*l*).

Near the *Union Railway Station,* in the centre of the town, stands the handsome *City Hall,* with a medallion of Roger Williams on the façade (*View from the tower). In front is a *Soldiers' & Sailors' Monument,* and facing this, at the other end of Exchange Place, is a *Statue of General Burnside* (1824-81). *Westminster Street,* the chief business-thoroughfare, runs hence towards the S.W., and from it an *Arcade,* 225 ft. long, leads to the left to Weybossett St. Among the other prominent buildings are the *Post Office,* the *Roman Catholic Cathedral,* and the *Rhode Island Hospital.* — The most interesting part of the town, however, lies on the E. side of the Providence River, reached by a bridge near the Union Depot. Just beyond the bridge, at the corner of College St. and Benefit St., is the *County Court House,* next to which is the *Athenaeum,* containing a library of 50,000 vols. and some interesting portraits (one by Sir Joshua Reynolds) and a small painting on ivory by Malbone ('The Hours').

About $1/4$ M. up the hill (cable-car on College St.) are the buildings of BROWN UNIVERSITY, founded in 1764, in a campus shaded with fine old elms (250-300 students). *University Hall*, the oldest part, dates from 1770. Some of the new buildings are handsome. The *Ladd Observatory* stands on Tip-Top Hill. To the N., at the corner of Waterman St. and Prospect St., is the *University Library* (72,000 vols.), and next to it is the hall of the *Rhode Island Historical Society*, with interesting relics. — *Prospect Hill Terrace*, near the University, commands a fine *View of Providence.

Among the interesting old buildings in Providence are the *Friends' Meeting House* (1759); the *Ives House*, at the corner of Brown St. and Power St., near the University, with an interesting portico; the *Tillinghast House* (1710); the *Hopkins House* (1750); the old *John Brown House*, Power St., cor. of Benefit St., a fine example of its date (1786); the *Whipple House*, in Abbott St. (ca. 1660); and the *Betsy Williams House* (1775), in the Roger Williams Park.

At the S. end of the town is the *Roger Williams Park*, containing a statue of Roger Williams (1559-1683). On the Seekonk River, near the E. end of Power St., enclosed by a railing, is the *What Cheer Rock*, the first landing-place of Roger Williams.

Among the pleasant points in the environs of Providence are *Cranston*, 4 M. to the W., with the Narragansett Trotting Park ; *Mount Hope*, seat of King Philip, near (7 M.) *Bristol*, on the E. shore of Narragansett Bay; *Hunt's Mill* (3 M.); *Pawtucket, Silver Spring* (clam-bakes), *Rocky Point* (clam-bakes), and other places on Narragansett Bay. — The sail down *Narragansett Bay* to Newport (there and back 75 c.) is very attractive (comp. p. 72).

FROM PROVIDENCE TO WORCESTER, $43^1/2$ M., railway in $1^1/4$-$1^3/4$ hr. — This line ascends the pretty industrial valley of the *Blackstone*. At (7 M.) *Lonsdale* are the grave and monument of *William Blaxton* (see p. 75; to the right). 16 M. *Woonsocket* (pop. 20,830). — $43^1/2$ M. *Worcester*, see p. 60.

From Providence to Boston we follow the tracks of the Old Colony R.R. 191 M. *Pawtucket*, a city with 27,633 inhab. and large thread and other mills, was the place where cotton-manufacturing was introduced into the United States by Samuel Slater in 1790. The Slater Mill is still standing. — 199 M. *Attleboro*, in Massachusetts, with manufactories of plate and jewellery; $216^1/2$ M. *Canton Junction* (p. 72). The train approaches Boston (Park Square Station) through the suburbs of *Hyde Park* and *Roxbury*.

231 M. *Boston*, see R. 5.

d. Viâ Long Island and Eastern States Line.

253 M. This new route, opened in 1891, starts from *Flatbush Avenue Station*, Brooklyn, crosses Long Island Sound by steamer, and runs from Hartford along the N. Y. & N. E. R. R. (fares as above). Flatbush Ave. Station is reached from New York viâ the Bridge and Brooklyn Fifth Ave. Elevated R. R., or Flatbush Ave. tramway, or by tramway from South, Wall, Fulton, and Catherine ferries, and from Pennsylvania R. R. Annex.

Brooklyn, see p. 52. At (19 M.) *Mineola* the line turns to the

N. At (34 M.) *Oyster Bay*, a favourite summer-resort, the train is run bodily on board the large transfer-steamer and is ferried across *Long Island Sound* (see below) to (48 M.) *Wilson's Point* in about $3/4$-1 hr. The next section of the journey, as far as (79 M.) *Hawleyville* (p. 62), is over the tracks of the Housatonic R. R., passing (51 M.) *South Norwalk*, (53 M.) *Norwalk*, and (72 M.) *Bethel.* The route from Hawleyville to (136 M.) *Hartford* is described at p. 62, that from Hartford to (253 M.) *Boston* in R. 4 a.

e. By Steamboat.

1. STEAMBOAT to *Newport* and *Fall River* in 10-11 hrs. (Pier 28, foot of Murray St.); RAILWAY thence to *Boston* in $1^1/3$ hr. (through-fare $ 4; state-room $ 1-2).

2. STEAMBOAT to *Stonington* in 8-10 hrs. (Pier 36, N. River) and RAILWAY thence to Boston in $2^3/4$-$3^3/4$ hrs. (fares as above). Passengers need not leave their state-rooms at Stonington till 7 a.m.

3. STEAMBOAT of 'Norwich Line' to *New London* in 10-12 hrs. (Pier 40, N. River) and RAILWAY thence to *Boston* in 4-5 hrs. (fares as above).

4. STEAMBOAT to *Providence* in 10-12 hrs. (Pier 29, N. River; in summer only) and RAILWAY thence to *Boston* in $1^1/4$ hr. (fares as above).

The steamers on all these lines are well fitted up and contain good restaurants, etc.; those of the Fall River Line ('Plymouth', 'Puritan', 'Pilgrim', and 'Providence') are especially large and luxurious (comp. p. 7). All run at night, leaving New York about 5 or 6 p.m., and all proceed through Long Island Sound, so that one general description suffices. Each line runs directly to its terminus, without intermediate stoppages. Cabin-berths are included in the fares on all night-steamers, but state-rooms are extra. Fares are reduced 25 per cent. in winter. The trains in connection are timed to reach Boston about 7-8 a.m. The hours in the reverse direction are similar.

The steamers of all the lines start in the North River (p. 23) and proceed round the Battery (p. 25), affording fine views of the city and harbour. To the right lie *Ellis*, *Liberty*, and *Governor's Islands* (p. 3). Passing the last, we bend to the N., enter the *East River* (p. 23), and pass under the stupendous **Brooklyn Bridge* (p. 30), which is seen to great advantage from the steamer's deck. Beyond the bridge, to the right, opens *Wallabout Bay*, with the *U. S. Navy Yard* (p. 54). On both sides are wharves crowded with shipping. Farther up we pass between *Blackwell's Island* (p. 50) and *Long Island City* (p. 55), and then thread *Hell Gate* (p. 50), with *Ward's Island* and *Randall's Island* (p. 50) to the left.

We now leave the East River and enter **Long Island Sound,** which extends for a distance of 115 M. between *Long Island* (see p. 55) on the right and the coasts of New York and Connecticut on the left. Its width varies from 3 M. to 30 M. As we enter the Sound we pass *Berrian's Island*, the *Brothers*, and *Riker's Island*. To the right is *Flushing Bay*, with the town of *Flushing* (p. 57). The steamer threads a narrow channel, passes *Throgg's Neck* (with Fort Schuyler; to the left), and enters a wider part of the Sound. *Little Neck Bay*, to the right, is famous for its clams. Among the islands which conceal the mainland-coast here are *City Island*, *Hart's Island* (with the paupers' cemetery of New York), and *Hunter's Island*.

Glen Island, near *New Rochelle* (p. 57), is a favourite picnic-resort
(see p. 22). On *Sand's Point*, to the right, is a lighthouse (revolving white light). Among the chief points on the mainland farther
on are *Greenwich* (p. 57), *Norwalk* (p. 57), *Bridgeport* (p. 57),
New Haven (p. 58), and *Saybrook* (p. 62), at the mouth of the
Connecticut River. The lights passed are *Captain's Island* (fixed
white), *Stratford Lightship* (flash white), *Falkner's Island* (revolving white), and *Cornfield Lightship* (fixed red), to the left; and
Eaton's Neck (fixed white), *Plum Island* (revolving white), and *Little
Gull Island* (fixed white) to the right. We are here about 7 hrs. out
from New York. The NORWICH STEAMER now heads for shore, enters
the Thames, and stops at *New London* (p. 63), where passengers
disembark and proceed by train to Boston (see below).

FROM NEW LONDON TO BOSTON, 108 M., railway in 4-5 hrs. The train
follows the bank of the *Thames* (view to the right). 8 M. *Allyn's Point.*

13 M. **Norwich** *(Wauregan Ho.*, \$ 2-2¹/₂; *Union Square; Buckingham)*, an
attractive manufacturing city with 16,156 inhab., pleasantly situated between
the *Yantic* and *Shetucket*, which here unite to form the Thames. Among
its chief buildings are the *Court House*, the *Free Academy*, and *St. Patrick's
Cathedral*. The old *Indian Cemetery*, in Sachem St., has been the burial-
ground of the Mohicans or Mohégans from time immemorial, and contains
an obelisk to their famous chief Uncas (d. 1683). On *Sachem's Plain*, near
Greenville (1³/₄-2 M. from Norwich), another monument marks the spot
where Uncas captured and executed Miantonomoh, Sachem of the Narra-
gansetts (1643). About 5 M. to the S. of Norwich is *Mohegan*, with a handful
of half-breeds who represent the 'last of the Mohicans'. Steamers run
from Norwich to New York (twice weekly), Watch Hill (p. 63), Block Island (p. 63), Fisher's Island, and other points.

At Norwich our line diverges to the right from the New London and
Northern R. R., which runs to *Brattleboro*, etc. (comp. p. 63). 14¹/₂ M.
Greenville (see above). At (29 M.) *Plainville* we intersect the Providence
division of the N. Y. & N. E. R. R. About 4 M. to the W. of (38 M.)
Danielsonville is *Brooklyn*, the home of General Israel Putnam (see p. 91).
At (47 M.) *Putnam* (p. 62) we join the main line of the N. Y. & N. E. R. R.
Hence to (108 M.) *Boston*, see R. 4b.

The STONINGTON STEAMER passes the mouth of the Thames,
runs inside *Fisher's Island*, and reaches its landing-place at *Stonington* (see p. 63), while the NEWPORT and PROVIDENCE STEAMERS
keep on their course outside of Fisher's Island.

From Stonington to *Boston* (95 M., in 2³/₄-3³/₄ hrs.), see R. 4c.

We now pass out of Long Island Sound, *Montauk Point* (p. 57)
lying nearly due S. of us. On a point to the left, beyond Fisher's
Island, is *Watch Hill* (p. 63; fixed white light), while *Block Island* (p. 63; light) lies off to the right as we begin to bend
towards the N. The revolving white light of *Point Judith*, 5 M. to
the S. of Narragansett Pier (p. 63), next shows ahead, to the
left; and in rounding this headland, if anywhere, we may experience a little rough weather. Passing *Narragansett Pier* (p. 64;
left), we keep to the right of the *Beaver Tail Light* (fixed white),
on *Conanicut Island* (p. 71), steer between *Goat Island* (with
Fort Wolcott; left) and the mainland (*Fort Adams;* right), and
enter Newport harbour.

Newport. — **Hotels.** *Ocean House, Bellevue Ave., from $4, omn.
50 c., closes Oct. 1st; *Cliffs Hotel, with view of the sea; Aquidneck
House, Pelham St., $4; Clifton, $3; Perry House, Washington Sq., commercial, $3. Few of the hotels of Newport compare favourably with those
of other large watering-places, as the fashionable visitors reside almost
entirely in the so-called 'Cottages'. — There are numerous *Boarding-Houses*
(Pelham St., Church St., etc.) from $10 per week upwards.

Electric Tramways run from Commercial Wharf and Broadway to
Easton's Beach (5 c.), passing near Washington Sq.; also to Morton Park
and Middletown. *Public Brakes* run from Washington Sq. (also from rail.
stat. and wharves) along Bellevue Ave. to *Bailey's Beach* (10 c.); also from
Bailey's Beach round the *Ocean Drive* (50 c. each). — *Hack* (bargaining
advisable) about $1 per hr.; round the Ocean Drive (1-4 pers.) $3; from
the wharf or station to the hotels 50 c. (1-2 pers.). *Hotel Omnibus* 50 c.

Bathing. The use of bathing-cabin and costume at *First* or *Easton's Beach*
costs 25 c. Full costume obligatory when white flag up. The popular hour
is 11-12. Beach reserved for gentlemen, 1-3 p.m. (red flag; demi-costume).

Boats may be hired at Kinsley's, Long, and Spring Wharves. Newport
is a favourite port for *Yachts* and *Yacht Racing.*

Steamboats ply frequently to *Block Island*, *Conanicut Island*, *Narragansett Pier*, *Providence*, *Wickford*, etc., starting from the Commercial
Wharf. The *New York* steamer starts at the Old Colony Wharf.

Railway Station (for Boston, etc.), West Marlborough St., below
Washington Sq. Another route to Boston (and also to New York) is by
steamer to *Wickford* and thence by rail viâ *Wickford Junction* and the
Shore Line (comp. p. 64).

Casino, Bellevue Ave. Concerts 11 a.m. to 1.30 p.m. (50 c.), and on
Sun. 8-10 p.m. (25 c.); music and dancing on Mon. & Frid., 9.30 p.m. to
11.30 p.m. ($1); adm. at other times 25 c.

Principal Attractions. Those who have but one day to spend at Newport should make their way to the *First Beach* (p. 69), viâ *Touro Park*
and the *Old Mill* (p. 69); !walk hence by the *Cliff Walk* (p. 70) to *Bailey's] Beach* (p. 71); and then take the *Ocean* or *Ten Mile Drive* (p. 71).
Other interesting points are *Purgatory* (p. 70), the *Hanging Rocks* (p. 70),
and *Second Beach* (p. 70).

Newport, the undisputed 'Queen of American seaside-resorts',
occupies a low plateau near the S.W. extremity of *Rhode Island*
(see p. 71), rising from a fine harbour which opens on the E. side
of Narragansett Bay. It is one of the two capitals of the State of
Rhode Island (comp. p. 64) and contains (1890) 19,457 inhabitants. This population is, however, very largely increased in summer (June-Sept.), when visitors flock to the town from all parts of
the United States, taking up their abode for the most part in the
luxurious country-houses and private villas known here as 'Cottages'. The older part of the town adjoins the harbour, but the
new and fashionable quarters lie higher up and farther back, extending across to the ocean side of the narrow island.

The chief reason of Newport's popularity is said to be its balmy and
equable climate, but the natural beauty of its cliffs and surroundings
would alone justify its reputation. The fashionable people of the whole
N.E. part of the United States spend the early months of summer here
as regularly as they pass the later amid the Berkshire Hills (p. 136).

Newport was settled in 1639 by William Coddington and other dissent-
ers from the Puritan church of Massachusetts, and a century later had
about 5000 inhabitants. In 1770 Newport was surpassed by Boston only
in the extent of its trade, which was considerably greater than that of
New York. It suffered greatly during the Revolution, however, and never
recovered its commercial importance, so that in 1870 its population was

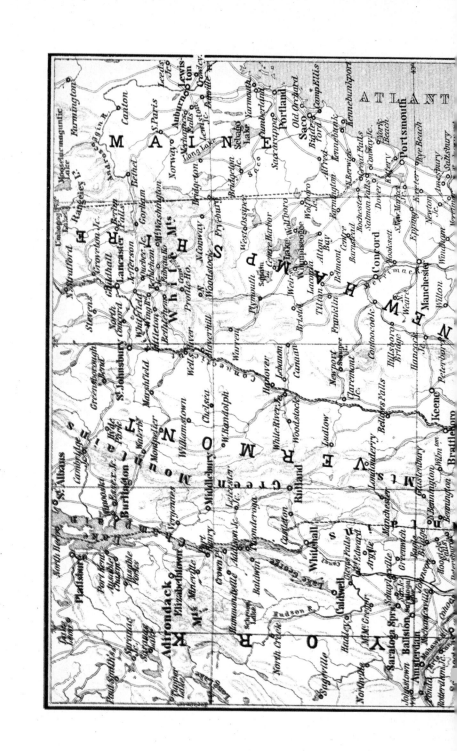

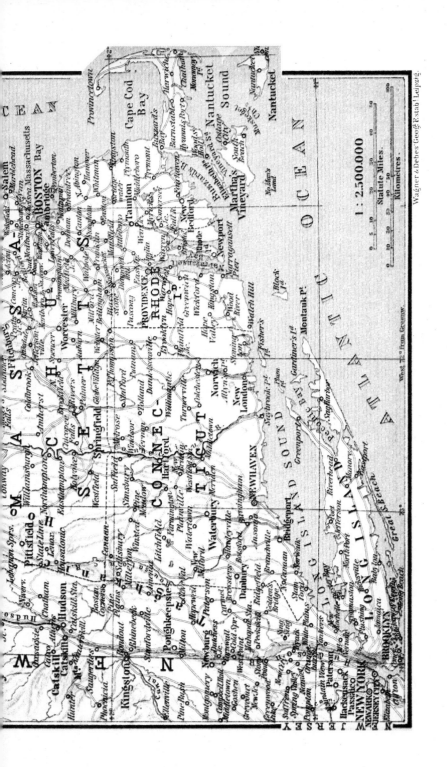

Wagner & Debes Geogr Estab Leipzig.

no larger than in 1770. During part of the Revolutionary struggle Newport was occupied by the French allies of the Americans, who were so favourably impressed with Rhode Island, that they sought to have it ceded to France. *Wm. Ellery Channing* (1780-1842) was a native of Newport, and *Bishop Berkeley* (1684-1753) lived here from 1729 to 1731 (see p. 70).

The central point of Old Newport is WASHINGTON SQUARE or the PARADE, within a few minutes' walk of the railway-station and steamboat-wharf. Here are the *State House* (1738-43; with portrait of Washington, by Stuart), the *City Hall*, a *Statue of Commodore O. H. Perry* (1785-1819), the hero of Lake Erie (p. 267), the *Perry Mansion*, and the *Roman Catholic Church* (with an Ionic portico).

Following Touro St. to the E., we pass (left) the *Synagogue* (1762; said to be the oldest in the United States), the *Newport Historical Society* (10-4; interesting relics), and (5 min.) the picturesque *Hebrew Cemetery*. Touro St. ends here and BELLEVUE AVENUE, the fashionable promenade, begins, running to the S. (right). To the right is the *Newport Reading Room*. A little farther on, to the left, is the *Redwood Library* (1748), a Doric building, containing 40,000 vols. and some sculptures and paintings (open 12-2). The fine *Fern-leaf Beech*, at the corner of Bellevue Ave. and Redwood St., should be noticed. Nearly opposite this is **Touro Park**, given to the town by Judah Touro (1775-1854), one of the numerous wealthy Hebrews who at one time lived in Newport. In this park stands one of the most interesting relics of Newport, the **Round Tower* or *Old Stone Mill*, the origin of which is still somewhat of a mystery, though the inferential evidence is pretty strong that it was built by Gov. Arnold in the 17th cent. and not by the Norsemen in the 11th. Arnold certainly describes it in his will as 'my stone-built wind-mill', and there is no doubt that it was used in this capacity, though Longfellow treats it more respectfully in his 'Skeleton in Armor'. The park also contains statues of *M. C. Perry* (1794-1858) and *W. E. Channing* (see above; erected in 1893); and on its S. side stands the *Channing Memorial Church*.

A few hundred paces farther on *Bath Road* (electric tramway) leads to the left from Bellevue Ave. to the (10 min.) First Beach.

Bellevue Avenue soon passes the *Casino* (left), a long, low, many-gabled building, containing a club (introduction necessary), a theatre, etc. (concerts, see p. 68). The Lawn Tennis Championship of America is decided in the courts attached to the Casino (Sept.). A little farther on, on the same side, is the *Ocean House* (p. 68). The avenue then passes between a series of magnificent villas (see *New York Book Co.'s* Plan of Newport, 25 c.), among which the white marble house and wall of *Mr. W. K. Vanderbilt* are conspicuous to the left (about 1 M. farther on). The avenue then turns sharply to the right and ends at *Bailey's Beach* (p. 71).

First or **Easton's Beach**, a strip of smooth hard sand, 1 M. long, affords some of the best and safest surf-bathing on the Atlantic coast. Besides the bathing-houses (see p. 68) there is a handsome pavilion, containing a restaurant and hot and cold baths. Behind the beach lies *Easton's Pond*, and at its farther (E.) end is a group of cottages. *Easton's Point*, forming the E. barrier of the beach, affords an excellent view of Newport.

From the E. end of the beach a path leads along the cliffs to (³/₄-1 **M.**)
"**Purgatory,** a curious fissure in the conglomerate rocks, 150 ft. long,
7-14 ft. wide, and 50 ft. deep, resembling the so-called Chasms, near Manor-
bier in S. Wales (see *Baedeker's Great Britain*). Numerous legends attach to
it, one relating how a youth leaped it at the challenge of his lady-love and
then renounced her in the spirit of the hero of 'The Glove' by Schiller:
'Not love it is, but vanity, sets love a task like that'. Just beyond Purgatory is *Sachuest* or *Second Beach*, where the surf is much heavier than
at Easton's Beach. To the N. of Sachuest Beach is *Paradise Valley*, with
the picturesque *Paradise Rocks*, ending in the *Hanging Rocks*, below which
Bishop (then Dean) Berkeley was wont to sit. Here, it is said, he composed his 'Alciphron, or the Minute Philosopher' and also the lyric containing the much-quoted verse: —

> 'Westward the course of empire takes its way,
> 'The first four acts already past,
> 'A fifth shall end the drama with the day,
> 'Time's noblest offspring is the last.'

Bishop Berkeley's residence, now a farm-house, in Berkeley Ave.,
to the N. of Paradise Road, is not far off. Those who have come thus
far by carriage (the road passes near the beaches) may continue along
Indian Avenue to *Boothden* (Edw. Booth's house) and (7 M.) the *Glen*, and
return by the N. end of the town.

At the W. end of Easton's Beach begins the famous ***Cliff Walk,**
which runs along the winding brow of the cliffs for about 3 M., with
the ocean on one side and the smooth lawns of the costliest and
handsomest 'cottages' in the town on the other (fine views). No
fences intervene between the walk and the cottage-grounds. Passing
two groups of smaller cottages, clustered round a central hotel (Cliffs
Hotel), we pass a vacant lot and reach the finely kept enclosure
of *Mrs. Gammell*, containing three villas. At the end of it are the
'*Forty Steps*', descending to the beach, with an outlook platform
commanding a fine ***View** (to the E. Easton's Point, Sachuest Point,
and West Island in the distance; below, to the right, *Ellison's
Rocks*). Crossing *Narragansett Avenue*, which leads from this point
to Bellevue Ave. (p. 69), we enter the *Goelet Place*, which contains
one pretty villa and one pretentious and inappropriate mansion. A
little farther on we pass the **Lorillard-Wolfe Cottage*, a long many-
gabled red building, in which the low rambling style of architecture
developed in the Newport cottage is seen to great advantage. The
next house is that of *Mr. Cornelius Vanderbilt* (rebuilt in 1893),
with its rustic summer-house on *Ochre Point*, where we turn to
the right (W.). Farther on we cross *Marine Avenue*, and enter
the grounds of the late *Mr. August Belmont*, adjoining which is
the enclosed rose-garden of the late *George Bancroft* (1800-91),
the historian. Beyond the red villa of *Mrs. William Astor* we pass
the white marble palace of *Mr. William K. Vanderbilt* (see p. 69),
a magnificent dwelling, but hardly in keeping with the *genius loci*.
It is the only place on the Cliff Walk screened from the vulgar
gaze by a fence. Passing *Sheep Point*, the path descends to a lower
level. Opposite the picturesque stone house of *Mr. F. W. Vanderbilt* we cross a small rocky bridge. To the left is *Rough Point*.
We then cross the *Ledge Road*, leading from Bellevue Ave. to the

Land's End, off which lies *Coggeshall's Ledge*. Crossing the hill and passing the wooden *Look-Out Tower*, we finally reach **Bailey's Beach**, a small bay with a long row of bathing-houses, which has of late years become the most fashionable bathing-resort of the Newport cottagers.

From Bailey's Beach we either return to town by one of the drags running along Bellevue Ave. (p. 68), or we may begin the beautiful ***Ocean Drive**, which skirts the coast of the peninsula to the S. of the town for about 10 M., commanding magnificent views (2-2½ hrs.; comp. p. 68). *Ocean Avenue*, forming the first part of the drive, begins at Bellevue Ave. and runs to the W. past Bailey's Beach. To the left, at the W. arm of the beach, is the *Spouting Rock*, where the water, after a storm, sometimes rises to a height of 40-50 ft. To the right lies *Lily Pond*, where we turn to the left (S.). Looking over the bay to the left, we see *Gooseberry Island*, with the house of the *Newport Fishing Club*. We now cross a bridge over a small inlet and see to the left, on *Price's Neck*, the *United States Life-Saving Station*. At *Brenton's Point* (*View) the road turns to the right and runs towards the N., soon passing *Castle Hill*. We then turn again to the right, with the ocean behind us, and soon turn to the left into *Harrison Avenue* or the *Fort Road*. On the point to the left, projecting into Narragansett Bay, stands *Fort Adams* (see below), and ahead of us lies Newport Harbour. On a rocky islet to the left, a little farther on, is the *Lime Rock Lighthouse*, in charge of Ida Lewis, the 'Grace Darling' of America. Turning again towards the bay, we follow the road skirting the harbour, and regain the Parade (p. 69) through *Thames Street*, the chief business-street of the old town.

The so-called '*Neck*', embracing the district between the Ocean Drive and the S. part of the island, has been laid out in numerous winding drives. — Among other points of interest in or near Newport may be mentioned *Trinity Church*, in Church St., dating from 1725 and often preached in by Bp. Berkeley; the *First Baptist Church*, in Spring St. (1644); *Vernon House*, cor. Clarke St. and Mary St., headquarters of Count Rochambeau, the French commandant in 1780; the *U. S. Naval Training Station*, on *Coaster Harbor Island* (3 p.m. till sunset); *Fort Adams*, near Brenton's Cove, 3 M. from the town by road, but easily reached by boat across the harbour, one of the strongest forts in the United States, with room for a garrison of 3000 men (guard-mount and dress-parade at 9 a.m. daily, except Sun.; battalion drill, Wed. 4-5; band-practice, Mon., Wed., & Frid. at 3 p.m.); *Fort Wolcott*, with the *U. S. Torpedo Station*, on Goat Island (no admission); *Morton Park* and the *Polo Grounds*, at the S. end of Thames St.; and *Miantonomoh Hill* (view), on the N. side of the city (1½ M.; at the end of Malbone Road). — The steamer to *Wickford* (see p. 64; 12 M., in 1 hr.) passes between *Conanicut Island* to the left and the islands of *Prudence, Hope*, and *Despair* to the right. *Jamestown* (Bay View Ho., $2½), on Conanicut, is a growing summer-resort; the headland nearest Newport, known as the *Dumplings*, is crowned with a ruined fort. From Wickford to *Boston* (2¾-3 hrs.) and to *New York* (5-8 hrs.), see p. 64. *Fall River* (see p. 72) is 18 M. from Newport by railway.

Rhode Island, the Indian *Aquidneck* ('Isle of Peace'), which was bought from the Indians in 1639, is about 15 M. long and 3-4 M. wide, with a population of 22,560. Its present name, which is supposed to have been given to it from a fancied resemblance to the Isle of Rhodes, has been extended to the whole state, far the larger portion of which is on the mainland. † It is fertile and well farmed, and much of its surface is picturesque. The island is connected with the mainland by a railway-bridge and an ordinary road-bridge.

Leaving Newport, the FALL RIVER STEAMER steers between *Prudence Island* (p. 71) and Rhode Island, and enters *Mount Hope Bay*, opening off the N.E. corner of Narragansett Bay. On the peninsula to the left lies *Bristol*, connected by rail with Providence (comp. p. 65). In 1 hr. we reach **Fall River** (*Wilbur House, Mellen Ho.*, $ 2-3), which lies to the right. The river to which it owes its name rises a little to the E. and falls about 140 ft. in $1/2$ M., affording admirable water-power to the mills which make the town one of the chief cotton-manufacturing places in New England. Total value of industrial products in 1890, $ 31,335,000 (four-fifths cotton goods). Pop. (1890) 74,398. Passengers for Boston here disembark and finish their journey by railway.

FROM FALL RIVER TO BOSTON, 51 M., railway in $1^{1}/_{3}$-$1^{3}/_{4}$ hr. — The train skirts the E. side of Mt. Hope Bay and then crosses it to (6 M.) *Somerset.* 13 M. *Taunton* (City Hotel), an industrial town with 25,448 inhab., is the junction of several local lines. 32 M. *Stoughton Junction* (see below); 40 M. *South Braintree*, junction of a line to Plymouth (see p. 86); 41 M. *Braintree;* 43 M. *Quincy*, a thriving suburban city (16,723 inhab.), famous as the home of the Adams and Quincy families. Beyond (45$1/2$ M.) *Atlantic* the train crosses the *Neponset River* and various arms of Boston Harbour, traverses *Dorchester* and *South Boston*, crosses the *Fort Point Channel*, and enters the Kneeland St. Station at (51 M.) *Boston* (see below). — Trains also run from Fall River to (54 M.) Boston viâ (20 M.) *Middleboro* and (27 M.) *Bridgewater* (p. 88), connecting with the above-mentioned line at *South Braintree.* — The express-trains running in connection with the steamers diverge from the above line at (32 M.) *Sotughton Junction*, join the Providence division at (37 M.) *Canton* (p. 65), and run into the Park Sq. Station (see below).

FROM FALL RIVER TO NEW BEDFORD, 14 M., railway in 35 min. *New Bedford*, see p. 89.

The PROVIDENCE STEAMER, on entering Narragansett Bay, steers to the left of *Beaver Tail Light* and *Conanicut Island* (see p. 71), rounds *Warwick Neck*, and proceeds through the beautiful *Narragansett Bay* to *Providence* (p. 64). From Providence to *Boston* by railway (45 M., in $1^{1}/_{4}$ hr.), see p. 65.

5. Boston.

Railway Stations. *Boston & Albany* (Pl. D, 4), Kneeland St.; *Old Colony* (Pl. D, 4), Kneeland St., close to the last; *Providence* or *Park Square Station* (Old Col. R. R.; Pl. C, 4, 5), at the head of Columbus Ave.; *New York & New England* (Pl. D, 3), Atlantic Ave., at the foot of Summer St.; *Boston & Maine, Western Division* (Pl. C, 2), Haymarket Sq.; *Boston & Maine, Southern Division* (Pl. B, 2), and *Boston & Maine, Eastern Division* (Pl. B, 2), Causeway St.; *Fitchburg*, Causeway St. (Pl. B, 2), adjoining the last; *Boston, Revere Beach, & Lynn* (Pl. D, 3), Atlantic Ave.

Hotels. *VENDOME (Pl. a; B, 5), cor. of Commonwealth Ave. and Dartmouth St., from $ 5; *BRUNSWICK (Pl. b; B, 5), cor. of Boylston and

---

† The full official title of the state, however, is *Rhode Island and Providence Plantations.*

Clarendon Sts., from $ 5; *VICTORIA (Pl. c; B, 5), at the cor. of Dartmouth and Newbury Sts., R. from $ 2, these three in the pleasantest part of the city; *PARKER HOUSE (Pl. d; C, 3), School St., R. from $ 1$^1/_2$; *YOUNG'S (Pl. e; C, 3), Court St., near the head of State St., R. from $ 1$^1/_2$; ADAMS HOUSE (Pl. f; C, 4), 553 Washington St., R. from $ 1; TREMONT (Pl. g; C, 3), cor. of Beacon and Tremont Sts., $ 4, R. from $ 1; *UNITED STATES (Pl. h; D, 4), near the Albany and Old Colony Stations, from $ 2$^1/_2$, R. from $ 1; THORN-DIKE (Pl. i; C, 4), Boylston St., opposite the Public Garden, R. from $ 1; COPLEY SQUARE HOTEL (Pl. k; B, 5), $ 4-5, R. from $ 1$^1/_2$; REVERE HOUSE (Pl. l; C, 3), Bowdoin Sq.; BELLEVUE (Pl. m; C, 3), Beacon St., R. from $ 1; AMERICAN HOUSE (Pl. n; C, 3), Hanover Sq., $ 2$^1/_2$, R. from $ 1; QUINCY HOUSE (Pl. o; C, 3), Brattle Sq., $ 3-5; LANGHAM (Pl. p; C, 7), 1679 Wash-ington St., at the S. End, R. from $ 1; REYNOLDS (Pl. 4), 623 Wash-ington St, R. from $ 1; GRAND HOTEL (Pl. q; B, 6), 417 Columbus Ave., $ 3, R. from $ 1; BOSTON TAVERN (Pl. r; C, 3), R. from $ 1, for men. — *Boarding Houses* are numerous and comfortable, especially on Beacon Hill (Pinckney St., Mt. Vernon St., etc.) and in Columbus Ave. and other streets at the S. End; rates from $ 8 a week. *Furnished Apartments* are also easily obtained, from $ 4 a week.

Restaurants. At the *Parker House, *Young's,* the *Adams House,* the *Thorndike,* the *Victoria,* the *United States* (meals 75 c.), the *Reynolds,* and most of the other hotels mentioned above; *Ober,* Winter Place, off Winter St., good cuisine (men only); *Vercelli,* 200 Boylston St., opposite the Public Garden, D. $ 1, luncheon 75 c., incl. wine; *Weber, Dooling,* Temple Place; *Copeland,* 128 Tremont St.; *Mieusset Frères,* Van Rensselaer Place, off Tre-mont St., table d'hôte 60 c.; *Marliave,* Bosworth St., table d'hôte with wine 75 c.; *The Moulton,* 24 Summer St.; *McDonald,* 132 Tremont St. (fre-quented by ladies); *Boston Tavern* (see above), *Park's Chop House,* Bos-worth St. (musty ale, broiled live lobster, game, etc.), these two for men; *Marston's,* 23 Brattle St.; *Thompson's Spa, The Silver Grill*(luncheon counters), Washington St. (Nos. 219, 263); restaurants at the *Providence* (upstairs room) and other railway-stations. — *Huyler's,* 146 Tremont St., for ices, etc.

Steamers ply from Boston to *Liverpool* (Cunard Co., wharf at E. Boston, Pl. E, 1; every Sat.), *New York, Philadelphia, Baltimore, Savannah, Portland, Halifax, Bangor, Mt. Desert, Provincetown, Plymouth, Isles of Shoals, Nahant* (from Battery Wharf), *Revere Beach, Gloucester,* etc. (wharves on the W. side of the harbour). Steamers also run from Rowe's Wharf (Pl. D, 2) to *Nantasket Beach, Hull, Hingham,* and other points in Boston Harbour. — **Ferries** ply to *Chelsea* (5 c.) and *East Boston* (1 c.; see Map).

Tramways (electric and horse) traverse all the principal streets and run to the various suburbs (fare 5 c., transfers 8 c.). The system is an excellent one as far as outlying points are concerned, but the extraordinary congestion of the main business-streets of Boston makes the electric tram-way somewhat of an absurdity in the centre of the city. The electric cars stop only at points indicated by a white band on the posts. — **Carriages.** Per drive within the city proper, each pers., *Hacks* 50 c., *Herdics* and other *Cabs* 25 c.; from points S. of Dover St. or W. of Berkeley St. to points N. of State, Court, and Cambridge St., 1 pers. $ 1, each pers. addit. 50 c. (herdics 35 c., 25 c.); longer distances in proportion. Double fares from midnight till 6 a.m. Ordinary luggage free. Fare per hour $ 1-1$^1/_2$, with two horses $ 1$^1/_2$-2$^1/_2$.

Places of Amusement. *Tremont Theatre* (Pl. C, 4); *Boston Theatre* (Pl. C, 4), the largest in New England; *Boston Museum* (Pl. C, 4), including the oldest theatre in the city (good stock-company) and a museum of relics (adm. 25 c.); *Globe Theatre* (Pl. C, 4); *Hollis Street Theatre* (Pl. C, 4); *Columbia Theatre* (Pl. 7; D, 5); *Park Theatre* (Pl. C, 4); *Grand Opera House* (Pl. 11; D, 5), Washington St.; *Gaiety & Bijou* (Pl. C, 4); *Bowdoin Square Theatre* (Pl. 3; C, 3); *Howard Athenaeum* (Pl. C, 3), *Arena* (Pl. C, 5), *Palace Theatre* (Pl. 16; C, 3), *Lyceum,* variety performances at low prices; *Turnhalle* (Pl. C, 5), 29 Middlesex St. (occasional performances in German); *Italian Theatre,* North St. — The celebrated *Boston Symphony Concerts* are held in the *Music Hall* (Pl. C, 3; Frid. afternoon and Sat. ev'g. in winter). Other good concerts are given in the same hall and in the *Tremont Theatre*, *Tremont Temple*, *Bumstead Hall*, and the *Mechanics'* *Hall* (Pl. B, 6; for large gatherings). Good *Smoking Concerts* are given at the Music Hall in summer. The *Cecilia*, *Philharmonic*, *Apollo*, and *Orpheus* are among the best of the musical societies. — The free lectures of the *Lowell Institute* (tickets on previous application) are delivered in winter in the *Institute of Technology* (p. 79). — *Art Exhibitions* are held regularly in the rooms of the *Boston Art Club* (Pl. B, 5), Dartmouth St. — Good *Flower Shows* are held in *Horticultural Hall* (Pl. C, 3). — The *Baseball Grounds* are in Walpole St., at the S. End. — A *Lawn Tennis Tournament* is held annually at the grounds of the *Longwood Club*. — *Horse Races* at *Beacon Park* and *Mystic Park*.

Clubs. *Somerset* (Pl. B, 4), 42 Beacon St.; *Algonquin* (Pl. A, B, 5), 217 Commonwealth Ave.; *St. Botolph* (Pl. B, 5), 2 Newbury St., with Sat. evening reunions in the style of the Century Club at New York (p. 18) and frequent art-exhibitions; *Union* (Pl. C, 3), Park St.; *Temple* (Pl. C, 3), 35 West St.; *Puritan* (Pl. 18; B, 4), cor. of Beacon and Spruce Sts.; *University Club* (Pl. 21; A, 5), Beacon St.; *Century*, 146 Boylston St.; *Elysium*, Huntington Ave. (Hebrew); *Suffolk*, 4¹/₂ Beacon St.; *Paint & Clay Club*, 419 Washington St.; *Tavern Club* (Pl. 20; C, 4), 4 Boylston Place; *Boston Athletic Association* (Pl. B, 5), Exeter St.; *New England Women's Club*, 5 Park St.; *Press Club*, 61 Court St.; *Women's Press Club*; *Appalachian Mt. Club*, Park St.; *Camera Club*, 50 Bromfield St.; *New Riding Club*, Parker St., near Back Bay Park; *Country Club*, Clyde Park, Brookline. — Among the numerous *Dining Clubs*, which are a characteristic Boston institution, are the *Saturday Club* and the *Papyrus*, besides several of a political, commercial, or professional complexion; while other good clubs, meeting periodically at the members' houses, are the *Wednesday Evening Club* (founded 1777), *Thursday Evening Club*, and the *Round Table* (sociological).

Post Office (Pl. C, 3), Devonshire St., open from 7.30 a.m. to 7.30 p.m., Sun. 9-10 a.m. (see p. 78). *Branch-Offices* at Copley Sq. (p. 79), at Washington St., cor. of Brookline St. (Pl. C, 6), etc.

British Consul, *Montague Yeats Brown*, 13 Exchange Place (Pl. C, 3).

Bibliography. For details see *Edwin M. Bacon's* 'Boston in Little' (25 c.) and 'Dictionary of Boston' (75 c., in cloth $ 1); also *Henry Cabot Lodge's* 'Boston' ('Historic Towns Series').

Boston, the capital of Massachusetts, the chief town of New England, and one of the oldest and most interesting cities in the United States, lies at the head of *Massachusetts Bay*, about 200 M. to the N.E. of New York. Boston proper occupies a peninsula between the Charles River and the arm of the bay known as *Boston Harbour* and was originally founded on three hills, *Beacon, Copp's*, and *Fort*, which, however, have been materially cut down. The city limits also include *East Boston*, on *Noddle's* or *Maverick Island*, on the other side of the harbour; *South Boston*, separated from the old city by an arm of the harbour; *Charlestown*, on the other side of the river; and the suburban districts of *Brighton* (W.), *Roxbury* (or *Boston Highlands*), *West Roxbury*, and *Dorchester* (S.). Boston is connected with the city of Cambridge (see p. 83) by several bridges across the Charles. The old town is cramped and irregular, and its streets are narrow and crooked; but the new parts, especially the district known as the *Back Bay* (see p. 82), formed by filling in the tidewater flats on the Charles, are laid out on a very handsome and spacious scale. The chief retail business-streets are *Washington Street* and *Tremont Street*, both of which, and especially the former, rank among the most crowded thoroughfares in Christendom. Among the finest residence streets are *Commonwealth Avenue* (p. 82), *Beacon Street* (p. 82), *Marlborough Street, Newbury Street,* and *Mt. Vernon Street.* A characteristic feature of the residence quarters is seen in the luxuriant vines of 'Boston ivy' *(Ampelopsis Veitchii),* which cover many of the buildings (especially beautiful in autumn). The population of Boston in 1890 was 448,477, including a large proportion of Irish Roman Catholics.

History. The Indian name of the peninsula on which Boston lies was *Shawmut* ('Sweet Waters'), and the early colonists called it *Trimountaine* or *Tremont.* The first English settler was a recluse Anglican clergyman, the *Rev. William Blaxton* or *Blackstone* (ca. 1623), but soon after the arrival of the Salem Colonists, who migrated to this peninsula in 163) (see p. 91), he transferred his rights to them (1634) for 30*l.* and moved into the wilderness (comp. p. 65). The new settlers named the place *Boston* in honour of the native city of some of their leaders, and Gov. Winthrop made it the capital of the colony. The little town increased with some rapidity and soon carried on a considerable sea-going trade (first wharf built in 1673). In the middle of the 18th cent. Boston was probably the largest and most important town in America, containing about 25,000 inhab., and outstripping New York and Philadelphia. The first American newspaper ('Boston News-Letter') was published here in 1704. Boston's share in the Revolution is well known. The 'Boston Massacre' (see p. 77) occurred on Mar. 5th, 1770, and the 'Boston Tea-Party' on Dec. 16th, 1773. During the war Boston was occupied by British troops, but on Mar. 4th, 1776, Washington crossed from Cambridge, took possession of *Dorchester Heights* (now a part of South Boston, p. 74), and compelled the evacuation of the city (Mar. 17th). Since the Revolution Boston's upward course has continued steadily, with a few interruptions, of which the embargo of 1807-15 was perhaps the most important. It received its city charter in 1822, having then a population of about 50,000. In 1840 this number had risen to 93,383, in 1860 to 177,840, and in 1880 to 362,839. In 1872 the chief business portion of the city was devastated by a fire, which destroyed property to the value of $ 70,000,000 (14,000,000*l.*). From 1830 to 1860 Boston was the headquarters of the Abolition Party, led by *William Lloyd Garrison* and *Wendell Phillips.*

It is of great interest to study a plan of Boston, showing the original area of the peninsula and the extent to which it has been increased by filling in the tidal flats all round it (see, e. g., *H. C. Lodge's* 'History of Boston'). This process has more than doubled the area of the peninsula (780 acres ; now about 1900 acres), while the total area now comprised within the municipal limits is nearly 24,000 acres (37 sq. M.). The hills have been partly levelled, and indeed the whole face of the ancient city has been entirely altered, with the exception of three old burial-grounds and a few buildings. The original peninsula was connected with the mainland on the S. by a narrow 'Neck', little wider than the present Washington St., which runs along it. Boston has often been described as the most English of American cities, and in many respects this is true, though it must not be understood to indicate a conscious or voluntary imitation of English standards. Mere wealth probably counts for less in Boston than in any other large American city. As a literary centre Boston was long supreme in the United States and still disputes the palm with New York. A list of its distinguished literary men would be endless; but it may not be invidious to mention *Hawthorne, Emerson, Longfellow, Holmes, Lowell, Everett, Agassiz, Whittier, Motley, Bancroft, Prescott, Parkman, Ticknor, Channing, Theodore Parker, Henry James, T. B. Aldrich,* and *Howells* among the names more or less closely associated with Boston. Among the most eminent of its sons in other spheres are *Benjamin Franklin* (born at No. 17 Milk St., the site of which is now covered by an office-building, with a bust of Franklin), *Daniel Webster* (138 Summer St.; in-

scription), and *Charles Sumner* (20 Hancock St.). *Paul Revere* lived at
No. 19 North Sq. (Pl. C, 2). *Prescott* wrote his 'Conquest of Peru' and
'Philip II' at No. 55 Beacon St., where he spent the last 14 years of his
life; and *George Ticknor* occupied part of the house at the corner of Park
St. and Beacon St. where *Lafayette* lodged in 1824. The *Atlantic Monthly*
is published at Boston (Houghton, Mifflin, & Co., 4 Park St.).

Commerce and **Industry.** Boston is, perhaps, the wealthiest city in
America in proportion to population. Its total valuation in 1892 was
$ 911,000,000 (188,200,000*l.*). Boston capital has been very largely in-
strumental in the development of the West. Its foreign commerce is very
extensive; the total value of its exports in 1891 was $ 81,439,568, of its im-
ports $ 70,659,669. Among the chief articles are grain, live-stock, fish, wool,
sugar, hides, chemicals, and coals. In the same year its harbour was entered and cleared by 4833 vessels (exclusive of coasters), of 2,525,700 tons
burden. Its manufactures are very varied, employing (1890) 95,000 hands
and producing goods to the value of $ 215,850,000. Among the staples
are leather, boots and shoes, hardware, machinery, and cotton. Boston
is the second wool market of the world (coming after London only), its
sales in 1891 amounting to 158,155,460 lbs.

***Boston Common** (Pl. B, C, 3, 4), a park of 48 acres in the heart
of the city, shaded by fine elms and other trees and crossed by many
pleasant walks, has been reserved for public use since 1634 and is
carefully guarded for this purpose in the charter of 1822. Perhaps
no other city-park in the world is more closely entwined with the
historic interests and warm affections of the surrounding population.

The *Soldiers' Monument*, on a hill near the centre of the Common,
was designed by Martin Milmore and erected in 1871-77. It stands near
the site of the *Old Elm*, which was older than the city and was blown
down in 1876. The adjoining sheet of water is known as the *Frog Pond*.
On the Mall abutting on Tremont St. is a monument in memory of
Crispus Attucks and others killed in the *Boston Massacre*. The 'Long Path'
(see 'The Autocrat of the Breakfast Table') extends from Joy St. (Pl. C, 3)
to Boylston St. (Pl. C, 4).

On the S. side of the Common is the *Central Burying Ground* (Pl. C, 4),
laid out in 1756 and containing the graves of Gilbert Stuart (1754-1828),
the portrait-painter, and Julien (d. 1805), the restaurateur (after whom
the well-known soup is named). — To the N. of the Common, adjoining
Tremont St., is the ***Old Granary Burial Ground** (Pl. C, 3), which contains
the graves of several early governors of Massachusetts, the parents of
Benj. Franklin, the victims of the Boston Massacre, *Samuel Adams* (1722-
1803), *John Hancock* (1737-93), *Paul Revere* (1735-1818), and numerous other
Boston worthies (permit at the City Hall).

On the S.W. side the Common is bounded by Charles St., on the other
side of which is the ***Public Garden** (Pl. B, 4), 24 acres in extent, the site
of which half-a-century ago was a tidal flat. The show of flowers here
in spring and summer is very fine. Among the monuments in the Public
Garden are an equestrian *Statue of Washington*, by Ball, statues of *Edward
Everett* (1794-1865; by Story), and *Sumner* (1811-74; by Ball), and a group
commemorating the *Discovery of Ether*, by J. Q. A. Ward. [Few either
of these or of the other statues in Boston do credit to its taste for art.]
Pleasure-boats ply on the artificial sheet of water in the centre. — At
the S.W. corner of the Public Garden stands the **Arlington Street Church,**
built in 1859 by the congregation of which *Dr. W. E. Channing* (p. 69) was
pastor from 1803 to 1842.

Near the N.W. angle of the Common, on *Beacon Hill*, stands
the ***State House** (Pl. C, 3), an imposing building by *Charles Bul-
finch*, surmounted by a huge gilded dome and preceded by a Corinthian portico. A large extension in the rear is now approaching

completion. On the terrace in front are statues of *Daniel Webster* (1782-1852) and *Horace Mann* (1796-1859).

Interior. We first enter the *Doric Hall*, containing a statue of Gov. Andrew (by Ball), busts of Lincoln, Sumner, and Henry Wilson, and a collection of flags carried by Massachusetts regiments in the Civil War. — The *Rotunda*, opening off the Doric Hall, contains a statue of Washington (by *Chantrey*) and facsimiles of the memorial stones of the Washington family at Brington, Northamptonshire. — The *House of Representatives*, reached by the staircase to the left, has a codfish hanging from the roof as an emblem of one of the former chief sources of the State's prosperity. — The *Senate Chamber*, on the other side, has portraits of early governors. — The *State Library* (70.000 vols.) is in the W. wing. — The *Dome* (open when the 'General Court', as the State Legislature is called, is not sitting) commands a very fine and extensive *View.

The new part of the State House will accommodate the House of Representatives, the Library, and the leading executive departments. The Senate is to be transferred to the present Hall of Representatives.

Opposite the State House the ***Shaw Monument,** by *St. Gaudens*, is to be erected in 1893 in honour of Col. Shaw and his regiment (the first coloured regiment raised in the Civil War).

In Beacon St., just below the State House, stood the old *Hancock Mansion* (site indicated by a tablet on the fence).

We now follow Beacon Street towards the N., passing (left), at the corner of Bowdoin St., the *Unitarian Building* (Pl. C, 3), the hedaquarters of the American Unitarian Association. To the right is the *Boston Athenaeum (Pl. C, 3), an institution founded in 1807 and now containing a library of 220,000 vols. (open to members olny). On the ground-floor are the rooms of the *American Academy of Arts and Sciences*. — In Somerset St., which diverges to the left, are the large **New County Court House** (Pl. C, 3); the general building of *Boston University* (Pl. C, 3), the various departments of which are attended by 900 students; and the *New England Historic-Genealogical Society*, with valuable collections of books and MSS. We, however, proceed to the right, through *School Street*, in which, to the left, at the corner of Tremont St., stands *King's Chapel* (Pl. C, 3), built in 1754 on the site of the first Episcopalian church of Boston. The adjoining burial-ground, the oldest in Boston, contains the graves of *Gov. Winthrop* (1588-1649) and other worthies. To the N. of the graveyard are the rooms of the *Massachusetts Historical Society*, with many interesting relics. In School St., to the left, is the **City Hall** (Pl. C, 3), behind which is the *Old Court House* (Pl. C, 3). In front of the City Hall are statues of *Franklin* (1706-1790), by Greenough, and *Josiah Quincy* (1772-1864; mayor for six years in succession), by Ball.

School St. ends at Washington Street (Pl. C, D 2-7), the most crowded thoroughfare in Boston, with many of the best retail-shops. To the left is the *Old Corner Book-Store*, a favourite haunt of literary men, past and present. Following Washington St. to the left, we soon reach, at the corner of State St., the ***Old State House** (Pl. C, 3), an unpretending edifice, dating from 1748 and restored as far as possible to its original appearance, even to the figures of the British lion and unicorn on the roof.

The 'Boston Massacre' (p. 75) was the result of an encounter between a British sentry here and the crowd. The old *Council Chamber* and *Hall of Representatives*, on the upper floor, contain an interesting collection of historical relics and paintings (9.30-5; free). On the top-floor is the Curtis Collection of Photographs of Ancient Boston Buildings. The main facts of the building's history are given in appropriate inscriptions.

Opposite are the tall *Sears* and *Ames Buildings.*

STATE STREET (Pl. C, D, 2, 3), the headquarters of financial life, leads hence to the N.E. to the **Custom House** (Pl. D, 2), a massive granite building in the shape of a Greek cross, surmounted by a dome. State St. ends at *Atlantic Ave.* and *Long Wharf* (Pl. D, 2).

Change Alley, diverging to the left from State St., leads to *****Faneuil Hall** (Pl. C, 2, 3; open 9-5), the 'cradle of American liberty', originally built and presented to the city in 1742, by Peter Faneuil, a Huguenot merchant, but rebuilt after a fire in 1761.

The Hall proper, on the upper floor, is 76 ft. square and has no seats. It is used for public meetings and was the scene of numerous important gatherings in Revolutionary, Abolition, and later times. The British officers used it as a theatre in 1775-76. It contains portraits of eminent Americans (copies).

Adjacent is *Quincy Market* (Pl. C, 2). — The new *Chamber of Commerce* (Pl. 5; D, 2, 3) stands at the corner of Atlantic Ave. and India Wharf.

Devonshire Street leads to the right (S.) from State St. to the **Government Building** (Pl. C, 3), a huge edifice by *Mullet*, in his usual Mansard-roof style, occupying the entire block between Milk St., Devonshire St., Water St., and Post Office Sq. The *Post Office* occupies the ground-floor, the basement, and part of the first floor, while the rest of the building is devoted to the *U. S. Sub-Treasury* (10-2) and the *U.S. Courts* (2nd floor). The allegorical groups above the main entrance are by *D. C. French* (p. lxxxvi).

The Post Office, though it itself escaped, adjoins the district destroyed by the fire of 1872 (p. 75) and now covered with substantial business-blocks. The financial quarter is crowded into the small territory bounded by *State, Washington, Milk,* and *Broad Sts.* (Pl. C, D, 3); the wool trade is centred in *Federal* and *High Sts.* (Pl. D, 3); the leather and boot and shoe trade spreads over *Summer, Bedford, Lincoln,* and *South Sts.* (Pl. C, D, 4), and also part of *Pearl St.* (Pl. D, 3) and *Atlantic Ave.* (Pl. D, 2, 3); while the whole sale drygoods business affects *Winthrop Sq.* and *Franklin, Chauncy, Kingston,* and *Bedford Sts.* (Pl. C, D, 3, 4). The large retail dry-goods stores of Boston rank with those of New York (p. 18). Among the most noted are *Jordan & Marsh* and *R. H. White* (Washington St.), *Hollander* (Boylston St.), *Houghton & Dutton* (Tremont St.), and *Hovey* (Summer St.).

We now follow *Milk Street* (Pl. C, 3), to the E., back to Washington St. At the corner stands, perhaps, the most sacred shrine in Boston, the *****Old South Meeting House** (Pl. C, 3), built in 1729 on the site of an earlier church of wood, which lay near Gov. Winthrop's house.

Benjamin Franklin was baptised in the original church in 1706, and here Judge Sewall made his confession of repentance for his share in the witchcraft delusion of 1692. Some of the most stirring meetings of the Revolutionary times were held here, and from its doors the disguised Bostonians who threw the tea into the harbour in 1773 (p. 75) started for their enterprise. The British turned it into a riding-school in 1775, but it was afterwards restored to its sacred uses. The annual Election

Sermon was delivered here, with few interruptions, from 1712 to 1872. It barely escaped the fire of 1872 and was afterwards used as a post-office. It now belongs to a patriotic society and contains an interesting collection of historical relics (9-6; adm. 25c.). Lectures on local history are delivered in the Old South in winter.

BOYLSTON STREET (Pl. A-C, 4-7), diverging from Washington St. to the right (W.), skirts the Common and Public Garden and leads to the *Back Bay* (p. 82). Facing the Common is the ***Public Library** (Pl. C, 4), which is the largest free public library in the world (ca. 600,000 vols.), circulating 1,812,106 books in 1891.

The Boston Public Library combines a great collection of books to be used only in the building itself, with a circulating library open freely to all citizens. Among its numerous and valuable special collections are the Ticknor Collection of Spanish and Portuguese Books, the Barton Library (with, perhaps, the finest existing collection of Shakspeariana, including both the early folios and the early quartos), the Bowditch Mathematical Library, the Theodore Parker Library, the Prince Library (MSS. and early New England books, including two copies of the Bay Psalm Book, p. 36, and two copies of Eliot's Indian Bible, 1663-85), the Franklin Collection, the collection of works on early American history (including a Latin copy of the letter of Columbus to the King and Queen of Spain in 1493), the John A. Lewis Library (books printed in Boston), and the Tosti Collection of Engravings. — For the new building, see p. 80.

Also to the left, at the end of Columbus Ave., a short distance from Boylston St., we see the tower of the handsome **Providence Station* (Pl. C, 4, 5). In front of this station is the *Emancipation Group*, by Ball. At the corner of Berkeley St., to the right, stands the **Museum of Natural History** (Pl. B, 5; 9-5, 25 c.; free on Wed. & Sat.), containing a library of 20,000 vols. and good zoological, ornithological, entomological, and mineralogical collections. Opposite is the *Young Men's Christian Association*. Adjacent is the ***Massachusetts Institute of Technology** (Pl. B, 5; President, *Gen. Francis A. Walker*), the leading institution of the kind on the W. side of the Atlantic (1000 students; fine apparatus and collections). — Opposite is the large *Brunswick Hotel* (p. 72).

Boylston St. now reaches ***COPLEY SQUARE** (Pl. B, 5), which offers perhaps the finest architectural group in Boston, including Trinity Church, the Museum of Fine Arts, the new Public Library, the Second Church (Unitarian), and the New Old South Church.

*Trinity Church (Pl. B, 5), on the N. side of the square, the masterpiece of *H. H. Richardson* and a typical example of 'Richardsonian' architecture, is deservedly regarded as one of the finest buildings in America. It was completed in 1877 at a cost of $800,000 (160,000*l.*). Its style may be described as a free treatment of the Romanesque of Central France (Auvergne).

The building is in the form of a Latin cross, surmounted by a massive central **Tower*, 210 ft. high. The completed design includes two towers on the W, façade, which have not yet been built. The interior is very elaborately decorated by La Farge. The **Stained-glass Windows include fine specimens of La Farge, Burne Jones and William Morris, Henry Holiday, and Clayton & Bell. It is interesting to compare the painted English windows with La Farge's work, in which only the faces and hands are painted, the rest being in coloured glass. Adjoining the chancel is **a** bust of *Dean Stanley* (1815-81). The adjacent *Chapel* is connected with the church by very effective open cloisters, in which is preserved the tracery from a window of the ancient church of St. Botolph, Boston, England. — The *Rev. Phillips Brooks* (d. 1893), late Bishop of Massachusetts, was rector of Trinity Church for 22 years.

The new *Public Library (Pl. B, 5), on the S. side of the square, designed by McKim, Mead, & White, is a dignified and imposing, simple and scholarly edifice, which forms a worthy mate to its vis-a-vis, Trinity Church. Its style is that of the Roman Renaissance. The exterior is practically completed, and the whole building will be ready for use in 1893 or 1894. It is 228 ft. long, 225 ft. wide, and 68 ft. high (to the cornice), and encloses an open court, 140 ft. long and 100 ft. wide.

EXTERIOR. Among the chief features of the exterior are the reliefs over the main entrance (arms of the Library, City, and State; by *Augustus St. Gaudens*), the medallions below the cornice representing the bookmarks of famous printers, and the inscribed names of eminent men. The platform in front of the entrance is to be embellished with two groups of statues by *A. St. Gaudens*.

The *INTERIOR is excellently arranged and equipped and affords accommodation for 2½ million volumes. The marble and mosaic decorations and mural paintings are very tasteful. The books are kept in huge stacks, whence they are expeditiously transferred to the delivery room by ingenious mechanical appliances. The principal room is the *Bates Hall* (so called in honour of an early benefactor of the library, a member of the firm of Baring Bros.), which is 217½ ft. long, 42½ ft. wide, and 50 ft. high; it is used as the general reading-room. The *Delivery Room*, the *Periodical Room*, the *Patent Department*, the *Lecture Room*, and the *Exhibition Hall* are also spacious apartments. The special collections mentioned at p. 79 are to be housed on the top floor. The fine marble *Staircase*, 20 ft. wide, is embellished by figures of lions, in Siena marble, by *Louis St. Gaudens*. A unique feature is the *Central Court*, with its turf, fountain, arcade, and open-air walk, where readers may establish themselves in hot weather.

The *Second Church* (Pl. B, 5), rebuilt on its present site on the N. side of Copley Sq. in 1873-74, was the church of the three Mathers (p. 82) and of Ralph Waldo Emerson (1829-32).

The *Museum of Fine Arts (Pl. B, 5), on the E. side of Copley Sq., a somewhat restless piece of architecture, of red brick, with terracotta details, contains some valuable collections (open daily 9-5, Mon. 12-5, Sun. 1-5; adm. 25 c., free on Sat. & Sun.; catalogue of sculptures 50 c., of paintings, etc., 25 c.).

The **Ground Floor** is mainly devoted to a large and excellent collection of *Casts*, chronologically arranged and surpassed in importance by those of Berlin and Strassburg only. — The two rooms to the right of the main staircase contain a *Collection of Egyptian Antiquities* (including many fine specimens from the Egypt Exploration Fund), while a room to the left contains *Greek and Graeco-Roman Vases and Glass*, *Terracottas*, a few *Bronzes*, *Reliefs from the Temple of Assos*, *Etruscan Sarcophagi*, *Cypriote Antiquities*, etc.

First Floor. The N. side contains the *Collection of Paintings*, most of which are on loan and frequently changed. — On the wall of the staircase is the Mosque of the Great Moguls at Delhi, by *Verestchagin*. — Turning to the right at the head of the main staircase, we enter the FIRST PICTURE GALLERY, which contains works of the Italian, French, and Spanish Schools, including specimens of *Palma Vecchio*, *Garofalo*, *Antonello da Messina*, *Pinturicchio*, *Guercino*, *Tintoretto*, *Watteau*, *Greuze*, *Boucher*, *Salvator*

Rosa, etc. The door to the right leads to the Print Rooms (see below); that in front to the —

ALLSTON ROOM (American and English Schools), which contains works by *Washington Allston*, *Gilbert Stuart*, *Copley*, *Trumbull*, *Benjamin West*, *Kneller, Reynolds, Lely,* etc. No.* 120 (unfinished) is one of the three portraits of Washington painted by Stuart from life. No. 121 (Martha Washington) and No. 122 (Washington at Dorchester Heights) are also by *Stuart.* There are many other interesting portraits.

DUTCH ROOM. Dutch, Flemish, and German Schools, including works by *Teniers, Maas, Rubens, Van Dyck, Matsys,* etc. — This room also contains a *Collection of Miniatures.*

The FOURTH and FIFTH PICTURE GALLERIES contain Modern Works, including specimens of *Corot, W. M. Hunt, Regnault, George Fuller, Elihu Vedder,* etc. We now reach the —

SOUTHERN CORRIDOR, which contains a few *Paintings, Illuminated MSS., Japanese Armour,* the fine *Fenollosa Collection of Japanese Paintings,* and the highly valuable *Morse Collection of Japanese Pottery.* [By far the larger part of the Japanese paintings, prints, and designs are stored away downstairs, where they are accessible to students.] — From the other end of the corridor we enter the —

JAPANESE ROOM, containing one of the finest collections in the world of *Japanese Bronzes, Enamels, Lacquer-Work, Weapons, Ivory and Wood Carvings, Gold and Silver Ornaments,* etc. — The right door leads to the —

COIN ROOM, which contains collections of *Coins, Electrotype Reproductions of Coins, Gold and Silver Ware, Watches, Rings, Fans,* etc. — The —

METAL ROOM contains *Italian Bronzes* (Renaissance), *Oriental Metal-Work, Electrotype Reproductions,* etc. — The —

POTTERY AND PORCELAIN ROOM contains extensive collections of *Majolica, Faience, Sèvres and English China, Indian and Mexican Pottery, German and Venetian Glass, Chinese and Japanese Porcelain, Enamels,* etc. — The first door to the right leads to the —

LAWRENCE ROOM, fitted up with carved oak in the style of the 16th cent. and containing some old cabinets. It is adjoined by the ROOM OF WOOD CARVING, ARMS, AND ARMOUR, from which we enter the —

TEXTILE GALLERY, containing Gobelins, Beauvais, and other tapestry, Italian embroideries, laces, etc. — We have now made the circuit of the building and regained the hall at the head of the staircase.

The three PRINT ROOMS (see above) contain varying selections of *Prints and Engravings,* a visitors' guide to which is hung on the walls. The Third Print Room is adjoined by the —

ROOM OF WATER-COLOURS AND DRAWINGS (communicating with the Fifth Picture Gallery (see above), among the contents of which are 21 drawings and water-colours by *J. F. Millet,* 27 water-colours by *Wm. Blake,* and a drawing by *Michael Angelo* (No. 480).

The **Second Floor** and the **Basement** are occupied by the *School of Art.* The fine *Art Library* is also on the basement.

The ***New Old South Church** (Pl. B, 5), so called as the successor of the Old South Church (p. 78), is a fine building in an Italian Gothic style, with a tower 248 ft. in height. It was built in 1874-75. The marbles and ornamental stone-work are fine.

Among other noteworthy buildings in this part of the city are the *Boston Art Club* (Pl. B, 5), at the corner of Newbury and Dartmouth St. (exhibitions, see p. 74); the *Hotel Vendome* (Pl. a, B 5; p. 72), at the corner of Dartmouth St. and Commonwealth Ave.; the *Boston Athletic Association* (Pl. B, 5; p. 74), Exeter St.; the *University Club* (Pl. A, 5), Beacon St.; the *Harvard Medical School* (p. 83), at the corner of Exeter and Boylston Sts.; the **First Baptist Church* (Pl. B, 5), at the corner of Clarendon St. and Commonwealth Ave, generally known as the *Brattle Square Church,* a fine building by *H. H. Richardson,* with a Florentine tower embellished with bas-reliefs and figures of angels; the **Central Congregational Church* (Pl. B 5), Berkeley St., a beautiful building; the **First Church (Unitarian;* Pl. 9, B, 4),

Berkeley St., cor. of Marlborough St.; *Emmanuel Church* (Pl. B, 5), Newbury St.; the *Normal Art School* (Pl. B, 5), at the corner of Newbury and Exeter Sts.; the *Horace Mann School for the Deaf*, Newbury St.; the *Spiritual Temple* (Pl. B, 5), at the corner of Newbury and Exeter Sts.; and the *Mt. Vernon Church*, at the corner of Beacon St. and West Chester Park (Pl. A, 6).

*Commonwealth Avenue (Pl. A, B, 4-6), which runs parallel with Boylston St., is one of the finest residence-streets in America, with its double row of trees and handsome houses. It is 240 ft. wide and is adorned with statues of *Alex. Hamilton* (Pl. B, 4, 1757-1804; by Rimmer), *John Glover* (Pl. B, 5; 1732-97; by Milmore), *William Lloyd Garrison* (Pl. B, 5; 1805-79; by Warner), and *Leif Ericson*, the leader of the Norsemen who are supposed to have landed at Point Allerton (p. 85) in the 11th cent. (Pl. A, 6; by Miss Whitney).

*Beacon Street (Pl. A-C, 3-6), beginning on Beacon Hill, skirting the W. side of the Common, and then running parallel with Commonwealth Ave., is the aristocratic street of Boston *par excellence.* Its back-windows command a fine view of the Charles River. No. 296 is the home of *Dr. Oliver Wendell Holmes.*

The **Back Bay** (Pl. A, B, 4-6), the fashionable W. end district traversed by the above-named streets, was at the beginning of the present century occupied by dreary mud-flats, salt-marshes, and water, and its reclamation was a work of immense toil and expense (comp. p. 74). The **Back Bay Park* (Pl. A, 7) has been skilfully laid out by Mr. F. L. Olmsted on the site of the unsightly fens which formerly lay here and forms the first link in the chain of parks and boulevards, of which Franklin Park is the chief ornament. — **Franklin Park* is 500 acres in extent and lies in W. Roxbury (reached by electric car). Its natural beauties have been skilfully taken advantage of by Mr. F. L. Olmsted, and many of its drives and walks are very beautiful (park-carriages 25 c. each).

The **North End** (Pl. B, C, 1-2) of Boston, embracing the site of *Copp's Hill* (p. 74), now one of the poorer districts and occupied mainly by foreigners, contains some points of considerable historical interest. The **Copp's Hill Burial Ground** (Pl. C, 2; key kept by sexton; see notice on gate), dating from 1660, contains the graves of Increase, Cotton, and Samuel Mather (1639-1723, 1663-1728, 1706-1785). Adjacent, in Salem St., is **Christ Church** (Pl. 6; C, 2), the oldest church now standing in the city (1723), on the steeple of which the signal-lanterns of Paul Revere were displayed on April 18th, 1775, to warn the country of the march of the British troops to Lexington and Concord (p. 112).

Boston has long been famous for its **Charitable Institutions.** The **Perkins Institute for the Blind*, in South Boston (p. 74), indissolubly associated with the names of Laura Bridgman and Helen Keller, is one of the best known of these and has a large library of raised-letter books (visitors admitted on Thurs. at 11 a.m.; 15 c.). Others are the *Massachusetts General Hospital* (Pl. B, 3); the *New England Women's Hospital* in Roxbury, entirely managed by women; the *Eye & Ear Infirmary* (Pl. B, 3); the *Old Ladies' Home* (Pl. B, 5); the *City Hospital* (Pl. D, 7); the *Children's Hospital;*

the *Carney Hospital*, in South Boston; and the *Homeopathic Hospital* (Pl. D, 7). The *Criminal* and *Reformatory Institutions* are mainly on the harbour islands (p. 85) or in S. Boston.

Among other points of interest in Boston proper are the **Cathedral of the Holy Cross** (R. C.; Pl. D, 6), a large edifice in Washington St. (365 ft. long), in front of which is a *Statue of Columbus*, erected in 1892; the *Church of the Immaculate Conception* (Pl. 13; D, 7), Harrison Ave. (good music); the *Church of the Advent* (Pl. 1; B, 4), Brimmer St. (high-church Epis.; good music); the *New England Conservatory of Music* (Pl. 8; C, 6), Franklin Sq. (1800 pupils); the *Boys' English High & Latin School* (Pl. 4; C, 6), between Montgomery St. and Warren Ave. (the oldest school in America, dating from 1635, and the largest building for public school purposes in the country); the *Girls' High & Latin School* (Pl. 10; C, 6), W. Newton St.; the *Youth's Companion Building* (Pl. C, 5), at the corner of Columbus Ave. and Berkeley St.; the *Pope Cycling Co.'s Building* (Pl. 10; C, 5), adjoining the last; the *Charles River Embankment* (Pl. A, B, 2, 3); and the *Marine Park* at South Boston, with two large piers, one of which leads to *Castle Island* (p. 85). *Liverpool Wharf* (Pl. D, 3), formerly Griffin's Wharf, was the scene of the Boston teaparty (p. 77). The statues not yet mentioned include those of *Samuel Adams* (p. 76), by Miss Whitney, in Adams Sq. (Pl. C, 3); *Gov. Winthrop* (p. 75), Scollay Sq. (Pl. C, 3), by Greenough; and small figures of *Columbus* and *Aristides* in Louisburg Sq. (Pl. B, 4).

The **Warren Museum of Natural History**, 92 Chestnut St. (Pl. B, 4), is of special interest to anatomists (adm. on application to Dr. Warren, 58 Beacon St., or Dr. Dwight, 235 Beacon St.). It contains the only perfect skeleton of the mastodon.

Cambridge (no good hotels), an academic city with 70,028 inhab., lies on the N. bank of the *Charles River*, opposite Boston, with which it is connected by several bridges traversed by electric and other tramways. Its interest centres in the fact that it is the seat of **Harvard University*, the oldest, richest, and most famous of American seats of learning.

Harvard College was founded in 1636, mainly with a legacy of 800*l.* bequeathed for the purpose by the *Rev. John Harvard*, a graduate of Emmanuel College, Cambridge. Its growth through public fostering and private endowment has been continuous; and it is now attended by about 2900 students, taught by 290 professors and instructors. The faculty of Arts and Sciences includes Harvard College proper, or the academic department (1500 students), the Lawrence Scientific School (science, mining, engineering), and the Graduate Department. The Professional Schools embrace divinity, law, medicine, dentistry, veterinary medicine, and agriculture. The list of distinguished alumni includes the names of John Adams (class of 1755), John Quincy Adams (1787), W. E. Channing (1798), Edward Everett (1811), W. H. Prescott (1814), George Bancroft (1817), R. W. Emerson (1821), O. W. Holmes (a native of Cambridge; 1829), Sumner (1830), Motley (1831), Lowell (a native of Cambridge; 1838), E. E. Hale (1839), and Thoreau (1837). Among its presidents and professors have been Josiah Quincy, Edward Everett, Jared Sparks, Asa Gray, Jeffries Wyman, Benj. Peirce, Agassiz, Longfellow, Holmes, and Lowell.

The main buildings of the University are grouped near the centre of old Cambridge, about 3½ M. from Boston, and enclose two spacious quadrangles, shaded by fine elms. They include *University Hall* (1815), with the college-offices; *Massachusetts Hall* (1720), the oldest college building now standing; *Harvard Hall* (1766); *Gore Hall* (1841), with the *University Library* (400,000 vols.; numerous interesting relics and autographs); the *Boylston Chemical Laboratory;* **Sever Hall* (1880), a good example of H. H. Richardson; *Appleton Chapel;* the tiny and outgrown *Holden Chapel* (1744); and several dormitory buildings (*Stoughton, Hollis, Matthews, Holworthy,* etc.). To the N., beyond Cambridge St., is the handsome **Memorial Hall*, by Van Brunt and Ware, erected in memory of the members of the University who fell in the Civil War. It includes a *Vestibule*, with tablets of marble bearing the names of the fallen; the *Sanders Theatre*, in which the graduation ceremonies are held, with a statue of *President Josiah Quincy* (1772-1863); and a large *Hall*, containing numerous interesting portraits, and used daily as a dining-hall by 1000 students. To the W. of the building is a *Statue of John Harvard* (1607-38), by D. C. French. The *University Museums (9-5), a little to the N. of the Memorial Hall, contain valuable collections of natural history (*Agassiz Museum*) and archæology (*Peabody Museum*). The collection of *Glass Flowers* in the former is of unique interest. Opposite is the *Divinity Hall*. The *Lawrence Scientific School*, the *Hemenway Gymnasium*, the *Jefferson Physical Laboratory*, *Hastings Hall* (the most elegant of the College dormitories), and the *Law School* (*Austin Hall*; by H. H. Richardson) all lie to the W. of Memorial Hall. The *Botanical Garden* and the *Observatory* are ³/₄ M. to the N.W. The buildings of the *Medical, Dental,* and *Veterinary Schools* are in Boston (comp. p. 81), and the *Bussey Institution* is at Jamaica Plain (p. 85). — The *Athletic Grounds* of Harvard include the *Jarvis* and *Holmes Fields* (10 acres), near the Museums, the latter with the fine *Carey Athletic Building;* the *Norton Field* (7 acres), behind the Divinity Hall; and the *Soldiers' Field* (20 acres), on the S. bank of the Charles. The *Boat Houses* lie on the N. bank of the Charles.

The **Common**, to the W. of the University buildings, contains a *Soldiers' Monument* and a *Statue of John Bridge* (1578-1665). Near its N.W. angle is the venerable *Washington Elm*, under which Washington assumed command of the American army on July 3rd, 1775. To the S. of the Elm is *Fay House*, the home of the so-called *Harvard Annex*, where about 300 young women receive instruction from Harvard professors and are granted testimonials certifying that they have successfully passed tests equivalent to those of the University. Adjacent is the *Shepeard Memorial Church*. To the W. of this is the *Episcopal Theological School*. — Opposite the S. end of the Common stand the *First Parish Church*, with a Gothic steeple, and *Christ Church*, built of materials brought from England and containing a fine set of chimes. Between them is an old burying-ground.

'Like Sentinel and Nun, they keep
'Their vigil on the green;
'One seems to guard, and one to weep
'The dead that lie between' (*O. W. Holmes*).

A little farther on, in Brattle St., facing towards the Charles River, is *Craigie House, built in 1759 by Col. Vassall and occupied by Washington in 1775-6, but winning its chief interest from the fact that it was the home of *Henry W. Longfellow* from 1837 till his death in 1882. It contains many interesting relics of the poet. In Elmwood Ave., which leads to the left from Brattle St. farther on, is *Elmwood*, the home of *James Russell Lowell* (1819-91). In Brattle St., near Elmwood, in the house of *Mr. W. W. Newell*, is a portrait of Paul III., believed to be by Titian.

Following Brattle St. for about 1 M. (horse-car), we reach the entrance to *Mt. Auburn Cemetery, which is very beautifully laid out and contains the graves of Longfellow, Lowell, Sumner, Everett, Channing, Motley, Agassiz, Prescott, Phillipo Brooks, and many other distinguished men. Fine view from the tower on the highest point.

Among the other important buildings of Cambridge are the *City Hall, Main St., designed by A. W. Longfellow; the *Public Library*, at the corner

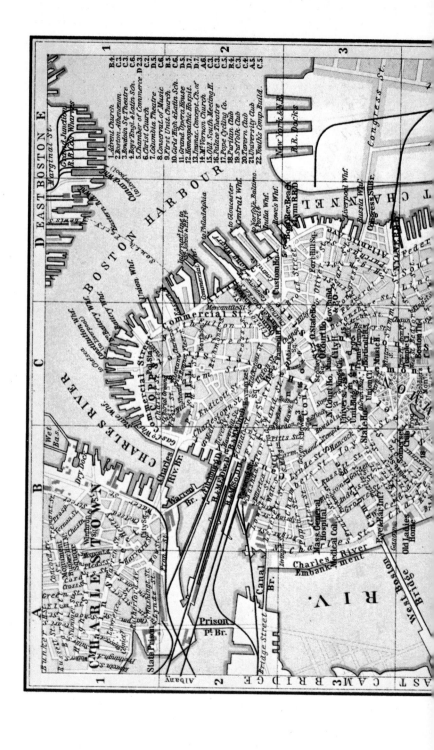

1. Advent Church. B.4.
2. Boston Athenæum. C.3.
3. Bowdoin Sq.Theatre. C.3.
4. Boys' Prof.& Latin Sch. C.6.
5. Chamber of Commerce. D.23.
6. Christ Church. C.2.
7. Columbia Theatre. D.5.
8. Conservat. of Music. D.5.
9. First Unit. Church. C.6.
10. Girls' High.& Latin Sch. C.6.
11. Grand Opera House. D.5.
12. Homœopathic Hospit. D.7.
13. Instruc. Concept. Ch. of. D.7.
14. M.Vernon Church. A.6.
15. Old South Meeting H. C.3.
16. Police Theatre. C.2.
17. Pope Cycling Co. R.4.
18. Purity Club. C.4.
19. Norfolk Club. C.4.
20. Tavern Club. A.5.
21. University Club. C.3.
22. Youth's Comp.Build. C.5.

E EAST BOSTON

BOSTON HARBOUR

CHARLES RIVER

C CHARLESTOWN

Prison
Pt. Br.

Charles River
Embankment

RIV.

CAMBRIDGE

BOSTON.

1 : 25,600

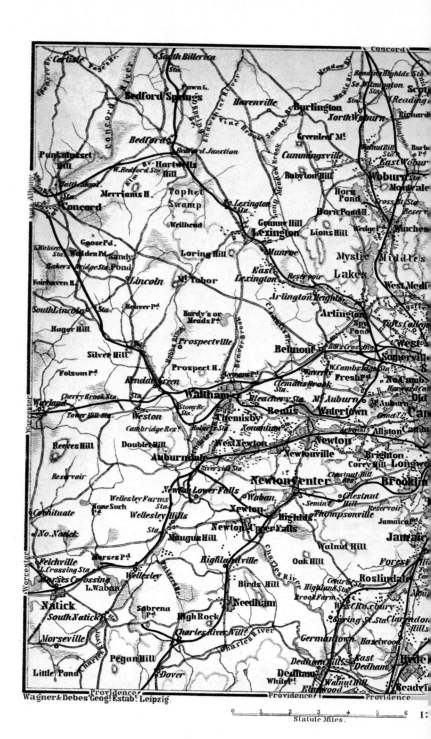

Wagner & Debes' Geog! Estab! Leipzig.

Statute Miles.

Pillings Pd.
Suntaug L.
Peabody
No. Salem
Salem Neck
Pt. Pickering Light
Eagle Id.
Lowell St. Sta.
Lynnfield
Cedar Pd.
Salem
Salem
Sta.
Codson
Hill
Lowells Id.
inapowill L.
Montrose
So. Lynnfield
Needhams Corner
So. Peabody
So. Salem
Salem
Harbour
Marblehead
Wakefield
North Saugus
Mt. Spickett
Spring Pd.
Devereaux Sta.
Marblehead
Neck
Nashua
Wakefield
Junct.
Saugus River
Wyoma L.
Wyoma
Clifton Sta.
Greenwood
Birch Pd.
Wenuchust.
Beach Bluff Sta.
Phillip's Beach Sta.
Tinker's Id.
ham
Prankers Pd.
Breed's Pd.
East Lynn
Phillip's Beach
Highds.
Saugus
Lynn
Ram Id.
Crystal L.
Swampscott
Melrose
East Saugus
Lynn
Nahant Bay
Fells Sta.
Franklin Pk.
Cliftondale
Harbour
Lynn Beach
Maplewood
Linden
Point of Pines
Little Nahant
Malden
Egg Rock Light
Revere Beach Sta.
Nahant
Everett
Mt. Washington
Revere Beach
Bass Pt.
East Point
Bass Pt.
Shag Rocks
Crescent Beach
Sta.
MASSACHUSETTS
Chelsea
Belle Isle
Beachmont
Mystic River
Breeds Hill
Grover's Cliff
East
Boston
Winthrop
Maverick
Winthrop Beach
Sta.
Snake Id.
Winthrop Head
The Graves
Boston
Apple Id.
Point Shirley
BAY
Pt. Winthrop
Governor's Id.
Deer Island
Green Id.
Harbour
Great Calf
Id.
Outer Brewster
So. Boston
Ft. Independence
President Roads
Middle Brewster
City Point
Castle Id.
Lovell's Id.
Great Brewster
Washington Vill.
Long Island Light
Little Brewster
Old Harbour
Spectacle Id.
Gallop's
Id.
Boston Light
Long
Thompson's Id.
Island
Pt. Warren
George's Id.
Nantasket Roads
Dorchester B.
Moon Id.
Rainsford Id.
Windmill Pt.
Pt. Allerton
Commercial Pt.
Hog
Id.
Harding's Ledge
Squantum
Peddock's
Id.
Hull
Sagamore Head
Neponset
Quincy Bay
Strawberry Hill
No. Quincy
Prince's Id.
Bumkin Id.
Atlantic Sta.
Nut Id.
Sheep Id.
Little Black Rock
Lower Mills
Half Moon
Id.
Hough's Neck
Grape Id.
World's End
Black Rock
Wollaston
Heights
Downer Landg.
Nantasket
ton Mills
Vill.
Hingham
Harb.
Jerusalem
in Creek
Quincy Center
Germantown
Hingham
Old Colony Ho.
Sta.
No. Cohasset Sta.
amsville
W. Quincy
Quincy Pt.
No. Weymouth
W. Hingham

0 1 2 3 4 5 6 7 8 9 10
Kilomètres.

of Broadway and Irving St. ; and the *Manual Training School*, opposite the last — all three presented to the city by *Mr. F. H. Rindge*, a native of Cambridge. The *Epworth Methodist Church*, near Austin Hall, may also be noted. A visit should be paid to the *Riverside Press* (Houghton, Mifflin, & Co.), one of the finest publishing houses in America; it lies on the Charles River, 3/4 M. to the S.E. of Harvard College. At *Cambridgeport* are the famous telescope-makers, *Alvan Clark & Co.* The total value of the industrial products of Cambridge in 1890 was $ 36,000,000.

Charlestown (Pl. A, B, 1), on the right bank of the Charles River, a city of about 40,000 inhab., is now incorporated with Boston, with which it is connected by numerous railway and other bridges. The most prominent feature of Charlestown is the **Bunker Hill Monument** (Pl. A, 1), a granite obelisk 221 ft. high, erected in 1825-42 to commemorate the battle of *Bunker* or (more properly) *Breed's Hill* (June 17th, 1775). The *View from the top (adm. 20 c.) includes Boston, Boston Harbour, the Charles and Mystic Rivers, Cambridge, the Blue Hills etc. Adjacent is a bronze statue of *Col. Prescott*, by Story, and in the building at the base of the monument is one of *Gen. Warren* (killed in the battle). Charlestown also contains a *Navy Yard* (Pl. B, 1 ; 87 acres), a *Soldiers' Monument*, and a *Monument to John Harvard* (p. 83, in the old burial-ground).

The **Environs** of Boston are very attractive and afford opportunity for many pleasant excursions. First in point of interest is the beautiful *Harbour*, dotted with numerous islands. It is about 20 M. long from N. to S. and 8 M. wide from E. to W. and has a minimum depth of 23 ft. at low water. The Main Ship Channel, or entrance to the harbour, is between *Point Allerton* on the S. and the *Brewsters*, with *Boston Light*, on the N. Steamers ply regularly from *Rowe's*, *Forster's*, and *India Wharves* to the favourite resorts. Among these are Hull (*The Pemberton*, $ 4 ; *Oregon Ho.*), with the headquarters of the *Hull Yacht Club*; *Hingham* (see p. 86); and *Nantasket Beach* (*Rockland Ho.*, $ 4; *Atlantic House*, $ 3-4 1/2; *Nantasket Hotel*, from $ 2, frequented by day-trippers), a fine strip of beach, 5 M. in length, which offers a scene of great animation on Sundays and holidays. A narrow-gauge railway runs from Hull along Nantasket Beach to *Old Colony House* (see p. 86). Among the chief islands in the harbour are *Castle Island* (p. 82), with the old Fort Independence; *Governor's Island*, with Fort Winthrop; *Deer Island*, with the House of Industry; *Long Island*, with the City Poorhouses; and *George's Island*, with the strong Fort Warren. The lights and beacons include *Deer Island Light*, *Long Island Light*, *Nix's Mate*, *Bug Light*, and *Boston Light*, at the entrance to the Harbour.

Steamers also ply regularly in summer to *Nahant* (p. 90), while excursion-trips are made to the *North Shore* (p. 92), *Provincetown* (p. 88), *Plymouth* (p. 86), and other points in *Massachusetts Bay*.

The most beautiful of the suburban neighbours of Boston is *Brookline*, which lies to the S.W. of the city and contains many very handsome residences embowered in trees. It is connected with Boston by railway and electric tramway. Near Brookline is the large *Chestnut Hill Reservoir*, the drive round which is a favorite one from Boston. To the S. of Brookline lies *Jamaica Plain*, with *Jamaica Pond* and the *Arnold Arboretum*, one of the finest institutions of the kind in the world. A little farther to the S. is the pretty *Forest Hills Cemetery*, which abuts on *Franklin Park* (see p. 82). All these places may be easily combined in one afternoon's drive and are accessible by electric car. The *Martin Luther Orphan Home*, in the district of *West Roxbury*, occupies the **Brook Farm**, where a small group of cultivated people, led by George Ripley, made their famous attempt to found a socialistic community (1841-47). Hawthorne, Margaret Fuller, and Channing were among those connected with this experiment

— **Chelsea,** to the N. of E. Boston, on the *Mystic River*, contains a Soldiers' Monument, a Soldiers' Home, a Marine Hospital, a Naval Hospital, and well-known Art-Tile Works. — Those who are fond of rowing and canoeing should go by the Boston & Albany R. R. to (11 M.) *Riverside* (boat-houses, etc.), situated on a lovely reach of the *Charles River*. On the river-bank, about 1 M. below, is a tower erected by Prof. Horsford on what he believed to be the site of the ancient *Norumbega*.

Other favourite resorts within easy reach of Boston are *Newton* (see p. 61); the *Blue* or *Milton Hills* (views), 8 M. to the S.; *Revere Beach* (p. 90); and the *Middlesex Fells* (p. 116). Longer excursions may be made to *Concord* and *Lexington* (p. 112), *Providence* (p. 61), *Newport* (p. 68), etc. From Boston to *New York*, see R. 4; to *Portland*, see R. 9; to the *White Mts.*, see p. 121; to *Nantucket and Martha's Vineyard*, see p. 87; to *Plymouth*, see R. 6; to *Cape Cod,* see R. 8; to *Campobello and Grand Manan*, see R. 13; to *Albany*, see R. 17; to *Canada*, see R. 15.

6. From Boston to Plymouth.

a. Viâ Abington.

37 M. OLD COLONY R. R. (*Kneeland St. Station*) in 1½-1¾ hr. (fare 90 c.). From Boston to (11 M.) *South Braintree*, see p. 72. 15 M. *South Weymouth;* 19 M. *Abington.* From (21 M.) *Whitman* a branch-line runs to (7 M.) *Bridgewater* (p. 88). 30 M. *Plympton*, at the S. end of *Silver Lake;* 33 M. *Kingston.* The monument at Duxbury (see below) is now seen to the left, as the train skirts *Plymouth Bay.* 37 M. *Plymouth*, see below.

b. Viâ South Shore.

46 M. OLD COLONY R. R. (*Kneeland St. Station*) in 1¾ hr. (fare 90 c.). From Boston to (10 M.) *Braintree*, see p. 72. Our train turns to the left (E.). 12 M. *Weymouth*, — 17 M. *Hingham* (Cushing Ho., $ 2), a quaint village on Boston Harbour, settled in 1635, with the oldest occupied church in New England (1681). In the graveyard (*View) is the grave of *J. A. Andrew* (d. 1867), the famous 'War Governor' of Massachusetts, marked by a statue. — 18 M. *Old Colony House* is the junction of a branch-line to *Nantasket Beach* and *Hull* (see p. 85). — 22 M. *Cohasset* (Black Rock Ho.), a delight-ful shore-resort, with numerous fine villas lining the beautiful *Jerusalem Road.* — 27 M. *Scituate*, an old fishing village, frequented for sea-bathing. About 4 M. offshore is the *Minot's Ledge Lighthouse.* — 34 M. *Marshfield* was the home of *Daniel Webster*, where he died in 1852. — 38 M. *Duxbury* (Standish Ho., $ 2½) was the home of *John Alden* and *Miles Standish*, and a monument 110 ft. high, sur-mounted by a statue, has been erected near the site of the latter's house. — 42 M. *Kingston*, and thence to (46 M.) *Plymouth*, see above.

Plymouth (*Samoset Ho.*, $ 2½; *Plymouth Rock Ho.*, unpretend-ing, $ 2; *Hotel Pilgrim*, $ 2½-3, 3 M. to the S.E., reached by electric tramway), an industrial village and summer-resort with 7314 inhab., lies on the sheltered bay of the same name, opening off the W. side of the larger *Cape Cod Bay* (p. 89). It is of abiding interest as the landing-place of the Pilgrim Fathers (Dec. 20th, 1620) and the site of the first settlement in New England.

On leaving the railway-station we proceed to the W. to *Court St.,* which we follow to the left. At the corner of Chilton St., to the left, is ***Pilgrim Hall** (open daily; 25 c.), containing numerous interesting relics of the Pilgrims, paintings of their embarkation and landing, old portraits, etc. — Farther on, to the right, at the corner of Russell St., is the *Court House.* North St., to the left, leads to the ***Plymouth Rock,** on which the landing was made, a granite boulder, now enclosed by a railing and covered with a canopy. The retrocession of the sea has left the rock at some distance above the water. *Cole's Hill,* opposite the rock, was the burial-place of the early settlers (1620-21), and some human bones found here are now preserved in a chamber in the canopy over the Rock.

We now follow *Water Street* to *Leyden Street,* which we ascend to the right, passing (left) the site of the first house. On reaching *Town Square* we ascend by the path to the right to the ancient ***Burial Hill,** with the graves of many of the early settlers, including Gov. Bradford (d. 1667).

A fortified church was erected here in 1622. The *View embraces Plymouth Bay, with the Gurnet Lighthouse; Duxbury, with its monument (p. 85); Cape Cod; the Pilgrim Monument (see below); the Manomet Hills (to the S.), etc. — To the S. is *Watson's Hill,* where the Pilgrims made a treaty with Massasoit in 1621.

We may now descend on the N.W. side of Burial Hill and follow *Allerton Street* to the N. to (1/4 hr.) the ***National Monument to the Pilgrims,** consisting of a granite pedestal 45 ft. high, surmounted by a figure of Faith, 36 ft. high, and surrounded by seated figures, 20 ft. high, representing Law, Morality, Freedom, and Education. The monument was completed in 1888. It is about 1/4 M. from the railway-station, which we regain by following Cushman St. to the E.

The *Environs of Plymouth contain hundreds of small lakes and ponds, of which *Billington Sea* is the largest. Large quantities of the trailing arbutus or Mayflower (*Epigaea repens*) are found here in spring. — *Manomet Bluffs,* to the S.E. of Plymouth, are frequented in summer.

7. From Boston to Martha's Vineyard and Nantucket.

Old Colony Railroad to (72 M.) *Wood's Holl* in 2½ hrs.; Steamer thence to *Cottage City* in ½ hr. (through-fare $2.35, return-fare $3), to *Nantucket* in 3 hrs. (through-fare $3.35, return-fare $4).

From Boston to (55 M.) *Buzzard's Bay,* see R. 8. — The train here diverges to the right from the line to Provincetown and runs to the S. along the shore of *Buzzard's Bay.* 57 M. *Monument Beach;* 59 M. *Pocasset;* 68 M. *Falmouth* (Menauhant Hotel, $2½-3), the station for *Falmouth Heights* (Tower's Hotel, $3).

72 M. **Wood's Holl** (*Dexter Ho.,* $2) is a small maritime village with a Marine Biological Laboratory and a station of the U. S. Fish Commission. It is reached from New York viâ Fall River. Steamers ply hence at frequent intervals to (7 M.) *Cottage City,* on *Martha's Vineyard.*

Martha's Vineyard is an island off the S. coast of Massachusetts, 23 M. long and 10 M. across at its widest part. Its inhabitants, (4500) were formerly occupied in the whale-fisheries, but now owe most of their prosperity to the summer-visitors. The chief resort of the latter is **Cottage City** (*Naumkeag*, $ 2½-4; *Narragansett*, $ 2-4; *Pawnee*, $ 3; *Wesley*, $ 2½; *Highland Ho.*, $ 2-2½, etc.), pleasantly situated on the N.E. side of the island. At the large *Camp Meeting Grounds* 20,000 Methodists assemble every August. A narrow-gauge railway runs to the S. to *Edgartown* (Harbor View Hotel, $ 2½-3½) and (8 M.) *Katama* (Mattakeset Lodge); and there are also summer-settlements at *Vineyard Haven* (Tashmoo Ho., $ 2), with a fine harbour, and *West Chop* (The Cedars, $ 3). *Gay Head*, the W. extremity of the island, commands a fine view; the cliffs are 200 ft. high (lighthouse). Part of this end of the island is reserved for the remnant of the Indian inhabitants.

Steamers ply daily from Cottage City to *Nantucket* (see below) and *New Bedford* (p. 89) and weekly to *Portland* (p. 96) and *New York* (p. 6).

The sandy, treeless island of **Nantucket** lies 12-15 M. to the E. of Martha's Vineyard, but the steamboat course from Cottage City to the quaint town of **Nantucket** (*Nantucket*, $ 3-3½; *Ocean Ho.*, *Bay View*, $ 2½-3; *Springfield*, $ 2-2½; *Veranda*, $ 2½-3), on the N. side of the island, is about 30 M. Nantucket, like Martha's Vineyard, was once a great whaling-place, but now depends mainly on fishing, farming, and summer-visitors. Catching bluefish is one of the chief amusements of the last. A narrow-gauge railway runs to (2½ M.) **Surfside** (*Surf Side Ho.*, $ 4), where a splendid surf rolls in after a storm, and to (10 M.) **Siasconset** (pron. 'Sconset'; *Atlantic Ho.*, *Ocean View Ho.*, $ 3), at the E. end of the island. *Sankoty Head* (90 ft.), 1 M. to the N. of Siasconset, bears a lighthouse and affords a fine ocean-view. In 1890 the island contained 3268 inhabitants. Both Martha's Vineyard and Nantucket were settled in the 17th cent. and possess buildings and relics of considerable historical interest. Nantucket, in particular, is very quaint and picturesque.

8. From Boston to Provincetown.
Cape Cod.

120 M. OLD COLONY RAILROAD (*Kneeland St. Station*) in 4-4½ hrs. (fare $ 2.95, return-fare $ 4.80). — *Steamers* also ply daily to Provincetown in summer from *Battery Wharf* (50 M. in 4 hrs.; return-fare $ 1).

From Boston to (11 M.) *South Braintree*, see p. 72. 20 M. *Brockton*, an industrial city with 27,294 inhab.; 27 M. *Bridgewater*, a pleasant village, with 4249 inhab., a large State Normal School, foundries, and iron-works. — 35 M. *Middleborough*, a manufacturing town with 6065 inhab., is the junction of lines to *Fall River* and *Newport* (see p. 72), etc. — From (46 M.) *Tremont* a branch-line runs, viâ *Marion* and *Mattapoisett*, to (15 M.) *Fairhaven*, opposite *New Bedford*.

New Bedford (*Parker Ho.*, $ 2¹/₂-3¹/₂; *Bancroft Ho.*, $ 2), a pleasant little city at the mouth of the *Acushnet*, was formerly an important whaling port and still possesses a number of vessels engaged in this business. Its cotton manufactures were valued at $ 8,185,286 in 1890. Pop. (1890) 40,733. It contains many fine old mansions and other mementoes of its former prosperity. It is reached direct from Boston (56 M.) in 1¹/₂ hr.

Our train now runs to the E. 49 M. *Wareham.* 51 M. *Onset Junction*, for the line to (1¹/₂ M.) *Onset Bay*, a seaside-resort. 55 M. *Buzzard's Bay*, near which are the seaside homes of President Cleveland and Mr. Joseph Jefferson, is the junction of the line to *Wood's Holl* (see R. 7).

At (62 M.) *Sandwich* begins **Cape Cod**, which stretches hence towards the E. for 35 M. and then to the N. and N.W. for 30 M. more.

The Cape gradually tapers in width from 8 M. to about 1 M. and consists almost entirely of sand, with few rocks or large trees. It encloses *Cape Cod Bay* (comp. p. 86 and see Map). The inhabitants, genuine descendants of the Pilgrims, are still very quaint and primitive in many of their ways. They form excellent seamen. The *Cranberry Bogs* produce one of the most lucrative crops of the Cape, and the scene at the cranberry harvest (Sept.-Oct.) is not unlike hop-picking in England. Fast pickers can earn $ 4-5 a day at the rate of 10 c. per 'measure' of 6 quarts. Some use an ingenious picking-machine.

69 M. *West Barnstable* is the station for (7 M.) *Osterville*, a sea-bathing resort on the S. shore of the Cape. 73 M. *Barnstable.* 76 M. *Yarmouth*, junction of a short line to (3 M.) *Hyannis*. 85 M. *Harwich* is the junction of a branch-line to (7 M.) *Chatham*, whence stages run to *Hotel Chatham* ($ 3-5). The line now turns to the left (N.). 89 M. *Brewster;* 94 M. *Orleans;* 97 M. *Eastham;* 111 M. *Truro*, with a dangerous beach guarded by *Highland Light*.

120 M. **Provincetown** (*Gifford Ho.*, $ 2; *Central*, $ 1¹/₂-2) is a quaint old fishing-town (cod and mackerel) with 4642 inhab. and a fine land-locked harbour formed by the final crook of Cape Cod. The *Mayflower* anchored here on Nov. 11th, 1620. Good view from *High Pole Hill*. There is a lighthouse on *Race Point*.

9. From Boston to Portland.

a. By the Eastern Division of the Boston and Maine Railroad.

108 M. RAILWAY in 3¹/₂-5 hrs. (fares $ 2¹/₂-3). This line runs near the E. coast of Massachusetts, New Hampshire, and Maine, affording frequent views of the ocean (seats to the right). Beyond Portland it runs on to (244 M.) *Bangor* and (450 M.) *St. John* (Canada); comp. R. 10 a.

Leaving the station in Causeway St. (see p. 72), we cross the *Charles River*, with the Fitchburg and the Boston & Maine (W. Division) railways to the right and the Boston & Lowell line to the left. To the right lies *Charlestown*, with the Bunker Hill Monument (p. 85). At *Prison Point*, with the *State Prison* to the right and the *McLean Insane Asylum* to the left, we intersect the Fitchburg

R. R., and at (2 M.) *Somerville* we cross the Western Division of the B. & M. and a branch of the B. & L. Beyond Somerville the train crosses the *Mystic*. — From (5 M.) *Chelsea* (see p. 86) a tramway runs to *Revere Beach* (several hotels), a popular holiday resort of Boston's lower classes. It is also reached by the narrow-gauge *Boston, Revere Beach, and Lynn R. R.*, which runs along the beach to *Point of Pines* (Hotel) and (9¹/₂ M.) Lynn (see below). The train traverses salt-marshes, crosses *Chelsea Creek* and the *Saugus*, and reaches —

11 M. **Lynn** (*Sagamore, Kirtland*, $ 2¹/₂), an industrial city of 55,727 inhab., with a handsome *City Hall* and a *Soldiers' Monument*. It is one of the largest boot and shoe manufacturing towns in the world, producing 12-15 million pairs annually, valued at 25 million dollars. View from *High Rock*. Fine *Public Forest Park*.

Omnibuses run from Lynn to *Lynn Beach* (Red Rock Ho.) and (4 M.) **Nahant** (*Hood's Hotel*, from $ 3; *Hotel Nahant*, $ 2¹/₂-3), a curious rock-built promontory, with fine cliffs and beaches, connected with the mainland by a narrow neck of sand. Nahant contains the seaside homes of so many leading Bostonians as to have been called 'Cold Roast Boston'. Steamboat, see p. 85.

13 M. **Swampscott** (*Lincoln Ho., Ocean Ho.*, $ 3-4), a fashionable seaside-resort of the Bostonians, with charming combinations of rocky bluffs and sandy beaches. The main line station is about 1¹/₂ M. from the sea, and carriages from the hotels meet the chief trains.

A small branch-line diverging here runs along the beach to *Marblehead* (17 M. from Boston), passing *Phillips Beach*, *Beach Bluff* (Hotel Preston, $ 3¹/₂-4), *Clifton* (Clifton Ho., $ 3; Crowninshield, $ 2-2¹/₂), and *Devereux* (Devereux Mansion, $ 2¹/₂- 3), all frequented for sea-bathing.

Marblehead (Hotels at Clifton, Devereux, and Marblehead Neck), a seaside town with 8202 inhab., dates back to early in the 17th cent. and is one of the oldest and quaintest places in New England. It lies on a rocky peninsula and has a fine harbour. Its ancient days of maritime commerce are, however, long since gone, and its chief industry now is the making of shoes. Fishing is also carried on. Among the most noteworthy of the old colonial buildings is the *National Bank*, built as a mansion for Col. Lee in 1768, with materials brought from England. The *Old Fort*, to the S. of the town, commands an excellent view. *St. Michael's Church* dates from 1714. *Abbot's Hall*, with its lofty tower, contains the town-offices and a public library. A granite monument near the station commemorates the capture of a British ship in 1776 by a Marbleheader. Marblehead was the birthplace of *Elbridge Gerry* (of 'Gerrymander' fame; 1744-1814) and is the scene of *Whittier's* poem 'Skipper Ireson's Ride'. The famous encounter between the 'Chesapeake' and the 'Shannon' took place off the coast here, and most of the crew of the 'Constitution' were recruited in the town. See *Samuel Roads'* 'History of Marblehead' and *Bynner's* historical novel 'Agnes Surriage'.

Marblehead Neck (Nanepashemet House, $ 3-4), forming the outer arm of the harbour and connected with the mainland by a narrow causeway, is a popular bathing-place and the headquarters of the Eastern and Corinthian Yachting Clubs. The Marblehead course is one of the favourite yacht-racing resorts on the coast, and the little harbour is no stranger to such famous boats as the 'Volunteer', the 'Mayflower', and the 'Puritan'.

As we approach the next station the notorious *Witch Hill* (comp. p. 91) is seen to the left.

16 M. Salem (*Essex House*, $ 2), the mother-city of Massachusetts, is a quiet and ancient town with 30,800 inhab. and a good harbour flanked by two crumbling forts. Its former commerce with the East Indies has now given way to a small coasting-trade, and a few manufactures are also carried on.

Naumkeag, on the site of Salem, was first visited by Roger Conant, one of the Cape Ann immigrants, in 1626, and a permanent settlement was made here by Gov. Endicott two years later. Gov. Winthrop landed here in 1630, and for a time Salem was the capital of Massachusetts. In 1692 Salem was the scene of the extraordinary witchcraft delusion, of which mention is made below. The legislature of Massachusetts met at Salem in 1774 (the last time under the English Crown) and issued a call for a Continental Congress. Privateersmen from Salem were very active during the war. After the war Salem engaged in the East India trade, and many of its citizens attained great wealth and influence. Indeed it is said that about 1810 a Salem merchant was the largest ship-owner in the world. Among the famous natives of Salem are *Nathaniel Hawthorne* (1804-1864), who was Surveyor of the Port here from 1846 to 1850; *W. H. Prescott* (1796-1859), the historian; *Maria S. Cummins* (1827-66), author of 'The Lamplighter'; *Peirce* (1809-80), the mathematician; *Count Rumford* (1753-1814); and *W. W. Story*, the sculptor (b. 1819). Comp. *Osgood and Batchelder's* 'Historical Sketch of Salem' and *Hunt and Robinson's* 'Visitors' Guide' (1893).

Essex Institute, 132 Essex St., contains interesting collections of historical paintings, portraits, and relics (open 9-5); and Plummer Hall, next door, on the site of Prescott's birthplace, contains the *Salem Athenaeum Library*. Behind Plummer Hall is the *First Church*, the oldest Protestant church in America (1634; apply to the Secretary, Essex Institute). The Peabody Academy of Science, also in Essex St. (No. 161), contains ethnological and natural history collections and the *East India Marine Museum*.

At the head of *Derby Wharf*, at the S. end the city, is the old *Custom House* in which Hawthorne was employed for four years (see above) and the scene of the introduction to 'The Scarlet Letter'. The quaint gambrel-roofed house in which he was born is No. 21 Union St., a narrow side-street extending from Essex St. to Derby St. The *Turner House*, 34 Turner St., is pointed out sa the 'House of the Seven Gables'.

The *Roger Williams House*, 310 Essex St., in which Roger Williams resided in 1635-6, is said to have been the scene of the preliminary examinations of some of the witches in 1692. The *County Court House* contains original records of these trials. *Gallows* or *Witch Hill*, on which the witches were put to death, is 1 M. to the W. of the city (near the tramway to Peabody; see p. 92).

Salem Village, the actual scene of the outbreak of the witchcraft delusion of 1692, lies 5 M. to the W. of Salem, on the old Andover high-road. Twenty innocent persons were put to death through the denunciations of eight girls (varying in age from 11 to 20), who met in the house of Samuel Parris, the too credulous minister of the parish. The house has been pulled down, and its site is marked only by a slight depression in the soil. Other spots that became memorable during this Reign of Terror are still pointed out; and a good account of it will be found in books by *Upham* and *Nevins* (1893). They all lie in the township of Danvers. The farm-house in which *Gen. Putnam* was born stands about 1 M.

beyond Salem Village, at the intersection of the Andover and Newburyport roads.

About 2 M. to the N. of Salem (railway) is **Peabody,** the birthplace of
the philanthropist George Peabody (1795-1869). The *Peabody Institute,* which
he founded and endowed, contains the jewelled portrait of Queen Victoria
given by her to Mr. Peabody. He is buried in *Harmony Grove Cemetery,*
a little to the W. A tramway-trip may also be taken to (20 min.) *The
Willows,* a picnic resort overlooking the North Shore and the outer harbour.

A charming *DRIVE may be taken from Salem along the 'North Shore'
to (2 M.) *Beverly,* (9 M.) *Manchester,* (12 M.) *Magnolia,* and (15 M.) *Gloucester*
(comp. below), traversing beautiful woods, passing numerous fine country-
houses, and affording views of the sea. The drive in the opposite direction
to (4 M.) *Swampscott* and (6 M.) *Lynn* is also attractive.

A short branch-line runs from Salem to (4 M.) *Marblehead* (p. 90), and
it is also the junction of lines to *Lawrence, Wakefield, Lowell,* etc.

On leaving Salem the train passes through a tunnel, 200 yds.
long, and crosses the North River.

18 M. **Beverly** (*Trafton Ho.*, $ 2), another ci - devant seaport,
now given over to the making of shoes, is the junction of a branch-
line to Gloucester and Rockport.

FROM BEVERLY TO GLOUCESTER AND ROCKPORT, 17 M., railway in
3/4-1 hr. This line follows the so-called **North Shore,** with its fine series
of beaches and the innumerable sea-side villas of well-to-do Bostonians,
to the extremity of *Cape Ann.* Among the numerous authors and artists
who have frequented this lovely bit of sea-coast are Longfellow, Holmes,
Whittier, Bayard Taylor, W. M. Hunt, J. Freeman Clarke, Susan Hale,
and James T. Fields. Passing *Montserrat, Pride's Crossing, Beverly Farms,*
and *West Manchester,* all with handsome country-houses, we reach (7 M.)
Manchester-by-the-Sea (*Masconomo,* $ 4-5; *Manchester Ho.,* $ 2½), described
by William Black as 'a small, scattered, picturesque-looking watering-
place, overlooking Massachusetts Bay, the Swiss-looking cottages of wood
dotted down everywhere on the high rocks above the strand'. One of its
special features is the *Singing Beach,* the white sand of which emits a musical sound when stirred. The *Coolidge Memorial Library* is interesting. —
From (9 M.) *Magnolia Station* omnibuses run to (2½ M.) **Magnolia** (*Magnolia,* $ 3-3½; *Ocean Side, Hesperus,* $ 3; *Oak Grove,* $ 2½), another pleasant
little watering-place on a rocky bluff, adjoined by the fine *Crescent Beach.*
The beautiful woods round Magnolia are among its special charms. A
little to the E. is the wonderful *Rafe's Chasm* (60 ft. deep and 6-10 ft. wide),
opposite which is the black reef of *Norman's Woe,* immortalized by Longfellow in 'The Wreck of the Hesperus'. A handful of Penobscot Indians
generally camp near Magnolia in summer and sell baskets, etc. The plants
which have given name to the place (in bloom in July) grow in a swamp
near the station.

13 M. **Gloucester** (*Pavilion,* $ 3; *Ocean,* $ 2), a quaint and foreign-
looking city with 24,651 inhab., is said to be the largest fishing-port in
the world, employing 5-6000 men in its fleets. Among the foreign vessels
which put into its safe and capacious harbour are several Sicilian barques,
bringing salt for the fish-curers. Gloucester is a great resort of artists, owing partly to the picturesqueness of the town itself and partly to
the fine scenery of *Cape Ann* (p. 93). The outer harbour is protected by
Eastern Point, with a lighthouse at its extremity. Here lies (2½ M.) *East
Gloucester* (Beachcroft; The Hawthorns, $ 2; Harbor View, $ 1½-2), reached
by electric tramway from the station, a pleasant little sea-bathing resort,
affording a striking *View, across the harbour, of many-spired Gloucester.
Elisabeth Stuart Phelps (Mrs. Ward) has her summer-home here (see her
'Old Maid's Paradise'). The *Bass Rocks* and *Good Harbor Beach* (Bass Rock
Ho., $ 3), lie a little to the N.E., facing the twin lighthouses on *Thatcher's
Island.* A favourite outing from Gloucester is that '*Round the Cape*' (14 M.),
and excursions may also be made to (3 M.) *Rafe's Chasm* (see above) and
to *Norman's Woe* (see above; by boat).

The railway ends at (17 M.) *Rockport*, where a huge breakwater is being constructed by the U. S. Government. Stages run hence, passing large granite quarries, to (2 M.) *Pigeon's Cove* (Pigeon Cove Ho., $ 2½), a bathing-resort near the end of *Cape Ann*. Omnibuses also run from Rockport to the (1½ M.) *Land's End* (Turk's Head, $ 3-4). To complete the round of the Cape we go on to *Lanesville, Bay View, Annisquam,* and *Riverdale,* and so back to Gloucester.

Returning to the mainland, we soon reach (23 M.) *Wenham,* with its lake known almost all over the world for its supplies of ice. The ice-houses are seen to the left. 28 M. *Ipswich* (Agawam Ho.), a quaint little town, with 4439 inhab. We cross the *Parker River*.

37 M. **Newburyport** (*Wolfe Tavern*, $ 2-2½), 'an ancient sea-blown city at the mouth of the *Merrimac*', with 13,947 inhab., like other old New England coast-towns, has turned from maritime commerce to manufactures (boots, cotton, silver, etc.). The *Public Library* (State St.) occupies an old colonial mansion in which Washington and Lafayette were entertained. The *Marine Museum,* in the same street, contains oversea curiosities. In High St. is a good *Statue of Washington,* by J. Q. A. Ward. George Whitefield (1714-1770), the famous preacher, is buried in the *Old South Church* (Federal St.), behind which is the house in which William Lloyd Garrison (1805-1879) was born. The old mansion of the eccentric *Lord Timothy Dexter* (High St.) is another of the town's lions.

OMNIBUSES and STEAMBOATS (on the Merrimac) ply daily from Newbury-port to (4 M.) **Salisbury Beach** (*Seaside Ho.*), which extends for 6 M. to the N. of the Merrimac. A tramway runs to (2½ M.) **Plum Island** (*Plum Island Ho.*, $ 2½-3), a long sand-dune running S. from the mouth of the Merrimac for 9-10 M. A steamboat also ascends the Merrimac to (11 M.) *Haverhill.* Other points of interest in the neighbourhood are (3½ M.) *Indian Hill Farm,* the home of Ben. Perley Poore (1820-87 ; relics); the *Devil's Den,* a cave 2 M. to the S.; the *Chain Bridge* and *Hawkswood,* on the Merrimac, 3 M. to the N.

A branch-railway from Newburyport runs to (5 M.) *Amesbury,* long the home of John G. Whittier (1807-92), who has celebrated this whole neigh-bourhood in his poems and ballads.

In leaving Newburyport we cross the *Merrimac* by a bridge 500 yds. long (view). Beyond *Salisbury* we traverse the *Folly Hill Woods* and enter *New Hampshire* ('Granite State'). Farther on we cross salt marshes. 47 M. *Hampton* (Whittier Ho., $ 2) is the station for **Hampton Beach** (*Boar's Head, $ 2-3; Hampton Beach Ho., $ 1½-2½), 3 M. to the S.E. (stages at the station), and from (49 M.) *North Hampton* stages run to (3½ M.) **Rye Beach** (*Farragut,* $ 3½-4; *Sea View,* $ 3½, etc.), the most frequented of the New Hampshire beaches. A charming shore-road runs N. from Rye Beach to (4 M.) *Straw's Point,* a station of the sub-marine cable to England. — 53 M. *Greenland* is the station for (2½ M.) the N. end of Rye Beach.

57 M. **Portsmouth** (*Rockingham,* $ 4; *Kearsarge,* $ 2-3   *Webster,* $ 1½), the only seaport of New Hampshire, is situated on a penin-sula 3 M. from the mouth of the *Piscataqua*. It is a quaint and quiet old town, with 9827 inhab. and pleasant tree-shaded streets. Many of the old colonial houses are interesting. The *Athenaeum* contains a

library and museum. On *Continental* or *Fernald's Island*, in the river, is the *Kittery U. S. Navy Yard* (ferry from Daniel St.). where the 'Kearsarge' was built and the old 'Constitution' is now laid up. T. B. Aldrich (b. 1836), James T. Fields (1817-81), and B. P. Shillaber ('Mrs. Partington'. b. 1814) were born at Portsmouth, In Vaughan St. (No. 32) is the house to which Daniel Webster brought his young bride in 1808.

Stages run daily to (2½ M.) *Newcastle* (*Wentworth Ho., $ 4½), a summer-resort on an island at the mouth of the harbour. Close by, at *Little Harbor*, is the interesting old mansion of the Wentworth family (1750).

FROM PORTSMOUTH TO THE ISLES OF SHOALS, 10 M., steamer several times daily in 1 hr. The *Isles of Shoals are nine rocky islands, 6-9 M. from shore, frequented as summer-resorts on account of their pure sea-air and immunity from mosquitoes. The chief are *Appledore* (Appledore Ho., $ 3½, 700 beds) and *Star Island* (Oceanic Ho., $3½, 700 beds). On *White Island*, to the S.W., is a powerful lighthouse. See *Celia Thaxter's* 'Among the Isles of Shoals' and *Lowell's* 'Appledore'.

FROM PORTSMOUTH TO YORK BEACH, 10 M., railway in ¾ hr. — York Beach (*Marshall*, $ 3-3½; *York Harbor Ho.*, $ 2-4, and *Harmon*, $ 2½-3, station York Harbor; *Bartlett*, *Garrison*, $ 2-2½, at the Long Sands, Long Beach station; *Ocean Ho.*, $ 2-3, *Atlantic*, $ 1½-2, etc., York Beach station) is another long stretch of sand, with numerous hotels and summer-cottages. At its N. end is *Cape Neddick*, with the rocky 'Nubble' (lighthouse) off its extremity; and 4½ M. farther to the N. is *Bald Head Cliff (85 ft. high). To the N. of this is *Ogonquit Beach* (Maxwell Ho., $ 2). Inland from York Beach rises (6 M.) *Mt. Agamenticus* (680 ft.; *View).

On leaving Portsmouth we cross the Piscataqua and enter *Maine*. At (67 M.) *Conway Junction* diverges a line to North Conway (p. 123). At (74 M.) *North Berwick* the Eastern Division of the Boston and Maine R. R. crosses the Western Division, and becomes in reality the W. or inland route. [The stations on both routes are the same, but as most of them lie near the sea they are better described in R. 9 b (see below). In fact one of the E. Division trains runs hence to Portland on the W. Division tracks.]

108 M. *Portland*, see p. 96.

b. By the Western Division of the Boston and Maine Railroad.

115 M. RAILWAY in 3-8 hrs. (fares as above).

The train starts from the *Haymarket Station* (p. 72) and follows practically the same course as the E. Division till beyond the *Mystic* (comp. p. 90). It then keeps due N., while the E. Division turns to the N.E. 97 M. *Melrose*, with a winter-resort named the *Langwood Hotel;* 10 M. *Wakefield*, the junction of a line to (30 M.) *Newburyport* (p. 93).

23 M. Andover (*Mansion Ho.*, *Elm Ho.*, 2½-3), an academic town with 6142 inhab., is best known through the *Andover Theological Seminary*, the chief educational institution in America of the Congregationalists (about 50 students). The *Phillips Academy*, the *Punchard High School*, and the *Abbott Female Seminary* also enjoy a considerable reputation. Mrs. Beecher Stowe moved to Andover while publishing 'Uncle Tom's Cabin' (comp. p. 97); and Mrs. Ward

(Eliz. Stuart Phelps) was born here and wrote 'The Gates Ajar' in the still-standing *Phelps House.* At *North Andover* (on the Peabody & Lawrence branch) are the large Stevens Cotton Mills. — 26 M. *South Lawrence* lies on the right bank of the *Merrimac,* opposite **Lawrence** (*Franklin Ho.,* $2-3; *Central Ho.* $2), one of the largest industrial cities of New England, with 44,654 inhabitants. Its numerous large and substantial *Cotton* and *Woollen Mills,* employing 13,000 hands and producing annually 160 million yds. of cloth, line both sides of the Merrimac and are driven by water-power supplied by the construction of a huge dam in 1845 (fall of 28 ft.; 10,000 horsepower; value of manufactures in 1890, $26,400,000).

Beyond South Lawrence we descend along the right bank of the Merrimac ‡ to (32³/₄ M.) *Bradford* (with an old and famous academy for girls) and (33¹/₄ M.) **Haverhill** (*Webster,* $2¹/₂), a shoe-manufacturing town with 27,412 inhab. (manufactures in 1890, $25,340,000). The poet Whittier was born in 1807 near *Lake Kenoza* (the scene of 'Snowbound'), 1 M. to the N.E. of Haverhill. A branch-line runs from Haverhill to (16 M.) *Newburyport* (p. 93).

We now enter *New Hampshire* (p. 92) and leave the Merrimac. 41 M. *Newton Junction,* for *Amesbury* (p. 93). 51 M. *Exeter* (Rail. Restaurant; pop. 4284), with another Phillips Academy, which has numbered among its pupils Daniel Webster, George Bancroft, and Edw. Everett. — 68 M. *Dover* (American Ho., $2¹/₂), a cotton and woollen manufacturing city, with 12,790 inhab., settled in 1623.

Dover is the junction of lines to (28 M.) *Alton Bay,* on Lake Winnepesaukee (p. 118), and to *Portsmouth* (p. 93).

Entering *Maine,* we cross the *Salmon Falls River* at (72 M.) *Salmon Falls,* with cotton-mills; and at (78 M.) *North Berwick* the W. Division intersects the E. Division (see p. 94). 85 M. *Wells Beach* (Bay View Ho., $1-2). To the right we have a view of the sea. From (90 M.) *Kennebunk* a line runs to (5 M.) **Kennebunkport** (*Ocean Bluffs Ho.,* $3-5; *Parker Ho.,* $2-3; *Glen Ho.,* $2-4), an old maritime village at the mouth of the *Kennebunk,* now in repute among summer visitors, who congregate chiefly on *Cape Arundel.*

99 M. *Biddeford* (Biddeford Ho., $2-2¹/₂) and (100 M.) *Saco* (Saco Ho., $2), two busy little towns (14,443 and 6075 inhab.), on opposite sides of the *Saco River,* which here falls 55 ft. and furnishes water-power for cotton-mills, saw-mills, and machine-shops.

Steamers descend the Saco to (8 M.) *Biddeford Pool* (Sea View Ho.) at its mouth, connecting at *Camp Ellis* with *Orchard Beach Railway* (see below).

104 M. **Old Orchard Beach** (*Old Orchard Ho.,* $4; *Ocean Ho., Fiske, Seashore,* etc., $2-3; *Belmont,* $1¹/₂-3), one of the best and most popular bathing-beaches in New England. The train runs close to the beach, with the large hotels to the left. The beach extends from the Saco to (10 M.) *Scarborough;* the beach-railway runs from *Camp Ellis* (see above) to *Old Orchard Beach Junction,* on the E. Division.

---

‡ Some trains cross the Merrimac and enter Lawrence proper.

From (109 M.) *Scarborough* omnibuses run to (3 M.) *Scarborough Beach* (Atlantic, Kirkwood, $ 2¹/₂-3), 2 M. to the S. of which is *Prout's Neck* (Southgate Ho.). — Farther on the train crosses the *Fore River* and enters the Union Station at —

116 M. **Portland.** — **Hotels.** FALMOUTH HOUSE, Middle St., in the centre of the town, $ 3-4; PREBLE HOUSE, Monument Sq., $ 3-3¹/₂; UNITED STATES, Monument Sq., $ 2-2¹/₂; CITY, $ 2-2¹/₂.

Steamboats run regularly from Portland to *Boston* (daily, in 8 hrs.; $ 1, stateroom $ 2), *New York* ($ 5, including stateroom), *Eastport* and *St. John*, *Mt. Desert* and *Machias* (see p. 101), and the *Kennebec River*. Small steamers ply frequently from the Custom - House Wharf to *Harpswell*, *Peak's Island*, *Cushing's Island*, and other points in *Casco Bay*. In winter Portland is the American port of the Allan Ocean Steamers.

Tramways run through the principal streets, and to the railway stations and suburbs.

Portland, the largest city in Maine, with (1890) 36,425 inhab., is finely situated on a hilly peninsula projecting into *Casco Bay*. Its harbour is deep and well protected, and its commerce with the West Indies and Great Britain is considerable. The number of trees in its streets have earned for it the name of 'Forest City'.

The town was originally founded in 1632 and was at first named *Machigonne* or *Casco* and afterwards *Falmouth*. It suffered severely at the hands of the French and the Indians and in 1775 it was almost entirely destroyed by the British. After the war it was rebuilt and in 1786 received the name of Portland. Among the distinguished natives of Portland are Longfellow (1807-82), N. P. Willis (1807-67), 'Fanny Fern' (Mrs. Parton; 1711-'2), Neal Dow (b. 1803), and Commodore Preble (1761-1807), of Tripolitan War fame.

Most of the principal buildings are in CONGRESS STREET, which runs the whole length of the peninsula, from the *Western Promenade* on *Bramhall's Hill* (175 ft.) to the *Eastern Promenade* on *Munjoy's Hill* (160 ft.). The *Observatory* (fee) on the latter affords an excellent *View of the city, the bay, the White Mts. (p. 121), and the Sandwich Mts. (panorama by Abner Lowell). Near the middle of Congress St. is the *City Hall*, a large light-coloured building, with a dome; and hard by, in Middle St., is the tasteful *Post Office*, with a Corinthian portico. A little to the E. of the City Hall, Congress St. passes *Lincoln Park* (right) and the *Roman Catholic Cathedral* (left), and a little farther on is the *Eastern Cemetery*, with the graves of Commodore Preble (see above) and Commanders Burrowes and Blythe of the 'Enterprise and 'Boxer' (p. 99). At the intersection of Congress St. and State St. (see below) is a good *Statue of Longfellow*, by Franklin Simmons. The *War Monument* in Monument Sq. is by the same artist.

Among the other chief buildings are the *Custom House*, near the Boston steamboat-wharf; the *Marine Hospital*; and the buildings of the *Natural History Society* and the *Maine Historical Society* and *Public Library*. *Deering's Oaks*, the city park, lie a little to the N. of the W. end of Congress St. — *State Street*, a broad and shady street, leading from the W. part of Congress St. to the harbour, contains some good specimens of old Colonial houses and two fine churches *(St. Luke's Cathedral* and *St. Dominic's).* — The house in which *Longfellow* was born stands at the corner of Fore St. and Hancock St., close to the Grand Trunk R. R. Station. The *Wadsworth Mansion*, in which he afterwards lived, is next door to the *Preble Hotel* (see p. 96).

The *Environs* of Portland are attractive. Pleasant drives may be taken to *Evergreen Cemetery* (2½ M.; tramway); to *Falmouth Foreside*, 6 M. to the N.; and to (3 M.) *Cape Cottage Hotel* ($ 3), the (8 M.) *Ocean Home* ($ 3), and (9 M.) the *Twin Lighthouses*, all on **Cape Elizabeth*, to the S.

*Casco Bay is crowded with pretty wooded islands (said to be 365 in all), many of which are favourite summer-resorts, especially (3 M.) *Cushing's Island* (*Ottawa House, $ 3-4, much frequented by Canadians; fine cliffs), *Peak's Island* (2½ M.; Oceanic Ho., Avenue Ho., $ 2-2½, and many others), *Long Island* (4 M.; Casco Bay Ho., Granite Spring Ho., $ 1½-3), and *Little Chebeaque* (6 M.; Waldo, $ 3).

10. From Portland to Mount Desert. Moosehead Lake.
a. Viâ Bangor.

186 M. MAINE CENTRAL RAILROAD to (178 M.) *Bar Harbor Ferry* in 5½-10 hrs.; steam-ferry thence to (8 M.) *Bar Harbor* in 40 min. (through-fare $ 5; parlor-car $ 1.25, sleeper $ 2). From Boston to *Bar Harbor* by this route in 9 hrs. (fare $ 6½, parlor-car $ 1½, sleeper $ 2).

Portland, see p. 96. The line runs to the N., affording a good retrospect of the city, and soon crosses the *Presumpscot*. 11 M. *Cumberland Junction* (p. 105). We cross the Grand Trunk Railway at (15 M.) *Yarmouth Junction* (comp. p. 108). — 29 M. **Brunswick** *(Tontine*, $ 2-2½; *Rail. Restaurant)*, a flourishing town of 6012 inhab., lies at the head of the tidal waters of the *Androscoggin*, which forms three small falls here. It is the seat of *Bowdoin College* (near the station), one of the leading institutions of learning in New England (2-300 students). The *Picture Gallery* of the college contains about 150 paintings, including some good portraits and works attributed to Hogarth, Brouwer, Berghem, Hondekoeter, Van Dyck (*Portrait), Rubens, and Teniers. 'Uncle Tom's Cabin' was written at Brunswick, while Mrs. Stowe's husband was a professor at Bowdoin (pron. 'Bowden') College (1851-2).

Brunswick is the junction of the line to *Bath* and *Rockland* (see R. 10 b). Lines also run hence to *Lewiston* (p. 105) and *Leeds Junction* (p. 106).

Beyond Brunswick we cross the Androscoggin and run to the N. along the *Kennebec* (to the right). 50 M. *Iceboro*, with the largest ice-houses in the world (on the river; 1,000,000 tons of ice are shipped from the Kennebec yearly to all parts of the world); 56 M. *Gardiner*, a city with 5491 inhab., engaged in wood-sawing in summer and ice-cutting in winter.

62 M. **Augusta** *(Augusta Ho., Cony Ho.,* $ 2½), the capital of Maine, with 10,527 inhab., lies on both sides of the Kennebec, about ½ M. below the huge *Kennebec Dam*, which affords ample water-power for its factories. The principal buildings are the *Post Office* and the solid granite **State House*, the dome of which commands a beautiful **View*. On the E. side of the river are the huge

State Insane Asylum and the *Kennebec Arsenal.* Augusta was the home of *Mr. J. G. Blaine* (d. 1893). Steamers ply from Augusta to Gardiner (p. 97), connecting with large boats for Portland, Boston, etc.

In leaving Augusta we cross the Kennebec, which now runs to our left. Beyond (80 M.) *Winslow* we cross it again, near its confluence with the *Sebasticook.* 81 M. *Waterville* (Rail. Restaurant), with 7107 inhab., large cotton-mills, and a Baptist college (Colby University), is the junction of the Lewiston division of the Maine Central R. R. (see p. 105) and of a branch-line to (18 M.) *Skowhegan* (5068 inhab.). On the Kennebec near Waterville are the *Taconic Falls.* — The train now crosses and leaves the Kennebec, and passes over the watershed between that river and the Penobscot. From (95 M.) *Burnham* a branch-line runs to (34 M.) *Belfast* (5294 inhab.), on Penobscot Bay; and from (102 M.) *Pittsfield* another runs to (8 M.) *Hartland.* To the right flows the *Sebasticook.* 109 M. *Newport* is the junction of a line running N. to *Dexter, Dover,* and *Moosehead Lake* (p. 99).

136 M. **Bangor** *(Bangor Ho., $2¹/₂; Penobscot Exchange, Bangor Exchange, $2; Rail. Restaurant),* the third city in Maine, with 19,103 inhab., is commandingly situated on the *Penobscot,* at the head of navigation and 60 M. from the ocean. Its chief industry is the sawing and shipment of lumber, about five million ft. of lumber being annually floated down to it from the vast forests of Northern Maine. Among its chief buildings are the *Custom House,* the *Theological Seminary,* and *Norombega Hall.*

From Bangor to St. John (in New Brunswick), 204 M., railway in 7-10 hrs. (from Boston to St. John, 450 M., in about 20 hrs). This line is a continuation of that described above from Portland to Bangor, and passes through a district of great importance to the sportsman. The following are the chief stations : — 13 M. *Oldtown,* the junction of the line to Moosehead Lake (see p. 99). The second railway in the United States, opened in 1836, ran from Oldtown to Bangor. — 59 M. *Mattawamkeag,* the junction of a line to Greenville (Moosehead Lake) and thence to Lake Megantic and Sherbrooke (comp. p. 99). — Beyond (114 M.) *Vanceboro* (Rail. Restaurant) the train crosses the *St. Croix,* enters *New Brunswick* (Canada), and passes on to the Canadian Pacific Railway. 120 M. *McAdam Junction,* for the line to (43 M.) *St. Andrews* (*Algonquin Hotel, $3-5). — 159 M. *Fredericton Junction,* for (22 M.) **Fredericton** *(Queen's, Barker, $2-2¹/₂; pop. 6502),* the capital of New Brunswick, finely situated on the *St. John River,* with an E. E. *Cathedral, a University, and handsome Parliament Buildings. From Fredericton we may descend the St. John River (fine scenery) by steamer to (84 M.) *St. John* (fare $1). — 204 M. **St. John** *(Dufferin, Royal, $3; Victoria, $2-2¹/₂; New Victoria, $2),* the commercial metropolis of New Brunswick (pop. 39,179) and sixth city of the Dominion of Canada, finely situated at the mouth of the St. John River. Among the most prominent buildings are the *Roman Catholic Cathedral, Trinity Church,* and the *Custom House.* The *Falls of the St. John,* formed where the river rushes through a narrow gut just above the bridges, are remarkable from the fact that they are 'reversible', the strong and high tide from the Bay of Fundy (which rises 23 ft.) having a fall of 15 ft. into the river at high water and the river having a like fall into the sea at low water. The falls are well seen from the *Suspension Bridge* (214 yds long and 70 ft. above high-water) Steamers ply from St. John to Eastport, Portland, Boston, etc.

From Bangor to Greenville (*Moosehead Lake*), 89 M., *Bangor & Pis-*

cataquis Railway in 3³/₄-8 hrs. This line diverges to the left from the Maine Central R. R. at (13 M.) *Oldtown* (see p. 98) and traverses a sparsely peopled district, with some picturesque scenery. Branch-lines diverge to various shooting and fishing resorts. 52 M. *Dover* is the junction of the line from Pittsfield and Dexter (see p. 98). 89 M. Greenville (*Moosehead Inn*, $2¹/₂; *Lake Ho.*, $2-2¹/₂), at the S. end of Moosehead Lake. [Another railway-route from Bangor to Greenville runs viâ *Newport* and joins the above route at *Dover.*]

*Moosehead Lake, the largest in Maine, with 400 miles of shore-line (35 M. long, 1-15 M. wide), lies about 1000 ft. above the sea and is drained by the Kennebec River. Its waters abound in trout and other fish, and the forests surrounding it are well stocked with moose, caribou, deer, and ruffled grouse. See *L. L. Hubbard's* 'Guide to Moosehead Lake'. Black flies and mosquitoes are very troublesome here in summer. — From Greenville a small steamer plies in summer to (17 M.) *Mt. Kineo* (1760 ft.; *View), which projects into the lake on the E. side, so as to narrow it down to a channel 1 M. across. The **Mt. Kineo Hotel* ($2-4¹/₂; 500 beds) is a favourite resort of anglers and their families. The steamer goes on from Mt. Kineo to (18 M.) the N. end of the lake, whence a portage of 2 M. leads to the upper waters of the *Penobscot River.* Enterprising travellers may descend this river and the lakes along it in birch-bark canoes (with guides) to *Mattawamkeag* (p. 98; 6-8 days). A good view is obtained to the E. of *Mt. Ktaadn* or *Katahdin* (5200 ft.) which is also visible from Moosehead Lake (to the N.E.) in clear weather. Greenville is also a station on the Canadian Pacific Railway from St. John, viâ *Mattawamkeag* (comp. p. 98), to *Lake Megantic* (84 M. from Greenville; frequented by sportsmen) and *Sherbrooke* (151 M. from Greenville; see p. 109). This line traverses an excellent sporting district.

The Bar Harbor branch crosses the *Penobscot* and runs from Bangor toward the S.E. The chief station is (166 M.) *Ellsworth*, a ship-building place with 4804 inhab., at the head of navigation of *Union River.* We pass *Green Lake* (well stocked with landlocked salmon and trout) on the left and another small lake on the right. At (172 M.) *Franklin Road* we have our first view of Mt. Desert (right). 177 M. *Mt. Desert* or *Bar Harbor Ferry* (Bluffs Hotel, $3-4). The train runs alongside the steamer, which crosses **Frenchman's Bay* to (186 M.) *Bar Harbor* (see p. 102), usually calling first at *Sorrento* (Sorrento Hotel, $3-5, with good café-restaurant), a pleasant resort on the mainland.

b. Via Rockland.

156 M. Maine Central Railroad to (86 M.) *Rockland* in 3¹/₂ hrs.; Steamer from Rockland to (70 M.) *Bar Harbor* in 5 hrs. (through-fare $4).

As far as (29 M.) *Brunswick* this route coincides with that above described. Here we diverge to the right and soon reach (38 M.) *Bath* (Sagadahoc Ho.), a small ship-building town with 8723 inhab., on the Kennebec, 12 M. from the sea.

Small steamers ply from Bath down the Kennebec to *Popham Beach* (Ocean Ho.; Eureka), *Boothbay* (Menawarmet, $3), *Squirrel Island* (Chase Ho., $2), and other points in the charming archipelago at the mouth of the river. A little to the E. of the estuary of the Kennebec is the historic peninsula of *Pemaquid*, off which the American brig 'Enterprise' captured the British brig 'Boxer' after a hard contest (Sept. 4th, 1814). Both commanders were killed (see p. 96).

Through-carriages for Rockland are carried across the river to (39 M.) *Woolwich.* 56 M. *Newcastle & Damariscotta.* To the left

7*

lies *Damariscotta Lake.* — 88 **M. Rockland** (*Thorndike Hotel*, $3; *Bay Point*, $2), a ship-building and lime-burning city, with 8174 inhab., is situated on *Owl's Head Bay*, an inlet of *Penobscot Bay*. Steamers ply hence to Boston, Portland, Bangor, Mt. Desert, and several of the islands in Penobscot Bay. We here leave the railway and embark on the Mt. Desert steamer.

About 8 M. to the N. (reached by stage or steamer) lies **Camden** (*Bay View*, from $2; *Mountain View*, $2), a favourite seashore-resort, backed by fine hills (Mt. Megunticook, etc.) rising to a height of 1300-1450 ft.

Two steamers, following somewhat different routes, ply at present from Rockland to Bar Harbor.

That of the *Boston & Bangor Steamship Co.* leaves Rockland in the morning, on the arrival of the steamer from Boston to Bangor, and steers to the E., between the islands of *North Haven* on the left and *Vinal Haven* and *Calderwood's Neck* on the right, passing through the so-called *Fox Island Thoroughfare*. It then crosses *Isle-au-Haut Bay*, with the *Isle au Haut* (so named from its height) lying at some distance to the right. We next enter the *Deer Island Thoroughfare*, threading our way amid the archipelago of small islands to the S. of Deer Isle and touching at *Green's Landing*, on *Deer Isle* itself (small steamers hence to Isle au Haut). Farther on we pass *Swan Island* and the *Placentia Isles* (both to the right), while the mountains of Mt. Desert come in sight ahead. Passing *Bar Harbor Head* (lighthouse), at the S. end of Mt. Desert (left), we soon turn to the N. (left) and steer between Mt. Desert and *Cranberry Island*. After calling at *South West Harbor* and *North East Harbor* (see p. 104), on opposite sides of the entrance to *Somes Sound* (p. 105), the steamer steers to the E., with *Greening's Island* and *Bear Island* (lighthouse) to the left and *Sutton Island* to the right. It then turns again to the N. and runs along the fine E. coast of Mt. Desert, passing *Otter Cliffs*, *Great Head* (p. 103), etc. *Egg Rock Lighthouse* lies at some distance to the right. About 5-6 hrs. after leaving Rockland we reach *Bar Harbor* (see p. 102), passing the pretty little *Porcupine Island*.

The steamer of the *Portland, Mt. Desert, & Machias Co.* leaves Rockland every Tues., Thurs., & Sat. at 6 a.m., or on arrival of the 7 p.m. train from Boston. It first steers to the N. through the beautiful archipelago of *Penobscot Bay*, leaving *North Haven* (see above) to the right, and passing the long *Islesborough* to the left. To the left, too, on the mainland, rise the *Camden Hills* (see above). About 2 hrs. after leaving Rockland we reach **Castine** (*Acadian Hotel*, $2¹⁄₂-3; *Castine*, $2), a pleasant little town on a peninsula projecting into the bay, now a favourite summer-resort. The steamer next retraces its course for a time, turns to the left (E.), and enters the narrow *Eggemoggin Reach*, between the mainland on the left and *Little Deer* and *Deer Islands* on the right. It touches here at *Sargentville* and *Sedgwick*, two resorts on the mainland, and at *Deer Isle*. Quitting this sound we steer first to the N.E. round *Naskeag*

Wagner & Debes Geogl Estabt Leipzig

Hadley Pt

Eastern Bay

Sand Pt

The Ovens

Frenchman

Narrows

Thomas I.

Mt Desert Narrows

Thomsons I.

Thomas North Eastern Cr.

Eden

B.

tness Pt

Hull Cove

Bay

Mt Desert

Negro Pt

Lake Wood

Burnt Porcupine I.

Sheep

Clark Cove

Town Hill

The Pond of Witch Hollow

Bar I.

Indian Pt

Bar Harbor

Round Porcupine I.

M O U N T

Interlaken

Duck Brook

BAR HARBOR

Cromwell's Harbor

Hill

761

McFarland Mt

Great Hill

Mt Kebo

405

Little Round Pd

Somesville

Eagle

925

The White Cap

Bear Br.

Oak Hill

Somes Harbor

Lake

Cr. Mt.
Chain

Mt Dry Mt

1268

Green

Newport Mt

Black Pd.

Somes Pond

Somes

Bar I.

1527

1060

Schooner Hd.

D E S E R T

Sargent Pt

1344

Turtle Lake

Anemone Cave

Somes Sound

Sargent Mt

325

The Bubbles
780

Long

Echo L.

Falls

Jordan Pond

Pemetic Mt
1262

Great Head

Beech Hill

Robinsons Mt
680

Browns Mt
660

Newport Cave

Carter's Nubble

Upper Hadlock Pond

Tibbets

The Triad
720

Thunder Cave

Lake

Beech Mt

Dog Mt
670

Lower Hadlock Pd

Jordan Mt

Otter Creek

Otter Cliffs

Western Mt
1073

I S L A N D

Valley Cove

Mt Asticou

The Cleft
610

Cove of Stone'd B.

West Peak

Flying Mt

Asticou

Long Pond

Seal Harbor

Seal Harbor

Fernald Pt

N.E. Brook

Brazy Cove

Manchest Pt

N.E. Harbor

Norwood Cove

Light

Bear I.

A T L A N T I C

S.W. Harbor

Greening I.

Clarke Pt

Sutton I.

South West Harbor

Mt Gilboa
160

Islesford

Burnt Mt
175

Sperling Pt

Cranberry or Little Cranberry

Great Harbor

Island

Bass Harbor

Great

Duck Cove

Sea Wall Pt

Cranberry

The Pool

Deadman

Baker Island

Mitchell C.

Island

Light

O C E A N

Lopaus Pt

Bass Harbor

Race Pt

Bass Harbor

Light

Head

The Nubble

Locust Reach

Point and then to the S.E. between some small islands, and join the steamer-route above described near the *Placentia Islands* (p. 100). We reach *Bar Harbor* (p. 102) about 5 hrs. after leaving Castine. Beyond Bar Harbor the steamer goes on to (4 hrs.) *Machias* (p. 102).

11. Mount Desert.

The island of ***Mount Desert**, the Indian *Pemetic*, lying just off the coast of Maine, in Frenchman's Bay, about 110 M. to the E. of Portland, is 14 M. long, 4-12 M. wide, and 100 sq. M. in area. In 1890 it contained 5337 inhab., but this number is immensely increased during summer. Within a moderate compass it contains a considerable variety of picturesque scenery, and its mountains, or rather hills, rising abruptly from the sea, have no parallel along the whole Atlantic coast of the United States and are much more imposing than their moderate elevation would suggest.

History. Mount Desert (accent on the first syllable) was first sighted in 1604, by Champlain, who gave it the name of '*Isle des Monts Déserts*'. In 1613 a small French colony, sent out by Mme. de Guerchville, to convert the Indians, planted the settlement of *St. Sauveur* on Somes Sound (see below), but it was soon destroyed by the English (see Parkman's 'Pioneers of France in the New World'). In 1688 Louis XIV. granted the island to M. de la Motte Cadillac; but it was not till 1786 that his granddaughter, Mme. de Gregoire, came over to claim the property, — a claim that was allowed by the State of Massachusetts in 1787. The island has, however, long since passed out of the possession of this family. It was about 1850 that Mt. Desert was first visited by artists and other summer-guests, but it was not till ten or fifteen years later that Bar Harbor (see p. 102) began to be what it now is — one of the most frequented and fashionable summer-resorts in the United States.

Physical Features. The mountains of Mt. Desert are mainly confined to the S. part of the island, where they run N. and S. in roughly parallel ridges, separated by narrow, trough-like valleys. The place of one of these valleys is taken by *Somes Sound*, which penetrates to the heart of the island. Thirteen main peaks are reckoned, the highest of which is Mt. Green (1527 ft.) in the S.E. corner. Numerous small mountain lakes and streams afford good fishing. Prof. Shaler finds evidence that even the highest summits of Mt. Desert were submerged beneath the sea for some time after the disappearance of the ice of the glacial epoch. — The *Climate* of Mt. Desert is usually cool and refreshing in summer, but fogs are rather frequent. The water is too cold for much bathing. There are several good roads and numerous well-marked footpaths (especially in the vicinity of Bar Harbor), but much might still be done, by a society formed for the purpose, to open up the interior of the island by the formation of paths, the erection of sign-posts, and the like. On the N. the island is connected with the mainland by a bridge.

Approaches. Most of the usual approaches to Mt. Desert are indicated in R. 10. We may also go from Boston to Bar Harbor by a steamer of the Boston & Bangor Steamship Co., which starts daily at 5 p.m. and connects at *Rockland* early next morning with the Bar Harbor boat of the same company (see p. 99); through-fare $4, stateroom $1-2). There is also a passenger steamer (Mallory Line) in the S.E. corner. from New York (Pier 20 or 21, East River; 36 hrs.; fare $9½, stateroom $1-5, D. $1, B. or S. 75 c.). — Comp. *Chisholm's* 'Mount Desert Guide' and *Sherman's* 'Bar Harbor Guide'.

As nine-tenths of the visitors to Mt. Desert land at Bar Harbor, it is convenient to begin with that watering-place.

Bar Harbor. — **Hotels.** Louisburg, Atlantic Ave., $ 4¹/₂-5; Malvern, Kebo St., $5; West End, West St., $3-4, a large house overlooking Frenchman's Bay; The Eden, cor. Main St. and Mt. Desert St., the largest, $ 2¹/₂-3; *St. Sauveur, Mt. Desert St., with views of mountains and bay, $ 3¹/₂; Lynam's, Belmont, Mt. Desert St., $2-3; Newport House, with its annex the Rockaway, nearest the steamer-wharf, $3; Hôtel des Isles, Marlborough, Main St., $2-2¹/₂; Porcupine, Main St., R. from $1. Decreased rates by the week or month, and before or after the height of the season. — *Boarding Houses,* $4-10 per week; *Furnished Lodgings* from $2-3 upwards. — *Sproul's Restaurant,* Main St.

Carriages. With one horse $1¹/₂ per hr., with two horses (1-6 pers.) $ 2¹/₂. To the different places of interest on the island by tariff. — The favourite carriage is the 'Buckboard', an excellent easy-riding conveyance for hilly roads, made here to hold 2-12 persons.

Steamers to *Rockland*, see p. 99; *Boston*, p. 97; *New York*, p. 101; *Machias*, p. 101; *Eastport*, p. 107; *Bar Harbor Ferry*, p. 99. Steamers also ply to *Bangor*, to *Sorrento* (p. 99) and *Sullivan*, to (4 M.) *Winter Harbor* (Hotel Cleaves, $ 2-3), on the other side of the bay, etc.

Boats for rowing, sailing (cat-boats), and fishing can be hired at moderate rates; also steam-launches. Row-boat 35c. per hr., with man 75c.; canoes, with Indians to paddle, 75 c. per hr. — *Yachts* frequent the harbour in large numbers, and regattas take place here in summer. — A visit of the *Atlantic Squadron* of the U. S. Navy is generally one of the events of the season at Bar Harbor, and is accompanied by a round of gaieties.

Kebo Valley Club, Eagle Lake Road; *Mount Desert Reading Room and Club*, Birch Point; both open to strangers on introduction by a member. — *Eden Swimming Pool Club*, Eden St. — *Indian Encampment*, at Eddy Brook (see below; curiosities for sale).

Comp. the current issue of the *Bar Harbor Record* (5c.).

Bar Harbor, a popular watering-place frequented by 10-20,000 visitors every summer and almost vying in importance with Newport (p. 68), lies on the E. coast of Mt. Desert, in *Frenchman's Bay,* opposite the pretty little *Porcupine Islands* and within 2 M. of the N.E. base of Green Mt. (p. 103). Its name is derived from the sandy bar, uncovered at low water, which connects it with *Bar* or *Rodick's Island.* The principal street is *Main Street* (running S. from the steamboat-wharf), from which West St., Cottage St., and Mt. Desert St. run to the W. A fine view is enjoyed, across the harbour, of the hills on the mainland, and numerous pleasant walks and drives may be made in the neighbourhood. A huge breakwater, now in construction, will render the harbour one of the best on this coast.

The following Walk of 4¹/₂ M. shows most of the points of interest in Bar Harbor itself. Starting at the steamboat-wharf and passing the *Rockaway Hotel*, we enter the *Shore Walk or Tow Path*, which, like the Cliff Path at Newport (p. 70), runs between the sea on one hand and beautiful villas and lawns on the other. The *Mt. Desert Club* (see above) stands at the beginning of the walk. A little farther on, off the shore, is the *Poised Rock*. The stone tower farther on is at the end of a bowling-alley belonging to the *Villa Edgemere*. From *Reef Point* a path runs to the E. towards Main St. Just before reaching *Wayman Lane*, also leading to Main St., we pass the handsome house of *Mr. J. M. Sears* of Boston. Adjacent is *Kenarden Lodge*. Beyond *Redwood*, the second house past the lane, we reach (³/₄ M.) the pretty little *Cromwell Harbor*, where we follow the path through the trees on its N. shore to (¹/₄ M.) Main St., which we reach near its S. end. Turning to the right, we follow Main St. to (10 min.) the *Grand Central Hotel*, where we turn to the left into *Mt. Desert St.* At the (10 min.) end of this street we descend *Eden St.* or the *Ellsworth Road* to the right to (5 min.) the bridge over the *Eddy Brook.* Continuing to follow this

road for about 1 M., with villas on both sides, the grounds on the right
extending down to the bay, we reach the *Duck Brook Bridge*, whence a
pleasant *Footpath ascends to the left along the brook and through the
trees to (2 M.) *Eagle Lake* (see below). The so-called *Bay Drive* begins at
the Duck Brook Bridge. In the meantime, however, we turn at the
bridge and retrace our steps along the Ellsworth Road to (1/2 M.) *Highbrooke
Road*, which diverges to the right and runs circuitously over the hill,
rejoining the Ellsworth Road (Eden St.) about 1/2 M. farther on. In Highbrooke road, to the left, is *Stanwood*, the summer-home of Mr. James
G. Blaine (d. 1893). We finally return (10 min.) to Main St. through *West
St.* or *Cottage St.*, which both run to the left from the Ellsworth Road.

EXCURSIONS. The ascent of *Green Mountain (1527 ft.) is, perhaps, the
best excursion to begin with. We may drive the whole way to the top
(4 M.) by a somewhat rough road (toll 25 c. for each horse and for each
passenger, 10 c. for each walker), diverging to the left from the road to
Eagle Lake (the prolongation of Mt. Desert St.) about 1¼ M. from the
village. Walkers may ascend by the same route (1½-2 hrs.), but will
do better to follow the *Path ascending the gorge between Green Mt. and
Newport Mt. (comp. Map; sign-posts). The *Green Mountain Railway* (cog-
wheel; disused at present) is reached by following the road to (2 M.) *Eagle
Lake* (2 M. long, 1/2 M. wide, and 275 ft. above the sea) and crossing the
lake. At the top is a small *Hotel* (meal $ 1). The *View includes Bar Har-
bor, Frenchman's Bay, almost the whole of Mt. Desert, the ocean, and
the coast of Maine. Many visitors stay overnight to see the sunrise. Good
walkers may descend along the ridges by compass (no path) to (1-2 hrs.)
the *Otter Creek Road* (see below) and return by it to Bar Harbor. — **Newport Mt.** (1060 ft.), to the E. of Green Mt. and close to the sea, is ascended
from the Schooner Head Road in 1 hr. The path (sign-post) leads through
trees, then over the ledges by cairns. *View less extensive but more
satisfactory than from Green Mt. The descent may be made viâ the *Beehive*. — **Mt. Kebo** (405 ft.), between Green Mt. and Bar Harbor, is ascended by a road (2½ M.). — A very pleasant trip for walkers is to go
to (2 M.) *Eagle Lake* (see above; trout and salmon fishing); traverse it by
boat; follow a forest-path from its S. end, below the *Bubbles* (p. 104),
to (1 M.) *Jordan's Pond;* cross by boat to the lower end of Jordan's
Pond; and walk thence to (2½ M.) *Seal Harbor* or (2½ M.) *Asticou* (comp.
p. 104). The boat may be ordered by telephone from *Tibbett's* (Rfmts.), at
the lower end of Jordan's Pond, or (less certain) may be signalled for
with the flag and horn provided for the purpose at the N. end.

*Ocean Drive to *Schooner Head*, *Great Head*, and the *Otter Cliffs*, returning
through the *Gorge*, is a fine round of 12 M. ($ 1½ for each passenger). We
leave Bar Harbor by Main St. and drive towards the S. At (3 M.) *Schooner
Head*, named from a white stain resembling the sails of a schooner, are the
Spouting Horn (seen to advantage in rough weather only) and the *Anemone
Cave*. About 1 M. farther on we diverge to the left from the road to visit the
bold and massive promontory of *Great Head*, towering 140 ft. above the
water and affording a fine view. To the S. lies *Newport Beach*, with *Thunder
Cave*, near which our road runs to (2 M.) Otter Cliffs, with the *Peaks of Otter*
(506 ft.) rising to the right. To visit the *Otter Cliffs* (180 ft.; *View), we
again diverge to the left from the road (small fee). We now turn to the
right (N.) and drive back to (6 M.) Bar Harbor through the fine *Echo Gorge*,
between *Newport Mt.* on the right and *Dry Mt.* (1268 ft.) on the left.

Another favourite drive is to (1¼ M.) *Duck Brook* (see above) and
thence by the high and winding *Bay Drive* or *Corniche Road* (*View) to
(1¼ M.) *Hull's Cove*, the former home of Mme. de Gregoire (p. 101). We
may return viâ *Eagle Lake* and the so-called *Breakneck Road* (5 M.); and
we may extend the drive beyond Hull's Cove to (3 M.) the *Ovens* (caves;
visited by boat at high water), with the archway known as the *Via Mala*.
— The so-called *Twenty-Two Mile Drive* leads viâ the Eagle Lake Road to
(6 M.) the N. end of *Somes Sound* (p. 105); then runs on the E. side of the
Sound to (4 M.) *North East Harbor;* follows the coast thence viâ Seal
Harbor to (6 M.) *Otter Creek;* and returns to (6 M.) *Bar Harbor* viâ either

Echo Gorge (p. 103) or the *Ocean Drive* (p. 103). — *Somesville* (p. 105) is about 8 M. from Bar Harbor.

Short STEAMBOAT EXCURSIONS may be made to *Seal Harbor*, *N.E. Harbor*, *S.W. Harbor*, *Winter Harbor* (p. 102), *Sorrento* (p. 99), etc. The voyage *Round the Island* (1 day) is recommended.

Seal Harbor (*Glencove*, *Seaside*, $ 2), in a cove on the S. side of the island (8 M. from Bar Harbor), is a small hamlet, with the largest sand-beach on the island. It is a good centre for walkers. About $2^{1}/_{2}$ M. (road) to the N. is *Jordan's Pond*, $1^{1}/_{4}$ M. long and $^{1}/_{4}$ M. wide (trout-fishing; boating), between *Sargent's Mt.* on the W. and *Pemetic Mt.* on the E. At its N. end rise the *Bubbles* (780 and 845 ft.). *Green Mt.* (p. 103) and *Sargent's Mt.* (see below) are often ascended from Seal Harbor.

North East Harbor is a narrow inlet, penetrating the S. coast for 1 M. about 2 M. to the W. of Seal Harbor, and the group of cottages and hotels (*Kimball Ho.*, $ 2-3; *Clifton Ho.*, *Rock's End*, nearest the wharf, $ 2) that bears its name lies on the promontory between it and Somes Sound. Like Seal Harbor and South West Harbor, it is a favourite resort of those who prefer quieter and less fashionable quarters than Bar Harbor offers. The steamboat-landing is on the E. side of Somes Sound (see p. 105). Opposite the mouth of N.E. Harbor is *Bear Island* (with a lighthouse), and a little farther out are *Sutton's Island* and the two *Cranberry Islands*. At the head of the cove, $1^{1}/_{2}$ M. from the steamboat-landing, lies the prettily-situated *Asticou* or the *Harbor Cottages* (Savage's, Robert's Ho., $ 2), at the base of *Mt. Asticou* (*View).

Sargent's Mt. (1344 ft.), the highest but one on the island, rises about 2 M. to the N. of Asticou. We follow the road leading N. to the (1 M.) *Upper Hadlock Pond*, diverge here to the right, and follow the brook (path indicated by shingles and red paint). Beyond ($^{1}/_{4}$ hr.) a small waterfall the route to ($^{3}/_{4}$-1 hr.) the top is indicated by 'blazes' on the trees and by small cairns on the ledges. Sargent's Mt. may also be ascended on the S. side by a path diverging to the left from the path to Jordan's Pond (see below) and crossing *Cedar Mt.* (comp. Map). The *View includes a great part of the island, with the Bubbles, Green Mt., and Pemetic to the E., and Brown's Mt. and the hills beyond Somes Sound to the W.; also the sea, with numerous islands. The descent may be made by a somewhat rough scramble viâ the pretty little *Lake of the Clouds* to Jordan's Pond (see above). — The trail or path from Asticou to ($2^{1}/_{2}$ M.) *Jordan's Pond* (see above) is pretty distinct. From Jordan's Pond to *Eagle Lake*, see p. 103. — Drives may be taken to *Bar Harbor* (see p. 102; $ 2 each), to (7 M.) *Somesville* (p. 105; $ $1^{1}/_{4}$ each), etc. Rowing and sailing trips are made to the above-mentioned Islands and to *S.W. Harbor*. *Somes Sound* may be visited by steam-launch ($ 5-10); or we may drive to (7 M.) *Somesville*.

South West Harbor (*Island Ho.*, *Claremont Ho.*, *Dirigo Ho.*, near the steamboat-wharf, $ $2-2^{1}/_{2}$; *Ocean Ho.*, *Stanley Ho.*, on the opposite side of the harbour, $ 2; *Freeman Ho.*, $ 2), on the W. side of the entrance to Somes Sound, is the largest summer-resort on Mt. Desert after Bar Harbor, and is called at by nearly all the regular steamers. Boating, deep sea-fishing, and fine sea views are its chief attractions. About 3 M. to the S. is the *Sea Wall* (Hotel, $ $1^{3}/_{4}$), a curious pebble ridge, 1 M. long and 15 ft. high. Off the harbour lies *Greening's Island*, a favourite spot for picnics.

The road to (6 M.) Somesville (see below) runs N., between *Dog Mt.* (670 ft.) and *Robinson Mt.* (700 ft.) on the right and *Beech Mt.* (855 ft.) and *Carter's Nubble* (480 ft.) on the left. About 1¼ M. from the village, beyond *Norwood's Cove*, a road to the right descends between Dog Mt. and *Flying Mt.* (300 ft.) to (1 M.) *Fernald's Point*, on Somes Sound, believed to be the site of the French colony of St. Sauveur (see p. 101). 'Father Biard's Spring' (see 'The Jesuit's Ring', by *A. A. Hayes*) is shown here. Farther on the Somesville road skirts *Echo Lake* (left) for (1¾ M.) *Somesville*, see below. — *Dog Mt., Beech Mt.*, and *Flying Mt.* are good points of view, easily ascended from S.W. Harbor. — Favourite drives lead to (14 M.), *Bar Harbor* (p. 102), viâ Somesville, and to *Bass Harbor*, 4 M. to the S.W.

Perhaps the finest boating excursion from S.W. Harbor is to *Somes Sound* (see below), which may be conveniently made by steam-launch (to Somesville and back in half-a-day). — A small steamer makes daily trips from S. W. Harbor and N. E. Harbor to *Isleford (Little Cranberry)* and *Great Cranberry Island* (fine surf at Deadman's Point).

*Somes Sound runs into the S. part of Mt. Desert Island for about 6 M., with an average width of ½-1 M. Its scenery is fine, and no one should fail to ascend it by small steamer or row-boat (sailing dangerous on account of sudden squalls).

As we enter the Sound proper we have *Fernald's Point* (see above) on the left and *Manchester Pt.* or *Indian Head* (Indian Head Ho.) on the right. The finest point on the fjord is *Thunder Cliff*, the wall-like front of *Dog Mt.* (to the left), rising sheer from deep water to a height of 5-600 ft. (good echo). Farther on, between *Robinson's Mt.* (left) and *Brown's Mt.* (right), the Sound narrows to ⅓ M., expanding again higher up. To the right opens a fine view of *Sargent's Mt.* (p. 104). To the left are *Granite Quarries*, which supplied the material used in the piers of Brooklyn Bridge (p. 30). At the head of the Sound we enter *Somes Harbor* and reach the village of *Somesville* (see below).

Somesville (Central Ho., Somes Ho., $2), a small village, is frequented mainly by driving parties from Bar Harbor, S.W. Harbor, or N.E. Harbor, who ascend Beech Hill (see below), dine or sup at one of the hotels (famous for their broiled chicken and 'popovers'; meals $1), and return in the afternoon or evening.

Beech Hill (ca. 500 ft.), 2 M. to the S.W. of Somesville (road to within 10 min. of the top), commands a splendid *View*, with *Echo Lake* (see above) lying sheer below its precipitous E. face. To the W. is *Long Pond* (4 M. long), beyond which rises the double-peaked *Western Mt.* (1073 and 971 ft.).

12. From Portland to Lewiston, Farmington, and the Rangeley Lakes.

139 M. MAINE CENTRAL RAILWAY to (92 M.) *Farmington* in 3¼ hrs. NARROW GAUGE RAILWAY thence to (18 M.) *Phillips* and (47 M.) *Rangeley* in 4 hrs. (through-fare $5.25).

From *Portland* to (11 M.) *Cumberland Junction*, see p. 97. Our train diverges here to the left and runs parallel with the Grand Trunk Railway (p. 108), which it intersects at (29 M.) *Danville Junction* (p. 108). At (35 M.) *Auburn* we cross the *Androscoggin*, obtaining a good view of the *Lewiston Falls* (52 ft.). Just across the river is (36 M.) **Lewiston** (*De Witt Ho.*, $2½), the second city in Maine, an important manufacturing place (cotton and woollen goods, etc.), with 21,701 inhabitants. The *City Hall* and *Bates College* (150 students) are among the chief buildings.

The train now follows the *Androscoggin* for some distance. To the right are the buildings of the *Maine Agricultural Society.* 46 M. *Leeds Junction,* where the Androscoggin Division of the Maine Central Railway, which we follow, diverges to the left.

The main line goes on viâ *Oakland* (junction for *Norridgewock, Madison,* and *Anson*) to (34 M.) *Waterville,* where it joins the route described at p. 98. *Lake Maranacook* is, perhaps, the prettiest of the numerous sheets of water passed on this line. — A branch-line also connects Leeds Junction with (27 M.) *Brunswick* (p. 97).

The train to Farmington runs through a pleasant hilly country, following the general course of the Androscoggin, which it nears at (75 M.) *Livermore Falls.* From (84 M.) *Wilton* coaches run to (13 M.) *Weld Pond,* frequented by trout-fishers. At (91 M.) *West Farmington* we cross the *Sandy River* on a long curved trestle. — 92 M. **Farmington** (*Stoddard Ho., The Willows,* $ 2), a prosperous village of 1200 inhab., where we change carriages for Rangeley.

The narrow-gauge SANDY RIVER RAILWAY runs through a picturesque district, with *Blue Mt.* to the left, to (11 M.) *Strong* (junction of a line to *Kingfield,* 15 M.) and (18 M.) *Phillips* (Elmwood, $ 3; Barden Ho., $ 2). Thence we continue by the PHILLIPS & RANGELEY RAILWAY to (47 M.; 139 M. from Portland) *Rangeley* (Rangeley Lake Ho., $ 2), on the N. bank of Rangeley Lake. To the right of this line rises *Saddleback Mt.* (4000 ft.; *View).

The *Rangeley or Androscoggin Lakes, a group of half-a-dozen small lakes, 1200-1500 ft. above the sea, connected with each other by water-ways, and covering a total area of about 80 sq. M., are a veritable sportsman's paradise and also offer the attraction of beautiful scenery and pure air. Large trout (up to 10 lbs.) abound in the lakes, and moose, deer, and other game in the forests. There are numerous hotels and camps round the lakes, with simple and inexpensive accommodation; expert guides ($ 2¹/₂-3 a day) are easily procured. Several clubs for fishing and hunting have their headquarters here. Mosquitoes and black flies are not troublesome after July. Warm clothing is desirable. Small steamboats afford almost continuous passage from Rangeley Lake to Lake Umbagog (p. 109). For other routes to the lakes, see pp. 108, 109.

Rangeley Lake or Lake Oquossoc, the north-easternmost of the group, is 9 M. long and 1-3 M. wide. Besides Rangeley (see above), *Greenvale* (Greenvale Ho., $ 2), at the E. end of the lake (3 M. from Rangeley), is a favourite resort on this lake. A steamer plies to *Mountain View Ho.* ($ 2) and the *Outlet,* at the foot (W. end) of the lake, 1¹/₂ M. to the N. of which is *Indian Rock,* with the headquarters of the Oquossoc Angling Association. — **Lake Mooselucmaguntic** (8 M. × 2 M.) is next in order, with inns or camps at *Haines Landing, Camp Bemis,* and the *Upper Dam* (S. end). Connected with this lake on the N. is the smaller *Lake Cupsuptic.* — Below the Upper Dam are *Lakes Molechunkamunk (Upper Richardson;* 5 M. × 1-2 M.) and *Welokenebacook (Lower Richardson;* 5 M. × 1¹/₂ M.). From the S. arm of the latter to *Andover* and *Bryant's Pond,* see p. 108. — From the *Middle Dam* (Inn), on the W. side of Lake Welokenebacook, a road leads to (6 M.) **Lake Umbagog** (1256 ft.), 9 M. long and 1-2 M. wide, at the S. end of which lies the *Lakeside Hotel.* The White Mts. (p. 121) are visible from this lake.

Coach hence to *Bethel*, see p. 108; steamer to *Errol's Dam*, see p. 109, coach from Errol's Dam to *Berlin Falls*, see p. 109; to *Colebrook*, see p. 111.

Steamers also run from Lakeside and Errol's Dam up the *Magalloway River* to (30 M.) **Lake Parmachenee** (*Camp Caribou*), another favourite sporting resort, 2500 ft. above the sea.

13. From Boston to Campobello. Grand Manan.

Routes. (1). STEAMER of the *International Steamship Co.* thrice weekly to (300 M.) *Eastport* in 17 hrs. ($4; stateroom $2-4; meals extra); STEAM FERRY thence to (2½ M.) *Campobello* in ½ hr. (fare 25 c.).

(2). BOSTON & MAINE RAILROAD to (402 M.) *St. Andrews* in 17-19 hrs.; STEAMER thence down the St. Croix to (15 M.) *Eastport* in 1 hr. (through-fare $9); FERRY as above to Campobello. — The ferry-boats for Campobello connect at Eastport with all steamers.

The STEAMER calls at *Portland* up to June; afterwards it proceeds direct from Boston to *Eastport* and *St. John* (p. 98). It sails at night (5 p.m. to 10 a.m.), but affords views of the coast in the evening and morning.

RAILWAY from Boston to *St. Andrews*, see R. 10a. The trip down the *St. Croix* to *Eastport* is pleasant.

Eastport (*Quoddy Ho.*, $2-3), the easternmost settlement of the United States, with 4908 inhab. and an abandoned fort, lies on a small island in *Passamaquoddy Bay*, connected with the mainland by a bridge. Its inhabitants are mostly fishermen and keepers of summer boarding-houses.

STEAM-FERRIES run at frequent intervals to (3 M.) *Lubec* (Hillside Ho., $2-3) and (2½ M.) *Campobello* (see below). A steamer runs regularly to (18 M.; 2 hrs.) *Grand Manan* (p. 103).

Campobello (**Tyn-y-Coed Hotel*, with its annex the *Tyn-y-Maes*, $3½-5), an island 9-10 M. long and 2-3 M. wide, lies between *Passamaquoddy Bay* and the *Bay of Fundy*, just on the Canadian (New Brunswick) side of the international boundary. It is irregular in shape, and its shores abound in picturesque cliffs, chasms, fjords, and beaches. The interior is covered with a dense growth of firs and larches, affording a pleasant shade for the numerous walks and drives that have been made through it in all directions. The climate is cool in summer, ranging from 50° to 75° Fahr. The island is now owned by a syndicate of New Yorkers and Bostonians, who have spent large sums on its development, and it has lately become a favourite summer-resort.

Excursions. To *Herring Cove Beach*, 1¾ M. The shady road crosses *Lake Glensevern* by a bridge 600 ft. long. The crescent-shaped beach is 3 M. long. We may return from its farther end by the Herring Cove road, or by a bridle-path diverging to the left from that road and traversing the wood. — To **Head Harbor*, 10 M. The road leads partly along the coast and partly through the well-wooded interior. It passes the famous *Cold Spring*, with a uniform temperature of 44°, and *Bunker Hill* (300 ft.), the top of which, reached by a bridle-path, affords a *View of Grand Manan, the *Wolves*, and (on very clear days, with a telescope) *Nova Scotia*. A detour may be made from this road to (2 M.) **Schooner Cove*, whence a path (good for ¾ M., when the Head comes in sight; difficult trail thence) leads to (2 M.) *Nancy Head*, a fine cliff, 210 ft. high, with a pretty beach at its foot. Following the Head Harbor road a little farther, we may diverge to the right to *Mill Cove.* (If we include this point, it is wise to bring luncheon and devote the whole day to the excursion.) — *Nine Mile Drive* (3 hrs.). We follow the *Glen Severn* road for 1 M. and then the Raccoon Beach road to the (1¹/₂ M.) *Raccoon Beach,* whence we may visit the wild *Southern Head* on foot (5 min.). Returning to the road, we follow it to the right for 5 M. and return by either the *Fitzwilliam Road* or the *Narrows Road.* — To **Man-of-War Head* (3¹/₄ M.; fine views). We proceed through *Welchpool,* the largest hamlet on the island, and then bear to the right over the *North Road.* The head is a high rocky bluff at the entrance of *Harbor de Lute,* commanding a good view. — *Eastern Head.* From the end of the Herring Cove road we descend rapidly to the left and cross a beach. A few minutes farther on we follow a path to the right which leads to (20 min.) the summit (300 ft.; *View). — Other points of interest are *Robinson's Ravine, Jacob's Ladder, Meadow Brook Cove,* etc.

EXCURSIONS BY WATER may be made to *Dennysville, Calais, St. Andrews,* up the *Magaguadavic River* to *St. George, Grand Manan* (see below), *St. John* (p. 98), and *Mt. Desert* (p. 101).

Sailing, Rowing, and *Canoeing* are safe, and the *Fishing* is excellent.

Grand Manan (*Marble Ridge Ho.*, $ 1¹/₂), a Canadian island, 22 M. long and 3-6 M. wide, lies at the entrance of the *Bay of Fundy*, 9 M. from the American coast. It is also a frequented summer-resort and is reached by steamer from *Eastport* (p. 107), in 2 hrs. Some of its cliffs and headlands are very fine.

14. From Portland to Montreal and Quebec.

a. Viâ the Grand Trunk Railway.

GRAND TRUNK RAILWAY to (297 M.) *Montreal* in 10-12 hrs. (fares $ 7¹/₂, drawing-room car $ 1¹/₂, sleeping-berth $ 2); to (317 M.) *Quebec* in 15¹/₂-18 hrs. (fares $ 8¹/₂, $ 2, $ 2¹/₂). This route forms a pleasant approach to Canada, skirting the N. margin of the White Mts. (p. 121; views to the left). From Boston to Canada by this route takes 4 hrs. more.

Portland, see p. 96. The train crosses (3 M.) the *Presumpscot River* (*View of *Casco Bay* to the right). At (11 M.) *Yarmouth* we intersect the Maine Central R. R. (comp. p. 97) and then turn to the left (N.W.). As far as (27 M.) *Danville Junction* the Maine Central R. R. (see p. 110) runs parallel to our line (to the left).

From Danville six-horse coaches run to (5 M.) **Poland Springs** (800 ft.; **Poland Springs Ho.*, $ 3¹/₂-5, 500 beds; *Mansion Ho.*, $ 2¹/₂), the chief inland watering-place of Maine, with good mineral water. Fine views.

We now again cross the Maine Central R. R. and turn towards the W. 29 M. *Lewiston Junction,* for *Auburn* and (6 M.) *Lewiston;* 36 M. *Mechanic Falls;* 47 M. *South Paris,* the station for (2 M.) *Paris Hill* (830 ft.), to the E. of which is *Mt. Mica*, where mica, beryls, tourmaline, and other minerals are found. From (62 M.) *Bryant's Pond* (700 ft.) coaches run to (15 M.) *Rumford Falls,* where the *Androscoggin* descends 160 ft. in three leaps.

A coach also runs from Bryant's Pond to (21 M.) *Andover* (Andover, French's, $ 2), whence connection is made by buckboard with the foot of *Lake Welokenebacook* (Rangeley Lakes; comp. p. 106).

We have now fairly left the level coast districts and entered the the mountains. 70 M. *Bethel* (1000 ft.; Bethel Ho., $ 2), a small summer-resort, with mineral springs, pleasantly situated above the 'intervales' of the *Androscoggin*.

Coaches (fares $ 2¹/₂) run regularly from Bethel to (26 M.) *Lakeside Hotel*, at the S. end of *Lake Umbagog* (p. 106). The road leads through wild and picturesque scenery, ascending the valleys of the *Androscoggin* and *Bear River* and affording distant views of the White Mts.

Beyond Bethel we obtain numerous fine views of the *White Mts.* (p. 121; to the left), while the Androscoggin runs on the right. Near (86 M.) *Shelburne* (725 ft.), in *New Hampshire*, we have views of *Mt. Madison* and *Mt. Moriah* to the left and *Mt. Hayes* to the right.

91 M. **Gorham** (860 ft.; meal-station), see p. 125.

Beyond Gorham our train turns to the N.W. and ascends along the Androscoggin, affording a good view of Mt. Adams to the left, to (98 M.) *Berlin Falls* (Berlin Ho., $ 2; Wilson Ho., $ 1¹/₂-2), where the river pours tumultuously through a narrow pass, descending 200 ft. within a mile. Coaches run hence to (22 M.) *Errol Dam* (Umbagog Ho., $ 2), whence steamers ascend the Androscoggin to (3 M.) *Lake Umbagog* (p. 106). — The train now leaves the Androscoggin, which turns to the N. Beyond (103 M.) *Milan* (view) we follow the *Upper Ammonoosuc* to (122 M.) *Groveton* (Melcher Ho., $ 2), the junction of the Concord & Montreal R. R. (to the White Mts. and Wells Junction; see p. 119). This is the starting-point for an ascent of the *Percy Peaks* (3150 ft. & 3335 ft.; 2¹/₂-3¹/₂ hrs.). The line now passes into the *Connecticut Valley* (to the right the white Percy Peaks). From (134 M.) *North Stratford*, where our line intersects the Maine Central R. R. (see p. 111), coaches run to (1¹/₂ M.) *Brunswick Springs*. We now cross the Connecticut, enter *Vermont* (the 'Green Mountain State'), and run through forest. 149 M. *Island Pond* (1500 ft.; Stewart Ho., $ 2; Rail. Restaurant), with the frontier custom-house (baggage examined). At (166 M.) *Norton Mills* we enter *Canada* and begin to descend the *Coaticooke*. 193 M. *Lennoxville*, at the confluence of the *St. Francis* and *Massawippi*, is the junction of the Passumpsic Division of the Boston & Lowell R. R. (p. 120). — 196 M. **Sherbrooke** (*Albion*, $ 2), a town of 10,110 inhab., near which are the *Rapids of the Magog*, is the junction of the Canadian Pacific R. R. to *Lake Megantic*, *Moosehead Lake*, and *St. John* (see p. 99) and of the Quebec Central R. R. to *Quebec* (comp. p. 111). *Lake Memphremagog* (see p. 120) lies 16 M. to the S.W. of Sherbrooke. We now follow the St. Francis to (221 M.) *Richmond* (2056 inhab.), where our line forks, the left (main) branch running to (76 M.) Montreal and the right to (96 M.) Quebec.

The line to Quebec traverses a thinly peopled district, with some pleasant scenery. 12 M. *Danville*. From (32 M.) *Arthabaska* a branch-line runs to (35 M.) *Three Rivers*. 55 M. *Ste. Julie*. We cross the *Chaudière* (2¹/₂-3 M. from the Falls) at (87 M.) *Chaudière Junction*. The railway ends at (96 M.) *Point Levi* (see p. 112), and passengers are ferried across the St. Lawrence to *Quebec* (see *Baedeker's Canada*).

The main line crosses the St. Francis and runs due W. from Richmond to Montreal, through a sparsely peopled forest-region.

Farther on it crosses the *Yamaska* and reaches (262 M.) *St. Hya-cinthe* (Yamaska, $2), a French-Canadian town of 7,016 inhab., with a cathedral and a large Jesuit college. We next traverse a flat and fertile country, inhabited by an industrious French peasan-try. To the N. rise the *Yamaska Mts.* Near (276 M.) *Beloeil* we pass *Beloeil Mt.* and cross the *Richelieu.* Beyond (292 M.) *St. Lam-bert* the train crosses the *St. Lawrence* by the wonderful *Victoria Bridge* and enters the Bonaventure Station at —

297 M. **Montreal** (see *Baedeker's Handbook to Canada*).

b. Via the Maine Central Railway.

To (286 M.) *Montreal* in 12-16½ hrs. (fare $ 7½; parlor-car $ 1; berth $2); to (322 M.) *Quebec* in 14½ hrs. (fare $ 8½). This line traverses the centre of the White Mts. (seats to the right; observation-cars attached to the trains in the mountain-district). Through-cars are run from Portland to Montreal, and passengers for Quebec may join the through-train from Boston at N. Conway, Fabyans, Lancaster, Colebrook, or Beecher's Falls, or they may connect viâ North Stratford, with the Grand TrunkRailway (R. 14a).

Portland, see p. 96. The train starts from the Union Station, crosses the *Presumpscott* twice, and runs towards the W. 5 M. *Cumberland Mills.* 17 M. *Sebago Lake Station*, at the S. end of **Sebago Lake** (265 ft.), a pleasant, islet-dotted sheet of water, 13 M. long, 10 M. wide, and 100 ft. deep in its deepest part.

Steamers ply from this point across Sebago Lake, through the *Songo River* (6 M.), and across *Long Lake* (13 M. long and 2 M. wide), to (32 M.) *Harrison* (Elm Ho., $1; there and back in 8 hrs.; a pleasant trip). From Harrison coaches run to (14 M.) *South Paris* (p. 108).

Beyond (25 M.) *Steep Falls* we follow the valley of the *Saco*, the falls of which are seen near (34 M.) *West Baldwin.* From (35 M.) *Bridg-ton Junction* a narrow-gauge line runs to (16 M.) *Bridgton*, on Long Lake (see above), the usual starting-point for an ascent of (10 M.) **Pleasant Mt.** (2020 ft.; *Mt. Pleasant Ho.*, on the top, $2), which commands a splendid *Panorama of the White Mts. — 49 M. **Frye-burg** (420 ft.; *Fryeburg Ho.*, $1½), a summer-resort, is 10 M. to the N. of Pleasant Mt. (see above). — We now enter *New Hamp-shire* (p. 93). Beyond (55 M.) *Conway Centre* we cross the Saco, and enter the district of the *White Mountains* (R. 16). 60 M. *North Conway* (520 ft.; see p. 123), the junction of the Boston & Maine R. R. We now ascend more rapidly. To the right are Middle Mt., Hurricane Mt., and Mt. Kearsarge (comp. pp. 123, 124); to the left the long ridge of Moat Mt. (p. 124), with the 'Ledges'. 62½ M. *Intervale* (p. 123). The train traverses the beautiful Conway 'inter-vales'. From (66 M.) *Glen Station* (p. 124) coaches run to (3 M.) *Jackson* and (14 M.) the *Glen House* (p. 125). The train turns to the left and crosses the Saco. Beyond (72 M.) *Upper Bartlett* (Bart-lett Ho., $2; Rail. Restaurant), where an 'observation-car' is added to the train, we twice cross the Saco, then turn to the N. and cross *Sawyer's River* (station) and *Nancy's Brook.* To the left rises the triple-peaked *Mt. Carrigain* (4700 ft.). 78 M. *Bemis.* To the right are *Mt. Crawford* (3130 ft.), *Mt. Resolution* (3436 ft.), and the *Giant's Stairs* (3512 ft.); to the left is *Mt. Nancy* (3944 ft.). — The line now bends to the N.W. and enters the famous **Crawford or White Mountain Notch*, a narrow defile, about 3-4 M. long, with the towering walls of *Willey Mt.* (4313 ft.) on the left and *Mt. Webster* (3928 ft.) on the right. The train ascends rapidly (1 : 44), at a height of 100-350 ft. above the river, and affords, perhaps, better views than the road (comp. p. 126). The deep ravine below (82 M.) *Frankenstein Cliff* (stat.) is crossed by a dizzy trestle, 80 ft. high and 500 ft. long. 83 M. *Willey House* (p. 126). To the right (ahead) we have a good view of Mt. Washington. The *Willey Brook* is crossed by another lofty trestle (80 ft. high). To the right are the *Silver* and *Flume Cascades* (p. 126). The train skirts the E. slope of *Mt. Willard* (2570 ft.; p. 126), leaves the Notch by its narrow *Gateway* (p. 126), and reaches the plateau on which lies the (87 M.) *Crawford House* (1890 ft.; p. 126). We now begin the descent, with the *Ammonoosuc* to the right. 89 M. *Mt. Pleasant House.* At (91 M.) *Fabyan's* (p. 127) we connect with the railway to the summit of *Mt. Washington* (see p. 131). Just beyond Fabyan's we cross the Ammonoosuc and descend along its left bank. 92 M. *White Mt. House;* 94 M. *Zealand,* the junction for the narrow-gauge line to *Bethlehem Junction, Maplewood, Bethlehem Street,* and the *Profile House* (see p. 129); 95 M. *Twin Mountain House* (p. 127). We now skirt the shoulder of *Cherry Mt.*

101 M. *Quebec Junction,* where the Quebec (Upper Coos) Division of the Maine Central R. R. diverges to the right, connecting with the Canadian Pacific and the Quebec Central Railways.

FROM QUEBEC JUNCTION TO QUEBEC, 221 M., in 10 hrs. We pass *Cherry Pond,* cross the *Whitefield & Jefferson R. R.,* and reach (4 M.) *Jefferson* (see p. 130), situated on a spur of *Mt. Starr King* (4030 ft.), which rises to the right. The railway skirts the *Israel River.* — 11 M. **Lancaster** (870 ft.; *Lancaster Ho.,* $2-3; *Williams Ho.,* $1½), pleasantly situated on the Israel River, with 3373 inhab., is a favourite summer-resort and commands distant views of the White Mts. *Mt. Prospect* (2090 ft.; Prospect Ho., $3), 2 M. to the S.E., is a good point of view. To the E. are the *Pilot Mts. Jefferson Hill* (p. 130) is 7 M. to the E.S.E. — We now pass from the White Mt. district and enter the *Coos District.* The train crosses the *Concord & Montreal Railway* at Lancaster, and farther on twice crosses the *Connecticut,* which here forms the boundary between Vermont and New Hampshire. At (31 M.) *North Stratford* our line intersects the *Grand Trunk Railway* (see p. 109). We ascend to the N. through the valley of the *Connecticut.* From (44 M.) *Colebrook* (1030 ft.; Nirvana, $4-7; Monadnock Ho., $2) a coach runs to (10 M.) the **Dixville Notch* (*Dix Ho.,* at the entrance, $2), a fine ravine, 2 M. long, with its most striking points (Table Rock, etc.) marked by sign-posts. Coaches run from the Notch to (11 M.) *Errol's Dam* (p. 109). — At (54 M.) *Beecher's Falls,* whence stages run to the (15 M.) *Connecticut Lakes* (2550 ft.; Connecticut Lake Ho., $1½-2), the source of the Connecticut, we enter Canada (luggage examined). We traverse a heavily-timbered and scantily-settled region. At (72 M.) *St. Malo* we cross the watershed between the Connecticut and the St. Lawrence. 83 M. *Sawyerville,* with a large saw-mill. At (90 M.) *Cookshire Junction* we cross the Canadian Pacific R. R. between Sherbrooke and Lakes Megantic and Moosehead (comp. pp. 99, 109). Farther on we cross the *St. Francis River.* — 103 M. *Dudswell Junction* is the point of intersection with the *Quebec Central*

R. R. from Sherbrooke to Quebec (comp. p. 109; the Upper Coos R. R. goes on to *Lime Ridge*, 4 M. farther on). The intermediate stations are unimportant. From (220 M.) *Point Levi* passengers are ferried across the St. Lawrence to *Quebec* (see *Baedeker's Handbook to Canada*).

From Quebec Junction the main line descends along the Ammonoosuc to (109 M.) *Scott Junction*, where it crosses the Concord & Montreal R. R. It then crosses the *Connecticut* and enters Vermont. At (111 M.) *Lunenburg* (Maple Grove Ho., $2) we pass on to the lines of the St. Johnsbury & Lake Champlain Division of the Boston & Maine R. R. A little beyond (118 M.) *Miles Pond* we meet the *Passumpsic* and follow it down to (133 M.) *St. Johnsbury* (p. 119), where we join the main route of the Boston & Maine R. R. to Canada. Thence to (286 M.) *Montreal*, see R. 15c.

15. From Boston to Montreal.

a. Viâ Rutland and Burlington.

335 M. FITCHBURG RAILROAD from Boston to (114 M.) *Bellows Falls* in 3¹/₄ hrs.; CENTRAL VERMONT RAILROAD from Bellows Falls to (194 M.) *St. John's* in 7 hrs.; GRAND TRUNK RAILWAY thence to (27 M.) *Montreal* in ³/₄-1 hr. (through-fare $9; parlor-car $1¹/₂; sleeper $2¹/₂).

Boston, see p. 72. Leaving the Fitchburg station (p. 72), the train crosses the *Charles*, affording a view to the right of the *Hoosac Tunnel Docks*, the *U. S. Navy Yard*, and *Bunker Hill Monument* (p. 85). At the *State Prison* (right) the line wheels to the left (W.) and crosses a backwater to *Somerville*. It then traverses *Cambridge* (p. 83), with a glimpse of the Harvard College buildings to the left. — 10 M. **Waltham** (*Sanderson Ho.*, $2¹/₂), a city of 18,707 inhab., with extensive cotton-mills and the interesting works of the *American Waltham Watch Co.* (the largest in the world, producing 550,000 machine-made watches annually). We have our last view of the Charles here, to the left. To the right is *Prospect Hill* (480 ft.). A little farther on we pass *Lake Walden* (right), a favourite haunt of Thoreau (1817-1862; see 'Walden'), but now frequented by picnic parties instead of recluses.

20 M. **Concord** (*Thoreau House Ho.*, $2¹/₂), a village with 4427 inhab. situated on the *Concord River*, here formed by the junction of the *Sudbury* and the *Assabet*, is of abiding interest as the home of Hawthorne and Emerson, Thoreau and the Alcotts. It may be fittingly described as the American Weimar or Stratford-on-Avon and has kept its literary association less tainted by commercialism than either of these places. The following brief account should be supplemented by *Mr. George B. Bartlett's* interesting little volume on 'Concord: Historic, Literary, and Picturesque' (with plan).

On leaving the *Fitchburg Railway Station* we proceed to the right along *Thoreau Street* to *Sudbury Street*, which we follow to the left. To the left, where Sudbury St. joins *Main Street*, stands the *Free Public Library*, containing many interesting autographs. Following Main St. to the right, we cross the *Mill Brook* and reach a square whence several streets radiate.

If we follow *Lexington Street* to the right, which was the route of the

British retreat in 1775 (see below), we reach (5 min.), to the right, at the point where Lincoln St. diverges, the white *House of R. W. Emerson*, still occupied by his daughter. Here the 'Sage of Concord' was visited by *Frederika Bremer*, *Margaret Fuller* (Countess d'Ossoli), etc. A little farther on, to the left, is *Orchard House*, long the home of the Alcott Family, of which *Louisa M. Alcott* (1832-88), author of 'Little Women', is the most widely known member. To the W. of the house is the building used by the *Concord School of Philosophy*, which was established by *A. Bronson Alcott* (1799-1888) in 1879 and counted Emerson, Ben. Peirce, Dr. W. T. Harris, and Col. T. W. Higginson among its lecturers. The next house (left) is *The Wayside*, the home of *Nathaniel Hawthorne* in 1852-64, with the tower-study in which he wrote 'Septimius Felton' and other works.

We now return to the above-mentioned square and follow *Monument Street* to the N., crossing the Lowell R. R. and reaching (12 min.; to the left) the *Old Manse*, built for the *Rev. Wm. Emerson* in 1765 and occupied after him by the *Rev. Dr. Ripley* and many other eminent divines. This was the birthplace of R. W. Emerson, and in the study above the dining-room he wrote 'Nature' and Hawthorne his 'Mosses from an Old Manse'. Adjoining the grounds of the Old Manse is the bridge over the Concord River, where the 'minute-men' of the neighbourhood encountered the British soldiers on April 19th, 1775, and 'where the embattled farmers stood and fired the shot heard round the world'. Beyond the bridge is a fine commemorative statue of the *Minute-Man*, by Dan. C. French.

Bedford Street, running to the E. from the central square, leads to (10 min.) *Sleepy Hollow Cemetery*, one of the most romantic burial-grounds in America. Among the illustrious dead buried here are *Ralph Waldo Emerson* (1803-82; grave marked by a huge block of pink quartz), *Nathaniel Hawthorne* (1804-68; grave surrounded by a low hedge of arbor vitæ), *Henry Thoreau* (comp. p. 112), and the *Alcotts* (see above).

The Concord rivers are very picturesque and a row on one or other of them may fitly wind up the visit.

A line runs from Concord to (10 M.) Lexington (*Russell Ho.*, $2; also reached direct from Boston by the Boston & Maine R. R., 11 M.), where, on April 19th, 1775, the first battle between the British and Americans took place (comp. above). A monument has been erected to the eight militia-men who fell here.

At (22 M.) *Concord Junction* we cross the Old Colony line to Lowell (p. 116) and the Concord and Montreal R. R.; to the right is the *State Reformatory*. 25 M. *South Acton;* 36 M. *Ayer Junction.*

50 M. **Fitchburg** (*Fitchburg Ho.*, *Derby Ho.*, $2-2¹/₂), a busy industrial city on the *Nashua River*, with 22,037 inhab., the junction of lines to Worcester (p. 60) and South Framingham (p. 61).

The train now begins to ascend. To the right runs the Nashua. From (53 M.) *Wachusett* coaches run to the S. to (6 M.) **Mt. Wachusett** (2108 ft.; *Summit Ho.*, $2-2¹/₂; *View), which may also be reached from *Princeton Centre* (*Wachusett Ho.*, $2-2¹/₂), on the Worcester line (see above). At (60 M.) *South Ashburnham* the Cheshire branch diverges to the right (N.) from the main line (which goes on to the Berkshire Hills and Troy, N. Y.; see p. 134). At (68 M.) *Winchendon* we cross the Monadnock branch to *Peterboro.*

From Peterboro a stage runs to (4 M.) the lovely summer-resort of **Dublin** (*Appleton*, *Boulderstone*, $2-3), finely situated near the N.W. base of Mt. Monadnock. It is also reached viâ *Harrisville*, on the Boston & Maine R. R.

The train now enters *New Hampshire.* From (82 M.) *Troy* a coach (fare 50 c.) runs to (5 M.) the *Mountain House*, about halfway up **Monadnock Mt.* (3186 ft.; *View), one of the finest mountains in New England. Beyond (104 M.) *Westmoreland* the train begins to descend into the valley of the *Connecticut.* 110 M. *Walpole* (Dinsmore Ho., $2½), a charming summer-resort on the Connecticut. We now cross the river to —

114 M. **Bellows Falls** (250 ft.; *Island Ho* , $2½; *Rail. Restaurant*), in *Vermont*, a picturesque summer-resort. The wooded *Mt. Kilburn*, on the New Hampshire bank, affords a fine view of the village and the rapids in the river (fall of 40 ft.). At Bellows Falls we intersect the *Connecticut River R. R.* (see p. 143) and pass on to the tracks of the *Central Vermont R. R.*

Some of the trains from Bellows Falls to Burlington (see below) run viâ *White River Junction* (comp. p. 143).

We now traverse the pretty valley of the *Williams River* and soon begin to ascend the E. slope of the *Green Mts.* (see p. 117). Near (136 M.) *Cavendish* (920 ft.) are valuable quarries of serpentine marble. From (148 M.) *Summit* (1360 ft.) we descend rapidly to —

167 M. **Rutland** (525 ft. ; *Berwick Ho.*, $2½-3½; *Bates Ho.*, $2-3), a town of 11,760 inhab., largely built of fine white marble. It is the junction of the *Delaware & Hudson R. R.* (to Saratoga, etc.) and of the *Bennington & Rutland R. R.* (Troy, Albany, etc.).

Excursions may be made from Rutland to (7 M.) *Clarendon Springs* (Hotel; coach); to (10 M.) *Killington Peak* (4240 ft.; Hotel near the top, $2½; *View), the highest of the Green Mts.; to *Mt. Ida*, etc. — Vermont produces three-fourths of the marble quarried in the United States, and Rutland is the centre of the industry, which employs many thousand men. The *Sutherland Falls Quarry*, at *Proctor*, 5 M. to the N.W., is the largest single quarry in the world. The marble of Vermont is said to be whiter and more durable than that of Carrara.

176 M. *Pittsford* (475 ft.), with marble quarries; 183 M. *Brandon* (365 ft.), with marble quarries, rich deposits of bog-iron, and mines of kaoline, used here in making mineral paint. From (188 M.) *Leicester Junction* a branch-line runs to (17 M.) *Ticonderoga* (p. 185). About 5 M. to the E. of (193 M.) *Salisbury* (stage) is the pretty *Lake Dunmore* (Lake Dunmore Ho., $2½ -3), surrounded by the *Green Mts.*, of which we have good views to the right. 199 M. *Middlebury* (335 ft.; Addison Ho., $2-2½), the seat of a college, is a good centre for excursions to (11 M.) *Breadloaf Inn* (1600 ft.; $3), *Snake Mt.* (1310 ft.; *View), and other points among the Green Mts. We descend along the *Otter Creek* to (213 M.) *Vergennes* (170 ft.; Stevens Ho., $2½), 8 M. from Lake Champlain, of which we obtain views, backed by the Adirondacks (R. 25), to the left.

243 M. **Burlington** (*Van Ness Ho.*, $2½-3½; *Burlington*, $2; *Chittenden*, small, $1-2), beautifully situated on a hill rising from the E. shore of *Lake Champlain* (p. 184), is the chief city of Vermont and one of the largest lumber-marts in America, the lumber coming chiefly from Canada. Pop. (1890) 14,590. Near the public square in the centre of the town, which is well built and laid out, are the *Post Office*, the *City Hall*, the *Court House*, and the *Young*

Men's Christian Association. The *Roman Catholic Cathedral* and *St. Paul's Episcopal Church* are conspicuous among the churches.

The UNIVERSITY OF VERMONT, on a hill 365 ft. above the lake, is attended by 450-500 students.

The handsomest of its buildings is the *Billings Library*, designed by H. H. Richardson, and containing a fine collection of books in the Scandinavian languages. The University Tower commands a magnificent *View (best at sunset) of the city, Lake Champlain (with *Juniper Island* opposite Burlington), the Adirondacks (incl. Mt. Marcy, Mt. Mansfield, and Whiteface), and the Green Mts. (to the E.; Mt. Mansfield, Camel's Hump, etc.). In the University Park is a *Statue of Lafayette*, by J. Q. A. Ward.

Col. Ethan Allen (see p. 117; monument) is buried in *Green Mt. Cemetery*, and *Lake View Cemetery*, to the N.W., is also worth visiting.

Pleasant walks and drives may be taken along the *Winooski*, to *Shelburne Point, Mallett's Bay* (8 M.), etc., and longer excursions to *Mt. Mansfield* (p. 117), *Camel's Hump* (p. 117), and other Green Mt. peaks. Steamers on Lake Champlain to *Port Kent* (Ausable Chasm), *Plattsburg*, etc., see R. 27.

Beyond Burlington our train runs to the N., passing the picturesque gorge and falls of the *Winooski*, to (251 M.) *Essex Junction* (Rail. Restaurant), where we join the line from *White River Junction* (comp. p. 117). We have constant views of the Green Mts. to the right and peeps of Lake Champlain and the Adirondacks on the left.

266 M. **St. Albans** (400 ft.; *Welden Ho.*, $ 2-3; *American Ho.*, $ 2; *Rail. Restaurant*), a pleasant village with 7771 inhab., finely situated on rising ground, 2¹/₂ M. from Lake Champlain. It contains the car-shops of the Central Vermont R. R. and is an important market for butter and cheese. The elm-shaded square in the centre of the village is embellished with a handsome fountain.

Aldis Hill (500 ft.), ³/₄ M. to the N.E. of St. Albans, and *Bellevue Hill* (1300 ft.), 2 M. to the S.W., command *Views of the Green Mts., Adirondacks, and Lake Champlain (afternoon light best). — *St. Albans Bay* (Lake View Ho., St. Albans Point Ho., $ 2) affords good bass and pike fishing.

FROM ST. ALBANS TO RICHFORD, 28 M., railway in 1¹/₄-2¹/₄ hrs., along the *Missiquoi River*. — 10 M. Sheldon Springs (*Congress Hall*, $ 2¹/₂; *Portland*, 1¹/₂ M. from Sheldon station, $ 2), with alkaline and mineral springs used for cutaneous diseases, dyspepsia, and liver complaints. The Missiquoi forms rapids here. — 28 M. *Richford* (American Ho., $ 2), see p. 120.

From (272 M.) *Swanton Junction* a branch-line runs to (14 M.) *Rouse's Point* (p. 145; passing *Alburgh Springs*) and (132 M.) *Ogdensburg* (p. 207). 279 M. *Highgate Springs* (Franklin Ho., Lakeside, $ 2¹/₂-3), near the Missiquoi Bay (muskalonge, black bass, pickerel; duck-shooting), with effective alkaline springs. A little farther on the train passes into *Canada* (Province of Quebec). Beyond (290 M.) *Stanbridge* we see the *Rougemont* and *Beloeil* to the right (p. 110). Crossing the *Richelieu* at (308 M.) *St. John's* (p. 120), we join the Grand Trunk Railway. Hence to —

335 M. *Montreal* (Bonaventure Station), see *Baedeker's Canada*.

b. Viâ Lowell and Concord.

335 M. BOSTON & LOWELL RAILROAD to (145 M.) *White River Junction* in 4¹/₂-6¹/₄ hrs.; CENTRAL VERMONT RAILROAD thence to (190 M.) *Montreal* in 6-7 hrs. (through-fare $ 9; parlor-car $ 1¹/₂; sleeper $ 2).

Boston, see p. 72. The train starts from the *Lowell Station*

(Causeway St.; p. 72), crosses the *Charles* and the Fitchburg R. R. (p. 72), and runs to the N.W. through *Somerville*, *Medford*, and the picturesque *Middlesex Fells. To the left lies *Mystic Pond.* Farther on we cross the *Concord River* and reach (26 M.) **Lowell** (*Merrimac Ho.*, *St. Charles*, *American Ho.*, $2-2½), at the confluence of the *Concord* and *Merrimac*, the third city of Massachusetts (pop. 77,696) and one of the most important industrial cities in the United States. In 1890 its huge mills and factories, run mainly by the water-power furnished by the Pawtucket Falls on the Merrimac (32 ft.; seen from the bridge), employed 29,000 hands and produced goods (woollen cloth, carpeting, etc.) to the value of $40,600,000 (8,120,000 l.). Dickens gives a graphic description of Lowell in his 'American Notes' (chap. 4), but many of its features have changed since his day, and the mill-operatives are now mainly French Canadians and Irish.

Beyond Lowell the line follows the Merrimac (seats to the right), and beyond (33 M.) *Tyngsboro* (*View) it enters *New Hampshire.* — 40 M. **Nashua** (*Tremont*, $2½; *Laton Ho.*, $2), a pleasant town of 19,311 inhab., at the confluence of the Merrimac and the *Nashua*, with manufactures of iron, cotton, carpets, etc. — The train now runs to the N. through the pretty valley of the Merrimac.

57 M. **Manchester** *(New Manchester Ho., Windsor*, $2½-3½; *Rail. Restaurant)*, the largest city in New Hampshire (44,126 inhab.), with manufactures of cotton goods and prints (value in 1890, $19,000,000). Its water-power is furnished by the *Amoskeag Falls*, on the Merrimac. — At (66 M.) *Hooksett* and other points we cross and recross the Merrimac. To the W. is *Pinnacle Mt.* (view).

75 M. **Concord** (250 ft.; *New Eagle*, $2½-4½; *Phoenix*, $2½-3½; *Rail. Restaurant*), the capital of New Hampshire, with 17,004 inhab., is a pleasant tree-shaded city on the W. bank of the Merrimac, with carriage-works and quarries of fine granite. Among the chief buildings are the *State Capitol*, the *City Hall*, and the *Insane Asylum.* Count Rumford (p. 91) lived here for some years.

FROM CONCORD TO CLAREMONT JUNCTION, 57 M., railway in 2½ hrs. From (7 M.) *Bradford* coaches run to (5 M.) *Bradford Mineral Springs* (Hotel). 34 M. *Newbury* lies at the S. end of **Lake Sunapee** (950 ft.), a pretty sheet of water, 9 M. long and 1-3 M. wide, on which a small steamer plies. 55 M. *Claremont.* — 57 M. *Claremont Junction* (see p. 143).

At Concord our present route diverges to the left from the main line of the Concord & Montreal R. R., which runs viâ *Lake Winnepesaukee* and *Plymouth* to *Wells River Junction* (see pp. 117, 119). As we cross the *Conticook*, near (82 M.) *Fisherville*, we see on *Duston's Island*, to the right, a colossal *Statue of Mrs. Hannah Duston* of Haverhill, who here killed 10-12 of her Indian captors and made her escape. — *Daniel Webster* (1782-1852) was born 2 M. to the S.W. of (94 M.) *Franklin.* Farther on we pass *Webster Lake* (right) and *Highland Lake.* From (106 M.) *Potter Place* coaches run to (4 M.) the *Winslow House*, high up on the slope of *Mt.*

Kearsarge (2943 ft.; not to be confounded with Mt. Kearsarge in the White Mts., p. 123), the top of which (*View) is reached thence by a bridle-path. Beyond (126 M.) *Canaan* (955 ft.), to the left, lies *Mascoma Lake*, with a Shaker village on its S. bank. At (142 M.) *W. Lebanon* we cross the *Connecticut* to —

144 M. **White River Junction** (365 ft.; *Rail. Restaurant; Junction Ho.*, $ 2), where we cross the Passumpsic Division of the Boston & Maine R. R. and join the Central Vermont R. R.

From White River Junction to *New York* and to *Quebec*, see p. 143. — A branch-line runs to (14 M.) *Woodstock*, the birthplace of *Hiram Powers* (1805-73), the sculptor, and *Geo. P. Marsh* (1801-82), the diplomatist and Norse scholar.

Our line ascends through the picturesque **Valley of the White River*, which flows down through the *Green Mts.* Beyond (153 M.) *West Hartford* we cross the river (*View). 159 M. *Sharon* (500 ft.), the birthplace of *Joseph Smith* (1805-1844), founder of Mormonism. At (177 M.) *Randolph* (680 ft.) the scenery becomes wilder and the higher summits of the Green Mts. come into sight. At (192 M.) *Roxbury* (1015 ft.) we cross the watershed and begin the descent to Lake Champlain. On a hill to the right, at (199 M.) *Northfield*, is *Norwich University*, a military college.

209 M. *Montpelier Junction*, whence a short branch-line runs to **Montpelier** (520 ft.; *Pavilion*, $ 2-3), the capital of Vermont, on the *Winooski*, with 4160 inhab. and a handsome *State House, surmounted by a dome 124 ft. high. In the portico is a *Statue of Ethan Allen* (1737-89; p. 115). — Near (213 M.) *Middlesex* (535 ft.) the Winooski passes through the *Middlesex Narrows*, a rocky gorge $1/4$ M. long, 60 ft. deep, and 30 ft. wide. —217 M. *Waterbury* (430 ft.; Waterbury Ho., $ 2) is a good centre for excursions.

Coaches run from Waterbury to the N. to (10 M.) *Stowe* (*Brick Hotel*, $ 2), a favourite summer-resort amid the Green Mts. **Mt. Mansfield** (4070 ft.), long supposed to be the highest of the Green Mts., is ascended hence by a good road (9 M.) and affords a splendid *View. It has three distinct peaks, the *Forehead*, *Nose*, and *Chin*, of which the last is the highest. The road ends at the base of the Nose (Summit Ho., $ 2-3), whence a path ascends to the Chin ($3/4$-1 hr.). The view from the Nose is, however, almost as good, including Lake Champlain and the distant Adirondacks. — Excursions may also be made from Stowe to *Moss Glen Falls*, the *Smuggler's Notch*, the *Camel's Hump* (see below), etc.

Camel's Hump (ca. 4000 ft.) is now seen to the S.W. (left) and may be reached from (222 M.) *North Duxbury* (road 3 M., path 3 M.). To the N. (right) we see the *Bolton Falls*. At (236 M.) *Williston* we cross the *Winooski* (view of Mt. Mansfield and Camel's Hump). Lake Champlain is seen to the left.

From (241 M.) *Essex Junction* to (335 M.) *Montreal*, see R. 15a.

c. Viâ Concord, Plymouth, Wells River, and Newport.

344 M. Boston & Maine Railroad to (235 M.) *Newport* in 7¹/₂-8 hrs.; Canadian Pacific Railway thence to (109 M.) *Montreal* in 4-4¹/₂ hrs. (fares as above). — This route runs viâ *Lake Winnepesaukee* (p. 118) and also forms one of the approaches to the *White Mts.* (p. 121; views to the right).

From Boston to (75 M.) *Concord*, see R. 15 b. Our present line crosses the *Merrimac* and runs towards the N. About 4 M. from (84 M.) *Canterbury* is a large Shaker village. To the left rises *Mt. Kearsarge* (p. 117). On the hill above (93 M.) *Tilton* is a *Memorial Arch* (55 ft. high), erected in honour of the Tilton family. Beyond Tilton, where we leave the Merrimac, we cross and recross the *Win-nepesaukee River* and skirt *Lake Winnisquam*. Ahead (left) rise the *Sandwich Mts.* 102 M. *Laconia* (Eagle). — 104 M. *Lake Village* (Mt. Belknap Ho., $ 2), at the extremity of *Long Bay*, an inlet of Lake Winnepesaukee, is the junction of a branch-line to (17 M.) *Alton Bay* (see below), at the S. end of Lake Winnepesaukee.

*Lake Winnepesaukee or Winnepiseogee (470 ft.; 'Smile of the Great Spirit' or 'Beautiful Water in a High Place'), the largest lake in New Hampshire, is an irregularly shaped sheet of water, 25 M. long and 1-7 M. wide, surrounded by picturesque hills and dotted with innumerable islands. Its waters (10-300 ft. deep) are singularly clear and are well-stocked with fish. The villages on the shores of the lake are favourite summer-resorts, and are centres for numerous charming excursions. Small steamers traverse the lake (see below), which is generally reached either at *Alton Bay*, *Weirs*, or *Wolfeborough* (see below).

Alton Bay (*Winnepesaukee House*, $ 2¹/₂) lies at the end of the narrow fjord, 5 M. long, forming the S. extremity of the lake. Among the excursions made from this point is the ascent of *Belknap Mt.* (2395 ft.; *View; afternoon light best), 12 M. to the N.W. (carriage-fare there and back $ 1¹/₂). Nearer points of view are *Mt. Major*, *Prospect Hill*, and *Sheep Mt.* *Merry Meeting Lake* lies 3 M. to the E. Besides the above-mentioned route, Alton Bay is reached viâ Lawrence and Dover (see p. 95).

From Alton Bay a small steamer plies to (9 M.) **Wolfeborough** (*Kings-wood*, $ 2¹/₂-3¹/₂; *Glendon*, *Bellevue*, $ 2-3; *Lake*, $1¹/₂-2; many boarding-houses), the largest village on the lake (3020 inhab.), pleasantly situated on the E. bank. The favourite excursion is to *Copple Crown Mt.* (2100 ft.), 6¹/₂ M. to the S.E. (carriage, $ 1¹/₂ each), the *View from which includes Mts. Ossipee and Chocorua to the N. (with Mt. Washington in the distance on a clear day) and extends to the ocean on the S.E. *Tumble Down Dick*, to the N. of Copple Crown, also affords a good view. Wolfeborough may also be reached viâ Salem, Portsmouth, and Wolfeborough Junction (see p. 121).

From Wolfeborough steamers run across the lake to (14 M.) *Weirs* (comp. below; 80c.) and up the lake to (17 M.) *Centre Harbor* (80c.), both routes affording beautiful views, including Mt. Washington.

Weirs (*Sanborn's*, *Lakeside*, *Winnecoette*, $ 3-3¹/₂; *Story's*, $ 2), on the W. side of the lake, is a popular summer camping-ground of various ecclesiastical and other bodies. It is a station on the Concord & Montreal R. R. (see below), and steamers run to *Lake Village* (see above).

Centre Harbor (*Senter Ho.*, $ 3-4; *Moulton*, $2; boarding-houses), at the N.W. extremity of the lake, is, perhaps, the pleasantest point to sojourn. About 4 M. to the N.W. (carr. to the foot, bridle-path to the top 1¹/₂ M.) rises *Red Hill* (2038 ft.), commanding a splendid *View, with the Sandwich Mts. (Chocorua, etc.) to the N. and N.E. To the W. of Red Hill, about 3 M. from Centre Harbor, lies *Squam Lake, a smaller edition of Lake Winnepesaukee (*Asquam Ho.*, on Shepherd Hill, on the W. bank. *Centre Harbor Hill* (1 M.) is a good point of view. Drives may be taken 'Round the Ring', to *Ossipee Park*, *Plymouth* (p. 119), etc. — Coaches run from Centre Harbor to (18 M.) *West Ossipee*, whence *Mt. Chocórua* (3508 ft.; *View), one of the most finely shaped mountains in New England, may be ascended viâ *Tamworth*.

From Lake Village (see above) the train runs to the N. along the bays on the W. side of Lake Winnepesaukee. 109 M. *Weirs* (see above); 112 M. *Meredith*, 5 M. from *Centre Harbor* (see above).

To the right is *Lake Waukewan*. We now turn away from Lake Winnepesaukee. 121 M. *Ashland*. At (123 M.) *Bridgewater* we cross
the *Pemigewasset* (g soft; 'place of crooked pines').

126 M. **Plymouth** (**Pemigewasset Ho.*, $ 2-4, meal-station; *Ply-
mouth Ho.*, $ 2), in the beautiful valley of the Pemigewasset, 7 M.
to the W. of Squam Lake (p. 118). A good view is obtained from
Walker's Hill, close to the village: and **Mt.* **Prospect** (2070 ft.),
4 M. to the N.E., commands a splendid panorama of the Franconia
Mts. (N.), Sandwich Mts., and Lake Winnepesaukee. Plymouth is
known for its buckskin gloves, and contains the old court-house
where Daniel Webster made his first plea.

FROM PLYMOUTH TO NORTH WOODSTOCK, 21 M., railway in ³/₄ hr. This
line ascends the *Valley of the Pemigewasset and leads to the heart of the
Franconia Mts. (see p. 128). Fine views. — 21 M. **North Woodstock** (**Deer
Park Hotel*, $ 3; *Fair View*, $ 2) is finely situated at the S. end of the **Franconia Notch*, 10 M. from the *Profile House* (see p. 128; stage).

Our train now ascends the valley of the *Baker River*. Small stations. 146 M. *Warren* (Langdon Ho., $ 1¹/₂) is the starting-point
of the stage to the (10 M.) top of **Mt.* **Moosilauke** ('bald place';
4790 ft.), which has been conspicuous to the right for some time
(*Tip-Top Ho.*, at the top, $ 2-4; *Moosilauke*, at the base, $ 3; *Mountain Ho.*, halfway up, $ 1¹/₂-2). The **View of the White Mts., the
Franconia Mts., and the Connecticut Valley is very fine. — Near
(150 M.) *Warren Summit* (1060 ft.), the highest point on the line
(path to the top of Mt. Moosilauke, 5 M.), the train passes through
a deep rock-cutting. At (168 M.) *Woodsville*, at the mouth of the
Ammonoosuc (p. 126), we cross the *Connecticut* to —

169 M. **Wells River Junction** *(Rail. Restaurant)*, where our
line joins the Passumpsic Division of the Boston and Maine Railroad. Wells River is also the junction of lines to the *White Mts.* and
Montpelier (see below).

FROM WELLS RIVER JUNCTION TO GROVETON JUNCTION, 52 M., railway in
2¹/₂-3 hrs. This line runs into the heart of the White Mts. (see R. 16) and
forms part of one of the regular through-routes from New York and
Boston (comp. p. 121). The White Mt. expresses from the latter city do
not cross the river at Wells Junction. — The train ascends along the
Ammoosuc. 4 M. *Bath*. From (9 M.) *Lisbon* coaches run to *Sunset Hill Ho.*
(p. 130). 20 M. *Littleton* (Oak Hill, Chiswick, $ 3; Thayer's, $ 2-3; The
Maples), a pleasant resort, from which stages run to (6 M.) *Franconia*
(p. 130). — 25 M. *Wing Road* is the junction of the line to (4 M.) *Bethlehem Junction*, (8 M.) *Twin Mt. House*, (11 M.) *Zealand*, (12 M.) *White Mt.
House*, and (13 M.) *Fabyan's* (comp. p. 127). [From Bethlehem Junction a
narrow-gauge railway runs to (2 M.) *Maplewood*, (3 M.) *Bethlehem Street*,
and (10 M.) the *Profile House;* see p. 111.] — 31 M. *Whitefield* (p. 126),
the junction of the Maine Central line to Jefferson (see p. 111); 42 M.
Lancaster (see p. 111). — 52 M. *Groveton Junction*, see p. 109.

FROM WELLS RIVER JUNCTION TO MONTPELIER, 39 M., railway in 1³/₄ hr.
— 23 M. *Marshfield*. 39 M. *Montpelier*, see p. 117.

Beyond (181 M.) *Barnet* we leave the valley of the Connecticut,
which bends to the N.E., and ascend along the *Passumpsic*, which
we cross 25 times in 24 M. — 190 M. **St. Johnsbury** (*St. Johnsbury
Ho.*, *Avenue Ho.*, $ 2-2¹/₂), a busy little town of 6567 inhab., with

the *Fairbanks Scales Works*, a *Soldiers' Monument*, and an *Art Gallery.* It is the junction of lines to (22 M.) *Lunenburg* (p. 112) and (96 M.) *Swanton* (p. 115). — 199 M. *Lyndonville*, with the *Great Falls of the Passumpsic.* At (213 M.) *Summit Station* (1050 ft.), we cross the watershed between the Connecticut and the St. Lawrence.

235 M. **Newport** (700 ft.; **Memphremagog Ho.*, $ 2¹/₂ - 3 ; *Newport Ho.*, $ 1¹/₂-2), a village with 3000 inhab., is prettily situated at the head (S. end) of *Lake Memphremagog* and is a good centre for excursions. Good view of the lake from *Prospect Hill*. *Jay Peak* (4018 ft.), 12 M. to the W., commands a wide prospect.

**Lake Memphremagog* ('beautiful water'; 470 ft.), a lovely sheet of water, 30 M. long and 2-4 M. wide, lies one-fifth in Vermont and four-fifths in Canada. It is enclosed by rocky shores and wooded hills, and its waters abound in lake-trout (*salmo confinis*), pickerel, perch, and bass.

A small steamer plies daily between Newport (see above) and *Magog*, at the N. end of the lake (there and back about 6-7 hrs.). Passing *Indian Point* and the *Twin Sisters*, we cross the Canadian line near *Province Island*. On the W. (left) shore we stop at (12 M.) the *Mountain House* ($ 2-3), at the foot of the prominent **Owl's Head** (3270 ft.), which is ascended hence in 1¹/₂-2¹/₂ hrs. The *View includes, on a clear day, Montreal and the Green, White, and Adirondack Mts. Farther on the steamer passes *Long Island* and calls at some small landings. On the E. shore are the country-houses of several wealthy Montrealers, and on the W. rises *Mt. Elephantis* (Revere Ho.). *Georgeville* (Camperdown Hotel), on the E. bank, 20 M. from Newport, is a quiet and inexpensive watering-place. — **Magog** (*Park's House*), at the N. end of the lake, at its outlet through the *Magog River*, is a good fishing-station and is connected by railway (C. P. R.) with (19 M.) *Sherbrooke* (p. 109). *Mt. Orford*, 5 M. to the W., affords a good view of the Canadian pine-forests to the N. and W.

From Newport there are two routes to Montreal : viâ *Sherbrooke* (p. 109) and the Grand Trunk Railway, and viâ *Richford* and the Canadian Pacific Railway. In the mean time we follow the latter.

At first we run W. to (266 M.) *Richford*, whence a branch-line diverges on the left to *Sheldon Junction* and *St. Albans* (p. 115). At Richford we cross the Canadian frontier and proceed N. to (278 M.) *Sutton Junction.* Here we turn again to the W. 314 M. *St. John's*, and thence to (344 M.) *Montreal*, see *Baedeker's Canada.*

The other line from Newport to Montreal (see above) crosses an arm of Lake Memphremagog (see above), enters Canada, and traverses the picturesque '*Eastern Townships*'. 241 M. *Stanstead Junction;* 256 M. *Massawippi*, near the pretty lake of that name, which lies to the left. Thence we ascend along the *Massawippi* to (272 M.) *Lennoxville*. 275 M. *Sherbrooke*, and thence to (383 M.) *Montreal* and to (418 M.) *Quebec*, see p. 109.

d. Viâ Portsmouth and North Conway.

365 M. BOSTON AND MAINE RAILROAD to (138 M.) *North Conway* in 5³/₄-6¹/₂ hrs.; MAINE CENTRAL RAILROAD thence to (51 M.) *Lunenburg* in 2³/₄ hrs.; ST. JOHNSBURY & LAKE CHAMPLAIN RAILROAD thence to (22 M.) *St. Johnsbury* in 1 hr.; BOSTON AND MAINE RAILROAD thence to (45 M.) *Newport* in 1³/₄ hr.; CANADIAN PACIFIC RAILWAY thence to (109 M.) *Montreal* in 4 hrs. (through-fare $ 10.50). Passengers for *Quebec* (fare $ 11) may travel either viâ *Quebec Junction* and the *Upper Coos R. R.* (see p. 111) or viâ *Sherbrooke* and the *Quebec Central R. R.* (see p. 109). — This line forms the shortest and quickest approach to the White Mts. (R. 16) and is also one of the regular routes to Lake Winnepesaukee (see pp. 118, 121).

From Boston to (57 M.) *Portsmouth* and (67 M.) *Conway Junc-tion,* see R. 9a. — Our line here diverges to the left (W.) 69 M. *South Berwick;* 70 M. *Salmon Falls* (p. 95); 73 M. *Great Falls.* — 79 M. **Rochester** (*Dodge's, Cascade, Mansion Ho.*, $2), a small manufacturing town with 4683 inhab., is the junction of lines to (29 M.) *Portland* (see p. 96) and to (18 M.) *Alton Bay*, on *Lake Winnepesaukee* (see p. 118). — 87 M. *Milton.* From (97 M.) *Wolfe-borough Junction* (Rail. Restaurant) a branch-line runs to (11 M.) *Wolfeborough*, on Lake Winnepesaukee (see p. 118). Beyond (115 M.) *Ossipee Centre* we have a view of *Lake Ossipee* to the right. 121 M. *West Ossipee.* To the left are seen the *Ossipee Mts.* and the *Sand-wich Mts.* (p. 118), with the finely-shaped *Chocorua* as their Eastern flanksman. We pass between *Elliot Pond* (left) and *Silver Lake* (right). Near (125 M.) *Madison* is the largest erratic boulder (granite) known in the United States, and probably in the world (75 ft. long, 40 ft. wide, 30-37 ft. deep; prob. weight 7-8000 tons). 132 M. *Conway* (Conway Ho., $2-3; Pequawket Ho., $1½-2½), on the *Saco River*, is a quieter centre than N. Conway for the many pleasant excursions of this region. *Moat Mt.* (p. 124) is conspicuous on the left, and *Mt. Kearsarge* (p. 123) on the right.

138 M. *North Conway*, see p. 123. From North Conway to (211 M.) *St. Johnsbury*, see R. 14b; from St. Johnsbury to — 365 M. **Montreal**, see R. 15c.

16. The White Mountains.

The chief ROUTES FROM BOSTON to the White Mts. are given at pp. 117, 120. The main gateways are *North Conway* (p. 123), reached in 4½-8 hrs. (return-fares $6½-9¾ acc. to route); *Bethlehem* (p. 128; 7 hrs.; $10¾-11¾); and *Plymouth* (p. 119; 3½ hrs.; $6½).

The chief direct ROUTE FROM NEW YORK is viâ *Wells River* to *Fabyan's* or *Bethlehem* (comp. R. 20a; 10½ hrs.; return-fare $17), but many travellers approach viâ *Boston* and *North Conway* or *Plymouth* (comp. RR. 15c, 15d; 12 hrs.; return-fare $17.50).

Travellers from MONTREAL and QUEBEC generally approach viâ *Gorham* (p. 125), but may also proceed viâ *St. Johnsbury* to *Bethlehem* (comp. R. 15c).

EXCURSION (*i.e.* RETURN) TICKETS at reduced fares are issued in summer and autumn in all cases, giving alternative routes in going and returning, ample 'stop-over' privileges, and a liberal allowance of time. Through-carriages are run to the principal points in the Mts., and parlor or sleeping cars are attached to all the chief trains (about $1½-2½ extra). The variety of combinations in which the trip is possible is too great to be detailed here, but full information, with maps, time-tables, and illustrated guidebooks, may be obtained on application from the railway companies interested (comp. p. xxi). *Circular Tour Tickets* are also issued by Raymond & Whitcomb and Thos. Cook & Co. (p. xxv).

SEASON. The *White Mts.* may be comfortably visited any time from June to October inclusive, and pedestrians will find the earlier and later months preferable to the warmer and more crowded months of July and August. The colouring of the autumn-leaves is an additional attraction in Sept. and October. Black flies and mosquitoes are somewhat trouble-some in June. The larger hotels do not open before July.

TIME. The chief points of the White Mts., including *Mt. Washington*, the *Crawford Notch, Bethlehem*, and the *Profile House*, may be visited in a week or even less; but it is highly desirable to spend at least 2-4 weeks in the district. A visit to *Lake Winnepesaukee* (p. 118) may be conveniently combined with one to the White Mts.

HOTELS. The hotels vary from the large and fashionable summer-caravanserais down to small, unassuming, and inexpensive inns and board-ing houses. As a general rule they are good of their kind; and a special word of praise is due to the waiting of the students (male and female) at some of the larger houses. The rates vary from $ 1½ to $ 5 a day and from $ 5 to $ 25 a week.

OUTFIT. Walkers should be provided with the plain outfit suggested at p. xxv, and should be prepared for both rain and cold, especially at the higher elevations. In July and August, however, the temperature in the valleys is pretty high, and light clothing suffices. Frequent change of dress has become all too usual at the larger hotels, but those whose object is rather outdoor exercise than indoor frivolity need not yield to this custom more than they choose.

GUIDES are seldom found in the White Mts., as most of the main routes are easily followed. They are, however, sometimes useful for the less well-known excursions (fee $ 2-3 a day); and the pedestrian should, at any rate, refrain from visiting the less-frequented routes alone. *C. E. Lowe* and *Hubbard Hunt*, of Randolph, are trustworthy guides for the Great Range ($ 3-4). A good pocket-compass is useful, especially in the woods.

CARRIAGES ('Buckboards', etc.) are easily obtained at all the chief resorts. Those obtained from the hotels are expensive, but more reason-able terms may be obtained from livery-stable keepers and farmers.

BIBLIOGRAPHY. The fullest guidebook to the White Mts. is that by *M. F. Sweetser* (Houghton, Mifflin, & Co.; $ 1½). *Chisholm's White Mt. Guidebook* (25 c.) is by the same author. Comp. *T. Starr King's* 'White Hills', *S. A. Drakes's* 'Heart of the White Mts.', and *J. H. Ward's* 'White Mts'.

The **Appalachian Mountain Club** (9 Park St., Boston), founded in 1876 and now numbering 800 members, has done good service in the White Mts. in making paths, setting up sign-posts, and preparing maps. Its quarterly periodical, *Appalachia*, contains much valuable information. Admission fee $ 5, annual subscription $ 3.

The **White Mountains** form the central portion of the Atlantic system of mountains extending from the peninsula of Gaspé to the Carolinas. In the ordinary use of the term, they cover an area of 1300 sq. M. in the state of New Hampshire, extending from the Androscoggin and Upper Ammonoosuc on the N. to the base of the Sandwich Range on the S. (a distance of 30 M.), and from the Maine frontier on the E. to the valley of the Connecticut on the W. (45 M.). The higher mountains rise from a plateau about 1500-1600 ft. above the sea, and attain an extreme elevation of 5-6000 ft. They are roughly divided into two main groups, the White Mts. proper to the E. and the Franconia Mts. to the W., but with numer-ous subordinate groups. In the original and narrowest sense the name of White Mts. is restricted to the *Great* or *Presidential Range*, extending for about 13 M. from Mt. Madison on the N.E. to Mt. Webster on the S.W. The summits of this range culminate in *Mt. Washington* (6293 ft.), the highest point to the E. of the Rockies and to the N. of N. Carolina. The great mass of the White Mts. con-sists of granite, overlaid by mica slate. The scenery of the White Mts. is of a very beautiful and varied nature; and though few of the summits are sharp enough to deserve the name of peaks, many of them (such as Mt. Washington and Mt. Lafayette) are of very noble outline. They are now visited annually by many thousands of summer-guests, and all the chief points are of easy access. The first white visitor is said to have been Darby Field, in 1642.

The following account notices the chief tourist centres.

a. North Conway.

North Conway (520 ft.; **Kearsarge Ho.*, $ 3-4; *Sunset Pavilion, McMillan Ho.*, $3; *North Conway Ho.*, $2; numerous boarding-houses), charmingly situated on a low terrace above the 'inter-vales' of the winding *Saco River* (pron. 'Sawco'), is a favourite resort with those who like to combine the softer beauties of the valley with excursions into the mountains. To the W. rises *Moat Mt.*, to the E. the *Green Hills*, and to the N.E. *Mt. Kearsarge* and *Hurricane Mt.*, while to the N. and N.W. more distant views are obtained of Mt. Washington and other lofty summits. About 1 1/2 M. to the N. lies the pretty and sequestered little hamlet of *Intervale* (550 ft; **Intervale Ho.*, $3; *Bellevue*, $2; stat., p. 110); and near the foot of Mt. Kearsarge (see below), 1 M. to the N.W., is *Kearsarge Village* (The Ridge, $ 2-2 1/2; *Merrill Ho.*, $1 1/2).

To ECHO LAKE AND THE LEDGES, 2-2 1/2 M. From the *Kearsarge Ho.* we follow the road to the N. to (7 min.) the *Sunset Pavilion*, take the road to the left here (which soon passes below the railway), and cross the (7 min.) Saco by a covered bridge. A few hundred paces farther on we cross a branch of the river. About 8 min. farther on, at another brook, the road forks, the left branch leading to Echo Lake, the right to the Cathedral (see below). We follow the former. At the (12 min.) cross-roads we continue in a straight direction. 3 min. **Echo Lake* (925 ft.), a tiny lake, finely situated at the base of a bold rocky bluff which has been prominent during most of our walk. This is the *White Horse Ledge* (so called from a patch of white rock), one of a series of so-called *Ledges* (100-900 ft.), or cliffs, in which Moat Mt. ends on this side. Following the bank of the lake towards the N. and disregarding roads leading back to the right, we reach (7 min.) a path leading through wood to the left, which ultimately crosses a fence and reaches (8 min.) a road. We follow the road in the same direction past a quarry, just beyond which are a small refreshment hut and the *Devil's Den*, under an overhanging slab of rock. A stony path clambers up the cliff to (3 min.) the *Cathedral*, a cavity in the granite rock, 60 ft. high, 40 ft. deep, 20 ft. wide, and 167 ft. above the river (view). We now return to the point whence we emerged from the forest-path, and follow the road to the left. At (6 min.) the high-road (white farm-house) we turn to the right. 10 min. *Bridge*, where we diverged to the left for Echo Lake (see above). [By turning to the left on regaining the high-road and following it for 3/4 M., we reach a sign-board pointing to *Diana's Baths*.]

To ARTISTS' FALLS, 1 3/4 M. We proceed to the S. from the Kearsarge Ho., past the Maine Central R. R. Station, to (10 min.) the bridge over *Artists' Brook;* then turn to left and follow the road, crossing another bridge, to (12 min.) the *North Conway Keeley Institute* (formerly *Artists' Falls Hotel*). A path to the right leads to (5 min.) the *Forest Glen Mineral Spring* (alkaline). To reach the falls we take the right branch of the fork opposite the spring, and in 5-6 min. more hear their roar. The *Artists' Falls* are small, but pretty in wet weather.

*ASCENT OF MT. KEARSARGE (5-6 hrs. there and back). Going N. from the Kearsarge Ho., we take the (3 min.) second turning to the right (sign-post 'to Kearsarge Village'), cross the railway, and (5 min.) turn to the left. This road leads through *Kearsarge Village* (see above) to (1 1/4 M.) a small church, where we turn to the right. 1/3 M. *Farm-house* (carr. to

this point, 50 c. a head; horse hence to the top $2; guide, unnecessary, $2; ascent hence in 1³/₄-2¹/₄ hrs.). The path, which is steep and stony at first, comparatively easy in the middle, and steep towards the top, begins behind the farm-house, crosses fields, and enters (8 min.) the wood. 25 min. Path leading back to the right to *Prospect Ledge* (*View of Saco Valley, Moat Mt., etc.). About 10 min. farther up we pass a small spring (to the right). In 10 min. we emerge from the wood and reach the rocky ledges, and soon see a small cairn a little to our right. It is not easy to give directions from this point, but by noting the worn part of the rocks and keeping a look-out for the cairns, we reach the top in about 1 hr. more. At first we keep to the right and then swing round to the left to approach the summit from the W. The noble *View from the pyramidal **Mt. Kearsarge**, *Kiarsarge*, or *Pequawket* (3270 ft.; Rfmt. Hut at the top) includes the Saco Valley to the S. and W.; Mt. Chocorua and the bare ridge of Moat Mt. to the S.W.; Moosilauke (p. 131; in the distance), Mt. Hancock, Mt. Carrigain, and Mt. Lafayette, to the W. and W.N.W.; and most of the main summits of the White Mts., including a grand view of Mt. Washington, to the N.W., and the Wild-Cat and Carter Mts., with the Carter Notch between, to the N.; several lakes and ponds, including Lake Sebago, to the E. and S.E. The other Mt. Kearsarge (p. 117), 60 M. off, is seen to the left of Chocorua. The descent may be made to Bartlett (p. 110). In descending to N. Conway a little care is necessary to follow the route over the ledges. In the wood we keep mainly to the right, as nearly as possible straight down the incline.

    Moat Mountain (N. peak, 3217 ft.; *View) may be ascended in 3-4 hrs., from North Conway by a path (sign-posts and cairns) beginning near (3 M.) *Diana's Baths* (see p. 123). — *Middle Mt.* (1500 ft.), another good point of view, is ascended in 1 hr. by a path beginning near the Forest Glen Mineral Spring (see p. 123). The adjoining *Peaked Mt.* (1 hr.) and *Sunset Hill* (855 ft.), a 'cub' of *Hurricane Mt.*, are also easily ascended.

    Among the favourite Drives from N. Conway are those '*Around the Square*' (5 M.), the '*Dundee Drive*' (12 M.), and to *Jackson Falls* (9 M.; see below). The distance through the *White Mountain Notch* (p. 126) to the *Crawford House* (p. 126) is 26 M.

    Coaches run regularly from N. Conway to (9 M.) *Jackson* (see below) and (20 M.) the *Glen House* (p. 125), passing (5 M.) *Glen Station* (p. 110).

b. Jackson and the Glen House.

    Jackson (760 ft.; *Wentworth Hall, Arden Ho.*, and *Thorn Mt. Ho.*, $4-5; *Gray's Inn*, $2-3; *Jackson Falls Ho.*, $2¹/₂-3; *Glen Ellis Ho.*, $2¹/₂; boarding-houses) is a small hamlet overshadowed by *Iron Mt.* (2740 ft.) and *Thorn Mt.* The *Jackson Falls*, on the *Wild-Cat River*, near the hotels, are pretty. Good fishing.

    Excursions are made hence to *Goodrich Falls*, 1¹/₂ M. to the S. (fine after heavy rain only); up the glen of the *Wild-Cat Brook* to the (8 M.) *Carter Notch* (3320 ft.), between *Wild-Cat Mt.* (4415 ft.) and the *Carter Dome* (4856 ft.); to the top of (1 hr.) *Thorn Mt.* (ca. 2300 ft.); to (4¹/₂ M.) *Fernald Farm* (view of Mt. Washington); to the (3 M.) *Winneweta Falls*, etc.

    Coaches ply to (4 M.) *Glen Station*, (11 M.) the *Glen Ho.*, and (9 M.) *N. Conway*. Carriage to (20 M.) the top of *Mt. Washington* $6 each, incl. toll; there and back $7.

    The road from Jackson to (11M.) the Glen House runs to the N. along the *Ellis River*, passing through the wooded *Pinkham Notch* (2018 ft.) and affording glimpses to the left of the deep ravines of Mt. Washington. About 4 M. from the Glen Ho. a path to the right (sign-board) leads to the (¹/₄ M.) *Glen Ellis Falls* (70 ft.), and a little farther on, to the left (sign-board), diverges that to the (³/₈ M.)

Crystal Cascade (80 ft.). A steep road to the left farther on joins the
(1¹/₂ M.) carriage-road from the Glen Ho. to Mt. Washington (p. 132),
2 M. above the toll-house. The path to (¹/₄ M.) *Thompson's Falls* and
Emerald Pool (guide-board) leads to the right, 1¹/₂ M. farther on.

The *Glen House (1630 ft. ; $ 4¹/₂), a large summer-hotel, is
finely situated on the *Peabody River*, at the N.E. base of Mt. Washington, with Mts. Clay, Jefferson, Adams, and Madison forming a
grand line of summits to the N. of it. It is a good centre for some
of the finest excursions in the White Mts.

The chief excursion is, of course, the *Ascent of Mt. Washington*, described
at p. 132, either by road or on foot through Tuckerman's Ravine.
Short excursions may be made to (3³/₄ M.) the *Crystal Cascade*, the
(4¹/₄ M.) *Glen Ellis Falls*, and the (2¹/₄ M.) *Thompson's Falls* and *Emerald
Pool* (see above); to *Garnet Pools*, on the Peabody, ³/₄ M. to the N.; and
to the *Osgood Cascades*, 1¹/₄ M. to the N.W. By following the Gorham
road (see below) for about 2 M., crossing the bridge over the Peabody, and
turning to the right, we reach a point whence we see the profile on *Imp Mt.*
Carter Dome (4856 ft.; to the *Carter Notch*, 3-4 hrs.; thence to the top
1¹/₂-2¹/₂ hrs.) is a good point of view and may be ascended with a guide.
— The ascent of *Mt. Wild-Cat* (4280 ft.; *View of Mt. Washington) is
shorter and easier (1-1¹/₂ hr.). — Good walkers may reach the top of
Mt. Washington viâ Mts. Madison, Adams, Jefferson, and Clay in 9 hrs.
(with guide); and the Appalachian Club has also constructed a blazed path
along the whole *Carter Range* (8 M.; fine views) to *Mt. Moriah* (see below).
— *Tuckerman's Ravine*, see p. 132.
The *Drive from the Glen House to Gorham (8 M.; coach $ 1¹/₂)
descends the valley of the *Peabody* and affords fine views.

c. Gorham.

Gorham (810 ft.; *Alpine House*, $ 2¹/₂-3¹/₂ ; *Eagle Ho.*, $ 2),
the N. gateway to the White Mts.., is a village with about 2000
inhab., finely situated at the confluence of the *Androscoggin* and the
Peabody and commanding a charming view of hill and valley. To
the S. is the Peabody valley, with Mts. Moriah and Carter to the
left; to the N.E., Mt. Hayes; to the N.W., the Pilot Mts. The
peaks of the Presidential Range (see p. 122) are concealed by *Pine
Mt.* (2380 ft.), which rises in the S.W. foreground, but they are
well seen from adjacent points. Numerous delightful excursions
can be made in the neighbourhood (see below).

A good point of view in the immediate vicinity is the *Lary Farm*
(³/₄ M. to the N.). — Perhaps the best of the shorter walks is that to
the top of **Mt. Hayes** (2600 ft.), 2 M. to the N.E. The easy and well-
marked path begins at the N. end of the suspension-bridge over the Androscoggin and ascends directly, through wood, to (1¹/₂ M.) the ridge and (¹/₂ M.)
the summit. The *View includes (from left to right) Mt. Moriah, Imp Mt.,
and Carter Mt. to the S.; the valley of the Peabody (Pinkham Notch), a
little to the right; to the S.W., Mt. Washington, the low Pine Mt. (in
the foreground), Mt. Madison, and Mt. Adams; to the W., Cherry Mt., Owl's
Head, and (more to the right) Randolph Mt. and Mt. Starr King; to the
N.W., the Pilot Mts., Deer Mt., and the twin Percy Peaks. Some authorities consider this the best view of Mt. Washington.
Mt. Surprise (2030 ft.), a spur of Mt. Moriah, to the S.E. of Gorham,
may be ascended in 2 hrs. by a path through wood (boy to show its
beginning desirable), and commands a fine *View of the Presidential
Range. — A seldom-used path (guide necessary) leads hence to the (2-3 hrs.)
top of *Mt. Moriah* (4065 ft.; *View).

Randolph Hill (1700 ft.; Randolph Hill Ho.), 5 M. to the W. of Gorham, is reached by a good road, affording fine views of the Presidential Range.

Stage-coaches run daily from Gorham through the Peabody Valley to the (8 M.) *Glen House* (see p. 125) in 1¹/₂ hr. (fare $ 1¹/₂). It is possible by this route to ascend Mt. Washington from Gorham in one day (comp. p. 132).

Pleasant drives may also be taken along the S. bank of the Androscoggin to (11 M. to the E.) *Gilead Bridge*, returning on the N. bank by the *Lead-Mine Bridge* (3¹/₂ M. from Gorham; *View); to the N., along the 'Milan Road' to (6 M.) the *Berlin Falls* (p. 109) and (14 M.) *Milan Corner*; and W. to (37 M.) the *Crawford House* (see below) and the *White Mt. Notch* (see below) viâ (17 M.) *Jefferson Hill*, by the 'Cherry Mt. Road', the *White Mt. House* (p. 127), and the *Fabyan House* (p. 127; splendid views). A grand walk for a good pedestrian would be to ascend *Mt. Madison* (p. 125) and proceed thence viâ *Mts. Adams* and *Jefferson* (see p. 125) to *Mt. Washington* (guide necessary; 1-2 days).

Gorham is a station on the Grand Trunk Railway from Portland to Montreal (see p. 109), and a new line is in progress hence to *Jefferson* and *Whitefield* (comp. p. 119, and see Map, p. 120).

d. Crawford House and the Notch.

The *Crawford House (1900 ft.; $ 4¹/₂ a day, $ 21-28 a week), one of the most deservedly popular hotels in the White Mts., occupies a solitary site on a small plateau, ¹/₄ M. above the N. entrance to the White Mt. Notch. The small pool in front of the house is the source of the *Saco River*, flowing to the S. through the Notch to Maine and the sea, while the *Ammonoosuc*, also rising close to the hotel, flows N. (and then W.) to the Connecticut. The railway station (p. 111) is near the hotel. To the W. rises *Mt. Tom* (p. 127) and to the E. *Mt. Clinton* (p. 127), while in front, enclosing the Notch, are *Mt. Willard* (p. 127; r.) and *Mt. Webster* (p. 127; l.)

The railway route through the *White Mountain Notch (1915 ft.) has been described at p. 111 and affords some of the finest, though most fleeting, views of it. The Notch is seen to greater advantage in descending. The road and river enter the Notch through a rocky *Gateway*, 25 ft. wide, while a separate cutting has been made for the railway (above, to the right). To the left is the rock known as the *Elephant's Head* (*View). Within the Notch various fantastic names have been given to rocks supposed to resemble human faces, etc. About ³/₄ M. from the Crawford Ho., to the left, the *Flume Cascade* descends, in three leaps, from a height of 250 ft.; and ¹/₄ M. farther on is the graceful *Silver Cascade*, with a total fall of 900 ft., of which about 300 ft. are seen from the road. The *Willey House* (1325 ft.), a small inn 3 M. from the Crawford Ho. and 300 ft. below the railway, was the scene of a terrible disaster in Aug., 1826. The whole Willey family, 9 in number, rushing from the house to escape a land-slip, apparently descending directly upon it, were overtaken and crushed, while the house escaped harm through the splitting of the land-slide by a rock. The Notch proper ends just below the Willey Ho., but it is well worth while to continue the walk or drive to Bemis, whence if necessary we may return by railway. At the (1¹/₄-1¹/₂ M.) *Cow* or *Avalanche Brook* (the second

brook below the Willey Ho.), we may cross the railway and ascend
to the right to (1³/₄ M.) the *Ripley or *Sylvan Glade Falls* (110 ft.),
about 1 M. above which is the *Sparkling Cascade.* Continuing to
follow the road along the Saco we reach (2 M.; 6¹/₂ M. from the
Crawford Ho.) *Bemis Brook,* whence an ascent of 1 M. along its
course brings us to the picturesque *Arethusa Falls* (175 ft.). *Bemis*
(rail. stat., p. 110) is 2 M. farther down. The Mts. to the left at
this part of the road are the *Giant's Stairs* (3512 ft.), *Mt. Resolution* (3436 ft.), and *Mt. Crawford* (3130 ft.), while *Mt. Nancy*
(3944 ft.) towers to the right. Drivers may go on from Bemis to
(18¹/₂ M.) *North Conway* (p. 123).

*Mt. Willard (2570 ft.), easily ascended by a carriage-road (2 M.), crossing
the railway below the station, commands a splendid *View of the Notch
(afternoon light best). Near the top (S. side) is a cavern known as the
Devil's Den, accessible by ropes only. The *Hitchcock Flume,* 350 ft. long
and 50 ft. high, is reached by a path to the left, ¹/₄ M. from the summit. —
Ascent of *Mt. Washington,* see p. 133. — Ascents of *Mts. Clinton* (4330 ft.),
Pleasant (4780 ft.), *Franklin* (5013 ft.), and *Monroe* (5379 ft.), see p. 133. —
The ascents of *Mt. Webster* (3923 ft.) and *Mt. Jackson* (4076 ft.) are fatiguing and unremunerative. — The views from *Mt. Tom* (4078 ft.) and *Mt.
Field* (4355 ft.) are also obscured by trees. — A better view is obtained
from *Mt. Willey* (4313 ft.; 2-3 hrs.; well-marked path beginning a little to
the S. of *Moore's Brook Station,* 3¹/₄ M. from the Crawford House).

Pleasant short walks may be taken to (³/₄ M.) *Beecher's Falls* (path crossing a foot-bridge over the railway and ascending through wood on the left bank
of the stream), *Bugle Cliff* (³/₄ M.), *Red Bench* (¹/₂ M.; view of Mt. Washington),
and the *Shapleigh Path* (1 M.). *Gibbs Falls* (¹/₂ M.) are reached by turning
to the left and ascending through wood and along a brook.

Between the Crawford House and (4 M.) *Fabyan's* (see below) the road
and railway descend 330 ft. (80 ft. per mile).

e. Fabyan House, Twin Mt. House, and Zealand.

The *Fabyan House (1570 ft.; $ 4¹/₂ a day, $ 21-25 a week), a
large and popular hostelry, stands on the site of the *Giant's Grave,*
a drift-mound on the Ammonoosuc river, 4 M. to the N. of the
Crawford House and near the S. base of *Mt. Deception* (3722 ft.). It
commands fine views of the mountains and is the junction of the
railway to the top of Mt. Washington (see p. 132; comp. pp. 111,119).

The *Mt. Pleasant House* ($ 3), ¹/₂ M. to the S.E., and the old *White Mt.
House* ($ 2¹/₂), ³/₄ M. to the N.W. (rail. stat., see p. 111), are smaller and
cheaper hotels, which send conveyances to meet the trains at Fabyan's.

UPPER FALLS OF THE AMMONOOSUC, 3¹/₄ M. We cross the railway in
front of the house and follow the road to the right (notice about key on
gate refers to carriages only). ¹/₄ hr. (left) *Monument to E. A. Crawford,*
one of the earliest settlers in the White Mts. The *Falls* (30-40 ft. high)
are picturesque, with their grey granite walls and grand mountain-back-
ground. — The (1¹/₄ M.) *Lower Ammonoosuc Falls,* near the White Mt. Ho.,
have been spoiled by a saw-mill. — A path leads from the Fabyan Ho. to
a view-point on the S. spur of *Mt. Deception* (see above).

The **Twin Mountain House** (1375 ft.; $ 4; rail. stat., p. 111)
is pleasantly situated on the Ammonoosuc, 5 M. to the W. of the
Fabyan House, but does not command so fine a view. The mountains opposite it are *Mt. Hale* (4100 ft.; left) and the *North Twin*
(4783 ft.; right), the latter concealing the *South Twin* (4922 ft.).

The path to the top of the *North Twin Mt.* is now in good order and marked with sign-boards (3-4 hrs.). The continuation thence to the *South Twin* is reported as still easy to follow.

From **Zealand** (p. 111), 1 M. to the E. of the Twin Mt. Ho., a lumber railroad (not used by passengers) runs to (7 M.) *Zealand Pond* and (9 M.) *Thoreau Falls*, which descend 200 ft. in ¹/₂ M., in the deep valley between *Mt. Bond* on the right and the Willey Mt. (p. 127) on the left. The narrow-gauge line to *Bethlehem* and the *Profile House* (see below) also begins at Zealand, running along the standard-gauge line to *Bethlehem Junction*.

f. Bethlehem and Maplewood.

Bethlehem and *Maplewood* are reached by a short narrow-gauge railway from *Bethlehem Junction*, which passengers from the E. take at *Zealand* (comp. p. 111 and above).

The train from *Bethlehem Junction* (p. 111) soon reaches —

2 M. **Maplewood**, a small station for a group of hotels and summer-cottages. The *Maplewood* (1490 ft.; $4¹/₂; 500 guests), one of the handsomest and most fashionable hotels in the White Mts., commands a splendid distant *View of Mt. Washington. Adjacent is an annexe, the *Maplewood Cottage* ($2¹/₂-3 a day; from $10 a week). Public conveyances run frequently to Bethlehem (10 c.). *Mt. Agassiz* (see below; 2 M.) is ascended by a path beginning behind the Maplewood Hotel and proceeding through wood past (1 M.) a view-tower. The Bethlehem excursions (see below) may all be made from Maplewood.

3 M. **Bethlehem** (*Sinclair House*, $3¹/₂; *Mt. Agassiz Ho.*, $2; *Highland Ho.*, $2¹/₂; *Alpine Ho.*, well spoken of, $2-2¹/₂; *Ranlet Ho.*, $3; *Turner Ho.*, $2; and many others), with 1000 inhab., finely situated 1460 ft. above the sea and 260 ft. above the Ammo-noosuc, is visited annually by 10-15,000 summer-guests. Its lofty situation makes it cool in summer, and it commands magnificent views of the White Mts., while the Green Mts. are visible to the W. The 'White Mountain Echo' is published here.

Mt. Agassiz (2400 ft.), which rises at the back of the village, is ascended in ³/₄-1 hr. We follow the road leading S. from the Sinclair Ho. to (25 min.) a house with a sign referring to the toll to Mt. Agassiz (25 c., payable only by those who wish to enter the view-tower). Here we turn to the left and follow the path through wood to (25 min.) the top. The *View includes mountains on every side, the names of which are given by rough mountain-indicators on the top of the view-tower. Mt. Washington is seen to the E., Mt. Lafayette to the S., the Green Mts. to the W. The descent may be made to *Maplewood* (see above; not advisable in waning light, as the 'trail' through the woods is not very distinct). — *Cruft's Ledge*, 2 M. to the E. (reached by a path beginning beyond the Maplewood Hotel), and *Wallace Hill*, 3¹/₄ M. to the W., are other good points of view. — Favourite drives are the *Cherry Valley Drive* (5 M.), *Around the Heater* (6 M.; views of Franconia Mts.), to (7 M.) *Twin Mt. Ho.*, to (7¹/₂ M.) *Sugar Hill*, to (10 M.) *Profile House* (also reached by train, see p. 129), to (15 M.) *Jefferson Hill*, and to (17 M.) *Crawford House*. To reach the top of *Mt. Washington* viâ Fabyan's takes 2-2¹/₂ hrs. by train.

g. The Franconia Mts. Profile House.

The **Franconia Mts.**, included in the wider acceptation of the name White Mts. (see p. 121), is the small group of summits between the Twin Mt. Range on the E. and the Pemigewasset Range on the

W. The sharp-peaked *Mt. Lafayette* (see below) is the monarch
of the group, and the *Profile House* is the chief tourist centre.   On
the W. the range is bounded by the Franconia Notch (see below),
though in popular speech the term includes the mountains to the W.
of this valley. Most of the Franconia Mts. are densely wooded.

The *Profile House* is reached from *Bethlehem Junction* by a narrow-gauge
railway, 10 M. long, which runs through wood and affords little view. To
the right, as we approach the terminus, lies *Echo Lake.* — Route to the
Profile House from *Plymouth*, through the *Pemigewasset Valley*, see p. 119.

The **Profile House** (1974 ft.; $ 4-5), perhaps the largest of the White
Mt. hotels, stands, with its group of cottages, at the N.end of the
Franconia Notch (see below), to the W. of Mt. Lafayette.

About 1/2 M. to the N. of the hotel, to the right (E.) of the road, is
the pretty little *Echo Lake*, where fine echoes are aroused by bugle
(small fee; steam-launch round the lake, 1-5 pers. 75 c., each addit. pers.
15 c.). At the foot of the lake is *Artists' Bluff*, a good point of view. —
Eagle Cliff (1470 ft. above the hotel), close to the hotel on the E., is a
fine specimen of rock-formation (well seen from Profile Mt.). — **Profile
Mt.** or **Mt. Cannon** (4107 ft.), opposite the Eagle Cliff, is ascended in 2-
2 1/2 hrs. by a somewhat steep path beginning to the S. of the hotel and
running first through wood and then over rocky ledges. *View of Mt.
Lafayette. The *Cannon Rock* lies a little below the summit, on the E.
side. The *Profile Ledges* (see below), reached from above by a somewhat
steep scramble (no path), afford one of the best points of view. — *Bald
Mt.* (2310 ft.), to the N. of Echo Lake, is easily ascended in 1/4 hr. by a
cart-track diverging to the right from the road, 1 M. to the N. of the
hotel (*View; afternoon light best). — **Mt. Lafayette** (5270 ft.) is ascended
in 2 1/2-3 1/2 hrs. by a steep bridle-path diverging to the left from the road
in front of the hotel and skirting the S. side of Eagle Cliff (to *Eagle Lakes*,
1 1/4-1 3/4 hr.; thence to the top about as long). The sharp pyramidal
summit commands a splendid *View, including the Pemigewasset Valley
to the S., the Connecticut Valley and the Green Mts. to the W., and Mt.
Garfield (close at hand) and the Presidential Range to the N.E.

Most of the excursions from the Flume House (see p. 30) can be
made from the Profile House at a small additional expenditure of time.

The *Franconia Notch is a narrow wooded defile, 5 M. long,
traversed by the Pemigewasset River and flanked by the Franconia
Mts. on the E. and the Pemigewasset Range on the W. It lies about
2000 ft. above the sea, and the enclosing mountains rise 1500-
3000 ft. higher. Frequent coaches run through the Notch to (5 M.)
the Flume Ho. and thence to (5 M.) *North Woodstock* (p. 119).

Starting from the Profile House to walk or drive through the
Notch to (5 M.) the Flume House (p. 130), we soon reach a
sign-board by the roadside marking the best point of view for the
* *Profile* or *Old Man of the Mountain*, a curious freak of nature
formed by three protruding and disconnected ledges, 1200 ft. above
us, on the side of Cannon or Profile Mt. (right; see *Hawthorne's* 'Great
Stone Face'). Below the Profile, to the right of the road, 1/2 M. from
the hotel, is *Profile Lake* (boats). The road for the most part runs
through wood and affords no views. About 2 1/2 M. from the hotel, to
the right, a bridle-path diverges to (1 1/4 M.) *Lonesome Lake*, on
Cannon Mt., 1000 ft. above the road. To the left, 1/2 M. farther on,
is a sign-post indicating the way to *Walker's Falls* (1/2 M.) and *Cataract*

(1 M.). These lie in the *White Cross Ravine*, below Mt. Lincoln (5098 ft.), to the S. of Mt. Lafayette. To the right, 1 M. farther on, is the *Basin*, a small pool by the roadside, where the imaginative see the form of a human foot and leg in the rocks. A small brook coming in here may be ascended to ($^3/_4$ M.) the *Tunnel Falls.*

5 M. The *Flume House (1430 ft.; $ 3$^1/_2$), at the S. end of the Franconia Notch, is smaller, quieter, and cheaper than the Profile House, and well situated for excursions. It lies at the base of *Mt. Pemigewasset*, opposite *Mt. Liberty* and *Mt. Flume.*

A sign-post in front of the hotel indicates the route to ($^3/_4$ M.) the *Flume, a fine rocky gorge, 700 ft. long, 60-70 ft. high, and 10-20 ft. wide. It is traversed by a foaming stream, up which the path is carried by wooden galleries and bridges (waterproofs useful on account of the spray). Extensive traces are still discernible of the landslip of 1883, which carried away the boulder formerly suspended in the narrowest part of the ravine. — Another sign-post in front of the hotel points to ($^1/_2$ M.) the *Pool*, a basin in the solid rock, 150 ft. wide and 40 ft. deep, overshadowed by cliffs 150 ft. high. — The fine (3 M.) *Georgianna* or *Harvard Falls* (two leaps of 80 ft.) are reached by a path leaving the highroad to the right at a farm-house (guide), 1 M. to the S. of the Flume House. — *Mt. Liberty* (4472 ft.; view) may be ascended in 3-4 hrs. (descent 2-3 hrs.) by an Appalachian Mt. Club path viâ the Pool and *Langton's Falls*. This path is continued to the (2 M.) top of *Mt. Haystack*. A comparatively easy walk leads along the ridge from Mt. Liberty to Mt. Lafayette. — The ascent of *Mt. Flume* (4340 ft.; *View) is somewhat arduous. — *Mt. Pemigewasset* (2560 ft.), ascended by a steep bridle-path in $^1/_2$-1 hr., is a good and easily reached view-point.

Franconia (920 ft.; *Forest Hills*, $ 3$^1/_2$; *Elmwood*, $ 2, etc.), situated on the *Gale River*, 6 M. to the S. of Littleton (p. 119; daily coaches), 4 M. to the S.W. of Bethlehem, and 4 M. to the N.E. of the Profile Ho., is frequented by many summer-visitors. It affords good views of the Franconia Mts. and is a fair centre for excursions.

Sugar Hill (1350 ft.; *Sunset Hill Ho.*, $ 3; *Goodnow*, $ 2$^1/_2$; *Hotel Look Off*, etc.), 2$^1/_2$ M. to the S.W. of Franconia, is reached by daily coach from (7 M.) *Lisbon* (p. 119). The *View from the summit of the ridge (1780 ft.) from which the village takes its name is superb.

h. Jefferson Hill.

Jefferson Hill (1440 ft.; *Waumbek*, $ 2$^1/_2$-4; *Plaisted Ho., Starr King Mt. Ho., Jefferson Hill Ho.*, $ 2$^1/_2$-3; *Stalbird Ho., Grand View Ho.*, $ 2), situated on a spur of *Mt. Starr King*, above the *Israel River*, is a station on the Concord and Montreal R. R. and lies about 2 M. from Jefferson station on the Maine Central line (p. 111; hotel-omnibuses to meet the trains), 12 M. to the N. of Fabyan's, and 17 M. to the W. of Gorham (comp. p. 126). It commands what many consider the finest general *View of the White Mts.

Mt. Starr King (4030 ft.), the southernmost summit of the *Pilot Range*, is ascended by a well-marked path from the Waumbek Ho. in 1$^1/_2$-2$^1/_4$ hrs. The *View embraces the White Mts., the Franconia Mts., the Green Mts., the valley of the Connecticut, and the Pilot Mts. (to the N.). — **Owl's Head** (3270 ft.; view) is generally ascended from its W. side by a path (1$^1/_2$ hr.; fee) beginning at *King's Farm*, 6 M. from Jefferson Hill. — About 5 M. to the S.E. of Jefferson Hill, on the road to Gorham, is the *Mt. Adams House* ($ 2), 3$^1/_2$ M. beyond which begins 'Lowe's Path' up *Mt. Adams (5820 ft.; *View; 2$^1/_2$-3$^1/_2$ hrs.). [A path diverging

to the left from Lowe's ascends through *King's Ravine.*] — *Bray Hill*, a
low eminence 6 M. to the S.W. of Jefferson Hill, affords a good view.

The *Drive from Jefferson Hill to (17 M.) *Gorham* (comp. p. 126) or
(19 M.) the *Glen House* affords a splendid, unimpeded *View of the N.
side of the Presidential Range; and that to (16 M.) the *Crawford House*
(p. 126) is also fine. Other favourite drives are the rounds viâ *Stag Hollow* and the *Valley Road* (9 M.), and viâ *Blair's Mills*, the *Valley Road*,
and *Cherry Mt. Road* (18 M.). *Lancaster* (p. 111) is 7 M. to the W.N.W.

i. Mount Washington.

Mt. Washington (6293 ft.), the highest mountain in the United
States to the E. of the Rockies and N. of N. Carolina, deserves its
rank as monarch of the White Mts. as much for the grandeur of its
form as for its height. On the N. and E. it is furrowed by several
huge ravines, of which Tuckerman's (see p. 132) is the best-known. —
See *W. H. Pickering's* 'Walking Guide to the Mt. Washington Range'.

The group of buildings at the top includes the **Summit House**, a comfortable inn in which the night may be spent ($5 a day, meal or bed
$ 1¹/₂); a *U. S. Signal Service Station;* a view-tower (small fee); the office
of *'Among the Clouds'*, a daily paper published here in summer; the old
Tip-Top House (disused); stables; an engine-house, etc. The summit is now
annually visited by about 10,000 people. Warm clothing should be brought,
as even at midsummer the temperature is very low (30-50°). A temperature
of 60° below zero has been observed in winter. A powerful electric light,
placed on Mt. Washington in 1892, is visible for 100 M. round.

Botanists will find much to interest them in the flora of Mt. Washington,
the plants on and near the summit being identical with those of the Arctic
Circle. The happiest hunting-ground is the so-called *'Alpine Garden'*, a
terrace to the E. of and below the cone. See the *Geology of New Hampshire.*

The ordinary starting-points for the ascent of Mt. Washington are the
Fabyan House, the Crawford Ho., and the Glen Ho., while the route over
the Northern Peaks (p. 133) is a favourite one with tried pedestrians. Travellers should ascend one way and descend another. The routes from the
Glen Ho. (p. 132) are, perhaps, the finest. A good walker can ascend from
the Crawford Ho. and descend to the Glen Ho. in one day.

The **View from Mt. Washington is one of the finest and most
extensive in the Eastern States, reaching into Canada on the N. It
is particularly grand at sunrise or sunset, but the summit is sometimes swathed in mist or clouds for days at a time. The atmospheric
phenomenare often very interesting.

View. To the N., across the 'Great Gulf', rise Mts. Clay, Jefferson,
Adams, and Madison; a little farther to the right are Mt. Hayes, the Androscoggin Valley, and Mt. Moriah. Gorham is hidden by Pine Mt. To
the N.E. we look over the deep valley in which the Glen House lies to
Mt. Carter, to the right of which follow the Carter Dome, Carter Notch,
and Mt. Wild-Cat. In the distance, towards the N.E., are the Rangeley
Lakes and mountains on the Canadian border. To the E. we see Baldface, Mt.
Pleasant (with its hotel), and other lower mountains, in the State of Maine.
To the S.E. are the pyramidal Mt. Kearsarge and other hills round North
Conway, with the Ellis River flowing down to join the Saco. Directly
below us is Tuckerman's Ravine. Lake Sebago is also seen, while Portland and the ocean are visible on a clear morning. To the S. are Ossipee
Lake and Lake Winnepesaukee, with Mt. Chocorua between them, while
more in the foreground are the Giant's Stairs, and Mt. Webster, rising
over the White Mt. Notch. The stream seen here is the Mt. Washington
River. On the other side of the Notch (S.W.) rise Mts. Nancy, Carrigain,
Willey, and Field, while Mt. Moosilauke appears on the horizon a little
more to the right. The Lakes of the Clouds lie below Mt. Monroe, in

9*

the S.W. foreground. To the S. of W. the finely-shaped Mt. Lafayette is
seen among the other Franconia Mts.; while almost due W. opens the
valley of the Ammonoosuc (with the Fabyan Ho.), with the Green Mts.
and even the Adirondacks visible in the distance. To the N.W. are Cherry
Pond, Jefferson Hill, and the Israel River, with Mt. Starr King and the
Percy Peaks in the distance. The most' distant points said to be visible in exceptionally favourable weather are Mt. Beloeil (p. 110), 135 M. to
the N.E.; Mt. Wachusett (p. 113), 126 M., and Mt. Monadnock (p. 114),
104 M. to the W. of S.; and Mt. Whiteface (p. 172), 130 M. to the N.W.

ASCENT OF MT. WASHINGTON BY RAILWAY. A branch-line runs
from the Fabyan House (p. 127) to (6 M.) *Marshfield* or *Ammonoosuc
Station* (2670 ft.; Marshfield Ho.), the starting-point of the **Mt.
Washington Railway,** which was constructed on the cog-wheel
principle in 1866-69 and ascends on the W. side of the mountain.
The distance to the summit $(3^1/_{10}$ M.) is accomplished in $1^1/_2$ hr.
(fare $3; return-fare $4); the average gradient is 1 : 4, the maximum
gradient is $1 : 2^2/_3$. The season begins in July, and two or more trains
run daily. This is by far the most frequented ascent.

The train ascends steeply through wood. $^3/_4$ M. *Cold Spring*. Beyond
(1 M.) *Waumbek Junction* (3910 ft.; water-station) the trees become thinner.
At *Jacob's Ladder* (5470 ft.; water-tank), a long trestle-work, 30 ft. high
in the middle, the gradient is at its steepest. We now pass the forest line
and enjoy fine views. To the left are the 'humps' of *Mt. Clay*, with the
'Great Gulf' yawning below them and the peaks of Mts. Jefferson and Adams
above. From the $(2^1/_4$ M.) *Gulf Tank* (5800 ft.) to the summit the ascent
is easier. We see the carriage-road to the left, and pass the monument
(right) erected on the spot where Miss Bourne died of exhaustion in 1855.
3 M. *The Summit House* (see above). — It is possible, but rough and fatiguing,
to ascend on foot from Marshfield to the top along the railway (3-4 hrs.).

ASCENT FROM THE GLEN HOUSE (p. 125). An excellent carriage-
road (average gradient 1 : 8) was constructed from the Glen House
to $(8^1/_2$ M.) the *Summit House* in 1854, and mountain-carriages ascend twice daily in 3 hrs. (return-fare $5 each, incl. toll; descent
$3). Toll for foot-passengers 17c. — Pedestrians may also ascend
from the Glen Ho. through *Tuckerman's Ravine* in 4-6 hrs.

a. BY ROAD. The road at first ascends rapidly through wood, and
2 M. up is joined by the new road mentioned at p. 125. $3^1/_2$ M. *Halfway
House* (3840 ft.). At (4 M.) the *Ledge* we emerge from the trees and obtain a fine *View of the 'Great Gulf', with the other peaks of the Presidential Range beyond it. The road now ascends, less steeply, along the
edge of the Great Gulf. It then turns sharply to the left (S.S.E.) and
ascends along a shoulder, making another loop to the right ('Cape Horn')
farther up (*Views). The final ascent of the cone is steep.

b. ON FOOT THROUGH TUCKERMAN'S RAVINE ($4^1/_2$-6 hrs.; a fatiguing
route, but guide not necessary for mountaineers). We reach the ravine
either by a footpath made by the Appalachian Club from the *Crystal Cascade*
($3^3/_4$ M. from the Glen Ho.; see p. 125), or by a path, diverging to the left
from the Mt. Washington road, 2 M. from the Glen House (sign-post), and
joining (2 M.) the Crystal Cascade path.

*Tuckerman's Ravine is a huge gorge on the S.E. side of Mt. Washing-
ton, enclosed by towering rocky walls 1000 ft. high. Following the Appalachian path from the Crystal Cascade, through wood, we reach the
($1^1/_2$ M.) *Hermit Lake*, a small tarn, commanding magnificent views. A
rough walk of $^3/_4$ M. ($^1/_2$-$^3/_4$ hr.) brings us hence to the *Snow Arch*, in the
ravine proper, formed by the stream flowing under the huge masses of
snow piled up here in winter. The arch is generally to be seen till August.
From the Snow Arch we may reach the summit by a hard climb of 1-$1^1/_2$ hr.;

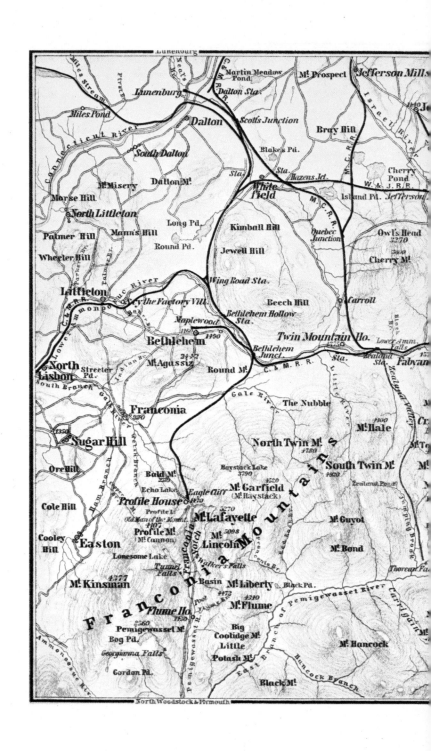

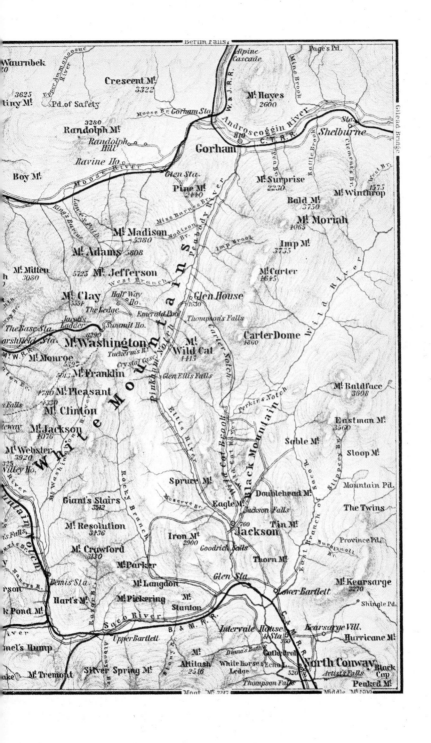

the route is marked by white paint on the rocks. Tuckerman's Ravine is often visited as an excursion from the Summit Ho. (there and back 3 hrs.); the descent to the Glen Ho. takes 3-3½ hrs. (view best in descending).

ASCENT FROM THE CRAWFORD HOUSE (4-6 hrs.; guide unnecessary in clear weather). The path is well marked and commands very extensive views.

The path begins to the E. of the Crawford House and ascends through wood on the W. side of Mt. Clinton (to the left the path to *Gibbs's Falls*, p. 127). In 1½-2 hrs. we reach the summit of **Mt. Clinton** (4330 ft.; view) and have behind us the worst part of the route. The path now leads along a ridge to the N.E., descends about 270 ft., and then re-ascends. The regular path leads to the right over the S.E. shoulder of **Mt. Pleasant** (4780 ft.), but a less distinct trail to the left leads to the (³/₄-1 hr.) top (*View), where the footpath from the Fabyan Ho. comes in (see below). We now descend in the same general direction to the *Red Pond*, on the plateau (4400 ft.) between Mt. Pleasant and Mt. Franklin. To the right, beyond the pond, is *Oakes Gulf* (3000 ft.; care necessary here in foggy weather). **Mt. Franklin** (5013 ft.), reached in ½ hr. from Mt. Pleasant, is another good point of view. Between Mt. Franklin and Mt. Monroe the path runs along a ridge, without much change of level. It leads round the S. peak of Mt. Monroe and bends to the N. To the E. is *Boott's Spur*, to the left the small *Lakes of the Clouds* (5050 ft.). ³/₄-1 hr. **Mt. Monroe** (5379 ft.), reached by a detour of ½ hr. from the main path, commands one of the best near views of Mt. Washington. The path next passes the gap (5100 ft.) between Mt. Monroe and Mt. Washington, and ascends over the rocky ledges on the S. side of the latter (the last part, up the cone, steep) to (1-1½ hr.) the top of *Mt. Washington* (see p. 131).

The *Davis Path* (6-8 hrs.) from the Crawford Ho., ascending between *Mts. Crawford* and *Resolution* and over the *Giant's Stairs*, is now seldom used and is not easily found without a guide.

ASCENT FROM THE FABYAN HOUSE (4³/₄-5½ hrs.).

This path diverges to the right from the railway, halfway between the Fabyan House and the Base Station, follows an old 'logging road' for some distance, and ascends the W. side of *Mt. Pleasant*, at the (1½-2 hrs.) top of which it joins the Crawford Path (see above).

ROUTE OVER THE NORTHERN PEAKS (1-1½ day, with guide).

The *Walk over Mts. Madison, Adams, Jefferson, and Clay to the summit of Mt. Washington forms a fine but trying excursion for good mountaineers with trustworthy guides. It is possible to do it in one long day, but it is preferable to take two days and pass the night in the *Madison Spring Hut* of the Appalachian Mt. Club (4900 ft.; open to all).

The *Views are very grand. **Mt. Madison** (5380 ft.) may be ascended from the Glen House by a somewhat overgrown path in 3-4 hrs.; it may also be ascended on the N. side by a path beginning at the Ravine House, 6½ M. to the W. of Gorham (comp. p. 125). In passing from Mt. Madison to Mt. Adams, we dip about 450 ft., and the *Madison Spring Hut* is in this depression, near *Star Lake*. **Mt. Adams** (5820 ft.) may also be ascended by the path ('Lowe's Path') mentioned at p. 130. *Storm Lake* (4940 ft.) lies in the hollow between Mt. Adams and **Mt. Jefferson** (5736 ft.; *View of Mt. Washington). Between Mt. Jefferson and **Mt. Clay** (5554 ft.) we descend 735 ft., and between Mt. Clay and *Mt. Washington* (p. 131) 940 ft.

17. From Boston to Albany.

a. By Boston & Albany Railroad.

202 M. RAILWAY in 5³/₄-7½ hrs. (fare $4½). To (38 M.) *Saratoga* in 1¼ hr. more (see p. 180). Through-trains run by this route to *Pittsburg*, *Chicago*, *Cincinnati*, etc.

From *Boston* (p. 72) to (99 M.) *Springfield*, see R. 4a. The

line to New York (see p. 6) diverges here to the left (S.), while
our line crosses the *Connecticut* and runs nearly due W. through the
valley of the *Agawam*. 108 M. *Westfield*, with manufactures of whips
and cigars. The train now begins to ascend along the *Westfield
River* and the hills grow higher. Beyond (126 M.) *Chester* the line
climbs rapidly through a rocky and wooded valley, contracting at
places to a wild ravine. Deep rock-cuttings. Numerous small lakes.
Near (135 M.) *Becket* (Claflin Ho.) we reach the flat top of the
Housac Range (ca. 1400 ft.), and farther on we begin to descend
again into the *Berkshire Valley*. For a description of the *Berkshire
Hills*, see R. 19. The descent to (146 M.) *Dalton* (Irving Ho.) is
rapid and the scenery picturesque. — 151 M. **Pittsfield**, junction
of the Housatonic R. R., see p. 136.

From Pittsfield to North Adams, 20 M., railway in ³/₄ hr. 9 M.
Cheshire; 14 M. *Adams*, the nearest station to *Greylock* (p. 141; ascent
arduous from this side). — 20 M. *North Adams*, see p. 141.

To the N. (right), at some distance, rises the double-peaked Greylock (p. 141). The train now crosses the *Housatonic*, turns to the
left (S.), passes (155 M.) *West Pittsfield* (with a settlement of Shakers),
and at (162 M.) *State Line* enters the *State of New York*. We leave
the Berkshire Valley by crossing the *Taghkanic* or *Taconic Range*
(ca. 2000 ft.) and then traverse an undulating wooded district. 185 M.
Niverville, with a fine park, much resorted to from Albany. Beyond
(200 M.) *Greenbush* we cross the *Hudson* by a fine bridge (view).
202 M. **Albany**, see R. 22.

b. Viâ the Hoosac Tunnel.

197 M. Fitchburg Railroad to (191 M.) *Troy* in 6-8 hrs.; New York
Central Railroad thence to (6 M.) *Albany* in ¹/₄ hr. (fares as above). *Saratoga* (p. 180) is reached by this line, viâ *Johnsonville*, in 6 hrs. Through-
trains run to the Western cities. The line skirts the N. margin of the
Berkshire Hills (R. 19; views to the left).

From Boston to (60 M.) *South Ashburnham*, see p. 113. Beyond
(97 M.) *Miller's Falls* we see Mt. *Toby* (1275 ft.) to the left. We
then cross the *Deerfield* and the *Connecticut* and reach (105 M.)
Greenfield (*Mansion Ho.*, $ 3; *American Ho.*, $ 2), a favourite summer-resort and the junction of the Conn. River R. R. Excursions
may be made hence to (3 M.) *Deerfield* (p. 142), *Turner's Falls*
(4¹/₂ M.), the *Coleraine*, *Leyden*, and *Shelburne Gorges*, etc.

The train now follows the pretty valley of the Deerfield, with
Arthur's Seat to the right, and beyond the *Deerfield Gorge* reaches
(119 M.) *Shelburne Falls* (Hotel), where the river descends 150 ft. in
two or three distinct falls. To the N. (right) of (128 M.) *Charlemont*
rises *Pocomtuck Mt.* (1890 ft.). The stream is crossed repeatedly,
and the scenery becomes wilder. A little farther on we penetrate
the *Hoosac Mt.* (2270 ft.) by the (135 M.) *Hoosac Tunnel* (765 ft.),
which is 4³/₄ M. long (transit of 9 min.; Mt. Cenis Tunnel 7¹/₂ M.)
and was constructed in 1855-74 at a cost of $ 16,000,000 (3,200,000*l.*).

143 M. *North Adams*, see p. 141. The train descends the valley of the Hoosac. To the left rises *Greylock* (p. 141), to the right *East Mt.* (2270 ft.). 148 M. *Williamstown*, see p. 141. We turn to the N.W. (right), cross a corner of *Vermont*, and enter *New York State*. 164 M. *Hoosick Falls*; 166 M. *Hoosick Junction*, for a branch-line to (6 M.) *Bennington* (p. 145).

At (175 M.) *Johnsonville* the railway forks, the left branch leading to Troy (see below), and the right to (189 M.) *Mechanicsville* (p. 144) and (212 M.) *Rotterdam Junction* (p. 195).

From (188 M.) *East Saratoga Junction*, on the latter branch, a line runs to (18 M.) *Saratoga* (p. 180).

191 M. **Troy**, see p. 145. Thence to (197 M.) **Albany**, see R. 20 c.

18. From New York to Pittsfield *(Berkshire Hills)*.

166 M. NEW YORK, NEW HAVEN, AND HARTFORD RAILROAD to (56 M.) *Bridgeport* in 1¹/₂-2¹/₂ hrs.; HOUSATONIC RAILROAD thence to (110 M.) *Pittsfield* (through-fare $3.40) in 4-4¹/₂ hrs. The 'Berkshire Hills Limited Express' diverges at (41¹/₂ M.) *South Norwalk* and joins the Bridgeport line at *Hawleyville* (to *Pittsfield* in 4¹/₂ hrs.).

From New York to (41¹/₂ M.) *South Norwalk* and (56 M.) *Bridgeport*, see R. 4a.

From South Norwalk one branch of the *Housatonic Railroad* runs to the N. through a pretty wooded country, becoming hillier as we proceed. 43 M. *Norwalk* (p. 57); 49 M. *Wilton;* 55 M. *Branchville*, the junction of a short line to *Ridgefield*, the birthplace of 'Peter Parley' (S. G. Goodrich; 1793-1860); 59 M. *Redding*, the birthplace of Joel Barlow (1755-1812), author of the 'Columbiad'; 63 M. *Bethel*, a prosperous little place with 2335 inhabitants. At (66 M.) *Hawleyville* we join the main line from Bridgeport (see below).

From Bridgeport the *Housatonic R. R.* ascends the valley of the *Pequonnock*. At (71 M.) *Botsford* it unites with the branch from New Haven (p. 58) and leaves the river. At (75 M.) *Newtown* the 'hills begin to show mountainous symptoms'. At (79M.) *Hawleyville* (see above) we cross the N. Y. & N. E. R. R. (p. 66).

The SHEPAUG RAILROAD runs from Hawleyville to (33 M.) Litchfield (*U. S. Hotel*, $2), a summer-resort in a pretty, hilly district, near *Bantam Lake*. Pop. (1890) 2246. It was the birthplace of *Henry Ward Beecher* (1813-1887) and *Mrs. Beecher Stowe* (b. 1812).

83 M. *Brookfield Junction*, for Danbury (p. 62), etc. At (85 M.) *Brookfield* the *Housatonic*, the beautiful valley of which we henceforth follow, comes into view on the right. We cross the river as we near (101 M.) *New Milford* (Weantinaug Inn, $3¹/₂-4; New Milford Ho., $2) and thereafter have it to the left. 104 M. *Kent* (Elmore Ho.), a prettily situated village; 113 M. *Cornwall Bridge*. To the left rises the *Sharon Ridge*. — 123 M. *Falls Village* (Dudley Ho.), near the **Falls of the Housatonic* (60 ft.). A coach runs hence to *Salisbury*. To the left (2¹/₂ M.) rises *Mt. Prospect*, a good point of view. — 129 M. *Canaan* (670 ft.; Dudley Ho., Warner Ho., $2), also a station on the Hartford & Connecticut Valley R. R., a good centre for excursions.

Canaan Mt. (1500 ft.), 1 M. to the S.E., affords a view of the Housatonic Valley, the Twin Lakes, and the Berkshire Hills (R. 19). The *Twin Lakes* lie 2½ M. to the W. Excursions may also be made to *Campbell's Falls* (7½ M.;), *Sage's Ravine* (9 M.; p. 137), etc.

We now pass from Connecticut into *Massachusetts* and enter the district of the *Berkshire Hills* proper (R. 19).

The *Taghkanic* or *Taconic Mts.* rise to the left, and the *Hoosac Range* to the right. Beyond (131 M.) *Ashley Falls* we cross the Housatonic. 135 M. *Sheffield* (see below); 141 M. **Great Barrington** (p. 137). — 143 M. *Van Deusenville* is the junction of a line to *West Stockbridge, State Line*, and *Albany* (p. 154). *Monument Mt.* (p. 138) rises to the right. — 145 M. *Housatonic*; 148 M. *Glendale*. We cross the river once more and bend to the right (E.). — 149 M. **Stockbridge** (p. 137). In the next few miles we cross the Housatonic several times. 151 M. *South Lee*; 155 M. *Lee* (p. 139); 157 M. *Lenox Dale*. At (159 M.) *Lenox Station* omnibuses from the hotels at (2½ M.) **Lenox** (p. 139) meet the trains. 162 M. *New Lenox*. We cross the river for the last time in entering —

166 M. **Pittsfield** (p. 140; *Rail. Restaurant*).

From Pittsfield to (20 M.) *North Adams*, see p. 141.

19. The Berkshire Hills.

The district known as the *Berkshire Hills, corresponding practically to *Berkshire County* (pop. 81,108) in the W. part of Massachusetts, is about 50 M. long from N. to S. and 20-25 M. wide from E. to W., covering an area of about 1300 sq. M. On the W. it is bounded by the Taconic Mts. and the State of New York; on the E. by the Hoosac Mts., a S. prolongation of the Green Mts.; on the S. by Connecticut; and on the N. by Vermont. The region confined between the two mountain-ranges is broken up into a number of smaller valleys, interspersed with isolated hills; and for the gentle loveliness of a hill-country, as contrasted with a mountain-country, it is unsurpassed in the United States and has few rivals elsewhere. The *Hoosac* flows through the district towards the N. to join the Hudson, and the *Housatonic* flows S. towards Long Island Sound, while innumerable small lakes and brooks add to its attractions. The praises of the Berkshire Hills have been repeatedly sung by Longfellow, Bryant, Whittier, Hawthorne, Beecher, and others. — The name of the Taconic Mts. is well known in geology, as the non-fossiliferous Taconic formations are regarded as a distinct system, intermediate between the Archæan rocks and the Potsdam sandstone. — Perhaps the best SEASON to visit the Berkshires is in autumn, as the brilliant autumnal tints of the American woods are seen here to perfection. Fashion has decreed that the seaside sojourn at Newport should be followed ere returning to town by a 'fall' visit to the Berkshire Hills, and many people stay here till well on in November. *Lenox* (p. 139) is the most fashionable resort, but *Stockbridge* (p. 137), one of the loveliest villages in America, is perhaps an equally good centre for casual travellers; while *Pittsfield* (p. 140), *Great Barrington* (p. 137), and other places also form good headquarters. The *Hotels* are usually good and not exorbitant. The *Roads* are good and well-adapted for driving and cycling. *Carriage Hire* is lower than at Newport or in the White Mts.

Pittsfield is reached from *New York* in 4½ hrs. (fare $ 3¼-3½; see R. 18) and from *Boston* (see R. 17a) in 4½-5 hrs. (fare $ 3.40).

The S. half of the district has hitherto been the best known, and the following description enumerates the chief points in order from S. to N. Comp. the 'New Book of Berkshire', by *Clark W. Bryan*.

Sheffield (675 ft.; *Conway Ho.*, $ 2; rail. stat., see above), a quiet little village on the *Housatonic*, attracts a few summer-visitors and is known for its marble-quarries, which supplied the material for Girard College (p. 217). Pop. (1890) 1954.

Mt. Washington (2625 ft.; view), sometimes called the *Dome* or *Mt. Everett*, one of the highest of the *Taconic Mts.*, rises 5 M. to the W. and is frequently ascended hence (road to the base; path to the top 1/2 hr.). — The *Sheffield Elm*, mentioned in the 'Autocrat of the Breakfast Table', is 1 M. to the S. of the centre of the village. — Other pleasant points are *Bear's Den*, 1 M. to the W.; *Sage's Ravine*, 4 M. to the S.W.; *Twin Lakes*, 7 M. to the S.; and *Ashley Falls* (4 M.). The *Bashbish Falls* are also visited hence.

From Sheffield we may proceed to the N., along the *Housatonic*, either by road (a pleasant drive) or railway, to (6 M.) —

Great Barrington (720 ft.; *Berkshire Inn*, Main St.; *Miller Ho.*; *Collin's Ho.*, $ 2; rail. stat., p. 136), beautifully situated in a hollow surrounded by hills, the slopes of which afford good views of the picturesquely-spired town and the valley. Pop.(1890) 4612.

The railway-station lies to the W. of *Main Street*, shaded by fine elms into which we turn to the S. (right). We pass the *Post Office* (l.) and *Town Hall* (r.) and in a few minutes reach (r.) the *Episcopal Church*, built of blue limestone, and the large new *Berkshire Inn*. Opposite, concealed by a massive stone wall and trees, is **Kellogg Terrace**, a magnificent mansion of blue limestone, with red-tiled roofs, erected by the late Mrs. Hopkins-Searles, in a French Gothic style, at a cost of $ 1,500,000 (300,000*l.*). It is most elaborately fitted up (no admission). A good distant view of it is obtained from the hill on the opposite side of the river. The *Grounds* contain a fine fountain (jet 80 ft. high). — The handsome **Congregational Church** and the Hopkins Memorial Manse (cost $ 300,000) are on the same side of the street, a little to the N. of the Post Office. The former contains a magnificent organ (3954 pipes, 60 speaking stops) and an 'echo' organ, concealed in the walls and operated by 2½ M. of electric wire. The parsonage is said to be the finest in the United States.

William Cullen Bryant (1794-1878), the poet, was for many years (1815-25) town-clerk of Great Barrington, and many of the town records are in his handwriting. His house (the 'Henderson Place') stood in the site occupied by the Berkshire Inn, but has been moved farther back and is now an annex of the hotel. *Dr. Samuel Hopkins*, the hero of Mrs. Stowe's 'Minister's Wooing', lived at Great Barrington for 25 years.

A few hundred yards to the N.W. of the station is the pretty little *Mansfield Pond*. The *Berkshire Heights* (980 ft.), 1½ M. to the N. of the station, command a fine *View*. About 3/4 M. to the S. is *Mt. Peter*, a good point of view. To the E., across the river, rise *Mt. Bryant* (1450 ft.) and *East Mt.* (1740 ft.). *Belcher's Cave* lies at the N. end of the village.

To the S.E. (5½ M.) lies *Lake Buel*, in the hill on the W. side of which is a chasm known as the *Ice Gulf*, where ice is found nearly all summer. — *Long Lake* lies 3 M. to the N.W. — *Monument Mt.* (p. 138) is 4½ M. to the N.

The direct road from Great Barrington to (7½ M.) *Stockbridge* (railway, see p. 136) runs on the E. side of the *Housatonic*, with *Monument Mt.* (p. 138) to the left and *Bear Mt.* (p. 139) to the right.

Stockbridge (830 ft.; *Stockbridge Inn*, $ 3, a comfortable old-fashioned house, with old china and other curiosities; *Edwards Hall*, p. 138, $ 2; boarding-houses), one of the most typical and charming of New England villages, with its immemorial elms and immaculate neatness, 'sleeps along a level plain just under the rim of the hills'. Pop. (1890) 2132.

The *Stockbridge Inn* stands in Main St., at the corner of the road leading to (1/2 M.) the railway-station (p. 136). Opposite is the

tasteful *Episcopal Church*, adjoining which is a *War Monument.*
Following Main St. towards the left (W.) we pass, on the left, the
Sedgwick Mansion, the old home of the Sedgwick family. To the
right, nearly opposite, is *Edwards Hall*, now a boarding-house,
where *Jonathan Edwards* (1703-58) wrote his famous treatise on
'The Freedom of the Will'. It is recognizable by the three little
windows above the ponderous old door.   Beyond Edwards Hall is
the *Casino*, with tennis - courts, etc.   Nearly opposite (left) is the
Congregational Church, in front of which is a *Bell Tower*, erected by
David Dudley Field to the memory of the Indian Mission and his
deceased grandchildren. The most interesting part of the *Cemetery*
(right) is the enclosure of the Sedgwick family, with the grave of
the authoress Catherine M. Sedgwick (1789-1867). The *Edwards
Monument*, also to the right, was erected in 1871 by the descendants
of Jonathan Edwards. To the left is the beautiful *Dwight Place*,
beyond which, on the same side, is the interesting *Old Burial Ground
of the Stockbridge Indians, with an appropriate monument (*View).
The road diverging to the right at the Edwards Monument leads to
a *Park*, laid out and presented to the town by Cyrus W. Field (view).

In the part of Main Street to the E. of the Stockbridge Inn is the
Jackson Library and Reading Room (10,000 vols.; open to strangers).
A little farther on is the *Academy*, with *Laurel Hill* behind it.

To Ice Glen, 1¹/₄ M. From the railway-station we follow the track
to the left (E.) to (6 min.) a style to the right, where we cross the fence.
The path to the glen runs to the right (up the hill). *Ice Glen, a cleft in
Bear Mt. (see p. 139), is a wild, cold, and narrow rocky ravine, in the
caverns of which ice may be found in midsummer and which forms a
startling contrast to the surrounding scenery. At (15-20 min.) the upper
end of the glen we pass through a gate into a pasture, across which we
descend by a faint path to (5 min.) the road (gate here marked 'Path to
Ice Glen'). Following the road to the right, we regain the station in ¹/₄ hr.

*From Stockbridge to Monument Mt. (there and back 9-10 M., or
3-4 hrs.). From the Stockbridge Inn we descend Main St. to the left. It
bends to the left, passes the Indian Burial Ground (see above), and (²/₃ M.)
crosses the *Housatonic*. We then turn to the left and in a few hundred
paces cross the railway. Avoiding the road to the right here, we continue in a straight direction to (³/₄ M.) the cross-roads, where we keep
to the left. The road soon dwindles to a lane and begins to ascend.
³/₄ M. *Smith's Farm*, 325 ft. above Stockbridge (view). Here we should
ask the way across the pasture, which ascends to the left to (8 min.) a
gate leading into the wood. The route through the forest is by an old
and winding cart-track, now seldom used for driving. In 20 min. it is
joined by another track from the right. A few yards beyond this, to the
left, is a small patch of grass, with a slab of rock. A steep footpath
ascends hence over rocks to (5-10 min.) the chaotic, rocky top of *Monument Mt. (1250 ft.), which commands a magnificent *View of the Housatonic Valley and the Berkshire Hills. The rock-formations (white quartz)
are very fine, especially one huge detached pinnacle known as the 'Pulpit'.
Ladies or others who object to scrambling should now return to the cart-
track and either retrace their steps or follow it to the left to (25 min.)
the Great Barrington road. A little time is saved, however, by descending
the indistinct path on the other side of the summit, which merges (¹/₄ hr.)
in a grassy wheel-track, that joins (3 min.) the above-mentioned cart
track about 10 min. from the Great Barrington road. Here we turn to
the left for (3³/₄ M.) *Stockbridge*, a dusty high-road walk which we may

.avoid by having a carriage to meet us. About 1 M. from Stockbridge we pass the stump (32 ft. in girth) of a huge willow.

From Stockbridge to Lenox viâ Lake Mahkeenac and Bald Head, 8-9 M. We follow the road leaving Main St. at the Episcopal church and take the first road to the left (sign-post 'to Lenox 6 M.'). The road ascends *Prospect Hill* (*View of Stockbridge) and for a mile or two is lined with handsome 'places'. To the right is *Rattlesnake Hill.* After about 3 M. we see *Lake Mahkeenac or the Stockbridge Bowl (ca. 920 ft.) below us to the left. At the (1 M.) fork near the N. end of the lake, we follow the left branch ('to Lenox and Pittsfield'). At ($^3/_4$ M.) the next fork we again keep to the left, passing (on the lake, to the left) the scanty remains of the house in which Nathaniel Hawthorne lived in 1849-51, and wrote the 'House of the Seven Gables' and other works. $^3/_4$ M. Opposite the pretty home of Mr. Higginson, we take the central of three roads (driving to this point advisable in hot or dusty weather), and immediately afterwards follow the road to the left between two private roads. A very little farther on we ascend to the right by a steep lane. In 20-30 min. we see the bare grassy top of **Bald Head** or *Mt. Prospect* (1585 ft.) to the right, which we reach by crossing the fence and grass to (5 min.) the cairn. *View to N. and S., including Lenox, the Stockbridge Bowl, and Monument Mt. We may now return to the lane and follow it round a wooded hill and down to ($2^1/_2$ M.) Lenox. Or we may descend the cart-track in the hollow between Bald Head and the wooded summit to the N., which leads toward Lenox but soon dwindles to a trail and finally disappears (this route not advisable for ladies or elderly people). At (10-15 min.) the foot of the hill we emerge from the wood on a field, where we climb the fence and continue in the general direction of ($1^1/_2$ M.) Lenox, which is seen in front. There are so many private roads here, that it is impossible to give precise directions, but it is scarcely possible to go far wrong. *Lenox*, see below.

Excursions are also made from Stockbridge to *Mohawk Lake,* $2^3/_4$ M. to the W.; *Lake Averic,* 3 M. to the N.W.; *Eldon's Cave,* in *Tom Ball Mt.,* $3^1/_2$ M. to the W.; over the old *Burgoyne Road* (*Bear Mt.;* views); *Lee* (4 M.); *Great Barrington* ($7^1/_2$ M.); *West Stockbridge* (5 M.), etc.

Lee (865 ft.; *Morgan Ho.*), 4 M. to the N.W. of Stockbridge, is a village with paper-mills and quarries of marble (used for the Capitol at Washington, etc.). Pop. (1890) 3785. A fine drive may be taken through the *Hopbrook Valley* to *Fernside* (1160 ft.; Hotel), *Tyringham,* and *Monterey* (12 M.). *Highlawn Farm,* a famous horse-breeding establishment, lies $^3/_4$ M. to the N.W., on *Laurel Lake* (p. 140).

Lenox (1270 ft.; *Curtis House,* $ 4; *Bellevue House,* with fine view from the back-windows, $ 3; numerous boarding-houses), beautifully situated on a ridge, $2^1/_2$ M. to the W. of the railway-station (p. 136) and 6 M. to the N. of Stockbridge, is the Newport of the Berkshires and makes an even greater impression of wealth and luxury than the real Newport. The main street, shaded with elms, contains the hotels, a *Club,* a *Public Library,* etc., while the slopes and crests of the surrounding hills are covered with large and often beautiful country - houses. Driving, riding, and lawn tennis (tournament in Oct.) are the favourite amusements; horse-races are held in the Lee Pleasure Park, and the annual 'Tub Parade' (of carriages) is a regular institution. *Fanny Kemble* (1811-93) and *Henry Ward Beecher* (1813-87) are among the most famous of former Lenox residents.

The best way to see Lenox is to hire a carriage, with an intelligent driver, and spend 2-3 hrs. in driving about the network of excellent private roads (open to light vehicles only) of which the place consists. The grounds of many of the houses are open to the carriages of visitors. The

*Sloane and *Lanier Places* adjoin each other and command a superb *View. Perhaps the finest grounds are those of the *Rathbone Place.* The *Stokes House* is built round a tree. The *Westinghouse Mansion* is a costly and pretentious structure of white marble.

The DRIVES and WALKS round Lenox are very attractive, and one can scarcely go wrong in any direction. Among the favourite excursions are those to the top of *Bald Head* (2¹/₂ M.; see p. 139); the *Stockbridge Bowl* (2¹/₂ M.; p. 139) and *Stockbridge* (6 M.; p. 137); *Laurel Lake* and the *Highlawn Farm* (p. 139), 2³/₄ M. to the S.E.; *North Lenox Mt.* and *Yokun's Seat* (2080 ft.), 4-4¹/₂ M. to the N.W.; *Pittsfield* (6 M.; see below); the settlement of the *Lebanon Shakers* (see below) and *Perry's Peak* (2080 ft.; view), 9 M. to the N.W.; *October Mt.,* 4 M. to the N.E. *Richmond,* 4¹/₂ M. to the W., is celebrated for its parallel trains of boulders, described by Sir Chas. Lyell. Short walks may be taken to (³/₄ M.) the *Ledge,* the (1 M.) *Pinnacle,* the *Lily Pond* (1¹/₂ M.), the *Schermerhorn Woods,* etc.

Pittsfield (1010 ft.; **Maplewood*, North St., $ 3; *Springside; American Ho.*, open all the year, $2¹/₂-3; *Burbank Ho.*, commercial, $2-3; *Rail. Restaurant*), the chief city of Berkshire County, with (1890) 17,281 inhab., is finely situated on a plateau surrounded by hills. It was named in 1761 in honour of the elder Pitt.

The public green in the centre of the city, named the 'heart of Berkshire', bears the original statue of the *Massachusetts Colour Bearer*, by Launt Thompson, which has been reproduced at Gettysburg (p. 239). Among the buildings round the green ar two Churches, the white marble *Court House*, and the *Berkshire Athenaeum* (with the *Berkshire Historical Society*). The *Bishop Training School for Nurses*, the *House of Mercy*, the *Old Ladies Home*, and the small *R. C. Cathedral of St. Joseph* may also be mentioned. Pittsfield is the headquarters of the *Agassiz Association* for the study of natural history, which has 1000 local 'chapters' in different parts of the world and over 20,000 members (president, H. H. Ballard). Among the many interesting and attractive private residences are the *Appleton* or *Plunkett House*, in East St., where Longfellow wrote 'The Old Clock on the Stairs' (clock still in the house); the quaint old *Kellog Place*, also in East St.; and *Elmwood*, Broad St., with its beautiful grounds. The *Cemetery* contains fine old trees and a large red granite obelisk. *Oliver Wendell Holmes* lived for some time at a small villa, 2 M. to the S., on the road to Lenox; and the *Rev. Dr. John Todd* (1800-1874), author of the well-known 'Lectures to Children', was long pastor of the Congregational Church. Electric cars traverse the principal streets.

About 2 M. to the W. of Pittsfield lies *Lake Onota*, on the E. shore of which a public park has been laid out. The excursion may be continued in the same direction, across the *Taconic Mts.*, to (7 M.) *Lebanon Springs* (Columbia Hall, $3-4), the waters of which are useful in cutaneous and liver complaints. The Shaker village of *Lebanon* is 2 M. to the S. of the Springs (interesting Sunday services). — *Pontoosuc Lake*, reached by electric car, lies 2¹/₄ M. to the N. of Pittsfield, on the road to (20 M.) *Williamstown* (p. 141). *Lanesboro*, 2¹/₂ M. farther on, was the birthplace of 'Josh. Billings' (H. W. Shaw; b. 1818). — On the slopes of the Taconic Mts., to the N.W. of Lake Onota, are the *Lulu Cascade* (4 M.) and *Berry Pond* (5 M.). — Among the 'Opes', or view-commanding vales, in this neighbourhood, is the '*Ope of Promise*', affording a view of the '*Promised Land*'. — The *Balanced Rock* is 2 M. to the N. of Lake Onota and 2 M. to the W. of Pontoosuc Lake. — *South Mt.* (1870 ft.), 2 M. to the S., commands a view of Pittsfield, Lake Onota, Greylock, etc. — Other favourite points for excursions are *Potter Mt.*, 8 M. to the N.W.; the *Wizard's Glen*, 4 M. to the N.E.; the *Wahconah Falls*, 8 M. to the N.E.; *Lake Ashley* (1800 ft.), 6 M. to the S.E.; *Perry's Peak* (see above; 8 M.), etc.— A little to the N.E. of the city is the fine *Allen Stock Farm* (trotting-horses).

The N. part of Berkshire County is much less known than the S., and there is no important centre for visitors between Pittsfield and North Adams and Williamstown, 20 M. to the N.

North Adams (700 ft.; *Wilson Ho.*, $ $2^1/_2$-3; *Richmond Ho.*, *Mansion Ho.*, $2), a manufacturing city in the narrow valley of the *Hoosac*, with (1890) 16,074 inhab., is a station on the Fitchburg Railway (see p. 135) and the terminus of a branch of the Boston & Albany R.R. (see p. 134). It is connected with (6 M.) *Adams* (p. 134) by an electric tramway.

About 1 M. to the N.E. of North Adams is the *Natural Bridge*, a rocky narrow archway spanning the Hudson Brook at a height of 50-60 ft. — The W. end of the **Hoosac Tunnel** (p. 134) is 2 M. to the S.E. of N. Adams, and a favourite excursion is over the *Hoosac Mt.* (2270 ft.) to (9 M.) the E. end of the tunnel and *Hoosac Tunnel Station* (Hotel).

ASCENT OF GREYLOCK (8 M.; road). We follow the Williamstown road (to the W.) for a short distance and then turn to the left into the road through the *Notch* (views), passing ($1^1/_2$ M.) the *Notch Brook Cascade*, 30 ft. high. About 3 M. from N. Adams the new road, constructed by the *Greylock Park Association*, diverges to the right and leads through wood to (5 M.) the summit (easy gradient). About halfway up we have a view into the *Hopper* (1000 ft. deep). At the top are refreshment booths and a view-tower (40 ft. high). The *View from **Greylock** (3535 ft.) includes Adams, N. Adams, Pittsfield, the valleys of the Hoosac and Housatonic, and most of the Berkshire Hills. Farther off are the Catskills to the S.W., the Green Mts. to the N., Mts. Monadnock and Wachusett to the E., and Mts. Tom and Holyoke to the S.E.

Williamstown (595 ft.; *Greylock, Taconic Inn*, $ 3-$3^1/_2$), 5 M. to the W. of N. Adams and 1 M. to the S. of the rail. station (p. 135; omn. 25 c.), lies on the *Green River*, an affluent of the Hoosac. Pop. (1890) 4221. It is the seat of *Williams College* (350 students), the buildings of which are the chief feature of the village. The most modern is the *Mark Hopkins Memorial Hall* (1890); the *President's House* is a good specimen of Colonial architecture. President Garfield, a graduate of the college, is commemorated by a window in the chapel. The streets are prettily laid out and shaded by fine trees.

In *Flora's Glen*, 1 M. to the W., Bryant is said to have composed his 'Thanatopsis', at the age of eighteen. — The *Hopper* (see above), a huge gorge enclosed by Mt. Prospect, Bald Mt., and Greylock, is 5 M. to the S. — The top of *Greylock* is 10 M. distant by the new road (see above). — The **Taconic Range** rises about 3 M. from Williamstown, and good views are afforded by *Mt. Belcher, Mt. Hopkins (Berlin Mt.; 2790 ft.)*, and other summits. The chief passes over this range are the *Petersburg Pass* (2075 ft.), the *Berlin Pass* (2190 ft.), the *Kidder Pass* (bridle-path), and the *Johnson Pass.* — The *Snow Glen* is 7 M. to the N.W., 2 M. to the N. of the Petersburg Pass. — Among the favourite drives are the '*Short Oblong*' (2 M.) and '*Long Oblong*' (10 M.). Longer drives may be taken to ,*Pittsfield* (20 M.), *Lebanon Springs* (20 M.), *Hoosac Falls* (17 M.); etc.

20. From New York to Montreal.
a. Viâ Connecticut Valley.

450 M. NEW YORK, NEW HAVEN, & HARTFORD RAILROAD to (136 M.) *Springfield* in $3^3/_4$ hrs.; CONNECTICUT RIVER R. R. thence to (50 M.) *South Vernon* in $1^1/_4$-2 hrs.; CENTRAL VERMONT R. R. thence to (10 M.) *Brattleboro* in $1/_2$ hr.: CONNECTICUT RIVER R. R. thence to (50 M.) *Windsor* in $1^1/_2$-2 hrs.; CENTRAL VERMONT R. R. thence to (204 M.) *Montreal* in $6^3/_4$-$7^1/_4$ hrs. (throughfare $ 10; sleeper from Springfield $2; express from New York to Montreal in 14-16 hrs.). — Trains run to *Quebec* by this route in 21-22 hrs. (fare $ 12). Through-trains run to *Fabyan's* in the White Mts. (R. 16) in $10^1/_2$ hrs. (fare $7; parlor-car $ 2).

From *New York* to (136 M.) *Springfield*, see R. 4a. We here
join the *Connecticut River R. R.*, which ascends the beautiful *****Valley
of the Connecticut** (views mainly to the right). The train crosses
the river by a long bridge. 140 M. *Chicopee*, a manufacturing town
of (1890) 14,050 inhab., with cotton-mills, a bronze-foundry, etc.
Chicopee Falls, 2 M. to the E., also with cotton-mills, is the home
of *Edward Bellamy*, author of 'Looking Backward'. Tobacco is grown
in this part of the valley. — 144 M. **Holyoke** (95 ft.; *Windsor*,
Hamilton, $2^1/_2$-3), an industrial city with (1890) 35,637 inhab.,
has the greatest water-power in New England and is said to be the
chief paper-making place in the world (200 tons daily; value of
manufactures in 1890, $ 24,500,000). The river has a fall of 60 ft.
and is bridled by a huge dam, 1000 ft. across. — Beyond (149 M.)
Smith's Ferry we pass between *Mt. Holyoke* (see below) on the right
and *Mt. Tom* (see below) on the left and cross the river.

153 M. **Northampton** (125 ft.; *Norwood*, $2^1/_2$-3; *Mansion Ho.*,
$ 2^1/_2$) 'the frontispiece of the book of beauty which Nature opens
wide in the valley of the Connecticut', is a lovely elm-shaded city
of (1890) 14,900 inhab., on the W. bank of the Connecticut. It is
widely known as an educational centre.

The chief of its educational institutions is **Smith College**, one of the
leading colleges for women (450-500 students). It possesses an art-gallery,
a music hall, a gymnasium, etc. Other large buildings are *Memorial Hall*
(with the Public Library), the *State Lunatic Asylum* (1 M. to the S.W.),
and the *Clarke Institution for Mutes*. The last stands on *Round Hill*, which
commands a good view of the town.

The chief of the numerous delightful excursions from Northampton
is that to the top of *****Mt. Holyoke** (955 ft.; *Prospect Ho.*, at the top, $ 2^1/_2$),
2 M. to the S.E. A carriage-road leads to a small mountain-railway which
surmounts the last 600 ft. (return-fare $ 1; toll for walkers 50 c.). The ex-
quisite *View from the summit includes the Connecticut Valley, the Hoosac
Mts. and Greylock (W. and N.W.), Mt. Tom (S.W.), Springfield and the
E. and W. Rocks at Hartford (S.), Mt. Wachusett (E.), Amherst (in the
distance) and Monadnock (N.E.), and the Green Mts. (N.). — The main
summit of *Mt. Tom* (1335 ft.), 4^1/_2$ M. to the S., is seldom visited, but *Mt.
Nototuck* (850 ft.; Eyrie Ho.), its N. peak, is easily accessible from Mt.
Tom station (see above; *View). — **Hadley** (*Elmwood Ho.*), a beautiful
New England village, 2^1/_2$ M. to the N.E. of Northampton, is celebrated
for its magnificent *Avenue of elms. The regicides Goffe and Whalley
lived in concealment at Hadley for 15 years (1664-79). At *South Hadley*,
^{1}/_2$ M. to the S., is the *Mt. Holyoke Seminary for Girls* (250-300 pupils). —
Amherst (p. 63) is 7 M. to the N.E. of Northampton (coach daily).

Beyond Northampton the train passes near the *Great Bend of
the Connecticut* and then leaves the river. *Hadley* (see above) is seen
to the right. 157 M. *Hatfield* (150 ft.). From (164 M.) *South Deerfield* (205 ft.) we may ascend *Sugar Loaf Mt.* (500 ft.), which rises
to the right. A little farther on, to the right, is a monument marking
the battlefield of *Bloody Brook*, where Capt. Lathrop and 80 young
men, 'the flower of Essex Co.', were killed by Indians in 1675.
169 M. *Deerfield* (220 ft.), a pretty village at the foot of *Deerfield Mt.*
(700 ft.), with (1890) 2910 inhabitants. *Mt. Toby* (see p. 134) may
be ascended hence. — The train crosses the *Deerfield* and at (172 M.)

Greenfield (see p. 134) intersects the Fitchburg R. R. Beyond (179 M.) *Bernardston* the Connecticut again comes into sight on the right, and this part of the valley is very picturesque. Tobacco and maize are cultivated. At (186 M.) *South Vernon*, the junction of a line to *Concord* (p. 116), we pass on to the *Central Vermont R. R.*

196 M. **Brattleboro** (*Brooks Ho.*, $2¼-3; *American Ho.*, $2), a large village with (1890) 5467 inhab., charmingly situated on the W. bank of the Connecticut, is the centre of the maple-sugar industry of Vermont. The *Estey Organ Works* here turn out 20,000 organs yearly. In the *Cemetery* (view) is an elaborate monument to the notorious *Jim Fisk* (1835-72). — 220 M. **Bellows Falls,** see p. 114. — We now cross to the E. bank of the river and leave Vermont for *New Hampshire.* Beyond (238 M.) *Claremont Junction* (line to *Concord*, see p. 116) we cross the deep gorge of the *Sugar River* by a bridge 105 ft. high. We recross the Connecticut River to (246 M.) *Windsor* (Windsor Ho., $2), the station for an ascent of *Mt. Ascutney* (3320 ft.; *Rfmt. Ho.*, at the top; *View).

260 M. **White River Junction** *(Rail. Rest.)*, see p. 117. The shortest route to Montreal diverges to the left here and runs viâ *Montpelier* and *St. Albans* (see R. 15b). Trains for *Quebec* and *Montreal* viâ *Sherbrooke* continue to follow the Connecticut Valley to *Wells River* (see below). The next station on the latter route is (265 M.) *Norwich*, whence omnibuses run to *Hanover* (The Wheelock, $2), ¾ M. to the S.E., the seat of **Dartmouth College** (400-450 students), the *alma mater* of Daniel Webster, George Ticknor (author of a History of Spanish Literature), G. P. Marsh (the philologist), Rufus Choate, and Chief-Justice Chase. The *College Park* is pretty and its *Art Gallery* contains some interesting portraits.

The train crosses the *Ompompanoosuc.* 296 M. *Newbury*, a pretty village in the *Ox Bow* 'intervales' of the Connecticut.

300 M. **Wells River Junction** *(Rail. Rest.)*, see p. 119. Route hence to *Montreal* and *Quebec*, see R. 15c.

b. Viâ Albany (or Troy), Saratoga, and Lake Champlain.

384 M. New York Central & Hudson River Railroad to (142 M.) *Albany* in 2¾-4¾ hrs.; Delaware & Hudson Railroad thence to (242 M.) *Montreal* in 8-10 hrs. (through-express in 11½ hrs.; through-fare $10, parlor-car $2, sleeper $2; seats to the left).

This is the shortest and most direct route from New York to Montreal, Lake George, and Lake Champlain. Those who have not seen the *Hudson* should go by Steamer to Albany (see R. 146); and they may also leave the train for the steamer on *Lakes George* and *Champlain.*

From New York to (143 M.) *Albany*, see R. 21. Beyond Albany we follow the tracks of the *Delaware and Hudson Railway*, which traverses a very interesting district, skirting *Lake George* (p. 182), *Lake Champlain* (p. 184), and the *Adirondack Mts.* (p. 165). — The line passes the *Rural Cemetery* and reaches (149 M.) *West Troy*, with a large United States Arsenal, situated on the Hudson, opposite *Troy* (p. 145). — 152 M. *Cohoes* (Harmony, $2-2½), a prosperous manufacturing city with (1890) 22,509 inhab., situated at the *Falls of the Mohawk River* (75 ft. high, 900 ft. wide), which the train crosses here by a long bridge (view of falls to the left). — **154 M.** *Waterford.* At (155 M.) *Albany Junction* the Albany division unites with the main line coming from (6 M.) *Troy.* — At (159 M.) *Mechanicsville,* where the *Fitchburg Railroad* joins ours (see p. 135), we turn to the N.W. (left) and quit the Hudson. 166 M. *Round Lake* (Wentworth, $2^1/_2$), with a well-known Methodist camp-meeting ground and summer-schools (lake to the right). — 173 M. *Ballston Spa* (The Lincoln), with mineral springs, now little visited, is the junction of a line to *Binghamton* (see p. 197).

180 M. **Saratoga Springs** *(Rail. Restaurant),* see p. 179.

Beyond Saratoga the train runs to the N.E. and crosses the Hudson at (197 M.) *Fort Edward* (St. James, $2), where, however, all traces of the fort, built in 1755, have disappeared. Passengers for the Lake George steamer diverge here (see below).

FROM FORT EDWARD TO CALDWELL, 16 M., railway in 3/4-1 hr. The railway ascends the Hudson, which here makes numerous falls. — 6 M. **Glens Falls** (700 ft.; *Rockwell Ho.,* $3; *American Ho.,* $2), an industrial city with (1890) 9509 inhab., where the Hudson forms a picturesque *Fall of 50-60 ft. The island below the fall is the scene of some well-known incidents in *Cooper's* 'Last of the Mohicans'. — Beyond Glens Falls the train descends rapidly through a wooded defile, affording fine views of lake and mountain. To the left, 2 M. from Caldwell, is the *Williams Rock*, a boulder marking the spot where Col. Ephraim Williams was killed and his 1200 men were defeated by the French and Indian army of Dieskau, which was in turn defeated, also with the loss of its commander, by Sir William Johnson (Sept. 8th, 1755). Hard by is the *Bloody Pond*, into which the dead bodies were thrown. — 16 M. **Caldwell** (400 ft.), see p.183.

Beyond Fort Edward our train leaves the Hudson and descends the valley of *Wood Creek.* 209 M. *Fort Ann,* the site of a fort of 1757, near which Gen. Putnam was defeated and captured by the French and Indians in 1750. — 219 M. **Whitehall** (*Hall Ho.,* $2), the junction of a line to *Rutland* (p. 114), is a lumbering village of (1890) 4434 inhab., situated at the foot of *Mt. Skene* and at the S. extremity of *Lake Champlain* (p. 184).

The train crosses the *South Bay* and follows the W. bank of Lake Champlain, which is at first more like a river than a lake. — 241 M. *Fort Ticonderoga* (see p. 185), at the foot of *Mt. Defiance* (800 ft.), is the junction of a line to (5 M.) *Baldwin*, on Lake George (see p. 184), and the starting-point of the steamer on Lake Champlain to *Plattsburg,* etc. (see p. 185). — The train threads a tunnel. 243 M. *Addison Junction*, for a line to *Leicester* and *Rutland* (p. 114); 250 M. *Crown Point* (p. 185); 259 M. *Port Henry* (p. 185). The *Adirondack Mts.* now rise prominently to the left. From (270 M.) *Westport* (p. 170) coaches run to *Elizabethtown, Keene Valley,* and *Lake Placid* (see p. 171). The train passes behind *Split Rock Mt.* (right) and emerges on the wider part of Lake Champlain (views). The rocks to the left rise precipitously. — 283 M. *Willsborough.* — 296 M. *Port Kent* (p. 186), the

junction of a line to (3 M.) *Ausable Chasm* (p. 170) and *Keeseville.*
— 306 M. *Hotel Champlain* and *Bluff Point* (see p. 186).
309 M. **Plattsburg** (p. 167; *Rail. Restaurant*) is the junction
of lines to *Saranac Lake* (p. 167) and *Ausable* (p. 167). Our line
now leaves Lake Champlain and traverses a somewhat monotonous
district. 319 M. *West Chazy* is the junction of an alternative route
to Montreal. — 334 M. *Rouse's Point* (Windsor, $3), at the N. end of
Lake Champlain, is the frontier-station. We then descend along
the left bank of the *Richelieu* to (357 M.) *St. John's.* Hence to —
384 M. **Montreal**, see *Baedeker's Canada.*

c. Viâ Troy, Rutland, and Burlington.

400 M. NEW YORK CENTRAL & HUDSON RIVER RAILROAD to (148 M.)
Troy in 4¹/₄-5 hrs.; FITCHBURG R. R. thence to (30 M.) *White Creek,* in
1 hr.; N. BENNINGTON & RUTLAND R. R. thence to (54 M.) *Rutland* in
2 hrs.; CENTRAL VERMONT R. R. thence to (168 M.) *Montreal* in 5¹/₂-6 hrs.
(through-trains in 14 hrs.; fares as above). — This line is the direct route
from New York to *Burlington* (p. 115) and the *Green Mts.* (p. 117).

From New York to (142 M.) *Greenbush,* see R. 21b.
148 M. **Troy** (*Troy Ho.*, $3; *American Ho.*, *Revere Ho.*, *Man-
sion Ho.*, $2-2¹/₂), a busy industrial city of (1890) 60,956 inhab.,
at the head of the steam-navigation of the Hudson. Its chief products are iron, Bessemer steel, railway rolling-stock, cotton and
woollen goods, collars and shirts. Some of its charitable and other
public buildings are handsome. Its laundries are famous.

Troy is an important railway-centre, lines diverging in all directions
(New York; Burlington and Montreal; Boston viâ the Hoosac Tunnel, etc.).
The main line of the Del. and Hudson R. R. begins here and unites with
the Albany division at *Albany Junction* (p. 144).

Our train turns to the right (N.E.) and runs over the *Fitchburg
R. R.* to (180 M.) *N. Bennington.* We then run towards the N.,
with the *Green Mts.* at some distance to the right. 201 M. *Manchester* (Equinox Ho, $4), a summer-resort at the base of *Mt.
Equinox* (3847 ft.), the *View from which includes the Catskills,
the Berkshire Hills, Lake George, and Lake Champlain.

232 M. *Rutland* (Rail. Restaurant), and thence to —
400 M. **Montreal**, see R. 15a.

d. Viâ Herkimer and Malone.

474 M. NEW YORK CENTRAL & HUDSON RIVER RAILROAD to (224 M.)
Herkimer in 6 hrs.; ADIRONDACK & ST. LAWRENCE RAILWAY thence to (173 M.)
Malone in 6 hrs.; CENTRAL VERMONT RAILROAD thence to (40 M.) *Coteau
Junction* in 1 hr.; GRAND TRUNK RAILWAY thence to (37 M.) *Montreal* in
1 hr. (through-express in 13 hrs.; fares as in R. 20b). — This new route,
opened in 1893, crosses the *Adirondacks* (comp. p. 178), and forms the
most convenient approach to many points in that district.

From *New York* to (224 M.) *Herkimer,* see R. 28; from Herkimer
to (397 M.) *Malone,* see R. 25e. The train then turns to the E. (right)
and follows the Central Vermont R. R. (from Ogdensburg to Rouse's
Point; comp. p. 188) to (437 M.) *Coteau Junction.* Thence to —
474 M. **Montreal**, see *Baedeker's Canada.*

21. From New York to Albany.

a. By Steamer.

144 M. The finely-equipped steamers of the Hudson River Line ('Albany Day Line') leave New York every morning (except Sun.) in summer (May-Oct.) from *Vestry Pier* at 8.40 and *22nd St.* (N. R.) at 9 a.m., and reach *Albany* about 6 p.m., calling at seven or eight intermediate points (fare $2, return-fare $3½). The largest steamer of this line is 311 ft. long and has a speed of 25 M. an hour. — The **People's Line Steamers** leave *Pier 41* (foot of Canal St.) every week-day at 6 p.m., reaching *Albany* at 6 a.m. next day and making no intermediate stops (fare $1½, return $2½, berth 50 c.). — The **Citizen's Line Steamers** leave *Pier 46* daily, except Sat., at 6 p.m. and reach *Troy* about 6 a.m., calling at *Albany* on Sun. only (fare $1½, return $2½, berth 50 c.). — The '**Mary Powell**' plies every afternoon from the foot of Desbrosses St. to (95 M.) *Rondout* and *Kingston* (6 hrs.; fare $1, return-fare $1½).

Those who wish to see the beauties of the Hudson should, of course, select the 'Day Line'; but the night-boats afford a comfortable and easy mode of travel. Good restaurants on board all the steamers (meals à la carte). Through railway-tickets to Albany by the N. Y. C. R. R. or the West Shore R. R. are available on the Day Line steamer, and vice versâ.

The **River Hudson** rises in the Adirondack Mts., 4000 ft. above the sea (comp. p. 166), and flows into the Atlantic Ocean at New York after a nearly due S. course of 300 M. Its chief tributary is the *Mohawk*, which joins it on the W., a little above Troy. The mountains of the Hudson are part of the Appalachian system, the Highlands (see p. 148) being a continuation of the Blue Ridge. The Hudson has sometimes been called the 'American Rhine', but this title perhaps does injustice to both rivers. The Hudson throughout a great part of its course is three or four times as wide as the Rhine, and its scenery is grander and more imposing; while, though it lacks the ruined castles and ancient towns of the German river, it is by no means devoid of historical associations of a more recent character. The vine-clad slopes of the Rhine have, too, no ineffective substitute in the brilliant autumn-colouring of the timbered hillsides of the Hudson. The E. bank, for many miles above New York, is sprinkled with handsome country-houses. The effect of the tide is perceptible as far as Troy, and the river is navigable for large steamers for 150 M. Sailing-vessels and yachts are abundant in the lower part of its course, while numerous 'tows' of coal-barges, grain-barges, and lumber-rafts are also encountered. Beyond the influence of salt water the Hudson freezes solid in winter, affording an ample harvest to the ice-cutter and a magnificent field for the exciting sport of ice-boat sailing. Its name is derived from *Henry Hudson*, a British navigator in the Dutch service, who in 1609 ascended the river in the 'Half Moon' as far as Albany, in search of a water-passage across the Continent. According to Ruttenber ('Indian Tribes of the Hudson River') the E. bank of the Hudson and part of the W. bank were occupied by the Mohicans, while the W. bank below the Catskills belonged to the Lenni Lenapes (Delawares) and above Cohoes to the Mohawks (Iroquois). The first steamboat that plied regularly for passengers was the 'Clermont' of Robert Fulton, which ran between New York and Albany in 1807.

The *Photo-Panorama of the Hudson*, published by the Bryant Literary Union (Evening Post Building, New York; price $1), shows both sides of the river from Albany to New York, 'accurately represented from 800 consecutive photographs'.

In the following description the terms right (R., r.) and left (L., l.) are used with reference to persons ascending the river.

As the steamer starts from its dock, we enjoy a good view of New York Harbour to the S. On the right lies *Manhattan Island*, with the city of *New York*, while to the left, in the *State of New Jersey*, are *Jersey City* (p. 51), *Hoboken* (p. 51), and *Weehawken*

(p. 51). Among the most conspicuous points to the right are the spire of Trinity Church (p. 27), the dome of the 'World' Office (p. 29), the Post Office (p. 29), the Dakota Flats (p. 40), the Orphan Asylum (p. 48), Riverside Park (p. 48), the Convent of the Sacred Heart (p. 48), and *Ottendorfer's Pavilion.* To the left are Stevens Castle (p. 51), the Elysian Fields (p. 51), *Union Hill Observatory, St. Michael's Observatory,* the West Shore Railroad Station (p. 6), the Guttenberg Brewery (p. 51), and *Pleasant Valley.* Near the end of Manhattan Island, 10-11 M. from the Battery, we pass between *Fort Lee* (p. 51), with its hotel, on the left, and the site of *Fort Washington,* captured by the British on Nov. 15th, 1776, on the right. At Fort Lee begin the *Palisades, an extraordinary ridge of columnar basaltic rocks, not unlike the Giant's Causeway, rising almost vertically to a height of 200-500 ft. and extending along the W. bank of the Hudson for about 15 M. The width of the mountains of which they form the E. escarpment is $1/2-1^1/2$ M., and the W. slope is quite gentle. To the right (13 M.) is *Spuyten Duyvil Creek* (p. 150).

16$^1/_2$ M. (r.) *Mt. St. Vincent Convent,* the buildings of which include *Fonthill,* formerly the home of Edwin Forrest, the actor.

17 M. (r.) **Yonkers** (p. 150), with the old *Phillipse Manor House* (recognisable by its square tower).

21 M. (r.) *Hastings* (p. 150). Opposite is **Indian Head** (*View), the highest point of the Palisades. About $1/2$ M. farther on (l.) is the boundary between New Jersey and New York, both banks henceforth belonging to the latter. — 23 M. (r.) *Dobbs Ferry* (p. 150).

24 M. (r.) *Irvington* (p. 150). *Sunnyside,* Irving's house, $3/4$ M. above, can scarcely be distinguished from the steamer. Opposite (l.) lies *Piermont,* with the long pier of the Erie Railroad. About 2 M. to the S.W. of Piermont is the old village of *Tappan,* where André was executed (Oct. 2nd, 1780). — The Palisades here lose their wall-like character, and the Hudson expands into the lake-like expanse of the **Tappan Zee,** 10 M. long and 3-4 M. wide.

25 M. (r.) *Lyndehurst* (see p. 150), the residence of the late Mr. Jay Gould (d. 1892), loftily situated, with a tall tower.

27 M. (r.) *Tarrytown* (p. 150), whence a steam-ferry plies across the Tappan Zee to (3 M.) **Nyack** (*Tappan Zee Ho.,* \$4), a brisk little village, the terminus of the Northern Railroad of New Jersey. The *Dutch Church* in *Sleepy Hollow* (p. 150) may be distinguished about $3/4$ M. above Tarrytown.

30-32 M. (l.) *S. Hook Mt.* (730 ft.) and *N. Hook Mt.* (610 ft.). *Rockland* lies just beyond the latter.

32 M. (r.) *Sing-Sing* (p. 151), with the low white-marble prison at the water's edge.

33 M. (r.) Estuary of *Croton River* and *Croton Point* (p. 151). Opposite is *Teller's Point,* off which the 'Vulture' anchored when she brought André to visit Arnold (p. 148).

The steamer now enters **Haverstraw Bay**, which is 4 M. wide.
37 M. (l.) **Haverstraw** (p. 151), at the N. base of *High Torn*
(820 ft.). The *Highlands* (see below) are visible in the distance.
40 M. (l.) *Stony Point*, at the N. end of Haverstraw Bay, now
marked by a lighthouse, was the site of a fort taken by the British
on June 1st, 1779, and re-captured at the point of the bayonet by
Gen. Wayne (p. 231) six weeks later. The river here is only $1/2$ M.
wide, and on the E. bank is *Verplanck's Point*, the site of *Fort
Lafayette*. — 41 M. (l.) *Tompkin's Cove*, with limestone quarries. —
43 M. (l.) *Kidd's Point* or *Caldwell's Landing; r. Peekskill*.

The river makes an abrupt bend to the left here, and the Dutch
mariner Jan Peek is said to have followed the *Peekskill* (r.) under the
idea that it was the Hudson, until his ship ran aground. Above
Caldwell's Landing rises the **Dunderberg** (1090 ft.), and to the N.
of Peekskill is *Manito Mt.*, with the camp of the *New York State
National Guard*. — We here pass through the S. gate of the ***Highlands**, the beautiful hill-girt section of the river extending from
this point to near Newburg (see below).

46 M. (r.) **Anthony's Nose** (1230 ft.), a lofty summit, deriving
its name, according to Diedrich Knickerbocker's familiar and
humorous account, from the 'refulgent nose' of the Dutch trumpeter,
Anthony van Corlear. Nearly opposite are *Iona Island, Bear Hill*
(1350 ft.) and the sites of *Forts Clinton* and *Montgomery*.

50 M. (r.) *Sugar-Loaf Mt.* (865 ft.), near the S. base of which
is *Beverley House*, Arnold's headquarters, where he received the
news of André's capture and whence he made his escape to the
'Vulture'. Opposite are the *Buttermilk Falls*, 100 ft. high (insignificant except after heavy rain), on the bluff above which is the
large and finely situated *Cranston's Hotel* ($ 5).

52 M. (l.) **West Point** (p. 152), the site of the well-known *Military Academy*, of which the domed library and other buildings are
visible. To the N. is the *West Point Hotel* (p. 152) and above the
'Post' rises *Fort Putnam* (575 ft.). Steam-ferry to *Garrison* (p. 151).

Passing West Point, the steamer turns sharply to the left. To
the right, on the point known as *Constitution Island*, was long the
home of *Miss Warner* (1818-85), author of the 'Wide, Wide World'.

$54^{1}/_{2}$ M. (l.) *Crow Nest* (1430 ft.). — r. *Cold Spring* (p. 151),
at the foot of *Mt. Taurus* (1440 ft.).

56 M. (l.) ***Storm King** or *Butter Mt.* (1530 ft.), with *Cornwall* (p. 153) at its N. base. — r. *Breakneck Mt.* Between these hills
is the *N. Gate of the Highlands*, issuing from which we pass the
little *Polipel's Island* (r.). The mountains now trend to the N.E.

59 M. (l.) *New Windsor*. — r. *Dutchess Junction* (p. 151).

61 M. (l.) **Newburg** (see p. 153). *Washington's Headquarters*
(see p. 153), a one-storied stone building, with a timber roof, surrounded by trees and distinguished by a flag-staff, are seen just below the town. Steam-ferry to *Fishkill Landing* (p. 151).

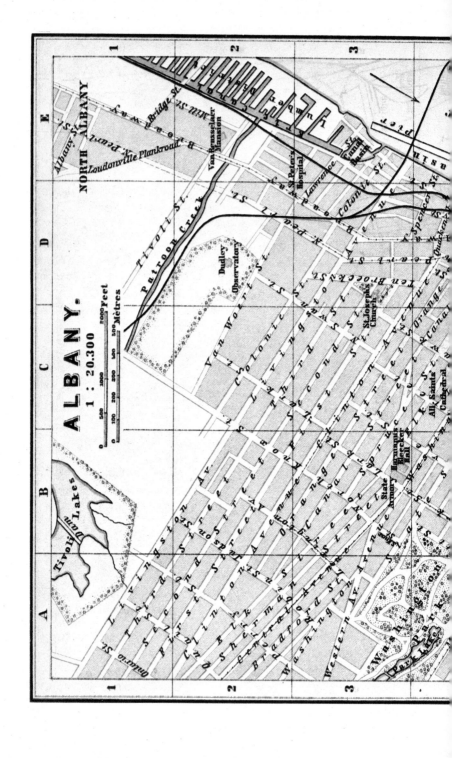

Wagner & Debes'Geogl Estab! Leipzig.

67 M. (l.) *Duyvil's Dans Kammer*, a low flat rock on a promontory.

70 M. (l.) *Marlborough*, with fine Arbor Vitæ trees.

75 M. (r.) **Poughkeepsie** (see p. 151). *Vassar College* (p. 151) is not visible. — l. *New Paltz Landing.*

The *Poughkeepsie Railway Bridge, which here spans the Hudson, constructed on the cantilever principle, is 2260 yds. long ($1^1/_4$ M.) and 80 ft. above high-water.

77 M. (r.) *Hudson River State Hospital for the Insane.* Numerous handsome residences are passed on the right, and large ice-houses on the left. Many of the estates on both banks are still in the hands of the 'Knickerbocker' families to which they were originally granted. — 82 M. (r.) *Hyde Park* (p. 151).

87 M. (r.) *Dinsmore Point*, with the house of *Wm. B. Dinsmore*, long president of the *Adams Express Co.*, which began in 1840 with two men, a boy, and a wheel-barrow, and now has 8000 men and 2000 waggons and carries parcels over 25,000 M. of railway.

91 M. (l.) **Kingston** and **Rondout** (see p. 153), at the mouth of the *Delaware and Hudson Canal* (p. 153). Opposite lies *Rhinecliff Landing* (p. 151).

99 M. (r.) *North Bay* (above *Cruger's Island*), where Fulton built the 'Clermont' (p. 146), with the aid of Chancellor Livingston, a member of the influential New York family of that name.

100 M. (r.) *Tivoli*, whence a ferry runs to —

102 M. (l.) *Saugerties* (p. 153), with a lighthouse.

The **Catskill Mts.** (R. 24) now bound the view on the left. *Overlook Mt.* (3300 ft.), with its hotel, rises nearly opposite Tivoli, and next to it is *Plattekill* (3200 ft.), above Saugerties.

103 M. (r.) *Clermont*, the original seat of the Livingston family, descended from the Earls of Linlithgow (comp. above). Nearly opposite is *Malden*, above which rises *Kaaterskill Mt.* (3800 ft.), with the *Kaaterskill Hotel* and the *Catskill Mt. House* (p. 161).

104 M. (r.) *Germantown Station.* Just beyond this point we have the best view, to the left, of the supine figure of the '*Man in the Mountain*', whose knee, breast, and face (from S. to N.) are formed by different peaks of the Catskills. *Round Top* (3500 ft.), one of the highest of the Catskills, rises to the N. of the man's head.

112 M. (l.) *Catskill* (p. 160), at the mouth of the *Kaaterskill Creek*, with the large *Prospect Park Hotel*. This was the highest point reached by the 'Half-Moon' (p. 146), but Hudson sent small boats up as far as *Waterford* (p. 114), 4 M. above Troy. Numerous large *Ice-houses* to the left.

116 M. (r.) **Hudson** (p. 151). Steam-ferry to *Athens* (l.). The scenery is now less attractive. — 124 M. (l.) *Coxsackie* (ferry). — 125 M. (r.) *Stuyvesant*. Numerous flat islands are passed. — 134 M. (r.) *Schodack.* — l. *Coeymans* (p. 153), behind which rise the *Helderberg Mts.* (p. 158). — 137 M. (r.) *Castleton.* Extensive dykes have been made from this point onwards to improve the channel.

143 M. (r.) *Van Rensselaer Place* (1642).

145 M. (r.) **Albany** (see p. 154), with the *Capitol* towering above the other buildings, is connected by three bridges with *Green-bush* (p. 151).

150 M. (r.) **Troy**, see p. 145.

b. Viâ Railway on the East Bank.

143 M. NEW YORK CENTRAL AND HUDSON RIVER RAILROAD in $2^3/_4$-$4^3/_4$ hrs. (fare $ 3.10; parlor-car $ 1). This line affords good views of the W. bank of the Hudson (seats to the left).

New York, see p. 6. The train leaves the Grand Central Depot, traversesr the Park Avenue tunnel (comp. p. 37), passes *125th Street Station*, crosses the *Harlem River*, turns to the W. (left) at (5 M.) *138th Street*, and skirts the Harlem to *High Bridge* (p. 49) and (11 M.) *Spuyten Duyvil*, on *Spuyten Duyvil Creek* (p. 22), so named, says the legend, from the Dutch trumpeter *Anthony van Corlear*, who 'swore most valorously that he would swim across it in spite of the Devil (en spuyt den duyvil)', but 'sank for ever to the bottom' (see *W. Irving's* 'Knickerbocker History of New York'). The creek formed the S. boundary of the 'Neutral Ground' in the Revolutionary War. — Spuyten Duyvil lies on the E. bank of the *Hudson*, which we now follow closely, obtaining good views of the *Palisades* (p. 147), on the opposite side. The line passes several of the riverine suburbs of New York, but runs at too low a level to afford views of them (comp., however. R. 21c). 14 M. *Mount St. Vincent*, with a large convent. — 16 M. **Yonkers** (*Getty Ho., Mansion Ho.,* $ $2^1/_2$-3$) a thriving town, with (1890) 33,033 inhab. and the residences of many New Yorkers. It occupies the land of the Phillipse estate (comp. p. 147), and the manor-house (1682) is now the city-hall. — 20 M. *Hastings.* — 21 M. *Dobbs Ferry* (Glen Tower Ho., $ 3), a picturesque suburban village, affording fine views of the N. end of the Palisades, was the first place appointed for the meeting of Arnold and André. — 23 M. *Irvington*, on the bank of the *Tappan Zee*, with 'Sunnyside', the home of Washington Irving, the E. end of which is covered with ivy, grown from a slip given to Irving at Abbotsford by Sir Walter Scott. The *Paulding Manor* (*Lyndehurst;* see p. 147) is a fine old building. *Nevis* is a stately mansion built in 1836 by a son of Alex. Hamilton and named in honour of his father's birthplace. — 26 M. **Tarrytown** (*Franklin Ho.,* $ 2-3; *Cosmopolitan,* $ 2), on a hill rising from the river.

This was the scene of Major André's capture in 1780 (spot marked by a monument) and is the centre of a district rich in reminiscences of the Revolutionary War. It is, perhaps, still better known from its connection with *Washington Irving* (1783-1859), who was churchwarden of *Christchurch* here and is buried in the graveyard of the old *Dutch Church*, $3/_4$ M. to the N., built in 1699 with bricks brought from Holland. The latter church lies in '*Sleepy Hollow*', which is traversed by the *Pocantico* or *Mill Brook*, with the bridge across which 'Ichabod Crane' rushed helter-skelter from the pursuit of the 'Headless Horseman'. Opposite Tarrytown lies Nyack (p. 147).

31 M. **Sing Sing** (*American Hotel*, $2¹/₂), a prettily situated town with (1890) 9352 inhab., is the seat of the *State Prison*, the large buildings of which are seen to the left. The train then crosses the mouth of the *Croton River* (6 M. up which is the *Croton Reservoir*, p. 49) and intersects *Croton Point*. Across the Hudson, which is here at its widest (*Haverstraw Bay*, 4 M.), is the village of *Haverstraw* (p. 148). Farther on the train is frequently carried across creeks and bays on low trestle-work. — 42 M. **Peekskill** (*Eagle*, $2-3), a pretty little town with (1890) 9676 inhab., on *Peek's Kill*, opposite the *Dunderberg* (p. 148; ferry to *Caldwell's Landing*). The train penetrates *Anthony's Nose* (p. 148) by a tunnel 70 yds. long, passes (47 M.) *Highlands Station* (view of the hills across the Hudson), and reaches (50 M.) *Garrison's* (Highland Ho., loftily situated), opposite *West Point* (p. 152; ferry). About 1 M. to the S. is *Robinson House*, where Arnold heard of André's arrest. 54 M. *Cold Spring* (ferry to *Cornwall-on-the-Hudson*, p. 153); 56 M. *Storm King*, opposite the hill of that name (p. 148); 58 M. *Dutchess Junction*.

59 M. **Fishkill Landing**, the W. terminus of the N. Y. & N. E. R. R. (see pp. 148, 153), lies at the mouth of the *Matteawan Creek*, opposite *Newburg* (p. 153), and 5 M. to the W. of the small town of *Fishkill* (Mt. Gulian Hotel, $2-3; 3617 inhab.).

74 M. **Poughkeepsie** (200 ft. above the river; *Nelson Ho., Morgan Ho.*, $2¹/₂-3¹/₂; *Rail. Restaurant*), a city of (1890) 22,290 inhab., was settled by the Dutch in 1698 and contains some handsome buildings, including a large *State Insane Asylum*. The name is a corruption of the Indian *Apo-keep-sinck* ('safe harbour'). The *Eastman Park* is pleasant y laid out.

About 1¹/₂ M. to the E. lies **Vassar College** (400 students), perhaps the most famous of the American colleges for women, founded and endowed by Matthew Vassar, an Englishman, at a cost of $1,000,000 (200,000*l.*). Its main building, 500 ft. long, is modelled after the Tuileries. — The fine *Cantilever Bridge* (see p. 149) was built in 1873 to provide direct communication between New England and the coal-fields of Pennsylvania.

80 M. *Hyde Park;* 85 M. *Staatsburg.* The river-banks are now much less precipitous. — 89 M. *Rhinecliff,* terminus of the Central New England and Western R. R. About 2 M. to the E. lies *Rhinebeck* (Rhinecliff Hotel, $2). A steam-ferry plies hence to *Kingston* (p. 153). The *Beekman House*, near Rhinecliff, is a good specimen of a Dutch house of the 17th century. — From (99 M.) *Tivoli* a ferry plies to *Saugerties* (p. 153). The Catskills (p. 149) are now prominent on the other side of the Hudson. From (111 M.) *Catskill Station* a steam-ferry runs to the town of *Catskill* (p. 160), the chief avenue of approach to the *Catskill Mts.* (R. 24).

115 M. **Hudson** (*Worth Ho.*, $2¹/₂; *Waldron Ho.*, $2), a small city with (1890) 9970 inhab., lies on the slope of *Prospect Hill* (200 ft.), at the head of ship-navigation (steam-ferry to *Athens*, p. 153). — 142 M. *East Albany* or *Greenbush* (comp. p. 150). Our train here crosses the Hudson, while trains for Troy and

other points to the N. (comp. R. 20c) continue on the E. bank of
the river.

143 M. **Albany** *(Rail. Restaurant)*, see p. 154.

c. Viâ Railway on the West Bank.

142 M. WEST SHORE RAILROAD in 4¹/₂-5¹/₂ hrs. (fare $3.10; parlor-car
$1). This line affords better views than that on the E. bank, but starts
from *Weehawken* (p. 51; ferry from Franklin St. ¹/₂ hr., from 42nd St. ¹/₄ hr.).

The train starts from the station at *Weehawken* (see p. 51) and
passes through a long tunnel into the valley of the *Hackensack*, which
runs through marshes to the left. As far as Nyack our line runs
parallel with the *Northern New Jersey Railroad* (to the right). All
view of the Hudson is at first cut off by the *Palisades* (p. 147).

10 M. *West Englewood;* 19 M. *Tappan* (p. 147); 24 M. *West
Nyack*, 1¹/₂ M. to the W. of *Nyack* (p. 147). At (26 M.) *Valley Cottage* the *S. Hook Mt.* (p. 147) rises to the right. 28¹/₂ M. *Conger's*
is the station for *Rockland Lake* (150 ft.), 1 M. to the S.E., an important source of New York's ice-supply. The train now threads a
tunnel and emerges on *Haverstraw Bay* (p. 148; *View of the
Hudson). To the left is *High Torn* (p. 148). 32 M. *Haverstraw*, with
extensive brick-fields. The line now hugs the river. 41 M. *Iona
Island* (p. 148); 43 M. *Fort Montgomery* (p. 148); 46¹/₂ M. **Cranston's**, a large summer-hotel ($5), 250 ft. above the river (*View).

47¹/₂ M. **West Point** (*West Point Hotel*, adjoining the Parade
Ground, $3-4), the seat of the well-known *Military Academy* for
training officers for the U. S. army, is finely situated on the W. bank
of the Hudson, overlooking the Highlands (p. 148). The railway-
station is on the level of the river, but the parade-ground and the
principal buildings of the 'Post' occupy a plateau about 180 ft. above.

West Point was first fortified in 1778, and this 'Gibraltar of the Hudson' was an important point in the Revolutionary War, though no actual
fighting took place here. Arnold was commander of the post at the time
of his treason. Washington recommended the site for a military academy,
but it was not till 1802 that it was established.

The ***West Point Military Academy** usually contains about 300 cadets,
who are nominated, between the ages of 17 and 22, by Members of Congress and appointed by the President. The discipline is essentially military, and the course of instruction (4 years) is very thorough. The instructors are officers of the army. The cadets go into camp in July and
Aug., but the most interesting drills are held in April, May, Sept., and
Oct.; dress-parades are held all the year round, weather permitting.

Visitors will find an introduction convenient, but can see most of
the points of interest without one.

Ascending from the landing by a good road cut in the cliffs, we pass,
on the right, the *Riding School* (visitors admitted to the galleries). The
horsemanship of the senior cadets is wonderfully good, and no one should
neglect an opportunity to see their exercises. On the higher ground
immediately to the W. of the Riding School is the *Headquarters Building*,
and farther on we reach in succession the *Library* (with a dome), the
Chapel (allegorical painting by Weis), the *Academic Building*, the *Cadet
Barracks*, and the *Gymnasium*. To the S. of the Academic Building is the *Cadet
Mess Hall*, with portraits of Grant, Sherman, Sheridan, and other officers.

All military excercises take place on the fine *Parade Ground*, 40 acres
in area. In the N.W. corner is a statue of *Gen. Sedgwick*, in the S.E. corner

one of *Col. Thayer*. To the N.E., in an angle of *Fort Clinton*, is a monument to *Kosciuszko*. Just below the crest of the hill, to the N. of the library, is a monument to *Dade's Command* (p. 364).

The so-called 'Flirtation Walk', on the river-side, leads to *Kosciuszko's Garden*, a spot frequented by that heroic Pole. The *Officers' Quarters* are on the N. side of the Parade Ground; and the *Soldiers' Barracks* are on a lower level, below and to the W. of the West Point Hotel.

The views from different parts of the Post are beautiful, but the visitor with a little time to spare should ascend to **Old Fort Putnam** (596 ft.). We follow the road ascending the hill behind the new Gymnasium and at (3 min.) the cross-roads take the third road to the left (second to the right), which brings us in 10-15 min. to the ruins of the Old Fort. Here we can walk round the ramparts, obtaining a magnificent *View in all directions: up and down the Hudson, nearly the whole of the Highlands, Newburg, the buildings of the Post (at our feet), the red-domed observatory on a lower hill to the S., Cranston's Hotel (p. 152), etc. — A fine road (*Views) leads from West Point to (7 M.) *Cornwall* (see below) over the slopes of *Crow Nest* (p. 148) and *Storm King* (p. 148), and the energetic visitor may easily ascend one or both of these mountains (*Views).

Leaving West Point the train tunnels under the Parade Ground and skirts the bases of *Crow Nest* (p. 148) and *Storm King* (p. 148), commanding fine views of the mountains on the other side of the Hudson.   52 M. *Cornwall* (Union, $2), a popular summer-resort, with *Idlewild*, for 15 years the home of *N. P. Willis* (1807-67).

57 M. **Newburg** (*U. S. Hotel*, $2¹/₂-3; *Merchants'*, $2), a city and coaling port of (1890) 23,087 inhab., finely situated on the W. bank of the Hudson, 130-300 ft. above the water. The chief point of interest here is the old *Hasbrouck Mansion*, to the S. of the city, which was Washington's headquarters in 1782-83 and dates in part from 1750 (interesting relics; adm. free). It was here that Washington was offered the title of king by the officers of the army.

Newburg is the junction of a branch of the *Erie Railway* (running into Pennsylvania) and connects across the Hudson with the *N. Y. & N. E. R. R.* (comp. p. 151).

The line continues to follow the Hudson closely. — 72 M. *Highland* is the station for the steam-ferry to *Poughkeepsie* (p. 151).

88 M. **Kingston** (*Eagle, Mansion Ho.*, $2-2¹/₂) and *Rondout*, the one on the heights a little back from the river and the other at the mouth of the *Rondout Creek*, have been united in one city with (1890) 21,381 inhab., manufactures of cement, and a trade in coal.

Kingston is the junction for the *Ulster & Delaware R. R.*, one of the approaches to the Catskill Mts. (see R. 24c), and connects by steam-ferry with *Rhinecliff* (p. 151). — Rondout is the termination of the **Delaware and Hudson Canal**, which was constructed in 1825-28 to tap the Pennsylvania coal-fields and runs to (108 M.) *Honesdale*. About 2¹/₂ million tons of coal are annually brought over it.

The train now runs at some little distance from the river.   99 M. *Saugerties*, at the mouth of the *Esopus Creek* (rail. stat., 1 M. from the river), near the *Plattekill Clove* (p. 164).

110 M. *Catskill*, the junction of the *Catskill Mt. Railway* and another portal to the *Catskill Mts.*, see p. 160. 115 M. *West Athens;* 120 M. *Coxsackie*. At (128 M.) *Coeyman's Junction* the line for Buffalo and the West diverges to the left.

142 M. **Albany,** see R. 22.

22. Albany.

Hotels. *Kenmore (Pl. a; D, 4), N. Pearl St., $4; Delavan (Pl. b; D, 4), Stanwix Hall (Pl. c; D, 5), Broadway, near railway-station, $2¹/₂-3¹/₂; American, Globe, State St., $2.

Tramways (chiefly electric; fare 5 c.) run through the main streets and to *Troy* (p. 145), *West Albany*, and *Greenbush*.

Steamers ply to *New York* (see R. 21a), *Newburg* (p. 148), *New Baltimore, Troy* (p. 145), *Greenbush* (p. 151), *Bath*, etc.

Cabs. For each pers., 1 M. 50 c., 2 M. 75 c., 3 M. $1.

Theatres. *Leland Opera House, Music Hall*, S. Pearl St. (Pl. C, 5).

Post Office (Pl. D, 5), Broadway, corner of State St.

Albany, the capital of the State of New York, is a thriving commercial city with (1890) 94,923 inhab., finely situated on terraced hills rising from the W. bank of the *Hudson*, at its confluence with the Erie and Champlain Canals. It is well built on the whole, with many really handsome buildings, and retains much of the clean, comfortable, and easy-going character of its original Dutch foundation. Brewing and stove-making are its chief industries, and it has a large timber market. Albany is united with the E. bank of the Hudson by a road-bridge and two railwaybridges (comp. p. 150).

Albany was founded by the Dutch in 1614, and was thus, next to Jamestown in Virginia (p. 331), the oldest European settlement in the Thirteen Original States. A stockade was erected here in 1624 and named *Fort Orange*, but in 1664, when the place passed into the hands of the British, it was re-christened Albany in honour of the future James II. The small town long carried on a lucrative fur-trade with the Indians, but did not contain more than 5000 inhab. at the beginning of the present century. It received a city charter in 1686 and became the State capital in 1798.

In 1629 the 'Patroon' system of Holland was established on the Hudson. The first Patroon was *Killian van Rensselaer*, of Amsterdam, a director of the Dutch West India Co., who, along with others, received from the States General a grant of land extending along the Hudson for 24 M. from the Mohawk River to Beeren Island, below Albany, and running inland for 24 M. from each bank. The Patroon was practically a feudal lord, with the absolute title to the soil, and his tenants were little more than serfs. The property was created a manor in 1685, and soon after the Van Rensselaer heir bought out the other co-proprietors. The manor was not entailed, but its descent was regulated by the law of primogeniture. The patroonship was inherited through five generations but became obsolete after the Declaration of Independence. The last patroon, *Gen. Stephen van Rensselaer*, died in 1839. After the Revolution the obligation of paying rent to the Patroon produced the so-called 'Anti-Rent War', which convulsed the State of New York and caused the troops to be called out several times. The rights of the Van Rensselaers were sustained by all the State Courts. *Col. Church* purchased the rights of the Van Rensselaers in 1853, and most of the tenants have acquired the fee-simple of their lands.

The **Erie Canal**, which connects Lake Erie at Buffalo with the Hudson at Albany, was constructed in 1817-25 at an original cost of $7,500,000 (1,500,000*l.*), since increased to $45,000,000 (9,000,000*l.*), including enlargement, feeders, and connections (Champlain Canal, etc.). It is a monument of the foresight of *Gov. De Witt Clinton* (p. 55), who pushed on the work in spite of all opposition, and gave New York its start as the commercial metropolis of America. The canal is 360 M. long, 7 ft. deep, 56 ft. wide at the bottom, and 70 ft. wide at the surface. It descends 570 ft. by means of 72 locks. It is chiefly used for the conveyance of grain, salt, and timber; and the annual amount of goods carried over it is 6,000 000 tons, valued at $ 300,000,000 (60,000 000*l.*).

Albany has long been an important political centre. In 1754 a provincial congress that met here formed a plan of union that made possible the concerted action of the Colonies a little later; and in more recent times the little knot of Albany politicians has practically determined the nomination and election of several Presidents of the United States. The 'Albany Regency' was the name given by Thurlow Weed to a powerful junto of Democratic politicians here in 1824-37, including Martin van Buren.

Bret Harte was born at Albany in 1839.

The *Railway Stations* (Pl. D, 4) are both close to *Broadway*, the chief commercial thoroughfare, running nearly parallel with the Hudson. A little to the S., at the corner of State St., stands the *Post Office* (Pl. D, 5).

*STATE STREET, 150 ft. wide, ascends directly from the river to the (¹/₄ M.) Capitol (see below), crossing *Pearl St.* (N. and S.), which runs parallel with Broadway and contains the best shops. To the right, at the corner of James St., is the *Mechanics' and Farmers' Bank*, with an inscription stating that it occupies the site of the house of *Anneke Jans*, whose heirs made such valiant and long-continued efforts to recover from Trinity Church (p. 27) the old family property in New York. On the same side, just below N. Pearl St., is the *New York State National Bank*, bearing an inscription to the effect that it is the oldest bank-building continuously used as such in the United States (since 1803).

The chief buildings in *N. Pearl Street* (Pl. D, 4) are the *Young Men's Christian Association* and the *Kenmore Hotel* (both to the left, *i.e.* W. side). A house at the corner of *Columbia St.*, built of Dutch bricks and dated 1710, is the oldest in Albany.

S. Pearl St. ends at (2¹/₄ M.) *Norman's Kill.* — Schuyler St., ³/₄ M. from State St., runs to the right from S. Pearl St. to the interesting old *Schuyler Mansion (Pl. C, 6), now a R. C. asylum, built for Gen. Philip Schuyler in 1760-61. Alex. Hamilton was here married to Elizabeth Schuyler in 1780, and a dent in the old staircase is said to have been made by the tomahawk of one of a party of Indians who tried to carry off Gen. Schuyler in 1781. Gen. Burgoyne was entertained here with his staff after his capture at Saratoga. Washington, Franklin, Carroll of Carrollton, etc., were also guests of this house, and Pres. Millard Fillmore was married here.

A little farther up State St., to the left, is the *State Museum of Natural History* (Pl. C, 4; daily, 9-6), containing zoological, botanical, mineral, and agricultural collections, mainly illustrative of the State of New York. Opposite stands *St. Peter's Episcopal Church* (Pl. C, 3).

The ***Capitol** (Pl. C, 4), commandingly situated at the top of State St. hill, with a small park in front of it, is a huge structure in the French Renaissance style, built in the form of a quadrangle, 300 ft. wide and 400 ft. deep, with a central tower (to be 300 ft. high) and Louvres towers at the angles. The central court is 137 ft. long and 92 ft. wide; above the dormer windows are the arms of the Stuyvesant, Schuyler, Livingston, Jay, Clinton, and Tompkins families. The building is one of the largest in the United States and covers an area of three acres (comp. p. 253). It is built of a light-coloured granite, which contrasts pleasantly with the red-tiled roofs. It was begun in 1869, and is only now approaching completion, though it has been partly occupied for some time. Its total cost, when complete, is estimated at $ 25,000,000. The original design was by *Tho-*

mas Fuller, but this has been considerably modified in construction. 'If anyone had come up to me and told me in French, old or new, that the new Capitol was 'le château de Monseigneur le duc d'Albanie', I could almost have believed him' *(Prof. E. A. Freeman)*.

Interior (guidebooks and photographs for sale at stall inside N. entrance; guides obtainable on application at the Superintendent's Office).

The GROUND-FLOOR, which is occupied by offices and committee-rooms, is connected with the upper floors by elevators and by two handsome staircases. The *Assembly Staircase*, on the N. side, built of brown freestone, is fine but ill-lighted and somewhat gloomy. It leads to the *Golden Corridor* (140 ft. long, 20 ft. wide, and 25 ft. high), extending along the courtside of the N. wing. The *Senate Staircase*, in the S.E. part of the building, is of warm red sandstone, with round and pointed arches and much fine tracery and decoration.

The FIRST FLOOR is also mainly occupied by offices. In the S.E. corner is the *Governor's Room* or *Executive Chamber* (80 ft. × 40 ft.), with mahogany wainscoting and ceiling and hangings of Spanish leather. The elaborate coloured marble decorations of the *S. Corridors* are very effective. Near the E. end of the N. side (below the Assembly Chamber) is the *Old Court of Appeals* (now containing the valuable *State Library* of 150,000 vols.), opening off the Golden Corridor (see above).

SECOND FLOOR. The **Assembly Chamber** (towards E. end of N. side), 140 ft. long and 84 ft. wide (including the galleries), is a fine example of a civic Gothic interior. It is covered by the largest groined arch in the world (56 ft. high), supported by four massive columns of red granite. The N. and S. walls were decorated with two monumental frescoes by *Wm. M. Hunt*, but these, as well as the arched roof itself, are concealed by a wooden ceiling, added to improve the acoustics of the chamber. Visitors admitted to the galleries when the house is in session. — The *Court of Appeals*, at the E. end of the S. side, is a fine room (53 ft. long and 35 ft. wide), adorned with red oak, marble, and Mexican onyx. Next to it is the *Senate Chamber, one of the most sumptuous legislative halls in the world, the elaborate design of which is due to *Mr. H. H. Richardson* (p. xci). It is 100 ft. long, 60 ft. wide, and 50 ft. high (including lobbies and galleries). Among the chief decorative features are the oaken ceiling, the panelling of Mexican onyx and Tennessee marble, the gilded frieze, the open fireplaces, the chandeliers, and the stained-glass windows. The galleries are supported by arches of yellow Siena marble, borne by dark-red granite columns. 'When I say that the arches in the Senate Chamber seemed to me, as far as their general conception goes, worthy to stand at Ragusa, some will understand that I can say no more' *(Freeman)*. — The *Lieut. Governor's Room* is entered from the W. lobby of the Senate Chamber.

Third or Gallery Floor (reached by elevator or small staircase). On the N. side are Committee Rooms and entrances to the Galleries of the Assembly Room. On the S. side are Committee Rooms, the entrances to the Senate Galleries, and the *Bureau of Military Statistics* (W. end; open 9-5), with a collection of State flags used in the Civil War, photographs, memorials of Lincoln, and other relics.

To the N.E. of the Capitol Park, at the corner of Eagle St. and Maiden Lane, is the *City Hall (Pl. C, 4), a striking and beautiful building by *H. H. Richardson* (1881-83), in a free S. French Gothic style, with a fine tower. It is adjoined on the N. by the *State Hall*, to which the collections of the Natural History Museum (p. 155) are to be removed. Opposite are the *Academy Park* and the *Albany Academy* (for boys), where Joseph Henry first demonstrated the theory of the magnetic telegraph by ringing a bell by electricity transmitted through a mile of wire strung round the room.

By following *Eagle Street* towards the S. we reach the *Albany Medical College* (good museum) and, at the corner of Madison Ave., the R. C. **Cathedral of the Immaculate Conception,** a large Gothic building, with spires 210 ft. high. The elaborate interior is lighted by numerous stained-glass windows. A little farther on, below Elm St., is the *Governor's Mansion.*

To the W. of the Capitol State St. is continued (street-cars) to (¹/₂ M.) *Washington Park (Pl. A, B, 3, 4), which, though not very large (81¹/₄ acres), is beautifully laid out (views of Catskills and Helderbergs). It contains a small lake. In Willett St., on the E. side of the park, is the *State Normal College* (Pl. B, 4), an imposing building.

In WASHINGTON AVENUE (Pl. B, C, 3, 4), is the handsome new *Harmanus Bleeker Hall,* for public meetings, concerts, etc. Adjoining, at the corner of Lark St., is the *State Armoury* (Pl. B, 3), with its great round arches.

In S. Swan St., a little to the N. of Washington Ave. and only a few minutes' walk from the Capitol, is the new Episcopal *Cathedral of All Saints (Pl. C, 4), the first regularly organised Protestant cathedral erected in the United States.

In its present condition the building dates from 1884-87; but the towers, the transepts, and the courses above the triforium (at present replaced by a temporary wooden roof) have still to be added. With its noble proportions (length 270 ft.) and tasteful details, it promises to be one of the most beautiful churches in America. Its style is English Gothic. The architect is *Mr. R. W. Gibson.*

Following Broadway (see p. 155; electric tramway) towards the N. from the railway-stations we reach, on the right, near the corner of Manor St., the (³/₄ M.) **Van Rensselaer Mansion** Pl. E, 2), the former residence of the Patroon (p. 154), erected in 1765, but now dilapidated and neglected. It has a pseudo-classical porch, and the paper in the front hall was imported from Holland. Opposite rises the hill crowned with the **Dudley Observatory** (200 ft.; Pl. D, 2), a well-equipped and well-endowed institution, which has done good astronomical work (visitors admitted on Tues. evening, on previous written application to the Director). A fine view is obtained from the Observatory Hill, including the vast lumber-yards adjoining the river. The Observatory is soon to be removed to a new building in Lake Ave., near Washington Park.

We may go on from here by electric car (5 c.) to (20 min.) the *Rural Cemetery* and (¹/₂ hr.) *West Troy* (p. 143). Visitors to the *Rural Cemetery have ¹/₂ M. to walk (to the left) after leaving the car, when they reach the tasteful lodge of the cemetery to the right and the gate of the *St. Agnes R. C. Cemetery* to the left. The chief lion of the Rural Cemetery is the figure of the *Angel at the Sepulchre,* by E. D. Palmer, to reach which we turn to the left at the lodge and follow, as nearly as possible, the railing of the St. Agnes Cemetery, until we reach the top of the *S. Ridge* (*Views). Close by is the tomb of *Gen. Schuyler* (p. 155) and a little to the N. is that of *President Arthur.*

Among the other buildings of Albany may be mentioned *St. Joseph's Church* (R. C.), at the corner of Ten Broeck St. and Second St.; the *Child's Hospital;* the *Penitentiary;* the *County Hospital;* and the *Alms Houses.*

The old *Vanderheyden Palace* (1725), mentioned in 'Bracebridge Hall', stood near 'Elm Tree Corner' (cor. of State St. and Pearl St.), on a site

now occupied by the Perry Building; and at the N.E. corner af State and
Pearl St. was the quaint *Lydius House.*
  Among points of interest within easy reach of Albany, besides the
Hudson River places of R. 21, are *Saratoga* (p. 179), the *Catskills* (p. 159),
the *Adirondacks* (p. 165), *Howe's Cave* (see below), *Sharon Springs* (see
below), *Cooperstown* (see below), and *Lake George* (p. 182). *Shakers*, 7 M.
to the N.W., was the original Shaker settlement in America (1774) and is
the burial-place of Mother Ann Lee (d. 1784).

23. From Albany to Binghamton.

142 M. DELAWARE AND HUDSON RAILROAD in 4³/4-5¹/4 hrs. (fare $ 4.25).

  The line ascends towards the W. 7 M. *Voorheesville* (p. 195).
To the left are the *Helderberg Mts.,* whence the Helderberg limestone
formations are named. At (27 M.) *Quaker Street,* where the line
from Mechanicsville and Saratoga joins ours, we see to the right the
singular trestle-work of the *Dodge Coal Storage Apparatus.*
  39 M. *Howe's Cave* (780 ft.; *Pavilion Hotel, $ ¹/2) is the station
for one of the most remarkable caverns in America.
  *Howe's Cave, an old underground water channel, in the Lower Hel-
derberg limestone, is entered from the Pavilion Hotel (adm. $1, incl.
guide and dress; time of visit 3-4 hrs.) and is named from its discoverer
Lester Howe (1842). The stalactite and stalagmite formations are often
very beautiful, and appropriate names have been given to the chief points
of interest, which include the 'Stygian Lake', crossed by boat. Visitors
are conducted to a point about 3 M. from the entrance, but the cave extends several miles farther.
  45 M. *Cobleskill* (Hotel Augusta) is the junction of a branch-
line to (13 M.) *Sharon Springs* and (22 M.) *Cherry Valley.*
  Sharon Springs (*Pavilion*, finely situated, $ 3¹/2; *Union*, $ 3; *Sharon
House*, $ 2¹/2-3; *American, Mansion Ho.*, *Fethers, Howland, Vanderbilt*, $ 2),
charmingly situated in a pretty little wooded valley, 1350 ft. above the
sea, has frequented sulphur and chalybeate springs, chiefly used for bathing.
Just below the *Baths*, at the old bridge to the N., the stream forms a
pretty waterfall, 60 ft. high. The piazza at the back of the Pavilion Hotel
commands an extensive *View over the *Mohawk Valley* (p. 186), with the
Adirondacks in the background. The view from *Prospect Hill*, 3¹/2 M. to
the N.W., on the road to Cherry Valley, is still finer.
  22 M. *Cherry Valley* (1320 ft.), another little summer-resort, with hotels
and boarding-houses. In 1778 the inhabitants were all massacred or taken
prisoner by the Tories and Indians. A pleasant drive may be taken to
(14 M.) *Richfield Springs* (p. 188; stage).
  50 M. *Richmondville;* 67 M. *Schenevus.* — 75 M. *Cooperstown
Junction,* for a short line to (16 M.) *Cooperstown.*
  Cooperstown (1240 ft.; *Fenimore Ho.*, $ 2-3; *Central, Carr's, Ballard's,*
$ 2), a village of 2657 inhab., prettily situated at the lower (S.) end of
Otsego Lake, was founded in 1798 by *Wm. Cooper*, father of *J. Fenimore
Cooper* (1789-1851), the novelist, who lived and died here and immor-
talized the district in his romances. *Otsego Lake (the 'Glimmerglass' of
Cooper), 9 M. long and ³/4-1¹/2 M. wide, is one of the prettiest of the
New York lakes. The *Susquehanna* issues from it at the foot of Main St.
  To reach the site of the old *Cooper Mansion*, where the novelist lived
from 1834 to his death in 1851, we descend Main St. and turn to the right
at Fair St. (first cross-street beyond Ballard's Hotel). It is marked by a
stone with an inscription. Cooper is buried in the Episcopal graveyard,
reached by turning to the left beyond the site of the house.
  Two small steamers ply regularly on Otsego Lake, connecting at the

N. end with coaches for (7 M.) *Richfield Springs* (p. 188). The drive or walk round the lake (ca. 20 M.) is a pleasant excursion. Crossing the Susquehanna at the foot of Main St., we reach (5 min.) cross-roads, where walkers may ascend the steps to the right through wood. In 13 min. we cross a road and, keeping to the left, reach (3-4 min.) the summer-house on *Prospect Rock* (1440 ft.), commanding a splendid *View of Cooperstown and the lake. Returning to (3-4 min.) the road we crossed, we descend it to (10 min.) the above-mentioned fork. We then continue our route along the lake, the pretty tree-shaded road recalling that along the W. bank of Windermere. 7 min. *Cemetery,* containing a monument to Fenimore Cooper. About 2-3 min. farther on a path descends to the left to the *Fairy Spring. Point Judith,* with Kingfisher's Tower, is 1½ M. farther on.

In following the W. shore of the lake we pass many of the places mentioned in *Cooper's* 'Deerslayer'. ½ M. *Hannah's Hill* and *Musk-rat Cove;* 2½ M. *Leatherstocking Falls;* 3 M. *Three Mile* or *Wild Rose Point,* where Hetty Hutter landed. Adjacent is *Mohican Glen.* From *Five-Mile Point* a road ascends to the top of *Mt. Otsego* (2800 ft.; Inn and view-tower), commanding an extensive *View. 6 M. *Hutter's Point,* near which take place the final scenes of the story. A white buoy in the lake marks the site of 'Hutter's Castle'. The *Steamboat Landing* is about 2 M. farther on.

Numerous other walks and drives may be made from Cooperstown. It is 13 M. from *Cherry Valley* and 20 M. from *Sharon Springs* (p. 158).

82 M. *Oneonta* (1085 ft.), with railway-workshops and a trade in hops; 119 M. *Nineveh,* the junction of a branch to *Wilkesbarré* (p. 228); 127 M. *Tunnel Station,* where we thread a tunnel ½ M. long.

142 M. **Binghamton** (860 ft.), see p. 197.

24. The Catskill Mts.

The chief gateways to the Catskill Mts. are *Rondout* (p. 149) and *Catskill* (p. 149), both situated on the W. bank of the Hudson and both reached from New York by *Steamer* (R. 21a; fares $1, $1½), by *West Shore Railroad* (R. 21c; $2.18), or *N. Y. C. & H. R. Railroad* (R. 21b) and ferry ($2.18). Through-tickets are issued on these routes to the chief resorts in the mountains (*e.g.* to *Catskill Mt. Ho.,* $2.75 to $3.93), and prompt connections are made. The Mts. may be approached from the N.W. vià *Stamford* (p. 165).

The *Catskills, the Indian *Onti Ora* or '*Mts. of the Sky*', are an outlying group of the great Appalachian system, running parallel with the Hudson for about 12-15 M., at a distance of 8-9 M. from its W. bank. They lie mainly in Greene Co., New York, and cover an area of about 500 sq. M. Their name is derived through the Dutch name of *Katzbergs,* applied to them on account of the numerous wild-cats that infested them (kill = stream, gorge). Towards the E. their declivity is very abrupt, and as seen from the Hudson they appear like an almost vertical wall 2000-3000 ft. high. On the other sides the slopes are more gradual. Deep ravines, known as 'Cloves', are cut into many of the mountains by mountain-torrents. The highest summits are *Slide Mt.* (4205 ft.; p. 164) and *Hunter Mt.* (4050 ft.; p. 163). An additional attraction of the Catskills is the part they play in the scant legendary lore of America (comp. p. 160). Their picturesque scenery, cool and healthy atmosphere, and easy accessibility have made them a favourite summer-resort; and numerous good hotels and boarding-houses (mostly open June-Sept.) now sprinkle the entire district (see below). The most frequented of these are the *Kaaterskill Hotel* and the *Catskill Mountain House* (see pp. 161, 162). A glimpse at the chief points of interest may be obtained in a day by a round-trip from Catskill to either of the above hotels and thence vià *Stony Clove* and the *Kaaterskill Railroad* to *Tannersville, Phoenicia,* and *Kingston* (or in the reverse direction); but a stay of 1-3 weeks is desirable for a closer acquaintance with the mountains. The Catskill railways generally cease running in winter. Fair trout-fishing is obtained in the mountain-streams. The red sandstone to which the name Catskill has been attached belongs to the latest Devonian formations of America.

a. From Catskill to the Catskill Mountain House and the Hotel Kaaterskill.

Catskill (95 ft.; *Prospect Park Hotel,* with view of the Hudson, $ 3-4; *Grant House,* 1 M. to the W., with view, $ 3; *Windsor, Irving Ho.,* $ 2-3), a village with 4920 inhab., is finely situated on the W. bank of the Hudson, at the mouth of the *Catskill Creek.* There are numerous pleasant walks and drives in the vicinity, and boating and fishing may be enjoyed on the two rivers.

Catskill is the starting-point of the narrow-gauge CATSKILL MOUNTAIN RAILROAD, which runs hence to (13 M.) *Cairo* (35-45 min.) and to (16 M.) *Palenville* ($^3/_4$-1 hr.). The railway ascends the Catskill Creek to (8 M.) *South Cairo* and (10 M.) *Cairo Junction,* where the Cairo branch (3 M.) diverges to the right.

Cairo (345 ft.; *Columbian,* $ 3; *Winter Clove Ho.,* $ 2) is an unpretending little summer-resort, commanding a good view of the Catskills.

Beyond Cairo Junction the train skirts the base of *Cairo Round Top Mt.* 12 M. *Lawrenceville.* 14 M. *Mountain House Station,* where the road to the (4 M.) *Catskill Mt. House* (p. 161) begins.

The *ROAD FROM THE MOUNTAIN HOUSE STATION TO THE MOUNTAIN HOUSE ($4^1/_4$ M.) ascends very rapidly, and good walkers can accomplish the distance almost as fast as the carriages. After passing through ($^1/_2$ M.) the toll-gate at the foot of the mountain, we turn to the left and ascend to *Sleepy Hollow,* the scene of Rip van Winkle's famous adventure, and to (1 M.) the *Rip van Winkle House* (1275 ft.). A slab of rock is pointed out as the actual spot of his twenty years' slumber! Farther on the road toils up the 'Dead Ox Hill', rounds 'Cape Horn', passes the 'Short Level', again turns abruptly to the left, climbs 'Featherbed Hill', traverses the 'Long Level', and leads through a final brace of curves to the W. or rear entrance of the *Catskill Mt. Ho.* (see p. 161).

$15^1/_4$ M. *Otis Junction,* the starting-point of the OTIS ELEVATING RAILWAY, which leads directly to the *Catskill Mt. House* in 10 min., ascending 1600 ft. in its length of $1^1/_3$ M. (fare 75 c.). This new route, opened in 1892, reduces the time between Catskill and the Mountain Ho. by more than 1 hr. The *Hotel Kaaterskill* (p. 162) is 1 M. from the top of the railway.

16 M. **Palenville** (*Stony Brook Ho.,* $ 2-3; *Maple Grove Ho., Pine Grove Ho., Winchelsea,* $ 2; *Palenville Ho.,* 1 M. from the station, $ 2),, finely situated at the entrance to the Kaaterskill Clove (see below), lies 3 M. from the Kaaterskill Hotel (omnibuses meet the train here; see below). Palenville is much frequented by artists, and many pleasant walks and drives may be made from it. Coaches run hence to *Haines's Falls* and *Tannersville* (p. 164; $ 1).

Some travellers prefer to drive all the way from Catskill to (12 M.) the *Mountain House* or the (14 M.) *Kaaterskill Hotel.*

The *Kaaterskill Clove is a narrow wooded ravine, like the 'Notches' of the White Mts. (pp. 126, 129), enclosed by *South Mountain* (p. 161) on the right and *High Peak* (p. 163) and *Round Top* (p. 162) on the left. A rough road ascends through the Clove, crossing the creek near the Palenville Hotel, 1 M. from the station. $^1/_3$ M. *Artist's Grotto* and *La Belle Falls.* A little farther on are two landslips. At (1 M.) *Profile Rock* we cross the creek (profile seen by looking back from the bridge). ¹/₄ M. *Fawn's Leap;* ¹/₄ M. *Buttermilk Falls;* ¹/₄ M. Bridge over *Lake Creek.* Here we may either turn to the right and follow the lateral ravine to (1 M.) the *Kaaterskill Falls* or take the path up the Clove proper to (1¹/₄ M.) *Haines's Falls* (p. 164). The road ascends to (1¹/₄ M.) the *Haines House* (p. 164).

The **Catskill Mountain House** (2225 ft.; $ 2-4 per day, $ 14-25 per week, acc. to room and season; 400 beds) is magnificently situated on the ridge of *South* or *Pine Orchard Mountain* (2500 ft.). The **View from the rocky ledges in front of the hotel is of a unique beauty and interest.

The E. escarpment of the mountain rises so abruptly from the plain that the effect is almost as if we were leaning out of the car of a balloon or over the battlements of a castle 2000 ft. high. The plain between the mountains and the Hudson, 10 M. off, is spread out at our feet like a low-relief map, with checkerboard squares of fields, patches of woodland, villages, and farm-houses. Catskill is distinctly seen due E., and Athens (p. 149) and Hudson (p. 151) may be made out a little more to the N. The moving trains on the banks of the Hudson are curiously distinct and minute. The E. background is formed by the blue Berkshire Hills (p. 136), over which the shadowy White Mts. (p. 121) are sometimes visible.

Walks. By following the road leading towards North Mt. and North Lake and taking the first path to the right, we soon reach (10 min.) the *Artist's Rock*, on the E. ledge of N. Mt. (view), beyond which the path ascends some steps and reaches (3 min.) *Prospect Rock*, which commands a very extensive *View. The ledge-path next leads to (5 min.) *Sunset Rock*, beyond which it bends to the left to (7 min.) *Jacob's Ladder* and the *Bear's Den* (*View). The ledge-path ends at *Newman's Ledge* (view of Sleepy Hollow, p. 160), 10-12 min. beyond the Bear's Den. — The path to the *left* at the fork, 5 min. beyond the Bear's Den, ascends towards the crest of **North Mountain** (3450 ft.), a walk round which takes in all 4-5 hrs. The path crosses the '*Burnt District*' to (20 min. from Bear's Den) the cavity called the *Cellar.* Here we bend towards the left and walk round the crest to (¹/₂ hr.) the so-called *First Outlook, at the top of the mountain, and (10 min.) the *Second Outlook*. The trail descending from this point through the trees is sometimes a little difficult to follow; but there is little danger of being lost if the general direction of the hotel be taken at the Outlook and followed by compass. An additional help in case of doubt is the water-pipe leading to the hotel (1¹/₂-2 hrs.). It is advisable not to try this walk alone. — By following the path to the left at the entrance to the North Mt. walk, passing the E. end of North Lake, and ascending along the stream, we reach (¹/₂ hr.) *Mary's Glen*, with small waterfalls. We may return by crossing the stream above the falls and following a path leading S.W. to (¹/₄ hr.) the main road, which we reach at the *Charcoal Pit*, ¹/₃ M. from the hotel.

The Catskill Mt. House is about 1 M. to the N.E. of the Kaaterskill Hotel (p. 162), and the excursions made from the latter (see p. 162) can all be made from the former also.

The *ROAD FROM PALENVILLE TO THE HOTEL KAATERSKILL (3 M.; see above; coach-fare $ 1¹/₂, trunk 50 c.) runs from the station to the W. through the village, then turns to the right and ascends along the N. side of the Kaaterskill Clove (p. 160). In 1¹/₂ M. we cross the so-called *Gulf*, with the *Point of Rocks* and *Indian Head* high above us to the right, and about ¹/₂ M. farther on we bend back on our course and proceed for some distance to the E., climbing towards (¹/₂ M.) the head of the Gulf, several hundred feet above the point where we crossed it below. To the left diverges the *Ledge Drive* (p. 162). In ¹/₂ M. more we reach the —

BAEDEKER's United States.

*Hotel Kaaterskill (2495 ft.; $ 4-5 per day, $ 21-25 per week;
1500 beds, including dépendances), the most fashionable resort in
the Catskills, situated on one of the highest points of *South Mt.* (see
p. 161) and commanding a view little, if at all, inferior to that from
the Mountain House (see p. 161). Immediately to the S.W. rise
High Peak (3665 ft.) and *Round Top* (3500 ft.), thickly clad with
timber from top to bottom, and due W. is *Hunter Mt.* (4050 ft.).
Kaaterskill Station (p. 164) lies about 3/4 M. to the W., at the end
of South Lake (p. 164).

Walks. Most of the paths, roads, and points of interest are clearly
indicated by sign-posts and arrows painted on the rocks.

1. To the *Catskill Mt. House*, 1-1¼ M. Different paths, indicated by
sign-posts, begin in front (E.) and to the N. of the hotel, and lead viâ the
Fairy Spring, the *Mossy Path*, the *Druid Rocks*, the *Lemon Squeezer*, and
the *Ledge Path*. The last skirts the E. edge of the mountain, affording fine
views of the Hudson Valley, the best from the so-called (½ M.) *Grand
View*. A short digression may be made to the left to the top of *South
Mountain* (2500 ft.; *View). — A pleasant round may be made by going
viâ the Ledge Path and returning viâ the Druid Rocks, making a complete circuit of South Mt.

2. *Palenville Overlook*, 1¾ M. The path leads to the E. from the hotel.
The *Overlook (1660 ft.) commands a fine view of Kaaterskill Clove (p. 160).

3. *Inspiration Point and Sunset Rock*, 1 M. A path beginning at the
hotel-stables (to the S. of the hotel) leads through low wood, crossing a
road, to (⅓ M.) a point on the Ledge Drive, where stands a sign-post indicating the path to (¼ M.) *Inspiration Point* (*View), overlooking Kaaterskill Clove. Thence we follow the path along the brink of the Clove to
(¼ M.) *Sunset Rock (2120 ft.), which commands a magnificent view of
the Clove and of the tree-clad mass of High Peak (see above). — We may
continue this walk to *Kaaterskill Falls* (see below), either by the paths
on the level of the rock or by descending the ladder-steps to the bottom
of the Clove. The easiest route to follow is the path to the extreme right
('To Hotel Kaaterskill'), which ascends to (5 min.) the *Ledge Drive*. We
follow this road to the left, and in about 1 M., turning twice to the left,
reach the *Laurel House* and the *Falls* (see below).

4. *Laurel House and Kaaterskill Falls*, 1 M. We may either follow the
road leading to the S.W. from the front of the Hotel and joining (¾ M.) the
Ledge Drive (see above), or we take a path leading W. from the Annex to
(4 min.) an old 'logging road', which leads to the left and joins the Ledge
Drive near the Laurel House. — The Laurel House ($ 2½-4 per day,
$ 15-25 per week) is situated at the head of the Kaaterskill Falls, 300 yds.
from the railway-station mentioned at p. 164. — The *Kaaterskill Falls,
in an imposing rocky amphitheatre, reached by a flight of steps behind the
hotel (adm. 25 c.), are 260 ft. in height, in two leaps of 180 ft. and 80 ft.
In dry weather the water is dammed up at the head of the falls and turned
on for visitors like the Lichtenhain Waterfall in the Saxon Switzerland.
A little lower down are the *Bastion Falls* (40 ft.). — A good view of the
Falls is obtained from *Prospect Rock*, on the S. side of the Clove, reached
by a path (½ M.) from the Laurel House.

5. To *Haines's Falls*, 2½-3½ M. The most direct route is by a forest-
path from Prospect Rock (see above), which comes out on (1 M.) *Featherbed Lane* (see below), about ½ M. from the Falls. This route is a little
difficult to find unaided, but the following is quite distinct. To the *Laurel
House*, as above, 1 M. Hence we follow the road to the W., crossing the
railway. On reaching the (½ M.) main road we follow it to the left for
1¼ M. We then descend to the left by *Featherbed Lane* to the (½ M.)
bottom of the Clove, turn to the right, and reach the (¼ M.) *Haines's Falls
House* (p. 164), where a placard indicates the way to the *Falls* (p. 164).

Other short walks may be made to (½ M.) the *Boulder* and to the
points mentioned in connection with the Mountain House at p. 161.

The ascent of *North Mt.* (p. 161) takes about 1 hr. — That of **High Peak** (3665 ft.) takes 1¹/₂-2¹/₂ hrs. from the Haines's Falls House (see p. 162) and is rather toilsome, but the view is very fine.

Longer Excursions, by railway or carriage, may be made to *Tannersville* and *Onteora Park* (p. 164; 5-8 M.), *Stony Clove* (see below), *Catskill* (p. 160), *Sleepy Hollow* (p. 160), *Overlook Mt.* (see below), *Plattekill Clove* (p. 164), etc.

b. From Kingston (Rondout) to the Hotel Kaaterskill.

49 M. Railway in 2¹/₂-3 hrs. (fare $ 2.71).

We at first follow the Ulster and Delaware Railroad, which traverses the S. and W. sides of the Catskill Mts. The train starts at *Rondout* (p. 153) and then stops at (2 M.) the Union Station in *Kingston* (p. 153). The line ascends gradually through the beautiful valley of the *Esopus.* 8 M. *Stony Hollow* (410 ft.). — 9 M. *West Hurley* (530 ft.) is the starting-point of the road (coach $ 1.50) to (9 M.) the top of **Overlook Mt.** (3150 ft.), near which stands the *Overlook Mt. House* ($ 3; 2980 ft.; 300 beds), a favourite resort, the *View from which, embracing the Hudson, the Highlands (p. 148), and the Catskills, is considered by some authorities the finest in the district. *Mead's Hotel* ($ 2), about halfway up the mountain (7 M. from the railway), is well spoken of. — Near (18 M.) *Shokan* (535 ft.) *High Point Mt.* (3100 ft.) is conspicuous to the left. The train now turns to the N., disclosing, to the left, a fine semicircle of mountains, sending off radiating spurs to a common centre (the two most to the right are *Mt. Cornell,* 3680 ft., and *Mt. Wittenberg,* 3775 ft.). Near (21 M.) *Boiceville* we twice cross the Esopus. — Beyond (24 M.) *Mt. Pleasant* (700 ft.) the valley contracts; to the left rises *Panther Mt.* (3825 ft.). *Indian Head* (3580 ft.) and other high mountains are seen to the right.

27 M. **Phoenicia** (800 ft.; *Tremper House,* $ 3¹/₂-4; *Broas House,* unpretending, $ 2), the junction of the Stony Clove Railroad (see below), is pleasantly situated and a good centre for excursions (to the top of *Mt. Wittenberg, Stony Clove, Woodland Valley, Big Indian Valley,* etc.). — We now leave the Ulster and Delaware line and ascend by a narrow-gauge railway (views to the left) through *Stony **Clove,** a beautiful wooded ravine between *Mt. Sheridan* (2490 ft.) and *Hunter Mt.* (4040 ft.) on the left and *Mt. Tremper* (3840 ft.) and *Stony Mt.* (3850 ft.) on the right. — 29 M. *Chichester,* with a chair-factory; 32 M. *Lanesville,* with a fine view (left) of the *Diamond Notch, Hunter Mt.,* and *Big West Kill Mt.* (3900 ft.; to the W.). To the left are deep ravines between the spurs of Hunter Mt. At (37 M.) *Stony Clove* we reach the top of the pass (2070 ft.) and begin to descend. — 39 M. *Kaaterskill Junction* (1700 ft.), whence the *Kaaterskill Railroad* diverges to the right (through-cars).

The Stony Clove R. R. goes on to (41 M.) **Hunter** (1645 ft.; *St. Charles,* $ 2¹/₂-4; *Prospect Ho.,* $ 2¹/₂), close to the base of the *Colonel's Chair* (3040 ft.) and 2 M. to the N. of *Hunter Mt.* (see above), both of which summits may be ascended hence. Fine drives may be taken to the *Overlook Mt. Ho.* (14 M.) and the *Hotel Kaaterskill* (11 M.); and nearer points of interest are *Mossy Brook* (1 M.), *Onteora Park* (p. 164), and *Stony Clove.*

11 *

The KAATERSKILL RAILROAD ascends towards the E. — 42 M. **Tannersville** (1860 ft.; *Roggen's Mountain Hotel*, $ 2-2¹/₂, open all the year; *Blythewood, Fabian Ho., Campbell Ho.*, $ 2¹/₂) occupies one of the most conveniently central situations in the Catskills.

Clum Hill (2370 ft.), ³/₄ M. to the S., easily ascended in ¹/₂ hr., affords a good view, including the Kaaterskill Falls (p. 162). — About 2 M. to the N. is *Onteora Park*, a cottage colony belonging to a club which includes several well-known writers (Mrs. Mary Mapes Dodge, etc.). The enclosure is private, but visitors will generally be allowed, on application at the gate, to ascend to (20 min.) the top of *Onteora* or *Parker Mt.* (2735 ft.), the *View from which includes High Peak, Round Top, the Kaaterskill Hotel, Twin Mt., Sugar Loaf, Plateau Mt., Hunter Mt., Round Hill, Thomas Cole Mt., Black Dome, and Black Head. — Parker Mt. is separated by the *Parker Notch* from *Star Rock* (2545 ft. to the W.), another good point of view. — The **Black Dome** (4000 ft.), about 3 M. to the N.W. of Parker Mt., affords a fine panorama of the valley in which Tannersville lies and the mountains enclosing it. *Slide Mt.* (4205 ft.; p. 165), the highest of the Catskills, is seen to the right, over the shoulder of Hunter Mt. — To the S. of Clum Hill (see above) extends the fine *Plattekill Clove* (road), between *Round Top* and *High Peak* (p. 163) to the left and *Sugar Loaf* or *Mink Mt.* (3805 ft.), *Twin Mt.* (3650 ft.), and *Indian Head* (3580 ft.) to the right. About 6 M. from Tannersville are the *Plattekill Falls* (60 ft.), near which is the *Plattekill Mt. House*. A new road (*Views) ascends to the right to (6 M.) the *Overlook Mt. House* (p. 163). — About 3 M. to the S. of Tannersville, on the slope of Sugar Loaf Mt., is *Elka Park*, the property of the *Lieder-Kranz* ('L. K.') of New York, with a nice club-house. — Among other points within easy reach of Tannersville are *Haines's Falls* (see below), *Kaaterskill Falls, Clove*, and *Hotel* (pp. 160, 162), and *Stony Clove* (p. 163).

Beyond Tannersville the train soon reaches (44 M.) **Haines's Corner** (1920 ft.; *Haines's Falls House, Hilton Ho., Holbert Ho.*, $ 2), the nearest station to (1/₂ M.) *Haines's Falls* (see below).

*Haines's Falls, at the head of Kaaterskill Clove (p. 160), consist of two main leaps, 150-160 ft. and 80 ft. high, with other plunges lower down, making in all a descent of 475 ft. in ¹/₄ M. The water is dammed up in dry weather and the sluices opened for visitors (fee 25 c.). The environment of the falls is very picturesque. The bridge above the falls leads to *Twilight* or *Haines's Falls Park*, another cottage-colony like Onteora Park (see above). — From Haines's Falls to the *Kaaterskill Falls* and *Hotel*, see p. 162.

The train now traverses wood to (46 M.) *Laurel House Station* ⁀065 ft.), 300 yds. from the *Laurel House* and the *Kaaterskill Falls* (᠁ p. 162). The falls are seen to the right just before we reach the station. — The railway ends at (47 M.) *Kaaterskill Station* (2145 ft.), situated at the W. end of *South Lake*, a pretty little sheet of water. The road to the (³/₄ M.) *Hotel Kaaterskill* crosses the bridge to the S. and leads through wood. The road to (1 M.) the *Catskill Mt. House* (p. 161) skirts the N. side of the lake and then turns to the right and passes up between South Lake and the still smaller *North Lake*.

c. From Rondout (Kingston) to Bloomville.

87 M. ULSTER AND DELAWARE RAILROAD in 3¹/₂-4 hrs. (fare $ 2.61). This line skirts the S. and E. sides of the Catskills, and gives access to many interesting points. Through-cars from New York, comp. p. 159.

From *Rondout (Kingston)* to (27 M.) *Phoenicia*, see p. 163. To

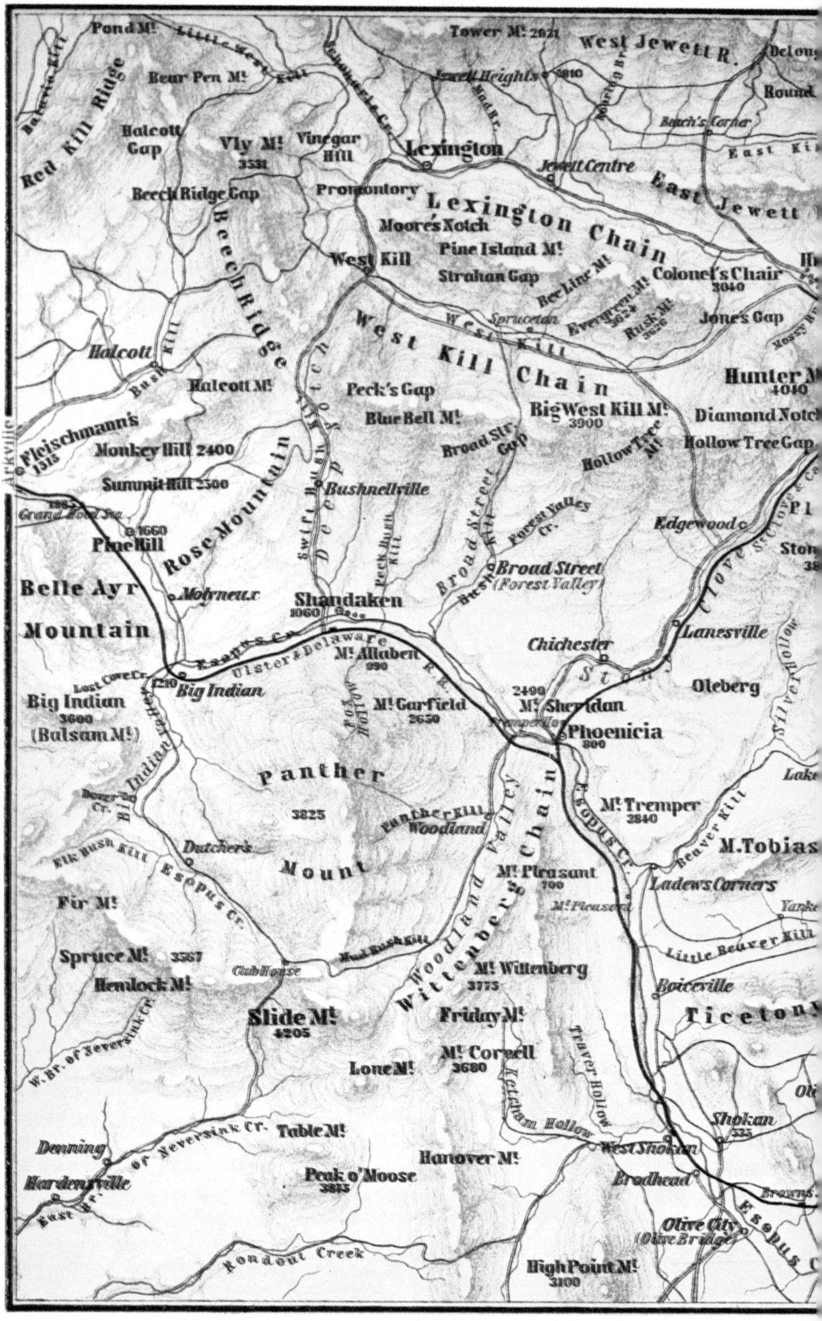

Pond Mt.
Tower Mt. 2921
West Jewett R.
Bear Pen Mt.
Jewett Heights 3810
Red Kill Ridge
Halcott Gap
Vly Mt. 3531
Vinegar Hill
Lexington
Jewett Centre
East Jewett
Beech Ridge Gap
Promontory
Lexington Chain
Moore's Notch
Pine Island Mt.
West Kill
Strahan Gap
Colonel's Chair 3040
Beech Ridge
Bee Line Mt.
Evergreen Mt. 3624
Rusk Mt. 3626
Jone's Gap
West Kill Chain
Halcott
Hunter Mt. 4040
Halcott Mt.
Peck's Gap
Big West Kill Mt. 3900
Diamond Notch
Blue Bell Mt.
Fleischmann's 1515
Broad St. Gap
Hollow Tree Mt.
Hollow Tree Gap
Monkey Hill 2400
Rose Mountain
Summit Hill 2300
Bushnellville
Deep Notch
Arkville
Grand Hotel Sta.
Edgewood
Pine Hill
Broad Street Kill
Forest Valley Cr.
Belle Ayr Mountain
Molyneux
Broad Street (Forest Valley)
Shandaken 1060
Stony Clove
Lanesville
Esopus Cr.
Ulster & Delaware R.R.
Chichester
Mt. Allaben 990
Lost Cove Cr.
Big Indian
Oleberg
Big Indian 3600 (Balsam Mt.)
Fox Hollow
Mt. Garfield 2650
2400 Mt. Sheridan
Phoenicia 800
Silver Hollow
Panther Mountain 3825
Panther Kill
Woodland
Mt. Tremper 3840
Beaver Kill
M. Tobias
Dutcher's
Elk Bush Kill
Esopus Cr.
Woodland Valley
Wittenberg Chain
Mt. Pleasant 700
Ladews Corners
Fir Mt.
Little Beaver Kill
Spruce Mt. 3567
Club House
Mt. Wittenberg 3775
Hemlock Mt.
Boiceville
Slide Mt. 4205
Friday Mt.
Ticetonyk
W. Br. of Neversink Cr.
Mt. Cornell 3680
Lone Mt.
Traver Hollow
Ketcham Hollow
Shokan 535
Table Mt.
Denning
Hanover Mt.
West Shokan
Hardenville
Peak o'Moose 3843
Brodhead
East Br. of Neversink Cr.
Olive City (Olive Bridge)
Rondout Creek
High Point Mt. 3100
Esopus Cr.

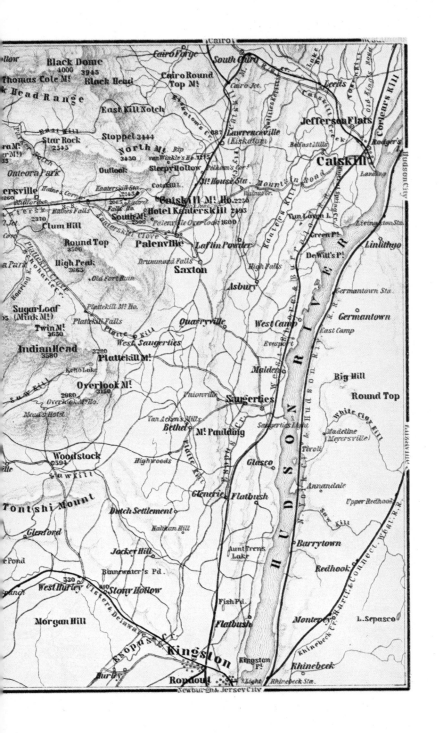

Jo Indian Pd

Stillwater

Wolf Pd
Long Pond

Indian Rock

Rainbo

Whitney

Buck Mt

Barnum
Follensby Jr
Paul Smith's Sta.

Osgood Pd
St Regis L. Ho.
Paul Smith's

Bay Pd

Spitfire Pd

Lower St Regis L.
Upper-
Paul Sm

Mc Donald Pd

St Regis Mt
2890

Kickabuck Sta.

Fish Pd

St Regis Pd

Amber L.

East
Saranac Inn
Sta.

Big Clear Pd Ho.

Jordan Ho.

Jordan L.

Willis Pd

Long

Little-
Clear

Sta.

Big-
Clear

Saranac
Junction
Colby

Kildare Sta.

Raquette R.

Bloodwood Pd

Saranac Inn

Ampersand Hot.
Saranac L. Ho.
1539

James town Falls

Moosehead Mt

Rollins Pd

Upper

Lower
Saranac
Lake

Lonesc

Childwold Park Ho.

Matumbla Mt

Big-
Wolf Pd

Saranac

Massawepie L.

Childwold Sta.

Little

Lake

Milf

Tupper L. Junct.

Wawbeck Lod.

1542

Round
Lake

Childwold R. R. Sta.

Raquette Pd

Tupper Lake

Simons Pd

Bartlett
Rustic Lodge
Stony Creek Pds

Ampersand Mt
3330

Gull Pd

Arab Mt

Mt Morris H.

Follensby
Pd

Ampersan

Silver L.

Horseshoe Pd

Tupper L. Ho.

Mt Morris

Little Symons Pd

Raquette Falls
Raquette Falls Ho.

Mt Seward
4384

Graves Mt
Hitchins

Silver Mt

Bog R.

Tupper Pd

Bog Falls

Jenkins Pd

Moose Creek

Cola R.

Preston Ponds

Trout Pd

Bear Pd

Cone Mt

Duck Pd

Santanoni Mt

L. Henc
Pan
4645

Robbins Ho.

Round Pd

Sperry Pd

Handsome Pd

Buck Mt
1612

Round Pd

Moose Pd
Moose Mt

And

Little
Tupper
Lake
1730

Mohegan Pd

Grampus L.

Kempshall

Catlin
Lake

Catlin Mt

Wolf Pd

L. Delia

Stony Pd

Lit. Slim Pd

Slim Pd

Mud Pd

Big Brook

Baldwin Mt

Rock Pd

Clear Pd

Pickwocket Pd

Rich L.

L. Harris

Salmon

Bottle Pd

Sidton Pd

Owls Head
2825

Long Lake Ho.

The Sagamore

Goodenow Mt

Newcomb

Carry Pd

Moose Pd

Mt Sabattis
Grove House

MOU

Brandreth L.

Little Forked Pd

South Pd

Mt Joseph

Forked Lake
1750

Buttermilk Falls

Tirrell Pd

7 Chain Lakes

Forked L. Ho.

Sargent Pds

Minnow Pd

Blue Mt
L. 1800

Blue Mt
3760
Blue Mountain

L. Bonney

Eagle's Nest
Marion Eagle L.
Otowina L.

Prospect Ho.

Rock River

Cedar R.

The Hemlocks
Camp Fine Knot
Hathorn

Antlers

Raquette Lake

Golden Beach

Rock L.

Club Ho.

Brown Tract Inlet

Indian R.

Trenton Falls

North Branch Adirondack

South Branch Adirondack

Dead Creek

St Lawrence

Tupper Lake

Long Lake

Raquette R.

Hudson R.

North or Hudson R.

ADI

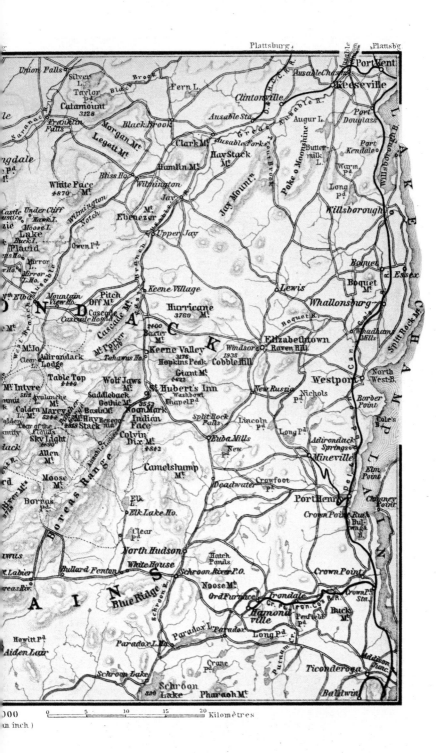

the left, beyond Phoenicia, rises *Mt. Garfield* (2650 ft.). 32 M. *Alla-ben* (990 ft.). From (33 M.) *Shandaken* (1060 ft.; Palace Hotel, $3; Whitney, $2) coaches run through the *Deep Notch* to *West Kill* and *Lexington.* — 36 M. *Big Indian* (1210 ft.; Joslyn Ho., $2) lies at the mouth of *Big Indian Valley*, with the headwaters of the *Esopus.*

This is the starting-point for a visit to (11 M.) *Slide Mt.* (see below). A road ascends Big Indian Valley, with *Big Indian* or *Balsam Mt.* (3600 ft.) to the right and *Panther Mt.* (3825 ft.) to the left. Several small hotels are passed. 5 M. *Dutcher's Panther Mt. House* (2000 ft.; unpretending, $1½), the nearest hotel to Slide Mt., where a guide may be obtained. In 3 M. more we reach the head of the valley, whence a path (steep at first, then easy; 1-2 hrs.) ascends to the left to the top of **Slide Mt.** (4205 ft.), the highest of the Catskills. The *View from the tower here is very extensive, em-bracing about 70 peaks in the Catskills, Mt. Everett in Massachusetts (due E.; p. 137), etc. Slide Mt. is included in a large State Reservation. — A road leads across from the head of Big Indian Valley into (4½ M.) *Woodland Valley*, near *Phoenicia* (p. 163).

The gradient here is very steep. 39 M. **Pine Hill** (1660 ft.; *Rip van Winkle Ho.*, *Grampian*, $3; *Alpine*, $2½, etc.), pleasantly situated below the railway to the right. — 41 M. *Grand Hotel Station* (1885 ft.) is the culminating point of the line, on the watershed between the Hudson and the Delaware. To the right stands the *Grand Hotel ($4½), one of the most fashionable resorts of the Catskills, finely situated on the slope of *Summit Hill* (2500 ft.). It commands a splendid *View, including Belle Ayr, Big Indian, and Slide Mts. Adjacent are several smaller hotels.

The train now descends, making a bend to the left, to (44 M.) *Fleischmann's* (formerly *Griffin's Corners*; 1515 ft.), which lies like a toy-town in the valley to the right. 48 M. *Arkville* (1345 ft.; Commercial Ho., $1½; *Ackerley Ho.*, at Margaretville, 1 M. from the station, $2). We now descend along the E. branch of the *Delaware.* — 59 M. *Roxbury* (1500 ft.); 65 M. *Grand Gorge* (1570 ft.), between *Bald Mt.* (left) and *Irish Mt.* (right); 70 M. *South Gilboa.*

74 M. **Stamford** (1765 ft.; *Churchill Hall*, $2½-3; *Bancroft Ho.*, $2; *Hamilton Ho.*, *Delaware Ho.*, $2, unpretending), pleasantly situated near the source of the W. branch of the *Delaware*, is a quiet and inexpensive summer-resort. The favourite excursion is to the top of *Mt. Utsayantha* (3365 ft.; view; 2½ M. by road).

Travellers bound for *Cooperstown* (see p. 158) may drive from Stam-ford, through the beautiful *Charlotte Valley*, to (22 M.) *West Davenport*, where they reach the railway.

78 M. *Hobart* (1600 ft.; Commercial, $1-2). — 87 M. *Bloomville* (Bloomville Ho., $1½) is the terminus of the railway.

Numerous other points on the N. and W. sides of the Catskills are frequented as summer-resorts.

25. The Adirondack Mountains.

APPROACHES. The principal gateways to the Adirondack Mts. are *Plattsburg* (p. 167), *Port Kent* (p. 186), *Westport* (p. 170), *Herkimer* (p. 187), *Malone* (p. 179), and *Saratoga* (p. 179); and in the following description it will be most convenient to follow the routes leading from these points into the heart of the mountains. The Adirondacks are within 10-14 hrs. of New York by railway (comp. RR. 20b, 20d), and the additional time required to go from the nearest railway-station to any point mentioned below can be easily calculated from the data in the text. *Plattsburg* is 12 hrs. from Boston viâ Burlington (comp. R. 15a). Fare from New York to *Plattsburg* $ 8, parlor-car $ 2, sleeper $ 2; to *Port Kent*, $ 7.60; to *Westport*, $ 6.80; to *Saratoga*, $ 4.20; to *North Creek* (p. 177), $ 5.95.

GENERAL FEATURES. The *Adirondack Mountains, in the N. part of the State of New York, stretch from near Canada on the N. to near the Mohawk River on the S. (120 M.), and from Lakes George and Champlain on the E. to an indefinite and irregular line on the W. (ca. 80 M.), covering an area of about 8-10,000 sq. M. The mountains, which run in five parallel ranges from S.W. to N.E., rise from an elevated plateau and many of them are over or nearly 5000 ft. high. The highest range, or Adirondacks proper, is on the E. side of the district; and the loftiest peaks are *Mts. Marcy* (5345 ft.), *McIntyre* (5200 ft.), *Haystack* (5005 ft.), *Dix* (4915 ft.), *Basin* (4905 ft.), *Gray Peak* (4900 ft.), *Skylight* (4890 ft.), and *Whiteface* (4870 ft.). The whole of the district (the so-called '*Adirondack Wilderness*'), except the highest peaks, is densely covered with forest, much of which is still virgin and almost unexplored. Lumbering is carried on very extensively, and huge quantities of spruce, hemlock, and other timber are annually sent down to the Hudson and St. Lawrence. The geological formations of the Adirondacks are mainly granitic and other primary rocks. In the valleys lie more than 1000 lakes, varying in size from a few acres to 20 sq. M. (*Schroon Lake*) and in height from 830 ft. (*Schroon Lake*) to 4320 ft. (*Tear of the Clouds*). The *Hudson River* rises in the Tear of the Clouds (p. 175), and the *Raquette, Saranac, Ausable*, and numerous other rivers and streams connect the labyrinth of lakes. This combination of mountain, lake, and forest is, perhaps, unrivalled elsewhere, and the scenery is of great and varied attraction. The fauna of the district includes catamounts or 'panthers' (*Felis Concolor;* rare), black bears, wild-cats, numerous deer, otters, badgers, rabbits, black eagles, hawks, loons, wild ducks, partridges, herons, etc.; while the lakes and streams are well stocked with trout and bass. There are no rattlesnakes or other venemous serpents. — A movement is on foot to set apart about 4000 sq. M. of the Adirondacks as a State Park like the Yosemite (p. 454), but all but 800 sq. M. of this are still in private hands.

RESORTS. The most frequented and fashionable region is the district of the *Saranac* and *St. Regis Lakes* (pp. 168, 169), which are closely environed by hotels and summer-camps. *Lake Placid* (p. 171) is now almost as frequented, while *Keene Valley* (p. 172), perhaps the gem of the district, is daily growing in favour. The *Blue Mt.* and *Raquette Lake* region (p. 177) is somewhat more remote from the ordinary run of travel; while the less mountainous districts to the W. are rarely penetrated by visitors except in search of sport.

A fair general idea of the attractions of the Adirondacks may be obtained by the following tour. From *Plattsburg* (p. 167) to *Paul Smith's* (p. 168); thence, viâ the *St. Regis* and *Saranac Lakes*, to *Saranac Village* and *Lake Placid*, as described at pp. 168-170; from Lake Placid to *Adirondack Lodge* (p. 175); thence to *Summit Rock* in the *Indian Pass* (p. 176) and back; from Adirondack Lodge to *Keene Valley* (p. 172), either by road or (preferable for good walkers) over *Mt. Marcy* (see p. 174); thence to *Elizabethtown* (p. 171) and *Westport* (p. 176). This tour may be accomplished in 8-10 days. Those who have longer time may add the *Tupper, Long, Raquette*, and *Blue Mountain Lakes* in the ways suggested at pp. 169, 177-179.

SPORT. *Deer*, which are the chief object of the Adirondack sportsman, are generally killed by the somewhat unsportsmanlike practice of driving them into the water by hounds and shooting them from a boat. 'Still-hunting' and 'jack-hunting' (with a light at night) are also employed. The State Game Laws, which the visitor should study carefully, impose various limitations on the indiscriminate massacre of the deer, and there are now various reservations (comp. pp. 173, 176) in which the game is strictly preserved. An occasional shot at a bear may be had in the remoter recesses, but the visitor need scarcely count on this as among the possibilities. The shooting of *Partridges* (ruffed grouse, *Bonasa umbellus*) is carried on with the aid of dogs. Good *Fishing* is obtained in many of the lakes and ponds. The intending sportsman should put himself at once into communication with the local talent. His outfit should be as plain, strong, and limited in extent as possible. Comp. also p. xxv.

CAMPING is one of the chief features of Adirondack life; the camps varying from the luxurious permanent 'Camp' of the regular visitor down to the makeshift lean-to's of the sportsman. *Camping Parties* of ladies and gentlemen are frequently organized, and, with good guides, a cook, and efficient equipments, afford a very pleasant variation of ordinary summer pleasures. — Flies and mosquitoes are troublesome in June and July.

GUIDES are to be found at all the chief resorts, and the regular charge is $ 3 a day, which includes the use of their boats and cooking and table ware. Their keep is also paid by the traveller. When a guide is dismissed at a distance from his home, he expects the full daily fee and allowance for food on his return-journey. For short trips one guide and boat can take two persons, but for longer expeditions there should be a guide to each traveller. The boats are small and light, so that they are easily transported over the 'carries' between the lakes on the guide's shoulders. When horses are used for the carries the employer pays for the transportation. Nothing but small hand-baggage can be taken in the boats. — The *Adirondack Guides' Association*, organized in 1891, issues certificates and badges to its members. In the absence of a graduated tariff, the same fee is demanded for a short walk as for a severe day's work.

The HOTELS of the Adirondacks are generally comfortable, and some of the larger ones may even be termed luxurious. Prices vary greatly according to the style of the house and its situation.

EXPENSES. The expenses of a rapid tour through the Adirondacks are apt to be somewhat high, as the guide's fee ($ 3) and keep ($ 1-1½) have to be added to the traveller's personal expenses ($ 3-5). Camping and sporting parties live, of course, much more cheaply than hotel-guests.

The information in the following pages will suffice for a rapid tour through the Adirondacks, but those who contemplate a prolonged stay or shooting and camping parties should procure the guidebook of *S. R. Stoddard* (with maps; price 25 c.), which contains details of routes, outfit, and supplies.

a. From Plattsburg to St. Regis, Tupper, and Saranac Lakes.

Plattsburg (100 ft.; *Fouquet Ho., Cumberland, Witherill*, $ 2-3; *Rail. Restaurant*, meals 75 c.), a small town with 7010 inhab., is pleasantly situated on the W. shore of *Lake Champlain* (comp. p. 186), at the mouth of the *Saranac River*. It is a convenient starting-point for excursions on the lake, and it is the junction of branch-railways to *Ausable* and *Saranac Lake*. It is 12 hrs. from New York by express-train (comp. R. 20 b).

FROM PLATTSBURG TO AUSABLE, 20 M., railway in 1½ hr. (fare $ 1). — The line runs to the S.W. through the valley of the *Little Ausable*. From (20 M.) *Ausable* coaches run to *Wilmington* ($ 1) and *LakePlacid* ($ 2½).

FROM PLATTSBURG TO SARANAC LAKE, 73 M., *Chateaugay Railroad* in 4¼ hrs. (fare $ 3.35). — From New York to *Saranac Lake* in 16 hrs. (fare $ 11.75).

The train passes the *U. S. Barracks* and runs to the W. through the valley of the *Saranac*. It crosses the river before and after (12 M.) *Cadyville* and then ascends to the right, leaving the river.

Beyond (17 M.) *Dannemora* (1810 ft.), with *Clinton Prison*, we make a wide sweep to the left, round *Johnson Mt.* To the left is *Lyon Mt.* (3810 ft.). — 28 M. *Chazy Station* (1500 ft.; Chazy Lake Ho., $ 2¹/₂, boat from station 50 c.), at the S. end of *Chazy Lake* (4 M. long, 1 M. wide; trout-fishing).

From (34 M.) *Lyon Mountain*, an iron-mining village, coaches run to (3¹/₂ M.) *Ralph's* ($ 3 a day ; fare 50 c.) and (4¹/₄ M.) *Merrill's* ($ 3; fare 50 c.), on the E. side of *Upper Chateaugay Lake* (4 M. to 1 M.). A small steamer plies on the Chateaugay Lakes and a coach runs from the N. end of the *Lower Lake* (3¹/₂ M. × ³/₄ M.) to (6 M.) *Chateaugay Station*, on the Ogdensburg and Lake Champlain R.R. — The railway now bends to the S. (left), affording a good view of Chateaugay Lake to the right. 54 M. *Loon Lake Station*, at the N. end of *Loon Lake* (2 M. long), connects by stage (50 c.) with (2¹/₂ M.) *Loon Lake House* ($ 3¹/₂-5), at the S. end. To the right are *Loon Lake Mt.* and *Long Pond*. At (61 M.) *Rainbow* we see *Rainbow Lake* (p. 179) to the right. — 66 M. *Bloomingdale* is the station for *Paul Smith's*, 7 M. to the W. (sandy, uninteresting road; stage $ 1; see below). — 73 M. *Saranac Lake* (see p. 169).

The **St. Regis Lake House**, known as *Paul* (properly *Apollos*) *Smith's*, a hotel (500 beds; $ 4-5 a day, $ 21-30 a week) on the N. bank of the *Lower St. Regis Lake* (1620 ft.; 2 M. × 1 M.), is one of the most fashionable resorts in the district and may be made the starting-point for a guide-boat tour of the N. Adirondack lakes. It is only 4 M. from *Paul Smith's* on the Adirondack & St. Lawrence R.R. (see p. 179). Both the St. Regis Lakes are surrounded by numerous camps, and good fishing and shooting are obtained in the neighbourhood.

The following *Round Trip is frequently made from Paul Smith's, and affords an excellent idea both of the attractions of the Adirondacks and of the ordinary methods of travelling.

The circuit is about 40-45 M., and 3 days should be allowed for it, though more may profitably be spent, especially if any digressions are made. Those who make the round trip quickly should engage their guide and boats for the whole journey; others may hire from place to place (comp. p. 167). The guides should be expressly instructed to go by the distinctly preferable 'Seven Carry Route', as otherwise they will select the 'Big Clear Route', on which two horse-carries ($ 1 and $ 1¹/₂) save them some work and add to the tourist's expenses. If desired, heavy baggage may be sent to Saranac Village by railway.

Leaving Paul Smith's, we cross the *Lower St. Regis Lake* by boat (¹/₂ M.); row or 'carry' to (³/₄ M.) *Spitfire Pond;* cross this pond (¹/₂ M.), and row or carry to the (¹/₂ M.) *Upper St. Regis Lake* (1625 ft.), which we cross to (2 M.) its S. end. To the W. rises *St. Regis Mt.* (2890 ft.).

Here begins the carry to (1¹/₂ M.; fee for horse $ 1) *Clear Lake* ('*Big Clear*'), a pretty little lake, well stocked with fish, on the N. bank of which stands the *Big Clear Pond Hotel* ($ 3; well spoken of). Clear Lake is 2 M. long, and a carry of 4 M. leads from its S. end to *Saranac Inn* (horse for boat $ 1¹/₂; seat in a carriage 50 c.).

On the Seven Carry Route we traverse six short carries and six small ponds and reach (3 M.) *Little Clear Pond,* which is 1 M. long and 2 M. from Saranac Inn (9 M. from Paul Smith's). In either case we cross the Adirondack & St. Lawrence R. R.

*Saranac Inn ($ 4; telegraph-office) lies at the N. end of Upper Saranac Lake, 1³/₄ M. from *Saranac Inn Station* on the Adirondack and St. Lawrence R.R. (see p. 179).

*Upper Saranac Lake (1575 ft.), 7¹/₂ M. long and ¹/₂-3 M. wide, is one of the largest sheets of water in the district. It is dotted with islands and surrounded by thickly wooded and hilly banks. Good fishing and shooting. A small steamer plies on the lake (fare 75 c., round-trip $ 1), calling at the *Sweeny Carry* (Wawbeek Lodge, $ 3¹/₂, with tel. office), on the W. bank, *Indian Carry* (Rustic Lodge, $ 2), at the S. end, and *Bartlett's* or the *Saranac Club,* on the E. side.

Wawbeek Lodge is 8 M. to the E. (stage $ 1¹/₂) of *Tupper Lake Village,* on the N. Adirondack R.R. (see p. 179). — The *Sweeny Carry* (3 M.; horse for boat $ 1¹/₂, seat in buckboard 75 c.) leads to *Raquette River* (Tromblee's Inn), which may be ascended, with the help of a horse-carry ($ 1¹/₂, seat in carr. 50 c.) round the *Raquette Falls* (Raquette Falls Hotel), to (ca. 20 M.) the N. end of *Long Lake* (p. 178). Or we may descend the river to (11 M.) *Tupper Lake* (p. 179).

Indian Carry crosses to (1 M.) the *Stony Creek Ponds* (1640 ft.; Hiawatha Hotel) and to (3 M.) the *Raquette River* (about 8 M. from Tromblee's).

A short carry from the landing for Bartlett's (¹/₄ M.; horse, unnecessary, 50 c.) leads to the stream flowing into the (¹/₂ M.) *Middle Saranac Lake,* more often called *Round Lake* (1545 ft.), a nearly circular sheet of water, 2¹/₂ M. in diameter. This little lake is sometimes lashed by violent squalls coming down from the hills, and it is advisable to keep an eye on the weather. To the S.E. rises *Ampersand Mt.* (3430 ft.; *View), the trail to the top of which (ca 2¹/₂ M.) leads through the woods and is not easy to follow without a guide. At the N.E. corner of Round Lake we enter its pretty outlet, descending to (2¹/₂ M.) the lower lake and passing about halfway a series of rapids, where a short carry is necessary.

*Lower Saranac Lake (1540 ft.), 5 M. long and ³/₄-1¹/₄ M. wide, is one of the prettiest of the Adirondack lakes, surrounded by wooded hills and thickly sprinkled with islands, said to number fifty-two. Near the lower (N.E.) end of the lake lies Saranac Lake Village, the terminus of the Chateaugay R. R. (p. 167), and one of the chief centres of the district for hotels, guides, and outfits.

The *Ampersand Hotel ($ 3-5) is pleasantly situated on high ground on the N. bank of the lake. The Saranac Lake House (*Miller's;* $ 3-4) lies close to the S. shore of the lake, 1¹/₂ M. from the railway-station (omn. 50 c.). The Algonquin ($ 3-4) is a little farther to the W. (omn. from station 50 c.). Smaller hotels, in the village, are *Martin's* ($ 2¹/₂), the *Berkeley ($ 2¹/₂), and the *Adirondack* ($ 2). The *Adirondack Sanitarium* (for consumptives) lies 1 M. to the N.E. — *H. H. Miner,* taxidermist, near the Saranac Lake House, has excellent stuffed specimens of the fauna of the Adirondacks.

Saranac Lake is 10 M. by road (coach $ 1¹/₄) from *Lake Placid* (see p. 171). The road turns to the right in the village, at the Adirondack Ho., 1¹/₂ M.

from the lake, and passes (2¹/₂ M.) the *Ray Brook House* ($ 3). At (3 M.) the fork the left branch leads to (3 M.) *Lake Placid*, the right to (5 M.) *North Elba* (p. 171).

We may now return to Paul Smith's by railway (see p. 179).

b. From Port Kent to Ausable Chasm and Lake Placid.

Port Kent lies on the W. shore of *Lake Champlain* (see p. 186), nearly opposite *Burlington* (p. 114; steamer), and within 11 hrs. by railway of New York (comp. R. 20b: fare $ 7.80).

A short branch-railway runs in 20 min. from Port Kent to (2¹/₂ M.) *Ausable Chasm* (*Lake View House, finely situated, $ 3) and to (6 M.) *Keeseville*.

The ****Ausable Chasm** is, perhaps, the most wonderful piece of rock-formation to the W. of the Rockies, and should not be omitted by any traveller who comes within a reasonable distance of it. The *Ausable River*, a large and rapid stream, here flows through a rocky gorge only 20-40 ft. wide, between perpendicular walls of Potsdam sandstone, 100-175 ft. high. Waterfalls and rapids add to the attractions. A visit to the chasm has been facilitated by paths and bridges; and the boat-ride through the rapids affords a novel and exciting but perfectly safe experience. Numerous interesting fossils *(lingula antiqua, trilobites)* have been found here.

The ENTRANCE to the chasm (adm. 50 c., boat-ride 50 c.) is a little to the N. of the *Trestle Bridge*, a few minutes from the Lake View House. At the head of the chasm (to the left) are the *Rainbow or Birmingham Falls*, 70 ft. high, while near the point where we enter are the lower **Horse-shoe Falls**. Following the path to the right over the ledges (smooth as if made artificially), we round the *Elbow*, beyond which, across the stream, rises the *Pulpit Rock* (135 ft.). Below the *Split Rock* (l.) we cross the stream. Farther on more or less appropriate names are attached to the various phenomena, such as the *Devil's Oven* (r.), *Hell Gate*, *Jacob's Ladder* (r.), the *Devil's Punch-Bowl* (l.), *Jacob's Well* (l.), *Mystic Gorge* (l.), *Shady Gorge* (r.), the *Long Gallery*, *Point of Rocks* (l.), *Hyde's Cave* (r.), *Column Rocks* (r.), and the *Post Office* (l.; so-named for very obvious reasons). We are now in the *Upper Flume*, at the lower end of which we cross to the flat *Table Rock*, where the boat-ride begins and where many visitors turn back. Here, to the right, tower the *Cathedral Rocks* and the *Sentinel*, 100 ft. high. The boat at first passes through the *Grand Flume*, the rocky sides of which are 175 ft. high, while at one place the river is 60 ft. deep and only 12 ft. wide. Emerging from the Flume, we pass through a quiet pool and enter the *Rapids*, through which we sweep swiftly to the landing-place at the foot of the chasm. We may now either walk or drive back to the (1¹/₂ M.) hotel.

COACHES run daily in summer from the Lake View House to (32 M.) *Lake Placid* (p. 171; fare $ 4), viâ (3¹/₂ M.) *Keeseville*, (13 M.) *Ausable Station* (p. 167), and (21 M.) *Wilmington* (p. 172).

c. From Westport to Elizabethtown, Keene Valley, and Lake Placid.

Adirondack Lodge. Indian Pass.

Westport (*Westport Inn, overlooking the steamboat-wharf, $ 2¹/₂-3; *Gibbs Ho.*, $ 2; *Pleasant View Ho*, at the rail. station, $ 2, quite unpretending) is a village of 563 inhab., on the W. shore of Lake Champlain, 25 M. to the S. of Port Kent (p. 170) and 10 M. to the N. of Port Henry (p. 185). It is the chief gateway to, perhaps, the finest part of the Adirondacks, coaches running hence, viâ (9 M.) *Elizabethtown* ($1), to *Keene Valley* (24 M.; $2½), *Lake Placid* (36 M.; $4), and *Adirondack Lodge* (36 M.; $4½). It is within 10 hrs. of New York by fast train (comp. R. 20b).

The ROAD TO ELIZABETHTOWN (9 M.) is pleasant, but calls for no special remark. — **Elizabethtown** (600 ft.; *Windsor*, $3; *Mansion Ho.*, $2½; *Maplewood Inn*, open the whole year, $2), a village with 573 inhab., is prettily situated on the *Boquet River*, in the well-named *Pleasant Valley*.

Among the points of interest in the neighbourhood are *Cobble Hill* (1935 ft.), just to the S.W. of the town; *Raven Hill* (1980 ft.), to the E.; and *Hurricane Mt.* (3760 ft.), 5 M. to the W. (cart-road; path to the summit 2 M. more), a fine point of view. — A road leads S., viâ the (8 M.) *Split Rock Falls*, (10 M.) *Euba Mills*, and (23 M.) *Schroon River P. O.*, to (32 M.) *Schroon Lake* (p. 177; coach thrice weekly, $2½). — To the N. a road leads to (22 M.) *Keeseville* (p. 170), viâ *Poke o' Moonshine Mt.* and *Augur Lake.*

The *ROAD FROM ELIZABETHTOWN TO LAKE PLACID (28 M.; from which the roads to Keene Valley and Adirondack Lodge diverge) passes through one of the most beautiful parts of the Adirondacks. It leads to the W., passing between *Hurricane Mt.* (see above) on the right and several lower hills on the left. 10 M. *Keene Valley* (see p. 172) opens to the left. Our road turns N. to (2 M.) *Keene Village* or *Keene Centre* (1000 ft.; Hotel, D. 75 c.). Beyond Keene the road turns sharply to the left (S.E.) and ascends to the (4 M.) beautiful *Cascades Lakes* (2040 ft.; well stocked with trout), with *Pitch Off Mt.* (3520 ft.) rising so abruptly to the right as barely to leave room for our passage. *Long Pond Mt.* rises equally sheer on the other side of the lakes. The *Cascade Lake House* (6 M. from Keene; $3, D. $1) is a favourite resort of fishermen and others. Ahead of us we now obtain a fine *View of the mountains enclosing Lake Placid. — 4 M. *Ames's Mountain View House* ($2). Among the mountains seen to the S. (left) are *Mts. Marcy* and *McIntyre* (see pp. 174, 175), the two loftiest peaks in the district. About 1 M. farther on the road to (5 M.) *Adirondack Lodge* (see p. 175) diverges to the left, and after 1 M. more the road through the *Wilmington Notch* (see p. 172) leads to the right. Just beyond this point we cross the *Ausable River*, and on the left, ½ M. farther on, is a sign pointing to (½ M.) *John Brown's Farm* (see p. 172). 1 M. *North Elba Post Office*, where the road to (2 M.) *Lake Placid* diverges to the right from the main road, which goes on to (10 M.) *Saranac Lake Village* (see p. 169).

*Lake Placid** (1860 ft.), 4 M. long and 2 M. broad, is surrounded by finer and higher mountains than any other of the larger Adirondack lakes, and numerous hotels and cottages have been built on its banks. It contains three islands, *Hawk*, *Moose*, and *Buck*. At its S. end it is closely adjoined by the small *Mirror Lake* (1858 ft.), 1 M. long and ⅓ M. wide. Boating and fishing are carried on on both lakes. The beautifully-shaped *Whiteface Mt.* (see below) is conspicuous at the N.E. end of Lake Placid, while *McKenzie Mt.* rises to the W. The *View to the S. includes the following peaks (named from left to right): Gothic, Saddleback, Basin, Marcy, Colden, and McIntyre, with Indian Pass (p. 174) to the right of the last.

Most of the hotels and other houses are clustered round the S. end of Lake Placid and Mirror Lake. *Stevens House* (1965 ft.; $3-4), on the ridge between the two lakes; *Mirror Lake House* ($3-4), at the S. end of Mirror Lake; *Grand View House* ($3-4), to the S. of the Stevens Ho.; *Lake Placid House* (*Brewster's;* $2½), a small and comfortable house, to the E. of the Stevens Ho., with view of both lakes; *Ruisseaumont Ho.*, to the N. of the last ($3); *White Face Inn*, in a sequestered site on the S.W. side of Lake Placid, $3; *Castle Rustico, Undercliff*, W. bank of Lake Placid. The *Summer Camp of Mr. E. D. Bartlett*, near the White Face Inn, is one of the finest in the Adirondacks.

EXCURSIONS. The path to (3 M.; ca. 2 hrs.) the top of *Whiteface Mt.* (4870 ft.) begins at the N. end of Lake Placid (guide desirable; road in progress). The *View includes the main Adirondack peaks (S.), Lake Champlain (E.), and the Saranac and Tupper Lakes (W.), while on the N. it reaches to Canada and the St. Lawrence. The descent may be made by bridle-path and cart-track to (6 M.) *Wilmington* (see below). — *McKenzie Mt.* (3190 ft.) may be ascended in 2 hrs. (no path). — *John Brown's Farm* (route, see p. 171) is in a lonely spot, 3 M. from Lake Placid. The sturdy old Abolitionist (comp. p. 265) had his home here from 1849 till his death (1859), and now lies buried in a small enclosure near the house, with a huge boulder marking the spot (shown by the present occupant of the house, who has photographs for sale). Walkers may cut off 2 M. of the route to *Adirondack Lodge* (see below) by descending to the *Ausable* from John Brown's, crossing the river by stepping-stones, and following a path through the woods, which joins the road in 2 M.

The *ROAD THROUGH THE WILMINGTON NOTCH TO AUSABLE FORKS (26 M.) AND AUSABLE STATION (29 M.) diverges to the left (N.) from the road to Elizabethtown, at a point 4 M. from Lake Placid (see p. 171; coach $2½). The *Notch* (10 M.) is a defile on the W. flank of *Mt. Whiteface* (see above), through which flows the W. branch of the Ausable, scarcely leaving room for the road. *Wilmington* (Bliss House, Storrs Ho., $2), 6 M. farther on, is a good starting-point for an ascent of Whiteface (see above; saddle-horse $4, guide $3). At *Ausable Forks* (10 M. farther on) the two branches of the *Ausable* unite. At (29 M.) *Ausable Station* we reach the railway (see p. 167).

Among the numerous other excursions made from Lake Placid are those to *Adirondack Lodge* (10 M.; see p. 173) and *Keene Valley* (21 M.; see below).

****Keene Valley** (approaches, see pp. 171, 175), extending for 8 M. to the S. from *Keene Village* (p. 171), is, in its combination of the gentler and the sterner beauties of scenery and its convenience as a centre for all kinds of excursions, perhaps the most desirable headquarters in the Adirondacks. It is watered by a branch of the *Ausable*, and is enclosed by two mountain ranges, including *Hopkins Peak*, the *Giant of the Valley*, and *Noon Mark* on the E., and *Mt. Porter, Twin Mts.*, and the *Wolf's Jaws* on the W. The autumn colouring of the trees is often rich beyond expression.

The valley is traversed by a good road, which passes various hotels and (5 M.) *Keene Valley Village* (1030 ft.). The following list of the hotels names them in consecutive order from N. to S., as we penetrate the valley; but the tourist is advised to fix his quarters as near the head of the valley as possible. *Estes House* ($2), on the E. bank of the river, at the foot of Prospect Hill; *Adirondack House* ($2½), to the W. of the village; *Tahawus House* ($2), in the village, to the right; *Maple Grove House* ($1½-2); *St.*

Hubert's Cottage ($ 2¹/₂), to the right, near the head of the valley, an annex of St. Hubert's Inn. *St. Hubert's Inn (1350 ft.; $ 3-4) is a large and well-managed house at the head of the valley, occupying the site of the well-known Beede House, which was burned down in 1890. It is surrounded by groups of private cottages, many of the occupants of which take their meals at the hotel. The *View from this point is superb. Immediately facing St. Hubert's Inn, to the S.E., rises Noon Mark, with the long ridge of the Giant and Hopkins Peak to the left and the conical Mt. Colvin to the right. To the N. we look down the Keene Valley, and to the S.W. is the road to the Ausable Lakes, between Mt. Colvin and Mt. Resegonia.

The following EXCURSIONS are described with St. Hubert's Inn as centre, but it will be easy to make the necessary rectification for other start-ing-points in the valley. — Keene Valley has an excellent *Guides' Union*, a list of the members of which may be obtained at the hotels. The regular fee is $3 a day for any excursion; a graduated tariff is an obvious desideratum which has not yet been adopted.

*Ausable Lakes, ca. 15 M. (there and back). This is the favourite ex-cursion from Keene Valley and should on no account be omitted. The lakes are included in the *Adirondack Mountain Reserve*, a tract of about 40 sq. M. to the S. of Keene Valley, bought and controlled by a New York company. Ordinary tourists, however, are freely admitted to the Reserve, though none but the authorized guides are permitted to have boats on the upper lake. The entrance to the Reserve is a little to the S.W. of St. Hubert's Inn (toll for carr. $ 1/2-1, walkers free). A good road, con-structed by the company, leads hence to the (3¹/₂ M.) *Lower Ausable Lake (1960 ft.; Boat-house, with rfmts., boats to hire, etc.), a small sheet of water, about 2 M. long, surrounded by beautifully wooded mountains de-scending sheer to the water. To the left rises *Indian Head* (2535 ft.; *View), a knob of Mt. Colvin; to the right are the finely formed *Gothics* and *Mt. Resegonia* or *Sawteeth*. [From the boat-house we may make a trip by boat (1-3 pers. 15 c., each pers. addit. 5 c.) to (10 min.) the landing for *Rain-bow Falls*, a veil-fall of about 100 ft. (rainbow 12-2 p.m.). From the upper end of the lake a good trail leads to (1¹/₄ M.) the *Upper Ausable Lake (1990 ft.), which is 1¹/₂ M. long. 'In the sweep of its wooded shores, and the lovely contour of the lofty mountains that guard it, this lake is probably the most charming in America' (*Warner*). To the right (named from left to right) are *Skylight, Haystack, Mt. Bartlett, Saddleback, Gothic,* and *Resegonia;* to the left, *Colvin* and the *Boreas Range*. (Mt. Marcy is not seen from either lake.) The lake is surrounded with camps belonging to the guides, where meals are usually cooked and eaten before returning. Many parties also spend days here in one of the camps, the charge being 25c. per night for each person. Before returning, we may row up the inlet of the lake as far as (1/2 hr.) the *Elk Lake Trail* (see below) and then follow the general course of the stream (avoiding paths to the left) to (20 min.) *Panorama Bluff*, which commands a splendid *View of the mountains (from left to right: Allen, Skylight, Marcy, Haystack, Bartlett, Basin, Saddleback, Gothics, Resegonia). Route to *Mt. Marcy*, see p. 174.
— A trail beginning about 1³/₄ M. above the Upper Ausable Lake, a little beyond the Marcy trail (p. 174), leads to the E. over the *Boreas Mt. Range* to (5¹/₂ M.) *Elk Lake* (1980 ft.), whence a road leads S. to (5 M.) the road from Tahawus (p. 176) to *Schroon River P. O.* (p. 176; 5 M. to the E.).

SHORT WALKS. The *Russell Falls* are reached in 10 min. by a path descending from the back (S.W. corner) of St. Hubert's Inn. — The foot of *Roaring Brook Falls*, descending for about 300 ft. over a cliff on the W. side of the Giant, is about ³/₄ M. to the E. of the hotel. We follow the Port Henry road to (10 min.) the fork, turn to the left, cross a small bridge, and then cross a field to the right to bars leading into the wood. The cart-track in a straight direction leads to the foot of the falls. By following the Port Henry road for 1¹/₂ M. farther, we reach *Chapel Pond* (1600 ft.; right). A steep path, a little farther on, to the left, ascends to (20-30 min.) the *Giant's Washbowl* (2250 ft.), a solitary mountain-tarn at the foot of a gigantic cliff. A new trail (marked by 'blazes' on the trees) leads hence to the W. to (1 M.) the top of Roaring Brook Falls (see above),

whence we regain the road by descending on the right side of the stream
(a round in all of 4-5 M., taking 2-3 hrs.). — With the last-mentioned
walk may be combined a visit (2 hrs. more) to *Round Pond* and *Boquet
Falls* (trails hard and indistinct; guide necessary). — To reach the (3 M.)
Cathedral Rocks we follow the Ausable Lake road for 2 M. and then cross
a rustic bridge to the right. With this may be combined a visit to the
small *Cathedral Falls* (someone to point out the way desirable). — *Artist's*
or *Chapel Brook*, 1¹/₂ M. We proceed as in the Roaring Brook Walk to
(20 min.) the bars leading into the wood, and follow the first path to the
right. The scenery somewhat resembles the Torrent Walk at Dolgelley.

ASCENTS. The following ascents are condensed, by permission, from
papers by *Mr. Frank W. Freeborn* in 'Appalachia' (p. 122). Experts may dis-
pense with guides in the first six. — *Noon Mark* (3550 ft.; 1³/₄-2¹/₂ hrs.).
We diverge to the right from the Chapel Pond road, just beyond the last
cottage on the right (Prof. Felix Adler's), and follow the broad path, which
soon climbs along the left side of a ravine to (35-45 min.) a bare ledge
(view). The path then follows a gentle ridge and (in 25-35 min.) begins
to ascend steeply to (30-40 min.) the top. The *View includes Keene Valley and its bounding mountains, Mt. Dix, with its curious knob (S.), Nippletop, and the Marcy group. — **Mt. Colvin** (4140 ft.; 2-3 hrs.). The path
leaves the Ausable Lakes road to the left, about ¹/₄ M. on this side of the
lower lake, and ascends the left side of *Indian Head* (p. 173; sign-boards).
35 min. Path to (5 min.) *Wizard's Washbowl*, to the left. ¹/₂ hr. (l.) Path
to (6 min.) *High Falls*. 5 min. (l.) Trail to *Fairy Ladder Falls* and *Nippletop* (4685 ft.). 35 min. (r.) High white cliff, a little beyond which are a
large rock and a small spring (r.). 20 min. Top (highest point reached by
ladders). The *View to the N. includes the Ausable Lakes and the highest
peaks of the Adirondacks (named from left to right: Skylight, Marcy,
Haystack, Basin, Saddleback, Gothic, with Sawteeth in front, and Wolf's
Jaws). — *Giant of the Valley (4530 ft.; 2¹/₂-3¹/₂ hrs.). The path diverges
to the left from the track to Roaring Brook Falls, just beyond the bars
(1250 ft.) mentioned at p. 173. 12-15 min. We follow the path to the left.
15-20 min. *Corduroy Bridge*, beyond which we follow 'blazes' through
the wood to the left and reach (3 min.) the brook. A foot-worn trail, also
indicated by blazes, ascends hence steadily for 1-1¹/₄ hr. (The right branch
at the fork is of easier gradient.) Then follows ¹/₂-³/₄ hr's scramble over
rocks to the end of the S. spur. Hence to the top ¹/₂ hr. more. (A little
to the N.E. of the Signal is a small pool of water.) The *View includes
Lake Champlain and the Green Mts.; and Mt. Washington (p. 131) is said
to be visible in clear weather. — **Hopkins Peak** (3135 ft.; 2¹/₂-3 hrs.). We
follow the road down the valley for about 3 M., and before reaching the
Tahawus Ho. (p. 172) turn to the right and cross the *Ausable*. We then
turn to the right and follow the road to (10 min.) a house, at the back of
which the path begins. 1¹/₂-1³/₄ hr. Spring, a little beyond which the path
emerges on the bare ledges. (It is well to mark this point in some way
as a guide in returning.) 35-45 min. Top. Good view of the Giant, etc. — **Mt.
Baxter** (2600 ft.; 1¹/₂-2¹/₂ hrs.). The path begins about ³/₄ M. to the W.
of the cottage of 'Old Mountain Phelps,' which is ³/₄ M. from the Tahawus
Ho. The *Balcony*, a bare ledge on the W. summit, commands a splendid
*View of Keene Valley, and it is hardly worth while to climb (20 min.
more) to the top of the highest (middle) peak. — The **Gothics** (4745 ft.;
2¹/₂-3¹/₂ hrs.). The trail begins to the right of the Ausable Lake road,
2 M. from St. Hubert's Inn. It is not very clear at first, but, after crossing
(¹/₄ hr.) the Ausable, improves. 3 min. Cascade. 1¹/₂ hr. Ridge at right
angles to our course, which the trail skirts to the right. ¹/₂ hr. Hollow,
with swampy pool. The (15-20 min.) top commands a good near *View
of Mt. Marcy, with Mt. McIntyre to its right. Lake Placid and Whiteface
are seen in the distance (N.). Dix Mt., with its singular notch, is conspicuous to the E. — *Mt. Marcy or *Tahawus* ('Cloud-splitter'; 5345 ft.;
two days; guide necessary), the highest of the Adirondacks. This is a
grand but somewhat fatiguing excursion, which should not be lightly undertaken. The night is spent in Boulder Camp (see p. 175), and the descent may be made to Adirondack Lodge (p. 175). Campers on the Upper

Ausable Lake can make the trip in one day (ascent 4-5 hrs., descent 3-4 hrs.). The path (7 M. long) begins at the little bay called 'Cold Slough' in the inlet of Upper Ausable Lake, about 1^1/$_2$ M. beyond its S. end, and at first crosses boggy ground. 25 min. Path diverging to the left (our path straight on). ^{3}/$_4$ hr. *Lookout Point*, a high sandy bank. The path becomes steeper and in 40 min. crosses *Marcy Brook*. 10 min. Path leading to the right to (5 min.) *Boulder Camp* (see p. 174). The main path becomes steep and wet. 40 min. Col between *Skylight* (l.; 4890 ft.) and Mt. Marcy, with a spring of good water and the remains of *Summit Camp*. The trail crosses a tract of low balsams to (25 min.) the open ledges, beyond which there is no trail. The top is reached in ^{1}/$_4$ hr. more. The *View from the top embraces the whole of the Adirondacks, with Lake Champlain and the Green Mts. to the E. To the S.E., between us and the dark *Haystack*, lies the deep and narrow *Panther Gorge* (3350 ft.). At our feet (S.W.) lies the *Tear of the Clouds*, a small lake 4320 ft. above the sea, which is the highest source of the Hudson. The trail from the top to *Adirondack Lodge* is 7^1/$_2$ M. long. (see below). — Among other mountains that may be ascended from Keene Valley, with guides, are *Dix Mt.* (4915 ft.; one long day), *Haystack* (5005 ft.; one day), *Nippletop* (4685 ft.; 8 hrs.), and *Mt. Porter* (E. end, 3700 ft.; 3^1/$_2$-4^1/$_2$ hrs.).

Schroon Lake (p. 177) is reached from Keene Valley by the Port Henry road (see p. 173) to (8 M.) *Euba Mills*, and thence as at p. 171. — There is no very direct or easy route connecting Keene Valley with the *Long Lake* and *Blue Mountain* district. Perhaps the best route is by the trail over the *Boreas Mt. Range* (p. 173) or by the *Tahawus Trail* (p. 176). Or we may go viâ *Saranac Lake* as described at p. 169. Lastly, we may return by train, viâ Westport, to *Saratoga*, and proceed thence as in R. 25d.

Adirondack Lodge (2160 ft.; $ 4 a day, from $ 16 a week), a comfortable little hotel, completely hidden in the dense forest to the N. of Mt. McIntyre and 5 M. from the high-road (transfer-coach $ 1; comp. p. 171), is a favourite resort of anglers, sportsmen, and pedestrians. It is tastefully built in the style of a rustic log-house, while the internal fittings are in a corresponding style, the bark being left intact on part of the furniture. In front of the house lies the pretty little *Clear Lake*, reflecting the form of *Mount Jo*, opposite Mt. McIntyre. The view from the tower extends over an ocean of forest, with not a sign of human habitation. Beyond the hotel (to the S.) all roads cease, and the only means of communication are 'trails' through the virgin forest, sometimes followed by the 'blazes' only (guides generally desirable). — *Indian Pass*, see p. 176.

EXCURSIONS. To *Avalanche Lake*, 5 M. The trail leads to the S., through the woods. This pretty little lake (2855 ft.) lies between Mt. McIntyre and Mt. Colden. The trail is continued along its W. side to (1^1/$_2$ M.) *Lake Colden* (2770 ft.; log-camp). From Lake Colden a trail leads to the W. to (7 M.) the Adirondack Club (see below), viâ (2 M.) *Calamity Pond*. — *Mount Jo* is climbed in ^{1}/$_2$-^{3}/$_4$ hr. and affords a good view. — *Mt. McIntyre* (5200 ft.), the highest but one of the Adirondacks, is ascended hence in 2-3 hrs. (descent 1^1/$_2$-2 hrs.; path steep, esp. towards the top; guide desirable, but may be dispensed with by an expert who has received a few directions). The trail winds round the W. side of *Mt. Wright* (to our left). About halfway up are the small *Crystal Falls*. The *View includes Mt. Marcy (close by, to the S.E.), Lake Colden (but not Avalanche Lake), Avalanche Mt., Saranac Lakes, the finely formed Gothics, the noble form of Whiteface, the splendid precipice of Wallface (see p. 176), Mt. Seward, etc. Lake Champlain is said to be visible in clear weather. — *Mt. Marcy (p. 174) is climbed hence by a trail 7^1/$_2$ M. long, in 4-5 hrs. (descent 2^1/$_2$-3^1/$_2$ hrs.; guide necessary). The first half of the ascent is generally very muddy and fatiguing. Those who mean to descend to Keene Valley telegraph for a boat to meet them at the inlet of Upper Ausable Lake (comp. p. 175), and should arrange to pass the night in Boulder Camp (p. 175). *View, see p. 175. — A trail leads through the woods from Adirondack Lodge to (5-6 M.) *John Brown's Farm* (p. 172). — The *South Meadow Trail* (easy to follow) diverges to the right from the road to the high-road, 1 M. from the Lodge, and leads to the W. viâ the *South Meadow Marshes*, and then to the N. to the high-road, which it reaches about 2 M. to the W. of the *Cascade Lakes* (p. 171). This is the shortest route for walkers to Keene Valley, but is uncomfortable in wet weather.

FROM ADIRONDACK LODGE THROUGH THE INDIAN PASS TO THE ADIRONDACK CLUB, LAKE HENDERSON, AND TAHAWUS, 23 M. (9-10 hrs.; guide necessary).

The trail begins at the S. end of *Clear Lake* and leads through the woods. A divergence of a few hundred yards on either side of the path would bring us into virgin forest, where, perhaps, no white man had ever been before. After about 5 M. (2 hrs.) we reach a small open camp, where meals are sometimes cooked by the guide. The next mile involves a good deal of rough clambering over rocks (no danger) and leads us to (1/2 hr.) *Summit Rock*, in the centre of *Indian Pass (2940 ft.), a magnificent ravine between Mt. McIntyre and Mt. Wallface. In front of us the *View stretches over a sea of forest to (5 M.) Lake Henderson, 1300 ft. below us, while to the right the majestic rocky wall of **Wallface (3890 ft.) rises sheer to a height of 1300 ft., one of the grandest cliffs in the New World. The headwaters of the *Hudson*, flowing to the S., and the Ausable, flowing to the N., rise here so close to one another that they are said to mingle in time of flood. [Those who do not wish to go on by this route to the Blue Mt. country may turn back here, as this view commands the entire pass and the trail farther on is rough and neglected. Good walkers, however, may go on to Lake Henderson and return to Adirondack Lodge by the Lake Colden route (see p. 175), spending a night, if desired, at the Adirondack Club (see below).] Our path then begins to descend rapidly, at first over rocks. Farther on it is easier and more gradual. In 5 M. (2 hrs.) from Summit Rock we reach *Lake Henderson* (1875 ft.), the E. bank of which we follow to (2 M.; 3/4 hr.) the deserted hamlet of **Adirondack** or the *Upper Iron Works*, where accommodation may be procured in the house of the *Adirondack Club* ($ 3), which holds 40 sq. M. of the surrounding country as a game and fish preserve. *Mt. Marcy* (see p. 174) may be ascended hence in 5-6 hrs. by a trail (12 M.) leading viâ *Calamity Pond* to *Lake Colden* (as described at p. 175) and then striking to the right and passing the *Tear of the Clouds* (p. 175; guide necessary). To the W. rises (4 M.) *Mt. Santanoni* (4645 ft.), and to the N.W. (8 M.) *Mt. Seward* (4385 ft.). The Iron Works were established in 1826 by a Mr. Henderson, who was killed by an accident at Calamity Pond (p. 175) in 1845, after which they were abandoned. — From the Adirondack Club a fair road leads to the S., passing *Lake Sanford* (1800 ft.; 3½ M. long), to (21 M.) *Tahawus Post Office*. Hence we may either drive to the right (W.) to (19 M.) the *Sagamore*, at *Long Lake* (p. 178), or to the left (E.) to (19 M.) *Schroon River Post Office*, M. to the N. of *Schroon Lake* (p. 177).

d. From Saratoga to North Creek.

Schroon Lake. Blue Mountain Lake. Raquette Lake. Long Lake.

FROM SARATOGA TO NORTH CREEK, 59 M., *Adirondack Railway* in 2½ hrs. ($ 2; sleeping-cars from New York to North Creek without change $ 2; from Saratoga to *Blue Mt. Lake* $ 4¾).

Saratoga, see p. 179. The train runs to the N., passing *Hilton Park* (p. 181; r.). Near (17 M.) *Jessup's Landing* we reach (r.) the *Hudson*, the pretty upper valley of which we follow. At (22 M.) *Hadley* we cross the *Sacandaga* (bridge 96 ft. high).

Hadley is the station for **Luzerne** (*Wayside*, $3¹/₂-4), a pleasant summer-resort beyond the Hudson, on the pretty little *Lake of Luzerne*.

The wooded sugarloaf hill to the right, beyond Hadley, is known as the *Potash Kettle* (1735 ft.). The valley contracts, and the hills are prettily wooded. — 50 M. *Riverside* (815 ft.) is the starting-point of the stage-coaches for (7 M.) *Schroon Lake* (see below).

The coaches run viâ (6 M.) the *Pottersville House* ($2, D. 75c.) to the landing at the lower end of the lake, whence a small steamer plies to the hotels at its (9 M.) head (fare from Riverside $2), touching at the *Watch Rock Hotel* ($2-3), on the E. shore, and the *Taylor House* ($2¹/₂-3), on the W. shore. — **Schroon Lake** (830 ft.), 10 M. long and 1-2 M. wide, is surrounded by rugged hills and affords good fishing. Near its head lies the village of *Schroon Lake*, with numerous hotels, the largest of which are the *Leland House* ($3-3¹/₂), the *Lake House* ($2¹/₂), the *Ondawa* ($2¹/₂), and the *Windsor* (2-2¹/₂). The road (stages) to the N. runs hence viâ *Schroon River Post Office* (p. 171) to (22 M.) *Euba Mills* (p. 171), where it forks, one branch going to (6 M.) *Keene Valley* (p. 172), the other to (10 M.) *Elizabethtown* (p. 171).

59 M. North Creek (975 ft.; *American Ho.*, $2) is the terminus of the railway and the starting-point of the coaches to Blue Mt. Lake.

From North Creek to Blue Mountain Lake, 30 M., coach in 6-7 hrs. (fare $3). This is not a very attractive drive, especially as the road is bad and passes through an extensive 'burnt district'. — To the left rises *Gore Mt.* (3540 ft.). 5 M. *North River Hotel* (Roblee's; D. 75c.). The road now quits the Hudson and ascends rapidly. *Mt. Marcy*(p. 174) may be seen in the distance to the right. We cross (17 M.) *Indian River* (Hotel, $2). 18 M. *Indian Lake* (Ordway Ho., $2); 20 M. *Cedar River* (Hotel, $2). We cross the watershed (1760 ft.) between the Hudson and the *Raquette*. 25 M. *Forest House* ($2). — 29 M. *Blue Mountain Lake* (see below).

Blue Mountain Lake (1800 ft.), 3 M. long and 2 M. wide, |lies at the base of *Blue Mt.* (3760 ft.), which rises to the N.E.

The hotels on the lake are the *Prospect House* (500 beds; $4-5), on the S. shore; *Holland's Lake House* ($3), at the E. end; *Blue Mt. House* (225 ft. above the lake; $2¹/₂), at the foot of Blue Mt. — **Blue Mountain** (3760 ft.) is ascended by a bridle-path in 2 hrs. — A road leads N. from Blue Mt. Lake, through the woods, to (10 M.) *Long Lake Village* (p. 178).

From Blue Mountain Lake to Raquette Lake, 12 M., steam-launch in 3 hrs. (fare to Marion Carry 75c., to the Hemlocks or the Antlers $1.25, to Forked Lake Carry $1.75). — The little steamer traverses *Blue Mt. Lake*, affording a good view of *Blue Mt.*, passes through a small outlet into *Eagle Lake* (with *Eagle's Nest*, a solitary farm-house on the N. bank, formerly the home of 'NedBuntline', the author), and then threads another connecting stream and reaches the narrow *Utowana Lake*, 2¹/₂ M. long. At the W. end of this lake we leave the boat and pass across a short carry (¹/₂ M.) to the *Marion River*, the intricate course of which we descend in another steam-launch to (6 M.) *Raquette Lake*, where we disembark at the *Hemlocks* or the *Antlers*.

*Raquette Lake (1775 ft.), the most irregularly shaped of the Adirondack lakes, with numerous promontories and bays, is about 10 M. long (5 M. in a direct line) and 1-2¹/₂ M. wide. It is surrounded by low hills, and the environing forests teem with game.

The following are the Lake Raquette hotels : *Antlers ($3½), on the
W. bank; *The Hemlocks ($3), near the Marion River Outlet; *Whitney ($2),
S. end; *Blanchard's Wigwam ($2), W. bank. — The **Private Camps** round
Raqette Lake are the most elaborate in the whole district, and *Camp
Pine Knot* (W. W. Durant, Esq.), on the S. side of the promontory below
the Marion River, is, perhaps, the most beautiful place of the kind in
America, if not in the world. An introduction to the owner of one of
these camps will double the pleasure of a visit to the lake.

To the S.W. of Raquette Lake stretches the **Fulton Chain of Lakes**
(1680-1800 ft.), eight in number, a favourite resort of sportsmen and anglers.
They are reached hence viâ the *Brown Tract Inlet*, and a small steamer
plies on some of the lakes. They may be approached from *Herkimer* by
the Adirondack & St. Lawrence Railway (see below). — Other parts of this
W. district of the Adirondacks are frequented by sportsmen; but the means
of locomotion are scanty and the accommodation somewhat primitive.

FROM RAQUETTE LAKE TO LONG LAKE, 12 M., by small boat,
with guide. From the N. end of Raquette Lake we cross a short
carry (½ M.) to **Forked Lake** (1750 ft.; *Forked Lake House,* closed),
a picturesque sheet of water, with several private camps.

Those who are bound for the *Tupper Lakes* (p. 179) cross Forked Lake
(pron. 'Forkéd') to the N., pass through the outlet into (6 M.) *Little Forked
Lake*, and thence proceed, by boat (2½ M.) and carries (5½ M.), viâ *Carry
Pond*, *Bottle Pond*, and *Rock Pond*, to (8 M.) *Little Tupper Lake* (see p. 179).

We turn to the right (E.) on Forked Lake and from its E. end
descend through the picturesque *Raquette River* to (8 M.) Long Lake,
about 2 M. of the route being the 'carries' required to pass the
Buttermilk Falls and other unnavigable parts of the river.

Long Lake (1615 ft.), 14 M. long and ½-1 M. wide, is pretty,
though tamer than many of the other lakes. To the right and left
as we enter it are *Mt. Sabattis* and the *Owl's Head* (2825 ft.). On
the right (E.) bank, about 2 M. below the head, is the *Grove House*
($2½), a great hunting and fishing resort; and about 1 M. farther
on, on the same side, is *Long Lake Village*, with the *Sagamore
House* ($3-4) and *Long Lake House* ($2).

Nearly opposite Long Lake Village begins a boat and portage route
to *Little Tupper Lake* (p. 179) viâ *Clear Pond*, *Little* and *Big Slim Ponds*,
and *Stony Pond*.

Farther on Long Lake expands. At its lower end (W. bank) is
the small *Island House*. To the right rises *Mt. Seward* (p. 176).

From Long Lake to *Upper Saranac Lake*, see p. 169.

e. From Herkimer to Malone viâ the Tupper and Saranac Lakes.

173 M. ADIRONDACK AND ST. LAWRENCE RAILWAY in 6-7 hrs. (fare
$5.22; parlor-car $1.25). Through-carriages run from New York to all
points in the Adirondacks reached by this railway (to *Tupper Lake Junction*
in 10 hrs., $8.14; to *Saranac Inn* in 10½ hrs., $8.59; to *Malone* in 12 hrs.,
$9.60; parlor-car or sleeper $2). The line traverses the whole of the
Adirondack Wilderness from S. to N. Through-carriages will also be run
from New York and from Boston viâ Malone.

Herkimer, see p. 187. — The line runs towards the N.W. 20 M.
Trenton Falls, see p. 188. We cross the *West Canada Creek*. 28 M.
Remsen, see p. 188. At (50 M.) *McKeever* we cross the *Moose River*.
— 58 M. *Fulton Chain* is 1¼ M. from *Old Forge* (Forge Ho., Cedar
Isle Ho., $2), whence a small steamer ascends the **Fulton Lakes**

(see p. 178) to the head of *Fourth Lake.* Thence we may ascend by small boat and 'carries' to (3-4 hrs.) *Raquette Lake* (p. 177). — 69 M. *Big Moose;* 80 M. *Little Rapids;* 91 M. *Bog Lake.* — 107 M. *Childwold,* the station for (5 M.; coach $1) the *Childwold Park House* ($ 3-4), on *Lake Massawepie.*

113¹/₂ M. *Tupper Lake Junction* is 1¹/₂ M. (stage) from *Tupper Lake Village* (Altamont, $2¹/₂-5), the terminus of the Northern Adirondack R. R. (see below), situated on *Raquette Pond,* 2 M. below the foot of Tupper Lake (see below). In summer a steamer plies hence to the head of the lake, calling at the various hotels. The station is 8 M. from *Wawbeek Lodge* (p. 169), on Upper Saranac Lake.

Tupper Lake (1555 ft.), 7 M. long and 3 M. wide, is surrounded by low but wild hills and is much frequented by sportsmen. It contains several islands. The chief hotel is the *Tupper Lake House* ($3), near its head (S. end). *Moody's* ($2), near the N. end, is a smaller house. — From the head of Tupper Lake we may proceed by boat and portages to (4¹/₄ M.) *Round Pond,* cross this (2¹/₂ M.) by boat, and carry to (1 M. Little Tupper Lake. — Little Tupper Lake (1730 ft.) is 4 M. long and 1 M. wide. On its W. bank is the *Robbins House,* an unpretending resort of sportsmen. — From Little Tupper Lake to *Long Lake,* see p. 178; to *Raquette Lake,* see p. 178.

The line now passes several small lakes. — 128¹/₂ M. *Saranac Inn Station,* 1¹/₂ M. from *Saranac Inn* (p. 169). From (131¹/₂ M.) *Lake Clear* (1¹/₂ M. from Big Clear Ho., p. 168) a branch line runs to the right to (5 M.) *Saranac Village* (see p. 169). To the left lies *Clear Lake* (p. 168). — 136 M. *Paul Smith's* is 4 M. from the *St. Regis Lake House* (see p. 168; stage). A stage also runs hence to (16 M.) *Meacham Lake House.* To the left, at (139 M.) *Rainbow Lake Station* (Rainbow Inn, $2), we see *Rainbow Lake* (3 M. long; trout). 148 M. *Loon Lake Station* is 3¹/₂ M. from *Loon Lake House* (p. 168; stage). The line now runs parallel to the Chateaugay Railway (p. 167) for some distance and then skirts the *Salmon River.*

173 M. **Malone** (*Flanagan, Howard,* $ 2-2¹/₂), an industrial village with (1890) 4896 inhab., is a station on the Central Vermont Railway from *Rouse's Point* to *Ogdensburg* (see p. 189).

The *Tupper Lakes* and the *St. Regis Lake House* may also be reached by the *Northern Adirondack R. R.,* starting from *Moira* (p. 189), another station on the Central Vermont line to Ogdensburg, 14 M. to the W. of Malone.

26. Saratoga.

Railway Stations. *Delaware and Hudson Station,* Division St., near the back of the U. S. Hotel, for New York, Albany, the Adirondacks, etc.; *Mt. McGregor Railway Station,* Catherine St.; *Saratoga Lake Railway Station* (Fitchburg R. R.), Henry St., for Saratoga Lake, Boston, etc.

Hotels. GRAND UNION, occupying the square between Broadway, Congress, Federal, and Washington Sts., and enclosing a large tree-shaded court, with 2400 ft. of street-front and 2000 beds, $5; UNITED STATES HOTEL, Broadway, cor. Division St., an enormous structure 300 yds. long, with nearly 2000 beds, $5; CONGRESS HALL, Broadway, between Spring St. and East Congress St., with 1000 beds, $3-4; WINDSOR, Broadway, cor. E. William St., a fashionable house, from $5; CLARENDON, Broadway, cor. William St., frequented by Southerners, $4; *WORDEN, Broadway, cor.

Division St., $3, open all the year round; ADELPHI, next door to the
U. S. Hotel, $3; AMERICAN, adjoining the last, $3-3¹/₂; COLUMBIAN, near
the Clarendon, from $2¹/₂; KENSINGTON, Union Ave.; MANSION HOUSE,
Excelsior Park, $2¹/₂; VICTORIA ($2¹/₂-3¹/₂), HUESTIS, ALBEMARLE ($2-3),
and many other small hotels and boarding-houses, at all prices. —
Dr. Strong's Sanitarium, Circular St., with good baths.

Horse Races in July and Aug. at the *Race Course*, Union Avenue.
Post Office, in the *Arcade*, opposite the U. S. Hotel.

Saratoga Springs (300 ft.), the most noted inland watering-
place in the United States and in some respects the most remarkable
in the world, is situated on a level and monotonous plateau near
the E. edge of the State of New York, 180 M. to the N. of the city
of New York and 12 M. to the W. of the Hudson. The saline
mineral springs which have made the fame of the place are about
30 in number (see below). The permanent population of the town
is about 12,000, but in the height of the season (July and Aug.)
this is often more than doubled.

The name is supposed to be derived from Indian words meaning
'place of the swift water'. The springs were known to the Indians for
centuries, and *Jacques Cartier* heard of their virtues in 1535. The first
white man to use them is believed to have been *Sir William Johnson*
(p. 187), the adopted sachem of the Mohawks, who was brought hither
by these Indians in 1767 and recovered his health by drinking the High
Rock Spring (p. 181). Hotels and boarding-houses began to be erected
early in the present century, and since then the progress of the place
has been very rapid, in spite of its want of fine scenery or commercial
advantages. No more effective picture of the wealth of the United
States can be seen anywhere than at Saratoga during July or Aug.,
though Newport (p. 68) and Lenox (p. 139) show a greater refinement of
luxury. Saratoga is also a popular place for 'conventions' of politicians,
lawyers, bankers, etc. — Large quantities of the water are exported to
all parts of the United States and Europe. — The battle of Saratoga
(Oct., 1777), resulting in the surrender of Sir John Burgoyne to the
Americans, was fought some distance to the S. of the Springs (see p. 182).

The **Hotels** of Saratoga afford accommodation for about 20,000 visitors.
The two at the head of the list are among the largest, if not the very
largest, hotels in the world; and a visit to their enormous ball-rooms,
dining-rooms, and piazzas should not be omitted. The dining-room of
the Grand Union is 275 ft. long.

Most of the **Springs** lie in a shallow valley stretching to the N.E.
from Broadway (see pp. 181, 187), and rise through a fault in the underlying
rock (slate, limestone, and sandstone), the S. strata being tilted above
those to the N. Some are chalybeate, others contain iodine or sulphur,
and all are strongly impregnated with carbonic acid gas. Their temperature is usually 46-50° and most of them are pleasant to drink. They
are both tonic and cathartic in working, and are considered efficacious in
dyspepsia, liver complaints, calculus, rheumatism, etc. They should not
be too freely indulged in without medical advice.

Broadway, the principal street of Saratoga, containing the chief
hotels, the best shops, and the finest private residences, runs N.
and S. for a distance of 3 M. and is shaded by fine elms. Most of
the springs are in or near it. Proceeding to the right (S.) from
the *U. S. Hotel* we soon reach, to the left, Spring St., just to the
N. of *Congress Hall* (p. 180), with the *Hathorn Spring*, a saline
spring containing bicarbonate of lithia. To the S. of Congress Hall
is **Congress Spring Park,** a prettily laid out little park (adm. 5 c.),

with a small deer-paddock. Near the entrance are *Congress Spring*
(saline, with magnesia; resembling the Kissingen Racoczy) and
Columbian Spring (chalybeate), the former the most widely known
of the Saratoga waters and extensively used as a cathartic in
bilious disorders. A band plays in the park thrice daily, and
Sunday and other concerts are given. — Behind Congress Hall is
the *Hamilton Spring* (similar to the Columbian), and a little to the
N., in Philadelphia St., are the *Putnam Spring and Baths.* Continuing to follow Broadway towards the S., we reach (left) the
Convention Hall erected for the conventions mentioned at p. 180
(5000 seats). Adjacent is the **Pompeia* (adm. 50 c.), a unique and
interesting reproduction of the House of Pansa at Pompeii (destroyed A. D. 79), erected by Mr. Franklin W. Smith (comp. p. 357).

The *Art Gallery* annexed to the Pompeia contains a painting of Rome
in the time of Constantine (50 ft. ✕ 7 ft.) and many illustrations of art
and history.

Washington Spring rises opposite, in the court of the Clarendon Hotel. — Ballston Avenue, a little farther on, leads to the
right, passing an *Indian Camp* (baskets, etc., for sale), to (1¹/₄ M.)
Geyser Park and *Lake*, with the *Geyser* or *Spouting Spring* (rising
from a depth of 132 ft.) The *Saratoga Vichy*, the *Saratoga Kissingen* (both alkaline), the **Champion Spouting Spring* (throwing its
water to a height of 30 ft.), the *Carlsbad Spring* (saline and cathartic),
and the *Lafayette Spring* are in the same neighbourhood.

Following North Broadway to the left (N.) from the U. S. Hotel,
we pass the *Town Hall* (right) and reach a part of the street lined with
handsome private residences. At (³/₄ M.) *Third Street* we turn to
the left and reach the entrance to **Woodlawn Park*, a fine expanse
of 1200 acres, belonging to Judge Hilton and containing his house,
but freely open to the public.

The park is traversed by walks and drives in all directions. The
trimmer part near the houses, ornamented with dubious statuary, is less
attractive than the wilder part, to the N. Views are obtained of the
Catskills (S.), the Green Mts. (E.), and the foothills of the Adirondacks
(N.). — We may continue our walk through the park to (2¹/₂ M.) *Glen
Mitchell*, with a Roman Catholic college, and return by Broadway.

Returning along Broadway, we turn to the left at Rock St.,
cross the railway, and reach a group of springs in *Spring Avenue.*

The *High Rock Spring*, the earliest known (comp. p. 180), bubbles
from a conical rock, 3¹/₂ ft. high, formed by its deposits. Below is the
Star Spring. To the S. are the *Seltzer Spring*, the *Magnetic Spring* (baths),
the *Flat Rock* or *Imperial Spring* (behind the Town Hall), the *Pavilion
Spring*, and the *Royal Spring* (600 ft. deep). To the N. are the *Empire Spring*,
the *Red Spring* and *Bath-House* (with a large proportion of iron; useful for
affections of the skin), and the *Saratoga 'A' Spring.*

Following Spring Avenue towards the N.E., we reach (³/₄ M.) the
Mansion House Hotel (p. 180 ; left), opposite which is the entrance
to the *Excelsior Spring and Bottling Works*, prettily situated in
Excelsior Park, near which is the *Union Spring.* — About ¹/₄ M. to
the E. are the *White Sulphur Spring* (baths) and *Eureka Spring.*

— We may now return towards Broadway by one of the paths through the pretty patch of woodland to the S.W. of the Excelsior Spring, emerging (10 min.) upon *East Avenue.* Here we turn to the left and then follow *Lake Avenue* (right), past the handsome *Armory* and the *Fitchburg Railway Station,* to (6 min.) Broadway.

Environs. The favourite short *Drive* from Saratoga is that to *Saratoga Lake,* 4 M. to the S.E. We follow *Union Avenue,* which leads to the left from Broadway at Congress Hall. On the left we pass another *Indian Camp* and on the right the *Racecourse,* one of the best tracks in the United States, and *Yaddo,* the residence of Mr. Spencer Trask, to the beautiful grounds of which visitors are admitted, The lake, on which a small steamer plies, is 7 M. long and is frequented for boating and fishing. Near its N. end is *Thomas's Hotel* (formerly *Moon's*), a favourite resort for game and fish dinners and for 'Saratoga Chips' (fried potatoes; sold in paper packets or served with meals). *Riley's,* on *Little Lake,* 1/4 M. to the S.W., is a similar resort. An electric tramway (fare 25 c.) runs from the Grand Union Hotel to Saratoga Lake. — *Gridley's Ponds,* a fishing-preserve near the racecourse, are much frequented by ladies and others (fee $1 per pound of trout caught). — *Ballston Spa* (7 M.; p. 144), *Round Lake* (12 M.), and *Lake Luzerne* (see p. 177; 20 M.) may be reached by road or railway; and longer excursions may be made to the *Adirondacks* (p. 165), *Lake George* (see below), *Lake Champlain* (p. 184), etc.

A branch of the FITCHBURG RAILWAY runs to (12 M.) *Schuylerville,* whence the *Battlefield of Saratoga* (p. 180), with its national monument, may be visited. Memorial tablets mark the chief points of the battle-ground.

FROM SARATOGA TO MT. MCGREGOR, 10 M., railway in 3/4 hr. (return-fare $1). — At the top of the hill (1200 ft.) lies the **Balmoral Hotel** ($3-4), commanding an exquisite *View and standing in a large park, with fishing-lakes, drives, etc. The cottage in which *Gen. Ulysses Grant* died in 1885, near the hotel, is now State property and is shown to the public.

27. Lake George and Lake Champlain.

*Lake George (345 ft.), a picturesque sheet of water in the State of New York, to the S.E. of the Adirondack Mts. (p. 156), is 33 M. long from N. to S. and 3/4-3 M. wide. It is flanked on both sides by wooded mountains, sometimes descending to the water in bold crags, and is dotted with pretty islands (220 in all). It is sometimes called, perhaps with more zeal than discretion, the Como, the Windermere, or the Loch Lomond of America. At the N. end it discharges into Lake Champlain, 245 ft. below it, from which it is separated by a ridge 4 M. wide.

Lake George has long been a favourite summer-resort, and there are many hotels, large and small, on its banks, while camp-life is also in high favour. It is usually approached by the route to *Caldwell* described at p. 144; and a steamer plies twice daily thence in 3-3¹/₂ hrs. to *Baldwin,* at the foot of the lake (return-fare $1.50; restaurant on board, meals 75 c.). Fair fishing for lake-trout, perch, and bass is obtained in the lake (boat with fisherman $3 a day). — See *S. R. Stoddard's* 'Lake George and Lake Champlain' (25 c.); and comp. *Francis Parkman's* 'Historic Handbook of the Northern Tour'.

Lake George was first seen by white men in 1642, when three Frenchmen, including the Jesuit Jogues, were brought hither as captives of the Iroquois. Father Jogues named it the *Lac du Saint Sacrement;* the Indian name was *Andiatarocte* ('place where the lake closes'), and Cooper tried in vain to attach to it the romantic title of *Lake Horican* ('silvery waters'). The present name was given to it in honour of

George II. The position of Lake George on the highway between the English colonies and Canada gave it a prominent rôle in the Anglo-French struggles of the 17-18th cent., and more than one battle has been fought on or near its waters (comp. below and p. 184). Its associations with the romances of Cooper lend it an additional interest.

Caldwell (**Fort William Henry Hotel*, a large house with 800 beds, $4-5; *Lake House*, $3-3$\frac{1}{2}$; *Central Hotel*, *Carpenter Ho.*, $2-3), the terminus of the railway mentioned at p. 144, is a small village, beautifully situated at the head (S. end) of Lake George, at the foot of *Prospect Mt.* (1735 ft.; Inn), and much frequented as a summer-resort (good boating and fishing). To the E. rises *French Mt.*

The *Fort William Henry Hotel* stands near the site of the old *Fort William Henry*, built by the English in 1755 to command the head of the lake. Two years later it was captured by General Montcalm at the head of 8000 men; and the massacre of 1500 helpless men, women, and children by his Indian allies has left an indelible stain on the memory of that gallant Frenchman (see the descriptions in *Cooper's* 'Last of the Mohicans' and in *Parkman*). A few relics of the fort subsist. — About $\frac{1}{2}$ M. to the E. are the picturesque ruins of *Fort George*, dating from 1759. — It was at this spot that the army of Gen. Abercrombie started in a fleet of boats for its disastrous expedition against Fort Ticonderoga (1758; see *Cooper's* 'Satanstoe'), and a year later Lord Amherst set out hence with the army that finally expelled the French from Lakes George and Champlain.

The STEAMER down the lake leaves Caldwell after touching at various hotel-landings and crosses to the *Crosbyside Hotel* ($3-3$\frac{1}{2}$), at the foot of French Mt. On the same side, 1 M. to the N., is *St. Mary's Convent*, the summer-retreat of the Paulist Fathers of New York. We pass *Tea Island*, *Diamond Island*, and *Long Island*. To the right are *Kattskill Bay* and *Pilot Mt.*, at the foot of which are some small hotels frequented by anglers (1\frac{1}{2}$-2 per day). Opposite is the *Marion House* (3\frac{1}{2}$).

8$\frac{1}{3}$ M. *Buck Mt.* (2010 ft.). — The steamer steers between *Dome Island* (r.), in the widest part of the lake, and *Recluse Island* (l.), connected by a bridge with the tiny *Sloop Island*.

9$\frac{1}{2}$ M. (left). **Bolton** (**Sagamore*, situated on an island connected with the mainland by a bridge, $4; **Mohican Ho.*, *Bolton Ho.*, $3; *Lake View Ho.*, 2\frac{1}{2}$-3), the largest village on the lake after Caldwell, is a good centre for excursions. Black Mt. (see below) stands out well to the E.N.E. Above Bolton extends *Ganouskie* or *North West Bay*, 5 M. long, formed by a tongue of land jutting out southwardly into the middle of the lake.

11-12 M. (r.) **Shelving Rock Mt.** (*Hundred Island House*, *Pearl Point Ho.*, $3), descending abruptly into the lake.

Off the shore is *Fourteen Mile Island* (The Kenesaw, 2\frac{1}{2}$), at the entrance to the **Narrows*, between *Tongue Mt.*, *Three Mile Mt.*, and *Five Mile Mt.* to the left, and *Mt. Erebus* and the sombre *Black Mt.* (2660 ft.; **View*) to the right. The Narrows are crowded with islands, through which the steamboat holds a devious course.

14 M. (r.) *Black Mt. Point* (to top of Black Mt., 1$\frac{1}{2}$-2$\frac{1}{2}$ hrs.).

17 M. *Harbor Islands,* where a body of 400 English were surprised by the Indians in 1757 and nearly all killed or captured.

18 M. (l.) *Deer's Leap Mt.* — (r.) *Hulett's Landing* (Hotel, $2¹/₂-3), whence Black Mt. is ascended from the N.

18¹/₂ M. (l.) *Bloomer Mt.,* forming, with Deer's Leap Mt., the *Twin Mts.,* as seen from the N.

19 M. (l.) *Sabbath Day Point, a fertile cape at the outlet of the Narrows, was the scene of a battle between the Colonists and the Indians and French in 1756 and between the Americans and the Indians in 1776, in both of which the first-named won. Generals Abercrombie and Amherst (see p. 183) both landed here. Good view up and down the lake.

24 M. (l.) **Hague** (*Phoenix Hotel,* $ 2; *Hillside Ho., Rising Ho., Trout Ho.,* $ 1¹/₂-2), a favourite fishing-resort, backed by the ridge of the *Three Brothers.* — The lake again contracts.

27 M. (r.) *Anthony's Nose,* rising abruptly from the water's edge.

28 M. (l.) *Rogers' Slide* (600 ft.) and **Rogers' Rock Hotel* ($ 3-3¹/₂).

30 M. (l.) **Baldwin** (*Baldwin Ho.,* $ 2), where we leave the steamer for the train. *Lord Howe's Point,* just to the N., was the landing-place of the English army in 1758. Offshore lies *Prisoners' Island,* where the French are said to have confined their captives.

FROM BALDWIN TO FORT TICONDEROGA, 5 M., railway in ¹/₂ hr. (fare $ 75 c.). This short railway, connecting Lake George with Lake Champlain, descends rapidly (245 ft.) round the slope of *Mt. Defiance* (p. 185). At the village of *Ticonderoga* (Burleigh Ho., $ 2), about halfway, the outlet of Lake George forms a picturesque waterfall (left). — *Fort Ticonderoga,* see below and p. 185.

***Lake Champlain** (100 ft.), 120 M. in length, ¹/₄-12 M. in width, and 50-400 ft. deep, lies between New York on the W. and Vermont on the E. and extends on the N. for a short way into Canada. Its shore-line is indented by numerous bays and inlets, and there are about fifty islands, one of which is 30 sq. M. in extent. The Vermont shore is generally level and fertile, with the Green Mts. in the background, while the W. shore is broken and diversified by the foothills of the Adirondacks. Besides the city of Burlington (p. 114) there are numerous towns and villages on its banks. A considerable navigation is carried on on its waters, and it communicates with the Hudson by a canal and with the St. Lawrence by the river Richelieu.

The name of the lake recalls Samuel de Champlain, Governor of Canada (see below), who discovered it in 1609. Its Indian names were *Caniaderi Quaranti* ('gate of the land') and *Petoubouque* ('waters that lie between'). Like Lake George, it was for a century and a half the scene of repeated conflicts between the English and the French; and in 1759 it finally passed into the possession of the former. The most interesting contests are mentioned below in connection with their scenes of action.

STEAMBOATS (good restaurants on board) ply regularly from *Fort Ticonderoga* (see p. 185) to *Plattsburg* (p. 167), calling at all important intermediate points; from *Westport* (p. 170) to *North Hero* (p. 186); and from

Westport to *Vergennes* (p. 114; woman-pilot). — For the RAILWAYS along its banks, see RR. 15, 20.

The S. extremity of Lake Champlain, from *Whitehall* (p. 144) to (24 M.) *Fort Ticonderoga*, is so narrow as to resemble a river rather than a lake, and has been sufficiently described in R. 20 b. Steamboat- navigation begins at Fort Ticonderoga.

Fort Ticonderoga (*Fort Ticonderoga Hotel*, near the old fort, $ 2) is a railway-station and steamboat-landing on the W. side of Lake Champlain, at the foot of *Mt. Defiance* (850 ft.; *View). The village of *Ticonderoga* (p. 184) lies 2 M. inland, while the ruins of *Fort Ticonderoga* (see below) crown a high bluff 1½ M. to the N.

Fort Carillon, the first regular fortification here, was built by the French in 1755. In 1758 General Abercrombie (see p. 183) made an unsuccessful effort to capture it, and had to retreat up Lake George, with the loss of Lord Howe and 2000 men. The following year, however, the French evacuated it on the approach of Lord Amherst (see p. 183), and the English considerably strengthened and enlarged it, changing its name to **Fort Ticonderoga**. In 1775 the fort was taken by Green Mountain Boys led by Col. Ethan Allen of Vermont, who surprised the unsuspecting commandant in his bed and called on him to surrender 'in the name of the Great Jehovah and the Continental Congress'. Gen. Burgoyne, however, recaptured it in 1777 with the aid of a battery posted on the top of Mt. Defiance. The fort was dismantled in 1780 and allowed to fall into decay. It long formed a quarry for the buildings of the neighbourhood; but its scanty remains, from which a fine view is obtained, are now preserved as a national memorial.

At Fort Ticonderoga the lake is barely ½ M. wide, and it does not widen materially till beyond Crown Point. The STEAMER makes its first stop at *Larrabee's Point* (right) and then crosses the lake to (10 M.) the landing of *Crown Point* (left), 1 M. to the E. of the village. A short railway runs to (13 M.) *Hammondville*, connecting by stage with *Schroon Lake* (p. 177). About 5½ M. farther on we thread the narrows between *Chimney Point*, on the right, and *Crown Point, on the left, the latter surmounted by a lighthouse and the ramparts of the old fort.

The French *Fort Frederick*, erected on this point in 1731, was abandoned at the same time as Fort Ticonderoga (see above). The English constructed a much larger and more formidable fortification, which, like Ft.Ticonderoga, was taken by Ethan Allen in 1775 and by Burgoyne in 1777. — A dancing pavilion, restaurant, etc., have been erected here.

Beyond the narrows the lake widens to 2 M. Behind Crown Point is *Bulwagga Bay*, the shore of which is, perhaps, the point where Champlain fought with the Iroquois in 1609.

19 M. (l.) **Port Henry** (Lee House, $ 2-3), a prettily situated village, whence a railroad runs to (7 M.) *Mineville*, 19 M. from *Schroon River Post Office* (p. 177). A fine view of Mt. Dix (p. 174) and other Adirondack peaks is now obtained to the left.

30 M. (l.) **Westport**, in *North West Bay*, one of the approaches to the Adirondacks (see p. 170). — Farther on *Split Rock Mt.* (lighthouse) rises to the left, while opposite is the mouth of the *Otter Creek*, up which a small steamer plies to (8 M.) *Vergennes* (p. 114).

40 M. (l.) **Essex**. The steamer now soon enters the widest part

of the lake and steers to the N.E., passing the *Four Brothers* and *Juniper Island* (lighthouse). To the left lies *Willsborough Point* (Green Mt. View Ho., $2), where the American Canoe Association holds its annual meeting.

54 M. (r.) **Burlington,** see p. 114. This beautiful city is seen to great advantage from the lake. — From Burlington the steamer runs nearly straight across the lake to —

64 M. (l.) *Port Kent,* the station for the **Ausable Chasm* (see p. 170). The *Ausable River* enters the lake 2¹/₂ M. farther on.

70 M. (l.) *Port Jackson,* on the narrow channel between the mainland and *Valcour Island,* where a hotly contested naval battle took place between Arnold and Pringle in 1776, resulting in the destruction of the American fleet.

Beyond this point the lake is divided into two branches by the large islands of *Grand Isle* or *South Hero* (30 sq. M.) and *North Hero* and the promontory of *Alburgh.* Our steamer follows the left (W.) arm. On *Bluff Point* (l.), 3¹/₂ M. beyond Port Jackson, stands the magnificently situated **Hotel Champlain** ($5), one of the most luxurious hotels in the United States, commanding fine views of the Adirondacks, Lake Champlain, and the Green Mts.

77 M. (l.) **Plattsburg** (see p. 167), in *Cumberland Bay,* one of the main gateways to the Adirondacks.

In 1814 Cumberland Bay was the scene of the *Battle of Plattsburg,* in which Commodore Macdonough defeated the British fleet under Commodore Downie. At the same time Gen. Macomb, in command of the land-forces, repelled Sir George Prevost's attempt to capture Plattsburg.

Plattsburg is the terminus of the Lake Champlain Transportation Co.'s steamer from Fort Ticonderoga, but the Westport steamer (comp. p. 185) ascends to *North Hero,* touching at various landings on the islands. The fishing at this end of the lake is excellent, and accommodation may be had at various small hotels, farm-houses, and camps.

28. From New York to Buffalo and Niagara Falls.
a. Viâ New York Central and Hudson River Railway.

462 M. RAILWAY to (440 M.) *Buffalo* in 8³/₄-13 hrs. (fare $9.25; sleeper $2; parlor-car $2); to (462 M.; 446 M. by direct route, see p. 192) *Niagara Falls* in 11¹/₄-16¹/₂ hrs. (fares the same). Seats to the left. The 'Greased Lightning Train', leaving New York about 2 p.m., runs at the rate of over 50 M. an hour, including stops.

From *New York* to (143 M.) *Albany,* see p. 154. The train now turns to the left (W.) and leaves the *Hudson.* 146 M. *West Albany.*

160 M. **Schenéctady** (245 ft.; *Edison,* $2¹/₂-4; *Gilmore Ho.*), a quaint old town of Dutch foundation, situated on the right bank of the *Mohawk,* with various manufactories and a trade in broom-corn, hops, and butter. Pop. (1890) 19,902. It was the scene of two horrible massacres in the Colonial wars. *Union College* (1795) stands to the E. of the city. At Schenectady we intersect the Del. & Hudson R. R. (N. to Saratoga, S. to Binghamton; comp. p. 197).

The train now crosses the river and the *Erie Canal* (Union College to the right) and ascends the smiling pastoral **Valley of the Mohawk*, formerly the stamping-ground of the Indian tribe of that name (see below). Evidences of rustic comfort and fertility abound on every side. The Catskills are visible in the distance to the S., and the outliers of the Adirondacks appear to the N. Broom - corn is one of the characteristic crops, the brooms being made mainly by the Shakers, who have several settlements in the lower valley.

176 M. *Amsterdam* (280 ft.), a city of 17,336 inhab., with various industries; 182 M. *Tribe's Hill*, a former meeting-place of the Indians. — From (187 M.) *Fonda* a branch runs to (26 M.) *Northville.*
Johnstown, on this railway, 3 M. to the N., was the residence of *Sir William Johnston* (d. 1774; comp. p. 130), one of the pioneers of the valley, who acquired great influence with the Mohawks and was made one of their sachems. He was created a baronet for his victory at Lake George (see p. 144), and received a large grant of land here for his subsequent services. He was the father of 100 children by his Indian and white mistresses, one of whom was a sister of the famous Mohawk chief, Joseph Brant. His strong stone mansion still stands.

The *Mohawks* were, perhaps, the best known of the Indian tribes which formed the confederation known as the *Five Nations*, occupying the great Lake District of New York. The other members of the league, named from E. to W., were the *Oneidas, Onondagas, Cayugas,* and *Senecas.* The *Tuscaroras* from Carolina were afterwards admitted to the league, which then took the name of the *Six Nations.* The confederacy had about 15,000 members, and perhaps 10-12,000 still exist, the majority in Canada, the others in reservations in New York, where they live as peaceable farmers.

From (198 M.) *Palatine Bridge* (305 ft.) coaches run to (14 M.) *Sharon Springs* (see p. 158).

217 M. **Little Falls** (375 ft. ; *Girvan Ho.,* $ 2-2¹/₂), a small manufacturing town with 8783 inhab., romantically situated in a narrow **Gorge* cut by the Mohawk through a spur of the Adirondacks. The river, the N. Y. C. and West Shore railways, and the Erie Canal can barely make their way through the pass side by side. The Mohawk here descends 45 ft. in ¹/₂ M., forming a series of pretty little falls, and the houses cling picturesquely to the steep rocky sides of the defile. This gorge affords an excellent opportunity of studying the crystalline rocks of the Laurentian formation, part of the oldest dry land on the face of the globe. *Richfield Springs* (p. 188) is 12 M. to the S. — Farther on we cross the *Canada Creek* and reach (224 M.) *Herkimer* (Palmer Ho., $ 2-2¹/₂; 4000 inhab.), junction of the *Adirondack & St. Lawrence Railway* (see p. 178).

Beyond *Ilion* (400 ft.), a pretty village to the left, with an important small-arms factory, the train crosses the river and canal.

238 M. **Utica** (410 ft.; *Baggs,* $ 4; *Butterfield,* $ 2¹/₂-3 ; *St. James,* $ 2-3; *Rail. Restaurant*), a prosperous town and headquarters of the American cheese trade, with 44,007 inhab., lies on the S. bank of the Mohawk, on the site of *Fort Schuyler* (1756). To the W. is the *State Lunatic Asylum. Genesee Street* is a handsome thoroughfare.

FROM UTICA TO OGDENSBURG, 134 M., railway in 5¹/₂-6 hrs. (fare $ 4.21). This line runs to the N., connecting Utica with Lake Ontario and the St. Lawrence, and forming part of a favourite through-route from New York to the Thousand Islands (p. 206). — The train crosses the Mohawk. 17 M. *Trenton Falls Station* (840 ft.; Moore's Hotel, $ 3-3¹/₂; Kauyahoora, $ 2), is about ¹/₂ M. from the *Trenton Falls, a scene of mingled grandeur and beauty, which is by no means so well or widely known as it deserves. The *West Canada* or *Kahnata* ('amber-water') *Creek*, the *Kauyahoora* ('leaping water') of the Indians, here forms a highly picturesque ravine, with abrupt rocky sides, through which, within 2 M., the water descends 310 ft. in a charming series of five main falls and innumerable rapids. The stratification of the limestone rocks is very clearly defined, exposing the geological and the fossil organic remains to full view; and an abundance of interesting fossils, including innumerable trilobites, have been found. The name of the Trenton formation is taken from this place. We descend (fee 25 c.) to the floor of the ravine by a staircase near Moore's Hotel and walk up past the singular *Sherman Falls* (35 ft.), the *High Falls* (80 ft.), the *Mill-dam Falls* (15 ft.), the rocky amphitheatre called the *Alhambra*, the curious formation named the *Rocky Heart*, and the *Prospect Falls* (20 ft.). We may then return to the hotel (2¹/₂ M.) by a path along the top of the cliffs, affording fine *Views of the chasm. — 21 M. *Remsen* (see p. 178); 35 M. *Boonville*. We ascend the valley of the *Black River*. 45 M. *Lyons Falls* (845 ft.; falls to the right, 70 ft. high); 58 M. *Lowville* (Rail. Restaurant). — 74 M. *Carthage* (740 ft.) is the junction of lines E. to *Benson Mines* in the Adirondacks (near *Cranberry Lake*) and W. to *Watertown* and (30 M.) *Sackett's Harbor* (455 ft.), on Lake Ontario. — At (87 M.) *Philadelphia* we cross the line from *Rome* (see below) to *Massena Springs* (p. 207). 92 M. *Theresa Junction*, for the line to (16 M.) *Clayton* (p. 206), on the St. Lawrence. — 123 M. *Morristown* (p. 207). — 134 M. **Ogdensburg** (250 ft.), see p. 207.

FROM UTICA TO BINGHAMTON, 95 M., railway in 3-3³/₄ hrs. (fares $ 2.85). — From (13 M.) *Richfield Junction* a branch-line runs to *Richfield Springs* (see below). — 95 M. **Binghamton**, see p. 197.

[*Richfield Springs** (1700 ft.; *Spring House*, *Earlington*, $ 4; *Davenport*, *Tuller Ho.*, $ 2-3; *Tunnicliff Cottage*; *Kendallwood*, etc.), a group of hotels and cottages, 1 M. from the head of the pretty little *Candarago Lake* (boating and fishing), is much frequented both for its picturesque scenery and for its sulphur springs (through drawing-room cars from New York). The latter, 17 in number, are especially efficacious in cutaneous disorders, and are used both for drinking and bathing. The *Bath-house, completed in 1890, is excellently fitted up and includes a swimming-basin. Among the favourite drives are those round *Candarago Lake* (12 M.), to (5 M.) *Mt. Otsego*, to (3 M.) *Allen's Lake*, to (13 M.) *Cooperstown* (p. 158), and to (14 M.) *Cherry Valley* (p. 158). Coaches run regularly to (7 M.) the head of *Otsego Lake* (p. 158), connecting with the steamer to Cooperstown. Horseback exercise is, perhaps, the favourite amusement here, and the surrounding country is admirably adapted for it.]

Beyond (244¹/₂ M.) *Oriskany* (420 ft.) a notice-board to the left calls attention to the battle-ground of Aug., 1777, when Gen. Herkimer was defeated and slain by the Indians. An obelisk on the hill marks the ground. — We cross the river and the canal.

252 M. **Rome** (*Stanwix Hall*, *Arlington*, $ 2-3), a town of 14,991 inhab., with cheese-factories and rolling-mills, occupies the site of the Revolutionary *Fort Stanwix*. It is an important railway-junction, and the Erie Canal is joined here by the *Black River Canal* from Lyons Falls (see above).

From Rome the *Rome*, *Waterstown*, *& Ogdensburg R. R.* runs to the N. to (73 M.) *Waterstown*, (141 M.) *Ogdensburg* (p. 207), and (160 M.) *Mas-*

sena Springs (p. 207), connecting at (147 M.) *Norwood* with the Central Vermont line to *Moira* (p. 159), *Malone* (p. 159), and *Rouse's Point* (p. 145).

265 M. *Oneida.*

About 6 M. to the N.W. is Oneida Lake, 28 M. long and 5-6 M. wide, in a rich dairy region. The *Oneida Community*, a communistic society founded by J. H. Noyes in 1847, lies 3 M. from the village, but is now simply a business-corporation. To the S. is the *Oneida Indian Reservation.*

Beyond (270 M.) *Canastota* (425 ft.) we cross the Erie Canal.

276 M. *Chittenango* (White Sulphur Springs Hotel, $2½), at the entrance of the narrow valley through which Cazenovia Lake drains into Lake Oneida. — 283 M. *Manlius.* The train now enters Syracuse, passing along the main-street, without fence or barrier.

291 M. **Syracuse** (400 ft.; *The Yates*, $4-5; *Vanderbilt Hotel, Globe*, $2½-4; *Rail. Restaurant*), a thriving industrial city of (1890) 88,143 inhab., situated at the S. end of *Onondaga Lake* (365 ft.; 6 M. long, 1½ M. wide), owes a great part of its wealth to the saltsprings in the marshes bordering the lake, which have been exploited since 1650 and now yield about 3 million bushels annually. A visit to the evaporating houses, brine-conduits ('salt logs'), and pumping-houses is interesting. The *Erie Canal* runs through the middle of the town, a little to the N. of the railway, and affords scenes of almost Venetian effect by moonlight.

Among the most noteworthy buildings are the *Town Hall*, Washington St., in the Richardsonian style; the *Post Office*, in Fayette St., a pleasing relief to the stereotyped Mansard-roofed Government buildings; the **Syracuse Savings Bank*, on the Canal; *St. Paul's Cathedral; St. John's Cathedral* (R. C.); the *First Presbyterian Church;* the *State Hospital for Feebleminded Children;* and the *Court House.* In the S.E. part of the town are the handsome buildings of SYRACUSE UNIVERSITY (800 students), including the *Crouse Memorial Hall for Women*, the *Hall of Languages*, the *Library* (45,000 vols., incl. Leopold v. Ranke's historical collection), and the *Holden Observatory* (open to the public on the 2nd and 4th Tues. of each month). The hill on which the University stands commands a splendid *View of the city, lake, and hills. Adjacent lies *Oakwood Cemetery.* — The handsomest residence street is JAMES STREET, leading to the N.E. from the centre of the town. — A BOULEVARD, 100 ft. wide, is being constructed round Onondaga Lake.

Railways radiate from Syracuse to *Oswego, Richland, Ithaca* (p. 190), etc. The *Oswego Canal* here joins the Erie Canal. — Oswego (*Doolittle Ho.*, $2-3) is a busy flour-making city and port, with 21.826 inhab., on the shore of Lake Ontario.

Between Syracuse and Rochester (p. 191) the N. Y. C. & H. R. R. R. has two routes: — the *Direct Route* (80 M.), used by through trains, and the *Old Route* (104 M.) viâ Auburn, Geneva, and Canandaigua. Both are described below.

a. DIRECT ROUTE FROM SYRACUSE TO ROCHESTER. As we leave Syracuse, we have a good view to the right of Lake Onondaga and the Salt Works (see above). The line runs through a pleasant pastoral

district, repeatedly crossing the Erie Canal and passing numerous
small towns. Beyond (312 M.) *Weedsport* we cross the *Seneca River*.
At (349 M.) *Palmyra* (440 ft.) Joseph Smith, the Mormon prophet,
claimed to have found the golden plates of the Mormon Bible
(p. 425). Large crops of peppermint are raised here.
371 M. *Rochester*, see p. 191.

  b. FROM SYRACUSE TO ROCHESTER VIÂ CANANDAIGUA ('Auburn
Road'). We cross the Erie Canal and run to the S. of W. From
(308 M.) *Skaneateles Junction* (610 ft.) a branch-line runs to (5 M.)
Skaneáteles (five syllables), situated on *Lake Skaneateles* (860 ft.),
a pretty sheet of water, 15 M. long and 1/2-11/2 M. wide, traversed
by a small steamboat. — 317 M. **Auburn** (715 ft. ; *Osborn Ho.*, $ 2-3;
Avery, $ 2), a manufacturing city of 25,858 inhab., situated on the
outlet of *Owasco Lake* (11 M. × 1 M.), which lies 3 M. to the S.
The *Auburn State Prison*, with accommodation for 1200 convicts,
is well known for its 'silent system' of discipline. *W. H. Seward*
(1801-72), Secretary of State during the Civil War, long lived here
and is buried in *Fort Hill Cemetery*, which is supposed to occupy
an eminence raised by the Mound Builders (p. lxiv). — At (327 M.)
Cayuga (Rail. Restaurant) the train crosses the lower end of Cayuga
Lake (see below) by a bridge more than 1 M. long.

  *Cayuga Lake (390 ft.), 38 M. long and 1-4 M. wide, is enclosed by
hills rising 600-700 ft. above the water-level, and affords good fishing,
boating, and bathing. Steamers ply upon the lake, and a railway runs
along its E. bank to (38 M.) *Ithaca*, passing (6 M.) *Union Springs* and (12 M.)
Aurora, the seat of the Wells College for Women.

  Ithaca (400 ft.; *Ithaca Ho.*, $ 21/2-3; *Clinton Ho.*, $ 2), a flourishing city
with 11,079 inhab., lies amid picturesque scenery at the head of Cayuga
Lake and is best known as the seat of *CORNELL UNIVERSITY*, one of the
leading colleges of America (146 teachers, 1600 students). The university
is munificently endowed, and its buildings, splendidly situated 400 ft.
above the lake (*View), are handsome and capacious. It owes its foundation to the bounty of the State of New York and of *Mr. Ezra Cornell*
(1807-74), whose large house stands in the town, below the Campus. Besides
the usual academic and professional branches, the educational course includes agriculture, the mechanic arts, and military tactics. The library
contains 115,000 vols., and the grounds embrace 250 acres. — The romantic
gorges near Ithaca contain, perhaps, a greater number of pretty waterfalls and cascades than can be found in any equal area elsewhere. *Fall
Creek*, in *Ithaca Gorge*, forms eight waterfalls within 1 M., one of which,
the *Ithaca Fall*, is 160 ft. high. The *Cascadilla Creek*, a little to the S.,
also forms several cascades. The finest waterfall, however, near the head
of Cayuga Lake, is the *Taughanic Fall*, which is about 9 M. to the N.
of Ithaca and 11/2 M. to the W. of the lake. The stream here forms a
ravine, with rocky sides 200-400 ft. high, and plunges perpendicularly over
a table-rock to a depth of 215 ft., presenting the highest waterfall E. of
the Rockies (50 ft. higher than Niagara). There is a hotel near the fall,
and it may be reached by road, railway, or water.

  332 M. *Seneca Falls*, situated at the falls of *Seneca River*, the
outlet of *Seneca Lake* (see p. 191); 335 M. *Waterloo*. — 342 M.
Geneva (450 ft.; *Franklin Ho., Kirkwood Ho.*, $ 2-21/2), a pleasant
little city with 7557 inhab. and extensive nurseries for seeds and
flowers, is situated at the N. end of *Seneca Lake* (see p. 191). *Hobart*

College here is a well-known Episcopal institution. Geneva is the junction of lines to *Watkins, Ithaca, Lyons,* etc.

°**Seneca Lake** (440 ft.), one of the most beautiful of the New York lakes, is 38 M. long and 2-6 M. wide. It is surrounded by hills, is very deep (over 500ft.), and never freezes. At a depth of 300 ft. the temperatur is constant at 39° Fahr. Only a narrow ridge divides it from Cayuga Lake (p. 190). Steamers ply in summer thrice daily from Geneva to *Watkins* (see below), calling at intermediate points (fare 25 c.).

Watkins (Glen Park Hotel, near the entrance to the Glen, $2-3; *Glen Mt. Ho.,* in the Glen, open in summer only, $3; *Jefferson, Fall Brook, Kendal,* unpretending, $2), a pleasant village of 2604 inhab. with tree-shaded streets, is frequented by thousands of visitors to Watkins and Havana Glens. It is also reached viâ RR. 28c, d.

The entrance to *Watkins Glen (adm. 50 c.; free to guests of the Glen Mt. Ho.) is ½ M. from the lake, to the right, just on this side of the bridge. The glen, which may be described as a somewhat less imposing edition of the Ausable Chasm, is 2½-3 M. long, and is traversed by paths, steps, and bridges (stout shoes and waterproofs desirable). The points of interest are indicated by sign-boards. Among the finest are the *Cathedral* (with its wonderfully smooth floor, and rocky sides 300 ft. high), *Glens Alpha* and *Omega, Elfin Glen,* and *Pluto Falls.* At the *Mt. House* (see above) we do not need to cross the bridge but remain on the same side of the ravine and almost immediately descend a flight of steps to the left. Farther on the path passes behind the small *Rainbow Falls,* where a rainbow is generally visible about 4 p.m. The head of the glen is spanned by a spider-web-like railway bridge, 165 ft. high. Here a steep path ascends to the right to *Glen Watkins Station* (Rfmts.), on the Syracuse, Corning, & Geneva R. R. Opposite, on the other side of the track, is a gap in the fence, where begins the short path back to the village along the top of the cliffs on the left side of the glen. It leads through wood for 10-12 min. and then emerges on a plateau commanding a splendid *View of the lake and village. We descend through the cemetery in 15-20 min. more.

Visitors to Watkins should not fail to visit also the *Havana Glen,* about 3 M. to the S.E. (entr. through the Fair Grounds at Havana, near the large *Cook's Academy;* adm. 50 c.). This glen is about 1¼ M. long, and its most striking feature is the wonderful rectangularity of the rocks in its lower part. This is specially evident in the square *Council Chamber,* not far from the entrance. The prettiest falls are, perhaps, those descending from the Council Chamber; farther up are the *Bridal Veil, Jacob's Ladder,* and the *Curtain Falls.* The stream, which contains more water than that in Watkins Glen, may be followed up (no path) beyond the glen proper. — There are other pretty glens in the neighbourhood.

Beyond Geneva the line makes a wide sweep to the N. 355 M. *Clifton Springs* (620 ft.; Sanitarium, $3-3½; Hotel, $1½), with sulphurous springs. 366 M. *Canandaigua* (740 ft.: Canandaigua Ho., $2-3), a village with 5868 inhab., at the N. end of **Canandaigua Lake** (670ft.), which is 15 M. long and 1 M. wide.

STEAMERS ply on the lake to various points of summer-resort. — Canandaigua is the N. terminus of the *Northern Central R. R.,* which runs hence to Philadelphia, Washington, and Baltimore. It is also the junction of a line to Buffalo viâ *Batavia.*

The stations hence to (394 M.) *Rochester* are unimportant.

Rochester (510 ft.; *Powers Hotel,* $4; *Livingston,* $2-3, R. from $1; *New Osburn,* $2-2½; Rail. Restaurant), a city of 133,896 inhab., situated on both sides of the *Genesee,* 7 M. from Lake Ontario, makes flour, beer, clothing, boots, and other articles to the annual value of $75,000,000. Near the middle of the city the river forms a perpendicular *Fall,* 90-100 ft. high (best seen from the new Platt

St. Bridge, reached from the Powers Hotel by following Main St. to the left, State St. to the left, and Platt St. to the right). The river forms two other falls to the N. within the city limits, the *Middle Fall*, 25 ft. high, and the *Lower Fall*, 85 ft. high. — *Main St.* crosses the river by a concealed bridge, lined on both sides with houses in the style of old London Bridge. A little to the N. of this, the Erie Canal is conducted over the river by an *Aqueduct*, 850 ft. long and 45 ft. wide, a fine piece of engineering. — The POWERS BUILDING, part of which is occupied by the *Powers Hotel*, contains (upstairs) the *Powers Gallery of Paintings* (adm. 25 c.), embracing many ascribed to masters of the first rank. A fine *View of the city is obtained from the tower (204 ft.). — The *University of Rochester* (200 students), in the E. part of the city, has good geological collections. — The *Warner Observatory*, East Avenue, a well-known private institution, with a 16-inch telescope, is open to visitors, if clear, on Tues. and Frid. (7-9 in winter, 8-10 in summer) by cards obtained at 60 N. St. Paul St. The *City Hall*, near West Main St., has a tower 175 ft. high. — *Mt. Hope Cemetery* is pretty, and the *Public Parks* are well laid out. — Interesting visits may be paid to the large *Flour Mills* and *Breweries* (lager-beer), lining the river, and to the extensive *Nurseries* in the outskirts of the city. Rochester is a great centre of Spiritualists and supporters of Woman's Rights.

Railways radiate from Rochester to Elmira and New York, Niagara Falls, *Ontario Beach* (on Lake Ontario; 7 M.), Pittsburg, etc. — A fine drive may be taken along the *Boulevard* to (7 M.) Lake Ontario.

The direct RAILWAY TO NIAGARA FALLS (74 M.) runs viâ *Lockport* to *Suspension Bridge* (p. 199) and the *Falls* (p. 199).

The train crosses the Genesee above the falls (not seen from the line). — 404 M. *Batavia*, with 7221 inhab. and the *State Blind Asylum*, is the junction of various railways. To the right is seen the monument to *William Morgan*, believed to have been murdered by the Free Masons in 1826 to prevent the publication of his book on the secrets of the craft. — 436 M. *East Buffalo.*

440 M. **Buffalo.** — Hotels. *HOTEL IROQUOIS (Pl. a; C,7), a well-built and finely equipped fire-proof structure, at the corner of Main and Eagle Sts., $ 4-5, R. from $ 1½; *NIAGARA HOTEL (Pl. b; B, 5), pleasantly situated in Prospect Park (with *View), about 2 M. from the rail. stations (electric cars), and sumptuously fitted up, with a winter-garden, $ 4-5; these are two of the finest hotels in the country. — GENESEE HO. (Pl. c; C, D, 6), TIFFT HO. (Pl. d; D, 7), Main St., $ 2½-4; STAFFORD (Pl. e; C, 7), $ 2; BROEZEL HO. (Pl. f; D, 7), close to Union Depot, $ 2½-3.

Railway Stations. *Union Depot* (Pl. D, 7), Exchange St., for trains of the N. Y. C., West Shore, Michigan Central, Lake Shore, W. N. Y. & P., Grand Trunk, and Buffalo and Pittsburg R. R.; *Erie Depot* (Pl. D, 7), Exchange St., a little to the E., also used by Lehigh Valley and N. Y. C. & St. L. R. R.; *Delaware & Lackawanna Depot* (Pl. C, 8), at the foot of Main St.

Steamboats ply regularly to the chief points on Lake Erie and the other Great Lakes.

Cabs. For 1 pers. for 1 M. 50 c., each pers. addit. 25 c., 2 M. 50 c. each, above 2 M. $ 1 each; per hour 1-4 pers., $ 1½; one article of luggage free, each addit. article 5-10 c. — Street Cars (*Tramways*) traverse all the principal streets (5 c.). — A Belt Railway Line, starting at the Union Depot, makes the circuit of the city (15 M.) in 3/4 hr. (fares 5-30 c.).

Post Office (Pl. C, D, 7), cor. of Seneca St. and Washington St.

Theatres. *Academy of Music* (Pl. C, 7), 245 Main St.; *Star Theatre* (Pl. C 7), cor. Pearl St. and Mohawk St.; *Corinne Lyceum* (Pl. C, 7), Washingto St., near Broadway; *Court St. Theatre* (Pl. C, 7); *Germania*, 331 Elliot St., performances in German.

Buffalo, the third in size of the cities of New York State, with (1890) 255,664 inhab., lies at the E. end of *Lake Erie*, at the mouth of the *Buffalo River* and head of the *Niagara River*, 20 M. above the *Niagara Falls*. It is well built, and many of its wide streets are shaded with trees and smoothly paved with asphalt.

The name of the city is supposed to be derived from the herds of buffalo which frequented the creek here entering the lake. The first dwelling for a white man was erected here in 1791, but it was not till after the construction of the Erie Canal in 1825 that the place increased with any great rapidity. Between 1880 and 1890 it added 100,000 souls to its population. The commerce of Buffalo is very great, as its situation makes it an emporium for much of the traffic with the great North-West. Its lake-harbour is safe and capacious, and it has several miles of water-front. Lumber, grain, coal (5-6 million tons), and cattle are among the chief articles of trade. The grain elevators have an aggregate capacity of 13-14 million bushels. The industries of Buffalo include brewing, distilling, oil-refining, car-building, and the manufacture of metal goods, soap, and starch. They employ 55,000 hands, while their produce in 1890 was valued at $ 101,000,000. The population includes a large proportion of Germans and many Poles and Italians.

Lake Erie (485 ft.), the second (counting from the E.) of the chain of Great Lakes between the United States and Canada, is 290 M. long and 65 M. wide. It is by far the shallowest of all, having an average depth of only 84 ft. It communicates with Lake Huron by the Detroit River (see p. 275) and pours its waters into Lake Ontario by the Niagara River (see p. 201). It is the scene of a very busy navigation. The first vessel to navigate the lake was built on the Niagara River by La Salle in 1679, and the first steamboat was launched in 1818.

To reach MAIN ST. (Pl. C-F, 1-8) from the *Union Depot* (Pl. D, 7), we proceed to the left (W.). Following Main St. to the right (N.), we soon reach the *Weed Block*, at the corner of Swan St., in which President Cleveland lived when in Buffalo. On the left is *St. Paul's Church* (Pl. C, 7), one of the most successful Gothic (E. E.) churches in America. A little back from the church, fronting on Franklin St., is the substantial *City Hall*, with a tower 200 ft. high (view). To the right, at the corner of Eagle St., is the imposing *Iroquois Hotel* (p. 192; view from roof). A little farther on the street crosses *Lafayette Square* (Pl. C, D, 7), with a *War Monument*. Here, to the right, at the corner of Broadway, stands the handsome *Public Library* (Pl. D, 7), which contains 65,000 vols. and various collections.

The spacious *Reading Room* on the ground-floor contains E. A. Poe's watch and a very interesting *Collection of autograph MSS. (Howells, G. E. Craddock, etc.). In one case is a *Manual of Arithmetic* published at Raleigh, N. C., during the Civil War (1863), open at a curious example.

On the first floor is the *Fine Arts Academy*, with a picture-gallery. — The *Buffalo Historical Society* (second floor) has interesting collections of relics. — In the basement is the museum of the *Society of Natural Sciences*.

Opposite the Public Library is the *Grosvenor Library* (40,000 vols.).

At the corner of Niagara St. stands the *Erie Co. Savings Bank*. Main St. then intersects the wide *Genesee Street* (Pl. C-F, 5-7). To the left, $^1/_2$ M. farther on, at the corners of Edward St., are the large *Music Hall* and the R. C. **Church of St. Louis* (Pl. D, 6).

The finest residence-street in Buffalo is **DELAWARE AVENUE* (Pl. C, D, 3-7), which begins at *Niagara Square* (Pl. C, 7) and runs to the W. of and parallel with Main St. At the corner of Niagara Sq. and Delaware Ave. is the house of *President Millard Fillmore* (1800-74), now a boarding-house. Among the other buildings in this street are *St. Joseph's College*, cor. of Church St.; the *Methodist Episcopal Church*, cor. of Tupper St.; **Trinity Church*, between Tupper and Edward Sts.; and the *Synagogue*, between Allen and North Sts.

Delaware Ave. leads to ($2^1/_2$ M.) *Forest Lawn Cemetery* (see below), but in the meantime we may turn to the left at ($1^1/_4$ M.) *North Street* (Pl. C-E, 5), another handsome residence-street, and follow it to ($^1/_2$ M.) the *Circle* (Pl. C, 5), containing the **First Presbyterian Church*. Beyond the Circle we follow *Porter Avenue*, which leads to ($^1/_4$ M.) the small *Prospect Park* (Pl. B, 5; with the *Niagara Hotel*, p. 192) and ($^1/_4$ M.) the **Front* (Pl. A, B, 5), a bold bluff on the Niagara River, affording a fine view of Lake Erie, the river, and the Canadian shore (1 M. distant). A little to the N. is *Fort Porter*, a small military station, now of no great importance. Continuing to follow *Niagara Street* along the river, we pass the *Waterworks* (with a 'crib' in the river) and *Fort Erie Ferry* (Pl. A, 4) and reach (2 M.) the **International Bridge** (Pl. A, 2), $^3/_4$ M. long, which crosses the river with the aid of *Squaw Island* and was completed in 1873 at a cost of $ 1,500,000 (300,000*l.*).

Retracing our steps to *FOREST AVENUE* (Pl. B-D, 2), we follow it towards the E., passing (left) the large grounds and buildings of the **State Insane Asylum** (Pl. C, 2; open on Mon., Wed., & Frid.). In $1^1/_2$ M. we reach one of the entrances to the **Park* (Pl. D, E, 1, 2), which is prettily laid out and contains a boating lake. Adjoining the park on the S. and E. is **Forest Lawn Cemetery* (Pl. D, E, 2, 3), with the grave of *President Fillmore* (see above). Near the S.W. entrance are a statue of the Indian chief *Red Jacket* and the *Nelson Blocher Monument*, the latter a piece of crude realism which has strong local admirers. Near the same entrance is a handsome *Crematorium* (Pl. D, 3).

On the S.E. Forest Lawn Cemetery is bounded by Main St., whence we may return to our hotel by tramway. Or we may follow it out for about $^1/_2$ M. to the HUMBOLDT PARKWAY (Pl. E, F, 2-4). This passes the *Driving Park* and *Fair Grounds* (Pl. E, F, 3, 4) and leads to ($1^1/_2$ M.) the **Parade** (Pl. F, 5), another portion of the park system, with the *Parade House* (Restaurant, with concerts, etc.) in the S.E. corner. Thence we may now return to Main St. by Genesee St. (tramway). — Those who have time may take a car on *Broadway* (Pl. D, F, 6, 7) and proceed through a German and Polish district, passing the *State Arsenal* (Pl. D, 7), to (3 M.) the terminus of the line. A little way farther out, to the left, are the **Wagner Palace*

Car Works, in which the wood-carving machines and other processes are interesting (visitors generally admitted on application). — Farther on in the same direction, beyond a labyrinth of railway-tracks, are a series of gigantic **Coal Elevators,** 1 M. long and 200 ft. high. — Among other buildings may be mentioned the *Post Office* (Pl. C, 7), cor. of Seneca and Washington Sts.; the *Board of Trade* (Pl. C, 7; view from roof), cor. of Seneca and Pearl Sts.; *St. Joseph's Cathedral* (R. C.; Pl. C, 7), Franklin St.; *Canisius College* (Pl. D, 6), Washington St., and several other R. C. institutions; and the *Erie County Almshouse,* N. Main St.

EXCURSION STEAMERS run from the foot of Main St. to *Fort Erie* (Canada) and other points of interest on the lake. Excursions may be also made to *Chautauqua* (p. 278), *Lakewood* (p. 278), etc.; but the favourite is, of course, that to **Niagara Falls* (p. 199), which may be made by railroad (see below) or steamer (return-fare 50c.). — Buffalo is an important railway-centre, lines radiating hence in all directions (see RR. 34, 46 etc.).

The N. Y. C. line from Buffalo to Niagara Falls descends along the right bank of the *Niagara River.* 444 M. *Black Rock;* 451 M. *Tonawanda;* 462 M. **Niagara Falls,** see p. 199.

Beyond the Falls station the line goes on to (2 M.) *Suspension Bridge* and (7 M.) *Lewiston* (p. 206), where it connects with the steamer to *Toronto.*

b. Viâ West Shore Railway.

452 M. RAILWAY to (428 M.) *Buffalo* in 11¹/₂-16 hrs. ($8); to (452 M.) *Suspension Bridge* in 12¹/₂-17 hrs. ($8). The through-cars do not run through Albany, but holders of unlimited tickets may go viâ Albany, on notice to the conductor. From Schenectady onwards this line follows almost the same route as the N. Y. C. R. R., having been constructed as a rival line and afterwards bought up by the N. Y. C. R. R. Co.

From New York to (128 M.) *Coeyman's Junction,* see R. 21 c. The Buffalo line here diverges to the left from that to *Albany* (R. 54). 142 M. *Voorheesville,* junction of a line to *Cobleskill,* etc. (R. 23); 152¹/₂ M. *South Schenectady* (see p. 186); 159¹/₂ M. *Rotterdam,* junction of the Fitchburg R. R. (see p. 135). Our line follows the S. bank of the *Mohawk,* parallel with the N. Y. C. R. R. on the N. bank. From (190 M.) *Canajoharie* coaches run to (8 M.) *Sharon Springs* (p. 158). 209 M. *Little Falls* (p. 187). From (216¹/₂ M.) *Mohawk* coaches run to (10 M.) *Richfield Springs* (p. 188). — 232 M. **Utica,** see p. 187. — At (259 M.) *Oneida Castle* we intersect the *N. Y., Ont., & W. R. R.* (from New York to *Oswego,* 326 M.). — 278 M. **Syracuse,** see p. 189. — 324 M. *Lyons.* Beyond (349 M.) *Fairport* the trains viâ (359 M.) *Rochester* (see p. 191) diverge to the right, while others keep on viâ (362 M.) *Genesee Junction.*

428 M. **Buffalo,** see p. 192.

From Buffalo to (452 M.) *Suspension Bridge,* Niagara, see above.

c. Viâ Delaware, Lackawanna, & Western Railway.

409 M. RAILWAY to *Buffalo* in 11¹/₂-12¹/₂ hrs. (fare $8; sleeper $2; parlor-car $1.50). The trains start from *Hoboken* (ferries from Barclay St. and Christopher St.; comp. p. 6).

13*

Hoboken, see p. 51. The train threads the *Bergen Tunnel* ($^7/_8$ M.) 11 M. *Passaic,* a town of 13,028 inhab., at the head of navigation on. the *Passaic River.* — 15 M. **Paterson** (*Franklin Ho.*, $2), an industrial city with 78,347 inhab. and large silk and cotton mills. The *Passaic Falls* here are 50 ft. high. — 34 M. *Denville* (520 ft.).

Another route of the same railway to this point leads viâ (8 M.) *Newark* (p. 208); 12 M. *Orange,* a pretty little suburban city of 18,844 inhab.; and (20 M.) *Summit* (380 ft.). — 37 M. *Denville,* see above.

From (48 M.) *Hopatcong* coaches run to (4 M.) *Lake Hopatcong* (725 ft.), $8^1/_2$ M. long and $3^1/_2$ M. wide, with several summer-hotels. — 51 M. *Stanhope* (870 ft.) is the station (stage) for ($2^1/_2$ M.) the pretty little *Budd's Lake.* — From (57 M.) *Hackettstown* (570 ft.) stages run to *Schooley's Mountain* (1200 ft.), another summer-resort (*Dorincourt Ho.*, *Heath Ho.*, $ $2^1/_2$-3). — 66 M. *Washington* (500 ft.) is the junction of a line to (14 M.) *Easton* (p. 227) and *Philadelphia.* Farther on our line penetrates the *Manunka Chunk Mt.* by the *Voss Gap Tunnel,* 330 yds. long. 77 M. *Manunka Chunk,* the junction of the Belvidere Division of the Penna. R. R. (for Philadelphia, etc.).

88 M. **Delaware Water Gap** (320 ft.; **Kittatinny House,* **Water Gap Ho.*, $ 3-4; *Glenwood,* $ 2-3), a group of hotels and cottages, at the **Water Gap,* or gorge, where the Delaware forces its way through the *Kittatinny* or *Blue Mts.*, the *Minsi* rising to the W. (in Pennsylvania) and *Tammany* (comp. p. 32) to the E. (in New Jersey). The gorge is about 2 M. long, with rocky sides 1500 ft. high, and is so narrow as barely to leave room for the railway and the river.

'Whether this immense chasm has been caused by one mighty eruption, or by a gradual yielding of stratum after stratum, by the immense pressure of the waters of a lake thousands of acres in area . . . is of course a subject of mere conjecture. . . . The evidences of the action of water and rocks hundreds of feet above the present level of the river-bed, and the masses of drift forming isolated hills and alluvial banks, indicate lake-like repose in the country now drained by the tributaries of the stream above the great gate in the mountain barrier' (*L. W. Brodhead's* 'Delaware Water Gap'). The Indian name of *Minisink* ('the water is gone'), applied to the country above the Gap, points to the traditional existence of this lake. Several other gaps in the Blue Mts. are of similar late formation (comp. pp. 227, 229). — The Gap should be seen from the river, the road, Table Rock, and Lovers' Leap.

WALKS (comp. Map supplied at the hotels). To *Eureka Falls,* the *Moss Grotto,* and *Rebecca's Bath,* by the carriage-road through the Gap to ($^2/_3$ M.) the first creek. — *Hunters' Spring,* $^1/_3$ M. farther up the **Eureka Glen,* is also reached by a white-marked path diverging to the right from the Mt. Minsi path (see below). — The *Silvan Way,* beginning at the small lake near the Water Gap House and indicated by white marks, leads viâ *Cooper's Cliff* and *Table Rock* (500 ft. above the river), to ($^1/_2$ M.) *Caldeno Falls,* the *Moss Cataract,* and *Diana's Bath.* — By turning to the left 200 yds. farther on we can descend to the ($^1/_4$ M.) *Ledge Path* (red marks) and follow it to the left, past the *Lovers' Retreat,* back to ($^1/_2$ M.) the hotel. — To ascend **Mt. Minsi** (1500 ft.; $1^1/_2$-2 hrs.) we follow the *Ledge Path* (see above; red marks), passing the *Lovers' Retreat* and *Winona Cliff,* and making a slight digression (path with yellow marks) to **Prospect Point* (1 M. from hotel; 700 ft. above the river; view). The top, 2 M. farther on, commands an extensive **View.* The summit is also known as the *Sappers' View,* from the *Honourable Corps of Sappers and Miners,* an association of New Yorkers and Philadelphians, which had about 100 officers of various grades to

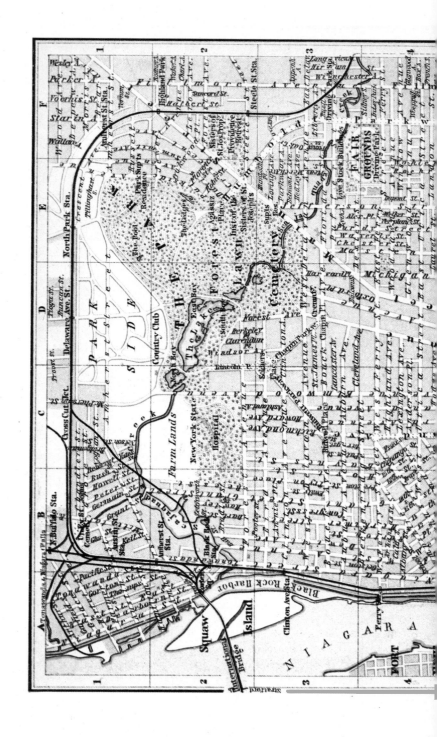

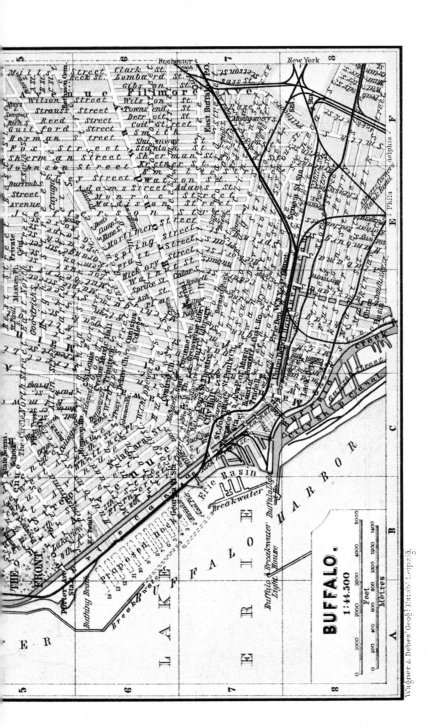

BUFFALO.

1:44.500

Wagner & Debes Geogr. Estab. Leipzig

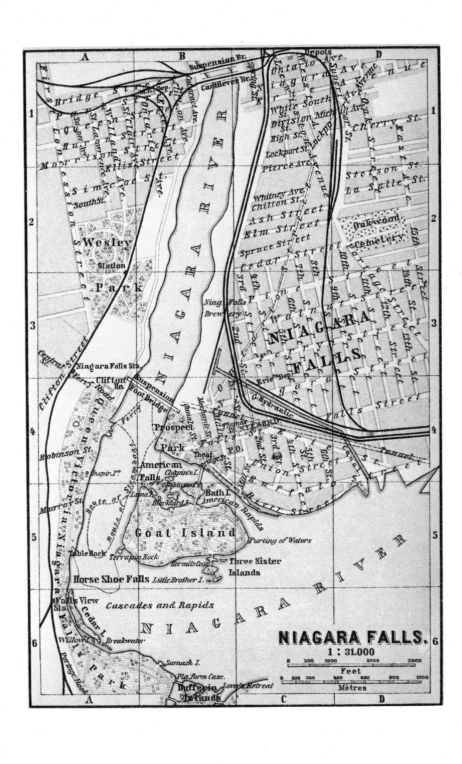

NIAGARA FALLS.

1 : 31.000

command a single individual known as the 'High Private'. This body
made many of the paths and roads in the vicinity. — On the top of
Winona Cliff is the *Lovers' Leap*, reached by a blue-marked path diverging
from the Ledge Path. — To ascend *Mt. Tammany* (1480 ft.; 1¹/₂-2 hrs.) we
cross the river and start below the slate-factory.

Among the favourite DRIVES are those to *Stroudsburg* (4 M.), *Deer Park*
and *Cherry Valley* (a round of 10 M.), *Buttermilk Falls* (3 M.), *Falls of
Winona* (12 M), *Marshall's Falls* (7 M.), and *Castle Rock* (4 M.).

A small STEAMER plies on the Delaware, and BOATS may be hired for
rowing or fishing. Among the places visited along the river are the *Indian
Ladder Bluff*, *Mather's Spring*, and the *Point of Rocks*.

From *Philadelphia* (p. 210) the Delaware Water Gap is reached by the
Pennsylvania R. R. in 3¹/₂ hrs., viâ *Trenton* (p. 209).

In leaving the Water Gap the train crosses *Brodhead Creek* and
penetrates *Rock Difficult* by a narrow cutting. — Beyond (92 M.)
Stroudsburg (400 ft.) we soon begin to ascend the steep slope of
Pocono Mt., passing through a tunnel near the top (view). At (118 M.)
Tobyhanna (1930 ft.) we begin to descend the W. slope of the
Allegheny Mts., at places very rapidly.

144 M. **Scranton** (1060 ft.; *Wyoming Ho.*, $2¹/₂-3¹/₂; *West-
minster*, $2-3), a city of (1890) 35,005 inhab., at the confluence
of the *Roaring Brook* and the *Lackawanna*, owes its importance to
the vast fields of anthracite coal in the neighbourhood. Its iron industries are extensive. — Beyond Scranton we pass several small
stations and enter *New York State* ('Empire State').

207 M. **Binghamton** (845 ft; *Arlington*, $2¹/₂-4; *Hotel Bennett*,
$2-3), a manufacturing town of 35,005 inhab., is the junction of
railways to Albany (D. & H. R. R.; p. 159), Richfield Springs
(p. 188), Syracuse (p. 189), Utica (p. 187), etc., and of the Erie
Railway (R. 28 d). — Our line here turns to the W. and follows the
same course as the Erie Railroad (p. 199), the one on the right
and the other on the left bank of the *Susquehanna*. 228 M. *Owego*
(815 ft.; Ahwaga, $2), at the confluence of the *Owego* and the
Susquehanna, is the junction of a line to Ithaca (p. 190).

263 M. **Elmira** (855 ft.; *Rathbun*, 2¹/₂-3; *Frasier, Delevan*, $2¹/₂;
Elmira Water-Cure), an industrial town with 30,893 inhab., contains
large rolling mills, the car-shops of the Erie Railroad, a Female
College, and an Academy of Science. The *Elmira Reformatory* has
played an important part in the reformatory treatment of criminals.

Railways radiate hence to *Watkins Glen* (p. 191) and *Rochester* (p. 191),
to *Ithaca* (p. 190) and *Canastota* (p. 189), to *Harrisburg* (p. 232) and *Philadelphia* (p. 210), and through the *Lehigh Valley* (p. 227).

278 M. **Corning** (930 ft.; Dickinson Ho., $2), with 8850 inhab.,
is the junction of lines to Rochester (p. 191) and Williamsport
(p. 230). At (324 M.) *Wayland* (1360 ft.) we part company with
the Erie line, which here turns to the N. 332 M. *Dansville* (1040 ft.;
Dansville Sanitarium, $3¹/₂-5); 363 M. *Rochester & Pittsburg Junc-
tion*, for lines to the N. to Rochester and to the S. to Pittsburg.

409 M. **Buffalo**, see p. 192.

From Buffalo to *Niagara Falls*, see p. 195 or p. 199.

d. Viâ Erie Railway.

444 M. NEW YORK, LAKE ERIE, AND WESTERN R. R. to (423 M.) *Buffalo*
in 12½ hrs. (fare $ 8; parlor-car or sleeper $ 2); to (444 M.) *Suspension
Bridge* in 13¼-17 hrs. (fares as above).
The train start from *Jersey City* (comp. p. 6; ferries from 23rd St.
and Chambers St.). — This line, constructed in 1836-52, passes some fine
scenery in penetrating the Allegheny Mts.

Jersey City, see p. 52. The train threads the *Bergen Tunnel*
(p. 196) and traverses the *Salt Marshes of the Hackensack.*

These extensive marshes, are covered with reeds and sedge grass,
growing in soft mud, which is sometimes 40 ft. deep. They are overfl-
owed at high tide.

Beyond (9½ M.) *Rutherford* we cross the *Passaic.* 12½ M.
Passaic (p. 196); 17 M. *Paterson* (see p. 196). At (32 M.) *Suffern*
(300 ft.) we enter *New York State* (p. 197). — 34 M. *Ramapo*, in
the picturesque valley of that name. — 38 M. *Tuxedo.*

About 1½ M. to the W. is **Tuxedo** Lake, the property of the *Tuxedo
Park Association*, a club of wealthy New Yorkers, who have made this
one of the most fashionable pleasure-resorts and game-preserves in the
country. On the shores of the lake are the club-house and the cottages
of members. This is a delightful place for visitors with an introduction.

48 M. *Turner's* (558 ft.; Rail. Rest.) is the junction of a line
to Newburg (p. 153). — 50 M. *Monroe* (Seven Springs Mt. Ho.).

About 9 M. to the S. lies *Greenwood Lake (1000 ft.), a favourite
resort, 10 M. long and 1 M. wide, also reached by a direct railway from
Jersey City. The chief hotels are the *Brandon House* ($ 3) and the *Winder-
mere* ($ 2½), in *Greenwood Lake Village*, at the N. end of the lake.

60 M. *Goshen*, junction of a line to Kingston and Rondout
(p. 153); 67 M. *Middletown* (Russell Ho., $ 2-3), with 11,977 in-
hab., junction of the New York, Ontario, & Western R. R. to *Oswego*
(comp. R. 28 b). Beyond (71 M.) *Howells* the line ascends the
Shawangunk Range, and the scenery improves. Beyond (76 M.)
Otisville the train reaches the summit (870 ft.) by a long rocky
cutting and begins to descend rapidly into the valley of the *Delaware.*

88 M. **Port Jervis** (440 ft.; *Delaware Ho., Fowler Ho.*, $ 2),
situated at the junction of the Delaware and the *Neversink*, is a village
of 9327 inhab., frequented as a summer-resort.

The *Tri-States Rock*, to the S. of the town, marks the meeting of New
York, New Jersey, and Pennsylvania. — Among the numerous picturesque
resorts within easy reach of Port Jervis are *High Point* (1960 ft.; The Inn,
$ 3) and *Lake Marcia*, 4 M. to the E., on the ridge of the *Kittatinny* or
Shawangunk Mts.; Milford (numerous inns), 7 M. to the S.W. (daily coach);
Dingman's Ferry (High Falls Ho., $ 2½), 15 M. to the S. (coach); and the *Falls
of the Sawkill*, not far from Milford. *Point Peter*, one of the twin mountains
overlooking the town, is a good point of view. The neighbourhood abounds
in good fishing streams. — A branch-line runs to (24 M.) *Monticello.*

Beyond Port Jervis the train crosses the Delaware into *Pennsylvania* ('Keystone State') and runs along its right bank, high above
the river. Great engineering difficulties were overcome in making
this part of the line, where the river-gorge is deep and tortuous. At
(111 M.) *Lackawaxen* (650 ft.) the Delaware and Hudson Canal
crosses the Delaware by an aqueduct. Like most of the other small

stations in the '*Delaware Highlands*' this is a summer-resort with several unpretending hotels and boarding-houses.

At (116 M.) *Mast Hope* we recross the river and re-enter New York. At (122 M.) *Narrowsburg* the valley is very narrow. Beyond (177 M.) *Deposit* (1010 ft.) we quit the Delaware, turn to the left (S.W.), and begin to ascend the ridge separating it from the Susquehanna. Fine scenery. From (184 M.) *Summit* (1375 ft.) we descend rapidly, soon obtaining a fine *View of the *Susquehanna* (right). We cross the *Cascade Bridge* (180 ft. high) and the *Starrucca Viaduct*, 1200 ft long and 110 ft. high. 193 M. *Susquehanna* (915 ft.), with railway repair-shops, lies on the left bank of the river. — The line now descends through the Susquehanna Valley. Beyond (215 M.) *Binghamton* (870 ft.; see p. 197) it runs parallel with the Lackawanna Railway (R. 28 c), on the opposite (right) bank. 237 M. *Owego* (p. 197); 274 M. *Elmira* (p. 197). At (291 M.) *Corning* (940 ft.; p. 197) a branch-line to Rochester (p. 191) runs to the right (N.), while the main line leaves the river and runs towards the E.

At (332) M. **Hornellsville** (1160 ft.; *Osborne Ho.*, *Page Ho.*, $2; *Rail. Restaurant*), a town of 10,996 inhab., with railroad-works, the Buffalo branch diverges to the right from the main line, which goes on to (414 M.) *Salamanca* and (460 M.) *Dunkirk* (see p. 278). — 362 M. *Portage* (1315 ft.; Ingham Ho., $2) is the station for the beautiful *Portage Falls*, formed here by the *Genesee River*.

The *Upper* or *Horseshoe Falls*, 70 ft. high, are 3/4 M. below the village. About 1/4 M. farther down are the *Middle Falls*, 110 ft. high, with a cave called the 'Devil's Oven' in the rocks near the foot of the precipice. For 2 M. farther the river descends through a narrow rocky defile and then reaches the *Lower Falls* (150 ft.).

The train crosses the Genesee by a bridge 235 ft. high, affording a view of the Upper and Middle Portage Falls. 365 M. *Castile* (1400 ft.); 368 M. *Silver Springs*, 6 M. from *Silver Lake*; 392 M. *Attica* (1000 ft.); 421 M. *East Buffalo* (610 ft.).

423 M. **Buffalo**, see p. 192.

The trains for Niagara Falls follow practically the same route as the N. Y. C. R. R. (p. 195). 432 M. *Tonawanda*; 438 M. *La Salle*; 442 M. *Niagara Falls* (see below); 444 M. *Suspension Bridge*. The trains cross the bridge in full view of the Falls (comp. p. 270) and connect at *Clifton* (p. 270) with the Grand Trunk Railway of Canada.

29. Niagara Falls.

Hotels. *CATARACT HOTEL, close to the river, with good cuisine, $4; INTERNATIONAL HOTEL, $4; KALTENBACH, well spoken of, with view of the river, $3; PROSPECT HOUSE, $31/2-51/2. The first two are open in summer only. These are all on the American side, in the city of *Niagara Falls*. — *CLIFTON HOUSE, on the Canadian side, near the end of the Suspension Bridge, with distant view of the Falls, $3-5 (open in summer only).

Railway Stations. *New York Central*, cor. of Falls St. and Second St., also used by the Michigan Central and the R. W. & O. railways; *Erie Station*, cor. of Niagara St. and Second Sts., also used by the Lehigh Valley R. R. — The Canadian lines make connection for Niagara Falls

at *Suspension Bridge*, 2 M. to the N.; and there are also stations on the
Canadian side at *Clifton* (see p. 270), *Niagara Falls, Ontario* (for the Clifton
House), and *Falls View* (comp. p. 271). — Niagara Falls, N. Y., is also
connected with Suspension Bridge by tramway (5 c.).

Carriages. The former extortionate charges and impertinent demeanour
of the Niagara hackmen have been greatly abated. The rates are $1¹/₂ for
the first and $1 for each addit. hr., with two horses $2 and $1¹/₂; but
it is always advisable to make a distinct bargain with the driver, and
lower terms than the legal rates may often be obtained, especially by a
party. It should be expressly stipulated who is to pay the tolls in crossing the bridges, etc.; and the driver should be strictly enjoined not to
stop at any of the bazaars or other pay-places unless ordered to do so.
A single-horse conveyance should not cost more than $3 for half-a-day
or $5 for a whole day. — *Park Vans* make the round of the American
Reservation at frequent intervals (fare 25 c., for Goat Island 15 c.), and
passengers are entitled to alight at any number of points and finish the
round by any subsequent vehicle on the same day. — *Omnibus* from the
station to the hotels 25 c.

Fees. Since the establishment of the American and Canadian National
Parks and Reservations, most of the former extortionate fees have been
abolished; and any visitor who is able to walk a few miles can see all
the chief points at very little cost. Goat Island and all the best views
of the Falls are free; and the only extra expenses which the visitor is
advised to incur are the trip in the '*Maid of the Mist*', including the visit
to the Canadian side (50 c.), the *Cave of the Winds* ($1), and the view of the
Grand Rapids from the Canadian side (50 c.) A visitor who 'does' *Goat
Island* and *Queen Victoria Park* and takes these three trips may safely
disregard all other attacks on his pocket. At present a toll (20 c., incl.
return) is exacted for crossing the bridges, but there is some hope that this
may be abolished and a real International Park formed. Driving is quite
unnecessary on the American side.

Bazaars. While the hackman nuisance has been abated, the bazaar
nuisance continues in full force; and it is so serious an annoyance that
many travellers hurry through their visit and leave Niagara much sooner
than they intended. It is impossible to walk through the streets or look
into the shop-windows without being annoyed by the most impudent and
persistent solicitations. A stony disregard of all such importunity is im-
peratively necessary, especially in the bazaars through which one approaches the inclined railways. The 'No charge for admission' is almost as
impudent a fraud as the 'Entrée Libre' of the Parisian cafés-chantants. No
purchases should be made at places to which tourists are taken by hackmen.
Those who wish Indian curiosities should buy from the Indians themselves.

Reservations. The *New York State Reservation at Niagara* comprises
107 acres and was opened in 1885. It includes *Prospect Park*. — The
Queen Victoria Niagara Falls Park, on the Canadian side, covers 154 acres
and was opened in 1888. — The New York Commissioners issue a folder
of useful 'Suggestions to Visitors', which may be obtained (free) at any
of the hotels or from the officers of the Reservation.

Plan and Season of Visit. The description in the text follows the
best order in which to visit the Falls. The American side is seen to
greatest advantage in the morning, the Canadian side in the afternoon,
the sun being then at our backs as we face the Falls. The Grand Rapids
are best seen from the Canadian side. It is possible to see all the chief
points in one day, but it is better to allow 2-3 days for the visit. May,
the first half of June, the second half of Sept., and Oct. are good seasons
to visit Niagara, which is hot and crowded in midsummer. No one who
has an opportunity to see them should miss the Falls in the glory of
their winter dress.

The **Falls of Niagara** ('Thunder of Waters'), perhaps the
greatest and most impressive of the natural wonders of America,
are situated on the *Niagara River*, 22 M. from its head in Lake Erie

and 14 M. above its mouth in Lake Ontario. This river forms the outlet of the four great Western lakes (Erie, Huron, Michigan, and Superior), descending about 330 ft. in its course of 36 M. and affording a channel to a large part of the fresh water in the globe. Its current is swift for about 2 M. after leaving Lake Erie, but becomes more gentle as the channel widens and is divided into two parts by *Grand Island*. Below the island the stream is $2^1/_2$ M. wide. About 15 M. from Lake Erie the river narrows again and the rapids begin, flowing with ever increasing speed until in the last $^3/_4$ M. above the Falls they descend 55 ft. and flow with immense velocity. On the brink of the Falls, where the river bends at right angles from W. to N., the channel is again divided by *Goat Island*, which occupies about one-fourth of the entire width of the river (4750 ft.). To the right of it is the **American Fall**, 1060 ft. wide and 167 ft. high, and to the left of it is the **Canadian** or **Horseshoe Fall**, 158 ft. high, with a contour of 3010 ft. The volume of water which pours over the Falls is 15 million cubic ft. per minute (about 1 cubic mile per week), of which probably nine-tenths go over the Canadian Fall.[†] Below the Falls the river contracts to 1000-1250 ft., and rushes down foaming and boiling between lofty rocky walls. Two miles farther down it is barely 800 ft. wide, and at the Whirlpool (see below) the huge volume of water is compressed into a space of 250 ft. Within 7 M. these lower rapids descend over 100 ft., but at Lewiston the river once more becomes wider and smoother.

The gorge through which the river runs has been formed by the action of the vast body of water rushing through it, and the Falls themselves are receding up the river at a rate which in 1842-90 averaged $2^1/_5$ ft. per annum on the Canadian side and $^2/_3$ ft. on the American side. The rocks passed through by the receding falls are sandstone, shale, and limestone. At present the formation over which the water pours is limestone, with shale lying 80-90 ft. below it; and the frequent fall of great masses of limestone rock is probably occasioned by the erosion of the underlying shales. At the Whirlpool the continuity of the rock-formation is interrupted, and the whole wall of the ravine is formed of drift. Geologists tell us that a farther retrocession of about 2 M. will cut away the layers of both limestone and shale and leave the falls stationary on the sandstone, with their height reduced about 50 per cent.

Niagara Falls appear under the name of Ongiara in Sanson's Map of Canada (Paris, 1657), but the first white man known to have seen Niagara Falls was *Father Hennepin*, a member of La Salle's party in 1678. He described them as 'a vast and prodigious Cadence of Water, which falls down after a surprizing and astonishing manner, insomuch that the Universe does not afford its Parallel' . . . The Waters which fall from this horrible Precipice do foam and boyl after the most hideous manner imaginable, making an outrageous Noise, more terrible than that of Thunder; for when the Wind blows out of the South, their dismal roaring may be heard more than 15 leagues off'. The sketch he made of the Falls shows several points of difference from their present state.

The Indians have a tradition that the Falls demand two human victims every year; and the number of accidents and suicides is perhaps large enough to maintain this average. Many lives have been lost in foolhardy attempts to cross the river above Goat Island.

---

† The international boundary passes through the middle of the so-called Canadian Fall.

The American city of *Niagara Falls* closely adjoins the river and contains (1890) 5502 inhabitants. The chief source of its prosperity has long been the influx of sightseers; but it now carries on many manufactures and when the great tunnel (see below) is completed, it expects to take a high place among the industrial centres of the country. It is estimated that about 400,000 tourists visit the Falls yearly. The *Museum* and *Cyclorama* need not detain the visitor.

A *Tunnel, 29 ft. deep and 18 ft. wide, is being excavated through the solid rock from a point just below the Suspension Road Bridge to a point about 1¼ M. above the Falls, where it will still be 165 ft. below the level of the river. It passes below the village at a depth of about 200 ft. A short canal will divert a portion of the river to the head of the tunnel, where a maximum of 120-150,000 horse-power will be attained by the descent of a stream of water which will not perceptibly diminish the volume of the Falls. The district upon which the mills are to be erected is quite out of sight of the Falls, the picturesque grandeur of which will not be any way marred by signs of intrusive utilitarianism. It is expected that the tunnel will be finished in 1893.

We may begin our visit to the Falls by entering **Prospect Park,** 12 acres in extent, which adjoins the gorge close to the American Fall. At *Prospect Point*, protected by a stone wall, we stand on the very brink of the Fall and see it dash on the rocks below. *Hennepin's View*, a little to the right (N.), commands a good general *View. The *Library Building* in the Park contains maps and charts. Near the point is the *Superintendent's Office*, whence an *Inclined Railway* (5 c.) and a *Flight of Steps* descend to the bottom of the gorge and the dock of the 'Maid of the Mist' (see below).

Following the parkway to the left (W.) from Prospect Point, we reach (3 min.) the *Goat Island Bridge* (360 ft. long), crossing the right arm of the river, a little above the American Fall. It commands a fine view of the *Upper Rapids*. To the right are several little rocky islets, including *Avery's Rock*, where an unfortunate man found foothold for 18 hrs. before being swept over the fall by the impact of a boat let out with ropes in an attempt to save him. The bridge ends at *Bath Island*, whence another short bridge crosses to *Goat Island** (80 acres in extent). Here we follow the path to the right to (4 min.) *Luna Island*, a rocky islet between the main American Fall and the *Centre Fall*, named from the lunar rainbows seen here at full moon. The continuation of the path along the W. side of Goat Island leads in a minute or two more to the *Biddle Stairs* (free) and the office where a guide and dress are obtained for a descent to the **Cave of the Winds** (fee $ 1; small gratuities expected by the guide and the boy who helps you to dress).

Everyone should descend the stairs and follow the path along the foot of the cliffs towards the base of the Horseshoe Falls; but only those of strong nerves should attempt the trip through the Cave of the Winds, which, however, is said to be safe and is often made by ladies †. For those who can stand it the experience is of the most exciting and pleasurable de-

---

† The first fatal accident here occurred in 1892 and seems to have been due to the unfortunate victim's own rashness.

scription. After passing over the gangways and bridges amid the rocks and spray in front of the Centre Fall, we are conducted through the 'Cave of the Winds' behind it, where the choking, blinding, and deafening tumult of wind and water defies description. The visitors grasp each other by the hand and sidle through on a narrow ledge, with a perpendicular wall of rock within an inch of their noses and the mighty volume of the fall at their backs.

Beyond the Biddle Stairs the path on Goat Island leads to (4 min.) *Porter's Bluff*, overlooking the Horseshoe Fall, the Canadian Rapids, and the ravine below the Falls. A staircase and bridge descend hence to *Terrapin Rock, on the edge of the Horseshoe Falls, affording the best view of these from this side. The tower which used to be here has been removed as unsafe.

'The river here is evidently much deeper than the American branch, and instead of bursting into foam where it quits the ledge, it bends solidly over and falls in a continuous layer of the most vivid green. The tint is not uniform, but varied, long strips of deeper hue alternating with bands of brighter colour ... From all this it is evident that beauty is not absent from the Horseshoe Fall, but majesty is its chief attribute. The plunge of the water is not wild, but deliberate, vast, and fascinating' *(Tyndall).* — A condemned warship sent over the Fall in 1829 drew 18 ft. of water, but passed without touching the ledge.

Our path next leads along the S. side of Goat Island to (7-8 min.) the series of bridges leading to the **Three Sister Islands*, which afford the best view of the imposing ***Canadian Rapids**, running at the rate of 30 M. an hour. The Third Sister is adjoined by a smaller rock known as the *Little Brother*.

We may now return through the centre of Goat Island to (5 min.) the bridge leading to the mainland, but those who have time should follow the path to (4 min.) the 'Parting of the Waters' at the head of Goat Island, where we obtain a good view of the broad and quiet river above the cascades, with *Grand Island* (p. 205) in the background. Thence the path leads back along the N. side of Goat Island, affording a view of the *American Rapids*, to (5-6 min.) the bridge.

We may now cross to the Canadian side of the river by the ***New Suspension Bridge**, about 250 yds. below the Falls (see p. 200).

The present graceful structure, which has a span of 1268 ft. between the towers, was erected in 1889 in place of a similar bridge which was carried away bodily by the tremendous storm of Jan. 10th in that year. It is 190 ft. above the level of the water.

'Of all the bridges made with hands this seems the lightest, most ethereal; it is ideally graceful, and droops from its slight towers like a garland ... In front, where tumbled rocks and expanses of naked clay varied the gloomier and naked green, sprung those spectral mists; and through them loomed out, in its manifold majesty, Niagara, with the seemingly immovable white Gothic screen of the American Fall, and the green massive curve of the Horseshoe, solid and simple and calm as an Egyptian wall; while behind this, with their white and black expanses broken by dark-foliaged little isles, the steep Canadian rapids billowed down between their heavily wooded shores' ('Their Wedding Journey', by *W. D. Howells*). On the American shore is seen the so-called *Bridal Veil*, the 'end of a poor but respectable mill-race, which has devoted itself strictly to business, and has turned mill-wheels instead of fooling round water-lilies' *(Howells).* Above are the few mills and manufactories that have been left in the neighbourhood of the Falls. Below is the mouth of the tunnel described at p. 202.

On reaching the Canadian end of the bridge, we turn to the left, pass the Clifton House (p. 199), and reach (3 min.) the entrance to the *Queen Victoria Niagara Falls Park, which extends along the river for 2¹/₂ M. Splendid general views are obtained as we proceed of the Falls and the gorge, especially from the (3 min.) **Rambler's Rest* and (4 min.) **Inspiration Point*. To the right, 3-4 min. farther on, are *Picnic Grounds* and a *Restaurant;* and in 3 min. more we reach the *Table Rock House* and **Table Rock, which affords an indescribably grand view of the Horseshoe Falls. Beautiful rainbows are seen on the spray in the afternoon. The roar of the water is deafening.

The name of Table Rock still adheres to this point, though the last portion of the overhanging ledge that gave rise to it fell into the abyss in 1850. — An elevator here affords an opportunity to those who wish to go under the Falls (25c, with dress 50c.). This trip is not so interesting as that to the Cave of the Winds, but may be taken by those who wish to exhaust the sensations of the Falls.

Visitors with time to spare may extend their walk through the Park above the Falls to (3-4 min.) *Cedar Island* and (1 M.) *Dufferin Islands, enjoying good views of the Canadian Rapids (p. 203). On the mainland, just beyond the Dufferin Islands, is the interesting *Burning Spring* (adm. 50c.), highly charged with sulphuretted hydrogen gas, which burns with a pale blue flame. — *Falls View Station* of the Michigan Central R.R. (see p. 271), lies just outside the Park, opposite the lower end of Cedar Island. — A road diverging near Table Rock leads to the battlefield of *Lundy's Lane*, where the Anglo-Canadian forces defeated the Americans after a bloody struggle on July 25th, 1814.

No one should omit to take the **Trip in the little steamer the *Maid of the Mist*, which starts near the foot of the Inclined Railway descending from the Library (see p. 202), steams up the river nearly to the foot of the Horseshoe Fall, and touches at a wharf on the Canadian side (fee 50c., incl. water-proof dress). The **View it affords of the Falls is one of the best to be had; and the trip is perfectly safe. Passengers may disembark on the Canadian side (where a steep path ascends to the National Park) and return by any later trip of the steamer the same day.

The river and its banks below the New Suspension Bridge are not included in the National Reservations, but offer many points of great interest. The Lower Rapids and the Whirlpool (see p. 205) are both seen to greatest advantage from the Canadian side.

From the N. end of the bridge we follow the road descending along the edge of the cliff to (2 M.) the *Cantilever Bridge of the *Michigan Central Railroad*, one of the first examples of this method of construction, completed in 1883. It is entirely of steel and has a total length of 900 ft. The two cantilever arms, 395 ft. and 375 ft. long, are connected in the centre by a fixed span of 125 ft. It is 245 ft. above the water. About 100 yds. below this bridge is the **Railway Suspension Bridge*, finished in 1855, with a roadway below the railroad track (toll 10 c. for each pers., incl. return). and 245 ft. high, and is used by the Grand Trunk and Erie Railroads. It commands a fine view of the Whirlpool Rapids, but the

It is 825 ft. long view of the Falls is obstructed by the Cantilever Bridge.

A little below the Suspension Bridge is the entrance to the so-called *Rapids Park*, where we descend an Inclined Railway (50 c.) to view the **Whirlpool Rapids*, which in their own way are as wonderful as the Falls. The immense volume of water is here forced to flow through so narrow a channel (300 ft.) that it actually assumes a convex form, the centre of the river being 20-30 ft. higher than the edges. Three other elevators (each 50 c.) descend to the Rapids on the American side.

The impression of force is overwhelming. 'The surges did not look like the gigantic ripples on a river's course, as they were, but like a procession of ocean billows; they rose far aloft in vast bulks of clear green, and broke heavily into foam at the crest' (*Howells*).

It was in an effort to swim down these Rapids that Capt. Webb lost his life in 1883, but since then several persons have passed through them safely in barrels. The old 'Maid of the Mist' was successfully piloted through the Rapids to Lewiston in 1861. Blondin and others have crossed the gorge above the Rapids on ropes of hemp or wire.

We may now cross the railway Suspension Bridge and return along the American side (tramway, see p. 200).

About 1 M. below the Railway Suspension Bridge is the **Whirlpool*, of which we get a good distant view from the top of the cliff, while we may descend to its margin by an inclined railway (50 c.). The river here bends suddenly at right angles to its former course, and the Whirlpool is occasioned by the full force of the current impinging against the cliffs of the left bank.

'Here within the compass of a mile, those inland seas of the North, Superior, Huron, Michigan, Erie, and the multitudes of smaller lakes, all pour their floods, where they swirl in dreadful vortices, with resistless undercurrents boiling beneath the surface of that mighty eddy. Abruptly from this scene of secret power, so different from the thunderous splendours of the cataract itself, rise lofty cliffs on every side, to a height of two hundred feet, clothed from the water's edge almost to their crests with dark cedars. Noiselessly, so far as your senses perceive, the lakes steal out of the whirlpool, then, drunk and wild, with brawling rapids roar away to Ontario through the narrow channel of the river. Awful as the scene is, you stand so far above it that you do not know the half of its terribleness; for those waters that look so smooth are great ridges and rings, forced, by the impulse of the currents, twelve feet higher in the centre than at the margin. Nothing can live there, and with what is caught in its hold, the maelstrom plays for days, and whirls and tosses round and round in its toils, with a sad maniacal patience' (*Howells*).

The RIVER ROAD ascends along the American side of the river from Goat Island Bridge to (1 M.) the *Old French Landing*, where La Salle and Father Hennepin are said to have embarked in 1678 after their portage from Lewiston. Nearly opposite, on the Canadian shore, is the village of *Chippewa*, where the Americans defeated the English in 1814. About 1 M. farther up is the *Schlosser Landing*, fortified by the French in 1750 and by the English in 1761. *Navy Island*, near the Canadian shore, gave shelter to the insurgents of the 'Mackenzie War' (1837-38). Just above is *Grand Island* (26 sq. M. in area), which obtained some notoriety in 1820, when Major Noah proposed to found here the city of Ararat, as a universal refuge for the Jews. Opposite Grand Island, on the American shore, 5 M. above the Falls, is the mouth of the *Cayuga*, where La Salle launched the 'Griffon', the first vessel to navigate the Great Lakes (1679).

The *Observation Trains* of the N.Y.C.R.R. between *Niagara Falls* and
(7 M.) *Lewiston* (return-fare 25 c.) afford admirable *Views (to the left) of
the gorge of the Niagara. — *Lewiston*, a pleasant little village, is the
starting-point of the steamers across Lake Ontario to *Toronto*. — On the
opposite shore, on the Michigan Central R.R., is *Queenston*, where Gen.
Brock fell on Oct. 11th, 1812 (spot marked by a monument 195 ft. high).
— About 8 M. to the N.E. of Niagara Falls is the *Reservation of the Tuscarora Indians* (p. 187; baskets, etc., for sale). — *Fort Niagara*, at the
(14 M.) mouth of the river, first established in 1678, is now garrisoned by
U.S. troops. Opposite is the watering-place of *Niagara-on-the-Lake*.

30. The St. Lawrence River and the Thousand Islands.

Passengers who make the St. Lawrence trip from American soil usually join the steamer at *Clayton* (see below), which is reached from New
York (346 M.) viâ the *N. Y. C. R. R.* to (238 M.) *Utica* and the *Rome,
Watertown, & Ogdensburg R. R.* thence (10 hrs.; through-carriages; fare
$ 8.27; comp. R. 28 a). — The Montreal steamer of the *Richelieu & On-
tario Navigation Co.* leaves *Toronto* in the evening, and *Kingston* (where
it receives most of its passengers) about 5 a.m., calling at Clayton 1 hr.
later (fare from Clayton to Montreal $5.25). — Those who wish merely
to visit the Thousand Islands may do so by the steamer 'St. Lawrence',
which makes daily round trips from Clayton (fare 50 c.). Comp. *Baedeker's
Handbook to Canada*.

The **St. Lawrence**, the outflow of the Great Lakes, has a length (from
Lake Ontario to its mouth) of 500 M. and pours more fresh water into the
Ocean than any other river except the Amazon. It is navigable for large
vessels to Montreal and for small steamers all the way, though some of
the rapids have to be avoided by means of canals by boats ascending the
river (comp. p. 207). During 4-5 months, however, the navigation of the
lower St. Lawrence is stopped by ice. Comp. *Baedeker's Canada*.

Distances in the following route are calculated from Kingston.

Kingston (*British American Hotel*, $ 2-3), a city of 19,264 inhab.,
with picturesque fortifications, situated at the point where the St.
Lawrence issues from *Lake Ontario*, is described in *Baedeker's Canada*. A small steamer plies regularly to *Cape Vincent*.

On leaving Kingston our steamer almost at once begins to traverse
the expansion of the St. Lawrence known as the ***Lake of the Thousand Islands**, which is 40 M. long and 4-7 M. wide and contains
about 1700 islands, big and little. Many of these islands are favourite
summer-resorts, with hotels and boarding-houses, while others are
private property, with the country-houses of rich Americans and
Canadians. The voyage through them is picturesque, and many of
the islands are illuminated at night. Our course at first lies between
Wolfe or *Long Island* (r.) and *Howe Island* (l.).

25 M. (r.) **Clayton** (*Hubbard, Walton, Windsor*, $ 2½), a vil-
lage and summer-resort with 1748 inhab., is the terminus of the R.,
W., & O. R. R. from (103 M.) Utica (comp. p. 108). Opposite is the
large *Grindstone Island*, behind which, on the Canadian shore, lies
Gananoque.

28 M. (r.) *Round Island*, with the large *Hotel Frontenac* ($ 3-4).

31 M. (l.) **Thousand Island Park** (*Columbian*, $ 3; *Thousand
Island Park Ho.*, $ 2½), a great Methodist resort, at the W. end of
Wells Island.

39 M. (r.) **Alexandria Bay** (*Crossmon*, $4; *Thousand Isle Ho.*, $3-5; *Central Park Ho.*, $2-3), the chief resort among the Thousand Islands, lies on the American shore opposite Wells Island, and counts pretty scenery and good boating and fishing among its attractions. Among the most prominent villas on the neigbouring islets are those of *George M. Pullman* (p. 286) and *H. H. Warner* (of the 'Safe Cure'). — *Westminster Park* (Hotel Westminster, $2-3) lies at the E. end of Wells Island, opposite Alexandria Bay.

Farther on we pass the *Summerland Islets* (l.) and the long *Grenadier Island* (l.), leave the Lake of the Thousand Isles, and reach the open river, here about 2 M. wide. For some distance now the voyage is monotonous and uninteresting.

63 M. (r.) *Morristown* (Terrace Park Hotel, $2-3).

64 M. (l.) **Brockville** (*Revere*, *St. Lawrence Hall*, $2½) is a Canadian city with 8793 inhab. and good fishing.

76 M. (l.) *Prescott* (Daniels Ho., $2-3).

77 M. (r.) **Ogdensburg** (*Seymour Ho.*, $2), a city with 11,662 inhab. and a trade in grain. From Ogdensburg to *Rouse's Point*, see p. 115; to *Rome* and *Utica*, see p. 188.

About 10 M. below Ogdensburg we pass through the *Galoup Rapids*, which are followed, 10 M. lower, by the *Rapid du Plat*. Neither of these is very noticeable, though each is avoided by a canal (Canadian side) in going up stream. Between the two rapids we pass the narrowest point in the river (500 ft.). Numerous islands.

97 M. (l.) *Morrisburg*, just below the Rapid du Plat.

102 M. (r.) *Louisville Landing*, whence stages run to (7 M.) *Massena Springs* (Hatfield Ho., $1½; Harrowgate Ho.; comp. p.189).

113 M. (l.) *Dickinson's Landing*, at the head of the *Long Sault Rapids, between the Canadian shore and *Long Sault Island*. The rapids are 9 M. long and are tumultuous enough to give a slight suggestion of danger to the process of 'shooting' them. They are avoided in ascending by the *Cornwall Canal*, 12 M. long.

125 M. Cornwall (*Rossmore Ho.*, $2-2½), a town of 6805 inhab., at the foot of the Long Sault Rapids. — The boundary between the United State and Canada bends away from the river here, and the Indian village of *St. Regis*, opposite Cornwall, is in the *Province of Quebec*. The *Adirondack Mts.* (p. 165) are now visible to the right.

140 M. *Lancaster* lies on the expansion of the river named *Lake St. Francis*, 28 M. long and 5-7 M. wide. — Beyond (155 M.) *Port Louis* (r.) both banks are in Quebec.

At (165 M.) *Coteau Landing* the river is crossed by a railway swing-bridge (comp. *Baedeker's Canada*). We now enter a series of rapids which follow each other at short intervals, with a combined length of 20 M.: *Coteau Rapid*, *Cedar Rapid*, *Split Rock Rapid*, and the *Cascades. The large Roman Catholic churches of the villages that line the banks are now very conspicuous.

173 M. (r.) *Beauharnois*, at the foot of this series of rapids, lies

opposite the mouth of the *Ottawa River*, which enters the St. Lawrence by two channels, enclosing the island of *Perrot*. The village of *Ste. Anne*, on the E. bank of the E. branch, is the scene of Tom Moore's well-known 'Canadian Boat Song'. — The *Lake of St. Louis*, which we now traverse, is 12-15 M. long.

198 M. (l.) *Lachine* (Lake View, Hanna, $2) lies at the head of the famed *Lachine Rapids, the shortest (3 M.) but most violent of all, forming an exciting and dramatic close to our voyage. The rapids begin just below the fine bridge of the *Canadian Pacific Railway*. Soon after leaving the rapids we pass under the *Victoria Tubular Bridge*. To the left lies —

207 M. **Montreal** (see *Baedeker's Handbook to Canada*).

31. From New York to Philadelphia.

a. Viâ Pennsylvania Railroad.

90 M. RAILWAY in 2¼-2½ hrs. (fare $ 2½; parlor-car 50 c.). The huge railway-station is in *Jersey City* (p. 6; ferries from Desbrosses St. and Cortlandt St. and from Brooklyn).

The **Pennsylvania Railroad** has, perhaps, the strongest claim to the title of the leading railway of the United States in right of its combination of extent of system, punctuality of service, excellence of road-bed, civility of employees, and comfort of equipment (comp. p. 247).

Jersey City, see p. 51. The train runs to the W. to (9 M.) **Newark** (*Continental*, *Park*, $ 2-3), a prosperous but uninteresting city on the *Passaic*, with 181,830 inhab., large breweries, and extensive manufactures of jewelry, iron goods, celluloid, paper, and leather (value in 1890, $ 82,000,000). *Thomas A. Edison*, the inventor, has his home and workshop here. The line passes through the town 'at grade'. — At (14½ M.) *Elizabeth* (Sheridan Ho., $ 2-2½), a well laid-out city with 37,764 inhab., we cross the Central R.R. of New Jersey. — 19½ M. *Rahway*, with 7105 inhab. and considerable trade and manufactures. 24 M. *Menlo Park*, the rural home of Thomas A. Edison, the 'Wizard of Menlo Park'. — 31½ M. **New Brunswick** (*Palmer Ho.*, $ 2½), on the *Raritan*, a manufacturing city of 18,603 inhab., is the site of *Rutgers College* (seen to the right), a well-known institution of the Dutch Reformed Church, chartered in 1770 (250 students). In entering the city we cross a bridge over the river, the *Delaware & Raritan Canal*, and the road. — At (41 M.) *Monmouth Junction* diverges the line to Long Branch, etc. (R. 33 c.) — 47 M. *Princeton Junction*, for the branch to (3 M.) *Princeton* (The Nassau, $ 3), with 3422 inhabitants.

Princeton College or *College of New Jersey*, founded at Elizabeth (see above) in 1746 and transferred to Princeton in 1757, ranks high among the American universities and is attended by about 800 students. It is under the control of the Presbyterians, and the *Princeton Theological Seminary* is considered one of the bulwarks of orthodoxy. The college buildings, among the chief of which are *Nassau Hall*, *Dickinson Hall*, the *School of Science*, *Marquand Chapel*, the *Art Museum*, and the *Library* (80,000 vols.), stand in a beautiful tree-shaded 'campus'. — The *Battle of Princeton* (Jan.

3rd, 1777), in which Washington defeated the British, was one of the most important in the early part of the Revolutionary struggle.

The line now descends towards the *Delaware.* 57 M. **Trenton** (*Trenton, Windsor,* $2^1/_2$-$3^1/_2$; *American,* $2-3$), the capital of New Jersey, is a well-built town, situated on the Delaware, at the head of navigation. Pop. 57,458. Its chief industry is the making of pottery (value in 1890, $4,500,000), the material for which is found on the spot. The *State House* is a handsome edifice overlooking the river; the *State Lunatic Asylum* and *Penitentiary* are large buildings. The *Delaware & Raritan Canal* intersects the city.

On Dec. 26th, 1776, Washington crossed the Delaware here and surprised and routed the Hessians under Rall, following up this success by the battle of Jan. 2nd, 1777, in which he maintained his ground against Lord Cornwallis. — Trenton is the junction of a branch to *Manunka Chunk* and the *Delaware Water Gap* (see R. 28 c).

Bordentown (*Bordentown Ho.,* $2), about 5 M. to the S. of Trenton, was from 1815 till 1832 the home of Joseph Bonaparte, ex-king of Spain, whose fine park is still shown.

Crossing the Delaware, we now enter the 'Keystone State' of *Pennsylvania* and traverse a rich farming country. To the right is the canal. At (58 M.) *Morrisville* the French general Moreau lived from 1806 to 1813, in a house built by Robert Morris, the 'banker of the Revolution'. 67 M. *Bristol.* As we approach Philadelphia we leave the Delaware and traverse a district full of mills, manufactories, and artizans' dwellings. 85 M. *Germantown Junction,* an important suburban railway-centre (comp. p. 221).

As we enter Philadelphia we cross and recross the *Schuylkill* ('Skoolkill'). *Views of the city and Fairmount Park (p. 220).

90 M. **Philadelphia** (Broad Street Station), see p. 210.

b. Viâ Royal Blue Line.
(Bound Brook Route).

89 M. CENTRAL R. R. OF NEW JERSEY and PHILADELPHIA & READING R. R. in 2-4 hrs. (fares as above). The route is much the same as the Penna. R. R. — Station in *Jersey City* (see p. 6; ferry from Liberty St.).

Jersey City, see p. 5. The train crosses *Newark Bay* by a bridge 2 M. long, with views of *Newark* (p. 208) to the right and *Staten Island* (p. 50) to the left. 11 M. *Elizabethport,* the junction of branches to Newark and to the New Jersey seaside-resorts (R. 33), is the site of the Singer Sewing Machine Co. (3300 hands). 13 M. *Elizabeth* (see p. 208). — 24 M. *Plainfield* (Albion, $2), an industrial town with 11,267 inhab. On the *Orange Hills,* to the right, is *Washington's Rock,* whence that general is said to have observed the movements of the British troops. — At (30 M.) *Bound Brook,* on the *Raritan,* we pass on to the tracks of the *Philadelphia & Reading R. R.* In 1777 the Americans were defeated here by Lord Cornwallis. The line now traverses cornfields and orchards. — From (48 M.) *Trenton Junction* a short branch-line runs to (4 M.) *Trenton* (see above). Our line crosses the *Delaware* by a fine bridge (views) at (50 M.)

Yardley. 67 M. *Langhorne*, a summer-resort of the Philadelphians;
79 M. *Jenkintown*, the junction of a line to Bethlehem (p. 226).
From (85 M.) *Wayne Junction* lines radiate in all directions.
89 M. **Philadelphia** (Reading Terminal Station; see below).

32. Philadelphia.

Railway Stations. *Broad Street Station* (Pl. F, 6), facing the City
Hall, for the trains of the Pennsylvania R. R. to New York, Balti-
more, Washington, Pittsburg, Chicago, and numerous local lines; *Reading
Terminal Station* (Pl. F, 6), of the Philadelphia and Reading R. R., for
New York (R. 31b), Washington, Baltimore, Gettysburg, Lehigh Valley,
etc.; *Baltimore & Ohio Station* (Pl. E, 6), cor. of Chestnut St. and 24th St.,
for Washington, the West, etc.; *Market St. Ferry Station* (Pl. H, 6) and
West Jersey Railroad Station (Pl. I, 6), Camden, reached by ferry from
Market St., for Cape May and the Amboy Division of the Penna. R. R.;
Camden & Atlantic Station (Pl. I, 5), Camden (ferries from Market, Vine,
and Shackamaxon Sts.), for trains to Atlantic City, Cape May, and other
New Jersey points; *Philadelphia & Atlantic City Railroad Station* (Pl. I, 8),
Camden (ferry from Chestnut St. or South St.), for Atlantic City, etc.
Aslo numerous *Suburban Stations.* — *Tramways* run from all these stations
or ferries to the chief centres of the city, and *Hotel Omnibuses* (25 c.) meet
the principal trains. *Cabs*, see below.

Hotels. *STRATFORD (Pl. a; F, 6), Broad and Walnut Sts., handsomely
furnished, R. from $2; *BELLEVUE (Pl. b; F, 6), at the opposite cor. of
Broad and Walnut Sts., R. from $2, good cuisine; LAFAYETTE (Pl. c; F, 6),
Broad and Sanson Sts., $4; COLONNADE (Pl. d; F, 6), Chestnut and 15th
Sts., $3¹/₂, R. from $1; ALDINE (Pl. e; E, 6), 1910 Chestnut St., a good
family hotel, $3¹/₂-5; CONTINENTAL (Pl. f; G, 6), GIRARD HOUSE (Pl. g; G,
6), 9th and Chestnut Sts., $3-4; GREEN'S (Pl. h; G, 6), 8th and Chestnut Sts.,
R. from $1, for men; BINGHAM (Pl. i; F, 6), 11th and Market Sts., $2¹/₂.

Restaurants. *Bellevue Hotel*, see above, somewhat expensive; *Boldt*,
Bullet Building, 4th St., below Chestnut St.; *Schafer*, Library St.; *Colonnade Hotel*, see above; *Dooner*, 10th St., above Chestnut St.; *Green*, see
above; *Reisser*, 5th St., above Chestnut St., for men, with a 'Rathskeller'
downstairs; *Boothby*, Chestnut St., near 13th St. (oysters); *Partridge*,
19 S. 8th St.; *Wanamaker's*, see p. 213; *Dennett's Lunch Rooms*, 529 Chestnut St., 13 S. 9th St., and 1313 Market St. (low prices).

Tramways (*Street Cars*). Electric, Cable, or Horse Cars traverse all
the principal streets (fare 5 c., transfer-tickets 8 c.). Cars run to the E.
on Columbia Ave., Jefferson, Girard Ave., Wallace, Green, Spring Garden,
Callowhill, Race, Arch, Filbert, Market, Chestnut, Spruce, and Lombard
Streets; to the W. on Columbia Ave., Master, Girard Ave., Poplar, Fairmount Ave., Spring Garden, Callowhill, Vine, Arch, Market, Sansom,
Walnut, Pine, and South Streets; to the N. on 3rd, 5th, 8th, 9th, 11th,
13th, 16th, 18th, 19th, and 23rd Streets; to the S. on 2d, 4th, 6th, 7th,
10th, 12th, 15th, 17th, 19th, 20th, and 23rd Streets. — *Omnibuses* ply up
and down Broad St. and in Diamond St. (5 c., transfers 6 c.).

Cabs. — (1). *Pennsylvania R.R. Service.* Hansoms (1-2 pers.) 1¹/₂ M., 25 c.,
each 1 M. addit. 15 c., per hr. 65 c., each addit. ¹/₄ hr. 20 c.; no trunks
carried. Four-wheelers: 1-2 pers., 40 c., 20 c., 75 c., 20 c.; each addit. pers.
10 c.; each trunk 25 c., small article carried outside 10 c. — (2). *Reading R.
R. Service.* Four-wheelers, 1-2 pers. 50 c., 25 c., 75 c., 25 c.; each addit. pers.
25 c. — (3). *City Service.* Carriages (two horses): 1 pers., 1 M. 75 c., 2 pers.
$1.25, each addit. pers. 25 c.; 2 M., $1.25, $1.75, 25 c.; each 1 M. addit.,
each pers. 50 c.; per. hr., 1-2 pers., $1.50, each pers. addit. 25 c. One trunk
or valise free, each extra article of luggage 6 c.

Ferries cross the Delaware to *Camden* (p. 221) from Market, Vine,
South, Chestnut, and Shackamaxon Sts. (3 c.), and to *Gloucester* from
South St. (10 c.).

Steamers. Steamers ascend the Delaware to *Burlington* and other points. Steamers also ply to *Liverpool* (Wed.; 'American Line'), *Antwerp*, *New York, Boston, Baltimore, Savannah, Charleston, Florida*, etc.

Theatres. *Academy of Music* (Pl. F, 7), Broad St., cor. of Locust St. (2900 seats), used for operas, concerts, balls, etc.; *Chestnut Street Opera House* (Pl. G, 6), 1023 Chestnut St.; *Chestnut Street Theatre* (Pl. F, 6), 1211 Chestnut St.; *Broad St. Theatre* (Pl. F, 7), near Locust St.; *Arch Street Theatre* (Pl. G, 6), 613 Arch St. (1800 seats); *Park Theatre* (Pl. F, 4), Broad St., cor. of Fairmount Ave. (2200 seats); *Grand Opera House* (Pl. F, 3), N. Broad St., cor. of Montgomery Ave.; *Eleventh Street Opera House* (Pl. F, 6), near Chestnut St. (minstrel entertainments); *Germania*, 526 N. 3rd St. (German); *Empire Theatre* (Pl. F, 7), cor. of Broad and Locust St.; *National Theatre* (Pl. G, 5), 10th St. and Callowhill St. (varieties).

Post Office (Pl. G, 6), cor. of Chestnut St. and 9th St.; also several sub-stations and numerous letter-boxes.

Exhibitions of Art. *Academy of Fine Arts*, Broad St., cor. of Cherry St. (adm. 25 c.; free on Sun. & Mon.; concert on Thurs. afternoon); *Memorial Hall*, Fairmount Park, see p. 220; *Art Club*, see p. 218. — Among the finest private collections of art are those of *Mr. William B. Bement*, 1814 Spring Garden St., and *Mrs. Henry C. Gibson*, 1612 Walnut St., to which properly accredited visitors may obtain entrance. The former includes examples of Cabanel, Cot (The Coming Storm), A. Achenbach, Verboeckhoven, Herzog, Koekkoek, Tenkate, Bouguereau, Boughton, Van Marcke, W. T. Richards, Troyon, and Harnett (wonderfully realistic still-life piece). The Gibson Collection includes works of Clays, Gérôme, Jules Breton, Munkacsy, Detaille, Cabanel, Henner, De Neuville, Rosa Bonheur, Millet, Leys, Van Marcke, Meissonier, Troyon, etc.

British Consul, *Capt. R. C. Clipperton*, 708 S. Washington Sq.

Philadelphia (the 'Quaker City'), the third city of the United States in population (1,046,964 inhab. in 1890), lies mainly upon a broad plain between the *Delaware* and the *Schuylkill*, 96 M. from the Atlantic Ocean. In extent it is the second-largest city in America, being 22 M. long from N. to S. and 5-10 M. wide, and covering 130 sq. M., or about the same area as London proper, though, of course, not so completely built over. It probably contains a larger proportion of small houses than any other large city in the world (5.79 inhab. per house; New York 16.37) and is sometimes called the 'City of Homes'. It is laid out with chessboard regularity (see p. 212) and contains 1150 M. of streets, of which 750 M. are paved. The characteristic Philadelphia house is a two-storied or three-storied structure of red pressed brick, with white marble steps and white or green window-shutters. The two rivers give it about 30 M. of water-front for docks and wharfage, and it is the headquarters of two of the greatest American railways (the Pennsylvania and the Reading). Its commerce by sea and land is very large, and as a manufacturing centre it ranks next to New York. The great wholesale business-thoroughfare is MARKET STREET, running E. and W. between the two rivers, while CHESTNUT STREET, parallel with it on the S., contains the finest shops, the newspaper offices, etc. BROAD STREET is the chief street running N. and S. Among the most fashionable residence-quarters are the W. parts of *Walnut, Spruce, Pine, Arch, Race*, and *Vine Streets*. *Eighth Street* is the great district for cheap shops.

14*

History. Philadelphia, the 'City of Brotherly Love' or 'Quaker City', was founded in 1682 by a Quaker colony under William Penn (1644-1718), who purchased the site from its Indian owners. [A Swedish colony, however, settled on the Delaware, a little lower down, in 1638 (comp. p. 219), and many of Penn's original patentees were descendants of these settlers.] The city attracted large numbers of immigrants and received its charter from Penn in 1701, when it had about 4500 inhabitants. From about that time to the present century it rivalled Boston as the leading city of the country, and it was the scene of the most important official steps in the Revolution. The first Continental Congress assembled here in 1774; the *Declaration of Independence* was signed here on July 4th, 1776; the *Constitution of the United States* was drawn up and promulgated here in 1787; the first President of the United States resided here; and here Congress assembled till 1797. From Sept., 1777, to June, 1778, the city was in the possession of the British. During the present century its history has been one of quiet and rapid growth in size and prosperity. In 1876 Philadelphia was the scene of the *Centennial Exhibition*, held in honour of the 100th anniversary of the Declaration of Independence, which was visited by ten million people. — After William Penn, the man whose name is most intimately associated with Philadelphia is *Benjamin Franklin* (pp. 214, 219), who came here in 1723 at the age of eighteen. The *Friends* or *Quakers* still form a very important element in Philadelphia, many of the oldest, wealthiest, and most esteemed families belonging to this sect.

Industry and Commerce. The value of the manufactures of Philadelphia in 1890 was $570,000,000 (114,000,000*l.*), the number of hands employed being 259,000. The chief products are machinery, locomotives, iron wares, ships, carpets, woollen and cotton goods, sugar, drugs, and chemicals. The value of its foreign trade in 1891 was $105,300,000. In 1891 5652 vessels entered and 5710 cleared the port.

Streets. In planning his city Penn laid out two wide thoroughfares crossing it at right angles (High, now Market St., and Broad St.), with an open space at their intersection and four other squares (Washington, Franklin, Logan, and Rittenhouse Squares) near the outer corners of his plan. The other streets were all laid out parallel to the two above-named, and this rule has also been observed in the subsequent extensions of the city. Those parallel to Market St. have names (often taken from trees), while those parallel with Broad St. are numbered (Front, Second, etc.). The prefixes North and South distinguish respectively the numbered streets to the N. and S. of Market St. The houses on the N. or E. side of the street have odd numbers, and those on the S. or W. side even numbers. The numbers of the E. and W. streets begin at the Delaware, those of the N. and S. streets at Market St. With each new block a new century of numbers begins, although there are seldom more than 40 numbers in a block. With this system a very slight familiarity with the city enables one to find his way to any house. Thus, *e.g.*, 1521 Arch St. must be between N. 15th St. and N. 16th St.

In *City Hall Square* (Pl. F, 6), at the intersection of Broad St. and Market St., in the centre of the city, stands the new **City Hall** (Pl. F, 6), generally known as the *Public Buildings*, a huge pile with a granite basement-story and white marble superstructure, begun in 1874 and still unfinished. It is 486 ft. long from N. to S. and 470 ft. in breadth, covering a greater area (4$^1/_2$ acres) than any other building in the United States (Capitol at Washington, 3$^1/_2$ acres; St. Peter's at Rome, 4$^5/_6$ acres; Palais de Justice at Brussels, 6$^1/_4$ acres). The *Tower* is to be 510 ft. high, and is to be surmounted by a statue of William Penn, 37 ft. in height, which now stands in the interior court. The style of the building is modified French Renaissance; the architect was *John McArthur Jr.* (d. 1890).

PHILADELPHIA

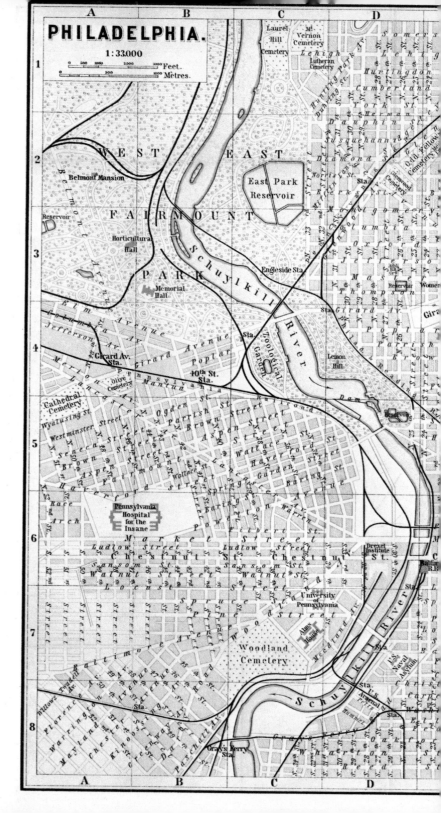

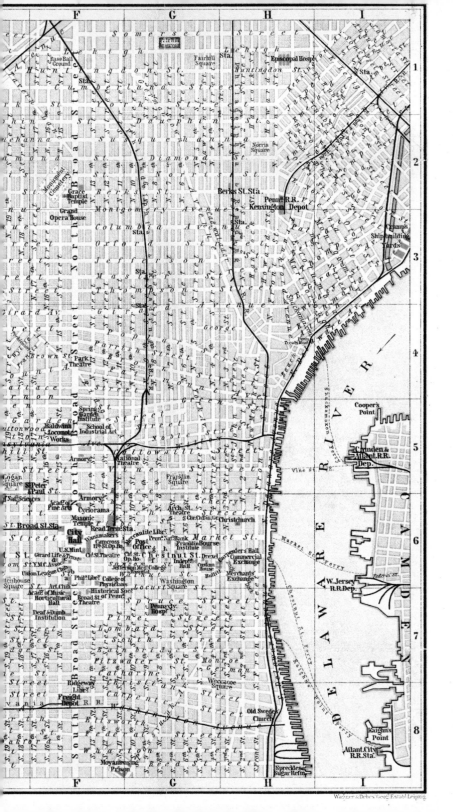

The building contains 750 rooms. On the first floor are the *Council Chamber* and other offices of the municipal government. The S. part of the third floor is devoted to the *Supreme Court of Pennsylvania*.

On the W. side of City Hall Sq., opposite the City Hall, is the handsome *Broad Street Station* (Pl. F, 6) of the Penna. Railroad, the spacious dimensions of which have become all too small for the immense traffic carried on here. — On the N. side of the square, at the corner of Broad St. and Filbert St., is the *Masonic Temple (Pl. F, 6), a huge granite structure in the Norman style, erected in 1868-73 at a cost of $1,500,000 (300,000*l.*). Among its most prominent features are the tower, 250 ft. high, and the elaborately carved Norman porch. The lodge-rooms are finished in accordance with seven different styles of architecture (Egyptian, Ionic, Corinthian, Norman, Gothic, Renaissance, and Oriental). — On the E. side of the square, occupying the block bounded by the square, Market St., 13th St., and Chestnut St., is *Wanamaker's Store* (Pl. F, 6), the Bon Marché or Whiteley's of Philadelphia, with 4500 employées. — On the S. side of the square is the tall *Betz Building*, completed in 1893. — At the S.E. angle of the square (entr. from Chestnut St.), adjoining the last, is the *United States Mint* (Pl. F, 6; adm. 9-12, free), a white marble building with an Ionic portico. The Mint was established in 1792; the present building dates from 1829-33.

This is the parent mint of the United States. The various processes of coining are interesting. The total value of the pieces coined here from 1793 to 1891 was: gold $676,389,759, silver $356,001,000, minor coins $23,946,941. In 1891 the silver dollars issued here numbered 8,694,206. In a room upstairs is a *Collection of American and other Coins*. The most interesting are the *Selections* in the case at one end of the room, including the 'Widow's Mite' (No. 3116), found among the ruins of the Temple at Jerusalem. A new Mint is to be erected facing Independence Square.

Chestnut Street (Pl. A-H, 6), on which the Mint fronts, is the chief street of Philadelphia, containing many of the handsomest and most interesting buildings; and we now follow it towards the Delaware (E. or left), passing the Mint (left, see above). The S. side-pavement is the fashionable promenade of the Quaker City. To the W. of the Mint is the *Girard Life Insurance Building*. At the corner of 12th St. (r.) is the *Beneficial Saving Fund Society*, and at the corner of 10th St., to the left, is the *New York Mutual Life Insurance Co.*

In 12th St., to the N., is the *William Penn Charter School*, founded in 1689. In 10th St., also to the N., is the *Mercantile Library* (Pl. G, 6), with 160,000 vols. and a large free reading-room (9-10). — In the same street, to the S., is the *Jefferson Medical College* (Pl. G, 6).

At the corner of 9th St., extending on the N. to Market St., is the *Post Office (Pl. G, 6), a large granite building in the Renaissance style, erected at a cost of $5,000,000 (1,000,000*l.*). It also contains the *United States Courts* and the offices of various Federal officials. — The *Singerly Building* (Nos. 915-917; left) and the adjoining *Penn Mutual Life Building* have very elaborate façades. This neighbourhood contains a large number of newspaper offices.

At the corner of 6th St., on the *Public Ledger Building*, is a *Statue of Benjamin Franklin* (1706-90).

In N. 7th St. is the *Franklin Institute* (Pl. G, 6), with a library, museum, and lecture-hall. Opposite is the free exhibition of the *Builders' Exchange*.

We now reach, on the right, between 5th and 6th Sts., **Independence Hall* (Pl. G, 6), or the old *State House* (adm. 9-4), a modest brick edifice erected in 1729-34, which is in some respects the most interesting building in the United States. The steeple was added afterwards. It was here that the Continental Congress met during the American Revolution, and here, on July 4th, 1776, the Declaration of Independence was adopted.

Passing through the door in the centre, we first enter (left) the *East Room* or *Independence Hall* proper, the actual scene of the deliberations of those statesmen of whom William Pitt wrote: 'I must declare that in all my reading and observation, for solidity of reasoning, force of sagacity, and wisdom of conclusion, under such a complication of difficult circumstances, no body of men could stand before the National Congress of Philadelphia'. With the exception of a new flooring, the room is substantially in the same state as when the Congress sat, and the old furniture has been replaced in it, including the table on which the Declaration of Independence was signed. On the back of the chair of the President of the Congress (John Hancock) is the emblem of which Franklin said that he had often wondered, before the success of the Revolution was assured, whether it was the *rising* or the *setting* sun. On the E. wall hangs a facsimile of the Declaration of Independence, of which the original is preserved at Washington (see p. 260). On the walls hang portraits of all but twelve of the signers of the Declaration, and also the original 'Rattlesnake' flags of the Union, with the motto 'Don't tread on me'.

In the *National Museum* or *West Room* (to the right of the entrance-hall) are the painting of Penn's Treaty with the Indians, by *Benj. West;* a portrait of George III., by *Allan Ramsay;* the silver inkstand used in signing the Declaration of Independence; the original Charter of the City of Philadelphia (1701); and many other portraits, autographs, and relics.

At the head of the *Stairway*, supported by a chain of 13 links (emblematical of the 13 Original States), hangs the famous **Liberty Bell*, the first bell rung in the United States after the Declaration of Independence. It was afterwards used on various occasions of national importance, but was cracked in 1835, and since 1843 has never been sounded. It was originally cast in England, but was recast in Philadelphia.

In the building to the W. of the State House, Washington was inaugurated in 1793 and Adams in 1797. That to the E. is occupied by city offices. — In front of the State House is a *Statue of Washington*, by Bailey, erected in 1869. — Behind the State House lies *Independence Square*, an open space 4 acres in extent.

Opposite Independence Hall is the picturesque gabled building of the *Pennsylvania Co. for Life Insurance and Annuities*.

In 5th St., just below Chestnut St., is the **American Philosophical Society**, an outgrowth of the *Junto Club*, founded by Franklin in 1743. It contains a library of 60,000 vols. and many interesting relics.

Beyond 5th St., Chestnut St. is flanked on both sides with handsome banks and insurance offices. At the corner of 5th St., to the right, is the white marble **Drexel Building* (Pl. G, 6), in which is the *Stock Exchange* (visitors admitted to the gallery, 10-3). [The new *Bourse* is now building in 5th St., a little to the N.] Adjacent is the *Custom House* (Pl. G, 6), with a Doric portico, originally erected in 1819-24 for the United States Bank. — A little lane

lane diverging to the right between 4th and 3rd Sts., opposite the *Fidelity Safe Deposit Co.*, leads to *Carpenters' Hall (Pl. G, 6 ; open to visitors), where the First Colonial Congress assembled in 1774. It contains the chairs used at the Congress, relics of Washington and Jefferson, etc. — Chestnut St. ends at the Delaware River.

At 134 South Second Street is the *Commercial Exchange* (Pl. H, 6), on the site of the 'Slate-roof House', the home of William Penn.

WALNUT STREET (Pl. A-H, 6) runs parallel to Chestnut St., a little to the S. In this street, at the intersection of Dock St. and 3rd St., is the *Merchants' Exchange* (Pl. H, 6), with a semicircular portico facing towards the river, near which (in 3rd St.) is the *Girard Bank*, originally built for the first U.S. Bank and long owned by Stephen Girard (p. 217). At 4th St. is the fine building of the *Manhattan Insurance Co.* — Between 6th and 7th Sts. Walnut St. passes *Washington Square* (Pl. G, 6 ; p. 212), with a great variety of trees.

Two blocks to the S. of Walnut St., bounded by Spruce, Pine, 8th, and 9th Sts., stands the *Pennsylvania Hospital* (Pl. G, 7), the oldest in the city. — At the corner of Locust St. and 13th St., one block to the S. of Walnut St., stands the building of the "Historical Society of Pennsylvania (Pl. G, 7; adm. 10-6), founded in 1824, which contains highly interesting historical relics, paintings, and autographs. In the FIREPROOF ROOM on the ground-floor are a letter of *President Lincoln* (1864) and the play-bill of the theatre on the night he was assassinated; the *Bradford Almanack* of 1686 (printed 1685), the first book printed in the Middle States; many other examples of *Bradford, Franklin*, and other printers of the Middle States before 1800; *William Penn's* Wampum Treaty Belt, Bible, and razor; the original *Instructions of Penn* regarding Pennsylvania; the *News of the Battle of Lexington*, passed on to Philadelphia in the manner of the 'Fiery Cross' (Ap. 19-24th, 1775), with attestations of the persons through whose hands it passed; first copy of *Poor Richard's Almanack*; one of the *Stamp Act* stamps; *German Bible* and other works printed by Christopher Saur, including the *First Bible printed in America*. — On the UPPER FLOOR are the *Tower Collection of Colonial Laws down to 1789*; portraits of *Penn, Washington, Franklin, Robert Morris, Steuben*, etc.; relics of Robert Morris; old charter of Philadelphia; and part of *Franklin's Printing Press* (front room).

At the N.E. corner of Locust St. and 13th St. is the College of Physicians (Pl. F, 6), incorporated in 1780, with a fine medical library, second only to that of the Royal College of Physicians in London. The large hall, in which the *Anatomical Museum* is displayed, contains a fine chimney-piece.

The Philadelphia Library (Pl. F, 6), also in this neighbourhood, at the corner of Locust St. and Juniper St., was founded by Dr. Franklin and others in 1731 and contains 160,000 vols., a clock said to have belonged to Cromwell, part of Franklin's electrical machine, and other relics.

Walnut St. now crosses Broad St., to the W. of which it consists mainly of private residences. Between 18th and 19th Sts. we pass *Rittenhouse Square* (Pl. E, 6; p. 212), a fashionable residence-quarter.

On reaching 24th St. we may follow it to the right to the spacious Baltimore and Ohio Railway Station (Pl. E, 6), which lies on the river, at the end of Chestnut St. Following the latter street towards the E., we pass the *Second Reformed Episcopal Church*, on the right, and the *First Unitarian Church* and the *Swedenborgian Church* (cor. 22nd St.) on the left. At 15th St. are the *Church of the Epiphany* (left), the *Colonnade Hotel* (p. 210; right), and the *Young Men's Christian Association* (Pl. F, 6; r.), containing a fine hall.

We now again reach our starting-point at Broad St. (comp. p. 212), where we may either turn to the left and proceed past the City Hall and up North Broad St., or follow South Broad St. to the right.

NORTH BROAD STREET (Pl. F, 6-1), beginning on the N. side of City Hall Square, a handsome street, 113 ft. wide, contains in its upper portion many of the finest private residences in Philadelphia. To the right, at the corner of Filbert St., is the *Masonic Temple* (see p. 213), which is adjoined by the handsome *Arch Street Episcopal Church*. Opposite are the Lutheran *Church of the Holy Communion*, of green serpentine, and the brown-stone *First Baptist Church*. — To the left, a little farther on, at the corner of Cherry St., is the *Academy of Fine Arts* (Pl. F, 6), a tasteful building in the Venetian style of architecture (admission, see p. 211). The Academy was founded in 1805 and besides its collections supports an excellent art-school. Its collections include 300 paintings, numerous sculptures, several hundred casts, and 60,000 engravings. Annual exhibitions of the works of living artists are held here in autumn and spring. Some of the most notable possessions are given below.

Paintings. No. A 5. *C. W. Peale*, Portrait of himself; A 13. *John Neagle*, Pat Lyon at the forge; A 19. *W. Bouguereau*, Orestes and the Furies; A 20. *P. Janssen*, Peter's Denial; A 23. *John Vanderlyn*, Ariadne in Naxos; A 27. *C. R. Leslie*, Murder of Rutland by Clifford (*Henry VI.*, Part 3, I, 3); A 34. *Gilbert Stuart*, George Washington (replica of 'Lansdowne Portrait'); A 38. *E. May*, Dying brigand; A 40. *Washington Allston*, Dead Man resuscitated by the bones of Elisha (2 Kings, xiii, 20); A 50. *T. Sully*, G. F. Cooke as Richard III.; A 59. *G. Stuart*, Mrs. Blodgett; A 77. *Rich. Wilson*, Falls of Tivoli; A 130. *Poelenburg*, Nymphs; A 183. *Krimmel*, Fourth of July; A 185. *C. Schuessele*, Queen Esther denouncing Haman; A 187. *Van der Helst*, Violinist; A 189. *C. W. Peale*, Robert Morris ('the financier of the Revolution'); A 191. *J. B. Wittkamp*, Deliverance of Leyden (1594); A 194. After *Kneller*, John Locke; A 196. *Guffens*, Rouget de Lisle singing the Marseillaise for the first time (1792); A 206. *Gastaldi*, Duke of Arno meditating the death of his wife Parisina; A 207. *Farufini*, Cæsar Borgia and Macchiavelli; A 208. *Joseph Vernet*, Cardinal and friends; A 253. *Ben. West*, Rejection of Christ; A 256. *W. L. Picknell*, On the borders of the marsh; A 257. *Snyders*, Dead game and fruit; A 258. *T. B. Read*, Sheridan's ride; A 261. *R. Koehler*, Holiday occupation; A 262. *Robt. Wylie*, The story-teller; A 266. *C. Hermans*, Masked ball at the Opera; A 269. *Trego*, Light artillery; A 271. *F. A. Bridgman*, Roumanian lady; A 273. *Carolus-Duran*, Mme. Modjeska; A 285. *T. Hill*, Yosemite Valley, from Bridal Veil Meadows (see p. 453).

Sculptures. B 13. *W. W. Story*, Jerusalem; B 34. *Hiram Powers*, Proserpine; B 49. *A. Kiss*, Amazon attacked by panther; C 11. *John Lough*, Battle of Centaurs and Lapithæ (cast from original model).

Nearly opposite the Academy is a *Circus*, and farther on (No. 145) is the *Armoury of the State Fencibles* (Pl. F, 5, 6).

Race Street (Pl. E-H, 5) leads to the left to LOGAN SQUARE (Pl. E, 5; p. 212), on the E. side of which stands the Roman Catholic **Cathedral of SS. Peter & Paul** (Pl. E, F, 5), a large edifice, with a Corinthian portico and a dome 210 ft. high. The interior is adorned with mural paintings, and over the high-altar is a Crucifixion by *Brumidi*. — On the S. side of the square, at the corner of 19th St., is the *Academy of Natural Sciences* (Pl. E, 5, 6), erected in 1875 (adm. 9-5, free). The society was founded in 1812. Its museum contains valuable and extensive *Collections of Natural History*, among which may be specified the Morton Collection of Crania (1200) and the Ornithological Cabinet, which furnished Audubon with many of his types. The library contains 35,000 volumes.

In Broad St., beyond the *First Regiment Armoury* (Pl. F, 5), we cross the line of the *Reading Railway.* To the right, at the corner of Spring Garden St., is the *Spring Garden Institute* (Pl. F, 5), for instruction in drawing, painting, and the mechanic arts (750 students). Opposite are *Baldwin's Locomotive Works, one of the most interesting industrial establishments in Philadelphia, employing 3000 men and turning out two locomotives daily (adm. after previous application, supported by an introduction).

SPRING GARDEN STREET, a pleasant residence-street, leads to the W. to (1 M.) the S. end of *Fairmount Park* (see p. 220). At No. 1336, a little to the E. of Broad St., is the **Pennsylvania School of Industrial Art* (Pl. F, 5), incorporated in 1876, with a special view to the development of the art industries of Pennsylvania, and now attended by 300 students. One of its most characteristic features is the Department of Weaving and Textile Design. The Industrial Museum in Memorial Hall (p. 220) is connected with this excellent institution. — The *Assembly Hall of the German Society of Pennsylvania*, to the E., at the corner of Marshall St., is said to contain the best German library in America (35,000 vols.).

A little farther on are the *Boys' Central High School* and the *Synagogue Rodef Shalom.*

FAIRMOUNT AVENUE (Pl. D-H, 4), 1 M. from the City Hall, leads to the left to (¹/₂ M.) the *Eastern Penitentiary (Pl. E, 4; warden, Mr. M. J. Cassidy), a large and well-managed prison (1100-1200 inmates), rendered widely known by a somewhat sensational passage in *Dickens's* 'American Notes' (adm. by ticket from one of the Board of Inspectors). The penitentiary, which covers 11 acres of ground, is built on the radiating plan, and is conducted on the so-called 'individual' system, in which an attempt is made by discriminating treatment to bring about a reform of the criminals. There is about 1 warder to 30 prisoners (1 to 10 in similar English prisons); and most European visitors will be struck with what may seem the unreasonable comforts of the cells (many containing pictures, flowers, birds, etc.), the abundant rations, and the large amount of liberty granted to the prisoners. Knitting, carpentry, and the making of cigars, brushes, etc., are actively carried on. Dickens's criminal served 12 sentences in the penitentiary and was finally, at his own request, brought here to die. — *Girard College* (see below) lies about ¹/₂ M. to the N.

Farther up Broad St. are numerous handsome private houses, churches, and other edifices. The *Grace Baptist Temple* (Pl. F, 2) has accommodation for 6000 worshippers. Opposite is the entrance to *Monument Cemetery* (Pl. F, 2), and ³/₄ M. farther out are the *Base Ball Grounds* (Pl. F, 1). Beyond this Broad St. runs out to Germantown (see p. 221), 6 M. from the City Hall.

GIRARD AVENUE (Pl. D-H, 4) runs to the W. from N. Broad St. to (¹/₂ M.) *Girard College (Pl. E, 3, 4), one of the richest and most notable philanthropic institutions in the United States, founded in 1831 by *Stephen Girard* (1750-1831), a native of France, for the education of poor white male orphans (adm. on previous application to the Director or Secretary; no clergymen admitted). It now accommodates about 1600 boys, and the value of Mr. Girard's bequest of $2,000,000 has increased to about $16,000,000 (3,200,000*l.*).

The *Main Building is a dignified structure in the Corinthian style by T. U. Walter, resembling the Madeleine at Paris. In the vestibule are a statue of Stephen Girard, by *Gevelot*, and his sarcophagus; and a room on the ground-floor contains several relics of him. The other buildings, about a dozen in all, include school-rooms, dormitories, dining-halls (one for 1000 boys), a swimming-bath, a technical institute, and a chapel. The services in the last are conducted by laymen, as Mr. Girard's will forbids the presence of a clergyman within the college enclosure. The *Grounds*, which are 41 acres in extent, are lighted by seven electric masts, 125 ft. high, and contain a monument to former pupils who fell in the Civil War.

Opposite Girard College are the *Mary J. Drexel Home* and the *German Hospital* (Pl. E, 4). To the N. of Girard College are the *Women's Medical College* and *Hospital.* — In Stiles St., to the E., between 17th and 18th Sts., are the large *Church of the Gesù* and various Roman Catholic colleges and hospitals.

SOUTH BROAD STREET (Pl. F, 6–8) leads to the S. from City Hall Square. To the right, at the corner of Sansom St., stands the substantial building of the *Union League Club (Pl. F, 6), the chief Republican club of Pennsylvania (1400 members). On the same side are the *Lafayette, Bellevue,* and *Stratford Hotels* (p. 210). Beyond these is the *Art Club (Pl. F, 7), a good example of the Renaissance style, in which exhibitions of paintings, concerts, and public lectures are held. At the corner of Locust St., also to the right, is the *Academy of Music (p. 211), below which are the *Horticultural Hall* (flower-shows) and the *Beth-Eden Baptist Church.* At the corner of Pine St. (r.) is the *Deaf and Dumb Asylum* (Pl. F, 7), with a portico. Below Pine St., Broad St. contains few buildings of importance. The visitor, however, should go as far as the *Ridgeway Library (Pl. F, 8; open 9–5), which stands to the left, between Christian St. and Carpenter St., nearly 1 M. from the City Hall. This handsome building was erected, with a legacy of $1^{1}/_{2}$ million dollars left by Dr. Rush in 1869, as a branch of the Philadelphia Library (p. 215), and contains some interesting relics and rare books. — Broad St. ends, 4 M. from the City Hall, at *League Island,* in the Delaware, on which is a *United States Navy Yard.*

MARKET STREET (Pl. A–H, 6), the chief wholesale business thoroughfare of the city, is somewhat mean-looking in its general aspect and contains little of interest to the visitor. A little to the E. of City Hall Sq. it passes the new *Terminal Station of the Reading Railroad* (Pl. F, 6). The *Penn National Bank* (Pl. G, 6), at the corner of S. 7th St., occupies the site of the house in which Jefferson wrote the Declaration of Independence. The street ends at the Delaware, in a busy quarter of wharves, railway-stations, and ferry-boat docks.

In N. Second St., a block above Market St., is **Christ Church** (Pl. H, 6; Epis.), erected in 1727–37, in the style of St. Martin's in the Fields, London, on the site of an older church of 1695, and attended by the Royal officers and early officials of the American Republic.

No. 239, ARCH STREET (Pl. E–H, 6), a little to the N., between 2nd and 3rd Sts., is the *House* (now a shop) in which the first American flag (13 stars and 13 stripes) was made by Mrs. John Ross in 1777 (visitors welcome). At the corner of Arch St. and 5th St. (l.) is the *Apprentices' Library* (30,000 vols.). At 5th St. is the *Christ Church Burial Ground* (Pl. G, 6), with many interesting tombs. A railed opening in the wall (in Arch St.) shows the flat tombstone of *Benjamin Franklin* (1746-1790) and his wife.

One of the most interesting historical buildings in Philadelphia is the old *Swedes' Church* (Pl. B, 8; reached by 2nd St. tramway), in Swanson St., near the Delaware end of Christian St., erected in 1700, on the site of an old wooden church of 1646 (comp. p. 212), now used for divine service in the English language (interesting tombstones). Adjacent is the *Cooper's Shop* where the ladies of Philadelphia provided meals for the troops passing S. during the war. In the neighbourhood is the huge *Spreckels Sugar Refinery.* — At *Shackamaxon*, in Beach St., is the small *Penn Treaty Monument* (Pl. H, 4), supposed to occupy the spot where Penn made his treaty with the Indians in 1682, under an elm that has long since vanished (a compact, in the words of Voltaire, 'never sworn to and never broken'). The island in the river here is known as *Treaty Island.* — A little farther to the N., at the foot of Ball St., are **Cramp's Ship-building Yards* (Pl. I, 3), one of the chief American yards for the building of iron and steel ships (U.S. war-vessels, etc.). — The *U.S. Naval Asylum* (Pl. D, 7) accommodates 150 old soldiers. A little to the S. is the *Schuylkill Arsenal* (Pl. D, 8), now devoted to the manufacture of army clothing.

West Philadelphia, the extension of the city beyond the Schuylkill, contains many of the chief residence streets and several public buildings and charitable institutions.

The **University of Pennsylvania* (Pl. C, 7) occupies a group of spacious buildings bounded by Pine St., Woodlands Ave., and 34th St. (reached by Market St. or South St. cars). It is now attended by about 1800 students and has acquired a special reputation for the excellence of its schools of medicine, biology, and political economy.

The *College Hall* is built of serpentine, with grey stone facings. The new **Library*, designed by Mr. Frank Furness and opened in 18.0, is one of the most beautiful and most convenient library-buildings in the world. It contains 90,000 vols. and numerous interesting relics, and is open to the public. The *University Collections* are of considerable value.

To the S. of the University are the large *Blockley Almshouses* (Pl. C, 7) and the *Philadelphia Hospital.* — A little to the N. E., at the corner of Chestnut St. and 32nd St., is the new **Drexel Institute* (Pl. D, 6), founded by A. J. Drexel at a cost of $1,500,000 and opened in Dec., 1891. Visitors are admitted.

The chief object of the institution is 'the extension and improvement of industrial education as a means of opening better and wider avenues of employment to young men and women.' It also provides free lectures and evening classes and contains a free library and a museum. The latter includes collections of wood and metal work, ceramics, embroideries, and textiles. The library contains a fine **Collection of Rare Prints, MSS., and Autographs*, presented by Mr G. W. Childs (incl. MSS. of Thackeray's lecture on George III., and Dickens's 'Our Mutual Friend', a vol. containing autograph-letters of every President of the United States, MSS. of Hood and Leigh Hunt, etc.). The institute is already attended by 1500 students.

To the N. of Market St., between 42nd St. and 49th St., is the enormous **Pennsylvania Insane Asylum** (*Kirkbride's Hospital;* Pl. A, B, 6), situated in large grounds and containing *West's* picture of 'Christ healing the sick' (no adm. on Sat. or Sun.).

Philadelphia prides herself on few things more than on ***Fairmount Park** (Pl. A-D, 1-5), the largest city park in the world, which covers an area of about 2800 acres (Prater 2500, Richmond 2250). The park proper extends along both banks of the Schuylkill for about 4 M., and the narrow strip along the Wissahickon (see below), 11 M. long, is also included in the park limits. Its natural beauties are considerable, but so far little has been done to it by art. Several statues have been erected. The principal entrances are at the end of *Green St.* (Pl. D, 5) and *Girard Ave.* (Pl. C, D, 4).

Entering by the Green St. Gate, we have to our left the original *Fair Mount* from which the park takes its name. On the top of the hill (*View) is a huge *Reservoir*, to which the river-water is pumped up by the adjoining *Water Works* (Pl. D, 5). A little farther on we cross a plaza, with a statue of *Abraham Lincoln*, beyond which is *Lemon Hill* (Pl. D, 4), crowned by the old house of Robert Morris, now a restaurant. Adjacent is the *Lemon Hill Observatory*, a high iron-work tower, the top of which (elevator 10 c.) commands a good view. At the foot of the hill, on the bank of the Schuylkill, are several picturesque boathouses belonging to different clubs. On reaching the handsome GIRARD AVENUE BRIDGE (Pl. C, 4), one of the widest in the world (120 ft.), at the end of which is a *Statue of Humboldt*, we cross it to the larger portion of the park on the W. bank of the river. To the left we see the *Zoological Garden* (see p. 221). Following the *Lansdowne Drive*, we pass (to the left) the *Penn House*, the old home of William Penn, transferred hither from Letitia St., near Market St. and Second St. A little farther on we cross a ravine by a rustic bridge and soon reach ***Memorial Hall** (Pl. B, 3), built as part of the Centennial Exhibition of 1876, at a cost of $1,500,000 (300,000 *l.*) and now containing a permanent collection of art and industry (*Pennsylvania Museum of Industrial Art;* open from 9, on Mon. from 12, to ¹/₂ hr. before sunset; 281,473 visitors in 1892). In front of the building are two colossal winged steeds in bronze. The collections include paintings, sculptures, casts, stoneware, majolica, pottery, metal work, ivory carvings, electroplate reproductions, tapestry, furniture, models, Japanese work, objects from British India, embroideries, etc. A little to the N. is the large **Horticultural Hall* (Pl. A, 3), another survival of the Centennial, finely situated above the Schuylkill and forming a large winter-garden. In the vicinity are the picturesque *St. George's House* (the English building) and a few other Centennial buildings. [Those who wish may now return to the city by tramway from Elm Avenue, a little to the S. of Memorial Hall; Pl. A, B, 4.] A little to the W. of the Memorial Hall is an allegorical *Fountain*, which lies at the base of *George's Hill* (*View). About 1 M. to the N. of this hill is the old *Belmont Mansion* (now a restaurant), and about 1¹/₄ M. farther on we reach *Chamounix* and the N. boundary of the W. Park. The bridge here crosses the river to the village of *Schuylkill Falls*.

By turning to the right on the E. bank, we may follow the river-drive through the E. Park back to (3¹/₂ M.) the Green St. entrance (see above). In this case we skirt *Laurel Hill Cemetery (Pl. C, 1; entrances in Ridge Ave.), which here occupies the high bank of the river, containing many handsome monuments and affording fine views. Near the main entrance is a group, by *Thom*, of Old Mortality and Sir Walter Scott.

By turning to the left on crossing to Schuylkill Falls, we may follow the ***Wissahickon Drive**, which ascends the romantic valley of the *Wissahickon Creek*, an Alpine gorge in miniature, with sides 200-300 ft. high, to (6 M.) *Chestnut Hill*, affording a scene of singular loveliness to be included within the limits of a city. The gorge is crossed by several bridges, including the lofty viaduct of the Reading Railway (70 ft. high),

near the entrance, and the curious *Pipe Bridge* (100 ft. high), the chords
of which are formed by the pipes conveying water to Germantown (see
below). Near the summit of the gorge (to the right) is a *Statue of William Penn*, inscribed 'Toleration'. Along the stream (on both banks) are
several inns, frequented in summer for 'catfish and waffles'.

The *Zoological Garden (Pl. C, 4), to the S. of West Fairmount
Park, is perhaps the best collection of the kind in America (adm.
25 c., children 10 c.). It occupies a tract of ground formerly owned
by John Penn, grandson of William Penn, and contains his house,
the *Solitude* (1785). The garden may be reached by train from
Broad St. or by tramway (25th St. or Girard Ave.).

Camden (*West Jersey Ho.*, $ 2), an industrial and commercial city with
58,313 inhab., lies on the left bank of the Delaware, opposite Philadelphia
(see Pl. I, 5-8; ferries, see p. 210). It was long the residence of the poet,
Walt Whitman (1819-92). — It is the terminus of the *West Jersey*, the
Camden & Atlantic, and the *Phil'a & Atlantic Railways* (comp. pp. 210, 225).

FROM PHILADELPHIA TO GERMANTOWN AND CHESTNUT HILL, 12 M., railway from Broad St. Station in 35 minutes. — Beyond (5½ M.) *Germantown
Junction* (p. 209) the line turns to the N.W. and traverses *Germantown,
the principal residential suburb of Philadelphia, stopping at several stations,
of which (8 M.) *Chelton Avenue* is, perhaps, the nearest to the best parts
of the district. Germantown is very prettily laid out, with fine trees
and gardens, and contains some interesting old houses. The battle of
Germantown, in which Washington was defeated by Lord Howe, was
fought on Oct. 4th, 1777. The old *Chew House* (with marks of cannon-balls)
and *Johnson House*, the quaint old *Mermaid Inn*, and the picturesque *Wakefield Mills* are interesting relics. Germantown is also reached by the Reading R. R. and by tramway. — 11 M. *Wissahickon Heights*, with the *Wissahickon
Inn.* 12 M. *Chestnut Hill*, another pleasant residence suburb.

FROM PHILADELPHIA TO WEST CHESTER, 27 M., railway from Broad St.
Station in 1-1½ hr. This line crosses the Schuylkill, runs to the S. along
its W. bank, turns to the right beyond *Woodlands Cemetery*, and runs
towards the S.W. through a pleasant district. — 11 M. *Swarthmore*, the
seat of *Swarthmore College* (right), an important Hicksite Quaker establishment, attended by 250 male and female students. *West House*, now occupied
by one of the professors, was the birthplace of *Benjamin West* (1738-1820).
— 14 M. *Media* (370 ft.), a pleasant little town (2736 inhab.) in a pretty
hilly district, much affected by Philadelphians as a residence. — 16 M.
Williamson, the site of the *Williamson Free School of Mechanical Trades*, founded in 1888 by Mr. I. V. Williamson at an expense of $ 2, 125,000 (425,000l.).
It stands in pretty grounds of 200 acres (permission to visit obtained at 119 S.
4th S., Philadelphia). — 27 M. *West Chester*, a town with 8028 inhabitants.

O ther attractive points within easy access of Philadelphia are *Bryn
Mawr* (p. 231), *Long Branch* (p. 223), *Cape May* (p. 225), and *Atlantic City* (p. 226).
From Philadelphia to *Reading*, see R. 35; to *Baltimore*, see R. 40;
to *New York*, see R. 31; to *Buffalo*, see R. 34; to *Pittsburg*, see R. 37;
to *Erie*, see R. 36.

33. Summer and Winter Resorts of New Jersey.

a. From New York to Long Branch and Point Pleasant by Rail.

63 M. NEW YORK AND LONG BRANCH RAILROAD in 2¼-2½ hrs. (fare to
Long Branch $1, to *Point Pleasant* $1.45; return-fares $1.50 and $2.35).
Tickets by this route are also available by the Sandy Hook route (p. 222).
— Passengers start in Jersey City, either from the *Pennsylvania R. R.
Station* (p. 6; ferries from Desbrosses and Cortlandt St.) or from the *Cen-
tral R. R. of New Jersey Station* (p. 6; ferry from Liberty St.).

The *Central R.R. of New Jersey* branch crosses *Newark Bay* to

(12¹/₂ M.) *Elizabethport* and then runs to the S. to (25 M.) *Perth Amboy,* where it is joined by the *Penn. R. R.* train, coming viâ *Rahway.* We then cross the *Raritan River* to (27 M.) *South Amboy.* 32 M. *Matawan,* the junction of lines to *Freehold* and to *Keyport* and *Atlantic Highlands.* — 42 M. **Red Bank** (*Globe, Prospect Ho.,* $ 2), on the estuary of the *Navesink* (view to the right), is the junction of the New Jersey Southern R. R. (for *Atlantic Highlands,* etc.). Farther on we cross the *Shrewsbury River.* — 42 M. *Branchport.*

48 M. **Long Branch,** see p. 223. The two following stations, *Hollywood & West End* (49 M.) and *Elberon* (50¹/₂ M.) are practically parts of Long Branch and are described with it at p. 223.

The line now skirts the shore, affording good views of the ocean to the left. — 46³/₄ M. *Deal Beach* (Hathaway Ho., $ 3, well spoken of). — 53 M. **Asbury Park** (*Coleman Ho.,* $ 3¹/₂-4; *West End, Atalanta, Ocean Ho.,* $ 3-4; *Continental,* $ 2¹/₂, and many others; numerous boarding-houses), a prosperous town with about 20,000 annual visitors, is largely frequented by those who object to the religious management of Ocean Grove (see below), but appreciate the 'no licence' policy of its sister-town. It has a good beach, skirted by a plank-walk 1 M. in length, and is divided from *N. Asbury* on the N. by *Sunset Lake* and from Ocean Grove by another narrow lake.

54 M. **Ocean Grove** (*Sheldon,* $ 3-4; *Arlington,* $ 2¹/₂-3; *La Pierre,* $ 3; *Atlantic,* $ 2-3; many other hotels and boarding-houses), a seaside-resort established in 1870 by an Association of the Methodist Episcopal Church and now frequented yearly by 20-25,000 people.

This extraordinary settlement, possible only in America, in which many thousands of persons, young and old, voluntarily elect to spend their summer vacations under a religious autocracy, which is severe both in its positive and negative regulations, is curious enough to repay a short visit. It is bounded by the sea on the E., by lakes on the N. and S., and by a high fence on the W.; and its gates are closed at 10 p.m. daily and all day on Sunday. The drinking of alcoholic beverages and the sale of tobacco are strictly prohibited, and no theatrical performances of any kind are allowed. No bathing, riding, or driving is permitted on Sunday. Innumerable religious meetings of all kinds are held daily, the chief place of assemblage being a huge *Auditorium,* which can hold 5000 people. The annual *Camp Meeting* is the great event of the season. Near the Auditorium is a large *Model of Jerusalem.* The excellent bathing-beach is skirted by a plank-walk, ³/₄ M. long.

We now pass several small seaside-resorts. 60 M. *Sea Girt* (p.223).

63 M. **Point Pleasant** (*Resort Ho.,* $ 2¹/₂-3; *Ocean Ho., St. James,* $ 2-3; *Arnold Ho.,* $ 2-2¹/₂), a frequented watering-place, forming the terminus of the *New York & Long Branch Railroad.*

Beyond this point we may go by the *Pennsylvania Railroad* to *Bay Head, Seaside Park,* and other points on *Barnegat Bay* (comp. R. 33 d).

b. From New York to Long Branch viâ Atlantic Highlands and Sandy Hook.

30¹/₂ M. STEAMER from *Rector St.* (Pl. A, 2, 3) to (20 M.) *Atlantic Highlands* in 1¹/₄ hr.; RAILWAY thence to (11 M.) *Long Branch* in ¹/₂ hr. (through-fare $ 1). — This is the pleasantest route to Long Branch in fine weather.

The steamer affords an excellent view of *New York Harbour*

(comp. R. 1) and lands at (20 M.) **Atlantic Highlands** (*Grand View*, $ 3¹/₂; *Windsor*, $ 2¹/₂), a modern watering-place at the base of the *Navesink Highlands* (200-300 ft.), often the first land seen on approaching New York by ocean steamer. — 24 M. *Highland Beach* (Swift Ho., $ 3-4; Pavilion, $ 2-3), a small bathing-place, on the narrow strip of sand connecting *Sandy Hook* (p. 2) with the mainland. Adjacent is the *Navesink Lighthouse* (250 ft.), with two castellated towers, the light of which is visible for 40 M. Farther on life-saving stations occur at frequent intervals, as vessels mistaking the entrance to New York harbour in foggy weather are often wreck- ed on this coast.

26¹/₂ M. **Sea Bright** (*Normandie-by-the-Sea, $ 4-5; *Octagon, Sea Bright Ho.*, $ 4; *Shrewsbury, Peninsula Ho.*, $ 3¹/₂), one of the liveliest resorts on the coast. The numerous ice-houses show that fishing is extensively carried on here. — 28¹/₂ M. *Galilee*, a quaint fishing-village. — 29 M. *Monmouth Beach*, a group of private cot- tages, with a club-house and a casino.

30¹/₂ M. *Long Branch*, see below.

c. From Philadelphia to Long Branch.

95 M. PENNSYLVANIA RAILWAY in 3¹/₂ hrs. (fare $ 2.25).

From Philadelphia to (50 M.) *Monmouth Junction*, see R. 31. The Long Branch line here diverges to the right. 56 M. *James- burg;* 67 M. *Freehold;* 75 M. *Farmingdale* (p. 225), 83 M. *Sea Girt* (p. 222); 89 M. *Ocean Grove* (p. 222); 95 M. *Long Branch* (see below).

Local trains also run from the West Jersey R. R. Station in Camden (p. 221) to (82 M.) *Long Branch*, viâ *Whiting* (p. 225) and *Tom's River* (p. 224).

82 M. Long Branch. — There are railway-stations at *Long Branch* proper, for the old village, the pier, and the E. end (omn. to the best hotels 50 c.); at *West End & Hollywood*, near the best hotels; and *Elberon*, the fashion- able cottage part of Long Branch. The trains stop at all these stations.

Hotels. °HOLLYWOOD, finely situated among trees, near the Hollywood station and ¹/₂ M. from the sea, one of the most luxurious and expensive hotels in America, with French management and waiters, and excellent cuisine, R. from $ 5 a day, food *à la carte*, open all the year. Connected with the hotel is a large tidal *Salt Water Swimming Bath* (50 c.). — WEST END, a huge caravanserai on the sea, HOWLAND, SCARBORO, $ 4; these nearest West End Station. — ELBERON, at Elberon. — OCEAN HOTEL; UNITED STATES, $ 3-3¹/₂; BRIGHTON; IAUCH; SHELBURNE, small; these near the pier and E. end. — Numerous *Boarding Houses*, $ 10-15 per week. — Cottages (*i.e.* vil- las) $ 400-4000 for the season.

Bathing. Hours for bathing announced by the hoisting of a white flag at the hotels (not hoisted in dangerous weather).

Long Branch, one of the most popular watering-places in the United States (50,000 summer-guests) and also one of the most fashionable, in the sense in which the word is used by those who 'fondly imagine that lavish display of wealth is evidence of high social position' (Kobbe), takes its name from the 'long branch' of the *Shrewsbury River*. The original village lies about 1 M. inland, but the modern watering-place occupies a bluff, which here faces the sea, at a height of 20-35 ft. above the beautiful sandy beach. Along the edge of the bluff, which is being gradually worn away by the action of the sea in spite of the protection of strong bulk-heads, runs the *Ocean Avenue, a wide road 5 M. long, which presents a scene of wonderful animation on summer afternoons and evenings, being crowded with vehicles of every description. At the E. end of the Avenue is a long *Iron Pier*. Most of the hotels (see above) face the Avenue, which turns slightly inland beyond the West End Hotel and is thenceforward bordered with houses on both sides. The finest villas are at *Elberon*, but being mostly of timber hardly vie with the Newport cottages (see p. 68). Among the most interesting are that which was General Grant's summer-home for 16 years and the reddish brown house, a little to the W. of the Elberon Hotel, in which President Garfield died in 1881. The leading show-place of Long Branch is *Hollywood*, the estate of the late Mr. John Hoey (d. 1892), a little inland from the West End Hotel, the somewhat meretricious attractions of which, however, scarcely satisfy a fastidious taste. The flower-gardens and conservatories (open to visitors) are fine. Near Hollywood is *Norwood*, a group of cottages with a casino. A *Grand Carnival* and *Lawn Tennis Tournament* are held at Long Branch in August.

About 3 M. to the W. of Long Branch is **Monmouth Park** (*Monmouth Park Hotel*), one of the principal American race-tracks, with a grand-stand accommodating 10,000 persons (see p. 17).

Numerous pleasant drives may be made, the favourite being the Beach Drive between Highlands (p. 223) and Pay Head (p. 222; 20 M.), of which Ocean Avenue is a part. — *Eatontown*, 4 M. inland, is visited for its picturesque old mill. Farther on are *Shrewsbury* and the *Tinton Falls* (p. 225).

d. Barnegat Bay.

Barnegat Bay, 27 M. long and 1-4 M. wide, extends from Point Pleasant (p. 222) to a point a little to the N. of Atlantic City (p. 225). It is more like a lake than a bay, being separated from the ocean by two long strips of sandy beach, and entered by a narrow inlet between them. The bay is a great resort of sportsmen, affording excellent fishing and wild-fowl shooting. Among the places chiefly resorted to are *Mantoloking* (Albertson, $2-3), *Seaside Park* (Seaside Park Ho., $2½), *Barnegat City* (Oceanic Ho.), and *Beach Haven* (Engleside, Baldwin, $3), on the island-strips; and *Forked River* (Lafayette Ho., $2), *Tom's River* (Magnolia, $3), *Waretown*, and *Barnegat* (Clarence, $2), on or near the mainland-coast. The last are the special haunts of sportsmen. All the places named above are reached either by the Penn. or Cen. New Jersey R. R.

e. From New York to Lakewood and Atlantic City.

137 M. Central Railroad of New Jersey to (60 M) *Lakewood* in 1½ hr. (fare $1.45); to (137 M.) *Atlantic City* in 5½-5¾ hrs. (fare $3.25). — The train starts from *Jersey City* (see p. 6; ferry from Liberty St.).

From *Jersey City* to (42 M.) *Red Bank*, see R. 33a. Our line here

diverges to the right from the line to Long Branch (p. 223). 42 M.
Shrewsbury, a small town dating from 1665, with some old buildings. About 2½ M. to the S. are *Tinton Falls*. — At (43½ M.)
Eatontown, we enter the *Jersey Pine Plains*, a stretch of forests,
broken only by the settlements along the railway. The district has
lately been coming into reputation on account of the health-giving
odour of the pines. — At (53 M.) *Farmingdale* we cross the line
from *Freehold* to *Sea Girt* (p. 222).

60 M. **Lakewood** (**Laurel House*, **Laurel in the Pines*, belonging
to the same proprietors, with 700 beds, $4; **Lakewood*, with 600
beds, $5; *Palmer House*, $3), a pleasant little settlement in the heart
of the pine woods, has recently become a frequented winter-resort
on account of its sheltered situation and comparatively high temperature (10-12° warmer than in New York). It is the property of an
association, which has laid out pleasant drives and walks through
the woods, the most popular being that through *Pine Park*. The
village is adjoined by two pretty little lakes, *Carasaljo* and *Manetta*.

68 M. *Manchester*, the junction of a line to *Tom's River* (p. 224)
and *Barnegat* (p. 224). At (73 M.) *Whiting* we cross the line from
Philadelphia to Long Branch (see p. 223). — 106 M. *Winslow
Junction*, where we reach the Camden & Atlantic Railroad from Philadelphia to Atlantic City. Hence to (137 M.) *Atlantic City*, see below.

The line we have been following goes on to (122 M.) *Vineland* (Baker
Ho., $2), a glass-making and fruit-growing town, with 3822 inhab.;
134 M. *Bridgeton*, also a glass-making town (11,422 inhab.); and (144 M.)
Bay Side, on the N. bank of the estuary of the Delaware.

f. From Philadelphia to Atlantic City.

1. READING RAILROAD (*'Atlantic City Line'*) from *Kaighn's Point, Camden*
(ferry from Philadelphia, see p. 210), to (56 M.) *Atlantic City* in 1¼-2¼ hrs.
(fare $1). — 2. CAMDEN & ATLANTIC RAILROAD (59 M.; ferry from Market
St., Philadelphia, see p. 210) in 2-2½ hrs. (fare $1). — 3. WEST JERSEY
RAILROAD (ferry to *Camden*, see p. 210), 64 M., in 1½-2½ hrs. (fare $1).

The two lines first mentioned follow practically the same route
and touch many of the same stations. Both pass through *Winslow
Junction* (see above), 24 M. from Camden by the first route and 27 M.
by the second. 38 M. (41 M.) *Egg Harbor*, with manufactures of
native wine. — 56 M. (59 M.) *Atlantic City*, see below.

The West Jersey route runs farther to the S. 8 M. *Woodbury*;
30 M. *Newfield*; 59 M. *Pleasantville*. 64 M. *Atlantic City*, see below.

Atlantic City. — Hotels. TRAYMORE, BRIGHTON, $3-5; SEASIDE, DEN-
NIS, UNITED STATES, SHELBURNE, ISLEWORTH, CHALFONTE, HADDON HALL,
MANSION HOUSE, all $3-4; ALBION, HOFFMANN, IRVINGTON, KENILWORTH,
$3-3½; CONGRESS HALL, ELBERON, $2½-3; BERKSHIRE INN, $2-3, etc. —
Boarding Houses, $10-25 a week. — *Cottages* from $200 for the season.

Carriages from the railway-stations to the hotels, 1-2 pers. 50c., each
addit. pers. 25c.; per. hr. $1½. — *Tramway* along Atlantic Ave.

Atlantic City, the 'Coney Island' of Philadelphia, lies on *Absecon
Island*, a small sand-strip, separated from the New Jersey Coast by
5 M. of sea and salt-meadows. It contains a permanent population

of (1890) 13,055, which is increased fivefold to tenfold in summer.
It is also frequented as a winter-resort. The beach is one of the
finest in America, and 50,000 people have bathed here in one day
(bath, with dress, 25 c.). It is bordered by a *Board Walk*, 24 ft.
wide and 4 M. long, and there are three *Piers*, 600-1000 ft. long.

Among the favourite EXCURSIONS are the *Beach Drive*, 10 M.; to *South
Atlantic City*, with an Elephant like that at Coney Island (p. 55), 5 M.; to
(7 M.) *Longport* (Aberdeen Hotel), near the S. end of the island, by road
or railway; to *Brigantine Beach* (Hotel) and *Peter's Beach* (Hotel), by boat;
and to *Barnegat Bay* (p. 224). — *Absecon Lighthouse* (160 ft. high) is open
to visitors, 9-12. — *Boating* and *Sailing* are carried on mainly in the *Inlet*,
at the upper end of the island (sail-boat $ 5 10 per day; sailing excursions,
25 c. each). — *Fishing* and *Wild-fowl Shooting* are other attractions.

g. From Philadelphia to Cape May City.

82 M. WEST JERSEY RAILROAD in 2¹/₄-3 hrs. (fare $ 2¹/₂). The trains
start from Camden (ferry from Philadelphia, see p. 210). — STEAMERS also ply
in summer down *Delaware Bay* to Cape May (6 hrs.; return-fare $ 1).

From Philadelphia to (30 M.) *Newfield*, see R. 33 f. Our line
here diverges to the right. 34 M. *Vineland*, see p. 225. — From
(61 M.) *Sea Isle Junction* a branch line runs to (5 M.) *Sea Isle City*
and (16 M.) *Ocean City*, two small sea-bathing resorts.

81 M. **Cape May City.** — Hotels. LAFAYETTE, $ 3-5; STOCKTON HOUSE
(1200 beds), CONGRESS HALL (1000 beds), $ 3-4; COLUMBIA; ARLINGTON,
CHALFONTE, WINDSOR, $ 2¹/₂-4, etc. — *Boarding Houses* $ 10-20 a week.

Cape May City, at the extreme S. point of *Cape May*, the E. arm
of *Delaware Bay*, a village with 2136 inhab., a popular sea-bathing
resort of the Philadelphians and also frequented to some extent by
Southerners and Westerners, is a somewhat more fashionable edition of Atlantic City (see above). Its beach, 5 M. long, is hard and
smooth, and the surf-bathing is excellent. The *Esplanade*, skirting
the sea-front, is most thronged between 11 and 1 and between 5 and
8. Excursions may be made to *Cape May Point*, *Cold Spring*, *Sewell's Point*, along the beach, etc. The cape is named after a Dutch
navigator, *Carolis Jacobsen Mey*, who visited Delaware Bay in 1623.

For farther details, see *Kobbe's* 'New Jersey Coast and Pines'.

34. From Philadelphia to Buffalo.

418 M. PHILADELPHIA AND READING RAILROAD SYSTEM *(Lehigh Valley
Division)* in 11-13¹/₂ hrs. (fare $ 10).

. Another through-route from Philadelphia to Buffalo (422 M. in 15-19 hrs.;
fare as above) is by the PENNSYLVANIA RAILROAD to (301 M.) *Emporium* and
thence by the BUFFALO, NEW YORK, AND PHILADELPHIA RAILROAD to (121 M.)
Buffalo. As far as Emporium this route is described in R. 36; the remaining portion calls for no special description.

Philadelphia, see p. 210. The train traverses the N. part of the
city and passes several suburban stations. 4¹/₃ M. *Wayne Junction*
(p. 210); 9 M. *Ogontz*, with a large girls' school. Beyond (33 M.)
Sellersville we penetrate the *Landis Hills* by a tunnel, ¹/₂ M. long.

56 M. **Bethlehem** (*Fountain Hill Ho.; Eagle*, $ 2¹/₂-3; *Sun*, a
relic of last century, $ 2), a thriving town of 17,064 inhab. (incl.

South Bethlehem), lies on the *Lehigh*, a small stream which joins the *Delaware*, 12 M. lower down. It is noted as the chief American centre of the Moravian Brothers, who settled here under Count Zinzendorf in 1740-41. Many of the old Moravian schools and other buildings are still extant; more recent institutions are the *Lehigh University* (above the town; 420 students) and *Bishopsthorpe*, a girls' school. The chief industries are the making of brass, zinc, and iron.

Easton (*Paxinosa Inn*, $4; *United States Ho.*, $2¹/₂-3), at the *Forks of the Delaware*, 12 M. to the N.E. of Bethlehem, an industrial town of 14,481 inhab., is the site of *Lafayette College*, a well-known institution (3-400 students), founded in 1826. It is an important railway-centre (p. 196).

The train now ascends the *Lehigh Valley*, with the tortuous stream to the right. Numerous iron-works are passed. 62 M. *Allentown* (Allen, American Ho,, $ 2-3), an iron and silk making town with 25,228 inhabitants. — 64 M. *Catasauqua*; 65 M. *Hokendaugua*; 66 M. *Coplay*, all with iron-works, blast-furnaces, and heaps of slag. The iron-works now disappear for a time and the scenery improves. 77 M. *Slatington* is the outlet for the most extensive slate-quarries in America. About 2 M. farther on we penetrate the *Blue Mts.* by the *Lehigh Water Gap*, in which two railways, the river, and a canal are compressed between the perpendicular cliffs of a narrow gorge. Beyond this point the valley expands somewhat, and the iron-works re-appear at (85 M.) *Parryville*. — At (89 M.) *Packerton* are the workshops of the Lehigh Valley R.R. and huge scales in which cars of coal are weighed while in motion. A little farther on the valley contracts and our line crosses to the N. bank of the river.

90 M. **Mauch Chunk** (530 ft.; *Mansion Ho.*, American, $ 2¹/₂-3¹/₂), a small town with 4000 inhab., picturesquely situated on a rocky shelf on the brink of the river, in one of the narrowest parts of the valley, with mountains towering overhead, is visited annually by thousands of travellers. It has but two streets, one running along the river and the other extending at right angles to it up a cleft in the mountains; while the slope is so abrupt that the man who enters his front-door on the street-level may step into his back-yard from the second story window. The *Bear Mt.* (Indian, *Mauch Chunk*) from which it takes its name rises to a height of 700 ft. immediately above the town. Mauch Chunk lies in the midst of a rich coal-district, and an immense traffic in coals is carried on by the railways and canals.

The chief lion of Mauch Chunk is the *Switchback or Gravity Railroad, originally built in 1827 to bring the coals out from the mines to the river, but now used by pleasure-seekers only (round trip in 1¹/₂ hr., fare 75 c.; omn. to foot of railway 25 c.). The train is first drawn by a powerful stationary engine to (¹/₂ M.) the top of *Mt. Pisgah* (1500 ft.; view), whence it descends by gravity to (6¹/₂ M) the foot of *Mt. Jefferson* (1660 ft.; *View). It is drawn up another inclined plane (gradient 1 : 4¹/₂) on this hill, and then runs on a level to (1 M.) *Summit Hill* (1485 ft.), a mining village with 2816 inhab., frequented by summer-visitors. One of the points of interest here is a *Burning Mine*, which has been smouldering for 60 years. The descent to *Upper Mauch Chunk*, near our starting-place, a distance of 9 M., is made by gravity in 25 minutes. — Good views are also obtained from *Prospect Rock* and *Flag-staff Peak* (950 ft.).

Beyond Mauch Chunk the railway continues to follow the narrow winding gorge of the river. — 92 M. *Glen Onoko* (Hotel Wahnetah, $ 2½-3), a beautiful little glen, traversed by a stream forming a series of falls. — At (115 M.) *White Haven* (1140 ft.) we leave the river and ascend the mountains to the left. — 126 M. *Glen Summit* (1730 ft.; Hotel, $ 3, meal-station), on the watershed between the Delawarè and the Susquehanna, commands a distant view of the main ridge of the Alleghenies (W.). We now descend rapidly into the *Wyoming Valley* (see below), a beautiful *View of which, with the *Susquehanna River*, is suddenly disclosed to the right.

144 M. **Wilkesbarré** (550 ft.; *Wyoming Valley Hotel*, $ 2-3; *Exchange, Luzerne*, $ 2), the chief town in the Wyoming Valley, on the E. bank of the Susquehanna, contains 37,718 inhab., who owe their prosperity to the rich coal-mines of the district. It is connected by a bridge with *Kingston* (2381 inhab.) on the opposite bank.

The *Valley of Wyoming (a corruption of the Indian *Maughwauwama* or 'large plains'), the name given to this expansion of the Susquehanna Valley, is about 20 M. long and 3-4 M. wide and is inclosed by two parallel ranges of hills, 800-1000 ft. high. The *Susquehanna* ('broad and shallow river'), which has a total length of 400 M. from Otsego Lake (see p. 158) to Chesapeake Bay, enters the valley through the *Lackawannock Gap* and leaves it through the narrow *Nanticoke Gap.* Within the valley its course is generally placid, but it forms two sets of rapids (the *Wyoming* and *Nanticoke Falls*) and receives several tributaries from the mountains. Numerous coal pits, culm-heaps, and smoking chimneys testify to the prevailing industry of the valley. A good *View of the valley is obtained from *Prospect Rock* (750 ft.), 2 M. from Wilkesbarré. *Campbell's Ledge*, on the E. side of the Lackawannock Gap, is also a good point of view. — A steamer descends the Susquehanna from Wilkesbarré to (8 M.) *Nanticoke.*

The name of the valley is widely known from the harrowing incidents narrated by Campbell in his 'Gertrude of Wyoming'. In June, 1778, a force of British troops and Indians entered the valley and defeated the settlers in a battle fought on July 3rd. The battle was followed by an atrocious massacre, in which the British officers were unable to set any bounds to the butchery of their savage allies, who, it is estimated, slew 300 men, women, and children. *Fort Forty*, the scene of the battle, 4 M. above Kingston (see above), is marked by an *Obelisk*, 60 ft. high; and about 3 M. farther up is *Queen Esther's Rock*, where the half-breed queen of the Senecas tomahawked 14 defenceless prisoners.

The train now ascends along the E. bank of the Susquehanna. The Wyoming Monument (see above) is seen across the river to the left. — 153 M. *Pittston* (570 ft.), with 10,302 inhab., lies near the point where the *Lackawanna* pours into the Susquehanna. Above rises *Campbell's Ledge* (see above). — A line leads hence to the N. E. to *Scranton* (p. 197) and *Carbondale.*

Beyond Pittston the scenery is less interesting. At (236 M.) *Athens* we cross the *Chemung River.* — Beyond (238 M.) *Sayre Junction* (for lines to Auburn, Owego, Elmira, etc.) we cross the Erie R. R. (R. 28 d). At (253 M.) *Van Etten* the line forks, the left branch running to Geneva (see below) viâ *Watkins* (p. 191) and *Seneca Lake* (p. 191), while that traversed by most through-trains runs to the N. to (274 M.) **Ithaca** (p. 190) and skirts the W. side of *Cayuga Lake* (p. 190). 297 M. *Hayt's Corners.* — 315 M. **Geneva,**

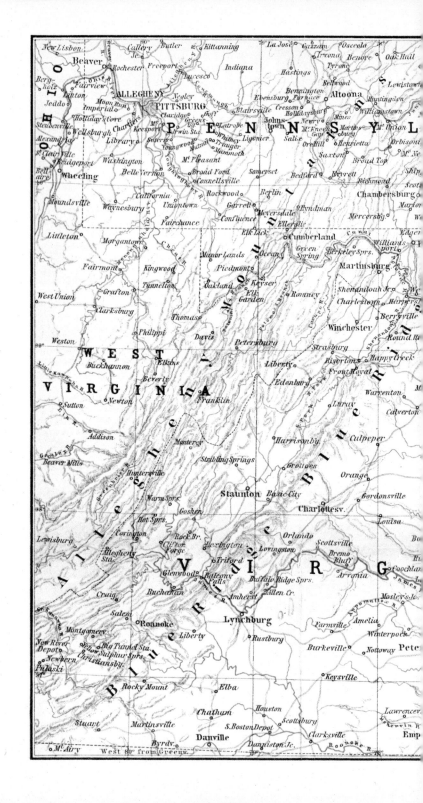

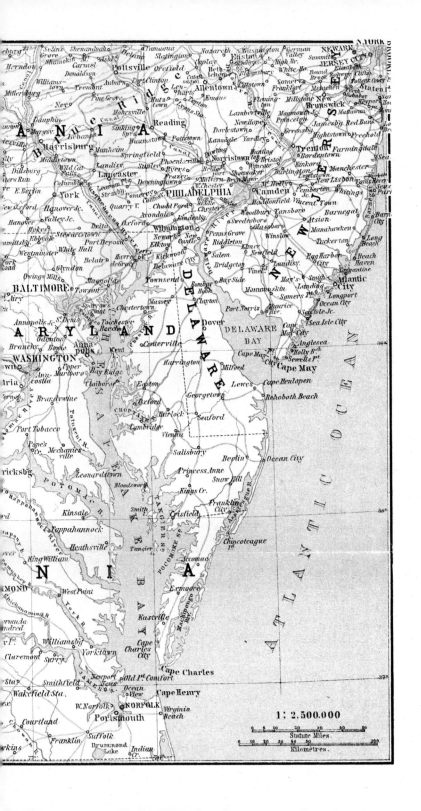

see p. 190. — 330 M. *Manchester;* 349 M. *Rochester Junction*, for
(13 M.) *Rochester* (p. 191). At (378 M.) *Niagara Junction* the branch
for Niagara Falls (p. 199) diverges to the right. 380 M. *Batavia*
(p. 192); 413 M. *East Buffalo* (p. 199).
418 M. **Buffalo,** see p. 192.

35. From Philadelphia to Reading and Williamsport.

198 M. PHILADELPHIA & READING RAILROAD in 6-10 hrs. (fare $ 5.78).
— The PENNSYLVANIA RAILROAD (Broad St. Station) is also available, the
trains following nearly the same route (fare as above). — Both lines traverse
the Schuylkill Valley and connect the great anthracite coal-fields of Pennsylvania with the ocean.

Philadelphia, see p. 210. The train crosses the *Schuylkill* (p. 211),
touches the N. end of *Fairmount Park* (p. 220), and ascends the
right bank of the river, parallel with the Schuylkill Valley Division
of the Pennsylvania Railroad on the opposite bank. The valley is
thickly populated and presents a scene of busy industry, with its
numerous factories and mills. — 17 M. *Bridgeport* lies opposite
Norristown (*Windsor Ho.*, $2), a thriving manufacturing city
(19,791 inhab.). — 23¹/₂ M. *Valley Forge*, the headquarters of Washington and the American army during the trying winter of 1777-78.
The farm-house in which Washington had his quarters is still preserved (to the left of the railway). — Beyond (27¹/₂ M.) *Phoenixville*, at the foot of *Black Rock*, with 8514 inhab. and the huge
Phoenix Iron and Steel Works, we thread a tunnel nearly ¹/₂ M.
long. Our train then crosses the river, changing sides with the Pennsylvania line. We are now in the district of the so-called 'Pennsylvania Dutch', a hard-working race of Teutonic origin, who speak
a curious dialect compounded of German, Dutch, and English. Near
(40 M.) *Pottstown*, another busy iron-making place (13,285 inhab.),
we cross the *Manatawny* by a long bridge.

58 M. **Reading** (270 ft.; *Mansion Ho.; American,* $2¹/₂), a busy
manufacturing city with 58,661 inhab., lies on a comparatively
level plateau hemmed in by *Penn's Mt.* on the E. and *Neversink Mt.*
on the S. The *Court House* is a handsome building, with a portico
borne by six columns of the old red sandstone found in the adjacent mountains. The chief industry is iron-making, and the shops
of the Reading Railway give employment to about 3000 men.

The "*White Spot*, on Penn's Mt., 1000 ft. above the river, is a favourite resort commanding a fine view. It is a remnant of Potsdam sandstone lying unconformably on Laurentian rock. — Reading is an important
railway-centre, lines radiating hence in all directions.

Beyond Reading our line continues to follow the Schuylkill Valley, and the long ridge of the *Blue Mts.* looms up ahead of us, changing
from gray to blue as we approach it. — At (78 M.) *Port Clinton*
(410 ft.), at the mouth of the *Little Schuylkill*, we pass through a
gap in the ridge, similar to, but less picturesque than, those mentioned at pp. 227, 196. Port Clinton stands on the S. edge of the

great anthracite coal-region, and has a busy traffic in coal. Our railway forks here, the left branch going on to *Pottsville* (see below), the right to Williamsport viâ the Catawissa Valley (see below).

FROM PORT CLINTON TO POTTSVILLE, 15 M., railway in $1/_2$-$3/_4$ hr. — The line follows the Schuylkill. — 5 M. *Auburn;* 11 M. *Schuylkill Haven.* — 15 M. *Pottsville* (615 ft.; Merchants', $2), a city with 14,117 inhab., in the gap where the river breaks through *Sharp Mt.* (1395 ft.), lies in the great S. or Schuylkill Coal Basin, which produces 10,0 0,000 tons of anthracite coal annually, or one-fourth of the total production of Pennsylvania (45,544,970 tons in 1889). The surrounding district is a network of railways.

The Williamsport train ascends the valley of the Little Schuylkill and traverses a busy coal-mining district. — $103^1/_2$ M. *East Mahanoy Junction.* Farther on we traverse the picturesque *Catawissa Valley.* At (145 M.) *Catawissa* (475 ft.) we cross the *Susquehanna.* 198 M. *Williamsport*, see below.

36. From Philadelphia to Erie.

446 M. PENNSYLVANIA RAILROAD in 16 hrs. (fare $ 10.35).

From Philadelphia to (105 M.) *Harrisburg*, see R. 37. Our line here diverges to the right from the line to Pittsburg and runs to the N. along the *Susquehanna.* — 159 M. *Sunbury* (450 ft.; 5930 inhab.), on the left bank of the wide *Susquehanna*, is an important outlet for the *Shamokin Coal District.* — At (161 M.) *Northumberland*, at the confluence of the N. and S. branches of the Susquehanna, *Dr. Joseph Priestly*, discoverer of oxygen gas, lived from 1794 till his death in 1804. He is buried in the cemetery here. — 171 M. *Milton.* Farther on our line runs parallel with the Reading line.

198 M. **Williamsport** (*Park, Updegraff*, $ $2^1/_2$-$3^1/_2$), a city on the right bank of the S. (or W.) branch of the Susquehanna, with 27,132 inhab., chiefly engaged in the timber-trade. The huge 'Boom' on the river here can contain 300 million feet of timber.

FROM WILLIAMSPORT TO NORDMONT, 40 M., *Williamsport & North Branch R. R.* in $1^3/_4$ hr. This line traverses a picturesque district which has been ambitiously dubbed the 'Adirondacks of Pennsylvania'. — The chief resorts are *Highland Lake* (2000 ft.; Grand View Hotel, Essick, Highland Ho.), reached by coach ($1^1/_2$ hr.) from (18 M.) *Picture Rocks* (670 ft.); **Eagles' Mere** (2300 ft.; *Hotel Eagles' Mere, Lakeside, Raymond*, $ 3-4; *Allegheny*, $ 2), reached by coach ($1^1/_2$ hr.) from (29 M.) *Muncy Valley;* and *Lake Mokoma* (La Porte Hotel), 4 M. from (40 M.) *Nordmont.*

From Williamsport to *Elmira*, see p. 197.

We turn to the left (W.), cross the *Lycoming Creek* and the Susquehanna, and ascend on the right bank of the latter. 223 M. *Lock Haven*, another lumbering town (7358 inhab.), situated on the right bank of the Susquehanna. The scenery here and as we advance farther up the river is picturesque. We cross and recross the stream. — 251 M. *Renovo* (670 ft.; *Renovo Hotel*, $ 2), a summer-resort, finely situated in the Susquehanna valley, among hills 800-1000 ft. high.

At (263 M.) *Keating* (720 ft.) the train leaves the Susquehanna, after following it for 160 M., and begins to ascend the *Sinnemahoning.*

The somewhat dreary and unsettled district we now traverse is known as the *Great Horseshoe of the Alleghenies.* — 278 M. *Driftwood,* junction of a line to Pittsburg (p. 240). — 297 M. *Emporium* (1030 ft.; St. Charles, $ 2), a hill-surrounded village with 2147 inhab., is the junction of the Western New York and Pennsylvania R.R.

FROM EMPORIUM TO BUFFALO, 121 M., railway in 5 hrs. — This line runs to the N. to (25 M.) *Port Allegheny*, and then follows the *Allegheny River* to (51 M.) **Olean** (*Olean Ho.*, $ 2), on the Erie R. R. (p. 278), one of the largest petroleum s'oring places in the world. Pop. 7308. — To the left, near (72 M.) *Franklinville*, is *Lime Lake*. — 121 M. *Buffalo*, see p. 192.

318 M. *St. Mary's* (1670 ft.), in a lumbering and bituminous coal producing district, has a large German Benedictine college and convent. — 342 M. *Wilcox* (1525 ft.), with a large tannery. — 351 M. *Kane* (2020 ft.; Thomson Ho., $ 2), a small town with 2944 inhab., frequented for deer-shooting and fishing. We now begin to descend on the Lake Erie side of the ridge. — 380 M. *Warren* (1195 ft.), pleasantly situated at the confluence of the *Allegheny* and the *Conewango*, is the junction of a line to Dunkirk (p. 267). — 409 M. *Corry* (1445 ft.), an industrial town (5667 inhab.).

From Corry to *Pittsburg* and to *Buffalo*, see p. 243. Corry is also the junction of lines to *Jamestown* (p. 278), etc.

428 M. *Waterford* (1190 ft.), on the *Le Boeuf Lake.* Beyond (433 M.) *Jackson* (1225 ft.) we cross the watershed between the Ohio and Lake Erie, here only 8 M. from the latter.

446 M. **Erie**, see p. 267.

37. From Philadelphia to Harrisburg and Pittsburg.

354 M. PENNSYLVANIA RAILROAD to (105 M.) *Harrisburg* in 2³/₄-4 hrs. (fare $ 3.15, parlor-car $ 1.50); to (354 M.) *Pittsburg* in 9-13 hrs. (fare $ 10, parlor-car $ 2, sleeper $ 2). This line, forming part of the fine through-route from New York to Chicago (see R. 47a), traverses the beautiful valleys of the Susquehanna and Juniata.

Leaving the handsome *Broad St. Station* (p. 213) the train crosses the *Schuylkill* and runs to the N.W. through *W. Philadelphia* (p. 219), passing various suburban stations, most of which are tasteful little buildings surrounded with flower-gardens. 9 M. *Haverford College*, with the most important college of the Orthodox Quakers, situated in a finely wooded park to the left. — 10 M. *Bryn Mawr* (415 ft.; Welsh 'great ridge'; Bryn Mawr Ho.), is the site of *Bryn Mawr College, one of the youngest and best colleges for women in the United States (130 students). The tower of the main building is conspicuous to the right. — 12 M. *Villa Nova* has a R. C. college, monastery, and farm. To the left, at (16½ M.) *Devon*, is the large *Devon Inn* ($ 4-5), a favourite summer-resort. At (20 M.) *Paoli* (535 ft.) the British defeated the Americans on Sept. 20th, 1777 (monument). It was the birthplace of '*Mad' Anthony Wayne* (1745-96; p. 148).

The train now leaves the region of suburban homes and enters the '*Garden of Pennsylvania*', one of the richest and most carefully cultivated farming districts in America. A splendid *View of the peaceful *Chester Valley* is disclosed to the right as we cross the ridge (550 ft.) of a S. outlier of the Alleghenies and emerge on the hillside. We follow the ridge for some time and then descend to the valley. — 32½ M. *Downingtown.* Iron-works and lime-kilns now appear. — At (38½ M.) *Coatesville* (380 ft.; 3680 inhab.) we cross the *West Brandywine* by a bridge 73 ft. high. — 51 M. *Gap* (560 ft.) lies in an opening in *Mine Hill,* on the watershed between the Delaware and the Susquehanna, and the train now descends into the *Pequea Valley,* with its fields of wheat, maize, and tobacco. — Crossing the *Conestoga Creek,* which preserves the name of the Conestoga Indians, we reach (69 M.) **Lancaster** (360 ft.; *Stevens Ho.,* $2½; *Lancaster*), a prosperous manufacturing town of 32,011 inhab. and an important market in tobacco and farm produce.

The *Franklin & Marshall College* and the *Theological Seminary* here both belong to the German Reformed Church. *Woodward Hill Cemetery* contains the grave of President Buchanan (1791-1868). The district is largely peopled by the descendants of German colonists. A railway runs hence to *Hanover* and *Gettysburg* (p. 235).

Beyond (87 M.) *Elizabethtown* the train enters the picturesque defiles of the *South Mountain.* At (90 M.) *Conewago* we cross the stream of that name (view) Farther on we reach the W. bank of the *Susquehanna,* a wide, shallow stream, thickly strewn with rocks. 96 M. *Middletown,* at the mouth of the *Swatara,* with 5080 inhab., is an iron-making place. — At (102 M.) *Steelton* (pop. 9250) are the huge works of the Pennsylvania Steel Co., employing 4500 men.

105 M. **Harrisburg** (320 ft.; *Lochiel Ho.,* $3; *Commonwealth,* $3; *Bolton,* $2½-3), the capital of Pennsylvania, is finely situated on the E. bank of the Susquehanna, here about 1 M. wide. Pop. 39,385. Except when the legislature is in session it is a somewhat dull place. The *Capitol,* surmounted by a dome and conspicuously situated on a hill, contains a good library. In State St. is a *War Monument,* 110 ft. high. A small enclosure in *Harris Park* contains the grave of John Harris, father of the founder of the town, and the stump of the tree to which he was tied by drunken Indians (1718), who intended to burn him alive. The Susquehanna is crossed here by four bridges, one of which is the quaint old covered bridge described by Dickens in his 'American Notes'.

FROM HARRISBURG to GETTYSBURG, 47 M., railway in 1¾-2hrs. — The train crosses the Susquehanna, just below the old bridge (see above), and runs to the S.W. — 21 M. *Carlisle Junction,* for a branch-line to (6 M.) *Carlisle* (see below). Near (22 M.) *Mt. Holly Springs* we pass through a gap (1000 ft) in the *South Mountain.* As we approach Gettysburg we traverse the field of the first day's battle (see p. 237). — 47 M. **Gettysburg,** see p. 235.

FROM HARRISBURG TO WINCHESTER, 116 M., railway in 4-4½ hrs. This line traverses the fertile *Cumberland Valley,* between the *Blue Mts.,* on the right, and the *South Mountain,* on the left. — The train crosses the Susquehanna as above. — 18 M. *Gettysburg Junction,* for the line to Gettysburg (see above). — 19 M. **Carlisle** (480 ft.; *Mansion Ho.,* $2), a pleasant little town of 7620 inhab., with a *Government Indian Training School,* in which about 800 Indian children are taught the arts and methods of civilisation. Carlisle was Washington's headquarters during the 'Whiskey War'

of 1794, and it was captured by Gen. Lee in 1863. — About 5 M. beyond
(63 M.) *Greencastle* the train crosses the famous *Mason and Dixon's Line*
(see p. 236) and enters *Maryland* ('Old Line State'), the northernmost of
the old slave-holding states. — 74 M. **Hagerstown** (570 ft.; *Baldwin*, $ 2-3),
a town of 10,118 inhab., on the *Antietam*, is the junction of lines to Washington (see p. 251), Harper's Ferry (viâ Weverton; see p. 265), and the
Shenandoah Valley (R. 70 b). It was a centre of military operations in the
Civil War. — 81 M. *Williamsport* is the point where Gen. Lee crossed the
Potomac on his retreat after the battle of Gettysburg (p. 238). We here
enter *West Virginia* ('Pan-handle State'). — At (94 M.) *Martinsburg* (635 ft.),
on the *Tuscarora*, we intersect the Baltimore & Ohio R.R. (p. 266). —
116 M. *Winchester*.

FROM HARRISBURG TO READING, 54 M., railway in 1¹/₂-2 hrs. — The
chief intermediate station is (26 M.) *Lebanon*. — 54 M. *Reading*, see p. 229.

FROM HARRISBURG TO WILLIAMSPORT, 93 M., *Northern Central Railroad*
in 3-3¹/₄ hrs. This railway ascends on the E. bank of the Susquehanna to
(54 M.) *Sunbury* (p. 230). Thence to (93 M.) *Williamsport*, see p. 230.

From Harrisburg to *Baltimore*, see p. 250.

Beyond Harrisburg the Penn. R. R. runs to the N. on the left bank
of the Susquehanna to (110 M.) *Rockville*, where it bends to the W.
and crosses the river by a bridge ²/₃ M. long (*View). It then turns
to the N. again and passes the *Dauphin Gap* (350 ft.). The river, now
to the right, is wide, shallow, and nearly choked with grassy islets.

Beyond (119 M.) *Duncannon* the line leaves the Susquehanna
and begins to ascend to the left through the valley of the 'beautiful
blue' *Juniata, 'which has been the theme of more song and romance
than almost any other American river' (Cook).

The *Scenery along this river, as we cross ridge after ridge of the
Alleghenies, is of the most picturesque character; and the entire geological formation of Pennsylvania is exhibited to the student, as the river
cuts its way through a stratification 6-7 M. in thickness. The line follows
the windings of the river (views chiefly to the right). The district traversed
is full of historical reminiscences of the struggles of the early Scoto-
Irish colonists with the Indians and of the enterprise of *David Brainerd*
and other missionaries. An immense traffic in coal and iron is carried
on by this line, and the coal-trains are sometimes of extraordinary length.

At (137¹/₂ M.) *Millerstown* (410 ft.) we thread the *Tuscarora Gap,
where the railway, river, road, and canal squeeze their way side by
side through a narrow defile. This lay in the land of the Tuscarora
Indians (see p. 187). Beyond (154 M.) *Mifflin* we pass through the
picturesque *Lewiston* or *Long Narrows*, where the railway runs
for several miles along one side of the stream, with the road and
canal on the other. The slopes of the hills (1000 ft.) are covered
with slate debris. — 167 M. *Lewiston* (500 ft.), a prosperous little
place with 3273 inhab., lies at the mouth of the *Kishicoquillas Valley*.

In this valley, a little above Lewiston, was the home of the famous
Mingo chief *Logan*, whose friendship for the white man was changed to
hatred by the cruel massacre of his family.

191 M. *Mt. Union* lies at the entrance of *Jack's Narrows (600 ft.),
made by the river forcing its way through *Jack's Mt.* — 202 M.
Huntingdon (*Brunswick*, $ 2), the largest town on the Juniata (5729
inhab.), occupies the site of the 'Standing Stone', where the Indians
assembled for centuries to hold their grand councils.

The *Broad Top Mt. Railroad* runs hence to (53 M.) *Bedford,* near which are *Bedford Springs* (Bedford Springs Ho., $ 3-4 ; Arandale, $ 2-3).

At (209 M.) *Petersburg* (680 ft.) we leave the canal, which follows the Franktown branch of the river, and ascend the *Little Juniata.* — At (222 M.) *Tyrone* (905 ft.), where we reach the E. base of the main range of the Alleghenies, the line turns sharply to the left (S.W.), leaves the Juniata, and enters the *Tuckahoe Valley. Bald Eagle Valley* opens to the N.E.

Tyrone is the outlet for the important *Clearfield Coal Measures,* which in 1859 produced 5,224,500 tons of bituminous coal. — About 3 M. to the E. is the *Sinking Valley,* which takes its name from the *Sinking Spring,* a singular underground watercourse.

From Tyrone the train runs along the base of the Alleghenies (right) to (237 M.) **Altoona** (1180 ft.; *Logan Ho.,* $ 3; *Wopsonock Inn; Rail. Restaurant*), a busy town of 30,337 inhab., founded in 1850 by the Pennsylvania R. R. and consisting almost wholly of its workshops and workmen's houses.

Altoona is, perhaps, the most representative railway-town in America. The works cover 120 acres, employ 6.00 men, and produce 300 locomotives, 200 pa senger cars, and 5000 freight cars annually. Some of the locomotives made here weigh 125 tons. — Those who wish to see the fine 'passage of the Alleghenies by daylight may pass the night here. Good views are obtained from *Prospect Hill* to the S. and *Gospel Hill* to the N.

Beyond Altoona the train gradually ascends to the summit of the mountains, climbing a gradient of 90 ft. to the mile. At (242 M.) *Kittaning Point* (1595 ft.) the line is carried round the famous **Horseshoe Curve* (views to the left), a wonderful piece of engineering, where the line crosses two ravines on a lofty embankment and cuts away the promontory dividing them. The sides of the curve are parallel, so that trains travelling the same way seem to be moving in opposite directions. A little farther on we pass through a *Tunnel,* $2/3$ M. long and 2160 ft. above the sea, crossing the Alleghenies and the watershed between the Atlantic and the Mississippi. The top of the ridge is 210 ft. above the tunnel.

The descent on the W. slope of the mountains is less abrupt. 248 M. *Gallitzin,* at the W. end of the tunnel, is named in honour of *Prince Demetrius Gall tzin* (d. 1840), who laboured as a missionary in this district for 40 years. — 252 M. **Cresson Springs** (2015 ft.; *Mountain House,* $ 4), a favourite summer-resort. Coaches ply hence to *Loretto,* founded by Prince Gallitzin (see above). — We descend along the upper waters of the *Conemaugh,* and the scenery increases in attractiveness. Numerous vestiges are seen of the old *Portage Railroad,* which formerly served the traffic across the Alleghenies by a series of inclined planes, communicating at each end with canals. — Near (269 M.) *Mineral Point* (1415 ft.) we cross the Conemaugh. *Conemaugh Lake* (1460 ft.), the bursting of the dam at which caused the terrible disaster of 1889 (see p. 235), lies a little to the left. 273 M. *Conemaugh* (1275 ft.).

275 M. **Johnstown** (1185 ft.; *Morrell Ho.,* $ 2$1/2$), an iron-making city at the confluence of the Conemaugh and *Stony Creek,* was

founded in 1791 by a German pioneer, named Joseph Jahns. It contains 21,805 inhab. and has to a great extent recovered from the effects of the inundation. The huge *Cambria Steel Works*, on the N. side of the river, were partly destroyed by the inundation in 1889, but have been restored and again give employment to 8000 men.

A glance at the deep narrow valleys with their high enclosing walls, at the junction of which the city lies, goes far to expl in the possibility of so tremendous a catastrophe as that which overwhemed Johnstown on May 31st, 1889. *Conemaugh Lake* (see above), $2^1/2$ M. long and $1^1/2$ M. wide, was reserved as a fishing-ground by a club of Pittsburg anglers, and its waters were restrained by a dam 1000 ft. long, 110 ft. high, 90 ft. thick at the base, and 25 ft. thick at the top. A continuance of violent rains filled the lake to overflowing, and all efforts to save the dam were fruitless. The break occurred about 3 p.m., a gap of 300 ft being at once formed. The water that burst through swept down the valley in a mass $1/2$ M. wide and 40 ft. high, carrying away everything in its way and completely destroying Johnstown and the other towns and villages in its track. The distance of 18 M. between Johnstown and the lake was traversed in about 7 min. The mass of houses, trees, machinery, railway iron, and human bodies was checked by the massive railway-bridge below Johnstown, and soon caught fire, probably burning to death some hundreds of persons imprisoned in the wreckage. The estimates of the total loss of life vary from 2250 to 5000. The vaue of property destroyed was at least $ 10,000,000 (2,000,000*l.*).

The train descends along the left bank of the Conemaugh. 295 M. *Bolivar* (1030 ft.) lies at the entrance to the beautiful *Packsaddle Narrows*, where the river breaks through the *Chestnut Range*, the W. ridge of the Alleghenies, which tower 1200 ft. above the water. At (300 M.) *Blairsville Intersection* (1115 ft.) the line forks, the main line leaving the Conemaugh and running direct to Pittsburg, while the right branch runs viâ *Blairsville* to *Allegheny City* (p. 243).

The district we traverse as we approach Pittsburg is a veritable 'Black Country', full of coal-pits, coke ovens, and smelting furnaces. 313 M. *Latrobe;* 322 M. *Greensburg* (1090 ft.). We approach the *Monongahela* at (343 M.) *Braddock's* (8561 inhab.), which marks the scene of the memorable defeat of General Braddock on July 9th, 1755, on his expedition against Fort Du Quesne (see p. 240). It was in rallying the defeated British forces that Washington won his first military laurels. The huge *Edgar Thomson Steel Works* are now situated here (see p. 242). — 346 M. *Wilkinsburg* (926 ft.), with two fine *Homes for Aged Persons*.

354 M. **Pittsburg**, see R. 39.

38. Gettysburg.[†]

Gettysburg is reached from New York viâ the Pennsylvania or the Reading R. R. in $7^1/2$ hrs. (fare $ 6.50), from Philadelphia viâ the same railways in 5 hrs. (comp. p. 232; $ 4), and from Washington viâ Baltimore in $6^2/3$ hrs. by the Western Maryland or the Northern Central R. R. (comp. p. 250).

† This account of Gettysburg was prepared for *Baedeker's Handbook to the United States* by Mr. *Joel Cook*, of the 'Philadelphia Public Ledger', who was present at the battle as a special correspondent.

Gettysburg (*Eagle* $2-3; *McClellan Ho.*, $1¹/₂-2), a small town with (1890) 3221 inhab., lies about 40 M. to the S.E. of *Harrisburg* (p. 232) and 7 M. to the N. of the boundary between Pennsylvania and Maryland, the famous *Mason and Dixon's Line* (p. 233), which, before the war, marked the N. limit of slavery. On July 1st-3rd, 1863, the vicinity of this town was the scene of what is regarded as the chief contest of the American Civil War and as the 'turning-point of the Rebellion'.

The battle-ground covers about 25 sq. M. and lies mainly to the S.W. of the town. The *Gettysburg Battlefield Memorial Association*, an organisation representing the soldiers engaged, has marked all the important points by monuments placed on ground acquired for the purpose. The tracts along the lines, aggregating 450 acres, are the land upon which the most important movements were executed. There are nearly 400 monuments on the field, erected with the utmost care in the exact localities, and standing in woods or open fields, by the roadside, on the stony ridges, in gardens, and being of all designs, executed in bronze, marble or granite. Over $1,000,000 has been expended on the grounds and monuments. The battlefield is probably better marked, both topographically and by art, than any other battlefield in the world.

There were engaged in the battle about 80,000 men on each side, the Union army having 3.9 cannon and the Confederates 293. Generals *George Gordon Meade* and *Robert Edward Lee* were the respective commanders, and it was among the most hotly contested battles of the war and the largest in actual numbers engaged. The Union loss was 3072 killed, 14,497 wounded, and 5434 prisoners, a total of 23,003; and the Confederate loss, 2592 killed, 12,709 wounded and 7467 prisoners, total 23,768.

The long curving ridges and deep intervening valleys of the Allegheny mountain ranges cross Central Pennsylvania, the South Mountain ridge passing to the W. of Gettysburg, with the Cumberland Valley beyond it, having two prominent towns, Chambersburg in Pennsylvania and Hagerstown on the Potomac river, in Maryland. Two parallel ridges border the plain on which Gettysburg stands. The long '*Seminary Ridge*', stretching from N. to S. about a mile to the W. of the town, gets its name from the Lutheran Theological Seminary standing upon it; and the *Cemetery Ridge*, to the S. of the town, which runs up its slopes, has, on its N. flat-topped hill, the village cemetery, wherein the chief grave was that of James Gettys, after whom the town was named. An outlying eminence known as *Culp's Hill* is farther to the E., making, with Cemetery Ridge, a formation bent round not unlike a fish-hook, with the cemetery at the bend and Culp's Hill at the barb, while down at the S. end of the long straight shank with the intervening rocky gorge of the 'Devil's Den', nearly 3 M. away, are two peaks formed of tree-covered crags, known as *Little Round Top* and *Big Round Top*. These long ridges with the intervale and the country around them are the battlefield, a topographical configuration displaying the ground to great advantage, the many monuments marking the respective lines of battle. Comp. Plan.

After their victory at Chancellorsville (p. 326) in May, 1863, the Confederates determined to carry the war to the N. into the enemy's country. Lee gathered nearly 90,000 men at Culpeper (Va.) including J. E. B. Stuart's cavalry force of 10,000 men. The Union army, commanded by General Hooker, was then encamped along the Rappahannock river, opposite *Fredericksburg* (p. 326), 150 M. to the S. of Gettysburg. Lee started to the N. across the *Potomac*, but Hooker did not discover it for some days, and then followed him. The Confederates crossed between June 22nd and June 25th and concentrated at *Hagerstown* (p. 233), in the *Cumberland Valley*, up which they made a rapid march, overrunning the entire country to the *Susquehanna River* (p. 228). Hooker was late in movement and crossed the Potomac to the E. of Lee on June 28th, thus making a northern race, with Lee in advance but on the longer route of the outer

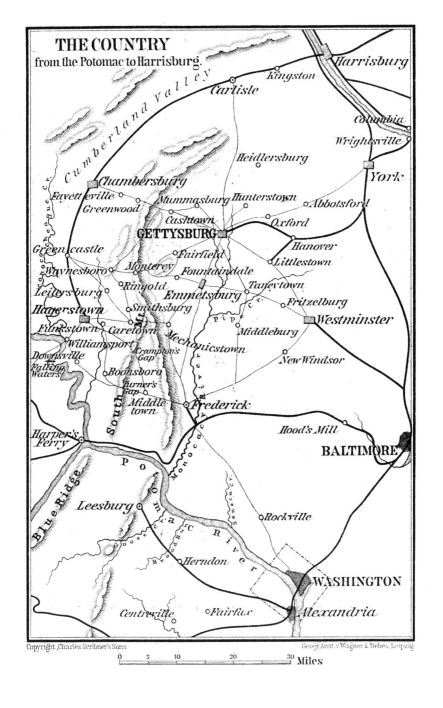

THE COUNTRY
from the Potomac to Harrisburg.

Harrisburg

Kingston

Cumberland Valley

Carlisle

Columbia

Wrightsville

Heidlersburg

York

Chambersburg

Fayetteville

Mummasburg   Hunterstown

Greenwood

Abbotsford

Cashtown

Oxford

GETTYSBURG

Hanover

Greencastle

Fairfield

Littlestown

Waynesboro

Monterey

Fountaindale

Leitersburg

Ringold

Taneytown

Fritzelburg

Hagerstown

Emmetsburg

Westminster

Smithsburg

Funkstown   Caretown

Mechanicstown

Middleburg

Williamsport

Crampton's
Gap

Downsville

New Windsor

Falling
Waters

Boonsboro

Turner's
Gap

Harper's
Ferry

Middle
town

Frederick

Hood's Mill

BALTIMORE

Blue Ridge

South Mt.

Potomac

Leesburg

Rockville

Monocacy River

Seneca Cr.

Herndon

River

WASHINGTON

Centreville

Fairfax

Alexandria

Copyright, Charles Scribner's Sons

Geogr. Anst. v. Wagner & Debes, Leipzig

0   5   10   20   30   Miles

GETTYSBURG

Final Attack of the First Day, and Battle of the Second Day.

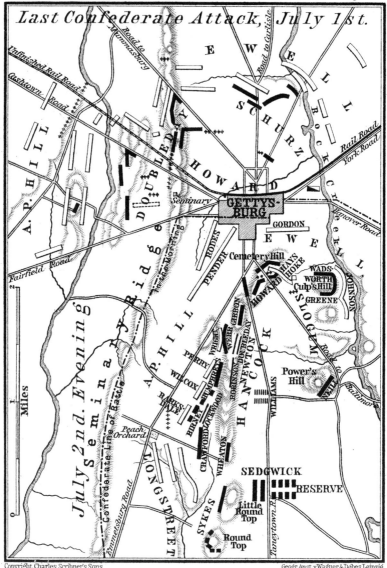

Last Confederate Attack, July 1st.

Copyright, Charles Scribner's Sons   Geogr.Anst.v.Wagner & Debes,Leipzig

The first day's battle is represented north of the Fairfield and Hanover roads.
The second day's battle south of the same roads.

■■■ *Union troops*   ☐ *Confederate troops.*

circle. There were 10,000 Union troops in the garrison at *Harper's Ferry* (p. 265) on the Potomac, and Hooker asked that they be added to his army; but the government declined, and Hooker immediately resigned his command. He was succeeded by Gen. Meade, who thus on the eve of the battle became the Union commander. This was on June 28th, when Meade was near the Potomac, and Ewell with Lee's advance guard had gone up the Cumberland Valley as far as *Carlisle* (p. 232) and was threatening *Harrisburg* (p. 232). The main body of Confederates lay at *Chambersburg*, with nobody opposing them. Lee, then hearing of the Union pursuit and being far from his base, determined to face about and cripple his pursuers, fixing upon Gettysburg as the point of concentration. He ordered Ewell to march to the S. from Carlisle and the others to the E. from Chambersburg through the mountain passes. Meade's cavalry advance under Buford reached Gettysburg on June 30th, ahead of the Confederates, and Meade's army was then stretched for 60 M. back towards the Potomac. When he heard of Lee's changed tactics, Meade concluded that his extended formation was too risky and decided to concentrate in a strong position upon the *Pipe Creek Hills* in Maryland, about 15 M. to the S. of Gettysburg. Thus the battle began with each army executing a movement for concentration.

The battle opened on July 1st, the Union Cavalry to the W. and N. of Gettysburg becoming engaged with the Confederate advance approaching from the passes through the *South Mountain*. The cavalry was at first victorious but was afterwards overwhelmed by superior numbers, and with their infantry supports under Gen. Reynolds, who was killed, were driven back through Gettysburg to the cemetery and Culp's Hill. These were manned by fresh troops that had come up. Meade was at Pipe Creek, laying out a defensive line, when he heard of Reynolds' death and the defeat, and he sent Hancock forward to take command, who determined that the Cemetery Ridge was the place to give battle. Ewell in the meantime had extended his wing round to the E. of Culp's Hill and held Gettysburg; but active operations were suspended, and both sides spent the night getting their forces up.

The second day opened with the armies confronting each other in line of battle, the Union forces along the Cemetery Ridge, and the Confederates upon the Seminary Ridge to the W. and also stretching round through Gettysburg, to the N. of the Cemetery, 2 M. to the E. along the base of Culp's Hill. In the long intervening valley and upon the ravines and slopes of the Cemetery Ridge and Culp's Hill, the main battle was fought. Lee opened the attack by Longstreet advancing against the two Round Tops, but after a bloody struggle the Unionists held them. Sickles, who held the line to the S. of Little Round Top, thought he could improve his position by advancing 1/2 M. towards Seminary Ridge, thus making a broken Union line with a portion thrust out dangerously. The enemy fell upon Sickles, front and flank, almost overwhelming his line in the 'Peach Orchard' and driving it back to the adjacent 'Wheat Field.' Reinforcements were poured in and there was a hot conflict, Sickles being seriously wounded and his force almost cut to pieces.

Ewell then made a terrific charge from out of Gettysburg upon the Cemetery and Culp's Hill with the 'Louisiana Tigers' and other troops, effecting a lodgement, although the defenders wrought great havoc with their heavy cannonade. The Union guns on Little Round Top having ultimately cleared the 'Wheat Field', the combatants rested; Lee, inspirited by his partial successes, determining to renew the attack next morning.

On the third and last day Gen. Meade opened the combat by driving Ewell's forces from Culp's Hill early in the morning. Lee did not hear of this, but had an idea that both the Union centre and right wing had been weakened the previous day, and during the night, he planned an attack in front to be aided by a cavalry movement round that wing to assail the rear, thus following up Ewell's supposed advantage. To give Stuart with his cavalry time to get around to the rear, the front attack was not made till afternoon. Each side got cannon in position during the morning, Lee having 120 guns along Seminary Ridge, and Meade 80 in the

Cemetery and along a low irregular stone pile, forming a sort of rude wall along the Taneytown road leading to the S. from Gettysburg. About 1 p.m. the Confederates opened fire, and the most terrific artillery duel of the war followed across the intervening valley, six guns being discharged every second. The troops, lying low, suffered little, but several Union guns were dismounted. After two hours, deafening cannonade, Lee ordered his grand attack, the celebrated charge by Gen. Pickett, a force of 14.000 men with brigade front advancing across the valley. They had a mile to go, marching swiftly, but before they got halfway across, all the Union guns were trained upon them. The attack was directed at an umbrella-shaped clump of trees, at a low point of the Cemetery Ridge, where the rude stone wall made an angle with its point outside, this being the famous 'Bloody Angle'. Hancock commanded this portion of the Union line, and while the grape and canister of the cannonade ploughed furrows through Pickett's ranks, when the column got within 300 yds., Hancock opened musketry fire with terrible effect. Thousands fell, and the brigades broke in disorder, but the advanceheaded by Gen. Armistead on foot continued, and about 150 men leaped over the stone piles at the angle to capture the Union guns. Lieut. Cushing, mortally wounded in both thighs, ran his last serviceable gun towards the wall, and shouted to his commander 'Webb, I will give them one more shot'. He fired the gun and died. Armistead put his hand on the cannon, waved his sword and called out, 'give them the cold steel, boys'; then pierced by bullets, he fell dead along side Cushing. Both lay near the clumps of trees about 30 yds. inside the wall, their corpses marking the farthest point to which Pickett's advance penetrated, where the 'High Water Mark Monument' now marks the top of the flood tide of the rebellion, for afterwards there was a steady ebb. There was a hand to hand conflict. Webb was wounded and also Hancock, and the slaughter was dreadful. The Confederates were overwhelmed, and not one-fourth of the gallant charging column composed of the flower of the Virginia troops escaped, the remnant retreating in disorder. Stuart's cavalry failed to coöperate, having unexpectedly met the Union cavalry about 4 M. to the E. of Gettysburg, and the conflict that ensued prevented their attacking the Union rear. After Pickett's retreat, there was a general Union advance which closed the combat. During the night Lee began a retreat, and aided by the heavy rains usually following great battles, the Confederates next day withdrew through the mountain passes towards Hagerstown, and afterwards escaped across the Potomac. The day of Lee's retreat, Vicksburg surrendered to Gen. Grant (see p. 321) and these two great events were the beginning of the Confederacy's downfall.

This battlefield is now covered with monuments and marking posts designating the positions of the opposing armies. Its survey is best begun by a tour to the N. and W. of the town, the scene of the first day's fight. The more interesting tour, however, is to the S. from Gettysburg. Ascending Cemetery Hill we pass by the roadside the house of Jenny Wade, the only woman killed in the battle, accidentally shot while baking bread. The rounded Cemetery Hill is a strong and elevated position bearing many monuments, and here, alongside the little village graveyard, the Government has a National Cemetery of 17 acres, where 3572 soldiers are buried, over 1000 being the unknown dead. A magnificent battle monument rises above them, surmounted by a statue of Liberty, and having figures of War, History, Peace, and Plenty, at the base of the shaft. This charming spot was the centre of the Union line, then a rough, rocky hill. This cemetery was dedicated on Nov. 19th, 1863, Edward Everett delivering the oration; the monument was dedicated on July 1st, 1869. The cemetery cost $ 150,000. At the ceremony of its dedication, President Lincoln was present, and made the famous 'twenty line address', which is regarded as the most immortal utterance of the martyr. The *Westminster Review* described it as an oration having but one equal, in that pronounced upon those who fell during the first year of the 'Peleponnesian War' and as being its superior, because 'natural, fuller of feeling, more touching and pathetic, and we know with an absolute certainty that it was really was really delivered'. The President, when requested to say a few words by way of dedication, drew from his pocket a crumpled piece of paper, on which he had written some notes, and thus he spoke: —

'Fourscore and seven years ago our fathers brought forth upon this continent a new nation, conceived in liberty, and dedicated to the proposition that all men are created equal. Now we are engaged in a great civil war, testing whether that nation, or any nation, so conceived and so dedicated can long endure. We are met on a great battlefield of that war. We are met to dedicate a portion of it as the final resting place of those who here gave their lives that that nation might live. It is altogether fitting and proper that we should do this. But, in a larger sense, we cannot dedicate, we cannot consecrate, we cannot hallow this ground. The brave men, living and dead, who struggled here have consecrated it far above our power to add or detract. The world will little note nor long remember what we say here, but it can never forget what they did here. It is for us, the living, rather to be dedicated here to the unfinished work that they have thus far so nobly carried on. It is rather for us to be here dedicated to the great task remaining before us—that from these honoured dead we take increased devotion to the cause for which they here gave the last full measure of devotion—that we here highly resolve that the dead shall not have died in vain—that the nation shall, under God, have a new birth of freedom, and that government of the people, by the people, for the people, shall not perish from the earth.'

From the cemetery the Lutheran seminary is seen a mile across the valley, the most conspicuous landmark of the Confederate line. Culp's Hill is to the S.E., strewn with boulders and timber-covered, the trees still showing marks of the fighting. The Emmettsburg road goes down the valley, gradually diverging from the Union line and crossing the fields that were the battle-ground on the 2nd and 3rd days. Many monuments line the road, some of great merit, and it leads to the 'Peach Orchard', where the line bends sharply back. Peach-trees are constantly replanted here as the old ones fall. The 'wheat-field' alongside is now a meadow; and beyond we go down among the crags and boulders of the 'Devil's Den', a ravine through which flows a stream coming from the orchard and wheat-field and separating them from the rocky 'Round Tops', the beetling sandstone crags of 'Little Round Top' rising high above the ravine. The sloping fields along the stream above the Den are known as the 'Valley of Death'. Many monuments among these rocks have been made with the boulders that are so numerous. 'Big Round Top' beyond is mounted by a toilsome path, and an Observatory on the summit gives a good view over the surrounding country and almost the entire battlefield. The summit, more than 3 M. to the S. of Gettysburg, has tall timber, preserved as in the battle. Cannon surmount the 'Round Tops' representing the batteries there during the battle. To the W., across the valley, is the long fringe of timber that masked the Confederate position on Seminary Ridge. A picnic ground has been located alongside the 'Round Tops', with access by railway; and large parties frequently visit this spot during the tourist-season. The lines of breastworks are retained, and not far away is the 'Bloody Angle', upon the lower ground, where the stone walls are preserved and the little umbrella-shaped grove of trees. The 20th Massachusetts Regiment have brought hither a huge conglomerate boulder from their New England home and set it up as their monument. Their colonel, Paul Revere, was killed in the battle. Crossing the valley, the tourist returns to the N. along the Confederate line, where, however, there was no fighting until the scene of the first day's conflict is reached, to the W. of Gettysburg. Here a plain granite stone marks where Reynolds fell, just within a grove of trees. Reynolds, from his untimely death, is regarded as the Northern hero of the battle, as Armistead was the Southern. Near by the 'Massachusetts Colour-bearer' holds aloft the flag of the 13th Mass. Regiment, standing upon a slope alongside the railway, this striking monument marking the spot where he fell at the opening of the battle.

39. Pittsburg. [†]

Hotels. MONONGAHELA (Pl. a; C, 3), pleasantly situated at the river-end of Smithfield St., well spoken of, $ 3-6; ANDERSON (Pl. b; C, 3), centrally situated but somewhat noisy, $ 3 5; *DUQUESNE (Pl. c; C, 3), Smithfield St., R. from $ 1½; SCHLOSSER (Pl. d; C, 3), R. from $ 1; CENTRAL (Pl. e; C, 3); ST. CHARLES (Pl. f; C, 3), SEVENTH AVENUE (Pl. g; D, 3), $ 2-3.

Restaurants. *Hotel Duquesne, Hotel Schlosser (see above); Hagan, 607 Smithfield St.; Newell, 99 Fifth Ave.; Reineman, 505 Wood St., for men.

Railway Stations. The chief are the Union Depot (Pl. D, 3), of the P. R. R., for trains to Cincinnati, St. Louis, Chicago, New York, etc., and the Monongahela Station (Pl. C, 4), for the B. & O. lines.

Tramways (electric, cable, and horse) run through the chief streets and to the suburbs. — **Inclined Railways** (10 in all), a characteristic feature of Pittsburg, lead to various points on the enclosing hills

Post Office (Pl. C, 3), Smithfield St., cor. 4th Ave.

Pittsburg (745 ft.), the second city of Pennsylvania and one of the chief industrial centres of the United States, occupies the tongue of land between the *Monongahela* and the *Allegheny*, which here unite to form the *Ohio*, and also a strip of land on the S. side of the Monongahela. The sister city of *Allegheny* lies on the N. bank of the Allegheny and extends down to the Ohio. Pop. (1890) of Pittsburg 238,617, of Allegheny City 105,387. For all practical purposes the two cities may be regarded as one (like Manchester and Salford), though they have separate municipal governments. The point of the tongue is quite flat, and also the immediate river-banks; but the tongue rises rapidly towards its root, and there are only narrow strips of level ground between the rivers and the abrupt heights on the S. side of the Monongahela and the N. side of the Allegheny. The residential quarters are mainly on the highlands of Pittsburg to the E. and those of Allegheny to the N. The rest of the delta and the river-banks are given over to manufacturing and are generally covered with a pall of dense black smoke. The two cities are substantially built, and the rivers are crossed by numerous bridges.

Pittsburg occupies the site of the French *Fort Duquesne*, erected in 1754 and abandoned on the advance of Gen. Forbes in 1758. Its place was taken by the English *Fort Pitt* (see p. 242), and the laying out of the town of Pittsburg may be dated from about 1765. Its early importance was due to its trade with the Indians, and its commercial advantages are still conspicuous; but the great basis of the prosperity of the 'Iron City' has been the fact that it stands in the centre of one of the richest coal districts in the globe, the four counties immediately adjoining Pittsburg yielding 20,600,000 tons of coal in 1889. Pittsburg also stands in the centre of the chief natural gas district (see p. 241), and the use of this as fuel gave a great impetus to its manufacturing industry, though it is now mainly used for domestic purposes. The iron ore, of which Pittsburg furnaces and mills used 2,500,000 tons in 1892, comes chiefly from Lake Superior (pp. 296, 297). The Pennsylvania, New York, W. Virginia, and E. Ohia oil-fields lie mainly in the basin of the Allegheny and Ohio Rivers to the N.E., S., and S.W. of Pittsburg and in 1891 yielded 37,423,347 barrels of petroleum. The staple manufactures of Pittsburg are iron, steel, and glass (comp. pp. 241, 242).

---

† Pittsburg itself keeps *Eastern Time*, but trains starting here for the W. do so on *Central Time* (see p. xviii). Thus a train timed to start for Chicago at 11 p.m. starts at midnight by the clocks in the hotels.

Natural Gas† is one of the gaseous members of the paraffin series (of which petroleum is a liquid member) and consists mainly of marsh gas, the 'fire damp' of the miner. Its origin is the decomposition of forms of animal or vegetable life, and it is stored under pressure below strata of rock, being set free when those are pierced. Usually it has but little odour. Natural gas has been known to exist in America for over a century, but the first economical use of it was made in 1821, when the town of Fredonia, New York, was lighted with the product of a small well. Its use in iron-making in Western Pennsylvania began in 1875 at the mills of *Etna Borough*, 6 M. above Pittsburg. It was first used in Pittsburg itself in 1886, when the gas from the Haymaker Well in *Murrysville*, the chief field of supply for Pittsburg, was conveyed in pipes to the city, a distance of 19 M. The annual consumption of natural gas at Pittsburg at present may be estimated at about 50,000,000,000 cubic ft., of which about two-thirds is used for domestic purposes and one-third for manufactures. Its price is 20-22¹/₂c. per 1000 cubic feet to private individuals, and 15 c. to manufacturers. There is no question but that the supply is gradually giving out; and it is already too high-priced for the rolling mills, which are reverting to coal and other forms of fuel gas. The illuminating power of natural gas is low. About 1200 M. of piping are used in leading the gas to Pittsburg, in about 15 different lines. The pressure at the wells averages 100 ft. per sq. inch and has been measured up to 700 ft. In fuel value 12 cubic ft. of gas are equal to 1 lb. of coal. The process of drilling for gas is similar to that of drilling for petroleum. Those who wish to visit a gas-well (of no great interest) should apply at the office of the *Philadelphia Co.*, cor. of Penn Ave. and 9th St.

SMITHFIELD STREET (Pl. C, 3), diverging from *Liberty Avenue* (Pl. C-F,1-3), near the *Union Station*, leads to the river Monongahela; and the visitor is recommended to begin by following this street to the (¹/₂ M.) bridge (tramway) and crossing it to obtain the view of the city from *Washington Heights*. On the way we pass, to the right, the **City Hall** (Pl. C, 3); on the staircase is an inscribed tablet from Fort Pitt (p. 242), bearing the date 1764. A little farther on, to the left, is the handsome new *Post Office* (Pl. C, 3). At the bridge are the *Monongahela Hotel* (r.) and the *Baltimore & Ohio Station* (l.).

Crossing the *Monongahela Bridge* (Pl. C, 3; toll 1 c.), we should ascend to the top of *Mt. Washington* (370 ft.) by one of the three *Inclined Railways* (5 c.) on this side. These interesting, but at first somewhat startling pieces of apparatus, are worked by ropes (not cog-wheels) and transport horses and carriages as well as persons. The *View from the top of the busy cities of Pitt-burg and Allegheny, the three rivers, and the encircling hills, all more or less enveloped in smoke, is highly imposing and picturesque. At night, when the cold gleam of the electric lights vie with the lurid glare of the furnaces and smelting-works, the effect is still more weird and fascinating. The deep basin in which Pittsburg lies has suggested the name of 'Hell with the lid off'. The Court House and Post Office are conspicuous.
Those who have time to spare may, while on this side of the river, ascend *Carson St.* (Pl. C-F, 4; electric car) to *S. 10th St.* (Pl. D, 4) and visit the interesting *Glass Works of Macbeth & Co.* (producing 40-50,000 doz. of lamp-chimneys per week) or the *United States Glass Works* (table glass).

The finest building in Pittsburg and one of the best in the United States is the ***Allegheny County Court House** (Pl. C, D, 3),

---

† Most of the data in this paragraph were kindly furnished by *Mr. Jos. D. Weeks*, of the 'American Manufacturer & Iron World'.

in Grant St., a splendid example of *Mr. H. H. Richardson's* treatment of Romanesque, erected in 1888 at a cost of $2,500,000 (500,000*l*.). The massive *Gaol* is connected with the Court House by a finely handled stone bridge. The main tower (*View) is 320 ft. high. The three entrances in the chief façade seem somewhat low and depressed for the size of the building. — Near the Court House is the R. C. *Cathedral of St. Paul* (Pl. C, 3).

The only remnant of Fort Pitt (p. 240) is an old and dilapidated *Block House* (Pl. B, 3), in Fort St., near Point Bridge, which will be pointed out by one of the urchins of the squalid neighbourhood (soon to be restored). Hard by, on the Allegheny River, are the *Exposition Buildings* (Pl. B, 3), in which annual exhibitions are held.

The *Penn Incline* (Pl. E, 2), 17th St., is interesting from the manner in which it is led down over the top chord of the bridge spanning the Pennsylvania Railroad at its foot. — Other buildings of importance are the *Pittsburg Library*, 613 Penn Ave.; the *German National Bank;* the *National Bank of Commerce;* the *Duquesne Club; Trinity Church;* the new *Carnegie Library*, Forbes St.; and the *School of the Ursuline Nuns*, Fifth Avenue.

To see the pleasant residence-quarters on the hills, we take a *Highland Avenue Electric Car*, alight at its terminus (where it turns to go back to town by a different route), and walk up to (1/2 M.) *Highland Park*, with the town-reservoirs, which commands a fine *View, especially of the Allegheny. — *Schenley Park* is also fine.

No one should leave Pittsburg without visiting one at least of the great iron and steel works which have made its prosperity and reputation. Among these are the *Edgar Thomson Steel Works*, the *Homestead Steel Works*, the *Jones & Laughlins Works*, the *Oliver Iron & Steel Co.*, the *Crescent Steel Works*, and the *Keystone Bridge Co.*

Those who wish to visit the two first-named works apply for a pass at the office of the Carnegie Steel Co., 42 and 48 Fifth Ave. (Pl. C, 3). Half-a-day at least should be allowed for the visit. Perhaps the best way is to go to *Bessemer*, on the Pennsylvania R. R. (from Union Station); visit the *Edgar Thomson Works;* proceed thence by B. & O. R. R. to *Salt Works* (10 c.); cross the river by small-boat ferry (5 c.) to *Munhall;* walk to (3/4 M.) the *Homestead Works;* and return to Pittsburg by the P. R. R. to Fourth Ave. or Union Station. The **Edgar Thomson Works** have an annual capacity for the production of 600,000 tons of metal, their chief product being steel rails. The **Homestead Steel Works**, perhaps the more interesting of the two, produce annually 400,000 tons of steel and make large quantities of steel and nickel armour-plates. Natural gas is largely used for fuel at both works. The two works employ about 6000 men. The name of Homestead became widely known in 1892 in connection with the disastrous strike of its workmen, which finally necessitated the intervention of the State militia.

The *American Iron & Steel Works (Jones & Laughlins)* are on the S. bank of the Monongahela, opposite Pittsburg. The *Keystone Bridge Works*, which have produced some of the finest steel bridges in the world, cover 7 acres of ground at the corner of 51st St. and Railroad St.

The *Pittsburg Reduction Co.*, at *Kensington* (20 M. from Pittsburg, on the Allegheny Valley R. R.), produces about 1000 lbs. of pure aluminium daily.

The *Pittsburg Plate Glass Works* are at *Tarentum, Creighton*, and *Ford City*, the first two on the Western Pennsylvania R. R., the last on the

Allegheny Valley R. R. The *Phoenix Glass Works* are at *Phillipsburg*, on the Pittsburg & Erie R. R.

Allegheny City *(Hotel Federal)*, on the N. bank of the Allegheny, offers few attractions to the visitor. The value of its manufactures in 1890 was $ 20,500,000. Taking a tramway-car in 6th St. (Pl. C, 3), we cross the river and follow *Federal St.* to the *Town Hall* and the *****Carnegie Free Library** (Pl. C, 2). Thence we may follow Ohio St. to the S.W., passing *St. Peter's Church*, to the *Park* (Pl. B, 2). To the left rises a hill crowned by the *Soldiers' Monument* (Pl. B, 2), to which we should ascend for its *****View** of the two cities. Walkers may descend on the other side and return to Pittsburg viâ the old covered *Union Bridge* (Pl. B, 2, 3).

River Navigation. Through the Monongahela, Allegheny, and Ohio more than 20,000 M. of inland navigation are open to the steamers of the cities of Pittsburg and Allegheny, and regular communication is thus kept up with *New Orleans* (p. 366), 2000 M. distant. The tonnage of the river-craft of Pittsburg (1,360,000 tons) is said to be greater than that of New York or all the Mississippi ports put together. This is owing to the enormous coal traffic, and stern-wheel tug-boats may frequently be seen conveying a train of barges with a total cargo of 20,000 tons of coal. — The *Davis Island Dam* (movable), on the Ohio, 4 M. below the city, was constructed at a cost of nearly $ 1,000,000 (200,000*l.*) and has one lock 500 ft. long and 110 ft. wide.

A trip up the *Monongahela* by steamer, as far as *Monongahela City* or *Brownsville*, is very picturesque.

FROM PITTSBURG TO CONNELLSVILLE, either by the *S. W. Pennsylvania R. R.* (56 M.) or by the *B. & O. R. R.* (58 M.), in 2-2¹/₂ hrs. — *Connellsville* (Gough Ho., $ 2), a town of 5329 inhab., on the *Youghiogheny*, lies in the midst of one of the two chief coke regions in the world, the other being that of Durham, England. About 6,000,000 tons of coke are produced here annually.

FROM PITTSBURG TO BUFFALO, 269 M., in 12-14 hrs. (*Allegheny Valley R. R.* to *Oil City*, 132 M.; *Western New York & Pennsylvania R. R.* thence to *Buffalo*, 137 M.). This line runs through one of the chief petroleum districts, and numerous oil-wells, in operation or deserted, are passed. Petroleum is obtained from oil-bearing sands by pipes of varying diameter, sunk to a depth of 300-3000 ft. The oil is transmitted to the large storage tanks of the Pipe Line Companies by pipe lines, which are sometimes hundreds of miles long. — The railway at first follows the *Allegheny River*. — 132 M. Oil City (*Arlington*, $ 3), a city of 10,932 inhab., is the great centre of the Oil District, and all the processes of procuring, preparing, and shipping the oil may be conveniently observed here. In 1892 Oil City was the scene of a terrible disaster, caused by the catching fire of a large petroleum tank. The burning oil, overspreading the water in the creek, set fire to many buildings and caused the loss of many lives. — The train now follows the valley of *Oil Creek*, with many abandoned wells. 148 M. Titusville (*European*, $ 2), with 8073 inhab., is another busy oil-centre. — 175 M. *Corry* (5677 inhab.). — 205 M. *Mayville*, at the head of *Chautauqua Lake* (1300 ft.), is the junction for (4 M.) *Chautauqua* (see p. 278). — 219 M. *Brockton*, and thence to (269 M.) *Buffalo*, see R. 46a.

FROM PITTSBURG TO ERIE, 148 M., *Pennsylvania Railway* in 5³/₄-6 hrs. — 25 M. *Rochester* (see below); 47 M. *Lawrence Junction*; 92 M. *Jamestown* (p. 278); 133 M. *Girard*, and thence to (148 M.) *Erie*, see R. 46a.

FROM PITTSBURG TO CLEVELAND, 150 M., *Penna. R. R.* in 4¹/₂-6¹/₄ hrs. — This line diverges from that to Erie at (25 M.) *Rochester*. 48 M. *Wellsville*; 93 M. *Alliance*; 124 M. *Hudson*. — 150 M. *Cleveland*, see p. 267.

FROM PITTSBURG TO WHEELING, 66 M., railway in 2¹/₄-2¹/₂ hrs. — *Wheeling*, see p. 266.

From Pittsburg to *Columbus* and *Cincinnati*, see R. 44b; to *Chicago*, see R. 44b.

40. From Philadelphia to Baltimore.

96 M. PENNSYLVANIA RAILWAY in 2-4 hrs. (fare $2.80; parlor-car 50c.).
From New York (186 M.) in 4-7 hrs. (fare $5.30). — The BALTIMORE &
OHIO R. R. follows almost the same route (same times and fares).

Philadelphia (Broad St. Station), see p. 210. The train crosses
the *Schuylkill* and runs to the S.W., not far from the W. bank of the
Delaware. The *University of Pennsylvania* (p. 219) and the *Blockley
Almshouses* (p. 219) are seen to the right. 13½ M. *Chester* (20,226
inhab.) was settled by the Swedes in 1643. Between (17 M.) *Linwood* and (19 M.) *Claymont* we cross a small stream and enter the
State of Delaware ('Diamond State'). Farther on we cross the *Brandywine* (see below) and reach —

27 M. **Wilmington** (*Clayton Ho.*, $3), the chief city of Delaware, situated at the confluence of the Delaware, Brandywine, and
Christiana, with 61,643 inhab. and extensive manufactures, including the making of iron (Diamond State Iron Works, etc.), carriages,
railway-carriages, iron and wooden ships, gunpowder, morocco and
other leather, and cotton goods (total value in 1890, $20,500,000).
The most interesting point is the old *Swedish Church* (seen to the
right as we enter the station), which dates from 1698 and marks the
site of the first Swedish colony in America and the first permanent European settlement in the valley of the Delaware (1638).

Picturesque walks may be taken in the **Glen of the Brandywine*, which
is kept as a public park. — The *Battle of the Brandywine*, in which Washington was defeated by the English in Sept., 1777, was fought about 13 M.
to the N.W.

FROM WILMINGTON TO CAPE CHARLES, 192 M., railway in 6 hrs. This
line, which descends the narrow peninsula to the E. of Chesapeake Bay
(p. 249), is of some importance as forming part of a through-route from
New York to *Old Point Comfort* (p. 332; 11-12 hrs.) and as a means of
bringing fruit and vegetable supplies to the Northern cities. It runs
through the famous peach district of Delaware. One perfectly straight
section of this line, 90 M. long, is said to be the longest tangent in the
United States From (192 M.) *Cape Charles* steamers ply to (24 M.) *Old
Point Comfort* (p. 332) and (36 M.) *Norfolk* (p. 331).

Beyond (39 M.) *Newark* the train crosses the famous *Mason &
Dixon's Line* (p. 236) and enters *Maryland* ('Old Line State'). Near
(51 M.) *North-East* we see *Chesapeake Bay* (p. 249) to the left. At
(60 M.) *Perryville* and (61 M.) *Havre-de-Grace* we cross the wide
Susquehanna, which here enters the head of Chesapeake Bay. Farther
on we cross several wide shallow rivers or arms of the Bay.

96 M. **Baltimore** *(Union Station)*, see below.

41. Baltimore.

Railway Stations. *Union* or *Charles Street Station* (Pl. C, D, 2, 3), for
all points reached by the Pennsylvania Railroad and its branches, incl. the
N. Central and Bal. & Pot. RR.; *Camden Station* (Pl. C, 5, 6), Camden St., for
the B. & O. lines; *Calvert Station* (Pl. D, 4), for trains of the Northern
Central and Baltimore and Potomac lines; *Hillen St. Station* (Pl. D, 4), for
the West Maryland R. R.; *North Avenue Station* (Pl. C, 2), for local trains
(Baltimore & Lehigh R. R.). — *Cab* to hotel 25 c. for each person.

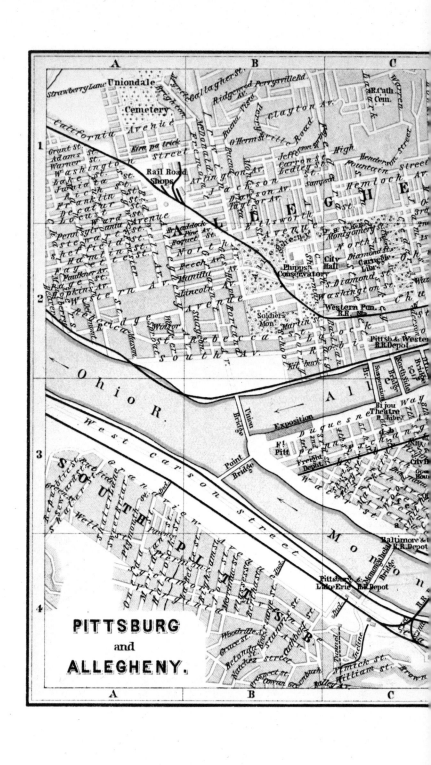

PITTSBURG
and
ALLEGHENY.

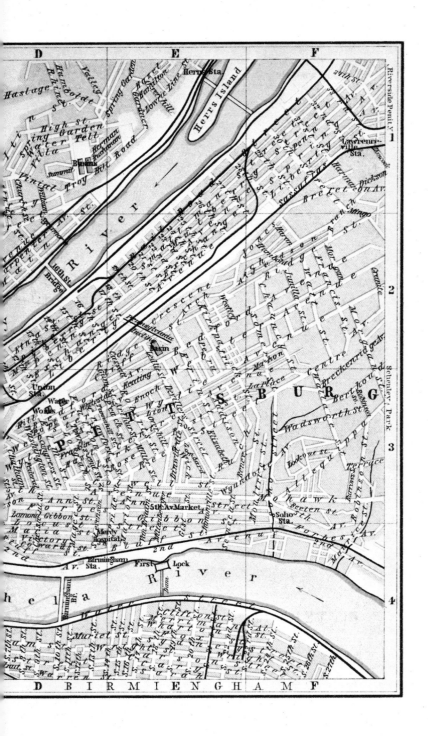

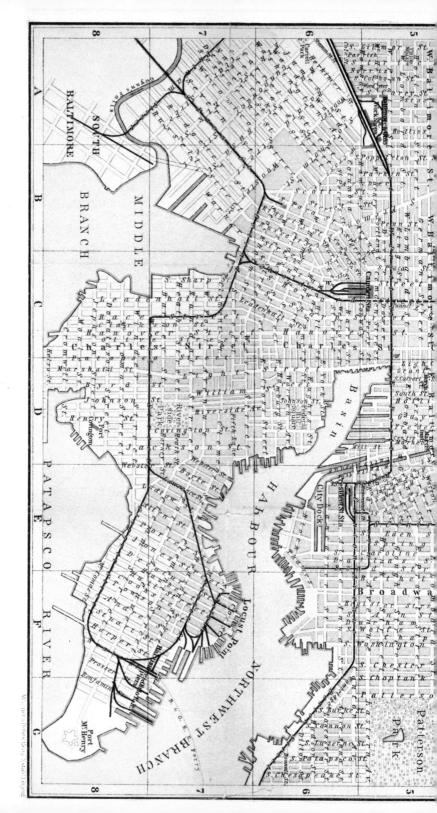

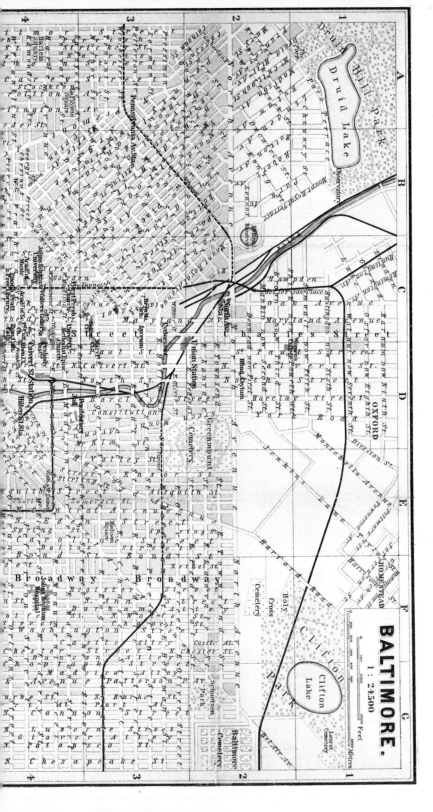

BALTIMORE.

1 : 24,500

Hotels. *Hotel Rennert (Pl. a; C, 4), cor. Saratoga & Liberty Sts., R. from $1½; *Altamont (Pl. b; B, 3), well situated in Eutaw Place, with view, $3-4½; *Mt. Vernon (Pl. c; C, 4), a quiet and comfortable house in a central situation, R. from $1 (E. P.); Eutaw House (Pl. d; C, 5), Eutaw St.; St. James (Pl. e; C, 4), cor. Charles and Centre Sts., R. from $1½; Carrollton (Pl. f; D, 5), a large down-town house, frequented by businessmen, $3-4; Albion (Pl. g, C 3; $3½-5), a quiet family hotel; Imperial, Monument Sq., opposite the Post Office (Pl. D, 5); Maltby (Pl. h; C, 5), near the steamboat-wharves.

Restaurants. At *Hotel Rennert and the *St. James*, see above; *Dorsey & Thomas*, cor. Calvert and German Sts.; *Brawner*, 226 E. Baltimore St.; *Women's Exchange*, cor. Charles and Pleasant Sts. (for ladies); *Boss' Café*, 108 E. German St. (German beer and wines); *Green Ho.*, 12 E. Pratt St., moderate (these two for men); *New York Confectionery Store*, Lexington St.

Tramways (5 c.) traverse the chief streets and run to various suburbs.

Cabs. Within district bounded by Jones's Falls, Pratt, Carey, and Mosher Streets, each pers. 25 c.; beyond the above district and within city-limits 35 c. By time 75 c. per hr. To *Druid Hill Park*, 1-2 pers. $1½, 3-4 pers. $2. *Hacks* (with two horses) 75 c. for 1 pers., each pers. addit. 25 c., per hr. $1½.

Theatres. *Academy of Music* (Pl. C, 4); *Ford's Opera House* (Pl. C, 5); *Lyceum* (Pl. C, 3); *Holliday Street Theatre* (Pl. D, 5); *Howard Auditorium* (Pl. C, 4). — *Cyclorama* (Pl. C, 3).

Post Office (Pl. D, 5), Monument Sq.

British Consul, W. T. Seagraves, 415 Water St.

Baltimore (the '*Monumental City*'), the chief city of Maryland and one of the great seaports of America, is finely situated on the broad estuary of *Patapsco River*, 14 M. from *Chesapeake Bay* (p. 249) and 204 M. from the Atlantic Ocean. The city, which is well laid out and built mainly of a cheerful red brick, is divided into two nearly equal sections by a stream named *Jones's Falls*, toward which the ground slopes rapidly on either side. In 1890 Baltimore contained 434,439 inhabitants. The Roman Catholic Archbishop of Baltimore (Card. Gibbons) is Primate in the United States.

Baltimore was first laid out as a town in 1729, and received its name from the title of the Barons of Baltimore (Co. Longford, Ireland), founders and proprietaries of the Maryland Colony. In 1780 it had grown sufficiently in importance to be made a port of entry, and it was incorporated as a city in 1796. After the conclusion of the war of 1861-65, its population rapidly increased, and of late years several populous suburbs have been incl- led in its limits, so that now (1893) its population is about 500,000. Baltimore has been in one respect more fortunate than other cities of the Southern States. During the War of Independence it was threatened, but not attacked; in the war with Great Britain in 1814 it successfully resisted a combined attack by water and land; and in the war between the States it lay outside the area of actual combat. Its history i- therefore an almost unbroken chronicle of peace and prosperity. — Dr. Holmes has remarked that three short American poems, each the best of its kind, were all written at Baltimore: *viz.* Poe's 'Raven', Randall's 'Maryland, my Maryland', and Key's 'Star-Spangled Banner'. The last was written in 1814, while its author was a prisoner on one of the British ships bombarding Fort McHenry (p. 249). Jerome Bonaparte, brother of Napoleon I., married a Miss Patterson of Baltimore, and their descendants still live in the city.

The total value of the manufactures of Baltimore in 1890 was $148,000,000 (29,600,000*l.*), in the production of which 87,000 hands were engaged. It is the chief seat of the canning industry of the United States, the materials being the famous oysters of Chesapeake Bay and fruits from its shores. The annual product is 50,000,000 cans, and about 15,000 hands are employed in this industry. Iron, steel, and copper are produced; and the Bessemer Steel Works at *Sparrow's Point* (9 M. from Baltimore) have a daily capacity of 2000 tons, equal to about one-third of the total produce of the United Kingdom. The cotton-duck mills in and near Baltimore run 150,000 spindles, employ about 6000 hands, and produce three-fourths of the sail-duck made in the United States. In brick-making Baltimore ranks fourth among American cities, producing annually 150,000,000. Next to New York it is the largest grain-market on the Atlantic coast, its annual receipts being 40-60 million bushels. The value of the imports of Baltimore in 1891 was $18,270,000, of exports $79,500,000. In 1890 its harbour was entered and cleared by 1651 vessels of 2,127,247 tons burden.

The water-supply of Baltimore is furnished by the Gunpowder River and Jones's Falls, and is stored in 8 reservoirs with an aggregate capacity of 2275 million gallons, capable of a daily supply of 300 million gallons, the daily consumption being 45 millions. The water from Gunpowder River is brought through a tunnel almost 7 M. long.

Before the days of railway transportation Baltimore was the principal centre for the trade with the West, the produce from which was carried in huge 'Conestoga' wagons across the mountains and over the national turnpike to this city. As curious relics of that period there still remain in the older portion of the city, near Jones's Falls, in a neighbourhood locally known as 'Old Town', a few old inns or taverns with spacious yards attached, where stabling was found for these wagons and their long teams of mules. Though now falling into decay, they preserve the type of the old-fashioned post-houses. For visiting them, and a few quaint streets containing houses characteristic of the last century, the guidance of a resident is required.

The natural centre for the visitor to Baltimore is *Mt. Vernon Place (Pl. C, 4), a small square, prettily laid out and suggesting Paris in its tasteful monuments and surrounding buildings. In the centre of the square rises the **Washington Monument** (Pl. C, 4), a column 130 ft. high, resting on a base 35 ft. in height and surmounted by a colossal statue of George Washington. The *View from the top (open from 9 a.m. till dusk; adm. 15 c.) forms the best introduction to the city.

The monument stands at the intersection of Charles St. (p. 247), running N. and S., and Monument St., running E. and W. To the S. lies the harbour. The dark-grey building to the E., just beyond the railway, is the *Gaol* (Pl. D, 4). Johns Hopkins Hospital (p. 248) is conspicuous to the E.

The other monuments in the square include *Bronzes of Peace, War, Force, Order, and a Lion, by *Barye* (p. 247); a statue of Chief Justice Taney (p. 250), by *Rinehart;* a statue of Peabody (p. 91), by *Story* (a replica of the one in London); and a figure of Military Courage, by *Dubois*.

On the N. side of the square is the handsome *Mt. Vernon Methodist Episcopal Church* (Pl. C, 4). On the S. side of the square stands the **Peabody Institute** (Pl. C, 4), founded and endowed by Mr. George Peabody (p. 91), for the encouragement of science, art, and general knowledge.

The *Library* (9-10.30), on the ground-floor, contains 110,000 well-selected vols.; the *Reading Room* is large and handsome.

The **Art Gallery** (10-4; catalogue 15 c.), on the first floor, contains collections of casts, American paintings, etc. The *Rinehart Collection* consists of casts (Nos. 116-139, 163-167, 168-182) of the works of *William H. Rinehart* (1825-74), a native of Maryland. No. 106 (Clytia) is an original. The institution also includes a *Conservatorium of Music*.

Also on the S. side of the square (No. 5) is the house of *Mr. W. T. Walters*, containing the celebrated **Walters Collection**, one of the finest private collections of art in America, if not in the world (open to the public on Wed., in Feb., March, and April, on Sat. also in April; tickets 50 c., sold for the benefit of the poor, at the Mt. Vernon Hotel, etc.; also at 1113 Pennsylvania Ave., Washington).

The **Collection of Paintings** (250), in a beautiful gallery lighted from the roof, consists mainly of masterpieces of modern French masters and is remarkable for its uniformly high rank of excellence, almost every canvas being good of its kind. Among the most noted pictures are the following: 8. *Charles Gleyre* (1807-74), Lost illusions; 12. *Alma Tadema*, Triumph of Titus; *13. *J. B. Corot* (1796-1875), Martyrdom of St. Sebastian (a large canvas, 8 ft. × 4 ft.); 19. *Briton Rivière*, Syria (the Night Watch); 24. *Gilbert Stuart* (1755-1828), George Washington; *32. *Alma Tadema*, Sappho; *46. *Mariano Fortuny* (1838-74), Hindoo snake-charmers; *48. *H. Leys* (1815-69), Edict of Charles V.; *58. *C. Troyon* (1810-65), Cattle drinking; *60. *Millet* (1814-75), Potato harvest; 63. *Gérôme*, Last prayer of Christian martyrs; *74. *Eugène Delacroix* (1798-1863), Crucifixion; *85. *Paul Delaroche* (1797-1856), 'Hémicycle du Palais des Beaux-Arts', a reduced replica of the mural painting in the Palais des Beaux-Arts at Paris, with figures of great artists and allegorical figures of art, etc.; 86. *E. van Marcke* (d. 1891), The approaching storm; 92. *J. J. Henner*, Nymph; 101. *Horace Vernet* (1789-1863), Italian brigands surprised by papal troops; *103. *Th. Rousseau* (1812-67), Le Givre (winter solitude); *109. *Gérôme*, The duel after the masquerade; 111. *J. L. E. Meissonier* (1816-91), The jovial trooper; 118. *Alma Tadema*, A Roman Emperor (Claudius); 119. *A. de Neuville* (1836-85), Attack at dawn; 135. *C. F. Daubigny* (1817-78), Sunset; 136. *Jules Breton*, Returning from the fields; *141. *Millet*, Sheepfold; 145. *Eugène Delacroix*, Jesus on the Sea of Galilee; **154. *Meissonier*, '1814' (Napoleon on the retreat from Moscow).

WATER-COLOURS, DRAWINGS, etc., in small rooms: *200. *Millet*, The Angelus (original design for the well-known painting); 201. *Millet*, Shepherd at the fold; 208. *Rosa Bonheur*, Andalusian bulls; 209. *E. Detaille*, Ready to march; 212-217. Water-colours by *Félix Ziem*; 221. *Meissonier*, Courtyard of the artist's studio; 224. *Rosa Bonheur*, Conversation; *226. *Millet*, The Sower; 236. *O. Achenbach*, Posilipo; 238. *Fred. Walker* (1840-75), Fishmarket; 248. *Alex. Bida*, Religious fanatics; *Alma Tadema*, 245. 'Twin Venus and Bacchus, 246. Xanthe and Phaon; 248. *Millet*, Shepherdess; 25 251. *Meissonier*, Portraits of himself.

HALL. *300. *W. H. Rinehart* (p. 246), Woman of Samaria; *E. D. Palmer*, 301. First Disappointment, 302. Infant Flora.

The ORIENTAL ROOM contains a magnificent **Collection of Chinese and Japanese bronzes, enamels, porcelain, ivory-carvings, paintings, etc.

A room upstairs (not usually shown) contains an extensive series of *Bronzes and Drawings, by *A. L. Barye* (1796-1875).

The other treasures of the collections, many of them stowed away in closed cabinets or in rooms not shown to visitors, include art-furniture, European porcelain and metal-work, mosaics, Limoges enamels, and objects of bric-a-brac of all kinds in endless profusion.

CHARLES STREET (Pl. C, 1-8), one of the chief thoroughfares of the city, leads to the N. from the Washington Monument past the *Union Station* (Pl. C, D, 2, 3; p. 244). Following it to the S., we pass (right) the *First Unitarian Church* (Pl. C, 4) and the back of the **Roman Catholic Cathedral** (Pl. C, 4), which faces Cathedral St. It is surmounted by a dome, 95 ft. high, and contains some interesting paintings. Three plenary councils have been held here. Adjacent is the residence of the Archbishop (p. 245).

In E. Mulberry St., a little to the W. of the Cathedral, is the *Pratt Free Library (Pl. C, 4), a white marble building, containing 70,000 books.

At the corner of Charles St. and Saratoga St., to the right, is the

Y. M. C. Association (Pl. C, 4; right). Opposite is the *New Mercantile Library* (40,000 vols.).

In W. Saratoga St. stands the **Athenæum** (Pl. D, 4), with the *Maryland Historical Society* (10-4), containing a library and some interesting portraits and relics.

In W. Fayette St., in the graveyard of the *Westminster Presbyterian Church* (Pl. C, 5), is the tomb of *E. A. Poe* (1809-49), with a small monument. Near this point, at the corner of Lombard and Greene Sts., is the **University of Maryland** (Pl. C, 5).

The °**Lexington Market** (Pl. C, 5), a little to the N. of this point, should be visited for its picturesque illustrations of Southern produce and manners (best on Sat. night).

Farther on Charles St. passes the *Masonic Temple* (Pl. C, 4, 5; left), intersects BALTIMORE STREET (Pl. A-G, 5), the chief business-street of the city, and is continued to S. Baltimore.

In the meantime, however, we may follow E. Fayette St. to the left to the *Post Office & U. S. Court House* (Pl. D, 5), a large granite building, in front of which rises the *Battle Monument*, erected in 1815 in memory of the struggles of the previous year. To the E. of the Post Office is the *City **Hall** (Pl. D, 5), a large and handsome building, with a dome 260 ft. high (view; open, 9-3).

A little farther along E. Fayette St., just beyond the stream, is the *Merchants' Shot Tower*, a curious relic of 1828, 246 ft. high.

A little to the W. of Mt. Vernon Place, between Howard St. and Eutaw St., are the unpretentious buildings of the ***Johns Hopkins University** (Pl. C, 4; *President Gilman*).

This institution, which forms the highest expression of the phenomenal development of education in Baltimore since the Civil War (comp. above and pp. 247, 249), was founded in 1876 with a legacy of 3½ million dollars (700,000 *l.*), bequeathed by *Johns Hopkins* (d. 1873), a Baltimore merchant, and offers special advantages for post-graduate work. It is now attended by 5-600 students, three-fifths of whom are graduates of other colleges and universities. Its success and influence, however, cannot be measured by the number of its students; and its system of instruction, publications, etc., have been of the greatest importance in stimulating the higher learning and original research. Its laboratories and other institutions are well equipped, and its library contains 60,000 volumes.

The ***Johns Hopkins Hospital** (Pl. F, 4; tramway viâ Centre St.), opened in 1889, is also due to the liberality of Mr. Hopkins, who bequeathed over $ 3,000,000 (600,000*l.*) for its foundation.

Both as a scientific and charitable institution, this hospital is a worthy pendant to the University; and in the completeness of its equipments and excellence of its system, it ranks with the foremost hospitals in the world.

Among the numerous other **Charitable Institutions** of Baltimore, many of which are of great interest, are the *Bay View Asylum* or *City Alms-House*, for paupers; the *State Blind Asylum* (Pl. D, 2); the *Children's Aid Society* (Pl. D, 4); the *City Hospital* (Pl. D, 4); the *Church Home*; *St. Joseph's Hospital* and other noble charities of the R. C. church; and the ** Wilson Sanitarium*, 5 M. from Baltimore, for affording change of air to sick children and their mothers in summer.

The *Wells & McComas Monument* (Pl. E, 4), passed on the way to the Johns Hopkins Hospital, is to the memory of two youths who killed the British commander, Gen. Ross, at the battle of North Point (Sept. 12th, 1814), and were themselves killed immediately afterwards.

Persons interested in the higher education of women should not

omit to visit the *Woman's College (Pl. D, 2), St. Paul St., and the
*Bryn Mawr School (Pl. C, 3), Cathedral St., two admirable insti-
tutions, with the most complete and most modern educational
equipments. The tasteful Bryn Mawr building is by *H. R. Marshall*
(New York). — The *First Presbyterian Church (Pl. C, 4), Park St.,
is a good specimen of Dec. Gothic, with a spire 250 ft. high.

Baltimore prides itself with justice on *Druid Hill Park (Pl.
A, B, 1), a pleasure-ground of about 700 acres, which owes its
beauty in great part to the fact that it had been preserved as a private
park for 100 years before passing into the hands of the city. Its hills
afford beautiful views. *Druid Lake*, $1/2$ M. long, is one of the
reservoirs of the city waterworks (p. 246). The old *Mansion House*
contains a restaurant; and there is a small zoological collection near
by. The *Main Entrance* may be reached by tramway viâ Madison
Ave. or Druid Hill Ave. Those who drive should choose the route
through *Eutaw Place (Pl. A, B, 2, 3). — *Greenmount Cemetery*
(Pl. D, E, 2, 3) contains the graves of Mme. Patterson Bonaparte
(d. 1879; see p. 245), Junius Brutus Booth (d. 1852), the actor
(father of Edwin Booth), Johns Hopkins (p. 248), etc. — The best
view of the water-front is obtained from *Federal Hill Park* (Pl. D, 6),
in S. Baltimore.

The **Harbour**, 3 M. long and $1/2$-$3/4$ M. wide, consists of an outer
bay accessible to the largest vessels and an inner basin for vessels
of lighter draught. Its entrance is commanded by **Fort McHenry**
(Pl. G, 8), which offers little to repay the long and tedious journey
to it (tramway) beyond its historical interest (see p. 245).

The elaborate system of **Tunnels** by which the railways traverse
Baltimore deserves the attention of the engineer. The Pennsylvania R. R.
crosses the city from E. to W. by the *Union Tunnel* ($2/3$ M.) and the *Baltimore & Potomac Tunnel* ($1^3/8$ M.), with an open stretch of $3/4$ M. (containing
the Union Station) between them. The new *Baltimore & Ohio Tunnel*, now
in progress, runs from N. to S. ($1^2/3$ M.), and when finished will obviate
the necessity of the B. & O. trains being ferried across the harbour as they
are at present. The trains in this tunnel are to be worked by electricity.

Excursions from Baltimore.

Chesapeake Bay is the largest inlet on the Atlantic coast, with a
length of 200 M. and a breadth of 10-20 M. It receives the waters of the
Susquehanna, Potomac, James, and other rivers, and is navigable for the
largest vessels. The bay is a favourite resort of sportsmen, and its game
(canvas-back ducks, etc.), fish, terrapins, and oysters have a wide reputation. The E. shore is not much frequented, but there are several summer-resorts on the W. shore, among which may be mentioned *Bay Ridge*
(32 M.), with fair hotels and other accommodation. *Tolchester Beach* (25 M.)
is on the E. shore. In summer steamers run regularly to different points
in the Bay (see daily papers), and the visitor is recommended to make a
day-trip on one of these, the numerous inlets into which they penetrate
with the mails imparting constant variety to the scenery. *Annapolis*
(p. 250), *Old Point Comfort* (p. 332), *Norfolk* (p. 331), etc., may be reached
by steamer on Chesapeake Bay.

Lake Roland (225 ft.), 8 M. to the N. (N. Cen. R. R.), one of the chief
reservoirs of the Baltimore Waterworks, is frequently visited; and *Gunpowder River*, another source of the water-supply, is also attractive.

Among other favourite resorts of the Baltimoreans are those in the
Blue Ridge Mts. (see below); and excursions may also easily be made to
Gettysburg (p. 235), *Harper's Ferry* (p. 265), *Washington* (p. 251), the *Shenandoah Valley* (p. 338), etc.

FROM BALTIMORE TO WILLIAMSPORT, 93 M., *Western Maryland Railroad*
(Hillen St. or Union Station) in 4¹/₃-4¹/₂ hrs. This line leads to several
favourite resorts in the *Blue Ridge Mts.* and to *Gettysburg*. — The train
runs to the N.W. 8 M. *Mt. Hope*, with a large Retreat for the Insane;
12 M. *Mt. Wilson*, with the Sanitarium mentioned at p. 248; 20 M. *Emory
Grove*, the junction of a branch-line to (51 M.) *Gettysburg* (see p. 235);
34 M. *Westminster* (700 ft.); 49 M. *Frederick Junction* (415 ft.), for (17 M.)
Frederick (p. 265). 69 M. *Blue Ridge* (1375 ft.), where the line crosses the
summit of the Blue Ridge Mts., is the station for *Monterey Springs* (Hotel).
70 M. *Buena Vista*, connected by tramway with (2 M.) *Buena Vista Spring
Hotel*. — 71 M. **Pen-Mar** (1200 ft.; *Cascade Ho.*), named from its situation
on the boundary between Pen(n)sylvania) and Mar(yland), is one of the
most popular resorts in the Blue Ridge Mts. A fine view of the *Cumberland*
and *Shenandoah Valleys* (pp. 232, 338) is obtained from (2 M.) **High Rock*
(2000 ft.), and **Mt. Quirauk* (2500 ft.) is another good view-point. — 72 M.
*Blue Mountain House ($ 3¹/₂), a large and excellent hotel, is, perhaps, the
best point for those who wish to stay a few days in the neighbourhood,
being less invaded by the excursionist than Pen-Mar. — 75 M. *Edgemont* is
the junction of the Cumberland Valley branch to *Chambersburg* (p. 237).
87 M. *Hagerstown*, see p. 233. — 93 M. *Williamsport*, see p. 230.

FROM BALTIMORE TO HARRISBURG, 85 M., *Northern Central R. R.* in
3-3¹/₂ hrs. — 7 M. *Hollins;* 46 M. *Hanover Junction;* 57 M. *York;* 83 M.
Bridgeport. — 85 M. *Harrisburg*, see p. 232.

FROM BALTIMORE TO MARTINSBURG, 100 M., *B. & O. R. R.* (Old Line)
in 4-5 hrs. — 9 M. *Relay Station* (p. 251); 58 M. *Frederick Junction*, for
(4 M.) *Frederick* (p. 265); 69 M. *Washington Junction* (p. 265); 79 M. *Weverton* (p. 265); 81 M. *Harper's Ferry* (p. 265); 89 M. *Shenandoah Junction*
(p. 265). — 100 M. *Martinsburg*, see p. 266.

FROM BALTIMORE TO ANNAPOLIS, 26 M., *Annapolis & Baltimore Short
Line* in 1 hr. — This line skirts *Chesapeake Bay* (left), crossing several of
its arms. The intermediate stations are unimportant.

26 M. **Annapolis** (*The Maryland*, $ 3; board, even for one night, at *Mrs.
Kennedy's*, 78 Prince George St., and *Mrs. Handy's* and *Mrs. Iglehart's*, Church
Circle), the quaint and quiet little capital of Maryland, with 7604 inhab.,
is pleasantly situated at the influx of the *Severn* into Chesapeake Bay.
It carries on a considerable trade in oysters. The traveller is advised to
begin his visit with the *View from the dome (200 ft. high) of the *State
House* (apply to janitor), near the centre of the town. The Senate Room
(to the right on entering) was the scene of Washington's surrender of his
commission in 1783 and of the First Constitutional Convention in 1786.
In front of the State House is a colossal *Statue of Chief Justice Taney*
(1777-1864), by Rinehart. To the left is a *Statue of Gen. De Kalb* (1721-
1780). The *Old City Hotel* was once frequented by George Washington
(adm. on application to janitor). Some of the old colonial houses and
churches are interesting (comp. p. lxxxix), but the chief lion of Annapolis
is the *United States Naval Academy*, founded in 1845 for the education of
officers for the navy, as West Point (p. 152) was for army officers. The
cadets, of whom there are about 250, are nominated in the same way as
the West Point cadets and are under similar discipline. The course of
instruction comprises four years at the Academy and two at sea. Among
the chief points of interest for visitors are the *Old Ships;* old *Fort Severn*,
now a gymnasium; the *Boat-House*, with its rigging-loft ballroom; the
Seamanship House, with its models; the *Steam House*, for instruction
in everything connected with steamships; the *Armoury;* and the *Cadet
Quarters*, with mess-rooms, etc. The drills, parades, and fencing take place
after 4 p.m., when the 'recitations' (classes) end.

42. From Baltimore to Washington.

a. Viâ Baltimore & Potomac Railroad.

43 M. Railway in 1-1½ hr. ($1.20; parlor-car 25 c.). This forms part of the Pennsylvania line from New York to Washington (228 M.; express in 5-6½ hrs., $6.50; sleeper or parlor-car $2).

The trains start from the *Calvert* and *Union Stations* (see p. 244) and pass below the N.W. quarters of the city by a tunnel 1⅓ M. long. The country traversed is flat and uninteresting. 19 M. *Odenton* is the junction of a line to (14 M.) *Annapolis* (see p. 250) and (18 M.) *Bay Ridge* (p. 249). 40½ M. *Navy Yard* (p. 261). In approaching Washington we thread a tunnel 300 yds. long. Fine view of the Capitol to the right.

43 M. **Washington**, see below.

b. Viâ Baltimore & Ohio Railroad.

40 M. Railway in ¾-1 hr. (fares as above). Express from New York in 6 hrs. (fares as above).

Baltimore, see p. 244. At (9 M.) *Relay Station* the train diverges from the Old Route (see p. 250) and crosses the fine *Washington Viaduct* over the *Patapsco River*. From (19 M.) *Annapolis Junction* a line runs to (20 M.) *Annapolis* (see p. 250). 34 M. *Hyattsville*.

40 M. **Washington**, see below.

43. Washington.

Railway Stations. *Baltimore & Potomac* (*Pennsylvania*) *Railroad* (Pl. E, 4), cor. of Sixth and B Sts., for trains in all directions; *Baltimore & Ohio* (Pl. F, 3), cor. of New Jersey Ave. and C St., for B. & O. trains to the N., N. W., and W. — *Hotel Omnibuses* meet the chief trains (25 c.). *Cab* into the town, each pers. 25-35 c. (see below).

Hotels *Arlington (Pl. a; D, 3), Vermont Ave., $4-5; Shoreham (Pl. b; D, 3), 15th St., $4-5, R. $1-3; Arno (Pl. c; C, 3), 916 16th St., $4-5, R. from $1; Normandie (Pl. d; D, 3), McPherson Sq., from $5, R. $1-3; The Cochran, 14th and K Sts. (Pl. D, 3); Willard's (Pl. e; D, 3), cor. of Pennsylvania Ave. and 14th St.; Ebbit Ho. (Pl. f; D, 3), F St., near 14th St.; Riggs Ho. (Pl. g; D, 3), cor. G and 15th Sts.; Wormley's (Pl. h; D, 3), cor. H and 15th Sts.; Metropolitan (Pl. i; E, 4), Pennsylvania Ave., 6th and 7th Sts.; these five old-established houses on the American plan, much frequented by politicians, $4; Welcker (Pl. k: D, 3), Chamberlain (Pl. l: D, 3), R. from $1; Congressional (Pl. n; F, 4), near the Capitol, $2-2½; St. James (Pl. o; E, 4), R. from $1. Also numerous small *Family Hotels* and *Boarding Houses* ($10-20 a week).

Restaurants. At the hotels on the European plan, see above; *Losekam*, F St.; *Harvey*, 1016 Pennsylvania Ave. (steamed oysters, etc.); *Hancock*, 1234 Pennsylvania Ave., a quaint little place (men only), with a collection of relics; *Capitol Restaurants*, see p. 255; *Shoemaker*, Pennsylvania Ave., a drinking-bar frequented by politicians, journalists, etc.; *Fussell*, 1425 New York Ave. (ice-cream, etc.).

Tramways (horse and electric) and **Omnibuses** ('*Herdics*') traverse many of the principal streets.

Cabs (*Hacks* and *Hansoms*). For 15 squares each pers. 25 c., each addit. 5 squares 10 c., at night (12.30-5 a.m.) 40 and 15 c.; per hr., 1-2 pers., 75 c., each addit. ¼ hr. 20 c., 3-4 pers. $1 and 25 c., at night $1, 25 c., $1¼, 35 c. Two-horse Hacks, 1-4 pers., per. hr. $1½, each addit. ¼ hr. 25 c. To *Arlington* $5, *Soldiers' Home* $5, *Great Falls of the Potomac* $20.

Steamers ply daily from 7th St. Wharf (Pl. E, 5) to *Mt. Vernon* (see p. 262) and other river-landings; also, at irregular intervals (see daily papers), to *Norfolk* (p. 331), *Old Point Comfort* (p. 332), *Baltimore* (p. 244), *Philadelphia* (p. 210), *New York* (p. 6), *Boston* (p. 72), etc. *Steam-Ferry* hourly from 7th St. Wharf to *Alexandria* (p. 262; fare 15 c.).

Places of Amusement. *Albaugh's Opera House* (Pl. D, 3), 15th St.; *New National Theatre* (Pl. D, 3), E St.; *Academy of Music*, cor. of D and 9th Sts. (Pl. D, 4); *Bijou* (Pl. E, 4), 9th St.; *Kernan's* (Pl. D, 4; varieties, etc.), cor. of C and 11th Sts.; *Metzerott Music Hall.* — *Panorama of the Battle of Gettysburg* (Pl. D, 3, 4), 15th St.

Art Collections. *Corcoran Gallery*, see p. 260; *Waggaman's Private Gallery* (from Jan. to April, 11-4; fee 50 c., devoted to charity; tickets at 1003 Pennsylvania Ave.).

Clubs. *Metropolitan* (Pl. C, 3); *United Service; Cosmos* (scientific; Pl. D, 3); *University; Columbia Athletic*, with fine gymnasium, etc.; *Gridiron Club; National Press Club.*

General Post Office (Pl. E, 3), cor. of 7th and F Sts. — **City Post Office** (Pl. E, 3), G St., between 6th and 7th Sts., open 6-11, Sun. 8-10 and 6-7. **British Embassy** (Pl. C, 2), Connecticut Ave.; *Sir Julian Pauncefote*, G. C. M. G., K. C. B., Ambassador.

Bibliography. Visitors should procure the *Congressional Directory* (50 c.); a good guidebook is that of *De B. Randolph Keim* (25 c.).

The *City of Washington*, the capital of the United States, lies on the left bank of the *Potomac*, at the confluence of the main stream with the E. branch, 156 M. from Chesapeake Bay and 185 M. from the Atlantic Ocean. It covers an area of about 10 sq. M., and in 1890 had 188,932 inhab. (with *Georgetown*, 202,978). The city is in many respects one of the most beautiful in the United States, being finely laid out, with wide asphalted streets, opening up vistas of handsome public buildings, monuments, or leafy squares, with the Capitol and the Washington Monument dominating the entire view. Its plan may be described as that of a wheel laid on a gridiron, the rectangular arrangement of the streets having superimposed upon it a system of radiating avenues, lined with trees and named for the different states of the Union. The streets running N. and S. are numbered, those running E. and W. are named by the letters of the alphabet. The *Circles* formed by the intersection of the streets and avenues are one of the most charming features of the city. *Pennsylvania Avenue*, between the Capitol and the White House (a distance of 1 1/3 M.), is the chief thoroughfare, and other important business-streets are *7th St., 14th St., 9th St.*, and *F St.* Among the finest residence-streets are *Massachusetts Ave., Vermont Ave., Connecticut Ave.*, and *16th St.*

The present site of the national capital of the United States was selected in 1790, mainly through the agency of George Washington; and the **Federal District of Columbia**, 100 sq. M. in area, was set apart for this purpose, on territory ceded by Maryland and Virginia. The Virginia portion of the district was, however, retroceded in 1846, and the present area of the District of Columbia is 65 sq. M. Its population in 1890 was 230,392 (75,927 coloured). The district is ruled directly by the President and Congress, through a board of Commissioners appointed under an act of 1874; and its inhabitants belong to no state and have no voice either in national or local government. The plan of the city of Washington was due to *Major l'Enfant*, a French officer of engineers; and the intention was to make the Capitol (see p. 253) its centre, with streets and avenues radiating from it in all directions. It was at first proposed to call it *Federal City*, but this name was changed to Washington in 1791.

The foundation-stone of the Capitol was laid in 1793; the seat of government was removed to Washington in 1800; and in 1802 the city received its charter. In 1810 the population was 8208; in 1840 it was 23.364; in 1870 it was 109,199; and in 1880 it was 147,307. In 1871 the city was still in a very backward condition; but the substitution in that year of a territorial for a municipal government inaugurated a series of reforms, which completely revolutionized the appearance of the city and left it one of the most comfortable and beautiful in the world. The commerce and manufactures of Washington are unimportant, and its prosperity depends on its position as the seat of Congress and the Government Offices. There are probably 40,000 army and navy officers and civil servants in Washington, and these with their families make a large proportion of the population. The sobriquet of 'City of Magnificent Distances', applied to Washington when its framework seemed unnecessarily large for its growth, is still deserved, perhaps, for the width of its streets and the spaciousness of its parks and squares.

The best time to visit Washington is during the sitting of Congress, which lasts from the first Mon. in Dec. to March 4th in the odd-numbered years, and till June, July, or later in the even-numbered years. The city itself is seen to greatest advantage in May or October. In summer (July-Sept.) it is very hot and is deserted by many of its inhabitants. The Public Offices are all open to the public, free, between 9 or 10 and 2; and the attendants will show on application any rooms not actually occupied.

The ****Capitol** (Pl. F, 4), finely situated on a hill 90 ft. above the level of the Potomac, dominates the entire city with its soaring dome and ranks among the most beautiful buildings in the world. It is 751 ft. in length and 121-324 ft. wide, and consists of a main edifice of sandstone, painted white, and of two wings of white marble. It covers an area of $3\frac{1}{2}$ acres. The main building, with its original low-crowned dome, was completed in 1827; the wings and the new iron *Dome*, 288 ft. high, were added in 1851-65. Numerous architects have been employed on the building, of whom it may be enough to mention *Mr. T. U. Walter*, designer of the extensions and the dome. The general style is classic, with Corinthian details. The principal façade looks towards the E., as the city was expected to spread in that direction, and the Capitol thus turns its back upon the main part of the city and on the other government buildings. A fine marble **Terrace* (view), 884 ft. long, approached by two broad flights of steps, has, however, been constructed on the W. side of the Capitol and adds great dignity to this view of the building. The dome is surmounted by a figure of Freedom, by *Crawford*, $19\frac{1}{2}$ ft. high (comp. p. 257). The total cost of the building up to the present time has been $ 16,000,000 (3,200,000 *l.*).

The Capitol stands in a park of about 50 acres in extent, laid out by *Olmsted*. In the plaza on the E. side, opposite the central portico, is a colossal *Statue of George Washington*, by *Greenough*.

The *Front* or *East Façade* is preceded by three porticos, the main entrance being in the centre. To the right of the central portico is the *Settlement of America*, a marble group by *Greenough;* to the left is the *Discovery of America*, a figure of Columbus by *Persico*. In the pediment above the portico is a relief of the *Genius of America*, by *Persico;* and in the pediment above the N. portico is a group representing the *Civilization of the United States,* by *Crawford.* The inauguration of the Presidents of the United States takes place on the broad steps in front of the main doorway.

*Interior (open, 9-4; guide, unnecessary, 60c. per hr.). The beautiful *Bronze Doors* are adorned with reliefs by *Randolph Rogers*, representing events in the life of Columbus (cast at Munich, 1851). To the right and left are statues of *Peace and War,* by *Persico.* — We first enter the — Rotunda, below the Dome, 96 ft. in diameter and 180 ft. high. The walls are adorned with eight historical paintings (named from right to left): 1 (to the right) Landing of Columbus in 1492, by *Vanderlyn;* 2. Embarkation of the Pilgrims at Delfthaven in 1620, by *Wier;* 3. Washington resigning his commission at Annapolis in 1783, by *Trumbull;* 4. Surrender of Cornwallis in 1781, by *Trumbull;* 5. Surrender of Burgoyne at Saratoga in 1777, by *Trumbull;* 6. Signing the Declaration of Independence (1776), by *Trumbull;* 7. Baptism of Pocahontas (1613), by *Chapman;* 8. Discovery of the Mississippi by De Soto in 1541, by *Powell.* Above these paintings is a band of frescoes, in imitation of relief, by *Brumidi,* representing scenes from American history from the Landing of Columbus to the Celebration of the Centennial of Independence at Philadelphia. The ceiling-painting, also by *Brumidi,* depicts the Apotheosis of Washington, with figures of Liberty, Victory, the 13 Original States, and other allegorical groups. The reliefs above the doors represent the Landing of the Pilgrims, Penn's treaty with the Indians, Pocahontas and Capt. Smith, and Daniel Boone and the Indians. — A staircase at the N.W. corner of the Rotunda ascends to the *Whispering Gallery,* in the interior of the dome, and to the lantern on the top of the dome (288 ft.), which commands a splendid *View of Washington. Pennsylvania Avenue (r.) and Maryland Avenue (l.) diverge like the spokes of a fan, and between them is the Mall, a broad enclosure containing the Smithsonian and other public institutions, with the tall Washington Monument towering above all. The Pension Office is conspicuous to the N.W. The White House is almost concealed by the Treasury (at the end of Pennsylvania Ave.). The door on the W. side of the Rotunda leads to the *Library of Congress (9-4), the largest library in the United States, containing about 900,000 volumes and pamphlets. It is, however, terribly straightened for want of room, and a large new building is now being erected for it (see p. 256).

The door on the S. side of the Rotunda leads to the Old Hall of Representatives, now the *National Hall of Statuary, a semicircular apartment, containing statues of eminent Americans, each State being allowed to send 'effigies of two of her chosen sons'. Among the other sculptures are statues of Washington (cast of *Houdon's* statue, p. 327), Lincoln (by *Miss Ream,* now *Mrs. Hoxie*), Jefferson (by *David d'Angers*) and Hamilton (by *Stone*). There are also a few portraits. The allegorical *Clock* is by *Franzoni.* A brass plate in the S.W. corner of the floor marks the spot where *John Quincy Adams* fell on Feb. 21st, 1848, two days before his death. This room has some curious 'whispering gallery' properties, which, however, require the aid of an habitué to discover.

Leaving the Statuary Hall by the corridor on its S. side, we next enter the wing devoted to the House of Representatives.

The **Hall of Representatives** (open to visitors before noon, when the House meets; galleries open at all times), occupying the centre of this wing, is a plain and business-like apartment, 139 ft. long, 93 ft. wide, and 36 ft. high. It contains desks for 352 members and 4 delegates. To the right of the Speaker is the pedestal on which the mace is placed when the House is called to order. To the right and left are portraits of Washington (by *Vanderlyn*) and Lafayette (by *Ary Scheffer*). The walls are adorned by two pictures by *Bierstadt* (Landing of Hudson and Discovery of California) and a fresco by *Brumidi* (Washington demanding the surrender of Cornwallis at Yorktown). Like the House of Commons, the hall is lighted through glass-panels in the ceiling. The *Galleries* round the Hall can seat 2500 people; different sections are reserved for ladies (with their escorts), gentlemen, the press, the diplomatic corps, and the families of members and officials. The general proceedings of the House are roughly similar to those of the House of Commons, but the noise and confusion are greater and it is a rare thing for a speaker to receive the attention of the whole House. The Republicans affect one side of the hall, and the Democrats the other (seats of members shown in Keim's Diagram, price 10c.). The Speaker has no distinguishing dress, and members do not wear their hats in the House. A novel feature to the European visitor is the presence in the House of a number of page-boys, who are summoned by the clapping of hands.

The Hall is surrounded with corridors, affording access to *Committee Rooms* and the *Rooms of Officials*.

On the E. and W. are *Staircases* ascending to the *Galleries*. On the wall of the E. staircase is a large painting, by *Carpenter*, of the Signing of the Proclamation of Emancipation, with portraits of Lincoln and his Cabinet (Sept. 22nd, 1863); and at its foot is a Statue of Jefferson, by *Powers*. On the W. staircase is *Leutze's* large painting of Westward Ho., with a view of the Golden Gate, by *Bierstadt*, below. The upper floor also contains various *Committee Rooms*. — The basement-floor, below the House of Representatives, contains a good *Restaurant*.

The door on the N. side of the Rotunda (see above) leads into the N. wing of the original Capitol (see p. 253), on the right (E.) side of which is the **Supreme Court Room**, formerly the *Senate Chamber*, which is open to visitors. The Supreme Court of the United States consists of a Chief Justice (Hon. M. W. Fuller) and eight Associate Justices. It holds its sessions from Oct. to May (12-4). The judges wear robes but no wigs; the counsel wear neither gowns nor wigs. — In the *Robing Room* are portraits of former Chief Justices.

We now pass through a corridor leading to the Senate Wing. The *Senate Chamber* is smaller (113ft. long, 80ft. wide, and 36ft. high) and more ornate than the House of Representatives. The general arrangements of the seats, galleries, etc., are like those of the House, and the Senate also meets at noon. The Vice-President of the United States is the official President of the Senate. The proceedings in the Senate are much more dignified and orderly than those in the House; and the late Mr. E. A. Freeman describes it as 'as much superior to the House of Lords as the House of Representatives is inferior to the House of Commons'. The Senators are 90 in number. To the N. of the Senate are the *President's Room*, richly adorned with frescoes and gilding; the *Marble Reception Hall;* and the *Vice-President's Room*, with a fine portrait of Washington by Rembrandt Peale. When the Senate is in session visitors to these rooms require the permission of a Senator; at other times they may enter them, if open, and apply to the messengers if closed. Several of the *Senate Committee Rooms* are also handsomely decorated. — At the foot of the *E. Staircase,* ascending to the *Galleries,* is a statue of Franklin by *Powers;* on the wall is Perry's Victory on Lake Erie (1813), a large painting by *Powell*. At the foot of the *W. Staircase* is a statue of John Hancock, by *Stone;* on the wall is the Storming of Chapultepec, Mexico (1847), by *Walker*. The rooms and corridors of the *Upper Floor* contain various portraits and paintings. In the basement is a *Restaurant*.

The *Bronze Doors* of the Senate Wing, opening on the N.E. portico, represent various scenes of American history, in relief, by *Crawford*.

The **Basement** of the Capitol contains *Committee Rooms, Library Rooms, Storage Rooms, Restaurants* (see above), etc. The walls and ceilings of the corridors are frescoed, and some of the Committee Rooms are also handsomely decorated (admission on application to the messengers). The *Ventilating and Heating Apparatus* is also interesting. In the centre, below the Dome, is the *Crypt*, with 40 Doric columns. In a small vestibule, reached from the outside by the door under the colonnade to the right of the main steps, are *Six Columns*, in the form of stalks of Indian corn, said to have been designed by Jefferson (comp. p. xc).

We may leave the building by the W. terrace and steps (see p. 253).

To the S.E. of the Capitol is the building of the **New Congressional Library** (Pl. F, 4), now in course of construction. This enormous structure, 470 ft. long and 365 ft. wide, promises to be one of the finest library-buildings in the world. Its estimated cost is $6,000,000 (1,200,000 *l.*), and it will accommodate 4-5 million volumes.

At the foot of the flights of steps descending from the terrace on the W. side of the Capitol is a colossal *Statue of Chief Justice Marshall* (1755-1835), by Story. The broad walk to the N. (r.) leads to the *Naval* or *Peace Monument*, by Simmons. The walk to the S. (l.) leads to the *Statue of President Garfield* (1831-81), by J. Q. A. Ward.

The first part of the Reservation is occupied by the **Botanic Gardens** (Pl. E, F, 4; 9-6), with palm-houses, conservatories, and the handsome *Bartholdi Fountain*.

We may now walk through the two small parks to the W. of this point, cross the railway, and visit the building of the *United States Fish Commission* (Pl. E, 4; entr. in 6th St.; 9-4), where the processes of fish-breeding may be inspected (aquarium). — A little farther to the W., beyond 7th St., stands the *Army Medical Museum* (Pl. E, 4; 10-3), containing a pathological collection, a collection of army medical supplies, and a library of 200,000 volumes.

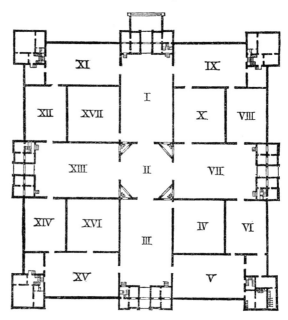

Immediately to the W. of the Medical Museum is the *National Museum* (Pl. E, 4), a large brick building 327 ft. square, containing valuable and excellently arranged collections of natural history, ethnology, antiquities, geology, arts, and industry. It is under the direction of the Smithsonian Institute (see below). Over the entrance is a group of Columbia as protectress of Science and Industry. Admission 9-4.30; catalogue (non-official) 25 c.

The NORTH HALL (Pl. I), which we first enter, contains relics of eminent Americans (to the left) and a miscellaneous collection of china, bronzes, Japanese curiosities, etc. (to the right). The wall-cases contain musical instruments and other objects. Above, on the walls, hangs some fine Flemish tapestry. Over the entrance is a large panel of Limoges fayence, representing man's triumphs over the material universe. — The *Rotunda* (Pl. II) contains the original model of the statue of Freedom on the Dome of the Capitol (p. 253), a Monument to *Daguerre* (1789-1851), the Haviland Memorial Vases, a Mosaic Lion from Tunis, etc. — The SOUTH HALL (Pl. III) is devoted to the fine collection of *Mammalia*, in which the buffalo and other American animals are represented in well-mounted groups. — We may now pass to the left into the SOUTH EAST COURT (Pl. IV), which is devoted to *Fossils*. — Returning through the South Hall, we again pass to the left into the EAST SOUTH RANGE (Pl. V), with its collection of *Comparative Osteology*. Off this room open the '*Public Comfort Rooms*' for ladies and gentlemen. — The SOUTH EAST RANGE (Pl. VI) contains *Drugs and Medicines.* — The EAST HALL (Pl. VII) contains collections illustrative of *Transportation and Engineering*. The W. part of the room belongs to the Ethnological Department. In the S.E. corner is a small *Restaurant.* — NORTH EAST RANGE (Pl. VIII). *Naval Architecture.* — EAST NORTH RANGE (Pl. IX). *Fishery Exhibition.* The pavilion opening off this room contains *Birds' Eggs.* — NORTH EAST COURT (Pl. X). *Arts and Textile Industries.* — We now regain the North Hall, which we cross obliquely to the WEST NORTH RANGE (Pl. XI), or lecture-hall, the walls of which are covered with an interesting °Collection of Paintings by *George Catlin*, illustrating the manners and custom of the North American Indians. Mr. Catlin spent 8 years (1832-40) among the Indians, visiting 48 different tribes and painting all of the 600 paintings from nature. — The NORTH WEST RANGE (Pl. XII) is devoted to the *Graphic Arts.* — WEST HALL (Pl. XIII). *Ethnological Collections.* — SOUTH WEST RANGE (Pl. XIV). *Minerals.* — WEST SOUTH RANGE (Pl. XV), *Rocks and Physical Geology.* — SOUTH WEST COURT (Pl. XVI). *Metallurgy and Economic Geology.* — We now retrace our steps through R. XV and then pass through R. III and the Rotunda to the NORTH WEST COURT (Pl. XVII), containing the *American Aboriginal Pottery.*

Just to the W. of the National Museum stands the *Smithsonian Institution (Pl. D, 4), a handsome red-stone building in the late-Norman style, erected in 1847-56 at a cost of $ 450,000 (90,000 *l.*). The loftiest of the nine towers is 150 ft. high. In front of it is a Statue of Prof. Joseph Henry (1799-1878), the first secretary of the Institution, by *Story*. The Institution is open free, 9-4.30; catalogue as above. Secretary, Dr. S. P. Langley; Assistant Secretary, Dr. G. Brown Goode. The part of the Mall in which the Smithsonian stands is 52 acres in extent.

The Smithsonian Institution was founded with the proceeds of a legacy of $ 535,000 bequeathed by an Englishman, *Mr. James Smithson* (1754-1829), a natural son of the Duke of Northumberland, 'for the increase and diffusion of knowledge among men'. So far as is known Mr. Smithson, who was distinguished as a chemist, never visited America, and had no personal relations with that country; and his choice of Washington for the establishment of his institution is supposed to be due to his sympathy with the democratic principles represented by the Western Republic. The policy of the Institution is to encourage research, and it has been the chief promotor of the scientific investigation of the climate, products, and antiquities of the United States. It possesses a library of 100,000 vols. (deposited in the Library of Congress) and issues three series of publications ('Contributions to Knowledge', 'Miscellaneous Collections', and 'Annual Reports') of great scientific value. The Museum issues Reports, Proceedings and Bulletins.

Ground Floor. The MAIN HALL contains the *Collection of Birds* (about 70,000 specimens) and also the *Collection of Shells*. A room to the right contains *Fish*, and one to the left contains *Corals and Sponges*.

The **First Floor** is devoted to the *Archaeological Collections*, which, as regards American antiquities, are the finest and most extensive in the world. Three distinct American civilizations are represented: — I. *Mexican and Central American Collections*, including numerous casts of stone monuments (Aztec Calendar Stone, in entrance hall; Sacrificial Stone; objects from Palenque, etc.) and also original articles of smaller size (stone collars from Porto Rico, clay vases from Nicaragua, etc.). — 2. *Cliff Dwellers and Pueblo Indians*. Models of cliff-dwellings and pueblos in New Mexico and Arizona, including Zuñi (p. 413), the largest and most interesting of the latter. Details are given by labels attached to the objects. There is a tradition that the Toltecs of Mexico came from the N.W. about the 6th cent. A.D. and were followed about 500 years later by the Aztecs, who drove the Toltecs before them into Central and S. America. It is thus *possible* that there may be some connection between the Pueblo Indians and the Toltec and Aztec races. — 3. *North American Indians*, such as are found throughout the whole of the United States. (The objects here are prehistoric, the historical period of these Indians being illustrated in the National Museum.) Models of Indian Mounds. Numerous cases of small antiquities. To the left (E.) of the entrance are cases giving a Synoptical View of European and American Prehistoric Antiquities, forming an interesting index or type-museum of the general collection. Next comes a series of cases containing American antiquities arranged by States. — The E. end of the room is occupied by the *Wilson Collection of Antiquities* (chiefly European). — To the W. are a fine collection of *Copper Implements of the United States* and the *Moorehead Collection of Objects found in Mounds* (Ohio).

The SOUTH HALL on this floor (no adm.) contains relics of Smithson.

The next part of the Mall, beyond 12th St., contains the building of the **Department of Agriculture** (Pl. D, 4; 9-4), which may be visited by those interested in scientific agriculture and horticulture. It includes a library, museum, herbarium, and conservatories of economic plants; and the grounds in front of it are devoted to an arboretum arranged by families.

In B St., near the S.W. corner of the Agricultural Grounds, is the **Bureau of Engraving and Printing** (Pl. D, 4), where the highly interesting processes of the manufacture of paper money and bonds are shown to visitors (Sat., 10-2).

We have now reached the open grounds in which the **Washington Obelisk** (Pl. D, 4), a unique monument of dignity and simplicity, rears its lofty form to the skies.

The Washington Obelisk, a worthy memorial of a great man, was begun in 1848, abandoned in 1855, resumed in 1877, and finished in 1884, at a total cost of $1,300,000 (260,000l.). It is constructed of white Maryland marble and is 555 ft. high, a height greater than any other structure of masonry in the world (Philadelphias City Hall, 510 ft.; spires of Cologne Cathedral 511 ft.). The walls are 15 ft. thick at the base and 1½ ft. at the top. The pyramidal roof is 55 ft. high and is capped with a piece of aluminium. The monument is open from 9 to 5.30, and may be ascended either by the 900 steps (fatiguing; 20-25 min.) or by the elevator (8 min.), which runs at intervals of about ½ hr. Stone tablets presented by different States and corporations are inserted in the walls.

The top commands a magnificent *View of the city of Washington and its surroundings. Arlington (p. 262) is seen to the E. across the Potomac. Among the points at a little distance are the new Observatory (p. 261; N.W.), the Soldiers' Home and Howard University (p. 262; N.), the R. C. University (p. 262; N.E.), and Alexandria (p. 262; S.). On a clear day the Blue Ridge Mts. are seen to the N.W., the prominent Sugarloaf being about 50 M. distant.

To the S. of the Washington Monument are the *Propagating Gardens* and (farther off) the *Long Bridge* (Pl. E, 5), over which the N. troops marched into Virginia during the Civil War. To the W. are the *U. S. Fish Ponds* (Pl. C, D, 4).

We may now ascend 15th St., skirting the *President's Grounds* (band in summer) on the left and passing the *Panorama*, the *Light Infantry Armoury*, and *Albaugh's Opera House* on the right. — To the left, opposite F St., stands the *Treasury Building (Pl. D, 3; 9-2), an immense edifice, 510 ft. long and 280 ft. wide, with an Ionic colonnade on the E. front and porticos on the other three sides.

Among the chief objects of interest shown to visitors are the *U. S. Cash Room*, in the N. corridor; the *Redemption Division*, in the basement; the *Silver Vaults*, containing coin to the value of hundreds of millions of dollars; the *Portraits of Secretaries of the Treasury* in the Secretary's Department, on the first floor; and the *Secret Service Division*, W. side of 2nd floor, with its collection of forged money and portraits of forgers.

The Swiss-looking little building to the S. of the Treasury is the *Photograph Office* of the Architect of the Treasury.

In Pennsylvania Ave., to the N. of the Treasury, stands the *Department of Justice* (Pl. D, 3); and a little farther to the N., at the corner of 15th and H Sts., is the *Columbian University* (Pl. D, 3; 7-800 students). — Following Pennsylvania Ave. towards the W., we reach (to the right) LAFAYETTE SQUARE (Pl. C, D, 3), with a bronze *Statue of Gen. Andrew Jackson* (1767-1845), by Clark Mills, and the *Lafayette Monument*, by Falguière and Mercié. On the E. side of the square is the house in which an attempt was made to assassinate *Secretary Seward* in 1865 and since occupied by *Mr. James G. Blaine* (d. 1893).

Opposite is the entrance to the *Executive Mansion of the President of the United States (Pl. D, 3), popularly known as the *White House*.

The Executive Mansion is a two-storied stone building, painted white, 170 ft. long and 86 ft. deep, with an Ionic portico. To the W. is a range of conservatories. It was founded in 1792, occupied by President Adams in 1800, burned by the British in 1814, and rebuilt in 1818. The large *East Room* (80 ft. ×40 ft. ×22 ft.) is open to the public from 10 to 2. Two or three times a week the President receives all comers here at 1 p.m., shaking hands with each as they pass him in single file. The *Reception Rooms*, which contain portraits of Presidents and their wives, are shown by special order only. The *Executive Office* and *Cabinet Room* are in the E. part of the upper floor. The W. part of the ground-floor and the upper floor are private. The *Grounds* surrounding the house are 75 acres in extent.

To the W. of the White House is the building that accommodates the **State, War, and Navy Departments** (Pl. C, 3; 10-2), a huge parallelogram, enclosing two courts and measuring 567 ft. in length by 342 ft. in breadth.

The N. and W. wings are occupied by the **War Department**, where the Secretary's Apartments and the adjoining corridors contain a collection of *Portraits of Secretaries of War and Generals*, including one of Washington by D. Huntington. The *Library*, on the 4th floor, contains a fine collection of books on military science and the late Civil War.

The **Navy Department** is in the E. part of the building and contains models of war-ships, portraits, etc. The *Library*, on the 3rd floor, is a fine room with 25,000 volumes.

The *Department of State (corresponding to the Foreign Office in London) occupies the S. part of the building. Among the rooms usually shown to visitors are the *Diplomatic Reception Rooms*, containing portraits of the Secretaries of State from 1789 to the present day, and the *Library* (2nd floor), with Jefferson's original copy of the Declaration of Independence and other relics.

To the S. of the State Building are the old *Van Ness House* and the cottage in which *Davy Burns* entertained *Tom Moore*. — To the S.W. is a grey painted house which was General Grant's headquarters during the Civil War.

At the corner of Pennsylvania Ave. and 17th St., to the N. of the State Building, is the *Corcoran Gallery of Art (Pl. C, 3), built and endowed by the late *Mr. W.W. Corcoran* (open daily, from 9 or 9.30 till 4; on Tues., Thurs., & Sat. free; on Mon., Wed., & Frid. 25 c.). Niches on the front and side of the building contain statues of famous artists. The collections, of somewhat unequal merit, include paintings, sculptures, and ceramics. Catalogue 25 c.

Ground Floor. To the left is the *HALL OF BRONZE AND CERAMICS, including many bronzes by *A.L. Barye*, electrotype reproductions, and large English and Japanese vases. At the back is the HALL OF ANTIQUE SCULPTURE (casts). To the right are the HALLS OF MODERN AND RENAISSANCE SCULPTURE (casts). The hall at the back communicates with the CORCORAN SCHOOL OF ART and the TAYLOE COLLECTION (paintings, books, and bric-a-brac).

Upper Floor. The MAIN PICTURE GALLERY contains works by *Cole*, *Le Roux*, *Boughton*, *Rousseau*, *O. Achenbach*, '*Sully*, *Troyon*, *Huntington*, *F. E. Church*, *Gérôme*, *Raphael Mengs*, *Breton*, *Renouf*, *Becker*, *Otto van Thoren*, *Kensett*, *Ary Scheffer*, *Müller*, *Morland*, *Detaille* (Passing Regiment), *Ziem*, *Corot* (Wood-gatherers), *Knaus*, *Bierstadt*, *Van Marcke*, *Henner* (Joan of Arc), *Eliott* (Portrait of Mr. Corcoran), *Diaz*, *Isabey*, *Inness*, *Daubigny*, *Vibert*, *Morot*, *Cazin*, *Rico*, *Max Weyl*, *Harrison*, and *Aivasovsky*. In the centre is *Vela's *Last Days of Napoleon, in marble. — W. GALLERY. Small paintings, some of great merit. Group of sleeping children, by *Rinehart* (p. 250). — OCTAGON ROOM. *Greek Slave, by *Hiram Powers* (1805-73). — S.W. and S.E. GALLERIES. Pictures, chiefly on loan. — E. GALLERY. Portraits of Presidents and others, including specimens of *Gilbert Stuart*, *Eliott*, *Healy*, *Sully*, *Malbone*, *R. Peale* and *Duplessis*.

We may now return to the Treasury (p. 259) and follow F St. towards the E. To the right, between 8th and 7th Sts., is the **General Post Office** (Pl. E, 3; 9-2), a handsome building in the Corinthian style. Opposite stands the *Department of the Interior (Pl. E, 3; 9-2), generally known as the *Patent Office*, a huge building 453 ft. long and 330 ft. deep, with a Doric portico. The centre is of stone, and the wings of marble.

This building contains the rooms of the Secretary of the Interior, the Indian Office, the General Land Office, etc., which may be viewed on application to the attendants. The upper floor is occupied by four halls containing a huge *Collection of Patents and Models*, some idea of the extent of which may be gathered from the fact that about half-a-million of patents

WASHINGTON.

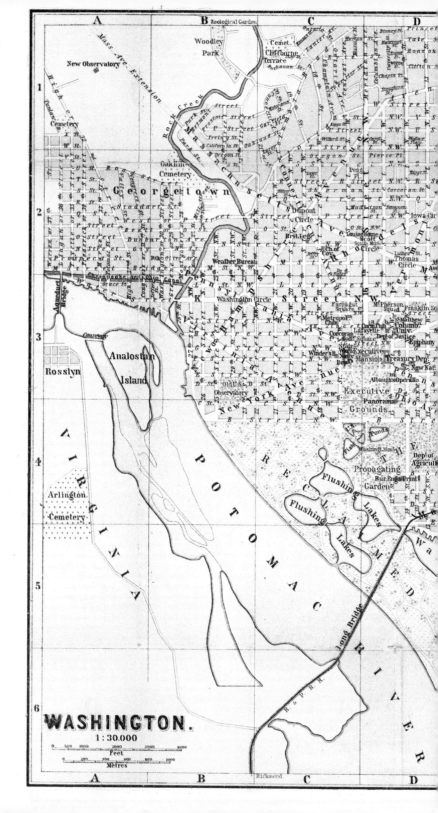

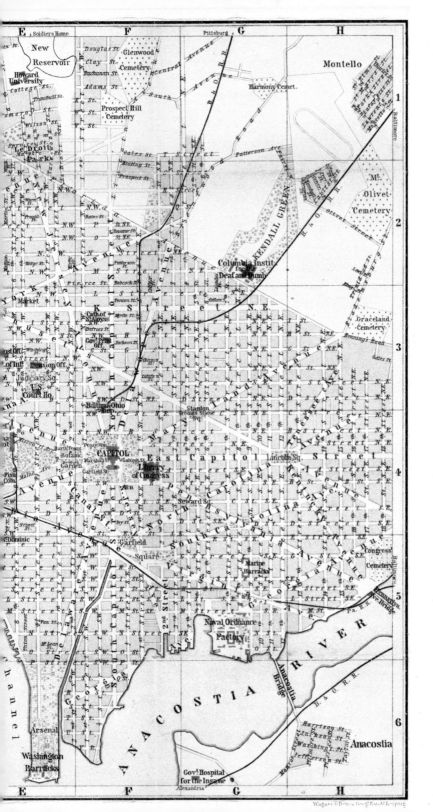

have been granted in the United States since 1836 (compared with 150,000 in Great Britain since 1621). Some of the most interesting have been removed to the National Museum (p. 257).

At 5th St. F St. reaches JUDICIARY SQUARE (Pl. E, 3), on the N. side of which stands the **Pension Building,** an enormous barn-like structure of brick, 400 ft. long and 200 ft. wide. It is surrounded by a terracotta frieze, illustrating military and naval operations. The interior, with its mammoth columns, is rather imposing, and can accommodate about 20,000 people at an inauguration ball. — On the S. side of the square stands the *United States Court House* (or *City Hall*), occupied by the U. S. Courts and the offices of the Civil Service Commissioners. In front is a column bearing a *Statue of Lincoln,* by Flannery.

A little to the N.E. of this point, at the corner of North Capitol St. and H St., is the *Government Printing Office* (Pl. F, 3; 9-4). — *Ford's Theatre* (Pl. D, 3; now used by Government), in which President Lincoln was assassinated by Wilkes Booth on April 14th, 1865, is in 10th St., between F St. and E St. A house opposite (No. 576) bears a tablet stating that Lincoln died there. — The *Baltimore & Potomac Railway Station* (Pl. E, 4) was the scene of Garfield's assassination by Guiteau (July 2nd, 1881), and the spot where he fell is marked in the pavement.

A visit may be paid (tramway along 7th St.) to the *Washington Barracks* (Pl. E, 6), now used as an artillery station (drill 9-11 a.m.). Mrs. Surratt and others implicated in the murder of Lincoln were hanged in front of the Guard House here. — About 1 M. to the E. (tramway on M St.), on the *Anacostia* or E. branch of the Potomac, is the **Washington Navy Yard** (Pl. G, 5; open from sunrise to sunset), which contains a museum and other points of interest. Ships are not built here, but the gun-foundry is very important and large quantities of naval stores are made. — A little to the N. are the *Marine Barracks* (Pl. G, 5), where the band plays in the Armoury from Jan. to May (Mon., 1.30-3) and on the Parade in summer (Thurs., 4.30-6 p.m.). — Farther to the E. are the *Congressional Cemetery* (Pl. H, 5), containing the graves of many Members of Congress; the *U. S. Jail* (10-4); and the *Alms House.* — On the S. side of the Anacostia is the large *Government Insane Asylum* (Pl. G, 6; 1500 inmates). — From the Jail we may return through Massachusetts Ave. to (3/4 M.) *Lincoln Square* (Pl. G, H, 4), with *Ball's* Emancipation Group (Lincoln and a freed slave), whence tramways and omnibuses run to the Capitol and the city.

The new **Naval Observatory** (Pl. A, 1; 9-4), in the N.W. part of the city, should be visited by all interested in astronomical work. Its equipments and instruments are excellent.

On the site of the *Old Observatory* (Pl. B, 3) Mr. Franklin W. Smith (comp. pp. 181, 357) hopes to see realised his scheme for a grand National Gallery, with eight courts for architectural reproductions and galleries for historic representation of past nationalities.

The *Signal Office and Weather Bureau* (Pl. B, 2; 9-2), at the corner of M and 24th St., is also well worth a visit. The arrangements for forecasting the weather are most interesting.

Many of the Circles formed by the intersection of the streets and avenues (see p. 252) are adorned with statues, among which are the following: *Washington* (equestrian), by Clark Mills, in Washington Circle (Pl. B, 3); *Admiral Dupont*, by Launt Thompson, in Dupont Circle (Pl. C, 2); *Gen. Winfield Scott* (equestrian), by H. K. Browne, in Scott Circle (Pl. C, D, 2); *Adm. Farragut*, by Mrs. Hoxie (Vinnie Ream). in Farragut Sq. (Pl. C, 3); *Gen. McPherson* (equest.), by Rebisso, in McPherson Sq. (Pl. D, 3); *Gen. Thomas* (equest.), by J. Q. A. Ward, in Thomas Circle (Pl. D, 2); *Martin Luther* (just to the N. of the last), a replica of the figure by Rietschel, in the Reformation Monument at Worms; *Ben. Franklin*, by Plassman and Juvenal, at the intersection of Pennsylvania Ave. and 10th St. (Pl. D, 3); *Gen. Rawlins*, by Bailey, at the crossing of Louisiana Ave. and Pennsylvania Ave. (Pl. E, 4); *Gen. Greene* (equest.), by Browne, in Stanton Sq. (Pl. G, 4).

The **Columbia Institute for the Deaf and Dumb** (Pl. G, 2), in *Kendall Green*, incorporates what is said to be the only college for deaf-mutes in the world.

One of the favourite Drives in Washington is that to the *Soldiers' Home*, a large asylum for old soldiers (600 inmates), situated in a beautiful park to the N. of the city, 3 M. from the Capitol. On the way to it we pass the *Howard University* (Pl. E, 1), founded in 1867 for the education of youth irrespective of colour or sex. The grounds of the Soldiers' Home afford fine views ('Capitol Vista', etc.) and contain a *Statue of Gen. Scott*, founder of the Home, by Launt Thompson. President Lincoln spent part of the summers of his last term in one of the cottages at the Soldiers' Home. — To the N. lies the *National Military Cemetery*, with the graves of Gen. Logan and 5400 soldiers. — To the E. of the Soldiers' Home Park is the large *Roman Catholic University* (200 students). We may now return viâ *Glenwood Cemetery* (Pl. F, 1).

Georgetown, or *West Washington* (tramway), beyond *Rock Creek*, lies at the head of the Potomac navigation and is the port of entry for the District of Columbia. It contains large flour-mills, the handsome buildings of *Georgetown College*, an old Jesuit institution founded in 1789 (500 students; fine library), and the *Convent of the Visitation*. In *Oak Hill Cemetery* (Pl. B, 2) is the grave of J. Howard Payne (1792-1852), author of 'Home, Sweet Home'. A large *Park* and *Zoological Garden* have been constructed on Rock Creek, to the N. of Georgetown (comp. Pl. B, 1).

*To Arlington and National Cemetery. This interesting trip should not be omitted. Those who do not drive all the way (carr. $5) may go by tramway to the *Georgetown Aqueduct* (Pl. A, 3) and either take the electric car or cross the bridge here and follow the road to the right, passing (1 M.) *Fort Myer* and soon after reaching (1/3 M.) the rear-gate of the **National Cemetery** (Pl. A, 4, 5). which contains the graves of about 16,000 soldiers. *Arlington House*, in the middle of the grounds, 200 ft. above the river, was once the residence of *George Washington Parke Curtis* (grandson of Washington) and afterwards of *Gen. Robert Lee*, the famous Confederate commander, who married Miss Curtis. It affords a fine 'View of Washington, but now contains little of interest. Near the house are the graves of *Gen. Sheridan, Gen. Sherman*, and other distinguished officers. To the S. is a tomb containing the remains of 2110 unknown soldiers. The return may be made (longer) viâ the Long Bridge (p. 259).

*From Washington to Mount Vernon, 15 M., steamer daily from 7th St. Wharf (Pl. E, 5) at 10 a.m, allowing 2 hrs. at Mt. Vernon, and regaining Washington about 3.30 p.m. (return-fare $1, including admission to Mt. Vernon). [Mt. Vernon may also be reached by electric tramway viâ Alexandria; fare 70 c. incl. adm.] This highly interesting trip to the old home of George Washington should on no account be omitted. — The steamer descends the *Potomac*. 6½ M. **Alexandria** (*Braddock Ho.*, $2), a quaint and somewhat decayed old Virginian city of 14,339 inhab., with the church (Christchurch) which Washington used to attend (pew still pointed out). The old *Carey House* was the headquarters of Gen. Braddock in 1755. Adjoin ing the city is another *National Cemetery*, with 4000 graves. — 8¹/₂M. *Fort Foote*, Maryland, an abandoned earthwork of the Civil War; 12 M. *Fort Washington*, an old stone fort.

15 M. **Mt. Vernon**, an old-fashioned wooden mansion, 96 ft. long, stands on a bluff, 200 ft. above the river, and commands a splendid view. The estate, originally named *Hunting Creek* and comprising 8000 acres, was inherited by George Washington in 1752 from his brother Lawrence, who had changed the name in honour of his former commander, Adm. Vernon of the British navy. The central part of the house was built by Lawrence, and the wings were added by George Washington. The house and 200 acres of land around it were bought by the *Mt. Vernon Ladies Association* in 1859 for $ 200,000 (raised in great part through the exertions of Mr. Edward Everett) and have been restored as nearly as possible to their condition in George Washington's lifetime. — In ascending from the wharf to the house we pass the plain brick *Tomb of George Washington*, containing, behind an iron grating, two sarcophagi with the remains of the General (1732-1799) and his wife Martha (1730-1801). The House contains an abundance of interesting relics, of which, perhaps, the key of the Bastille is the most notable. The room in which Washington died is at the S. end of the first floor, and Mrs. Washington died in the one immediately above it. The room marked *Mrs. Washington's Sitting Room* was more probably *George Washington's Business Room*. The tiles in the piazza were brought from the Isle of Wight. The brick *Barn*, dating from 1733, is probably the oldest part of the buildings. The *Negro Quarters* are to the W. of the house. The *Garden* contains trees planted by Washington.

Among other favourite points for drives are the *National Chautauqua* at *Glen Echo* (7 M.); *Cabin John Bridge*, 10 M. to the N.W.; and the *Great Falls of the Potomac*, 5 M. farther on in the same direction. In summer a small steamer plies from Georgetown to these points (return-fare 50 c.). — RAILWAY EXCURSIONS may be easily made to *Annapolis* (p. 250), *Harper's Ferry* (p. 265), the *Shenandoah Valley* (p. 338), etc. — From Washington to *Chicago*, see R. 45; to *Baltimore*, see R. 42; to *New York*, see R. 42; to *Richmond*, see R. 67; to *New Orleans*, see R. 70.

44. From Pittsburg to Chicago.

a. Viâ Crestline and Fort Wayne.

468 M. PENNSYLVANIA CO.'s LINES in 13-19 hrs. (fare $12, sleeper $2¹/₂). — From New York to *Chicago* by this route, see p. 47 a.

Pittsburg, see R. 39. The train crosses the *Allegheny River* (p. 243), runs through *Allegheny City* (p. 240), and follows the right bank of the *Ohio* for some distance. 25 M. *Rochester* (710 ft.), at the confluence of the Ohio and the *Beaver River*, which we now follow towards the N. (right). 30 M. *Beaver Falls*. Farther on we turn again to the W. (left) and beyond (45 M.) *Enon* (995 ft.) we enter *Ohio* (comp. p. 267). — 83 M. *Alliance* (1100 ft.) is the junction of a branch-line to *Cleveland* (p. 267). — 101 M. *Canton* (26,189 inhab.), in a fine wheat-growing district; 175 M. *Mansfield* (13,473 inhab.). — 189 M. *Crestline* (1170 ft.) is the junction of lines to Toledo, Cleveland, Cincinnati, Indianapolis, etc. — 201 M. *Bucyrus* (5974 inhab.), on the *Sandusky River*. Beyond (288 M.) *Van Wert* we enter *Indiana* (p. 269).

320 M. **Fort Wayne**, an important railway-centre (comp. p. 270). From this point the route is substantially the same as that described

at p. 270. — 360 M. *Warsaw*, on the *Tippecanoe River*; 384 M. *Plymouth*; 415 M. *Wanatah*; 424 M. *Valparaiso* (p. 275). We now approach *Lake Michigan* (right). Various suburban stations. 468 M. **Chicago** *(Canal St. Station)*, see R. 48.

b. Viâ Columbus and Logansport.

507 M. PITTSBURG, CINCINNATI, CHICAGO, & ST. LOUIS RAILROAD (Pennsylvania Co.'s 'Pan Handle Line') in 19-20 hrs. (fares as above).

Pittsburg, see R. 39.. This line runs at first almost due W., crossing the narrow arm of *West Virginia* (p. 264), which is interposed between Pennsylvania and Ohio. Beyond (42 M.) *Wheeling Junction* we cross the *Ohio River* and enter *Ohio* (p. 263). 43 M. *Steubenville* (730 ft.; U. S. Hotel, $2-2½), an industrial city of 13,394 inhab. on the W. bank of the Ohio. 93 M. *Dennison;* 124 M. *Coshocton;* 138 M. *Trinway*, the junction of a line to Cincinnati. 193 M. **Columbus.** — Hotels. *Chittenden, Neil Ho.*, $3-5; *American Ho., Park Hotel, United States*, $2. — Tramways traverse the principal streets. — Post Office, Capitol Sq., cor. of State St. and Third St.

Columbus (745 ft.), the capital of Ohio, is a thriving city of 88,150 inhab., situated on the E. bank of the *Scioto River*. Its commerce is important, and it has manufactures of iron and steel goods, carriages, and agricultural implements (value in 1890, $20,000,000). Its streets are broad and much better paved than is usual in American cities. *Broad Street*, in particular, affords a delightful drive of 7 M. over an asphalted roadway shaded with trees. — The *State Capitol* is a large and somewhat odd-looking building, surrounded with a small park full of tame gray squirrels. Other important buildings are the *Ohio State University* (700 students), the *Central Ohio Lunatic Asylum*, the *Deaf and Dumb Asylum*, the *State Penitentiary*, the *U. S. Barracks* (in a pretty park), the *Court House*, the *Starling Medical College*, the *Idiot Asylum*, the *Blind Asylum*, and the *Board of Trade.* *Goodale Park*, at the N. end of the city, is prettily laid out.

From Columbus to *Cincinnati*, see p. 303. Railways also run hence to *Toledo, Cleveland, Indianapolis*, etc.

Beyond Columbus we pass numerous unimportant stations. 240 M. *Urbana* (3511 inhab.), a railway-centre; 266 M. *Piqua* (9090 inhab.). At (276 M.) *Bradford Junction* the railway forks, the left branch leading to Indianapolis (p. 302) and St. Louis (p. 311) while the Chicago line keeps to the right. At (297 M.) *Union City* we enter *Indiana*. 350 M. *Marion* (8769 inhab.). 385 M. *Anoka Junction* (p. 303). — 390 M. **Logansport** (605 ft.; *Murdock, New Barnett*, $2½-3), a city of 13,328 inhab., at the confluence of the *Wabash River, Eel River*, and *Wabash & Erie Canal*, is an intersecting point of several important railways (comp. p. 303). — 466 M. *Crown Point*.

507 M. **Chicago** *(Canal St. Station)*, see R. 48.

45. From Baltimore to Chicago.

853 M. BALTIMORE & OHIO RAILROAD in 27 hrs. (fare $17, sleeper $5). This line passes some fine scenery. — From New York to *Chicago* by this route, see p. 279.

From Baltimore to (40 M.) *Washington*, see R. 42. A good view of Washington is enjoyed as we leave it. The line runs towards the N.W. through *Maryland* (p. 233). Beyond (76 M.) *Dickerson's* the *Potomac* comes into sight on the left. At (83 M.) *Washington Junction*, or *Point of Rocks* (230 ft.), the train threads a tunnel below a promontory of the *Catoctin Mts.*, a prolongation of the Blue Ridge.

This is the junction of a line to (15 M.) *Frederick* (8193 inhab.), the scene of Barbara Frietchie's exploit with the flag and Stonewall Jackson (see Whittier's poem and Mrs. Caroline Dall's book).

Farther on the valley contracts and the hills grow higher. Near (92 M.) *Weverton* (250 ft.), the junction of a line to *Hagerstown* (p. 233), took place the battle of South Mountain (Sept. 14th, 1862). The scenery here is very picturesque. The train soon crosses the Potomac and enters *West Virginia* at —

93 M. **Harper's Ferry** (270 ft.; *Conner's*, $2; *MorrellHo.*, *Hill Top Ho.*, *Lockwood Ho.*, on the hill), magnificently situated on the point of land formed by the confluence of the Potomac and *Shenandoah*, with the *Maryland Heights* on the one side and the *Virginian* or *Loudoun Heights* on the other. Pop. 1762, including *Bolivar*. The name of this little place is widely celebrated through the famous raid of John Brown (see below), practically the first scene of the Civil War. The armoury and arsenal, destroyed during the Civil War, have not been rebuilt.

John Brown of Ossawattomie, at the head of a party of about 20 armed Abolitionists, entered Harper's Ferry by the bridge on the night of Oct. 16th, 1859, and took possession of the Arsenal, intending to liberate the negro-slaves and occupy the Blue Ridge as a base of hostilities against the slave-owners. The negroes, however, did not rise, and Brown and most of his companions were killed or captured, after two days' fighting, by a squad of U. S. Marines that had come to the aid of the Virginia militia. The small engine house in which John Brown made his last stand has been removed to Chicago (p. 280). John Brown and six of his associates were afterwards hanged at Charlestown, 7 M. to the S.W.

The visitor should ascend from the station to (5-10 min.) the top of the promontory (about 300 ft. above the river), which commands a fine *View of the confluence of the rivers and of the gap made in the Blue Ridge by their combined waters bursting through it. Just below, on the Shenandoah side, is a curious pile of rocks known as *Jefferson's Rock*. We may follow the path along the Shenandoah (high above it) and then go on by road, passing the large *Storer College*, to (1 M.) the top of the ridge called *Bolivar Heights*, which commands a splendid *View of the rich and fertile *Valley of Virginia (Shenandoah Valley)*, backed by the Alleghany Mts., 30 M. away. To the N. lies the battle-field of *Antietam* (p. 338). — A fine drive may be taken on the road round the promontory at the foot of the cliffs. — The ascent of **Maryland Heights** (1455 ft.; view) takes 1½ hr. (bridle-path). We cross the bridge over the Potomac and turn to the left. About ⅔ of the way up, we take the less promising path to the left.

Beyond Harper's Ferry the line leaves the Potomac for a time.

103 M. *Shenandoah Junction* is the junction for the railway through

the Shenandoah Valley (see R. 70 b). 114 M. *Martinsburg*, the junction for Harrisburg, see p. 233. Farther on we cross *North Mt.* (550 ft.) and rejoin the Potomac (right), on the other side of which are the ruins of *Fort Frederick* (1755). The line hugs the winding stream, with the hills rising abruptly on each side. Beyond (184 M.) *Patterson's Creek* we cross the Potomac and re-enter Maryland. — 192 M. *Cumberland* (640 ft.; Queen City Hotel, with rail. restaurant, $ 2-3), a city of 12,729 inhab., with large rolling-mills and glass-works.

Cumberland is the junction of a line to (150 M.) *Pittsburg* (p. 240), running viâ the picturesque *Youghiogheny Valley*, *Connelsville*, and *McKeesport*.

Our line turns to the S.W. and continues to follow the Potomac. The scenery is rugged and picturesque. Near (215 M.) *Keyser* (800 ft.) we cross the river into West Virginia, but soon recross it. At (220 M.) *Piedmont* (930 ft.) we leave the river and begin the steep ascent of the *Allegheny Mts.* 228 M. *Franklinville* (1700 ft.); 234 M. *Swanton Water Station* (2280 ft.); 237 M. *Altamont* (2620 ft.), the highest point of the line. The descent is more gradual, and we pass at first through a comparatively level district known as the *Glades*, on the crest of the Alleghenies and containing the headwaters of the *Youghiogheny*. 240 M. *Deer Park Hotel* (2440 ft.), a large summer-resort ($ 3); 243 M. *Mountain Lake Park;* 246 M. *Oakland* (2370 ft.; Oakland, $ 3-4; Glades, $ 3), another summer-resort amid beautiful scenery; 256 M. *Terra Alta* (2550 ft.). We now descend, passing through numerous cuttings and tunnels, to the *Cheat River Valley*, crossing the river at (267 M.) *Rowlesburg* (*View to the right). We now begin another steep ascent to the crest of *Laurel Hill*, crossing numerous wild gorges. 274 M. *Cassidy's Summit* (1855 ft.). Beyond (275 M.) *Tunnelton* (1820 ft.) we pass through the *Kingwood Tunnel*, 3/4 M. long. 282 M. *Newburg* (1215 ft.). At (294 M.) *Grafton* (990 ft.; 3159 inhab.), on the *Tygart's Valley River*, we leave the mountains.

Our line (to Wheeling and Chicago) here diverges to the right from the line to Parkersburg, Cincinnati, and St. Louis (see R. 58 d) and runs towards the N.W., down the Tygart's River. Beyond (316 M.) *Fairmount* (875 ft.), at the head of navigation on the *Monongahela*, we ascend the picturesque ravine of *Buffalo Creek*, passing through the head of the pass (1150 ft.) by a tunnel. We then descend along a branch of *Fish Creek*, threading several tunnels. At (382 M.) *Moundsville* (640 ft.) we approach the *Ohio* (to the left).

The place takes its name from an *Indian Mound*, 70 ft. high and 820 ft. in circumference at the base, in which two sepulchral chambers were found, containing three skeletons (comp. p. 309).

At (389 M.) *Benwood* we cross the river and enter *Ohio*. Beyond this point we run by Central Time (p. xviii).

Wheeling (645 ft.; *Windsor*, $ 2¹/₂-4; *McClure Ho.*, $ 2¹/₂-3), on the Ohio, 4 M. above Benwood, is the largest city in West Virginia (34,522 inhab.) and has manufactures of nails, iron, pottery, and glassware (value in 1890, $ 11,540,000). It is an important railway-centre (to Pittsburg, see p. 243).

390 M. *Bellaire* (655 ft.) lies on the Ohio side of the river, opposite Benwood (see above). — 468 M. *Zanesville* (710 ft.; Clarendon,

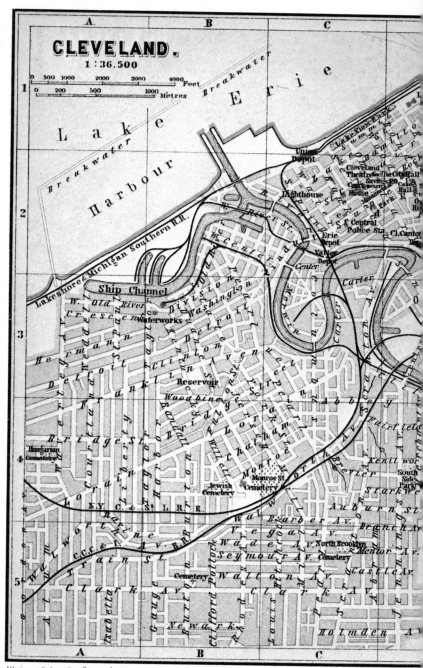

CLEVELAND.

1:36.500

Wagner & Debes Geogᵗ Estabᵗ Leipzig.

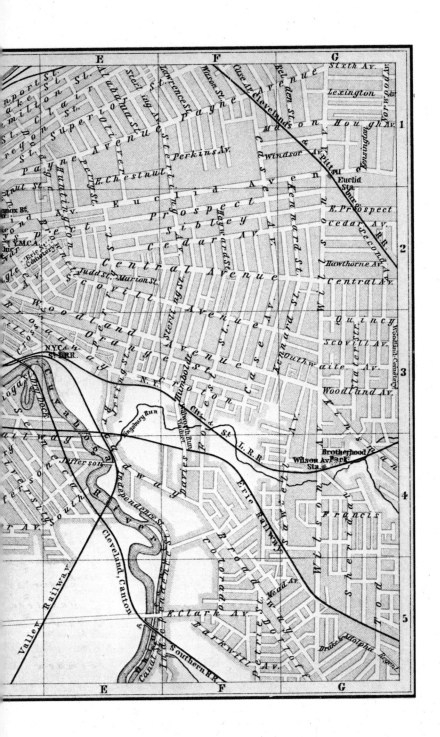

$2^1/_2$; Kirk Ho., $2), a manufacturing city with 21,009 inhab., at the confluence of the *Muskingum River* and the *Licking River*. We cross the former river by a bridge 170 yds. long. — At (494 M.) *Newark* (820 ft.; Warden, $ 2), an industrial place with 14,270 inhab., we cross the Pittsburg, Cincinnati, and St. Louis R. R. (see p. 264). Our line runs to the N.W. to (556 M.) *Mansfield* (see p. 263) and (582 M.) *Chicago Junction*, where it forks, the left branch leading to Chicago, the right to *Sandusky* (p. 269). The stations beyond this point are unimportant. 670 M. *Defiance;* 823 M. *Miller's.* 853 M. **Chicago** *(Monroe St. Station)*, see p. 279.

46. From Buffalo to Chicago.

a. Viâ Lake Shore & Michigan Southern Railroad.

540 M. RAILWAY in 14-20 hrs. (fare $ 14; sleeper or parlor-car $ 3). This line skirts the S. shore of Lake Erie. From *New York* to *Chicago* by this route, see p. 47 d.

Buffalo, see R. 39. The first important station is (40 M.) *Dunkirk*, where connection is made with the Erie R. R. (comp. p. 306). Pleasant views of Lake Erie to the right. 49 M. *Brocton Junction* (for Chautauqua, etc.), see p. 278. At (68 M.) *State Line* we pass into *Pennsylvania*. — 88 M. **Erie** (*Reed Ho.*, $2-3; *Moore*, $ 2; *Ellsworth; Massasauga Point*, on the lake), a lake shipping-port with a good harbour (enclosed by *Presque Isle*) and 40,464 inhab., occupies the site of a French fort built in 1749 and was the headquarters of Commodore Perry when he defeated the Anglo-Canadian fleet in 1813. It contains some handsome buildings. It is the junction of lines to Philadelphia (see p. 210), Pittsburg (see p. 240), etc. — 103 M. *Girard* (p. 243). Beyond (108 M.) *Springfield* we enter *Ohio* (the 'Buck-eye State', so-called from the buckeye-tree, *Æsculus flava* or *glabra*). 129 M. *Ashtabula* is the junction of a line to Oil City, Pittsburg, etc. 155 M. *Painesville* is also the junction of a line to Pittsburg.

183 M. **Cleveland.** — **Railway Stations.** *Union Depot* (Pl. C, 1, 2), at the foot of Bank St.; *Erie Depot* (Pl. C, 2), near the Viaduct; *New York, Chicago, & St. Louis Railroad* (Pl. E, 3), Broadway; *Cleveland & Canton Railroad* (Pl. D, 2), Ontario St.; *Valley Railway* (Pl. C, 2), S. Water St.

Hotels. HOLLENDEN (Pl. a; D, 2), Superior St., cor. of Bond St., a large house, Amer. plan $ 3-5, R. on Europ. plan from $ 1; *STILLMAN (Pl. b; D, 2), pleasantly situated in Euclid Ave., good cuisine, $ 3^1/2-5; WEDDELL (Pl. c; C, 2), Superior St., commercial, $ 3-5; FOREST CITY (Pl. d; C, 2), Monument Park, $ 2^1/2-3; KENNARD (Pl. e; C, 2), $ 3; AMERICAN (Pl. f; C, 2), $ 2-2^1/2; PENCE, $ 2.

Restaurants. *Hollenden*, see above; *Lennox*, Euclid Ave. and Erie St.; *De Klyn*, *Heyse & Weissgerber*, Euclid Ave.; *Stranahan*, in the Arcade.

Tramways traverse the chief streets in all directions. — **Cab** from station to hotel, each pers. 50 c., incl. baggage; per hour, $1^1/2; other fares in proportion; 50 per cent. more after 11 p.m.

Places of Amusement. *Opera House* (Pl. D, 2), Euclid Ave.; *Music Hall* (Pl. D, 2; 5000 seats); *Lyceum Theatre* (Pl. C, 2); *Star Theatre* (Pl. D, 2); *Cleveland Theatre* (Pl. C, 2).

Post Office (Pl. D, 2), East Public Sq.

Cleveland (580 ft. above the sea), the second city of Ohio, with (1890) 261,353 inhab., lies on the S. shore of Lake Erie, at the mouth of the small *Cuyahoga River*, and, with its broad and well-paved streets, its green lawns and squares, and its numerous trees ('Forest City'), makes a favourable impression on the visitor. Its important iron and steel works produce goods to the annual value of $ 36,000,000; it is the seat of the Standard Oil Co. ; and it carries on a very extensive trade through its excellent harbour. Most of its factories are tucked away in the river-valley below the level of the plateau on which the city lies, or are in West Cleveland and along the river-front.

Cleveland was founded in 1796, but did not begin to grow with any rapidity until the completion of the Ohio Canal, connecting Lake Erie with the Ohio (1834). Its pop. in 1830 was 1000, in 1860 it was 43,417, and in 1880 it was 160,142. In the decade 1880-90 it increased by 60 per cent. Cleveland is one of the chief ship-building cities in the United States, building vessels of 71,322 tons in 1889 and 1890. The value of its manufactures in 1890 was $ 105,500,000 (21,100,000*l.*); 50,000 hands were employed.

The chief business-street is Superior Street (Pl. C-F, 2, 1), a really fine and wide thoroughfare, the W. end of which is lined with substantial business blocks, such as the *Perry-Payne Building* (Nos. 103-109). A little farther on the street expands into **Monumental Park* or the *Public Square* (Pl. C, D, 2), containing monuments of *Commodore Perry* (p. 267) and *Gen. Moses Cleaveland* (1754-1806), founder and godfather of the city. At the N.E. corner of the square stands the **Post Office and Custom House** (Pl. D, 2), and at the N.W. corner is the *Old Court House* (Pl C, 2). On the N. side of the square, at the corner of Ontario St., is the handsome building of the **Society for Savings* (Pl. C, 2), established in 1849 and now containing upwards of 20 million dollars (four millions sterling). There are no stock-holders, the entire profits going to the 45,000 depositors (**View from the top of the building). In Superior St., just beyond the Post Office, is *Case Hall* (Pl. D, 2), with a library of 30,000 vols., and next to it is the massive **City Hall** (Pl. D, 2).

*Euclid Avenue (Pl. D-G, 2, 1), which begins at the S.E. angle of the Public Square, is at its E. end also an important artery of business and farther out becomes one of the most beautiful residence-streets in America, with each of its handsome houses surrounded by pleasant grounds and shady trees. To the left is the ***Arcade** (Pl. D, 2), 400 ft. long, 180 ft. wide, and 144 ft. high, with a fine five-balconied interior, running through to Superior St. Near Erie St. is the *Public Library* (70,000 vols.), and at the corner is the *Lennox Building* (Pl. D, 2). Farther on are several fine churches. About 4 1/2 M. from the square (street-car), Euclid Ave. reaches the beautiful ***Wade Park,** opposite which are the buildings of the **Western Reserve University** *(Adelbert College* and *Cleveland Medical College)* and the *Case School of Applied Sciences*. About 1 1/2 M. farther on the avenue ends at ***Lake View Cemetery,** containing the handsome ***Garfield Memorial** (adm. 10 c. ; erected in 1890 at

a cost of $130,000), the top of which (165 ft. high) affords a splendid *View of the city and its environs.

Prospect Street (Pl. D-G, 2), which runs parallel to Euclid Ave. on the S., is little inferior to it in beauty. At the corner of Erie St. is the handsome building of the *Young Men's Christian Association* (Pl. D, 2). Another favourite resort is *Gordon's Park, to the N.E. of the city, on the lake, open to the public on Tues. and Sat. — The huge new *Market* (Pl. D, 2), in Ontario St., is one of the largest and finest in the country.

Cleveland is connected with *West Cleveland*, on the other side of the Cuyahoga Valley, by an enormous *Viaduct (Pl. C, 2), 1070 ft. long, completed in 1878 at a cost of $2,200,000 (440,000*l*.) and deservedly regarded as a wonderful feat of engineering. The main portion of the viaduct is of stone, but the central part is of iron lattice-work and swings open to allow the passage of vessels. The *View of the manufacturing quarters in the valley from this viaduct is very imposing, especially at night. There are three other similar viaducts at different parts of the city (see Pl. D, 2; F, 3).

Driving parties may cross the Viaduct and follow *Lakeside Ave.* and *Detroit St.* to (8 M.) *Rocky River*, a favourite supper resort in summer.

A visit may also be paid to the great OIL DISTRICT at the S. end of Wilson Ave. (comp. Pl. G, 5), where the enormous tanks and refining works of the *Standard Oil Co.* are situated.

The huge ORE DOCKS of the N. Y. P. & O. R. R., on the W. side of the city, sometimes contain 2,000,000 tons. — The HARBOUR (Pl. A, B, 1, 2) and BREAKWATER (2 M. long) also repay inspection.

Cleveland is, naturally, an important RAILWAY CENTRE, from which lines radiate, more or less directly. to *Pittsburg* (p. 240), *Marietta, Columbus* (p. 264), *Cincinnati* (p. 307), *Toledo* (see below), *Chicago* (p. 279), etc. — STEAMERS ply to all important points on the Great Lakes.

At (209 M.) *Elyria* the line forks, the branches reuniting at *Millbury* (see below). The chief station on the right branch is (243 M.) **Sandusky** (*West Ho., Sloane Ho.*, $2-3), with a good harbour and a large trade in fish and fruit (see p. 275). Pop. 18,471. — The left or inland line runs viâ (218 M.) *Oberlin* (with a college open to both sexes, white or coloured; 1200 students) and (239 M.) *Norwalk.* 288 M. *Millbury.*

296 M. **Toledo** (*Boody Ho.*, $2½-4; *Madison, Jefferson, Burnett*, $2-2½), a city and important railway-centre on the *Maumee River*, 6 M. from Lake Erie, with 81,434 inhab., has a large trade in grain, coal, iron-ore, and timber, and numerous manufactures (value in 1890, $15,000,000). Among the handsomest of its buildings are the *Public Library* (35,000 vols.), the *Soldiers' Memorial*, and the *Toledo Club House*. One of its newspapers is named the *Toledo Blade*. Many pleasant excursions may be made on the Maumee River.

FROM TOLEDO TO DETROIT, 65 M., railway in 2-3 hrs. The chief stations are (25 M.) *Monroe* and (44 M.) *Trenton.* 65 M. *Detroit*, see p. 271.

Beyond Toledo the line forks, the branches rejoining each other at Elkhart (see below). The 'Air Line' (followed by through-trains) enters *Indiana* (the 'Hoosier State') at (337 M.) *Archibald* and runs through that state to (429 M.) *Elkhart.* The 'Old Line' enters *Michi-*

gan ('Wolverine State') beyond (307 M.) *Sylvania* and passes (329M.) *Adrian* (810 ft.; 8756 inhab.), the centre of a rich farming country, (362 M.) *Hillsdale*, a fine summer-resort, and (420 M.) *White Pigeon*, the junction of a line to *Kalamazoo, Grand Rapids* (p. 273), and *Mackinaw* (p. 273).

439 M. *Elkhart* (735 ft.) is a busy little city, with 11,360 inhabitants. 454½M. *South Bend* (725 ft.; Arlington, $ 2-2½), a city with 21,819 inhab., on the *St. Joseph's River*, is known for its carriages and wagons (Studebaker's works). — 481 M. *La Porte*, with 7126 inhab., is the junction of a line to *Indianapolis* (p. 302). 491 M. *Otis. Lake Michigan* (p. 276) soon comes into sight on the right, and we enter *Illinois* ('Prairie State') at (499 M.) *Chesterton.* Various surburban stations are passed before we reach the Van Buren St. Station at —

540 M. **Chicago** (see p. 279).

b. Viâ New York, Chicago, and St. Louis Railroad.

523 M. RAILWAY (*'Nickel Plate Line'*) in 18 hrs. (fares as above).

Buffalo, see p. 192. As far as (184 M.) *Cleveland* (p. 267) this line runs parallel with the one above described and passes the same stations. Beyond Cleveland it follows the shore of Lake Erie pretty closely. 210 M. *Lorain*, the junction of a line to *Elyria* (p. 269). Beyond (221 M.) *Vermillion* the line bends to the left and runs inland. 240 M. *Kimball*; 248 M. *Bellevue*; 280 M. *Fostoria*, the junction of several railways; 300 M. *McComb.* Beyond (349 M.) *Payne* we enter *Indiana.*

371 M. **Fort Wayne** (775 ft.; *Aveline Ho., Wayne Ho.*, $ 2½-3), an industrial city of 35,393 inhab., on the *Maumee River*, here formed by the confluence of the *St. Joseph* and the *St. Mary*, occupies the site of an old fort (first built in 1764), which plays a considerable part in Colonial history. It is a railway-centre of great importance (comp. p. 263). — Near (424 M.) *Tippecanoe* Gen. Harrison ('Old Tippecanoe') defeated Tecumseh, at the head of the Miamis and Shawnees, in 1812. 514 M. *Grand Crossing.*

523 M. **Chicago** *(Van Buren St. Station)*, see p. 279.

c. Viâ Michigan Central Railroad.

536 M. RAILWAY (*North Shore Line* or *'Niagara Falls Route'*) in 15-22 hrs. (fares as above). This line runs on the N. side of Lake Erie, through the Canadian province of Ontario. It affords a good view of *Niagara Falls* (see below). Luggage checked to United States points is not examined; small packages examined in crossing the Cantilever Bridge (p. 204).

Buffalo, see p. 192. The train descends along the right bank of the *Niagara River* (comp. p. 195) to (24 M.) *Niagara Falls*, N. Y. (p. 199), and (26 M.) *Suspension Bridge* (p. 203). It then crosses the river by the **Cantilever Bridge* described at p. 204 (*View of rapids) to (26¼ M.) *Clifton* (p. 199). From Clifton it runs to the S., along the *Victoria Park* (p. 204), to (27 M.) *Niagara Falls*

(Ont.) and (28 M.) *Falls View*, where all trains stop five minutes to allow passengers to enjoy the splendid **View of Niagara Falls* (p. 204). We then turn to the right (W.). 40 M. *Welland*, a small town with 2035 inhab., lies on the *Welland Ship Canal* (27 M. long) uniting Lake Ontario with Lake Erie. It is the junction of a direct line to Buffalo and of a line to *Port Dalhousie*. From (82 M.) *Hagersville* a branch-line runs to Hamilton (p. 274). 141 M. **St. Thomas** (*Grand Central*, $ 2-2¹/₂), a thriving town with 10,370 inhab., is the junction of lines to Toronto, London (p. 274), St. Clair (p. 273), and *Port Stanley*, the last, the chief harbour on the N. side of Lake Erie, lying 8 M. to the S. — 196 M. *Fargo;* 222 M. *Comber;* 236 M. *Essex Centre.* At (250 M.) *Windsor* (International Hotel, $ 1-2) the train is run on to a large steamferry and carried across the *Detroit River* to (251 M.) *Detroit.*

Detroit. — Hotels. CADAILLAC, Michigan Ave., $ 2¹/₂-4; RUSSELL HOUSE, Campus Martius, $ 3-3¹/₂; THE WAYNE, opposite the M. C. R. R. Depot, $ 2-3¹/₂; LEIDERS, Congress St., $ 2-3. — *Swan's Restaurant*, 87 Woodward Ave.

Tramways traverse the principal streets (5 c.). — Cabs: drive within the city limits, each pers. 50 c.; first hour 1-4 pers. $ 1¹/₂, each. addit. hr. $ 1; trunk 15 c.

Ferries ply from the foot of Woodward Ave. to *Belle Isle* and to *Windsor* every ¹/₄ hr., and from the foot of Joseph Campau Ave. to *Belle Isle* and to *Walkerville* every ¹/₂ hr. — Steamboats ply to *Put-in-Bay Islands* (p. 275), *St. Clair, Cleveland, Buffalo, Port Huron, Sault Ste. Marie, Mackinaw*, and other points on the Great Lakes.

Post Office, Griswold St.

Detroit (580 ft.), the chief city of Michigan, with 205,876 inhab., is situated 18 M. from Lake Erie, on the N. bank of the *Detroit River*, which connects that lake with the small *Lake St. Clair* (530 ft.), just above the city, and so with Lake Huron (p. 276). It is a well-built town, with numerous trees, carries on a large traffic in grain, wool, pork, and copper, and has many important manufactures. Most of its streets are laid out on the rectangular plan, but several avenues radiate from a centre like the spokes of a wheel. The city is lighted by electricity by a system of lofty steel towers (150-175 ft. high).

The site of Detroit was visited by Frenchmen in 1670 and 1679 (La Salle), and in 1701 the Sieur de la Motte Cadaillac (p. 101) founded *Fort Pontchartrain* here. In 1760 it passed into the hands of the English, and in 1763-6 it was successfully defended for 15 months against the Indian chief Pontiac. It was nominally ceded to the United States in 1783, but the Americans did not become masters of it till 1796. The fort was taken by the British in 1812 and retaken by the Americans in 1813. Detroit was incorporated as a city in 1824, with about 1500 inhabitants. In 1850 the population was 21,019, in 1880 it was 134,834.

Some idea of the volume of traffic on the Great Lakes may be gathered from the fact that the aggregate tonnage of the ships passing Detroit in the seven months during which navigation is open (36 million tons in 1890) nearly equals that of the vessels annually entering and clearing at London and Liverpool (37¹/₂ million tons in 1890).

The staples of its manufactures, the value of which in 1890 was $ 80,000,000 (16,000,000*l.*), are iron and steel goods, cars and car-wheels, stoves, drugs, and tobacco.

WOODWARD AVENUE, running N. and S. from the river and

dividing the city into two nearly equal parts, is the main business-thoroughfare and the chief centre of life. Most of the principal buildings are on or near it. Near its foot (S. end) are the chief *Steamboat Wharves* and the *Ferry to Windsor* (p. 271). About ¹/₂ M. from the river the street expands into the CAMPUS MARTIUS, from which *Michigan* and *Gratiot Avenues* diverge to the left and right. To the left stands the **City Hall**, the tower (view) of which contains a clock with a dial 8¹/₂ ft. in diameter. In front of the City Hall is the *Soldiers' Monument*, by Randolph Rogers.

In Gratiot Ave., near the Campus Martius, is the **Public Library**, containing 100,000 vols. and some historical relics. In Griswold St., running parallel with Woodward Ave. on the W., is the **Post Office** (new one in progress in Fort St.). At the corner of Griswold St. and Grand River Ave. is the *Young Men's Christian Association.*

A little farther on Woodward Ave. reaches GRAND CIRCUS PARK, a square with trees and fountains. At the corner of Edmund Place, ¹/₂ M. farther on, are the **First Unitarian* and *First Presbyterian Churches*, two fine Romanesque buildings of red stone. To the right, at the head of Martin Place, is the handsome *Harper Hospital;* and *Grace Hospital* is also seen to the right (cor. of Willis Ave. and John R. St.) a little farther on. To the left, a little higher up, is the *Detroit Athletic Club.* The N. end of Woodward Avenue and the adjoining streets form the principal residence quarter of the town.

JEFFERSON AVENUE, which runs at right angles to Woodward Ave., crossing it ¹/₅ M. from the river, contains many of the chief wholesale houses, and towards its S. end has also many pleasant residences. The site of Fort Pontchartrain (see above) was at the corner of Jefferson Ave. and Shelby St., two squares to the W. of Woodward Ave. To the E., on the left side of the street, are the *Academy of the Sacred Heart*, the R.C. *Cathedral of SS. Peter and Paul*, and the *Jesuit College.* Nearly opposite, at the corner of Jefferson Ave. and Hastings St., about ¹/₂ M. to the E. of Woodward Ave., stands the ****Museum of Art** (9-4, 25 c.: Sun., 2-4, free).

The chief contents of the Museum are the *Scripps Collection of Old Masters* and the *Stearns Collection of Japanese, Chinese, and East Indian Curiosities.* The former contains a painting by *Rubens* (David and Abigail), pen-and-ink drawings by *Raphael* and *Michael Angelo*, and works ascribed to *Lippi, Pinturicchio, Masaccio, Bellini, Da Vinci, Matsys, Titian, Del Sarto, Correggio, Carracci, Guido Reni, Cuyp, Rembrandt, Teniers, Murillo, Corn. de Vos, De Hoogh*, etc.

At Nos. 1022-1056 Jefferson Ave., near Elmwood St., are the large *Michigan Stove Works*, in the yard of which (facing the avenue) is the stump of a tree surmounted by a figure of *Pontiac* (p. 271), which is said to mark the spot where that chief surprised and slew Capt. Dalzell and his troops in 1763.

In Atwater St., near this point, is the huge *Drug Manufactory of* Messrs. *Park, Davis, & Co.*

About 3 M. from Woodward Ave., we reach the bridge crossing an arm of the river to **Belle Isle*, which is about 700 acres in extent and forms a beautiful public park, with fine trees and still retaining many of its natural features unimpaired. In summer park-carriages take visitors round for a small fee. Fine view of Lake St. Clair from its E. end. *Ferries*, see p. 271.

Among other points of interest in Detroit are *Elmwood Cemetery, in the E. part of the city, about ¹/₂ M. to the N. of Jefferson Ave.; *Fort Wayne*, on the river, 3¹/₂ M. to the W. of Woodward Ave. (tramway through Fort St.), garrisoned by a few companies of U. S. troops; and the *Exposition Buildings*, ¹/₂ M. farther to the W. (annual exhibitions). — A wide BOULEVARD is being constructed round the entire city, beginning and ending at the river-front.

Among favourite resorts in the vicinity are *Grosse Pointe*, on Lake St. Clair, 9 M. to the E., with the country-houses of many of the citizens; St. Clair Flats, a frequented shooting and fishing resort, with its hotels and cottages built on piles; *Windsor* (p. 272); *Mt. Clemens* (see below); St. Clair Springs (Oakland Hotel, $ 3); and *Put-in-Bay Islands* (p. 275).

From Detroit to *Toledo*, see p. 269.

FROM DETROIT TO LANSING AND GRAND RAPIDS, 150 M., railway in 4-5 hrs. — 23 M. *Plymouth*. — 85 M. **Lansing** (*Downey, Hudson*, $ 2), the capital of the State, is a manufacturing city of 13,102 inhab., on the *Grand River*. — 150 M. **Grand Rapids** (*Morton Ho.*, $ 2¹/₂-4; *Sweet's*, $ 2-3), a busy city of 60,278 inhab., with fine water-power afforded by a fall of 18 feet on the Grand River (value of manufactures in 1890, $ 20,000,000).

FROM DETROIT TO PORT HURON, 59 M.; railway in 1³/₄ hr. — 22 M. *Mt. Clemens* (Sherman, Avery, $ 2-3). — 59 M. *Port Huron*, see p. 275.

FROM DETROIT TO MACKINAW CITY (*Mackinac Island*), 290 M., railway in 13 hrs. — This railway traverses nearly the entire length of Michigan from S. to N., passing through one of the greatest 'lumbering' regions in America. 60 M. *Lapeer;* 87 M. *Vassar*, the junction of a line to (22 M.) *Saginaw City* (46,322 inhab.). — 108 M. **Bay City** (*Fraser Ho.*, $ 2¹/₂-3), situated near the point where the *Saginaw* empties into Saginaw Bay, with 27,839 inhab. and a large trade in timber, fish, and salt. — 142 M. *Alger;* 227 M. *Gaylord*. — 290 M. *Mackinaw City* (Wentworth, $ 2), with 333 inhab., lies at the N. extremity of Michigan, on the *Straits of Mackinac* (4 M. wide), which connect *Lake Michigan* (p. 276) and *Lake Huron* (p. 276). Steamers run hence, in connection with the trains, to *St. Ignace* (p. 297), on the opposite side of the Straits, and to (8 M.) *Mackinac Island* (see below), while others run to *Sault Ste. Marie* (p. 276), *Manistique*, etc.

***Mackinac Island**, a rocky and wooded little islet, 9 M. in circumference, contains a good deal of picturesque scenery in its narrow limits and has become a favourite place of summer-resort. Its fresh breezes, clear water, excellent fishing, and romantic legends are additional attractions. It is a military post of the United States and is reserved as a National Park. On the S. side of the island lies the picturesque village of *Mackinac*, with 750 inhabitants. On the cliff above it stands *Fort Mackinac*, and a little farther inland are the ruins of *Fort Holmes* (300 feet; *Views), built by the British. The largest hotel on the island is *Plank's Grand Hotel* (1300 beds; $ 3-5), on a bluff near the village; and good accommodation may also be obtained at the *Astor House* ($ 2-3), the *Mission House* ($ 2-3), the *New Murray* ($ 2-3), the *Island House* ($ 2¹/₂-3), the *Grand Central* ($ 2-3), and other smaller inns and boarding-houses. Among the chief points of interest on the island are the *Arch Rock, on the E. side, 150 ft. high; the *Lover's Leap*, 145 ft. high; *Robertson's Folly*, the *Giant's Causeway*, *Sugar Loaf Rock*, *Scott's Cave*, the *British Landing* (1812), etc. Excursions may be made to *St. Ignace* (p. 297), the *Cheneaux Islands*, *Bois Blanc Island*, etc. A steamboat tour round the island should also be made. The island was frequently visited by the early French travellers and remained in possession of France from 1610 to 1761, when it was ceded to Great Britain. It came into the hands of the United States in 1796, was taken by the English in 1812, and was restored to the United

States in 1815. The Astor House (see p. 273) was the headquarters of the *Astor Fur Co.*, founded by John Jacob Astor, in 1809-1850. Comp. the 'Annals of Fort Mackinac', by *D. H. Kelton*, and 'Anne', by *Constance Fenimore Woolson*. — Mackinac Island is also reached from Detroit by steamer.

Beyond Detroit the line runs almost due W., across the State of Michigan. 269 M. *Wayne Junction;* 281 M. *Ypsilanti*, a paper-making town of 6129 inhab., on the *Huron River*, which we now follow. — 288 M. **Ann Arbor** (770 ft.; *Cook's, Arlington, Germania,* $ 2), a flourishing, tree-shaded city of 9431 inhab., situated on both sides of the Huron River, is the seat of MICHIGAN UNIVERSITY.

This university, one of the most important educational institutes in the United States, is attended by about 2800 students, of whom $1/5$ or $1/6$ are women. It differs from the large Eastern universities in being a State institution. It is richly endowed and has several fine buildings, good museums and laboratories, and a library of about 80,000 volumes.

327 M. *Jackson* (925 ft.; Ashley, $ 2), an industrial town on the *Grand River*, with 20,798 inhab., is the junction of lines to Lansing (p. 273), Grand Rapids (p. 273), etc. Beyond (337 M.) *Parma* we follow the wheat-growing valley of the *Kalamazoo River.* 372 M. *Battle Creek.* 395 M. *Kalamazoo*, an agricultural centre with 17,853 inhab. and a Baptist College, is the junction of lines to Grand Rapids (p. 273) and *South Haven.* — Our line now runs to the left (S.) to (443 M.) *Niles*, on the *St. Joseph River* (4197 inhab.). — 469 M. *New Buffalo.* Lake Michigan now lies to the right. 515 M. *Hammond.* 536 M. **Chicago** *(Illinois Central Station),* see R. 48.

d. Viâ Grand Trunk Railway.

543 M. RAILWAY in $16^3/4$-$19^1/4$ hrs. (fares as above). This line passes through the peninsular part of the province of Ontario, one of the most fertile districts in Canada. — Hand-baggage examined in crossing the Niagara and St. Clair Rivers. — For fuller details, see *Baedeker's Canada.*

Buffalo, see p. 192. The train descends the E. bank of the Niagara to (24 M.) *Suspension Bridge* and crosses the river by the Suspension Bridge (p. 199). From the Canadian village of (24 1/4 M.) *Niagara Falls* the line runs almost due W. At (34 M.) *Merritton* we pass through a tunnel below the *Welland Ship Canal* (p. 271), the vessels in which may be seen sailing above our heads as we emerge. — 36 M. *St. Catharine's* (Stephenson Ho., $ 3), a prettily situated little town (9170 inhab.) on the Welland Canal, with mineral springs. *Lake Ontario* is now frequently in view to the right. 50 M. *Grimsby Park*, with a Methodist camp-meeting ground, lies in a district producing immense quantities of peaches and other fruit.

68 M. **Hamilton** (255 ft.; *Royal*, $ 2 1/2-4; *St. Nicholas*, $ 2), finely situated at the W. end of Lake Ontario, a busy industrial and commercial city of 50,348 inhab., is the junction of the railway to Toronto, which may also be reached by steamer. — 87 M. *Harrisburg* (735 ft.), the junction of various lines; 115 M. *Woodstock* (960 ft.). — 144 M. **London** (805 ft.; *Tecumseh Ho.*, $ 2-3; *Grigg Ho.*, $ 1 1/2-2), an important agricultural and railway centre, with 31,977 inhab. and a considerable trade. — 205 M. *Sarnia* (Bell

Chamber, $ 1$^1/$_2-2^1/$_2$), a port on Lake Huron, with 6693 inhabitants. The train now passes from Canada to the United States (Michigan) by a *Tunnel, 1$^1/$_6$ M. long, under the *St. Clair River.*

This is the longest river-tunnel in the world and was constructed in 1889-90 at a cost, including approaches, of $ 2,700,000 (540,000 *l.*). It consists of a cast-iron tube, with an inside diameter of 20ft., and was designed by *Mr. Joseph Hobson.*

Central time is now the standard. **208 M. Port Huron** (*Huron Ho.*, $ 2-2$^1/$_2$), with 13,543 inhab., lies on Lake Huron, at the mouth of the *Black River*, and carries on a trade of considerable importance (lumber, fish, etc.). The train now runs to the S.W. through Michigan. 253 M. *Lapeer* (p. 273). From (290 M.) *Durand* a line diverges to *Grand Haven*, on Lake Michigan, whence a steamer plies in connection with the trains to *Milwaukee* (p. 287). 312 M. *Lansing* (p. 273); 367 M. *Battle Creek* (p. 274); 396 M. *Schoolcraft;* 442 M. *South Bend* (p. 270); 487 M. *Valparaiso;* 522 M. *Blue Island Junction.*

543 M. **Chicago** (*Dearborn Station*), see R. 48.

e. By Steamer.

It is possible to go the whole way from Buffalo to Chicago by water, through Lakes Erie, Huron, and Michigan (through-fare $ 20). The steamers of the LAKE SUPERIOR TRANSIT Co , leaving Buffalo (Atlantic Dock, foot of Evans St.) on Tues., Thurs., & Sat. at 7 p.m. , ply to *Cleveland* (fare $ 4), *Detroit* ($ 6$^1/$_2$), *Port Huron* ($ 7), and *Sault Ste. Marie* ($ 13), which they reach in 4 days. Here they connect with steamers of the LAKE MICHIGAN AND LAKE SUPERIOR TRANSPORTATION Co., which ply to *Milwaukee* ($ 20) and *Chicago* ($ 20; 5$^1/$_2$ days). — The steamers are reasonably comfortable, and the above fares include meals and berths. The whole journey is apt to be rather tedious, but the traveller who is wearied of railway-travelling may be glad to make part of the distance by water. Stop-over checks available for 15 days are given by the Purser on application. Warm wraps should be taken even in midsummer.

Buffalo, see p. 192. The steamer plies to the W. through **Lake Erie**, a description of which has been given at p. 193. The following are the points usually called at by all steamers, and ample time to go ashore is generally allowed (consult the captain).

80 M. (ca. 6 a.m., central time) **Erie**, see p. 267. The picturesque harbour is protected by *Presque Isle*. It was hither that Commodore Perry brought his prizes after defeating the English fleet in 1813. — Beyond Erie the steamer runs near the well-wooded shore. *Ashtabula* (p. 267) is seen about noon.

175 M. (4 p.m.) **Cleveland** (see p. 267), one of the most beautiful cities on the great lakes, is seen to advantage from the steamer. The *Garfield Memorial* (see p. 268) is conspicuous as we approach. Several hours are usually spent here. — Beyond Cleveland the coast becomes more picturesque. *Sandusky* (p. 269) is the chief place passed in the night. The **Put-in-bay Islands*, near the mouth of the Detroit, are a favourite summer-resort (several hotels).

Detroit River, which ascend we on leaving Lake Erie, is 25 M. long and varies in width from 4 M. at its mouth to $^1/$_2$ M. opposite of Detroit. It generally presents a very animated scene (comp. p. 271)

285 M. (8-10.30 p.m.) **Detroit**, see p. 271.

The boat now passes *Belle Isle* (p. 272) by the Canadian channel and soon enters **Lake St. Clair** (530 ft.), a shallow lake, 25 M. in diameter and about 20 ft. deep. The intricate navigation of the shallow upper end is avoided by a canal $1\frac{1}{2}$ M. long. The lake is connected with Lake Huron by the *St. Clair River*, a strait 40 M. long, with prettily wooded banks.

355 M. (4-6 a.m.) **Port Huron**, see p. 275. Opposite, on the Canadian shore, lies *Sarnia* (p. 274). We pass above the tunnel mentioned at p. 275. Between *Fort Gratiot* and *Fort Edward*, just above Port Huron, the strait narrows to 330 yds.

Lake Huron, which we now enter, is 270 M. long, 160 M. wide, 20,000 sq. M. in area, 580 ft. above the sea, and 300-1800 ft. deep. It contains about 3000 islands, and is often visited by violent storms. The steamer generally keeps within sight of the Michigan shore, but makes no stop before reaching —

575 M. *Detour*, a small fishing and lumbering port, where connection may be made with the Chicago steamer. Most passengers, however, will prefer to go on, through the beautiful *St. Mary's River* (55 M. long), connecting Lakes Huron and Superior, to —

635 M. (8 a.m.) **Sault Ste. Marie** (see p. 298), where the Chicago steamer starts. The steamer on which we have been travelling hitherto goes on through Lake Superior to *Duluth* (p. 295; through-fare from Buffalo $ 25). Sault Ste. Marie is a convenient point from which to visit *Mackinac* (p. 273).

The Chicago steamer takes us back viâ (60 M.) *Detour* (see above) and (100 M.) *Mackinac Island* (p. 273), passes through the *Straits of Mackinac* (p. 273), and enters **Lake Michigan** (590 ft. above the sea), the largest lake lying wholly within the United States (360 M. long, 108 M. wide; greatest depth 900 ft.). The only stop made by the through-steamers is at —

360 M. (midnight) **Milwaukee** (see p. 287). In about 8 hrs. ($5\frac{1}{2}$ days from Buffalo) we reach —

450 M. (from Sault Ste. Marie; 6 a.m.) **Chicago** (see p. 279).

47. From New York to Chicago.

a. Viâ Philadelphia and Pittsburg.

912 M. PENNSYLVANIA RAILROAD in 24-33 hrs. (fare $ 26.50; limited ticket, good for three days, $ 20; sleeper $ 5). The *Pennsylvania Limited Vestibule Train* on this route (fare $ 28, incl. sleeper), starting from New York at 10 a.m. and reaching Chicago at 9.45 a.m. (central time) next day, consists entirely of Pullman vestibuled cars and offers every imagi nable comfort to the traveller. It is provided with a dining-car, a library, a smoking and outlook car, a barber's shop, a bath, a ladies' maid, and a stenographer. Through-cars on the other trains also.

The various sections composing this route have been already described. From New York to (90 M.) *Philadelphia*, see R. 31; from Philadelphia to (444 M.) *Pittsburg*, see R. 37; from Pittsburg to

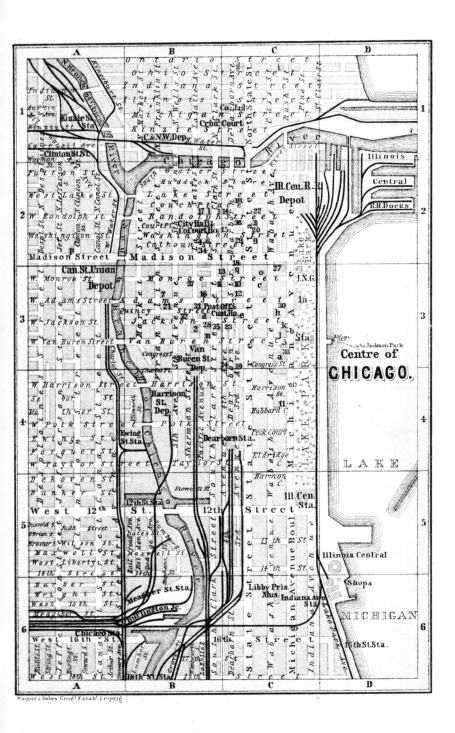

Centre of **CHICAGO.**

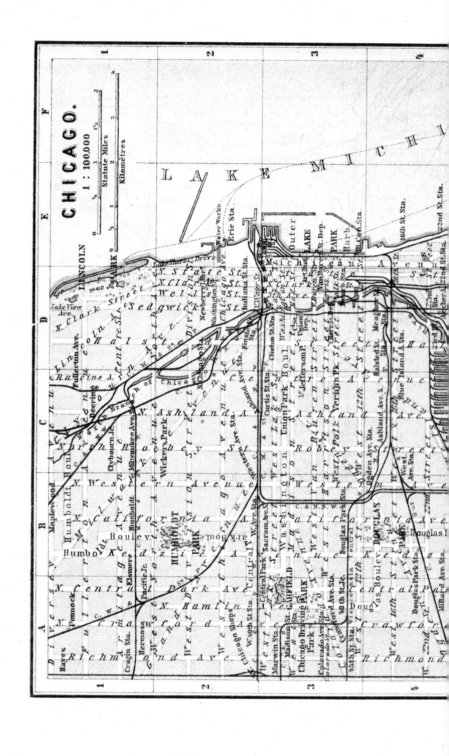

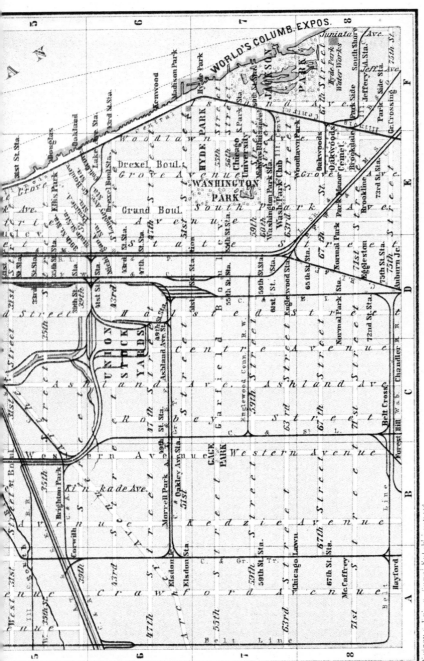

(912 M.) *Chicago*, see R. 44. The most beautiful part of the route is that between Philadelphia and Pittsburg, most of which is traversed by the Vestibule Limited Train by daylight.

b. Viâ Buffalo and Detroit.

There are various combinations by which this route can be effected. Through-carriages are run on the following: —

(a.) 976 M. NEW YORK CENTRAL AND HUDSON RIVER R. R. to (440 M.) *Buffalo* and MICHIGAN CENTRAL R. R. thence to (976 M.) *Chicago* in 24-35 hrs. (fare $ 20, sleeper $ 5). The *North Shore Limited*, leaving New York at 4.30 p.m. and reaching Chicago at the same time next day, is a train similar to the 'Pennsylvania Vestibule Limited' described at p. 276 (fare $ 28, incl. ticket for Wagner Palace Car).

(b.) 979 M. WEST SHORE RAILROAD to (428 M.) *Buffalo*, GRAND TRUNK RAILWAY thence to (683 M.) *Detroit*, and WABASH R. R. thence to (J79 M.) *Chicago* in 28-35 hrs. (fares as above).

(a.) From New York to (440 M.) *Buffalo*, see R. 28 a; from Buffalo to (976 M.) *Chicago*, see R. 46 c. This line affords a good view of *Niagara Falls* (see p. 199).

(b.) From New York to (428 M.) *Buffalo*, see R. 28 b; from Buffalo to (683 M.) *Detroit*, see R. 46 c. — The WABASH RAILROAD from Detroit to Chicago runs to the S.W., passing through a rich farming country. 741 M. *Adrian*, see p. 270; 779 M. *Montpelier;* 807 M. *Auburn;* 843 M. *South Whitley.* From (856 M.) *Laketon Junction* the line runs W. to (979 M.) *Chicago* (see p. 279).

c. Viâ Buffalo and Hamilton.

(a.) 976 M. NEW YORK CENTRAL R. R. to (440 M.) *Buffalo* and GRAND TRUNK RAILWAY thence to (976 M.) *Chicago* in 27-34 hrs. (fares as above).

(b.) 964 M. WEST SHORE RAILROAD to (428 M.) *Buffalo* and GRAND TRUNK R. R. thence to (964 M.) *Chicago* in 26-33 hrs. (fares as above).

(c.) 963 M. ERIE RAILWAY to (423 M.) *Buffalo* and GRAND TRUNK RAILWAY thence to (963 M.) *Chicago* in 27-35 hrs. (fares as above).

(a.) From *New York* to (440 M.) *Buffalo*, see R. 28 a; from Buffalo to (976 M.) *Chicago*, see R. 46 d.

(b.) From *New York* to (428 M.) *Buffalo*, see R. 28 b; from Buffalo to (964 M.) *Chicago*, see R. 46 d.

(c.) From *New York* to (423 M.) *Buffalo*, see R. 28 d; from Buffalo to (963 M.) *Chicago*, see R. 46 d.

These routes afford distant views of *Niagara Falls* (see p. 199) and good views of the *Niagara Rapids* (see p. 205).

d. Viâ Buffalo and Cleveland.

980 M. NEW YORK CENTRAL RAILROAD to (440 M.) *Buffalo* and LAKE SHORE & MICHIGAN SOUTHERN R. R. thence to (980 M.) *Chicago* in 24-34 hrs. (fares as above). The *Vestibule Limited Train* (comp. p. 276) on this route leaves New York at 10 a.m.

From *New York* to (440 M.) *Buffalo*, see R. 28 a; thence to (980 M.) *Chicago*, see R. 46 a. This line runs along the S. shore of Lake Erie.

e. Viâ Salamanca and Marion.

!88 M. Erie Railway in 29½-36 hrs. (fares as above). The solid through-train leaves New York at 3 p.m.

From *New York* to (332M.) *Hornellsville* (1160 ft.), see R. 28 d. Our line here diverges to the left from the line to Buffalo (see p. 192). Beyond Hornellsville we traverse a farming district. 358 M. *Wellsville* (1525 ft.). At (383 M.) *Cuba* (1700 ft.) we pass the culminating point of the route and begin to descend. From (395 M.) *Olean* (1440 ft.) to *Buffalo*, see p. 231. 407 M. *Carrollton* (1400 ft.).

414 M. **Salamanca** (185 ft.; *Arlington, Dudley,* $2), with 3692 inhab., is the junction of a line to (43 M.) *Dunkirk* (p. 267). Central time here becomes the standard. — 448 M. **Jamestown** (1320 ft.; *Sherman Ho.,* $2-2¼; *Humphrey Ho.,* $2), a city of 16,038 inhab., near the S. outlet of Lake Chautauqua (see below), and (453 M.) **Lakewood** (*Kent,* $4-6; *Sterlingworth,* $3½-7; *Ermin,* $2), at the S. end of the lake, are frequented as summer-resorts.

*Lake Chautauqua (1290 ft. above the sea; 725 ft. above Lake Erie), 18 M. long and 2 M. wide, is only 8 M. from Lake Erie but empties its waters into the Atlantic through the Conewango, Allegheny, Ohio, and Mississippi. It is surrounded by low hills. Steamers ply regularly from *Jamestown* and *Lakewood* to *Mayville* (p. 243), *Chautauqua* (see below), and *Point Chautauqua* (Grand Hotel).

Chautauqua (*Hotel Athenaeum,* 500 beds, $2½-4; numerous small hotels and boarding-houses), a pretty little place on the W. bank of the lake, is famous as the summer meeting-place (July & Aug.) of the **Chautauqua Assembly**, a huge system of home-reading circles and correspondence classes, which has spread all over the United States since its foundation by Bishop Vincent in 1878. It has had about 200,000 members. The *National Home Reading Union* of England has been founded on the same model. The public buildings of Chautauqua include assembly-halls, lecture-rooms, club-houses, a museum, a gymnasium, and a model of Palestine, 500 ft. long. The Summer School has classes in language, literature, science, art, and music, taught by upwards of 50 instructors from various American colleges and universities. A so-called '*Citizen Tax*' is levied on all frequenters of the Chautauqua Summer Assembly (above twelve years of age): 25-40 c. per day, $1-2 per week, $5 per season. The tuition-fees are $5 for one department, $10 for two or more. The office of the Assembly is at 455 Franklin St., Buffalo, where full information may be obtained. — The *Chautauqua Lake R. R.* runs from Jamestown to Chautauqua and Mayville (comp. p. 243).

About 15 M. beyond Jamestown we enter Pennsylvania. Beyond (475 M.) *Corry* (1430 ft.; p. 243) we descend the valley of *French Creek*, passing several important petroleum-wells. 516 M. *Meadville* (1080 ft.; 9520 inhab.). Near (555 M.) *Orangeville* we enter *Ohio*. 579 M. *Leavittsburg* (890 ft.), the junction of a line to (48 M.) *Cleveland* (p. 267); 599 M. *Ravenna,* an agricultural and industrial town, with 3417 inhab.; 616 M. *Akron* (1005 ft.), a flour and woollen making city of 27,601 inhabitants. At (683 M.) *Mansfield* (1155 ft.; see p. 263) we intersect the New York, Chicago, & St. Louis R. R. 718 M. *Marion* (960 ft.) is the junction for (85 M.) *Dayton* (p. 306) and (144 M.) *Cincinnati* (p. 307). 770 M. *Lima;* 814 M. *Decatur;* 902 M. *Monterey;* 968 M. *Hammond;* 982 M. *Englewood*.

988 M. **Chicago** (Dearborn Station), see p. 279.

f. Viâ Baltimore and Washington.

1048 M. BALTIMORE & OHIO RAILROAD in 32-36 hrs. (fare $26.50; limited ticket $17; sleeper $5). The *Vestibule Limited Train* (fare $28) leaves New York at 12.15 a.m. and arrives in Chicago at noon of the following day. From *New York* to (90 M.) *Philadelphia*, see R. 31b; from Philadelphia to (186 M.) *Baltimore*, see R. 40; from Baltimore to (226 M.) *Washington*, see R. 42; from Washington to (1048 M.) *Chicago* (Grand Central Station), see R. 45.

48. Chicago.

Plans. In the subjoined *General Plan* of Chicago (scale 1 : 100,000), referred to as Gen. Pl., clearness is aimed at by the omission of some of the streets. The important central section of the city is also given in a *Special Plan* (1 : 28,500, referred to in the text as Pl.).

Railway Stations. *Illinois Central R. R.* (Pl. C, 2), at the foot of Lake St., also used by the C. C. C. & St. L. R. R. and the M. C. R. R. (new station almost completed, Pl. C, 5); *Canal St. Union Depot* (Pl. A, 3), for the C. & A., C. B. & Q., C. M. & St. P., C. St. L. & P., and P. Ft. W. & C. R. R.; *Van Buren St. Depot* (Pl. B, C, 3), for the C. R. I. & P., the L. S. & M. S., and the N. Y. C. & St. L. R. R.; *Dearborn Station* (Pl. C, 4), cor. of Dearborn and Polk Sts., for the C. & G. T., A. T. & S. F., C. & E., C. & E. I., L. N. A. & C., C. & W. I., Chicago & Atlantic, & Wabash R. R.; *Grand Central Depot* (Pl. B, 4), Harrison St., for the C. & N. P., the Chic. Gt. West., and Wis. Central lines; *Baltimore & Ohio* (Pl. C, 3), at the foot of Monroe St.; *Chicago & North-Western* (Pl. B, 1), cor. of Wells & Kinzie Sts. — Cab to the principal hotels, 1-2 pers. 50 c.; hack (1-2 pers.) $1 (comp. p. 280). *Parmelee's Omnibuses*, 50 c. each.

Hotels. *AUDITORIUM (Pl. a; C, 3), a large building on Michigan Ave., facing the lake, with a very elaborate interior, from $5, R. from $1¹/₂; opposite is the CONGRESS HALL, a large annex opened in 1893; *RICHELIEU (Pl. b; C, 3), Michigan Ave., a small but luxurious and expensive house on the European plan, R. $2-5; GREAT NORTHERN (Pl. e; C, 3), 237 Dearborn St.; *HOTEL METROPOLE (Gen. Pl. f; D, E, 4), Michigan Ave., cor. of 23rd St., $4-8; GRACE, next door to the Union League Club (Pl. B, C, 3), R. from $1¹/₂; PALMER HOUSE (Pl. c; C, 3), State St., a largehouse, frequented by business-men and politicians, $3-6; GRAND PACIFIC (Pl. d; B, 3), cor. of Clark St. and Jackson St., $3-5; THE HAMPDEN, cor. of 39th St. and Langley Ave., R. $3-6; ONTARIO (Pl. g; C, 1), Ontario St., $3-5; WELLINGTON (Pl. h; C, 3), cor. of Wabash Ave. and Jackson St., R. from $2; HYDE

---

† Legend of Special Plan.

1 Ashland B. . . . BC 2	Post Office . . B C 323	Monadnock . . . . C 3
1a Art Institute . . . C 3	11 Cyclorama . . . . C 424	Monon . . . . C 3
Auditorium (see	12 Fair Building . . . C 327	Panorama (Chic.
Pl. a) . . . . C 3	13 First National	Fire) . . . . C 3
2 Board of Trade . . B 3	Bank . . . . C 328	Phenix B. . . . . . B 3
3 Central Music Hall C 2	14 German (Schiller) 29	Portland B. . . . . C 2
4 Chamber of Com-	Theatre . . . . . C 2	Post Office & Cus-
merce . . . . . B 2	15 Grand Opera	tom House . . B C 3
5 Chicago Club . . . C 3	House . . . . . B C 230	Pullman B. . . . . C 3
6 „ Opera House B 2	16 Home Insurance B. B 331	Rookery . . . . . . B 3
7 „ Burl. & Quincy	17 Hooley's Theatre . B 232	Royal Insurance
R. R. Office . . . B 3	18 McVickers The-	Co. . . . . B 3
City Hall & County	atre . . . . . C 2, 333	Studebaker B. . . C 3
Court House . . B 2	19 Manhattan . . . . C 434	Tacoma B. . . . . B 2
8 Columbia Theatre BC 2	20 Marshall Field's 35	Union League
9 Columbus B. . . . C 2	Store . . . . . . C 2	Club . . . . . . B C 3
10 Commercial Bank	21 „ „ Wholesale . B 336	Unity B. . . . . . . C 2
Custom House &	22 Masonic Temple . C 237	Women's Temple . B 3

PARK (Gen. Pl. r; F, 6), cor. of 51st St. and Lake Ave., $ 2¹/₂-4; LEXINGTON (Gen. Pl. s; E, 4), Michigan Ave., cor. 22nd St., $ 3-5; VIRGINIA (Pl. i; C, 1), Ohio & Rush Sts., from $ 3¹/₂; PLAZA, North Ave., cor. of Clark St. (Gen. Pl. D, 1, 2), with a fine view of Lincoln Park and the Lake; VICTORIA (Pl. j; C, 3), Michigan Ave., $ 3-5; LELAND (Pl. k; C, 3), Michigan Ave., $ 3-5; SHERMAN (Pl. 1; B, 2), cor. Randolph & Clark Sts., $ 3-4; TREMONT (Pl. m; C, 2), Lake St., $ 3-4¹/₂; McCOY'S (Pl. n; B, 3), GORE'S, Clark St. (Nos. 278, 266), R. from $ 1; CLIFTON (Pl. o; C, 3), cor. of Monroe St. and Wabash Ave., $ 2¹/₂-3; GAULT (Pl. p; A, 2), W. Madison St., $ 2-2¹/₂; SOUTHERN (Pl. t; Gen. Pl. D, 4), Wabash Ave., cor. 22nd St., $ 2¹/₂-4; WINDSOR (Pl. q; C, 3), 145 Dearborn St., R. from 75 c. — *Board* may easily be obtained in any part of the town from $ 5 to $ 15 per week.

It is estimated that at the opening of the World's Fair the Chicago hotels will have accommodation for 500,000 people.

Restaurants. *Richelieu Hotel*, see p. 279, high charges; *Kinsley*, 105 Adams St.; *Auditorium*, see p. 279; *Rector*, cor. of Monroe St. and Clark St. and 31 Adams St.; *McCoy*, see above; *Lassange*, 77 S. Clark St., D. 75 c.; *Kern*, 108 La Salle St.; *Boston Oyster House*, 112 Madison St.; *Lakeside*, Adams St., cor of Clark St.; *Thompson*, 145 Dearborn St. (moderate charges); *McEwan's Coffee House*, 93 West Madison St. (cheap); *Vienna Bakery*, 36 Washington St. (ladies); *Kohlsaat's Luncheon Rooms*, 196 Clark St. 59, Washington St., etc.; also at most of the other hotels and at *Marshall Field's*, *The Fair*, and other large dry-goods stores. — For men: *Billy Boyle's Chop House*, 5 Calhoun Place, behind 120 Dearborn St.; *Schlogl*, Fifth Ave., between Madison St. and Washington St.; *Schimpferman*, 172 Madison St. — BEER SALOONS: *Lentz, Stein, Kretschmar*, N. Clark St. (Nos. 21, 649, 625); *Meyer*, cor. Madison and Dearborn Sts. — WINE ROOMS: *Jansen*, 163 Washington St.; *Wilken*, 49 La Salle St. (Californian wines); *Faulhaber*, 78 Fifth Ave. and 526 N. Clark St.

Tramways (cable, electric, and horse-cars) traverse the chief streets and run to suburban points (fare 5 c.). Cars stop at the farther street-crossings or at other places indicated by signs. Lines of '*Carettes*' (5 c.) also traverse various streets. — *Parmelee's Omnibuses* run between the hotels and railway-stations (50 c.). — The *South Side Elevated Railroad* runs from Congress St. to the World's Fair (p. 285); others are projected.

Cabs. With one horse: 1-2 pers. per mile 50 c.; per hr., 1-2 pers., 75 c., each addit. ¹/₄ hr. 20 c., in the parks and beyond the city limits $ 1 and 25 c.; each trunk carried outside 10 c. With two horses (*Hacks*): 1-2 pers. 1 M. $ 1, 2 M. $ 1¹/₂, each addit. pers. 50 c., per hr. $ 2, each addit. hr. $ 1, per day $ 8; ordinary baggage free. Each vehicle is bound to exhibit a tariff inside, but it is well to come to a clear understanding beforehand.

Steamers ply from Chicago to all the points on the Great Lakes and (in summer) to points on the St. Lawrence River. Among the chief lines are the *Goodrich*, the *Seymour*, the *Lake Michigan & Lake Superior Transportation Co.*, and the *Graham & Morton Transportation Co.* Steamers to *Milwaukee* (p. 287) run 2-3 times daily (steamer 'Virginia' of the Goodrich Line the best). Small steamers ply at frequent intervals (esp. on Sun. and holidays) to *Jackson* and *Lincoln Parks* (pp. 285, 284); and during the World's Fair the service to Jackson Park will be very frequent (comp. p. 285). The steam-boat-wharves are on the Lake Front, mainly in the *Outer Harbour* (Gen. Pl. E, 3).

Theatres and Places of Amusement. *Auditorium Theatre* (Pl. a; C, 3), Congress St. (comp. p. 282), splendidly fitted up and accommodating 4-5000 people; *Schiller Theatre* (Pl. 14; C, 2), Randolph St.; *Chicago Opera House* (Pl. 6; B, 2), 118 Washington St.; *Columbia* (Pl. 8; B, 2, 3), Monroe St.; *McVicker's Theatre* (Pl. 18; C, 2), Madison St.; *Hooley's Theatre* (Pl. 17; B, 2), Randolph St.; *Haymarket*, West Madison St.; *Grand Opera House* (Pl. 15; B, 2), Clark St.; *Alhambra*, State St.; *Havlin's*, Wabash Ave.; *Jacobs' Academy of Music*, South Halsted St.; *Timmerman Opera House*, in Englewood (S. Side); *Criterion* Sedgwick St., N. Side. — *Central Music Hall* (Pl. 3; C, 2), cor. State and Randolph Sts. — *Cyclorama of the Battle of Gettysburg* (Pl. C, 4), Wabash Ave., cor. of Panorama Place; *Panorama of the Chicago Fire* (Pl. 27; C, 3), Michigan Ave. — *Libby Prison Museum* (p. 328, Pl. C, 6), Wabash Ave., between,

14th and 16th Sts. (9-10; adm. 50 c., children 25 c.). — *John Brown's Fort* (see p. 265; removed to Chicago in 1892), 134 Wabash Ave. (adm. 50 c., children 25 c.). — The*Concerts of Thomas's Orchestra* are held in the Auditorium (p. 282).

Post Office (Pl. B, C, 3), see p. 283; open 7 a. m. to 10 p. m., on Sun 11.30-12.30. There are also 22 sub-stations and numerous letter-boxes.

British Consul, *Hayes Sadler*, *Esq.*, 72 Dearborn St.

Chicago (pron. *Shekáhgo;* 590 ft. above the sea, 15-75 ft. above the lake), the second city and largest railway-centre of the United States, is situated on the W. shore of *Lake Michigan* (p. 2ɩ6), at the mouths of the rivers *Chicago* and *Calumet.* It is 850 M. from Baltimore, the nearest point on the Atlantic, and 2415 M. from San Francisco. It covers an area of 181 sq. M. (more than any other city in the country), and in 1890 contained 1,099,850 inhab., an increase of 118 per cent. in ten years, and actually as well as relatively greater than that of London proper in the same period. The city has a waterfront on the lake of 22 M. and is divided by the Chicago River and its branches into three portions, known as the *North, South,* and *West Sides.* The site of the city is remarkably level, rising very slightly from the lake; and its streets are usually wide and straight. Among the chief business-thoroughfares are *State, Clark, Madison, Dearborn,* and *La Salle Streets,* and *Wabash Avenue.* Perhaps the finest residence-streets are *Michigan Avenue* and *Drexel* and *Grand Boulevards,* on the S. side, and *Lake Shore Drive,* on the N. side. It is estimated that not more than 300,000 of the inhabitants are native Americans; nearly 400,000 are Germans, 220,000 are Irish, 90,000 Scandinavians, 50,000 Poles, 50,000 Bohemians, and 45,000 English and Scottish.

History. The growth of Chicago has been phenomenal even among American cities. The river *Chicago* (the Indian *Checagua,* meaning 'wild onion' and 'pole-cat') was, indeed, visited by the Frenchmen Joliet and Marquette in 1673, but it was not until 1804 that the United States Government erected *Fort Dearborn,* the first permanent settlement in the swamp that was afterwards Chicago. The garrison of the fort was massacred by Indians in 1812, but the fort was rebuilt and re-occupied two years later. In 1831 the little village contained about 100 inhab., and in 1837 it had attained to the dignity of an incorporated city and a population of 4170. In 1850 its population had increased to 29,963 and its commercial energy had begun to attract attention. A signal instance of the energy of the citizens was given in 1855, when the level of the entire city was raised 7 ft., huge buildings being elevated bodily without interruption to business. By 1860 its population was almost quadrupled (109,206), while its trade in bread-stuffs had increased tenfold. By 1870 Chicago contained 306,605 inhab., and had become one of the leading commercial centres of the New World. In 1871 (Oct. 8-10th) the flourishing city was the scene of a terrible conflagration, which originated in the W. side (at No. 137 De Koven St.; Pl. A, 5), crossed to the N. of the river, swept over an area of 3½ sq. M., destroyed 17,500 buildings and property to the value of nearly $ 200,000,000 (40,000,000*l.*), and left 100,000 people homeless. About 200 people perished in the flames. The recovery from this disaster was rapid and complete; and in a few years the only trace of it was the improved character of the streets and buildings. The fire found Chicago of wood and left it of brick and stone. In 1880 the population was 503,185. — Great injustice is done to Chicago by those who represent it as wholly given over to the worship of Mammon, as it compares favourably with many American cities in the efforts it has made to beautify itself by the creation of parks and boulevards and in its encouragement of education and the liberal arts (comp. below and p. 285). At present Chicago is exciting more than usual interest as the site of the Columbian Exhibition, celebrating the four-hundredth anniversary of the discovery of America by Columbus (comp. p. 285). — Chicago has long been the favourite meeting-place of the conventions held by the great political parties to nominate candidates for the office of President. Lincoln (1860), Grant (1868), Garfield (1880), Cleveland (1884 and 1892), and Harrison (1888) were all nominated here.

Commerce and Industry. The trade of Chicago is second to that of New York alone among American cities, and in 1892 amounted in value to 1540 million dollars (308 millions sterling). The staples are grain (250 million bushels yearly), lumber, live-stock, and packed meat, in which branches it is the largest market in the world. The value of its manufactures in 1892 was $ 586,000,000 (117,000,000*l.*), including iron and steel wares, agricultural implements, railway-cars, textiles, leather, beer, spirits, chemicals, etc. In 1892, the number of vessels entering and clearing Chicago Harbour was 21,123, or about 25 per cent more than New York. — Among the leading industrial establishments may be mentioned the *Illinois Steel Co.*, which has five plants in different parts of the city (including the largest rolling mills in the world at South Chicago), has a capital of $50,000,000 (10,000,000*l.*), and employs 12,000 men; the *McCormick Harvesting Machine Co.*, in the S.W. part of the city, employing 2000 hands and producing 120,000 machines annually; the *Grant Locomotive Works;* and the *Chicago Cold Storage Exchange.* Comp. also p. 286.

Architecture. Chicago has become identified with the erection of enormously tall office-buildings, the upper stories of which are made accessible by rapid-running elevators. The architectural beauty of these is often questionable, but no one can fail to admire the wonderful skill of their architectural engineering. These 'sky-scrapers' are now erected on the 'steel-frame system', the walls forming no support to the edifice but merely forming a kind of veneer to the actual structural frame. The interiors are often admirably fitted up and adorned (comp. p. xci). A recent municipal ordinance limits the height of future buildings to 150 ft.

The visitor to Chicago cannot, perhaps, better begin his examination of the city than by ascending to the top of the *Tower* (270 ft. high; adm. 25 c.) of the *Auditorium (Pl. a; C, 3), which affords a splendid view. This huge building, erected in 1887-89 at a cost of $ 3,500,000, includes a large hotel (p. 279) and one of the handsomest theatres in the world (p. 280; 4100 seats). The tower is occupied by a U. S. Signal Service Station. The longest front of the building, towards Congress St., is 360 ft. — The *Studebaker Building* (Pl. 33; C, 3), adjoining the Auditorium, is one of the show buildings of Chicago, but, though in several respects not unworthy of its situation, it is too palatial in character to fairly represent the severity of this city's commercial architecture *(Schuyler).* — The beautiful Romanesque building to the N. of the last is the *Chicago Club* (Pl. 5; C, 3). Until lately it was the home of the **Chicago Art Institute,** which possesses some very interesting and valuable collections, and will ultimately occupy the fine new building erected on the site of the old Industrial Exhibition and temporarily used for the Congresses of the Columbian Exposition (Pl. 1, a; C, 3).

On the N., Michigan Ave. ends at the *Chicago River,* near the *Illinois Central Station* (Pl. C, 2; p. 279). Fort Dearborn (p. 281) stood to the left, on the river, at the end of the avenue (tablet at the corner of River St.).

The *Chicago River*, a narrow and uninviting looking stream, has a frontage within the city of nearly 60 M., of which one-third are navigable. As Chicago derives its drinking-water from Lake Michigan (see p. 284), the disposal of the river-drainage was a serious problem, until the current of the river was reversed by skilful engineering and the stream made to flow through the Illinois & Michigan Canal into the Illinois and Mississippi. The river is crossed by numerous bridges and undermined by three tunnels, traversed by tramway-lines. — The **Harbour** is 16 ft. deep and has an area of about 450 acres; and there is also an external breakwater, 1 M. long, to shelter the mouth of the river.

To see something of the business-quarters of Chicago and the lofty office-buildings for which it is famous, we may now follow *Randolph St.* (see Pl. A-C, 2) to the W. to the **City Hall and County Court House** (Pl. B, 2), a huge twin-building occupying an entire square and erected at a cost of nearly $5,000,000. On the top floor of the City Hall (entr. from La Salle St.) is the *Public Library*, with 175,000 vols. (new building in progress). On the ground-floor are the headquarters of the *Fire Department (1000 men). — Adjacent is the new *Drake Fountain*, with a statue of Columbus.

La Salle Street (Pl. B, 1-3), leading to the S. from this square, contains some of the finest office-buildings in the city. Among these are the **Chamber of Commerce* (Pl. 4, B 2; 14 stories), at the corner of Washington St. (left); the *Tacoma Building* (Pl. 34, B 2; 13 stories), at the corner of Madison St.; the oddly-shaped *Women's Temperance Temple* (Pl. 37, B 3; 13 stories), at the corner of Monroe St. (right); the *Home Insurance Co. Building* (Pl. 16, B 3; 11 stories); and the *Rookery (Pl. 31, B 3; 10 stories), the last two at the corner of Adams St. (left). The *Interior (600 rooms) of the last, lined with white marble, is worth inspecting, and visitors should ascend by one of the 'express' elevators to the rotunda at the top. At the end of La Salle St. stands the **Board of Trade** (Pl. 2, B, 3; *View from the tower, 322 ft. high). Visitors are admitted to the gallery (businesshours, 9.30-1.15), and the scene on the floor is, perhaps, even wilder than that in the New York Stock Exchange (p. 26).

Jackson St. leads hence to the E. to the *Custom House & Post Office* (Pl. B, C, 3), which occupies an entire block. Close by are five very large buildings (16 stories): the *Great Northern Hotel* (Pl. 2, C 3; Dearborn St.), the *Fair Building* (Pl. 12, C 3; cor. of Dearborn St. and Adams St.), the *Manhattan* (Pl. 19, C 4; Dearborn St.), the *Monon* (Pl. 24, C 3; Dearborn St.), and the *Monadnock-Kearsarge* (Pl. 23, C 3; Jackson St.). Adjoining the last is the *Union League Club* (Pl. 35; B, C, 3).

Going on to State Street (Pl. C, 1-6) and following it to the left, we pass the *Columbus Building* (Pl. 9, C 2; 14 stories), at the corner of Washington St. (right); *Marshall Field's Store* (Pl. 20, C, 2), the Whiteley's of Chicago, at the opposite corner of Washington St. (r.); and the enormously tall *Masonic Temple* (Pl. 22, C 2; 21 stories), at the corner of Randolph St. (r.; view from top, 25c).

Among other buildings of interest in this Business Quarter are the new *Unity Building* (Pl. 36, C 2; 18 stories), Dearborn St., near Randolph

St.; the *Rand-McNally Building*, in Adams St., near La Salle St., one of the largest and finest publishing and printing houses in the world (700 hands; built almost entirely of steel; partly occupied at present by the offices of the Columbian Exposition); the *General Offices of the Chicago, Burlington, & Quincy Railroad* (Pl. 7; B, 3), Adams St., cor. Franklin St.; the *Wholesale Establishment of Marshall Field & Co.* (Pl. 21; B, 3), Adams St., designed by H. H. Richardson ('one of the most individual examples of American commercial building'; in it 'the vulgarity of the commercial palace is gratefully conspicuous by its absence, and it is as monumental in its massiveness and durability as it is grimly utilitarian in expression'); the *Royal Insurance Co.* (Pl. 32; B, 3), Jackson St., nearly opposite the Board of Trade; the *First National Bank* (Pl. 13; C, 3), at the cor. of Dearborn & Monroe Sts., with the largest banking-room in the world; the *Pullman Building* (Pl. 30; C, 3), cor. of Michigan Ave. and Adams St.; the *Ashland Block* (Pl. 1, B 2; 16 stories); the *Schiller Building* (*German Theatre*; Pl. 14, C 2); the *Opera House Block* (Pl.-25; C, 2); the *Chicago Opera House* (Pl. 6; B, 2); the *Grand Opera House* (Pl. 15; B, 2); the *Phenix Building* (Pl. 28; B, 3), 128-150 Jackson St., by Burnham & Root, with a fine *Entrance; and the *Owings Building*, 213 Dearborn St.

The *Public Parks of Chicago, with a total extent of 1795 acres, form, with their connecting boulevards, a nearly complete chain round the city, affording from Lincoln Park (see below) to Jackson Park (p. 285) a drive of 37 M. — On the N. side is *Lincoln Park* (see below), reached by tramways on N. Wells, N. Clark, and N. State Streets. On the way to it walkers or drivers should pass the *Water Works* (Gen. Pl. E, 2), near the foot of *Chicago Ave.*, the tower of which, 175 ft. high, commands an extensive view.

The water-supply of Chicago is derived from Lake Michigan, being conducted to the city through tunnels from a '*Crib*' 2 M. out in the lake. A new tunnel, to a crib 4 M. out, has just been constructed, as there is reason to believe that the water at a distance of 2 M. from shore is not altogether uncontaminated by the city drainage. The old tunnel is to be extended 2 M. farther out.

A little farther on begins the *Lake Shore Drive (Gen. Pl. E,2), one of the finest residence-streets in Chicago, containing some very handsome houses, including specimens of H. H. Richardson (not in his happiest manner) and R. M. Hunt (next door). On the N. it ends at *Lincoln Park (Gen. Pl. D, 1; 250 acres).

Among the attractions of this park are the conservatories, palm-house, lily-ponds, and flower-beds; a small zoological collection; a fountain illuminated at night by electric light; the statues of *Lincoln (by *St. Gaudens*), Grant (by *Rebisso*), Schiller, La Salle, and Linnæus; and the boating lake. Park-phaetons 20 c. per drive.

A new *Breakwater Carriage Drive has been constructed in the lake alongside of Lincoln Park, whence it is to be prolonged by the *Sheridan Boulevard* to Fort Sheridan (27 M.). The strip of water between this drive and the park will be used as a regatta-course for small boats. *Graceland* and *Rosehill Cemeteries*, also in the N. Side, deserve a visit.

The S. Side parks are also fine. They may be reached by the Illinois Central R. R. or by the Cottage Grove Ave. cable-line; but the best plan is to drive through *Michigan Boulevard (Pl. E,4,5) and *Drexel Boulevard (Gen. Pl. E, 6), two fine residence-streets, with tasteful houses and ornamental gardens. Michigan Boulevard also contains several churches, the *Calumet Club* (cor. 20th St.; rebuilding), numerous large hotels and apartment houses, and the

First Regiment Armoury (cor. 16th St.; entrance wide enough for a whole company to march abreast). In Drexel Boulevard is the handsome *Drexel Memorial Fountain.* We may return by *Grand Boulevard (Gen. Pl. E, 6).

Prairie Avenue (Gen. Pl. E, 4-7), contains the residences of *P. D. Armour, Marshall Field, George M. Pullman,* and others of Chicago's magnates; but few of them are of architectural importance.

*Washington Park (Gen. Pl. E, 7; 371 acres) and *Jackson Park (Gen. Pl. F, 7, 8; 586 acres) are connected by a wide boulevard known as the *Midway Pleasance* (Gen. Pl. E, F, 7; park-phaetons, 25 c. each pers., children 15 c.).

Washington Park is notable for its fine trees, its *Flower-gardening, its large circular stable, and its conservatory. — Jackson Park has been chosen as the main site of the **World's Columbian Exposition** (comp. p. 282), which also overflows into the Midway Pleasance and Washington Park. — The World's Fair Grounds may be reached by the Illinois Central R. R. to 60th Str. (1/4 hr.; 15 c.); by the B. & O. R. R. and Belt Line to the terminal station in the grounds, near 64th St.; by the South Side Elevated R. R. to 63rd St. (25 min.; 5 c.); by the cable-cars on Wabash Ave. and State St. (1 hr.; 5 c.); by steamboats on Lake Michigan (from Van Buren St. Pier to Casino Pier in 35 min.; 15 c.); or by carriage (7 1/2 M.). — It is still undecided which of the buildings of the World's Fair are to be permanent, though it is probable that the *Art Building* and the *Japanese Building* (on the wooded islet) will be among those left standing.

The W. Side parks: *Douglas Park* (Gen. Pl. B, 4; 180 acres), *Garfield Park* (Gen. Pl. A, 3; 186 acres), and *Humboldt Park* (Gen. Pl. B, 2; 200 acres), are little inferior to those of the N. and S. Sides.

Some of the most prominent educational, scientific, and charitable institutions, of which Chicago is justly proud, are noted below. The new **University of Chicago** (Gen. Pl. E, 7), between 56th and 59th Sts., opened its doors in 1892 with an attendance of 600 students. It has a total endowment of over $7,000,000 (1,400,000*l.*), of which $3,600,000 were given by Mr. Rockefeller. — The *Newberry Library (Gen. Pl. D, 2), endowed by the late Mr. Newberry with $3,000,000 (600,000*l.*), at present occupies temporary premises in State St., until the large and handsome building being erected for it in Ogden Square is finished. It already possesses 110,000 vols., including the best musical collection in the country.

Mr. *John Crerar* (d. 1890) has bequeathed $2,225,000 (445,000*l.*) for the establishment of a similar library on the S. Side.

The **Churches** of Chicago are comparatively uninteresting. Among the most important are the R. C. *Cathedral of the Holy Name*, at the cor. of Superior and N. State Sts. (N. Side); the *Third Presbyterian Church*, cor. of Ashland and Ogden Aves. (Gen. Pl. C, 3), with good stained glass; the *Church of the Epiphany*, at the cor. of Ashland Ave. and Adams St., not far from the last; the *Second Presbyterian Church*, Michigan Ave., cor. 20th St. (Gen. Pl. E, 4); and *Plymouth Church*, Michigan Ave., near 25th St. (Gen. Pl. E, 4).

The interesting 'Medical District', in the W. Side, has for its nucleus the large *County Hospital*, near which are the *Rush Medical College*, the *College of Physicians and Surgeons*, the *Presbyterian Hospital*, the *Training School for Nurses*, the *Chicago Homeopathic Medical College*, and the *Women's Medical College.*

The **Chicago Historical Society** (142 Dearborn St.) lost its library and collections in the Great Fire (p. 281) but again contains many objects of interest. — The **Armour Mission**, at the corner of Butterfield and 33rd Sts., is one of the most interesting of the Chicago charities, including a mission hall, a crèche, a library, a kindergarten, a free dispensary, etc. The *Armour Institute*, the principal feature of which is manual training, has been endowed by its founder with $1,400,000.

The **Libby Prison** (Pl. C, 6), in Wabash Ave. , built at Richmond in 1845 as a tobacco warehouse, was converted into a prison during the Civil War and confined more than 12,000 Union prisoners. In 1889 it was transferred bodily to Chicago, where it has been fitted up as a Museum of the Civil War (adm., see p. 280). A little farther to the N. is *John Brown's Fort* (see p. 280).

Few travellers will leave Chicago without a visit to the famous **Union Stockyards** (Gen. Pl. C, D, 6). The yards are in South Halsted St., $5^1/_2$ M. to the S.W. of the City Hall, and may be reached by the South Halsted St. tramway or by the State St. line, with transfer at 35th St. or 43rd St. Visitors are freely admitted to the yards and will be shown round by a guide (25 c. each); but it is advisable to be provided with an introduction to one of the great packing-houses.

The yards proper cover an area of about 400 acres, and have 50 M. of feeding-troughs and 20 M. of water-troughs. The annual receipts of cattle are between 3 and 4 million head, besides 8-9 million hogs, 2-3 million sheep, and 100,000 horses, with a total value of 200-250 million dollars. From two-thirds to three-fourths of the cattle and hogs are killed in the yards, and sent out in the form of meat. About 25,000 workers are employed by the packing-houses, and the annual value of their products is nearly 150 million dollars. The largest and best known packing-house is that of *Armour & Co.*, which in the year ending April 1st, 1891, slaughtered 712,000 cattle, 1,711,000 hogs, and 413,000 sheep, employed 7900 men, and sold goods to the value of $ 66,000,000, including canned meats, fertilizers, glue, etc. — The processes of killing the cattle and hogs are extremely ingenious and expeditious, and will interest those whose nerves are strong enough to contemplate with equanimity wholesale slaughter and oceans of blood. The guide should be asked to point out 'Old Bill', the 'bunko steer', who acts as a decoy for his mates.

An interesting visit may be made to one of the large **Grain Elevators**, of which there are about 30, with an aggregate capacity of nearly 30 million bushels. They are all situated on the river.

A visit to **Pullman** (*Florence Hotel*, D. $ 1), 14 M., to the S. of the Court House, on the Illinois Central Railroad ($^3/_4$ hr.), should also be included by all who can spare half-a-day. An order for admission to the Pullman Car Works may be obtained at the Pullman Building, Michigan Ave., cor. of Adams St. (Pl. C, 3), but no guide is provided for visitors. Pullman was built and is owned by the *Pullman Palace Car Co.*, and is a model little town, consisting mainly of neat workmen's houses. To the left of the tasteful station are the **Pullman Car Works*, the various processes of which are full of interest. About 200 Pullman cars, 500 ordinary passenger-cars, and 10,000 freight-cars are manufactured annually, with a total value of 10-12 million dollars. The Pullman Car Co. now owns and operates 2500 cars. Among the chief features of the town is the *Arcade*, a building which includes shops, a tasteful theatre, and a free library (8000 vols.; M. Duane Doty, custodian). The population of the town in 1890 was about 11,000, most of whom are connected with the Pullman Car Works, though the 5-6000 operatives employed there are not compelled to live in Pullman.

Other favourite points for short excursions from Chicago are *Evanston*, *Michigan City*, *St. Joseph*, *Kenosha*, *Grand Haven*, *Kewaunee*, *Sturgeon Bay* (all reached by steamer), *Glen Ellyn Springs*, *Lake Forest*, *Highland Park*, *Winnetka*, etc.

49. From Chicago to Milwaukee.

a. Viâ Chicago & North-Western Railway.

85 M. Railway in 2¹/₂-3 hrs. (fare $2.55; chair-car 35 c.).

Chicago, see p. 279. The line runs to the N. along *Lake Michigan*, passing many small stations forming suburban homes for Chicago merchants. — 12 M. *Evanston*, with the buildings of the *North-Western University*, a Methodist institution with 1000 students (incl. 600 in the preparatory school). A little beyond (36 M.) *Waukegan* we enter *Wisconsin* (the 'Badger State'), a fertile agricultural and lumbering state, with numerous interesting Indian mounds and large deposits of iron. More prehistoric copper implements have been found here than in any other state. A very large number of the inhabitants are of German or Scandinavian stock. — 51 M. *Kenosha*, with 6532 inhab. and a flourishing trade and industry. — 62 M. *Racine* (Commercial, Merchants', $2), the fourth city of Wisconsin, with 21,014 inhab., has a good lake-harbour and carries on considerable trade and manufactures.

85 *M. Milwaukee*, see below.

b. Viâ Chicago, Milwaukee, & St. Paul Railroad.

85 M. Railway in 2¹/₂-2³/₄ hrs. (fares as above).

Chicago, see p. 279. This line runs nearly parallel with that above described, but a little more inland. 9 M. *Mayfair;* 32 M. *Rondout;* 43 M. *Wadsworth.* — 85 M. *Milwaukee*, see below.

Milwaukee. — Hotels. *Plankinton House, Grand Ave., cor. of West Water St., $2¹/₂-5; *Pfister*, Wisconsin St., cor. of Jefferson St., $2¹/₂-5; *Schlitz Hotel*, Grand Ave., cor. 3rd St., R. from $1; *Republican Ho.*, cor. Cedar & 3rd Sts., $2-3; *Pabst*, 464 Market Sq., $2-3¹/₂. — *Railway Restaurant*, D. 75 c. In the suburbs are numerous pleasant *Beer Gardens*, in the German style.

Tramways (fare 5 c.) traverse the principal streets.

Steamers ply regularly to all the chief places on the Great Lakes, and to various summer-resorts near Milwaukee.

Theatres. *Davidson's*, 3rd St., near Grand Ave.; *Bijou*, 2nd St.; *People's*, West Water St.; *Opera Ho.*, Oneida St.

Post Office, cor. of Wisconsin St. and Milwaukee St.

Milwaukee (580 ft. above the sea), the largest city in Wisconsin and one of the chief manufacturing and commercial centres of the N.W., occupies a pleasant undulating site on the W. shore of Lake Michigan, at the mouth of the river *Milwaukee*. An excellent harbour has been formed by the erection of huge breakwaters, and the river admits the largest lake-vessels to the doors of the warehouses. The Milwaukee receives two tributaries, the *Menomonee* and *Kinnick-innic*, within the city. The city is well built, largely of a light-coloured brick, and many of its streets are lined with shade-trees. Fully one-half of its (1890) 204,468 inhab. are Germans, which may account for its successful cultivation of music and art.

Milwaukee was founded in 1835 and received a city-charter in 1846. Its growth has been rapid, particularly in the last 10 years.

The chief articles of its extensive commerce are grain, flour, and

lumber. Its flour-mills are very large, and its grain-elevators have a
capacity of 6 million bushels. Milwaukee lager beer (Pabst, Schlitz, Blatz,
etc.) is known all over the United States, and in 1892 was produced to
the amount of 2¹/₄ million barrels. Pork-packing is extensively carried on,
and the other staple manufactures include leather, machinery (Reliance
Works), iron and steel goods, and tobacco (total value in 1890, $ 95,000,000).

Grand Avenue, which runs E. and W., contains many of the
chief buildings and best shops, while *Wisconsin Street* and *East
Water Street* are also busy thoroughfares. Among the most prominent
buildings are the *Custom House & Post Office*, at the corner of Wisconsin and Milwaukee Sts.; the *County Court House* (view from
dome), in the square bounded by Jefferson, Jackson, Oneida, and
Biddle Sts.; the *Chamber of Commerce*, Michigan St.; and *St. Paul's
Church* (Epis.), Marshall St. The *Exposition Building*, in Cedar St.,
contains a museum of natural history (open every afternoon, all
day on Sat.), and the *Layton Art Gallery, at the corner of Jefferson
and Mason Sts., has some interesting pictures (open daily; adm.
on Wed. and Frid. 25 c.). The *Public Library*, 408 Grand Ave.,
possesses 70,000 vols. (reading-room open 9-9). A large new *City
Hall* is contemplated.

*Juneau Park, laid out on a bluff overlooking the river, con-
tains statues of *Solomon Juneau* (1793-1856), the earliest white
settler, and *Leif Ericson* (p. 81); it commands fine views. A pleasant
drive may be taken to the N. along the river to (5 M.) *Whitefish
Bay*. The *Forest Home Cemetery* lies at the S.W. corner of the city.

Visitors to Milwaukee should not fail to inspect one of the great
Breweries, such as *Pabst's*, which produces over 1,000,000 barrels
of beer annually; and the *Grain Elevators* and *Flour Mills* will
also repay a visit.

About 3 M. to the W. of the city is the *National Soldiers' Home*, with
accommodation for 2000 disabled soldiers and a fine park (open to the
public on week-days). — One of the favourite resorts of Milwaukians is
Waukesha (*Fountain Spring Ho.*, $ 3-5), a village 20 M. to the W., with the
well-known *Bethesda Spring*, the water of which (efficacious in diabetes
and Bright's disease) is exported all over the United States and to Europe.

Milwaukee is an important railway-centre, lines radiating hence to
all points in Wisconsin. Those running to the N. and N.W. reach *Marquette, Ashland, Duluth*, and other points on Lake Superior (comp. p. 296),
but hardly fall within the scope of this Handbook. From Milwaukee to
Madison and *St. Paul*, see R. 50.

50. From Chicago to St. Paul and Minneapolis.
a. Viâ Chicago, Milwaukee, & St. Paul Railroad.

420 M. RAILWAY to (410 M.) *St. Paul* in 13-14 hrs. and thence to (10 M.)
Minneapolis in ¹/₂-³/₄ hr. more (fare $ 11.50; parlor-car $ 1, sleeper $ 2).
The fast mail line of this service is the route viâ La Crosse, described
below; but some trains run viâ *Madison* and *Prairie du Chien* or viâ *Dubuque*.

From Chicago to (85 M.) *Milwaukee*, see R. 49. The line now
turns to the W. 99 M. *Brookfield*; 118 M. *Oconomowoc*. At (130 M.)
Watertown our route diverges to the right from the line viâ *Madison*
(p. 289) and *Prairie du Chien* (see p. 291 and above).

Beyond Watertown our line runs to the N.W. 150 M. *Columbus;*
178 M. *Portage City* (Rail. Restaurant), a trading city with 5143
inhab., at the head of the navigation of the *Wisconsin.* 195 M.
Kilbourn City (Finch Ho., $2-2½) is the starting-point for a visit
to the fantastic *Dalles of the Wisconsin* (comp. p. 394). 240 M. *Tomah;*
257 M. *Sparta.* — 283 M. **La Crosse** (650 ft.; *Cameron Ho.*, $2½; *Rail.
Restaurant*), a flourishing city of 25,090 inhab. on the E. bank of the
Mississippi, with large saw-mills and an extensive timber-trade.

We now cross the Mississippi, here ⅓ M. wide, enter *Minnesota* (the 'North Star State'), and ascend on the W. bank of the
river, through picturesque scenery (views to the right). 307 M.
Winona, with 18,208 inhab. and a trade in timber and grain. 340 M.
Wabasha lies near the foot of the beautiful expansion of the Mississippi known as *Lake Pepin* (30 M. long and 3-5 M. wide). 352 M.
Lake City and (359 M.) *Frontenac* are two favourite resorts in this
beautiful district (comp. p. 323). 369 M. *Red Wing;* 390 M. *Hastings.*
410 M. **St. Paul,** see p. 291. — 420 M. **Minneapolis,** see p. 293.

b. Viâ Chicago & North-Western Railway.

421½ M. RAILWAY to (409½ M.) *St. Paul* in 13-14 hrs.; to (421½ M.)
Minneapolis in ¾ hr. more (fares as above).

Chicago, see p. 279. The train runs to the N.W., passing various
suburban stations. 63 M. *Harvard Junction.* We enter *Wisconsin* a
little farther on. Beyond this point some trains run viâ (91 M.)
Beloit (important college) and others viâ (91 M.) *Janesville,* re-uniting at (116 M.) *Evansville.*

138½ M. **Madison** (845 ft.; *Park Hotel,* $2½-3; *Capitol, Ogden,* $2-2½; *Tonywatha Springs Hotel,* 3 M. from the city, $2-3),
the capital of Wisconsin, a pleasant city of 13,426 inhab., situated
between the beautiful *Lakes Mendota* and *Monona.* The *State Capitol*
is a handsome building and contains a good library. The S. wing is
occupied by the *Wisconsin Historical Society,* the most important
institution of the kind beyond the Alleghenies, which possesses a
library of 150,000 vols., an art-gallery, and a valuable museum.
The *University of Wisconsin,* finely situated on *University Hill,* overlooking Lake Mendota, is attended by 1000-1200 students. Its observatory (the *Washburn Observatory*) is one of the best in America.

Beyond Madison we pass to the N. of the pretty *Lake Mendota*
(see above). At (213 M.) *Elroy* we diverge to the left from the line
to *La Crosse* (see above) and traverse a district of pine-forests. At
(321½ M.) *Eau Claire* (17,415 inhab.) we cross the *Chippewa River.*
345 M. *Menomonee.* 390½ M. *Hudson,* with the *O. W. Holmes
Sanitarium* ($1½-2½), pleasantly situated on the E. bank of *Lake
St. Croix.* An excursion may be made to the *Dalles of the St. Croix.*
We now cross the *Mississippi* and enter *Minnesota* (see above).

409½ M. **St. Paul,** see p. 291. — 421½ M. **Minneapolis,** see
p. 293.

c. Viâ Albert Lea Route.

529 M. CHICAGO, ROCK ISLAND, & PACIFIC R. R. to (222 M.) *West Liberty* ; BURLINGTON, CEDAR RAPIDS, & NORTHERN R. R. thence to (413 M.) *Albert Lea;* MINNEAPOLIS & ST. LOUIS R. R. thence to (521 M.) *Minneapolis* and (529 M.) *St. Paul* (21 hrs. ; fares as above).

Chicago (Van Buren St. Station), see p. 279. The train runs at first to the W.S.W. through a great prairie region, which offers comparatively little of interest to the stranger, except the sight of the growing wheat. 40 M. *Joliet* (540 ft.), an agricultural and industrial centre with 23,364 inhab., on the *Des Plaines River.* 84 M. *Ottawa* (9985 inhab.); 99 M. *La Salle* (9855 inhab.); 159 M. *Geneseo.*

181 M. **Rock Island** (470 ft.; *Harper Ho.*, $2-3; *Rock Island Ho.*, $2; *Rail. Restaurant*), an important railway-centre and industrial town of 13,634 inhab., on the E. bank of the *Mississippi.* It lies at the foot of the *Moline Rapids*, which afford good water-power. The island in the river from which it takes its name, 970 acres in area, is occupied by a large **United States Arsenal.*

The train now crosses the river by a fine bridge, enters *Iowa* (the 'Hawkeye State'), and reaches (182 M.) **Davenport** (*Kimball Ho.*, *Lindell Ho.*, $2-3), a grain-shipping city opposite Rock Island, with 26,872 inhab. and considerable manufactures. It is the junction of a line to *Kansas City* (p. 400). — Our train diverges to the right (N.) from the main line to Omaha at (222 M.) *West Liberty* (Rail. Restaurant) and traverses the great wheat-fields of N. Iowa. 259 M. *Cedar Rapids* (710 ft.; Pullman Ho., Grand, $2-2½) is a thriving town and railway-centre on the Cedar River, with 18,020 inhab. and large pork-packing houses. 316 M. *Cedar Falls.* Beyond (396 M.) *Northwood* we enter *Minnesota.* 413 M. *Albert Lea* (1230 ft.; Gilbert Ho., $2) is a thriving little city (3305 inhab.). 512 M. *Hopkins.*

521 M. **Minneapolis**, see p. 293. — 529 M. **St. Paul**, see p. 291.

d. Viâ Chicago Great Western Railway.

420-430 M. RAILWAY in 13-14 hrs. (fares as above).

Chicago (Harrison St. Station), see p. 279. The train runs at first a little to the N. of W. 52 M. *Sycamore;* 126 M. *Stockton.* We reach the *Mississippi* at (167 M.) **Dubuque** (600 ft.; *Julien Ho.*, $3-4; *Lorimier*, $2-3), the third city of *Iowa*, with 30,311 inhab. and a large trade in grain, lumber, and lead. — 197 M. *Dyersville.* At (240 M.) *Oelwein* (1040 ft.) we diverge to the right (N.) from the main line to *Kansas City* (p. 401). 348 M. *Dodge Centre.*

420 M. **St. Paul**, see p. 291. — 430 M. **Minneapolis**, see p. 293.

e. Viâ Chicago, Burlington, & Quincy Railroad.

431-442 M. RAILWAY in 13½-20 hrs. (fares as above).

Chicago (Canal St. Station), see p. 279. 37 M. *Aurora* (650 ft.; Bishop Ho., $2-2½), an industrial city with 19,688 inhab., claims to have been the first to light its streets by electricity (1881). We diverges to the right (comp. p. 390) from the line to Kansas City (p. 400), Omaha (p. 388), and Denver (p. 406). 99 M. *Oregon.* From (146 M.) *Savanna* (Rail. Restaurant) the line runs to the N. along the E. bank of the *Mississippi*, affording numerous fine views to the left. 172 M. *Galena Junction*, for (6 M.) *Galena*, a thriving little city (5635 inhab.) in an important lead-mining district. At (185 M.) *East Dubuque*, on the E. bank of the river, opposite Dubuque, we enter *Wisconsin* (p. 287). — 239 M. **Prairie du Chien** (620 ft.; *Commercial, Depot*, $2), a flourishing shipping-port, with 3131 inhab., just above the mouth of the *Wisconsin River.* 299 M. *La Crosse* (Rail. Restaurant), see p. 289; 326 M. *East Winona*, opposite Winona (p. 289). Numerous small stations.

431 M. **St. Paul**, see p. 291. — 442 M. **Minneapolis**, see p. 293.

f. Viâ Wisconsin Central Railroad.

462-472 M. RAILWAY in 14 hrs. (fares as above).

Chicago (Harrison St. Station), see p. 279. This line runs towards the N.E. and enters *Wisconsin* beyond (55 M.) *Antioch.* 98 M. *Waukesha* (p. 288). At (118 M.) *Rugby Junction* we join the Wisconsin Central line from Milwaukee (p. 287). — 156 M. *Fond du Lac*, a city with 12,024 inhab., and a trade in lumber, lies at the S. end of *Lake Winnebago* (30 M. long and 10 M. wide), the W. shore of which we now follow. 174 M. *Oshkosh*, a city of 22,836 inhab., with saw-mills and factories. At (187 M.) *Neenah* we turn to the left (W.) and leave the lake. 250 M. *Stevens Point;* 303 M. *Abbotsford;* 358 M. *Chippewa Falls*, on the *Wisconsin*, with 8670 inhab. and a trade in lumber; 423 M. *New Richmond.*

462 M. **St. Paul**, see p. 291. — 472 M. **Minneapolis**, see p. 293.

51. St. Paul and Minneapolis.

St. Paul and *Minneapolis*, the 'Twin Cities' of the West, are so intimately associated with each other in all ways, that it is convenient to treat of them together. Though their centres are 10 M. apart, they have extended towards each other so as almost to form one large city with 300,000 inhabitants.

St. Paul. — *Union Depot* (Pl. E, 2, 3), on the river, at the foot of Sibley St., used by most of the railways; *Broadway Depot* (Pl. E, 2), foot of 4th St., for the Minneapolis & St. Louis R. R. and trains to St. Croix Falls.

Hotels, *RYAN (Pl. a; D, 2), cor. Robert & 6th Sts., $3-6, with good café-restaurant; ABERDEEN, cor. of Dayton and Virginia Sts., from $3½; MERCHANTS (Pl. c; C, 3), cor. E. 3rd & Jackson Sts., commercial, $2-3½; WINDSOR (Pl. d; E, 3), cor. 5th & St. Peter Sts., $2½-5, a family house; CLIFTON (Pl. e; C, 3), R. from $1; CLARENDON (Pl. f; C, 3), $2. — *Magee's Restaurant*, 341 Jackson St.

Tramways. St. Paul is traversed in all directions by an excellent system of electric and cable cars (fare 5 c.), not a single horse being used for tramways in either of the Twin Cities. — *Interurban Electric Tramway* to (10 M.) *Minneapolis*, starting at Wabasha & 5th Sts. (fare 10 c.; ³/₄-1 hr.).

Cabs. For 1 pers., 1 M. 50 c., 1½ M. 75 c., 2 M. $1; each addit.

peis. 50 c. for the whole hiring; per hr. $1, each addit. hr. 50c., with two horses $1¹/₂ and $1.

Steamers ply to all points on the Mississippi (comp. p. 322).

Places of Amusement. *Metropolitan Opera Ho.* (Pl. D, 2); *Grand Opera House* (Pl. C, 3), 6th & St. Peter Sts.; *Park Theatre* (Pl. B, 3).

Post Office (Pl. C, 3), cor. Wabasha & 5th Sts. (7-7; Sun. 9-10 a.m.).

St. Paul (700-800 ft. above the sea), the capital of Minnesota, is finely situated at the head of navigation on the *Mississippi*, mainly on a series of terraces rising from the E. (or rather N.) bank. The business part of the town is well-built and regularly laid out, and the suburban quarters contain many fine streets and handsome residences. St. Paul is a great railway-centre, and by rail and river carries on an immense wholesale and retail trade. The value of its industrial products in 1890 was $32,600,000 (6,520,000*l.*). The population in 1890 was 133,156, including many Scandinavians.

The first white settler, a Canadian voyageur, built a house here in 1833, and in 1841 the place received its name from a French priest. In 1854, when it received a city charter, it contained 3000 inhab., and since then its growth has been very rapid. — A fine **Ice Carnival* is generally held here in winter.

The traveller in St. Paul may begin his visit by ascending to the top of the **Pioneer Press Office* (Pl. D, 2, 3), a 13-story building at the corner of 4th and Roberts Sts. (elevator). Another good view is obtained from the dome of the **Capitol** (Pl. C, 2; hard to climb; key on ground-floor). The library of the *State Historical Society*, in the Capitol, contains 20,000 volumes. — A little to the S. of the Capitol are the *Post Office* (Pl. C, 3) and the **City Hall** (Pl. C, 3), the latter a large and handsome building, erected at a cost of $1,000,000 and containing the *Public Library*. — Among other important buildings in the business-quarter are the *New York Life Insurance Building* (Pl. C, 2), cor. 6th & Minnesota Sts.; the R. C. *Cathedral of St. Paul* (Pl. C, 3), 6th St., cor. of St. Peter St.; the *High School* (Pl. C, 1), cor. 10th & Minnesota St.; the *National Guard Armoury* (Pl. B, 3), opposite the last; the *Globe Building* (Pl. D, 3), 4th St., cor. Cedar St.; the *Germania Life Insurance Office* (Pl. D, 3), opposite the last; the *Bank of Minnesota* (Pl. D, 2); the odd-looking *People's Church* (Pl. A, 3); and the *Great Northern Railway Offices* (Pl. E, 2).

The finest residence-street is **Summit Avenue* (Pl. A, B, 1, 2), of which Mr. Schuyler writes that very few streets in the United States 'give in as high a degree the sense of an expenditure liberal without ostentation, directed by skill, and restrained by taste'. It begins at Wabasha St. and runs from *Summit Park* (Pl. A, 2) along a high ridge. The most prominent dwelling is the large brown-stone mansion of Mr. Hill, President of the G. N. Railroad. — Near Summit Ave. is the extensive new *Roman Catholic Seminary of St. Thomas Aquinas.*

From Summit Ave. the visitor may descend to the **High Bridge,** a sloping bridge rising rapidly from the low N. (E.) bank of the Mississippi to the high bluffs on the S. (W.) side. It commands an excellent **View.*

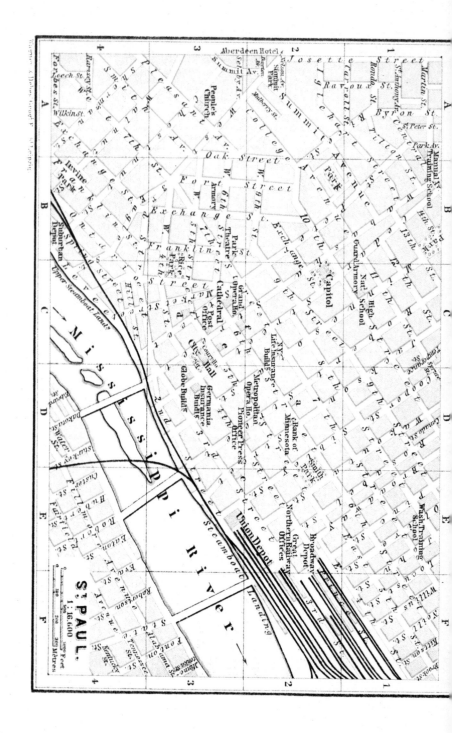

St. PAUL.
1:16,600

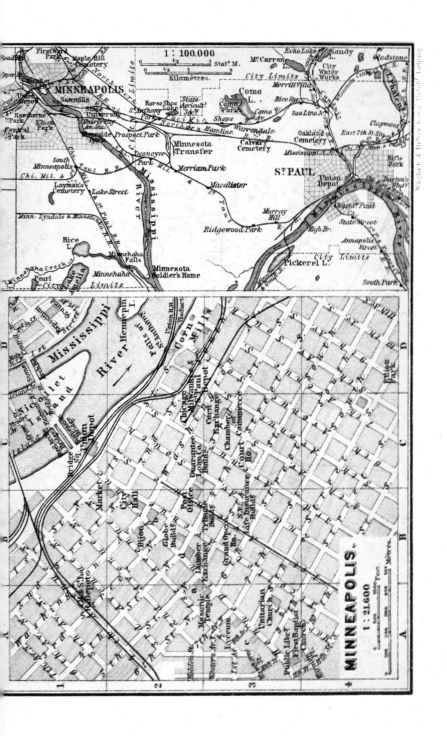

The *Indian Mounds*, at *Dayton's Bluff*, on the Mississippi, just to the E. of St. Paul, command a fine view of the city and river. *Carver's Cave*, in the bluff, was named from Capt. Jonathan Carver, who made a treaty with the Indians here in 1767. — *Lake Como* and *Como Park* lie about 3½ M. to the N W. of the centre of the city (tramway). Adjacent are the *State Fair Grounds*. — *Fort Snelling*, a U. S. military post, lies on the W. bank of the Mississippi, 6 M. above the city (C. M. & St. P. R. R.). — The **Minnehaha Falls* (see p. 295) may be reached from St. Paul by river (steamers in summer) or by the C. M. & St. P. R. R. — The State of Minnesota is thickly sown with lakes (7-10,000 in number, covering an area of 4160 sq. M.), and a number of these are within easy reach of St. Paul. Among the largest and most beautiful of these are *White Bear Lake* (10 M.; see p. 295), *Bald Eagle Lake* (11 M.; see p. 295), and **Lake Minnetonka* (20 M.; see p. 295).

From St. Paul down the Mississippi to *St. Louis*, etc., see R. 66.

Minneapolis (10 M.) may be reached from St. Paul by railway (½ hr.) or by the Interurban Electric Tramway (p. 291; ¾ hr.).

Minneapolis. — *Union Depot* (Pl. C, 1), Bridge Sq., used by several railways; *Chicago, Milwaukee, & St. Paul* (Pl. C, D, 2, 3), Washington Ave.; *Minneapolis & St. Louis Railway* (Pl. A, 1), N. 3rd St. and Fourth Ave.

Hotels. *WEST HOTEL (Pl. a; A, B, 2), Hennepin Ave., cor. 5th St., $3-5; NICOLLET HO. (Pl. b; B, 2), Washington Ave., $2½-4; THE HOLMES (Pl. c; A, 3), Hennepin Ave., $2½-4, R. from $1; BRUNSWICK (Pl. d; B, 2), from $2. — *Dietrich's Restaurant*, 316 Hennepin Ave.

Tramways and **Cabs** as in St. Paul (see p. 291).

Theatres. *Grand Opera* (Pl. B, 3), 6th St.; *Lyceum* (Pl. A, 3), Hennepin Ave.; *Bijou* (Pl. B, 2), Washington Ave.; *Hilton's*, Hennepin Ave.

Post Office (Pl. B, 2), 3rd St. (7-7; Sun. 9-10 a.m.).

Minneapolis (700-800 ft. above the sea), the largest city in Minnesota and the chief flour-making place in the world, lies on both banks of the Mississippi, a little above St. Paul, at the point where the river descends over the *Falls of St. Anthony*. The population in 1890 was 164,738, including many Scandinavians. Minneapolis covers a larger area (54 sq. M.) than St. Paul and is not so much built up; but it contains many individual edifices that are unexcelled in the sister-city, while numerous trees and lawns add to its attractions.

Minneapolis owes its prosperity and rapid growth to the extensive and fertile agricultural district tributary to it, and to the splendid water-power of the St. Anthony Falls, with an available perpendicular fall of 50 ft., yielding from 50,000 to 100,000 horse-power. The falls were named by Father Hennepin (p. 201) in 1680, but it was not till 1838 that the village of *St. Anthony*, now included in Minneapolis, was founded on the E. bank of the river. The settlement on the W. bank, which received the name of *Minneapolis* (from *minne*, the Sioux for water, and the Greek *polis*), was founded in 1852. In 1870 the population was 18,000, and in 1880 it was 46,000; while the last decade showed an increase of 252 per cent.

Its *Flour Mills*, about 25 in number, have a daily capacity of about 45,000 barrels and produce about 7 million barrels annually. Its *Lumber Mills* yearly cut 400-450 million ft. of timber. The total annual value of its manufactures, which also include iron goods, machinery, street-cars, etc., amounted in 1890 to about $80,000,000 (16,000 000l.). Its trade is also very large, the chief import being grain and the chief exports flour and timber.

At the corner of Second Ave. and N. 3rd St. stands the building of the **North-Western Guarantee Loan Co.* (Pl. C, 2), one of the best-equipped office-buildings in the United States, erected in 1888-90 at a cost of $1,000,000. The roof (172 ft. high, tower 48 ft.

more) is laid out as a garden (concerts in summer) and commands
an excellent *View of the city (*Restaurant on the 12th floor). Adjacent is the *Post Office* (Pl. B, C, 2), in a Romanesque style.

We may now follow 3rd St. to the W. to HENNEPIN AVENUE
(Pl. A-C, 1-3) and turn to the left. To the left, at the corner of N.
5th St., is the imposing *Lumber Exchange* (Pl. B, 2). To the right
are the *West Hotel* (Pl. a; A, B, 2) and the *Masonic Temple* (Pl. A, 3).
Farther on, at the corner of 10th St., is the ***Public Library and
Art Gallery** (Pl. A, 3), a handsome Romanesque structure, with an
ornate façade.

The *Library* (50,000 vols.) and *Reading Rooms* (open 8.30 a.m.-10 p.m.)
are on the first floor. Upstairs is the *Art Gallery* (8.30-12 & 1-6, also on
Frid. 7.30-10 p.m.; Sun., 2-10), containing pictures, casts, bric-a-brac,
etc. Among the pictures belonging to the Gallery is *De Neuville's* 'Storming of Tell el-Kebir'. — On the second floor are the collection of the *Minnesota Academy of Natural Sciences*. — The building also includes a
School of Art.

Adjoining the Public Library is the **First Baptist Church*
(Pl. A, 4). The **Unitarian Church* (Pl. A, 3), at the corner of Mary
Place and 8th St., is also a fine building.

At the other end of Hennepin Ave. are the *City Hall* (Pl. B, 2),
the *Market* (Pl. B, C, 1, 2), and the *Union Depot* (Pl. C, 1). The
bridge at its foot leads to the pleasant *Nicollet Island* (Pl. C, 1). —
Among other prominent buildings in the business-quarter are the
new *Court House* (Pl. C, 3; in progress), 5th St. and Third Ave.;
the **New York Life Insurance Building* (Pl. B, 3), 5th St. and Second Ave., with an elaborate interior (containing a double spiral
staircase inspired by the rood-screen of St. Etienne du Mont in
Paris); the *Bank of Commerce*; the *Globe Building* (Pl. B, 2); and
the *Chamber of Commerce* (Pl. C, 3), 3rd St. and Fourth Ave.

The **Flour Mills** of Minneapolis, perhaps its most characteristic
sight, are congregated on the banks of the Mississippi, near *St. Anthony's Falls* (Pl. D, 2; p. 293); and no one should leave the city
without a visit to them. Previous application will generally secure
admission to any of the larger mills. The 'roller' or Hungarian system is used here to the exclusion of the mill-stone.

Little is now to be seen of the *Falls*, which are 'cribbed, cabined, and
confined' by dams, retaining walls, and a huge wooden 'apron'. Among
the largest mills are those of the *Washburn-Crosby Co.*, on the right bank,
with a capacity of 9500 barrels a day. *The Pillsbury A Mill* (office in the
Guarantee Loan Building), on the left bank, with a capacity of 7000 barrels, is the largest single mill in the world. Comp. p. 293. — The *Grain
Elevators*, with a capacity of 16½ million bushels, are also interesting.
The *Union Elevator* alone has a capacity of 2½ million bushels.

A visit should also be paid to the **Lumber Mills,** the operations
of which are of an extremely interesting nature. Most of them are
on the river, above the town.

The mill of the *Bovey De Laittre Lumber Co.*, 3 M. above the city
(Camden Place electric tramway), is a good specimen of a modern mill,
cutting 25-30 million feet of timber yearly. The logs, each provided with
its owner's mark, are floated down the river and guided as far as possible

into their proper 'booms'. A certain mixture of logs is, however, inevitable; and this is adjusted by a sort of clearing-house arrangement by a class of State officials named 'scalers', who charge the stray logs against the yards they are found in. The logs are drawn up an inclined plane into the mill by an endless chain with large hooks, passed under the 'gangue' saw, and sawn into planks before they are well out of the water. Among the various improvements in machinery, with the object of minimizing the waste of sawdust, are the wonderfully delicate band-saws.

The **University of Minnesota** lies on the left bank of the river, between Eleventh and Eighteenth Avenues, S.E. It possesses various well-equipped buildings (*View from tower of main building) and is attended by about 1000 students (both sexes).

Among the finest residence-streets are *Summit Avenue* (to the S.W.), *Linden Avenue*, and *Harmon Place*.

Minneapolis is adjoined on the S.W. by several little lakes (*Lake Calhoun*, *Lake Harriet*, etc.), in connection with which a fine system of *Parks* and *Boulevards* has been constructed, affording opportunity for numerous pleasant drives. — About 5 M. to the S. (reached by C. M. & St. P. R. R. or by electric cars), in a pretty glen preserved as a town-park, are the graceful *Falls of the Minnehaha, 50 ft. high, immortalized by Longfellow and only wanting a little more water to be one of the most picturesque cascades in the country. The smaller fall below has been nicknamed the *Minnegiggle*. On the opposite side of the creek is the *Minnesota Soldiers' Home* (fine grounds). About 2 M. below the falls is *Fort Snelling* (p. 293). The most delightful resort near Minneapolis or St. Paul is *Lake Minnetonka (920 ft. above the sea), which lies about 10 M. to the S.W. of the former city and is easily reached from either by railway. The lake is singularly irregular in outline, and with a total length of 12-15 M. has a shore-line of perhaps 150 M. It is surrounded with low wooded hills, and affords good boating and fishing. Steamers ply regularly between all the chief points. The most frequented resorts are the **Hotel St. Louis* ($ 3-4), on the S. shore, reached direct by the C. M. & St. P. R. R. and also by the Minn. & St. L. R. R.; the *Hotel Lafayette* ($ 3-5), on the N. shore, reached by the G. N. R. R.; and the *Lake Park Hotel* ($ 3¹/₂). There are also small hotels and boarding-houses at *Excelsior*, *Wayzata* (p. 299; the nearest point to Minneapolis and the starting-place of the lake-steamers), and other points. The *Upper Lake* is wilder and less accessible than the Lower Lake, but has simple hotel and boarding-house accommodation. The *Minnehaha* (see above) flows out of Lake Minnetonka.

FROM MINNEAPOLIS AND ST. PAUL TO SAULT-STE-MARIE, 494 M., *M. St. P., & S. Ste. M. Railway* in 18-19 hrs. (fare $ 16.20; sleeper $ 2.50). — This line runs to the N.W. through *Wisconsin* and *Michigan*. Stations unimportant. — 494 M. *Sault-Ste-Marie*, see p. 298.

52. From St. Paul to Duluth.

152 M. St. Paul & Duluth R. R. in 5-7 hrs. (fare $ 4.30). — Other routes are the *Great Northern* and the *Chicago, St. Paul, Minneapolis, & Omaha Railways*.

St. Paul, see p. 291. The district traversed is comparatively uninteresting and most of the stations are unimportant. At first we traverse fields of Indian corn and afterwards tracts of unreclaimed forest. Soon after leaving St. Paul we pass between (12 M.) *White Bear Lake* (r.) and (13 M.) *Bald Eagle Lake* (l.), two favourite summer-resorts of the citizens of St. Paul (good hotels).

152 M. **Duluth** (610 ft.; *Spalding Hotel*, $ 3-5; *St. Louis*, $ 2-3; *Windsor, Merchants*, $ 2), ambitiously termed the 'Zenith City of the

Unsalted Seas', is finely situated on a bay at the W. end of *Lake Superior*, at the mouth of the *St. Louis River*, and contained 33,115 inhab. in 1890. In 1860 Duluth contained only 70 white inhabitants, and even in 1880 it had only 3470; it owes its rapid increase and its promise of future greatness to its situation at the head of the navigation of the Great Lakes and its extensive railway connections with the rich agricultural states of the West. It possesses a large harbour, entered by a short canal and lined with docks and ware-houses, and carries on a very large trade in grain.

It is estimated that the annual receipts of wheat at Duluth amount to 30 million bushels, and its elevators have a capacity of 12 million bushels. About 2000 vessels enter and clear its harbour annually, bringing coal and taking away flour and iron ore. The lumber trade is also important.

A great part of Duluth is well and substantially built. Among the most prominent buildings are the *Schools*, the *Lyceum Theatre*, the *Board of Trade*, the *Exchange*, and *St. Luke's Hospital*.

The **Boulevard Drive*, on the terrace at the back of the town (an old beach-line of Lake Superior), 4-500 ft. above the lake, affords splendid views of the town and lake.

About 100 M. to the N. of Duluth (reached by the Duluth & Iron Range R. R.) are the extensive iron deposits of the *Vermilion* and *Mesabi Ranges*, which produced about 1,000,000 tons of ore in 1891.

53. From Duluth to Sault-Ste-Marie.

a. By Railway.

410 M. DULUTH, SOUTH SHORE, & ATLANTIC RAILWAY in 17 hrs. (fare $15; sleeper $2.50).

Duluth, see p. 295. We cross a drawbridge, with *St. Louis Bay*, into which the St. Louis flows, to the right, and *Duluth Harbour* to the left, and enter *Wisconsin* (p. 287). 4 M. *West Superior*, with grain-elevators and ship-building yards, including those of the 'whale-back' steel ships, one of which carried its cargo from Duluth to Liverpool in 1891; 8 M. *Superior* (11,983 inhab., incl. W. Superior). Our line runs to the E., a little to the S. of *Lake Superior* (p. 297).

44 M. *Iron River*. 65 M. *Mason* (965 ft.) is the junction of a line to (22 M.) **Ashland** (*Chequamegon*, $3; 9956 inhab.), the shipping-port for the rich hematite Bessemer ore of the *Gogebic Range* (1,200,000 tons yearly). Beyond (98 M.) *Saxon* we pass from Wisconsin to *Michigan* (p. 269). 123 M. *Thomaston. Lake Gogebic* (1330 ft.) lies to the right, 15 M. farther on. 186 M. *Sidnaw*. 209 M. *Nestoria* (1650 ft.) is the junction of a line to (48 M.) *Houghton*, giving access to the valuable copper mines of *Keewenaw*. 217 M. *Michigamme* (1585 ft.), with the lake of that name to the right. The numerous mineral trains we meet bear witness to the richness of the iron-yielding land we are traversing. Our line now descends rapidly to the level of the lake. 240 M. *Ishpeming* (11,197 inhab.) and (243 M.) *Negaunee* (1440 ft.; 6078 inhab.) are two prosperous places, with large iron-mines. Gold is also profitably mined near Ishpeming.

255 M. **Marquette** (650 ft.; *Mesnard Ho.*, $ 2¹/₂-4; *Clifton*, $ 2-2¹/₂), named from Père Marquette, the French missionary and explorer, is a flourishing city of 9093 inhab., situated on *Iron Bay*, on the S. shore of Lake Superior, and forming the chief outlet for the great iron district of Michigan. The huge iron docks and wharves are seen to the left. — The train now commands glimpses of Lake Superior from time to time, but beyond (285 M.) *Au Train* runs more inland, through a heavily timbered region affording no views. 363 M. *Soo Junction*, for a line to (43 M.) *St. Ignace* (p. 273). As we approach Sault-Ste-Marie we skirt the *St. Mary's River* (left), connecting Lake Superior with Lake Huron.

410 M. *Sault-Ste-Marie*, see p. 298.

b. By Steamer.

436 M. STEAMER of the *Lake Michigan & Lake Superior Transportation Co.* or of the *Lake Superior Transit Co.* in two days (fare $ 13, including berth and meals) The steamers usually leave Duluth at 9 p.m. Regulations similar to those mentioned at p. 275. — Comp. *Baedeker's Canada.*

Lake Superior (600 ft. above the sea) is the largest body of fresh water on the globe, being 360 M. long, and 140 M. wide at its widest part, with an area of about 32,000 sq. M. The mean depth is about 900 ft. The lake receives the waters of 200 streams and contains numerous islands, chiefly near its E. and W. ends. Its coast-line (ca. 1500 M.) is irregular and generally rock-bound, some of its cliffs and mountains being very picturesque. The water is clear and very cold even at midsummer. Lake Superior whitefish *(Coregonus clupeiformis)* are excellent, and other varieties of fish are also abundant.

Duluth, see p. 295. The steamer steers towards the E. and early in the morning threads its way among the picturesque *Apostle Islands* (ca. 25 in all), which lie near the coast. The first stop is at —

80 M. (7 hrs.) *Bayfield* (Island View Ho., $ 2¹/₂), a seaside-resort, connected by railway and small steamer with *Ashland* (p. 296). About 50 M. farther on *Porcupine Mt.* (2025 ft.) rises conspicuously, and 20 M. beyond it lies the village of *Ontonagon*. The steamers are saved the long detour round *Keewenaw Point* by passing through *Portage Lake* (20 M. long, ¹/₂-2 M. wide) and the ship-canal in connection with it. The second stop is made here, at —

200 M. (19 hrs.) *Houghton* (Douglass House, $ 2¹/₂), a village of 2062 inhab. in a rich copper district (comp. p. 296). On emerging from the *Portage Entry*, as this passage is named, the steamer crosses *Keewenaw Bay* and steers S. E. by E., passing *Point Abbaye*, the *Huron Islands*, *Big Bay Point*, and *Granite Island*.

280 M. (37 hrs.) **Marquette**, see above.

About 4 hrs. (45 M.) after leaving Marquette the steamer passes *Grand Island* and then, if the weather permits, approaches as near shore as possible to afford a view of what is considered the finest piece of scenery on the trip, the so-called *****Pictured Rocks.**

These rocks are a series of sandstone bluffs, 300 ft. high, extending along the shore of Lake Superior for a distance of 5 M. and worn by frost and storm into the most fantastic and romantic forms. They owe their name to the vivid hues — red, blue, yellow, green, brown, and gray — with which they are stained. Cascades fall over the rocks at intervals. Among the chief points (named from W. to E.) are *Miner's Castle*, *Sail Rock* (like a sloop in full sail), the *Grand Portal*, and the *Chapel*. Those who wish to examine the Pictured Rocks satisfactorily should disembark at Marquette, proceed thence by railway to *Munising*, and there hire a small boat. This is the heart of the Hiawatha country, and Munising occupies the site of the 'Wigwam of Nokomis'.

About 20 M. farther on the steamer passes *Point au Sable* (light-house), 60 M. beyond which it rounds *Whitefish Point* (lighthouse) and steers to the S.W. across *Whitefish Bay* towards the mouth of the *St. Mary's River*. This river or strait, which connects Lake Superior with Lake Huron (comp. p. 276), is about 70 M. long and has several islands and lake-like expansions. In entering it we pass through *Waiska Bay*, with *Point Iroquois* to the right (U. S.) and *Gros Gap* to the left (Canada). The *St. Mary Rapids* are avoided by a ship-canal, adjoining which lies the town of *Sault-Ste-Marie*, generally pronounced 'Soo St. Mary' (see below).

The old *St. Mary's or Soo Ship Canal was constructed by the State of Michigan in 1853-5 and was 1800 yds. long, 100 ft. wide, and 12 ft. deep, with two locks, each 350 ft. long. The present canal, constructed by the U. S. Government, is 2330 yds. long, 108 ft. wide at its narrowest part (the movable dam), and 16 ft. deep. The lock is 515 ft. long, 80 ft. wide, and 39 1/2 ft. deep. It has a lift of 18 ft., can hold two large lake-steamers, and takes 11 min. to fill. Two minutes are required to open or close the lock-gates. The total cost of the canal enlargement was $ 2,150,000 (430,000 *l.*). A new lock now in construction on the site of the two old locks of 1855 will be still larger than the present one, having a length of 800 ft., a breadth of 100 ft., and a depth of 43 1/4 ft. The estimated cost of this new lock and the accompanying enlargement of the canal is $ 4,740,000 (958,000 *l.*). — A *Ship Canal* is now also being constructed on the Canadian side of the river.

The annual tonnage of the vessels passing through the Soo Canal is greater than that passing through the Suez Canal. In 1890 the canal was passed by 10,557 vessels with an aggregate tonnage of 8,454,433 (Suez Canal in the same year, 6,890,096 tons). The value of the freight carried was $ 102,214,848 (20,442,970 *l*).

Sault-Ste-Marie (615 ft.; *Iroquois*, $ 2-3; *Chippewa*, $ 2 1/2-3; *Michigan Exchange*, $ 2 1/2), a thriving little city with 5760 inhab., originated in a French mission established here in 1641. Its position on the Soo Canal and at the convergence of several railways gives it a considerable commercial importance. To the E. lies *Fort Brady*, a U. S. military post. The St. Mary's River is crossed here by the fine bridge of the Canadian Pacific Railway. Frequent steam-ferries cross to the Canadian *Sault-Ste-Marie* (International Hotel), which lags behind its American namesake in size and life.

One of the things to 'do' at the Soo is to shoot the *Rapids* in a canoe guided by an Indian, an exciting but reasonably safe experience (enquire at hotels). There is good trout-fishing above the Rapids and in the neighbouring streams, and the Indians catch whitefish with scoop nets below the Rapids. The island of *Mackinac* (p. 273) is easily reached from the Soo. From Sault-Ste-Marie to *Buffalo* by steamer, see R. 46 e.

54. From St. Paul to Winnipeg.

478 M. GREAT NORTHERN RAILWAY in 20 hrs. (fare $ 14.20, 2nd cl. $ 11.35; Pullman car $3; family tourist-car $1). Through-tickets are issued to points on the Pacific Coast over this route ('Manitoba-Pacific Route') in connection with the *Canadian Pacific Railway* (comp. *Baedeker's Canada*)

Harvest Excursion Trains from St. Paul to points in the Red River Valley are run at reduced rates in summer and autumn for visitors to the wonderful harvesting operations in this great wheat district (comp. p. 300).

St. Paul and (11 M.) *Minneapolis*, see R. 51. Our train now runs to the N.W. through the beautiful *Lake Park District* of Minnesota, thickly sprinkled with lakes (comp. p. 293). From (24 M.) *Wayzata*, at the E. end of *Lake Minnetonka* (see p. 295), a branch-line runs to *Hotel Lafayette* (p. 295) and (7 M.) *Spring Park*. Numerous small stations are passed, in a thriving farming district. 76 M. *Litchfield* (Brightwood, $2), a summer-resort on *Lake Ripley*. — 102 M. *Willmar* is the junction of a line to **Sioux** ('Soo') **Falls** (10,177 inhab.), in *South Dakota* ('Coyote State'), and **Sioux City** (37,806 inhab.), in Iowa. — From (132 M.) *Benson* a line runs to *Watertown* and *Huron*. Other lines diverge to the W. and E. at (197 M.) *Tintah Junction*. At (214 M.) *Breckinridge* we reach the *Red River* (p. 300), which we cross to (215 M.) *Wahpeton* (960 ft.; 1510 inhab.), in *North Dakota* (p. 371), with the Red River Valley University.

Two lines of the G. N. R. ascend the Red River Valley, one on each side of the river. Through-trains generally follow that on the W. bank, which they reach on crossing from (259 M.) *Moorhead* (p. 371) to (260 M.) *Fargo* (900 ft.; p. 371), where the G. N. R. intersects the Northern Pacific R. R. (R. 83). We are here joined by the line running viâ Barnesville (see p. 300). Fine fields of wheat are passed. — 338 M. **Grand Forks** (830 ft.; *Dacotah Hotel*, $ 2¹/₂- 3¹/₂; *Ingalls Ho.*, $2), with 4979 inhab., large lumber mills, and the *State University of North Dakota*, is the junction of the G. N. R. line to Montana described in R. 55. — 416 M. *Neche*, on the 49th parallel of N. lat., is the last station in the United States and (418 M.) *Gretna* is the first station in Canada (custom-house examination). We now run over the tracks of the *Canadian Pacific Railway*, through a district peopled with Scots, French half-breeds, and Mennonites.

478 M. **Winnipeg**, see *Baedeker's Handbook to Canada*.

55. From St. Paul to Everett and Seattle.

1803 M. GREAT NORTHERN RAILWAY to (1777 M.) *Everett* and (1803 M.) *Seattle* in about 3 days (fare $ 70; sleeper $ 13.50). This line, forming a new through-route to the Pacific Ocean, was opened in the beginning of 1893. Through-carriages also run by this route to (1180 M.) *Helena* in 43 hrs. (fare $40; sleeper $8) and to (1254 M.) *Butte* in 46 hrs. (same fares). Free *Colonist Sleeping Cars* are also attached to all through-trains. — *Harvest Trains*, see above.

St. Paul and (11 M.) *Minneapolis*, see p. 291. The train ascends on the E. bank of the *Mississippi*, parallel to a track on the other side used by trains running towards St. Paul. 29 M. *Anoka* (4252 inhab.);

40 M. *Elk River.* — At (75 M.) **St. Cloud** (*Grand Central, West Ho.,*
$2), a city of 7686 inhab., with large granite quarries, the two lines
from St. Paul unite with that from Duluth (p. 295). It is also the
junction of a line to Willmar (p. 299). — Farther on we pass through
a country so thickly sprinkled with lakes that the line has often had
to be led across them on trestles. From (117 M.) *Sauk Centre* a branch-
line runs to the N. to (91 M.) *Park Rapids.* 130 M. *Osakis* (Fair View,
Lake Ho., $2), on the pretty lake of that name, is a favourite resort
of summer-visitors and anglers. 142 M. *Alexandria* (Alexandria,
Geneva Beach Ho., $2), another summer-resort, has good fishing
and shooting. 168 M. *Ashby* (Hotel Kitson, $2½). At (187 M.)
Fergus Falls, with 3772 inhab., the descent of the infant Red River
is used by mills and factories. We now run through the interminable
wheat-fields of the fertile **Red River Valley,** one of the principal
wheat-growing regions of the world, its crop amounting in favourable
years to 30-40 million bushels. Numerous grain-elevators are seen
in all directions. 218 M. *Barnesville* is the junction of the line to
Moorhead and *Fargo* (p. 371). At (300 M.) *Crookston* we cross the
Red Lake River and turn to the left (W.).

At (326 M.) *Grand Forks* (p. 299) we cross the Red River and
the Manitoba-Pacific route (R. 54) and enter *North Dakota* (p. 299),
continuing to traverse a great wheat-country and passing numerous
small stations. — 415 M. *Devil's Lake* (Benham Ho., Cliff Ho., $2)
lies on the N. shore of the large lake of that name, 50 M. long and
2-8 M. wide, with good bathing and fishing (pickerel, etc.). On the
S. shore lie *Fort Totten*, a U. S. military post (reached by steamer),
and the *Cuthead Sioux Indian Reservation.* From (433 M.) *Church's
Ferry* and (472 M.) *Rugby* lines run N. to points in the *Turtle Mts.*
At (491 M.) *Towner* and again at (532 M.) *Minot*, where we change
to 'Mountain' time (p. xviii), we cross the *Mouse River.* At (654 M.)
Williston we reach the *Upper Missouri River*, which flows to the left.
674 M. *Fort Buford*, an important military station, lies on the Missouri, opposite the mouth of the *Yellowstone* (p. 378). A little farther
on we enter *Montana* (p. 372). 739 M. *Poplar*, a military post, with
a large Indian school. Beyond (795 M.) *Nashua* we leave the Missouri and follow the *Milk River*, through a grazing district. 866 M.
Bowdoin; 906 M. *Savoy.* Near (941 M.) *Chinook* the *Bear Paw Mts.*
and the *Little Rockies*, spurs of the Rocky Mts., are seen to the left.

From 960 M. *Pacific Junction* a line runs to the left (S.) to *Great
Falls, Helena,* and *Butte* (see below).

FROM PACIFIC JUNCTION TO (220 M.) HELENA AND (294 M.) BUTTE, *G. N.
Railway* in 8½-12 hrs. — 10 M. *Fort Assinaboine*, amid the foot-hills of the
Bear Paw Mts., is one of the largest and best-equipped military posts in
the United States, and has a garrison of nine companies. — 79 M. *Fort
Benton*, on the *Missouri*, which the line now follows. — 122 M. **Great Falls**
(3200 ft.; *Park Hotel*, $3; *Milwaukee Ho.*, $2) is a brisk and growing little
industrial city of 5000 inhab., with large smelting-works. It derives its
name and importance from the falls formed here by the Missouri, with a
total descent of 500 ft. The river contracts here from a width of upwards
of ½ M. to one of 300 yds. and descends over the *Black Eagle Falls* (50 ft.),

Colters Falls (12 ft.), *Crooked Falls* (20 ft.), *Rainbow Falls* (48 ft.), and *Great Falls* (92 ft.). Near Rainbow Falls is the *Giant Spring Fall*, formed by a spring or river bursting from the bank of the Missouri, 20 ft. above the channel. Branch-lines run S. from Great Falls to (64 M.) *Barker* and (67 M.) *Neihart* (Belt Mts.) and N. to (199 M.) *Lethbridge* (Canada). — About 40 M. beyond Great Falls the train enters the *Prickly Pear Cañon*, threading the *Gate of the Mountains, where the Missouri breaks through the rocky mountain wall. Farther on we leave the river. — 220 M. Helena, see p. 373. — From Helena to (294 M.) Butte, see p. 373. At Butte we make connection with the *Union Pacific Railway* for points to the W. (comp. p. 392).

Beyond Pacific Junction our line runs nearly due W. through a grazing country, with the *Sweet Grass Hills* to the N. 1068 M. *Shelby Junction*, for lines to *Great Falls* (p. 300) and *Lethbridge* (Canada). At (1152 M.) *Summit* (5230 ft.) we cross the *Rocky Mts.*, at an elevation 300-2500 ft. lower than that of any other American railway (comp. pp. 374, 391). The scenery on the W. slope of the Great Divide is imposing. We cross the *Flathead River* near (1213 M.) *Columbia Falls*. 1228 M. *Kalispell*, the chief town of the *Flathead Valley*. Farther on we cross the *Cabinet Mts.* and follow the *Kootenai River*, through a district of gold and silver mines. Near (1308 M.) *Jennings* we enter *Idaho* (p. 375). 1332 M. *Kootenai Falls*. At (1338 M.) *Troy* we pass from 'Mountain' to 'Pacific' time (p. xviii). From (1371 M.) *Bonner's Ferry* steamers ply to the *Kootenai Lake District* of British Columbia (comp. *Baedeker's Canada*). The line now bends to the S. 1405 M. *Sand Point*, on *Lake Pend d'Oreille* (p. 375). Farther on we cross the *Priest River* and *Clark's Fork of the Columbia*.

1479 M. **Spokane**, see p. 375. Beyond Spokane the line runs almost due W. through the *State of Washington* (p. 375), crossing the *Big Bend Wheat Region*. 1508 M. *Edwall;* 1524 M. *Harrington.* At (1640 M.) *Rock Island Rapids* we cross the *Columbia River* (p. 394), which we follow to (1653 M.) *Wenatchee*, whence steamers ply to *Lake Chelan*. The line then follows the *Wenatchee* for 40 M., crosses the *Cascade Mts.* (p. 376), and descends through vast forests to (1769 M.) *Snohomish* and —

1777 M. **Everett** (*Bay View, Everett*, $ 2¹/₂), on *Puget Sound* (p. 470), where we reach tide-water. From this point lines run to the N. to *Fairhaven* (p. 471) and *South Westminster* (British Columbia), and to the S. to —

1803 M. **Seattle** (see p. 470).

56. From Chicago to St. Louis.

a. Viâ Illinois Central R. R.

301 M. RAILWAY in 10¹/₂-11 hrs. (fare $ 7.50; sleeper $ 2).

From Chicago to (56 M.) *Kankakee*, see p. 302. Our line crosses the *Kankakee River* and runs towards the S. At (81 M.) *Gilman* the line forks, one branch leading to (232 M.) *Vandalia* viâ *Gibson City, Clinton, Decatur*, and *Pana*, and the other viâ (103 M.) *Paxton*, (128 M.) *Champaign*, (150 M.) *Tuscola*, (172 M.) *Mattoon*, (199 M.)

Effingham, and (211 M.) *Altamont*. From Vandalia we runs to the S.W., viâ (250 M.) *Greenville*, to (298 M.) *East St. Louis* and —
301 M. **St. Louis** (see p. 311).

b. Viâ Chicago and Alton R. R.

283 M. RAILWAY in 10½-11¼ hrs. (fares as above).

Chicago (Canal St. Depot), see p. 279. The line runs to the S.W. through the prairies of Illinois, passing at first several suburban stations. 33 M. *Lockport* (2449 inhab.); 37 M. *Joliet* (see p. 290); 74 M. *Dwight;* 124 M. *Normal*, with large nurseries. — 126½ M. **Bloomington** (825 ft.; *Windsor*, $ 2½-3), a busy manufacturing town of 20,484 inhab. and an important railway-centre.

185 M. **Springfield** (630 ft.; *Leland Ho.*, $ 2½-3; *St. Nicholas*, $ 2), the capital of Illinois, is a well-built and tree-shaded city of 24,963 inhab. ('Flower City'), the trade and industry of which are promoted by large coal-mines in the vicinity. The *State Capitol* is a large building, with a dome. *Oak Ridge Cemetery*, 2 M. to the N., contains the grave of Abraham Lincoln (1809-65), marked by a handsome monument, erected in 1874 at a cost of $ 200,000 (40,000 *l.*). 210 M. *Girard;* 251 M. *Godfrey*. — 257 M. **Alton** (470 ft.; *Madison*, $ 2½), an industrial city of 10,294 inhab., lies on high ground on the E. bank of the *Mississippi*, 3 M. above the mouth of the Missouri. The train descends along the Mississippi and at (280 M.) *East St. Louis* crosses it by a fine bridge (p. 314).
283 M. **St. Louis**, see R. 61.

57. From Chicago to Cincinnati.

a. Viâ Indianapolis.

306 M. CLEVELAND, CINCINNATI, CHICAGO, & ST. LOUIS RAILWAY (*'Big Four Line'*) in 9-11 hrs. (fare $ 8; sleeper $ 2; reclining-chair $ 1).

Chicago (Illinois Central Station), see p. 279. The train runs along the lake-front in full view of the *World's Fair Buildings* (p. 285), to (10 M.) *Grand Crossing* and then turns to the S. (inland). 34 M. *Monee* (800 ft.), on the watershed between Lake Michigan and the Mississippi; 56 M. *Kankakee* (625 ft.), a railway and industrial centre with 9025 inhab., on the *Kankakee River*. Our line now crosses the *Iroquois River* and runs to the S.E. Beyond (86 M.) *Sheldon* we enter *Indiana*. — 131 M. **Lafayette** (590 ft.; *Lahr Ho.*, $ 2-3), an industrial city of 16,243 inhab., at the head of navigation on the *Wabash River. Purdue College* has 400 students of agriculture, engineering, and other practical branches. The battle-field of *Tippecanoe* (see p. 270) lies about 7 M. to the N.

197 M. **Indianapolis.** — HOTELS. *Bates Ho.*, $ 3-5; *Denison*, $ 2½-6; *Grand*, $ 2½-5; *Spencer*, $ 2-2½. — *Tramway Cars* (5 c.) traverse the chief streets. — *Post Office*, cor. Pennsylvania St. and Market St.

Indianapolis (700 ft.), the capital and largest city of Indiana, with (1890) 105,436 inhab., lies on the W. branch of the *White*

River, in the midst of a wide plain. It is a great railway-centre, carries on an extensive trade in grain and live-stock, and produces manufactures to the value of 33 million dollars (6,600,000 *l.*) annually.

The *State Capitol* is a large building with a central tower and dome, erected at a cost of $2,000,000. The *Court House* is also an imposing edifice. In *Circle Park*, to the E. of the Capitol, is the *Soldiers' Monument*, 265 ft. high. Other large and important buildings are the *Blind Asylum*, a little to the N. of the Capitol; the *United States Arsenal*, on a hill to the E. of the city; the *Deaf & Dumb Asylum*, also to the E.; the *Propylaeum, a unique building, owned and controlled by a stock-company of women for literary purposes; the *Union Depot;* the *Classical School for Girls;* the new *City Library;* and several *Churches*. The *State Lunatic Asylum* lies $1^1/_2$ M. to the W. of the city. A visit may be paid to *Crown Hill*, 2 M. to the N., and to some of the large *Manufactories* (iron, terracotta pork-packers) and the *Stockyards* (to the S.W., beyond the river).

Beyond Indianapolis the train continues to run towards the S. E. 242 M. *Greensburg*. At (283 M.) *Lawrenceburg Junction* we reach the *Ohio*, which we follow to the E. to —

306 M. **Cincinnati** *(Central Union Station;* see p. 307).

b. Viâ Logansport.

293 M. PITTSBURG, CINCINNATI, CHICAGO, & ST. LOUIS RAILWAY in $9^1/_4$-11 hrs. (fares as above).

From *Chicago* to (117 M.) *Logansport*, see R. 44 b. At (122 M.) *Anoka Junction* the Cincinnati line diverges to the right from that to Columbus and Pittsburg (see p. 310). 175 M. *Anderson*. 224 M. *Richmond* (Arlington Ho., $2), with 16,608 inhab., is the entrepot of a rich agricultural district. At (240 M.) *Eaton* we turn nearly due S. 267 M. *Hamilton*, an industrial town with 17,565 inhab., on the *Miami*.

298 M. **Cincinnati** *(Pan Handle Depot)*, see p. 307.

58. From New York to Cincinnati.

a. Viâ Pennsylvania Railroad.

757 M. RAILWAY in 23-33 hrs. (fare $21.50; Pullman car $5). Through-carriages.

From New York to (90 M.) *Philadelphia*, see R. 31 a; from Philadelphia to (444 M.) *Pittsburg*, see R. 37; from Pittsburg to (637 M.) *Columbus*, see R. 44 b.

At Columbus our line diverges to the left (S.) from that to Chicago (comp. p. 264).— 692 M. **Xenia** (920 ft.; *Bradley*, $2-2$^1/_2$), a city of 7301 inhab., with paper-mills and twine manufactures, *Wilberforce University* (for coloured students), a large *Orphan's Home*, and other well-known educational and charitable institutions.

757 M. **Cincinnati**, see R. 59.

b. Viâ Chesapeake & Ohio Railroad.

844 M. Railway in 24-25 hrs. (fare $ 21.25; sleeper $4). The F.F.V. (Fast Flying Virginian) Vestibule Limited Train on this route leaves New York at 5 p.m. (no extra charge).

From New York to (90 M.) *Philadelphia* (Pennsylvania R. R.), see p. 208; thence to (186 M.) *Baltimore* (Penna. R. R.), see p. 244; thence to (246 M.) *Washington* (Baltimore & Potomac R.R.), see p. 251. From Washington the line follows the tracks of the Richmond & Danville R. R. (see R. 70) to (331 M.) *Orange.*

At (340 M.) *Gordonsville* (500 ft.) we are joined by the line from Richmond and Old Point Comfort.

359 M. **Charlottesville** (450 ft.; *Parrott's*, *Wright's*, $ 2-2¹/₂; *Rail. Restaurant*), a town of 5591 inhab., on *Moore's Creek*, is of interest as the home of Jefferson and the site of the University of Virginia.

The **University of Virginia**, founded in 1819, mainly through the exertions of Thomas Jefferson, lies 1¹/₂ M. to the W. of the town (street-car 5 c.) and is attended by 4-500 students. The original buildings erected from Jefferson's designs and under his supervision consist mainly of parallel ranges of one-story dormitories, the inner rows bordering a tree-shaded campus, at one end of which stands the *Rotunda* (view from roof). The new buildings include the *Lewis Brooks Museum of Natural History* (8-6; with a facsimile of the mammoth) and a good *Observatory.*

Monticello, the home of *Thomas Jefferson* (1743-1826), is finely situated on a view-commanding hill, 2¹/₂ M. to the S.E. of Charlottesville, and is an interesting example of the architecture of the period (visitors not admitted to the interior; adm. to grounds 25 c.). The great statesman is buried in a small private graveyard adjoining the road leading to the house.

A visit may be paid to the interesting cellars of the *Monticello Wine Co.*, where various good wines are produced from the grapes of the vicinity.

From Charlottesville to *Lynchburg* and the South, see R. 70 a.

Our line now runs towards the W. and begins to ascend among the *Blue Ridge Mts.* 384 M. *Afton* (1405 ft.; Afton Ho., $ 2), pleasantly situated near the top of the ridge (tunnel) and affording fine views of the *Piedmont Valley.* At (387 M.) *Basic City* (Brandon, $ 2¹/₂-4) we cross the Norfolk & Western R. R. (see p. 339). 380 M. *Staunton* (1385 ft.; Virginia Ho., $ 2¹/₂), an industrial town with 6975 inhab. and several large educational institutions, lies on the plateau between the Blue Ridge and the Allegheny Mts. It is the junction of a line to (36 M.) *Lexington.* — *North Mt.* (2075 ft.) rises to the right near (408 M.) *Swoope's* (1645 ft.). 432 M. *Goshen* (1410 ft.) is the junction of a branch-line to the (9 M.) *Rockbridge Alum Springs* (2000 ft.; Grand, Brooke, Central, $ 2-3). — 440 M. *Millboro* (1680 ft.) is the station for *Millboro Springs*, *Bath Alum Springs*, etc. — 457 M. *Clifton Forge* (1050 ft.; Rail. Restaurant), on the *Jackson River*, is the junction of the James River Branch of the C. & O. R. R. We now change from Eastern to Central time. — From (469 M.) *Covington* (1425 ft.) a new branch-line runs to *Healing*, *Hot*, and (23 M.) *Warm Springs.*

These thermal springs, situated in a mountain-girt valley 2000-2500 ft. above sea-level, are used both for drinking and bathing and are efficacious in gout, rheumatism, liver and cutaneous complaints, dyspepsia, scrofula, etc. All are provided with ample hotel and cottage accommodation, the transient rates being about $ 2-3 a day (cheaper by the week or longer). The Hot Springs have a temperature of 78-110° Fahr., the Warm Springs of 98°, and the Healing Springs of 84°. The scenery in the neighbourhood is picturesque, and numerous pleasant excursions can be made.

At (486 M.) *Allegheny* (2070 ft.), on the crest of the *Allegheny Mts.,* we thread a tunnel 1600 yds. long. Coaches run hence to (9 M.) *Sweet Chalybeate Springs* and (10 M.) *Sweet Springs* (2000 ft.; Hotel, $ 2$^1/_2$), one of the oldest and most popular of Virginian resorts (water good for dyspepsia, dysentery, etc.).

491 M. **White Sulphur Springs** (1920 ft.; **Grand Central Hotel*, $ 3-4 per day, $ 21 per week, $ 75 per month; numerous boarding-houses and cottages), the largest and most fashionable of the Virginian spas, is finely situated in the heart of the Alleghenies and is visited annually by thousands of guests.

For nearly a century the Greenbrier White Sulphur Springs have been the typical resort of the wealth and aristocracy of the South; and the pictures of Southern life, beauty, and fashion still seen here will be found of great interest by the European or Northern visitor.

The temperature of the water is 62° and its chief ingredients are nitrogen, oxygen, carbonic acid, hydro-sulphuric acid, sulphates of lime and magnesia, and carbonate of lime. It is used both internally and externally, and is efficacious in dyspepsia, liver complaints, nervous affections, gout, rheumatism, skin diseases, asthma, etc. Mud baths are also used. The spring yields 30 gallons per minute. Large swimming-baths.

Among the most prominent of the mountains enclosing the valley are *Kate's Mt.* (3500 ft.), 1 M. to the S.; *Greenbrier* (3500 ft.), 1 M. to the W., and the *White Rock*, 3 M. to the S.W.

The train now descends the valley of the *Greenbrier*. Coaches run from (508 M.) *Fort Spring* (1625 ft.; Inn) to (14 M.) *Salt Sulphur Springs* (Hotel, $ 2$^1/_2$), and from (525 M.) *Lowell* (1510 ft.) to (20 M.) *Red Sulphur Springs* (Hotel), resembling the Eaux Bonnes of the Pyrenees (54° Fahr.). Beyond (537 M.) *Hinton* (1375 ft.) we follow the *New River*, with its romantic falls. 558 M. *Quinnimont* (1195 ft.); 588 M. *Hawk's Nest* (830 ft.; Hotel), opposite a huge cliff 1200 ft. high; 597 M. *Kanawha Falls* (670 ft.), with a pretty waterfall on the *Kanawha River*, formed by the confluence (2 M. above) of the New River and the *Gauley*.

The train now leaves the picturesque scenery and reaches a more open district. Numerous coal-mines. To the right flows the Kanawha. 623 M. **Charleston** (600 ft.; *St. Albert*, $ 2), the capital of West Virginia, a city of 2287 inhab., with a new *State House*. At (678 M.) *Guyandotte* (560 ft.) we reach the *Ohio River*. 683 M. *Huntington* (Rail. Restaurant). At (693 M.) *Catlettsburg* (545 ft.) we cross the *Big Sandy* and enter *Kentucky* (the 'Blue Grass State'). The train now follows the left bank of the Ohio all the way to Cincinnati. 703 M. *Ironton* (10,930 inhab.), on the Ohio (right) bank of the river; 781 M. *Maysville;* 789 M. *South Ripley;* 843 M. *Covington* (p. 304). The train now crosses the Ohio to —

844 M. **Cincinnati** (*Central Union Station;* see p. 307).

c. Viâ Cleveland.

866 M. Railway in 24-30 hrs. (fare $21.25; sleeper $5). *N. Y. C. R. R.*
to (440 M.) *Buffalo; Lake Shore R. R.* thence to (623 M.) *Cleveland;* and
Cleveland, Cincinnati, Chicago, & St. Louis Ry. thence to (866 M.) *Cincinnati.*
Buffalo may also be reached by the routes mentioned at pp. 195, 198.
Through sleeping-cars on the express trains.

From New York to (440 M.) *Buffalo,* see R. 28a; from Buffalo
to (623 M.) *Cleveland,* see R. 46a.

From Cleveland the railway runs towards the S.W. Neither the
country traversed nor the stations passed are of special interest.
698 M. *Crestline* (p.263); 703 M. *Galion* (p.306); 737 M. *Delaware*
(925 ft.). — 761 M. **Columbus,** see p. 264. — 808 M. **Springfield**
(990 ft.; *Arcade,* $2¹/₂), a manufacturing city (agricultural machin-
ery, etc.) of 31,895 inhab., with fine water-power furnished by the
Lagonda Creek and *Mad River.* It has a large trade in farm products.

810 M. **Dayton** (745 ft.; *Beckel Ho.,* $2¹/₂-3), a city of 61,220
inhab., lies at the confluence of the *Mad River* with the *Great Miami*
and manufactures machinery, flour, paper, etc., to the value (1890)
of $22,500,000. On a hill 2 M. to the W. is the *Central National
Soldiers' Home,* with 5000 inmates.

866 M. **Cincinnati,** see p. 307.

d. Viâ Baltimore & Ohio Railroad.

780 M. B. & O. Railroad in 25 hrs. (fare $21.50; sleeper $5).

From New York to (226 M.) *Washington,* see R. 42b; thence to
(480 M.) *Grafton,* see R. 45.

From Grafton the line runs to the W. through a somewhat uninteresting district, with petroleum wells and coal-mines. 502 M.
Clarksburg, on the *Monongahela.* 584 M. *Parkersburg* (615 ft.; Blen-
nerhassett, $2¹/₂), a petroleum-trading city, with 8408 inhab., at
the confluence of the *Kanawha* and *Ohio.* The train crosses the
latter river by a fine bridge and enters *Ohio.* We now pass from
Eastern to Central time (p. xviii). 585 M. *Belpré.* — 621 M. *Athens*
(655 ft.), on the *Hocking,* with 2620 inhab. and *Ohio University.* In
the neighbourhood are several Indian mounds. — 681 M. *Chillicothe*
(635 ft.), a city of 11,288 inhab., with considerable manufactures,
is the centre of a rich agricultural district. 738 M. *Blanchester.*

780 M. **Cincinnati** *(Central Union Station),* see p. 307.

e. Viâ Erie Railway.

862 M. Railway in 26-33 hrs. (fare $21-25; sleeper $5). Through-cars.

From New York to (718 M.) *Marion Junction,* see R. 47e. From
this point the line follows much the same route as the C. C. C. &
St. L. Railway (R. 58c). 767 M. *Urbana* (1030 ft.), an industrial
city with 6510 inhab. and a Swedenborgian College. 782 M. *Springfield* (see above); 803 M. *Dayton* (see above); 837 M. *Hamilton* (p. 303).

862 M. **Cincinnati,** see p. 307.

59. Cincinnati.

Railway Stations. *Central Union Station* (Pl. D, 5), Central Ave. & 3rd St., used by the C. C. C. & St. L., the B. & O., Kentucky Central, and other lines; *Pan Handle Depot* (Pl. F, 4), Pearl & Butler Sts., for the Pennsylvania lines, etc.; *Cincinnati, Hamilton, & Dayton Depot* (Pl. C, 4, 5), 6th St.; *Chesapeake & Ohio Station* (Pl. D, 5), 4th St., near Smith St.; *Cincinnati, Lebanon, & Northern* (Pl. E, 3), Court St. and Broadway. — *Omnibuses* and *Cabs* meet the principal trains (to the hotels, 50 c. each).

Hotels. GRAND HOTEL (Pl. a; D, 4, 5), Central Ave., cor. 4th St., $2¹/₂-5, R. from $1; *ST. NICHOLAS (Pl. b; D, 4), Race St., cor. 4th St., R. from $1¹/₂; ST. CLAIR (Pl. c; C, 4), Mound St., cor. 6th St., $3-4; BURNET HO. (Pl. d; D, 4), Vine St., cor. 3rd St., $3-5; GIBSON HO. (Pl. e; D, E, 4), Walnut St., near 4th St., $3-4; EMERY (Pl. f; D, 4), $3-4, R. from $1; PALACE (Pl. g; D, 4), $2-2¹/₂; THE STAG, 170 Vine St. (for men), R. from 75c.

Restaurants. *St. Nicholas Hotel*, see above; *Hotel Emery*, see above (moderate prices); *Brock*, Mound St.; *Hunt*, 5th St.; *Women's Exchange*, cor. Race & George St.; *Glencairn*, in the Chamber of Commerce (luncheons); *Vienna Bakery*, Race St., cor. 7th St. (cheap). — *Beer Gardens*, in the German style (concerts in summer), on the hills round the city, at the top of the inclined planes (see below).

Tramways (electric, cable, and horse) traverse all the chief streets and cross to *Covington* and *Newport* (p. 309). — Cabs: per drive, each pers. 25-50 c.; with two horses, 1-2 pers. $1, each addit. pers. 50 c.; per hr. $2, each addit. hr. $1¹/₂; heavy luggage extra. — **Ferries** to *Covington* from the foot of Central Ave.; to *Ludlow*, from foot of 5th St. — **Four Inclined Planes** (similar to those at Pittsburg, p. 240) ascend to the tops of the surrounding hills (fare 5c.): (1). *Mount Adams & Eden Park* (Pl. E, 4); (2). *Mt. Auburn* (Pl. D, 2, 3); (3). *Cincinnati & Clifton* (Pl. D, 2); (4). *Price's Hill* (Pl. A, 4). Comp. pp. 308, 309. — **Steamers** ply to the chief ports on the Ohio and Mississippi.

Theatres. *Grand Opera Ho.* (Pl. D, 4), Vine St.; *Walnut St. Theatre*, Walnut St., between 6th and 7th Sts.; *Robinson's Opera Ho.* (Pl. D, 4), cor. Plum & 9th Sts.; *Heuck's* (Pl. D, 3), 437 Vine St.; *Vine St. Opera Ho.*; *Havlin's Theatre; Fountain Square Theatre*, Lodge Str., adjoining Fountain Sq. Some of these are open on Sunday. — *Zoological Gardens*, see p. 309.

Post Office (Pl. E, 4), 5th St. (6 a.m.-10 p.m.).

Cincinnati (430-550 ft. above the sea), the chief city of Ohio, the ninth in the United States, and one of the most important manufacturing and commercial centres of the Middle West, is finely situated on two terraces rising from the right (N.) bank of the Ohio and is surrounded by an amphitheatre of hills 400-500 ft. high. It has a frontage of 10-12 M. on the river. The main portion of the city is regularly laid out and its streets are well paved. The best residential quarters are on the surrounding highlands. In 1890 Cincinnati contained 296,908 inhab., of whom about a third were of German origin. These Germans reside mainly to the N. of the *Miami Canal*, and their district is known as 'Over the Rhine'. On the opposite bank of the Ohio, in Kentucky, lie the cities of *Covington* and *Newport* (p. 309), connected with Cincinnati by five fine bridges.

Cincinnati was settled in 1788 and named in honour of the Society of the Cincinnati (officers of the Army of the Revolution). Mounds containing relics seem to indicate that part of the site was occupied in prehistoric times. By the beginning of this cent. it contained about 7-800 inhab., and in 1814 it received its city charter. Its growth dates mainly from the construction of the Miami Canal (1830) and the advent of the railway system (1840). In 1850 it contained 115,436 inhab., in 1870 it had 216,239. and in 1880 it had 255,708.

Industry and Trade. The value of Cincinnati's manufactures in 1890 was $ 181,500,000 (36,300,000*l.*), produced by 92,000 hands. The staple articles include iron, machinery, carriages, boots and shoes, school-books, clothing, harness, furniture, pottery, beer, and whiskey. Pork-packing is also extensively carried on. Its trade, carried on by river and rail, is also very important.

*Fountain Square (Pl. D, E, 4), an expansion of *5th Street*, may, perhaps, be called the business-centre of the city and from it start many of the tramway-lines. In the middle of the square stands the *Tyler-Davidson Fountain, one of the most successful works of art in the United States, erected in 1871. It was designed by *August von 'Kreling* and cast at the Royal Bronze Foundry at Munich. To the N., at the corner of 5th St. and Walnut St., is the U. S. Government Building (Pl. E, 4), accommodating the *Post Office, Custom House*, and *U. S. Law Courts*.

By following 5th St. to the W. and turning to the left down Vine St. we pass the entrance to the *Emery Arcade* (Pl. D, 4) and reach, at the corner of the busy *4th Street*, the *Chamber of Commerce (Pl. D, 4), designed by *H. H. Richardson* (p. xci) and perhaps the finest building in the city.

Following 4th St. towards the W., we soon reach *Plum Street* (Pl.D, 4, 5),which we may follow to the right(N.) to **St.Paul's Church* (Pl. D, 4; Epis.), at the corner of 7th St.; the *R. C. Cathedral of St. Peter* (Pl. D, 4), at the corner of 8th St. (with a Murillo and other pictures); and the *Hebrew Temple* (Pl. D, 4), opposite the last. In 8th St., a little to the S., is the new *City Hall (Pl. D, 4), a large and handsome red building in a Romanesque style, with a lofty tower (*View). A little to the E., in Vine St., between 6th & 7th Sts., is the *Public Library* (Pl. D, 4 ; 190,000 vols.).

To the N. of this point, 'over the Rhine' (see p. 307), is Washington Square (Pl. D, 3), with the *Springer Music Hall* and the *Exposition Building*.

Among other buildings may be mentioned the *County Court House* (Pl. E, 4), the *University of Cincinnati* (Pl. D, 2; 120 students), *St. Xavier's College* (Pl. E, 4), the *Oddfellows' Hall*, the *Cincinnati Hospital* (Pl. D, 3, 4), and the huge *Workhouse* (Colerain Road).

The chief park of Cincinnati is **Eden Park** (Pl. E, F, 2, 3), 216 acres in extent, which lies on the hills to E. and affords fine views of the city and river (band on Sun.). It contains the Art Museum (see p. 309) and the main reservoir of the *City Water-works*.

We may reach the park by the light-green electric cars from Fountain Sq., which are elevated bodily by the inclined plane railway at *Highland House* (Pl. E, 3, 4; *View) and run through the park, past the door of the Art Museum (through-fare 5 c.) [Near the head of the inclined is the *Rookwood Pottery* (see p. 309; visitors admitted).] Or we may take the Walnut Hills cable-car to the Eden Park Entrance, 5 min. from the Art Museum. [*Elsinore*, a towered gateway standing in a curiously isolated position, a

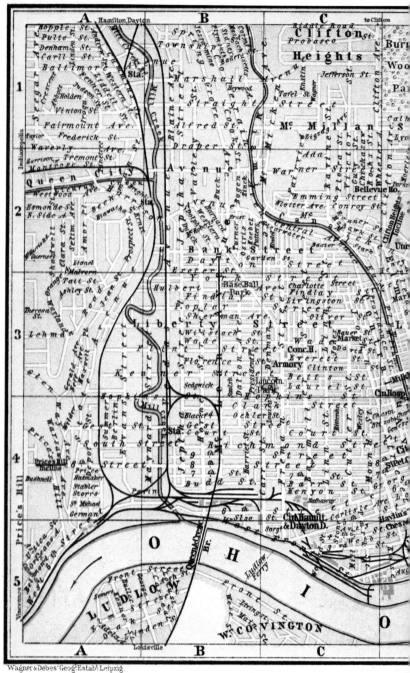

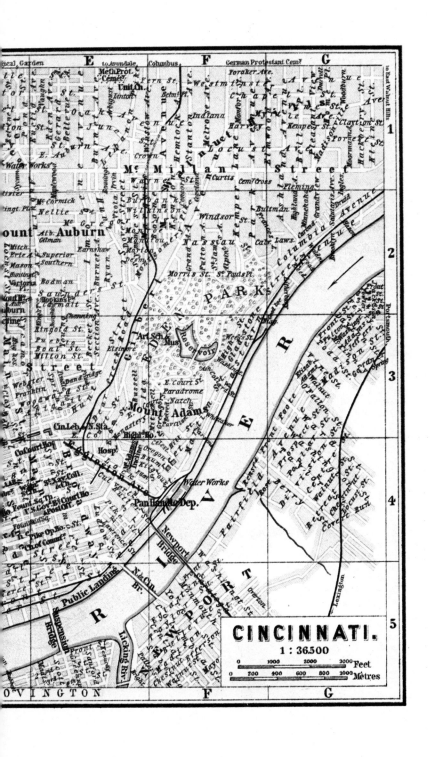

CINCINNATI.

1 : 36.500

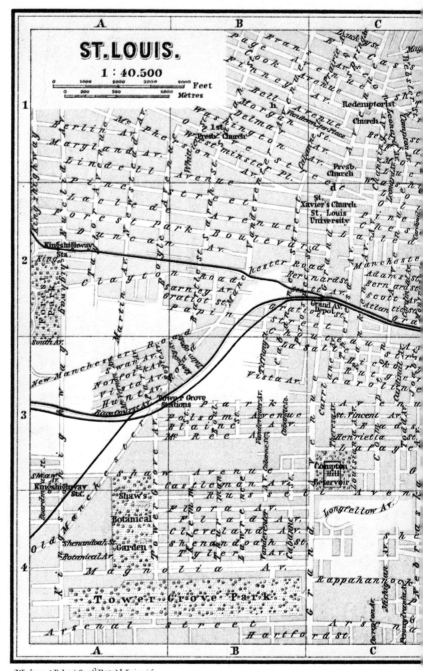

ST. LOUIS.

1 : 40.500

Wagner & Debes' Geogl Establ Leipzig.

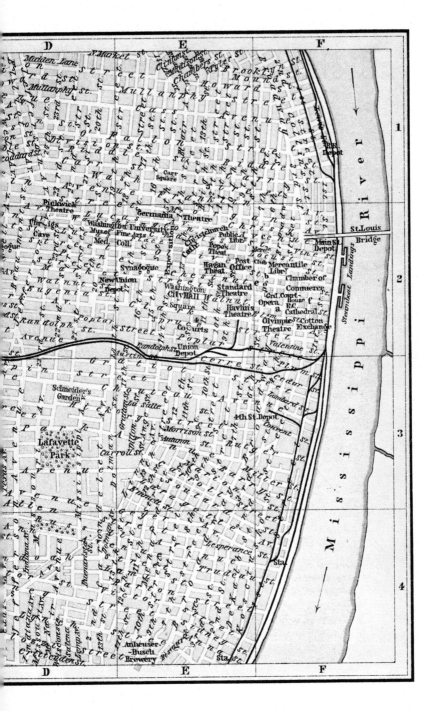

little farther down Gilbert Ave., on this route, was erected by the City Water-Works.]

The **Art Museum** (Pl. F, 3), a handsome building of rusticated masonry with a red-tiled roof, is open daily, 9-5 (Sun. 1-5; adm. 25 c., Sun. & Thurs. 10 c.; catalogues 10 c.). Adjacent is the *Art Academy* (400 students). Both are maintained by a private corporation.

The collections include *Paintings, Sculptures, Engravings, Etchings, Metal Work, Textile Fabrics, Pottery, American Ethnology and Archaeology,* etc. Among the pictures, on the upper floor, are specimens of Bol, Calame, Haydon, Lessing, Maratta, Rubens (No. 93) Tiepolo (105), Tintoretto (106), and modern French, German, and American masters. The art of *Wood-Carving* has been successfully revived at Cincinnati, and the specimens of this are worth attention. *Rookwood Pottery* (p. 308), another art-product of Cincinnati, is also well represented in the museum. The **Bookwalter Loan Collection* affords good illustrations of Oriental art.

One of the best views of Cincinnati is obtained from the *Lookout House,* the beer-garden at the top of the *Mt. Auburn Inclined Railway* (Pl. D, 2).

From the *Bellevue House,* at the top of the *Clifton Heights Inclined Railway* (Pl. D, 2), we may go by electric car to the *Burnet Woods Park* (Pl. D, 1), a new pleasure-ground. A good view is also obtained from the top of the *Price's Hill Inclined Plane* (Pl. A, 4). — The **Spring Grove Cemetery,* 5 M. to the N.W., is picturesque and contains some interesting monuments. — The **Zoological Garden** (Pl. D, 1; adm. 25 c.; open daily, Sun. included), reached by electric tramway along Main St., contains a fine collection of animals and is a favourite resort (restaurant).

The **Suspension Bridge** (Pl. E, 5), connecting Cincinnati with Covington, constructed by Roebling (p. 30) at a cost of $1,800,000, is 2250 ft. long (including the approaches; between the towers 1057 ft.), 36 ft. wide, and 103 ft. above low-water mark (toll 3 c.). The planks in the side-walks are uncomfortably laid an inch or so apart. The new **Newport Bridge* is also a handsome structure ; and there are besides four *Railway Bridges.* The *Levee* or *Public Landing* (Pl. E, 5, 4), below the Newport Bridge, 1000 ft. long, usually presents a busy and animated sight.

Covington (37,371 inhab.) and *Newport* (24,918 inhab.) are two uninteresting cities in Kentucky, which need not detain the stranger. They are separated from each other by the *Licking River* (crossed by a suspension bridge) and contain the residences of many Cincinnati merchants.

Pleasant drives may be taken to the *Walnut Hills, Avondale, Mt. Auburn, Clifton, Spring Grove, Price's Hill,* and *Fort Thomas,* in the highlands behind Newport (fine views of the river and city).

Cincinnati will probably be the most convenient point from which the scientific traveller can visit the famous **Serpent Mound**. This is situated on the bank of *Brush Creek,* in Adams County, Ohio, and the nearest railway-station is *Peebles,* 71 M. to the E. of Cincinnati, by the *Cincinnati, Portsmouth, & Virginia R. R.* (station at cor. of Court St. and Broadway). The mound, which is 7 M. from Peebles (omn. or carr.), is in the form of a serpent, 1000 ft. long and 5 ft. high, and is 30 ft. wide at the base. The tail ends in a triple coil, and the mouth is open, as if to swallow an oval mound which rests partly between the distended jaws. This oval is 4 ft. high, with diameters of 109 and 39 ft. The combined figure has been supposed to represent the Oriental cosmological idea of the serpent and the egg.

From Cincinnati to *Chicago,* see R. 57; to *St. Louis,* see R. 60 d; to *Louisville, Chattanooga,* and *New Orleans,* see R. 63.

60. From New York to St. Louis.

a. Viâ Cleveland and Indianapolis.

1171 M. Railway in 35-45 hrs. (fare $ 22.50; through-sleeper $ 5)·
N. Y. C. R. R. from New York to (623 M.) *Cleveland* and C. C. C. & St.
L. R. R. thence to (1171 M.) *St. Louis.*

From New York to (440 M.) *Buffalo*, see R. 28a; thence to (623 M.)
Cleveland, see R. 46 a; thence to (703 M.) *Galion*, see p. 306.
At Galion our line diverges to the right from that to Cincinnati
(see p. 306). 724 M. *Marion;* 764 M. *Bellefontaine* (1215 ft.);
804¹/₂ M. *Versailles;* 821¹/₂ M. *Union City* (1110 ft.), partly in Ohio
and partly in Indiana; 870 M. *Anderson.*
906 M. **Indianapolis** *(Rail. Restaurant),* see R. 57 a.
Beyond Indianapolis the train runs to the S. W. through Indiana.
945 M. *Greencastle* (780 ft.), with 4390 inhab. and a Methodist
University. — 978 M. **Terre Haute** (490 ft.; *Terre Haute Ho.*,
$ 2¹/₂-4), a busy commercial and industrial city of 30,217 inhab., on
the *Wabash River*, with some fine buildings and several educational
institutions. It is an important railway-centre, and steamers descend
the Wabash hence to Vincennes (p. 311). — The train now crosses
the Wabash and enters *Illinois.* 1035 M. *Mattoon* (p. 301); 1075 M.
Pana (p. 301); 1115 M. *Litchfield* (685 ft.). From (1153 M.) *Alton*
(470 ft.) the line runs to the S. along the fertile valley of the Mississippi. At (1168 M.) *East St. Louis* we cross the Eads Bridge (p. 314).
1171 M. **St. Louis**, see p. 311.

b. Viâ Philadelphia and Pittsburg.

1058 M. Railway (*Pennsylvania Lines*) in 32-36 hrs. ($ 31.30; sleeper $ 5).

From New York to (692 M.) *Xenia*, see R. 58 a. The St. Louis
line here holds on towards the W., while the Cincinnati line (see
p. 303) diverges to the left. 708 M. *Dayton* (see p. 306); 750 M.
Richmond (p. 303). 818 M. **Indianapolis** (p. 302). The 'Vandalia
Line', which we now follow, takes nearly the same course as the
line above described. 856 M. *Greencastle;* 890 M. *Terre Haute*
(see above); 958 M. *Effingham*, and thence to —
1058 M. **St. Louis**, see p. 302.

c. Viâ Wabash Railroad.

1172 M. Railway in 37-45 hrs. (fare $29.05). *N. Y. C. R. R.* to (440 M.
Buffalo; Michigan Central R. R. thence to (736 M.) *Toledo; Wabash R. R.*
thence to (1172 M.) *St. Louis.*

From New York to (440 M.) *Buffalo*, see R. 28 a; thence to (736 M.)
Toledo, see R. 46 a.
From Toledo the train runs towards the S.W., touching the
Maumee River at (772 M.) *Napoleon* (680 ft.) and crossing it at (786 M.)
Defiance (700 ft.). Beyond (807 M.) *Antwerp* we enter *Indiana.* At
(830 M.) *Fort Wayne* (see p. 270) we intersect the Pennsylvania R. R.
route from New York and Philadelphia to Chicago. 873 M. *Wabash*

(740ft.); 887 M. *Peru* (685 ft.); 903 M. *Logansport* (p 264); 940 M.
Lafayette (p. 302). At (961 M.) *Attica* we cross the *Wabash* and at
(978 M.) *State Line* we enter *Illinois.* 1060 M. *Decatur* (p. 278);
1120 M. *Litchfield* (p. 310); 1169 M. *East St. Louis.*

1172 M. **St. Louis,** see below.

d. Viâ Cincinnati.

1120 M. Baltimore & Ohio R. R. in 33-38 hrs. (fare $ 31.30; sleeper $ 5).

From New York to (779 M.) *Cincinnati*, see R. 58 d. Beyond
Cincinnati the train *(Ohio & Mississippi R. R.)* follows the N. (right)
bank of the *Ohio* for some distance, crossing the *Great Miami* and
entering *Indiana* beyond (794 M.) *North Bend.* At (805 M.) *Aurora*
(490 ft.) it leaves the river. — 852 M. *North Vernon* (725 ft.) is the
junction of a branch-line to (54 M.) *Louisville* (p. 315). At (929 M.)
Shoals we cross the S. fork of the *White River*, and beyond (952 M.)
Washington we cross the N. fork of the same river. 971 M. *Vincennes*,
a city with 8853 inhab., on the E. bank of the *Wabash* (steamers
to Terre Haute, see p. 310). We here cross the Wabash and enter *Illinois.* 1055 M. *Odin;* 1117 M. *East St. Louis.*

1120 M. **St. Louis,** see below.

61. St. Louis.

Arrival. The *Union Depot* (Pl. E, 2, 3), used by all except a few suburban trains, is in Poplar St., between 10th and 12th Sts., where hacks
(see below) and hotel-omnibuses (50 c.) are in waiting. A huge and much-
needed new Union Depot is in progress (Pl. D, 2). All trains from the
E. stop at the *Main St. Station* (Pl. F. 2), at the St. Louis end of the Eads
Bridge (p. 314); and this, being nearer the centre of the city, is convenient for travellers without luggage. — The *Steamboat Landings* (Pl. F, 2)
are near the Eads Bridge.

Hotels. Planters (Pl. b; F, 2), 4th St., between Chestnut & Pine
Sts., recently rebuilt, $ 2¹/₂-4¹/₂; Southern (Pl. a; F, 2), a huge caravan-
serai bounded by Walnut, Elm, 4th Sts., and Broadway, $ 3-5; Lindell
(Pl. c; F, 2), cor. Washington Ave. & 6th St., $ 2¹/₂-4¹/₂; *Hotel Beers
(Pl. d; C, 1), pleasantly situated in Olive St., cor. Grand Ave., a little
distant from the centre of the city, $ 3-5; *West End (Pl. h; B, 1), Van-
deventer Ave., R. from $ 1; Laclede (Pl. e; F, 2), Chestnut & 6th Sts.,
$ 2-3¹/₂; Barnum (Pl. f; F, 2), cor. Washington Ave. and 6th Sts.; Hurst
(Pl. g; F, 2), Chestnut St. and Broadway, R. from $ 1. — Accommodation
is difficult to procure at the time of the Fair (p. 312) and should be secured in advance. Application may be made to the *Hotel & Boarding Bureau.*

Restaurants. *Faust*, cor. Elm St. and Broadway; *Moser*, 811 Pine St.;
Delmonico, Lindell Boulevard, entr. of Forest Park; *Luncheon Rooms* of
the *Delicatessen Co.* in Olive St. (S. side, betw. 7th and 8th St.), 4th St.,
Lucas Pl., cor. 19th St. (near Museum), etc. *Schneider's* (Pl. D, 3) and other
Beer Gardens in the German style (concerts in summer).

Tramways (horse, electric, and cable) traverse the city in all directions and cross to East St. Louis (fare 5 c.). — **Carriages** (1-4 pers.) 1 M.
$ 1, per hr. $ 2, each additional hr. $ 1¹/₂. **Hansom Cabs** (1-2 pers.), 1 M.
25 c., each addit. ¹/₂ M. 15 c., per hr. 75 c. (beyond the three-mile limits
$ 1), each addit. ¹/₄ hr. 20 c., each article of baggage carried outside 10 c. —
Ferries to *East St. Louis* from foot of Market St., Carr St., and Spruce
St. — **Steamers** ply to points on the Mississippi, Missouri, Ohio, etc.

Theatres. *Grand Opera House* (Pl. F, 2), Market St.; *Olympic* (Pl.
F, 2), Broadway; *Pope's* (Pl. E, 2), Olive St.; *Havlin's* (Pl. E, 2), *Standard*

(Pl. E, 2), Walnut St.; *Hagan* (Pl. E, 2), cor. Pine and 10th Sts.; *Germania* (Pl. E, 2), Locust St. (German performances); *Pickwick*, Washington Ave., cor. Jefferson Ave.; *Uhrig's Cave*, a summer-theatre, near the last.

Post Office (Pl. E, 2), Olive St., open 7-6 (Sun. 9-12).

St. Louis (4-500 ft. above the sea), the largest city of Missouri and the fifth of the United States, lies on the W. bank of the *Mississippi*, about 20 M. below the mouth of the *Missouri*. It has a frontage of nearly 20 M. on the river and rises from it in three terraces, the third of which is about 200 ft. above the river-level. The city is regularly laid out, on the Philadelphia plan, Market St., running E. and W., being the dividing line between N. and S. The streets running N. and S. are numbered. *Broadway* or *Fifth Street* is the chief shopping thoroughfare, while other important business streets are *Fourth St.* (banks), *Olive St.* (retail trade), *Washington Ave.* (wholesale trade), *Third St.* (insurance offices), and *1st* (or *Main)* and *2nd Streets* (along the river; commission houses). The city is divided into a N. and a S. side by the valley of *Mill Creek* (now filled in), which is spanned by seven bridges, the finest of which is at the Grand Ave. Depot (Pl. C, 2). The population of St. Louis in 1890 was 451,770, including about 150,000 Germans.

History. The fur-trading station of *St. Louis* or *Pain Court* was established by the French in 1764, and it still bears traces of its French origin in the names of some of its streets and leading families. Louis XV. had just ceded the territory to the E. of the Mississippi to England, while at the same time he had made a secret treaty, transferring the W. bank to Spain. It was not till 1770, however, that Spanish authority was established at St. Louis. In 1804 St. Louis, the population of which was still below 1000, passed to the United States, with the rest of the territory then known as Louisiana. This was the signal for immigration from the States, and the English-speaking inhabitants soon outnumbered the French. St. Louis was incorporated in 1809 and by 1831 had 6000 inhabitants. In 1840 the population had swollen to 16,469, in 1859 to 185,000, and in 1880 to 350,522. — In the first week of October St. Louis is the scene of a popular *Fair*, which attracts many thousands of visitors. One of the chief features is the *Procession of the Veiled Prophet*, in the style of the Mardi Gras at New Orleans (p. 368), which is accompanied by an elaborate illumination of the city.

Trade and Industry. St. Louis' position in the centre of the great Mississippi Valley gives it an immense trade, among the staples of which are cotton (600,000 bales yearly), bread-stuffs, packed meats, tobacco, livestock, timber, grain, wool, furs, etc. In manufactures St. Louis ranks fourth among American cities, producing goods in 1890 valued at $228,715,000 (45,743,000 *l.*) and employing 93,600 hands. It is the chief tobacco-making city in the world, and also produces immense quantities of beer, flour, boots and shoes, hardware, stoves, railway and tramway cars, wooden wares, bricks, drugs, biscuits ('crackers'), etc. The *Anheuser-Busch Brewery* (Pl. E, 4), cor. of 9th and Pestalozzi Sts., employs 2000 men and produces 15 million gallons of beer annually; and the *Ligget & Myers Tobacco Co.* produces 25-30 million pounds of tobacco in the same period. Strangers may also be interested by visits to the *Horse & Mule Market* (N. Broadway; the greatest mule market in the world), to the *Simmons Hardware Store* (Washington Ave., cor. 9th St.; prob. the largest hardware shop in the world), and to the *Cupples Wooden Ware Co.* (Olive St., cor. 2nd St.). The *N. O. Nelson Manufacturing Co.* (supplies for sanitary engineering) is noteworthy as carrying on its immense business on a system of 'profit-sharing'.

The **Court House** (Pl. F, 2), in Broadway, between Market and

Chestnut Sts., is a large and substantial building in the form of a Greek cross. It is surmounted by a dome (300 ft. high), the gallery of which commands an excellent view of the city and river (open till 4 p.m.). The building contains some frescoes by *Wimar* (see below). A little to the W., in 3rd St., cor. of Chestnut St., is the **Chamber of Commerce** (Pl. F, 2), the main hall of which, with a painted ceiling, is 220 ft. long (business-hours 10-1; gallery open to visitors). The grand ball of the Veiled Prophet (p. 312) is held here. — The *Cotton Exchange* (Pl. F, 2) is at the corner of Main and Walnut Sts.

By following Market St. to the W. from the Court House we soon reach the square named *Washington Park*, in which the new **City Hall** (Pl. E, 2) is being erected. A little to the S., in the square enclosed by Clark Ave. and Spruce, 11th, and 12th Sts., are the so-called **Four Courts** (Pl. E, 2), built on the model of the Louvre, with a large semicircular gaol at the back. — A little to the N. of the City Hall runs the busy OLIVE STREET (Pl. C-F, 2), which we may follow to the left to the **Exposition Building** (Pl. E, 2), in which annual exhibitions are held; or to the right (E.) to Broadway, passing the **Post Office** (Pl. E, 2) on the left. In BROADWAY (Pl. E, F, 2-4), at the corner of Locust St., is the *Mercantile Library* (Pl. F, 2), which contains 80,000 vols., statues by Miss Hosmer, etc.

A street-car on Washington Ave. or Olive St. will bring us to *Washington University (Pl. D, E, 2), one of the most important of Western universities, the buildings of which are situated at or near the corner of Washington Ave. and 17th St.

This university is notable for the width of its charter, which includes an ordinary undergraduate department, schools of fine arts, law, medicine, dentistry, and botany, a manual training school, and schools for boys and girls. It is attended by about 500 University students and 1000 others.

Close to the University, at the corner of Lucas Place and 19th St., is the handsome *Museum of Fine Arts (Pl. D, 2; adm. 25 c.).

The contents include large collections of *Casts* (incl. the Ægina Marbles) and *Electrotype Reproductions* and well-chosen selecrions of *Pottery, Glass, Ivory Carvings, Lace, Wood* and *Metal Work*, etc. Among the pictures are several by *Carl Wimar* (1829-63), a St. Louis artist who painted characteristic Western scenes from nature.

Opposite the Museum stands the *St. Louis Medical College.

The **Parks** of St. Louis are among the finest in the United States, and their area (2100 acres) is exceeded by those of Philadelphia alone. All those named below are easily reached by tramway.

Forest Park (Pl. A, 2), on the W. side of the city, 4½ M. from the Court House, is the largest park in St. Louis (1370 acres). It has fine trees and drives, but is still in a somewhat unimproved condition. The muddy *Des Pères River* meanders through it, and it also contains several small lakes. The streets leading to, and adjoining, Forest Park contain many of the handsomest residences in the city. — *Tower Grove Park (Pl. A, B, 4), a long narrow oblong (276 acres) in the S.W. part of the city, is beautifully laid out and contains three fine bronze statues (Columbus, *Humboldt, and Shakspeare), by Ferd. v. Miller of Munich. Tower Grove Park is adjoined by Shaw's or the **Missouri Botanical Garden** (Pl. A, 3, 4), the finest garden of the kind in the United States, which was bequeathed to the city by *Mr. Henry Shaw* (b. at Sheffield, Eng., in 1800; d. 1889), the founder of the botanical school in Washington University and also the donor of Tower Grove Park (see p. 313). The garden (75 acres in extent), which is open to the public on week-days, is excellently equipped for the purposes of the student and is also a delightful resort for the layman. At one end of the garden is *Mr. Shaw's House,* near which is a mausoleum containing his remains. — *Lafayette Park (Pl. D, 3) is small (30 acres) but very beautiful. It contains a bronze replica of Houdon's *Washington* (p. 327) and a statue of *Senator Benton.* — Other parks are *Carondolet Park* (183 acres), in the S., and *O'Fallon Park* (158 acres) in the N. part of the city. Adjoining the latter are the extensive *Bellefontaine Cemetery* (350 acres) and *Calvary Cemetery* (415 acres). — The **Fair Grounds**, 140 acres in extent, contain an amphitheatre, a racecourse, etc. On the 'Big Thursday' of Fair Week (p. 312) they are sometimes visited by 125-150,000 people.

The great ***St. Louis Bridge*** (Pl. F, 2), across the Mississippi, is deservedly one of the lions of the city. The visitor is recommended to cross it on foot (toll 5 c.) for the sake of the views up and down stream, and to return by ferry (5 c.) for the view of the majestic arches of the bridge itself.

The bridge, which was designed by *Capt. James B. Eads* (p. 326), was constructed in 1869-74 at a cost of $ 10,000,000 (2,000,000 *l.*). It consists of three steel spans (centre 520 ft., others 502 ft. each) resting on massive limestone piers. The total length is 2070 yds. The bridge is built in two stories, the lower for the railway, the upper for the roadway and foot-passengers. Trains enter the lower track by a *Tunnel*, 1630 yds. long, beginning near the Union Depot. The highest part of the arches is 55 ft. above the water.

The **Merchants' Bridge**, 3 M. farther up the river, is a steel truss bridge, and was built in 1889-90, at a cost of $ 3,000,000. It is used by the railway only. It has three spans, each 500 ft. long and 70 ft. high.

The old **St. Louis Waterworks** adjoin the W. end of the Merchants' Bridge (fine view from the water-towers, 180 ft. high). New waterworks are being constructed farther up the river.

Among other buildings of importance in St. Louis are the *St. Louis University* (Pl. C, 2), a Roman Catholic institution in Grand Ave., with 200-300 students; the *Roman Catholic Cathedral* (Pl. F, 2), in Walnut St.; *Christ Church Cathedral* (Epis.; Pl. E, 2), Locust St., cor. of 13th St.; the *Church of the Redemptorists* (Pl. C, 1), Grand Ave.; the *Grand Avenue Presbyterian Church* (Pl. C, 1); the *First Presbyterian Church* (Pl. B, 1), Washington Ave., cor. of Sarah St.; the *Pilgrim Congregational Church* (Pl. D, 2), Washington Ave., cor. Ewing Ave.; the *Jewish Temple* (Pl. E, 2), Pine St., cor. 17th St.; the *Temple Israel* (Pl. D, 2), Pine St., cor. 28th St.; the new *Mercantile Club* (Pl. F, 2), S. E. cor. 7th and Locust Sts.; the new *Public Library* (Pl. E, 2), Locust St., cor. 9th St.; the *County Insane Asylum;* and the *U. S. Arsenal.*

Among the favourite pleasure-resorts near St. Louis are *Montesano*; *Jefferson Barracks*, 12 M. to the S. (grand parade on Sun., at noon); *Kirkwood*, 14 M. to the W.; *Crystal City* (see p. 324); *Creve Coeur Lake*, 20 M. to the N.W.; and *Florissant*, 16 M. to the N.W.

From St. Louis to Cairo, 150 M., railway in 5-6 hrs. — *Cairo*, see p. 320.

From St. Louis to *New Orleans* by railway, see R. 64; by steamer, see R. 66; to *St. Paul*, see R. 66; to *Chicago*, see R. 56; to *New York*, see R. 60; to *Louisville*, see R. 62; to *Denver* see R. 89; to *Texarkana*, see R. 90.

62. From St. Louis to Louisville.

273 M. LOUISVILLE, EVANSVILLE, AND ST. LOUIS RAILWAY in 10 hrs. (fare $8, sleeper $2½).

St. Louis, see p. 311. The train crosses the *Eads Bridge* (p. 314) and runs to the E. S. E. through *Illinois*. 16 M. *Belleville;* 64 M. *Centralia* (500 ft.; 4763 inhab.), the junction of several railways; 86 M. *Mt. Vernon* (405 ft.; Rail. Restaurant); 148 M. *Mt. Carmel.* We now enter *Indiana.* From (151 M.) *Princeton* and (172 M.) *Oakland* railways run to *Evansville* (see below). — 198 M. *Huntingburg* (495 ft.; Rail. Restaurant; 3167 inhab.) is the junction of branch-lines to (47 M.) *Evansville*, etc.

Evansville (380 ft.; *St. George*, $2½-3), a busy city of Indiana, with 50,756 inhab., lies on the *Ohio* and carries on an extensive trade in coal, timber, grain, pork, flour, and tobacco.

From (239 M.) *Milltown* we may visit (8½ M.) the *Wyandotte Cave* (see below).

The *Wyandotte Cave, second in size to the Mammoth Cave only, is its superior in the number and beauty of its stalactites and stalagmites. There is a small *Hotel* ($1½) at the mouth of the cave, and three regular routes are laid out through the latter (as at the Mammoth Cave), one 10-12 M. long (fee $1, all three routes $2). The cave may also be reached from (11 M.) *Corydon* (see below) or from (5 M.) *Leavenworth*, on the Ohio.

From (249 M.) *Corydon Junction* a short line runs to *Corydon* (see above). 267 M. *New Albany* (21,059 inhab.). The train now threads a tunnel, crosses a long bridge over the *Ohio*, and reaches (278 M.) *Louisville.*

Louisville. — **Hotels.** *Galt House*, Main St., cor. 1st St., $3-4; *Louisville Hotel*, Main St., betw. 6th and 7th Sts., $2½-3½; *Willard's*, $2½.

Railway Stations. *Union Depot*, on the river, between 7th and 8th Sts., for the Ohio and Mississippi, the Louisville Southern, and other railways; *Union Station*, 10th St., cor. Broadway (a handsome building), for the Louisville and Nashville, and other lines; *Louisville, Cincinnati, and Lexington Depot*, on the river, between 1st and 2nd Sts.; *Louisville, Evansville, & St. Louis Depot*, Main St., cor. 14th St.

Tramways traverse all the principal streets and run to the suburbs (5 c.). — **Cabs** from the stations or wharf into the town 25-50 c. each person; per hr. $2, each addit. hr. $1. — **Ferries** ply to *Jeffersonville* and *New Albany.* — **Steamers** run to Cincinnati, Evansville, and other places on the *Ohio.*

Theatres. *Macauley's*, Walnut St.; *Harris', Bijou*, 4th St.

Post Office, cor. of 4th Ave. and Chestnut St. (7-6; Sun. 9-10 a.m.).

Louisville (450 ft.; the 'Falls City'), the largest city of Kentucky and the entrepot of the lower *Ohio*, which here descends 26 ft. within 2 M., lies on a level plain and extends for 6 M. along the river. Pop. (1890) 161,129.

Louisville was founded by Col. George Rogers Clark in 1778 and named in honour of Louis XVI. of France. It received its city charter in 1828, when its population was about 10,000. In 1850 it contained 43,194 inhab., in 1870 it had 100,753; and in 1880 it had 123,758. In March, 1890, Louisville was visited by a terrific tornado, which swept through the heart of the city with a width of 600-800 ft., levelling almost everything that stood in its way, destroying property to the value of $3,000,000, and killing 76 persons.

Since the Civil War Louisville has rapidly grown in importance as one of the chief gateways to the S.W. Its trade, both by river and rail, is very large; and the value of its manufactures in 1890 was $46,500,000 (9,300,000*l.*). It is one of the largest tobacco markets in the world and handles one-third of the tobacco raised in America, or about 150,000 hogsheads. Its sales of Kentucky whiskey are also extensive. Other important industries are pork packing, brewing, and the making of iron, farm waggons, ploughs, cement, leather, flour, and cast-iron gas and water pipes. — Natural gas (p. 241) is used here to some extent.

The *Falls of the Ohio*, adjoining the Kentucky & Indiana Bridge (see below), are rapids rather than falls and are scarcely visible when the river is full. Vessels are enabled to avoid them by a canal 2½ M. long.

Louisville contains comparatively little to interest a stranger. Perhaps the most prominent building is the new CUSTOM HOUSE, on Chestnut St., between 3rd and 4th Sts. The *Court House* is in Jefferson St., between 5th and 6th Sts., and is adjoined by the *City Hall*, with its square clock tower. — The *Polytechnic Society of Kentucky*, in 4th St., contains 50,000 vols., an art gallery, and a small museum, including the *Troost Collection of Minerals. The *Farmers' Tobacco Warehouse*, in Main St., the centre of the tobacco trade, has a storage capacity of nearly 7000 hogsheads and sells about 30 million pounds of leaf tobacco yearly. Public auctions of tobacco take place here almost daily. — The *University of Louisville*, at the cor. of 9th and Chestnut Sts., is a handsome building.

No stranger in Louisville shoul domit to visit *CAVE HILL CEMETERY, which lies on the E. margin of the city (tramway) and is very prettily laid out. The high grounds in it command good views. The large building with a dome seen to the E. is the *State Blind Asylum*, containing the *American Printing House for the Blind*. A little nearer is the *Workhouse*. — Fourth Avenue (tramway), with many pleasant residences, leads to the S., passing the pretty little *Central Park*, to the *Racecourse*. Three new *Parks* are now being laid out.

The *Louisville Bridge*, 1 M. long, crossing to *Jeffersonville*, was built in 1868-72 and has 27 iron spans supported by limestone piers. The *Kentucky and Indiana Bridge*, leading to *New Albany* (p. 315), is ½ M. long (1886). A third bridge is in progress.

Zachary Taylor (1784-1850) is buried near his old home, 5 M. to the E. of Louisville.

From Louisville to the *Mammoth Cave, Nashville*, and *New Orleans*, see R. 63 b; to *Memphis* and *New Orleans*, see R. 65; to *Cincinnati*, see R. 63 b. — A visit to the *Wyandotte Cave* (p. 315) is easily made from Louisville by rail or steamer.

FROM LOUISVILLE TO LEXINGTON, 88 M., *Louisville Southern R.R.* in 4 hrs. The Lexington branch diverges at (63½ M.) *Lawrenceburg* from the main line to Chattanooga. — 88 M. *Lexington*, in the 'Blue Grass Country', see p. 317.

63. From Cincinnati to New Orleans.

a. Viâ Chattanooga *('Queen & Crescent Route').*

826 M. RAILWAY in 27-36 hrs. (fare $21; sleeper $5). *Cincinnati, New Orleans, & Texas Pacific Railway* to (335 M.) *Chattanooga; Alabama Great Southern R. R.* thence to (630 M.) *Meridian; New Orleans & North Eastern*

R. R. thence to (826 M.) *New Orleans.* This line traverses the famous *Blue Grass Region* of Kentucky.

Cincinnati, see p. 307. The train crosses the *Ohio* to ($1/2$ M.) *Ludlow* and runs to the S. through *Kentucky.* The country traversed is pleasant, but few of the stations are important. $17^1/2$ M. *Walton* (925 ft.); 67 M. *Georgetown* (880 ft.).

79 M. **Lexington** (975 ft.; *Phoenix,* \$ $2^1/2$-3), a thriving little city with 21,567 inhab., is the metropolis of the famous *Blue Grass Country* (see below) and one of the most important horse and cattle markets in the United States. It received its name from having been founded in the year of the battle of Lexington (1775). The city is well built and contains many pleasant residences. It is the site of the *University of Kentucky* (700 students, including the commercial college) and the *State Agricultural & Mechanical College,* and has large distilleries of 'Bourbon' whiskey. *Henry Clay* (1777-1852) is commemorated by a monument. The trotting-races held here are largely frequented.

Lexington may also be reached from Cincinnati by the *Kentucky Central R.R.* (100 M.), which also passes through part of the Blue Grass Region (see below).

The **Blue Grass Region,** which occupies about 10,000 sq. M. in N. Kentucky, is an undulating and fertile plateau surrounded by hills. The soil is very rich, and agriculture, especially the raising of tobacco and hemp, is carried on with great success. Its characteristic feature, however, consists of the celebrated pastures of 'Blue Grass' (*Poa pratensis*), which support the horses and other livestock for which Kentucky is famous. Stock-farms abound throughout the whole district, especially in the neighbourhood of Lexington. The American trotting horse was here brought to its present high state of excellence, the blood horses of Kentucky exhibiting a remarkable combination of speed and endurance. Among the most famous stock-farms near Lexington is *Ashland* ($1^1/2$ M.), formerly the home of Henry Clay and now the property of Maj. McDowell. 'Mambrino Chief', one of the most famous sires of the American stud-book, was an Ashland horse, and 'Jay-Eye-See' was sired here. *Woodburn,* 15 M. from Lexington, was the home of the famous thorough-bred 'Lexington' and the birthplace of 'Maud S.' who trotted a mile in 2 min. $8^3/4$ sec. 'Nancy Hanks', who trotted a mile in 2.4, the fastest time on record, was bred by Mr. Hart Boswell at *Poplar Hill,* 7 M. to the N. of Lexington. *Paris,* on the Ken. Central R. R., 19 M. to the N.E. of Lexington, is another centre of racing stock; and there are also important stud-farms near *Cynthiana,* 13 M. farther to the N.

At (100 M.) *High Bridge* (775 ft.), the train crosses the *Kentucky River* by a fine *Cantilever Bridge, 285 ft. high, with three spans of 375 ft. each. At (106 M.) *Burgin* we are joined by the line from Louisville (p. 315). 118 M. *Junction City* (1000 ft.). Beyond (136 M.) *King's Mountain* (1180 ft.) we pass through a tunnel 1300 yds. long. 158 M. *Somerset* (880 ft.). At (165 M.) *Burnside* we cross the *Cumberland River* (view). The line here runs high up on the cliffs. 176 M. *Greenwood* is the station for the ($2^1/2$ M.) *Natural Bridge* of Kentucky, which is 30 ft. high and has a span of 200 ft. From (179 M.) *Cumberland Falls Station* (1245 ft.) coaches run to (10 M.) *Cumberland Falls,* 60 ft. high. Beyond (194 M.) *Pine Knot* we enter *Tennessee* (the 'Volunteer State'), where the line traverses the picturesque district of the foot-hills of the *Cumberland Mts.*, among which are numerous pleasant summer-resorts. 206^1/$_2$ M. *Oneida* (1455 ft.) is the highest point on the line. 221 M. *Rugby Road* is the station for *Rugby* (7 M. to the W.; 1400 ft.), founded in 1880 by Tom Hughes (author of 'Tom Brown's School-Days') and partly colonized by Englishmen. 252 M. *Oakdale*, on the *Emory River*, along which the train descends. 256^1/$_2$ M. *Harriman*, an iron-making place, is 15 M. from *Alum Springs*, a favourite resort amid the Cumberland Mts. 280 M. *Spring City;* 297 M. *Dayton* (715 ft.). At (331 M.) *Boyce* (695 ft.) we cross the *Tennessee River*.

335 M. **Chattanooga,** and thence to —

826 M. **New Orleans,** see R. 70 b.

b. Viâ Louisville and Nashville.

921 M. RAILWAY in 29^1/$_2$ hrs. (fare $ 21 ; sleeper $ 5).

Cincinnati, see p. 307. The train crosses the *Ohio* to (1 M.) *Newport* (p. 311) and runs to the S.W. through *Kentucky*. At (21 M.) *Walton* we cross the route above described. 83 M. *Lagrange* is the junction of lines to *Lexington* (p. 317), etc. 98 M. *Anchorage*.

110 M. **Louisville,** see p. 315. The train now runs towards the S. From (132 M.) *Bardstown Junction* a line runs to (37 M.) *Springfield* (Ky.), and from (140 M.) *Lebanon Junction* another runs to *Lebanon* and *Knoxville* (p. 341). — From (201 M.) *Glasgow Junction* a short line diverges to *Mammoth Cave* (see below).

FROM GLASGOW TO MAMMOTH CAVE, 9 M., railway in ^{3}/$_4$ hr. At present there are two trains daily, at 9.30 a.m. and 6.10 p.m. (returning at 1.35 and 7.30 p.m.). — At the end of the railway, on the *Green River*, at a height of 735 ft. above the sea, stands the *Mammoth Cave Hotel* ($ 3), 250 yards from the cave. Guides, etc., are procured at the hotel. About 5000 tourists visit the cave yearly.

The **Mammoth Cave of Kentucky*, accidentally discovered by a hunter in 1809, is the largest cave known, extending below the earth for 9-10 M., while the various avenues already explored have a total length of about 175 M. The carboniferous limestone of Kentucky, in which the cave occurs, occupies an area of 8000 sq. M., and Prof. Shaler estimates that there are at least 100,000 miles of open caverns beneath it. The interior contains a vast series of halls, domes, grottoes, caverns, cloisters, lakes, rivers, and the like, to which more or less appropriate names have been given. There are comparatively few stalactites or stalagmites, but some of those found here are of great size. Two regular routes have been established, over which guides conduct visitors at stated times, but those who wish to make a more leisurely exploration can make special arrangements. The *Long Route* (ca. 20 M.; fee $ 3) includes the Rotunda, the Main Cave, the Giant's Coffin, the Pits and Domes, Echo River, and beyond to the end of the cave, with return by the Corkscrew. The *Short Route* (8 M.; $ 2) takes in the Rotunda, Main Cave, Gothic Gallery, Star Chamber, Pits and Domes, and Giant's Coffin. The pure air and even temperature (52-56° Fahr.) make these excursions much less fatiguing than they would be above ground. Visitors often accomplish the Short Route on the evening of their arrival (7-11 p.m.) and the Long Route on the following day (9 a.m.-6 p.m.). Luncheon is carried in from the hotel. Special fees ($ 1 each) are charged for visits to the Mammoth Dome and Chief City (500 ft. long, 200 ft. wide, and 120 ft. high). The fees include the fireworks necessary to illuminate the domes and chasms. The curiosities of the cave include eyeless fish *(Amblyopsis spelaeus)* and craw-fish. It contains large deposits of nitrous earth, from which saltpetre was made in 1811-15. A good account of the Mammoth Cave, by *H. C. Hovey*, is sold at the hotel (25 c.). — A visit may also be paid to the *White Cave* ($ 1), with fine stalactites.

224 M. *Bowling Green* (Rail. Restaurant; 7803 inhab.). At (228 M.) *Memphis Junction* the line forks, one branch running to the S.W. (right) to *Memphis* (p. 320), while the other holds on nearly due S. Near (251 M.) *Mitchelville* we enter *Tennessee* (p. 317). 285 M. *Edgefield Junction,* for the line to St. Louis (p. 311).

295 M. **Nashville** (550 ft. ; *Maxwell Ho.*, $ 2½-5; *Duncan*, $ 3-5; *Nicholson, Linck*, $ 2-3), the capital and largest city of Tennessee, with (1890) 76,168 inhab., occupies a somewhat hilly site on both banks of the *Cumberland River*. It contains extensive manufactories of hard-wood wares, large flour-mills, and various other industries (value of products in 1890, $ 14,090,000), and it is, perhaps, the most important educational centre in the South. Among the chief buildings are the *Capitol* (with a tower 205 ft. high), the *Court House*, the *Blind Asylum*, the *Custom House*, and the *City Hall*. At the head of the educational institutions stands the large *Vanderbilt University*, endowed by Cornelius Vanderbilt with $ 1,000,000 and attended by 7-800 students. The medical school of *Nashville University* has been incorporated with that of the Vanderbilt University, while its academic department has been converted into the *Peabody Normal College* (400 students). The *Fisk University* (400 students), the *Roger Williams University* (300 students), and the *Central Tennessee College* (600 students) are the leading seats of learning for coloured persons. The *Watkins Institute* contains a good library and interesting collections. — The home and tomb of *President Polk* (1795-1849) are in the city.

Among the places of interest near Nashville are the *Hermitage*, the home of *Gen. Andrew Jackson* (1767-1845), 12 M. to the E.; *Belle Meade*, a famous stock-farm, 5 M. to the W., now owned by Gen. W. H. Jackson; and the *National Cemetery*, 4½ M. to the N, containing 16,500 graves. — In the *Battle of Nashville*, fought on Dec. 15-16th, 1864, Gen. Hood, at the head of a Confederate army of 40,000 men, was completely defeated by Gen. Thomas. — Lines radiate from Nashville to *St. Louis* (p. 307), *Hickman* (p. 324), *Memphis* (p. 320), *Chattanooga* (p. 342), etc.

The line continues to run towards the S. 342 M. *Columbia*, on the *Duck River*. At (390 M.) *State Line* we enter *Alabama* (p. 336). At (417 M.) *Decatur* (see p. 343) we cross the *Tennessee*. 450 M. *Cullmans;* 504 M. *Birmingham*, see p. 343 ; 537 M. *Calera*.

600 M. *Montgomery*, and thence to (780 M.) **Mobile** and — 921 M. **New Orleans**, see R. 70 a.

64. From Chicago and St. Louis to New Orleans.

ILLINOIS CENTRAL R. R. from *Chicago* to (915 M.) *New Orleans* in 30 hrs. (fare $ 27.55); from *St. Louis* to (700 M.) *New Orleans* in 24⅓ hrs. (fare $ 21.25); through-sleepers. The St. Louis train traverses the ST. LOUIS & CAIRO SHORT LINE and joins the main line at (73 M.) *Du Quoin* (p. 320).

From Chicago to (199 M.) *Effingham*, see R. 56a. Our line now diverges to the left from that to St. Louis. 244 M. *Odin.* 252 M. *Centralia* is one of the chief outlets of a rich fruit-growing country (4763 inhab.). — At (288 M.) *Du Quoin* we are joined by the line from St. Louis (see p. 319). 308 M. *Carbondale*, a busy little industrial town (2382 inhab.). 329 M. *Anna* adjoins *Jonesborough*, a busy market for fruit and cotton.

365 M. **Cairo** (*Halliday*, $ 2^1/$_2$-3 ; *Planters'*, $ 2), a manufacturing city with 10,324 inhab., lies on a low flat tongue of land at the confluence of the *Mississippi* and *Ohio*. It has never, however, attained the commercial importance expected at its foundation. — The train crosses the Ohio by a fine bridge and enters *Kentucky.* 395 M. *Clinton.* Beyond (409 M.) *Fulton* (p. 323) we enter *Tennessee.* 420 M. *Martin.* At (451 M.) *Milan* the line forks, the right branch running to (93 M.) *Memphis* (see below). — 474 M. **Jackson** (*Arlington*, $ 2-2^1/$_2$; *Robinson*, $ 2), with 64,495 inhab., is a considerable cotton-market and carries on various industries. 503 M. *Bolivar.* Beyond (521 M.) *Grand Junction*, where we cross the E. Tennessee, Virginia, & Georgia R. R., we enter *Mississippi.* 546 M. *Holly Springs;* 621 M. *Grenada*, on the *Yalobusha River;* 674 M. *Durant;* 709 M. *Canton.* — 732 M. **Jackson** (*Edwards Ho.*, $ 2^1/$_2$-3), the small capital of Mississippi (5920 inhab.), has a handsome *State House* and other public buildings. Beyond (827 M.) *Osyka* we enter *Louisiana.* In approaching New Orleans we cross the outlet of *Lake Maurepas* (right) and skirt *Lake Pontchartrain* (left).

915 M. **New Orleans**, see p. 366.

65. From Louisville to Memphis and New Orleans.

847 M. NEWPORT NEWS & MISSISSIPPI VALLEY RAILWAY to (392 M.) *Memphis* in 14 hrs. and LOUISVILLE, NEW ORLEANS, & TEXAS RAILWAY thence to (847 M.) *New Orleans* in 13 hrs. (through-fare $ 11.25; sleeper $ 2^1/$_2$).

Louisville, see p. 315. The line runs at first towards the S.W. 47 M. *Cecilia;* 72 M. *Leitchfield.* Beyond (118 M.) *Rockport* we cross the *Green River.* 127 M. *Central City;* 180 M. *Princeton;* 194 M. *Kuttawa.* A little farther on we cross the *Cumberland* and soon after the *Tennessee*, which here (15-20 M. above their mouths in the Ohio) approach within 3-4 M. of each other.

226 M. **Paducah** (*Palmer Ho.*, $ 2^1/$_2$), a city of 12,797 inhab., lies on the left bank of the *Ohio*, a little below the influx of the Tennessee. It carries on a brisk trade in tobacco, grain, and pork. — Our line now turns abruptly to the S. (left). At (271 M.) *Fulton* we intersect the Illinois Central R. R. (see above) and enter *Tennessee.* — Beyond (296 M.) *Obion* we cross the *Obion River;* beyond (316 M.) *Dyersburg* the two branches of the *Forked Deer River;* and beyond (346 M.) *Henning's* the *Big Hatchie.* 354 M. *Covington.*

392 M. **Memphis** (200 ft.; *Peabody, Gayoso*, $ 2^1/$_2$-4; *Gaston, R.* from $ 1, *Luehrman's*, for men), the second city of Tennessee

and the most important on the *Mississippi* between St. Louis and New Orleans, is strikingly situated on the *Chickasaw Bluffs*, with a wide levee overlooking the river. It is one of the most progressive cities in the S., in spite of its former trouble with the yellow fever, and its population has increased from 33,593 in 1880 to 64,495 in 1890. It is of great importance as a distributing point for cotton (7-800,000 bales), groceries (annual value $ 25,000,000), shoes, hardware, lumber, and other commodities. Several railways converge here (comp. pp. 343, 404) and many lines of steamers ply up and down the Mississippi (comp. p. 325). The railway bridge, completed in 1892, is the only bridge across the Mississippi to the S. of St. Louis.

The *Cotton Exchange*, the *Merchants' Exchange*, the *Custom House*, the *Office of the Appeal-Avalanche*, the *St. Agnes Academy*, the buildings of the *Tennessee Club*, the *Chickasaw Club*, and the *Athletic Association*, and the *Cossett Free Library* are among the most conspicuous buildings. The *Levee* presents a busy and animated picture, and interesting visits may be paid to the various *Cotton Compresses* and *Cotton-seed Oil Mills*. *Court Square* contains a bust of Gen. Andrew Jackson and innumerable squirrels.

An electric tramway runs from Memphis to (5 M.) the *National Cemetery*, with the graves of 14,000 Union soldiers, and (8 M.) *Raleigh*, a pleasant resort with a large hotel. — Memphis also possesses a fine *Race Course*. — Steamers ply viâ the *White River*, *St. Francis River*, and *Arkansas River* to *Fort Smith* in Arkansas.

Soon after leaving Memphis the train enters *Mississippi*. 404 M. *Lakeview* (lake to the right). Beyond (437 M.) *Clayton* we pass *Beaver Dam Lake* and *Beaver Dam Bayou*. 448 M. *Lula*, near *Moon Lake;* 455 M. *Coahoma*. To the left lies *Swan Lake*. 531 M. *Leland*. We now follow the *Deer River*. — 601 M. *Redwood*, on the *Old River*.

612 M. **Vicksburg** *(Piazza,* $ 2½; *Washington ,* $ 2-3; *Vicksburg),* picturesquely situated on the Mississippi, amid the *Walnut Hills* (500 ft.), is the largest city in the state and a commercial and industrial place of some importance. Pop. (1890) 13,373.

The name of Vicksburg is well known from its prominence in the Civil War, when, as the key of the Mississippi, it was strongly fortified and garrisoned by the Confederates. After baffling Farragut and Sherman in 1862, it was finally captured by Grant in 1863 (July 4th), in a campaign which cost him 9000 of his troops (comp. p. xliii). The *National Cemetery* above the city contains 16,600 graves.

Near (635 M.) *Ingleside* we cross the *Big Black River*, and near (641 M.) *Port Gibson* the *Pierre*. From (661 M.) *Harrison* a line runs to *Natchez* (p. 325). Farther on we cross several small rivers. Near (718 M.) *Whitaker* we enter *Louisiana*. — 758 M. **Baton Rouge** *(Capitol Ho.,* $ 2-3), the capital of Louisiana, is a quaint old place with 10,478 inhab., on a bluff above the Mississippi. It contains the *Louisiana State University* and other State institutions. — Beyond Baton Rouge we skirt the Mississippi, with its low banks and levees, sugar-plantations, and picturesque planters' houses. 836 M. *Kenner*.

847 M. **New Orleans,** see p. 366.

66. From St. Paul to New Orleans by the Mississippi River.

The **Mississippi**, the 'Father of Waters', is one of the great rivers of the world, with a length of 2616 M. (or, reckoned from the source of the Missouri, of 4191 M.) and a drainage-basin nearly 1½ million sq. M. in area. It rises in the N. part of Minnesota, on the watershed between Hudson's Bay and the Gulf of Mexico, and is a stream 12 ft. wide and 2 ft. deep after issuing from *Lake Itasca*. At first it runs towards the N.E., but soon turns towards the S.E., and its general course afterwards runs nearly due S., though with many bends and curves. The principal tributaries are the *Missouri*, which joins it from the W. about 1330 M. from its source; the *Ohio*, which comes in from the E. 220 M. farther on; and the *Arkansas* (W.). The best scenery is between St. Paul and St. Louis, where the river frequently flows between lofty and picturesque bluffs, 100-600 ft. high and 1-5 M. apart. The finest reaches are between St. Paul and Dubuque. After its junction with the Missouri the waters of the Missisippi become yellow and turbid, and it flows mainly through a flat and monotonous alluvial plain. As we near the Gulf of Mexico the vegetation becomes more and more tropical in character, and the river finally loses itself in a wilderness of creeks, bayous, and swamps, reaching the gulf through several outlets. The width of the Mississippi from St. Paul to New Orleans seldom varies much from 3000 ft., except at the bends, where it sometimes expands to 1 M. or 1½ M. — The United States Government has spent many millions of dollars in improving the navigation of the Mississippi, which is still apt to be interfered with by shallows and mud-banks. The most important work was the construction of the famous *Eads Jetties* (see p. 326) at the mouth of the river. — The first European explorer of the Mississippi was *De Soto* (1541), who is supposed to have reached it a little below Helena (p. 325).

Though there is a considerable traffic of smaller vessels above the *Falls of St. Anthony* (p. 293), the navigation proper of the Mississippi begins at *St. Paul*, and travellers will find comfortable passenger-steamers plying all the way thence to (1917 M.) New Orleans. The steamers of the *Diamond Jo Line* leave *St. Paul* twice weekly in summer for *St. Louis*, which they reach in 4½ days (fare $ 16, incl. berth and meals). At St. Louis they connect with the *St. Louis and New Orleans Anchor Line*, the boats of which ply weekly and reach New Orleans in 7 days (fare $ 20). Reduced rates are charged for return-tickets. Comparatively few travellers will care to make the whole journey from St. Paul to New Orleans; but a day or two on the river will be found an agreeable change from the dusty railways. The boat-companies issue combination-tickets, allowing any part of the journey the traveller selects to be traversed by railway; and liberal 'stop-over' privileges are granted on all tickets.

The commerce carried on by the Mississippi is very large. In 1891 the vessels plying on that river and its tributaries numbered 7453, with an aggregate burden of about 3½ million tons, including 1114 steamers, of 210,771 tons' burden. The amount of merchandise carried was 29,505,000 tons.

In the following description of the voyage down the river, only the more important places on the banks are mentioned. The distances are reckoned from St. Paul.

St. Paul, see p. 291. The steamer passes under five bridges. For the first 25 M. or so both banks of the river are in *Minnesota* (p. 289), but beyond the mouth of the *St. Croix River* (left) the E. bank is in *Wisconsin* (p. 287).

27 M. (right bank) *Hastings* (swing-bridge), see p. 289.

30 M. (l.) *Prescott* (swing-bridge), at the foot of *Lake St. Croix*, an enlargement of the river of that name.

52 M. (r.) *Red Wing* (see p. 289)', with *Barn Bluff* (200 ft.).

A little farcher on the steamer traverses the beautiful expansion of the river known as *Lake Pepin (see p. 289). To the left rises the *Maiden Rock* (410 ft.), to the right is the bold round headland called *Point No Point.*

67 M. (r.) *Frontenac,* see p. 289. — 73 M. (r.) *Lake City* (p. 289). — 79 M. (l.) *North Pepin.* — 84 M. (r.) *Read's Landing* (pontoon-bridge), at the lower end of Lake Pepin and opposite the mouth of the *Chippewa.* — 87 M. (r.) *Wabasha,* see p. 289. — 117 M. (l.) *Fountain City.* The next stretch of the river abounds in islands, and the flanking bluffs are very picturesque in outline. — 125 M. (r.) *Winona* (two bridges), see p. 289. — 137 M. (l.) *Trempealeau,* at the mouth of the Black River. *Trempealeau Island,* 500 ft. high, commands a beautiful view. This is, perhaps, the most beautiful section of the Upper Mississippi.

156 M. (l.) **La Crosse** (two swing-bridges), see p. 291. The scenery continues to be attractive, while the towns and villages on the banks now follow each other in closer succession.

187 M. (l.) *Victory.* Nearly opposite is the boundary between Minnesota and *Iowa* (p. 290), where 'Black Hawk' met his final defeat. — 199 M. (r.) *Lansing* (Iowa). — 227 M. (l.) *Prairie du Chien* (pontoon-bridge), near the mouth of the *Wisconsin River* (see p. 291). — 230 M. (r.) *McGregor* (pontoon-bridge). — 252 M. (r.) *Guttenberg.* — 260 M. (l.) *Cassville.* — 289 M. (l.) *East Dubuque* (p. 291) lies in *Illinois* (p. 270), just beyond the frontier of Wisconsin. Nearly opposite rises *Eagle Point* (300 ft.).

290 M. (r.) **Dubuque** (two bridges), see p. 290. The bluffs now become lower and the scenery tamer. — 325 M. (l.) *Savanna* is connected with (327 M.; r.) *Sabula* (p. 388) by a railway-bridge.

345 M. (l.) *Fulton* (p. 320), *Lyons* (r.), and —

347 M. (r.) *Clinton* (p. 389) are connected by three bridges. — Beyond (381 M.; r.) *Le Claire* we shoot the picturesque *Upper Rapids,* which extend hence to Rock Island.

397 M. (l.) **Rock Island** (p. 290) and (398 M.; r.) **Davenport** are united by the fine bridge mentioned at p. 290. A good view is obtained of the *Government Island* and *Arsenal.* — 426 M. (r.) *Muscatine* (bridge), a thriving city with 11,432 inhab., carries on a brisk trade in timber, sweet potatoes, and melons. — 455 M. (l.) *Keithsburg* (bridge; 1484 inhab.).

480 M. (r) **Burlington** (bridge), see p. 390. — 494 M. (l.) *Dallas City.* — 504 M. (r.) *Fort Madison* (bridge), see p. 302. — 512 M. (l.) *Nauvoo,* a place of 1450 inhab., was once a flourishing Mormon city with a population of 15,000 (see p. 425). — 515 M. (r.) *Montrose* lies at the head of the *Lower Rapids,* which extend hence to (527 M.; r.) *Keokuk* (bridge), at the mouth of the *Des Moines River,* here forming the boundary between Iowa and *Missouri* ('Bullion State'). — 531 M. (l.) *Warsaw* (2721 inhab.). — 551 M. (r.) *Canton* (2241 inhab.).

568 M. (l.) **Quincy** (bridge), see p. 402. — 588 M. (r.) *Hannibal* (bridge), see p. 401. — 616 M. (r.) *Louisiana* (bridge; 5090 inhab.). — 626 M. (r.). *Clarkville.* — 641 M. (l.) *Hamburg.* — 663 M. (r.) *Cap au Gris.* — 690 M. (l.) *Grafton*, at the mouth of the *Illinois River.* — 706 M. (l.) *Alton*, see p. 302.

About 3 M. farther on we reach the confluence of the Mississippi and the **Missouri**. The latter river, flowing in from the N.W., has a longer course than the Mississippi up to their junction (2908 M., as compared with 1330 M.) and contributes a greater volume of water to the joint stream, so that it would seem that the name Mississippi in its application below this point has clearly usurped the place of the Missouri. The clear waters of the Mississippi long refuse to mingle with the turbid flood of the Missouri.

729 M. **St. Louis** and its two magnificent bridges are described in R. 61. This is the terminus of the Diamond Jo Line Steamers, and passengers continuing their journey by water are here transferred to one of the boats of the Anchor line (comp. p. 322).

The scenery of the Lower Mississippi differs materially from that of the Upper Mississippi (comp. p. 322), and the place of landscape beauty is taken to some extent by historic interest. The towns and villages on the banks usually follow each other rapidly, and innumerable islands are passed.

761 M. (32 M. from St. Louis; r.) *Crystal City* (see p. 314). — 789 M. (r.) *Ste. Genevieve* (1586 inhab.). — 809 M. (l.) *Chester* (2708 inhab.). — 849 M. (l.) *Grand Tower*, a favourite resort of the citizens of St. Louis. A little farther on we pass the island known as the *Devil's Tea-table.* — 879 M. (r.) *Cape Girardeau* (4297 inhab.). — 894 M. (l.) *Commerce*. The large island to the right, a little farther on, is *Power's Island.*

929 M. (l.) **Cairo**, at the mouth of the *Ohio*, see p. 320. — 951 M. (l.) *Columbus* (bridge), the first landing-place in *Kentucky* (p. 305), was strongly fortified by the Confederates in the Civil War, but was ultimately abandoned without attack. Just beyond is *Wolf Island* or *Island No. 5.* — 967 M. (l.) *Hickman* (1652 inhab.). — *Island No. 10*, off (986 M.; r.) *Donaldson Point*, was also strongly fortified in the war and was captured by the Federal gun-boats in April, 1862, after a month's bombardment. — 988 M. (l.) *Wades*, nearly opposite, is in *Tennessee* (p. 317). — 999 M. (r.) *New Madrid*, with 1193 inhab., was captured at the same time as Island No. 10. — 1017 M. (l.) *Tiptonville*. A little to the E. lies *Reelfoot Lake.* — Numerous small and unimportant landings are now passed. — 1074 M. (r.) *Hickman's* is the first station in *Arkansas* (p. 404). — 1119 M. (l.) *Fort Pillow*, situated on the *First Chickasaw Bluff*, evacuated by the Confederates in 1862, was the scene of what is known as the *Fort Pillow Massacre* (April 12th, 1864). The river now winds considerably and passes several islands, the largest of which are named *Centennial* and *Brandywine.*

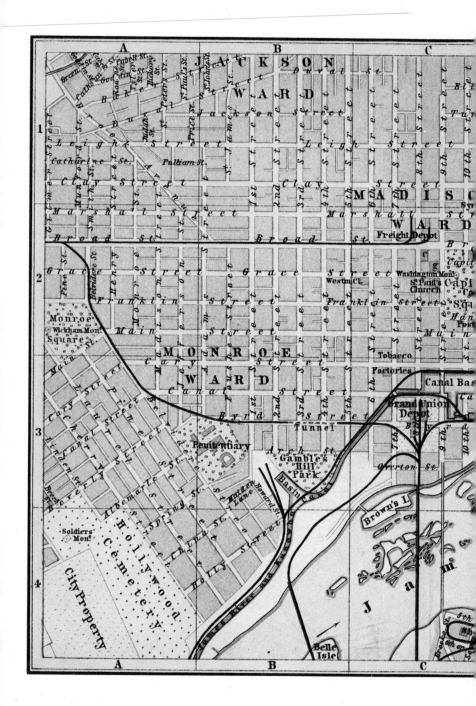

RICHMOND.

1 : 17.500

| 0 | 500 | 1000 | 2000 Feet |
| 0 | 100 | 200 | 300 | 400 | 500 | Mètres |

Wagner & Debes' Geogʰ Estabᵗ Leipzig.

1179 M. (l.) **Memphis** (bridge), see p. 320. Farther on numerous windings are threaded. — 1207 M. (l.) *De Soto* is the first station in *Mississippi* (p. 338). — 1261 M. (r.) *Helena* (railway-ferry) is a busy little city with 5189 inhab. and a trade in timber. — Numerous small stations. — 1352 M. (r.) Mouth of the *White River*, which rises in Missouri and joins the Mississippi after a course of 700 M.

1359 M. (r.) *Black Hawk* lies at the mouth of the *Arkansas River*. The **Arkansas River** rises in the Rocky Mts., to the W. of South Park (p. 409), and has a course of 1600 M., of which 800 M. are navigable.

Beyond the *Choctaw Bend* we reach (1396 M.; r.) *Arkansas City* (800 inhab.). — Passing *Rowdy Bend*, *Miller's Bend*, *Island 82* (1410 M.), and *Bachelor's Bend*, we reach (1435 M.; l.) *Greenville*, a small cotton-trading city with 6658 inhabitants. The banks are now lined with cotton-plantations, which afford a very interesting sight in time of harvest (Sept.-Nov.). The planters' houses, especially as we approach the S., are often roomy and quaint old mansions, surrounded with groves of fine trees. Many of the trees are fantastically draped with Spanish moss *(Tillandsia usneoides)*. — 1463 M. (r.) *Grand Lake* is the first station in *Louisiana* (p. 338). No places of any great size or importance are passed till we reach —

1555 M. (l.) **Vicksburg** (railway-ferry; see p. 321). — 1606 M. (r.) *St. Joseph.* — 1611 M. (l.) *Rodney.*

1639 M. (l.) **Natchez** *(Natchez Hotel)*, a city of 10,000 inhab., founded by *D'Iberville* in 1700, lies on and at the foot of a bluff rising 200 ft. above the river. It takes its name from a now extinct tribe of Indians, who were among the noblest specimens of Red Men in America. Some traces of the old French fort are still visible. A *National Cemetery* adjoins the city.

1709 M. (l.) *Fort Adams.* — 1719 M. (r.) *Red River Landing*, at the mouth of the *Red River*. Beyond this point both banks of the river are in Louisiana. — 1749 M. (l.) *Bayou Sara.*
The 'Swampers' of Bayou Sara are a peculiar community of wood-cutters, living on raft-houses floating in the swamps.

1783 M. (l.) *Baton Rouge*, see p. 321. The course of the river between this point and New Orleans is very circuitous. — 1835 M. (r.) *Donaldsonville* (3121 inhab.). — 1850 M. (l.) *Convent.* — 1855 M. (l.) *Belmont Plantation.* — 1875 M. *Fruit Plantation.* — 1879 M. (l.) *Bonnet Carré Point.* — 1890 M. *Red Church.* — 1899 M. (l.) *Kennerville.* — 1909 M. *Carrollton* (p. 370).

1917 M. **New Orleans,** see R. 82.

Below New Orleans the trees disappear, the river banks become less defined, and the river finally loses itself in a vast marsh, through which various 'passes' or channels lead to the Gulf of Mexico. About 70 M. from New Orleans the ocean-steamers pass between *Fort St. Philip* (left) and *Fort Jackson* (right) and soon after enter the *South Pass*, marked by lighthouses. At the lower end of the S. Pass are the wonderful *Eads Jetties, constructed by Capt. Eads in 1875-79 at a cost of $5,000,000 (1,000,000*l.*) and forming a channel 30 ft. deep where formerly the draught was not more than 10 ft. The jetties are, respectively, $2^1/_3$ and $1^1/_2$ M. long, and are constructed of willow rods, rubble, and concrete. The ends of the jetties, marked by two lights, may be called the mouth of the Mississippi, beyond which we are on the *Gulf of Mexico*.

67. From Washington to Richmond.

116 M. BALTIMORE & POTOMAC and RICHMOND, FREDERICKSBURG, & POTOMAC RAILROADS in $3^1/_2$-$4^1/_2$ hrs. (fare $3.50; parlor-car $1.50). This is part of the Penn. and Atlantic Coast line route to the S. (comp. R. 75a).

Washington, see p. 251. The train crosses the *Long Bridge* (p. 259), affording a view of *Arlington House* (p. 262) to the right, enters *Virginia* (the 'Old Dominion'), and skirts the right bank of the *Potomac* to (7 M.) *Alexandria* (p. 262) and (34 M.) *Quantico*. The line now edges away from the river and skirts the '*Wilderness*', a barren and unattractive district widely known from the terrible struggles of the Civil War that took place here in 1863-4 (p. xliv).

55 M. **Fredericksburg** (*Exchange Hotel*, $2^1/_2$), a quaint old city of 4528 inhab., on the *Rappahannock*, founded in 1727. It was the scene of a hardly-contested battle in 1862, when the Confederates under Lee defeated the Union troops under Burnside. The huge *National Cemetery*, on *Mayres Hill*, contains 15,000 graves, and there is also a large *Confederate Cemetery*.

Those who are interested in studying the campaigns of the Civil War will find much to occupy their attention in and around Fredericksburg. The *Battle of Chancellorsville* (May 2-4th, 1863), in which 'Stonewall' Jackson was mortally wounded, took place 11 M. to the W., resulting in another repulse to the Union forces, with a loss of 17,000 men. A little to the S. is *Spottsylvania Court House*, the centre of some of Grant's operations in 1864 (p. 329). The 'Battles of the Wilderness' between Grant and Lee were almost continuous during May, 1864; and the losses of the two armies exceeded 60,000. Comp. p. 329.

George Washington spent his boyhood near Fredericksburg. His mother died here in 1789 and is commemorated by a monument.

The train runs towards the S. At (67 M.) *Guinea* Stonewall Jackson died (see above). At (92 M.) *Bothwell* we cross the C. & O. R. R. (R. 58 b). *Henry Clay* (1777-1852) was born near (99 M.) *Ashland*.

116 M. **Richmond.** — **Hotels.** *Exchange* and *Ballard House* (Pl. a; D, 2), two houses on opposite sides of Franklin St., connected by a covered bridge, $3-4; *Ford's* (Pl. b; C, 2), Capitol Sq., $3; *Murphy's European Hotel* (Pl. c; C, 2), 801 Broad St., R. from $1, well spoken of; *Davis Ho.* (Pl. d; D, 2), R. from $1; *American Ho.* (Pl. e; C, D, 2), $2-3; *Dodson's* (Pl. f; D, 2), $2-3. — Richmond is much in need of a really good hotel. — *Ruger's Restaurant*, cor. 9th and Bank Sts.

Tramways traverse the chief streets (5 c.). — *Hacks* and *Omnibuses* meet the principal trains at the *Union Depot* (Pl. C, 3); fare into the town 50 c. each. — *Steamers* ply down the James to Norfolk, Old Point Comfort, Newport News, Philadelphia (Clyde Line), New York (Old Dominion Line), etc. — *Post Office* (Pl. C, 2), Main St., between 10th & 11th Sts.

Richmond, the capital of Virginia and one of the most interesting cities of the S., is situated on a series of low hills rising from the N. bank of the *James River*. In 1890 it contained 81,388 inhab., while *Manchester*, on the opposite bank of the river, with which it is connected by several bridges, had 9246. The city is regularly laid out, and most of the streets running N. and S. are denoted by numbers. Fine water-power is afforded by the James River, which descends 116 ft. in 9 M.

Richmond was founded in 1737, on the site of the home of the famous Indian Chief *Powhatan*, and had still only a few hundred inhabitants when made capital of the State in 1779. At various national crises it was chosen as the meeting-place of important conventions; and in 1861 it became the seat of government for the seceding states. The capture of Richmond became ultimately the chief objective point of the Union troops, and it was defended with great obstinacy by the Confederates, who threw up strong lines of earthworks all round it (comp. p. 329). When finally compelled to evacuate Richmond (April 2nd, 1865; comp. p. 328) the Confederates set fire to the tobacco warehouses and other stores; and a large part of the city was destroyed. All traces of this devastation have been removed, and the city is now in a thriving condition, carrying on a brisk trade (tobacco, etc.) and considerable manufactures (machinery, locomotives, flour, etc.; total value in 1890, $ 27,000,000). About 600,000,000 of the famous Richmond Straight Cut cigarettes are made here annually by the Allen & Ginter Branch of the American Tobacco Co.

The European visitor will probably be struck by the number of *Negroes*, who form nearly half of the population and contribute many of its most picturesque and romantic features.

Near the centre of the city, on *Shockoe Hill*, is **Capitol Square** (Pl. C, 2), a tree-shaded area of 12 acres, in which the wonderfully tame grey squirrels are interesting. The **Capitol** or **State House** (Pl. C, 2), partly designed after the Maison Carrée at Nîmes, occupies the highest point of the square and dates from 1785.

Interior (freely open to visitors). In the *Central Hall*, surmounted by a dome, are *Houdon's* *Statue of Washington and a bust of Lafayette by the same artist. The *Senate Chamber*, to the right, was used as the Confederate House of Representatives during the Civil War. The *House of Delegates*, to the left, contains portraits of Chatham and Jefferson, and was the scene of Aaron Burr's trial for high-treason (1807) and of the State Secession Convention (1861). — The *Rotunda Gallery* contains an interesting collection of portraits (early governors, Confederate generals, etc.) and a fine old stove, made in England in 1770. — The *State Library*, on the upper floor, contains 50,000 vols. and numerous interesting relics. — The platform on the roof affords a fine *View of Richmond, Manchester, the James River, and the battlefields of the vicinity (p. 329).

Capitol Square also contains a fine equestrian ***Statue of Washington,** by *Crawford*, with figures of Patrick Henry, George Mason, Thomas Jefferson, Thomas Nelson, Andrew Lewis, and Chief Justice Marshall round the pedestal; a *Statue of Stonewall Jackson* (1824-63), by Foley, 'presented by English gentlemen' (Rt. Hon. A. J. Beresford Hope and others); and a *Statue of Henry Clay* (1777-1852), by Hart. The curious old *Bell House*, on the W. side of the square, was formerly used by the Public Guard. At the N. E. corner of the square stands the *Governor's Mansion* (Pl. D, 2). — On the N. side, in Broad St., is the handsome new **City Hall** (Pl. C, 2). — In *St. Paul's Church* (Pl. C, 2), at the corner of 9th St. and Grace

St., on the W. side of Capitol Sq., Jefferson Davis was seated when he received a despatch from Gen. Lee, announcing that Richmond must be evacuated (April 2nd, 1865).

In 12th St., at the corner of Clay St., a little to the N. of Capitol Sq., is the *Jefferson Davis Mansion* (Pl. D, 1), or '*White House of the Confederacy*', occupied by Mr. Jefferson Davis as President of the Southern Confederacy. It is now fitted up as a Museum of Confederate Relics. — At the corner of Clay St. and 11th St. (Pl. C, 1) is the *Valentine Museum*, containing a large collection of Indian relics. In this house Aaron Burr was entertained when on his trial (see above).

Following Broad St. to the E. from Capitol Sq., we pass on the left, near the corner of College St., the *Monumental Church* (Pl. D, 2), erected on the site of the Richmond Theatre, at the burning of which in 1811 Gov. Smith and fifty-nine others lost their lives. Beyond the church, facing College St., is the *Medical College of Virginia*. — About ³/₄ M. farther on, at the corner of 24th St. (r.), is **St. John's Church** (Pl. F, 2), erected in 1740, but since much enlarged.

The Virginia Convention was held in this church in 1775, and the pew is pointed out in which Patrick Henry made his famous 'give me liberty or give me death' speech. The verger is in attendance to show the church and sell photographs, canes made of the sycamore which overshadowed the above-mentioned pew, etc.

Twenty-ninth St., ¼ M. farther on, leads to the right to *Marshall Park*, on *Libby Hill* (Pl. F, 2), embellished with a *Confederate War Monument* and affording a good view.

A little farther out is *Chimborazo Park*. About 1 M. to the N.E. is *Oakwood Cemetery*, where 16,000 Confederate soldiers are interred.

From Libby Hill we may descend to Main St. and follow it to the left, between tobacco warehouses and factories, to 20th St. In 20th St., to the left, at the cor. of Cary St., close to the railway and the canal, is an ice-house which occupies the site of the famous *Libby Prison* (Pl. E, 2, 3), removed to Chicago in 1889 (see p. 280). — In Main St. (N. side, near 20th St.) is the *Old Stone House* (Pl. E, 2), the oldest building in Richmond. The **Post Office** (Pl. C, 2), between 10th & 11th Sts., to the right, was one of the few buildings in this part of the city that escaped the fire of 1865 (p. 327). — At 7th St. we may diverge to the left to visit the *Allen & Ginter Cigarette Works* (Pl. C, 3; see p. 327), at the corner of Cary St. At the corner of Main St. and 5th St., to the left, stood (till 1891) the large red brick *Allan House*, in which Edgar Allan Poe spent his boyhood with his foster-father, Mr. John Allan. Fourth St. leads to the left from Main St. to *Gamble's Hill Park* (Pl. B, 3), which commands a *View of the river, with its numerous falls and islands. Below lie the great *Tredegar Iron Works*. To the E. is the *State Penitentiary* (Pl. B, 3). Passing the Penitentiary we come (10 min. more) to the entrance to ***Hollywood Cemetery** (Pl. A, 4).

Near the W. gate of the Cemetery is the *Confederate Monument*, a rude pyramid of stone 90 ft. high, erected as a memorial to the 12,000 Confederate soldiers buried here. On *President's Hill*, in the S.W. corner of the cemetery, overlooking the river, are the graves of *Monroe* (1758-1831) and *Tyler* (1790-1862; no monument), two of the seven Presidents born in Virginia ('Mother of Presidents'). *John Randolph* (1733-1837) of Roanoke, *Gen. J. E. B. Stuart* (1833-64), and *Commodore Maury* (1830-71) are also interred here. A good view is obtained of *Belle Isle*, which was a prison-camp during the war. — To the W. of Hollywood are the *Riverside* and *Mt. Calvary Cemeteries* and ($^3/_4$ M.) the *New Reservoir Park*.

In the meantime, however, we leave the cemetery by its W. gate and proceed to the right (tramway), through a poor district, to ($^1/_2$ M.) *Park Avenue*, at the beginning of which, in *Monroe Square* (Pl. A, 2), is a *Statue of Gen. Wickham* (1820-88), by Valentine. We follow Park Ave. to the left for $^1/_2$ M. more, when we come in sight of the equestrian *Statue of General Lee, by *Mercié* (1890), one of the most beautiful monuments in the United States. Adjacent, to the E., is *Richmond College*, and $^1/_2$-$^3/_4$ M. to the W. are the *Exposition Buildings* (in the *State Fair Grounds*) and the *Soldiers' Home*.

We may now return to the centre of the city by *Franklin St.* (tramway), No. 707 in which was the home of *General Lee* (1807-70)

Among other points of interest in Richmond may be mentioned the *Virginia Historical Society*, in the *Westmoreland Club* (Pl. C, 2), at the cor. of Grace and 6th Sts.; *Chief Justice Marshall's House*, at the cor. of 6th and Marshall Sts. (Pl. C, 2); *Valentine's Studio*, 809 E. Leigh St. (Pl. C, 1); the *Tobacco Exchange*, Shockoe Slip; and the *National Cemetery*, 2 M. to the N.E. of the city (6540 graves).

Battlefields round Richmond. During the last three years of the Civil War (1862-65) battles raged all round Richmond, and remains of the fortified lines constructed to protect the city are visible in various parts of the environs. Probably the best plan for the stranger is to hire a carriage with an intelligent driver and spend a day visiting the scenes of the principal battles. Guides may be obtained at the hotels. — The chief direct attack on Richmond was made on May 15th, 1862, when the Union fleet attempted, without success, to force its way past the batteries at *Drewry's Bluff*, on the James River, 7 M. below the city (easily visited by steamer, see p. 330). Simultaneously Gen. McClellan advanced with the land-forces up the peninsula between the York and James Rivers and invested Richmond on the E. and N. This led to the hardly-contested but indecisive battle of *Seven Pines* or *Fair Oaks* (May 31st, 1862), in which the Confederates under Gen. Joseph E. Johnston attacked McClellan's left wing, to the S. of the *Chickahominy*. Large cemeteries and a park now mark the spot, 8 M. to the E., reached by the West Point R. R. (p. 330). The district is swampy, and McClellan lost more men by pestilence than in fighting. Gen. Robert E. Lee now assumed command of the Confederate forces and made an attempt, in combination with Gen. Stonewall Jackson, to overwhelm McClellan's right wing, which was posted at *Mechanicsville*, on the Chickahominy, 5$^1/_2$ M. to the N. of Richmond, and thus began the famous **Seven Days' Battle** (June 26th-July 2nd, 1862). Mechanicsville was followed by the battles of *Gaines Mill*, *Cold Harbor*, *Savage's Station*, *Frazier's Farm*, and *Malvern Hill*. The upshot of this series of contests, in which 40,000 men fell, was the relief of Richmond, as the Union troops were compelled to retreat to Malvern Hill, 15 M. to the S.E., where they repelled the Confederates in their last attack but soon after withdrew to *Harrison's Landing*, on the James River. During 1863 there were no direct attacks on Richmond. In May, 1864, Gen. Ulysses S. Grant came down through the 'Wilderness' (see p. 326), attacked Lee in his entrenched position at Cold Harbor (June 3rd, 1864), and lost 15,000 men without making much impression on the enemy. He then transferred his army to the S. side of the James; and the later stages of the war were rather a siege of *Petersburg* than of Richmond (see p. 333). Gen. Butler captured *Fort Harrison*, opposite Drewry's Bluff, in Sept., 1864.

From Richmond to West Point and Yorktown, 65 M.; railway to (39 M.) *West Point* in 1¹/₃-1¹/₄ hr. and steamer thence to (26 M.) *Yorktown* in 1³/₄ hr. (through-fare $1¹/₂). The train runs to the E., passing some of the battlefields of the Civil War. Beyond (7 M.) *Fair Oaks* (see p. 329) it crosses the *Chickahominy.* 39 M. *West Point* (Terminal Hotel, $ 2¹/₂), with 2018 inhab., lies at the head of navigation of the *York River*, and we are here transferred to the steamer of the *Baltimore, Chesapeake, & Richmond Steamboat Co.* The trip down the river is pretty. The only intermediate stop is *Clay Bank.* — 65 M. **Yorktown** (*Cooper Ho., Yorktown Ho.*, $ 2), on the right bank of the river, 10 M. above its mouth, is memorable for the surrender of the British army under Lord Cornwallis on Oct. 19th, 1781, forming the final scene of the War of Independence. Remains of British intrenchments are still visible, and a monument commemorates the surrender. — From Yorktown the steamer ascends *Chesapeake Bay* to *Baltimore* (p. 244).

From Richmond to *Old Point Comfort*, see R. 68; to *Charleston*, see R. 72; to *Savannah*, see R. 74.

68. From Richmond to Norfolk and Old Point Comfort.

a. By Steamer.

Steamer down the James River to *Norfolk* and *Old Point Comfort* (116 M.) in 10 hrs. (fare $ 1¹/₂). This is a pleasant and interesting trip. The steamers of the *Virginia Steamboat Co.* start on Mon., Wed., & Frid. at 7 a.m. and run to Newport News, Old Point Comfort, and Norfolk. Those of the *Old Dominion Co.* (for New York) leave at 5 a.m. and call at Norfolk, but not at Old Point Comfort.

Richmond, see above. The course of the *James River* is very circuitous and the direct distance from Richmond to its mouth is only about 74 M. The water is of a muddy brown colour, telling of the rich tobacco-growing soil through which it flows. Its ancient name was *Powhatan* (comp. p. 327).

Just below Richmond, on the left bank, is the site of Powhatan's home, where Pocahontas is said to have saved the life of Capt. John Smith. Several old iron-clad monitors are anchored here. — Farther on, on both banks, are earthworks of the Civil War.

7 M. (r.) **Drewry's Bluff** (120 ft.), with remains of the old fortifications (see p. 329). — 8¹/₂ M. (l.) *Chaffin's Bluff*, behind which lay *Fort Harrison* (p. 329). — 14 M. *The Dutch Gap Canal*, constructed by Gen. Butler to avoid the Howlett House Batteries, saves a detour of 5¹/₂ M. — 15 M. (l.) *Varina* was the home of Pocahontas and her husband John Rolfe. — 22 M. To the left, opposite *Turkey Bend*, rises *Malvern Hill* (p. 329). — Farther on (right) are the lowlands of *Bermuda Hundred*, where, in Grant's significant phrase, Gen. Butler was 'bottled up'. — 30 M. (l.) *Shirley*, a plantation still owned by the *Carters* (here pron. 'Cyarter'), one of the 'F.F.V.' (first families of Virginia).

32 M. (l.) **City Point**, at the mouth of the *Appomattox River* (p. 333), with the house of Dr. Epps, the headquarters of Grant in 1864-65. City Point is 12 M. from *Petersburg* (p. 333; railway). — 38 M. *Berkeley* (l.), with *Harrison's Landing* (p. 329), was the birthplace of the first *President Harrison* (1773-1841). — 39¹/₂ M. (l.) *Westover*, the former home of the Byrds and Seldens, is, per-

haps, the finest old Colonial mansion on the James (comp. p. lxxxix).
— 46¹/₄ M. (r.) *Fort Powhatan*, a relic of the war of 1812. — 56 M.
The *Chickahominy* (p. 330) joins the James opposite *Claremont*,
a rising settlement of recent origin.

68 M. (l.) *Jamestown*, the earliest English settlement in America,
founded in 1607 by Capt. John Smith and Christopher Newport. The
only remains of the ancient town are the tower of a ruined church
(in which Pocahontas was married) and a few tombstones. The river
here expands into a wide estuary. Fleets of oyster-boats are seen.

80¹/₂ M. *Deep Water Light;* 89 M. *Point of Shoals Light.*

101 M. **Newport News** (*Hotel Warwick*, $4), a flourishing little
city, with 4449 inhab., large grain elevators, coal wharves, ship-
building yards (dry-dock 609 ft. long), and iron-works. — We now
enter **Hampton Roads,** one of the best harbours on the Atlantic coast.
It was in these roads that the Confederate iron-clad *Virginia* (the
old *Merrimac*) nearly annihilated the wooden fleet of the Union, until
it was itself disabled by the opportune arrival from New York of the
famous turret-ship *Monitor.*

110 M. *Old Point Comfort* and *Fortress Monroe*, see p. 332. To
the N. (left) opens *Chesapeake Bay* (p. 249). — To reach Norfolk the
steamer ascends the *Elizabeth River*, an arm of Chesapeake Bay.

116 M. **Norfolk** (*St. James Hotel*, $3, R. from $1; *Atlantic*,
$2¹/₂-4; *Purcell Ho.*, $2-3), with 34,781 inhab., the second city of
Virginia and excelled by Savannah alone among the Atlantic ports
to the S. of Chesapeake Bay, was founded in 1682. The staples of
its busy export-trade are cotton, coal, oysters, and early fruits and
vegetables (strawberries, 'goubers' or pea-nuts, etc.). The city is
irregularly laid out but contains some pleasant residence-quarters.
A visit may be paid to one of the large *Cotton Compresses*, in which
the bales of cotton are prepared for transport by being reduced by
hydraulic pressure to one-fourth their original size. *St. Paul's Church*,
dating from 1730, was struck by a British cannon-ball in 1776, but
the one now resting in the indentation is not the original.

On the opposite bank of the Elizabeth (ferry) lies **Portsmouth** (*Ocean
Ho.*, $2¹/₂), a city of 13,268 inhab., with an excellent harbour. At *Gos-
port*, the S. end of Portsmouth, is the *Navy Yard* (open 8-5), the most
important in the country, with a huge dry-dock. To the N. is a large
Naval Hospital. — The *Seaboard & Roanoke R. R.* runs hence to (79 M.)
Weldon (p. 346), where it connects with through-routes to the S.

From Norfolk a short branch-line runs to (18 M.) *Virginia Beach* (Princess Anne Hotel, $4-5), a seaside resort on the Atlantic coast, surrounded
by pine forest. — The *Dismal Swamp* (see p. 333) may be easily visited
from Norfolk. — *Currituck Sound*, 30 M. to the S. of Norfolk, offers splendid wild-fowl shooting. — Steamers ply from Norfolk to *Old Point Comfort*
(p. 332; ¹/₂ hr.), *Richmond*, *New York*, *Baltimore*, *Washington*, etc.

b. Viâ Chesapeake & Ohio Railroad.

RAILWAY to (85 M.) *Old Point Comfort* in 3 hrs. (fare $2.50). STEAM
FERRY from (75 M.) *Newport News* to (12 M.) *Norfolk* in ³/₄ hr. (through-
fare $2.50). — Norfolk is reached from Richmond by railway viâ *Peters-
burg* in 2¹/₂-3¹/₂ hrs. (see pp. 346, 333).

Richmond, see p. 326. The train runs to the S.E., down the peninsula between the *York River* and the *James River*, a flat region of swamps and pine forest. We skirt the *Chickahominy Swamp* (p. 329) and cross that river near (18 M.) *Roxbury*. 24 M. *Providence Forge.* — 48 M. *Williamsburg* (Spencer Ho., $ 2), the ancient capital of Virginia, a place of 1831 inhab., with a church of 1678, a magazine of 1741, and other venerable relics.

The old *College of William and Mary*, chartered in 1693 (buildings mainly modern) and now used as a normal school, was the earliest college in the New World after Harvard (p. 82) and was the Alma Mater of 17 governors, 7 cabinet ministers, 1 chief justice, and 3 Presidents of the United States. In the quiet 'campus' is an old statue of Lord Botetourt.

75 M. *Newport News*, see p. 331.

82 M. **Hampton** (*Barnes Hotel*, $ 2¹/₂), a pleasant little town with 2513 inhab., is the seat of a *National Soldiers' Home* (2000 inmates) and the **Normal and Agricultural Institute for Negroes and Indians.*

A visit to the latter is of special interest. The institute is attended by 5-600 Negroes and 100-150 Indians, of whom the former pay part of their expenses by working. The chief aim of the institute is to train teachers for the coloured schools, and in this, as well as in the education of the Indians, its success has been highly satisfactory. Visitors are welcome to the classes, parade, dinner, etc. (specimens of pupil's work for sale). Hampton also contains a *National Cemetery* (5000 graves), and the *Church of St. John*, built in 1660 with English bricks. It is connected with (3 M.) *Old Point Comfort* by a fine shell road and an electric tramway.

The train now crosses an arm of Hampton Roads and reaches —

85 M. **Old Point Comfort** or **Fort Monroe** (** Hygeia Hotel*, 1000 beds, $ 4-8; **Chamberlain's Hotel*, 1000 beds, $ 5, these two close to the sea; *Sherwood Ho.*, $ 2¹/₂), consisting mainly of two huge hotels, the most elaborate fortification in the United States, and a group of cottages, and situated on a small peninsula on the N. side of the entrance to *Hampton Roads* (p. 331), with the Atlantic Ocean in front and *Chesapeake Bay* (p. 249) opening to the N.

Point Comfort received its name from Capt. John Smith in 1608 and has long been a favourite seaside resort, frequented by the Northerners in winter and by the Southerners in summer. The *Hygeia Hotel* was originally founded, in a very modest way, in 1821, and has grown to be one of the largest and most popular houses in the country; the *Chamberlain* is of recent construction. The immediate proximity of Fort Monroe, with its large garrison, adds a characteristic feature to the gaiety of the place. Good bathing, boating, and 'crabbing' are among the attractions. In winter the temperature rarely falls below 40°, and in summer it seldom exceeds 80°.

Steamers ply hence to *Norfolk* (³/₄ hr.; 50 c.), *Baltimore*, *Richmond* (p. 330), *Washington*, and *New York* (Old Dominion Line, in 24 hrs.).

*Fort Monroe, 100 yds. from the Hygeia Hotel, was constructed in 1819 et seq. to command the mouth of the James River and the approach to the Norfolk Navy Yard and to furnish a base of operations against a hostile fleet attempting to enter Chesapeake Bay. The ramparts are about 2 M. in circumference, affording a fine walk, and enclose an area of 80 acres, which resembles a beautiful park. Outside the ramparts is a broad moat. Guard-mounting (8-9 a.m.) and dress-parade (1 hr. before sunset) are great attractions to the visitor. The fort is garrisoned by a battalion of heavy artillery and is the seat of the Artillery School of the U. S. Army. Jefferson Davis was confined here for a year and a half after the Civil War, and then released without a trial. Off-shore is the low island of the *Rip-Raps*, almost covered by the works of *Fort Wool*.

Pleasant excursions may be made from Old Point Comfort to *Norfolk* (p. 331), *Hampton* (3 M.), *Newport News* (p. 331), etc.

69. From Norfolk to Roanoke.

258 M. NORFOLK & WESTERN R. R. in 9-9½ hrs. (fare $7.70; sleeper $2). — This line traverses the district around *Petersburg* (see below), the seat of the final struggles of the Civil War.

Soon after leaving *Norfolk* (see p. 331) the train skirts the N. margin of the *Great Dismal Swamp*, which may be visited from (23 M.) *Suffolk* (55 ft.), at the head of the *Nansemond River*.

The **Dismal Swamp**, 40 M. long and 35 M. wide, is intersected by small canals and yields a large quantity of cypress, juniper, and other timber. At Suffolk we may hire a man and a canoe to paddle us as far as (10 M.) *Lake Drummond* and back by the *Jericho Run Canal*, a novel and interesting trip.

We now traverse a district of pine-forest. Beyond (68 M.) *Disputanta* (115 ft.) we approach the scene of the battles of 1864-65.

81 M. **Petersburg** (*Gary, Southern, St. James*, $2-3), a manufacturing town of 22,680 inhab., on the *Appomáttox*, is of interest as the centre of the final operations of the Civil War. The ivy-clad ruins of the old *Blandford Church* are picturesque. A large stone bowl, at the N. end of the railway-bridge over the Appomattox, is known as 'Pocahontas' Wash Basin'.

Battlefields. When Grant crossed to the S. side of the James River in June, 1864 (comp. p. 329), he made *City Point* his base of supplies and spread his lines towards the W., so as to shut up Lee and his Confederate forces in Petersburg. The so-called *Siege of Petersburg* lasted from June 16th, 1864, to April 2nd, 1865; and during its continuance 13 pitched battles were fought in the neighbourhood. The intrenchments of Lee and Grant still form conspicuous features in the landscape; Grant's lines extended from the Appomattox to *Fort Fisher*, and thence E. to *Fort Bross*, a distance of 23 M. One of the best-known engagements was that of the *Old Crater*, to the E. of the city, on *Griffith's Farm*, where a small museum of war relics is shown. Carriages ($1-1½ per hr.) and saddle-horses to visit the entrenchments and battlefields may be hired at the Petersburg hotels, and guides may also be obtained.

Petersburg was also the scene of important military operations in the War of Independence (1781).

From Petersburg to (23 M.) *Richmond*, see p. 346.

As we leave Petersburg, we see, to the right, the large *Virginia Normal & Collegiate Institute*, for coloured students. The country traversed is unattractive. 129 M. *Crewe* (425 ft.). Beyond (141 M.) *Rice* we cross the *Appomattox Valley* by a lofty iron bridge (view). At (149 M.) *Farmville*, with lithia springs, we enter a fruit, tobacco, and corn growing region. — Near (181 M.) *Appomattox*, at *Appomattox Court House*, the Civil War ended on April 9th, 1865, in the surrender of Lee and his forces to General Grant.

Farther on (198 M.) we cross the *James River* and approach

(204 M.) **Lynchburg** (525 ft.; *Norvell-Arlington, Lynch*, $ 2; *Rail. Restaurant*), an industrial and tobacco-exporting city of 19,709 inhab., picturesquely situated on the S. bank of the James. It is the junction of the Richmond & Danville R. R. (see below). — Beyond Lynchburg we pass through a tunnel and begin to ascend towards the Blue Ridge Mts. The finely-shaped **Peaks of Otter* (3875-4000 ft.) are seen to the right. 229 M. *Bedford City* or *Liberty* (950 ft.; Beechenbrook, $ 2) has 2897 inhab. and various industries. To the right, beyond it, is the handsome *Randolph-Macon Academy*. — At (246 M.) *Blue Ridge* (1240 ft.), with mineral springs and a hotel ($ 3), we begin to descend on the other side of the crest.

258 M. **Roanoke** (910 ft.; **Hotel Roanoke*, $ 3; *Ponce de Leon*, $ 2 1/2; *Rockledge*), finely situated on the *Roanoke*, among the Blue Hills, has grown, since 1880, from the insignificant hamlet of *Big Lick* (500 inhab.), to a busy city of 16,159 inhab., with large machine, iron, bridge, carriage, and other manufactories. It is the junction of various branches of the Norfolk & Western R. R., including that through the *Shenandoah Valley* (see R. 70 b).

70. From Washington to New Orleans.

a. Viâ Richmond & Danville Railroad.

1143 M. RAILWAY ('Piedmont Air Line') in 33 1/2 hrs. (fare $ 27.50; sleeper $ 7). Through vestibuled train (resembling that described at p. 276) from New York to New Orleans in 40 hrs. (fare $ 34; sleeper $ 9).

From *Washington* the line runs at first towards the S.W. 7 M. *Alexandria* (p. 262). 33 M. *Manassas* (315 ft.; Cannon Ho., $ 2) was the scene of two battles during the Civil War (monument to right).

In the first *Battle of Manassas* or *Bull Run* (July 21st, 1861) which was the first important conflict of the war, the Federals under McDowell were routed by the Confederates under Beauregard and thrown back on Washington. In the second battle (Aug. 29-30th, 1862), fought on almost the same ground, 3 M. to the right, Lee defeated the Federals under Pope.

At (57 M.) *Rappahannock* we cross the river of that name. 68 M. *Culpeper* was an important point during the Civil War and is now the site of a National Cemetery. The *Rapidan River*, which we cross at (80 M.) *Rapidan*, was another name frequently heard during the struggle in Virginia, 85 M. *Orange*. — At (113 M.) **Charlottesville** (p. 304; *Rail. Restaurant*) we intersect the C. & O. R. R. (R. 58 b). We continue to run thence towards the S.W., with the *Blue Ridge* at some distance to the right. — At (173 M.) **Lynchburg** *(Rail. Restaurant)* we intersect the Norfolk & Western R. R. (see above). Farther on we cross several streams and pass numerous small stations. — 238 M. **Danville** (420 ft.; *Normandie*, $ 2 1/2; *Rail. Restaurant*), a busy little town of 10,305 inhab., in the centre of tobacco-growing region, is the junction of the line from Richmond (p. 326) which gives name to the huge Richmond & Danville system.

A little beyond Danville we enter *North Carolina* ('Old North

State'). — 286 M. **Greensborough** (840 ft.; *Benbow*, $ 2¹/₂), a growing town of 3317 inhab., with a trade in tobacco, coal, and iron.

FROM GREENSBOROUGH TO RALEIGH AND GOLDSBOROUGH, 130 M., railway in 6¹/₂-12 hrs. This line passes through a cotton and tobacco growing country. — 17 M. *Elon College;* 22 M. *Burlington*, with cotton-mills. — 47 M. *University* is the junction of a branch-line to (10 M.) *Chapel Hill*, the site of the *University of North Carolina*, founded in 1795 (300 students). — 55 M. **Durham** (*Claiborne*, $ 2¹/₂), a city of 5485 inhab., is one of the chief tobacco-making places in America. *Duke's Factory* produces 250 million cigarettes annually. — 81 M. **Raleigh** (320 ft.; *Yarborough House*, $ 2¹/₂-3), the capital of North Carolina, with 12,678 inhab., lies on high ground near the centre of the state. The *State House* stands in *Union Square*, in the centre of the city. Among other large buildings are *St. Mary's College* (pleasant grounds), *Shaw University* (for coloured students), the *State Insane Asylum*, the *State Geological Museum*, and the *Post Office*. A drive may be taken to the *Old*, *Confederate*, and *Federal Cemeteries* (views). — 130 M. *Goldsborough* (100 ft.; St. James, $ 2), a small place with 4017 inhab., is connected by railway with **New Berne** (*Albert*, $ 2-2¹/₂), at the head of *Neuse River*, and (95 M.) *Morehead*, on the Atlantic coast.

A line also runs from Greensborough, viâ *Fayetteville*, to (179 M.) *Wilmington* (p. 346).

Just beyond Greensborough, to the right, is the battlefield of *Guilford Court House* (Mar. 15th, 1781), where the British under Cornwallis defeated the Americans under Greene. — We traverse many cotton-fields. Near Salisbury we cross the *Yadkin.* — 335 M. **Salisbury** (760 ft; *Mt. Vernon*, $ 2), with 4418 inhab., was the seat of one of the chief Confederate prisons in the Civil War, and the *National Cemetery* contains the graves of more than 12,000 soldiers who died here in captivity.

From Salisbury to *Asheville* and *Knoxville*, see R. 71.

Near (379 M.) **Charlotte** (725 ft.; *Buford, Central*, $ 2-3¹/₂), with 11,557 inhab., are some gold mines. It is the junction of lines to *Wilmington* (p. 346), to *Columbia* and *Charleston* (see R. 72 b), etc. — Beyond (407 M.) *All Healing Springs* we enter *South Carolina* ('Palmetto State'). Near (413 M.) *King's Mountain* (940 ft.) the Americans defeated the British on Oct. 7th, 1780, and near (445 M.) *Cowpens* is the scene of a more important victory of the patriots (Jan. 17th, 1781).

455 M. **Spartanburg** (790 ft.; *Merchants' Hotel*, $ 2-2¹/₂), the junction of lines to *Columbia* (p. 347) and *Asheville* (R. 71), is a thriving little city of 5544 inhab., in a district of iron and gold mines and mineral springs. — 487 M. **Greenville** (975 ft.; *Exchange Hotel*, $ 2-2¹/₂), a city with 8607 inhab., on the *Reedy River*, is the junction of a line to *Columbia* (p. 347). — Beyond (528 M.) *Seneca* (955 ft.) we cross the *Savannah* and enter *Georgia* ('Empire State of the South'). About 2 M. from (554 M.) *Toccoa* are the beautiful *Toccoa Falls* (185 ft. high). 568 M. *Mt. Airy* (1590 ft.; Mt. Airy Hotel, $ 2¹/₂) affords a fine view of *Yonah Mt.* (3025 ft.) and the Blue Ridge. — The line now descends. — 570 M. *Cornelia* is the junction of a short line to (8 M.) *Clarksville* and (20 M.) *Tallulah Falls.*

Clarksville (1480 ft.; *Eureka, Mountain View*, $ 2) is a convenient point from which to explore the fine scenery of the Georgia portion of the *Blue Ridge Mts.* — The *Tallulah Falls (Cliff House*, $ 2-3; *Robinson*, $ 2), 400 ft.

high, lie in the deep gorge of the *Tallulah* or *Terrora*, which here cuts across the Blue Ridge. — Other points of interest in this district are the *Valley of Nacoochee*, 8-10 **M.** to the N.W. of *Clarksville*, and th$_\circ$ *Falls of the Eastatoia*, 15 **M.** to the N. of Tallulah Fall α.

From (583 **M.**) *Lula* a branch-line runs to (39 **M.**) *Athens*, the seat of the *University of Georgia* (1200 students). — 595 **M.** *Gainesville* (1230 ft.; Arlington, Piedmont, $ 2¹/₂) is a small town of 3202 inhab., 20 **M.** to the N. of which lie the *Dahlonega Gold Mines* (deserted). — 618 **M.** *Suwanee* (1030 ft.). Farther on *Stone Mt.* (1685 ft.), a huge mass of granite, is seen to the left (in the distance).

650 **M. Atlanta** (*Kimball Ho.*, $ 3-5 ; *Weinmeister*, $ 3 ; *Markham*, $ 2-3 ; *Rail.Restaurant*), the capital of Georgia (the 'Gate City'), with 65,533 inhab., is a prosperous commercial and industrial city, and an important railway-centre, whence lines radiate in all directions. It is well situated 1000-1100 ft. above the sea, and enjoys a healthy and bracing climate.

The chief point of interest in the history of Atlanta, which was founded in 1840, is its siege and capture (Sept. 2nd, 1864) by Gen. Sherman, who, after holding the city for two months, here began his famous 'March to the Sea' (comp. p. 351). The business quarter was previously burned down, either by design or by accident, but has been rebuilt on a finer and more modern plan. The great staples of Atlanta's trade are tobacco and cotton. Among its industrial products are cotton, furniture, patent medicines, street-cars, flour, and iron (total value of products in 1890, $ 12,000,000).

The city is laid out in the form of a circle, of which the radius is 3¹/₂ **M.** and the large *Union Depot* the centre. A little to the S. of the station is the **New State Capitol*, which contains a library of about 50,000 vols. and an interesting *Geological Collection*. A little to the N.W. is the *New Court House ;* and farther to the N., beyond the railway, is the *Custom House*. The *City Hall*, the *Chamber of Commerce*, the *Opera House*, and the *Equitable Building* are handsome edifices. Among the chief educational establishments are the *Georgia School of Technology* (a branch of the University at Athens (see above), the *Atlanta University* (for coloured students), and the *Clark University*. — In the suburb of *West End* is the home of *Joel Chandler Harris* ('Uncle Remus'). To the S. of the city are the large *McPherson Barracks*.

Atlanta is the point of divergence for the Memphis and Florida trains of the Richmond & Danville R. R. and is also the junction of lines to *Chattanooga*, *Augusta* (p. 350) and *Charleston* (p. 347), etc.

Our train now passes on to the tracks of the *Atlanta & West Point R. R.* — 689 **M.** *Newnan* (960 ft.), the junction of a line to Macon (p. 342). At (737 **M.**) *West Point* (585 ft.) we cross the *Chattahoochee*, enter *Alabama* ('Cotton Plantation State'), and join the lines of the *Western Railway of Alabama*. 759 **M.** *Opelika* is the junction of branch-lines to (29 **M.**) *Columbus* (p. 264) and to *Birmingham* (p. 343). Farther on the *Alabama River* runs to the right.

825 **M. Montgomery** (160 ft. ; *Windsor, Exchange*, $ 2¹/₂-3 ; *Houston; Rail. Restaurant*), the capital and third city of Ala-

bama, lies on the high left bank of the Alabama, at the head of navigation. It contains (1890) 21,883 inhab. and carries on a large trade in cotton (150,000 bales annually) and various manufactures. The dome of the *State House*, in which the Confederate Government was organized in Feb., 1861, affords an extensive view. The *Post Office*, *Court House*, and *City Hall* are large buildings. Montgomery, which dates from 1817, is surrounded by many old-fashioned plantation residences. — We now pass on to the *Louisville & Nashville R. R.* 869 M. *Greenville;* 906 M. *Evergreen;* 944 M. *Flomaton*, the junction of a line to *Pensacola* (p. 366). Farther on we cross the *Mobile River* and skirt its estuary to —

1004 M. **Mobile.** — Hotels. *Battle House*, $ 2¹/₂-4; *Windsor*, $ 2-2¹/₂. — Tramways traverse the chief streets (5 c). — Steamers ply to points on the Alabama and Tombigbee; also to New York, Liverpool, Tampa, Havana, Vera Cruz, etc. — Post Office, at the cor. of Royal and St. Francis Sts.

Mobile, the largest city and only seaport of Alabama, lies on the W. side of the Mobile River, just above its entrance into *Mobile Bay*. It is situated on a plain, backed by low hills, and is well laid out. Its broad and quiet streets are shaded with magnolias and live oaks, and its gardens are fragrant with orange blossom and jessamine. The harbour is approached by a deep-water channel through Mobile Bay and now admits vessels of 23 ft. draught. At the entrance to the bay, 30 M. below the city, are two forts. Pop. (1890) 31,076.

Mobile was founded about 1710 by the Sieur de Bienville, who transferred the earliest French colony in this region from Biloxi (p. 338) to Mobile Bay. It was the capital of Louisiana down to 1723. In 1763 it passed, with part of Louisiana, to Great Britain; in 1780 it was handed over to Spain; and in 1813 it became part of the United States. It was incorporated as a city in 1819, with 2500 inhab., a number that had increased to 20,515 in 1850 and to 32,034 in 1870. In 1864 the harbour was attacked and closed by Adm. Farragut. The city itself did not surrender to the Federal troops till April 12th, 1865.

The chief articles of Mobile's commerce are cotton (250,000 bales annually), timber, coal, and naval stores. Its manufactures include shingles, barrel-staves, saddlery, bricks, cotton-seed oil, cordage, cigars, and beer.

The most prominent building in the city is the Custom House & Post Office, at the corner of Royal St. and St. Francis St., erected at a cost of $ 250,000 (50,000 *l.*). Other important edifices are the *Cotton Exchange*, the *Court House*, the *Barton Academy* (a large building with a dome), the *U. S. Marine Hospital*, the *City Hospital*, the *Medical College*, the *Southern Market and Armoury*, and the *Cathedral of the Immaculate Conception*. The *Guard House Tower* is a quaint old structure in the Spanish style. The most beautiful private residences are in the shady **Government Street*. The *Shell Road, extending for 8 M. along the Bay, is the favourite drive.

About 6 M. to the W. is *Spring Hill* (steam-tramway), with a large Roman Catholic College (100 students). — *Frascati* is a popular resort on the Shell Drive (also reached by tramway). At the S. end of the Shell Road is *Frederic's Restaurant* (fish, game, and oysters). — More distant resorts of the Mobilians are *Point Clear* (Grand Hotel, $ 2¹/₂), on the E. shore of the Bay, and *Citronelle* (Hygeia Hotel, $ 1¹/₂), 30 M. to the N.

Beyond Mobile the train runs near the Gulf of Mexico, of which
it affords occasional views to the left. It traverses a characteristic
Southern landscape, passing savannahs, cane-brakes, and pine-
forest, and crossing several 'bayous'. Beyond (1030 M.) *Grand Bay*
we enter *Mississippi* ('Bayou State'). At (1035 M.) *Scranton* we
pass *Pascagoula Bay* on a low trestle. At (1065 M.) *Biloxi*, where
we cross another trestle, the Sieur de Bienville erected a fort in
1690, before he transferred his colony to Mobile (p. 337). From
(1087 M.) *Pass Christian* (Mexican Gulf Hotel, $ 3-4), a pleasant
shore-resort, we cross a long trestle to (1093 M.) *Bay St. Louis*, a
flourishing little town with 1974 inhabitants. Beyond (1105 M.)
Claiborne we cross the *Pearl River* and enter *Louisiana* ('Pelican
State'). Farther on we cross the outlet of *Lake Pontchartrain* (p. 370)
and traverse the peninsula between it and *Lake Borgne*. *Lake Catherine* (r.) is an arm of the former. 1143 M. *Pontchartrain Junction.*
1145 M. **New Orleans**, see R. 82.

b. Viâ the Shenandoah Valley.

1163 M. BALTIMORE & OHIO R. R. to (63 M.) *Shenandoah Junction;* NOR-
FOLK & WESTERN R. R. thence to (430 M.) *Bristol;* EAST TENNESSEE, VIR-
GINIA, & GEORGIA R. R. thence to (670 M.) *Chattanooga;* ALABAMA GREAT
SOUTHERN R. R. thence to (967 M.) *Meridian;* and NEW ORLEANS & NORTH
EASTERN R. R. thence to (1163 M.) *New Orleans* (through-fare $ 27.50; sleeper
$ 7). — Passengers from New York are forwarded in through-sleepers
viâ *Harrisburg* (p. 232) and *Hagerstown* (p. 233; through-fare $ 34, sleeper
$ 9). The Washington sleeper runs through to *Memphis* (p. 320).
This line traverses the beautiful *Shenandoah Valley* and affords access
to two of the greatest natural wonders of America, the *Natural Bridge
of Virginia* and the *Luray Caverns.*

From Washington to (63 M.) *Shenandoah Junction*, see R. 70b.
[Travellers from the N. reach this point viâ *Harrisburg* and *Hagerstown* (pp. 232, 233).] We here turn to the S. (left) and begin to
ascend the lovely *Shenandoah Valley, which, in addition to its natural beauties, offers the interest of the campaigns of the Civil War.
The so-called *Valley of Virginia, stretching between the Blue Ridge
and the Allegheny Mts. for about 300 M., covers 7500 sq. M. of ground and
includes the whole or part of the valleys of the Shenandoah, James, Roanoke, and New River. It was the scene of many conflicts during the war,
including Stonewall Jackson's skilful operations against Pope, Banks, Fremont, and Shields (1862) and Sheridan's brilliant cavalry feats (1864).
Between Hagerstown (p. 233) and (23 M.) Shenandoah Junction the
Norfolk & Western R. R. traverses the battlefield of *Antietam* (p. xliii).
Lee's headquarters are seen from the train.

The Shenandoah runs at first to the left, at some distance. Beyond it rise the *Blue Ridge Mts.* 68 M. *Charlestown*, the scene of
John Brown's execution (p. 265). We cross the river at (99 M.)
Riverton (500 ft.), which lies at the confluence of the N. and S. forks
of the Shenandoah. We follow the S. fork (to our left). The Shenandoah Valley is here divided into two branches by *Massanutton
Mt.*, an offshoot of the Alleghenies, which is now conspicuous to the
right. 102 M. *Front Royal.*

128 M. **Luray** (820 ft.; *Mansion Inn*, $ 3-4; *Lawrance*, $ 2),
a small town of 1386 inhab., beautifully situated on the *Hawksbill*,
5 M. from the Blue Ridge and 3-4 M. from Massanutton. It is frequented by thousands of visitors to the **Luray Cavern**, justly ranked
among the most wonderful natural phenomena of America.

To reach the cave from the station (seat in vehicle there and back
35 c.) we ascend the main street of the village to (15-20 min.) the top of
the hill, where we see (to the right) the conical hill containing the caves
and the cottage at the entrance (adm. $ 1, after 6 p.m. $ 1½, electric lights
extra after 6 p.m.; description of the cave 25 c.). The ****Cavern of Luray**
is probably 'more completely and profusely decorated with stalactite and
stalagmitic ornamentation' than any other in the world, surpassing even
the celebrated Adelsberg Cave in this respect. Appropriate names have
been given to the more important formations, which are often as beautiful
in colour as in shape. Some of the chambers are very large and lofty.
Small lakes, rivers, and springs occur. The cavern has a pleasant uniform
temperature of 54-58°, is traversed by dry and easy paths, and is bril-
liantly lighted by electricity, so that a visit to it involves little fatigue.
It takes about 3-4 hrs. to see the parts usually shown to visitors.

Visitors to Luray may also ascend **Stony Man** (4030 ft.), one of the
highest of the Blue Ridge summits, which rises 5 M. to the E. and commands a fine view (one day; horses can go nearly all the way to the top).
— Luray is also a good centre from which to visit many of the battlefields of the Virginia Valley campaign.

Beyond Luray the scenery of the valley continues to increase in
picturesqueness. 146 M. *Shenandoah*, with iron-works and railway
workshops. — 169 M. *Grottoes* or *Shendun* (1120 ft.; Wright's Hotel)
is the station for a visit to the *Grottoes of the Shenandoah (Weyer* and
Fountain Caves), which lie ½ M. from the railway (tramway 5 c.).

The grottoes (adm. $ 1) are lighted by electricity and are easily ex-
plored (2-3 hrs.). The stalactites and stalagmites vie with those of Luray.

At (183 M.) *Basic City* (Brandon Hotel, $ 3-4), a new industrial
settlement, we intersect the C. & O. Ry. (see p. 304). Near (201 M.)
Vesuvius (1420 ft.) are the *Crabtree Falls*. 225 M. *Buena Vista*
(Hotel Buena Vista) is another of the busy little towns that have
recently sprung up to develop the mineral resources of the district.
We cross the *South River*. 235 M. *Glasgow* (Hotel), another young
iron-making town.

238 M. *Natural Bridge Station* (760 ft.), on the *James River*,
2½ M. from the *Natural Bridge*, the hotels at which send vehicles
to meet the trains. The C. & O. Ry. has also a station here.

The ****Natural Bridge of Virginia** (1500 ft. above the sea) is a huge
monolithic limestone arch, 215 ft. high, 100 ft. wide, and 90 ft. in span,
crossing the ravine of the *Cedar Brook*. It seems to be a remnant of a great
horizontal bed of limestone rock that entirely covered the gorge of the
brook, which originally flowed through a subterranean tunnel. The rest
of this roof has fallen in and been gradually washed or worn away. The
bridge is finely situated in a beautiful amphitheatre, surrounded by mountains. Adjacent is a group of not very first-class hotels (*Appledore*, *Pavilion*, *Forest Inn*, $ 3-4). A kind of *Park* has been formed, embracing the
five hills named *Lebanon*, *Mars Hill*, *Mt. Jefferson*, *Lincoln Heights*, and
Cave Mt.; and drives and bridle-paths have been constructed in all directions.

The pathway to the foot of the bridge (adm. 50 c.) descends along a
tumbling brook, overhung by grand old arbor vitæ trees. The *View of
the arch from below is very imposing. Among the names upon the smooth

side of the archway is that of George Washington (W. side, about 25 ft. up), which was the highest of all until a student named Piper actually climbed from the bottom to the top of the arch in 1818. We pass under the bridge and follow the path up the glen to (1 M.) the small but pretty *Lace Falls*, passing *Saltpetre Cave*, *Hemlock Island*, and the *Lost River*. We then return to the gate-house and follow the road crossing the bridge, so as to enjoy the *Views from the top (from *Pulpit Rock*, *Cedar Cliff*, etc.). A pleasant path leads from the bridge along the edge of *Rock Rimmond*, on the top of the right (W.) bank of the ravine of Cedar Brook (views). — Continuing to follow the road we soon come in sight of the (³/₄ M.) view-tower on *Mt. Jefferson*, which commands a splendid *View of the Blue Ridge (E.), the Peaks of Otter (S.E.; p. 334), Purgatory Mt. (S.), House Mt. (N.), and North Mt. (W.). — The view from *Mt. Lincoln* is said to be even better. — The *Balcony Falls* lie 7 M. to the E.

The line now follows the James (right), with the C. & O. Ry. on the opposite bank as far as (254 M.) *Buchanan*. Fine scenery.

279 M. **Roanoke** (see p. 334) is an important junction, lines diverging here to *Norfolk* (R. 69) and *Winston-Salem*. — 286 M. *Salem* (1005 ft.); 299 M. *Elliston* (1250 ft.); 303 M. *Shawsville* (1470 ft.), the station for (2 M.) *Allegheny Springs* and *Crockett's Arsenic Lithia Springs;* 307 M. *Montgomery*, for (1 M.) *Montgomery White Sulphur Springs;* 317 M. *Christiansburg* (2005 ft.), for (3 M.) *Yellow Sulphur Springs*. — 323 M. *Radford* (1770 ft.;Radford Inn), on New River, is the junction of the Ohio Extension of the N. & W. R. R.

FROM RADFORD TO COLUMBUS, 406 M., railway in 12 hrs. — This line descends through the Alleghenies along the left bank of the *New River*. 19 M. *Pembroke* (1620 ft.). At (39 M.) *Glen Lyn* it leaves the New River and ascends to (62 M.) *Bluefield*, beyond which it traverses the great *Pocahontas Coal Field*. Beyond (74 M.) *Cooper* we thread a tunnel the sides of which are of coal. We then descend to the *Elkhorn* and *Tug River*, passing below a corner of Kentucky by a long tunnel at (156 M.) *Hatfield*. From (180 M.) *Naugatuck* we descend the *Twelve Pole River* to (267 M.) *Kenova*, at the confluence of the *Ohio* and the *Big Sandy*. We cross the former river and enter *Ohio*. 279 M. *Ironton*. At (396 M.) *Portsmouth* we leave the Ohio and ascend the *Scioto Valley*, which is full of interesting remains of the 'Mound Builders' (comp. p. lxiv). Some of the most extensive of these are near Portsmouth, which is 35 M. by railway from *Peebles* (*Serpent Mound;* p.305). Near (330 M.) *Piketon* is a remarkable '*Graded Way*', 1080 ft. long. 356 M. *Chillicothe* (p. 306) also lies amid numerous mounds and circles. 276 M. *Circleville*. — 406 M. **Columbus**, see p. 264.

332 M. *Pulaski* (1920 ft.; Maple Shade Inn, $3), a busy little iron and zinc making town with 2118 inhab., is connected by a branch-line with the *Cripple Creek District*, with its rich deposits of brown hematite iron ore. 351 M. *Max Meadows* (2030 ft.; Inn); 359 M. *Wytheville* (2240 ft.; Hotels, $2), a frequented summer-resort. To the S. (left) are the *Lick Mts.*, here dividing the valley into two branches. 372 M. *Rural Retreat* (2575 ft.), the highest point on the line; 386 M. *Marion* (2135 ft.), with the State Insane Asylum.

430 M. **Bristol** (1690 ft.; *Hamilton*, *Wood's*, $2-3), an industrial city and tobacco market with 6226 inhab., lies on the boundary between Virginia and *Tennessee*. — The scenery continues picturesque. — 455 M. *Johnson City* (1640 ft.).

A narrow-gauge railway, known as the '*Cranberry Stem-winder*', ascends through the *Doe River Cañon* (1500 ft. deep) and up **Roan Mt.** to (26 M.) *Roan Mt. Station* and (34 M.) *Cranberry*. From Roan Mt. Station stages ($2) run to (12 M.) *Cloudland Hotel*, on the summit (6315 ft.), the highest human habitation to the E. of the Rocky Mts. The *View hence is very extensive, some authorities considering it the finest in Western North Carolina (comp. p. 345). The rhododendrons and azaleas are at their best between June 20th and July 10th. Excursions may be made hence over the mountain-roads to *Hot Springs* and (80 M.) *Asheville* (p. 344).

On a hill to the left as we leave (487 M.) *Greenville* is the grave-monument of *Andrew Jackson* (1767-1845), a resident of the district. — 519 M. *Morristown* (1280 ft.).

A short branch-line runs hence to *Bean's Station*, 1½ M. from which lie *Tate Springs* (Hotel, $2½-3½), among the *Clinch Mts.* (4200 ft.). — Another line runs from Morristown along the *French Broad River* to (50 M.) *Hot Springs* and (88 M.) *Asheville* (comp. R. 71).

Beyond Morristown we enjoy frequent glimpses of the *Holston River*, which we cross before reaching Knoxville.

560 M. **Knoxville** (900 ft.; *Vendome*, $2½-4; *Knox*, $2-4; *Palace*, $2-3), the chief city of E. Tennessee, is finely situated among the foothills of the *Clinch Mts.*, on the *Tennessee River*, formed 4 M. farther up by the junction of the *Holston* and the *French Broad*. It is the centre of the Tennessee marble district, in which 250,000-300,000 tons of this beautiful stone are annually quarried. It has a large trade in country produce and various manufactures. Among the chief buildings are the *University of Tennessee*, the *Agricultural College*, the *Custom House*, the *Court House*, and the *City Hall*.

Knoxville claims to have been besieged thrice, but never captured. *Fort Saunders*, on the outskirts of the city, was unsuccessfully attacked by the Confederates on Nov. 29th, 1863. Visits may also be paid to the *National Cemetery, Gray Cemetery, Island Home Park*, and *Luttrell Park*.

Mountaineers may go by train to (16 M.) *Maryville* (Jackson Ho., $2), 25 M. (drive) from **Thunderhead Peak** (5520 ft.), one of the finest of the *Great Smoky Mts.* (ascent, with guide, in 7-8 hrs.; *View).

The KNOXVILLE, CUMBERLAND GAP, AND LOUISVILLE R. R. runs from Knoxville to (69 M.) *Cumberland Gap (1665 ft.), the chief pass across the *Cumberland Mts.*, between Virginia and Kentucky, and to (72 M.) **Middlesborough** (*The Middlesborough*, $2½-4), a young iron-making town with 3271 inhab., of whose future vast hopes are entertained. In approaching the Gap the railway passes through a tunnel, 3750 ft. long, which begins in Tennessee, passes under a corner of Virginia, and comes out in Kentucky. Railways also run from Knoxville to *Louisville* (p. 318), etc.

The part of the Alleghenies bounding the S. horizon at this part of our route is known as the **Great Smoky Mts.** (5-6000 ft.), familiar to the readers of *George Egbert Craddock's* novels. At (590 M.) *Loudon* (815 ft.) we cross and quit the *Tennessee River*. 616 M. *Athens* (930 ft.), with Grant University (left).

At (643 M.) *Cleveland* (880 ft.; Ocoee Ho., $2), an industrial city with 2863 inhab., the railway forks, one branch running viâ Rome to Mobile or Atlanta (see below) and the other viâ Chattanooga to Birmingham and New Orleans. The latter is our present route.

FROM CLEVELAND TO MOBILE, 425 M., railway in 29 hrs. — This line enters *Georgia* at (15 M.) *Cohuttah*. 25 M. *Dalton*. — 68 M. **Rome** (*Armstrong Hotel*, $2½-4), one of the chief cities of N. Georgia, with 6957 inhab. and considerable manufactures, is the junction of the line to *Atlanta, Macon*, and *Brunswick* (see p. 342). — At (90 M.) *Prior* we enter *Alabama*. — 131 M. **Anniston** (900 ft.; *Anniston Inn*, $2¼-4), beautifully situated among the foot-hills of the Blue Ridge, has recently sprung into industrial prominence from the rich beds of brown iron ore which surround it. It is also a cotton mart. Pop. (1890) 9998. Among its chief buildings are the fine *Church of St. Michael & All Angels* and the *Noble Institutes for Boys and Girls.* — 264 M. Selma (*St. James Hotel*, $ 2¹/₂), an industrial city with 7622 inhab., on the *Alabama*, is the junction of a line to *Meridian* (p. 343). — 330 M. *Thomasville;* 36² M. *Jackson;* 400 M. *Mt. Vernon*, with large U. S. barracks. — 425 M. Mobile, see p. 337.

Farther on we cross the *Critico Creek* and thread a tunnel.

670 M. **Chattanooga** (685 ft.; *Read Ho.*, $ 2¹/₂-4; *Southern Hotel*, opposite the Central Station, $ 2-2¹/₂; *Brunswick, Merchants,* $ 2-2¹/₂; *Shipp*), the third city of Tennessee, with 29,100 inhab., lies on the left bank of the Tennessee, in the centre of a district rich in iron, coal, and timber. Its progress of late has been very rapid, and its manufactures (value in 1890, $ 9,500,000) and trade are of considerable importance. The river is navigable to this point during the greater part of the year, and railways diverge in all directions. The large *Grant University* (Methodist) is attended by 450-500 students (incl. those in the department at Athens, p. 341).

Chattanooga was a point of great strategic importance during the Civil War, and several battles were fought in the neighbourhood (comp. p.   ). The best general idea of the military operations is obtained from *Look Out Mt. (2125 ft.), which rises to the S. of the city and commands a superb *View, extending into seven states. The top may be reached by railway (10 M.), by road, or by inclined plane (the last beginning in the suburb of *St. Elmo*, reached by tramway). The railway winds through the suburbs of Chattanooga, passes the *Cravens Ho.* (headquarters of Gen. Walthall) and the old *Confederate Fort*, skirts the point where the 'Battle above the Clouds' took place on Nov. 24th, 1863, and ends at the large Look Out Inn ($ 4¹/₂; 1000 beds, incl. the cottages). A narrow-gauge railway (*Views) runs from the head of the inclined plane (restaurant) along the crest of the mountain to *Sunset Rock* and (3 M.) *Natural Bridge.* To the E. rises *Missionary Ridge* (also ascended by an electric tramway), which gave name to the battle of Nov. 25th, 1863. Beyond the ridge is the battle-field of *Chickamauga* (Sept. 19th-21st, 1863), perhaps the bloodiest battle of modern days (30,000 men killed or wounded out of 112.000 engaged), which has recently been laid out as a national park (*Park Hotel*, near Crawfish Springs). Other battle-fields lie a little farther to the E. The pretty *Lulu Fal's* are easily reached from Look Out Inn. — The *National Soldiers' Cemetery*, with 13,000 graves, lies to the E. of the city.

From Chattanooga to Brunswick, 430 M., railway in 15-17 hrs. At (27 M.) *Cohuttah* this line joins the line from Cleveland (see p. 341) and enters *Georgia*. At (80 M.) *Rome* (see above) we diverge from the Mobile line and run towards the E. The railway passes near several battle-fields. — 152 M. **Atlanta**, see p. 336. From (203 M.) *Florilla* a steam-tramway runs to *Indian Springs* (The Wigwam). — 240 M. **Macon** (*Lanier Ho.*, $ 2¹/₂-4; *Brown Ho.*, $ 2-3), a busy cotton-mart and railway-centre, with 22,746 inhab., lies on the *Ocmulgee River*. The *Wesleyan Female College* here (300 students) dates from 1836 and claims to be the oldest female college in the world. — 279 M. *Cochran;* 298 M. *Eastman* (Uplands Hotel; Ashland, $ 2-2¹/₂), a winter-resort; 317 M. *Helena.* At (388 M.) *Jesup* we intersect the Atlantic Coast Line from Savannah to the S. (see R. 75a). — 430 M. **Brunswick** (*Oglethorpe*, $ 2¹/₂-4), a rising cotton-shipping port and winter-resort, with 8459 inhab., is situated on the *Brunswick River*, near its embouchure in the Atlantic Ocean. The 'Wanderer', the last slave-ship to cross the ocean, landed her 500 slaves at Brunswick. The historic *St. Simon's Island* (Hotel) and other pleasant resorts are in this vicinity. Steamer to Savannah and Florida, see p. 353.

From Chattanooga to Memphis, 310 M., in 11-12 hrs. -- The line crosses the Tennessee and enters *Alabama* at (30 M.) *Bridgeport* and runs towards the W. 97 M. *Huntsville* (610 ft.; Huntsville Hotel, $ 3-4; Monte Sano, a summer-hotel on a spur of the Cumberland Mts., 1700 ft. above the sea, $ 3-4) was formerly the capital of the state. — We recross the Tennessee to (122 M) *Decatur* (570 ft.; The Tavern, $ 2-3), a rising little iron-making city with 6330 inhab. and various manufactures. 165 M. *Tuscumbia*, with the adjacent *Sheffield* and *Florence* (across the Tennessee), has an industrial population of 11,200. Beyond *Iuka* (555 ft.) we leave the Tennessee and enter *Mississippi*. — 217 M. *Corinth* was a place of some strategic importance in the War and was occupied by Gen. Beauregard after the two days' fight at Shiloh (10-12 M. to the N.; April 6-7th, 1862), in which Gen. Johnston lost his life and the Confederates were defeated by Grant and Buell. Afterwards Corinth was occupied by the Unionists under Rosecrans, who repelled a desperate attempt to take it (Oct. 3rd-4th, 1862). — 258 M. *Grand Junction.* — 310 M. Memphis, see p. 320.

From Chattanooga to *Lexington* and *Cincinnati*, see R. 63a.

Beyond Chattanooga the New Orleans train runs to the S.W. across Alabama on the tracks of the *Alabama Great Southern R. R.* (see p. 338). 722 M. *Fort Payne* (860 ft.); 756 M. *Attala* (580 ft.), the junction of lines to Decatur (see above) and Rome (p. 341).

814 M. **Birmingham** (580 ft.; *Caldwell*, $ 2½-6; *Florence, Wilson Ho.*, $ 2½-3; *The Oakley*, E. P.), a busy manufacturing city in *Jones Valley*, founded in 1871 and containing 26,178 inhab. in 1890, owes its rapid growth, phenomenal among southern cities, to the vicinity (6 M.) of *Red Mountain*, which contains inexhaustible stores of hematite iron ore in conjunction with abundant coal and limestone. Its activity is exhibited in large rolling mills, iron-furnaces, foundries, machine-shops, etc. (total value of products in 1890, $ 5,237,000). Alabama stands third in the list of iron-producing states, and three-fourths of Alabama iron is produced in the Birmingham district. Railways radiate hence in all directions. — 825 M. *Bessemer* (600 ft.; Montezuma Hotel), founded in 1887, contained 4544 inhab. in 1890 and is already an iron-making place of considerable importance. — 868 M. *Tuscaloosa* (160 ft.), at the head of steamboat-navigation on the *Black Warrior River*, has 4315 inhab. and is the site of the *University of Alabama* (250 students). — At (945 M.) *Cuba* we enter *Mississippi*. — 960 M. **Meridian** (320 ft.; *St. Charles*, $ 2-3), an industrial city with 10,624 inhab., is the junction of lines to *Vicksburg* (p. 321), *Corinth* (see above), and *Mobile* (p. 337). — We now follow the *New Orleans & N. E. R. R.* Unimportant stations. We reach *Louisiana* at (1115 M.) *Nicholson*. In entering New Orleans we cross *Lake Pontchartrain* (p. 370).

1163 M. **New Orleans**, see p. 367.

71. From Salisbury to Asheville and Paint Rock.

186 M. WESTERN NORTH CAROLINA RAILWAY in 8 hrs. (fare $ 4.60; sleeper 75 c.). From New York to *Asheville* in 24 hrs. (fare $ 21.45; sleeper $ 5).

This railway gives access to the beautiful scenery of **Western North Carolina** ('Land of the Sky'), which may be described as a plateau with an average altitude of 2000 ft., 250 M. long and 25 M. wide, bounded by the *Great Smoky Mts.* (p. 341) on the W. and by the *Blue Ridge* (p. 338) on the E. It is crossed by several spurs of the main chain, including the *Black*, the *Balsam*, the *Pisgah*, the *Cowee*, and the *Nantahala* ranges. Many of these are higher than the main chains, the Black Mts. alone containing 19 peaks over 6000 ft. in height. The district is watered by numerous rivers that rise in the Blue Ridge and flow with a steep decline and rapid current across this plateau, cutting through the Great Smokies on their way to the Mississippi. The *French Broad*, the *Pigeon*, the *Tuckaseegee*, and the *Little Tennessee* are the chief of these. In this way the country is cross-sectioned into many smaller valleys, affording endless variety of scenery. The fact that even the highest mountains are densely wooded to their tops adds much to the picturesqueness and softens the outlines of the landscape.

Salisbury, see p. 335. Beyond (26 M.) *Statesville* (955 ft.) we cross the *Catawba*. The main *Blue Ridge* (p. 338) soon comes into sight on the right, while various spurs are seen in the distance to the left. 38 M. *Newton* (1070 ft.). — 58 M. *Hickory* (1140 ft.; Hickory Inn, $ 3-4, meal 75 c.).

From Hickory a narrow-gauge railway runs to (20 M.) *Lenoir* (Jones Ho., $ 1½), whence a drive of 4 hrs. brings us to **Blowing Rock** (*Green Park Ho.*, *Blowing Rock Ho.*, $ 2-2½), 2 M. from the famous precipice and mountain of this name (4000 ft.). The *View from the latter is superb, including the *Grandfather* (5895 ft.) on the W., the *Pilot Mt.* (2435 ft.), 100 M. to the E., *King's Mt.* (1650 ft.) to the S., and *Mitchell's Peak* (p. 345) to the N. There are several pretty waterfalls and other points of interest in the vicinity.

To the left, at (79 M.) *Morgantown*, is the large State Lunatic Asylum. We enter the mountain-district proper at (112 M.) *Old Fort* (1450 ft.) and ascend abruptly through a romantic gorge, with its rocky mountain-walls overgrown by rhododendrons (in blossom in June). The engineering of the railway here is interesting, with its numerous loops, tunnels, cuttings, and bridges; at one point four sections of the line lie perpendicularly one above the other. At the head of the gorge we thread a long tunnel and reach the plateau of *Western North Carolina* (see p. 343). 139 M. *Biltmore*.

142 M. **Asheville.** — HOTELS. *Battery Park Hotel*, on a hill above the town, $ 4; *Kenilworth Inn*, 2 M. from Asheville, near Biltmore, see above, $ 5-7; *Oakland Heights*, $ 4; *Swannanoa*, $ 3; *Winyah Sanitarium*, $ 3; *Grand Central*, *Oaks*, $ 2. — *Electric Tramway* to the station (1½ M. from the centre of the town) and to the suburbs (5 c.).

Asheville (2350 ft.), finely situated at the junction of the *Swannanoa* and the *French Broad*, is the chief town of the district and is widely known as a health resort for patients suffering from pulmonary and other ailments. Pop. (1890) 10,235. About 70,000 persons visit Asheville annually, Southerners frequenting it for its comparative coolness in summer (mean temp. 72°) and Northerners for its mildness in winter (39°) and spring (53°; chief seasons, July and Aug., Feb. and March). Its climate is dry and bright, and there are usually few days in the year in which out-door exercise is not enjoyable. It is said to be pre-eminently suitable for early stages of phthisis, while sufferers from asthma, hay fever, nervous prostration, and the after-effects of fever all derive benefit from a sojourn in Asheville. The environs are full of scenic attractions and offer abundant opportunities for pleasant walks, rides, and drives.

WALKS. *Beaumont*, 1/2 M. to the E.; grounds open to visitors. — *Fernihurst*, 1 1/2 M. to the S., overlooking the junction of the Swannanoa and the French Broad (open daily, Sun. excepted). — *Richmond Hill*, 2 1/2 M. to the N.W. (always open). — *Gouche's Peak* (3 M.) and *Elk Mt.* (5 M.), to the N. of the town, are fine points of view. — The *Vanderbilt Estate*, near Biltmore (p. 344), with a new and palatial mansion, many miles of fine drives, and a wonderfully varied display of trees (views).

DRIVES. *Swannanoa Drive*, extending for several miles along the river, the banks of which are thickly wooded and covered with rhododendrons, kalmia, and other wild flowers. — *Tahkeeostee Farm*, 3-5 M. to the W. — The *Sulphur Springs*, 4 1/2 M. to the S., may be reached by electric car (fare 15 c.). — *Hickory Nut Gap*, a beautiful pass where the French Broad penetrates the Blue Ridge, lies 14 M. to the S.E., on the railway to *Rutherfordton*. About 9 M. beyond the entrance to the Gap is the curious *Chimney Rock*. On the opposite side rises *Bald Mt.* (5550 ft.), celebrated in *Mrs. Frances Hodgson Burnett's* 'Esmeralda'. There are two plain hotels not far from Chimney Rock. Other points of interest are the *Pools* and the *Hickory Nut Falls* (1300 ft.). — *Arden Park* (Hotel, $2), 10 M. to the S.

LONGER EXCURSIONS AND MOUNTAIN ASCENTS. *Mt. Mitchell* (6710 ft.), the highest peak in the United States to the E. of the Rocky Mts., rises in the Black Mts., 18 M. to the E. of Asheville. Its base may be reached by carriage along the Swannanoa or by railway to *Black Mt. Station*. The ascent (arduous but not dangerous) takes 5 hrs. The *View is very extensive. The night is sometimes spent in a shallow cave near the top. The name is derived from *Prof. Elisha Mitchell*, who lost his life here in 1857, while determining the height of the mountain, and is buried at the summit — *Mt. Pisgah* (5755 ft.), one of the loftiest peaks near Asheville, lies 18 M. to the S.W. and commands a splendid view of the French Broad Valley. Accommodation for the night can be obtained in a farmhouse at the base, and the ascent may be made on horseback in 2 hrs. — *Craggy Mt.* (6090 ft.), an outlier of the Blue Ridge, 14 M. to the E., may be ascended on horseback in 2 hrs. (best in June, when hundreds of acres of rhododendrons, kalmias, azaleas, and heather may be seen in bloom). — *Cæsar's Head* (3225 ft.), an outlier of the Blue Ridge, 45 M. to the S.W. of Asheville, may be reached either by carriage the whole way or by train to *Hendersonville* (see below) and carriage thence. On the S. side of the mountain is a precipice 1500 ft. high, overlooking the low country of South Carolina and Georgia for 100 M. At the summit stands a good hotel ($2). Various points of interest are passed on the way. — Other distant points which are visited from Asheville are *Hot Springs* (see below), *Highlands* (see below), *Roan Mt.* (p. 340), *Tryon*, and *Blowing Rock* (p. 344).

FROM ASHEVILLE TO SPARTANBURG, 70 M., railway in 3 1/4 hrs. — This line runs towards the S. 22 M. *Hendersonville* (2165 ft.; Hotel, $2-3) is the nearest railway station to (25 M.) *Caesar's Head* (see above). Farther on the train reaches the picturesque *Saluda Gap*, where it descends rapidly through a narrow gorge. Fine views (best to the left). Rhododendrons numerous. — 70 M. *Spartanburg*, see p. 335.

FROM ASHEVILLE TO MURPHY, 124 M., railway in 9-10 hrs. — The line runs towards the W. 23 M. *Waynesville* (2755 ft.; White Sulphur Springs Ho., $2) lies amid the *Balsam Mts.*, five of which in the immediate vicinity are over 6000 ft. high. — 49 M. *Dillsborough* is one of the nearest railway-stations to **Highlands** (3815 ft.; *Davis Ho.*, $2; *Highland Ho.*, $1 1/2), which lies 32 M. to the S. and is the highest village to the E. of the Rocky Mts. It is frequented for its bracing air and charming scenery.

Beyond Asheville the PAINT ROCK TRAIN runs to the N. through the beautiful valley of the *French Broad River*. Picturesque scenery (views to left). 153 M. *Alexander*.

180 M. **Hot Springs** (1325 ft.; *Mountain Park Hotel*, $4-5), situated in a beautiful little valley, 1 M. in diameter, surrounded by mountains 3-4000 ft. high, has long been frequented for its hot

springs and delightful climate (winter milder than at Asheville). The springs (temp. 84-104°) are efficacious in rheumatism, gout, sciatica, skin and blood affections, and nervous prostration. Pleasant walks may be taken among the hills, but the drives are limited to those up and down the river. *Round Top* (1840 ft.), to the N., across the river, is easily ascended in $1/2$ hr. and commands a good view.

Beyond Hot Springs we cross the French Broad and follow its S. bank.

186 M. **Paint Rock** (1275 ft.), the terminus of the Western North Carolina Railway, has railway communication with Knoxville, Chattanooga, Cincinnati, and other S. and W. points.

72. From Richmond to Charleston.

a. Viâ Weldon.

403 M. RAILWAY (*Atlantic Coast Line*) in 11-16 hrs. (fare $ 13.65; sleeper $ 3). This line forms part of the 'Atlantic Coast Line Route' from New York to Florida (see R. 75; from New York to *Charleston* in 22-30 hrs.; fare $ 21.55, sleeper $ 4.50).

Richmond, see p. 326. The train crosses the *James* and runs towards the S. 8 M. *Drewry's*, the station for *Drewry's Bluff* (p. 330); 13 M. *Chester*. Near (23 M.) *Petersburg* we see remains of the fortifications of the Civil War (see p. 333). Near (76 M.) *Pleasant Hill* we enter *North Carolina*. At (84 M.) *Weldon* (70 ft.) we are joined by the *Seaboard & Roanoke R. R.* from Norfolk (see p. 331). The train now traverses a flat region, clothed with endless pine-forests. 121 M. *Rocky Mount*, the junction of lines to *Norfolk* (p. 331) and to (75 M.) *Plymouth*, on *Albemarle Sound*. At (138 M.) *Wilson* the line forks, the new 'Short Cut' running in a straight direction, while the line to (23 M.) *Goldsborough* (comp. p. 335) and (107 M.) *Wilmington* diverges to the left.

Wilmington (*Orton*, $ 3-4; *Purcell Ho.*; *Island Beach Hotel*), the largest city of North Carolina (20,056 inhab.), lies on the *Cape Fear River*, 20 M. from the Atlantic Ocean. It has a large foreign commerce and regular steamship-communication with New York, Philadelphia, and Baltimore. It is a prominent market for naval stores. The *Atlantic Coast Line* (see above) has its headquarters here.

163 M. *Selma*, the junction of a line to *Raleigh* (p. 335); 212 M. *Fayetteville*, the junction of lines to *Greensborough* (p. 335), *Bennettsville*, and *Wilmington* (see above); 243 M. *Pembroke*, the junction of a line to *Charlotte* (p. 335). At (282 M.) *Pee Dee* we are rejoined by the Wilmington loop-line. — 797 M. *Florence* (Central Hotel, $ 2-3), with 3395 inhab., is a cotton-market and railway-centre of some importance. We here turn sharply to the left (S.). — 344 M. *Lane's* is the junction of a line to (37 M.) *Georgetown*, a quaint and old little seaport. At (396 M.) *Ashley Junction* we join the line from Columbia (comp. p. 347).

403 M. **Charleston,** see p. 317.

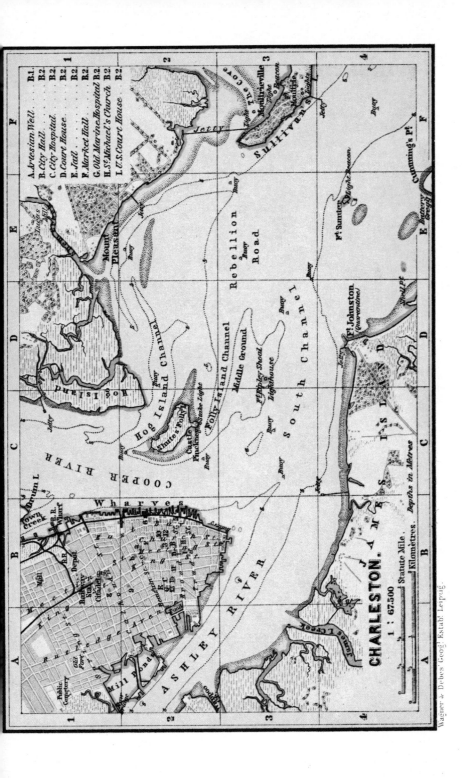

CHARLESTON.

1 : 67.500

Statute Mile.

Kilomètres. Depths in Mètres.

A. Artesian Well . . . . B.1.
B. City Hall . . . . . . B.2.
C. City Hospital . . . . B.2.
D. Court House . . . . B.2.
E. Jail . . . . B.2.
F. Market Hall . . . . B.2.
G. Old Marine Hospital B.2.
H. St Michael's Church B.2.
I. U.S. Court House . . B.2.

Wagner & Debes' Geogl Estabt Leipzig

b. Viâ Charlotte and Columbia.

519 M. RICHMOND & DANVILLE R. R. to (389 M) *Columbia* in 15 hrs.; SOUTH CAROLINA RAILWAY thence to (130 M.) *Charleston* in 4-4¹/₂ hrs. (fares as above).

Richmond, see p. 326. The train crosses the *James*, passes (1 M.) *Manchester* (p. 327), and runs to the S.W. through a tobacco-growing district. At (54 M.) *Burkeville* (520 ft.) we intersect the Norfolk & Western R. R. (R. 69). 74 M. *Keyville* (625 ft.). At (90 M.) *Randolph* we cross the *Roanoke*. From (109 M.) *South Boston* we follow the *Dan River* to (141 M.) **Danville** (p. 334).

From Danville to (282 M.) **Charlotte,** see p. 335. We here diverge to the left from the route to New Orleans (R. 70a). Beyond (279 M.) *Fort Mill* we cross the *Catawba River.* 327 M. *Chester.*

389 M. **Columbia** (300 ft.; *Grand Central,* $ 2¹/₂-3; *Jerome, Wright,* $ 2-2¹/₂), the capital of South Carolina, lies on the high banks of the *Congaree*, in the district of the *Pine Barrens*. Pop. (1890) 15,353. Its streets are wide and shady, and many of the public buildings are imposing. The most important is the new *State House*, in the grounds of which is a fine monument to the 'Palmetto Regiment', which served with distinction in the Mexican War (1846-7). Other large edifices are the *State Penitentiary*, the *Lunatic Asylum*, the *Court House*, and the *City Hall*. The *University of South Carolina* is attended by 250 students. The grounds of the *Executive Mansion* and *Arsenal Hill* command fine views of the valley. Pleasant drives may be taken in the *Fair Grounds* and *Sydney Park*. The city possesses large car, machine, and iron works.

Columbia became the state-capital in 1796. In 1832 the 'Nullification Ordinance' was passed by a convention sitting here; and on Dec. 20th, 1860, another convention announced the dissolution of the union between S. Carolina and the other states. The city was occupied by Gen. Sherman in 1865 and suffered severely from fire.

From Columbia to (67 M.) *Spartanburg.* see p. 335; to *Augusta*, see p. 350.

Beyond Columbia our line passes through a level, pine-clad district. 413 M. *Kingville;* 497 M. *Summerville* (Pine Forest Inn), frequented as a winter-resort; 512 M. *Ashley Junction* (p. 346).

519 M. **Charleston,** see below.

73. Charleston.

Hotels. *Charleston Hotel* (Pl. a; B, 2), Meeting St., $ 3-4; *St. Charles* (Pl. b; B, 2), Meeting St., $ 2¹/₂-4; *Osceola* (Pl. c; B, 2), King St., $ 2-2¹/₂.

Tramways traverse the chief streets (5 c.). — *Omnibuses* meet the principal trains (return-ticket 50 c.).

Steamers ply to *New York* (50 hrs.; fare $ 20), *Boston, Baltimore, Philadelphia, Savannah, Georgetown, Beaufort,* and *Florida* ports. A small steamer plies twice daily from Custom House Wharf to *Mt. Pleasant, Sullivan's Island,* and *Fort Sumter* (1¹/₂ hr., there and back; fare $ 1).

Post Office (Pl. 1; B, 2), East Bay. — *British Consul*, Mr. Charles L. St. John, Broad St. — *Grand Opera House*, Meeting St.; *Academy of Music*, King St.

Charleston, the largest city of South Carolina and one of the chief seaports of the Southern States, occupies the end of the narrow peninsula formed by the confluence of the *Ashley* and *Cooper Rivers*, about 6 M. from their embouchure in the Atlantic Ocean. It is a pleasant old-fashioned town, with its main streets well paved and numerous picturesque private residences embowered in semi-tropical flowers and trees. Pop. (1890) 54,955, more than half of whom are coloured. The land-locked harbour, since the completion of the new jetties, admits vessels of 20 ft. draught.

The small body of colonists under Col. Sayle, sent out by the lords-proprietors to take possession of the Carolinas in 1669, after calling at Port Royal, settled on the W. bank of the Ashley River, but soon (ca. 1680) transferred their town, named in honour of Charles II., to its present site. In 1685-6 numerous Huguenot emigrants were added to the population, and 1200 exiles from Acadia settled here in 1755. Charleston took a prominent share in the Revolution, repelled an attack on *Sullivan's Island* (Pl. F, 3) in 1776 (Col. Moultrie), and was captured by Sir Henry Clinton in 1780 after an obstinate defence. The Civil War began at Charleston with the bombardment of *Fort Sumter* (Pl. E, 4; April 12-13th, 1861), and the city was more than once attacked by the Unionists in the ensuing years, being finally evacuated in Feb., 1865. In 1886 Charleston was devastated by a severe earthquake, which has left numerous traces of its action in the form of ruined buildings, iron stays and clamps, and makeshift wooden fronts inserted in place of the destroyed brick ones.

Before the War Charleston was the chief cotton-shipping port of America, but its present prosperity is chiefly due to the discovery of extensive beds of excellent phosphates near the Ashley River; and the annual value of the exports of this article (including fertilizers) amounts to about $ 8,500,000. A visit to the phosphate-mines is interesting. Charleston also carries on a considerable trade in timber, rice, fruit, and vegetables, and manufactures cotton, flour, carriages, machines, and other articles (value in 1890, $ 9,294,200).

Following MEETING STREET (Pl. A, B, 1, 2), the chief wholesale business street, from the *Railway Station* (Pl. B, 1), towards White Point(see below), we pass the *Charleston* and *St. Charles Hotels* (p.347), the *Market* (left: interesting sight, 6-9 a.m.), and the *Circular Church* (Pl. 3; left), recently rebuilt in a handsome style. At the intersection of the street with BROAD STREET (Pl. B, 2) stands a group of public buildings: the *Court House* (Pl. D) and new *Post Office* (Pl. 1) to the right and the *City Hall* (Pl. B; with some interesting portraits) and **St. Michael's Church** (Pl. H; built in 1752-61; comp. p. lxxxviii) to the left.

St. Michael's was struck six times by the Federal cannon during the siege, was damaged by a cyclone in 1885, and nearly destroyed by the earthquake in 1886. Its fine tower commands an extensive view and contains a good set of chimes. In the churchyard, close to the iron gate in Broad St., is the tomb of a brother of Arthur Hugh Clough, with an epitaph by the poet, who spent part of his boyhood in Charleston, where his father was a cotton-merchant.

In front of the City Hall is a *Statue of William Pitt*, erected in 1770; the right arm was broken off by a British cannon-shot in 1780.

Farther on Meeting St. passes numerous private houses, embowered in roses, jessamines, and myrtles. It ends at *White Point Garden (Pl. 4; B, 3), shaded with beautiful live-oaks and commanding a fine view across the Ashley River. The *Jasper Monument* commemorates a gallant act in the defence of Fort Moultrie (June 28th, 1776). Ad-

jacent is a bronze *Bust of Wm. Gilmore Simms* (d. 1870). To the
E. extends the **Battery** (Pl. B, 2, 3), a broad esplanade, 500 yds.
long, affording a good view of the harbour and its forts.

On the island opposite the battery is *Castle Pinckney* and farther out is
Fort Ripley, while *Forts Moultrie* and *Johnston* stand opposite each other
on *Sullivan's Island* (left) and *James Island* (right). *Fort Sumter* occupies
a small island in the middle of the entrance to the harbour. The first
shot in the Civil War was fired by the Citadel cadets (see below), from a
battery thrown up on *Morris Island*, against a vessel trying to take reinforcements to the Union troops in Fort Sumter (Jan. 9th, 1861). On April
12th Fort Moultrie and the other batteries opened fire on Fort Sumter,
which had been occupied by Major Anderson with a small body of Union
troops, and its flag was hauled down on the following day. In 1863 the
Federal fleet invested the harbour and began a bombardment of the forts
and the city, which lasted, with scarcely an intermission, till the final
evacuation of Charleston in 1865. Morris Island had to be abandoned, but
Forts Sumter and Moultrie defended themselves successfully against all
attacks. Steamer to Fort Sumter, etc., see p. 350.

We now return along EAST BAY (Pl. B, 1, 2), passing the old *Post
Office*, to the new **Custom House** (Pl. 6), built of white marble (view
of harbour from back). A visit may also be paid to one of the *Cotton
Compresses* (no smoking) in this locality.

We may now return to Meeting St. and take the tramway to
MARION or CITADEL SQUARE (Pl. 7; B, 1), adorned with a statue of
John C. Calhoun (1782-1850), the famous S. Carolina statesman.
On the N. side of the square is the large **South Carolina Military
Academy,** usually known as the *Citadel*, the cadets of which took a
prominent share in the Civil War (see above).

Charleston prides itself, with some reason, on its charitable institutions. Perhaps the most prominent of these is the **Orphan House**
(Pl. 8; B, 1), founded in 1792 and said to be the oldest American
institution of the kind. The *Enston Home*, in King St., consists of a
group of 40 cottages, with a church.

Other important buildings are the *College of Charleston* (Pl. 9;
B, 2), founded in 1788; *St. Philip's Church* (Pl. 10; B, 2), Church
St., with Calhoun's grave in the churchyard (on the other side of the
street); *St. Finbar's Cathedral* (Pl. 11; R. C.), rebuilt in 1890; the
old *Huguenot Church* (Pl. 12; liturgy translated from the French);
the *Medical College* (Pl. 13); and the *Roper Hospital* (Pl. 14).

To the N. of the city, 3 M. from the City Hall (tramway 10 c.; carr.
there and back $5), lies *Magnolia Cemetery, which should be visited
for its fine live-oaks (draped with 'Spanish moss'), azaleas, magnolias,
camelias, almond-trees, etc. (best in May or June). The boughs of one
of the live-oaks have a spread of 100 ft., and the trunk of another is
17-18 ft. in girth.

No one in the season (Mar.-May) should omit to visit the (15 M.)
Gardens of Magnolia, on the Ashley (train at 10 a.m., returning at
1.15 p.m.), the chief glory of which is the gorgeous display of the azalea
bushes, which are sometimes 15-20 ft. high and present huge masses of
vivid and unbroken colouring. The live-oaks, magnolias, and japonicas
are also very fine.

The *Church of St. James's Goosecreek, an interesting relic of 1711, lies
in the heart of a forest 1 M. from (15 M.) *Otranto Station*. Otranto was
the residence of Dr. Garden, after whom Linnæus named the gardenia.

Near the church is a farm known as *The Oaks*, from a magnificent *Avenue *of Oaks* (200 years old) which leads to it.

Excursions may be made to *Mt. Pleasant* and *Moultrieville* (Pl. F, 3; New Brighton Hotel, $ 3-4), Sullivan's Island, near Fort Moultrie (p. 349), and to (22 M.) *Summerville* (p. 347). Osceola (p. 258) died as a captive at Fort Moultrie.

74. From Richmond to Savannah.

a. Viâ Charleston.

518 M. RAILWAY *(Atlantic Coast Line)* in 15 hrs. ($ 15.50; sleeper $ 4).

From Richmond to (403 M.) *Charleston,* see R. 72 a. The line *(Charleston & Savannah R. R.)* turns to the left (S.) at (410 M.) *Ashley Junction* (p. 346) and traverses a marshy district, with forests of moss-draped cypress and oak. Several muddy rivers are crossed. At (464 M.) *Yemassee* we intersect the railway from Augusta (p. 336) to *Beaufort* and *Port Royal.*

Beaufort *(Sea Island Ho.,* $ 2½-3; *Hotel Albemarle),* on *St. Helena Island,* is a fashionable Southern resort, with a fine shell-road and promenade. — Port Royal, with one of the finest harbours on the coast, was the first landing-place of the Charleston settlers (see p. 348).

We cross the wide and slow *Savannah* before reaching (504 M.) *Monteith,* and beyond it we cross the line from Augusta (p. 347).

518 M. **Savannah**, see p. 351.

b. Viâ Columbia and Augusta.

605 M. RICHMOND & DANVILLE R. R. in 22 hrs. (fares as above).

From Richmond to (389 M.) *Columbia,* see R. 72 b. Beyond Columbia the train runs to the W. through a flat, wooded region. 447 M. *Trenton.* — 460 M. *Graniteville* is the junction of the S. Carolina R. R. to *Charleston* (p. 347).

On this railway, 6 M. from Graniteville, lies **Aiken** (560 ft.; *Highland Park,* $ 4½; *Park Avenue,* $ 3; *Park Annex,* $ 2½), a popular winter-resort, much resorted to by consumptive and rheumatic patients and others. It lies in the 'sand hill' or 'pine barren' district of S. Carolina, and is surrounded by vast forests of fragrant pines, growing in a soil of white sand. The gardens of the town, thanks to careful cultivation and a liberal use of fertilizers, are full of jessamine, orange-trees, and other S. plants. The air is dry and balmy. The mean temperature of winter is 50° Fahr., of spring 57°, of autumn 64°.

Farther on the train crosses the *Savannah* and enters *Georgia.*

473 M. **Augusta** (180 ft.; **Bon Air Hotel,* at Summerville, see p. 351, $ 4-5; *Arlington,* $ 2½-4; *Planters,* $ 2½), the third city of Georgia (33,300 inhab.), pleasantly situated on the right bank of the Savannah, at the head of navigation, and connected by a bridge with *Hamburg* (S. C.) on the left bank. It carries on a large trade in cotton (200,000 bales yearly), and its cotton-mills, run by a system of *Water-power Canals,* produce more unbleached cotton goods than any other city in America (value of manufactures in 1890,$9,334,360). The main canal, bringing water from the Savannah, is 7 M. long, 150 ft. wide, and 14 ft. deep; it is owned by the city, and its revenues pay nearly the whole interest on the municipal debt. *Broad Street,*

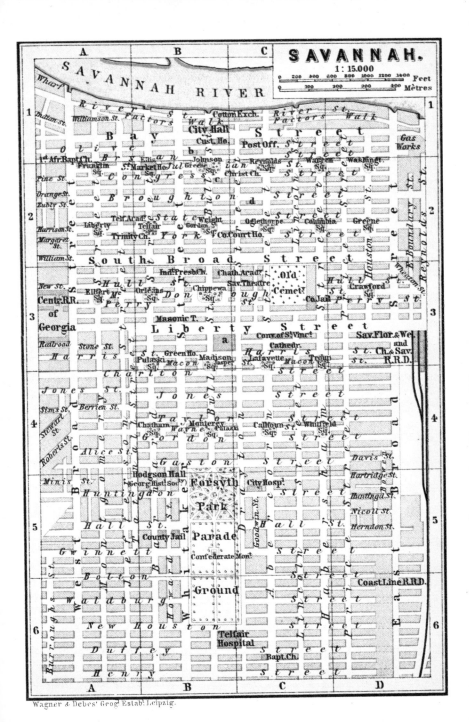

SAVANNAH.

1 : 15.000

Wagner & Debes' Geog. Establ. Leipzig.

120 ft. wide and paved with asphalt, is one of the handsomest business-thoroughfares in America; *Green Street*, with a fine double avenue of trees, is the most beautiful residence-street. In Broad St. is a handsome *Confederate War Monument*. Among the chief buildings are the *City Hall* and the *Exchange*. In 1892 a movement was started to erect a statue of *Eli Whitney*, who invented and perfected the cotton-gin in Georgia, in 1792.

On the hills 3 M. to the W. of Augusta (electric tramway) lies *Summerville* (2276 inhab.), with a U. S. Arsenal and the Bon Air Hotel (see p. 350). — *Schultz's Hill*, at Hamburg (see p. 350), and the *Fair Grounds* are favourite resorts.

Beyond Augusta the train runs to the S., soon leaving the river. At (526 M.) *Millen* (160 ft.) the railway forks, the right branch leading to Macon (p. 342). The left branch runs near the left bank of the *Ogeechee*. At (593 M.) *Bloomingdale* it turns to the left (S.E.) and soon reaches (605 M.) *Savannah*.

Savannah. — **Hotels.** **De Soto* (Pl. a; B, 3), Madison Sq., a large and handsome house, $ 3-5; *Pulaski* (Pl. b; B, 1), *Screven* (Pl. c; B, 2), Johnson Sq., $ 3-4; *Marshall* (Pl. d; C, 2), Broughton St., R. from $ 1; *Harnett* (Pl. e; B, 1), Market Sq., $ 2-2¹/₂.

Railway Stations. *Savannah, Florida, & Western*, and *Charleston & Savannah R. R. (Atlantic Coast Line)*, cor. E. Broad and Liberty Sts. (Pl. D, 3); *Central R. R. of Georgia*, cor. W. Broad and Liberty Sts. (Pl. A, 3). Stations of suburban lines, see p. 352. — **Tramways** traverse the chief streets (5 c.). — **Steamers** ply from the wharves on the Savannah, N. side of the city, to *New York* (55-60 hrs.; $ 20), *Boston, Philadelphia, Baltimore, Norfolk, Charleston, Florida*, etc.

Post Office (Pl. C, 1), Bay & Drayton Sts. — Savannah Theatre (Pl. B, C, 3), Chippewa Sq. (the oldest theatre in the United States; 1818). — British Vice-Consul, *Mr. Walter Robertson*, 89¹/₂ Bay St.

Savannah ('Forest City'), the second city and chief commercial centre of Georgia, lies on the S. bank of the river of the same name, on a bluff 40 ft. above the level of the river and 18 M. from its mouth. It is well built and regularly laid out, and the beautiful semi-tropical vegetation of its numerous parks and squares makes a very pleasing impression. *Bay Street* is the chief thoroughfare for wholesale business, while *Congress Street* and *Broughton Street* contain the best shops. *Bull Street* is the most fashionable promenade. Pop. (1890) 43,189.

Savannah was settled in 1733 by *Gen. Oglethorpe*, the founder of the youngest of the 13 original states, and owes much of its present beauty to the foresight of the plan he laid out. His object was to provide an asylum for the poor of England and the Protestants of all nations. John and Charles Wesley visited the settlement in 1736, and George Whitefield reached it in 1737. In the early troubles between the British and Spanish colonists Oglethorpe and his settlers played a prominent part, penetrating to the walls of St. Augustine (p. 357). In 1778 Savannah was captured by the British, who repulsed a Franco-American attempt to retake it the following year. The port of Savannah was closed to commerce by the Federal fleet from 1861 to 1865, and Sherman occupied the city in Dec.. 1864, at the end of his triumphant 'March through Georgia' (comp. p. 336). Since the war its progress has been rapid. Savannah contained 5195 inhab. in 1810; 15,312 in 1850; and 30,681 in 1880. — The first steamship to cross the Atlantic Ocean started from Savannah in 1819.

Savannah's export-trade is very extensive, the chief articles being cotton (second to New Orleans alone), timber, rice, and naval stores. Its manufactures (value $ 4,500,000 in 1890) include railway-cars, fertilizers, flour, and iron. A visit should be paid to one of the *Rice Mills* (River St.), and one of the *Cotton Compresses* (at the wharves).

The visitor may begin with a glance at the warehouses and wharves at the foot, and at the busy traffic of *Bay St.* (Pl. A-C, 1) on the top, of the bluffs overhanging the river. Among the buildings in this part of the city are the *City Exchange* or *City Hall* (Pl. B, 1; *View from tower), *Custom House* (Pl. B, 1), and *Post Office* (Pl. C, 1). We then follow *Bull Street (p. 351) towards the S., crossing Johnson Square (Pl. B, 1, 2), with a *Monument to Gen. Greene,* erected in 1829. In the building at the N.E. corner of Bull St. and Broughton St. the Ordinance of Secession was passed on Jan. 21st, 1861. In Wright Square (Pl. B, C, 2) is the handsome **County Court House,** built in 1889-91.

A little to the W. of this point, in Telfair Place, is the *Telfair Academy (Pl. A, B, 2; adm. 10-5, Sun. 1-5; 25 c.), which is well worth a visit (Director, *Carl L. Brandt*). It contains a collection of casts (incl. the 'Farnese Bull'), a selection of paintings, and various objects of art and historical interest. Among the paintings are good works by *Kaulbach, Julian Story, Dücker, Szymanowski, J. von Brandt,* and *C. L. Brandt* (Albrecht Dürer in his studio, Head of Christ). The picture-gallery is adorned with mural paintings by *Schraudolph* and panels by *C. L. Brandt.*

At opposite corners of *S. Broad Street* are the *Independent Presbyterian Church* (Pl. B, 3) and the *Chatham Academy* (Pl. B, 3).

In S. Broad St., a little to the E., is the interesting *Old Burying Ground* (Pl. C, 3).

We then cross *Chippewa Square* (Pl. B, 3) and reach *Liberty Street,* in which, a little to the E., are the *Roman Catholic Cathedral* and the *Convent of St. Vincent de Paul* (Pl. C, 3). In *Madison Square* (Pl. B, 3, 4) is the *Jasper Monument* (comp. p. 348), erected in 1879 in honour of Sergeant Jasper, who was killed at Savannah in 1779. The *Green House,* at the N.W. corner of the square, was the headquarters of Gen. Sherman (p. 350). *Monterey Square* (Pl. B, 4) contains the *Pulaski Monument,* in memory of Count Pulaski, who fell at the siege of Savannah in 1779 (see p. 351).

We now reach the beautiful *Forsyth Park (Pl. B, 4, 5), with its pines, roses, coleas, palmettoes, oleanders, jasmines, cacti, magnolias, etc. In the centre is a fountain. The *Parade Ground* (Pl. B, 5, 6), forming an extension of the park towards the S., contains a fine *Confederate War Monument* (Pl. B, 5). At the S. end of the Parade Ground is the *Telfair Hospital* (Pl. B, C, 6). At the corner of Whitaker and Gaston Sts., adjoining Forsyth Park on the W., is *Hodgson Hall* (Pl. B, 4), with the library and collections of the *Georgia Historical Society.* The *First African Baptist Church* (Pl. A, 1, 2), Franklin Square, has 5000 communicants.

Environs. *Bonaventure Cemetery, 4 M. to the S., reached by the *Coast Line R. R.* (station at the cor. of Bolton St. and E. Broad St., Pl. D, 3) or by the *Thunderbolt Shell Road,* is famous for its avenues of live-oaks, draped with Spanish moss. *Thunderbolt,* on the *Thunderbolt River,* 1 M. farther on, is a favourite resort. — Another fine shell-road leads W. to (9 M.) *White Bluff.* — The *City* and *Suburban Railway* (cor. Whitaker and 2nd St.), runs to (6 M.) *Isle of Hope*, on the *Skidaway River*, and (9 M.) *Mon. ʼmery* (return-ticket 50 c.), on the *Vernon River*. two pretty suburban resorts. Near the latter is *Beaulieu*. At (8 M.) *Bethesda*, on this line, is a large orphanage, established by George Whitefield in 1740. — At the mouth of the Savannah River lies (18 M.) **Tybee Beach** (*Hotel Tybee*, $ 3-4), one of the most popular sea-bathing resorts of the S. (reached by *Sav. & Atlantic R. R.*, from cor. of Randolph and President Sts.; return-ticket 50 c.). It has a fine beach. Adjacent, on *Cockspur Island*, is *Fort Pulaski*, which has been greatly strengthened since its capture by the Unionists in 1862. — A steamer plies twice weekly from Savannah to *Fernandina* (p. 355), calling at *Brunswick* (p. 342) and at several points on the *Sea Islands, on which large quantities of 'Sea Island' cotton used to be grown. They are covered with palmettoes and live-oaks.

75. From New York to Florida.

a. Viâ Atlantic Coast Line.

RAILWAY to (1034 M.) *Jacksonville* in 36 hrs. (fare $ 29.15; sleeper $ 6.50); to (1071 M.) *St. Augustine* in 39 hrs. (fare $ 30.65; sleeper $ 7); to (1274 M.) *Tampa* in 45 hrs. (fare $ 36.95; sleeper $ 8.50). The vestibuled through-train (similar to that described at p. 276) leaves New York at 12.15 a.m., but passengers may occupy their berths at 10 p.m. This is the most direct route from New York to Florida.

Florida, occupying the peninsula in the extreme S.E. corner of the United States, was the first portion of North America colonized by Europeans (comp. p. 356) and was named by its Spanish 'discoverers (1512) because first seen on Easter Sunday (*'Pascua Florida'*). Its mild and equable winter climate has made it a favourite resort of invalids and others who wish to escape the rigours of the North, while the beauties of its luxuriant semi-tropical vegetation and its excellent opportunities for shooting and fishing are additional attractions. The game on land includes deer, bears, pumas (*Felis concolor*), wild-cats, wild turkeys, and numerous other birds, while the fishing for 'tarpon' (*Megalops thrissoides*), the largest and gamiest of game-fish (sometimes 200 lbs. in weight), has its headquarters in this state (comp. pp. 362, 363). The orange is believed to have been introduced by the Spaniards, and about $3\frac{1}{2}$ million boxes (ca. 175 to a box) are now annually produced. Tobacco, cotton (including the valuable 'sea-island cotton'), rice, maize, oats, and sugar-cane are also grown, and extensive and valuable beds of phosphates have recently been discovered. Sponge and turtle fishing are other sources of wealth. The S. portion of the state is occupied by the *Everglades*, which may be described as a huge swamp, 8000 sq. M. in extent, covered with clear water and abounding in fish. A remnant of the Seminole Indians still linger here, but the district is without the pale of the ordinary tourist.

'The peninsula of Florida affords the most distinct field, in a physiographic sense, of any part of N. America. Including the N. portion of the State, it has a length of about 600 M., an average width of near 100 M., and a total area greater than that of New York, and nearly as great as that of New England. In all this great realm the maximum height above the level of the sea does not exceed about 400 ft. The whole of the soil is composed of materials recently brought together on the sea floor. About one fourth of the soil area is limy, due to the coral rock which underlies it. The remainder is nearly pure sand of a rather infertile nature. All the soil owes its value in the main to the admirable climate which the region enjoys ('Nature and Man in America', by *N. S. Shaler*).

The *Season* to visit Florida is from Dec. to April, when all the hotels are open and everything is seen to advantage. The communication with the North is excellent (comp. above and pp. 354, 355), and the hotels are much above the usual average of the South. Invalids should not visit Florida without medical advice, and all should remember that the climate varies considerably in different parts of the State. *Clothing* of medium thickness will be found most suitable, though it is advisable to be prepared for occasional great heat as well as for some really cool weather. Dust-coats will be found useful. *Walking Excursions* are not recommended, and most of the roads are too sandy for pleasurable *Driving*.

From New York to (228 M.) *Washington* (by the Pennsylvania R. R.), see RR. 31, 40, & 42; from Washington to (344 M.) *Richmond*, see R. 67; from Richmond to (862 M.) *Savannah*, see R. 74.

From Savannah we run towards the S. on the tracks of the *Savannah, Florida, and Western R. R.* The district traversed is rather featureless, but the traveller from the N. will be interested in the 'Spanish Bayonets' *(Yucca filamentosa)* and other vegetable evidence of a Southern clime. Near (878 M.) *Way's* we cross the *Ogeechee*, and beyond (908 M.) *Johnston* the *Ocmulgee*. At (919 M.) *Jesup* we intersect the line from Atlanta to Brunswick (see p. 342).

999 M. *Waycross* is a junction of some importance, lines running hence to Bainbridge (see below), Jacksonville (see p. 355), Brunswick (p. 342), and *Albany*. Numerous pear-orchards.

FROM WAYCROSS TO BAINBRIDGE, 141 M., *Savannah, Florida, & Western R. R.* in 4½-8 hrs. From (34 M.) *Dupont* a branch-line runs to *Live Oak* (p. 363) and *Gainesville* (p. 365). — 104 M. **Thomasville** (250 ft.; *Mitchell Ho., Piney Woods Hotel*, $4), a favourite winter-resort on a plateau covered with pine-forests. Pop. (1890) 5514. Its attractions include numerous walks and drives (Glen Arvern, Paradise Park, etc.), shooting, an opera-house, and comfortable hotels. It is supplied with water by an artesian well 1900 ft. in depth. Round the town are numerous orchards of the 'Le Conte' pear. — From (132 M.) *Bainbridge Junction* a branch-line diverges to (30 M.) *Chattahoochee*. — Beyond (141 M.) *Bainbridge* we may go on by the Albany Midland R. R. to *Montgomery* (p. 336).

From Waycross our line runs nearly due S. Beyond (993 M.) *Folkston* we cross the *St. Mary's River* and enter *Florida* (the 'Everglade State'). At (1014 M.) *Callahan* we cross the Florida Central R. R. from *Fernandina* (p. 355) to *Baldwin* and *Cedar Keys* (R. 79b).

1034 M. **Jacksonville**, see p. 355. Hence to (1071 M.) *St. Augustine*, see p. 356; to (1274 M.) *Tampa*, see R. 79.

b. Viâ Richmond & Danville Railroad.

RAILWAY to (1276 M.) *Jacksonville* in 40 hrs., to (1313 M.) *St. Augustine* in 43-44 hrs., to (1516 M.) *Tampa* in 48 hrs. (fares as above). The vestibuled train leaves New York at 4.30 p.m.

From New York to (228 M.) *Washington*, see R. 42; from Washington to (878 M.) *Atlanta*, see R. 70 a.

From Atlanta we follow the tracks of the *Central R. R. of Georgia* to (981 M.) *Macon* (p. 342), passing numerous unimportant stations. Here we turn to the right and take the S.W. division of the same railway. 1088 M. *Albany*, on the *Flint River*, is the junction of lines to *Montgomery* (p. 336) and *Thomasville* (see above).

We now turn to the left (E.) and follow the *Brunswick & Western R. R.* (unimportant stations) to (1200 M.) *Waycross*. Thence to —

1276 M. **Jacksonville**, see R. 75 a.

c. By Steamer.

There are various combinations for a sea-voyage on the way from New York to Florida.

Steamers of the *Clyde Steamship Co.* run thrice weekly from New York (Pier 29, E. River) to *Charleston* and *Jacksonville* (3 days; fare $ 25).

A steamer of the *Mallory Co.* plies every Friday at 3 p.m. from New York (Pier 21, E. River) to *Brunswick* (p. 342; 60 hrs.) and *Fernandina* (see below; 3½ days; fare $ 21). Fernandina is 1½ hr. from Jacksonville by railway (see below; through-fare $ 22.50).

Steamers of the *Ocean Steamship Co.* leave New York (Pier 35, N. River) four times weekly for *Savannah* (2-2½ days; fare $ 20, to Jacksonville $ 25), and Boston (Lewis' Wharf) once weekly for the same port (3 days; $ 22). From Savannah to *Jacksonville* by railway, see p. 354.

A steamer of the *Old Dominion Line* leaves New York (Pier 26, N. River) daily for *Norfolk* (p. 331; 22-25 hrs. ; $ 8), whence we may proceed to the S. by the Seaboard Line viâ *Weldon* (comp. p. 346).

Jacksonville. — **Hotels.** *Windsor, St. James,* $ 4; *Everett Ho., Carleton, Oxford,* $ 3; *Duval,* from $ 2½; *Glenada,* $ 2½-3½; *Grand View, Tremont,* $ 2-3. — *Boarding Houses,* $ 8-15 per week. *Furnished Rooms* $ 4-10 per week.

Tramways run through the chief streets and to the suburbs. *Cab* from the stations or wharves to the hotel, 25 c. each pers., each trunk 25 c. — **Steamers** ply up the *St. John's River* (p. 359) and to *Mayport, Charleston, Savannah, New York, Boston,* etc. — *Small Boats,* at the foot of Market St., 25 c. per hr. — *Post Office,* Bay St., corner of Market St.

Jacksonville, the commercial metropolis of Florida (17,201 inhab.), situated on the left bank of the *St. John's River*, 22 M. from its mouth, was founded in 1822 and named after Gen. Andrew Jackson. It is much frequented by visitors from the N. on account of its dry and equable winter-climate (mean winter temp. 55° Fahr.) but offers comparatively little of interest to the passing tourist, who will probably regard it merely as a stage on the way to St. Augustine and the more picturesque parts of Florida. It carries on a large trade in fruit, timber, and grain, and has some manufactures. The chief business-streets are *Bay Street* and *Forsyth Street*, parallel with the river, and *Laura Street* and *Ocean Street*, at right angles to it. The residence streets are generally shaded with bitter-orange and other trees. The chief streets are paved with wooden blocks.

The *Sub-Tropical Exhibition*, adjoining the *City Water Works*, ¾ M. from the river (tramway along Hogan St.), is open every second winter and affords a good idea of the products of Florida (adm. 25 c.). Pleasant drives may be enjoyed on the shell-roads to the N. and S. (across the river). Most of the other roads are too sandy for heavy wheeled traffic. Good views of the city and river are enjoyed from the bluffs to the N.E. and N.W.

FROM JACKSONVILLE TO FERNANDINA, 33 M., railway in 1½ hr. — Fernandina (*Strathmore,* $ 2½-4), a seaport with 2803 inhab., situated on the W. side of *Amelia Island*, at the mouth of the *Amelia River*, was settled by the Spaniards in 1632. It has the finest harbour S. of Chesapeake Bay, and carries on a trade in naval stores and timber, while steamers ply to New York (see above), Charleston, the Georgia ports, England, etc. Its population is much increased in winter by visitors from the N. A good shell-road leads to (2 M.) *Amelia Beach,* a fine expanse for bathing and driving.

23 *

Excursions are often made to *Cumberland Island.* — From Fernandina to *Baldwin* and *Cedar Keys*, see R. 79b.

FROM JACKSONVILLE TO PABLO BEACH, 17 M., *Jacksonville & Atlantic Railroad* (reached by ferry from foot of Newnan St.) in 1 hr. — **Pablo Beach** (*Ocean Ho.; Pablo*), one of the most popular summer and sea-bathing resorts in Florida, has a splendid beach and the usual seaside attractions. It is possible to drive along the beach to (6 M.) *Burnside* or *Mayport* (see below) and return thence by railway or steamer.

Mayport and *Burnside Beach*, at the mouth of the St. John, may be reached by steamer or by ferry from Pine St. and railway on the S. bank. From Mayport we may visit *Fort George Island* by small boat.

From Jacksonville to *St. Augustine*, see below; up the *St. John's River*, see p. 359; to *Pensacola* and *New Orleans*, see R. 81; to *Tampa*, see R. 79.

76. From Jacksonville to St. Augustine.

37 M. JACKSONVILLE, ST. AUGUSTINE, & INDIAN RIVER RAILWAY in 1-1¹/₄ hr. (fare $1.50). Station in Jacksonville at Bridge St. Viaduct.

Jacksonville, see p. 355. On leaving the station the train crosses the *St. John's River* by a steel bridge, 1320 ft. long, and traverses the suburb of *South Jacksonville*. Farther on we pass a few orange-groves, but most of the journey passes through pine-woods. Between (14 M.) *Sweetwater* and (16 M.) *Bayard* we cross the *Arlington*.

37 M. **St. Augustine.** — Hotels. **Ponce de Leon* (Pl. a; B, 4), from $5; *Alcazar* (Pl. b; B, 4), from $4; **Cordova* (Pl. c; C, 4), from $4, these under the same management; **San Marco* (Pl. d; B, 3), outside the city-gate. $4; *Florida Ho.* (Pl. e; B, 3), *Magnolia*, $3-4; *Valencia*, *Barcelona*, $2¹/₂. — Boarding Houses, $8-15 per week. — *Hotel Omnibuses* and *Carriages* at the station, ³/₄ M. from the town (25 c.; trunk 25 c.).

Carriages $1¹/₂-3 per hr., $4-5 per day; *Saddle Horses* $1 and $3. — *Boat*, with attendant, from 25 c. per hr., $2-5 per day (Central Wharf).

Post Office, Plaza de la Constitucion.

St. Augustine (accent on first syllable), one of the most picturesque and interesting little cities in America, lies on the Atlantic coast near the S. end of a narrow peninsula formed by the *Matanzas* and *St. Sebastian Rivers*, and opposite *Anastasia Island*. The surrounding country is flat, sandy, and overgrown with palmetto scrub. The older streets are all very narrow; the old Spanish houses are built of 'coquina' (a kind of shell limestone), and some of them have overhanging balconies. The gardens and squares are full of palmettoes, Spanish daggers, orange and citron trees, date palms, magnolias, and bananas. The permanent population of St. Augustine is (1890) 4742, but this is increased to at least 10,000 during winter. The climate is temperate and equable, the mean temperature for the year being about 70°, for winter 58°.

In 1512 the Spaniard Ponce de Leon landed near the Indian town of *Seloy* (on or near the site of St. Augustine), in search of the 'Fountain of Youth', but, not finding it, re-embarked. Half-a-century later (1564) a colony of French Huguenots, under René de Laudonnière, landed near the same spot, but soon migrated to the St. John's River. The settlement of a Protestant colony within his trans-Oceanic dominions aroused the indignation of Philip II. of Spain, who forthwith sent out an expedition under Don Pedro Menendez de Avilo to exterminate the invaders. Menendez landed at Seloy on Sept. 8th, 1565, found the Indians friendly, and erected the fort of *San Augustin*. St. Augustine is thus one of the oldest permanent settlements

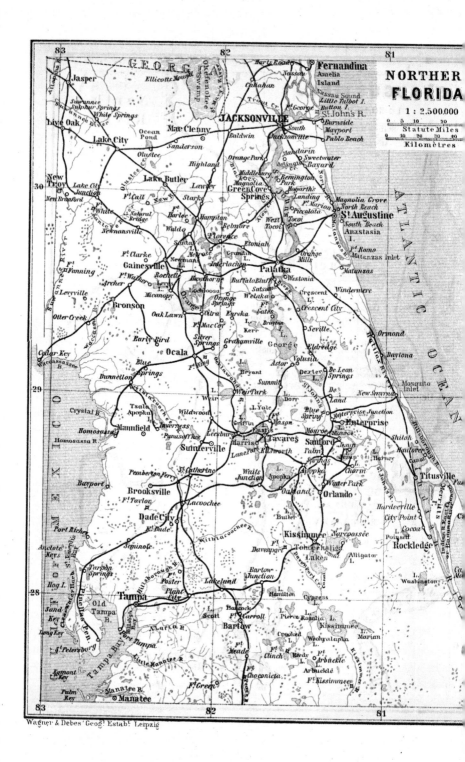

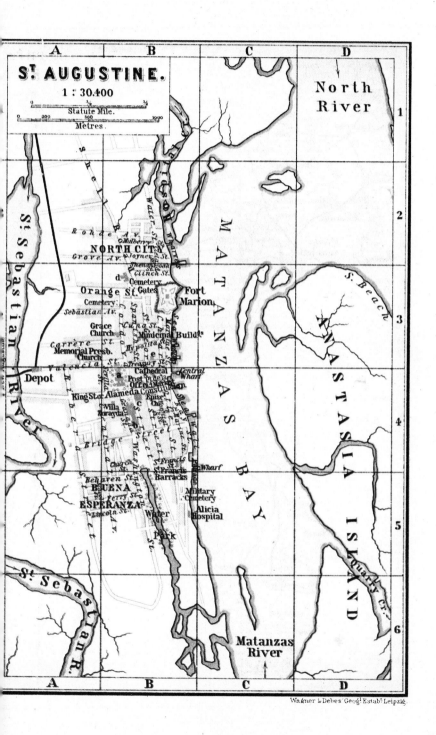

of Europeans within the territories of the United States (comp. p. 412). The Spaniards lost no time in carrying out the object of their coming by destroying the French *Fort Carolina* and massacring its inhabitants. During the next century St. Augustine led a very chequered existence. It was plundered by Sir Francis Drake in 1586 and by Capt. John Davis in 1665, and it was attacked on other occasions by the Indians, French, Carolinians, and Georgians (p. 351). In 1763 St. Augustine, with the rest of Florida, was yielded to Great Britain, but it was restored to Spain ten years later. Under the British it contained about 290 householders and 900 negroes. In 1821 Florida was ceded to the United States, and from this time may be dated St. Augustine's fame as a winter-resort, though it was not till after the termination of the troubles with the Seminole Indians (1842) that any large number of Northern visitors found their way hither.

There are now few persons of Spanish descent in St. Augustine, all having left the city on the British or American occupation; but some descendants of a colony of Minorcans, who arrived here in 1769, are still to be seen. Many of the older and more picturesque features of the place are disappearing, though a laudable effort has been made to erect new buildings in a style in harmony with the local atmosphere and traditions. The Tropical Lawn Tennis Championship is decided at St. Augustine.

In the centre of the city is the *Plaza de la Constitucion* (Pl. B, 4), extending on the E. to the sea-wall and the *Matanzas*, beyond which is seen the island of *Anastasia* (p. 356).

The *Monument* in the centre of the square was erected in honour of the Spanish Liberal constitution of 1812, from which it takes its name. On the E. side is the *Old Market*, erroneously known as the Slave Market. On the N. side is a *Confederate War Monument*. The *Roman Catholic Cathedral*, also on the N. side, was rebuilt on an enlarged scale after the fire of 1887. To the W. is the *Post Office*, to the S. the *Episcopal Church*.

Along the S. side of the Plaza runs the *Alameda (King St.)*, which brings us at once to a group of handsome modern buildings in a Spanish or Moorish style (Pl. B, 4). To the right is the huge *Ponce de Leon Hotel* (properly pron. 'Ponthe de Leōn', but usually called 'Pons dee Leeon'), to the left the *Córdova Hotel*, the *Alcazár*, and the *Villa Zorayda*, all adjoined by beautiful exotic gardens.

The *Ponce de Leon* (Pl. a), designed by Carrère & Hastings in the style of the Spanish Renaissance, is 380 ft. wide (façade) and 520 ft. long and encloses a large open court. The towers are 165 ft. high (*View). It is built of concrete, with red-tiled roofs and brick and terracotta details. The scheme of colour is very effective. The interior of the *Central Dome* or *Rotunda*, with its four galleries, is elaborately adorned with marble, carved oak, and allegorical paintings. The *Dining Room*, 150 ft. long and 90 ft. wide, is also embellished with scenes from the history of Florida, Spanish proverbs, etc. The whole building has been carried out with a rare attention to detail and every part of it will repay attention. — The *Alcazar* (Pl. b), opposite the Ponce de Leon, is by the same architects and also in the Spanish style. It includes a very large and magnificent *Swimming Bath*, supplied from a sulphurous artesian well. — The *Hotel Cordova* (Pl. c; formerly the *Casa Monica*), in a Hispano-Moorish style, was designed and built by *Mr. Franklin W. Smith* (see below and p. 181), who in this building and the Villa Zorayda (see below) first demonstrated the adaptability of the monolithic concrete architecture to modern buildings. It includes a fine sun-parlour, 108 ft. long. — The *Villa Zorayda*, the earliest of this group of buildings, was erected by Mr. Smith (see above) in 1883. It is in a Moorish style, with many suggestions from the Alhambra.

St. George Street (Pl. B, 3, 4), leading to the N. from the N.W. corner of the Plaza, is one of the quaintest and most picturesque streets in the city. It passes the new *Municipal Buildings* and ends at the remains of the old *City Gate (Pl. B, 3), consisting of two pillars, 20 ft. high, adjoined by fragments of coquina wall. On the inner side of the buttresses are two stone sentry boxes. The gate dates from the Spanish period, but its exact age is unknown. Outside the gate (to the left) are the old *Huguenot Graveyard* and the large *San Marco Hotel* (p. 356). We, however, turn to the right, to visit *Fort Marion (Pl. B, 3), the most interesting relic of the ancient city, which lies on the Matanzas, at the N. end of the sea-wall (open free, 10-4; fee to the sergeant who acts as cicerone).

Menendez (p. 356) erected a wooden fort *(San Juan de Piños)* on or near this spot. The present fort, which is made of coquina, was building for nearly 100 years and finished in 1756. The Spaniards named it *San Marco*, and it received its present name in 1821. The fort is laid out on the Vauban system, with bastions at the four chief angles, each protected by a watch-tower, and is surrounded by a moat and glacis. We enter by a drawbridge, over each end of which are the Spanish coat-of-arms and a Spanish inscription. Among the special features pointed out in the interior are the *Chapel*, the *Dungeon*, and the casemate from which the Seminole chief Coacoochee, who was confined here with Osceola, made his escape during the Seminole War (1835-42).

The SEA WALL (Pl. B, 3, 4), beginning at the water-battery of the fort and extending $3/4$ M. to the S.W., affords a fine promenade (views). It is made of coquina, capped with granite, and dates from 1835-42. — At the S. end of the sea-wall are the **St. Francis Barracks** (Pl. B, 4), named from occupying the site of the old Convent of St. Francis, some of the coquina walls of which are incorporated in the present structure. Guard-mount and dress-parade, with military music, attract many visitors. — A little farther S. is the *Military Cemetery* (Pl. B, 5), containing memorials of 'Dade's Command' (p. 364) and other soldiers who fell in the Seminole War (order of adm. necessary from the adjutant of the post). — A little to the S. is the new *Alicia Hospital* (Pl. B, 5).

Among the other buildings of interest in St. Augustine are *Grace Church* (Meth. Epis.; Pl. B, 3), by Carrère & Hastings, at the corner of Cordova St. and Carrère St., and the elaborate *Memorial Presbyterian Church* (Pl. A, 3), not far from the railway-station, designed by the same architects and erected by Mr. H. M. Flagler in memory of his daughter. — The museum of the *St. Augustine Institute of Natural Science*, 27 Alcazar Court, is open to visitors.

The harbour of St. Augustine is admirably adapted for *Rowing* and *Sailing*, and excursions may be made to *Matanzas* (to the S.), up the *North River*, etc. In the ocean, $3^{1}/2$ M. from Matanzas, is a hot *Sulphur Spring*. Among the points of interest on the island of *Anastasia* (ferry from Central Wharf; railway across the island) are the *South Beach*, the *Lighthouse*, and the old *Coquina Quarries*. *North Beach* is a favourite driving and riding resort. Fair sea-fishing (sea-bass, etc.) may be obtained here and at Matanzas.

77. The St. John's River.

STEAMERS of the *Clyde's St. John's River Line* leave Jacksonville daily (except Sat.) at 3.30 p.m. for *Palatka, Blue Springs, Sanford* (16 hrs. ; $2), and *Enterprise* (15½ hrs.; $2). Other steamers run to *Green Cove Springs, Palatka*, etc. — Travellers may save a little time by taking the railway from Jacksonville to Palatka (56 M., in 1¾-2 hrs.). Those who start from St. Augustine may also join the steamer at Palatka (railway from St. Augustine, 28 M., in 1¼-1½ hr.).

There is no great variety in the scenery of this trip, but visitors to Florida should make part of it at least for the sake of the picture it affords of luxuriant semi-tropical vegetation. The St. John's River is about 400 M. long, and its lower course resembles a series of lakes ½-6 M. wide.

The terms right (r.) and left (l.) in the following route are used with reference to travellers ascending the river.

Jacksonville, see p. 355. The following are some of the chief points passed.

10 M. (r.) *Black Point.* 14 M. (r.) *Orange Park* (rail. station). — 15 M. (l.) *Mandarin,* formerly the winter-home of Mrs. Harriet Beecher Stowe. — 24 M. (r.) *Magnolia Point,* one of the highest bluffs on the river. — 24½ M. (r.) Mouth of *Black Creek,* navigable for 8 M. — 25 M. (l.) *Remington Park.*

28 M. (r.) **Magnolia Springs** (*Hotel*, $3-5; rail. stat.), a favourite resort of consumptives, amid pines and orange-groves.

30 M. (r.) **Green Cove Springs** (*Clarendon*, $3-4; *St. Clair, St. Elmo*, $2-3), a favourite resort, with a copious sulphur-spring (78°), used both for bathing and drinking. A beautiful path leads along the river to (2 M.) *Magnolia.* — 38 M. (l.) *Hogarth's Landing.* — 44 M. (l.) *Picolata,* an old Spanish settlement. — 49 M. (l.) *Tocoi,* the junction of a (disused) railway to (18 M.) St. Augustine (p. 356). — 63 M. (l.) *Orange Mills,* with fine orange-groves.

75 M. **Palatka** (*Putnam Ho.*, $4-6; *Graham's*, $3; *St. George's*; tramway between railway-stations 5 c.), the largest town on the St. John's above Jacksonville (3030 inhab.), is pleasantly situated and attracts many winter-visitors. It is a railway-centre of some importance, and is the starting-point of the small steamers which ascend the *Ocklawaha* (see p. 360).

FROM PALATKA TO ORMOND, TITUSVILLE, AND ROCKLEDGE, 102 M., railway in 3 hrs.. This line forms the most direct connection between Jacksonville or St. Augustine and the Indian River (R. 80). — We cross the *St. John's River* to (2 M.) *E. Palatka* and (5 M.) *San Mateo.* — 25 M. *Windermere.* — 46 M. **Ormond** (*Ormond*, $4-5; *Coquina*, $3), a winter resort on the *Halifax River*, with fine beaches, may be made the starting-point of the Indian River voyage (comp. p. 364). Excellent fishing and deer-shooting. — 52 M. **Daytona** (*Palmetto*, $3-3½; *Ocean View, Fountain City*, $2-3) is another favourite resort on the Halifax River, with avenues of fine trees. — 67 M. **New Smyrna** (*Atlantic Ho., Ocean Ho.*, $3), on the *Hillsborough River* (comp. p. 364), frequented by sportsmen, was settled in 1767 by a colony of Minorcans under an Englishman named Trumbull (see p. 357). Railway to *Blue Springs*, see p. 360. — 82 M. **Titusville** (*Grand View, Indian River*, $3), near the head of *Indian River* (R. 80). is the most usual starting-point for the trip described at p. 364. — 88 M. *Hardeeville* (p. 364); 94 M. *City Point* (p. 364); 100 M. *Cocoa* (p. 364). — 102 M. **Rockledge**, the terminus of the railway, see p. 365.

From Palatka to *Sanford*, see p. 362; to *St. Augustine*, see above; to

Jacksonville (by railway), see p. 359. Lines also run hence to *Lake City* (p. 365) and to *Gainesville* (p. 363). A steamer plies to *Crescent City* (see below).

Above Palatka the vegetation becomes more luxuriant and exotic in character, including cypresses, orange-trees, magnolias, palmettoes, water-oaks *(Quercus aquatica)*, azaleas, vines of all kinds, etc. The river at first is narrow and winding.

76 M. (l.) *Hart's Orange Grove*, one of the most productive in Florida. — 84 M. (l.) *Westonia.* Just above is the mouth of *Deep River*, up which the *Crescent Lake* steamer plies to *Crescent City.* — At (87 M.) *Buffalo Bluff* the railway crosses the river (p. 361). — 93 M. (l.) *Satsuma*, with fine orange-groves. — 100 M. (l.) *Welaka* (McClure House, $ 3), on the site of Indian and Spanish settlements, is nearly opposite the mouth of the *Ocklawaha* (see below). — 106 M. (r.) *Fort Gates.* The river now expands into **Lake George*, 15 M. long and 5-6 M. wide. *Drayton Island* has fine orange-groves. To the right is the outlet of *Lake Kerr.* — On leaving Lake George we enter another narrow stretch of river. — 134 M. (l.) *Volusia*, on the site of an early Spanish mission. (r.) *Astor.* A little farther on we cross *Dexter Lake.* — From (162 M.) *De Land Landing* (l.) a short branch-line runs to *De Land* (Parceland, $ 2 1/2-3), with a (so-called) university. — From 168 M. (l.) *Blue Spring* (p. 361), with a singular spring, a railway runs to *New Smyrna* (p. 361). — 174 M. (r.) Mouth of the *Kissimmee River* (not to be confused with that at p. 362).

A little farther on the steamer passes another railway bridge and enters *Lake Monroe*, 5 M. in diameter, on the N. side of which lies (198 M.) **Enterprise** (p. 361) and on the S. (193 M.) **Sanford** (p. 362).

Above Lake Monroe the St. John's River is navigable for a considerable distance by steam-launches, and sportsmen and tourists occasionally go on as far as *Lake Harney* (guides, etc., obtainable in Sanford).

78. The Ocklawaha River.

STEAMERS leave *Palatka* every morning (10 a.m.) for (135 M.) *Silver Spring* (20 hrs., down stream 15 hrs.; fare $ 7, incl. meals and berth). The steamers, though necessarily small, are fairly comfortable.

This trip should not be omitted by any visitor to Florida. The ***Ocklawaha* ('dark, crooked water'), issuing from *Lake Griffin*, near the centre of Florida, joins the St. John's River (see p. 359) after a course of 280 M., of which about 200 M. are navigable by small steamers. It flows nearly all the way through a vast cypress-swamp, and has no banks except the tree-trunks rising from the water. The moss-draped cypresses produce a most weird and picturesque effect, especially when lighted up by the level rays of the rising or setting sun or by the flaming pine-knots used to help navigation at night. Alligators, snakes, turtles, water-turkeys, herons, egrets, and other birds of brilliant Southern plumage abound on its banks. No shooting is allowed from the steamers. The steering-apparatus is interesting. — The trip may also be made in the reverse direction.

From Palatka to (25 M.) *Welaka*, see above. Our steamer now leaves the St. John's River and turns to the right (W.) into the narrow *Ocklawaha*. The following are some of the chief landings, though none are of any size or importance.

32 M. *Davenport;* 48 M. *Blue Spring;* 56 M. *Fort Brooke.* — At (57 M.) *Orange Springs* the Ocklawaha is joined on the right by the *Orange Creek* and bends abruptly to the left (S.). — About 5 M. farther on we pass a double-headed palmetto. — 70 M. *Iola;* 74 M. *Forty Foot Bluff;* 85 M. *Eureka.* — At (85½ M.) the *Gate *of the Ocklawaha* we pass between two huge cypresses, barely leaving room for the steamer. About 5-6 M. farther on we pass a *Twin Cypress* (left), where two trees have grown into one. 97 M. *Hell's Half Acre* (island); 100 M. *Gore's;* 106 M. *Durisoe's;* 115 M. *Grahamville.*

Farther on (126 M. from Palatka) we leave the muddy Ocklawaha, emerge from the woods, and ascend the crystal-clear *Silver Springs Run* to the right.

135 M. **Silver Springs** *(Rail. Restaurant)*, the largest and one of the most beautiful of the springs of Florida, claims to be the 'Fountain of Youth' of which Ponce de Leon was in search (p. 356). The water is wonderfully transparent, small objects being distinctly seen at the bottom (60 ft. deep). The spring discharges thousands of gallons of water hourly. The visitor should row round the pool in a small boat.

Silver Springs is a station on the Florida Central & Peninsular Railway, by which connection can be made with all parts of the State. — *Ocala* (p. 364) *is* 6 M. to the W.

The upper part of the Ocklawaha, above Silver Springs Run (see above), is seldom visited by the tourist.

79. From Jacksonville to Tampa.
a. Viâ Sanford.

240 M. RAILWAY in 8 hrs. (fare $8; sleeper $2). *Jacksonville, Tampa, & Key West Railway* to (125 M.) *Sanford*, and *South Florida R. R.* thence to (115 M.) *Tampa. Port Tampa* (p. 363), the starting-point of steamers to Key West and Cuba, is 9 M. (³/₄ hr.) farther on. Through-carriages from New York to Port Tampa run on this route (comp. p. 353).

From *Jacksonville* (p. 355) to Palatka the line follows the left (W.) bank of the *St. John's River* (p. 359), which, however, is seldom in sight. 28 M. *Magnolia Springs* (p. 359); 29 M. *Green Cove Springs* (p. 359); 41 M. *West Tocoi* (comp. p. 359). — 56 M. **Palatka** (p. 359).

At (63 M.) *Buffalo Bluff* the train crosses to the E. bank of the St. John's. Numerous orange-groves are passed. 84 M. *Seville* (Seville, $3½), with a picturesque little station. *Lake George* (p. 360) lies 4 M. to the W. — 99 M. *De Leon Springs.* At (108 M.) *De Land Junction* we cross the short line from *De Land Landing* (p. 360) to *De Land* (p. 360), and at (113 M.) *Orange City Junction* we cross that from *Blue Spring* (p. 360) to *New Smyrna.* — 119 M. *Enterprise Junction*, the starting-point of the Indian River Division (see below).

FROM ENTERPRISE JUNCTION TO TITUSVILLE, 41 M., railway in 2½ hrs. — 4 M. Enterprise (*Brock Ho.*, $3-4), on the N. bank of *Lake Monroe*, opposite Sanford (p. 362), has considerable fame as a winter-resort. — 41 M. Titusville (see p. 359). Thence to (20 M.) Rockledge, see p. 365.

Our line now crosses the St. John's River as it issues from *Lake Monroe* (p. 360). 125 M. *Monroe.*

152 M. **Sanford** (*Sanford Ho.*, $ 3-4; *San Leon*, $ 2-2^1/$_2$; *Rail. Restaurant*), a thriving little city with 2016 inhab., is of some importance as the practical limit of navigation on the St. John's River and the junction of several railways. It lies on the S. side of *Lake Monroe*, in which fair fishing is obtained.

FROM SANFORD TO TARPON SPRINGS AND ST. PETERSBURG, 152 M., *Orange Belt Railway* in 7^1/$_2$ hrs. — 9 M. *Pine Forest Inn*, a winter-resort; 30 M. *Crown Point*, with lemon groves; 35 M. *Oakland*, on *Lake Apopka*, with large orange groves; 45 M. *Clermont*, on *Lake Mineola*, a tomato-growing centre; 75 M. *Lacoochee*, the junction of the F. C. & P. R. R. (R. 81). — 121 M. **Tarpon** Springs (*Tarpon Springs Hotel*, $ 3-4), a pleasant resort on the Gulf Coast, near the mouth of the *Anclote River*. The late Duke of Sutherland's manor lies 2 M. to the N.E. On the Anclote River, 3 M. to the W., is *Sponge Harbor*, whence large quantities of sponges are exported. — 126 M. *Sutherland* (Gulf View, San Marino, $ 2^1/$_2$-4), a favourite winter-resort. — 152 M. **St.** Petersburg (*Detroit*, $ 3), a good fishing-station. Steamers ply to *Port Tampa* (p. 363) and the *Manatee River*.

From Sanford to *Jacksonville* by steamer, see R. 77. Sanford is also connected by railway with *Lake Charm* and with *Tavares* (on *Lake Eustis*) and *Leesburg* (p. 364).

From Sanford we follow the track of the *South Florida R. R.*, which traverses a country thickly sprinkled with lakes. — 143 M. *Winter Park* (*Seminole Hotel, $ 4-5), a charming winter-resort, surrounded by numerous lakes (boating and fishing). — 147 M. **Orlando** (*San Juan*, $ 3-4; *Arcade*, $ 2-3; *Magnolia*, $ 2), a busy little city with 3560 inhab., affords good headquarters for guides and sporting supplies. — 165 M. *Kissimmee* (The Tropical, $ 3-4), on *Tohopekaliga Lake*, is another good hunting centre. It is the headquarters of the *Disston* or *Okeechobee Co.*, which has done much to reclaim the swampy land to the S.

The *Kissimmee River*, issuing from Tohopekaliga Lake, flows through *Lake Kissimmee* to the large *Lake Okeechobee*, which connects with the Gulf of Mexico by a canal and the *Caloosahatchee River*.

From (193 M.) *Bartow Junction* a branch-line runs to the S. to (17 M.) *Bartow* and (91 M.) *Punta Gorda*.

Punta Gorda (*Punta Gorda Hotel*, $ 4), on *Charlotte Harbor*, is the southernmost railway station in the United States and is called at regularly by the Morgan steamers from New Orleans to Key West and Cuba (comp. p. 363). It is resorted to by sportsmen and fishermen, who obtain good sport on the *Peace River* and in the harbour. The best fishing-ground for 'tarpon' is within easy reach.

208 M. *Lakeland* (215 ft.; Tremont Ho., $ 3), is the junction of another line to Bartow (and Punta Gorda) and also of one to the N. to Lacoochee, Pemberton, Leesburg (p. 364), Ocala (p. 364), etc. At (218 M.) *Plant City* we cross the Flor. Cen. R. (comp. p. 364).

240 M. **Tampa** (*Tampa Bay Hotel*, with 1000 beds, from $ 5; *Almeria*, $ 3^1/$_2$; *Plant Ho.*, $ 2^1/$_2$-3), the most important commercial city on the Gulf Coast of Florida, with 5532 inhab., lies at the head of *Hillsborough Bay* (the E. branch of Tampa Bay) and at the mouth of the *Hillsborough River*. It is surrounded with lemon and orange groves and has become one of the favourite health-resorts in Florida, especially since the opening (1891) of the huge and hand-

some Tampa Bay Hotel. The bay swarms with fish, including the 'tarpon' (p. 353), and with water-fowl, while deer and other game are found inland.

About 20 M. to the S.E. of Tampa, at *Indian Hill*, are some curious shell-mounds in which human remains were found.

249 M. **Port Tampa** (*The Inn, $4-5), on the peninsula separating Hillsborough Bay from *Old Tampa Bay*, is the starting-point of steamers to *Key West* and *Havana*, *Mobile*, *New Orleans*, *Central America, Jamaica*, and various points on *Tampa Bay*, the *Manatee River*, etc. To reach deep water the railway has to run into the bay on trestle-work for nearly 1 M., and at the end of this is the pier, with the inn and other buildings.

The Plant Line steamers for *Havana*, the capital of Cuba, run thrice weekly in winter and twice weekly in summer (32 hrs; fare $ 24.25). On the way they call at **Key West** (*Russell Ho.*, $ 3-4; tramways; carr. $1 per hr.), the most populous city in Florida (18,080 inhab. in 1890), situated upon one of the long chain of 'keys', or small coralline islands, which lie to the S. of the peninsula. The name is said to be a corruption of the Spanish *Cayo Hueso* ('Bone Island'), which took its rise from the finding of numerous human bones here by the Spanish mariners. Many of the inhabitants are Cubans, who have established cigar factories that now produce 125-150 million cigars annually. Other important industries are the sponge-fishery, turtle-catching, and deep-sea fishing (mullet, etc.). The city has some substantial public buildings. The fine harbour is protected by *Fort Taylor*, built on a small island. A visit may be paid to the *Banyan Tree* adjoining the *U. S. Barracks*. Key West is not so warm as many places to the N. of it (range 50-96°; mean for winter ca. 70°), and its pure air attracts many winter-visitors. Steamers ply regularly from Key West to *Cedar Key* (see below), *Tampa* (p. 362), *Punta Gorda* (p. 362), *Biscayne Bay* (E. coast of Florida), *New Orleans* (p. 366), *Galveston* (p. 467), *Baltimore* (p. 244), *New York* (p. 6), and *Havana* (9-12 hrs.; comp. above). *Sand Key*, 7 M. to the S.S.W. of Key West, is the southernmost point of the United States.

b. Viâ Waldo and Ocala.

212 M. FLORIDA CENTRAL & PENINSULAR R. R. in 9-11 hrs. (fares as above; to Ocala $ 3.90, to Cedar Key $ 5.10).

At (19 M.) *Baldwin* this line diverges to the left (S.) from the line to Tallahassee (and New Orleans; see R. 81) and joins the line from Fernandina (p. 355) to Tampa. 33 M. *Highland;* 38 M. *Lawtey*, with orange-groves and strawberry-farms. At (51 M.) *Hampton* we cross the railway from Palatka (p. 359) to Lake City (p. 365). — 56 M. **Waldo** (*Waldo Ho.*, $ 3) is the junction of a branch-line to Cedar Key (see below).

FROM WALDO TO CEDAR KEY, 71 M., railway in 4⅓ hrs. — 14 M. **Gainesville** (*Arlington*, *Rochemont*, $ 2½-3; *Brown Ho.*, $ 2-4), a city and winter-resort with 2790 inhab., is the junction of railways to Palatka, Ocala, Lake City, etc. Excursions may be made to the *Alachua Sink* and other natural curiosities. From *Archer* a branch-line leads through a rich phosphate district to *Eagle Mine* (phosphates). — 71 M. **Cedar Key** (*Suwanee*, *Schlemmer*, $ 2½-3½; *Bettelini*, $ 2), a city of 1869 inhab., lies on a small 'key' off the W. coast of Florida and has a harbour which admits vessels of 12 ft. draught. It carries on a trade in fish, turtle, oysters, and sponges, and cuts red cedar for lead pencils. Steamers ply hence to New Orleans, the Suwanee River, etc. — The **Suwanee River**, well known from the negro-song of 'The old folks at home' (by S. C. Foster), enters the Gulf of Mexico about 15 M. to the N.

At (70 M.) *Hawthorne* we intersect the line from Palatka to Gainesville (see p. 363). Farther on we skirt *Loch Loosa* and cross the E. branch of *Orange Lake*, on the S. shore of which we traverse, for nearly 1 M., the so-called *Mammoth Orange Groves*, with 70,000 trees. 83 M. *Citra*. From (98 M.) *Silver Springs Junction* a branch-line runs to (2 M.) *Silver Springs* (see p. 361). — 101 M. **Ocala** (*Ocala Ho.*, $ 3-4; *Montezuma*, $ 2-3), a thriving little city (2904 inhab.), in one of the most fertile districts of Florida. Large phosphate beds are worked in the vicinity. The *Semi-Tropical Exhibition* here is to be open every second year. Ocala is also a station on the Florida Southern R. R. and the starting-point of a line to *Dunnellon* (on the *Withlacoochee River*), *Crystal River*, and (48 M.) *Homosassa*, on the Gulf of Mexico. — From (127 M.) *Wildwood* a line runs to *Leesburg*, *Tavares*, etc. 135 M. *Panasoffkee*, at the S. end of the lake of that name. About 4 M. to the N. of (146 M.) *St. Catherine* (junction of the Florida Southern R. R.) is the spot where Major Dade and his detachment of 110 men were surprised and slain by the Seminoles on Dec. 28th, 1835, only three soldiers escaping alive. — 156 M. *Lacoochee* is the junction of the Orange Belt R. R. to (45 M.) *Tarpon Springs* (see p. 362). Near (164 M.) *Dade City* is the pretty *Pasadena Lake*, with a small hotel on its banks. 189 M. *Plant City*, see p. 362; 210 M. *Ybor*, with large tobacco-factories. 212 M. **Tampa**, see p. 362.

80. The Indian River.

The *Indian River* is, strictly speaking, a long and narrow sound or lagoon, running parallel with the Atlantic coast and separated from the ocean by a strip of land. It is connected with the ocean by several inlets, and its water is salt, tempered by an influx of much fresh water from its tributaries. From its head, 12 M. above Titusville, to the S. end at Jupiter Inlet it is about 160 M. long, while its breadth varies from about 50 yds. in the Narrows (p. 365) to 6 M. The banks are lined with luxuriant exotic vegetation, which affords cover to large and small game, including bears, pumas (p. 353), wild-cats, deer, and turkeys, while the water teems with fish. The water is often highly phosphorescent at night. The Indian River oranges (groves on the W. shore) are celebrated.

The steamers of the *Indian River Steamboat Co.* leave *Titusville* (see p. 359) daily about 6 a.m. for *Melbourne* (p. 365), arriving at 1 p.m., and thrice weekly for *Jupiter* (p. 365; fare $ 5.25) at about 7,30 p.m., arriving at 5.15 p.m. on the following day. The accommodation on board is good. Those who wish may begin their water-trip at *Ormond* (p. 359) or *Daytona* (p. 359), whence smaller steamers ply through the *Halifax* and *Hillsborough Rivers* (about 60 M.) to *Titusville* and *Rockledge*, passing *New Smyrna* (p. 359) and entering the Indian River through a short canal (fare $ 2.50).

Titusville, see p. 359. Opposite lies *Merritt's Island*, bisected by *Banana Creek*. This island divides the Indian River here into two branches, of which the E. is known as *Banana River*. To the E. of the island is *Cape Canáveral*, with a lighthouse.

12 M. (r.) *Hardeeville*. — 14 M. (l.) *Courteney*. — 14 M. (r.) *Faber's*. — 17 M. (r.) *Sharp's*. — 18 M. (r.) *City Point*. — 22 M. (l.) *Merritt*. — 24 M. (r.) *Cocoa*. — 25 M. (r.) *Hardee's*.

26 M. (r.) **Rockledge** (*Indian River Hotel*, $ 4; *Tropical*, $ 3;
New Rockledge, $ 2½), opposite the S. end of Merritt's Island, is
frequented by health-seekers and sportsmen. The Rockledge 'Hum-
mock' (a name applied to fertile land formed of vegetable mould)
abounds in fine orange groves. It is the terminus of the Jacksonville,
St. Augustine, & Indian River R. R. (p. 359).

31 M. (l.) *Georgiana.* — 42 M. (l.) *Tropic,* on the S. extremity
of Merritt's Island, between the Indian River and Banana River. —
50 M. (r.) *Eau Gallie.* — 51 M. (r.) *Melbourne*, with several small
hotels ($1½-2), where the river is about 2 M. wide. — 60 M. (r.)
Malabar. — 68 M. (r.) *Micco.* — 73 M. (l.) *Sebastian.* — 86 M. (l.)
Narrows. The vegetation becomes more tropical.

106 M. (r.) *St. Lucie.* Nearly opposite is *Indian River Inlet,* and
below is (109 M.) *Fort Pierce* (r.). The wide part of the river we
now traverse is named *St. Lucie Sound.* — 116 M. (r.) *Ankona.* —
123 M. (r.) *Eden.* Pine-apples are extensively grown here.

130 M. (r.) *Waveland.* — 133 M. (r.) *Sewell's Point*, at the
mouth of the *St. Lucie River.* — A little farther on we enter the
Narrows, where the river is sometimes not more than 100-150 ft. wide.

We reach the end of our journey at (154 M.) **Jupiter Inlet** (*The
Rockledge*, a large steamer used as a hotel, $3). Good fishing is
obtained here. The *View from the *Lighthouse* is very extensive.
About 1 M. to the S. is a *U. S. Life-Saving Station.* The mangrove-
thickets and curious arboreal forms are interesting.

A short railway runs to the S. from Jupiter to (8 M.) **Lake Worth,**
which is 22 M. long and ½-1 M. wide. It is frequented by visitors from
the N. and several villas have been built on its shores. Fish, including
the tarpon, abound in its waters. The vegetation is very luxuriant and
includes the cocoa-nut palm. A small steamer starting at *Juno,* the rail-
way-terminus, plies on the lake, calling at (6 M.) *Oaklawn* (Oaklawn Ho.,
$ 2½), the *Lake Worth Hotel* (8 M.; $ 4), *Palm Beach* (9 M.; Cocoa-nut
Grove Ho., $ 3), and other landings.

81. From Jacksonville to Tallahassee, Pensacola, and New Orleans.

614 M. FLORIDA CENTRAL & PENINSULAR R. R. to (208 M.) *River Junction* in 10-14 hrs.; LOUISVILLE & NASHVILLE R. R. thence to (406 M.) *New
Orleans* in 14-15 hrs. (through-carriages; fare $ 19.35; sleeper $ 3.50).

Jacksonville, see p. 355. The line runs nearly due W. At (19 M.)
Baldwin we cross the line from Fernandina to Cedar Key (see R. 79b).
Beyond (28 M.) *McClenny* we cross the S. fork of the *St. Mary's
River.* The Confederates defeated the Federals at (47 M.) *Olustee*
on Feb. 20th, 1864. — 59 M. *Lake City* (Central Ho., Gee Ho., $ 2),
embosomed in trees, is the seat of the State Agricultural College and
a U.S. Experimental Station and the junction of lines to *Palatka*
(p. 359), *Gainesville* (p. 363), *Macon* (p. 342), etc. It is surrounded
by numerous lakes and lakelets. — At (82 M.) *Live Oak* we intersect the Sav., Flor., & W. Railway, and at (95 M.) *Ellaville* we cross
the rushing *Suwanee River* (see p. 363). Beyond (124 M.) *Green-*

ville we cross the *Aucilla.* From (138 M.) *Drifton* a line runs N. to (4 M.) *Monticello* and *Thomasville* (p. 354). **147 M.** *Lloyd* (Rail. Restaurant, meals 75 c.). The country now becomes more hilly.

165 M. **Tallahassee** (*Leon,* $ 3-4; *St. James,* $ 2-3), the capital of Florida, is beautifully situated among trees, on a hill rising 280 ft. above the sea. Pop. (1890) 2984. The chief buildings are the *Capitol, Court House,* and *W. Florida Seminary.* The gardens are very beautiful, especially in the time of roses. The *Episcopal Cemetery* contains the grave of Prince Charles Murat (d. 1847), son of the King of Naples, who married a Virginian girl and settled near Tallahassee.

Pleasant drives may be taken to (6 M.) *Lake Jackson* (fishing), *Lake Iamonia* (12 M.), *Lake Miccosukie* (18 M.), *Bellair* (6 M.), and to the *Wakulla Spring* (15 M. to the S.). The spring (4¹/₂ M. from *Wakulla Station,* on the branch-line to *St. Mark's*) is 106 ft. deep and of wonderful transparency. It may be also reached by boat from St. Mark's (2 hrs.).

About 2 M. beyond Tallahassee the *Murat Homestead* (see above) is visible to the right. We cross the *Oclockonee River.* Magnolias grow here in great profusion. **189 M.** *Quincy,* with tobacco-plantations.

At (208 M.) *River Junction,* on the *Appalachicola River* (curious railway-station, erected on trestle-work above the river), we join the *Louisville & Nashville R. R.* Connection is also made here with the Appalachicola River steamers. Our train crosses a long trestle over the Appalachicola, formed by the junction of the *Flint* and *Chattahoochee,* 2 M. above. — **234 M.** *Marianna,* on the *Chipola.* **290 M.** *De Funiak Springs* (Chautauqua, $ 2-2¹/₂). Beyond (319 M.) *Crestview* we cross *Shoal River.* **349 M.** *Milton* lies at the head of *Blackwater Bay.* About 10 M. farther on we cross *Escambia Bay* by a trestle 3 M. long. Fine marine views to the left.

369 M. **Pensacola** (*Escambia,* $ 3-4; *Merchants'*), on the bay of the same name, 10 M. from the Gulf of Mexico, was founded by the Spaniards in 1696 and has now 11,750 inhab. and a large trade in fish and timber. The ruins of *Forts St. Michael* and *St. Bernard* date partly from the Spanish period.

Visits may be made (small steamer) to the *Navy Yard, Ft. Barancas,* and *Ft. Pickens (Santa Rosa Island).* Steamers also ply to *Havana.*

The train now runs to the N., along the *Escambia River,* and enters *Alabama* shortly before reaching (413 M.) *Flomaton.* From Flomaton to (472 M.) *Mobile* and —

614 M. *New Orleans,* see R. 70 a.

82. New Orleans.

Hotels. HOTEL ROYAL (Pl. a; F, 3), St. Louis St., E. P.; ST. CHARLES (Pl. b; F, 4), St. Charles St., $ 3-5; DENECHAUD (Pl. c; F, 4), at the corner of Perdido and Carondelet Sts.; LAFAYETTE, $ 2-2¹/₂; COSMOPOLITAN, E. P. A really good hotel is still a desideratum in New Orleans, and visitors for more than a day or two should hire lodgings and eat at the restaurants. — BOARDING HOUSES abound throughout New Orleans, and the numerous *Pensions* and *Chambres Garnies* of the French Quarter are carried on in genuine Creole style. During the Carnival (p. 368) a special bureau is established for giving information about lodgings.

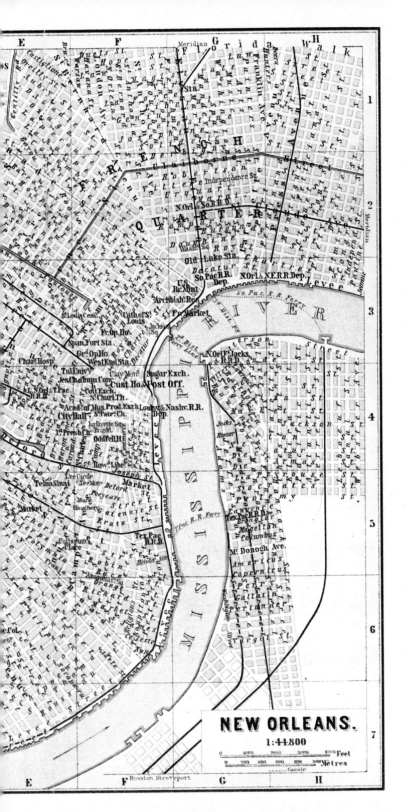

Restaurants. *Moreau*, Canal St.; *Bezaudon*, 107 Custom House St.; *Cassidy*, 174 Gravier St.; *Denechaud*, 8 Carondelet St. (see p. 366); *Acme*, 27 Royal St.; *Nicholl*, 44 Camp St.; *Antoine*, 65 St. Louis St. — *Cafés* abound in the French Quarter. — The markets of New Orleans are singularly well stocked with game, fish, fruit, and vegetables, and its restaurants have a good reputation. Among the Creole dishes for which New Orleans is famous is *Gumbo*, a kind of thick vegetable soup.

Tramways traverse the city in all directions (fare 5 c.). — **Carriages** about $1 per hour; from the railway-stations to the hotels 50 c. each person. — **Omnibuses** meet the principal trains (25 c.). — **Ferries** ply to *Algiers*, *Gouldsborough*, and *Gretna*, on the opposite side of the Mississippi. — **Steamers** ply to all points on the *Mississippi* (comp. R. 66), *Ohio*, and *Missouri*, and to *New York*, *Boston*, *Key West*, *Havana*, *Vera Cruz*, *Liverpool*, *Bremen*, and many other American and European ports.

Railway Stations. *Louisville & Nashville* (Pl. F, 4), on the Levee; *Louisville, New Orleans, and Texas (Mississippi Valley;* Pl. E, 4); *Illinois Central* (Pl. D, E, 4); *New Orleans & North Eastern (Queen & Crescent;* Pl. G, H, 3), on the Levee; *New Orleans & Southern* (Pl. G, 2), Elysian Fields; *Southern Pacific* (Pl. G, 3), *Texas Pacific* (Pl. F. 5), on the Levee, with ferries across the river; *Fort Jackson* (Pl. G, 3, 4). on the W. bank.

Places of Amusement. *French Opera House* (Pl. F, 3), corner of Bourbon and Toulouse Sts. (2000 seats); *Academy of Music* (Pl. F, 4), *St. Charles Theatre* (Pl. F, 4), St. Charles St.; *Grand Opera House* (Pl. F, 3), Canal St. — Comp. p. 370.

British Consul, *A. de Fonblanque*, 13 Carondelet St.

Post Office (Pl. F, 4), Canal St., open 6.30 a.m. to 7 p.m., Sun. 9-12.

New Orleans, the chief city of Louisiana, the twelfth city of the United States, and the largest to the S. of St. Louis, is situated on the *Mississippi*, 106 M. above its mouth in the Gulf of Mexico. The great bulk of the city lies on the left bank of the river, which is here $1/4$-$1/2$ M. wide and makes the bend from which New Orleans derives its appellation of 'Crescent City'. A great part of the city is below the level of the river at high water and is protected by a levee or embankment, 15 ft. wide and 14 ft. high. The municipal limits, which extend on the N. to *Lake Pontchartrain* (p. 370), enclose an area of 187 M., but about three-fourths of this is uninhabitable swamp. The city is laid out with considerable regularity, and many of the chief streets are wide and shaded with trees. The most important business-thoroughfare is *Canal Street*, which runs at right angles to the river and divides the *French Quarter*, or '*Vieux Carré*' (see p. 368), on the N.E., from the *New City*, or *American Quarter*, on the S.W. The finest residences are on *St. Charles Avenue*. In 1890 New Orleans contained 242,039 inhab., of whom about 18 per cent were of Anglo-American race, 17 per cent French, 15 per cent German, 14 per cent Irish, 8 per cent Italian, 2-3 per cent Spanish, and 25 per cent Coloured.

New Orleans was founded in 1718 by Jean de Bienville, governor of the settlement made in 1699 at Biloxi (see p. 438), and became capital of Louisiana in 1721, while still but little more than a village of trappers and gold-hunters (comp. *Miss Grace King's* 'Sieur de Bienville'). In 1762 it was ceded by France to Spain, but the inhabitants rebelled against this transference, established a government of their own, and were not suppressed till 1769. In 1732 the population was about 5000. From 1800 to 1803 New Orleans was again in the hands of the French, but in the latter year it was ceded, with the rest of Louisiana, to the United States. In 1804, when it had about 10,000 inhab., it received its city-charter. In 1815 the British were defeated here in an important battle by Gen. Andrew Jackson (see p. 369). In 1840 New Orleans was the fourth city of the United States, ranking after New York, Philadelphia, and Baltimore. New Orleans surrendered to the Unionists under Gen. Ben. Butler in 1862, after Adm. Farragut had succeeded in passing the forts at the mouth of the Mississippi and had the city under the guns of his fleet. By 1850 the population had increased to 116,375, by 1860 to 168,675, by 1870 to 191,418, and by 1880 to 216,140.

New Orleans is in many ways one of the most picturesque and interesting cities in America, owing to the survival of the buildings, manners, and customs of its original French and Spanish inhabitants. It has been described by *Mr. G. W. Cable* as 'a city of villas and cottages, of umbrageous gardens, intersected by 470 M. of unpaved streets, shaded by forest-trees, haunted by song-birds, fragrant with a wealth of flowers that never fails a day in the year, and abundant, in season, with fruit — the fig, the plum, the pomegranate, the orange'. The *French Quarter*, to the N.E. of Canal St., is inhabited almost exclusively by *Creoles*, 'a handsome, graceful, and intelligent race, of a decidedly Gallic type, whose name does not necessarily imply, any more than it excludes, a departure from a pure double line of Latin descent' (*Cable*). Among the foreign-looking features of this quarter are the walls of adobé, the limewashed stucco façades, the jalousies, the gratings, the small-paned windows, the portes-cochères, the arcades and balconies, the tiled roofs, and the inner courts — the whole embosomed in bright-flowering semi-tropical plants. Most of the streets bear French or Spanish names; and indeed the whole street-nomenclature of New Orleans is picturesque, though the Anglicised pronunciation will sometimes puzzle a stranger. — The famous *Carnival of Mardi-Gras* (Shrove Tuesday), celebrated here with great splendour, is, perhaps, the most picturesque festival in America. The city is taken formal possession of by Rex, the King of the Carnival; and the revels of his retinue, the Knights of Momus, the Mystic Crewe of Comus, and other societies are of the liveliest description. The processions are very elaborate (comp. 312). Those who mean to visit New Orleans at this season should secure rooms in advance (see p. 366).

Paul Morphy (1837-84), the famous chess-player, was a native of New Orleans and is buried in the old *St. Louis Cemetery* (Pl. F, 3).

New Orleans, as the outlet of the greatest agricultural valley in the world, is essentially a commercial city, and its foreign export trade is very important. It is the largest cotton-market in the world after Liverpool, and handles about two million bales annually. It also exports large quantities of sugar, molasses, rice, pork, Indian corn, wool, timber, hides, and tobacco, and imports fruits from Central and South America, including enormous quantities of bananas. Its manufactures (valued in 1890 at $ 35,000,000) include cotton-seed oil, machinery, barrel-staves, flour, rice, tobacco, and sugar. — In spite of the levees and embankments the lower Mississippi often breaks its bounds, and disastrous inundations are of frequent occurrence. Within the last 150 years the E. bank of the river at New Orleans has greatly advanced, the new land or 'batture' being at some points as much as 1500 ft. wide.

The visitor to New Orleans should be familiar with *George W. Cable's* romances ('Madame John's Legacy', 'Sieur George', 'Mme. Delphine', 'The Grandissimes', etc.). The house of 'Sieur George' is at the corner of Royal and St. Peter Sts. (Pl. F, 3). No. 253 Royal St. was the home of 'Mme. Delicieuse', and 'Mdme. Delphine's' is at 294 Barracks St. (Pl. F, 3), near Royal St. — Though not of much practical use as a guide, the 'Illustrated Guide and Sketch Book to New Orleans' contains much interesting matter about the quaint old city and its ways.

The tourist will do well to begin his exploration of New Orleans by taking his bearings from the roof of the *St. Charles Hotel* (Pl. b; F, 4) or the **Custom House** (Pl. F, 4). The latter is a large granite building in CANAL STREET, near the river, containing the *Post Office* (on the ground-floor) and the large *Marble Hall*.

Just below the Custom House, Canal St. ends at the *Levee (Pl.
G, H, 3-6), which extends along the E. bank of the Mississippi
for about 6 M. and presents a very animated and interesting scene.
Following it to the left (N.) we soon reach *JACKSON SQUARE (Pl.
F, 3), the old *Place d' Armes*, which contains a *Statue of Gen. Andrew
Jackson* (see p. 368) by Mills, and is adjoined by the **Cathedral of
St. Louis**, a good specimen of the Spanish-Creole style, built in
1792-94, on the site of the first church in Louisiana, but altered in
1850. It contains some paintings and interesting tombs. The build-
ings to the right and left are *Court Houses*, that to the S. having
been built for the *Cabildo*, or City Council, of the Spanish regime.
— On the Levee, just beyond Jackson Sq., is the **French Market**
(Pl. G, 3), a morning visit to which (best about 6 or 7 a.m.; on
Sun. 8 or 9 a.m.) reveals a scene of the greatest picturesqueness and
animation.—A little farther on, at the foot of Esplanade St., is the
U. S. Branch Mint (Pl. G, 3), a large building in the Ionic style.

We may now take an opportunity for a stroll in the picturesque
*Creole Quarter (see p. 368), among the chief promenades of which are
Esplanade Street (Pl. D-G, 1-3), *Rampart Street* (Pl. F, 2), and *Royal Street*
(Pl. F, 2). At the corner of Chartres St. and Hospital St. is the *Arch-
bishop's Residence* (Pl. F, G, 3), in the old Ursuline Convent (1787), to which
visitors are sometimes admitted.

Among other buildings adjoining the Levee are several *Railway
Stations* (comp. p. 367) and the *Ursuline Convent*.

In Canal St., a little above the Custom House (p. 368), is a
Statue of Henry Clay (Pl. F, 4). Following St. Charles St. to the
left, we pass the *St. Charles Hotel* (right) and the *St. Charles Theatre*
(right) and reach LAFAYETTE SQUARE (Pl. F, 4), with the *City
Hall*, the *Academy of Music*, *St. Patrick's Church*, the *First Presbyterian Church*, the *Odd Fellows Hall*, and a *Statue of Franklin*,
by Hiram Powers. Farther on is LEE CIRCLE (Pl. F, 5), with a monument to *Gen. Lee*. At the corner of Camp St. and Howard Ave.,
adjoining Lee Circle, stands the **Howard Library** (Pl. F, 4), the
last work of *H. H. Richardson*, who was a native of Louisiana. To
the S.W., in Carondelet St., is the Jewish *Temple Sinai* (Pl. E, 5).

We may now return to TULANE AVENUE (Pl. C-F, 2-4), in
which are situated most of the buildings of **Tulane University** (Pl.
E, F, 4). Opposite is the *Jesuits' Church*. Farther out in Tulane Ave.
stand the large *Charity Hospital* (Pl. E, 3), originally established
in 1784 (800 patients), and the *U. S. Marine Hospital* (Pl. D, 3).
The large **Cotton Exchange** (Pl. F, 4) is at the corner of Carondelet
St. and Gravier St.; the *Produce Exchange* (Pl. F, 4) is in Magazine
St.; and the *Sugar Exchange* (Pl. F, 4) is at the foot of Bienville
St. The *Church of the Immaculate Conception* (Pl. E, F, 4) is in a
singular Moorish style. The *Monument to Margaret Haughery* (Pl. F,
5), the 'Orphan's Friend', is said to be the only one of the kind to a
woman in the United States (comp., however, p. 116). — The *Shot
Tower* (Pl. F, 4, 5), at the corner of Constance St. and St. Joseph
St., commands a fine view (214 ft. high; elevator).

New Orleans is not well provided with parks. The **City Park** (Pl. B, C, 1), on the Metairie Ridge, is 150 acres in extent. The *Exposition Park* (Pl. A, B, 4-6), in which the Great Exhibition of 1884-5 was held, is a narrow strip extending for about $2^1/_2$ M. back from the river. Some of the exhibition-buildings are still standing. — The *Cemeteries of New Orleans are among its recognized sights, owing to the fact that the swampy nature of the soil prevents the digging of graves and requires the bodies to be interred in mounds above ground. Their magnolias and live-oaks are also picturesque. The *Cypress Grove Cemetery* (Pl. B, 1), near the City Park, is one of the most interesting. The *Metairie Cemetery* (Pl. A, 1), in the same district, contains the grave of *Gen. Albert Sydney Johnston* (1803-62), with an equestrian statue. In *Greenwood Cemetery* (Pl. B, 1) is a *Monument to the Confederate Dead*. — The old *French Graveyards*, near the *Jockey Club* (Pl. D, 1), in Esplanade St., are interesting.

Excursions. Among the favourite resorts of the New Orleaners is *Lake Pontchartrain*, which lies about 5 M. to the N. of the city and is 40 M. long and 25 M. wide. A fish or game dinner at one of the garden-restaurants here is a regular item of a visit to New Orleans. *Spanish Fort Park*, at the mouth of the *Bayou St. John*, marks the site of a fort erected by the Spaniards to guard this approach to the city. It is reached by railway (station at the corner of Canal and Basin Sts.) or by drive along the Shell Road. *West End* (West End Hotel), also reached by the Shell Road or by railway (cor. of Canal and Bourbon Sts.), is a favourite boating and yachting resort. *Milneburg*, to the E. of Spanish Fort, is reached by railway from *Old Lake Station* (Pl. G, 2, 3), at the corner of the Elysian Fields and Chartres St., or from the Louisville & Nashville Station (p. 367). — The site of the **Battlefield of New Orleans** (see p. 368) is at *Chalmette*, on the Mississippi, about 5 M. to the S. of Canal St., and may be reached by tramway or carriage. On the way we pass the *U.S. Barracks.* The site of the battle is marked by a monument. The *National Cemetery* contains 12,000 graves. — The *Carrollton Gardens* lie to the N. of the city (tramway). — A visit to one of the *Sugar Plantations* on the Mississippi will be found interesting. Among the finest are the Ames, McCall, and Kernochan Plantations. — Good wild-fowl shooting and fishing are obtained all round New Orleans.

Longer excursions may be made to *Pass Christian* (p. 338), *Bay St. Louis* (p. 338), *Mobile* (p. 337), the *Eads Jetties* (p. 326), etc.

From New Orleans to *New York*, see RR. 70 a, 70 b; to *Pensacola* and *Jacksonville*, see R. 70; to *Mobile*, see p. 337; to points in *Texas* and *California*, see RR. 101, 102; to *Cincinnati*, see R. 63; to *St. Louis*, see R. 64; to *Louisville*, see R. 65; to *Chicago*, see R. 64.

83. From St. Paul to Tacoma and Portland.

2055 M. NORTHERN PACIFIC RAILROAD to (1910 M.) *Tacoma* in 74-78 hrs. (fare $70; sleeper $13½) and to (2056 M.) *Portland* in 81-84 hrs. (same fares). Passengers bound for Portland direct (1887 M.) change cars at *Wallula Junction* (p. 376) and proceed thence by the UNION PACIFIC R. R. (R. 87). *Duluth* (p. 295) is also one of the E. termini of this line, the line thence uniting with the St. Paul line at Brainerd (see next page).

This important railway crosses a district of immense agricultural and mineral wealth and forms one of the main lines of communication between the E. and W. coasts of the United States, besides affording convenient access to British Columbia, Vancouver Island, and Alaska. Much of the scenery on the W. part of the line is very fine, and the branch-line from Livingston (see p. 373) affords the most direct route to the wonderful *Yellowstone Park* (R. 84). Through-carriages run over this route from Chicago to Portland (98-100 hrs.; fare $ 70; sleeper $ 13¹/₂), and travellers from New York to Portland (5 days; through-fare $ 106) change at Chicago only. Dining-cars (meals 75 c.) are attached to all through-trains.

St. Paul, see p. 291. The train follows the E. bank of the *Mississippi* (views to the left), passing the *State Fair Buildings* (p. 293) and *Hamline University*. At (11 M.) *Minneapolis* (see p. 293) we cross and recross the river. 29 M. *Anoka;* 41 M. *Elk River;* 76 M. *St. Cloud* (the city, with 7686 inhab. and large granite quarries, on the W. bank); 77 M. *Sauk Rapids*. At (108 M.) *Little Falls* (The Antlers, $ 2-3) the line forks, the right branch running to (138 M.) *Brainerd* (1600 ft.; 30 M. from Staples; see below), an industrial city of 5703 inhab., where it joins the line from *Duluth* (see p. 370). The through-trains from St. Paul follow the left branch, which crosses the Mississippi and runs direct (N.W.) to (142 M.) *Staples*. 159 M. *Wadena* is the junction of the Fergus and Black Hills branch. 172 M. *New York Mills*, with a large settlement of Finns. Many small lakes are passed. — 204 M. *Detroit* (Hotel Minnesota, from $ 2), on a pretty lake, is a summer-resort, with mineral springs and excellent shooting and fishing. About 25 M. to the N. is the *White Earth Reservation* of the Chippeway or Ojibway Indians. — 225 M. *Winnipeg Junction*, for a line to (257 M.) *Winnipeg* (p. 299). At (241 M.) *Glyndon* we cross the Great Northern R. R.

250 M. **Moorhead** (840 ft.; *Grand Pacific Hotel*, $ 2-3), a thriving flour-making city of 2088 inhab., lies on the E. bank of the *Red River of the North*, opposite (251 M.) **Fargo** (*Continental*, $ 2¹/₂-3; *Columbia*, $ 2-3), another busy grain-trading city (5664 inhab.), which lies in *North Dakota* ('Great Cereal State').

From Moorhead to *Winnipeg*, see R. 54.

In traversing N. Dakota we pass some of the huge prairie farms for which the 'Great North-West' is famous.

Some of these 'Bonanza' farms are 10-80 sq. M. in extent, and it is no unfrequent sight to see a row of 20 or more ploughs, harrows, seeders, or reapers at work at once. Continuous furrows have been ploughed for many miles in a straight line. Harvesting generally begins about Aug. 1st, and the vast expanses of yellow grain afford an extraordinary and very beautiful sight. A yield of 20-25 bushels per acre is often attained. North Dakota, in a good year, produces 60-65 million bushels of wheat.

Near (271 M.) *Casselton* is the great *Dalrymple Farm*, with an area of 75,000 acres (114 sq. M.). 293 M. *Tower City*, with a mineral artesian well (fountain near the railway-station). 309 M. *Valley City*, on the *Sheyenne River*. — 344 M. **Jamestown** (1395 ft.; *Gladstone*, $ 2-2¹/₂), a busy agricultural centre with 2296 inhab., the *N. Dakota Insane Hospital*, and a *Presbyterian College*, is prettily situated on the *James River*.

A branch-line runs hence to the N. to (90 M.) *Minnewaukan*, on *Devil's Lake* (p. 300), and (108 M.) *Leeds*.

The line now traverses the rolling district between the James and the Missouri known as the *Coteaux* (400 ft. above the rivers,

24 *

2000 ft. above the sea). Several small stations. — 445 M. **Bismarck** (1690 ft.; *Sheridan Ho.*, $ 2), the capital of N. Dakota, lies on the E. bank of the *Missouri*, here about 400 yds. wide. It is the head-quarters of navigation on the Upper Missouri and contains several U. S. institutions. The *State Capitol* is still unfinished. Pop. 2186.

The train crosses the river by a fine steel and iron truss-bridge, with three main spans of 400 ft. each, 50 ft. above high-water. 450 M. *Mandan* (Inter-Ocean, $ 3-4), on the W. bank. We change here from 'central' to 'mountain' time (1 hr. slower; see p. xviii). Fine mounted heads and fur-rugs are sold at the station. About 6 M. to the S. lies *Fort Abraham Lincoln.* Near Mandan are numerous prehistoric mounds and other remains. We cross the *Heart River* several times in rapid succession. The district we now traverse is very sparsely populated. Large numbers of prairie-dogs (a kind of marmot) are seen. Sharp conical elevations known as 'buttes' (pron. butes) rise from the plain in all directions. Near (549 M.) *Gladstone* we again cross the Heart River. 560 M. *Dickinson.* At (586 M.) *Fryburg* we enter the district known as **Bad Lands* or **Pyramid Park,** where the buttes have been carved by the action of fire and water into the most fantastic shapes. The colouring is also very variegated. The name 'Bad Lands' refers properly to the difficulty of travel and not to the soil, which affords excellent grazing. — From (599 M.) *Medora* (2265 ft.; Hotel), on the E. bank of the *Little Missouri*, we may visit Pyramid Park and the great Burning Mine (7 M.). About 16 M. farther on the curious *Sentinel Butte* is conspicuous to the left, and in 12 M. more we enter *Montana* ('Bonanza State'), the third-largest state of the Union, in which cattle-raising and mining are the chief industries. The native 'bunch-grass', which cures itself and stands as hay throughout the winter, forms excellent fodder. — 666 M. *Glendive* (2070 ft.) lies among picturesque scenery on the S. bank of the *Yellowstone River*, which the line now follows for a long distance. Numerous small tributaries of the Yellowstone are crossed. — 744 M. *Miles City* (2350 ft.), a busy little place at the confluence of the Yellowstone and the *Tongue.* 747 M. *Fort Keogh*, an important U. S. military post (9 companies); 776 M. *Rosebud*, at the mouth of the *Rosebud River;* 832 M. *Big Horn* (2690 ft.), at the mouth of the *Big Horn River*, the largest affluent of the Yellowstone, which we cross by a long bridge. We then thread a tunnel 1100 ft. long. About 30 M. to the S. of (838 M.) *Custer* (coach) is *Fort Custer*, and 15 M. farther to the S. is the spot where Gen. Custer and his command of over 250 men were annihilated by the Sioux (the 'Custer Massacre') in 1876. An extensive territory to the S. of this part of the Yellowstone has been set apart as a reservation for the Crow Indians (ca. 3000 in number). To the left, near Billings, is *Skull Butte*, so named from an Indian legend. Beyond (891 M.) *Billings* (3115 ft.) the scenery increases in grandeur, and snow-capped mountains appear in the distance.

The train crosses the Yellowstone and skirts its N. bank to (932 M.) *Stillwater*, where it returns to the S. side. 972 M. *Big Timber*, near the mouth of the *Big Boulder Creek* (good fishing); 987 M. *Springdale*, the station for (2¹/₂ M.) *Hunter's Hot Springs* (Hotel; 148-168° Fahr.), at the foot of the *Crazy Mts.* Fine views of the *Little Belt Mts.* to the right and the *Yellowstone Range* to the left.

1007 M. **Livingston** (4485 ft.; *Albemarle*, $3), a city of 2850 inhab., finely situated at the foot of the *Belt Range*, is the junction of the branch-railway to the *Yellowstone Park* (see p. 378). It is a good centre for shooting (elk, deer, antelope, bear, grouse, geese, ducks) and fishing (trout, grayling); and fine furs and stuffed animals may be bought at *Wittich's*, a little behind the railway-station.

The train now crosses and leaves the Yellowstone, which we have followed for 340 M. The line mounts rapidly (116 ft. per mile) to the *Bozeman Tunnel*, 1170 yds. long, which crosses the **Belt Mts.**, an outlying range of the Rocky Mts., at a height of 5570 ft. Beyond the tunnel we descend through the wild *Rocky Cañon into the wide valley of the *Gallatin*. 1031 M. *Bozeman* (4750 ft.; Hotel Bozeman, $3-4), a busy little city of 2143 inhab., on the *East Gallatin.* Large coal-fields lie within 8 M., and deposits of gold, silver, iron, and copper are also worked. — At (1056 M.) *Logan* (4100 ft.) the line forks, the right or main branch running viâ Helena and the left branch viâ Butte City. The two lines reunite at Garrison (see below).

Butte City (5485 ft.; *McDermott*, $3-4; *St. Nicholas*, $2¹/₂-3), 71 M. from Logan, may be described as a huge and bustling mining camp of 10,723 people, dating only from 1864, but already possessing many of the attributes of a large city. Including the settlements that are practically suburbs of Butte, the population is nearly 40,000. It is the seat of the great *Anaconda Copper and Silver Mine* and other gold, silver, and copper mining companies, producing ore to the annual value of at least $25,000,000 (5,000,000*l.*). A visit to one of the chief mines is very interesting (introduction desirable and in some cases necessary). — The smelting works at *Anaconda* (Montana Hotel, from $3¹/₂), 27 M. to the W., are said to be the largest in the world. — The line from Butte City to (51 M.) *Garrison* (see p. 374) runs through the picturesque *Deer Lodge Valley*, passing (40 M.) *Deer Lodge City* (4545 ft.; 1463 inhab.).

Beyond Logan the main line soon reaches (1060 M.) *Gallatin* (4030 ft.), the station for *Three Forks*, at the confluence of the *Madison*, *Jefferson*, and *Gallatin*, which unite to form the *Missouri*. Farther on we thread a wild cañon, with the Missouri to the left and precipitous walls of rock to the right. 1125 M. *Prickly Pear Junction*.

1130 M. **Helena** (3930 ft.; *Broadwater Hotel, 3 M. from Helena, see p. 374; *Grand Central*, $2¹/₂-4; *Helena*, from $3; *International*, $2¹/₂-3), the capital of Montana, is a mining city of 13,834 inhab., finely situated in the fertile *Prickly Pear Valley*, near the E. base of the main range of the Rocky Mts. The *State House* and some of the other official and commercial buildings are large and substantial, and the streets are lighted by electricity and traversed by electric tramways. A visit to the *U. S. Assay Office* is interesting.

Helena lies in the heart of one of the richest mining districts in the world. and claims to be the wealthiest city of its size in the world. It is said that gold to the value of at least $ 30,000,000 has been taken from the *Last Chance Gulch*, which runs through the city; and all round the city are valuable gold and silver bearing veins of quartz, besides deposits of copper, iron, and galena.

About 3 M. to the W. of Helena (reached by steam or electric tramway; fare 10 c.) are the *Broadwater Hotel* ($ 4-6) and a huge *Natatorium* (400 ft. long and 150 ft. wide; adm. 50 c.), fed by a hot spring, the temperature of which at its source is about 160° (in bath about 100°). The waters are good for rheumatism. — A visit to one of the *Gold* or *Silver Mines* in the vicinity is of great interest. The nearest are those at *Grizzly Gulch*, 4 M. to the S.W. One of the most famous is the *Drum-Lummon Mine*, 20 M. to the N., which has yielded $ 2,000,000 worth of gold and silver in a single year. Another important group of mines lies near *Jefferson City* and *Wickes*, about 20 M. to the S. (railway).

Helena is also a station on the Great Northern Railway (see R. 55) and a fine excursion may be made by taking the Montana Central Division of this line to (99 M.) *Great Falls* (p. 301).

About 21 M. beyond Helena we cross the main ridge of the **Rocky Mts.** by *Mullan's Pass*, where the train passes through a tunnel $2/3$ M. long and 5545 ft. above sea-level (summit of mountain over tunnel 5870 ft.). This is from 1800 to 2500 ft. lower than the passes of the Atlantic and Union Pacific Railroads (comp. pp. 391, 413). The contrast between the E. and the W. sides of the 'Great Divide' is very striking, as we at once pass from a scene of wild rocky grandeur to one of mild pastoral beauty. The line descends rapidly to the valley of the *Little Blackfoot River*. At (1180 M.) *Garrison* (4315 ft.), on the *Deer Lodge River*, we are joined by the line from *Butte* (see p. 373). Beyond Garrison we skirt the Deer Lodge River, which soon changes its name to *Hell Gate River*. The fine snow-clad pyramid of *Mt. Powell* (13,400 ft.) is seen to the left. Near (1189 M.) *Gold Creek* the last spike of the Northern Pacific Railroad was driven in 1883, the tracks advancing from the E. and the W. meeting here. Below (1214 M.) *Bearmouth* (3790 ft.) we pass through the *Hell Gate Cañon*, a picturesque mountain-flanked valley, 2-3 M. wide. At (1247 M.) *Bonner* the Hell Gate River is joined by the *Big Blackfoot River* (right), which we cross beyond the station. — 1254 M. **Missoula** (3195 ft.; *Missoula,* $ 2^1/$_2$-4; *Florence,* $ 3), finely situated on the *Hell Gate* or *Missoula River*, near its confluence with the *Bitter Root River*, is a rising little city of 3426 inhab. and the junction of the Bitter Root Valley branch. *Fort Missoula* lies 4 M. to the S. — At (1261 M.) *De Smet* our line diverges to the right from the Bitter Root Valley line and follows the *Jocko River*, crossing the *Marent Gulch* by a bridge 226 ft. high. We then traverse the *Reservation of the Flathead Indians*, a peaceful tribe whose boast is that they never killed a white man; their huts and 'teepees' are seen on both sides of the railway. The Agency Buildings are visible at the foot of the *Mission Mts.*, 5 M. to the N. Near (1299 M.) *Jocko* the Jocko joins the *Flathead* or *Pend d'Oreille*, which we now follow. Beyond (1313 M.) *Perma* (2490 ft.) we cross the river by a truss-bridge. About 8 M. farther on the Pend d'Oreille is joined by the Missoula, and the combined rivers take the name of *Clark's Fork of the Columbia.* The valley here is narrow and rocky, but at (1325 M.) *Paradise* and (1331 M.) *Horse Plains* (2460 ft.) it widens into two pleasant little plains, used by the Indians as wintering-places for their ponies. The white *Coeur d'Alène Mts.* rise to the left and the *Cabinet Mts.* to the E. 1357 M. *Thompson's Falls* (2435 ft.), at the falls of the Clark's Fork River. Picturesque scenery. Numerous bridges and cuttings. Near (1404 M.) *Heron* (2260 ft.) we enter *Idaho* ('Gem of the Mountains'), a mountainous state, the N. tip of which we now traverse. We cross the river and skirt the N. bank of its expansion, *Lake *Pend d'Oreille,* a beautiful sheet of water 45-50 M. long and 3-15 M. wide. — At (1427 M.) *Hope* (2110 ft.; Highland Ho., Lakeside Hotel, $2½), a railway division town and tourists' resort on the N. bank of the lake (boating and fishing), we pass from 'Mountain' to 'Pacific' time (1 hr. slower). 1438 M. *Kootenai.* At (1492 M.) *Sand Point* we cross an arm of the lake and then quit it. The scenery now becomes uninteresting. The line runs towards the S. as far as (1484 M.) *Rathdrum* (2210 ft.). 1491 M. *Hauser Junction,* for a line to (13 M.) *Coeur d'Alène City,* on the pretty lake of the same name. — We now enter *Washington* ('Evergreen State'), an important agricultural state, also remarkable for the splendid timber of its W. slopes. Beyond (1497 M.) *Otis* we cross the *Spokane River.*

1512 M. **Spokane** (pron. Spokán; 1910 ft.; *Spokane Hotel,* $3-4; *Cliff, Commercial, Grand Central,* $2-4; *Pacific Hotel,* E. P.), a thriving little city of 19,922 inhab., settled in 1878 and in great part rebuilt since a fire in 1889, lies on both banks of the Spokane River, in the centre of a district of great agricultural richness.

The two ***Falls,** both within the city, are 150 ft. in total height and furnish the water-power for numerous manufactories, for the electric lighting of the town, and for its system of cable and electric tramways. Visitors should descend to the foot of the lower falls and should also go to the bridge above the upper falls. Among the most conspicuous buildings, many of which are of extraordinary size and solidity for so small and young a city, is the **Opera House,* which has seats for 2000 people. The residence-quarter, on the hill above the railway (on the opposite side from the business-quarter), contains many houses of unusually good taste. The *High School,* in this quarter, is a handsome red building, with a tower. A fine *View of the city and valley is obtained from the *Cliff Heights* (reached by cable-cars and steam-tramway). — Several railways diverge from Spokane.

Beyond Spokane the line runs to the S.W. At (1521 M.) *Marshall Junction* diverges a branch-line that runs through the fertile *Palouse District* to (113 M.) *Genesee.* — From (1528 M.) *Cheney* (2340 ft.) a line runs to (124 M.) *Coulee City,* passing (10 M.) *Medical Lake,* a favourite invalid resort. — Beyond (1553 M.) *Sprague* (1910 ft.) we pass *Colville Lake* (left). We now traverse an unattractive district, overgrown with sage-brush. — 1657 M. *Pasco,* near the confluence of the *Columbia* and *Snake Rivers,* is the point of divergence of the Cascade Division of the N. Pacific R. R. (for Tacoma, etc.).

Passengers for Portland direct cross the Snake River by a long iron bridge and join the Union Pacific R.R. at (16M.) *Wallula Junction* (see p. 370).

Our line (Cascade Division) crosses the Columbia and follows the valley of the *Yakima* (river to the right) towards the N.W. Beyond (1698 M.) *Prosser* we traverse the *Yakima* or *Simcoe Indian Reservation.* The white cap of *Mt. Adams* (9570 ft.), one of the loftiest of the Cascade Mts. (see below), is seen to the left. — 1747M. *North Yakima* (990 ft.), with 1535 inhab., is the entrepot of the *Yakima Basin*, a district in which considerable quantities of fruit, vegetables, hops, and tobacco are grown by dint of irrigation. We now cross the river and have it to our left. Farther on we pass through the fine *Yakima Cañon* (15 M. long) and enter the *Kittitas Basin*, another fertile valley, bounded on the W. by the green *Cascade Mts.*, with the white peak of *Mt. Rainier* or *Tacoma* (p. 377) rising beyond. 1784 M. *Ellensburg* (1510 ft.; Horton, $ 2½-4) is a busy little city of 2768 inhab., with saw-mills and machine-shops. At (1822 M.) *Easton* the train begins to ascend the E. slope of the Cascade Mts. (see below) at a gradient of 116 ft. per mile. Fine views. The crest is penetrated by the *Stampede Tunnel* (2810 ft.; height of summit above the tunnel 3980 ft.), nearly 2 M. long, a length exceeded in America by the Hoosac Tunnel (p. 134) only.

The **Cascade Mts.** (a part of the Sierra Nevada; see p. 397) are a broad volcanic plateau, with many snow-peaks (9-11,000 ft.; average height 6000 ft.), running through Washington and Oregon from N. to S. and dividing the states into two regions differing widely in climate, surface, and vegetation. The region we now enter on the W. slope has a mild, moist climate (not unlike that of England) and is covered with dense forests, mainly of coniferous trees.

We now descend into the beautiful valley of the *Green River*, passing round winding curves, through tunnels, and over trestles, with numerous picturesque glimpses. 1847 M. *Hot Springs* (Hotel), a small health-resort; 1867 M. *Palmer.* After leaving the Green River we pass into the valley of the *White River* and then into that of the *Puyallup.* Frequent *Views of Mt. Tacoma are obtained to the left, sometimes to the S., sometimes to the E. of the line. — 1900 M *Meeker* is the junction of the line to (31 M.) *Seattle* (see p. 470). 1901 M. **Puyallup** (70 ft.; *Park Hotel*, $ 4), a town of 1732 inhab., is the centre of a rich hop-district, the numerous drying-kilns of which (very unlike the 'cowls' of Kent) have been visible for some time. It is also the headquarters of the *Puyallup Indian Reservation.* Expert hop-pickers, many of whom are Indians, can earn $ 1½-2 (6-8 s.) per day (compared with 3-4 s. in England).

1910 M. **Tacoma** (30 ft.; *Tourist Hotel*, to be ready in 1893; *Tacoma Hotel*, from $ 3½; *Grand Pacific*, *Fife*, E. P.; *Villard*, $ 2), a bustling industrial city and seaport of (1890) 36,006 inhab. (50,000 in 1892) and the W. terminus of the N. Pacific Railroad, is finely situated on a series of terraces rising from the head of *Commencement Bay*, the S.E. arm of *Puget Sound* (p. 470). It commands fine views of the Sound, the Cascade Mts., and the grand white cone of Mt. Rainier (S. E.; see below). Though scarcely 20 years old (300 inhab. in 1875, and 760 in 1880), Tacoma (the 'City of Destiny') already possesses numerous substantial streets and buildings, but it is still somewhat raw and uninviting in general appearance and contains few points of interest for the tourist. Its industrial establishments include large saw-mills (one with a capacity of 400,000 ft. per day), foundries, smelting-works, railway-workshops, iron and stove works, breweries, flour-mills, shingle-mills, etc. (value of products in 1890, $ 4,300,000); and it carries on a very extensive trade in grain ($1^1/_2$-2 million bushels annually), lumber, coal, tea, silk, and other articles. Among the principal buildings are the *Court House*, the *City Hall*, the *Opera House*, the *Chamber of Commerce*, the *Offices of the N. Pacific R. R.*, and the *Anna Wright Seminary*. Many of the private residences are large and handsome. A line of electric tramways connects the *Railway Station*, at the end of *Pacific Avenue*, the main business street, with the *Wharf;* and other electric, cable, or 'dummy' (steam) lines run to the suburbs, *Point Defiance, Puyallup* (p. 376), etc.

Tacoma is the starting-point of steamers to *Alaska* (see R. 103), *Seattle* (p. 470), *Port Townsend* (p. 471), *Olympia* (see below), *Victoria* (p. 471), and other points in Puget Sound; *San Francisco* (p. 428) and other Californian ports, etc. — Trains run to *Seattle* (p. 470) at frequent intervals (41 M., in $1^1/_2$ hr.).

A visit to *Mt. Rainier or Tacoma (14,445 ft.) takes about 3 days. The train is taken to (32 M.) *Wilkeson*, whence a bridle-path leads to (25 M.) a point about 9500 ft. above the sea, where a good view is obtained of two of the 14 living glaciers on the mountain. The hazardous ascent thence to the summit hould not be attempted except by experts. Mt. Tacoma, like the other isolated mountains of the Cascade Range, is an extinct volcano; and the craters at the summit still give off heat and sulphurous fumes. — Enquiry as to guides and horses should be made at the hotels.

FROM TACOMA TO OLYMPIA, 34 M., *Northern Pacific R. R.* in $1^1/_2$ hr. Some of the Portland trains run by this route, joining the route described below at (66 M.) *Centralia.* — **Olympia** (*Olympia*, $ $2^1/_2$-4; *Jefferson*), the capital of the State of Washington, is finely situated at the head of Puget Sound, in the midst of a thickly wooded district. Pop. (1890) 4698. It carries on a trade in agricultural produce, fruit, wool, and timber.

The Pacific Division of the Northern Pacific Railroad runs to the S. from Tacoma to Portland. Fine views of Mt. Rainier or Tacoma (40 M. distant) are obtained to the left, through breaks in the forest. 1920 M. *Lake View* (325 ft.) is the point of divergence of the above-mentioned line to Olympia. 1948 M. *Tenino* (315 ft.), the junction of another line to Olympia; 1960 M. *Centralia* (205 ft.; 2026 inhab.), see above; 1964 M. *Chehalis*, the junction of a line to *South Bend*, on the Pacific Ocean. Farther on we descend along the *Cowlitz*, and glimpses of *Mt. Adams* (p. 376) are obtained to the left. At (2015 M.) *Kalama* (33 ft.) the train is transferred across the wide *Columbia River* by a large steamer. Beyond (2030 M.) *Warren* we skirt the *Willamette* (p. 460), a tributary of the Columbia. In clear weather views are had to the left of *Mt. St. Helens* (9750 ft.; to the N.E.) and *Mt. Hood* (11,200 ft.; to the S.E., more distant).

2055 M. Portland, see p. 460.

84. The Yellowstone National Park.

The **Yellowstone National Park, which, by Act of Congress in 1872, was set apart as a public park or pleasure ground for the benefit and enjoyment of the people, originally covered a tract 65 M. long from N. to S. and 55 M. wide from E. to W., with an area of 3575 sq. M.; but to this has recently been added a forest-reservation of nearly 2000 sq. M. more on the S. and E., making a total area considerably larger than Connecticut or Belgium. The great bulk of the Park lies in *Wyoming*, but small portions of it are in *Montana* (N.) and *Idaho* (W.). The central portion of the Park consists of a broad volcanic plateau, with an average elevation of 8000 ft. above sea-level. Surrounding this on all sides are mountains with peaks and ridges rising 2000-4000 ft. above the general level. To the S. are the grand *Teton* and *Wind River Ranges*; to the E. the *Absaroka Mts.* To the N. E. a confused mass of mountains unites the Absarokas with the *Snowy Range*, which shuts in the Park on the N. The beautiful *Gallatin Range*, on the N. and N.W., lies partly within the national reservation. The whole district has been the scene of remarkable volcanic activity at a comparatively late geological epoch; and the traces of this activity, in the form of geysers, boiling springs, terrace and crater formations, cliffs of obsidian, deeply-cleft cañons, petrified trees, sulphur hills, and the like, are of the strangest and most startling description (see below). Its geysers are the largest in the world, excelling those of New Zealand or Iceland. Its lakes and waterfalls are also fine, and the marvellously coloured Cañon of the Yellowstone (p. 387) perhaps outstrips even the geysers as an attraction. A great part of the Park is covered with dense forests of yellow pine and Douglas spruce. An attempt has been made to make the Park a huge game-preserve, and large quantities of wild animals, including the last herd of buffaloes in America, elk, deer, bears, big-horn sheep, etc., are sheltered in its recesses. The ordinary tourist, however, will see little of these. No shooting is allowed within the Park precincts; but fishing is freely allowed, and excellent sport may be obtained in the Yellowstone, the Yellowstone Lake, and other waters (trout and grayling). The botanist will find much to interest him in the flora of the district, and it need scarcely be said that it is a peculiarly happy hunting-ground for the geologist. — The Park is under the exclusive control of the Secretary of the Interior, and troops of U. S. cavalry are stationed here in summer to protect the natural curiosities. The rules of the Park may be seen at the hotels, and any infringement of them is severely dealt with. — The Lower Geyser Basin was first explored by Capt. W.W. De Lacy in 1863, though trappers and hunters had previously brought home tales of its wonders. Since then the U.S. Government has sent various scientific topographical and geological expeditions into the Yellowstone, which has now been pretty thoroughly explored and mapped (comp. p. 380).

Geology of the Yellowstone Park (by *Arnold Hague*, U.S. Geological Survey). Geological evidence shows that the processes of mountain building were contemporaneous in all these ranges and took place near the close of Cretaceous time. By the upheaval of the mountains a depressed basin was formed, everywhere shut in by high land. Later, the pouring out of vast masses of lavas converted this depressed region into the Park plateau. Tertiary time was marked by great volcanic activity, lavas being piled up until the accumulated mass measured more than 2000 ft. in thickness. At least two centres of volcanic eruptions, Mt. Washburne and Mt. Sheridan, are known within this area. The plateau built up of these lavas embraces an area of 50 by 40 M., the volcanic flows resting against the steep spurs of the encircling mountains. Strictly speaking is is not a plateau; at least it is by no means a level region, but presents an undulating country characterized by bold escarpments and abrupt edge of mesa-like ridges. It is accidented by shallow basins of varied outline and scored by deep cañons and gorges. Evidences of fresh lava flows within recent times are wholly wanting; nevertheless, over the Park plateau the most unmistakable evidence of underground heat is every‘ where to be seen in the waters of innumerable hot springs, geysers-

and solfataras. A careful study of all the phenomena leads to the theory that the cause of the high temperatures of these waters is to be found in the heated rocks below and that the origin of the heat is in some way associated with the source of volcanic energy. Surface waters in percolating downward have become heated by relatively small quantities of steam rising through fissures in the rocks from much greater depths. Geysers and hot springs return these meteoric waters to the surface. They are in a sense volcanic phenomena and remain as evidence of the gradual dying out of volcanic energy. If this theory is correct, proof of the long continued action of thermal waters upon the rocks should be apparent, as they must have been active forces ever since the cessation of volcanic eruptions. Ascending currents of steam and acid waters have acted as powerful agents in rock decomposition and have left an ineffaceable impression upon the surface of the country. This is shown by numerous areas of altered lavas and extinct solfataras. No finer example of the action of steam upon lavas can be seen than along the walls of the Yellowstone Cañon. To-day the greatest activity is found in the geyser basins. The number of hot springs in the Park exceeds 4000. If to these be added the fissures and fumaroles from which issue large volumes of steam and acid vapours, the number of active vents would be greatly increased. There are about 100 geysers in the Park. Between a geyser and a hot spring no sharp line can be drawn, although a geyser may be defined as a hot spring throwing with intermittent action a column of hot water and steam into the air. A hot spring may boil incessantly without violent eruptive energy; a geyser may lie dormant for years without explosive action and again break forth with renewed force.

Bunsen's theory of geyser action, which he announced after investigating the geysers of Iceland, is undoubtedly correct in its essential principles, and has stood the test of careful study of the varied hydro-thermal phenomena in the Yellowstone Park, where they occur on so grand a scale. In the latter locality it may be shown that it is not necessary that the geyser conduit should be vertical or even straight. Bunsen's theory rests on the well-known principle that the boiling point of water increases with pressure and consequently the boiling point at the bottom of a long tube is much higher than at the top. When heat is applied to the bottom of a deep reservoir, explosive action is likely to follow, and in the case of a geyser the expansive force of steam which is generated drives out violently the water in the tube which leads to the surface.

The thermal waters of the Park may be classed under three heads: 1st, calcareous waters carrying calcium carbonate in solution; 2nd, silicious waters carrying free acid in solution; 3rd silicious alkaline waters rich in silica. Calcareous waters are confined almost exclusively to the Mammoth Hot Springs, which lie just to the N. of the Park plateau. Although the waters break out in close proximity to the lavas, and undoubtedly receive their heat from volcanic sources, they reach the surface through limestones. With a few exceptions silicious waters are found issuing from the lavas from which they derive their mineral contents. Acid waters may be recognized by efflorescent deposits of alum and soluble salts of iron, and frequently by the presence of delicate sulphur crystals. Alkaline springs present more of general interest than acid waters, as it is only in connection with the former that geysers occur. They are the principal waters of all the geyser basins and most hot spring areas. They deposit mainly an amorphous silicious sinter, but in an endless variety of forms, as is shown in the geyser cones and incrustations on the surface and edges of hot pools.

It is these unrivalled hydro-thermal manifestations and their varied phenomena that have made the Yellowstone Park famous throughout the world, and gained for it the distinction of America's Wonderland.

Approaches and Plans of Tour. The season for visiting the Yellowstone Park lasts from June 1st to Oct. 1st, and June and September are less crowded than July and August. The principal approach is viâ *Livingston* on the *Northern Pacific R. R.* (see p. 380 and R. 83). The railway company at present issues circular excursion tickets from St. Paul, Minneapolis, Duluth, Tacoma, Seattle, or Portland, good for 40 days, including all necessary living and travelling expenses, and allowing $6^1/_4$ days in the Park, for $120 (from Livingston $50). Those who desire can extend their stay in the Yellowstone at the rate of $3 a day for hotel-accommodation. Locomotion within the Park is carried on by the stage-coaches of the *Yellowstone Park Transportation Co.* The roads are by no means as good as they might be, and some of the drives between the chief points of interest are rather tedious. Carriages may be hired at $10-21 per day (3-7 pers.); saddle-horses $$2^1/_2$ per day. Messrs. Raymond & Whitcomb (p. xxv) conduct parties from Boston to the Yellowstone at rates proportional to those above mentioned. Camping parties may secure a complete outfit, guides, etc., at the Mammoth Hot Springs Hotel (p. 381). — The Yellowstone may also be approached from *Beaver Cañon*, on the *Union Pacific R. R.*, whence the Park (90 M.) is reached by stagecoach in two days, a night being spent on the way (comp. p. 392). The charge for a return-ticket from Omaha (p. 388) or Kansas City (p. 400) is $95. — *Warm Wraps* are very necessary in the Yellowstone, as however strong the sun is by day, the nights are apt to be very chilly.

Hotels. The hotels of the *Yellowstone Park Association* (headquarters at Mammoth Hot Springs) are comfortable and well managed. The uniform charge is $4 a day for the first week, then $3.

Guides. Men to point out the way to the various points of interest may be obtained at the hotels for a moderate fee; but really intelligent and efficient guides are still a desideratum. Mounted guide, for longer excursions, $5 per day.

Bibliography. The most detailed cacount of the Yellowstone is that of Prof. F. V. Hayden and his colleagues in the *Twelfth Annual U. S. Geological Report* (1878). See also *Arnold Hague's* 'Geological History of the Yellowstone Park' (1887) and *Richardson's* 'Wonders of the Yellowstone'. Small *Guides to the Yellowstone Park*, by *A. B. Guptill* (50 c.) and *W. C. Riley* (25 c.) may be bought at the hotels. Good *Photographs*, by F. Jay Haynes, are also on sale.

a. From Livingston to Mammoth Hot Springs.

NORTHERN PACIFIC RAILROAD to (51 M.) *Cinnabar* in 2 hrs. STAGE thence to (8 M.) *Mammoth Hot Springs* in $1^3/_4$ hr.

Livingston, see p. 373. — The train ascends the valley of the Yellowstone and soon passes through (3 M.) the *First Cañon of the Yellowstone* or *Gate of the Mts.*, a gorge about 1 M. long, with rocky walls 2000 ft. high. The wider reach then entered is known as *Paradise Valley.* 31 M. *Dailey's* (4915 ft.). To the left is *Emigrant Peak* (10,960 ft.), at the head of Paradise Valley. Near (41 M.) *Sphinx* (5070 ft.) we thread the fine *Middle* or *Yankee Jim Cañon*, 'a gigantic and perfect piece of ice-work, with rocky sides smoothly polished and striated from the bottom to the top' *(Geikie).* As we approach the end of the railway we see *Cinnabar Mt.* to the right, with the curious *Devil's Slide*, consisting of two dykes of hard sandstone, 30 ft. apart, ascending the mountain for about 2000 ft.

51 M. *Cinnabar* (5180 ft.) is the terminus of the railway and the beginning of the stage-line.

The coach passes (2 M.) *Gardiner*, at the confluence of the Yellowstone and the *Gardiner River*, where it enters the Yellowstone Park. It then ascends on the right bank of the Gardiner and in $1^1/_2$ M. more passes from Montana to *Wyoming* ('Equality State'). Between Cinnabar and Mammoth Hot Springs the road ascends 1200 ft.; the last part is steep.

8 M. ***Mammoth Hot Springs Hotel** (6385 ft.), the headquarters of the Park Association (300 beds, incl. annex; baths with water from Hot Springs), is finely situated on a plateau about 800 ft. above the Gardiner, with *Mt. Evarts* (7900 ft.) rising to the E. (beyond the river) and *Terrace Mt.* (8100 ft.) and *Bunsen Peak* (8775 ft.) to the S.

This is the starting-point and terminus of the circular tour round the Park, which may be made in either direction, though that followed below is preferable, as reserving the fine Yellowstone Cañon to the last. Trunks and other heavy luggage are left here. The drive through the Park is made in light vehicles holding 3-7 people, and the same carriage is retained throughout by those who perform the circuit within the usual time (6-7 days; fee to driver usual).

Guides to the Terraces (see below; 2-3 hrs.) charge $ 2-3, or 25 c. each for a large party. Their services are desirable but not absolutely necessary, as the hotel is scarcely ever out of sight. It is advisable to visit the Terraces, if possible, in the morning or late evening, as the heat reflected from the glaring white formations is very trying. Smoked glasses are a desirable protection to the eyes.

Opposite the hotel, on the slope of Terrace Mt., are the wonderful ***Formations** or **Terraces** formed by the calcareous deposits of the *Mammoth Hot Springs*. These deposits cover an area of nearly 200 acres, comprising 10-12 distinct terraces and 70 active springs, with a temperature varying from 65° to 165° Fahr. The main springs now active lie just above the Terraces, the total height of which is about 200 ft. The exquisite colouring of the formations (white, cream, salmon, red, brown, yellow, green, etc.), the singularly blue transparency of the water, and the striking arrangement of the terraces combine to form a scene that has no rival since the destruction of the famous Pink Terraces of New Zealand.

The first objects to attract the visitor's attention on leaving the hotel are the cones of two extinct geysers, named *Liberty Cap* (45 ft. high) and the *Giant's Thumb*. The path usually followed in visiting the Formations diverges from the main road about 200 yds. to the S. of the former; the path near the Giant's Thumb is generally taken in returning. Among the chief points of interest are the *Minerva Terrace*, the *Jupiter Terrace*, the *Pulpit Basins*, the *Pictured Terrace* (with the *Blue Pool*), the *Narrow Gauge Terrace*, the *Orange Geyser* (a hot spring, not a geyser proper), *Cupid's Cave*, and the *Devil's Kitchen*.

Those who stay more than a day at the Mammoth Hot Springs may walk or ride to the **Middle Gardiner Falls*, 4 M. to the S.E. They are about 150 ft. high and are in a cañon 1200 ft. deep. This excursion may be combined with an ascent of *Bunsen's Peak* (half-a-day; *View). — An ascent of *Mt. Evarts* (see above), including a visit to the *East Falls*, takes about a day. — A road leads to the E. from the Mammoth Hot Springs to (20 M.) *Yancey's Pleasant Valley Hotel* ($ 2), whence a trail ascends the Yellowstone to (4 M.) the **Tower Falls*, 110 ft. high. There is a small forest of *Petrified Trees*, 1½ M. to the S. of Yancey's. Fishermen and sportsmen will find Yancey's a good centre. Route thence to *Yellowstone Cañon*, see p. 387.

b. From Mammoth Hot Springs to the Lower Geyser Basin.

42 M. STAGE in about 10 hrs.

The road ascends to the S. through the cañon of the Gardiner River to (4 M.) the **Golden Gate*, where the W. branch of the river passes between Bunsen's Peak and Terrace Mt. The name is said

to be derived from the yellow moss which grows on the rocky walls
of the pass. The *Rustic Falls* here are picturesque. Fine retrospect. On issuing from the cañon we pass *Swan Lake* and cross
a somewhat bleak plateau. To the right rise the snow-peaks of the
Gallatin Range, including (from right to left) *Quadrant Mt.*
(10,125 ft.), *Bannock Peak* (10,330 ft.), and *Mt. Holmes* (10,528 ft.).
Behind us, to the N.W., is *Electric Peak* (11,155 ft.), the highest
mountain in the Park. About 2 M. beyond Swan Lake we cross
Indian Creek and *Obsidian* or *Willow Creek*, two affluents of the
middle fork of the Gardiner. To the left, 2 M. farther on, rise the
*Obsidian Cliffs, a ridge of volcanic glass, 300 yds. long and 150-
250 ft. high, once a favourite resort of the Indians, who made arrow-
heads of the obsidian. In the construction of the road the large
blocks of obsidian were shattered by being first heated by fires and
then douched with cold water. To the right lies *Beaver Lake*
(7415 ft.), so called from its numerous beavers' dams. The road
skirts the lake for about 1 M., crosses the *Green Creek*, and then
surmounts the watershed (7550 ft.) between the Gardiner, flowing
into the Yellowstone, and the *Gibbon*, flowing into the Madison.
We pass *Roaring Mt.* and the little *Twin Lakes*.

18 M. (from Mammoth Hot Springs) **Norris Hotel** (7260 ft.),
where a halt is generally made for luncheon, is merely an eating-
station. It lies in the **Norris Geyser Basin,** which, though not to be
compared with the larger basins described at pp. 383, 384, contains
features of considerable interest. Some of its active geysers are of
quite recent origin. Most visitors will see as much as they wish of
this basin by walking on about 1 M. ahead of their carriage. In this
way they may see a boiling spring to the left of the road; the *Black
Growler*, to the right; the *Hurricane*, a short way to the right of the
road (sign-post); and the *Constant Geyser.*

A path diverging to the left leads to the *Emerald Pool*, the *New Crater*,
and the (1/2 M.) *Monarch Geyser*. — Numerous other small geysers and
boiling springs are visible in various directions.

From Norris Hotel direct to the *Cañon of the Yellowstone*, see p. 388.

About 3 M. from the Norris Hotel the road enters a valley named
Gibbon Meadows, beyond which we descend the romantic **Gibbon
Cañon.*

About 1/2 M. to the E. (left) of the entrance to the cañon are the
Artists' Paint Pots, similar to those described at p. 383. — A path to the
right, 3/4 M. farther on, leads to the *Monument Geyser Basin*, 1000 ft. above
the road, which may be neglected by the non-scientific tourist.

About 2 M. from the entrance of the cañon, to the right, is the
*Beryl Spring, one of the most beautiful boiling springs in the Park
(15 ft. across). Near the end of the cañon, to the left, are the fine
*Gibbon Falls, 80 ft. high. The next part of the road is comparatively
uninteresting. The *Teton Mts.* (14,000 ft.), 75 M. to the S.W.,
are visible in clear weather. Farther on we descend gradually to
the valley of the *Firehole River*, the two branches of which unite to
form the Madison. At the forks of the Firehole and *Nez Percé*, 5 M.

from the Gibbon Falls, our road is joined by that from Beaver Cañon
(p. 392). We go on 2¹/₂ M. farther to the —

42 M. ***Fountain Geyser Hotel** (7250 ft.), the usual halting-place
for the first night after leaving Mammoth Springs. Hot mineral baths
may be obtained at the hotel.

The ***Lower Geyser Basin**, which we have now reached, has an
area of 3-4 sq. M. and a mean elevation of about 7250 ft. It is
known to contain about 700 hot springs, besides a score or so of
geysers, arranged in groups. Within a few hundred yards of the
hotel is the ***Fountain Geyser**, which spouts every 2-3 hrs.
Though not very high (30-50 ft.), the eruption of this geyser is so
wide, has so many interlacing jets shooting in all directions, and
rises and falls with so many variations, that it ranks among the most
beautiful in the Park. The approach of an eruption, which lasts 15-
20 min., is heralded by the gradual filling up of the crater. — Near
the Fountain Geyser are the very singular and curiously fascinating
*Mammoth Paint Pots, or *Mud Puffs*, a group of mud springs of
different colours (pink, yellow, etc.), within a crater about 40 ft. in
diameter. The mud is thrown up with a curious 'plopping' sound
and falls back into shapes resembling flowers, etc.

About 2 M. from the hotel, but somewhat difficult of access owing
to the marshy nature of the ground, is the **Great Fountain Geyser**,
which rises to a height of 150 ft. Adjacent are some interesting springs.

c. From the Lower Geyser Basin to the Upper Geyser Basin.

8 M. Stage-Coach in 3-4 hrs., including halt at the *Midway Geyser
Basin* (see below).

The road runs at first towards the W., then turns to the S. and
follows the *Firehole River*. In about 3 M. we are abreast of what is
known as the *Midway Geyser Basin*, on the W. bank of the river; and
a halt is generally made for a visit to it.

This group includes the great *Excelsior Geyser, the largest geyser
in the world, which, with a short exception in 1890, has not worked since
1888, when it threw a huge mass of water to a height of 200-300 ft. Its
crater is nearly 400 ft. long and 200-250 ft. wide, and its walls rise 15-20 ft.
above the level of the boiling water within. Its appearance amply justifies the name of *Hell's Half Acre*, which is sometimes applied to it. — A
little to the N. is the beautiful *Turquoise Spring, a pool 100 ft. in diameter,
remarkable for the intense blueness of its limpid water. — To the W.
lies *Prismatic Lake (400 ft. long and 250 ft. wide), the marvellous colouring of which is indicated by its name. The volumes of steam which rise
from it reflect those colours in a very beautiful way.

About 3 M. beyond the Middle Geyser Basin we reach the beginning of the *Upper Geyser Basin* (see p. 384), which the road to the
hotel traverses, following the course of the Firehole River. Among
the springs and geysers near the road as we proceed are the *Artemisia
Spring* (right), the ***Morning Glory** (left), the *Fan Geyser* (r.), and the
Mortar Geyser (r.). Beyond the bridge are the *Riverside* (l.), the *Grotto*
(l.), the *Giant* (l.), the *Splendid* (r.), the *Comet* (r.), the *White Pyra-*

mid (r.; at some distance), the *Oblong* (l.), the *Turban* (l.), the *Grand* (l.), the *Saw Mill* (l., thesethree beyond the river), and the *Castle* (l.).

The **Upper Geyser Hotel** is at present used as a luncheon-station only, travellers returning to the Fountain Geyser Hotel for the night.

The ****Upper Geyser Basin** (7395 ft.), which is about 4 sq. M. in area, contains about 40 geysers (including the largest, after Excelsior, and finest in the Park) and many beautiful hot springs. Most of the large springs and geysers are near the Firehole River. A good general view of the district is obtained from a mound near the hotel.

The chief points of interest in the Upper Geyser Basin may be seen in two rounds of about 3 M., one on either side of the river, and about half-a-day should be allowed for each. Hurried visitors will do well to engage a guide; in any case they should ascertain what geysers are 'due' and arrange their itinerary accordingly. A table at the hotel gives the periodic times of the different geysers, but few of them, with the exception of Old Faithful, can be trusted. Those who wish to see all the large geysers playing have to stay several days or even weeks; while some geysers intermit their eruptions for months and years at a time. Most of the chief geysers are marked by little wooden signs. Thick shoes or overshoes are desirable, as parts of the formations are almost constantly wet from the overflow of the geysers.

*Old Faithful, one of the most beautiful geysers in the Park, throws its stream, at intervals of 65 minutes, to a height of 125-150 ft. The eruption lasts about 4 minutes. — Crossing the foot-bridge in front of the hotel, we reach the *Beehive, so called from the appearance of its cone (4 ft. high), which throws a very compact stream of water from its nozzle-like opening to a height of 150-200 ft. To the E. of the Beehive is the *Giantess, the interesting exhibitions of which are due once a fortnight (150 ft.). A little to the N.W. of the Giantess is the *Sponge*, so called from the appearance of its crater. — A little farther to the N. are the *Lion, Lioness*, and *Cub*, to the E. of which is the *Beach*. The path next passes between *Spasmodic* (r.) and the *Sawmill (l., near a bridge over the Firehole) and reaches the *Turban* and the *Grand, the irregular eruptions of which last (200 ft. high) are very fine. Near this is the *Young Faithful* or *Minute-Man*, a small geyser which goes off every 5 min. and lasts for 1 minute. Continuing to follow the path towards the N., we pass *Beauty Spring, cross the river, pass the *Oblong Geyser* with its fine crater (to the right, close to the river), and reach (1 M. from the hotel) the *Giant Geyser, perhaps the finest geyser in the Basin, which plays irregularly, throwing its column to a height of 250 ft. The eruption lasts for 1½ hr. About 200 yds. to the N. of the Giant is the *Grotto, remarkable for its curiously-shaped cone. We recross the river by the carriage-bridge, just above which, by the river's bank, is the attractive *Riverside Geyser (thrice daily; 80 ft.). To the N., also adjoining the river, are the *Mortar* and the *Fan*, so called from the shape of its display, which usually follows that of Riverside. On the opposite side of the road is the exquisite *Morning Glory Spring, a most delicately tinted pool, so called from its resemblance to a convolvulus or morning glory. We may now return to the hotel (1½ M.) by the road passing the *Castle, named from the shape of its crater (every 30 hrs. or so; 75 ft.). Near the Castle is a fine spring known as the *Castle Well*.

For our second circular walk we leave the hotel by a path leading through trees to the N.W., with *Iron Spring Creek* a little to the left. We cross this stream to visit the beautiful *Emerald Pool and *Sunshine Pool, and then recross it and follow the path past the little *Mud Geyser*, to the curious *Black Sand Basin* and *Specimen Lake*, the latter a flat and dry expanse, with numerous semi-petrified trees. A waggon-road leads hence to the N. to the *Punch Bowl, about 1 M. from the hotel, and is continued, sweeping round to the E., to the main carriage-road, which it joins above the Oblong Geyser (see above). A digression to the left (N.) will take in the *White Pyramid* (the cone of an extinct geyser), the *Splendid Geyser (every 3 hrs. every alternate day; 200 ft.), and the *Comet Geyser*.

The *Biscuit Basin*, part of the Upper Basin about 2 M. from the hotel, is comparatively seldom visited. It includes the *Sapphire Pool*, the *Soda Geyser*, the *Black Pearl*, and the *Silver Globe*.

A Road, now comparatively seldom used, leads from the Lower Basin through the *Hayden Valley* to (25 M.) the road leading from Yellowstone Lake to the Grand Cañon. The road ascends *Mary's Mountain*, the watershed between the Missouri and the Yellowstone, by the rough and precipitous *Devil's Stairway*. Fine retrospect of the *Teton Mts.* (p. 382), about 100 M. distant, as we ascend. At the top of the hill lies *Mary's Lake* (8335 ft.). Farther on we pass and cross *Alum Creek*. To the left (N.) rises *Mt. Washburne* (10,345 ft.), while the *Absaroka Mts.* come into sight on the right front (E.). The road then descends gradually into *Hayden Valley*. The drive through the valley to the (25 M.) crossroads, where we turn to the right for (9 M.) Yellowstone Lake and to the left for (8 M.) the Cañon (comp. p. 386), is rather uninteresting. The herd of buffalo in the Park is said to winter here.

d. From Lower Geyser Basin to Yellowstone Lake.

43 M. Stage in 9-10 hrs., including a stoppage for luncheon.

From the Lower Basin to the (8 M.) *Upper Basin*, see above. The road then ascends to the S.E. along the *Firehole* or *Madison River* to (1½ M.) *Kepler's Cascades*, where the river descends for 130 ft. in a series of leaps. About 1 M. farther on it bends to the left and follows *Spring Creek*.

Near this turn is the *Lone Star Geyser*, which plays every ½-¾ hr. to a height of 75 ft. — About 5 M. farther to the S., at the W. end of *Shoshone Lake*, is the **Shoshone Geyser Basin**, with the *Union* and other interesting geysers and hot springs. **Lake Shoshone** (7830 ft.), 6½ M. long and ½-4 M. wide, consists of two expanses united by a narrow strait. It is surrounded by wooded hills.

Our road ascends steadily along Spring Creek, affording fine views of Shoshone Lake (see above), and at a point about 8 M. from the Upper Basin crosses the 'Continental Divide' or *Watershed* of the **Rocky Mts.** (ca. 8100 ft.). This 'Divide' here makes a curious sweep to the N. and then bends round again, so that we cross it a second time, at a height of 8500 ft., about 6 M. farther on, near *Lost Lake*. The road then descends, passing *Duck Lake*, to (3 M.) *Yellowstone Lake* (see below), which we reach at the *West Bay* or *Thumb* (Larry's Luncheon Station). The *Hot Spring Basin* here contains about 70 hot springs, many of which are remarkable for their brilliant colouring. One lies so close to the lake, that it is literally possible to catch a trout in the lake and cook it in the spring without changing one's position. About 150 yds. from the lake is a group of *Paint Pots*, which many visitors consider finer than those described at p. 383. A small *Steamer* plies from this point to (20 M.) the Yellowstone Lake Hotel (p. 386).

For the rest of the way the road skirts the W. bank of *Yellowstone Lake* (7740 ft.), one of the largest bodies of water in the world at so lofty an altitude, having an area of 140 sq. M., a shore-line of about 100 M., and a longest diameter of 18 M. Its shape is irregular and has been likened to a hand with three fingers and a thumb. The outlet is at the wrist (N.), near the Yellowstone Hotel. The lake is surrounded by lofty mountains. The *Yellowstone River* enters it on the S. and issues from it on the N. Before reaching the hotel we circle *Bridge Bay*, so called from a curious *Natural Bridge*, about 1¹/₂ M. from the lake.

The *Yellowstone Lake Hotel, 35 M. from the Upper Basin, is well situated on a bluff overlooking the lake and backed by a forest. It commands a fine view of the lake and of the **Absaroka Mts.** beyond. Among the chief of these (named from N. to S.) are *Mts. Cathedral* (10,700 ft.), *Chittenden* (10,190 ft.), *Silver Tip* (10,400 ft.), *Grizzly* (9700 ft.), *Doane* (10,715 ft.), *Langford* (10,780 ft.), *Stevenson* (10,420 ft.), *Atkins* (10,700 ft.), *Schurz* (10,900 ft.), *Eagle Peak* (10,800 ft.), and *Table* (10,800 ft.). Nearly S., considerably to the right of those just mentioned, are the **Red Mts.**, culminating in *Mts. Sheridan* (10,385 ft.) and *Hancock* (10,235 ft.). The numerous islands in the lake also enter pleasantly into the view.

Boats (50 c. per hour) may be hired for excursions on the lake, and the fishing is excellent, the trout being large and voracious (use of fishing-tackle 50 c. per hr.). — The bears in the adjoining forest are numerous and tame, and the early riser may chance to see one foraging for the refuse of the hotel. — To the E., among the Absaroka Mts. (see above), is the region known as **Hoodoo** or **Goblin Land**, where the extraordinarily grotesque forms of the rocks and crags will repay the lover of the marvellous who is prepared for a somewhat rough and trying expedition.

e. From Yellowstone Lake to Yellowstone Cañon.

17 M. Stage in 4 hrs.

The road leads to the N. and N.W., following the left bank of the *Yellowstone River*. About 7 M. from the hotel, to the left, is the *Mud Caldron or **Volcano**, one of the weirdest and most extraordinary sights in the Park. It consists of a circular crater about 20 ft. deep, the bottom of which is filled with boiling mud, constantly rising in pasty bubblings, interspersed with more violent eruptions. The horrible appearance of the muddy pulsations and the groaning sounds which accompany them suggest an entrance to Inferno, with the spirits of the damned making abortive efforts to escape. — About 2 M. farther on the road through *Hayden Valley* (see p. 385), joins ours on the left, and 2 M. beyond the cross-roads, to the right, rises the *Sulphur Mt.*, or the *Crater Hills* (150 ft.), where large amounts of sulphur have been deposited by the various vents. The large boiling spring, at the foot of the highest hill, is strongly impregnated with sulphur, and its fumes are very disagreeable. To the left are several small mud-springs.—As we approach the Hotel, about 4 M. farther on, we obtain glimpses of the *Upper Fall* and the *Cañon* (p. 387). Finally we cross a bridge over a small stream forming the *Crystal* or *Cascade Falls.*

The *Grand Cañon Hotel (7710 ft.) is finely situated on an elevated plateau, about ¹/₄ M. from the river and the upper end of the cañon. It is a good point to spend a few days, as the attractions of the cañon demand repeated visits, while good fishing may be enjoyed in the river above and below the falls.

The ****Grand Cañon of the Yellowstone**, in some ways the most marvellous and indubitably the most beautiful of the wonders of the Yellowstone, extends from the Great Falls (see below) to a point near the E. Fork, a distance of about 24 M. Its depth is from 600 to 1200 ft., and its width at the top varies from about 300 yds. to 1500 yds. The upper part of the cañon, where it is at its deepest and narrowest, is also the scene of its most gorgeous colouring, the tints of the enclosing cliffs including the most brilliant shades of red, orange, yellow, and purple, 'as if a rainbow had fallen from the sky and been shattered on the rocks'. The formation of the crags and cliffs is exceedingly bold and picturesque. Far below flows the river, a thread of the most exquisite blue. The margins of the cañon are fringed with dark-green pines.

Visitors should follow the trail which leads to the S.E. from the hotel across the grass (comp. map of cañon in hotel), enters the wood, and leads to the brink of the cañon, which we reach near ***Look-out Point**, affording one of the finest views of it. To the W. appear the *Lower Falls* (see below), at the head of the cañon. [The *Red Rock*, below Look-out Point, reached by a steep but safe trail, also affords a good view of the falls.] We now follow the path along the edge of the cañon towards the left (E.), passing various good points of view, among the best of which is *Hayden Point*. A small geyser may be observed sending up its column of steam far below on the side of the chasm, and a quick eye will easily detect some eagles' nests on the inaccessible peaks of the pinnacles of rock below us. In about 2 M. we reach ***Inspiration Point** (1500 ft. above the river), which commands a splendid view of the gorgeous colours of the upper part of the cañon (afternoon light the best) and of the more sombre hues of the pine-clad Lower Cañon. This is the limit of the walk in this direction and we may now retrace our steps. [Those who do not care to walk both ways can ride or drive to Inspiration Point and Look-out Point.]

The ****Great or Lower Falls of the Yellowstone**, as fine, though not so high, as the famous falls of the Yosemite (p. 450), plunge from a height of 310 ft. into the abyss of the chasm. The river suddenly contracts here from a width of 250 ft. to 75 ft. The falls are reached from the hotel in 10-20 min. either by a direct trail (steep) or by an easy trail diverging from the road at the bridge over the Cascade Falls (p. 386). The platform at the head of the falls commands a fine view of the cañon, with Look-out Point conspicuous to the left (Inspiration Point concealed). — To reach the ***Upper Falls**, which are 1/2 M. farther up and about 110 ft. high, we cross the above-mentioned bridge, follow the road for a few minutes more, cross a second bridge (to the left), and then follow the road through the wood. The rapids above the Upper Falls are picturesque; the stretch of water between the two falls is to all appearance calm and sluggish, though the current is really very rapid. — Some good views are also obtained from the opposite side of the cañon, which may be reached by crossing the river by boat above the Upper Fall. One of the best is had from *Artist's Point*, where Thomas Moran painted the picture of the Yellowstone in the Capitol at Washington.

Mt. Washburne (10,340 ft.), which rises to the W. of the Yellowstone Cañon, commands a splendid *View of a large part of the Park, including Yellowstone Lake and the Grand Cañon. It is easily ascended from the hotel on foot or on horseback in 4-5 hrs. (10 M.; guide desirable). The usual route is to follow the trail leading over the E. flank of the mountain to Tower Falls, and diverge from this to the left at its highest point (ca. 4000 ft. above the river). [It is intended to construct a carriage road over Mt. Washburne to Yancey's (p. 381), which will form part of the regular circuit of the Park and obviate the doubling of the route from the Norris Basin to Mammoth Springs (see below).] — The above-mentioned trail to *Tower Falls* (p. 381) is 16 M. long. Another trail leads to the Tower Falls viâ *Dunraven Peak* (8865 ft.) and the W. flank of Mt. Washburne. From the Falls to (4 M.) *Yancey's*, see p. 381.

f. From the Yellowstone Cañon to Mammoth Hot Springs.

30 M. STAGE in 7-8 hrs.

The road leads to the W. and is at first of no particular interest. Farther on it descends into the valley of the Gibbon, passing the pretty **Virginia Cascades*, which have a total fall of about 200 ft. Just beyond the cascades the road turns sharply round an angle known as 'Cape Horn' or the 'Bend in the Road'.

12 M. *Norris Basin Hotel*, and thence to (30 M.) *Mammoth Hot Springs Hotel*, see p. 381.

85. From Chicago to Council Bluffs and Omaha.

a. Viâ Chicago, Milwaukee, & St. Paul Railway.

490 M. RAILWAY in 15-16 hrs. (fare $12.50; sleeper $2.50).

Chicago, see p. 279. The line runs towards the W. through a farming district. 35 M. *Elgin* (700 ft.; Kelley Ho., $2), a busy city of 17,823 inhab. on the *Fox River*, with large watch and other factories. From (80 M.) *Davis Junction* a line runs to the N. to (13 M.) *Rockford*. — 137 M. **Savanna** (570 ft.; *Savanna Ho.*, $22¹/₂; *Occidental*, $2), on the E. bank of the *Mississippi*, is the junction of lines running N. to *Dubuque* (p. 290) and S. to *Rock Island City* (p. 290). Our line here crosses the river to (141 M.) *Sabula* and enters *Iowa* (p. 290). 173 M. *Delmar Junction* (810 ft.); 192 M. *Oxford Junction* (720 ft.); 227 M. *Marion*, the junction of a line to *Cedar Rapids* (p. 389); 281 M. *Tama City;* 347 M. *Madrid;* 394 M. *Coon Rapids;* 466 M. *Neola*. The line now bends to the left (S.).

487 M. **Council Bluffs** (980 ft.; *Grand Hotel*, $3; *Danforth Ho.*, $2-3; *Pacific Ho.*, $2), a flourishing city of 21,474 inhab., at the foot of the bluffs of the *Missouri*, 2¹/₂ M. to the E. of the river, owes its prosperity mainly to the fact that it is the principal E. terminus of the great Union Pacific Railway (see R. 86) and the converging point of the E. railways connecting with it. Many of the public buildings are large and substantial. *Fairmount Park* is prettily laid out and commands fine views. Council Bluffs is connected with Omaha by two railway-bridges and one road-bridge.

Our train now runs into the (488 M.) *Union Pacific Transfer Station* and then crosses the Missouri by a fine *Iron Bridge, more than ¹/₂ M. long, erected at a cost of $1,000,000.

490 M. **Omaha** (1030 ft.; *Paxton Ho.*, $3-5; *Millard*, $3-5; *Murray*, $3-4; *Dellone*, $2¹/₂-4), the largest city in *Nebraska* ('Antelope State') and on the Missouri, with (1890) 140,452 inhab., is sitated on a plateau rising from the W. bank of the river. The bus-

A map of Yellowstone National Park region showing the following labeled features:

Absaroka Range — The Trident

Mt. Chittenden 10190, Silver Tip Pk 10900, Avalanche Pk, Grizzly 9700 Pk, Mt. Doane 10715, Mt. Stevenson 10620, Mt. Langford 10780, Atkins Pk 10700, Mt. Selmira 10900, Coulter Pk, Eagle Pk 10800, Table Mt.

Mountain Cr., Cliff Escarpment, Bridger L.

Yellowstone River

Two Ocean Plateau, Continental Divide

Lake Butte, Clear Cr., Signal Hills, Signal Pt., South East Arm, Promontory Pt, South Arm, Steamboat Pt.

YELLOWSTONE LAKE

Stevenson I., Sand Pt., Dot I., Frank I., Breeze Pt., Plover Pt., Flat Mt.

West Arm 7740, Delusion L., Flat Mt. Arm, Surprise L., Chipmunk Cr.

Snake River, Mt. Hancock 10235, Continental Divide, Crooked Cr., Falls

Beaver Cr., Heart L., Mt. Sheridan 10385, Red Mts., Red Cr., Forrest Cr., Basin Cr.

Lewis L., Factory Hill, Ridgal L., Elk, Solitation Cr.

Lewis River, Union Falls, Spirea Cr., Falls

Shoshone Lake, Moose Cr., Shush Geyser B., Pitchstone Plateau

Lone Star Geyser, Kepler Cascade, Summit L., Hot Sprg.

Continental Divide, Heron Cr., Junipar Cr., Spruce Cr., Beach L.

Mammoth Hot Sprs, Lower Geyser B., Upper Geyser B., Old Faithful, Firehole River, Twin Buttes, Madison L., Beula L., Herring L., Birch Hills, Falls River, Boundary Cr.

iness-streets adjoin the river, while the pleasant residence-quarters occupy the high ground. Among the most important buildings are the *Post Office* (at the corner of Dodge and 15th Sts.), the *High School* (fine view from the lofty tower), the *County Court House*, the *Exposition Building*, the *City Hall*, several *Churches*, and the offices of the *Omaha Bee* and the *New York Life Insurance Co.*

Omaha (the 'Gate City') owes its commercial importance to its position as one of the chief gateways to the West and has grown rapidly since its foundation in 1854. Its industries include smelting, brewing, distilling, meat-packing (excelled only by Chicago and Kansas City), machine-shops, and the making of bricks and steam-engines. The total value of their products in 1890 was $38,961,523. It is a railway centre of great importance, being practically (comp. p. 395) the E. terminus of the Union Pacific Railway and in more or less direct communication with all the chief cities of the E. and S.

The *Art Collection of Mr. G. W. Lininger*, cor. of 18th and Davenport Sts. (open on Thurs. & Sun., to strangers at other times also), includes paintings by *Fra Angelico, Guido Reni* (*2), *Guercino, Del Sarto, Solimena, Giordano, Rembrandt, Zurbaran*, and several modern masters.

From Omaha to *Portland*, see R. 86; to *San Francisco*, see R. 87.

Fort Omaha, 4 M. to the N., is an important military post.

b. Viâ Chicago & North-Western Railway.

492 M. RAILWAY in 15-19 hrs. (fares as above).

Chicago, see p. 279. This line follows nearly the same general direction as that above described. Few of the stations are of great importance. Beyond (97 M.) *Dixon* (720 ft.) we follow the *Rock River* to (109 M.) *Sterling*, a small manufacturing city (5824 inhab.), with good water-power. — From (135 M.) *Fulton Junction*, on the E. bank of the *Mississippi*, lines run N. to *Savanna* (p. 388) and *Dubuque* (p. 290) and S. to *Rock Island City* (p. 290). We cross the river by a fine *Iron Bridge*, 3/4 M. long, enter *Iowa*, and reach (138 M.) **Clinton** (725 ft.; *Windsor*, $2-2 1/2; *Revere Ho.*, $2), a prosperous city with 13,619 inhab. and extensive lumber-mills. — 172 M. *Wheatland.* — 219 M. **Cedar Rapids** (745 ft.; *Clifton Ho.*, *Grand*, *Pullman Ho.*, $2-2 1/2), a city of 18,020 inhab., on *Red Cedar River*, is an important railway-centre (comp. p. 388), carries on a large trade, and contains large pork-packing establishments and several manufactories. — 270 M. *Tama*; 326 M. *Ames*, the junction of a line to (37 M.) *Des Moines* (p. 390). Beyond (340 M.) *Boone* (1155 ft.) we descend rapidly into the valley of the *Des Moines* and the scenery becomes more interesting. We cross the river near (345 M.) *Moingana*. Farther on we again traverse a rich prairie district. 362 M. *Grand Junction*. At (400 M.) *Maple River Junction* we bend to the left (S.). 405 M. *Arcadia* (1440 ft.; 870 above Lake Michigan) is said to be the highest point in the level state of Iowa. Beyond (423 M.) *Denison* we pass through the pretty *Boyer Valley*. Beyond (468 M.) *Missouri Valley* (1020 ft.), the junction of a line from *Sioux City* (p. 299), we have good views of the *Missouri* and its bluffs.

489 M. *Council Bluffs*, and thence to —

492 M. **Omaha**, see R. 85 a.

c. Viâ Chicago, Rock Island, and Pacific Railway.

501 M. RAILWAY in 15-20 hrs. (fares as above).

From *Chicago* to (181 M.) *Rock Island*, see R. 50 c. This line runs somewhat to the S. of those described above but through much the same kind of fertile prairie-lands. From Rock Island the train crosses the *Mississippi*, by a fine bridge, to (182 M.) **Davenport** (580 ft.; *Kimball Ho.*, *Lindell*, $2-3), the fourth city of Iowa, with 26,872 inhab.; an important trade in grain and coal, and numerous manufactories. It is finely situated on the slopes of a bluff rising from the river and contains many handsome and substantial buildings. — At (222 M.) *West Liberty* (665 ft.) we intersect the railway from Burlington to Minneapolis (p. 291). — 237 M. **Iowa City** (670 ft.; *Chicago Ho.*, $2), a city of 7016 inhab., on the *Iowa River*, with various manufactories, is the seat of the *State University* and the *State Historical Library* (4000 vols.). — 303 M. *Grinnell;* 335 M. *Colfax* (750 ft.), with mineral springs.

358 M. **Des Moines** (800 ft.; *Savery*, $2-4; *Aborn Ho.*, $3; *Kirkwood*, $2½-3; *Morgan*, $2-2½), the capital of Iowa, is a city of 50,093 inhab., situated at the confluence of the *Des Moines* and the *Raccoon*, at the head of navigation of the former river. It is an important railway-centre and carries on a considerable trade and several manufactures (value of products in 1890, $5,680,000). Among the finest buildings are the new *State Capitol* (erected at a cost of $3,000,000), the *Post Office*, the *City Hall*, the *Grand Opera House*, *Drake University*, and the *State Library* (16,000 vols.). — The train continues to run towards the W. Beyond (470 M.) *Neola* we descend to the level of the *Missouri*.

498 M. *Council Bluffs*, and thence to —
501 M. **Omaha**, see R. 85 a.

d. Viâ Chicago, Burlington, and Quincy Railway.

501 M. RAILWAY in 16-18 hrs. (fares as above).

Chicago, see p. 279. The line runs at first towards the S.W., through a rich farming district similar to those mentioned above.

38 M. *Aurora* (p. 290); 84 M. *Mendota* (750 ft.); 164 M. *Galesburg* (790 ft.; *Union*, $2-2½), a city of 15,264 inhab., with two flourishing colleges, various industries, and a trade in agricultural produce. — From (206 M.) *East Burlington* the train crosses the *Mississippi* to —

207 M. **Burlington** (525 ft.; *Duncan, Boston*, $2½; *Union*, $2), the fifth city of *Iowa*, with 22,565 inhab. and a considerable trade by river and railway. The city is regularly laid out, with the business quarters on the river bottom and the residence-quarters on the bluffs above. The *Burlington Institute*, the *Free Public Library* (28,000 vols.), and the *County Court House* are among the chief buildings. — The line now ascends towards the W. 235 M. *Mt. Pleasant* (725 ft.), with

two Methodist colleges and a large Insane Asylum; 282 M. *Ottumwa* (630 ft.), on the *Des Moines,* with 14,001 inhab. and considerable trade and industry; 307 M. *Albia* (945 ft.), the junction of a line to (68 M.) *Des Moines* (p. 390); 363 M. *Osceola* (1125 ft.). Beyond (397 M.) *Creston* (1250 ft.) the line descends towards the Missouri Bottom. 448 M. *Red Oak* (1030 ft.), the junction of a line to (50 M.) *Nebraska City; 482 M. Pacific Junction* (960 ft.).

498 M. *Council Bluffs* and thence to —

501 M. **Omaha,** see R. 85a.

86. From Council Bluffs and Omaha to Portland.

1825 M. UNION PACIFIC RAILWAY in 65 hrs. (fare $60; sleeper $13). Tickets by this route are also available viâ *Denver* (comp. R. 91a). Dining-cars are attached to through-trains (meals $1). For general remarks on the *Union Pacific System* and its connections, see p. 395.

Council Bluffs and *Omaha,* see p. 388. The train at first traverses the manufacturing suburbs of Omaha. Beyond (31 M.) *Elkhorn* (1165 ft.) we run along the left bank of the *Platte River,* through a farming and prairie district. At (42 M.) *Fremont* (1190 ft.) we are joined by a line from *Sioux City* (p. 299). 94 M. *Columbus* (1440 ft.), the junction of lines to *Sioux City* (p. 299) and other points; 156 M. *Grand Island* (1860 ft.), a railway-centre of some importance; 199 M. *Kearney* (2145 ft.); 234 M. *Lexington* (2385 ft.). At (294 M.) *North Platte* (2795 ft.; 3055 inhab.) we cross the *North Platte River* and pass from 'central' to 'mountain' time (p.xviii). — At (375M.) *Julesburg* (3455 ft.), the junction of the direct line to *Denver* (p. 410), an alternative route for holders of through-tickets (comp. above), the line dips into *Colorado* but returns almost at once to Nebraska. We now quit the Platte River, which we have followed for about 350 M. — Near (417 M.) *Sidney* (4090 ft.) the train passes from the farming district of Nebraska into the grazing district, in which immense herds of cattle are reared. Between (461 M.) *Adams* and (475 M.) *Pine Bluffs* we enter *Wyoming,* called the 'Equality State' because its men and women have equal voting rights. — 519 M. **Cheyenne** (pron. Shyénn; 6050 ft.; *Inter-Ocean Hotel,* $2½-5), with 11,690 inhab., is the junction of the Denver Pacific branch of the U. P. System (from Kansas City and Denver; comp. p. 410). It is one of the chief centres of the cattle industry of the N.W. Fort Russell lies 4 M. to the N. of Cheyenne. — The snow-clad peaks of the *Rocky Mts.* now come into sight on the left, including *Long's Peak* (p. 406) and the distant *Spanish Peaks* (p. 418). To the N. (right) are the *Black Hills.* The train ascends rapidly, passing (538 M.) *Granite Cañon* (7310 ft.), and at (552M.) *Sherman* (8245 ft.) reaches the culminating point of the line, where we cross the main ridge of the **Rocky Mts.,** the great 'Continental Divide'. To the left is the *Ames Monument,* 65 ft. high, erected to Oakes and Oliver Ames, to whom the completion of the U. P. Railway was mainly due. Farther on we cross the *Dale Creek* by a bridge 650 ft. long (in a single span) and 127 ft. high. To the left may be descried *Pike's Peak* (p. 417), 165 M. off. To the right are the *Red Buttes.* — 576 M. **Laramie** (7150 ft.; *Thornberg*, $2¹/₂-3), a city of 6388 inhab., lies on the *Big Laramie River*, in the midst of the so-called *Laramie Plains*, one of the best grazing districts in the United States. It is a wool-market of considerable importance.

In summer stages ply from Laramie to *North Park, which lies about 60 M. to the S. North Park is one of the great natural parks of Colorado, which consist of large elevated plains or upland valleys surrounded by lofty mountains. They offer considerable attractions to the adventurous traveller and to the sportsman in search of large game, but are somewhat beyond the range of the ordinary tourist. North Park has an area of 2000-2500 sq. M., with a mean elevation of 8-9000 ft. It may also be reached from Denver viâ *Fort Collins* (see p. 408). The other natural parks of Colorado are *Middle Park* (p. 407), *Estes Park* (p. 403), *South Park* (p. 409), and *San Luis Park* (p. 418).

Beyond Laramie the train continues to descend through rugged hilly scenery. To the right of (618 M.) *Miser* rises *Laramie Peak* (9000 ft.), to the left *Elk Peak* (11,510 ft.), the N. outpost of the *Medicine Bow Mts.* 625 M. *Rock Creek* (6700 ft.; Rail. Restaurant); 659 M. *Carbon* (6820 ft.). Beyond (697 M.) *Fort Steele* we cross the *North Platte*, which re-appears here, 300 M. from the point we last saw it (p. 391). We now begin to ascend again. 712 M. *Rawlins* (6745 ft.); 739 M. *Creston* (7050 ft.), beyond which the train descends to the plains; 808 M. *Point of Rocks* (6505 ft.). At (848 M.) *Green River* (6080 ft.) we cross the river of that name, and the scenery again improves.

878 M. **Granger** (6280 ft.) is the point at which the Portland line diverges to the right from the main San Francisco line described in the following route. — Our line now runs towards the N.W., at first on a level and then gradually descending. Stations few and unimportant. At (970 M.) *Border* (6080 ft.) we enter *Idaho* ('Gem of the Mountains'). 993 M. *Montpelier* (5945 ft.), near *Bear Lake* (left); 1024 M. *Soda Springs* (5780 ft.; Idanha Hotel, from $3), a favourite summer-resort, with numerous powerful springs.

1092 M. **Pocatello** (4465 ft.; *Union Pacific Hotel*, $3), a town of 2330 inhab., in the *Fort Hall Indian Reservation*, is the junction of lines running S. to (134 M.) *Ogden* and (171 M.) *Salt Lake City* (see p. 424), and N. to *Butte* and (351 M.) *Helena* (see p. 373). Circular tickets are issued by the U. P. Railway for tours from Pocatello to the *Shoshone Falls* (p. 393), the *Yellowstone Park* (p. 378), *Butte, Helena* (p. 373), etc.

On the line to Helena, 118 M. from Pocatello, is **Beaver Cañon** (6025 ft.), the starting-point of the stage-line to (90 M.) *Firehole Basin* in the *Yellowstone Park*, mentioned at pp. 380, 382, 383. The route traverses the *Camas Meadows* (with a view of the *Tetons*, p. 382, to the right) and *Antelope Valley*, fords the *Shot Gun River*, reaches the *Snake River* (halt for the night), skirts that river and *Lake Henry* (6440 ft.), climbs through the *Tyghee* or *Tahgee Pass* (7060 ft.), and descends along the *Madison* (p. 382).

Beyond Pocatello the train traverses the *Great Snake River Lava*

Fields, overgrown with sage-brush and greasewood; the snow-clad *Rocky Mts.* bound the distant horizon on the right. We cross the river at (118 M.) *American Falls Station* (4340 ft.) by a bridge, 600 ft. long, affording a good view of the **Falls.* To the N. rise the *Three Buttes of Lost River* and (farther to the W.) the *Saw-Tooth Mts.* In front, to the left, appear the snow peaks of the *Washoe Range.* — 1200 M. *Shoshoné* (3970 ft.), the starting-point for the stage to the (25 M.) *Shoshoné Falls* (3$^{1}/_2$ hrs.).

The road to the falls runs to the S. across a sage-brush plain, passes some lava ridges, and suddenly reaches the deep ravine of the *Snake River,* 1200 ft. below it. We cross the river by a substantial ferry and soon reach the small *Shoshoné Falls Hotel.* The *Great Shoshoné Falls, with a breadth of 950 ft., fall from a height of 210 ft. and deservedly rank with the waterfalls of the Yosemite or the Yellowstone. Just above the main cataract is the *Bridal Veil Fall* (80 ft.), and 3 M. higher are the *Twin Falls* (180 ft.). The bold volcanic formations of the deep cañon in which the falls occur are full of interest. About 5 M. below the falls, a little to the N. of the river, are the picturesque *Blue Lakes,* where boating and fishing may be enjoyed.

A branch-line runs to the N. from Shoshoné to (57 M.) *Hailey* (5340 ft.) and (70 M.) *Ketchum* (5820 ft.). The *Hailey Hot Springs* (Hotel), 1$^1/_2$ M. from the station (temp. 150°), are efficacious in rheumatism, dyspepsia, and other ailments. Near Ketchum are the *Guyer Hot Springs* (Hotel).

Near (1235 M.) *Ticeska* the railway again reaches the *Snake River,* the left bank of which we now skirt more or less closely. 1252 M. *Glenn's Ferry* (2565 ft.). Level plains give place to small rolling hills and bluffs, but the scenery continues to be uninteresting. 1337 M. *Nampa* (2490 ft.) is the junction of a branch-line to (19 M.) **Boisé City** (2885 ft.; *Capitol Hotel,* 2^1/_2$; *Overland Hotel,* $2), the capital of Idaho, a busy little mining city, with 2311 inhabitants. — 1346 M. *Caldwell* (2370 ft.). Between *Parma* and *Huntington* we cross the Snake River thrice, the last crossing bringing us into *Oregon* (p. 291). 1396 M. *Weiser* (2120 ft.) is the gateway of the district known as the *'Seven Devils',* named, apparently, from the hills seen to the right. Farther on the Snake River flows through a picturesque cañon (*View to right from the bridge). — At (1419 M.) *Huntington* (2110 ft.; Union Pacific Hotel, $2), we change from 'Mountain' to 'Pacific' time (1 hr. slower; see p. xviii). We now leave the Snake River and ascend the picturesque **Burnt River Valley,* crossing the stream repeatedly and threading rock-cuttings and tunnels. Near *Durkee* we leave the Burnt River. Beyond (1457 M.) *Baker City* (3440 ft.) we ascend across the *Blue Mts.* and then descend rapidly, passing several snow-sheds, into the fertile and beautiful ***Grande Ronde Valley,** watered by the river of that name. 1506 M. *Union* (2720 ft.); 1519 M. *La Grande* (2785 ft.); 1531 M. *Kamela* (2910 ft.); 1551 M. *Laka* (2918 ft.); 1591 M. *Pendleton* (1070 ft.), the junction of a branch-line to (251 M.) *Spokane* (p. 375); 1618 M. *Echo* (640 ft.). — 1637 M. *Umatilla Junction* (300 ft.) is the point where passengers for Portland direct over the Northern Pacific Railway reach the main line of the Union Pacific System (comp. p. 376; *Wallula* is 27 M. from Umatilla). Near

(1662 M.) *Castle Rock* (250 ft.) the train reaches the wide **Columbia River** (700-800 yds. across), the left bank of which we now follow all the way to Portland. The object of the shields and barricades noticed here is to prevent the fine loose sand, here bordering the river, from accumulating on the tracks, a cause by which trains are occasionally derailed. 1682 M. *Arlington* (230 ft.); 1713 M. *Grant's* (180ft.), with fine basaltic cliffs. Farther on we cross the *De Chutes River* (view to left). — 1724 M. *Celilo* lies at the beginning of the narrow and rapid stretch of the river known as the **Dalles of the Columbia,* extending to Dalles City (see below).

The name (derived from the sheets of lava well exhibited on or near the river here) is sometimes confined to the gorge just above Dalles City, where the river is compressed for about 2¹/₂ M. into a channel only 130 ft. wide. The river-valley here seems to have been obstructed during a recent geological period by a lava-flow, through which it has eroded this extraordinary channel. As we approach Dalles City we have a good view of *Mt. Hood* (see below), on the left front.

1736 M. **Dalles City** (105 ft.; *Cosmopolitan, Umatilla,* $2-3) is a small place of 3029 inhab., with a considerable trade and some manufactures. It stands at the head of the finest scenery of the Lower Columbia, which pierces the *Cascade Mts.* a little lower down.

Passenger-steamers ply regularly between this point and Portland and the traveller is advised to perform the rest of the journey by water (110 M.; railway-ticket available), as the scenery is seen to the best advantage from the deck of the steamer. The large 'fishing-wheels' are interesting. Comp. p. 461.

The scenery for the remainder of the journey to Portland is very grand, including beautiful river-reaches, fine rocks and crags, pleasant green straths, noble trees, romantic waterfalls, and lofty mountains. Beyond (1745 M.) *Rowena* we see (to the right) the island of *Memaloose,* the ancient burial-place of the Chinook Indians, with a tall shaft marking the grave of *Victor Trevet,* a pioneer and friend of the Indians. Beyond (1752 M.) *Mosier* (100 ft.) the railway and river pass through the gorge proper of the *Cascade Mts.* (p. 376). — 1758 M. *Hood River.*

From this station stages run in summer to (40 M.) *Cloud Cap Inn,* near the summit of **Mt. Hood** (11,200 ft.; comp. p. 462). The *View embraces an immense number of mountain-peaks, including Mts. St. Helens, Adams, Rainier, and (sometimes) Baker to the N., and the Three Sisters, Mt. Jefferson, Diamond Peak, Mt. Scott, and Mt. Pitt to the S. Mt. Shasta, 250 M. to the S., is said to be visible with a good glass. The glaciers of Mt. Hood are very extensive.

Near (1783 M.) *Bonneville* (55 ft.) are the *Cascade Locks,* where the river descends 25 ft. in a series of picturesque rapids.

At present steamboat-passengers are carried past this obstacle by a small railway on the N. shore and transferred to another boat. The U. S. Government is, however, constructing a canal (1 M. long) and two locks on the S. or Oregon shore, at a cost of about $4,000,000.

Among the numerous small waterfalls at this part of the line the most picturesque are the *Horse-Tail,* the **Multnomah* (850 ft. high), the *Latourelle* (not seen from the railwey), the *Bridal Veil,* and the *Oneonta,* all near the stations of (1789 M.) *Oneonta* and (1795 M.)

Bridal Veil. The towering crags passed below this include the *Castle Rock* (rising 1000 ft. from the river), *Rooster Rock* (in the river), *Cape Horn* (500 ft. high), and the *Pillars of Hercules*, forming a noble gateway for the railroad. Beyond (1821 M.) *East Portland* and (1822 M.) *Albina* the train crosses the *Willamette* (p. 460), a broad tributary of the Columbia. A fine view is obtained of Mts. Hood and St. Helens to the S. and Mts. Adams and Rainier to the N.

1824 M. **Portland** (35 ft.), see p. 460.

87. From Council Bluffs and Omaha to San Francisco.

1867 M. Union Pacific Railway to (1034 M.) Ogden in 35 hrs. and Central Pacific Railroad thence to (1887 M.) San Francisco in 33 hrs. (through-fare $60; sleeper $13). Through-carriages. Dining-cars attached to through-trains (meals $1). Passengers from New York to San Francisco by this route (4½ days; fare $90) change carriages at Chicago.

The opening of the Union Pacific and Central Pacific Railways in 1869 completed the first railway route from the Atlantic to the Pacific. The undertaking was performed with the aid of large subsidies in money and land from the U. S. Government. Though the Rockies and several other mountain-ranges are crossed, the gradients are seldom severer than 1:50, and no tunnels were necessary except in Utah and the Sierra Nevada.

From *Council Bluffs* to (878 M.) *Granger*, see R. 86.

The main line continues to run towards the W. through a somewhat monotonous country. Good views of the snow-clad *Uintah Mts.* to the left. 906 M. *Carter* (6510 ft.). We now ascend to the ridge of the **Wahsatch Mts.**, which we cross a little beyond (939 M.) *Aspen* (7395 ft.). At (944 M.) *Hilliard* (7245 ft.) we pass under a so-called 'V-flume', used for conveying timber from the mountains. 958 M. *Evanston* (6760 ft.). Beyond (960 M.) *Almy Junction* we enter the *Territory of Utah* ('Deseret'; sign to the S. of the track). The *Utah Enclosed Basin*, which we now traverse, is remarkable for the fact that its waters have no outlet to the sea, but flow into salt lakes which in summer get rid of their surplus by evaporation. At (978 M.) *Castle Rock* (6240 ft.), where an observation car is attached to the train, we enter the wild *Echo Cañon*, with its wonderful rock and mountain scenery. We emerge from this near (994 M.) *Echo* (5470 ft.), and a little farther on reach the *Weber Cañon*, wider and less confined than Echo Cañon but in its way equally imposing. Tunnels. One of the minor points of interest is the *One-thousand Mile Tree* (reckoned from Omaha; to the right). The *Devil's Slide* resembles that described at p. 380. Beyond (1017 M.) *Peterson* (4895 ft.) we descend into the *Valley of Salt Lake.*

1034 M. **Ogden** (4300 ft.; *Reed Ho., St. James,* $2-4; *Depot Hotel,* with rail. restaurant, $2-3, meals 75 c.; *Broom House,* $1½-2}), the W. terminus of the Union Pacific R. R. and the E. terminus of the Central Pacific R. R., is a prosperous industrial city of 14,889 inhab., situated on a lofty plateau surrounded by mountains. It is also the terminus of the *Denver & Rio Grande Western Railway* (see R. 92 a). *Salt Lake City* lies 37 M. to the S. (see p. 424).

FROM OGDEN TO POCATELLO, 134 M., *Union Pacific Railway* in 5 hrs.
— The line runs to the N., affording views of *Salt Lake* (p. 427) to the
left. Beyond (9 M.) *Utah Hot Springs*, at the base of the *Wahsatch Mts.*,
we see to the right some fine crag scenery with curious conical peaks.
From (15 M.) *Willard* a visit may be paid to the (3 M.) *Willard Falls* and
Cañon. Beyond this point the ancient bench-marks on the mountains are
very conspicuous. Between (21 M.) *Brigham* and (30 M.) *Honeyville* we cross
a small shallow lake. Farther on the scenery is very fine, with the deep
*Bear River Cañon to the left, while the rocky hills tower above us to
the right. We cross two lateral gorges on trestles. On the other side of
the cañon is an irrigating canal, a fine piece of engineering, tunnelled
at several points through the rock. 49 M. *Cache Junction;* 71 M *Logan*,
with a Mormon temple; 131 M. *McCammon*. — 134 M. **Pocatello**, see p. 392.
    Visitors may bathe in *Salt Lake* (see p. 427) by going by railway from
Ogden to (15 M.) *Syracuse Beach* , a pleasant little lake-resort. — Another
favourite point is the **Ogden River Cañon* (a drive of ½ hr.).

Beyond Ogden our line (the *Central Pacific R. R.*) runs at first
towards the N. parallel with the Pocatello line (see above), skirts
Bear River Bay, the N.E. arm of *Salt Lake* (p. 427), then bends to
the left, runs to the N. of the lake, and crosses the *Bear River*. 1059 M.
Corinne (4230 ft.), said to be the largest Gentile town in Utah. 1087 M.
Promontory (4905 ft.). Beyond (1120 M.) *Seco* we leave Salt Lake
and bend towards the S.W., traversing the N. part of the '*Great
American Desert*', with its arid brown hills and stretches of alkali and
sage brush *(Artemisia tridentata)*. Some crops have been raised here
by irrigation. 1158 M. *Terrace* (4550 ft.). To the S.W. rises *Pilot
Peak* (10,900 ft.). Just before reaching (1191 M.) *Tecoma* (4810 ft.)
we enter *Nevada* (the 'Sage Brush State'), the boundary being marked
by a stone monument. At (1227 M.) *Pequop* (6185 ft.) we cross the
ridge of the *Pequop Mts.* Snow-sheds. We then descend into *Independence Valley* and re-ascend to (1244 M.) *Moors* (6165 ft.), in *Cedar
Pass*. 1253 M. *Wells* (5630 ft.), with several springs, to some of
which no bottom has been found; 1286 M. *Halleck* (5230 ft.); 1309 M.
Elko (5065 ft.; Rail. Restaurant), with the State University. *Elko Mt.*
is seen first to the right and then to the left. Piute Indians now
begin to show themselves. 1333 M. *Carlin* (4900 ft.). 1342 M.
Palisade (4840 ft.), in a narrow cañon, is the junction of a narrow-
gauge line to (90 M.) *Eureka*, in a rich mining district. Farther on we
cross the *Humboldt River*, which we follow some time. To the N. are
the *Cortez Mts.* 1393 M. *Battle Mountain* (4510 ft.); 1453 M.
Winnemucca (4330 ft.). To the N. are the *Santa Rosa Mts.* 1493 M.
Humboldt (4235 ft.), a little oasis in the desert. A little farther on
we again cross the Humboldt River, which flows into the *Humboldt*
or *Carson Sink*, to the S. of the line. — 1554 M. *White Plains*
(3895 ft.), the lowest point on the line for 1300 M.; 1569 M. *Hot
Springs*. — At (1589 M.) *Wadsworth* (4085 ft.) we begin the long
ascent to the ridge of the Sierra Nevada, following the *Truckee River*.
The scenery becomes picturesque. Numerous snow-sheds are passed.
1603 M. *Clark's* (4260 ft.). — 1623 M. **Reno** (4500 ft.; *Arcade*,
Riverside, $ 2-2½*), a busy little town of 3563 inhab., with schools
and colleges, flour-mills and smelting mills.

FROM RENO TO VIRGINIA CITY, 52 M., railway in 3 hrs. The chief intermediate station is (31 M.) **Carson** (*Arlington*, $ 2; *Ormsby*, $ 1-2), the capital of Nevada, a prosperous city of 3950 inhab., with substantial buildings and fine residences. Stages run hence daily (fare $ 2) to (15 M.) *Glenbrook* (Adam's Spring Ho., $ 2-3), on *Lake Tahoe* (6700 ft.), a beautifully clear and ice-cold sheet of water, 22 M. long, 10 M. wide, and 1500 ft. deep. Though surrounded by snow-clad mountains, it never freezes. Small steamers ply to various points on the lake.

52 M. **Virginia City** (6205 ft.; *International*, $ 2¹/₂-3), a silver-mining city of 8511 inhab., will well repay a visit to all who are interested in mining. The famous *Comstock Lode* has produced (since 1859) gold and silver to the amount of $ 500,000,000 (100,000,000 *l.*) and still yields $ 4,000,000 annually. The *Sutro Tunnel*, which drains the lode, is nearly 4 M. long and cost $ 4,500,000. *Mt. Davidson* (7825 ft.) commands an extensive view. Tourists may leave Reno in the morning, spend the greater part of the day at Virginia City, return for the night to Carson, drive to Lake Tahoe next day, cross it by steamer from Glenbrook to *Tahoe City*, and go thence by stage to (14 M.) *Truckee* (see below). Either Virginia City or Lake Tahoe may be visited from Reno in one day.

Beyond Reno the train enters *California* ('El Dorado State'). From (1658 M.) *Truckee* (5820 ft.) stages run to (14 M.) *Tahoe City* (see above; fare $ 2). About 3 M. to the W. is the pretty *Lake Donner*, the name of which is associated with a sad tale of suffering and death in the early annals of the pioneers of California (1846-7). The train continues to ascend, through imposing scenery, and reaches the highest point of the pass across the **Sierra Nevada** at (1672 M.) *Summit Station* (7015 ft.), where we thread a tunnel 530 yds. long. About 4 M. to the N. is *Mt. Stanford* or *Fremont's Peak* (9175 ft.; *View).

The **Sierra Nevada** ('Snowy Range') is the name given in California to the magnificent range the N. continuation of which, in Oregon and Washington, is known as the *Cascade Mts.* (see p. 376). It forms the W. edge of the highest portion of the Cordillerean system (p. lxviii) and is, perhaps, on the whole the most conspicuous chain of mountains in the country. From Mt. San Jacinto to Mt. Shasta it is about 600 M. long; but some geographers consider that the Sierra proper ends at Lassen's Peak, 100 M. to the S. of Mt. Shasta. Its average elevation is 8-10,000 ft., and several of its peaks, such as *Mt. Whitney* (p. 441), *Mt. Shasta* (p. 459), and *Mt. Corcoran* (14,095 ft.), attain heights of over 14,000 ft. The *Yosemite Valley* (p. 453) and its enclosing peaks are, perhaps, the best-known part of the Sierra Nevada; but it abounds throughout in the grandest mountain-scenery and offers many opportunities for the Alpine explorer. There are some large glaciers in the N. part of the range.

As we descend on the Californian side of the range the scenery continues to be very picturesque, while the change in vegetation and the brilliance of the flowers announce the mild climate of the Pacific Slope. The descent is very rapid, and the transition from snow-wreaths to sub-tropical vegetation comes with startling swiftness.

At places the line runs along the face of precipices, on ledges barely wide enough to accommodate the tracks. Snow-sheds cut off much of the view at first. 1694 M. *Emigrant Gap* (5220 ft.); 1699 M. *Blue Cañon* (4695 ft.); 1709 M. *Alta* (3605 ft.); 1710 M. *Dutch Flat* (3395 ft.). Before reaching (1723 M.) *Colfax* (2420 ft.) we pass the rocky promontory known as *Cape Horn*. 1741 M. *Auburn* (1360 ft.). Orchards and vineyards are now numerous. Oranges grow at (1746 M.) *Newcastle* (955 ft.). 1759 M. *Roseville Junction* (165 ft.; p. 459).

1777 M. **Sacramento** (30 ft.; *Golden Eagle*, $2½-3; *Capitol*, $2-3), the capital of California, with 26,386 inhab., lies on the E. bank of the *Sacramento River*, just below its confluence with the *American River*. It is regularly laid out, with wide straight streets, shaded with trees and bordered by gardens. It is an important railway centre and carries on an active trade. The most conspicuous building is the *State Capitol*, a large and handsome structure containing a library of 90,000 vols. (fine view from dome). Other important edifices are the *Court House*, the *City Hall*, the *Free Public Library* (18,000 vols.), the *Roman Catholic Cathedral*, and other churches. The *Crocker Art Gallery* contains pictures, Californian minerals, and a school of art. The *State Agricultural Society* has a large exhibition building and spacious grounds. — A pleasant drive leads along the Sacramento to (4 M.) *Riverside*.

From Sacramento to *Portland*, see p. 459.

FROM SACRAMENTO TO LATHROP, 57 M., railway in 2¼ hrs. This line formed part of the old route from Sacramento to San Francisco. — 35 M. *Lodi* (55 ft.). — 48 M. **Stockton** (25 ft.; *Yosemite*, $2-3; *Grand Central*, $1½-2), a well-built and flourishing little city of 14,424 inhab., lies at the head of navigation on the *San Joaquin* ('Wahkeen') *River*. Among the most prominent buildings is the *State Insane Asylum*, seen to the right as we enter the station. From Stockton to the *Calaveras Grove*, see below. — At (57 M.) *Lathrop* we join the Southern Pacific line from San Francisco to the S. (comp. p. 441).

Stockton (see above) is the junction of a branch-line to (30 M.) *Milton*, whence stage-coaches run in 2¼ hrs. (incl. overnight halt) to (50 M.) the *Calaveras Grove of Big Trees*. The night is spent at *Murphy's Camp* (Mitchler Ho., $2). — The *Calaveras Grove (*Mammoth Grove Hotel*) is the northernmost of the Californian groves of big trees, and it is the nearest to San Francisco. It is, however, comparatively seldom visited, as the Mariposa Grove (see p. 452) is conveniently included in the usual route to the Yosemite. The *Sequoia* or *Wellingtonia gigantea*, the 'big tree' of California, is found only on the W. slope of the Sierra, while the *Redwood* or *Sequoia sempervirens*, belonging to the same genus, is confined to the Coast Ranges (see p. 441). The Calaveras Grove (4750 ft. above the sea) covers an area about 1100 yds. long and 70 yds. wide and contains about 100 trees of large size, besides many smaller ones. The tallest now standing is the *Keystone State* (325 ft. high, 45 ft. in girth). The *Mother of the Forest* (denuded of its bark) is 315 ft. high and has a girth of 61 ft., while the prostrate *Father of the Forest* measures 112 ft. in circumference. Two other trees are over 300 ft. high and many exceed 250 ft. A house has been built over a stump with a diameter of 24 ft. The bark is sometimes 1-1½ ft. in thickness. — About 5 M. to the S. is the *Stanislaus* or *South Grove*, also containing many fine trees, which may be visited on horseback. — Milton is the starting-point for one of the regular stage-routes to the *Yosemite Valley* (see p. 451), which may also be reached from the Calaveras Grove viâ Murphy's (see above), *Sonora* (34 M.), and *Chinese Camp* (45 M.; p. 451).

The train crosses the river at Sacramento and runs toward the W., passing (1790 M.) *Davis* and reaching at (1817 M.) *Suisun* ('Sooisoon') a swampy district overgrown with *tule*, a kind of reed. To the S. is *Suisun Bay*, with *Mt. Diablo* (3855 ft.) rising beyond it. —1834 M. *Benicia*, with 2361 inhab., a *U. S. Arsenal*, and large wharves, lies on the N. side of the narrow *Straits of Carquinez* (½ M.), uniting the bays of Suisun and *San Pablo*. It is accessible for ships drawing

23 ft. of water. The train crosses the strait on the 'Solano', the largest
ferry-boat in the world, 424 ft. long and accommodating a train of
24 passenger-coaches. — 1835 M. *Porta Costa*, on the S. side of the
strait, also has large wharves from which wheat is shipped direct to
Europe. — We now follow the S. shore of San Pablo Bay (views to
the right). 1838 M. *Vallejo Junction* ('Vallayho'), the starting-point
of the ferry to *Vallejo* (see p. 434), on the opposite shore. Farther
on we turn to the S. (left) and see the beautiful **Bay of San Francisco*
(p. 433) to the W. (right), with *Mt. Tamalpais* (p. 433) rising beyond
it. — 1856 M. *Berkeley*, with the *University of California*, situated
among trees to the left.

The ***University of California** has played a very important part in
the educational development of the Pacific Slope and will repay a visit.
It includes departments of Letters, Agriculture, Mechanics, Engineering,
Chemistry, Mining, Medicine, Dentistry, Pharmacy, Astronomy, and
Law. It is attended by about 800 students, and tuition is free except in
the professional departments (in San Francisco). Lick Observatory (p. 438)
is connected with the University. Some of the buildings are handsome, and
the college grounds, 250 acres in extent, are picturesque. The experimental grounds have been of great service to the farmers of California.
The museums, the **Bacon Art Gallery*, and the laboratories also deserve
attention. The University commands a splendid *View of the Golden Gate
(p. 429) and San Francisco. — The *State Deaf and Dumb Asylum* is also
at Berkeley.

1861 M. **Oakland** (*Juanita*, $2-4), the 'Brooklyn' of San Fran-
cisco, is a flourishing city of 48,682 inhab., pleasantly situated on
the E. shore of the Bay of San Francisco. It derives its name from
the number of live-oaks in its streets and gardens. The value of its
manufactures in 1890 was $6,335,000. The steam-railways which
traverse Oakland convey passengers free of charge within the
city-limits.

Visitors to Oakland are recommended to take the cable-car to *Blair
Park*, in order to enjoy the splendid *View of San Franciso, the Bay, and
the Golden Gate from *Inspiration Point* (especially fine at sunset). — Other
points of interest near Oakland are *Lake Merritt* (boating), *Brush Peak*
(1740 ft.), *Moraga Pass* (1400 ft.), *Alameda* (p. 434), and *San Leandro*.

The San Francisco train skirts the W. side of Oakland and runs
out into San Francisco Bay on a mole $1^1/_2$ M. long, at the end of
which we leave the train and enter the comfortable and capacious
ferry-boat which carries us across (4 M., in 20 min.) the bay. In
crossing we see *Goat*, *Alcatraz*, and *Angel* islands to the right, with
the *Marin Peninsula* beyond them and the *Golden Gate* opening to
the left of Alcatraz.

1867 M. **San Francisco**, see p. 428.

88. From Chicago to Kansas City.

a. Viâ Atchison, Topeka, and Santa Fé Railroad.

458 M. RAILWAY in 14-18 hrs. (fare $12.50; sleeper $2.50).

From *Chicago* (Dearborn Station) to (41 M.) *Joliet* this line follows
practically the same route as that described at p. 290. — Beyond

(54 M.) *Blodgett* we cross the *Kankakee.* 63 M. *Coal City.* — 93 M. *Streator,* a city of 11,414 inhab. and a railway-centre of some importance. At (100 M.) *Ancona* the line forks, the left branch running to *St. Louis* (p. 311). At (134 M.) *Chillicothe* we cross the *Illinois River* and the Rock Island Railway (R.50 c). — 182 M. *Galesburg,* an important railway-centre (comp.p.390). — At (229 M.) *Dallas* we reach the *Mississippi,* which we cross at (235 M.) *Niota.* — 237 M. **Fort Madison** (*Anthes, Florence, Metropolitan,* $2), on the W. bank of the Mississippi, in *Iowa* (p. 290), is a thriving little city with 7900 inhabitants. The line bends to the S.W. and near (256 M.) *Dumas* crosses the *Des Moines River* and enters *Missouri* (p. 323). — 305 M. *Hurdland;* 352 M. *Marceline.* From (416 M.) *Lexington Junction* a branch-line runs to *St. Joseph* (p. 401) and *Atchison* (p. 405). Our line now crosses the *Missouri.* 455 M. *Grand Avenue* (Kansas City).

458 M. **Kansas City** (730 ft.; *Coates, Midland, Brunswick,* $3-5; *Victoria,* $3-4$^1/_2$; *Bonaventure,* $3-4; *St. James,* 2^1/_2$-3; *Centropolis,* $2), the second city of Missouri, with (1890) 132,716 inhab., lies on the S. bank of the Missouri, just below the influx of the *Kansas River.* It has grown very rapidly since 1865, when it had only 3500 inhab., and is now an important industrial, commercial, and railway centre (value of manufactures in 1890, $32,700,000). Among the most prominent buildings are the *Court House,* the *Board of Trade Building,* the *Custom House,* the *Grand Central Depot,* the *Winner Office Building,* and several *Banks* and *Insurance Offices.* The Missouri is crossed here by three fine bridges.

On the opposite bank of the Missouri, at the mouth of the *Kansas River,* lies **Kansas City,** Kansas (*Ryan Ho.,* $2-3; *Carmo Ho.,* $2), the largest city in Kansas, with 38,316 inhab. and the second-largest stockyards and packing-houses (Armour, etc.) in the country (value of products in 1890, $44,000,000).

FROM KANSAS CITY TO (485 M.) DALLAS, (508 M.) FORT WORTH, AND (750 M.) HOUSTON, *Missouri, Kansas, and Texas Railway* in 21-23 hrs., 23-24 hrs., and 32-34 hrs. This railway affords a direct route to points in Texas, but is of no great interest to the tourist. Its extreme N. terminus is *Hannibal* (p. 401), and passengers from St. Louis may join it at *Sedalia* (p. 403). — Beyond (161 M.) *Chetopa* we enter *Indian Territory* (see p. 410). 254 M. *Muskogee* is the seat of the U. S. Indian Agency for the Five Tribes (p. 410), of an Indian University, and some Indian schools. At (412 M.) *Denison,* a railway-centre with 10,958 inhab., we enter *Texas* (p. 464). The line forks here, one branch running to (508 M.) *Fort Worth* (p. 469), the other to (485 M.) *Dallas.* The latter is continued to (750 M.) *Houston* (see p. 467).

b. Viâ Chicago and Alton Railroad.

488 M. RAILWAY in 14$^1/_2$-21 hrs. (fares as above). Dining-cars.

From *Chicago* to (126 M.) *Bloomington,* see R. 56 b. The Kansas City line diverges to the right from that to St. Louis. — 171$^1/_2$ M. *Mason City.* — 215 M. *Jacksonville* (620 ft.; Dunlap Ho., $3), a city of 12,935 inhab., with two flourishing colleges and several State asylums. — 236 M. *Roodhouse,* the junction of a line to *Godfrey* (p. 302). Beyond (242 M.) *Drake* we cross the *Illinois River,* and beyond (265 M.) *Pleasant Hill* we cross the Mississippi and enter

Missouri (p. 323). — 302 M. *Vandalia;* 325¹/₂ M. *Mexico* (800 ft.), the junction of a line to *Jefferson City* (p. 403). Beyond (380¹/₂ M.) *Glasgow* (630 ft.) we cross the *Missouri.* 433 M. *Higginsville* (645 ft.); 487 M. *Grand Avenue* (p. 400).

488 M. **Kansas City,** see p. 400.

c. Viâ Wabash Railroad.

512 M. RAILWAY in 19-21 hrs. (fares as above). Dining-cars.

From *Chicago* to (173 M.) *Decatur,* where our line diverges from that to *St. Louis* (p. 311), see R. 60 c. — The next important station is (211 M.) *Springfield* (see p. 302). 245 M. *Jacksonville,* see p. 400. At (266 M.) *Naples* we cross the *Illinois River.* Beyond (301 M.) *Kinderhook* we cross the *Mississippi* and reach (313 M.) **Hannibal** (470 ft.; *Union Depot Hotel,* $2¹/₂-3; *Park,* 2¹/₂), in *Missouri,* an important river-port and railway-centre (comp. pp. 324, 400), with 12,857 inhab., a brisk trade in tobacco, timber, and farm–produce, and numerous manufactories. — 383 M. *Moberly* (880 ft.; 8215 inhab.); 422 M. *Brunswick* (630 ft.). We now have a view of the *Missouri* to the left. 446 M. *Carrollton;* 470 M. *Lexington Junction* (p. 403). We skirt the N. bank of the Missouri and cross it at (510 M.) *Harlem.*

512 M. **Kansas City,** see p. 400.

d. Viâ Chicago and Rock Island Railway.

519 M. RAILWAY in 15-21 hrs. (fares as above). Dining-cars (meals 75 c.).

From *Chicago* to (182 M.) *Davenport,* see R. 50 c. Our line here diverges to the left from the Omaha line and runs towards the S.W. 212 M. *Muscatine* (545 ft.), on the W. bank of the *Mississippi,* is a river-port of some importance (lumber, etc.; comp. p. 323). At (232 M.) *Columbus Junction* (585 ft.) we cross the *Red Cedar River,* and at (295 M.) *Eldon* we cross the *Des Moines River.* At (376 M.) *Lineville* we enter *Missouri* (p. 323). 451 M. *Altamont,* the junction of a line to *St. Joseph* (see below). At (465 M.) *Cameron Junction* we diverge to the left from the line to *Leavenworth* (p. 405) and *Atchison* (p. 410). 493 M. *Kearney* (635 ft.); 517 M. *Harlem* (see above).

519 M. **Kansas City,** see p. 400.

e. Viâ Chicago Great Western Railway.

586 M. RAILWAY in 23 hrs. (fares as above). Dining-cars.

From *Chicago* to (240 M.) *Oelwein,* where we diverge to the left (S.) from the line to *Minneapolis* and *St. Paul,* see p. 290. 314 M. *Marshalltown.* — 372 M. **Des Moines,** see p. 390. — At (428 M.) *Afton Junction* we intersect the Burlington and Quincy Railroad. Beyond (463 M.) *Blockton* we enter *Missouri* (p. 323). 491 M. *Conception,* the junction of a line to *Omaha* (p. 388).

529 M. **St. Joseph** (*Pacific House, Union Depot Hotel,* $3), a city of 52,324 inhab., on the E. bank of the *Missouri,* is an important

railway-centre and has immense stock-yards, numerous factories (value of products in 1890, $11,400,000), and a large trade. The *City Hall* is a handsome building. — The train now descends on the E. bank of the Missouri. 539 M. *Dearborn*, the junction for *Atchison* (p. 405), on the other side of the river; 556 M. *Leavenworth* (p. 405).

586 M. **Kansas City,** see p. 400.

f. Viâ Burlington Route.

489 M. Chicago, Burlington, and Quincy Railroad in 15-19½ hrs. (fares, etc., as above).

From *Chicago* to (164 M.) *Galesburg*, see R. 85 d. Our line now diverges from that to *Omaha* (p. 388) and runs towards the S. 191 M. *Bushnell;* 241 M. *Camp Point.*

262 M. **Quincy** (*Newcombe*, $2½-3½; *Tremont Ho.*, $2-2½), the third city of Illinois, with 31,494 inhab., lies on a high bluff on the E. bank of the *Mississippi*. It carries on a brisk trade, and its manufactures in 1890 were valued at $10,262,000. — 264 M. *West Quincy*, on the opposite bank of the river, is in *Missouri* (p. 323). We now follow the tracks of the *Hannibal and St. Joseph Railroad.* 279 M. *Palmyra Junction*, for the line to (15 M.) *Hannibal* (p. 401); 334 M. *Macon;* 392 M. *Chillicothe* (p. 400). At (434 M.) *Cameron* the line forks, one branch leading to *St. Joseph* (p. 401). Our line runs to the S. by the route described above.

489 M. **Kansas City,** see p. 400.

g. Viâ Chicago, Milwaukee, and St. Paul Railway.

530 M. Railway in 21-22½ hrs. (fares, etc., as above).

From *Chicago* to (228 M.) *Marion*, see p. 388. Our line here diverges to the left (S.) from that to *Omaha* (p. 388). 234 M. *Cedar Rapids* (see p. 389); 288 M. *Webster*. At (324 M.) *Ottumwa* (p. 391) we cross the *Des Moines River.* Beyond (380 M.) *Buda* we enter *Missouri* (p. 323). 464 M. *Chillicothe;* 491 M. *Lawson*, the junction for *St. Joseph* (p. 401); 498 M. *Excelsior Springs* (The Elms, $3).

530 M. **Kansas City,** see p. 400.

89. From St. Louis to Kansas City and Denver.

1041 M. Missouri Pacific Railway to (283 M.) *Kansas City* in 10-12 hrs. (fare $7.50; sleeper $2); thence to (1041 M.) *Denver* in 27 hrs. (through-fare $25.65; sleeper $5.50). — Through-cars are run over this route, in connection with the *Union Pacific Railway* (see p. 395), to *Ogden* and *Salt Lake City* (where carriages are changed for *San Francisco*).

Kansas City may also be reached from St. Louis by the *Wabash R. R.* (277 M.), the *Chicago and Alton R. R.* (323 M.), and the *Chicago, Burlington, and Quincy R. R.* (337 M.); but none of these routes demand any detailed description. Through-sleepers to various large Western cities are attached to all the chief trains.

St. Louis, see p. 311. At (44½ M.) *Labadie* (600 ft.) we reach the *Missouri River*, which flows to our right for the next 80 M. —

125 M. **Jefferson City** (625 ft.; *Madison Ho.*, $2-2¹/₂; *Depot Hotel*, $2¹/₂), the capital of Missouri, is a prosperous place of 6742 inhabitants. The *State Capitol*, built in 1858-60, was enlarged in 1887-88. — A little farther on we leave the river. 188 M. **Sedalia** (890 ft.; *Sicher's Hotel*, $2-2¹/₂; *Kaiser*, $2) is a busy industrial city of 14,068 inhabitants.

The line forks at Sedalia, the right branch leading to Kansas City viâ Lexington (see below), while the left branch runs to (61 M.) *Pleasant Hill*. Here the line forks again, the right arm leading to Kansas City and the left affording an alternative route to Pueblo and Denver (1064 M. from St. Louis). Among the chief stations on this route are *Fort Scott*, *El Dorado*, *Wichita* (p. 410), and *Hutchinson*. At *Geneseo* (572 M. from St. Louis) it joins the route described below.

The Lexington line runs towards the N.W. 244 M. *Lexington* (735 ft.) is a place of 1075 inhab., on the S. bank of the Missouri, which we here rejoin. Our line keeps to the S. side of the river.

283 M. **Kansas City,** see p. 400.

Our line now runs towards the S., entering *Kansas* at (310 M.) *Newington*. At (343 M.) *Ossawattomie* (2662 inhab.), the Kansas home of John Brown, we turn to the right (W.). 364 M. *Ottawa* (900 ft.; Centennial, Hamblin, Sheldon, $2), a summer-resort with 6248 inhab.; 378 M. *Lomax*, the junction of a line to (39 M.) *Topeka* (p. 405); 396 M. *Osage City* (1075 ft.; 3469 inhab.); 435 M. *Council Grove* (1240 ft.; 2211 inhab.). — From (488 M.) *Gypsum City* a loop-line runs to (17 M.) *Salina* (1225 ft.; 6149 inhab.) and back to (42 M.) *Marquette* (see below). — 515 M. *Marquette* (see above). At (535 M.) *Geneseo* we are joined by the line mentioned above. We are now ascending the basin of the *Arkansas River*, which, however, flows far to the S. of the railway. At (568 M.) *Hoisington* we change from 'Central' to 'Mountain' time (1 hr. slower; see p. xviii). 626 M. *Brownell;* 692 M. *Scott;* 741 M. *Horace.* At (756 M.) *Towner* we enter *Colorado* (p. 405). Beyond (776 M.) *Brandon* we cross *Big Sandy Creek.* 831 M. *Arlington;* 886 M. *Boone.*

923 M. **Pueblo,** see p. 418. — Beyond Pueblo we follow the line of the *Denver and Rio Grande R. R.* (see R. 92 a).

1041 M. **Denver,** see p. 406.

90. From St. Louis to Texarkana.

490 M. St. Louis, Iron Mountain, and Southern Railway in 17-23 hrs. (fare $14.70, sleeper $3.50). Through-carriages run by this line to *Arkansas Hot Springs*, *Fort Worth*, *San Antonio*, *Laredo*, *Dallas*, *Houston*, *Galveston*, and *El Paso* (for *Los Angeles* and *San Francisco* viâ Texas Pacific Railway).

St. Louis, see p. 311. The line runs to the S. along the W. bank of the *Mississippi* as far as (27 M.) *Riverside*. It then leaves the river and runs to the S.W. through the great mineral district of E. Missouri. From (61 M.) *Mineral Point* (860 ft.) a branch-line runs to (4 M.) *Potosi*, with its numerous lead-mines. At (75 M.) *Bismarck* (1025 ft.) the railway forks, the left branch leading to *Columbus* (Ky.;

26*

p. 324), while the Texas line runs nearly due S. About 6 M. farther
on the famous **Iron Mt.** (1075 ft.) is seen to the left.

This is an irregular hill, consisting mainly of porphyry, intersected
by numerous mineral veins and capped with a deposit of specular iron
ore, 6-30 ft. thick and yielding nearly 70 per cent of pure iron. The
amount of mineral already taken from this hill exceeds five million tons.

Pilot Knob (1015 ft.), seen on the same side, 6 M. farther on,
also contains a wonderful bed of iron ore, 12-30 ft. thick. 88 M.
Ironton (910 ft.) uses the fine magnetic ore of *Shepherd Mt.*, which
is free from phosphorus and sulphur. 166 M. *Poplar Bluff* is the
junction of a line to (71 M.) *Bird's Point*, opposite *Cairo* (p. 320).
Beyond (181 M.) *Neelyville* (305 ft.) we enter *Arkansas* ('Bear State';
pron. 'Arkänsaw'). At (198 M.) *Knobel* (270 ft.) the through-carriages
to *Memphis* (p. 320) diverge to the left. 226 M. *Hoxie.* At (262 M.)
Newport (230 ft.) we cross the *White River* (p. 325). 288 M. *Bald
Knob*, the junction of a line to (91 M.) *Memphis* (p. 320).

345 M. **Little Rock** (260 ft.; *Capitol*, $ 2¹/₂-5; *Richelieu*, $ 3-4;
Deming, $ 2), the capital and largest city of Arkansas, with (1890)
25,874 inhab., is well situated on the wide *Arkansas River* and carries
on a large trade in cotton and other goods both by railway and
steamer. It is regularly laid out, and many of its streets are pleasantly shaded by magnolias. The principal buildings include the
State House, the *U. S. Court House*, the *County Court House*, the
State Insane Asylum, the *Deaf-Mute Institute*, the *School for the Blind*,
the *Post Office*, the *Board of Trade Building*, *Little Rock University*,
and the *Medical Department of Arkansas Industrial University*. Railways radiate hence in all directions.

388 M. **Malvern** (280 ft.; *Hot Springs, Commercial*, $ 2) is the junc-
tion of a branch-line to (25 M.) the famous *Arkansas Hot Springs*.

The town of **Hot Springs, Arkansas** (425 ft.; **Eastman*, about $ 3-5;
Park; Arlington; Plateau, $ 3¹/₂; *Avenue; New Sumpter Ho.*, $ 2-3¹/₂; *New
Waverley*, $ 3; *Argyle, Windsor, Josephine*, $ 2-3; *Southern Ho.*, $ 2-2¹/₂; and
many others), with (1890) 8086 inhab., is situated in a narrow gorge between *Hot Springs Mt.* and *West Mt.*, in the heart of the *Ozark Mts.*, and has
become one of the most frequented health and pleasure resorts in America.
The wide main street is flanked on one side with hotels and shops and on the
other with a row of handsome bath-houses. The *Springs*, of which there
are upwards of 70, rise on the W. slope of Hot Springs Mt., above the
town, vary in temperature from 76° to 158° Fahr., and discharge daily about
500,000 gallons of clear, tasteless, and odourless water. They are used both
internally and externally, and are beneficial in rheumatism, syphilis, nervous
ailments, and affections of the skin and blood. They contain a little silica
and carbonate of lime; but the efficacy of the water is ascribed mainly to
its heat and purity. The price for a single bath is 15-40 c., for 21 baths
$ 3¹/₂-8. The ground on which the springs rise is the property of the U. S.
Government, and a large *Army and Navy Hospital* has been erected here for
the use of officers, soldiers, and sailors. Among the numerous pleasant
points for walks, rides, and drives in the vicinity of the Hot Springs are
the *Valley of the Ouichita, Gulpha Gorge, Hell's Half Acre, Happy Hollow,
Ball Bayou, Crystal Mt.*, and *Whittington's Peak*. There are several other
mineral springs within easy reach, the chief of which are *Gillen's White
Sulphur Springs, Potash Sulphur Springs*, and *Mountain Valley Springs*, each
with a hotel. Good shooting and fishing are also obtainable.

409 M. *Daleville;* 426 M. *Gurdon;* 457 M. *Hope* (360 ft.).

490 M. **Texarkăna** (300 ft.; *Benefield, Collins, Cosmopolitan,* $ 2), a town with 6380 inhab., on the border of Texas and Arkansas, is an important railway-junction, from which connection can easily be made for all important points in Texas, viâ the Texas and Pacific and other railways (comp. p. 468).

91. From Kansas City to San Francisco.
a. Viâ Union Pacific Railway System.

2094 M. UNION PACIFIC SYSTEM in 82-84 hrs. (fare $ 60; sleeper $13). Through-carriages. Dining-cars on the through-trains.

Kansas City, see p. 400. The train at first follows the *Kansas River* towards the W. (views to the left). — 39 M. **Lawrence** (760 ft.; *Eldridge Ho.,* $ 2-2¹/₂), a pleasant little commercial city of 9997 inhab., situated on both banks of the *Kansas River,* is the seat of the *State University* (3-500 students) and also contains the *Haskell Institute,* a government training-school for Indians (400 boys and 150 girls). We are here joined by the line from (34 M.) *Leavenworth* (see below).

Leavenworth (750 ft.; *Delmonico, National,* $ 2-2¹/₂), on the W. bank of the *Missouri,* is a busy industrial and commercial city with 19,768 inhabitants. A colossal bronze statue of *Gen. U. S. Grant* was erected here in 1889. To the N. is *Fort Leavenworth,* an important military post.

We now traverse the great prairies of Kansas, an excellent farming and grazing country. — 67 M. **Topeka** (820 ft.; *Thorp, Copeland,* $ 3-4; *National,* $ 2; *Rail. Restaurant),* the capital of Kansas, is a flourishing city of 31,007 inhab., also situated on both sides of the Kansas River. The chief buildings include the *State Capitol,* the *Post Office and Custom House,* the *State Insane Asylum,* the *Reform School,* the *Free Library* (12,000 vols.), *Grace Church Cathedral, Washburn College,* and *Bethany College.* Topeka has large mills (value of products in 1890, $ 7,000,000) and a brisk trade. — 104 M. *Wamego* (930 ft.). We cross the *Blue River.* — 119 M. *Manhattan* (960 ft.), with the *State Agricultural College.* — 135 M. *Fort Riley,* an army post with an important military school. The *Ogden Monument* marks the geographical centre of the United States (excl. Alaska). — 139 M. *Junction City* (1020 ft.), for a line to *Clay Centre* and *Belleville,* etc. The *Smoky Hill River* now flows to the left. — 163 M. *Abilene* (1095 ft.; Rail. Restaurant). Large crops of wheat and other grains are raised here. — 186 M. *Salina* (p. 403). We now cross the river. 223 M. *Ellsworth* (1470 ft.); 289 M. *Hays City,* with *Fort Hays.* At (303 M.) *Ellis* (2055 ft.; Rail. Restaurant) we change to 'Mountain' time (p. xviii). 377 M. *Oakley* (2980 ft.); 420 M. *Wallace* (3285 ft.; Rail. Restaurant). We now begin to pass from an agricultural to a grazing district, where the useful 'bunch-grass' of the W. affords food, both summer and winter, to millions of cattle. Beyond (452 M.) *Arapahoe* we enter *Colorado* (the 'Silver State'). 462 M. *Cheyenne Wells* (4260 ft.; Rail. Restaurant). — At (473 M.) *First View* we obtain the first view of the *Rocky Mts.,* still about 170 M. distant. *Pike's Peak* (p. 417) is conspicuous, nearly due W. — Beyond (487 M.) *Kit Carson* (4275 ft.), named after a well-known trapper, we follow the *Big Sandy Creek* (left) towards the N.W. 535 M. *Hugo* (5025 ft.), on the middle fork of the *Republican River*. At (550 M.) *Limon* we cross the Rock Island Railway. 563 M. *Cedar Point* (5695 ft.) is the highest point on this part of the line. 596 M. *Byers* (5190 ft.); 618 M. *Watkins* (5515 ft.).

639 M. **Denver** (5270 ft.; *Metropole*, R. from $1¹/₂; *Palace*, $3-5; *Windsor, Albany*, $3-4; *St. James*, $2¹/₂-3¹/₂; *Broadway*, $2¹/₂-4; *Markham*, R. $1¹/₂; *American Ho.*, $3; *Glenarm*, $2-3), the capital and largest city of Colorado, lies on the S. bank of the *South Platte River*, about 15 M. from the E. base of the Rocky Mts., of which it commands a superb view. Denver, the 'Queen City of the Plains', was founded in 1858 and is a striking example of the marvellous growth of western cities, reaching a total of 35,630 inhab. in 1880 and no fewer than 126,713 in 1890 (150,000, incl. suburbs). Many of its buildings are large, handsome, and substantial, and the private residences and gardens are often very tasteful. Some of the business streets were paved with asphalt in 1892, but many are still very rough. It owes its prosperity to its position in the heart of a rich mining district and as the centre of numerous important railways (comp. pp. 414, 403, etc.); while in 1890 its manufactures, including cotton and woollen goods, flour, machinery, and carriages, were valued at $30,500,000.

The Union Depot lies at the foot of *Seventeenth Street*, one of the chief business-thoroughfares, and tramways start here for all parts of the city. The traveller is recommended to ascend 17th St. and 17th Ave. by cable car to the *City Park* (320 acres) and then walk across to Colfax or 15th Ave. and return by it. On the way out we pass the new *Equitable Building* (cor. of Stout St.), the top of which affords a superb *View.

The **Rocky Mts.** are seen to the W. in an unbroken line of about 170 M., extending from beyond *Long's Peak* (p. 408) on the N. to *Pike's Peak* (p. 417) on the S. Among the loftiest of the intervening summits are *Gray's Peak* (p. 408) and *Mts. Torrey* (14,335 ft.) and *Evans* (14,330 ft). The bird's-eye view of the city at our feet includes the new State Capitol (see below) and the fine residences of Capitol Hill to the E.

At the corner of 17th St. and Glenarm St. is the *Denver Club*, and at the corner of Sherman Ave. is the *Central Presbyterian Church*. — In returning through *Colfax* (or *15th*) *Ave.* we pass the new STATE CAPITOL, erected at a cost of $1,500,000. The COUNTY COURT HOUSE occupies the block bounded by Court Place and 15th, 16th, and Tremont Sts. — The CUSTOM HOUSE AND POST OFFICE, 16th St., is another imposing building. — A visit may also be paid to the *U. S. Branch Mint*, 16th St., where the processes of melting and assaying bullion may be witnessed (no coining).

The other important buildings of the city include the *Denver High School* (Stout St., betw. 19th and 20th Sts.), the *City Hall* (cor. 14th and Larimer Sts.), the *Mining Exchange* (cor. 15th and Arapahoe Sts.), the *Chamber of Commerce* (cor. 14th and Lawrence Sts., with the *Mercantile Library*), the *Presbyterian College* (Montclair), the *Tabor Opera House Block* (16th and Larimer Sts.), the *Broadway Theatre* (cor. 18th St. and Broadway), the *Bijou* (Curtis St.), *Trinity Church* (Broadway and 18th St.), *St. Mary's Cathedral* (R. C.; Stout St., between 15th and 16th Sts.), *St. John's Cathedral* (Epis.; at the head of Broadway), the *Westminster University of Colorado* (in progress), and the Jesuit *College of the Sacred Heart* (College Ave., cor. of Homer Ave.). — The *Art Museum*, in Montclair (see below), contains a collection of paintings and other objects of art.

A visit should also be paid to one of the great SMELTING WORKS of Denver, among which may be mentioned the *Colorado & Boston* (at *Argo*, see below), the *Omaha & Grant* (Larimer St.), and the *Globe*, all to the N. of the city. The value of the ores reduced here in 1891 amounted to $ 24,500,000.

A good idea of Denver's suburban growth is obtained by taking the electric tramway at the end of the 17th Ave. cable-line and going to the E. over *Capitol Hill* (fine residences) and through *Montclair* to *Aurora*. — Visits may also be paid by electric or cable cars to *Elitch's Zoological Garden* (adm. 25 c.), *Berkeley Lake* and *Park*, and *Sloan Lake*.

Denver is a good centre for numerous fine excursions, a few of which are enumerated below. Comp. also p. 415 (Colorado Springs), p. 414 (Denver & Rio Grande R. R.), and p. 403.

FROM DENVER TO GOLDEN, CENTRAL CITY, AND GRAYMONT, 60 M., *Union Pacific Railway* (narrow-gauge) in 4 hrs. Observation-cars are attached to the trains. — Beyond (2 M.) *Argo* (5215 ft.) and (3 M.) *Argo Junction* we have a good retrospect of Denver, with Pike's Peak (p. 417) in the distance. To the E. is the *Platte River*, to the W. rise the *Rocky Mts.* Farther on we descend into the *Clear Creek Valley*. At (7 M.) *Arvada* we turn to the W. — 15 M. **Golden** (5655 ft.; *Garbarew Ho.*, $3) at the base of the *Table Mts.*, is a busy little industrial and mining city, with 2383 inhabitants. We now ascend the picturesque *Clear Creek Cañon*, where the cliffs are sometimes 1000 ft. high. 24 M. *Beaver Brook*. — 29 M. *Forks Creek* (6830 ft.), at the confluence of the N. and S. branches of Clear Creek, is the junction of the line to *Central City* (see below). — The Graymont train follows the South Clear. 37 M. **Idaho Springs** (7540 ft.; *Colorado Hotel*, $2¹/₂-3), in the midst of a gold and silver mining district, is frequented for its hot and cold mineral springs (large baths). An excursion may be made to (13 M.) *Chicago Lakes* (11,000 ft.). — We continue to ascend rapidly, amid lofty mountains.

50 M. **Georgetown** (8475 ft.; *Barton Ho.*, $2), a silver-mining town with 1927 inhab., is also frequented as a summer-resort on account of its pure air and beautiful environment. Excursions may be made to (3 M.) *Green Lake* (10,400 ft.; Hotel), *Clear Lake* (3¹/₂ M.), *Elk Lake* (6 M.), etc. Four-horse coaches run thrice weekly from Georgetown, through the *Berthoud Pass*, to (56 M.) *Grand Lake* (Hotel), and (47 M) *Hot Sulphur Springs* (Kinney Ho., $2), in **Middle Park**, the second of the great Natural Parks of Colorado mentioned at p. 392. Middle Park, the only one on the W. side of the 'Continental Divide', has a mean elevation of about 7500 ft. and an area of 3000 sq. M. It is a fine resort for sportsmen in search of big game. The baths of Hot Sulphur Springs are efficacious in rheumatism, neuralgia, and cutaneous affections.

Above Georgetown the train threads the *Devil's Gate* and climbs up the mountains by means of the famous *Loop*, where it bends back on itself and crosses the track just traversed by a lofty bridge. A little higher up it makes two other sweeping curves, which nearly bring it back upon itself. 54 M. *Silver Plume* (9175 ft.). — 58 M. **Graymont** (9770 ft.; *Gray's Peak Hotel*), the terminus of the line, lies at the foot of *Gray's Peak (14,440 ft.), one of the loftiest of the Rocky Mts., which is easily ascended hence on horseback in 3-4 hrs. (return-tickets issued by the Railway Co. at Denver, incl. horse and guide to the top). The *View is superb, including in clear weather *Long's Peak* (see below) and *Pike's Peak* (p. 417). Adjacent is *Torrey's Peak* (14,335 ft.), which may also be ascended.

[The line from Forks Creek to Central City (see p. 407) ascends the *N. Clear Creek*, passing numerous quartz mines. Beyond (37 M. from Denver) *Black Hawk* (8030 ft.) it overcomes the heavy gradient by long 'switchback' curves. — 40 M. **Central City** (8500 ft.; *Teller*, $4), a busy little mining city, with 2480 inhabitants. An ascent may be made of *James Peak* (13,280 ft.; *View), and a pleasant walk or ride may be taken to (6 M.) *Idaho Springs* (see p. 407) viâ *Bellevue Hill* (fine view of the Front Range).]

FROM DENVER TO BOULDER AND FORT COLLINS, 71 M., *Union Pacific Railway* (narrow-gauge) in 3 hrs. Beyond (3 M.) *Argo Junction* (see p. 407) the train runs to the N. to (29 M.) **Boulder** (5335 ft.; *Brainard*, $2½-3; *Bowen*, $2-3), a small mining city and the site of the *University of Colorado* (150 students), at the mouth of *Boulder Cañon, which may be visited by carriage (to the *Falls*, 9 M., and back, $5). A branch-line runs from Boulder to (13 M.) *Sunset* (7695 ft.). — Beyond Boulder our line ascends to (40 M.) *Longmont* (4935 ft.) and (57 M.) *Loveland* (4970 ft.; Loveland Ho., $2-2½). From the latter a stage-coach runs to (28 M.) *Estes Park* (6810 ft.; *Estes Park Hotel*, $3; boarders taken at *James's* and other ranches), a smaller edition of the Great Natural Parks. [Estes Park is, perhaps, best reached from Denver by the Burlington & Missouri River R. R. to *Longmont* (see above) and (48 M.) *Lyons*, whence stages run to (20 M.) the Hotel.] **Long's Peak** (14,270 ft.) rises on the S. side of the park and may be ascended from the hotel in 4-6 hrs. (guide necessary; fatiguing); the *View includes a large section of the Rocky Mts. For the ascents of other mountains round Estes Park, see *F. H. Chapin's* 'Montaineering in Colorado.' A branch-line runs from Loveland to (8 M.) *Arkins* (5235 ft.). — Beyond Loveland the train runs on to (71 M.) *Fort Collins* (4970 ft.; views), which is connected by railway with *Greeley* (p. 410) and with *Colorado Junction*.

FROM DENVER TO LEADVILLE, 151 M., *Union Pacific Railway* (narrow-gauge) in 9¼ hrs. — The line runs to the S., crossing the *Platte River*. 7 M. *Sheridan* (5285 ft.), with *Fort Logan*. About 12 M. farther on we reach the *Platte Cañon (5490 ft.) and begin to ascend rapidly. 29 M. *South Platte* (6035 ft.); 31 M. *Dome Rock* (6200 ft.); 42 M. *Pine Grove* (6740 ft.). The gorge contracts. 51 M. *Estabrook* (7550 ft.), a summer-resort; 69 M. *Webster* (8980 ft.). The line curves nearly back upon itself as we approach the summit at (76 M.) *Kenosha* (9970 ft.). As we begin to descend we have a fine *View of *South Park* (p. 409). — At (88 M.) *Como* (9775 ft.; Rail. Restaurant) the Leadville line diverges to the right from that to Gunnison (see p. 409). We now again ascend rapidly, passing several old placer-workings. 93 M. *Halfway* (10,530 ft.). At (98 M.) *Boreas* (11,470 ft.), at the summit of the *Breckenridge Pass*, we reach the culminating point of the line, on the Continental watershed of the Rocky Mts. The descent is abrupt and tortuous. 110 M. *Breckenridge* (9525 ft.; Denver Hotel, $3), on the *Blue River*. To the W. and S.W. rise *Mts. Fletcher, Quandary, Buckskin*, and other peaks; to the N., *Mts. Gray, Torrey*, and *Powell*. Gold-mining is actively carried on all along this part of the route. — Beyond Breckenridge the train descends to the N., along the Blue River. 116 M. *Dickey* (8980 ft.) is the junction of a branch-line to (7 M.) *Keystone*. Farther on we bend to the left and pass through the *Ten Mile Cañon*. 134 M. *Robinson* (10,820 ft.), in a rich mining district. To the left towers *Mt. Fletcher* (14,265 ft.). To the N.W. rises the famous **Mt. of the Holy Cross** (14,175 ft.), so called from the cruciform appearance presented by two snow-filled ravines which cross each other at right angles (best seen from a point on the road to the W. of Robinson). — At (137 M.) *Climax* (11,290 ft.) we reach the top of Fremont's Pass and begin to descend. 144 M. *Bird's Eye* (10,635 ft.). — 151 M. *Leadville* (10,185 ft.), see p. 423. Leadville is also reached from Denver viâ the D. & R. G. and Col. Midland R. R. (comp. pp. 421, 423).

FROM DENVER TO GUNNISON, 202 M.. *Union Pacific Railway* (narrow-gauge) in 12 hrs. — From Denver to (88 M.) *Como*, see p. 408. Our line continues to run towards the S.W., through *South Park*, surrounding or flanking the rocky spurs sent out by the loftier mountains. 105 M. *Garos* (9170 ft.) is the junction of a branch-line to (10 M.) *Fairplay* (9885 ft.) and (15 M.) *London* (10,230 ft.), both near the centre of *South Park* (see below). — The valley widens. 112 M. *Platte River* (~935 ft.). From (119 M.) *Bath* or *Hill Top* (9460 ft.) we obtain a view of the *Sawatch* or *Saguache Range*, separating the Gunnison and San Juan country from the valley of the Arkansas and culminating in *Mt. Blanca* (14,165 ft.), the highest of the Rockies. We descend rapidly. 126 M. *McGee's* (8650 ft.). — 132 M. *Schwanders* (7815 ft.) is the junction of a line to (4 M.) *Buena Vista* (7945 ft.). About 8-10 M. to the W. of Buena Vista are the three 'Collegiate' peaks of the Saguache Range: *Mts. Yale* (14,185 ft.), *Princeton* (14,190 ft.), and *Harvard* (14,375 ft.). Near their bases are *Cottonwood Hot Springs* (6M. from Buena Vista; stage). — Beyond Schwanders we cross the Denver & Rio Grande R. R. (p. 421). 142 M. *Mt Princeton Hot Springs* (8170 ft.; mountain to the right); 149 M. *Alpine* (9245 ft.); 153 M. *St Elmo* (10,040 ft.). About 6 M. beyond (153 M.) *Romley* (11,520 ft.) we reach the *Alpine Tunnel (11,590 ft.), 590 yds. long, one of the highest pieces of railway in the world. We cross the Continental Divide in the middle of the tunnel and begin to descend towards the Pacific. The *View on emerging from the tunnel includes the *San Juan Mts.* (150 M. to the S.W.), the *Uncompaghre Range* (p. 422), the valley of the *Gunnison*, the *Elk Mts.* (right), and (in the foreground) *Mt. Gothic* and *Crested Butte*. The line runs along a narrow ledge, with perpendicular rocky walls on the one side and the deep valley on the other. The descent is very abrupt. 175 M. *Pitkin* (9180 ft.); 190 M. *Parlin's* (7910 ft.). — 202 M. Gunnison (7650 lt.), see p. 421. For other routes to the Gunnison district, comp. p. 421.

[*South Park (see above), separated from Middle Park (p. 407) by a range of lofty mountains, has a mean elevation of about 9000 ft. and an area of 2000 sq. M. Its climate is milder than that of the Parks to the N., and the railways make it more accessible. Numerous excursions may be made from *Fairplay* (see above), one of the finest of which is the ascent of **Mt. Lincoln* (14,295 ft.), easily accomplished (carriages available nearly to the top). The mountain-view is very grand and extensive. The beautiful *Twin Lakes (9330 ft.), at the E. base of the Saguache Range, are most easily reached from *Granite* (p. 421).

One of the finest excursions that can be made from Denver is that arranged by the *Denver & Rio Grande Railway* under the name of AROUND THE CIRCLE; OR 1000 M. THROUGH THE ROCKY MTS. (fare $28; tickets available for 30 days). On this round we cross and recross the Great Divide, thread four wonderful cañons, surmount four mountain-passes (one by coach), reach a height of 11,000 ft., and pass through some of the finest scenery in America. The round may be accomplished in 4 days, with halts for the night at Durango, Silverton, and Ouray; but it is better to spend a much longer time on it and make various side-trips. — The different sections of this circular tour are described elsewhere. From Denver to *Colorado Springs, Pueblo*, and (170M.) *Cuchara Junction*, see R. 92a; from Cuchara Junction to *Durango*, *Silverton*, and (345 M.) *Ironton*, see p. 418; from Ironton to (8 M.) *Ouray* (stage), see p. 420; from Ouray to (35 M.) *Montrose* and back to (353 M.) *Denver*, see pp. 422-414.

FROM DENVER TO LA JUNTA, 180 M., *Atchison, Topeka, and Santa Fé R. R.* in 6-7 hrs. Through-carriages run by this route to Kansas City, to Chicago, and to Californian and Mexican points. — From Denver to (117 M.) *Pueblo* this line runs parallel with the Denver & Rio Grande Railway (see R. 92a), passes the same stations, and enjoys the same scenery. — Beyond Pueblo it strikes off towards the S.E. 130 M. *Chico;* 170 M. *Rocky Ford.* — 181 M. **La Junta,** see p. 411.

At Denver the San Francisco line turns sharply to the right and runs to the N., along the *S. Platte River* and parallel with the Rocky Mts., 30-40 M. to the W. (fine views to the left). — From (658 M.) *Brighton* (4970 ft.) a branch-line runs to *Boulder* (see p. 408). — 686 M. *La Salle* (4665 ft.), the junction of a line to *Julesburg* (p. 391); 691 M. *Greeley* (4635 ft.; Oasis Hotel, $2-3), a thriving town of 2395 inhab., on the *Cache la Poudre River* (line to *Fort Collins*, see p. 408). Considerable quantities of 'alfalfa' or 'lucerne' (a kind of clover) and other crops are grown all along this line on land which is perfectly barren without irrigation.

746 M. *Cheyenne*, and thence to —

2094 M. **San Francisco**, see p. 391.

b. Viâ Atchison, Topeka, and Santa Fé Railway.

2118 M. ATCHISON, TOPEKA, & SANTA FÉ R. R. to (918 M.) *Albuquerque* in 38¹/₂ hrs.; ATLANTIC & PACIFIC R. R. thence to (818 M.) *Mojave* in 37¹/₂ hrs. ; SOUTHERN PACIFIC R. R. thence to (382 M.) *San Francisco* in 13¹/₂ hrs. (89¹/₂ hrs. in all; fare $60, sleeper $13). Through-carriages run from Chicago to San Francisco by this route (2577 M.) in 104 hrs. (fare $72.50; sleeper $15.50). A large part of the district traversed is semi-arid, but some points of considerable interest are passed (see below), while the wonderful ***Grand Cañon of the Colorado* is most easily reached from *Flagstaff* (p. 413).

Kansas City, see p. 400. The line runs to the W., along the S. side of the *Kansas River*, and ascends steadily. At (13 M.) *Holliday* (760ft.) we are joined by the branch from *Leavenworth* (p. 405). 40 M. *Lawrence* (p. 405). At (67 M.) **Topeka** (885 ft.; see p. 405) we are joined by the branch from *Atchison* (p. 401). We now pass through a prosperous district with many unimportant little towns. 93 M. *Burlingame* (1040 ft.); 147 M. *Strong City* (1170 ft.); 184 M. *Peabody* (1350 ft.). — 201 M. *Newton* (1440 ft.) is the junction of a line running S. to *Galveston*.

FROM NEWTON TO GALVESTON, 750 M., railway in 30 hrs. — Among the most important intermediate stations are (27 M.) *Wichita* (23,853 inhab.); 43 M. *Mulvane;* 65 M. *Winfield* (5184 inhab.); 79 M. *Arkansas City* (10.35 ft.), a flourishing place with 8347 inhabitants. We now cross the *Arkansas River* and enter **Indian Territory**, a tract of about 21 000 sq. M., set apart for the Indian tribes to the E. of the Mississippi. The chief civilised tribes located here are the *Cherokees, Chickasaws, Seminoles, Creeks*, and *Choctaws*, and these 'Five Nations' enjoy a considerable measure of Home Rule and meet occasionally in an International Council. Most of the Indians in the Territory are engaged in farming, and, when uninterfered with by whites of a low class, are promising and progressive. The Territory contains 220 schools, supported mainly by the tribes named above, and there are numerous churches, public buildings, etc. In 1890 the population was 186,390, including 177,6−2 members of the five civilised tribes and 8708 Reservation Indians. — The famous '*Cherokee Strip*' extends from Arkansas City to Wharton. To the right is the reservation of the *Nez Percés*.

Beyond (136 M.) *Wharton* we enter the **Oklahoma Territory** (the 'Boomers' Paradise'), formerly part of Indian Territory, but purchased from the Creeks in 1889 and opened to white settlers. It has an area of 39,034 sq. M. and a population of 61,701 whites and 5689 Indians. The rush across the border as soon as the new territory was opened has become historical, tent towns with thousands of inhabitants springing up in a single day (see 'The West from a Car Window', by *Richard Harding Davis*). The greater part of Oklahoma is still occupied by tribes of uncivilised Indians. — 168 M.

Guthrie (930 ft.; *Hotel*), the capital of Oklahoma, is a busy little place (2788 inhab. in 1890, prob. 8000 now). 199 M. *Oklahoma* (4151 inhab.). Near (232 M.) *Purcell* we cross the *Canadian River*. We now pass through the lands of the Chickasaw Nation, crossing the *Washita* two or three times. 268 M. *Washita.* Beyond (325 M.) *Thackerville* we cross the *Red River* and enter *Texas* (p. 464). 339 M. *Gainesville;* 405 M. **Fort Worth** (see p. 468); 432 M. *Cleburne,* the junction of a line to *Dallas* (p. 468); 531 M. *Temple Junction;* 576 M. *Milano,* the junction of a line to *Austin* (p. 466); 608 M. *Somerville;* 684 M. *Rosenberg Junction;* 721 M. *Alvin.* — 750 M. *Galveston,* see p. 467.

211 M. *Halstead* (1385 ft.); 236 M. *Hutchinson* (1525 ft.). We now follow the general course of the *Arkansas River* (left), passing through a good agricultural and cattle-raising district. 276 M. *Ellinwood* (1780 ft.); 333 M. *Kinsley* (2160 ft.). At (369 M.) *Dodge City* (2475 ft.; 1763 inhab.) we change from 'Central' to 'Mountain' time (1 hr. slower; comp. p. xviii). 469 M. *Garden City* (2825 ft.). — Beyond (485 M.) *Coolidge* (3360 ft.) we enter *Colorado* (p. 405). 519 M. *Lamar* (3600 ft.). Farther on the *Rocky Mts.* begin to come into sight in front, to the right. — 571 M. **La Junta** (pron. 'La Hunta'; 4060 ft.), a place of 1439 inhab., is the junction of the line from Denver described at p. 409. *Pike's Peak* (p. 417) is seen to the right. Our line runs towards the S. W. 599 M. *Iron Springs* (4675 ft.). — 652 M. **Trinidad** (5995 ft.; *Grand Union Hotel,* $ 3), the industrial and commercial centre of S.E. Colorado, is a thriving city of 5523 inhab., in which the characteristics of old Mexico and young America are inextricably mixed. It is the outlet of a district containing much coal and numerous other minerals, and is the terminus of a branch of the D. & R. G. R. R. (see p. 418).

At (663 M.) *Morley* (6745 ft.) we begin to ascend the *Raton Mts.*, which form a conspicuous feature in the views from Trinidad. The gradient is steep. Fine views, especially of the *Spanish Peaks* (p. 418; right). At the top of the pass (7620 ft.) we pass through a long tunnel and enter *New Mexico* (p. 419). The descent is also rapid. 686 M. *Raton* (6620 ft.). The line runs through the central valley of New Mexico, about 20 M. wide, which is traversed by the *Rio Grande del Norte* and several other streams, and flanked by mountains 6000-10,000 ft. high. Agriculture is carried on in the side-valleys and plains by careful irrigation, but the greater part of the Territory is better adapted for grazing. — 742 M. *Wagon Mound.* — 786 M. **Las Vegas** (6380 ft.; *Depot Hote, Plaza,* $ 3), a flourishing place with 2385 inhab., on a fork of the *Pecos River*, is an important wool-market. A branch-line runs hence to (6 M.) *Las Vegas Hot Springs.*

Las Vegas Hot Springs (6770 ft.; *Montezuma Hotel,* $ 2-5), about 40 in number, lie on the S.E. slope of the Santa Fé range of the Rocky Mts. and vary in temperature from 75° to 140° Fahr. The water closely resembles that of the Arkansas Hot Springs (p. 404) and has similar results. It is used both for bathing and drinking. Many fine excursions can be made in the vicinity. The mean annual temperature is 59° Fahr. (summer 73°).

Near (830 M.) *Rowe* we see the curious old *Pecos Church* (right), a relic of a Franciscan mission. Farther on we cross another ridge by the *Glorieta Pass* (7535 ft.) and descend to (851 M.) *Lamy Junction* (6460 ft.), where the line to (18 M.) *Santa Fé* diverges to the right.

    Santa Fé (7040 ft.; *Palace Hotel*, $ 3-3½; *Alamo*, $ 2½), the capital of New Mexico, is, perhaps, the most ancient town in the United States, having been founded by the Spaniards in 1605, while there seems good reason to believe that the site was occupied long before this by a city of the Pueblo Indians (p. lxv). It is in many ways a most quaint and interesting place, with its narrow streets, adobé houses, and curious mingling of American, Mexican, and Indian types. It lies in the centre of an important mining district and carries on a considerable trade. Pop. (1890) 6185. The focus of interest is the *Plaza*, or public square, with a *Soldiers' Monument*. On one side extends the *Governor's Palace*, a long low structure of adobé, which has been the abode of the Spanish, Mexican, and American governors for nearly 300 years. It harbours the *Museum of the New Mexico Historical Society*, containing old Spanish paintings, historical relics, and Indian curiosities. The *Cathedral of San Francisco*, a large stone building with two towers, incorporates parts of the old cathedral, dating from 1622. The *Church of San Miguel*, originally built about the middle of the 17th cent., was restored in 1710. Other points of interest are the new and the old *Fort Marcy*, *San Miguel College*, and the *Ramona Industrial School for Indian Children*. Among the chief modern buildings are the *State Capitol*, the *Post Office*, and the *Court House*. A visit should be paid to the makers of Mexican silver filigree-work, whose shops are mainly in or near the Plaza. Gen. Lew Wallace wrote 'Ben-Hur' in the Palace, while Governor of New Mexico (1879-80). — About 9 M. to the S.W. of Santa Fé is the interesting pueblo of the *Tesuque Indians*, who visit the city daily, bringing firewood on their 'burros' (donkeys). From Santa Fé to *Española* and *Antonito*, see p. 418.

    Near (882 M.) *Wallace* (5245 ft.), on the *Rio Grande*, are the pueblos of *Santo Domingo* (grand festival on Aug. 4th) and *San Felipe*. We now follow the bank of the large and rapid Rio Grande.

    918 M. **Albuquerque** (4930 ft.; *San Felipe Hotel*, $ 2-3½; *Armijo*, $ 2½-3, R. from $ 1; *International*, $ 3), a city of 5518 inhab., carrying on a brisk trade in wool and hides. This is the E. terminus of the *Atlantic & Pacific R. R.* and the connecting-point with the Atchison, Topeka, & Santa Fé line to *El Paso* and *Mexico*, though the actual point of divergence is 13 M. farther on (see below).

    FROM ALBUQUERQUE TO EL PASO, 254 M., railway in 9-10 hrs. Through-sleepers run viâ this route from Kansas City to El Paso, connecting with the Mexican Central Railway (comp. p. 464). — We diverge from the line to California at (13 M.) *Isleta Junction* (see below) and run towards the S. 30 M. *Belen* (4785 ft). The mezquite (*Prosopis jutiflora*) now begins to appear. 75 M. *Socorro;* 86 M. *San Antonio;* 102 M. *San Marcial;* 141 M. *Engle.* 177 M. *Rincon* (4015 ft.) is the junction of a line to *Deming* (p. 463). 210 M. *Las Cruces.* — 254 M. **El Paso**, see p. 464.

    We now follow the *Atlantic & Pacific R. R.*, from which the line to El Paso diverges to the left at (1390 M.) *Isleta* (see above), leave the Rio Grande, and run towards the W. through a semi-arid and monotonous country, which, however, makes some response to irrigation. The curious-looking *Yucca Palm* is now seen, often the only tree in the desert. At (985 M.) *Laguna* (5765 ft.) the railway runs through an Indian pueblo, the houses of which are built in terraces two and three stories high.

    A nearer visit to this pueblo demands (as the trains run now) the sacrifice of half-a-day, and the sleeping accommodation is not very good. The Indians, some of whom have been educated at Carlisle (p. 232) and speak

good English, welcome visitors and offer hand-made pottery for sale.
Their houses are of stone, plastered with adobé, and are usually entered,
with the aid of ladders, through the roofs. The Roman Catholic church is
nearly two centuries old. — About 16 M. to the S. of Laguna lies *Acoma*,
another interesting pueblo.

About 30 M. farther on we pass the Continental Divide (7300 ft.),
but there is nothing in the surroundings to suggest that we have
reached so high an elevation or are passing from the Atlantic to the
Pacific slope. 1055 M. *Coolidge.* 1065 M. *Wingate* (6715 ft.), 3 M.
from *Fort Wingate*, is the most convenient point from which to visit
the famous pueblo of Zuñi, which lies about 48 M. to the S. (stages).
At (1077 M.) *Gallup* (6480 ft.) are large coal-mines. 1085 M. *Navajo
Springs* (6350 ft.) is the supply station for *Fort Defiance* and the
Agency of the great *Navajo* ('Navaho') *Indian Reservation*. The last
lies at some distance to the N. of the line and is adjoined on the W.
by the smaller *Moqui Indian Reservation*. Indians may be seen at
the railway-stations, selling fine Navajo blankets, silver-work, and
other home-made articles. Beyond (1093 M.) *Manuelito* (6230 ft.)
we enter the *Territory of Arizona* (the 'Sunset Land'). — From
(1157 M.) *Carrizo* or (1172 M.) *Holbrook* (5050 ft.) a visit may be
paid to the extraordinary *Petrified Forests of Arizona*, which lie
about 20 M. to the S.E. 1204 M. *Winslow* (4825 ft.). Farther on we
cross a bridge, 540 ft. long and 222 ft. high, spanning a rift in the
ground known as the (1230 M.) *Cañon Diablo*.

1263 M. *Flagstaff* (6935 ft.; Hotels) is of importance as the
starting-point of the main stage-route to (65 M.) the *Grand
Cañon of the Colorado* (see below). To the N. rises *San Francisco
Mt.* (12,800 ft.), a fine extinct volcano, surrounded by a district of
cinder cones and lava beds, like the Phlegræan Fields of Italy.

The stage-coaches from Flagstaff to the (65 M.) *Grand Cañon* (fair road)
run tri-weekly (except in winter) in 12 hrs. (return-fare $20). Dinner
($1) is provided at a half-way house, and the road ends, near the cañon,
at *Hance's Camp*, with comfortable, wooden-floored tents (meals $1,
lodging $1; hotel to be built). — The **Grand Cañon of the Colorado, one
of the most stupendous natural wonders of the world, is 250 M. long and
3000-6500 ft. deep. Its walls, which are terraced and carved into a myriad
of pinnacles and towers, are tinted with various brilliant colours. Visitors
from Flagstaff reach it at the deepest part of the whole and obtain a
marvellous view into its depths, where the large and foaming river appears
as a mere thread. The bottom of the cañon may be reached by a new
and fatiguing trail (steady head necessary) beginning 1/2 M. from Hance's
(fee for each pers. $1; pack-animal $2; guide and pack-animals for 1-6
pers. $10). The cañon was first made specifically known to the world
by Major Powell, now Chief of the U. S. Geological Survey, who in 1869
descended it by boat from the Green River (p. 422) to the *Virgen River*, a
distance of 1000 M. He believes that the river was running here before the
mountains were formed, and that the cañon was formed by the erosion of
the water acting simultaneously with the slow upheaval of the rocks. The
geological student has unfolded to him in the sides of the cañon all the
strata from the carboniferous formations down to the Archæan granite.
Travellers should remain some days at the cañon to visit various points
on the rim (cliff-dwellings, etc.). Comp. *Major J. W. Powell's* 'Canyons
of the Colorado' (1893) and *Capt. Dutton's* 'Tertiary History of the Grand
Cañon District'. A good description of the cañon is given in 'Our Italy',

by *Chas. Dudley Warner.* — Visits may also be made from Flagstaff to the *Cliff Dwellings* in *Walnut Cañon*, 8 M. to the S. E., and to the *Cave Dwellings*, artificially excavated in the volcanic agglomerate of the *Coconino Butte*, 9 M. to the N.E.

From (1297 M.) *Williams* (6725 ft.; Rail. Restaurant) stages run to the *Grand Cañon of the Colorado* (see p. 413) in 24 hrs. (return-fare $ 24). To the left rises *Bill Williams Mt.* (9265 ft.), to the right (farther on) *Mt. Floyd.* Near (1320 M.) *Ash Fork* we thread the rocky *Johnson's Cañon.* From (1347 M.) *Prescott Junction* a branch-line runs to (74 M.) *Prescott* (5700 ft.). 1384 M. *Peach Springs* (4760 ft.; Rail. Restaurant) is only 23 M. from the *Grand Cañon of the Colorado* (stages), but the section reached hence is not so imposing as that reached from Flagstaff (see p. 413). 1407 M. *Hackberry* (3520 ft.), in a mining district. 1434 M. *Kingman* (3300 ft.); 1458 M. *Yucca* (1775 ft.); 1484 M. *Powell* (420 ft.).

We reach and cross the wide **Colorado River**, by a fine canti-lever bridge, 1110 ft. long, at (1497 M.) the **Needles** (480 ft.), so named from the curious pinnacles of purple porphyry and trachytic granite rising to the left. The train here enters *California* (p. 397) and runs to the W. across the great **Mojave Desert** ('Mo-havé'), an elevated sandy plateau, interspersed with salt lakes and alkali tracts, with little vegetation except yucca-palms, small piñons (nut-pines, *Pinus monophylla*), junipers, and sage-brush. Mountains are seen to the N., in the distance. 1520 M. *Homer* (2120 ft.); 1528 M. *Goff's* (2580 ft.); 1538 M. *Fenner* (2080 ft.); 1545 M. *Edson* (1730 ft.); 1588 M. *Bagdad* (785 ft.; Rail. Restaurant); 1612 M. *Ludlow* (1780 ft.).

1666 M. **Barstow** (2110 ft.) is the junction of the *Southern California R. R.* to *San Bernardino, Colton, Pasadena, Los Angeles,* and *San Diego* (see pp. 446-48). We change here from 'Mountain' to 'Pacific' time (1 hr. slower: comp. p. xviii). — 1676 M. *Hinckley* (2160 ft.); 1699 M. *Kramer* (2480 ft.).

At (1737 M.) **Mojave** (2750 ft.) we join the Southern Pacific Railway. Hence to —

2118 M. **San Francisco,** see pp. 442, 441.

92. From Denver to Salt Lake City and Ogden.

a. Viâ Denver and Rio Grande Railroad.

771 M. RAILWAY in 29 hrs. (fare $ 25; sleeper $5). Through-cars run on this line to San Francisco viâ Leadville (see p. 420), but lovers of the picturesque should choose the narrow-gauge route over *Marshall Pass*, uniting with the other line at Grand Junction (comp. pp. 421, 422).

The somewhat ambitious title of '*Scenic Line of the World*', adopted by this railway, is much more justified by facts than is usually the case with such assumptions, as the railway actually passes through part of the finest scenery in the United States (comp. also p. 409) and presents some features probably unequalled on any other railway.

Denver, see p. 406. The line runs towards the S., parallel with the Atchison, Topeka, and Santa Fé R. R. (p. 409). To the right flows the *Platte River*, while in the distance are the fine snowy peaks of the *Rocky Mts.* (comp. p. 406). 25 M. *Sedalia* (5835 ft.); 33 M. *Castle Rock* (6220 ft.), so named from a rock that rises from the plain to the left. Pike's Peak (p. 417) may now be seen in front, to the right. — 43 M. *Larkspur* is the station for *Perry Park*, with its fantastic rock-formations. To the right, about 8 M. farther on, rises the *Casa Blanca*, a huge white rock 1000 ft. long and 200 ft. high. — 52 M. *Palmer Lake* (7240 ft.; Rail. Restaurant), on the watershed between the *Platte*, flowing N. to the Missouri, and the *Arkansas*, flowing S. to the Mississippi. *Glen Park* (Hotel), 'Colorado's Chautauqua', lies $1/_2$ M. to the S. A new road leads to the S.W. from Palmer Lake to (35 M.) *Manitou Park* (Hotel, $3), another favourite resort (comp. p. 423). — The line traverses cattle and sheep ranches. The snowy mountains re-appear from their temporary concealment behind the foot-hills. — 62 M. *Husted* (6595 ft.). Several fantastic rocks are seen to the left. 67 M. *Edgerton* (6420 ft.) is the nearest station to *Monument Park* (p. 417). — As we approach Colorado Springs we have a splendid view, to the right, of Pike's Peak (p. 417) and the Gateway of the Garden of the Gods (p. 416).

75 M. **Colorado Springs** (6090 ft.; *The Antlers, pleasantly situated, $3-5; *The Thanet*, especially planned for health-seekers; *Alta Vista*, $3-4; *Alamo*, 2^1/_2-3^1/_2$; *St. James*, $2-3), a city of **11,140** inhab., on an elevated plateau, near the E. base of Pike's Peak, is pleasantly laid out, with wide tree-shaded streets, and resembles a well-kept and well-to-do New England country-town. It is the principal health-resort of Colorado, and has become the permanent residence of many who are unable to stand the changeable climate of England or the E. coast.

Colorado Springs was founded in 1871, though a settlement had been made somewhat earlier at *Colorado City* ('Old Town'), a small industrial colony, 2 M. to the N.W. (comp. p. 423). No manufacturing is carried on at Colorado Springs, which has been carefully kept as a residential and educational centre, and no 'saloons' are permitted. The name is somewhat of a misnomer, as the nearest springs are those at Manitou (p. 417); but this is decidedly the pleasantest headquarters for exploring the surrounding district (Manitou and Pike's Peak included).

The *View of the mountains from Colorado Springs, well seen from Cascade Avenue, near Colorado College, is very fine. *Pike's Peak* (p. 417) dominates the scene, while to the S. of it (named from right to left) rise *Cameron's Cone* (10,500 ft.), *Mt. Garfield*, *Bald Mt.* (ca. 12,500 ft.), *Mte. Rosa* (11,570 ft.), and *Cheyenne Mt.* (9950 ft.; p 416). To the right of Pike's Peak opens the *Ute Pass* (p. 423), and still farther to the right lies the *Garden of the Gods* (p. 416). The *Cheyenne Cañons* (p. 416) lie between Cheyenne Mt. and Monte Rosa. In the foreground is the high-lying plateau known as the *Mesa* (Span. 'table-land'). To the E. and S. of the town spreads the illimitable prairie, which in certain states of the atmosphere looks startlingly like the ocean — an illusion intensified by the moving shadows, the smoke of distant locomotives, and the outcrop of lines of rocks resembling breakers.

The **Climate** of Colorado Springs resembles that of Davos and like it is especially good for consumption or as a preventive for those predisposed to that disease. It is also well suited for persons suffering from nervous exhaustion, malarial poisoning, and other debilitating affections,

but is usually harmful to the aged and to those with organic affections of
the heart or nerves. It has more wind and dust than Davos, but also more
sunshine and dryness; and as the ground is bare most of the winter,
there is no period of melting snow to prevent the invalid staying all the
year round. Riding, driving, and the usual winter sports can be freely
indulged in. There is no rain from Sept. till April. In the winter (Nov.-
Mar.) of 1888-9 the average temperature at Davos was 26⁰ Fahr., of Colorado
Springs 30⁰; the latter had 300 hrs. more sunshine than the former. The
prevailing winds at Colorado Springs are S.E. and N.; the average per-
centage of humidity is 47. The town is sheltered by the foot-hills, except
to the S. E., where it lies open to the great plains; and, being situated
where they meet the mountains, it enjoys the openness and free supply of
fresh air of the sea-shore, without its dampness. The soil is dry sand
and gravel, with a shallow top-layer of garden soil. There are no springs
beneath the town-site. Good water is brought from the mountains, and
the sewerage system is excellent. The accommodation for invalids is
comfortable and there are several good physicians, one of whom is English
(Dr. Solly). No invalid should come or remain without medical advice.

Colorado Springs itself contains comparatively little to arrest the
tourist's attention, but it is a splendid centre for innumerable pleasant drives and excursions (see below). Among the most prominent
buildings are *Colorado College* and its preparatory school, *Cutler
Academy;* the *State Asylum for the Deaf, Dumb, and Blind;* the *Opera
House;* and the *Hotels* and *Sanitaria. Helen Hunt Jackson* ('H. H.';
1831-85) is buried in *Evergreen Cemetery.* Two small *Parks* have been
laid out. The principal clubs are the *El Paso Club,* the *Colorado
Springs Club,* the *University Club,* and the *Country Club,* the last
with pleasant quarters near the foot of Cheyenne Mt. (see below).

Excursions from Colorado Springs.

(1). **Austin Bluffs**, about 3¹/₂ M. to the N.E. of the city (reached by
carriage, tramway, or on foot), commands a magnificent *View of the
Rocky Mts., the city, and the plains. The Spanish Peaks, 100 M. to the
S., are clearly discernible. To the W. are the peaks mentioned at p. 415.
To the N. is the *Divide,* or watershed between Colorado Springs and Denver.

(2). CHEYENNE MT. AND THE CHEYENNE CAÑONS. The foot of **Cheyenne Mt.**
(9950 ft.), which rises 5 M. to the S.W. of Colorado Springs, is easily
reached by electric tramway (10 c.), passing near the pleasant quarters of
the *Country Club* (see above) and the *Broadmoor Casino.* The latter is a very
pleasant resort, with a boating lake, a good restaurant (table-d'hôte from
6 to 8, $ 1.25), ball-rooms, and orchestral concerts (afternoon and even-
ing). The *Cheyenne Mt. Road* leads across the flank of the mountain,
commanding exquisite views, in which the brilliant red rocks, the blue
sky, the green trees, and the dazzling white snow offer wonderful combinations of colour. The road is steep, narrow, and badly kept, so that
steady horses, driver, and head are desirable. It goes on to (22 M.) *Seven
Lakes* (10,350 ft.; Inn, sometimes closed), but most visitors turn back at
the (2¹/₂ M.) *Horseshoe Curve.* The summit of the mountain may be reached by
a path (1 M.) diverging to the left near the saw-mill. — The *Cheyenne
Cañons* are on the N. side of the mountain, and the terminus of the electric tramway is near their entrance. The *S. Cañon* (adm. 25 c.) may be
followed on foot to (1 M.) the *Falls,* which descend 500 ft. in seven leaps.
From the top of the flights of steps we may ascend to the left to the
brink of the cañon (*View) and go on thence to the above-mentioned road,
where our carriage may be ordered to meet us. The *N. Cañon* also contains fine falls, pools, and cliffs. It may be followed for 3-4 M.

(3). GARDEN OF THE GODS (5 M.). The road leads to the W. across the
Mesa (p. 415), passing (4 M.) the entrance to *Glen Eyrie,* a private estate
(visitors admitted) containing some fantastic rocky scenery (Cathedral

Rock, Major Domo, etc.). About 1 M. farther on we reach the *Gateway of the Garden of the Gods,* consisting of two enormous masses of bright red rock, 330 ft. high and separated just enough for the roadway to pass through. The *Garden of the Gods* is a tract of land about 500 acres in extent, thickly strewn with grotesque rocks and cliffs of red and white sandstone. Among the chief features are the *Cathedral Spires,* the *Balanced Rock,* etc. On reaching the road on the other side of the Garden we may either proceed to the right to (1¹/₂ M.) *Manitou Springs* (see below) or return to the left, viâ *Colorado City* (p. 423), to (4¹/₂ M.) Colorado Springs.

(4). **Manitou** (6370 ft.; *Mansion House, Manitou Hotel, Barker House, Iron Springs House,* $4; *Cliff Ho.,* $3-4; *Sunnyside, Ruxton,* $2-3), situated in a small valley among the spurs of Pike's Peak, and at the mouth of the *Ute Pass* (p. 423), is largely frequented for its fine scenery and its effervescing springs of soda and iron. It is reached from Colorado Springs by the railway (viâ Colorado City, 6 M.; 10 c.), by electric tramway (10 c.), or by driving across the Mesa or through the Garden of the Gods (ca. 5 M ; comp. above). The waters, which belong to the group of weak compound carbonated soda waters and resemble those of Ems, are beneficial in dyspepsia, diseases of the kidneys, and consumption. The chief springs are the *Navajo, Manitou, Shoshone, Little Chief,* and *Iron.* The water is very palatable and is used both for drinking and bathing; there is a well-equipped *Bath House.* Among the numerous pleasant points within reach of Manitou are the picturesque *Ute Pass* (comp. p. 423). with the fine *Rainbow Falls* (1¹/₂ M. from Manitou) and the *Grand Caverns* (adm. $1; fine stalactites and stalagmites); *Williams Cañon,* with (1 M.) the *Cave of the Winds* ($1); the (3 M.) *Red Cañon; Ruxton's Glen* and *Engleman's Cañon;* the (3 M.) *Garden of the Gods* (p. 416); *Monument Park* (see below); the *Cheyenne Cañons* (p. 416; 9 M.); and the *Seven Lakes* (p. 416; 9 M. by trail, 25 M. by road). Manitou is also the starting-point for the ascent of *Pike's Peak* (see below). *Manitou Park* (p. 423), at the head of the Ute Pass, is 20 M. distant.

(5). *Pike's Peak* (14,147 ft.), one of the best-known summits of the Rocky Mts., rears its snowy crest about 6 M. to the W. of Colorado Springs and just above Manitou. It is usually ascended by the *Manitou and Pike's Peak Railway,* which was built upon the Abt cog-wheel system and opened in 1891. The railway begins in Engleman's Cañon, a little above the Iron Springs Hotel. Its length is 8³/₄ M., with a total ascent of 7500 ft. or an average of 846 ft. per mile. The steepest gradient is 1 : 4. The ascent (return-fare $5) is made in about 2 hrs., including a stoppage at the *Half-way House* (meal 75 c.), a pleasant little hotel in *Ruxton Park,* frequented by summer-visitors. — The Carriage Road to the top of Pike's Peak, begins at *Cascade,* 6 M. from Manitou (railway; comp. p. 423). It is 17 M. long and has a comparatively easy gradient (carr. to the top and back in 8 hrs., $5 each). — The Bridle Path (6 hrs. on foot or on horseback; horse $5) begins near the railway-station and ascends through *Engleman's Cañon* (trail well defined; guide unnecessary for experts). Another *Trail,* 4¹/₂ M. long, now seldom used, ascends from the *Seven Lakes* (p. 416). — The summit is occupied by a *Weather Signal Bureau* (inhabited all the year round) and by a small *Inn,* open in summer (meals $1). The *View is superb, embracing thousands of square miles of mountain and plain. The Spanish Peaks (p. 418) and the extended line of the grand Sangue de Cristo Range (including Sierra Blanca) are seen to the S. and Long's Peak (p. 408) to the N., while the other peaks visible include Mt. Lincoln (N.), Mt. Gray, Mt. Bross, and the neighbouring mountains named at p. 415. Denver, Pueblo, Colorado Springs, and Manitou are all visible. The ascent of Pike's Peak can be safely made in summer only, owing to the snow; and the mountain-railway does not begin running till June.

(6). **Monument Park,** a tract of curiously eroded sandstone rocks, similar to those of the Garden of the Gods (see above), may be reached from Colorado Springs by road (9 M.; carr. $6-8) or by railway to *Edgerton* (p.415), from which it is ¹/₂ M. distant.

Among other points of interest near Colorado Springs are *Bear Creek Cañon,* 3 M. to the W; *My Garden* (so named by H. H.), 4 M. to the S.W., on the slope of Cheyenne Mt. (view); *Templeton's Gap* and *Colorado Springs Garden Ranch*, 4¹/₂ M. to the N. E.; and *Blair Athol*, a lovely glen to the N. of Glen Eyrie (see above).

Beyond Colorado Springs our line continues to run towards the S. To the right we see *Cheyenne Mt.* (p. 416); to. the left extends the boundless prairie. Stations unimportant.

120 M. **Pueblo** (4665 ft.; *Grand*, $3-4¹/₂; *Fifth Avenue*, R. from $1; *St James*, $2-3; *Railway Hotel and Restaurant*, $3-3¹/₂, meal 75 c.), situated at the confluence of the *Arkansas River* and the *Fontaine qui Bouille Creek*, is an active commercial and industrial city of 24,558 inhab., with smelting and steel works. It is the outlet of a rich mining district (coal, iron, etc.) and also trades in agricultural products.

Beyond Pueblo the D. & R. G. R.R. runs on to (210 M. from Denver) *Trinidad* (p. 411), where it joins the main line of the Atchison, Topeka, and Santa Fé R. R. (see R. 91 b).

Cuchara Junction (5940 ft.), 170 M. from Denver, is the point of divergence of the Silverton branch of the D. & R. G. R. R., forming part of the 'Around the Circle' tour mentioned at p. 417. Between Cuchara and (191 M.) *La Veta* (7025 ft.) the isolated **Spanish Peaks** (13 620 ft. and 12,720 ft.) are well seen to the left (S.). Beyond (199 M.) *Ojo* ('Oho') we begin to ascend the *Veta Pass*, the summit of which is 9390 ft. above the sea. Two engines are required to draw the train up the steep incline, and great engineering skill has been shown in overcoming its difficulties (maximum gradient 1 : 10). The most abrupt bend is known as the *Mule-Shoe Curve*. To the right rises *Veta Mt.* (11,175 ft.). We now begin to descend into the *San Luis Valley* or *Park*, the largest of the Great Parks of Colorado (p. 392). It is 100 M. long, 60 M. wide, and about 7000 ft. above the sea-level, and is surrounded by mountains 11-14,000 ft. high. 212 M. *Placer* (8410 ft.); 226 M. *Garland* (7935 ft.). To the right towers the triple-peaked *Sierra Blanca* (14,465 ft.), the southernmost of the Sangre de Cristo range and loftiest of the Rocky Mts. — 250 M. **Alamosa** (7545 ft.; *Victoria*, $ 3; *Rail. Restaurant*), a brisk little town of 1091 inhab., on the *Rio Grande del Norte*, is the junction of a branch-line to (70 M.) *Creede* and of another to *Villa Grove* and *Salida* (see p. 420). [The Creede branch ascends along the Rio Grande del Norte. 17 M. *Monte Vista* (7665 ft.; Hotel Blanco, $3); 31 M. *Del Norte* (7880 ft.; Richardson Ho., $3); 47 M. *South Fork*. Farther on (61 M.) we pass through the *Wagon Wheel Gap*, a picturesque mountain-pass, with *Hot Springs* (Hotel, $ 1¹/₂). 70 M. **Creede** (*Hotels*) is, perhaps, the most wonderful of the silver cities of Colorado, dating only from the discovery of the ore here in May, 1891, but already containing 7000 inhab. and producing silver to the value of $ 4,000,000 in 1892. The railway was extended from Wagon Wheel Gap to Creede in Oct.-Dec., 1891. The adventurous tourist in search of a real 'mining camp' should visit Creede.] From Alamosa our line runs towards the S. 265 M. *La Jara* ('La Hara'; 7610 ft.); 272 M. *Manassa*, a Mormon settlement. — 279 M. *Antonito* (7890 ft.; Belmont, $ 2) is the junction of a line running S. to (91 M.) *Española*.

[The Española branch enters *New Mexico* (p. 419) at (23 M.) *Palmilla* and traverses a district inhabited mainly by Spanish-speaking Mexicans. From (65 M.) *Barranca* a stage runs to (11 M.) the hot springs of *Ojo Caliente*. About 6 M. farther on the train enters the romantic *Comanche Cañon* ('Comanchay'). — 72 M. *Embudo* (5820 ft.), where we reach the Rio Grande del Norte (see above), is the starting-point for a visit to the (20 M.) *Pueblo de Taos* ('Tows'), one of the most interesting and complete of the cities of the Pueblo Indians (see p. lxv). A grand festival is held here on Dec. 27th. — 91 M. *Española* (5590 ft.), a small hamlet, is the S. terminus of the D. & R. G. R. R. On the opposite bank of the Rio Grande is the old Mexican town of *Santa Cruz*, with a church of the 16th century. Excursions may also be made to the (4 M.) *Pueblo of San Juan*, the *Pueblo of Santa Clara*, the *Pueblo de Taos* (p. 418), etc. Española is connected with (38 M.) *Santa Fé* (p. 412) by the Texas, Santa Fé, & Northern R. R.]

From Antonito the Silverton line runs towards the W., gradually ascending from the San Luis Valley towards the *Conejos Mts.* ('Conehos'). We repeatedly cross and recross the boundary between Colorado and *New Mexico* (the 'Sunshine State'). Beyond (305 M.) *Sublette* the railway bends round *Phantom Curve*, so called from the spectral sandstone rocks bordering the track. Below[us (left) lies the *Los Piños Valley*. The alignment of the railway here is of the most tortuous character. Beyond (309 M.) *Toltec* we thread a tunnel and enter the imposing *Toltec Gorge, the bottom of which lies 1500 ft. below us. The best view is obtained from the bridge, crossed just after emerging from the tunnel; and just beyond this, to the left, is a *Memorial of President Garfield.* At (329 M.) *Cumbres* (10,115 ft.) we reach the top of the pass across the *Conejos* or *San Juan Mts.* and begin the descent. 343 M. *Chama* (7860 ft.; Rail. Restaurant, meal 75 c.). From (365 M.) *Amargo* stages run to (28 M.) *Pagosa Springs* (7110 ft. ; Hotel; springs, 140° Fahr.). 402 M. *Arboles* (6015 ft.). At (424 M.) *Ignacio* we reach a reservation of the Ute Indians. — 450 M. **Durango** (6520 ft. ; *Strater House, Columbian*, $ 3-4; *National*, $ 2-2¹/₂), a progressive town of 2726 inhab., on the *Rio de las Animas*, is the commercial centre of S.W. Colorado.

[From Durango the tourist may, if he prefer, continue the 'Circle' by the *Rio Grande Southern R. R.*, rejoining the main route at *Ridgway* (p. 420). This line passes *Fort Lewis*, crosses the Animas watershed at (21 M.) *Cima* (8590 ft.), and descends the *Mancos Valley* to (40 M.) *Mancos*. This is the starting-point of the trail to the (20 M.) famous *Cliff Dwellings of the Mancos Cañon, which rank among the most important remains of the mysterious cliff-dwellers and should be visited by every student of the na tive races of America (guide and horses on application to the railroad agent at Mancos). Comp. p. lxv and 'The Land of the Cliff Dwellers', by *F. H. Chapin* (1892). — At (47 M.) *Millwood* (7640 ft.) we cross the *Chicken Creek Divide* and then descend through *Lost Cañon* to (60 M.) *Dolores* (6960 ft.; Hotel). Thence we ascend through the *Dolores Valley* and the narrow *Dolores Cañon* to (96 M.) **Rico** (8735 ft.; *Enterprise Hotel*, $ 2-3), a mining centre (pop. 1134) amid the *San Miguel Mts.* From Rico the train climbs (gradient 11 : 100) to (110 M.) the **Lizard Head Pass** (10,250 ft.), whence it descends on the other side of the San Miguel Mts., passing (113 M.) *Trout Lake* (9800 ft. ; Hotel). This descent, by means of the (117 M.) *Ophir Loop* (9220 ft.) and numerous zigzags, iron bridges, and rock-cuttings, taxed the skill of the engineer to the utmost. From (124 M.) *Vance Junction* (8115 ft.) a line runs to (8 M.) **Telluride** (8760 ft.; *American Hotel*, $ 4), a beautifully situated mining-town (pop. now about 4000), passing the large *Keystone Placer Mine.* Beyond (146 M.) *Placerville* (7295 ft. ; Hotel) we cross the *Horse-Fly Range*, a spur of the *Uncompaghre Mts.*, at the (149 M.) *Dallas Divide* (8990 ft.), and then descend into the fertile *Dallas* or *Pleasant Valley*, surrounded by snow-capped peaks. 154 M. *High Bridge* (7960 ft.). — 162 M. *Ridgway*, see p. 420.]

Beyond Durango the Silver or 'Rainbow' Route turns to the N. and follows the *Rio de las Animas.* Beyond (459 M.) *Trimble Hot Springs* (6645 ft. ; Hotel) the valley contracts and at (463 M.) *Rockwood* (7365 ft.) we reach the beautiful *Animas Cañon*, the walls of which rise 500 ft. above us on the one side and drop 1000 ft. below us on the other. A single mile of track here cost $ 140,000 (28,000 *l.*) to build. On issuing from the cañon we see the curious *Needle Mts.*, towering to the right. We then traverse the pretty little *Elk Park.* To the left rises *Garfield Peak* (12,135 ft.). — 495 M. **Silverton** (9225 ft.; *Grand Hotel*, $ 3), a mining town with 1214 inhab., and the terminus of this branch of the D. & R. G. R. R., is finely situated in *Baker Park*, near the base of *Sultan Mt.* (13,500 ft.), one of the grandest of the San Juan Mts.

We now follow the *Silverton Railway*, one of the most extraordinary feats of engineering in America, which ascends over *Red Mt.* (13,335 ft.) to (20 M.) *Ironton*, a small mining-town. The line winds backwards and forwards like the trail of a serpent and finally attains a height of 11,235 ft.

27*

(2000 ft. above Silverton). The scenery is of the grandest de- scription,
and the *View from the summit is superb. The descent is as wonderful
as the ascent. Numerous mines are passed.

At Ironton we leave the railway and proceed by stage to (8 M.; a
drive of 3 hrs.) *Ouray.* The road is good and the scenery magnificent. To
the left rises *Mt. Abrahams* (12,600 ft.). We pass the *Bear Creek Falls* (250ft.
high) and the *Uncompaghre Cañon.*

Ouray (7720 ft.; *Beaumont Hotel,* $ 3-4; *Dixon Ho.,* $ 2¹/₂-3), where we
again reach the D. & R. G. R. R., is a picturesque mountain - town with
2534 inhab., frequented for its grand scenery and its hot medicinal springs.
To the S. rise *Mt. Hardin* and *Mt. Hayden;* to the N.W. is *Uncompaghre
Peak* (14,420 ft.). — The distance from Ouray to *Montrose* (see p. 422) is
35 M. On the way the railway passes the confluence of the *Uncompaghre*
and the *Dallas,* (10 M.) *Ridgway* (7000 ft.; Mentone, $ 3-4; see p. 419), the
(22 M.) old *Los Piños Agency,* and (26 M.) *Fort Crawford,* a U. S. military
post. From Montrose to *Salida* and *Denver* and to *Salt Lake City,* see p. 422.

Our line now diverges to the right (W.) from the line running
S. to Trinidad (see p. 418). We follow the course of the *Arkansas
River* (left), crossing various tributaries. To the right fine views are
enjoyed of Pike's Peak (p. 417), towering above the lower mountains.
153 M. *Florence,* a collection of petroleum tanks and derricks. —
161 M. **Cañon City** (5345 ft.; *McClure, St. Cloud,* $2-3; *Hot
Springs Hotel,* 2 M. to the W., $ 2-3), a small health-resort (2,825
inhab.), frequented for its hot mineral springs, situated at the mouth
of the Royal Gorge, 2 M. to the W. Beyond Cañon City we pass between the Royal Gorge Hotel (left) and the *State Penitentiary* (right)
and enter the famous *Grand Cañon of the Arkansas,* 8 M. of
stupendous rocky scenery (granite). through which the railway barely
makes its way along the boiling river. At the narrowest point, known
as the *Royal Gorge,* where the train stops for a few minutes, the
rocks tower to a height of 2600 ft. and the railway passes over a
bridge hung from girders mortised into the smooth sides of the cañon.
Beyond the cañon we still follow the foaming Arkansas, passing numerous fantastic rocks and crags. Farther on we obtain a good view,
in front (generally to the left), of the fine snow-clad *Sangre de Cristo
Range.* To the left is the *Broadside Range.* As we near Salida the
Collegiate peaks, *Mts. Harvard, Yale,* and *Princeton* (see p. 409),
come into sight in front (N.W.).

217 M. **Salida** (7050 ft.; *St. Clair,* in the town, on the other side
of the river, $ 2¹/₂-3; *Monte Cristo,* at the station, indifferent, $ 3),
a small town (2586 inhab.), beautifully situated and commanding a
grand mountain-view (to the S., the lower N. peaks of the Sangre
de Cristo Range; to the S. W., Mts. Ouray and Shavano; to the
N.W., the Collegiate Peaks). The small hill in front of the station
(¹/₂ hr.; very steep path) is a most commanding point of view.

From Salida passengers by the Denver & Rio Grande R. R. have a
choice of two routes, uniting at *Grand Junction* (p. 422). The
narrow-gauge line (left) crosses *Marshall Pass* (p. 421), one of the
loftiest passes across the main ridge of the Rocky Mts., while the
standard-gauge line, with through-carriages (comp. p. 414), runs
viâ *Leadville* (p. 423). The latter route, which coincides to some

extent with the Colorado Midland Railway (p. 423), is here given in small type, while the Marshall Pass line is given as the main route.

FROM SALIDA TO GRAND JUNCTION VIÂ LEADVILLE, 239 M., railway in 9-10 hrs. — The train runs towards the N., with *Mt. Shavano* (14,240 ft.) to the left. 7 M. *Brown's Cañon;* 17 M. *Nathrop* (7695 ft.); 25 M. *Buena Vista* (see p. 409). To the left tower the *Collegiate Peaks* (p. 409). 42 M. *Granite* (8945 ft.; comp. p. 409) is the best point for excursions to the *Twin Lakes* (p. 409), one of the finest points in South Park (p. 409). — 56 M. *Malta* (9580 ft.) is the junction of the branch-line to (4 M.) **Leadville** (see p. 423). — 58 M. *Leadville Junction.* At (67 M.) *Tennessee Pass* (10,440 ft.) we cross the Continental watershed and begin to descend towards the Pacific Ocean. To the left rises *Mt. Massive* (14,300 ft.). Just before reaching (76 M.) *Pando* we have a good view (left) of the *Mountain of the Holy Cross* (14,175 ft.; see p. 408). A little farther on we pass through the short but fine *Red Cliff Cañon.* 83 M. *Red Cliff* (8670 ft.). About 5 M. farther on is the *Eagle River Cañon*, where the mining-shafts and miners' dwellings are seen clinging to the sides of the cliffs, 2000 ft. above our heads. Near (91 M.) *Minturn*, to the right, is a rock known as the *Lioness.* Beyond (133 M.) *Dotsero*, at the confluence of the *Eagle* and *Grand Rivers*, we enter the fine *Cañon of the Grand River*, which is 16 M. long and has rocky sides reaching a height of 2000-2500 ft. We pass through three tunnels, the last 444 yds. long. — 150 M. **Glenwood Springs** (5200 ft.), see p. 424. A branch-line runs hence to (41 M.) *Aspen* (see p. 424). To the S. E. towers *Mt. Sopris* (12,970 ft.). Beyond Glenwood we continue to follow the Grand River, which flows to the left. 162 M. *Newcastle*, and thence to (239 M.) **Grand Junction,** see p. 424.

Beyond Salida the narrow-gauge runs at first towards the S. W. — 222 M. *Poncha* (7480 ft.; Hot Springs Hotel, $2¹/₂-3), with hot springs (90 - 185°), is the junction of a branch-line to (11 M.) *Monarch.* — From (228 M.) *Mears Junction* (8435 ft.) a line runs S. to (75 M.) *Alamosa* (p. 418).

This line also runs through a picturesque district, affording fine views (left) of the **Sangre de Cristo Range**, including the *Three Tetons, Music Peak* (13,300 ft.), and the *Sierra Blanca* (p. 418).

We continue to ascend rapidly, the line winding backwards and forwards in a series of the most abrupt curves, and affording a striking spectacle of engineering skill. Lofty mountains rise on every side. The top of the ***Marshall Pass** is 10,858 ft. above the sea. The view (much obstructed by a long snow-shed) includes *Mt. Ouray* (14,400 ft.), rising close to the line on the right, and the *Sangre de Cristo Range* to the S. E. Snow lies here all the year round.

The first part of the descent is very rapid, and numerous abrupt curves are turned (no standing on the platform allowed). An almost continuous series of snow-sheds interferes sadly with the view. — 259 M. *Sargent* (8480 ft.). We now traverse a bleak moorland district. Beyond (279 M.) *Parlin* (7950 ft.) we repeatedly cross the meandering *Tomichi.* — 290 M. **Gunnison** (7680 ft.; *La Veta Hotel*, with railway-restaurant, $3-4, meal 75 c.), a town of 1105 inhab., is of considerable importance as the outlet of a rich mining district.

A branch-line runs from Gunnison to (28 M.) **Crested Butte** (8880 ft.; *Elk Mountain Ho.*, $2¹/₂-3), a small town, in a district rich in coal, silver, and gold. The *Crested Butte* is close to the town. The **Elk Mts.**, a little to the W., rise finely from the plain and afford good shooting.

Beyond Gunnison we follow the *Gunnison River*, at first on one

side and then on the other. — 316 M. *Sapinero* (7245 ft.) is the
junction of a line, running through **Lake Fork Cañon*, to (35 M.)
Lake City, near the beautiful *Lake San Cristobal*. An observation-
car is attached to the train for the passage of the **Black Cañon*, or
Grand Gorge of the Gunnison, which is 15 M. long and in some respects even finer than the Royal Gorge. Among the most prominent
individual features are the *Chippeta Falls* (right) and the **Currecanti Needle*, a lofty pinnacle of rock surmounted by a flag-staff
(about halfway down the cañon). The river, which we cross and recross, alternates between foaming rapids and pleasant quiet reaches.
Near the end of the cañon we diverge to the left from the Gunnison
and follow the cañon of its tributary, the **Cimarron*, one of the finest
pieces of the whole gorge. From (331 M.) *Cimarron* (6895 ft.; Rail.
Restaurant) we ascend rapidly to (336 M.) *Cerro Summit* (7965 ft.),
and then descend, nearly as rapidly, towards the Lower Gunnison.
The country now traversed is arid and unattractive. — 343 M. *Cedar
Creek* (6750 ft.). 353 M. *Montrose* (5790 ft.; Belvedere Hotel) is the
junction of the line to Ouray (see p. 420). The *Uncompaghre Mts.*,
culminating in *Uncompaghre Peak* (14,420 ft.), are seen to the S.W.
(left). Beyond (375 M.) *Delta* (4980 ft.) we pass through the *Cañon
of the Lower Gunnison*, where the smooth-faced sandstone cliffs are
striking. Beyond (399 M.) *Bridgeport* we thread a tunnel 722 yds.
long. In approaching Grand Junction we cross the *Grand River*, just
above the mouth of the Gunnison.

425 M. **Grand Junction** (4580 ft.; *Brunswick Hotel*, $3; *Rail.
Restaurant*) is of importance as the junction of the Denver and Colorado
Midland railways. We continue to follow the *Grand River* (left). To
the right are the fantastic *Little Book Cliffs*. We traverse the bare
'Colorado Desert'. At (460 M.) *Utah Line* we enter *Utah* (p. 425),
called by the Mormons *Deseret*. To the left ,in the distance, are the *La
Sal* and *San Rafael Mts.* To the right are the *Roan* or *Book Mts.* (7000-
9000 ft.), with their variegated cliffs. 480 M. *Cisco.* — At (531 M.)
Green River (4070; Hotel, with railway-restaurant, meals 75 c.) we
cross the river of that name and enter another stretch of desert.

Beyond Green River the train ascends steadily towards the Wahsatch Range. At (570 M.) *Lower Crossing* (4630 ft.) we cross the
S. fork of the *Price River.* 611 M. *Price* (5560 ft.). At (624 M.)
Castle Gate (6165 ft.) we reach the **Castle* or **Price River Cañon**,
the entrance to which is formed by two pinnacles of sandstone, 450-
500 ft. high, barely leaving room for the railway and river to pass
between them. 637 M. *Pleasant Valley Junction* (7185 ft.). At
(644 M.) *Soldier Summit* (7465 ft.) we reach the top of the pass
over the **Wahsatch Mts.** and begin to descend on the other side.
651 M. *Clear Creek* (6245 ft.); 669 M. *Thistle* (5040 ft.). A little
farther on we pass through the pretty little *Spanish Fork Cañon* and
emerge in the beautiful *Utah Valley* (p. 425). To the S. rises *Mt.
Nebo* (12,000 ft.). 684 M. *Springville* (4565 ft.). To the left lies

Utah Lake, with the *Oquirrh Mts.* rising beyond it.   689 M. *Provo* (4530 ft.), a thriving little Mormon city, with 5159 inhab., situated on the *Provo River,* a little above its mouth in Utah Lake.   706 M. *Lehi* (4545 ft.). Farther on we see (left) the small river *Jordan,* connecting Utah Lake with the Great Salt Lake (p. 427).   724 M. *Bingham Junction* (4380 ft.). As we approach Salt Lake City we have a view to the right of the Mormon Tabernacle and Temple.

735 M. **Salt Lake City** (4240 ft.), see p. 424.

Beyond Salt Lake City the train runs to the N., with Great Salt Lake generally in sight to the left. To the right rise the Wahsatch Mts. In the lake are the large and mountainous *Antelope Island* and (farther on) *Fremont Island.*   752 M. *Lake Park* (Hotel), a pleasant bathing-resort on Salt Lake, with excellent bathing arrangements (comp. p. 427).   764 M. *Hooper* (4390 ft.).

771 M. **Ogden** (4310 ft.), see p. 395.

b. Viâ Colorado Midland Railway.

712 M. Railway in 28-30 hrs. (fare $ 25; sleeper $ 5). Through-carriages to San Francisco. This line ('Pike's Peak Route') also traverses much fine scenery.

From *Denver* to (74 M.) *Colorado Springs* the train uses the tracks of the Atchison, Topeka, and Santa Fé Railway (see p. 409), practically coinciding with that above described (R. 92 a). From Colorado Springs the line runs towards the W.   77 M. *Colorado City,* see p. 415; 80 M. *Manitou,* see p. 417.   81 M. *Manitou Iron Springs* (6550 ft.), the starting-point of the Pike's Peak Railway (p. 417). Beyond Manitou the train ascends through the beautiful ***Ute Pass,** on the shoulder of Pike's Peak (p. 417), so called because formerly the regular route of the Ute Indians in passing across the mountains to the plains.   86 M. *Cascade Cañon* (7240 ft.; Hotel, $ 3-4), the starting-point of the carriage-road to the top of Pike's Peak (comp. p. 417); 87 M. *Ute Park* (7510 ft.; Hotel, $ 3-4); 89 M. *Green Mountain Falls* (7735 ft.; Hotel, $ 2½-3½); 94 M. *Woodland Park* (8485 ft.; Hotel), at the head of the Ute Pass, affording a splendid view of Pike's Peak. From (100 M.) *Manitou Park Station* (8465 ft.), a four-horse coach runs to (7 M.) **Manitou Park* (Hotel, $ 3-4). On leaving the Ute Pass we cross the (102 M.) *Hayden Divide* (9200 ft.), part of the Continental watershed, and descend, passing (111 M.) *Florissant* (8150 ft.), to the fine **Granite* or *Eleven Mile Cañon,* through which rushes the *South Platte River.* We are now traversing *South Park* (p. 409).   126 M. *Howbert* (8520 ft.); 132 M. *Spinney* (8630 ft.); 143 M. *Hartsel Hot Springs* (8890 ft.; Hotel, $ 2-2½), one of the chief resorts in South Park. After crossing the *Trout Creek Pass* (9345 ft.) we descend to (176 M.) *Buena Vista* (see p. 409), in the valley of the *Arkansas.*   193 M. *Granite Gate* (8960 ft.); 201 M. *Snowden* (9305 ft.).

209 M. **Leadville** (10,200 ft.; *Hotel Kitchen,* $ 3-4; *Hutchinson Ho.,* $ 2½; *Rail. Restaurant*), one of the highest cities and most

celebrated mining centres in the world, is finely situated amid towering mountains. Pop. (1890) 10,384. It is especially interesting in all points connected with mines and miners.

Leadville was founded in 1859 under the name of *California Gulch* and was for several years one of the richest gold-washing camps in Colorado. In 1876 the great carbonate beds of silver were discovered, and the population rose for a time to 30,000. The annual yield of silver in the Leadville mines amounts to about $ 13,000,000.

Among the favourite excursions from Leadville are those to the *Soda Springs* on *Mt. Massive*, 5 M. to the W. (reached by a fine boulevard), and to the *Twin Lakes* (p. 409), 14 M. to the S. — From Leadville to *Denver*, etc., by the Denver & Rio Grande R. R., see R. 92 a.

Beyond Leadville the train ascends rapidly towards the ridge of the *Saguache Mts.*, passing the 'Continental Divide' by the (226 M.) **Hagerman Pass** and **Tunnel** (11,530 ft.), the highest point reached by any railway in crossing the Rocky Mts. It then descends rapidly. 256 M. *Ruedi* (7570 ft.); 263 M. *Peach Blow* (7000 ft.). — From (271 M.) *Aspen Junction* (6615 ft.) a branch-line runs to (19 M.) *Aspen* (comp. p. 421).

Aspen (7950 ft.; *Jerome*, $ 2½-4; *Clarendon*, $ 2-2½), finely situated in the heart of the Rockies, is a prosperous mining town with 5108 inhabitants. Silver and lead are the chief sources of its wealth, but gold is also found in the vicinity. The annual value of the bullion yielded by the Aspen mines is about $ 8,000,000.

We continue to descend along the *Roaring Fork.* — 295 M. **Glenwood Springs** (5770 ft.; *The Colorado*, $ 3-5 new; **Hotel Glenwood*, $ 3-4), at the junction of the Roaring Fork and the *Grand River*, has of late come into prominence on account of its beautiful situation and hot salt mineral springs. The springs, rising on both sides of the Grand River, have a temperature of 120-140° Fahr., are highly mineralized, and are beneficial in rheumatism, gout, and most diseases of the blood and skin. The bathing arrangements are excellent, including a large swimming basin, 640 ft. long and 110 ft. wide (temp. 95°). A natural Turkish bath may be enjoyed in one of the *Vapour Caves* (105-110°).

307 M. *Newcastle* (p. 421); 321 M. *Rifle* (5100 ft.); 338 M. *Parachute*; 351 M. *De Beque*. At (384 M.) **Grand Junction** (p. 422) we pass on to the lines of the *Rio Grande Western Railway;* and the journey hence to (676 M.) **Salt Lake City** and (712 M.) **Ogden** is the same as that described in R. 92 a.

Salt Lake City. — Hotels. *Knutsford* (Pl. b; C, 2, 3), cor. of Third South and State St., R. from $ 1; *Templeton* (Pl. c; C, 2), corner opposite Temple Sq., $ 3-5; *Walker House* (Pl. d; B, 2), Main St., $ 2-3; *Cullen* (Pl. e; B, 2), $ 3-4; *Valley House* $ 1¼-1½.

Railway Stations. *Denver & Rio Grande* (Pl. A, 2, 3), cor. of 2nd S. and 5th W. Sts.; *Union Pacific* (Pl. A, 2), cor. of S. Temple and 3rd W. Sts.; *Utah Central* (Pl. B, 4), cor. of Main and 7th S. Sts.

Tramways (electric) traverse the principal streets (fare 5 c.).

Post Office (Pl. B, 2), W. Temple St., cor. 2nd S. St.

Streets. Salt Lake City is laid out on a rectangular plan, and its streets are named and numbered in such a way that it is easy to find any given point. The centre of the city is TEMPLE SQUARE (Pl. B, 1, 2), the streets

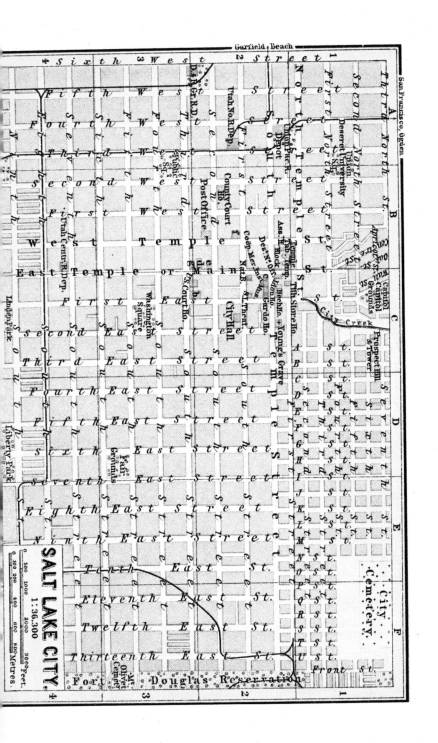

Garfield Beach

San Francisco, Ogden

SALT LAKE CITY.
1:36,300

0 500 1000 2000 3000 Feet.
0 100 200 400 600 800 Metres.

City Cemetery.

Fort Douglas Reservation

enclosing which are named *North Temple, West Temple, South Temple,* and *East Temple Streets.* The streets to the N. of N. Temple St. are known as 1st North, 2nd North, and so on; those to the W. of W. Temple St. as 1st W., 2nd W., etc.; those to the S. of S. Temple St. as 1st S., etc.; those to the E. of E. Temple St. as 1st E., etc. Each block is ¹/₈ M. long. First East St. was recently renamed State St. Popularly, East Temple St. is known as Main St., South Temple St. as Brigham St., and North Temple St. as Jordan St. On the bench in the N.E. part of the city, the blocks are smaller, and the streets narrower and named differently.

Salt Lake City (4230 ft.), the *Zion* of the *Latter Day Saints* or *Mormons* and the capital of *Utah Territory,* is finely situated in a spacious upland valley, encircled by mountains, which approach the city closely on the N. and E. (Wahsatch Range), while they are 20 M. distant to the S. and 15 M. distant to the S.W. *Great Salt Lake* (p. 427) lies 12 M. to the N.W. The city is regularly laid out and the streets are wide and shaded with trees. Each house in the residence-quarters stands in its own garden, the general effect being cool and pleasant. In 1890 the population was 44,843 (two-thirds Mormons and the rest 'Gentiles').

Salt Lake City was founded in 1847 by the *Mormons,* under *Brigham Young* (p. 426), who had been expelled from Nauvoo (Ill.; see p. 323) the previous year and had made a long and perilous journey across the Indian-haunted plains. The district was then a barren and unpromising desert, but the industrious Mormons set to work at once to plough and plant and began that system of irrigation which has drawn out the latent capabilities of the soil and made the Utah valleys among the most productive regions in the country. The *Territory of Utah* was organized in 1850, with Brigham Young as the first governor. A copious stream of Mormon immigrants soon set in from Europe; and, in spite of numerous collisions with the U. S. Government on the question of polygamy, the history of the city and territory has been one of steady progress and development. Of late years the proportion of 'Gentile' (*i.e.* Non-Mormon) inhabitants in Salt Lake City has increased very rapidly and introduced many new features and problems into the situation. Polygamy has been declared illegal by the U. S. Courts and has been discontinued.

† 'Early in 1820, at Manchester (N. Y.), *Joseph Smith,* then fourteen years old, became interested in a religious revival but was puzzled by the conflicting doctrines taught. He asked of God in prayer, which sect was right. In answer he saw a vision of God the father and his son Jesus Christ, and was told that all the sects were wrong. In subsequent visions he learned that he was to be the instrument in restoring the Gospel and the Holy Priesthood of the Son of God to men, and in establishing the Church and Kingdom of God upon the earth, never more to be overthrown; also where he would find the inspired history of the aborigines of America engraved in ancient characters on metal plates. This he afterwards translated into English, by the power of God, and published in 1830, as the Book of Mormon. It has been translated and published in Welsh, Swedish, Spanish, Dutch, Hawaiian, and Maori, and translated into Hindustani and Hebrew. On May 15th, 1829, John the Baptist appeared to Joseph Smith and *Oliver Cowdery,* laid his hands on them, and ordained them to the Aaronic or Lower Priesthood. The same year the apostles Peter, James, and John appeared to them and ordained them to the Apostleship of the Melchisedek or Higher Priesthood.

'The Church of Jesus Christ of Latter-day Saints was organized with six members, on April 6th, 1830, at Fayette (N. Y.), by Joseph Smith, by

---

† This statement of the origin and doctrines of Mormonism was drawn up for *Baedeker's United States* in the office of the President of the Church of Latter-Day Saints.

appointment and instruction from God. Twelve apostles, also seventies, high priests, elders, bishops, priests, teachers, and deacons, have been since ordained, now numbering many thousands. They have preached the Gospel to many nations, and hundreds of thousands of believers have been baptized. *Wilford Woodruff* is the present president of the Church, with *George Q. Cannon* and *Joseph F. Smith* as his counsellors, the three constituting the First Presidency.

'Driven from Missouri and Illinois, with their prophet and president, Joseph Smith. and his brother Hyram murdered in Carthage jail (Ill.) on June 27th, 1844, by an armed mob, the Latter-day Saints were led by *Brigham Young* to Salt Lake City in 1847, spreading since into the regions about. They now number about 200,000 and have built six Temples to the Lord, the most imposing of which is at Salt Lake City.

'The Latter-Day Saints believe in God the Father; his son Jesus Christ and his atonement; the Holy Ghost; the Gospel, the first principles being faith, repentance, baptism by immersion for remission of sins, and the laying on of hands for imparting the Holy Ghost; the resurrection of the dead, and the eternal judgments; the necessity of divine authority, by calling and ordination, to preach the Gospel and administer its ordinances; apostles, prophets, seventies, high priests, elders, bishops, priests, teachers, and deacons, for the work of the ministry; revelation from God; the Bible, Book of Mormon, and other inspired books; the gathering of Israel and the building up of Zion and Jerusalem; the sacredness and eternity of marriage; and the personal reign of Christ upon the earth as King of Kings and Lord of Lords.'

TEMPLE BLOCK (Pl. B, 1, 2), the Sacred Square of the Mormons, lies near the centre of the city and forms the chief object of interest to strangers. It is 10 acres in area, is surrounded by a high adobé wall, and contains the Tabernacle, the Temple, and the Assembly Hall. Visitors are admitted, by the W. gate, from 8 to 12 and 1 to 4.

The *Tabernacle (Pl. B, 2), built in 1864-67, is a huge and extraordinary structure, in the shape of an oval or ellipse, 250 ft. long, 150 ft. wide, and 70 ft. high. It is surmounted by a wooden roof with iron shingles, resembling the shell of a turtle or the inverted hull of a ship, supported by 44 sandstone pillars.

The Interior, presenting one of the largest unsupported arches in the world, has seats for over 8000 people and can accommodate about 12,000. Amorphous though it be, there is something imposing in its size and proportions, while it is well adapted for speaking and hearing. The building is surrounded by a gallery, except at the W. end, where there are a platform for speakers, with seats for the choir and others, and an immense and fine organ. Public religious services are held in the Tabernacle every Sunday at 2 p.m., and it is also used for lectures, concerts, and other meetings.

A little to the E. of the Tabernacle is the new *Temple (Pl. B, 2), a large and handsome building of granite, the corner-stone of which was laid in 1853 and the exterior completed in 1892. It is 186 ft. long from E. to W. and 99 ft. wide. At each end are three pointed towers, the loftiest of which, in the centre of the E. or principal façade, is 210 ft. high and is surmounted by a colossal gilded figure (12$^{1}/_{2}$ ft. high) of the Mormon Angel Moroni (by *C. E. Dallin*). The cost of the Temple so far has been about $4,000,000.

The Interior is elaborately fitted up and artistically adorned. The Temple will be used for the administration of ordinances, including marriage (for this world and the next, or for eternity alone) baptism for the dead, prayer, theological lectures, preaching, teaching, ordinations, etc.

The **Assembly Hall** (Pl. B, 2), to the S.W. of the Tabernacle, is
a granite building with accommodation for 3000 people, intended
for divine service. The interior is adorned with frescoes of scenes
from Mormon history. — The famous *Endowment House*, which stood
at the N. W. corner of the Temple Enclosure, has been pulled down.

We now follow SOUTH TEMPLE STREET towards the E. To the
left (N.) is the *Deseret News Office* (Pl. C, 2), behind which is the
Tithing Storehouse, where the Mormons pay their tithes in kind. A
little farther on, also to the left, are the *Lion House* (Pl. C, 2; with
a lion over the entrance), one of the residences of Brigham Young;
the *Office of the President of the Mormon Church*; and the *Beehive House* (Pl. C, 2; surmounted by a beehive, Utah's emblem),
another of Brigham Young's houses. On the opposite side of the
street (right) are the *Templeton Hotel* (Pl. c; C, 2); the huge warehouse of *Zion's Co-öperative Mercantile Institution* (Pl. C, 2); the
Museum (Pl. C, 2), containing Utah products and curiosities (adm.
25 c.); and the *Gardo House* (Pl. C, 2), opposite the Beehive House.

A little farther to the N.E. is *Brigham Young's Grave* (Pl. C, 2),
surrounded by an ornamental iron railing.

About ½ M. to the N. of this point is *Prospect Hill* (Pl. C, 1), with a
tower (adm. 15 c.) commanding an excellent *View of the city, its environs, and Salt Lake. Fort Douglas (see below) is seen to the E. — A still
more extensive view is obtained from *Ensign Peak* (5050 ft.), which rises
a little farther to the N. and may be ascended nearly all the way by carriage. To the N. lies *City Creek Cañon*, with some pretty scenery.

The other parts of the city call for no especial comment. The *Salt
Lake Theatre* (Pl. C, 2), at the corner of State and 1st S. Sts., is a
large building. The old *City Hall* (Pl. C, 2), is in 1st S. St., near
State St. A new and imposing *City and County Building* is in
course of erection in Washington Sq., at the corner of State and
4th S. Sts. (Pl. C, 3). A new *Capitol* is in contemplation in *Capitol Grounds* (Pl. C, 1), near Prospect Hill (see above). Among the
educational establishments is *Deseret University* (Pl. B, 1), in Union
Sq., attended by 3-400 students. The *Territorial Exposition Building* is in the Fair Grunds (Pl. D, 3).

On a plateau (500 ft.), 3 M. to the E. of the city, is **Fort Douglas**,
a U. S. military post, reached by the Utah Central Railway or by electric
tramway (fare 10 c.). Fine views from the post and from the road to it.
Parade and band-concert every afternoon.

***Great Salt Lake**, the nearest point of which is 12 M. to the N.W. of
Salt Lake City, is 80 M. long and 30 M. wide. Several rivers flow into
it, but it has no outlet and gets rid of its superfluous water by evaporation. Its water, which is extraordinarily buoyant, contains about 22 per
cent of pure salt (ocean 3-4 p. c., Dead Sea 24 p.c.). A bathe in it is very
exhilarating, but bathers should be careful not to get any of the brine into
their mouth or eyes. The lake contains several islands, the largest of which
are *Antelope* and *Stansbury*. It is very shallow in places, and the tints of
the water are often very beautiful. The lake may be conveniently visited by
taking the *Union Pacific R. R.* (p. 423; return-fare 50 c.) to (18 M.) **Garfield
Beach** (*Hotel*), with excellent bathing-arrangements. A small steamer sometimes plies hence to *Lake Park* (see p. 423). A railroad is in course of
construction to *Saltair*, the nearest bathing-place on the lake, and directly
to the W. of the city.

The *Warm Sulphur Springs*, just to the N. of the city, and *Beck's Hot Springs*, 2 M. farther on, are frequented for their medicinal qualities.

Among the chief points of resort among the *Wahsatch Mts.* are the *Big Cottonwood Cañon*, a day's drive from the city; the *Little Cottonwood Cañon*; the *City Creek Cañon*, close to the city; the *Weber Cañon*, to the N., and the *American Fork* and *Provo Coñons*, in Utah Valley, to the S.

93. San Francisco.

Arrival. *Railway Passengers* from the N., E., and S. leave the train at *Oakland* '(see p. 399) and reach San Francisco at the *Ferry Landing* (Pl. G, 2), at the foot of Market St., where cabs (50 c.), hotel-omnibuses (50 c.), and cable, electric, and horse cars (5 c.) meet the steamer. — Those arriving by *Steamer* also land in the same neighbourhood. — The only regular *Railway Station* in the city is that of the *Southern Pacific Railroad* (Pl. G, 5), at the cor. of 3rd and Townsend Sts., for Menlo Park, Santa Clara, Santa Cruz, San José, Tres Piños, Monterey, Paso Robles, etc. (comp. p. 436).

Hotels. PALACE (Pl. a; F, 3), at the corner of Market St. and Montgomery St., a huge building (1200 beds) surrounding an internal court; front-room and board from $5, court-room (undesirable) and board from $3½, front-room without board $3, court-room $1½. *CALIFORNIA (Pl. b; F, 3), Bush St., R. from $1; BALDWIN (Pl. c; F, 4), cor. of Market and Powell Sts., $2½-5; GRAND (Pl. d; F, 3), opposite the Palace, of which it is an annex, $3-5, R. $1-3; LICK HOUSE (Pl. e; F, 3), cor. of Montgomery and Sutter Sts.; OCCIDENTAL (Pl. f; F, 3), cor. of Montgomery and Bush Sts., $3-5; BELLA VISTA (Pl. g; E, 3), 1001 Pine St., a fashionable family hotel, for a long stay; RICHELIEU, Van Ness Ave., between O'Farrell and Geary Sts., $3-5; GOLDEN WEST, Ellis St., opposite the Baldwin, R. from $1; BERESFORD (Pl. h; F, 3), cor. of Bush and Stockton Sts., $2½-4; RUSS HOUSE (Pl. i; F, 3), cor. of Montgomery and Pine Sts., $1½-2½; PLEASANTON (Pl. j; E, 3), cor. of Sutter and Jones Sts., $3-5; *ELMER HOUSE (Pl. k; F, 3), 314 Bush St., a small but comfortable house.

Restaurants. At the *California, Palace*, and other hotels (see above); *Tortoni*, 107 O'Farrell St.; *Marchand*, 115 Grant Ave.; *Maison Dorée*, Kearny St.; *Maison Riche*, 104 Grant Ave. and 44 Geary St.; *Poodle Dog Rotisserie*, cor. Grant Ave. and Bush St.; *Viticultural Society*, 317 Pine St. (excellent Californian wines); *Wilson*, Post St. (low prices). — *Chinese Restaurants*, see p. 432.

Tramways. An excellent system of *Cable Cars* (fare 5 c.) traverses all the main thoroughfares and neutralizes the steepness of most of the streets (comp. p. 429). An elaborate system of transfers makes it possible to go from almost any point in the city to any other point for a single fare. The stranger should visit one of the 'Cable Power-houses' (*e.g.* at the cor. of Sutter and Polk Sts., or at the cor. of Mason and Washington Sts.). — '*Dummy*' *Steam Cars* run to the *Cliff House* (see p. 432). — **Cabs.** With one horse, 1-2 pers., 1 M. $1, with two horses (hacks) $1½; per hr. $1½, $2; each addit. hr. $1, $1½. Heavy baggage is usually transported by the transfer companies. — **Ferries**, plying from the foot of Market St., see p. 433.

Places of Amusement. *Baldwin Theatre* (Pl. F, 4), 936 Market St.; *California Theatre* (Pl. F, 3), 414 Bush St. (very tastefully fitted up); *Grand Opera House* (Pl. F, 3, 4), Mission St., near 3rd St.; *Bush Street Theatre* (Pl. F, 3 ; varieties), between Montgomery and Kearny Sts.; *Stockwell's Theatre*, Eddy St., opposite the Baldwin; *Alcazar* (Pl. F, 3), 114 O'Farrell St.; *Tivoli Opera House* (Pl. F, 4), Eddy St., near Powell St. (cheap but fair performances of opera; beer-drinking and smoking allowed); *Chinese Theatres*, see p. 432. — *Panorama* at the cor. of Market and 10th Sts. (Pl. E, 5). — *Race Course* (Pl. A, 5), near Golden Gate Park (meetings in spring, summer, and autumn); *Olympic Club Grounds*, for baseball, etc. — *Woodward's Garden* (Pl. E, 6), Mission St., between 13th and 15th St. (beer-garden, with concerts, a small zoological collection, etc.; adm. 25 c.). — *San Francisco Art Association*, 430 Pine St. (picture-gallery).

Clubs. *Pacific Union* (Pl. F, 3), at the cor. of Union Sq. and Stockton
St.; *Bohemian* (Pl. F, 3), cor. of Sutter and Mason Sts. (literary men,
actors, etc.); *Cosmos*, 317 Powell St; *Olympic*, Post St., near Mason St.;
University, Sutter St.; *Press*, 430 Pine St.; *Deutscher Verein*, Pioneer Building
(p. 430); *San Francisco Verein* (German), 219 Sutter St.; *Ligue Nationale
Française*, 305 Larkin St.; *Cercle Français*, 421 Post St. (these two French);
Concordia (Hebrew), at the cor. of Van Ness Ave. and Post St.; *California
Athletic*, 156 New Montgomery St.

Post Office (Pl. F, 2), at the cor. of Washington and Battery Sts. (8-8;
Sun. 9-10 a.m. and 2 p.m.); chief branch-office (Station D), at the foot
of Market St. Numerous letter-boxes.

British Consul, *Mr. Louis Donohoe*, 506 Battery St.

San Francisco, the largest city of California and the Pacific
Coast and the eighth city of the United States, is grandly situated
in 37° 47′ N. lat., at the N. end of a peninsula 30 M. long, separating the Pacific Ocean from *San Francisco Bay* (see below). The
city lies mainly on the shore of the bay and on the steep hills rising
from it, but is gradually extending across the peninsula (here 6 M.
wide) to the ocean. On the N. it is bounded by the famous *Golden
Gate*, the narrow entrance (1 M. across) to San Francisco Bay.
The city is on the whole well and substantially built but contains
fewer large buildings of architectural importance than any other
city of its size in the country. In 1890 it contained 298,997 inhab.,
including about 25,000 Chinese (comp. p. 431).

The *Mission of San Francisco* (see p. 431) was founded by the Mexicans in 1776, but the modern city nearly sprang from the village of Yerba
Buena ('good herb', *i. e.* wild mint), founded in 1835, about 3 M. to the E.
In 1846 Yerba Buena came under the American flag, and in the following
year its name was changed to *San Francisco*. In 1848, the year of the discovery of gold in California, its population was about 500. In 1850 it was
about 25.000, and each subsequent decade has seen an extraordinary increase (56,802 in 1860; 149,473 in 1870; 233,956 in 1880). San Francisco
received a city charter in 1850, but its corrupt municipal government led
in 1856 to the formation of a Vigilance Committee, which took the law
into its own hands and made a very thorough reformation. — To make
the present site of San Francisco suitable for a large city, an immense
amount of work had to be done in cutting down hills and ridges, filling up
gullies, and reclaiming the mud flats on the bay (comp. p. 75). The city,
however, is still remarkably hilly; and one of its most characteristic sights
is the cable cars crawling up the steep inclines like flies on a window-pane.

The **Climate** of San Francisco is wonderfully equable. The mean
annual temperature is about 57° Fahr., and no month varies to any great
extent from this average. September has the highest average (about 61°),
and a few hot days (80-90°) occur about midsummer. The mean temperature of January is about 50°. Visitors should always have warm wraps at
hand, especially in the afternoon, when a strong wind usually blows in
from the sea. The summer climate is not generally considered beneficial
for persons of weak lungs, owing to the wind and the dust; but the man
of ordinary health finds the air invigorating and stimulating all the year
round. The annual rainfall is about 25 inches. — *Earthquakes* occur occasionally in San Francisco but are never very destructive. The severest (Oct.,
1868) damaged some old and badly built structures considerably and caused
the loss of one life.

The **Commerce** of San Francisco is extensive, the value of its exports
and imports amounting to about $150,000,000. Among the chief exports are
gold and silver, wine, fruit, wool, and bread-stuffs; the imports include coal,
timber, rice, sugar, tea, and coffee. The **Manufactures** include iron, flour,
silk and woollen goods, canned fruits and vegetables, leather, liquors,

ship-building, meat-packing, carriages, silver-ware, sugar, glass, brass, machinery, cigars, cordage, etc., and had in 1890 a value of $ 134,000,000.

The **Population** is very heterogeneous, every European nationality being represented here, to say nothing of the Mexicans, Chinese (p. 431), Japanese, Africans, and other non-European races.

MARKET STREET (Pl. G-C, 2-7), the chief business-thoroughfare, extends to the S.W. from the *Ferry Landing* (Pl. G, 2) to a point near the twin *Mission Peaks* (925 ft.), a distance of about 3½ M. The visitor should begin his inspection of the city by ascending to the top of the tower of the **Chronicle Building** (Pl. F, 3), in Market St., nearly opposite the Palace Hotel (p. 428), which affords a good bird's-eye view of the city from a central point. He may then supplement this by following KEARNY STREET (Pl. F, 1-3), with many of the best shops, to *Telegraph Hill (Pl. F, 1; 295 ft.), which commands a good view of the Golden Gate (p. 429), the water-front of the City, the Bay, Mt. Tamalpais (N.W.; p. 434). Mt. Diablo (N.N.E.; p. 434), etc.

Following Market St. towards the S.W. from the Chronicle Building we pass between *Baldwin's Theatre* (Pl. F, 4; right) and the *Academy of Sciences* (Pl. F, 4; left), the latter with a fine inside staircase of gray Californian marble. A little farther on, at 8th St., a few steps to the right bring us to the large new **City Hall** (Pl. E, 4, 5; unfinished), a handsome and original structure, in *Yerba Buena Park*, a little to the N. of Market St., erected at a cost of over $4,000,000 (800,000l.). Near it are the large *St. Ignatius Church and College* (Pl. E, 5) and the *Mechanics' Pavilion* (Pl. E, 5; the property of the *Mechanics' Institute*, 31 Post St.), with a library of 50,000 volumes.

The **U. S. Branch Mint** (Pl. F, 4), in Fifth St., at the corner of Mission St., contains interesting machinery and a collection of coins and relics (adm. 9-12). In 1891 it coined bullion to the value of $ 32,115,007; in 1854-91, $ 951,000,000.

Among the other chief buildings in the business-quarter are the *Post Office* (Pl. F, G, 2), at the corner of Battery and Washington Sts.; the *Stock Exchange* (Pl. F, 3), 327 Pine St.; the *Merchants' Exchange* (Pl. F, 3) and the *Bank of California* (Pl. F, 3), California St.; the *First National Bank* (Pl. F, 3), at the corner of Bush and Sansome Sts.; the *Crocker Building* (Pl. F, 3); the lofty new *Mills Building* (Pl. E, 4); and the *Odd Fellows Hall* (Pl. E, 4), cor. Market and 7th Sts. — The *California Market* (Pl. F, 3), extending from California St. to Pine St., presents a wonderful show of fruits and vegetables (best in the early morning). — The *Mercantile Library* (Pl. E, 4), at the cor. of Van Ness and Golden Gate Avenues, is a handsome and well-equipped building, with an excellent collection of 70,000 volumes. — The *California State Mining Bureau*, in the building of the *Society of Californian Pioneers* (Pl. F, 4), 24 Fourth St., contains interesting collections of Californian minerals and relics (10-5). The *California Academy of Science* (see above; Market

St., near 4th St.), the *California Historical Society*, and the *Geo-graphiaal Society of the Pacific* offer much that is of interest to the scholarly visitor, and the historical student should also inspect some of the old Spanish grants in the *Surveyor General's Office* (610 Com-mercial St.).

One of the most interesting historical relics of San Francisco is the old **Mission Dolores** (Pl. D, 7; see p. 429) at the corner of Do-lores and 16th St. (Valencia St. cable-cars pass within two blocks). The old church, dating from about 1778, is built of adobe ('adóby'), and is adjoined by a tangled and neglected little churchyard. Adja-cent is a new church of no special interest.

Among the educational instutitions of San Francisco may be mentioned the *Cooper Medical College* (cor. Sacramento and Webster Sts.), the *Medical Department of the University of California* (Stock-ton St.; comp. p. 399), the *Cogswell Technical School* (cor. Folsom and 26th Sts.), the *Boys' High School* (Pl. D, 3), andthe *Girls' High Schoot* (cor. Geary and Scott Sts.). San Francisco possesses 24 free *Kindergartens*, attended in 1890 by 2133 children.

The **Presidio** (Pl. A, 1, 2), or *Government Military Reservation* (approached by the California St., Union St., or Jackson St. cable-cars), garrisoned by two regiments of U. S. troops, has an area of 1500 acres and stretches along the **Golden Gate* for about 4 M. Its walks and drives afford beautiful views, the finest, perhaps, being that from *Fort Point* or *Winfield Scott*. A military band plays at the Presidio nearly every afternoon. — There is another small military reservation at *Black Point* or *Point San José* (Pl. D, 1; reached by Union St. cars), with *Fort Mason*.

The part of CALIFORNIA STREET between Powell St. and Leaven-worth St. (Pl. E, 3) is known as '*Nob Hill*', as containing many of the largest private residences in San Francisco. Most of these are of wood, and no expense has been spared to make them luxurious resi-dences, but a great opportunity to develop something fine in timber architecture has been lost in an unfortunate attempt to reproduce forms that are suitable for stone buildings only.

Among the principal houses are the mansions of the *Stanford* (cor. of Powell St.), *Hopkins-Searles* (cor. of Mason St.), *Crocker* (cor. of Taylor St.), and *Flood* families (cor. of Mason St.; stone). Other large houses are found in Van Ness Avenue, Jackson St., etc.

The ***Chinese Quarter** is one of the most interesting and charac-teristic features of San Francisco, and no one should leave the city without visiting it. It may be roughly defined as lying between Stockton, Sacramento, Kearny, and Pacific Streets (comp. Pl. F, 2) and consists mainly of tall tenement buildings, divided by narrow alleys and swarming with occupants.

During the day strangers may visit *China Town* unattended without danger; but the most interesting time to visit it is at night, when every-thing is in full swing until after midnight, and it is then necessary to be accompanied by a regular guide. The guides, who are generally detec-tives, may be procured at the hotels and charge $5 for a party of not

more than 4-6 persons. One of the chief features of China Town is the
Theatres (adm. 10-25c.; for white visitors, who are taken on to the stage,
50c.), remarkable for the length of the performances (a single play often
extending over days or even weeks), the primitive scenery and absence of
illusion, the discordant music, the curious-looking audience, the gorgeous
costumes, and the seeming want of plot and action. No women appear
on the stage, and the female parts are taken by men. Among the other
points of interest usually visited by strangers are the *Joss Houses* (where
visitors are expected to buy bundles of scented incense-tapers), the *Opium
Joints*, the *Drug Stores* (extraordinary remedies), the *Curiosity Shops*, etc.
The visit is usually wound up at one of t e *Chinese Restaurants* in Dupont
St., where an excellent cup of tea and various Chinese delicacies may
be enjoyed.

China Town contains about 25,000 inhabitants. A large proportion of
these are men, and children are very scarce. There are several *Chinese
Missions* with schools, etc.

The largest of the public parks of San Francisco is **Golden Gate
Park* (Pl. A, 5, 6; reached by several lines of tramway), which extends
from Stanyan St. to (3 M.) the Pacific Ocean, with an area of 1013
acres and a width of ½ M. The landward end of the park is tastefully laid out and planted with trees (eucalyptus, Monterey cypress,
Monterey pine, etc.), but the seaward end is still in the condition
of bare sand-dunes characteristic of the entire peninsula. The
reclaimed portion of the park contains monuments to *Garfield*,
Francis Scott Key (author of the 'Star-spangled Banner'; by W. W.
Story), *Gen. Halleck*, and *Thomas Starr King* (p. 122; by D. C.
French; unveiled in 1892), a fine conservatory, and a children's
playhouse. Good views are obtained of the Golden Gate and (from
the W. end) of the surf rolling in on the ocean-beach. — The *Hill
Park* (Pl. B, C, 6), ½ M. from the E. end of Golden Gate Park,
commands fine views (highest point 570 ft.).

Near the N.E. corner of Golden Gate Park is a group of cemeteries, the largest of which is the **Laurel Hill Cemetery* (Pl. A, B,
4), containing many fine monuments. The adjoining **Lone Mountain*
(470 ft.), the top of which is marked by a large wooden cross, commands a splendid **View* of the city, the Ocean, San Francisco Bay,
the Golden Gate, Mt. Tamalpais, and Mt. Diablo. The *Yerba Buena*
(p. 429) grows on Lone Mt. — The *Presidio Reservation* (p. 431)
lies a little to the N. of Laurel Hill Cemetery.

EXCURSIONS. The most popular short excursion from San Francisco
is that to (6 M.) *Point Lobos*, with *Sutro Heights*, the *Cliff House*, and the
Seal Rocks, which may be reached by driving viâ the Golden Gate
Park or Geary St. (Point Lobos Avenue), by the Ocean Beach Railway along the S. side of Golden Gate Park, or by the Cliff Railway from
the N.E. corner of Laurel Hill Cemetery (Pl. B, 4). Those who are not
driving will find it a good plan to go by the Cliff Railway (reached by
Powell St. cars, with transfer at Jackson St.) and return by the Ocean
Beach Railway (returning by Haight St. car). The fare on each railway
is 5 c. The Cliff Railway skirts the rocks overhanging the *Golden Gate*
(p. 429), of which it affords a magnificent **View*, and ends near the entrance to **Sutro Heights Park*, the beautifully laid-out grounds of Mr.
Adolph Sutro (freely open to the public). The fine trees and plants
here grow luxuriantly on the originally sandy but now well-watered site.
The statuary could be dispensed with. Fine **View* from the terrace
over the Pacific Ocean, with the *Farralone Islands* 30 M. to the W. (light-

house). At our feet lies the *Cliff House, a hotel and restaurant, to which we now descend. The chief attraction here is the view from the piazza of the *Seal Rocks, a stone's throw from the land, which are covered with hundreds of huge sea-lions (Span. *lobos marinos*), basking in the sun. Some of the animals are 12-15 ft. long and weigh from 1000 lbs. upwards; and their evolutions in the water are very interesting. Their singular barking is easily audible amid the roar of the breakers. Large *Public Baths* have been built by Mr. Sutro near the Cliff House. — The station of the *Ocean Beach Railway* (see p. 432) lies on the beach, a little to the S. of the Cliff House. Drivers who have come by Geary St. or Golden Gate Park may vary the route in returning by following the beach for about 3 M. and then taking the San Miguel Toll or Mission Pass Road (comp. Plan; fine views). To the right, near the beginning of this road, lies *Lake Merced.*

Among the other short drives from San Francisco may be mentioned that to **Mt. San Bruno** (1325 ft.), 7 M. to the S. (2 M. from *Baden*, p. 437), a good point of view. — A drive along the water-front gives some idea of the commercial activity of San Francisco and may include visits to the large *Union Iron Works* at *Potrero Point* (Pl. H, 7; also accessible by tramway), where iron ships of war are built, and to the *Dry Dock* at *Hunter's Point* (Pl. H, 4).

The *Government Posts* in the Bay of San Francisco may be visited by the steamer 'McDowell', which sails several times daily from the foot of Clay St. (Pl. G, 2) to Alcatraz, Angel Island, Fort Mason (Black Point), and the Presidio (permit at the Military Headquarters, cor. of Market St. and O'Farrell St.). **Alcatraz Island** is strongly fortified and contains a military prison and a torpedo station. *Angel Island* is also fortified. The *Presidio* and *Fort Mason* are described at p. 431. — The largest naval station near San Francisco is at **Mare Island**, reached viâ *Vallejo Junction* and *Vallejo* (see p. 399). The island is the headquarters of the *U. S. Marine Corps* and contains a *Navy Yard*, with large dry docks and interesting machinery.

*San Francisco Bay, a noble sheet of water 50 M. long and 10 M. wide, gives San Francisco one of the grandest harbours in the world and affords numerous charming excursions. The various FERRIES start from the foot of Market St. (Pl. G, 2). Excursion steamers also ply sometimes through the Golden Gate to the Pacific Ocean, standing out to sea for a short distance and then returning.

(1). The steamer starting farthest to the N. plies to the N. across the Bay, affording a good view of the *Golden Gate* (left), to (6 M.) **Sausalito** or **Saucelito** (*Terrace Hotel*, $ 2-2½), a pleasant little yachting, bathing, and fishing resort, with fine laurels and other trees. A fine walk, affording good views of the Golden Gate, leads round the promontory viâ *Lime Point* to (4 M.) *Point Bonita*, the N. horn of the Golden Gate (lighthouse).

[From Sausalito the NORTH PACIFIC COAST RAILROAD (narrow-gauge) runs to the N. to (87 M.) *Cazadero*. — From (14 M.) *Ross*, **Mt. Tamalpais** (2606 ft.) may be ascended in 2½ hrs. (no livery stable nearer than San Rafael, see below). The *View from the top includes the Pacific Ocean, the Cascade Mts., the Sierra Nevada, the Santa Cruz Mts., the Contra Costa Hills (overtopped by Mt. Hamilton), Mt. Diablo, San Francisco, and San Francisco Bay. — 16 M. *San Anselmo*, the junction of a short line to *San Rafael* (see below); 30 M. *Taylorville*; 33 M. *Tocaloma*; 38 M. *Point Reyes*, a shooting and fishing preserve, at the head of *Tomales Bay*. Beyond (69 M.) *Howard's* (600 ft.) we pass through a fine redwood district. — 87 M. **Cazadero** (*Cazadero Hotel*, $ 1½-3), a favourite sporting and summer resort in the midst of the redwoods.]

(2). The second ferry plies to (6 M.) **Tiburon**, the starting point of the railway to *San Rafael*, *Petaluma*, and *Ukiah* (see below).

[FROM TIBURON TO UKIAH, 107 M., *San Francisco & North Pacific Railway* in 5 hrs. — 9 M. **San Rafael** (generally pron. 'San Raféll'; *Hotel Rafael*, $ 3-3½; *Central*, $ 1½-2), a charming little resort, affording a pleasant and balmy relief to the dusty winds of San Francisco, should be visited by every tourist, especially in the time of roses. It is a favourite point for an ascent of (11 M.) *Mt. Tamalpais* (see above), of which it affords an excellent view (carriages to the top in 3 hrs., descent in 2 hrs.). The drive may include the *Lagunitas Reservoir*. San Rafael may be easily taken in in conjunction with Sausalito (see p. 433). — 30 M. *Petaluma* (American Hotel, $2-3), with 3692 inhab., has a thriving trade in grain and fruit. 45 M. *Santa Rosa;* 50 M. *Fulton*, the junction of a branch-line to *Guerneville;* 51½ M. *Mark West*, with sulphur springs; 60 M. *Healdsburg*. From (68½ M.) *Geyserville* stages run to (8 M.) *Skaggs' Springs*, with a number of warm sulphur springs. — From (78 M.) *Cloverdale* (United States Hotel, $2) a stage-coach runs to (16 M.) the *Geyser Springs (2000 ft.; Hotel*, $3), a number of boiling springs in the *Devil's Cañon*, near the *Pluton River*. These springs vary greatly in temperature, appearance, and character, but there are no true geysers among them (comp. p. 379). The accepted theory ascribes them to chemical action. A guide is procured at the hotel to point out and name the most interesting features. The Geyser Springs may also be reached from Calistoga (see below). — Beyond Cloverdale the line continues to run towards the N., with *Russian River* at some distance to the right. 90 M. *Fountain;* 103 M. *El Robles*. It is proposed to extend the line from (107 M.) *Ukiah*, the present terminus, to *Eureka*, on *Humboldt Bay*.]

(3). The third ferry is that to *Oakland*, already mentioned at p. 399. This is the route for the chief railways to the N., S., and E.

(4). Another line runs to (3 M.) *Alameda Mole*, whence a railway runs to (6 M.) **Alameda** (*Yosemite Hotel*, $2), a pleasant suburban town (11,165 inhab.), adjoining Oakland on the S. This route connects with the narrow-gauge railway to San José and Santa Cruz (see p. 440).

FROM SAN FRANCISCO TO CALISTOGA, 73 M., railway in 3¼-3½ hrs. — From San Francisco to (29 M.) *Vallejo Junction*, see p. 399. We then cross the strait by steamer to (31 M.) *South Vallejo*. 32 M. *North Vallejo* ('Vallayho'), a small town of 6343 inhab., opposite *Mare Island* (p. 433). The train now runs to the N. through the fertile *Napa Valley*, which is especially rich in grapes and other fruits. From (38 M.) *Napa Junction*, a branch-line runs to (13 M.) *Suisun* (p. 398). From (46 M.) *Napa*, a busy little city of 4395 inhab., we may drive to the (6 M.) *Napa Soda Springs*. Beyond (55 M.) *Yountville* we traverse extensive vineyards. 64 M. *St. Helena*, with many fine vineyards, is the starting-point of stages to *White Sulphur Springs*, *Etna Springs*, and *Howell Mountain*. — 73 M. **Calistoga** (*Magnolia*, $2-2½), the terminus of the railway, is a pretty little town of 1200 inhab., with several warm mineral springs. About 5 M. to the W. is the curious *Petrified Forest*, a tract 4 M. long and 1 M. wide, over which are scattered the remains of about 100 petrified trees. — About 12 M. to the N.W. of Calistoga rises **Mt. St. Helena** (4345 ft.), an extinct volcano, which may be ascended on horseback and affords an extensive view. From Calistoga stage-coaches run daily to (27 M.) the *Geyser Springs* (see above).

FROM SAN FRANCISCO TO MOUNT DIABLO. — We proceed by ferry and train to (36 M.) *Martinez*, as described at p. 441, and go on thence by stage to (2 M.) *Clayton* (Clayton Hotel, $1½), whence the summit (6 M.) is easily reached on horseback or on foot. **Mt. Diablo** (3855 ft.), a conspicuous object for many miles round and well seen from San Francisco (28 M. distant as the crow flies), commands a very extensive *View*, including the valleys of the Sacramento to the N. and the San Joaquin to the S., the Sierra Nevada from Lassen's Peak on the N. to Mt. Whitney on the S. (325 M.), the Coast Range, and San Francisco.

Sonoma (*Union Hotel*, $2), a city of 1200 inhab., in the *Sonoma Valley*, to the N. of *San Pablo Bay*, is interesting as one of the chief seats of the Californian vine-culture. The wine is kept in tunnels excavated in the hills of volcanic sandstone. Sonoma is reached by railway (43 M.) from *Tiburon* (p. 433) or by stage (15 M.), from *Napa* (see above).

Californian Wine (communicated). — Wine-making in California dates from an early period, the European vine having been brought here by the early missionaries. No record has been found of the date of the event, nor can the species introduced be identified with any known sort.

It was probably brought from one of the Balearic Isles, the first missionaries having all been Catalans from Majorca, or it was, perhaps, a seedling raised on the spot. However this may be, it had attained a wide diffusion before the transfer of the country to the United States and was then found growing at almost all the Missions. Its fruit is abundant and quite palatable for the table, but makes a strong heady wine, not suited to the demands of commerce, though popular enough among a pastoral people, whose lives were spent out of doors and largely in the saddle. The first effort of the American emigration to improve the native wines did not meet with a distinguished success. They reasoned, justly enough, that California had within her borders every variety of soil and a climate decidedly superior to that of any part of Europe, because free from the unseasonable storms and inopportune frosts which so affect the viticulturists of the old world. They were, however, ignorant that besides soil and climate it was indispensable, in order to make a good wine, to have the proper sorts of grapes; for a fine wine can no more be made from a vulgar grape than the proverbial 'silk purse from a sow's ear'. In fact the most eminent French authority on the subject lays down the rule broadly that '*the brand of the wine is in the grape*'. The distinctive character of the wine of Burgundy is derived from the Pinot grape; and, in like manner, those of the Rhine, the Moselle, and the Medoc derive their essential characteristics from the particular sorts of grapes cultivated in those districts. But while the character of the wine depends on the grape from which it is made, its quality, within the range of that defined character, depends on soil, situation, exposure, and climate. All this is now recognized as elementary truth, but was little known even a decade ago.

The Germans were the first to improve the native wines. Finding the Mission grape did not make a wine suited to their national taste, they, at an early date, imported scions of the favorite stocks of their own country and propagated them. As a rule the Germans make white wine, and their choice of sorts was limited to those appropriate for such. Hence the white wines of California experienced a marked improvement twenty years ago, while her red wines continued to be still made of the mission grape. The late Col. Harasthy introduced many years since the Zinfandel and some other European vines for the production of red wine, but they were all what the French term '*cépages d'abondance*'. i. e. sorts which produced large crops. With the grape, however, as with many other things, quantity and quality go in inverse proportion. The Zinfandel grape was extensively propagated and became popular, for it was a decided improvement on the mission sort, had the advantage of being an early and abundant bearer, and made a wine which matured in two years. To the immigrants from the South of Europe — Frenchmen, Spaniards, Italians, Greeks, Dalmatians, etc., of whom such large numbers are to be found on the Pacific Coast — it was quite a boon, for it supplied them with their accustomed beverage, at a reasonable price, and it came just at the time when the devastations of the phyloxera in France rendered it almost impossible to obtain any ordinary claret of that country pure. Within the limits of the domestic demand, too, its production was profitable, by reason of its bountiful crops. But that limit was rigidly fixed. The product of the Zinfandel grape is essentially a peasant's wine; its consumption cannot be indefinitely extended by mere cheapness. No converts were ever made from whiskey or beer to wine by such a beverage, and those accustomed to the use of wine as a luxury — consumers of the better sorts of French wines — found it decidedly unpalatable. Hence production soon trod closely on the heels of consumption, and erelong outstripped it. For some years there has been no profit in the industry.

Meantime about 1880 and 1881 intelligent Americans had their attention directed to viticulture, and erelong learned, as the Germans had learned before them, with respect to white wines, that to make red wines, fit to compete with the products of the French vineyards, the first requirement was to have the proper sorts of grapes. They accordingly began about the date mentioned to import and propagate the sorts from which the

28*

great wines of France are made, and from that period dates the marked improvement of California red wines. A characteristic of these grapes, however, is the largely enhanced expense of cultivating them, the smallness of their crops, and the length of time necessary to bring their wine to maturity and render it fairly potable; so that the cost of the wine to the producer is enhanced in a degree quite proportioned to its increased value. The wine dealers who have become accustomed to the cheap blends made on a Zinfandel base are averse to the burden of carrying stocks for four or five years without an assured return for enlarged rents, quadrupled stocks of cooperage, and quadrupled care in handling. From this cause those in quest of the best California wines — especially red wines — have to seek them in the hands of the producers.

The principal districts of the state in which the vine has been extensively cultivated are: 1. The plain of which *Los Angeles* may be considered the centre and which was the centre of population in Spanish and Mexican days; 2. The *San Joaquin Valley;* 4. *Napa and Sonoma Counties,* to the N. of San Francisco Bay; 4. *Santa Clara County,* with the adjoining mountains of Santa Cruz to the S. of it. The Los Angeles and San Joaquin Valleys, from their great heat, are best able to produce wines of the Spanish and Portuguese types. From the proper sorts of grapes, grown in these districts, are made very fair ports and sherries, while brandy and very fine raisins are also produced there in considerable quantities. In Napa and Sonoma the vine is extensively cultivated, and excellent white wines of the Rhenish type are made. The prevailing use of the Zinfandel grape is, however, hostile to the production of red wines of any high quality, while the extensive diffusion of the phyloxera in both those counties threatens the extinction of the industry within a moderate time. The Santa Cruz mountains, and especially the adjoining foot-hills in Santa Clara County, are producing quite a considerable amount of excellent wine of the Bordeaux type, both red and white. Bordeaux stocks have been imported and extensively planted, and the local situation resembles so strikingly that of the Medoc as to suggest a natural correspondence in products. In fact Santa Clara and the S. part of San Mateo counties are thrust out between the waters of the Ocean and those of the Bay of San Francisco just as the Medoc is between the Bay of Biscay and the estuary of the Garonne, and the tempering effects of these large bodies of water on the climate and vegetation of the intermediate tongue of land must constitute an important factor in the quality of the viticultural products.

The production of wine in the State, according to the reports of the State Viticultural Commission. rose from about 4,000,000 gallons in 1877 to 22,000.000 gallons in 1890, declining again to 12,500,000 gallons in 1892.

94. From San Francisco to San José, Santa Cruz, and Monterey.

a. Viâ Standard-Gauge Railway.

SOUTHERN PACIFIC RAILWAY to (50 M.) *San José* in 2 hrs. (fare $1.25; parlor-car 25 c.); to (121 M.) *Santa Cruz* in 4-4¹/₂ hrs. ($3); to (125 M.) *Monterey* in 4-4¹/₂ hrs. ($3).

This excursion should not be omitted by any visitor to San Francisco. It is advisable to go one way and return the other; and in any case the section of the narrow-gauge railway between San José and Santa Cruz should be included. Perhaps the best plan is to go to *Monterey* (p. 439) by the standard-gauge railway, stopping off for visits to *Palo Alto* (p. 437), *San José* (p. 438), etc.; return viâ *Pajaro* (p. 439) to *Santa Cruz* (p. 441); drive thence to the *Big Trees* (p. 441); and thence take the narrowgauge line back to San Francisco. The drives across the *Sierra Morena* (see p. 437) are well worth taking.

San Francisco, see p. 428. The train starts from the station at the corner of 4th and Townsend Sts. (p. 428), stops again at the corner

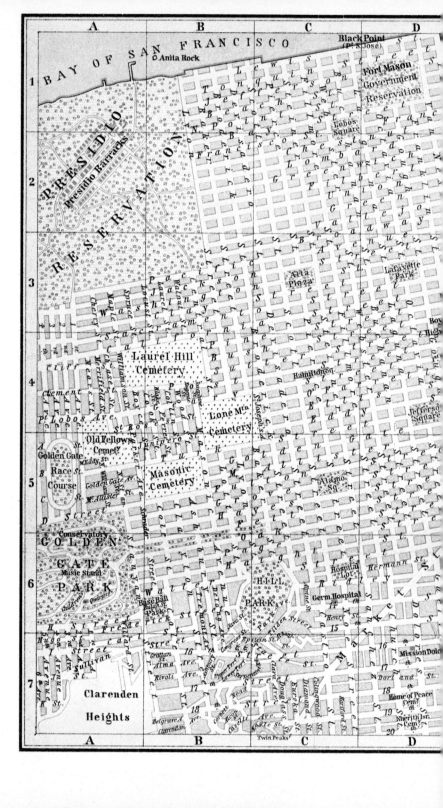

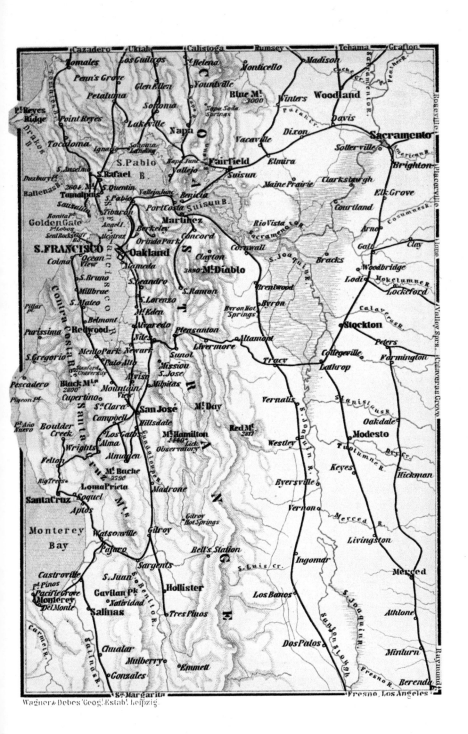

of 26th and Valencia Sts., and soon leaves the city behind. At (7 M.) *Ocean View* (290 ft.) we see the *Pacific Ocean* to the right. About 3 M. beyond (9 M.) *Colma*, a small wayside station, *San Francisco Bay*, which we skirt for 30 M., comes into view on the left. 12 M. *Baden;* 14 M. *San Bruno;* 17 M. *Millbrae*, with the large country-house of Mr. D. O. Mills (right). — 21 M. *San Mateo*, a pleasant little town, embosomed in live-oaks, is the starting-point of a stage-line to (32 M.) *Pescadero* (through-fare $3.10).

The road to Pescadero crosses the *Sierra Morena* (views), passing the interesting old village of *Spanishtown*. The *Cliffs at *Gordon's Landing* tower 250 ft. above the sea, recalling the Shakespeare Cliff at Dover. — **Pescadero** (*Swanton Ho.*, $1¹/₂-2), a small village on the Pacific coast, at the mouth of *Pescadero Valley*, is famous for its *Pebble Beach*, on which agates, opals, jaspers, and other similar stones are found.

25 M. *Belmont.* — 28 M. *Redwood* (Price's Hotel), so named from the trees in the timber of which it does its principal trade. A fine road runs hence across the Sierra Morena to *San Gregorio*, traversing a splendid redwood forest (*Views). — 32 M. **Menlo Park** (*Menlo Park Hotel, Oak Villa*, from $2) is a favourite residence of the wealthy merchants of San Francisco and contains many fine houses, surrounded by beautifully laid out grounds and noble trees. Beyond Menlo Park the red roofs of the *Stanford University* (see below) may be seen to the right. — 33 M. *Palo Alto* (Palo Alto taking its name ('tall tree') from a fine redwood to the left of Hotel), the railway, is the nearest station to the (1 M.) *University*.

*Leland Stanford Jr. University, founded by Mr. and Mrs. Leland Stanford in memory of their only son and endowed by them with upwards of $30,000,000 (6,000,000*l*.), was opened in Oct., 1891, with a staff of about 40 instructors and an attendance of 550 students, of whom 150 were women. It is finely situated on the Palo Alto stock-farm (a tract of 8400 acres, deeded to the University), on a plain near the foot of the coast mountains. The buildings were mainly designed by *H. H. Richardson*, who took the *motif* of their architecture from the cloisters of the San Antonio Mission. The material is buff, rough-faced sandstone, surmounted by red-tiled roofs, producing brilliant effects of colour in conjunction with the live oak, white oak, and eucalyptus trees outside, the tropical plants in the quadrangle, and the blue sky overhead. The main buildings at present form a low quadrangle, enclosing a court 586 ft. long and 246 ft. wide, the buildings of which are connected on the inner side by a beautiful colonnade; and there are besides two dormitories, an art museum, a mechanical department, and a little village of professors' houses. The completed scheme includes an outer, two-storied quadrangle, with cloisters on the outside, a memorial arch, and a chapel with a Richardsonesque tower. — Near the University are the celebrated *Palo Alto Stables and Paddocks* (Mr. Stanford's), where 1100 fine trotting horses and 500 running horses may be seen. Among the most famous horses bred at this stud are *Sunol* (who trotted a mile in 2 min. 7¹/₂ sec.), *Palo Alto* (2.8³/₄), *Arion, Electioneer, Electricity*, and *Advertiser*. The success of the Palo Alto stud is without parallel in the history of trotting horses.

39 M. *Mountain View* is the nearest station to (6 M.) *Cupertino*, the vineyard of Mr. John T. Doyle, where one of the finest red wines in California is produced *(Las Palmas)*. The railway now follows the *Santa Clara Valley*, one of the fairest and most fertile valleys in California, sheltered on either hand by mountains. Large quan-

tities of fruit (esp. grapes, prunes, and peaches) and wheat are grown here. At *Agnews*, as we approach Santa Clara, a large *Insane Asylum* is seen to the left.

47 M. **Santa Clara** (70 ft.; *Arguello Ho.*, $1¹/₂), a pretty little town with 2891 inhab., is the seat of *Santa Clara College*, a large institution founded by the Jesuits in 1851 and including a church belonging to an old mission of 1777 (150-200 students). Santa Clara is connected with (3 M.) San José (see below) by the **Alameda*, a fine avenue of willows, planted by the Mission Fathers in 1799 and now traversed by an electric tramway (fare 10 c.). It is well worth while, especially in the rose season, to leave the train at Santa Clara and drive (carr. or tramway) through the Alameda to San José.

50 M. **San José** ('Hosay'; 90 ft.; **Hotel Vendome*, with pleasant grounds and sun-parlour, $3-4; *St. James*, $2-2¹/₂; *Lick Ho.*, $2; *Auzerais*, E. P.), a beautiful little city of 18,060 inhab., is of importance as the chief place in the fruitful Santa Clara valley (see p. 437) and is also frequented on account of its delightful climate. The most conspicuous building is the *Court House*, the dome of which affords an extensive *View, including the Calaveras Mts. (with Mt. Hamilton) to the E., the Santa Cruz Mts. to the S., the Contra Costa Mts. to the W., and San Francisco Bay to the N. The *City Hall* and *Post Office* are large buildings. San José also contains several good schools and colleges.

San José is the starting-point for (26 M.) *Lick Observatory*, on Mt. Hammilton. Stages start every morning (except Sun.) and reach the Observatory about 1.30 p.m., halting 1 hr. and regaining San José at 6 p.m. (return-fare $3). On Sat., when visitors are allowed to look through the great telescope between 7 and 10 p.m., the stage starts at about 1 p.m. and returns about 9 or 10 p.m. (return-fare $5). Parties of four or more should hire a private carriage. The road, though uphill nearly all the way, is so well made and easily graded that a fair rate of speed is maintained, while the beautiful and ever-varying views prevent weariness. Innumerable wild-flowers line the way, while the manzanita, live oaks, and other trees are also interesting. The Observatory is in sight most of the time. We cross two intervening ridges. About 7 M. from San José we pass near the mouth of the *Penitencia Cañon* (so called because the monks of the San José Mission kept their retreats here), which has been reserved as a city park and contains *Alum Rock* and several mineral springs (Hotel). On crossing the second of the intervening ridges, we descend into *Smith's Creek* (2145 ft.), where a halt is generally made for dinner (75 c.) at the small hotel. The hotel lies at the base of Mt. Hamilton, 1¹/₂ M. from the Observatory in a direct line (footpath), but 7 M. by the road, which is said to make 365 bends. Visitors sometimes spend Sat. night here and return to San José on Sun. morning. — The *Lick Observatory (director, *Prof. Edward S. Holden*), founded with a legacy of $700,000 (140,000 *l.*) left by the late *Mr. James Lick* (1798-1876) of San Francisco, stands on the summit of *Mt. Hamilton* (4210 ft.), and is in point of situation, equipment, and achievement one of the leading observatories of the world. The *Great Telescope* is the largest and most powerful refracting telescope in existence; its object-glass, 36 inches in diameter, was made by Alvan Clark of Cambridge (p. 85). Mr. Lick is buried in the foundation-pier of the telescope. Visitors are received courteously at the Observatory and shown all the objects of interest (10-4, Sat. 7-10 in the evening; no admission on Sun.), but there is no inn or restaurant nearer than Smith Creek. The **View from the Observatory is very extensive, sometimes including wonderful effects of cloud and mist. It embraces, on a clear day, the Sierra Nevada, the Pacific Ocean, Santa Clara Valley, Angel Island (p. 433), Mt. San Bruno (p. 433), and Mt. Tamalpais (p. 433). Loma Prieta (see p. 441) is conspicuous to the S. Comp. 'Handbook of the Lick Observatory', by *E. S. Holden*.

About 13 M. to the S. of San José, in a spur of the coast range, are the interesting *Almaden Quicksilver Mines*, which may now be reached by railway (fare 35 c.). — An excursion may be made to the *Pacific Congress Springs* (700 ft.) 10 M. to the S.W. (6 M. from Los Gatos, p. 440), which are beneficial in rheumatism.

If they prefer, visitors may change carriages at San José and proceed to Santa Cruz viâ the narrow-gauge railway (comp. p. 440).

Beyond San José the *Lick Observatory* (see above), on the top of *Mt. Hamilton*, is seen to the left. 55 M. *Hillsdale* (150 ft.); 69 M. *Madrone* (340 ft.), 6 M. to the W. of the *Madrone Springs;* 80 M. *Gilroy* (190 ft.; Southern Pacific Hotel, $2) a busy little city of 1694 inhab., 14 M. to the W. of the frequented *Gilroy Springs* (stage daily). Beyond Gilroy the line goes on S. to (94 M.) *Hollister* and (101 M.) *Tres Piños*. Our line, however, turns to the right (W.) and runs towards the coast. 87 M. *Sargent's.* — 99 M. *Pajaro* ('Paharo'; 25 ft.) is the junction of the lines to *Santa Cruz* (right) and *Monterey* (left). For the journey from Pajaro to (121 M.) *Santa Cruz*, see p. 441, where it is described in the reverse direction.

The train to Monterey runs towards the S.W. 110 M. *Castroville* is the junction of a line running to the S. to (116 M.) *Santa Margarita*.

Among the chief places on this line are (33 M.) *Soledad*, with the remains of a mission, founded in 1791 (of no great interest); 62 M. *San Lucas;* 97 M. *San Miquel*, with a mission of 1797; and (106 M.) **El Paso de Robles** ('Pass of the Oaks': 720 ft.; *Hotel*, $2-4), frequented for its hot sulphur springs (95-110° Fahr.) and mud baths (122° Fabr.), which are good for rheumatism, gout, and cutaneous affections.

From *Santa Margarita* a stage runs daily to (10 M.; through-fare $7) **San Luis Obispo** (*Hotel Ramona*, $2-3), a pleasant little city of 2995 inhab., in the midst of a fine grazing country. It is the site of an old *Mission*, founded in 1772. San Luis Obispo is connected by the *Pacific Coast Railway* with (10 M.) *Port Harford*, which has regular steamer communication with San Francisco. To the S. this railway runs to (32 M.) *Santa Maria*, *Los Alamos* (54 M.), and (66 M.) *Los Olivos*, whence it is intended to prolong it to *Santa Barbara* (p. 444).

124 M. *Del Monte*, the station for the (1/3 M.) *Hotel Del Monte* (see p. 440). — 125 M. **Monterey** (*Hotel del Monte, see p. 440, $3-4; *Alta Vista*, $1 1/2-2; *El Carmelo*, at *Pacific Grove*, see p. 440, $2), situated on the S. side of the *Bay of Monterey*, 85 M. from San Francisco by sea, is one of the quaintest and most interesting towns in California (1662 inhab., largely of Spanish blood).

Its site was visited by the Spaniards in 1602, but it was not until 1770 that the *Mission de San Carlo de Monterey* was founded on this spot. Monterey was the capital of California until its conquest by the Americans in 1846, and with the removal of the seat of government went the commercial importance and life of the little town, which is now one of the quietest places in the State. It is, however, extensively visited on account of its balmy climate (warm in winter and cool in summer; mean temp. of Jan. ca. 50°, of June, July, and Aug. 60-64°), its beautiful sandy beach, and its charming surroundings. Many of its buildings are of adobé. Some remains of the old Spanish fort still remain, while the Roman Catholic Church occupies the site of the Mission, which was removed to Carmelo Valley in 1771 (see p. 440).

The *Hotel del Monte ('Hotel of the Forest'), one of the most comfortable, best-kept, and most moderate-priced hotels in America, lies in the midst of exquisite *Grounds, in some ways recalling the fine country-parks of England, though, of course, the vegetation is very different. Among the noble old trees which surround it are innumerable live-oaks and Monterey pines and cypresses, while the *Gardens offer a continual feast of colour. One section of the gardens, known as 'Arizona', is devoted to cacti of all kinds, and in another part of the grounds is a *Maze* of cypress hedges. A little to the N. of the hotel is the pretty little boating lake named the *Laguna del Rey*, while on the beach, ¹/₂ M. from the hotel, is a large *Bathing House*, including four swimming-basins. Nearly opposite the hotel is the *Hotel del Monte Club House*.

The chief excursion from Monterey is the so-called **Seventeen Mile Drive**, leading round the peninsula on which the town lies. As we leave the town, going towards the W., we see, on the hill to the left, a *Statue of Padre Junipero Serra*, the founder of the Mission, erected in 1891. To the right is the *Bay of Monterey*, with its white sandy beach. About 1 M. beyond Monterey is the summer settlement of *Pacific Grove* (El Carmelo Hotel, see p. 439), to which the railway has been extended. In 1 M. more we pass near the lighthouse on *Point Piños*, the S. headland of the Bay of Monterey, and turn to the left. The next part of the road lies mainly through trees, passing not far from the little *Lake Majella*. To the right is the *Moss Beach* (fine algæ, or sea-mosses). Farther on we have a fine unimpeded view of the Pacific Ocean, and about 7 M. from Monterey reach the *Seal Rocks*, where we enjoy a spectacle similar to that at p. 432. Another mile brings us to *Cypress Point*, with its flat, umbrella-like Monterey cypresses (*Cupressus macrocarpa*), a singular, crooked, mis-shapen tree indigenous to this locality. Beyond Cypress Point the road runs to the E., passing *Pebble Beach*, where agates, etc., may be picked up; *Chinese Cove*, with a small Chinese settlement; the nucleus of a small *Zoological Garden* (grizzly bear, buffaloes, etc.); and the sandy *Pescadero Beach*. The road then turns to the left (N.), and a short digression may be made to the right, to visit the old *Carmelo Mission*, where the original church has lately been supplied with a new roof. The remainder of the drive (5 M.) runs through wood.

Good fishing is obtained in the *Carmelo River* (reserved for guests of the Hotel del Monte), as well as in the bay. Deer and quail shooting may be enjoyed in the adjacent woods and mountains.

b. Viâ the Narrow-Gauge Railway.

FERRY to (9 M.) *Alameda;* RAILWAY thence to (43 M.) *San José* (fare $1.25, chair-car 25 c.), *Santa Cruz* (80 M.; $2.80), and (128 M.) *Monterey* ($3). Comp. remarks at p. 436.

From *San Francisco* to (3 M.) *Alameda Mole* and (9 M.) *Alameda*, see p. 434. The line skirts the E. shore of *San Francisco Bay* (views to right). 16 M. *San Lorenzo;* 24 M. *Alvarado;* 29 M. *Newark.* At (37 M.) *Alviso* we reach the smiling *Valley of Santa Clara* (p. 437). 43 M. *Santa Clara* (p. 438). — 46 M. **San José**, see p. 438.

The most picturesque part of the line soon begins now, as it ascends over the *Santa Cruz Mts.* (views). 55 M. *Los Gatos* ('The Cats'; 400 ft.), a pretty little town on the E. slope of the mountains, lies in the warm belt and grows oranges successfully. Farther on we ascend through a cañon with fine rock-scenery and towering redwood trees. 58 M. *Alma* (560 ft.); 61 M. *Forest Grove.* From (62 M.) *Wright's* (900 ft.) we descend rapidly, through similar scenery, towards the coast. 74 M. *Felton* (275 ft.). — 75 M. *Big Trees* (270 ft.), the station for the famous *Big Trees of Santa Cruz.

This grove (adm. 25 c.) contains about a score of the genuine *Redwood* (*Sequoia sempervirens;* comp. p. 452) with a diameter of 10 ft. and upwards. The largest is 23 ft. across; one of the finest, named the *Pioneer*, has a circumference of 70 ft. A large hollow tree is shown in which Gen. Fremont camped for several days in 1847. Another stump is covered with an arbour, which holds 12-14 people.

77 M. *Rincon* (300 ft.), 80 M. *Santa Cruz;* 81 M. *Santa Cruz Beach.*

Santa Cruz (*Pacific Ocean Ho.*, $2^1/_2$-3; *Pope Ho.*; *Sea Beach Ho.*, $2, at the beach, 1 M. from the town), a small city of 5596 inhab., is pleasantly situated at the N. end of the *Bay of Monterey* (p. 439) and is a favourite summer-resort. Its attractions include an excellent bathing-beach, fine cliffs, good fishing, caves and recesses abounding in sea-anemones, beautiful flower-gardens, and picturesque surroundings. A fine drive, affording splendid *Views of forest and mountain scenery, may be made to the (5 M.) *Big Trees* (see above). The town originated in the *Mission de la Santa Cruz* (1791).

The train for Monterey runs towards the S., passing *Santa Cruz Beach* (see above), to (86 M.) *Capitola* and (89 M.) *Aptos*, two other resorts on Monterey Bay. To the left rises the pointed *Loma Prieta* ('Black Mt'; 3790 ft.), one of the loftiest of the Santa Cruz Mts. At (102 M.) *Pajaro* we join the line described at p. 439.

95. From San Francisco to Los Angeles and Santa Barbara.

Southern Pacific Railway to (482 M.) *Los Angeles* in 22 hrs. (fare $15; sleeper $2.50); to (538 M.) *Santa Barbara* in 27 hrs. (same fares). Santa Barbara may also be reached by steamer direct (438 M.) or by a combination of railway-travelling and staging viâ Santa Margarita, San Luis Obispo, and Los Olivos (comp. p. 444). Los Angeles may be reached by steamer to (389 M.) San Pedro and railway (22 M.) thence (see p. 446).

From *San Francisco*, viâ *Oakland*, to (32 M.) *Porta Costa*, see p. 399. 36 M. *Martinez*, the usual starting-point for an ascent of *Mt. Diablo* (see p. 434), which rises to the right. At (50 M.) *Cornwall* we leave the *Suisun Bay* (p. 399) and turn towards the S. About 2 M. to the S. of (68 M.) *Byron* are the *Byron Hot Springs* (130° Fahr.; Hotel, $2-3). 83 M. *Tracy* (65 ft.) is the junction of the old route to San Francisco viâ *Livermore* and *Niles*. A little farther on we cross the *San Joaquin* ('Wahkeen') and reach (94 M.) *Lathrop* (25 ft.; Hotel, with rail. restaurant, $2-3, meal 75 c.), the junction of the old line to *Sacramento* viâ *Stockton* (comp. R. 87). We now ascend the great **San Joaquin Valley**, the granary of California, 200 M. long and 30 M. wide, producing endless crops of grain and fruit, including oranges, figs, and olives. 114 M. *Modesto* (90 ft.; 2402 inhab.); 152 M. *Merced* (170 ft.; 2000 inhab.). Various rivers are crossed. — 178 M. *Berenda* (255 ft.) is the junction of a branch-line to (22 M.) *Raymond*, forming the usual approach to the *Yosemite Valley* (see R. 99). The *Sierra Nevada* is visible to the left, including Mts. Lyell (13,040 ft.), Tyndall (ca. 14,000 ft.), Whitney (14,898 ft.), and

Goddard (ca. 14,000 ft.). — 185 M. *Madera* (280 ft.), a shipping-point for timber, brought from the mountains by a 'flume', 50 M. long. Near (197 M.) *Herndon* we cross the San Joaquin. — 207 M. **Fresno** (290 ft.; *Hughes Ho.*, $2¹/₂-3), a city with 10,818 inhab., is the centre of a large raisin-growing district, which in 1891 produced 1200 car-loads of raisins, valued at $1,500,000. The water necessary for irrigation is brought from the mountains by an extensive system of canals.

¶ |From Fresno a branch-line runs to (20 M.) *Sanger Junction*, the nearest station to the new **Sequoia National Park,** which lies in the High Sierra, 40 M. to the E. of the railway, and contains splendid forests of sequoias, besides most remarkable gorges, peaks, and caverns. This will probably become a popular resort when access to it is made easier. A tri-weekly stage runs from Sanger Junction to (45 M.) *Sequoia Mills.*

At (227 M.) *Kingsbury* (300 ft.) we cross the *King's River* by a trestle-bridge. 241 M. *Goshen* (285 ft.), the junction of a line to (60 M.) *Alcalde.* — 251 M. **Tulare** (280 ft.; *Grand Hotel*), a flourishing little town with 2697 inh. and a large trade in agricultural produce. The irrigation in this district is largely provided by artesian wells, the windmills of which are seen in all directions.

About 7 M. to the W. of (262 M.) *Tipton* (265 ft.) lies *Tulare Lake* (30 M. long and 25 M. wide). 282 M. *Delano;* 314 M. *Bakersfield* (415 ft.; 2626 inhab.). At (336 M.) *Caliente* (1290 ft.) we leave the San Joaquin Valley and begin to ascend the ***Tehachapi Pass,** which crosses the Sierra Nevada between this valley and the Desert of Mojave. The construction of the railway here is a very remarkable piece of engineering. The line winds backwards and forwards and finally, at the *Loop (3050 ft.), crosses its own track, at a height of about 80 ft. above the tunnel it has just threaded. Eight other short tunnels are passed through before the summit is gained at (362 M.) *Tehachapi* (4025 ft.), beyond which the train runs along a plateau for some miles, passing a small salt lake, before beginning the descent to the desert. 371 M. *Cameron* (3785 ft.).

382 M. **Mojave** ('Mohavé'; 2750 ft.; *Rail. Hotel,* $3), the junction of the *Atlantic and Pacific Railroad* (see p. 414), is a handful of wooden shanties on the edge of the cheerless *Mojave Desert* described at p. 414. The Los Angeles line runs towards the S. across the desert, forming an almost absolutely straight line for many miles. *Old Baldy* (p. 447) is seen in front, to the left, while the *San Bernardino Mts.* are faintly seen on the horizon (farther to the left). 396 M. *Rosamond* (2315 ft.). Beyond 407 M. *Lancaster* (2350 ft.) we quit the desert for a hilly and rocky country, passing through several short tunnels and crossing the *Soledad Pass* (3200 ft.). 417 M. *Harold* (2820 ft.); 427 M. *Acton* (2670 ft.). We now descend steadily, through cuttings and over bridges.

450 M. **Saugus** (1160 ft.) is the junction for the line to Santa Barbara (see below).

The Los Angeles line runs towards the S. and beyond (452 M.)

Newhall (Hotel) penetrates the *San Fernando Mts.* (ca. 3000 ft.) by a tunnel $1^1/_4$ M. long (1470 ft. above the sea). The *Valley of San Fernando*, which we now enter, is green with orange and olive groves and forms a strong contrast to the desert we have been traversing. 463 M. *Fernando* (1068 ft.); 475 M. *Sepulveda* (460 ft.).

482 M. **Los Angeles** (290 ft.), see R. 96.

FROM SAUGUS TO SANTA BARBARA AND ELWOOD. This line runs at first slightly to the N. of W. and descends towards the sea through the *Santa Clara Valley* (not to be confounded with that described at p. 437), with high mountains on either hand in varied and contorted forms. Numerous orchards and orange-groves are passed. To the left at first flows the *Santa Clara River.* 465 M. *Camulos* (285 ft.) was the home of 'Ramona' (see the story of that name by H. H.), and the ranch in which she was brought up may be seen to the left. We cross and leave the river near (468 M.) *Piru.* — 486 M. **Santa Paula** (285 ft.; *Pretolia Hotel*, $1^1/_2$-2), a busy little place with 1047 inhab., is the centre of the petroleum region of California. Coal also has been found in the vicinity. Fine orange-groves. — The hills now recede and the valley widens to a plain. The ocean comes into sight near (493 M.) *Saticoy* (145 ft.). The line turns to the right (N.). Distant islands are seen to the left, while the coast-hills rise to the right.

502 M. **San Buenaventura** (45 ft.; *Rose*, $3; *Anacapa*, $2-2^1/_2$; *Santa Clara Ho.*, $2), a city of 2320 inhab., pleasantly situated at the mouth of the valley of the *Ventura*, is the outlet of a fertile grain and fruit growing region and carries on a considerable trade in timber. It is also frequented as a health-resort. A Spanish mission was founded here in 1782; its present church dates from 1809.

Stage-coaches (fare $1) run from San Buenaventura to *Nordhoff* (Oak Glen Cottages), in the beautiful *Ojai* **Valley** ('Ohigh'), situated 15 M. to the N.W., at a height of 600-1200 ft. above the sea and surrounded by an amphitheatre of mountains, of which *Mt. Topotapa* (6000 ft.) is the chief. The valley is a favourite winter-resort for invalids, and is, perhaps, the best place in California for wild flowers.

Beyond San Buenaventura the train runs close to the sea, the mountains at places barely leaving room for its passage (views to the left). 517 M. *Carpinteria;* 521 M. *Ortega;* 524 M. *Montecito* (p. 444).

532 M. **Santa Barbara** (*Arlington*, $2-4; *San Marcos*, from $2; *Commercial*, $2), a city of 5864 inhab., the 'American Mentone', is charmingly situated on the coast-plain, at the base of the foot-hills, with the *Santa Ynez Mts.*, a little farther off, forming a fine screen against the cold N. and W. winds. It has a well-deserved reputation as one of the most attractive winter-resorts in California, due to its mild, dry, and equable climate (mean temp., winter 50-55°, summer 65-70°), the beauty of its surroundings, the luxuriance of its roses and other flowers, the excellent bathing beach, and its pleasant society. The main street, 2 M. long, is paved with asphalt and lined with substantial business blocks. Most of the private houses are surrounded

by delightful gardens. The chief lion of the place is the old *Mission,
founded by Padre Junipero Serra (p. 440) in 1786. It lies on a hill
³/₄ M. to the N. of the town and may be reached by following the
tramway which diverges to the right from Main St. at the Arlington
Hotel. The end of the tramway-line is near the Mission, with its
colonnaded front, red roof, and two-towered church.

Visitors are admitted 8.30-11 and 2-4, Sun. 3.30-4.30 (women to the
church only; small fee expected). The points shown include the plain,
whitewashed church (containing a few paintings), refectory, dormitory, and
garden. About a dozen of the old Franciscan monks still remain. The Mission commands a splendid *View (best from the church-tower) of Santa
Barbara and the Pacific, with the islands in the background. On the wall
about 100 yds. behind the Mission is a sun-dial with the inscription: 'Lux
dei vitæ vitam monstrat sed umbra horam atque fidem docet'.

After visiting the Mission we may ascend the picturesque *Mission Cañon*
behind it, crossing the bridge and turning to the left (sign-post 'Up the
Cañon'). The cañon contains some pretty waterfalls.

An excellent *View of the town, the ocean, the islands, the coast,
and the mountains is obtained from the pretty grounds of *Mr. Dibley's
House*, on the height to the W. of the bay (visitors freely admitted).

In a pretty valley, 4 M. to the E. of Santa Barbara, lies **Montecito**
(comp. p. 443), with numerous beautiful gardens. In one of these is *La
Parra Grande*, or the Great Vine, which covers a trellis 60 ft. square. has
a trunk 4 ft. in diameter, and produces annually 8000 lbs. of grapes (four
or five times as much as the famous vine at Hampton Court). The vine
is of the Mission variety (p. 435). — On a hill about 1 M. to the E. of
Montecito (sign-boards) are the *Hot Springs* (1400 ft.; temp. 114-118°), whence
a climb of ¹/₄ hr. brings us to *Point Look Out*, commanding one of the finest
views in the neighbourhood. — The *San Ysidro Ranche*, about 1 M. beyond
Montecito, has fine orange and lemon groves. — *La Piedra Pintada* ('painted
rock'), an interesting relic of aboriginal art, is on the Santa Ynez Mts.,
near the head of Montecito Valley.

Among other fine points near Santa Barbara are *Sycamore Cañon* (2 M.),
Bartlett's Cañon (10 M.), *Glen Annie* (13 M.), the *Cathedral Oaks* (6 M.), *Goleta*
(8 M.), *Ortega Hill* (5 M.), *Hollister's Ranche* (12 M.), with a beautiful avenue
of date-palms, *Cooper's Ranche* (15 M.), with a large olive-grove, and *Santa
Cruz Valley* (15 M.), with two old missions. Near the town we may notice
the Chinese vegetable gardens, the fields of Pampas grass (cultivated for
its plumes), and the groves of walnut. Flowers grow here most luxuriantly;
at a flower-show in Santa Barbara 160 varieties of roses were exhibited,
all cut from one garden the same morning. — The curious nest of the
Trapdoor Spider is often found near Santa Barbara.

OCEAN YACHTS make excursions, on a usually perfectly calm sea, to
various points on the coast and to the islands of *Santa Cruz* (26 M.) and
Santa Rosa (31 M.). The former is the larger of the two and is inhabited
by a few farmers. The beautiful *Abalone* shells are found in great abundance on these islands. — In the bed of the ocean, about 10 M. to the N.W.
of Santa Barbara and 1¹/₂ M. from shore, is a huge spring of petroleum, the
oil from which may be seen floating on the surface in calm weather.

STEAMERS ply regularly from Santa Barbara to *San Francisco* (p. 428),
San Diego (p. 449), *San Pedro* (p. 446), etc.

A STAGE runs daily from Santa Barbara to the N. to (45 M.) *Los Olivos*
(p. 439), starting about 8 a.m., stopping for dinner at the *Home Station*
(75 c.), and arriving about 4.30 p.m. (office at the Commercial Hotel; fare $ 4).
This fine route, crossing the *Santa Ynez Mts.* by the *San Marcos Pass*, is a
pleasant way of returning to San Francisco for those who do not wish to
go over the same ground twice.

Beyond Santa Barbara the railway goes on to (14 M.) *Elwood*,
whence it is intended to extend it to *Los Olivos* (p. 439).

96. Los Angeles.

Railway Stations. *Southern Pacific*, Fifth St.; *Southern California*, Santa Fé Ave.; *Los Angeles Terminal*, E. First St.; *Redondo*, cor. of Jefferson St. and Grand Ave., in the S.W. part of the city.

Hotels. *Hollenbeck*, from $3, R. from $1; *Westminster*, from $2¹/₂, R. from $1; *Nadeau*, $2¹/₂, R. from $1; *Hoffman*, $1¹/₂-2. — *Illich's Restaurant.*

Tramways (5 c.) traverse the chief streets and run to the suburbs.

Post Office, Main St., near Fifth St.

Los Angeles (g soft), or *La Puebla de la Reina de Los Angeles* ('City of the Queen of the Angels'), the metropolis of Southern California, lies on the *Los Angeles River*, 20 M. above its mouth and 15 M. in a direct line from the Pacific Ocean. It was founded by the Spaniards in 1781 and passed into American possession in 1846. It was, however, of no great importance till the ninth decade of the present century, when it underwent an almost unprecedentedly rapid increase in wealth and population. Its population rose from 11,183 in 1880 to 50,395 in 1890, and its adobé houses have given place almost entirely to stone and brick business blocks and tasteful wooden residences.

Los Angeles is a railway-centre of great importance and is the headquarters of the characteristic Californian industry of fruit-growing. The plains and valleys around it are covered with vineyards, orange-groves, and orchards. The total value of the fruit produced in S. California in 1891 was $6,000,000, and the value of the oranges exported from Los Angeles alone amounted $1,250,000. Los Angeles is also the centre of a district that produces petroleum and asphalt.

Though less specifically a health resort than some other places in Southern California, Los Angeles enjoys a mild and equable climate, with a tendency to coolness at night (mean annual temp., Jan. 52°, Aug. 70°). The city, especially the residential quarters, is embowered in vegetation, among the characteristic features of which are the swift-growing eucalyptus, graceful pepper-trees, an occasional palm, Norfolk Island pines, live-oaks, india-rubber trees, orange-trees, roses, geraniums, yucca-palms, century plants, bananas, calla lilies, and pomegranates.

Southern California, of which Los Angeles is the principal city, possesses, perhaps, an all-the-year-round climate that approaches perfection as nearly as any other known to us. It is a semi-tropical climate with little frost, no snow, and moderate winter rains, remarkable for its equableness and dryness. Winter and summer are terms that here lose their ordinary significance, their place being taken by what may almost be called a perpetual spring. Sea-bathing may be practised in Dec. or Jan., while the dryness of the atmosphere and the ocean breezes make the summer much less trying than in places farther to the E. The wild flowers of S. California, of which the golden poppy (*Eschscholtzia Californica*) is one of the most characteristic, are extraordinary in number, variety, and brilliancy. 'The greatest surprise of the traveller is that a region which is in perpetual bloom and fruitage, where semi-tropical fruits mature in perfection, and the most delicate flowers dazzle the eye with color the winter through, should have on the whole a low temperature, a climate never enervating, and one requiring a dress of woollen in every month' (Warner). Comp. 'Our Italy', by *Chas. Dudley Warner*, and 'California of the South', by *W. Lindley and J. P. Widney.*

MAIN STREET is the dividing line for E. and W. and contains many substantial buildings. Among these are the *Federal Building* and the *Post Office*. The *County Court House* is in Temple St., the *City Hall* in Broadway. Some of the *Schools* are handsome buildings. The *Viaduct of the Cable Tramway*, in San Fernando St., spanning the railway tracks on the E. side of the city, is an interesting piece of engineering. Los Angeles also contains two *Theatres*, six *Parks*, and two *Race-courses*. A visit may be paid to one of the open *Zanjas*, or irrigating canals, in the suburbs.

FROM LOS ANGELES TO SANTA MONICA, 15 M., *Southern Pacific Railway* or *Los Angeles and Pacific Railroad* in ³/₄ hr. — On the way we pass the large *National Soldiers' Home*. — **Santa Monica** (*Arcadia*, $2-3), a popular seaside resort, has a fine sandy beach, on which surf-bathing may be enjoyed all the year round.

FROM LOS ANGELES TO REDONDO BEACH, by the *Redondo Railway* (18 M.) or the *Southern California Railway* (23 M.) in ³/₄ hr. — 12 M. *Inglewood*, a pleasant town of suburban homes. — 23 M. **Redondo Beach** (**Redondo Beach Hotel*, $3-5; *Ocean View*, $2), another pleasant sea-bathing resort, has a beautiful beach and good facilities for boating and fishing. The large *Chautauqa Assembly Building* accommodates 4000 people. There is a deep-water pier, and Redondo is becoming of importance as a shipping-port.

FROM LOS ANGELES TO SAN PEDRO, 25 M., *Southern Pacific Railway* in 1 hr. — 6 M. *Florence*, the junction of the line to San Diego (see p. 449); 11 M. *Compton;* 21 M. *Thenard*, the junction of a branch-line to the bathing-resort of (4 M.) *Long Beach* (Bay View Ho.; Pavilion); 22 M. *Wilmington*, a small seaport. — 25 M. **San Pedro** (Hotel Metropole), with 1240 inhab., is the chief seaport of Los Angeles, with a harbour that has been improved at a cost of over $1,000,000 and admits vessels of 20 ft. draught. Steamers ply hence regularly to San Francisco, Santa Barbara, San Diego, etc. An excursion may be made by boat to (25 M.) **Santa Catalina Island* (Hotel at the village of *Avalon*), with its fine rocky coasts. Wild goats are hunted on Santa Catalina.

From Los Angeles to *Pasadena* and *San Bernardino*, see R. 97; to *San Diego*, see R. 98; to *Saugus* (for *Santa Barbara* and *San Francisco*), see R. 95; to *San Gabriel* and *Colton* (for *New Orleans*, etc.), see R. 101.

97. From Los Angeles to Pasadena, San Bernardino, and Barstow.

142 M. SOUTHERN CALIFORNIA RAILWAY to (10 M.) *Pasadena* in ¹/₂ hr. (fare 25 c.; return-fare 35 c.), to (61 M.) *San Bernardino* in 2-2¹/₂ hrs. (fare $1.75), and to (142 M.) *Barstow* in 6 hrs. (fare $6.60).

Pasadena may also be reached by the *Los Angeles Terminal Railway*, and *San Bernardino* by the *Southern Pacific Railway* viâ *Colton* (comp. p. 462).

Los Angeles, see p. 445. The railway ascends the valley of the *Arroyo Seco* ('dry river'). 9 M. *Raymond*, the station for the *Raymond Hotel* (see below).

10 M. **Pasadena** (830 ft.; **Raymond*, $4¹/₂, see below; *Hotel Green*, $3-5; *Carleton*, these two in the town; *The Painter*, $2¹/₂), a small city and health-resort, with a resident population of (1890) 4882, lies on the level floor of the fertile *San Gabriel Valley*, about 5 M. from the base of the *Sierra Madre Range* (2000-11,000 ft.). To the E. rises a small hill crowned by the huge *Raymond Hotel*, which stands in prettily laid out grounds and commands a splendid *View across the valley, with its glossy-green orange-groves, to the snow-topped wall of the Sierra Madre. *Mt. San Antonio* (p. 447), in the San Bernardino Range, is seen overtopping the Sierra Madre to the N.E., while the *San Jacinto Peaks* (p. 462) are visible on the S.E. horizon.

To the S. and S.W. lies the ocean, with the mountainous islands of *Santa Catalina* (p. 446) and *San Clemente.*

The city of Pasadena is well laid out and contains good *Schools, Churches,* a *Public Library,* an *Opera House,* and other substantial buildings. The *Museum of the Pasadena Academy of Sciences* contains an interesting collection of antiquities, fossils, and objects of natural history. The wealth of vegetation in the streets and gardens includes the eucalyptus, pepper-trees, olives, lemon and orange trees, cork and india-rubber trees, date and fan palms, bananas, guavas, Japanese persimmons, locust trees, and other trees and shrubs too numerous to name. The roads in the neighbourhood are good, and many pleasant drives may be made. Comp. 'All about Pasadena', by *C. F. Holder.*

One of the most interesting excursions from Pasadena is the ascent of *Wilson Peak (5600 ft.), which is generally accomplished by carriage or omnibus to the foot of the trail and thence to the summit by burro (burro $2 per day and feed; cable-line and hotel in contemplation). A good road, 9 M. long, beginning at *Eaton Cañon* (5 M. from Pasadena) ascends to the top of *Mt. Harvard* (5000 ft.; Camp Wilson, open throughout the year), an adjacent peak, whence the top of Mt. Wilson is easily reached. The *View is extensive and very beautiful. Wilson Peak has several times been used for important astronomical observations, and an observatory is to be erected here. The ascent of the two peaks is also often made from *Santa Anita* (see below). — The *San Gabriel Mission* (see p. 462) lies 3 M. to the S.W. of Pasadena; the road to it leads through large orange-groves. — Among other easily accessible points of interest near Pasadena are *Stoneman's Ranch,* with fine orange-groves, 1 M. to the S.; *Sunny Slope Winery,* 4 M. to the S.E.; the *Shorb* or *San Gabriel Winery,* 2 M. to the S., said to be the largest in the world; *Baldwin's Ranche,* 5 M. to the E., with a stud and race-course (station *Santa Anita,* see below); *Millard Cañon,* 4 M. to the N.; *Arroyo Seco Cañon* and the *Devil's Gate* (tramway), 4 M. to the N.W.; the *Ostrich Farm* (adm. 25 c.). 1½ M. to the N.W.; the *Sierra Madre Villa* (from $2½), 6 M. to the N.E., near the base of the Sierra Madre Range (view); *Linda Vista,* 2 M. to the N.E; and *La Canada Valley,* 4½ M. to the N.W. (tramway). *Mt. Disappointment* (5200 ft.) and *Brown's Peak* (5300 ft.) may be ascended (with guide) by those who are fond of mountain-climbing. *Mt. San Antonio (Old Baldy;* 10,140 ft.), 27 M. to the N.E., is best ascended from *N. Ontario* (see below).

The sportsman will find abundance of game for his gun in the vicinity of Pasadena, including bears in the remoter recesses of the mountains. Coursing is also practised, the hares or jack-rabbits affording good sport.

The *Los Angeles Terminal Railway* runs on to (6 M.) *Altadena* (1800 ft.), where immense tracts are covered in winter by brilliant poppies.

Beyond Pasadena the line runs towards the E. 13 M. *Lamanda Park* (735 ft.) is the nearest station to the (3 M.) *Sierra Madre* and the (1½ M.) *Sierra Madre Villa.* 15 M. *Santa Anita;* 19 M. *Monrovia* (Grand View Hotel); 25 M. *Azusa* (Hotel); 27 M. *Glendora;* 35 M. *Pomona* (comp. p. 462). — 41 M. *N. Ontario* (comp. p. 462) is a good starting-point for the ascent of *Mt. San Antonio* (p. 446). We drive through the *San Antonio Cañon* for 9 M. and then mount on burros.

61 M. **San Bernardino** (1100 ft.; *Hotel Stewart,* A. & E. P.; *Southern Hotel,* $1½-2; *Rail. Restaurant*), a busy little city with (1890) 4012 inhab., is finely situated near the E. margin of the valley of its own name and commands a good view of the *San Bernardino*

Mt. Range to the N., culminating in *Mt. San Bernardino* (11,600 ft.). The city was originally laid out by Mormons in 1851 and has had a prosperous career as the centre of a rich fruit-growing country. It is the junction of the Santa Fé line to *San Diego* and *National City* (see R. 98).

FROM SAN BERNARDINO TO (142 M.) SAN DIEGO AND (148 M.) NATIONAL CITY, railway in 5 1/2 hrs. — At (3 M.) *Colton* this line crosses the Southern Pacific Railway (see p. 462). — 6 M. *East Riverside* is the junction of a line to (24 M.) *Perris* (junction of another line to *San Jacinto*) and (51 M.) *Temecula.* — 9 M. **Riverside** (875 ft.; *Glenwood Hotel*, $ 2 1/2-3 1/2; *Arlington*, *Temescal*, $ 2-3), a city of 4683 inhab., is laid out on a very extensive scale, with beautiful avenues of ornamental trees. **Magnolia Avenue*, with its double rows of pepper-trees, is 8 M. long and 130 ft. wide. Riverside is the centre of the seedless navel orange culture, and the groves in its vicinity afford, perhaps, the most attractive picture of the orange-growing industry of California. It is a favourite resort of tourists and health-seekers. The San Bernardino Range is in full view. — 25 M. *South Riverside* (600 ft.). Beyond (28 M.) *Rincon* (490 ft.) we reach the *Santa Ana River* and run through the *Santa Ana Cañon*. At (47 M.) *Orange* we join the line to San Diego described in R. 98.

A loop-line, opening up some beautiful scenery, runs from San Bernardino to (9 M.) *Redlands*, (13 M.) *Mentone*, (19 M.) *Highlands*, (24 M.) *Arrowhead*, and so back to (27 M.) *San Bernardino*. — **Redlands** (1350 ft.; *Windsor*, $ 2-3; *Terrace Villa*, *Terracina Ho.*, $ 2), another flourishing orange-growing city, with 1904 inhab., is finely situated on the slopes of the foot-hills and commands good views of the *San Bernardino Mts.* (N.) and the *San Jacinto Mts.* (S.). — Arrowhead is the station for the **Arrowhead Hot Springs** (2035 ft.; *Hotel*, $ 2 1/2), which enjoy a considerable reputation.

Coaches (fine views) run from San Bernardino to (30 M.) *Bear Valley* (6400 ft.), where a gigantic reservoir has been formed by damming up a mountain-gorge.

The railway to Barstow runs to the N. from San Bernardino and ascends towards the summit of the pass over the San Bernardino Range (3820 ft.), which it reaches beyond (80 M.) *Cajon* ('Cahon'). On the other side we descend into the *Mojave Desert* (see p. 414), and beyond (105 M.) *Victor* we follow the course of the *Mojave River*. 121 M. *Point of Rocks;* 130 M. *Cottonwood*.

142 M. **Barstow**, see p. 414.

98. From Los Angeles to San Diego and National City.

Coronado Beach.

132 M. SOUTHERN CALIFORNIA RAILWAY to (126 M.) *San Diego* in 4 1/2 hrs. (fare $ 5, sleeper $ 1.50, chair-car 25 c.) and to (132) *National City* in 4 3/4 hrs. (same fares).

Los Angeles, see p. 445. 2 M. *Ballona Junction*, for the line to *Redondo Beach* (p. 446). The train runs at first through groves of oranges and walnuts and afterwards over meadows. A good view is obtained to the left, above the foot-hills, of the *Sierra Madre* (p. 446). Beyond (7 M.) *Bandini* we cross the *San Gabriel River*. 13 M. *Santa Fé Springs;* 26 M. *Anaheim* (Hotel del Campo), a pleasant little town, in one of the best orange-growing districts of the State. Before reaching (31 M.) *Orange* (180 ft.; Palmyra), the junction of the line

from San Bernardino (see p.447), we cross the wide sandy bed of the
Santa Ana River. This part of the line passes through numerous fine
orange-groves. — 34 M. *Santa Ana* is the junction of a short line to
Newport, on the coast. Near (41 M.) *Modjeska* is the winter-home
of Mme. Modjeska. Beyond (42 M.) *El Toro* (425 ft.) we descend
rapidly through a rolling green country, not unlike the fells near
Appleby and Carlisle. To the left, at (56 M.) *Capistrano,* are seen
the interesting ruins of the *Mission of San Juan Capistrano,* founded
in 1806 and overthrown by an earthquake in 1812. We reach the
ocean at (59 M.) *San Juan* ('Wahn'), and henceforward have it close
to us on the right. — 85 M. *Oceanside* (South Pacific Hotel, $2) is
the junction of a line to (13 M.) *De Luz.* A visit may be paid to
the (4 M.) remains of the *Mission of San Luis Rey de Francia.* —
From (86 M.) *Escondido Junction* a branch-line runs to (17 M.) *Escondido.* Fine views of the ocean to the right. 123 M. *Old Town of
San Diego* (see below).

126 M. **San Diego** (*Florence,* well situated on a hill above the
town, $2½; *Brewster,* $2½-5; *Horton,* in the town, commercial,
$2-3), a city of 16,159 inhab., has, like many other Californian towns,
been the subject of a 'boom' which has led it to lay out streets and
town-lots in places likely to be mere pasture-land for many years
to come. It lies on a bay of its own name and has the best harbour on
the Pacific Coast after that of San Francisco. Steamers ply regularly
to San Pedro (p.446), San Francisco, ports in Central and S. America,
etc., and sailing vessels to Hawaii, Australia, and numerous Californian
ports, while through-trains run over the Santa Fé route to Chicago
in 4 days. The climate is mild and equable (mean temp., Jan. 54°,
Aug. 69°), and the surrounding country is very fertile. The city
contains a U. S. garrison. The following excursions may be made
nearly as well from *Coronado Beach* (see below), as from San Diego.

About 8 M. to the N. of San Diego is the old *Mission of San Diego,* the
first settlement (1769) made by white men in California. Its olive-groves
are very prolific. The Mission may be reached by taking the electric car
to (5 M.) the hills overlooking the *Mission Valley,* and thence by burro; or
we may drive all the way, descending the curious and very steep '*Mission
Grade'.* Drivers should return by the *Old Town of San Diego* (the original
settlement), with its adobé buildings, Ramona's house (see *H. H.'s* 'Ramona'),
the Spanish church-bells (100 years old), and a mission-school attended by
Indian and white children. — Other favourite points are (6 M.) *Paradise
Valley; Pacific Beach,* reached by a steam-tramway (11 M.); the *Sweetwater
Dam* (13 M. to the E.), 396 ft. long, 90 ft. high, and 12-46 ft. thick, forming a reservoir with a capacity of 6,000,000,000 gallons; *La Jolla Cave* ('Holya'),
14 M. to the N.W.; and *El Cajon Valley* ('Cahon'), 15 M. to the N.E.

Coronado Beach, on a small peninsula immediately opposite
San Diego and forming the outer arm of San Diego Bay, is reached
from San Diego Railway Station by a tramway (5 c.) and ferry (5 c.),
connecting with a steam-tramway leading to the hotel (5 c.; hotel-
omnibus from the station to the hotel 50 c., incl. ferry and hand-baggage). Coronado Beach, about 12 M. in length, consists of a narrow

tongue of sand, running to the N. from the mainland and ending in the expansions known as the *South* and *North Beach*, each about $1^1/_2$ M. square. The latter, opposite Point Loma (see below), forms the S. horn of the entrance to San Diego Bay and is still mainly a waste of sand and chaparral. The South Beach, on the other hand, has been partly laid out as a city and contains some hotels, several hundred cottages, a motor railway, fine trees, beautiful gardens, and other attractions. Its permanent population is about 2000. The *Coronado Beach Hotel ($3-6) is one of the largest, finest, and most comfortable hotels in California, and is finely situated close to the ocean and an excellent sandy beach. Adjacent are bathing-tanks of salt-water, for summer and winter use, while steam-yachts, launches, and boats afford opportunity for excursions by water. Flowers thrive wonderfully on Coronado Beach, and the flower-beds adjoining the hotel are of astonishing brilliancy. The tower of the hotel commands a splendid *View. — The *Hotel Josephine* ($2) has no view of the sea.

The **Climate** of Coronado Beach is mild, dry, and equable (mean winter temp. 53°, spring 59°, summer 68°, autumn 65°). The daily range is singularly small, the difference between the lowest and the highest mean temperature of the 24 hrs. amounting in 1890 to only 10°. The average annual rain-fall is ten inches, and the average number of rainy days is thirty-four. The *Coronado Mineral Water*, now extensively exported, has been found efficacious in liver and kidney complaints.

Among the points of interest on South Beach are the *Ostrich Farm* (adm. 25 c.) and the beautiful **Botanical Gardens* ($2/_3$ M. from the Coronado Beach Hotel; station on the motor-line to the ferry). Opposite the hotel is a *Museum* of California relics and curiosities (adm. 25 c.). — A dummy or motor-line (steam-tramway) runs along the peninsula to (14 M.) *National City* (see below), returning along the shore to San Diego. — An excursion should be made to *Point Loma* (°View), the N. horn of the entrance to San Diego Bay, reached by boat to *Ballast Point* or by carriage from San Diego. The uppermost of the two lighthouses here, 500 ft. above the sea, is said to be the most loftily-situated lighthouse in the world. — Other excursions may be made to the places mentioned in connection with *San Diego* and *National City*. — Good fishing for mackerel, barracouda, halibut, and bluefish is obtained in the bay or ocean, while quail may be shot on North Beach and wild-fowl along the shore.

Beyond San Diego the railway soon reaches its terminus at (132 M.) **National City** (*International Hotel*, $2-3), with 1353 inhab., connected by a steam-motor line with (19 M.) *Tia Juana* ('Teea Wahna'), situated just beyond the Mexican frontier. About $1^1/_2$ M. to the N.E. of National City is *Mrs. Potts' Sanitarium*.

99. The Yosemite Valley.

Approaches. The usual and most convenient approach to the Yosemite Valley is that described below, viâ *Berenda* and *Raymond* (44 hrs.). The Valley is also sometimes entered viâ *Stockton* and *Milton* (31 hrs.; p. 398), and this route may used for a variation in returning to San Francisco. Circular tickets are issued by the *Yosemite Stage & Turnpike Co.* (office, 613 Market St.) for the journey from San Francisco to the valley and back for $50 ($40, if one goes viâ Stockton both ways), and similar tickets may be procured at Los Angeles, etc. Excursions to the principal points of interest in the Valley, including horse and guide for three days, cost $8. It is advisable to apply for tickets some days in advance, as the stage-accommodation in entering the Valley is limited; and the same precaution should be observed in leaving the Valley.

]Travellers approaching the Valley viâ the Stockton and Milton route take the train from San Francisco to (103 M.; 4 hrs.) *Stockton* (p. 398) and from Stockton to (30 M.; 1 hr.) *Milton* (p. 398), and go on thence by stage to (41 M.; 10 hrs.) *Priest's*, where the night is spent. An early start is made next morning, and the remaining 50 M. are driven over in 10 hrs. In leaving the Valley the night is spent at *Chinese Camp* (p. 398), 29 M. from Milton.]

Hotels. The two hotels in the Valley itself ($3-4 a day) are not so elaborate as those of the Yellowstone Park (see p. 380), but afford reasonably comfortable quarters. There are also fair hotels at the stopping-places of the stages on the way into the Valley, and two small inns at Glacier Point (p. 456) and the Nevada Falls (p. 457).

Season. Plan of Tour. The season of travel in the Yosemite begins about April 1st and ends about Nov. 1st. Perhaps the middle of May is on the whole the best time for a visit, as the roads are then generally free from snow or dust, the temperature is pleasantly warm by day and cool at night, the waterfalls are still full of water, the snow-effects on the mountains are fine, and the wild-flowers are in profusion. On the other hand some of the trails may still be closed by snow. Campers usually visit the Valley in June, July, or Aug., and suitable camping-places are set apart for their use. It is possible to see all the points usually visited in about three days, but it is advisable to spend at least a week in the Valley. Those who have time for one trip only should select that to Glacier Point, which gives a view of the Valley itself, the Sierra Nevada, and the Vernal and Nevada Falls. Next in importance come the Falls just named, Eagle Peak and the Yosemite Falls, and Cloud's Rest (the last for the more energetic). No one should fail to see the sun rise in Mirror Lake, which can be easily done on the same day as any of the other usual excursions except the very longest. The charges for horses, mules, carriages, and guides are reasonable and are fixed by the Board of Commissioners (tariff on application at the hotels). The roads on the floor of the Valley are good, and the mountain-trails are as a rule excellent bridle-paths, though nervous persons, or those inclined to dizziness, may find some of them rather trying to ride down. In this case, however, it is easy to dismount and go on foot, letting the mule follow. The *Guides* ($3) are usually pleasant and obliging, but do not compare in intelligence or knowledge of the country with the best Swiss guides. The trails are so unmistakable that their functions are mainly confined to looking after the horses.

Bibliography. The standard work on the Yosemite is the 'Yosemite Guide-book' by *Prof. J. D. Whitney* (published in three sizes, but at present unfortunately out of print). See also *J. M. Hutchings*' 'In the Heart of the Sierras'. A convenient small guidebook is that by *Lewis Stornoway* (Murdock & Co., San Francisco; price 50 c.). Excellent maps of the Yosemite Valley have been published by the U. S. Corps of Engineers (Wheeler Survey) and the Geological Survey of California. Good photographs may be obtained from Taber & Co., San Francisco, or from George Fiske, in the Valley itself. — The botanist will find the Yosemite Valley a place of great interest, and the number and variety of its wild flowers are especially remarkable. The singular snow-plant *(Sarcodes sanguinea)*, elsewhere rare, is frequently found in or near the Yosemite in May and June. It has the form of a bright scarlet column, 3-12 inches high, and grows on the edge of snow-drifts or in ground recently covered with snow. Good shooting and fishing may also be obtained.

According to the present time-tables the train leaves *Berenda* (see p. 441) early in the morning, runs towards the W., and reaches (22 M.) *Raymond* in time for breakfast at the Hotel ($1; rather dear). Here we change from the railway to the stages, in which the seats we are to retain till we reach our destination are assigned to

29*

us by number. The first part of the drive is comparatively uninteresting, as well as hot and dusty in summer; it is therefore hoped
that the railway may be extended to Grant's Springs (see below).
Beyond (14 M.) *Grub Gulch* we are accompanied for some time by
a long 'flume' for bringing timber down the mountains. To the right
is a *Gold Mine*, which is not worked at present.

25 M. **Grant's Sulphur Springs** (*Hotel*, $ 3, D. $ 1) is the dinner-
station. The springs are not of much importance. — The scenery
now improves. *Look-out Point* commands a fine retrospect, extending over the plain to the coast-hills. The timber along the road is
fine, including sugar-pines *(Pinus Lambertiana)*, cedars, firs, and
oaks, besides pretty blossoming trees like the dogwood *(Cornus Florida)*, buckeye *(Aesculus Californica)*, and California lilac *(Ceanothus
integerrimus)*. The curiously twisted and red-trunked manzanita
(Arctostaphylos glauca) is also abundant.

36 M. **Wawona** or **Big Tree Station** (3925 ft.; *Hotel*, $ 4, S.,
R., & B. $ 3¹/₂), the usual halting-place for the night, is beautifully
situated on the S. fork of the *Merced River* (p. 453) and forms pleasant headquarters for a prolonged stay. The principal point of interest in the vicinity is the *Mariposa Grove of Big Trees*, 7 M. to
the S.W., usually visited by Yosemite travellers on their way out of
the valley. — The roads from *Merced* (p. 442) and *Madera* (p. 442),
by which a few visitors approach the Yosemite, join ours at Wawona.

The *Mariposa Grove of Big Trees** (6500 ft.), so-called from its situation in Mariposa ('butterfly') county, occupies a tract of land, 4 sq. M. in
area, reserved as a State Park, and consists of two distinct groves, ¹/₂ M.
apart. The *Lower Grove*, which we reach first, contains about 100 fine
specimens of the *Sequoia gigantea* (see p. 398), including the 'Grizzly Giant',
the largest of all, with a circumference of 94 ft. and a diameter of 31 ft.
Its main limb, 200 ft. from the ground, is 6¹/₂ ft. in diameter. In ascending to the *Upper Grove*, which contains 365 big trees, the road passes
through a tunnel, 10 ft. high and 9¹/₂ ft. wide (at the bottom), cut directly
through the heart of a living Sequoia, 27 ft. in diameter. The road passes
close to nearly all the largest trees in the Grove, the names and dimensions of which will be supplied by the driver. About 10 of the trees exceed 250 ft. in height (highest 272 ft.) and about 20 trees have a circumference of over 60 ft., three of these being over 90 ft. The Calaveras Grove
(see p. 398) has taller trees than any in the Mariposa Grove, but the latter
has those of greatest circumference. Many of the finest trees have been
marred and reduced in size by fire. The wood of the *Sequoia gigantea*, like
that of the *Sequoia sempervirens* (redwood; comp. p. 441), is easily
worked, durable, and susceptible of a high polish. Small articles made
of it may be bought at the pavilion in the Upper Grove.

To the W. of the Wawona Hotel rises *Signal Peak* (7860 ft.), the top
of which (7 M.) may be reached by a good road. The *View embraces
the San Joaquin Valley (p. 441) and innumerable peaks of the Sierra Nevada. — The *Chilnooalna Falls* (300 ft. high), 5 M. to the N.I., are reached
by a good bridle-path and repay a visit.

Good fishing and shooting (with some chance for a bear) are obtainable round Wawona. — Close to the hotel is the Studio of *Mr. Thomas
Hill*, well known for his pictures of the Yosemite. Dried flowers, ex-
quisitely mounted by Mrs. Hill Jr., may be bought here.

Beyond Wawona the scenery traversed is of a very high order.
The road mounts rapidly, commanding a series of fine views, and

finally attains an elevation of 6500 ft. The descent is equally rapid. At (47 M.) *Eleven Mile Station* the horses are changed. At (51 M.) *Chinquapin Station* the direct road to *Glacier Point* diverges to the right (see p. 456). About 5 M. farther on we reach ****Inspiration Point** (5600 ft.), where we obtain the first view of the valley, with El Capitan to the left, Cathedral Spires and Sentinel Dome to the right, and the Half Dome and North Dome in the background. Farther on we descend a winding road, with rapid turns, 'hair-pin' bends, and glorious views of the valley. On reaching the floor of the valley we skirt the *Merced River* and pass near the foot of the *Bridal Veil Fall* (right, p. 455), while views of the *Virgin's Tears* and (farther on) of the *Yosemite Falls* (p. 454) are obtained to the left. The road from Milton (see p. 398) comes in from the N. and runs along the other (N.) bank of the river. — 63 M. *Yosemite Village* (4000 ft.), with *Barnard's Hotel* ($4) and the office of the Guardian of the Valley (p. 454).

64 M. *Stoneman House* ($4), the terminus of the stage-route, finely situated near the E. end of the valley. The stage arrives here about 1.30 p.m.

The ****Yosemite Valley** ('full-grown grizzly bear'; pron.'Yosémity') is a gorge or cañon on the W. slope of the Sierra Nevada, traversed by the *Merced River* and enclosed by rocky and almost vertical walls. The nearly level floor of the valley is 8 M. long and about 4000 ft. above sea-level, while the enclosing walls are 3000-5000 ft. higher. The width between the walls varies from $1/2$ M. to 2 M. At several points huge water-falls are precipitated over the face of the rocky walls into the valley below. The park-like floor of the valley is carpeted with fine flower-studded grass and freely sprinkled with beautiful trees and shrubs, while the emerald-green Merced flows through it in alternate reaches of calm and turmoil.

'The principal features of the Yosemite, and those by which it is distinguished from all other known valleys, are: first, the near approach to verticality of its walls; second, their great height, not only absolutely, but as compared with the width of the Valley itself; and finally, the very small amount of *talus* or *débris* at the base of these gigantic cliffs. These are the great characteristics of the Yosemite, throughout its whole length; but, besides these, there are many other striking peculiarities, and features both of sublimity and beauty, which can hardly be surpassed, if equalled, by those of any mountain valleys in the world' *(Whitney)*.

The visitor standing on the floor of the valley sees no outlet in any direction and feels curiously separated from the rest of the world. Perhaps no single valley in Switzerland combines in so limited a space such a wonderful variety of grand and romantic scenery.

The formation of the valley was at first ascribed to erosion or even to glacial action; but Prof. Whitney has proved to the satisfaction of most authorities that it was most probably due to a mighty convulsion of nature, caused by the subsidence of a limited area, marked by lines of 'fault' or fissure, crossing each other nearly at right angles. The ragged masses of rock that fell into the chasm were gradually covered up by the action of the river, ultimately producing the smooth level floor thatthe valley now presents. The geological formations are entirely granitic.

The Yosemite Valley was first seen by white men, so far as is know, in 1851, when a small party of soldiers came upon it suddenly when in pursuit of some Indians. The first settlement was made in 1857, and other buildings soon followed as the attractions of the Valley became known and tourists began to pour in. In 1864 an Act of Congress was passed, handing the valley itself, with the adjacent territory for a distance of about 2 M. all round it, to the State of California for the purposes of a *State Park*. This park is managed by the Governor and a board of State Commissioners, and these are represented on the spot by the Guardian of the Valley (Mr. Galen Clark), whose office is near Barnard's Hotel. The State Park is enclosed by the *Yosemite National Park*, which takes in the entire watershed of the rivers of the valley. About a score of the so-called *Digger Indians* (Shoshonians), who originally occupied the valley, still survive. They are one of the lowest types of red men, supporting themselves partly on roots and acorns and partly by fishing.

Perhaps the most striking object in the valley, to most visitors, is the cliff known as *El Capitan, which rises prominently as the N.W. buttress of the cañon. It is not by any means the highest part of the cañon-walls, though rising to a height of 3300 ft. above the floor of the valley, but produces its effect by its dominating position, its majestic form, the bareness and verticality of its face, and the narrowness of the valley in front of it. It has two faces, one looking W. and the other S., which join each other almost at right angles. The summit cannot be reached without a long and arduous journey, which is seldom undertaken. The *Ribbon Fall* or the *Virgin's Tears*, about 1000 ft. high, descends over the cliffs just to the W. of El Capitan. It is a beautiful fall in the early part of the season, but loses most of its water in summer. — To the E. of El Capitan are the fine peaks named the **Three Brothers,** the highest of which, known also as *Eagle Peak* (3830 ft. above the valley), is a favourite view-point (see p. 457). — In the recess to the E. of Eagle Peak, near the centre of the valley, are the **Yosemite Falls,** where the creek of that name descends to the valley in three leaps, with a total height of 2600 ft. The *Upper Fall* has a vertical descent of 1500 ft.; the *Middle Fall* consists of a series of cascades with a total descent of 626 ft.; while the *Lower Fall* is 400 ft. high. This is the highest waterfall in the world with anything like the same body of water. At the top it is about 35 ft. wide. Seen at its best, this fall is certainly one of the grandest features of the valley; but it dwindles considerably as the season advances. A splendid ice-cone, 500 ft. high, forms at the foot of the Upper Fall in winter. Trail to the top, see p. 457. — The projection to the E. of the

Yosemite Falls is named **Yosemite Point** (3220 ft.) and commands a splendid view (comp. p. 457). The ravine to the E. of this is known as *Indian Cañon.* The wall of rock on the other side of Indian Cañon is known as the **Royal Arches**, so called from the semicircular cavities on its front. Adjoining these, at the angle formed by the beginning of the Tenaya Cañon (see below), rises the *Washington Tower* or *Column* (2400 ft.), which is itself a cub or spur of the huge *North Dome* (3570 ft.).

We have now, in our survey, reached the head of the Yosemite Valley proper, where it splits into the three narrow cañons of the *Tenaya* or N. fork of the Merced to the N., the *Merced* proper in the middle, and the *Illilouette* or S. fork of the Merced to the S. (comp. p. 458). To the S. of the Tenaya Cañon, opposite the N. Dome and forming the E. terminus of the Yosemite Valley, rises the singularly shaped ****South** or **Half Dome** (4735 ft.), which disputes with El Capitan the place of the most remarkable single feature of the valley. 'It strikes even the most casual observer as a new revelation in mountain forms; its existence would be considered an impossibility if it were not there before us in all its reality; it is an unique thing in mountain scenery, and nothing even approaching it can be found except in the Sierra Nevada' *(Whitney).* The Half Dome was first ascended in 1875 by a man named Anderson, who scaled the summit on the S.E. side by means of a rope attached to pegs driven into the rock. Anderson's ladder has, however, been allowed to go to ruin, and at present the top of the Half Dome is inaccessible. — To the S.W. of the Half Dome, at the angle formed by the Tenaya and Merced Cañons, rises *Grizzly Peak*, a grim, wooded, and nearly inaccessible summit.

Passing over the Merced Cañon, which enshrines the *Vernal* and *Nevada Waterfalls* (see p. 456), we now come to the S. wall of the Yosemite Valley, the first (easternmost) peak of which is ****Glacier Point** (3250 ft.), the most frequently visited, and in many respects the finest, of the points of vantage from which to view the valley. A description of the trail to it and the view from it is given at p. 456. — For about 1 M. to the W. of Glacier Point the wall of the valley runs nearly in a straight line and is almost wholly covered with talus or debris. Above this, but a little back from the valley, rises the **Sentinel Dome** (4160 ft.), which commands a very extensive view (see p. 456). The front-wall just mentioned ends on the W. in the ***Sentinel Rock** (3045 ft.), the most conspicuous rock on the S. face of the valley. Its ascent is not difficult or dangerous for climbers. — Next in order, as we proceed towards the W., come the slender *Cathedral Spires* (2680 ft. and 2580 ft.), which are adjoined by the imposing ***Cathedral Rocks** (2660 ft.), directly opposite El Capitan. Over the W. side of the lower part of these rocks pours the ***Bridal Veil Fall,** which some visitors deem the finest in the valley. It has a clear vertical fall of about 630 ft., with a width of 50-70 ft.

The name is derived from the effect on it by the wind, which often makes it flutter like a white veil. Like most of the other falls, it loses much of its grandeur as the summer advances. A fine rainbow is generally visible on this fall between 4 and 6 p.m.

The above enumeration includes most of the principal points in the valley itself or in its immediate walls. Below follows a short description of the routes leading to these as well as to other points not included in the valley itself but generally visited thence. The Stoneman House (p. 453) is taken as starting-point. For information as to horses, guides, and so on, comp. p. 451.

(1.) *Lower Round Drive (12-20 M.), on the floor of the Valley (fare $2¹/₂ each; incl. Mirror Lake and Cascades, $3¹/₂). This drive gives a very good general idea of the Yosemite wonders, but, as most of them are almost as well seen on entering the valley by stage, it need not be taken by those whose time is limited. The points visited include the foot of the *Yosemite* and *Bridal Veil Falls* (pp. 454, 455), and it is well to time the drive so as to see the afternoon rainbow on the latter (see above). The *Cascade Falls* are about 3¹/₂ M. below the Bridal Veil Fall, beyond the limits of the valley proper. *Mirror Lake* (see p. 457) is about 2 M. to the N.E. of the Stoneman House.

(2.) Glacier Point (5¹/₂ M.; horse $3). The Glacier Point trail (well-made but somewhat trying on horseback for those liable to giddiness, esp. in descending; quite safe and not very steep for walking) begins near the foot of Sentinel Rock, about 1 M. to the W. of the hotel, which generally sends a carriage to the foot of it without extra charge. The trail ascends the steep face of the cliff in zigzags. *Union Point*, about two-thirds of the way up, commands a fine view. Close by is the singular *Agassiz Column*. **Glacier Point (3250 ft.), marked by a flagstaff, where an iron rail has been fixed between two rocks, commands a splendid view of most of the valley, the floor of which lies almost perfectly sheer below us. A little way from the edge of the cliff is the small and unpretending, but fairly comfortable *Glacier Point Hotel* ($3, meal $1), the porch of which commands a magnificent **View of the Merced Cañon, with the Vernal and Nevada Falls and the Cap of Liberty, the Half Dome, and the *High Sierra*, including (named from right to left) Mt. Starr King, Red Mt., Gray Mt., Mt. Clark, Mt. Ritter (in the extreme distance), Mt. Florence, Mt. McClure, Tenaya Peak, and Mt. Lyell (p. 458). Nearly every evening a fine display of fireworks (announced by a horn) is given here by throwing burning brands, etc., over the cliff (well seen from below). — Glacier Point is accessible, for those who can neither ride nor walk up the trail, by carriage-road from *Wawona* (p. 452), but this roundabout journey takes 2 days instead of 4-5 hrs. It may also be reached viâ *Nevada Fall* (comp. p. 457), and those who spend the night here should return by this route. — The top of *Sentinel Dome* (p. 455) is about 1¹/₄ M. from Glacier Point and is easily reached thence on foot or horseback (no extra charge). From Sentinel Dome the excursion may be extended to the (1¹/₂ M.) so-called *Fissures* (horse 75 c. extra; from Stoneman Ho. $3.75).

(3.) **Vernal and Nevada Falls (4¹/₂ M.; horse $3). The excellent *Anderson Trail*, which as far as Vernal Fall is so broad and easy as to give no cause for nervousness, begins about 1¹/₄ M. to the S.E. of the Stoneman Ho. and winds along the flank of *Grizzly Peak* (p. 455), with the beautiful *Merced River* rushing downwards on the right. A good distant view it obtained (right) of the *Illilouette Falls* (p. 458). About ¹/₄ M. below the Vernal Fall we cross the river by a bridge, which commands one of the best views of it. Beyond the bridge is the so-called *Register Rock*, where the trail forks, the left branch leading to the flat *Lady Franklin Rock*, near the foot of the Vernal Fall. The (2 M.) *Vernal Fall has a vertical descent of 350 ft., with a width of 70-80 ft. Behind rises the picturesque *Cap of Liberty* (7060 ft.). We may now ascend to the top of the fall by a series of iron *Ladders*, which climb the face of the rock close to the fall (waterproof desirable), but this route should not be tried by any except those of steady head. From Register Rock (see above) the trail (now narrower and steeper) makes a wide sweep to the right before reaching the top of Vernal Fall, where the flat rock, with a natural parapet, permits an approach to the verge of the water. Just above is the beautiful **Emerald Pool.* The trail recrosses the river about halfway between the top of the Vernal Fall and the bottom of the Nevada Fall. Above the bridge is the **Diamond Cascade* and below it is the **Silver Apron.* Near the foot of the Nevada Fall is the small *Casa Nevada* (Snow's; 1365 ft. above the valley), where refreshments and night-quarters may be procured. The hotel commands a fine view of the (3³/₄ M.) superb ***Nevada Fall*, which has a slightly sloping descent of about 600 ft. and ranks with the Bridal Veil and the Yosemite Falls. — Many visitors turn here, but those who have time and strength should certainly follow the steep trail to (³/₄ M.) the top of the Nevada Fall.

The trail to the *Little Yosemite* and *Cloud's Rest* (see below) diverges to the left before we reach the bridge above the falls.

Beyond the bridge the trail goes on, along the flank of *Mt. Starr King* (9020 ft.), to (12 M.; 17 M. from the hotel; horse $6) Glacier Point (see p. 456); and this route is recommended to those who have time. The night may be spent at Glacier Point Hotel (see p. 456). This trail crosses the *Illilouette* just above the falls (p. 458).

(4.) **Eagle Peak* and Yosemite Falls (7-7¹/₂ M.; horse $ 3). To reach Eagle Peak trail, a steep but well-made bridle-path (not so dizzy as the Glacier Point trail), we cross the bridge behind Barnard's Hotel (p. 453), turn to the left a little farther on, and cross the bridge over the creek descending from the Yosemite Fall. The trail diverges to the right about ¹/₄ M. beyond the last-named bridge (about 2 M. from the Stoneman Ho.), ascends round and up the ledges adjoining the Falls cañon, and then descends to (1¹/₂ hr.) a hitching-place near the foot of the ***Upper Yosemite Fall* (see p. 454) We clamber over the rocks and approach as near the fall as we care to penetrate through the clouds of spray, gaining an overwhelming impression of the stupendous power and volume of this marvellous waterfall. Continuing to follow the trail, we keep to the left, where a path to the right diverges to the top of the Yosemite Fall, and again to the left at the next fork, where the path to the right leads to Lake Tenaya (comp. p. 458). The **View* from Eagle Peak (p. 454) extends farther to the W. than that from Glacier Point and includes some peaks of the High Sierra. — If time allows, a visit to the top of the Yosemite Fall (see above) should certainly be combined with this trip. The **View* of the fall from above is as impressive in its way as that from below. A large boulder about 12 yds. below the bridge above the fall, on the left (E.) side of the stream, shakes or rather jerks perceptibly at irregular intervals, as may be felt by leaning against it. This movement is probably caused by the water of the fall entering some cavern far below. The trail crossing the above-mentioned bridge leads to *Yosemite Point* (p. 455), which commands a view similar to that from Eagle Point. If time and strength do not allow a visit to both, the top of the Yosemite Falls and Yosemite Point should be preferred to Eagle Peak.

(5.) Mirror Lake (carr. $1), a small piece of water, about 2 M. to the N.E. of the Stoneman House, at the mouth of the Tenaya Cañon, is visited for its wonderful reflections of the North and South Domes and Mt. Watkins. Its surface is generally most unruffled early in the morning, and visitors usually go to see the sun rise in it over the Half Dome (about 8 a. m. in summer). The reflections are also good by moonlight.

(6.) Cloud's Rest (10-11 M.; horse $ 5). This excursion is one in high favour among the more energetic visitors to the Valley. It may be accomplished in one long day (10-12 hrs.), but is made easier by passing the night at the *Casa Nevada* (see above). The trail is good and not difficult, but the upper part of it is apt to be buried in snow in the early part of the season. — From the Stoneman House to the point where the trail diverges from that to the top of the Nevada Fall, see p. 456. A little farther on the trail to the so-called *Little Yosemite* (6000 ft.) diverges to the right from the Cloud's Rest trail. Cloud's Rest (5780 ft. above the valley and

9770 ft. above the sea) commands a splendid *View of the walls of the Yosemite Valley and of the High Sierra. Immediately to the S.W. is the Half Dome; to the N., across the Tenaya Cañon, rises Mt, Watkins (see below). Among the most prominent peaks of the Sierra (named from N. to S.) are Mt. Hoffman, Tenaya Peak (with Tenaya Lake below it), the Cathedral, Mt. Dana, Mt. Gibbs, Mt. Lyell, Mt. Clark, and Mt. Starr King (p. 457).

(7.) FALLS OF THE ILLILOUETTE (2½ M.). The falls of the Illilouette or *Tululaweak* may be reached by a somewhat rough scramble up the cañon of the Illilouette, opening to the S. of the Merced Cañon (comp. p. 455). The total height is about 600 ft.; the main fall is 400 ft. high. They are also passed on the trail from Nevada Fall to Glacier Point (see p. 457). Most visitors will content themselves with the distant view from the Vernal Fall trail (see p. 456). A good echo is returned from *Echo Wall*, in the Illilouette Cañon.

(8.) Mt. Watkins (3570 ft. above the valley and 7570 ft. above the sea) rises on the N. side of the Tenaya Cañon and is sometimes ascended from the N.

Among the longer excursions in the High Sierra, which can be made by those who prolong their stay in the Yosemite Valley, are those named below. Guides are necessary in all cases, and a little experience in mountain-climbing is desirable for some of the ascents. Rough accommodation for the night can sometimes be procured, but in other cases camping out is necessary. — About 12 M. to the N. of Yosemite is the *Cañon of the Tuólumne (four syllables), a stream which, in this part of its course, runs nearly parallel with the Merced and is very attractive from the beauty and variety of its waterfalls and the grandeur of its overhanging cliffs. The upper part of the cañon can be easily reached on horseback by the *Virginia Creek Trail*, which leaves the trail to Mono Lake at Tenaya Lake (see below) and soon brings us to the first and uppermost of three picturesque groups of cascades, with a total descent of 2000 ft. within 1½ M. About 20 M. lower down is the *Hetch-Hetchy, a remarkable counterpart of the Yosemite, on a somewhat smaller scale, but closely resembling it in its main features, with similar high cliffs and fine waterfalls. It cannot easily be reached by descending the cañon, but is approached by a side-trail leaving the Milton road about 20 M. from Priest's Hotel (p. 451). Those who make this trip must provide their own food and camp accommodation. — Lake Tenaya, 17 M. from the Stoneman Ho., viâ the Eagle Peak trail (comp. p. 457), lies near the head of the Tenaya Cañon, in the midst of a grand mountain amphitheatre. *Tenaya Peak*, on its E. side, may be ascended with little difficulty. Beyond this lake the trail (to the left the Virginia Creek trail, see above) goes on to the (5 M.) *Tuólumne Meadows (8500 ft.), at the head of the Tuólumne Cañon (see above). The scenery here is very fine. Near the head of the Meadows are the (5 M.) *Soda Springs*, a favourite camping-ground for those making the ascent of Mt. Dana or Mt. Lyell (see below). The trail goes on to (20 M.) *Mono Lake*. — Mt. Dana (13,225 ft.; there and back, 3-4 days), the loftiest peak near the Yosemite, commands a very extensive view and is generally ascended from Soda Springs (see above; no particular difficulty). — Mt. Lyell (13,190 ft.) is more difficult and should not be attempted except by experts (3-4 days). It is also ascended from Soda Springs. — Mt. Hoffmann (10,870 ft.; *View) may be ascended from Tenaya Lake in half-a-day. — Visitors to the *Little Yosemite* (see above) may go through the gorge at its head, passing the *Silver Chain Cascade*, to the *Lost Valley* (there and back in one day).

100. From San Francisco to Portland.

772 M. SOUTHERN PACIFIC RAILWAY in 36 hrs. (fare $ 25; sleeper $ 5). This line traverses some fine scenery and affords good views of *Mt. Shasta* (p. 459); some of the engineering difficulties were very great.

STEAMERS of the *Pacific Coast Steamboat Co.* (agents, Goodall, Perkins, & Co., 10 Market St.) and of the *Union Pacific Co.* (1 Montgomery S.) leave

San Francisco every 4 days for Portland (2 days; fare $ 6, incl. berth and meals). The voyage is a pleasant one and usually calm in summer.

From *San Francisco* to (90 M.) *Sacramento* and (108 M.) *Roseville Junction*, see p. 397. Our line here diverges to the left from that to *Ogden* and runs to the N., ascending the valley of the *Sacramento River*, which flows at some distance to the left. 142 M. *Marysville* (65 ft.), a city of 3991 inhab., at the confluence of the *Feather* and *Yuba Rivers*. To the left rise the *Marysville Buttes* (1800-2100 ft.). At (163 M.) *Biggs* (100 ft.) we cross the Feather River. 186 M. *Chico* (195 ft.; 2894 inhab.). A fine fruit-growing country is traversed. Near (213 M.) *Tehama* (220 ft.) we cross the Sacramento.

Beyond (260 M.) *Redding* (555 ft.), near the he d of the Lower Sacramento Valley, we enter upon a stretch of very picturesque scenery (observation car), where the train crosses the winding Sacramento 18 times and threads 12 or more tunnels in 80 M. At (269 M.) *Copley* (600ft.) the Indians spear salmon. Between (277M.) *Kennet* (670ft.) and (282 M.) *Morley* (720 ft.) the Sacramento is joined by the *Pitt River*. To the right rise the *McCloud Mts.* The *McCloud River*, which flows into the Pitt River, is one of the finest trout-streams in California. 298 M. *Delta* (1140 ft.), a good fishing-station. Near (306 M.) *Gibson* (1390 ft.) we pass through fine pine-forest. To the left, near (320 M.) *Castle Crag* (2085 ft.; Castle Crag Tavern), rise the imposing *Castle Crags*, towering to a height of 4000 ft. above the river and forming one of the most striking pieces of scenery in the United States. Near (323 M.) *Chestnut* (2195 ft.) we obtain our first view of the huge snow-clad dome of *Mt. Shasta* (in front, to the right). To the right, near the (325 M.) *Upper Soda Springs* (2360 ft.), are the pretty *Mossbrae Falls*. A little farther on we cross the Sacramento for the last time and ascend rapidly, round the *Great Bend*, to (335 M.) *McCloud* (3350 ft.). — At (338 M.) *Sisson* (3555 ft.; *Sisson Tavern*, $ 1½-3; Depot Hotel, $ 2-2½), in *Strawberry Valley*, we enjoy a grand, unimpeded view of Mt. Shasta. To the left rise the *Scott Mts.* (*Mt. Eddy*, 9150 ft.).

The top of *Mt. Shasta (14,440 ft.) is 12 M. from Sisson and may be ascended thence (there and back) in 30-36 hrs. (guides, horses, etc., at Sisson's Hotel; total expense $ 15-20 each). The night is spent at *Sisson's Camp* (9000 ft.), just above the timber-line. There is a Geodetic Monument on the main peak. Mt. Shasta is a huge extinct volcano, and its volcanic character is clearly discernible in the *Crater* or *W. Peak* (12,900 ft.), where there is a crater ³/₄ M. in diameter and 2500 ft. deep. Hot springs and solfataric action are also visible near the top of the main peak. The *View from the summit is very extensive.

At (345 M.) *Black Butte Summit* (3900 ft.) the train reaches the summit of the pass across the N. part of the Sierra Nevada and begins its descent. To the right we obtain views of the five distinct cones of *Muir's Peak* or *Black Butte* (6500 ft.). The trees through which we run include the sugar pine (*Pinus Lambertiana;* with cones 12-18 inches long), the yellow pine *(P. ponderosa)*, the contorted pine *(P. contorta)*, the cembra pine *(P. flexilis)*, and the nut pine (*P. Sabiniana;* cones

12 inches long and 6 inches thick). 355 M. *Edgewood* (2955 ft.) commands a good retrospect of Mt. Shasta. We now ascend the *Shasta Valley*, with the *Shasta River* at some distance to the right. From (377 M.) *Montague* (2540 ft.) the *Siskiyou Mts.* (7660 ft.) are visible to the left. Near (395 M.) *Hornbrook* (2155 ft.) we cross the *Klamath River* and begin to ascend the Siskiyou Mts. (gradient 4 : 100). Beyond (404 M.) *Coles* (2905 ft.) we enter *Oregon* ('Webfoot State'). The line passes through a long tunnel just before reaching the summit at (414 M.) *Siskiyou* (4130 ft.). To the right is *Pilot Rock* (6430 ft.), the S. outpost of the *Cascade Mts.* (p. 376). — The train now descends rapidly, through tunnels and round curves, into *Rogue River Valley.* —431 M. *Ashland* (1900 ft.; 1784 inhab.). *Mt. Pitt* (9760 ft.) rises to the right. — 446 M. *Medford* (1400 ft.) is the nearest station to (85 M.) the curious *Crater Lake.*

^{c}**Crater Lake** (6800 ft.), not yet easily accessible to the ordinary tourist, lies in the heart of the Cascade Mts., occupying the crater of an extinct volcano. It is 7 M. long and 5 M. wide. Its most peculiar feature is the perpendicular enclosing wall of igneous rock, 1000-2000 ft. high, in which there is no opening. There is no visible affluent or outflow, but the water, though destitute of animal life, is fresh and sweet. The lake is over 2000 ft. deep. *Wizard Island*, in the centre of the lake, is a curious instance of a crater within a crater. The road to the lake is good, and the descent to the water's edge is easier than it looks. The district containing this lake has been set apart as the *Oregon National Park*.

Beyond Medford, to the right, stands *Table Rock*. 476 M. *Grant's Pass* (960 ft.); 510 M. *Glendale* (965 ft.); 552 M. *Myrtle Creek* (635 ft.); 574 M. *Roseburg* (490 ft.; 1472 inhab.), on the *Umpqua River*. To the right is *Mt. Scott* (7125 ft.), and farther on, on the same side, are the *Three Sisters* (8500 ft.). Beyond (649 M.) *Eugene* (455 ft.) we descend the pretty and well-wooded valley of the *Willámette* (left). 667 M. *Harrisburg* (335 ft.). — 692 M. *Albany* (240 ft.) is the junction of a line to (11 M.) *Corvallis* and (83 M.) *Yaquina*, on *Yaquina Bay* (p. 462). — 720 M. **Salem** (190 ft.; *Willamette Hotel*, $2), the capital of Oregon, a small city with 4515 inhab., the *State Capitol*, and various other State buildings and institutions. — 757 M. *Oregon City* (95 ft.), with 3062 inhab., possesses a fine water-power supplied by the *Falls of the Willamette* (40 ft.). — 771 M. *East Portland* (55 ft.). The train then crosses the Willamette and reaches its destination.

772 M. **Portland** (**The Portland*, from $3; *St. Charles, Gilman, Perkins*, on the European plan; *Esmond*, $2-2$^1/_2$; *Grand Central*), the business capital of the Pacific North-West, is advantageously situated on the *Willamette*, 12 M. above its confluence with the *Columbia* (see p. 394). Pop. (1890) 46,385, or, including *East Portland* and *Albina*, now incorporated with the city, 62,046. These figures include about 3000 Chinese. Its position at the head of deep-sea-navigation on the Columbia and Willamette and its extensive railway connections with the N., E., and S. have made Portland an important commercial centre, and it ranks among the wealthiest cities of

its size in the country. The streets are well laid out and have a more substantial look than those of many western towns.

Portland was first settled in 1843, and its growth since then has been rapid and uninterrupted. The annual value of its exports now amounts to about $ 15,000,000 (3,000,000 *l.*), the chief articles being wheat, flour, wool, fish (salmon, etc.), and timber. It manufactures pig iron, woollen goods, flour, furniture, beer, cordage, and other goods to the annual value of $ 25,000,000 (5,000,000 *l.*). It has steamship lines to San Francisco and other ports on the Pacific Coast, Puget Sound, British Columbia, Alaska, and Japan, while its sailing vessels ply to Great Britain, China, South America, and New York. — The annual rainfall at Portland is 53 inches.

The new Union Railway Station, at the corner of N. 5th and I Sts., will be a roomy and handsome building, with a tall clock-tower. A little to the S.W. of it, in the block enclosed by Jefferson, Madison, 4th, and 5th Sts., is the new City Hall, still uncompleted. Other important edifices in the business part of the city are the *Chamber of Commerce* (Stark St.), the *Post Office* and *Custom House* (5th St.), the *Court House* (4th St.), the *Opera House* (Morrison St.), the *Daily Oregonian Office* (cor. of 6th and Alder Sts.), and the *Marquam Block* (Morrison St.). The *Public Library*, 7th St., is a tasteful Romanesque building. The *Portland Hotel* (see p. 460), between 6th, 7th, Yamhill, and Morrison Sts., is a handsome structure. The *Portland Industrial Fair Building*, on the outskirts of the city, is used for annual exhibitions. Some of the *Churches, Schools*, and *Charitable Institutions* are worthy representatives of the city's wealth. Among other objects of interest are the huge *Pacific Coast Elevator* (capacity 1,000,000 bushels) and the fine *Steel Bridge* over the Willamette.

The visitor to Portland will, however, best use his leisure by ascending the *Portland Heights* on the W. side of the city (easily reached on foot or by tramway) for the sake of the magnificent *Mountain View they command. *Mt. Hood* (see below), 60 M. to the S.E., is the most prominent peak, but the rounded dome of *Mt. St. Helens* (p. 377; 50 M. to the N.), *Mt. Adams* (p. 376), and *Mt. Rainier* (p. 377) are visible, and the view also includes the *Coast Range* and the valleys of the *Columbia* and *Willamette*. The best point for this view is *Fairmount*, 1000 ft. above the city and about 1 hr.'s walk or $3/4$ hr.'s drive from its centre.

Excursions from Portland.

The favourite excursion from Portland is the voyage up the *Columbia River* to (60 M.) the *Cascades* and to the (110 M.) *Dalles* (fare $ 3 1/2; return-fare $ 5; comp. p. 394; Union Pacific Office, cor. of 3rd and Washington Sts.). The traveller may take the train to the Dalles, spend the night there, and return next morning by the steamer. If the trip is made only one way, the steamer should be preferred, as the scenery is not seen to the best advantage from the train. The boats leave early in the morning, but travellers can go on board the night before. On the way, 18 M. from Portland, we pass *Vancouver*, the military headquarters of the Department of the Columbia.

Steamers (office as above) also descend the **Lower Columbia** to (106 M.) *Astoria* (ca. 8 hrs.), affording a good view of the wide estuary of a great river. A visit to a *Salmon Cannery* may be combined with the trip. — **Astoria** (*Occidental Hotel*, $ 2 1/2), a small seaport with 6184 inhab., formerly famous for its fur-trade, has 3 M. of wharves on the Columbia. Excursions may be made hence to (16 M.) *Clatsop Beach* (Hotel) and *North Beach* (in Washington; return-ticket from Portland to either of the Beaches, $4¹/₂).

The **Willamette** affords another pleasant trip, steamers plying regularly to *Oregon City* (p. 460), *Dayton*, and *Corvallis* (p. 460).

*Mt. **Hood** is conveniently ascended from Portland by taking the train to (66 M.) *Hood River* (comp. p. 394).

Mt. St. Helens, *Mt. Adams*, *Mt. Jefferson*, and the *Three Sisters* may also be visited from Portland; but the trails are rough and camping out is necessary in each case.

Among other points of interest visited from Portland are the *Multnomah Falls* (p. 394), *Crater Lake* (p. 460), and *Yaquina* (p. 460), *Newport* (Ocean House), and other places on *Yaquina Bay* (8 hrs. by train; return-fare $6).

From Portland to *Tacoma* (for *Seattle*, *British Columbia*, *Alaska*, etc.), see R. 103; to *Omaha* and the *East*, see R. 86.

101. From San Francisco to New Orleans.

2496 M. SOUTHERN PACIFIC RAILWAY ('Sunset Route') in about 4 days (fare $67.50; sleeper $13). Through-carriages.

From *San Francisco* to (482 M.) *Los Angeles*, see R.95. On leaving Los Angeles the train runs to the E. through the fruitful *San Gabriel Valley* (p. 446). — 492 M. *San Gabriel* (410 ft.; Hotel San Gabriel, $2¹/₂-3¹/₂) is the site of the interesting *Mission **de San Gabriel Arcangel**, founded in 1771. The *Mission Church*, erected in 1804 with material imported from Spain, is seen to the left, just before we enter the station. The old Mission gardens and vineyards deserve a visit. *Pasadena* (see p. 446) lies about 3 M. to the N.W. To the N. and E. is the *Sierra Madre Range* (p. 446). — 515 M. *Pomona* (860 ft.; The Palomares, $2¹/₂), with 3634 inhab., is one of the prettiest and most prosperous of the fruit-growing towns in the *San Bernardino Valley* (p. 447). — 521 M. *Ontario* (980 ft.; Ontario, $2; South Pacific), a brisk little fruit-growing town with 1064 inhab., lies in the midst of a striking landscape, with the four highest mountains of S. California in sight (Mt. St. Bernardino and Grayback to the E., San Jacinto to the S.E., and Mt. San Antonio or Old Baldy to the N.). It is connected with (7 M.) *N. Ontario* (p. 447) by the beautiful *Euclid Avenue*, planted with eucalyptus and pepper trees and traversed by a gravity tramway.

540 M. **Colton** (965 ft.; *Trans-Continental Hotel*, $2¹/₂-3; *Marlborough Ho.*, $2), a town of 1315 inhab., is of importance as the junction of lines to *San Bernardino* (p. 447), on the N., and *San Diego* (p. 449), on the S. It grows large quantities of fruits of various kind and is widely known for its excellent black and white marble (comp. p. 430). — The train now begins to ascend rapidly towards the ridge of the *San Bernardino Mts.*, which we cross, at (563 M.) *Beaumont*, by the *San Gorgonio Pass* (2560 ft.). On the other side we descend as rapidly towards the Colorado Desert (see below). To the right are the striking *San Jacinto Mts.* (highest summit 10,990 ft.), to the left the San Bernardino Range. — The **Colorado Desert**, which we now traverse for about 150 M., is a

barren sandy wilderness, a great part of which actually lies below sea-level (see below). Almost nothing grows on it except cactus and yucca-palms. The Gulf of California would seem to have extended to the vicinity of the San Gorgonio Pass and when it receded left a large inland sea of salt-water, which finally dried up, leaving large deposits of salt near Salton (see below). — 569 M. *Banning* (2320 ft.); 575 M. *Cabazon* (1780 ft.); 583 M. *White Water* (1125 ft.). — About 7 M. to the S.W. of (589 M.) *Palm Springs* (585 ft.) lies *Palm Valley* (Inn), at the E. base of the San Jacinto Mts., with the only natural grove of date palms in California and a curious hot sand-spring. It is now frequented to some extent as a health-resort, and fruit-growing is also carried on. — At (612 M.) *Indio* (Rail. Restaurant) we are about 20 ft. below the level of the sea, and at (637 M.) *Salton* we reach the lowest point, 263 ft. below sea-level. In 1891 a lake, 30 M. long, 10 M. wide, and 4 ft. deep, was created near Salton by the Colorado River, the country thus partly reverting for a time to the physical conditions mentioned above. 661 M. *Volcano Springs* (225 ft. below sea-level). At (671 M.) *Flowing Well* we are again 5 ft. above sea-level. 703 M. *Cactus* (395 ft.) — Farther on we cross the *Colorado River,* and enter *Arizona* (p. 413).

731 M. **Yuma** (140 ft.; *Southern Pacific Hotel,* with *Rail. Restaurant,* $2½), one of the hottest places in the country, which was established by the Spanish missionaries in 1700 and lies on the Colorado just below its confluence with the *Gila* ('Heela'). The Mexican frontier is only 7 M. to the S. The *Yuma Indians,* specimens of whom sell bows and arrows, etc., at the railway-station, have a reservation adjoining the Colorado. The *Territorial Prison* is situated at Yuma. — The train now follows the course of the Gila (left) through an arid and unattractive district. Cacti are abundant, including many specimens of the giant cactus *(Cereus giganteus;* Mex. *sahuaro),* often 40 ft. high and 'looking like a Corinthian column surmounted by candelabra'. Mirages are often seen in crossing Arizona by this route. To the left rise the *Castle Dome Mts.,* to the right the *Gila Range.* Farther on other mountains are seen on both sides. 791 M. *Mohawk Summit* (540 ft.); 854 M. *Gila Bend* (735 ft.; Rail. Restaurant); 873 M. *Estrella* (1520 ft.). — From (896 M.) *Maricopa* (1175 ft.) a branch-line runs to the N. to (35 M.) **Phoenix** *(Commercial Hotel, Lemon Ho.,* $2½), the capital of Arizona, a city of 3152 inhab., in the *Salt River Valley.* The remains of several prehistoric towns have been found in the vicinity. — About 16 M. to the N. (2 hrs. by stage) of (917 M.) *Casa Grande* (1395 ft.; Fryer Hotel, $2) are the highly interesting remains of the pueblo of *Casa Grande* or *Chichitilaca,* with enormous adobé walls. — The line continues to ascend steadily.

982 M. **Tucson** (pron. 'Toosahn'; *St. Xavier,* $2½-3; *Palace; Rail. Restaurant,* $2-3), a quaint old Spanish-looking place with 5150 inhab., is the largest city of Arizona and carries on a considerable trade with Mexico. It contains the *Territorial University* and

an *Indian School.* About 9 M. to the S. is the old mission-church of *St. Xavier,* founded at the close of the 17th century. — Beyond Tucson the *Santa Rita Mts.* are seen to the right, culminating in *Mt. Wrightson* (10,315 ft.); to the left are the *Santa Catalina Mts.* — 1029 M. *Benson* (3580 ft.) is the junction of the Atchison, Topeka, and Santa Fé line to *Guaymas,* on the W. coast of Mexico (Gulf of California). At (1050 M.) *Dragoon Summit* (4615 ft.) we reach the highest point of this part of the line and begin to descend slightly. 1071 M. *Wilcox* (4165 ft.); 1079 M. *Railroad Pass* (4395 ft.); 1095 M. *Bowie* (3760 ft.). At (1125 M.) *Stein's Pass* (4350 ft.), in the *Peloncillo Range,* we enter *New Mexico* (p. 419). 1145 M. *Lordsburg* (4245 ft.), the junction of a branch-line to *Clifton;* 1175 M. *Wilna* (4555 ft.) — 1204 M. *Deming* (4335 ft.; Depot Hotel, $ 3), a place of 1136 inhab., is the junction of the A., T., & S. F. line to *Rincon* (for La Junta, Denver, etc.; see p. 409) and also of a short line to (48 M.) *Silver City.* — 1215 M. *Zuñi* (4185 ft.; not to be confused with the pueblo mentioned at p. 413). Beyond (1288 M.) *Rogers* we cross the *Rio Grande* and enter *Texas* ('Lone Star State'), the largest state in the Union (265,780 sq. M., or larger than France).

1293 M. **El Paso** (3715 ft.; *Vendome,* $ 2½-3½; *Pierson; Rail. Restaurant*), a city of 10,338 inhab., is situated on the left bank of the Rio Grande and has become a place of some industrial importance, with silver-smelting works and cattle-yards. It is the chief gateway of the trade between the United States and Mexico. Just across the river is the Mexican town of *Juarez* or *El Paso del Norte* (see p. 485), connected with El Paso by an 'international' tramway. El Paso is the S. terminus of the A. T. & S. F. line (R. 91 b), the W. terminus of the *Texas & Pacific Railway* (R. 102), and the N. terminus of the *Mexican Central Railway* (R. 106). — Railway time changes here from the 'Pacific' to the 'Central' standard (2 hrs. faster); local time accords with the 'Mountain' standard (comp. p. xviii).

Beyond El Paso the line follows the general course of the Rio Grande, here forming the boundary between Texas and Mexico. Antelopes are occasionally seen from the train. 1298 M. *Ysleta* (3665 M.); 1340 M. *Fort Hancock* (3520 ft.); 1377 M. *Sierra Blanca* (4510 ft.; Rail. Restaurant); 1446 M. *Valentine* (4425 ft.); 1481 M. *Marfa* (4690 ft.), the main depot for *Fort Davis,* a little to the N. — At (1495 M.) *Paisano* (5080 ft.) we reach the highest point on the Southern Pacific Railway between San Francisco and New Orleans (1055 ft. higher than the Tehachapi Pass, p. 442). Fine mountain scenery. — 1556 M. *Haymond* (3885 ft.); 1601 M. *Sanderson* (2780 ft.; Rail. Restaurant); 1674 M. *Langtry* (1320 ft.), a military post. The Rio Grande is again in sight. Beyond (1685 M.) *Shumla* (1420 ft.) we cross the *Pecos River* by a fine cantilever bridge, 2180 ft. long and 328 ft. high (one of the highest railway-bridges in the world). Near (1695 M.) *Painted Cave* (1005 ft.), in the cañon of the *Rio Grande,* is a large cavern with some curious and undeci-

phered Indian hieroglyphics. As we approach (1735 M.) *Devil's River*
(970 ft.) we see, to the left, the singular *Palisades*, in the *Castle
Rock Cañon.* Beyond (1749 M.) *Del Rio* (955 ft.; Hotel Val Verde,
$1¹/₂) we leave the Rio Grande and traverse a cattle-raising district.
— From (1786 M.) *Spofford Junction* (1015 ft.) a line runs to (34 M.)
Eagle Pass. the starting-point of the *Mexican International Railway*
route to Mexico. (see p. 484). 1826 M. *Uvalde* (930 ft.); 1879 M.
Dunlay (1010 ft.).

1919 M. **San Antonio** (685 ft.; *Menger,* $3-5; *Maverick,* $2¹/₂-4;
Southern, Mahncke, $2; *Rail. Restaurant*), the chief city of Texas
and the 'cradle of Texas liberty', is a well-built city, of a distinctly
Spanish cast, situated on the *San Antonio River*, which, with its
small affluent the *San Pedro*, divides the city into three parts.
San Antonio is a very important wool, horse, mule, and cattle
market, and is the centre of numerous railways (comp. p. 466). It is
also the headquarters of the Department of Texas, one of the most
important military posts in the United States (see below). Its population of (1890) 37,673 consists in nearly equal proportions of Americans, Mexicans, and Germans, with a few Coloured people. San
Antonio is one of the most interesting cities in the country and will
repay a day's halt. It is frequented as a winter-resort by persons of
weak lungs (mean temp., winter 52°, summer 82°).

San Antonio de Bexar was settled by the Spaniards about 1690-1700,
and like most of their settlements combined the character of a *presidio*,
or military post, with that of a mission *(San Antonio de Valero).* The most
outstanding event in its history is the 'Fall of the Alamo' in 1836. Texas
had just declared her independence of Mexico, and the latter sent an
army under Santa Ana to reduce the rebels. The advance-guard of
4000 men reached San Antonio on Feb. 22nd and found the fortified Church
of the Alamo (see below) garrisoned by a body of 145 Americans (afterwards joined by 25 or 30 more), under Travis, Bowie, and Davy Crockett,
who refused to surrender. After a siege of 12 days, the church was finally
carried by assault (Mar. 6th) and all the survivors of the gallant little band
of defenders were put to the sword. 'Remember the Alamo' became a
burning watchword in subsequent struggles. See 'San Antonio de Bexar',
a handsomely illustrated volume by *Wm. Corner*, including a sketch by
Sydney Lanier (price $2), and 'Remember the Alamo', a novel by *Mrs. Barr*.

The first object of interest for most visitors to San Antonio is the
*Church of the Mission del Alamo, situated in the Alamo Plaza,
in the quarter to the E. of the San Antonio River. The church, which
seems to have derived its name from being built in a grove of *alamo*
or cottonwood trees (a kind of poplar; Populus monilifera), is a low
and strong structure of adobe, with very thick walls. It was built in
1744, but has lost many of its original features. It is now preserved
as a national monument (visitors admitted free). — At the N. end
of the Alamo Plaza, in *Houston Street*, is the handsome new *Federal
Building.* On the W. side is the building containing the *San Antonio
Club* and the *Grand Opera House.*

Following Houston St. towards the left (W.), we cross the San
Antonio and reach *Soledad Street*, which leads to the left to the Main
Plaza *(Plaza de Las Yslas)*, pleasantly laid out with gardens. On its

W. side stands the CATHEDRAL OF SAN FERNANDO, dating in its present form mainly from 1868-73, but incorporating parts of the earlier building, where Santa Ana had his headquarters in 1836. — To the W. of the Cathedral is the MILITARY PLAZA *(Plaza de Armas)*, with the large new *City Hall.*

The *MILITARY POST *(Fort Sam Houston)*, with a garrison of about 600 men, is finely situated on *Government Hill*, 1 M. to the N. of the city, and deserves a visit (parades with music almost daily). A splendid *View of the city and its environs is obtained from the tower (88 ft. high), in the centre of the quadrangle.

No stranger in San Antonio should neglect to visit some of the other old Spanish Missions near the city. Those most often visited are the *First* and *Second Missions* (see below), but, if time allows, the *Third* and *Fourth Missions* should be included. They can all be seen by a drive of 5 or 6 hrs. The **Mission of the Conception,** or *First Mission,* lies about 2¼ M. to the S. of the city (reached via Garden St.), dates from 1731-52, and is well preserved. The church has two W. towers and a central dome. The sculptures on the W. door should be noticed. — The *Mission San Jose de Aguayo,** or *Second Mission,* 4 M. to the S. of the city, dates from 1720-31 and is the most beautiful of all. Among the points to be noted are the W. façade of the church and the doorway, window, and capitals of the small chapel or baptistry. To the W. of the church is the *Mission Granary,* with its arched stone roof and flying buttresses (now used as a dwelling). The line of the rampart of the Mission Square is now obscured by adobe huts erected on its ruins. — The **Mission San Juan de Capistrano,** or *Third Mission,* 6 M. to the S. of San Antonio, dates from 1731. The line of its square is well defined, and its ruined church, chapel, and granary are interesting. About ½ M. distant is a solid old *Aqueduct,* taking water to the Fourth Mission. — The **Mission San Francisco de la Espada,** or *Fourth Mission,* on the W. bank of the San Antonio River, 9 M. to the S. of the city, also dates from 1731. At the S.E. corner of the Mission Square is a well-preserved *Baluarte* or bastion. The *Church* has been restored and is regularly used for service by the Indians here.

About 3 M. to the S. of San Antonio are the *International Fair Grounds and Buildings,* reached either by the Aransas Pass Railway or by electric tramway. Adjacent is *Riverside Park,* with fine groves of pecan trees *(carya olivae formis). San Pedro Park,* 1 M. to the N. of the city, contains fresh springs and a zoological collection.

From SAN ANTONIO TO ROCKPORT or ARANSAS PASS, 159 M., railway in 6½ hrs. The line runs towards the S.E. 61 M. *Kenedy* is the junction of a line to (177 M.) *Houston* (see p. 467). — 138 M. *Gregory* is the junction of a line, crossing *Corpus Christi Bay,* to (11 M.) **Corpus Christi** *(St. James,* $ 2; *Constantine; Alta Vista),* a city of 4387 inhab., frequented as a summer-resort. It is the N. terminus of the *Mexican National Railroad,* which runs hence to *Laredo* (see p. 467), and has a considerable shipping-trade. The *King Ranche,* 45 M. to the S. of Corpus Christi, is the largest cattle-ranche in the United States owned by one person (Mrs. Richard King). It covers 700,000 acres (1090 sq.M.) and is stocked with 100,000 cattle and 3000 brood-mares. — 159 M. **Rockport** or **Aransas Pass** *(Shell Hotel,* $ 2½-3; *Aransas Hotel,* $ 2), a place of 1069 inhab., situated on *Aransas Bay,* is a favourite resort for bathing and for its fine tarpon and other fishing. It has a good harbour, entered by *Aransas Pass,* which is now being improved by the construction of stone jetties. The country round Aransas Pass and Corpus Christi is very fertile and produces large quantities of fruit.

FROM SAN ANTONIO TO AUSTIN, 81 M., *International and Great Northern R. R.* in 3½-4 hrs. — The chief intermediate station is (50 M.) *San Marcos.* — 81 M. **Austin** *(Driskill,* $ 3; *Avenue, Brunswick,* $ 2½), the capital of Texas, a pleasant little city, with 14,575 inhab., lies on the *Colorado River,* in full view of the *Colorado Mts.* Its handsome red granite *Capitol,* finely situated on high ground, was' built by Chicago capitalists in 1881-88, at a cost of 3¹/₂ million dollars, in exchange for a grant of 3 million acres of land. It is the largest capitol in America, after that at Washington, and is said to be the seventh-largest building in the world. Other prominent buildings are the *State University* (300 students), the *Treasury Building*, the *Land Office*, the *Court House*, and various *Asylums*. About 2 M. above the city is the *Austin Dam*, a huge mass of granite masonry, 1200 ft. long, 60-70 ft. high, and 18-66 ft. thick, constructed across the Colorado River for water-power and waterworks.

FROM SAN ANTONIO TO LAREDO, 153 M., *International and Great Northern R. R.* in 6¹/₃ hrs. The intermediate stations are unimportant. — Laredo *(Hotel)*, a busy commercial city with 11,319 inhab., lies on the left bank of the *Rio Bravo del Norte* or *Rio Grande*. — *Mexican National Railroad* hence to the *City of Mexico*, see R. 104.

Beyond San Antonio the New Orleans line passes a number of stations of no great importance. 1986 M. *Harwood* (460 ft.); 2049 M. *Columbus* (210 ft.); 2098 M. *Rosenberg* (110 ft.).

2133 M. **Houston** (65 ft.; *Capitol Hotel*, $2¹/₂-3¹/₂; *Hutchins Ho.*, $2-4; *Grand Central*, $2-3; *Tremont*, $1¹/₂), locally pronounced 'Hewston', the fourth city of Texas in population (27,557 in 1890), lies on the narrow but navigable *Buffalo Bayou*, 50 M. above Galveston. It is a characteristic specimen of a 'hustling', go-ahead, 'Western' city, with more than usually extravagant hopes of future development. In 1890 the value of the cotton handled here amounted to $20,000,000 (4,000,000 *l.*), while a large trade was also done in sugar, timber, and cotton-seed oil. The numerous manufactories employ about 8000 workmen. Among the principal buildings are the *Market* and *City Hall*, the *Cotton Exchange*, the *Court House*, the *Post Office*, and the *Masonic Exchange*. A visit to one of its large *Cotton Presses* is interesting. Houston is a railway centre of great importance, about a dozen lines radiating hence in all directions.

FROM HOUSTON TO GALVESTON, 50 M., railway in 1³/₄ hr. — Intermediate stations unimportant. As we approach our destination we cross a trestle, 2 M. long, leading over the channel between the two wings of *Galveston Bay* to *Galveston Island*. — 50 M. **Galveston** (*Girardin*, $3-4; *Tremont*, $2¹/₂-3¹/₂; *Beach Hotel*, see below; $3¹/₂-4; British Consul, *Mr. H. D. Nugent*), the third city of Texas in population (29,084 in 1890) and the first in commercial importance, lies at the N.E. extremity of the long and narrow Galveston Island, at the entrance to *Galveston Bay*. It is the third cotton-shipping port in the United States (700,000 bales yearly), and other important exports are wool, hides, flour, grain, and fruit. Regular steamer-lines ply to New York, New Orleans, Key West, Havana, Vera Cruz, Brazos, and various South American and European ports. Galveston Bay has a total area of about 450 sq. M. and is guarded at its entrance by a long bar, through which the U. S. Government is now constructing, at vast expense, a deep water-channel flanked by stone-jetties, 5 M. long. The streets, which are little above the level of the bay, are wide and straight, and the residence-quarters abound in luxuriant gardens, shaded with oleanders, magnolias, etc. Among the principal buildings are the new *Custom House and Post Office*, the *Cotton Exchange*, the *City Hall*, the *Court House*, the *Ball Free School* (a large building with a dome), the *Rosenberg Free School*, the *Free Public Library*, and the R. C. *University of St. Mary*. *Magnolia Grove Cemetery* may be visited. — The city of Galveston lies mainly on the inner side of Galveston Island, on the outer or seaward side of which is a splendidly smooth and hard *Beach*, 30 M. long, affording an unrivalled drive or walk. The *Beach Hotel* (see above), near which are good bath-houses, is about 1¹/₄ M. from the centre of the city (tramway). Good tarpon and other fishing is obtainable.   The mean temperature of winter here is about 62°, of summer 82°.

From Galveston to *Fort Worth* and *Newton*, see p. 410; to *Texarkana* (for *St. Louis*, etc.), see p. 403.

Beyond Houston our line continues to run towards the E., traversing the great timber-producing part of Texas. At (2176 M.) *Liberty* (40 ft.) we cross the *Trinity River*. 2218 M. *Beaumont* (30 ft.) is the junction of lines N. to *Rockland* and S. to *Sabine Pass*, with a harbour improved by the U. S. Government. Beyond (2239 M.) *Orange* (20 ft.) we cross the *Sabine River* and enter *Louisiana* (p. 338). 2278 M. *Lake Charles;* 2352 M. *Lafayette* (50 ft.). The line now bends towards the S. 2391 M. *Baldwin.* The features of the scenery are tree-lined 'bayous', magnolia groves, live-oaks and cypresses draped with Spanish moss *(Tillandsia usneoides)*, and plantations of sugar-cane, cotton, and tobacco. — 2416 M. *Morgan City* (City Hotel, $2; 2291 inhab.) may be made the starting-point of an interesting steamer-trip up the picturesque *Bayou Teche*, penetrating the district to which the Acadians were removed (comp. Longfellow's 'Evangeline'). — At (2495 M.) *Algiers* (p. 367) we cross the *Mississippi.* 2496 M. **New Orleans,** see p. 366.

102. From New Orleans to Dallas, Fort Worth, and El Paso.

TEXAS AND PACIFIC RAILWAY to (515 M.) *Dallas* in 20-23 hrs. (fare $15.30), to (547 M.) *Fort Worth* in 21-24¹/₂ hrs. ($15.30), and to (1163 M.) *El Paso* in 48-52 hrs. ($33.40). — Through-carriages run by this route to Los Angeles and San Francisco, following the tracks of the Southern Pacific Railway (R. 101) beyond El Paso.

New Orleans, see p. 366. The line at first ascends on the right bank of the *Mississippi*, finally parting company with the river near (85 M.) *Plaquemine.* From (89 M.) *Baton Rouge Junction* a short line runs to (12 M.) *Port Allen*, opposite *Baton Rouge* (p. 321). From (172 M.) *Cheneyville* a line runs to the S. to *Lafayette* (p. 467), on the S. Pacific Railway. — 196 M. *Alexandria* (Exchange Ho., $2) is a pleasant little town of 2861 inhab., on the *Red River.* Steamers ply hence to Shreveport (see below). — 326 M. *Shreveport Junction,* for (2 M.) **Shreveport** *(Phoenix,* $2¹/₂-3), a busy industrial and commercial city with 11,979 inhab., on the Red River. Its chief exports are cotton and live-stock. Steamers ply regularly to Alexandria and New Orleans. Shreveport is the junction of lines to *Vicksburg* (p.321) and *Houston* (p. 467). — Our line now bends to the left (W.) and enters *Texas* (p. 464) beyond (349 M.) *Waskom.*

368 M. **Marshall** (400 ft.; Capitol Ho., $3), a brisk little city with 7207 inhab., machine-shops, and other factories, is the junction of a line to (74 M.) *Texarkana* (p.405), connecting therewith the Iron Mountain Line (R. 90). — 391 M. *Longview* (335 ft.; Mobberly, Magnolia, $2-2¹/₂) is the junction of the International and Great Northern Railway to Austin (p. 466), San Antonio (p. 465), and Laredo (p. 467). — 314 M. *Big Sandy;* 337 M. *Mineola* (400 ft.).

515 M. **Dallas** (465 ft.; *McLeod Hotel,* $2¹/₂-5; *Grand Windsor* $2¹/₂-4¹/₂; *St. George,* $2; *Lakeside,* at Oak Cliff), the largest city in Texas, lies on the *Trinity River,* in the centre of a rich corn, wheat, and cotton producing district. Pop. (1890) 38,067. It is a railway-centre of great importance, lines branching off to all points of the compass; and the annual value of its trade is $25,000,000, of its manufactures about $4,000,000. The *Court House* and *City Hall* are large buildings. On the bluffs (200 ft.) to the S. of Dallas is the suburban town of *Oak Cliff,* with a large Female University.

547 M. **Fort Worth** (640 ft.; *Pickwick,* $2¹/₂-3¹/₂; *Vernon,* $2¹/₂-3; *Ginnochio, Mansion,* $2¹/₂), a city with (1890) 23,076 in-hab., on the Trinity River, is the chief railway centre of the South West, including lines to *Wichita* (p.410) and *Newton* (p. 410), *Austin* (p. 466), *San Antonio* (p. 465), and *Houston* (p. 467). This is the headquarters of the stock-men of the Texas 'Pan Handle' and has large stockyards, grain elevators. and flour-mills. The annual value of its trade is $30,000,000. To the W. are *Arlington Heights* (180 ft.; **Arlington Inn,* $3-4), a winter-resort commanding a splendid view of Trinity Valley.

Beyond Fort Worth the line traverses an interminable cattle-rais-ing district, with few points of interest for the traveller. Stations un-important. 578 M. *Weatherford* (865 ft.). 662 M. *Cisco* (1610 ft.) is the junction of the Houston and Central Texas R. R. 708 M. *Abilene;* 739 M. *Sweet Water;* 816 M. *Big Springs.*

To the N. of this part of the line extends the **Llano Estacado** or *Great Staked Plain,* a district of 50,000 sq. M., consisting of a vast elevated plateau nearly 5000 ft. above the sea, surrounded by an escarpment of erosion re-sembling palisades. On the N. it is bounded by the *Canadian River* and on the E. by the *Pecos.* The name is said to be due to the stakes driven into it by the Spaniards to mark their way. The soil is generally a brown loam, covered with grama grass *(Bouteloua digostachya)* and low mesquite shrubs, but there are also large tracts of sand. There is no other vegetation. The surface is almost perfectly level, except where a slight variation is afforded by the sandhills. There is no surface-water, except in a few scattered ponds, but numerous wells have been sunk, and the Staked Plain has thus now become a vast cattle pasturage. The geological condi-tions are interesting to the scientific visitor.

Beyond (876 M.) *Odessa* we see the *White Sand Hills* to the right. 948 M. *Pecos City,* on the *Pecos River,* is the junction of the Pecos Valley R. R. to (90 M.) *Eddy.* From (968 M.) *Toyah* stages run to *Fort Davis* and *Fort Stockton.* We now enter a mountainous district, with the *Guadaloupe Mts.* to the right and the *Apache Mts.* to the left. At (1048 M.) *Carrizo* the *Carrizo Mts.* rise to the right. From (1071 M.) *Sierra Blanca* to —

1163 M. **El Paso**, see p. 464.

103. From Tacoma to Puget Sound, Victoria, and Alaska.

The steamer 'Queen' of the *Pacific Coast Steamship Co.* (3000 tons burden) makes about six trips from Tacoma to *Sitka* and back every summer (June-Aug.), taking 12-14 days to the round journey (fare $100-250, according to position of berth and stateroom, the highest charge securing the sole occupancy of a large stateroom). This steamer carries passengers only and calls at Seattle, Port Townsend, Victoria, Nanaimo, Fort Wrangell, Juneau, Chilkat, the Muir Glacier, and Sitka. — The steamships 'City of Topeka' and 'Mexico' of the same company, starting from *Portland*, sail fortnightly the year round, carry freight as well as passengers, take 18-22 days for the round trip from Tacoma (fares $ 100-250), and call at more points in Alaska. Return-tickets are also issued from San Francisco (fare from $ 130), passengers travelling by sea between that city and Portland or Port Townsend (p. 471). The fares from Seattle, Port Townsend, or Victoria are slightly lower than those from Tacoma. — Other excursion steamers occasionally make the trip to Alaska in summer but cannot be recommended.

Passengers should secure their berths in advance. A pamphlet with all necessary information, including stateroom-plans of the steamers, may be obtained from Messrs. Goodall, Perkins, & Co., 10 Market St., San Francisco, or from any agent of the company. The arrangements of the Alaska trip resemble those on the trip to the North Cape (see *Baedeker's Norway and Sweden*), and it involves no greater hazard or fatigue. There are no hotels in Alaska, and passengers live entirely on the steamers. The weather is generally pleasant in June, July, or Aug., though rain and fog may be looked for at some part of the voyage, and forest-fires are apt to obscure the sky in the first part of the trip, especially in July and August. Warm winter clothing should! be taken, as the nights on board are often very cold, though the sun may be quite powerful during the day. Stout boots are desirable for the short excursions on land, and waterproofs are indispensable. Nearly the whole of the voyage is in the calm channel between the coast-islands and the mainland, so that sea-sickness need not be dreaded. The steamers, though not so luxurious as the Atlantic liners or the Fall River boats, are safe and reasonably comfortable. A little more variety and 'local colour' in the cuisine would be an improvement. The *Scenery passed en route* is of a most grand and unique character, such as, probably, cannot be seen elsewhere at so little cost and with so little toil or adventure. In the description of the text the usual route of the 'Queen' is followed. The approximate distances from Tacoma by this course are given in nautical miles (7 naut. miles = about 8 statute miles). Native curiosities can, perhaps, be best obtained at Sitka (p. 479), furs at Juneau (p. 477).

Tacoma, see p. 376. The first part of the voyage lies through *Puget Sound*, named from a lieutenant on Vancouver's vessel, one of the most beautiful salt-water estuaries in the world, surrounded by finely wooded shores and lofty mountains. Its area is about 2000 sq. M., while its extremely irregular and ramified shore-line is nearly 1600 M. long. The usual width is 4-5 M. The depth varies from 300 to 800 ft., and at many points 'a ship's side would strike the shore before the keel would touch the ground'. There are numerous islands. A very large trade is carried on in Puget Sound in timber, coal, and grain, the annual value of its exports amounting to about $10,000,000 (2,000,000*l.*). As we proceed *Mt. Rainier* or *Tacoma* (p. 377) is conspicuous to the S.E., while the *Olympic Mts.* (6-8000 ft.) are seen to the W.

25 M. **Seáttle** (three syllables; *The Rainier*, with fine view, $3-5; *Arlington*, $2-3, R. from $1; *Grand, Occidental*, R. from $1), finely situated in *Elliot Bay*, on a series of terraces rising from the shore of the Sound, is one of the largest and most energetic cities of the Pacific North-West. Founded in 1852 and named after an Indian chief, it had 4533 inhab. in 1880 and 42,837 in 1890. Its prosperity is the more remarkable as almost the whole of the business-

quarters was burned down in 1889; but this calamity seems, as in the case of Chicago (p. 279), to have served merely as an opportunity for rebuilding the city in a handsomer and more substantial manner. Among the best buildings are the *Court House*, the *Opera House*, the *High School*, the *Providence Hospital*, the *State University* (200 students), and the *Rainier Hotel*. The higher parts of the city command splendid views of the Olympic Mts. — The large and spacious *Harbour*, with its numerous wharves, is entered and cleared annually by about 1000 vessels, the chief exports being coal (600,000 tons), timber, hops, and fish. The value of its manufactures (1890) was $9,200,000. Iron has also been found in the neighbourhood.

About 2 M. to the E. of Elliot Bay lies *Washington Lake (easily reached by tramway) a beautiful sheet of fresh water, 20 M. long and 2-5 M. wide. Small steamers ply to various points on the lake, affording beautiful views of the *Cascade Mts.* (p. 376).

FROM SEATTLE TO VANCOUVER, 168 M., railway in 8 hrs. This line runs to the N. along the E. bank of Puget Sound and Washington Sound. 55½ M. *Stanwood;* 95 M. *Fairhaven,* a thriving little place (4076 inhab.) on *Bellingham Bay;* 98 M. *Whatcom* (Bellingham Ho.), also on Bellingham Bay (4059 inhab.). Beyond (119 M.) *Blaine* we enter *British Columbia.* 143½ M. *New Westminster* (Queen's Hotel, $2-3), with 6641 inhab., is the oldest settlement in this region. At (156 M.) *Port Moody* we join the main line of the *Canadian Pacific Railway.* — 168 M. Vancouver, see *Baedeker's Canada.*

From Seattle to *Tacoma* by railway, see p. 377; to *N. Yakima* and *Pasco Junction* (for the E.), see p. 376; to *Everett, Spokane,* and *St. Paul,* see R. 55. Lines also run to various other points.

Steamers ply to Tacoma, Victoria, and other ports in Puget Sound, on the Pacific Coast, and in Europe.

As the steamer continues to plough its way towards the N., we obtain a view of **Mt. Baker** (10,800 ft.), the last outlier of the Cascade Mts., far ahead of us (right). The steamer bends to the left into *Admiralty Inlet*, the main entrance to Puget Sound. To the right lies *Whitbey Island.*

65 M. **Port Townsend** *(Central,* $3; *Delmonico),* a picturesque little town of 4558 inhab., lies partly on the shore and partly on a steep bluff behind, reached by long flights of steps. It lies at the head of the *Strait of Juan de Fuca* and is the port of entry for Puget Sound. The large grey-stone building on the bluff is the *Custom House.* To the left lies *Fort Townsend,* with a large marine hospital.

Our boat now steers to the N.W. across the Strait of Juan de Fuca. To the left are the Olympic Mts., ahead lies Vancouver Island; to the right, in the distance, rises Mt. Baker. As we approach Victoria the little city presents a very picturesque appearance. The conspicuous building on the height to the right is the house of *Mr. Dunsmuir,* a wealthy coal-owner (comp. p. 472). To the left of the pier, among trees, are the barracks of *Esquimault* (see p. 472).

100 M. **Victoria** *(Dallas, Driard,* $3-5; *Victoria; Clarence; Poodle Dog Restaurant,* D. 75 c.; cabs cheap), the capital of British Columbia, is a quaint and quiet little city with 16,841 inhab., forming a strong contrast to the bustling and raw-looking cities we have just been visiting on the American shores of the Sound. Victoria, however, is

also of recent origin, having been founded as a station of the Hudson Bay Co. in 1843 and not beginning to develop into a town until the gold-mining excitement of 1858. The population includes about 3000 Chinamen. The export trade in 1891 was valued at $5,630,000 (1,126,000*l.*). The centre of the town (1$\frac{1}{2}$ M.) is reached from the wharf by tramway (5 c.). The *GOVERNMENT BUILDINGS, forming a tasteful group in a square adjoining James's Bay, include the *Parliament House*, a *Provincial Museum*, and the *Government Offices*. The monument in front commemorates *Sir James Douglas*, first governor of the colony. *Beacon Hill Park should also be visited. The streets are wide and clean, and most of the private residences stand in gardens rich in shrubs and flowers. The roads in the vicinity of Victoria are unusually good and afford charming drives through luxuriant woods of pine, maples, alders, arbutus, madronas, fern-trees, and syringas.

About 3 M. to the S.W. of Victoria (tramway; return-fare 25 c.) lies Esquimault, the headquarters of the British Pacific Squadron, with a good harbour, a dockyard (closed at 5 p.m.), a fine dry-dock, barracks, and a naval arsenal. Some British men-of-war may generally be seen here.

From Victoria to *Nanaimo*, see below. — Steamers ply regularly from Victoria to *Vancouver* (see *Baedeker's Canada*).

Vancouver Island, at the S. extremity of which Victoria lies, is 300 M. long and 25-70 M. wide, with an area of 18,000 sq. M. The greater part of its surface is covered with mountains, reaching an extreme height of 8-9000 ft., and but little has been reclaimed or settled by Europeans since its exploration by Vancouver in 1794. The two native tribes are the *Nootkas* and *Selish*, of whom a few degenerate specimens may be met in Victoria.

From Victoria our course lies to the N., through the *Canal de Haro*, which was decided by the arbitration of the King of Prussia in 1872 to be the line of demarcation between American and British possessions. To the left lies Vancouver Island, to the right the *San Juan Islands*, beyond which the cone of Mt. Baker is long visible. Looking backward, we see the Olympic Mts., on the other side of the Juan de Fuca Strait. On issuing from the archipelago of Haro Strait, we enter the broader waters of the Gulf of Georgia (20-30 M. wide). Various islands lie off the shore of Vancouver.

130 M. *Nanaimo*, a small town on the E. coast of Vancouver, with 4595 inhab., is of importance as the outlet of the extensive Wellington coal-mines (first exploited by Mr. Dunsmuir, p. 471). The Alaska steamers stop to coal here either in going or returning. The pretty, rose-gardened cottages of Nanaimo are very unlike the grimy abodes of coal-miners in England, and many of the miners own them in freehold. Nanaimo is connected with (70 M.) *Victoria* by the only railway on the island. — *Vancouver* (see *Baedeker's Canada*) lies on the mainland, directly opposite Nanaimo (steamer).

Farther on we see few settlements or signs of life. The shores are low and heavily wooded, but lofty mountains rise behind them on both sides, those on the mainland covered with snow. Long, deep, and narrow fjords, flanked with lofty mountains, run up into the land. To the right lie *Lesqueti Island* and the large *Texada Island*, covering the entrance to *Jervis Inlet*, one of the just-mentioned fjords. About 80 M. beyond Nanaimo we leave the Gulf of Georgia and enter *Discovery Passage, a river-like channel, 30 M. long and 1-2 M. wide, which separates Vancouver Island from *Valdes Island* and is flanked by mountains 3-6000 ft. high. Valdes Island, ending on the S. in *Cape Mudge*, occupies nearly the whole channel, and a scheme is now in consideration for running a railway from the mainland to Vancouver Island by bridges constructed over the narrow waterways here. About the middle of Discovery Passage are the famous *Seymour *Narrows*, 2 M. long and 1/2 M. wide, through which the water rushes with great velocity.

Discovery passage is succeeded by *Johnstone Strait, another similar channel, 55 M. long and 1-3 M. wide, between Vancouver Island on the left and the mainland itself or islands hardly distinguishable from it on the right. The *Prince of Wales Range*, on Vancouver Island, culminates in the snow-clad *Mt. Albert Edward* (6970ft.); and the white summits of the *Cascade Range* rise to the right beyond the lower intervening hills. The varied beauty of the scenery cannot easily be indicated in words; but few travellers will weary of the panorama unfolded before them as the steamer advances. — Beyond Johnstone Strait we thread the shorter *Broughton Strait* (15 M. long), between Vancouver and *Cormorant* and *Malcolm Islands*. On Cormorant Island lies the Indian village of *Alert Bay*, with a salmon-cannery and a native graveyard. The conical summit to the left is *Mt. Holdsworth* (3040 ft.).

On emerging from Broughton Strait we enter Queen Charlotte's Sound, which is 10-30 M. wide and contains many islands, mostly adjoining the mainland. On the shore of Vancouver lies *Fort Rupert*, an old post of the Hudson's Bay Co., with an Indian village. A little later we pass through *Goletas Channel* and then say farewell to Vancouver Island, the N. point of which, *Cape Commerell*, we leave to the left. For a short time (40 M.) we are now exposed to the swell of the Pacific Ocean, but this is seldom enough in summer to cause uneasiness even to bad sailors. To the N.W., in the distance, loom the large *Queen Charlotte Islands*.

Our course now hugs the mainland and leads at first through *Fitzhugh Sound, a deep and narrow channel, the W. shore of which is formed by a continuous series of islands. The sharp peak of *Mt. Buxton* (3430 ft.) rises on *Calvert Island*. As we near the N. end of the Sound the scenery becomes very grand, huge snowy peaks towering above the pine-clad hills that line the channel. Beyond the large *Hunter's Island* we turn sharply to the left and enter the extremely narrow and winding *Lama Passage, between it and *Denny Island*. On *Campbell Island*, to the left, is the Indian village of *Bella Bella*, opposite which is a graveyard, with totem-poles (comp. p. 475). Farther on we pass through the wider *Seaforth Channel* and reach *Millbank Sound*, the only other point on the voyage where we are exposed for a brief interval to the waves of the open sea. Beyond this sound we enter *Finlayson Channel,* 24 M. long and 2 M. wide, between the large *Princess Royal Island* (48 M. long and 25 M. wide) and the mainland. Numerous fjords, short and long, run into the mainland, and several high waterfalls descend from the cliffs. Finlayson Channel is continued by *Tolmie Channel, Graham Reach,* and *Frazer Reach,* beyond which we pass through *McKay Reach,* between the N. end of Princess Royal Island and *Gribbell Island,* into *Wright's Sound.* From this we enter *Grenville Channel,* which runs for 50 M. in an almost perfectly straight line between *Pitt Island* and the mainland. It is flanked on both sides with steep mountains 1500-3500 ft. high, while still higher mountains rise in the background to the right. At places the channel is only a few hundred feet wide. Signs of glacier action are seen on the more distant mountains, while the courses of long bye-gone avalanches may be traced by the light-green streaks of the younger growth of trees. Crossing an expansion of Grenville Channel, we next enter the short *Arthur Passage,* between *Porcher Island* (l.) and *Kennedy Island* (r.), which leads to *Malacca Passage* and the wide **Chatham Sound.** To the right is the mouth of the *Skeena River.* The E. side of the Sound is bounded by the large *Chim-sy-an* or *Tsimpsean Peninsula,* which is connected with the mainland by a very narrow neck of land. On this lies *Old Metlakatla,* the scene of Mr. Wm. Duncan's interesting experiences in educating the natives (see **p. 476**) and now a missionary station of the Episcopal Church of Canada. Higher up is *Port Simpson,* a station of the Hudson Bay Co., established in 1831. Our steamer, however, does not call at either of these points. To the left lie the *Dundas Islands,* opposite the northernmost of which opens *Portland Inlet.* Just here we cross the boundary-line between the British and American possessions (54° 40′ N. lat.; the famous 'fifty-four forty or fight' of 1842) and enter **Alaska.** To the left opens *Dixon Entrance,* between *Graham Island* (S.) and *Prince of Wales Island* (N.).

The territory of **Alaska** received its name from Charles Sumner in a speech addressed to the Senate in favor of the purchase of the territory. It is a corruption of an Aleut word referring to the continent as distinguished from the Aleutian islands. The boundaries of the territory comprise the continent and islands adjacent, to the W. of 141° W. lon., and also a strip to the W. of a line drawn parallel to the coast from the vicinity of Mt. St. Elias (p. 480) in a S.E. direction to the N. extreme of Portland Canal, through the canal in mid-channel, and westward to the ocean on the parallel of 54° 40′ N. lat. The W. limits of the territory, to the N. of the Pacific Ocean, include the Aleutian chain, the islands of Bering Sea, and the eastern of the two Diomede Islands in Bering Strait.

The territory is divisible by its physical characteristics into several diverse regions. The *Sitkan Region,* including the coast and islands to Cook's Inlet on the N. and the Kadiak group on the W., has a rough and mountainous topography with many glaciers, a bold sea-coast, numerous fjords and islands, a moist, cool, and equable climate, and a dense covering of chiefly coniferous forests. — The *Aleutian Region* includes the peninsula of Alaska, the Aleutian chain, and the Pribiloff or Fur-seal Islands. It also has a cool and equable climate, with much fog and wind but less rain than in the Sitkan region. It consists of broad level areas with numerous clusters of mountains, few glaciers, many volcanic cones, many harbours and anchorages; and, while totally destitute of trees, nourishes luxuriant crops of grass, herbage, and wild flowers. The Aleutian chain represents an old line of fracture in the earth's crust; and, contrary to the usual idea, a large proportion of the islands are not volcanic but composed of crystalline or sedimentary rocks. — The *Yukon Region* includes the mass of the continent to the N. of the great peninsula, which has on its N. border true Arctic conditions, on its W. shores a mild summer and an Arctic winter, and in the interior a hot short summer and a dry cold winter, much like that of Minnesota. It is a region of *Tundra*: low, undulating ranges of grassy mountains, and extensive, level, more or less wooded river valleys.

The products of the Sitkan region are timber, precious metals, salmon, halibut, and other sea-fish. Lignitic coal and extensive beds of marble exist in many places. The Aleutian region produces chiefly fox and sea otter fur, the fur-seal pelts, and a certain amount of coal. Extensive cod-fisheries are prosecuted along its shores. The Yukon region, except for a little placer-mining, produces nothing but furs and salmon. A remarkable characteristic of the Territory is that, though bordering on the Arctic Ocean and in the S. teaming with glaciers, it has still never been subjected to the action of a continental ice sheet, such as have ground down the coasts of the analogous fjord-regions of New England and Norway.

The native inhabitants of Alaska belong to four ethnologic stock races: the *Eskimo* or *Innuit*, with their special offshoot the *Aleutian* people; the *Haida Indians* of Alaska; the *Tlinkit* stock of the Sitkan region; and the *Tinneh* or *Athabascan Indians* of the great interior region. In all there are between twenty and thirty thousand of these natives, independent, self-sustaining, and mostly well disposed. They are in no direct way related to any of the present Asiatic races as is so often assumed, but, from the evidences of the prehistoric shell-heaps, have occupied the region for many centuries. They live by fishing and hunting; the moose, the caribou, and the salmon, in the interior, and the hair-seal, the beluga, the cod and other sea-fishes, the salmon, and wild fowl, on the coasts, furnish their chief supplies. The fjords and rivers are their roads; with hardly an exception they are canoe-men everywhere, and throughout the N. drivers of dogs and sledges.

Among the Tlinkit and Haida people one custom is forced on the attention of all who visit their villages. It is that of erecting what are called *Totem Poles*, which have various significations, the most common being that of a 'genealogical tree'. A man erects one of their large communal houses, and, in memory of this achievement, puts up in front of it a cedar pole carved with figures emblematic of the totems of himself and his ancestors, one above another. The door of the house is frequently cut through the base of the pole under the totem of the builder; while, above, the successive totems (which by their social laws must change with every generation) appear in the order of remoteness.

The estimated area of the territory is 580,000 sq. M. (thrice that of France); its total population about 35,000, of which one-seventh are accounted civilized; its chief archipelago, in the Sitkan region, is said to contain 11,000 islands; its total shore line amounts to some 18,200 M.; its principal commercial port is in about the same latitude as Liverpool; its southernmost islands lie on the parallel of Brussels; its westernmost village is as far W. from the mouth of the Columbia River, Oregon, as Eastport, Maine, is E. from that point; it includes within its boundaries the highest mountains, the most superb glaciers and volcanos in America to the N. of Mexico; and presents the anomaly of a territory with only about one inhabitant to 17 sq. M. which in 20 years has paid more than eight million dollars in taxes. It was transferred by Russia to the United States in 1867 for the sum of $7,250,000.

The most authoritative and complete work on Alaska is 'Alaska and its Resources' by *Dr. Wm. H. Dall*, who kindly drew up the above paragraphs for this Handbook. A good popular account is given in *Miss E. R. Scidmore's* 'Alaska and the Sitkan Archipelago'.

To the right, as we proceed, juts out *Cape Fox*, with the small station of *Fort Tongas*. The steamer now steers in a straight direction towards the N. and enters **Clarence Strait**, which is 100 M. long and 4-12 M. wide and is bounded on the W. by *Prince of Wales Island* (130 M. long and 30 M. wide). This is the home of the *Haidas*, the cleverest of the Alaskan tribes (comp. p. 475), and contains the best totem-poles, but the ordinary tourist has no opportunity of landing here. *Annette Island*, the largest of the Gravina group, is the seat of *Port Chester*, with the new *Metlakatla*, founded by Mr. Duncan on leaving his original station (see p. 474). We are now within what is known as the *Alexander Archipelago*, about 1100 of the islands of which appear on the U. S. charts, while innumerable small islets are disregarded. The mountains on each side of the strait are fine in size, proportions, and colouring. Near the head of Clarence Strait we steer to the right (E.), between *Etolin Island* (r.) and *Zarembo Island* (l.) and run into *Fort Wrangell*, usually the first stopping-place of the steamer 'Queen' after leaving Victoria.

790 M. (from Tacoma) **Fort Wrangell**, situated on the N. end of the island of the same name, opposite the mouth of the *Stikine River*, was formerly a place of some importance, as the outlet of the Cassiar Mines, but is now a dirty and dilapidated settlement inhabited by about 250 Tlinkits (p. 475) and a few whites. It was named from Baron Wrangell, Russian Governor of Alaska at the time of its settlement (1834).

To the tourist Fort Wrangell is of interest as containing the best collection of *Totem Poles* he is likely to see, though their execution is by no means so fine as that of the Haidas (see p. 475). The totems here are 20-40 ft. high. One is surmounted by a bear, another by a head with a 'Tyhee' hat, the badge of a *Shaman* or 'Medicine Man'. A specimen of such a hat, said to be 400 years old, is shown in one of the houses. The old *Graveyard* is so overgrown with vegetation as to be difficult of access and now contains little of typical interest. The carved figure of a bear (or wolf) which surmounted one of the graves now lies on the ground near two of the totem-poles.

The Tlinkits themselves will interest the visitors, who will at once notice such customs as the blackening of the faces of the girls (said to have for its object the preservation of the complexion) and the wearing of *labrets*, or small plugs of silver, ivory, wood, or bone, in the lower lip. Curiosities of various kinds, including labrets, silver bracelets, carved horn and wooden spoons, reed baskets, halibut hooks, gaily painted canoe-paddles, the carved rattles of the Shamans, and fine carvings in slate may be purchased from the natives; and the inquisitive may visit the imperfectly ventilated interior of one of the huts.

At the end of the village farthest from that with the totem-poles are the *Court House* and a *Mission School for Girls*, the teacher of which is glad to give information to interested visitors.

Soon after leaving Fort Wrangell we thread our way through the devious *Wrangell Narrows*, where the channel is marked by stakes and buoys. The shores here are well-wooded, and at places stretches of grass border the water like the lawns of an English country-house. Farther on, in *Soukhoi Channel*, the scenery is of a more majestic character. The mountains on either side, though apparently of no very great height, are covered with snow to within 1000 ft., or less, of the water; and their shapes are very varied and beautiful. One of the most striking is the *Devil's Thumb*, a peaked monolith recalling the Dolomites of Tyrol. We here see the first glaciers of the voyage (all to the right): the *Le Conte Glacier*, high up on the mountain-side; the larger *Patterson Glacier;* and the *Baird Glacier.* About this part of the trip, too, we may meet our first piece of floating ice; while the indescribably beautiful effects of the late sunsets (9-10 p.m.) will rouse even the most sluggish enthusiasm. The huge slopes of *névé*, or hardened snow, are very fine.

Soukhoi Channel widens into *Frederick Sound*, with *Kupreanoff Island* to the left; but our course soon leaves this sound and carries us to the N. through the long *Stephens Passage*, bounded on the W. by the large *Admiralty Island*. *Holkam Bay*, to the right, was at one time the scene of some placer-mining. Near the head of the passage, to the right, opens *Taku Inlet, with its fine glaciers, one of which has a sea-face ¹/₂ M. long and 100-200 ft. high. The muddy grey water of the inlet is filled with ice-floes and bergs. The surrounding mountains are of a fantastic, Dolomitic appearance. — Just beyond the mouth of the Taku Inlet we enter the pretty *Gastineau Channel*, between *Douglas Island* and the mainland.

990 M. **Juneau,** the largest town in Alaska, with (1890) 1253 inhab., about equally divided between whites and natives or half-breeds, is situated on the mainland, on a narrow strip of comparatively level ground between the sea and a precipitous, snow-seamed mountain (3300 ft.). Settled in 1880 and named after a nephew of the founder of Milwaukee (p. 287), it is occupied mainly by miners. It has a mission-school and publishes a weekly paper, the *Alaska Free Press.* The attractions of the town itself are limited, but it contains perhaps the best shops for the sale of Alaskan furs (sea-otter, seal, otter, beaver, bear, musk-rat, fox, etc.) and the famous *Chilkat Blankets.* The last are made of the hair of mountain-goats and coloured with native dyes, but genuine examples, worth $60-100, are now rare, and most of those offered for sale are made of wool and stained with aniline dyes.

About ¹/₂ M. to the N. of Juneau is a village of the *Auk Indians*, a curious and primitive, but very dirty settlement, which will repay a visit. The traveller may bargain here for a trip in an Indian canoe. Behind the village is a native *Cemetery*, with curious little huts containing the cremated remains and personal effects of the deceased.

Juneau possesses a few horses and carts and one of the only two roads in Alaska. This leads through the highly picturesque **Cañon of the Gold Creek*, with its waterfalls and small glacier, to (3¹/₂ M) **Silver Bow Mines,** and offers a trip well worth making if time allows. The Silver Bow Basin contains gold mines of great promise, and both quartz and placer mining are successfully prosecuted.

On Douglas Island, nearly opposite Juneau, is the famous ***Treadwell Gold Mine,** at which the steamers generally call. The mine, which is closn to the wharf and easily visited, has the largest quartz-crushing mill in the world, employing 240 stamps. The quartz does not produce more thae $4-6 of metal per ton, but is so easily and economically worked that the profits are said to be enormous. It is credibly stated that the company that owns it refused $16,000,000 for the mine, and the gold actually in sight is estimated to be worth 4-5 times as much as the price paid for the entire district of Alaska (p. 475). Many of the best workers in the mine are natives, who earn $ 2¹/₂ per day.

As Gastineau Channel has not been charted above Juneau, the steamer now returns to its S. end and then proceeds to the N. through *Saginaw Channel*, on the W. side of Douglas Island. This debouches on *Lynn Canal, a fine fjord extending for 60 M. towards the N. It is flanked with snow-mountains, rising abruptly from the very edge of the water, and presents, perhaps, the grandest scenic features we have yet encountered. About a score of glaciers, large and small, descend from the ravines into the fjord, among which the *Auk, Eagle* (r.), and *Davidson Glaciers* are conspicuous. The last-mentioned, near the head of the fjord and on its W. side, spreads out to a width of 3 M. as it reaches the water-level, its front being partly masked by a tree-grown moraine. Lynn Canal ends in two prongs, named the *Chilkoot* and *Chilkat Inlets*. The steamer usually ascends to *Pyramid Harbor*, at the head of the latter (the E. arm), and here we reach the highest latitude of the trip (59° 10′ 36″ N.; about that of the Orkney Islands, Christiania, and St. Petersburg). At midsummer there are not more than 3-4 hrs. of partial darkness here. Visitors who chose may land by one of the ship's boats and visit the small Chilkat village (80-100 inhab.), which possesses a prosperous salmon-cannery. There are also other settlements on the inlet. This is the district in which the fine Chilkat blankets (p. 477) are made. Good echoes may be wakened off the glaciers.

We now return to the S. end of Lynn Canal and then bend to the right (N.W.) into *Icy Strait*. Opening off this to the right is *Glacier Bay, which extends to the N. for about 30 M., with a width contracting from 12 M. to 3 M. The mountains immediately abutting on the bay are comparatively low (6000-7000 ft.), but as we ascend it we enjoy a magnificent **View to the left of the **Fairweather Range,** including (named from left to right) *Mt. La Perouse* (11,300 ft.), *Mt. Crillon* (15,900 ft.), *Mt. Lituya* (10,000 ft.), and *Mt. Fairweather* (15,500 ft.). The surface of the bay is full of small icebergs and floes detached from the large glaciers which descend into it, and the most careful navigation cannot avoid an occasional bump. As we near the head of the bay we have an excellent view of the wonderful **Muir Glacier, the grandest single feature of our Alaskan expedition (1270 M. from Tacoma by the course described). To the right is seen the small hut in which Prof. John Muir lived when making his explorations of the glacier in 1879. The steamer anchors as near the face of the glacier as prudence permits.

This stupendous glacier, throwing the large ice-fields of Switzerland entirely into the shade, enters the sea with a front 1 M. wide and 200-300 ft. high, probably extending twice as far below the water. From this wonderful wall of blue and white ice, which forms a striking contrast to the dirty terminal moraines of European glaciers, huge masses of ice, often weighing many hundreds of tons, detach themselves at frequent intervals

and fall into the bay with a reverberating roar, throwing up the water
in clouds of spray and creating waves that rock the huge steamer like
a cock-boat. Nine main streams of ice unite to form the trunk of
the glacier, which occupies a vast amphitheatre, 30-40 M. across. Seventeen
smaller arms join the main stream. The width of the glacier when it
breaks through the mountains to descend to the sea is about 2 M. Prof.
G. F. Wright, who explored the glacier in 1886, estimated its rate of
movement at 70 ft. per day in the centre and 10 ft. at the sides (an average
of 40 ft.), as compared with 1¹/₂-3 ft. at the Mer de Glace, but Prof. H. F.
Reid, of Johns Hopkins University, who spent the summer of 1889 here,
found the most rapid movement not more than 8-10 ft. per day. In August
about 200,000,000 cubic feet of ice fall into the inlet daily. Though the
glacier thus moves forward at a comparatively rapid rate, investigation
shows that it loses more ice in summer than it gains in winter and that
its front is retrograding steadily from year to year. It is evident from the
general appearance of the enclosing hills that the ice-stream once occupied
the whole of Glacier Bay; and numerous features of the moraines and
adjacent rocks give proof of more recent retrocession. Vancouver found
the bay blocked by a wall of ice in 1794.

Visitors are landed in small boats on one of the lateral moraines, and
by following this back for a mile or more may reach the surface of the
main glacier, which they may follow as far as time allows. The seaward
end of the glacier is so corrugated and seamed by vast crevasses as to be
quite inaccessible. The surface of the glacier commands a splendid view
of Glacier Bay and the Fairweather Range; and those who are good climbers
may obtain a still better view by ascending the stony conical mountain
(ca. 3000 ft.) on the left (N.W.) side of the glacier, about 2 M. from the
bay. Walking on the smooth surface of the glacier is generally easy in
summer; but the feet should be well protected against dampness, as the
strong summer-sun (which makes too warm clothing undesirable) has considerable effect on the surface-ice. The steamboat company provides alpen-
stocks for the use of passengers, and has constructed a plank-walk, with
guide-posts, leading up to the glacier. Those who make longer explorations should keep a good lookout for snow-covered fissures and avoid
wandering off alone.

The **Pacific Glacier**, which enters Glacier Bay to the W. of the Muir
Glacier, has a sea-front of 5 M., still higher than that of the Muir Glacier;
but it is not so easily approached and has not been explored.

The nearest way from Glacier Bay to Sitka would be through
Cross Sound and down the W. side of *Chichagoff Island*, but to avoid
the unpleasantness of an outside passage the steamer returns through
Icy Strait (p. 478) and Chatham Sound (p. 474). About one-third
of the way down the latter we diverge to the right through *Peril
Strait*, between the islands of *Chichagoff* (N.) and *Baranoff* (S.). This
strait is wide at first but ultimately contracts to a width of ¹/₂ M.,
where its wooded hills and islets recall the scenery of Loch Lomond.
As we approach Sitka we have a fine view, to the right, of *Mt. Edgecumbe* (see below), with its crater half filled with snow.

1420 M. **Sitka**, the capital of Alaska and seat of the governor,
is very beautifully situated on the W. side of Baranoff Island, with
a fine bay dotted with green islands in front and a grand range of
snow-mountains behind. The bay is sheltered by *Kruzoff Island*,
with the extinct volcano *Mt. Edgecumbe* (2800 ft.), while immediately to the E. of the town towers *Mt. Verstovaia* (3210 ft.). In
1890 Sitka contained 1190 inhab., of whom 293 were white, 31
Chinese, and 865 natives. The town was founded in 1804 by Alex.

Baranoff, the first Russian governor of Alaska (see *W. Irving's* ‚Astoria'). Sitka lies in 57° N. lat. (about the same as that of Aberdeen or Riga) and, owing to the *Kuro Siwo*, or Japanese current, has a milder winter climate than that of Boston, in spite of the propinqutiy of eternal snow (mean summer temp 54°, winter 32°). The tempeatrure seldom falls to zero. The rainfall is very high (ca. 110 inches).

On a height to the right of the dock stands **Baranoff Castle**, the residence of the Russian governors, a plain but somewhat quaint old wooden building, now in a very neglected condition. The roof commands a beautiful *View. — Near the head of the main street, leading from the wharf into the town, is the **Russo-Greek Church**, with its green roof and bulbous spire, which contains some interesting paintings and vestments. Many of the natives and half-breeds are members of the Greek church and are still ministered to by a Russian pope. Several of the substantial old *Log Houses* of the Russians are still in use. — Turning to the right at the head of the main street and following the road along the beach, we reach the buildings of the **Presbyterian Mission**, where visitors are welcome. The ***Sitka Museum**, a highly interesting collection of Alaskan products, is installed in a building in the mission-grounds, fitted up like the dwelling of a native chief, with a totem-pole at the entrance. — By passing up between these buildings we reach the ***Indian River Walk** (a round of about 2 M.), where the visitor with pre-conceived ideas of Sitka's arctic climate will be surprised to find luxuriant vegetation, fine trees, and a brawling brook, not unlike such typical English walks as the Torrent Walk at Dolgelley. One of the characteristic plant is the 'Devil's Club' (*Echinopanax horrida*). By turning to the right beyond the largest bridge we may see a specially fine group of cedars.

The **Native Village**, or *Rancherie*, lies to the left of the wharf and is occupied by 800-1000 Sitkans, including many interesting specimens such as 'Princess Tom' and 'Sitka Jack', who are always at home to steamboat-visitors. Tourists occasionally get up canoe races among the natives, and exhibitions of native dancing are often arranged for their benefit. Behind the village is the native and Russian cemetery.

Native curiosities may be bought at Sitka comparatively cheap, but furs are, perhaps, better obtained at Juneau (p. 477). A Russian samovar may still occasionelly be picked up here. Travellers should also visit the office of the *Alaskan* (10 c.), a weekly paper.

Sitka is the turning-point of our voyage, and we now retrace the way we have come (viâ Icy Strait, Chatham Sound, Frederick Sound, etc.). The distance to Tacoma is about 1200 M., taking 5-6 days. As a rule few stops are made on the homeward journey; but much fine scenery, previously passed at night, is now seen by daylight. Passengers for the *Canadian Pacific Railway* leave the steamer at Victoria and proceed thence by a smaller steamer to *Vancouver* (see *Baedeker's Handbook to Canada*).

Mt. St. Elias, the loftiest mountain in the United States (approximate height, acc. to the most recent calculations, 18,200 ft.) and vying with Mt. Orizaba (see p. 493) for the position of culminating point of the N. American Continent, is situated in Alaska, to the N. of 60° N. lat. and about 30 M. from the coast. It is nearly 300 M. to the W. N. W. of Glacier Bay (p. 478) and is not visible on any part of the trip above described.

MEXICO.

The **Republic of Mexico,** occupying the S. part of N. America, consists of a confederation of 27 States, two Territories, and a Federal District (in which is situated the city of Mexico). Its total area is about 770,000 sq. M. and its population in 1892 was estimated at 11,885,000. About 80 per cent of the inhabitants are of pure or mixed Indian blood, and only 20 per cent belong to the Spanish and other Caucasian races. With the exception of the flat and narrow strips along the coasts of the Gulf of Mexico and the Pacific Ocean, the country consists of a huge table-land bounded on each side by mountain-ranges, forming the N. prolongation of the Andes. The main range, bounding the W. side of the table-land, is named the *Sierra Madre.* The *Central Mexican Plateau* has a mean elevation of about 6000 ft.

Approaches. Plan and Season of Tour. Since the opening of the railways described in RR. 104-7, an excursion into Mexico can be easily added to a visit to the S. part of the United States, and affords a survey of so novel and picturesque a civilisation as amply to repay the time and trouble. Three weeks will suffice for the journey to and from the City of Mexico, with halts at many interesting places on the way, and also for a trip from the City of Mexico to Orizaba, or even Vera Cruz, and back. This excursion involves no serious hardships and is constantly made by ladies; but those who wish to visit the interesting remains of Yucatan, Chiapas, and Oaxaca, must be prepared to give more time and labour. The Mexican plateau may be visited at any season, and is, perhaps, at its pleasantest from June to Sept., when the dust is abated by the summer rains. For a general tour, however, winter or early spring is preferable; and March or April will be found as good months as any. Fairly light clothing is desirable for the heat of the day, but wraps should be at hand for the cool evenings and mornings. The rarefied air of the Mexican plateau is sometimes found rather trying at first. Those who intend to use the steamer (comp. p. 494) in one direction are advised to take it in going rather than in returning.

Travellers who do not speak Spanish cannot do better than join one of the *Raymond and Whitcomb Parties* (see p. xxv), which visit Mexico in winter and spring. Their usual route is from Eagle Pass to the City of Mexico (R. 105), and thence back to El Paso (R. 106), with excursions to Orizaba (R. 108), etc. The parties travel on a special vestibuled train, which serves them as their hotel (except in the City of Mexico) and has the additional advantage of reaching and leaving the stopping-places at convenient hours. Interpreters accompany each party.

Railways, etc. English is generally understood at the railway ticket-offices of the larger towns and by the conductors of the through-trains. Time-tables and 'folders' are also issued in English. The visitor to the parts of Mexico described below will scarcely come into contact with the system of *Diligences.* Most of the cities have complete systems of *Tramways* (drawn by mules), often with first-class and second-class cars. The tramways sometimes connect places 10-70 M. apart.

Hotels. Mexican hotels are apt to be poor, and their sanitary arrangements leave much to be desired. The ordinary charges are $ 2-2½ per day (higher in the City of Mexico). The place of chambermaids is usually taken by 'Mozos', or boys. Small fees are expected and efficacious. Neither soap nor matches are provided in the bedrooms. Wine and foreign beer are dear, native beer and pulque (p. 488) cheap.

Passports. Custom House. Passports are not necessary in Mexico, but may sometimes prove convenient. The custom-house examination is generally conducted courteously and leniently, and scarcely concerns things likely to be in the possession of the ordinary tourist. Articles purchased in Mexico are often liable to duty at the American frontier.

Money. Expenses. The legal unit of the Mexican monetary system is the *Peso* (dollar), divided into 100 *Centavos* (cents). The old expressions *Medio* (6½ c.) and *Real* (pl. *Reales;* 12½ c.) are still in constant use, though the coins they represent no longer circulate (*dos reales* = 25 c., *cuatro* *reales* = 50 c., *seis reales* = 75 c., *ocho reales* = $ 1). — The cost of a short tour in Mexico should not exceed $ 8-10 a day. A Mexican dollar is generally worth about 70 c. American gold. Mexican money may be bought cheaply in New York, but a fair rate of exchange (40-50 p.c.) can be obtained in the City of Mexico. American money may also be exchanged at the frontier. No bank-notes should be accepted except those of the Banco Nacional and the Bank of London, Mexico, and South America. Drafts on New York banks are a good form in which to carry large sums, and realize the highest rate of exchange in the City of Mexico.

Language. A slight acquaintance with Spanish will be found of great service in travelling in Mexico. The letters of the alphabet have the pronunciation of Continental Europe, with the following exceptions: c before e and i = th in then, before a, o, u, l, r, and at the end of a word = k; g before e and i = h; h is silent; ll = ly; y = ch in loch; z = th.

Postal Arrangements. A list of the insufficiently addressed letters received by each mail is usually exhibited at the post-office, and in applying for one of these it is necessary to give its number on the list as well as the name of the addressee. Letters addressed to the large hotels in the City of Mexico are delivered at the hotel-office. The postal rates for domestic letters is 10 c. per 1/2 oz., for letters to the countries of the Postal Union 5 c. per 1/2 oz. Letters from the U. S. to Mexico are sent at the U. S. domestic rate (2 c. per oz.).

Bull Fights may still be seen in some of the provincial cities, though they have been discontinued for some time in the national capital. Persons of delicate sensibilities will, however, do well to avoid these degrading and disgusting spectacles.

Bibliography. The best Mexican guidebook is that by *Thomas A. Janvier* (Scribner's Sons; 5th ed., 1893; price $ 1½), which, however, seems to contain no information more recent than 1889 or 1890. The Mexican routes in the present Handbook are therefore much more up to date. The traveller should be familiar with *Prescott's* 'Conquest of Mexico'. Other good books are by *David A. Wells, F. A. Ober*, and *F. Hopkinson Smith*. Gen. Lew Wallace's novel 'The Fair God' will also be found interesting. For the antiquities, see 'Report of an Archæological Tour in Mexico in 1881', by *A. F. A. Bandelier.*

104. From Laredo to the City of Mexico.

480 M. MEXICAN NATIONAL RAILROAD (*Camião de Fierro Nacional Mexicano*) in 41 hrs. (fare $ 31.25, U. S. currency; sleeper $ 9, Mexican currency).

The line affords the shortest and most direct route to the City of Mexico (from New Orleans 1570 M.) and passes through fine scenery. As, however, it is a narrow-gauge line, it cannot be traversed by the Raymond vestibuled trains (see p. 481). Baggage from the United States should be 'checked' to New Laredo, where the Mexican custom-house examination takes place and luggage is re-checked.

Laredo, see p. 467. The train crosses the *Rio Grande del Norte* into Mexico and halts at (1 M.) *Laredo Nuevo* or *New Laredo* (440 ft.; see above). The first part of the journey lies through a dreary plain of cactus and mezquite. To the right, beyond (73 M.) *Lampazos* (1030 ft.), rises the *Mesa de los Catujanos* (1500-2000 ft.).

160 M. **Monterey** (1790 ft.; *Hidalgo, Iturbide*, $ 2½), the capital of the *State of Nuevo Leon*, a city of 20,000 inhab., situated in a beautiful valley, between the *Cerro de la Silla* (4150 ft.) on the E. and the *Cerro de la Mitra* (3620 ft.) on the W., is frequented as a winter-resort. The *Topo Chico Hot Springs* (Hotel, $ 2½) lie 3 M. to the N.E. — Beyond Monterey the train ascends through the narrow valley of the *San Juan*, amid grand mountain-scenery (to the

right, the *Sierra de la Paila;* to the left, the *Sierra Madre*, p. 481).
— 235 M. *Saltillo* (5200 ft. ; Tomasichi, $ 2½; Rail. Restaurant,
meals $ 1), the capital of *Coahuila*, with 10,000 inhab., is famous for
its manufacture of *Serapes* (Mexican cloaks). Beyond Saltillo we
cross the battle-field of *Buena Vista* (Feb. 23rd, 1847). At (259 M.)
Carneros (6500 ft.) we reach the top of the central plateau of Mexico
(p. 481). The line descends a little and runs in a straight direction
across a level plain. 374 M. *Catorce* (Rail. Restaurant, D. $ 1) is the
station for the (8 M.) rich silver-mining town of the same name, accessible only on foot or on horseback. A little farther on we cross the
Tropic of Cancer and enter the Torrid Zone (pyramid to the right).

477 M. **San Luis Potosi** (6150 ft.; *American, San Fernando*,
$ 2½; *Rail. Restaurant*, meals $ 1), capital of the state of the same
name, a city of 60,000 inhab., owes its importance to the rich sil-
ver-mines in its vicinity.

The city is clean and well kept. Among the chief points of interest
are the *Cathedral* (with a clock given by Philip II. of Spain), the *Mint*,
the *Alameda*, the *Plaza Mayor*, the *Markets*, the *Governor's Palace*, the *City
Hall*, the *Palace of Justice*, and several *Churches*. The *San Pedro Mine*
should be visited. — Railways run hence to *Tampico* (p. 487), on the Gulf
of Mexico, and to *Aguascalientes* (p. 486).

563 M. *Dolores Hidalgo* is named in honour of the patriot Hidalgo
(p. 485), who was curé of this parish. — 585 M. *San Miguel de Allende*
(6000 ft.; Allende, $ 2), a city of 15,000 inhab., at the base of the
Cerro de Montezuma, contains several interesting churches and excellent public baths. It was the birthplace of the patriot Allende
(p. 485), for whom it is named. — The train now follows the valley
of the *Laja* (views to the right). Farther on the vegetation becomes
more tropical. — 619 *Celaya* (5770 ft. ; Solis), a city of 30,000 inhab.,
at the intersection of the Mexican National and Mexican Central railways (comp. p. 488), is a place of some importance, with fine old
churches (*Our Lady of Carmen*, etc.) and good baths. *Dulces*
(sweetmeats), strawberries, and opals are offered for sale at the station. — 642 M. *Salvatierra;* 662 M. *Acambaro* (6085 ft.), the junction of a line to *Morelia* and *Patzcuaro*. The line now turns to the
S.E. (right), and ascends through the valley of the *Lerma* (views to
the left). 700 M. *Maravatio* (6610 ft.) ; 723 M. *Tepetongo* (7650 ft.) ;
757 M. *Flor de Maria* (8500 ft. ; Rail. Restaurant, meals $ 1). We
thread a tunnel and enter the *Valley of Toluca*.

794 M. **Toluca** (**Leon d'Oro, Gran Sociedad*, $ 2), the capital
of the *State of Mexico*, is a prosperous and clean-looking city of
20,000 inhab., splendidly situated in a fertile valley, among lofty
mountains, at a height of 8650 ft. above the sea. Its attractions include the *State Buildings*, fine *Markets*, interesting *Churches*, and
quaint *Portales;* while linen 'drawn-work', pottery, and other sou-
venirs may be purchased.

The ascent of the **Nevado de Toluca* (15,155 ft.), a snow-clad volcanic
mountain rising to the S., takes about two days (there and back). The
view is superb.

The run from Toluca to Mexico reveals some of the finest scenery in Mexico, if not in the world. The train runs towards the E. and beyond the Indian town of (804 M.) *Ocoyoacac*, seen far below us to the right, begins to ascend the *La Cruz Mts.* (Sierra Madre; views to the right). We follow the windings of the *Rio Lerma*. To the right towers the *Nevado de Toluca* (see p. 483). 807 M. *Jajalpa* ('Hahalpa'; 8870 ft.). Much maguey (see p. 488) is cultivated in this district. 814 M. *Salazar*. At (815 M.) *La Cima* (10,200 ft.) we reach the summit and begin the descent, obtaining magnificent **Views of the *Valley of Mexico*, with its lakes, the City of Mexico in the centre, and the grand snow-clad volcanoes of Popocatepetl (r.) and Ixtaccihuatl (l.; see p. 492) in the background. At (822 M.) *Dos Rios* we cross the *Rio Hondo* by a lofty trestle. Numerous lateral ravines *(barrancas)* are also crossed. Farther on, Chapultepec (p. 491) is conspicuous to the right. 833 M. *Naucalpan*. Beyond (836 M.) *Tacuba* the tree of the Noche Triste (p. 492) is seen to the left.

839 M. **City of Mexico** *(Colonia Station)*, see p. 489.

105. From Eagle Pass to the City of Mexico.

1091 M. MEXICAN INTERNATIONAL RAILWAY *(Ferrocarril Internacional Mexicano)* in 62 hrs. (fare $51.40 for unlimited, $31.25 for limited tickets, sleeper $9; from Spofford Junction $32.30, New Orleans $52.70, New York $85.20). This is the most direct standard-gauge line from the East to the City of Mexico. Baggage is examined and re-checked at Eagle Pass (comp. p. 465).

Eagle Pass, a small town of 3000 inhab., lies on the N. or American bank of the *Rio Grande*. The train crosses the river by an iron bridge, 310 yds. long, and halts at *Ciudad Porfirio Diaz*, formerly called *Piedras Negras* (720 ft.; Hotel), a Mexican city of about 5000 inhab., in the *State of Coahuila*. Picturesque Mexican figures, the men in *sombreros* and scarlet *serapes*, the women in blue *rebozos*, appear at once. — The train ascends steadily towards the great Mexican tableland (p. 481), traversing at first an arid and mono-tonous desert. Few houses are seen except an occasional *hacienda*, of stone or adobe, and little vegetation except yucca-palms, mezquite, and cacti. 25 M. *Nava* (1065 ft.); 32 M. *Allende* (1230 ft.); 51 M. *Peyotes* (1595 ft.); 72½ M. *Sabinas* (1115 ft.), in a coal-producing district, the junction of a line to (11 M.) *Hondo; 82 M. *Soledad* (1215 ft.); 98 M. *Aura* (1485 ft.); 123 M. *Hermanas* (1300 ft.); 148 M. *Monclova* (1925 ft.; 10,000 inhab.); 159 M. *Castaño* (2455 ft.); 181 M. *Bajan* (2765 ft.); 209 M. *Reata* (2950 ft.); 223 M. *Treviño* (2920 ft.), the junction of a line to *Tampico* (p. 487) and *Monterey* (p. 482). — At (254½ M.) *Jaral* (3750 ft.), where we may be said to have fairly reached the great Mexican plateau, the line turns to the right (W.) and now runs at nearly the same level. A railway is in progress hence to *Saltillo* (p. 483). — 297 M. *Paila* (3900 ft.); 334½ M. *Bola* (3575 ft.), at the S. end of the large *Laguna de Parras;* 350 M. *Hornos* (3595 ft.), the junction for (14 M.) *San Pedro;* 369 M. *Matamoras* (3650 ft.).

At (383 M.) *Torreon* (3720 ft.; see below) we join the *Mexican Central Railway.* — To the (1091 M.) **City of Mexico,** see R. 106. The Mexican International Railway goes on to (540 M. from Eagle Pass) **Durango** (25,000 inhab.), the capital of the state of its own name.

106. From El Paso to the City of Mexico.

1224 M. MEXICAN CENTRAL RAILWAY *(Ferrocarril Central Mexicano)* in 62 hrs. (fare $61.40 Mex. currency; sleeper $9; return-tickets, valid for 6 months, to City of Mexico, from St. Louis $77, from Kansas City $71.20, from New Orleans $62.85 (all U. S. currency). Side-trip tickets are issued, to holders of through-tickets to California, from El Paso to Mexico and back to Eagle Pass viâ R. 105, or vice versâ, $40). This line is the direct route between the city of Mexico and California and the West (comp. R. 101). Baggage is re-checked at El Paso (comp. p. 464), and examined at Ciudad Juarez.

El Paso, see, p. 464. The train crosses the *Rio Grande* to ($3/4$ M.) *Ciudad Juarez* ('Wahrez'), formerly *El Paso del Norte* (3800 ft.; Rail. Restaurant), with the Mexican custom-house, an interesting old church, and a statue of Benito Juarez (p. 491). Our route at first lies through the *State of Chihuahua* ('Chee-wah-wah') and offers little of interest. 30 M. *Samalayuca* (4300 ft.); 96 M. *Ojo Caliente* (4090 ft.); 112 M. *Montezuma;* 139 M. *Gallego* (5450 ft.); 194 M. *Sauz* (5170 ft.). We cross the *Chubisca* to —

225 M. **Chihuahua** (4635 ft.; *Casa Robinson,* $2 1/2-3; *Palacio,* $2-2 1/2), the capital of the state of that name, a busy city with about 25,000 inhab., in a hill-girt plain. It was founded in 1539.

The chief object of interest is the fine *Parroquia,* or parish-church, dating from 1711-89. Behind the *Banco Minero Chihuahuense* is a monument marking the spot where *Miguel Hidalgo* and *Ignacio Allende,* leaders of the revolution of 1810, were executed in 1811. The patriots were previously imprisoned in the *Casa de Moneda* (Mint). The *Plaza* and *Alamedas* are pleasant, and the old *Aqueduct* is interesting. — A day's excursion may be made to the *Santa Eulalia Silver Mines.*

Beyond Chihuahua the line descends. We cross the *San Pedro* at (278 M.) *Ortiz,* and the *Conchos* near (325 M.) *Santa Rosalia* (4020 ft.; 6000 inhab.), with hot springs. — 370 M. *Jimenez* ('Heemenez'; 4530 ft.; Rail. Restaurant) is a city of 8000 inhab. on the *Florido.* The dust on this part of the route is very trying. From (416 M.) *Escalon* the Mexican Northern Railway runs to (78 M.) the great silver-mining district of *Sierra Mojada.* — Near (436 M.) *Saez* (3900 ft.) we enter the *State of Durango.* We now traverse the *Mapimi Basin,* in which cotton, sugar, maize, and wheat are produced. Beyond (514 M.) *Lerdo* (3725 ft.), a cotton-trading place of 10,000 inhab., we cross the *Rio Nazas.*

517 M. *Torreon* (3720 ft.; Rail. Restaurant) is the junction of the Mexican International Railway (R. 105). The country traversed is arid and sterile, and sand-spouts are frequently seen. The mountains become higher, one near (561 M.) *Jimulco* reaching a height of 10,280 ft. Numerous large haciendas are passed. The train ascends steadily towards the top of the great central plateau of

Mexico (p. 481). 614 M. *Symon* (5145 ft.). At (642 M.) *Camacho* (5400 ft.) we enter the *State of Zacatecas.* 695 M. *La Colorada* (6000 ft.); 749 M. *Fresnillo* (6860 ft.). Beyond (766 M.) *Calera* (7050 ft.; Rail. Restaurant) we begin to ascend rapidly and the scenery becomes very picturesque.

785 M. **Zacatecas** (8045 ft.; *Zacatecano*, $2), a city of 50,000 inhab., romantically situated in a narrow ravine, offers several points of interest to the stranger. It is one of the chief centres of the silver-mining of Mexico.

The *Market Place*, in the centre of the city (reached from the railway-station by tramway), presents a very picturesque appearance, with its large fountain, whence the water-carriers fetch their supplies for the city's use. Near by is the Cathedral (1612-1752), with an elaborately carved *Façade. The *Municipal Palace* (with its attractive court-yard) and the *Mint* are also within easy reach. — A visit may be paid to one of the *Silver Reduction Works*, in which the processes of reducing the ore are carried on after a highly primitive fashion, but a visit to a silver-mine is more conveniently managed at Guanajuato (p. 487). — A splendid *View is obtained from the *Bufa*, a mass of porphyry rising 500 ft. above the city and crowned with a small chapel, originally dating from 1728 but rebuilt in 1794. On March 2nd, 1871, the Revolutionary troops were defeated here by the Juarez forces after a sanguinary struggle.

Zacatecas is connected with (6 M.) Guadalupe by a tramway, down which the cars descend by gravity in 1/2 hr., while they are drawn up again by mules in 1-1¹/₄ hr. At Guadalupe is the fine *Church of Nuestra Señora de Guadalupe* (1721), with an elaborately decorated interior and a few fair paintings. The Chapel of the Purisima is especially gorgeous. The old convent adjacent contains a *College* and *Orphan Asylum*. — Good pottery may be bought at Zacatecas and Guadalupe.

On leaving Zacatecas the train again descends rapidly (seats to the left), affording striking *Views of the Oriental-looking city and the mountains. Numerous mines and smelting works are seen on both sides. The engineering difficulties overcome by the railway both in reaching and leaving Zacatecas are remarkable. 823 M. *Soledad.* Several lofty peaks are seen in the distance to the left.

860 M. **Aguascalientes** (6180 ft.; *Central, Plaza*, $2; *Rail. Restaurant*), a pretty little city with about 30,000 inhab., is the capital of the small state of the same name and is widely known for its hot springs.

The pretty *Alameda* leads to the E. from the station (tramway), which is itself 1 M. to the E. of the city (tramway), to the **Hot Springs** (ca. 95° Fahr.), each enclosed by a small bath-house (fee about 15 c.). The over-flow from the springs is carried off by a small canal skirting the Alameda; and here hundreds of the poorer inhabitants, of both sexes and all ages, may be seen bathing in full view of the passer-by. The best baths, fed by a conduit from a reserved spring, are close to the railway-station (fee about 25 c.). — Some of the *Churches* of Aguascalientes are interesting, and the *Public Squares* are gay with luxuriant vegetation.

FROM AGUASCALIENTES TO SAN LUIS POTOSI AND TAMPICO, 415 M., railway in 32 hrs. (including halt for the night, 7.30 p.m. to 6.30 a.m., at San Luis). This division of the Mexican Central Railway passes through some of the finest scenery in Mexico. — 68 M. *Salinas*, with large salt works. At (142 M.) San Luis Potosi (see p. 483) we cross the Mexican National Railway. — We now descend gradually by a series of terraces, traversing the *San Ysidro* and other beautiful valleys. Beyond (255 M.) *Cardenas* (3800 ft.; Rail. Restaurant) the line drops abruptly into the *Ca-*

noas Valley and then penetrates the fine *Tamasopo Cañon*, threading many tunnels. 298 M. *Rascon* (1000 ft.; Rail. Restaurant). Other fine cañons and waterfalls are passed farther on. — 415 M. Tampico (100 ft.; *Hotel Robins*), an old town of 7000 inhab., on the *Panuco*, 7 M. from its mouth into the Gulf of Mexico, has regular steamboat communication with New York, New Orleans, Mobile, and other ports.

Near (890 M.) *Encarnacion* (6090 ft.) we cross the *Rio Encarnacion* and enter the *State of Jalisco.* 928 M. *Lagos* (6150 ft.), a town with about 13,000 inhabitants. Beyond (945 M.) *Pedrito* we enter the *State of Guanajuato* ('Wahnawahto'). Fine scenery.

965 M. **Leon** (5865 ft.; *Hotel de Diligencias*, $ 2), a city of 60,000 inhab., with manufactures of saddlery and other leathern goods and of rebozos (p. 484), contains a *Cathedral* and several pretty *Plazas*. Visitors will notice the fences of the *Organ Cactus.* — 986 M. **Silao** (5830 ft.; *St. Julien; Rail. Restaurant*), a town of 15,000 inhab., with handsome churches and gardens.

From Silao a branch-railway runs through a cañon to (11 M.) *Marfil*, whence a tramway leads along a narrow gorge to (3 M.) **Guanajuato** (6835 ft.; *Union* $ 2), a highly interesting silver-mining city, founded in 1554. Pop. 50,000. The houses cluster in the bottom of the ravine or cling to its sides, while the fortress-like smelting works add to the general picturesqueness. Above the town rises a large square rock (view), forming a conspicuous landmark for many miles round. The chief source of interest in and near Guanajuato are the **Silver Mines**, including the *Veta Madre*, said to be the richest vein of ore in Mexico. The total annual output is now about 1,250,000*l.* The mines are more easily visited than those in other parts of Mexico, being entered by stone stairways; and orders of admission may be obtained from the *Administrador*. The *Reduction Works* are also interesting; almost all are worked by horse or mule power, with the primitive methods of 300 years ago. A visit may be paid to the large *Alhondigo de Granaditas*, dominating the city and now used as a prison. Other points of interest are the churches, numerous handsome private residences, and fine public and private gardens. The water-carriers bear curious long slender water-jars (almost peculiar to Guanajuato).

The district now traversed is fertile and diversified. At (1004 M.) *Irapuato* (5765 ft.) fine fresh strawberries are offered for sale every day in the year at the station (25-50 c. per basket).

From Irapuato to Guadalajara, 161 M., railway in 8 hrs. This line runs through the valley of the *Rio Lerma*, one of the most fertile districts in Mexico, and is to be continued to the Pacific coast. The large *Lake Chapala* lies a little to the S. of the line, but is not visible from it. — From (146 M.) *El Castillo* a tramway runs to (4 M.) the beautiful *Falls of Juanacatlan* ('Wahnacatlan'), on the Lerma, 70 ft. high and 600 ft. wide.

161 M. **Guadalajara** ('Wahdalahara'; 5055 ft.; *Cosmopolita*, $ 2), the second city of Mexico and capital of Jalisco (p. 486), is a rich and progressive place with about 95,000 inhab. and manufactures of fine pottery, rebozos, cotton, silk, and numerous other articles. It is cleaner and more regularly laid out than most Mexican cities and contains many points of interest for the stranger. Near the centre of the city stands the **Cathedral**, a fine edifice completed in 1618, with a dome and two lofty towers. In the sacristy is an Assumption ascribed to Murillo. To the S. of this, abutting on the *Plaza de Armas*, is the *Sagrario* (1808-43). On the E. side of the same square is the *Governor's Palace*, while on the S. and W. are the *Portales de Cortazar* and *de Bolivar*, containing many of the best shops. — The *Church of San Jose*, in the Plaza de Nunez, is a gorgeous modern edifice, elaborately adorned with gilding and painting and said to have cost $ 1,000,000. — On the N. side of the city is the interesting *Hospital de Belen*, and on the E. side, not far from the pretty *Alameda* (military

music), is the huge *Hospicio de Pobres* (1000 inmates), with its beautiful
flower-filled 'patios' and departments for men, women and children (incl.
a Kindergarten and a crèche), the deaf and dumb, and the blind ('drawn
work' and other articles for sale). On the opposite side of the town is
the *Penitentiary*, on the radiating principle (visitors admitted). The *Paseo*,
running to the S. from the Alameda, affords a fine walk or drive. — Other
important buildings are the *Bishop's Palace*, the *Mint*, the *City Hall*, and
the *Teatro Degollado*, one of the finest in Mexico. — *San Pedro* and other
points in the suburbs are also interesting.

1017 M. *Salamanca* is famous for its gloves. Beyond (1042 M.)
Celaya (5770 ft.; 30,000 inhab.), famous for its *dulces* or sweetmeats
(15-50 c. per box), we cross the Mexican National R. R. (R. 104),
and beyond (1060 M.) *Mariscala* we enter the *State of Querétaro*.

1071 M. **Querétaro** (5905 ft.; *Railway Hotel*), a picturesque
city of 36,000 inhab., is pleasantly situated in a fertile valley. The
domes and towers of numerous churches rise above the other buildings, the most interesting being the *Cathedral* and *Santa Clara*.
Opals are found in great abundance in the neighbourhood.

Perhaps the chief interest of Querétaro is its connection with the last
days of the unfortunate Emp. Maximilian, who was besieged here in 1867
by the Republican troops under Escobedo. The city surrendered on May
19th, and a month later Maximilian, with his adherents Miramon and
Mejia, was shot on the *Cerro de las Campanas*, a hill to the W. of the
town. The spot is now marked by three monuments and affords a fine
View of Querétaro, embowered in greenery. The *Capuchin Convent*, in
which Maximilian was confined before his execution, is now a private
house, but visitors are admitted to his room.

In leaving Querétaro the line passes under the fine *Aqueduct*
constructed in 1726-38 by the Marquis de Villar del Aguila to provide the city with water. Some of the arches are nearly 100 ft. high.
To the left, 2 M. from Querétaro, in a romantic ravine, is the large
Hercules Mill, the largest cotton-mill in Mexico (1800 workmen).

On this part of the journey we see immense fields of the *Maguey* or
Century Plant (Agave Americana), cultivated by the Mexicans for the sake
of its sap, which is converted into the national beverage *Pulque*. The
plants are sometimes 10-12 ft. high. A spirituous liquor named *Mescal*
is distilled from the leaves of the maguey, and another (*Tequila*) from its
roots, while its fibre and thorns are also turned to commercial uses.

Beyond (1105 M.) *San Juan del Rio* (6245 ft.; Rail. Restaurant;
15,000 inhab.) the line ascends rapidly, passing the plain of (1123 M.)
Cazadero and reaching its highest point (8135 ft.) just beyond
(1148 M.) *Marques*. The descent hence to Mexico is very fine. —
1174 M. *Tula* (6660 ft.; Hotel de Diligencias), a town of about
1500 inhab., is believed to have been founded by the Toltecs and
contains interesting remains ascribed to that people (guide at the
hotel). — Beyond (1185 M.) *El Salto*, where we join a branch of
the Mexican National R. R., we skirt the *Tajo de Nochistongo* (right),
a canal-cutting made by the Spaniards in 1607-8 to drain the lakes
in the Valley of Mexico (comp. p. 489). It is 12½ M. long, 130-
165 ft. deep, and 260-330 ft. wide. The majestic snow-capped peaks
of *Ixtaccihuatl* and *Popocatepetl* (p. 492) come into view ahead of us.
The line again ascends somewhat. 1195 M. *Huehuetoca* (7410 ft.).

1124 M. **City of Mexico,** see p. 489.

107. The City of Mexico.

Railway Stations. *Mexican Central Station* and *Mexican Railway Station* (Vera Cruz), Plazuela de Buena Vista, on the W. side of the city; *Mexican National Station*, Colonia Arquittectos, to the S.W.; *Interoceanic Station*, San Lazaro, to the E.; *Irolo Station* (Hidalgo & N.E. Railway), Peralvillo, to the N.E.

Hotels (comp. p. 481). ITURBIDE, Calle de San Francisco, a large house enclosing a large central court, once the residence of the Emp. Iturbide, R. $ 1-5 (elevator); HOTEL DEL JARDIN ('Hardeen'), Calle Primera Independenzia y Letran, well spoken of, $ 3-8; SAN CARLOS, Calle del Coliseo, R. $ 1-3; GUARDIOLA, R. $ 1-3; AMERICAN, GILLOW, $ 1-3; COMONFORT, $ 1-1¹/₂. — **Restaurants** at the above hotels; **Café de Paris; Recamier; Concordia; Café Anglais; Cantabro; Fonda San Agustin* (one of the best of the Mexican *fondas*, with genuine native cooking).

Tramways, drawn by mules, intersect the city in all directions (fare in first-class cars 6 c.; to suburban points 12-25 c.). — **Cabs** are divided into three classes, denoted by blue, red, and yellow flags; fares $ 1, 75 c., and 50 c. per hr., 50 c., 40 c., and 25 c. per ¹/₂ hr. or fraction thereof or per drive (each pers.). The fare from the railway-stations to the hotel, including hand-baggage, is about the same as the hourly rate. Double fares after 10 p.m. and on Sundays and holidays.

Baths. *Faehr* (38-75 c.); in the Iturbide Hotel (25-38 c.; see above); *Pane, Blasio, Osorio*, in the Paseo de la Reforma (25 c.-$ 1).

Theatres. *Teatro Nacional*, see p. 491 (good performances of opera in winter); *Teatro Principal*, Calle del Coliseo; *Arbeu*, Calle de San Felipe Neri; *Hidalgo*, Calle de Cocheras. — *Orrin's Circus*, Plaza Villamil.

Shops. Mexican curiosities, photographs, guide-books, maps, English books, periodicals, newspapers, etc., may be obtained at *Hoeck's*, Calle de San Francisco 5, *Spaulding's*, Calle de Cadena 23, and at *W. G. Walz's*, Calle de San Francisco 1 (English spoken at these; money exchanged). Other good shops are in the Calle de los Plateros and Calle de San Francisco, and the Calle de Cinco de Mayo (French, and sometimes English, spoken in the best). — 'The Two Republics', a daily paper in English (6 c.), contains many useful items for the tourist, including daily list of letters lying at the G. P. O. for English and American visitors (comp. p. 482).

Streets. The streets of the city of Mexico have been re-named since 1889. The town is divided into four quarters by the long street called *Avenida Oriente* and *Av. Poniente*, running from E. to W. past the N. side of the Plaza de la Constitucion and the Alameda, and by the *Calle Norte* and *Calle Sur*, running from N. to S. and intersecting the Avenida one block E. of the Alameda. All streets running E. and W. are called *Avenidas* (those to the E. of the dividing line *Av. Oriente*, to the W. *Av. Poniente*), while all the streets running N. and S. are called *Calles* (those to the N. of the central Avenida *Ca. Norte*, to the S. *Ca. Sur*). Each street has a number; in the N.W. quarter are the Avenidas Poniente with uneven and the Calles Norte with even numbers; N.E. the Av. Oriente and Calles Norte with even numbers; S.E. the Av. Oriente with even and Calles Sur with uneven numbers; S.W. the Av. Poniente and Calles Sur with even numbers. Most of the old names, however, are still constantly used.

Post Office, at the N. end of the Palacio Nacional (p. 490).

British Minister, *Sir Spencer St. John*, Puente Alvarado 15; consul, *Mr. Lionel Carden*, Calle de Gante 11. — **U. S. Minister**, *Isaac B. Gray*, Calle San Diego 2; U. S. Consulate, Calle de Gante 2.

Protestant Churches. Services in English are held at Calle de Gante 5 (Meth. Epis., 10.15 a.m.), Calle de San Juan Letran 53 (Epis., 10.30 a.m.), and *Union Church*, Calle de San Juan Letran 12 (11 a.m.).

Mexico (7400 ft.), the capital and by far the largest city of the Mexican Republic, lies in the centre of the Valley of Mexico, in part of the former bed of Lake Texcoco. It contains about 330,000 inhab., chiefly full-blooded Indians or mestizoes, and including some hundred natives of the United States and Great Britain. The streets are generally wide but badly paved and ill-kept. Most of the buildings are of stone, and several of the public edifices are very handsome. The public squares and gardens and the residential suburbs are very attractive. The climate is equable (50-70° Fahr.), but is rendered unhealthy by the exhalations from the lakes and the defective drainage.

The Spanish city of Mexico was founded in 1522 on the site of the ancient Aztec *Tenochtitlan*, the population of which is placed by tradition at from 300,000 to 500,000. Its growth has been steady and rapid. In 1600 it contained 15,000 inhab., in 1746 it had 90,000, and in 1800 it had about 120,000. Numerous ineffectual attempts have been made to drain the valley of Mexico (comp. p. 488), and large new works for that purpose were begun with English capital in 1890. The commerce of the city is mainly in transit. Its manufactures include cigars, gold and silver work, pottery, feather work, saddlery, paper, religious pictures, and hats.

The *Cathedral *(Church of the Asuncion de Maria Santisima),* stands on the N. side of the PLAZA DE LA CONSTITUCION or PLAZA MAYOR, 5-10 min. walk from the Iturbide and other chief hotels. This edifice, which occupies the site of the chief Aztec temple *(Teocalli),* was begun in 1573 and finally dedicated in 1667. The towers, 218 ft. high, were not completed till 1791. It is 425 ft. long (from N. to S.), 200 ft. wide, and 180 ft. high. In style it is similar to the Spanish Renaissance edifices of the same period.

The **Interior**, which is in the Doric style with traces of Gothic, has an imposing effect in spite of its huge and incongruous modern altars and the wooden flooring. The fine *Dome* is adorned with paintings. The *Choir* occupies the centre of the church and has richly carved stalls. The aisles are adjoined by rows of chapels, the most interesting of which are the *Capilla San Felipe de Jesus*, with the tomb of the Emp. Iturbide, the *Cap. de las Reliquias*, with paintings of martyrs by Juan de Herrera, and the *Cap. San Pedro*. The *Sacristy* and the *Chapter House* also contain interesting paintings. The heads of Hidalgo, Allende, Jimenez, and Aldama (comp. p. 485) are interred below the *Altar de los Reyes*, in the apse. — The visitor should not fail to ascend one of the towers for the sake of the *View of the city (fee 12½ c.).

On the E. the Cathedral is adjoined by the *Sagrario Metropolitano*, the first parish-church of the city, dating in its present form from 1749-69 and restored in 1858. It is in the florid style named after the Spanish architect Churrigera (close of 17th cent.). — In front of the Sagrario is the *Martinez Monument*, showing the geographical position of the city, the varying levels of Lake Texcoco, etc.

The centre of the Plaza Mayor is occupied by the pretty ZOCALO GARDEN, where a band generally plays in the evening. Many of the tramway-lines start in this square.

On the E. side of the Plaza Mayor stands the huge **Palacio Nacional, 675 ft.** long, containing many of the governmental offices (interior open to visitors on Sun. and Thurs.). The chief points of interest are the large *Hall of the Ambassadors* (with portraits of Mexican celebrities) and the *Senate Room*. — On the S. side of the Plaza are the *Disputacion* or *Palacio del Ayuntamiento* (City Hall) and the *Portales Flores* (shops). On the W. side are the *Portales Mercaderes*. — To the S.E. of the Plaza is the chief *Market* of the city.

Behind the Palacio Nacional and entered from the Calle de Moneda is the *National Museum (open daily, 10-12).
The most valuable and interesting collections are the **Mexican Antiquities* (from Yucatan, etc.), including the famous *Aztec Sacrificial Stone*
and the *Aztec Calendar. The *Historical Collections* are also of interest.
See Catalogue (Engl. trans. by *W. W. Blake).*
A little farther to the E., in the Calle Amor de Dios, is the *Academy of San Carlos (*Museum of Fine Arts;* 10-12), with good Italian and Flemish paintings and interesting collections of old and modern Mexican works (*Las Casas protecting the Indians, by *Felix
Parra,* etc.).
To the W. of the Cathedral, in the Calle del Empedradillo, is
the *Monte de Piedad,* or National Pawn Office, founded in 1775
Valuable objects may often be procured here at low prices.
The CALLE DE PLATEROS (now Avenida Oriente 4), forming with
its prolongation the CALLE DE SAN FRANCISCO (or Av. Poniente 4)
the principal business-street of the city, leads to the W. from the
Plaza Mayor to ($1/2$ M.) the *Alameda, a beautiful public garden,
with fine beeches and a great variety of flowering trees and shrubs
(band frequently; fashionable promenade on Sun. forenoon). — The
CALLE DE CINCO DE MAYO (or Av. Poniente 1) running parallel with
the Calle de San Francisco on the N., is also a fine street. It ends
on the W. at the *National Theatre (p. 489).
Near the Buena Vista stations (p. 489) and adjoining the *Guerrero Garden* is the *Church of San Fernando,* the interesting cemetery
attached to which contains the graves of Juarez (fine monument),
Miramon (p. 488), Mejia (p. 488), Zaragossa, Guerrero, Comonfort,
and other eminent Mexicans.

Among the numerous other interesting buildings in the city, of which
but a scanty selection can be named here, are the **Biblioteca Nacional**
(nearly 200,000 vols.), in the Calle St. Augustin, a little to the S.W. of the
Plaza Mayor, the *Casa de Moneda* (Mint), in the Calle de Apartardo; the
*Mineria (School of Mines), in the Calle de San Andres (29-51), near the
Alameda; the *House of Congress,* in the former Teatro Iturbide, at the
corner of the Calle Primera del Factor and the Calle de la Canoa; the
Church of Santo Domingo, in the plaza of the same name, a little to the
N. of the Cathedral; the *School of Medicine,* opposite the last, occupied
by the Inquisition for 250 years; the *Church of La Santisima,* with its finely
carved façade, $1^1/4$ M. to the E. of the Cathedral; and numerous other
churches and charitable institutions.

The fashionable drive of the Mexicans is the beautiful *PASEO
DE LA REFORMA, which begins near the Alameda and runs to the
S.W. to (2 M.) Chapultepec (see below). At the entrance is an
equestrian statue of Charles IV., and the 'Glorietas', or circles
(400 ft. in diameter), which occur at frequent intervals further on,
are adorned with monuments to *Columbus, Guatemotzin* (the last Indian Emperor), *Juarez,* etc. The Paseo commands fine views of
Popocatepetl and Ixtaccihuatl (p. 492).

Environs of Mexico.

The chief point of interest in the immediate neighbourhood of the City
of Mexico is the *Palace of Chapultepec, finely situated on a rocky hill

at the end of the Paseo de la Reforma (see above; also reached by the
Tacubaya tramway from the Plaza Mayor, 12½ c.). The present building,
which occupies the site of Montezuma's Palace, dates from 1783-5, with
later additions. It is occupied by President Diaz and by the National Military School (320 cadets). The fine old cypresses in the grove surrounding
the palace (*Cupressus disticha*) reach a height of 120 ft. and a girth of 30-
40 ft. A monument commemorates the cadets who fell in the defence of
the palace against the Americans in 1847. Beyond the hill is the battlefield of *Molino del Rey* (Sept. 8th, 1847). The *View from the ramparts
includes the city and valley of Mexico, with Popocatapetl and Ixtaccihuatl
in the background. — From Chapultepec the excursion may be extended
(tramway 1¼ M.) to *Tacubaya*, with the National Observatory, two churches, a secularised convent, and beautiful private *Gardens.

About 2¼ M. to the N. of the city (tramway from the Plaza Mayor;
12½ c.) is Guadalupe Hidalgo, with the sanctuary of the Virgin of Guadalupe, the patron-saint of Mexico and more especially of the Indians. The
Virgin is believed to have appeared to an Indian, Juan Diego, in 1531, on
the adjoining hill of Tepeyacac. At the foot of the hill is the large church
of *Nuestra Señora de Guadalupe*, completed in 1709, containing a mira-
culous picture of the Virgin, imprinted on Diego's *tilma* (blanket). At
the top of the hill is the *Capilla del Cerrito*, and close by is another chapel, covering a holy (chalybeate) spring. The singular monument on the
hill was erected by a grateful seaman.

The curious *Chinampas* or *Floating Gardens*, near the villages of (2 M.)
Santa Anita and (3 M.) *Ixtacalco*, are reached by the Viga Canal, leading
to the S. from the city (tramway from the Plaza to the Canal 6 c.; boat
to Santa Anita and back about $3/4-1, to Ixtacalco $2). This is a highly
interesting trip and should be made at least as far as Santa Anita (most
varied life seen on Sun.). The boats are a kind of rude parody of the
Venetian gondola. A visit may be paid on the way to the *Hacienda of
Don Juan Corona*, containing a collection of relics and a Charity school.
The 'floating gardens' are now small pieces of ground separated by narrow canals and used for growing vegetables. The canal ends at (8 M.) the
Lago de Xochimilico.

At *Popotla*, 2½ M. to the W. of the city (tramway from the Plaza;
12 c.), is the famous *Arbol de la Noche Triste*, or *Tree of the Dismal
Night*, under which Cortes is said to have wept on the night of the expulsion of the Spaniards from Mexico (July 1st, 1520). It is a kind of cypress (see above). The road to it passes the *Tlaxpana Aqueduct*. The tramway goes on to *Tacuba* and (2½ M. farther) *Atzcapotzalco* (18 c.).

Tramway excursions may also be made to *Dolores*, *Mixcoac* and the
Castañeda, *La Piedad*, *San Angel*, *Tlalpam*, and other points.

The two magnificent snow-capped volcanoes of Popocatepetl (17,780 ft.)
and Ixtaccihuatl ('Ixtaciwatl'; 16,060 ft.) are conspicuous features in the
environment of Mexico. The former is sometimes ascended from *Amecameca*, on the *Interoceanic Railway;* but the ascent is arduous and should
not be attempted except by experienced mountaineers in good condition.
Guides and horses may be obtained in Amecameca, but the bulk of the
provisions should be brought from Mexico. The trip takes 2-3 days and
costs about $40 for a single traveller and $25 for each member of a party.

Other excursions by railway may be made to *Texcoco* (25 M.; Inter-
oceanic Railway) on the site of the ancient city of the Chicimecs, with
Aztec remains; to *Toluca* (see p. 483); to *Orizaba*, *Cordoba*, or *Paso del
Macho* (see p. 494); to *San Juan Teotihuacan* (p. 493); to *Puebla* (p. 493), etc.

From Mexico to *El Paso*, see R. 106; to *Laredo*, see R. 104; to *Eagle
Pass*, see R. 105; to *Vera Cruz*, see R. 108.

108. From the City of Mexico to Vera Cruz.

263 M. MEXICAN RAILWAY (*Ferrocarril Mexicano*) in 11½ hrs. (fare
about $12-14). Only 33 lbs. of luggage are allowed free on this railway.
Visitors to Mexico should at least make a trip over this railway a

far as Orizaba or Paso del Macho for the sake of the magnificent scenery in the descent from the Mexican Plateau to the coast-level. Views to the right.

City of Mexico, see p. 489. The train ascends to the N. and N.E., passing *Guadalupe* (p. 491; left) and *Lake Texcoco* (right), and farther on crosses immense plantations of 'maguey' (see p. 488). Popocatepetl and Ixtaccihuatl are seen to the S. — 27 M. *San Juan Teotihuacan,* with two interesting 'Teocallis', or pyramids, dedicated to the Sun and Moon and believed to antedate the Toltecs (seen to the left, about 2 M. from the railway). The former is 216 ft. high, with a base measuring 760 ft. by 720 ft.; the other is smaller. — 34 M. *Otumba* was the scene of a crucial battle between the Spaniards and Aztecs (July 8th, 1520). 48 M. *Irolo* (8045 ft.) and (57 M.) *Apam* are two of the chief centres of the trade in 'pulque' (p. 488). Beyond Apam we pass from the *State of Hidalgo* to that of *Tlaxcala.* Near (77 M.) *Guadalupe* (8330 ft.), Mt. Orizaba and the Malintzi are visible to the S.E. — 86 M. *Apizaco* is the junction of a branchline to Puebla (see below).

FROM APIZACO TO PUEBLA, 29 M., railway in 1½ hr. — Good views are obtained of the *Malintzi* (13,460 ft., left) and, in clear weather, of Popocatepetl, Ixtaccihuatl and Orizaba. From (10 M.) *Santa Ana* we may make an excursion by tramway to (5 M.) the ancient city of *Tlaxcala,* with interesting churches, relics of Cortes and other early Spaniards (in the Casa Municipal), etc. — Beyond (22 M.) *Panzacola* the pyramid of *Cholula* (see below) is seen to the right.

29 M. **Puebla** (7200 ft.; *Diligencias, Universal,* $2), the capital of the state of the same name, with about 80,000 inhab., was founded in 1531 and is one of the most attractive cities in the country. The use of glazed and coloured tiles in external and internal decoration is a characteristic feature. Its most interesting products for tourists are the articles made of Mexican onyx, baskets and mats of coloured straw, and pottery. The *CATHEDRAL, dating from the middle of the 17th cent., with later additions, is scarcely inferior to that of Mexico in size and importance, while its interior is more richly decorated. It is in the Spanish Renaissance style, with a central dome, barrel vaulting, and two lofty towers (view). Among the points of interest in the interior are the onyx decorations, the marquetry work, the paintings, the tapestry, the altars, and the organ-cases. — Other interesting churches are those of *San Francisco, La Compania,* and *Nuestra Señora del Carmen.* — Near the railway station is a large new *Penitentiary.* — The *Paseo* along the *Rio Atoyac* affords a pleasant walk. — A visit should be paid to *Fort Guadalupe,* on the hill where took place the famous battle of the Cinco de Mayo (1862). The fort commands a splendid **View, including Mts. Popocatepetl, Ixtaccihuatl, Orizaba, and Malintzi.

About 8 M. to the W. of Puebla (railway) is *Cholula* (6910 ft., 5000 inhab.), with some interesting churches and the famous *Pyramid of Cholula, an artificial mound of sun-dried brick and clay, 204 ft. high, with a base about 1000 ft. square (approximately). It is built in terraces, three of which are distinctly recognizable. The top, consisting of a platform 165 ft. square, crowned by the *Church of the Virgin de los Remedios,* is reached by a winding stone-paved road, ending in a flight of steps. The *View is very fine. The construction of the pyramid is ascribed to the Olmecs or Toltecs, but its date and purpose are obscure.

137 M. *San Andres* is the starting-point for the difficult ascent of *Mt. Orizaba or Citlatepetl (18,245 ft.), now ascertained to be the highest mountain in Mexico and in N. America. The mountain is seen to the left. — At (152 M.) *Esperanza* (7980 ft.; Rail. Restau-

rant) begins a very rapid descent, to surmount which trains coming in the reverse direction require the aid of double-headed Fairlie locomotives. The scenery on this portion of the line is very grand, and its engineering is very remarkable. The vegetation becomes of tropical richness as we near the *tierra caliente*, or hot lands of the coast, including orange, lime, citron, banana, and pomegranate trees, sugar cane, palms, coffee plants, and a great variety of brilliant flowering trees and shrubs. — Beyond (156 M.) *Boca del Monte* (7925 ft.), where we look down into the valley 3000 ft. below us (right), the train runs along a terrace on the mountain-side, threading several tunnels and crossing several bridges. 166 M. *La Bota.* At (169 M.) *Maltrata* (5550 ft.) we reach the smiling valley of *La Joya* ('The Jewel'). A little farther on we pass the wild gorge named the **Barranca del Infiernillo* ('Little Hell'), with the *Rio Blanco* 600 ft. below us. Near Orizaba we round the *Cerro del Borrego*, where a small French force repulsed a large number of Mexicans in 1862. — 181 M. **Orizaba** (4090 ft.; *La Borda, Diligencias*, $2), a quaint little town of 15,000 inhab., the capital of the *State of Vera Cruz*, lies in a valley surrounded by mountains and contains some interesting churches, with numerous examples of the work of the local painter *Barranco*. Excellent fruit may be bought here very cheaply. The reed-thatched huts of this region are thoroughly tropical-looking. — Beyond Orizaba we cross the fine **Ravine of the Metlac* by a bridge, 92 ft. high, and other bridges and tunnels are passed (good engineering). 192 M. *Fortin;* 197 M. *Córdoba* (2710 ft.; fine fruit); 210 M. *Atoyac* (1510 ft.). A little farther on are the **Falls of the Atoyac.* 216 M. *Paso del Macho* (1500 ft.).

Beyond this point the scenery is uninteresting, and this may be made the turning-point for those who do not intend to take ship at Vera Cruz. Near (237 M.) *Soledad* we cross the *Jamapa* by a long bridge. 254 M. *Tejeria.*

263 M. **Vera Cruz** (*Diligencias*, $2¹/₂; *Hotel de Mexico*, $2), a seaport on the *Gulf of Mexico*, with 24,000 inhab., lies in a dreary sandy plain and contains comparatively little of interest to the tourist. Its commerce has declined since the opening of railway communication with the United States. The climate is hot and very unhealthy in summer.

Steamers ply regularly from Vera Cruz to New York, New Orleans, Galveston, and other American ports; and good sailors may prefer one of these routes in entering or leaving Mexico.

FROM VERA CRUZ TO JALAPA, 82 M., *Interoceanic Railway of Mexico* in 6 hrs. — Jalapa (4335 ft.; **Veracruzano, Mexicano*, $2), a quaint old city with 18,000 inhab., beautifully situated among the mountains, is, perhaps, the most charming summer-resort in Mexico, with a cool and refreshing climate. Many delightful excursions can be made from it. Jalapa derives its name from this city. The women of Jalapa are distinguished for their beauty.

INDEX.

Abbotsford 291.
Abilene 469. 405.
Abington 86.
Absaroka Mts. 386.
Acambaro 483.
Acton 442.
Adams (Mass.) 134.
— (Neb.) 391.
—, Mt. 133.
Addison Junction 144.
Adirondack Mts. 165.
— Lodge 175. 171. 172.
Adrian 270. 277.
Afton 304. 401.
Agassiz, Mt. 128.
Agawam Valley 134.
Agnews 437.
Aguascalientes 486.
Aiken 350.
Akron 278.
Alabama 336.
Alameda 434. 440.
Alamosa 418. 421.
Alaska 474.
Albany (Ga.) 354.
— (N. Y.) 154. 186.
— (Ore.) 460.
— Junction 144.
Albert Lea 290.
Albia 391.
Albina 395. 460.
Albuquerque 412.
Alcalde 442.
Allburgh Springs 115.
Alert Bay 473.
Aleutian Islands 474.
Alexander 345.
— Bay 476.
Alexandria (Minn.) 300.
— (Va.) 262. 326. 334.
— Bay 207.
Alger 273.
Algiers 367. 468.
All Healing Springs 335.
Allaben 165.
Allegheny City (Pa.) 243.
— (Va.) 305.
— Mts. 230. 266. 305 etc.
— Springs 340.
Allende 484.
Allentown 227.
Alliance 243. 263.
Allyn's Point 67.

Alma 440.
Almy 395.
Alpine Tunnel 409.
Alta 397.
Altadena 447.
Altamont (Ill.) 266. 302.
— (Mo.) 401.
Alton 202. 310. 324.
— Bay 118. 95. 121.
Altoona 234.
Alum Springs 318.
Alvarado 440.
Alvin 411.
Alviso 440.
Amargo 419.
Amecameca 492.
American Falls 393.
Ames 389.
Amesbury 92. 95.
Amherst 63. 142.
Ammonoosuc, the 109.
119.
— Falls 127.
Ampersand Mt. 169.
Amsterdam 187.
Anaconda 373.
Anaheim 448.
Anchorage 318.
Ancona 400.
Anderson 310.
Andover (Mass.) 94.
— (Me.) 108.
Androscoggin, the 97.
Anna 320.
Annapolis 250.
Ann Arbor 274.
Ann, Cape 92.
Anniston 341.
Anoka 299. 264. 300. 371.
Anson 106.
Anthony's Nose 148.
Antietam 233. 265. 338.
Antioch 291.
Antonito 418.
Antwerp 310.
Apam 493.
Apizaco 493.
Appalachia 366.
Appledore Island 94.
Appomattox 333.
Aptos 444.
Aransas Pass 466.
Arapahoe 405.

Arbol de la Noche Triste
492.
Arboles 419.
Arcadia 389.
Archer 363.
Archibald 269.
Arden 51.
Argo 407.
Arizona 413.
Arkansas (state) 404.
—, the 325. 415.
— Cañon 420.
— City (Ark.) 325.
— — (Kan.) 410.
Arkville 165.
Arlington (Col.) 403.
— (Ore.) 394.
— House 262.
Arrochar 51.
Arrowhead 448.
Arthabaska 109.
Arvado 407.
Asbury Park 222.
Ascutney Mt. 143.
Ashby 300.
Asheville 344. 341.
Ash Fork 414.*
Ashland.(Ky.) 317.
— (N. H.) 119.
— (Ore.) 460.
— (Va.) 326.
— (Wis.) 296. 297.
Ashley Falls 136.
— Junction 346. 347.350.
Ashtabula 267. 275.
Aspen 424. 395. 421.
Astoria 461.
Atchison 410.
Athens (Ga.) 336.
— (Ohio) 306.
— (Pa.) 228.
— (Tenn.) 341.
Atlanta 336. 342. 354.
Atlantic (Mass.) 72.
— City 225.
— Highlands 223.
Atoyac 494.
Attala 343.
Attica (Ill.) 311.
— (N. Y.) 199.
Attleboro 65.
Auburn (Cal.) 397.
— (Me.) 105.

Auburn (Mich.) 277.
— (N. Y.) 190. 228.
— (Pa.) 230.
Auburndale 61.
Augusta (Ga.) 350. 347.
Aura 484.
Aurora 290. 390.
Ausable 167.
— Chasm 170. 145. 186.
— Forks 172.
— Lakes 173.
Austin 466.
— Bluffs 416.
Au Train 297.
Avalanche Lake 175.
Ayer Junction 113.
Azusa 447.

Babylon 55. 56.
Baden 437.
Bad Lands 372.
Bagdad 414.
Bainbridge 354.
Bajan 484.
Baker City 393.
— Mt. 471.
Bakersfield 442.
Bald Eagle Lake 295.
— Head Mt. 138.
— Knob 404.
— Mt. (Col.) 415.
— — (N. C.) 345.
— — (N. H.) 129.
Baldwin (Fla.) 363. 365.
— (La.) 468.
— (N. Y.) 184. 144. 183.
Ballona 448.
Balsam Mts. 345.
Ballston Spa 144.
Baltimore 244. 278. 281. 304.
Bandini 448.
Bangor 98.
Banning 463.
Bardstown 318.
Bar Harbor 102. 99. 100.
— — Ferry 99.
Barker 301.
Barnegat 224. 225.
Barnesville 299. 300.
Barnet 119.
Barnstable 89.
Barranca 418.
Barstow 414. 448.
Bartlett 110.
Bartow 362.
Basic 339. 304.
Batavia 192. 191. 229.
Bath (Col.) 409.
— (Me.) 99. 97.
— (N. H.) 119.
Baton Rouge 321. 325. 468.

Battle Creek 274.
— Mt. 396.
Baxter, Mt. 174.
Bayard 356.
Bay City 273.
Bayfield 297.
Bayou Sara 325.
Bayridge 249. 251.
Bay St. Louis 338.
Bayside (N. Y.) 225.
Beach Bluff 90.
— Haven 224.
Bean's 34.
Bearmouth 373.
Bear Paw Mts. 300.
— Valley 448.
Beaufort 350.
Beauharnois (Can.) 207.
Beaumont 462. 466.
Beaver Brook 407.
— Cañon 392.
— Falls 263.
Becket 134.
Bedford (Va.) 334.
— Springs (Pa.) 234.
Bedloe's Island 2.
Beecher's Falls 111.
Belfast (Me.) 98.
Bella Bella 473.
Bellaire 266.
Bellefontaine 310.
Belle Island 272. 271. 276.
Bellows Falls 114. 143.
Belleville (Ill.) 315.
— (Kan.) 405.
Bellevue 315.
Belmont 437.
Beloeil 110.
Beloit 289.
Belpré 306.
Belt Mts. 373.
Bemis 110.
Benicia 398.
Bennettsville 346.
Bennington 135.
Benson (Ariz.) 464.
— (Minn.) 299.
— Mines 188.
Benwood 266.
Berenda 441. 451.
Berkeley (Cal.) 399.
— (Va.) 336.
Berkshire Hills 136.
Berlin Falls 109.
Bernardston 143.
Bessemer (Ala.) 343.
— (Pa.) 242.
Bethel (Ct.) 135. 66.
— (Me.) 108.
Bethlehem (N. H.) 128. 119.
— (Pa.) 226.
Beverly 92.

Biddeford 94. 95.
Big Horn 372.
— Indian 165.
— Moose 179.
— Sandy 468.
— — Creek 403.
— — Springs 469.
— Timber 372.
— Trees 452. 398. 440.
Biggs 459.
Billings (Mont.) 372.
Biloxi 338. 337. 367.
Biltmore 344.
Bingham 423.
Binghamton 197. 188.
Bird's Eye 409.
— Point 404.
Birmingham 343. 319. 336.
Bismarck 372.
Black Butte Summit 459.
— Cañon 422.
— Hawk (Col.) 408.
— — (Tex.) 325.
— Mt. (Lake George) 183.
— Point 359.
— Rock 194.
Blackstone 65.
Blackwell's Island 50. 66.
Blaine 471.
Blairsville 235.
Blanchester 306.
Block Island 63.
Blockton 401.
Blodgett 400.
Bloody Brook 142.
Bloomingdale (Ga.) 351.
— (N. Y.) 168.
Bloomington 302. 400.
Bloomville 165.
Blowing Rock 344.
Blue Cañon 397.
Bluefield 340.
Blue Mt. (Pa.) 227.
— — (Ore.) 393.
— — Lake 177.
Blue Ridge 334. 250.
— — Mts. 304. 339. 344. etc.
Blue Spring 360. 361.
Bluff Point 186. 145.
Boca del Monte 494.
Bog Lake 179.
Boiceville 163.
Boise City 393.
Bola 484.
Bolivar 235. 265.
Bolton 183.
Bonner 374.
Bonner's Ferry 304.
Bonneville 394.
Boone (Col.) 403.
— (Ia.) 389.
Booneville 188.
Bordentown 209.

Border 392.
Boreas 408.
Boston 72.
Back Bay 82.
Beacon Street 82.
Boston Art Club 81.
— Athenæum 77.
— Athletic Assoc. 81.
— Common 76.
— University 77.
Boylston Street 79.
Cambridge 83.
Cemeteries 76. 82.
Chamber of Comm. 78.
Charities 82.
Charlestown 85.
Churches:
Advent 83.
Brattle Sq. 81.
Cathedral of the Holy Cross 83.
Central Congreg. 81.
Christ 82.
Emmanuel 82.
First Baptist 81.
— Unitarian 81.
Mt. Vernon 82.
New Old South 81.
Second 80.
Spiritual Temple 83.
Trinity 79.
City Hall 77.
Commonwealth Ave. 82.
Conserv. of Music 83.
Copley Square 79.
Copp's Hill 82.
Country Court Ho. 77.
Custom House 78.
Faneuil Hall 78.
Franklin Park 82.
Gov. Building 78.
Harbour 74.
Harvard University 83.
Hist.-Gen. Society 77.
Instit. of Technology 79.
King's Chapel 77.
Massachusetts Historical Society 77.
Museum of Fine Arts 80.
— of Natural Hist. 79.
North End 82.
Old Granary Burial Ground 76.
— South Meeting House 78.
— State House 77.
Perkins Institute 82.
Post Office 78.
Public Garden 76.
— Library 79. 80.
Railway Stations 72.
School Street 77.
Shaw Monument 77.

Boston:
State House 76.
— Street 78.
Theatres 73.
Unitarian Building 77.
Warren Museum 83.
Washington Street 77.
Bothwell 326.
Botsford 135.
Boulder 408. 410.
Bound Brook 209.
Bowdoin 300.
Boyce 318.
Bozeman 373.
Braddock's 235.
Bradford (Mass.) 95.
— (Me.) 116.
— (Ohio) 264.
Brainerd 371.
Braintree 72. 86.
Branchport 222.
Branchville 135.
Brandon (Col.) 403.
— (Vt.) 114.
Brandywine 244.
Branford 62.
Brattleboro 143. 63. 67.
Bread Loaf Inn 114.
Breckinridge (Col.) 408.
— (Minn.) 299.
Brentwood 57.
Brewster (Ct.) 51. 62.
— (Mass.) 89.
Bridal Veil Falls 455.
Bridgeport (Ala.) 343.
— (Col.) 422.
— (Ct.) 57. 135.
— (Pa.) 229. 250.
Bridgewater (Mass.) 88.
— (N. H.) 119.
Brigantine Beach 226.
Brigham 396.
Brighton 410.
— Beach 56.
Bristol (R. I.) 65. 72.
— (Pa.) 209.
— (Tenn.) 340.
British Columbia 471.
Broadwater 374.
Brockton (Mass.) 87.
— (N. Y.) 243. 267.
Brockville 201.
Brook Farm 85.
Brookfield 135.
Brookline 85. 61.
Brooklyn (Ct.) 67.
— (N. Y.) 52.
Brownell 403.
Brown's Peak 447.
Brunswick (Ga.) 342.
— (Me.) 99. 106.
— (Mo.) 401.
— Springs 109.

Bryant's Pond 108.
Bryn Mawr 231.
Bucyrus 263.
Buda 402.
Budd, Lake 196.
Buena Vista (Col.) 421.
— — (Mex.) 483.
— — (Va.) 339.
Buffalo 192. 195. 197. etc
— Bluffs 360.
Bunker Hill 85.
Burgin 317.
Burkeville 347.
Burlingame 410.
Burlington (Ia.) 390. 323
— (N. C.) 335.
— (Vt.) 114. 186.
Burnham 98.
Burnside 317.
Bushnell 402.
Butte City 373. 300. 374.
Buzzard's Bay 89. 87.
Byers 406.
Byram 57.
Byron 441.

Cabazon 463.
Cabinet Mts. 301.
Cache Junction 396.
Cactus 463.
Cadyville 167.
Caesar's Head 345.
Cairo (Ill.) 320. 324.
— (N. Y.) 160.
Cajon 448.
Calaveras Grove 398.
— Mts. 437.
Caldwell (Idaho) 393.
— (N. Y.) 183. 144.
Calera 319. 486.
Caliente 441.
California 397. 414.
Calistoga 434.
Callahan 354.
Camacho 486.
Cambridge 83. 61. 112.
Camden (N. J.) 221.
— (Me.) 100.
Camel's Hump 117.
Cameron 442.
— Junction 401. 402.
Camp Ellis 95.
— — Point 402.
Campobello 107.
Camulos 443.
Canaan (Ct.) 135.
— (N. H.) 117.
Canajoharie 195.
Canandaigua 191.
Canastota 189.
Cañon City 420.
Canterbury 118.
Canton (Mass.) 65. 72.

Canton (Miss.) 320.
— (Mo.) 323.
— (Ohio) 263.
Cape Ann 92.
— Charles 244.
— Cod 89. 86.
— Girardeau 324.
— Horn 397.
— May 226.
Capistrano 449.
Capitola 441.
Carbondale (Ill.) 320.
— (Pa.) 228.
— (Wy.) 392.
Cardenas 486.
Carlin 396.
Carlisle 232. 237.
Carneros 483.
Carolina (R. I.) 64.
—, North 334.
—, South 335.
Carrizó 413. 469.
Carrollton (La.) 325.
— (Mo.) 401.
— (Pa.) 278.
Carson 397.
Carter 395.
— Mt. 125.
Carthage (Mo.) 432.
— (N. Y.) 188.
Casa Grande 463.
Cascade Cañon 423.
— Lake 171.
— Mts. 376. 471. 473.
Casco Bay 97.
Casselton 371.
Cassidy's Summit 266.
Cassville 323.
Castaños 484.
Castile 199.
Castine 100.
Castle Cañon 422.
— Crags 459.
— Gate 422.
— Rock (Col.) 415.
— — (Ore.) 394.
— — (Utah) 395.
Castleton 149.
Castroville 439.
Catasauqua 227.
Catawissa 230.
Cathedral Rocks 455.
Catlettsburg 305.
Catorce 483.
Catskill 160. 149. 151.
— Mts. 159. 149.
— Mt. House 161. 160.
Cavendish 114.
Cayuga Lake 190. 228.
Cazadero 433. 488.
Cecilia 320.
Cedar Creek 422.
— Falls 290.

Cedar Key 363.
— Point 406.
— Rapids 389. 290. 402.
— Swamp 64.
Celaya 483. 488.
Celito 394.
Central City 320.
Centralia (Ill.) 320. 315.
— (Wash.) 377.
Centre Harbor 118.
Cerro 422.
Chaffin's Bluff 330.
Chama 419.
Chambersburg 236. 250.
Champaign 301.
Champlain Hotel 186. 145.
—, Lake 185. 114. 144.
Chancellorsville 236. 326.
Chapala, Lake 487.
Chapel Hill 335.
Chapultepec 491.
Charlemont 134. 143.
Charles, the 83. 61. 86. etc.
Charleston (S. C.) 347. 346.
— (W. Va.) 265.
Charlestown (Mass.) 85.
— (W. Va.) 305.
Charlotte 335. 346.
— Valley 165.
Charlottesville 304. 334.
Chateaugay 168.
— Lakes 168.
Chatham (Mass.) 89.
— (N. Y.) 51.
— Sound 474.
Chattahoochee 366.
Chattanooga 342. 318.
Chaudière Falls 109.
Chautauqua 278. 243.
Chazy 168.
Cheat River Valley 266.
Chehalis 377.
Chelan Lake 301.
Chelsea 85. 90.
Cheney 375.
Cheneyville 468.
Cherry Valley 158.
Chesapeake Bay 249. 331.
Cheshire 134.
Chester (Ill.) 324.
— (Mass.) 134.
— (Pa.) 244.
— (S. C.) 347.
— (Va.) 346.
Chesterton 270.
Chestnut 459.
— Hill 221.
Chetopa 400.
Cheyenne 391. 410.
— Cañons 416.
— Mt. 416.
Chicago 279.
Chichester 163.

Chickahominy, the 330. 331.
Chico (Cal.) 459.
— (Col.) 409.
Chicopee 142.
Chihuahua 485.
Childwold 179.
Chilkat 478.
Chilkoot 478.
Chillicothe (Ill.) 402.
— (Idaho) 402.
— (Mo.) 402.
— (Ohio) 306. 340.
Chim-sy-an 474.
Chinese Camp 398. 451.
Chinook Mts. 300.
Chinquapin 453.
Chippewa Falls 291.
Chittenango 189.
Chocorua 118.
Cholula 483.
Christiansburg 340.
Church's Ferry 300.
Cima 419.
Cimarron 422.
Cincinnati 307.
Cinnabar 380.
Cisco 422. 469.
Citlatepetl 493.
City Point (Fla.) 364.
— — (Va.) 330.
Ciudad Juarez 485.
— Porfirio Diaz 484.
Claiborne 338.
Claremont 116.
Clarence Strait 476.
Clarendon Springs 114.
Clark's 396.
Clarksburg 306.
Clarksville 335.
Clarkville 324.
Clatsop Beach 462.
Clay 405.
—, Mt. 133.
Claymont 244.
Clayton (Cal.) 434.
— (Miss.) 321.
— (N. Y.) 188. 206.
Clear Creek 422.
— Lake 167. 179.
Clermont (Fla.) 362.
— (N. Y.) 149.
Cleveland (Ohio) 267.
— (Tenn.) 341.
Clifton (Can.) 199.
— (Mass.) 90.
— (N. Y.) 51. 270.
— Forge 304.
— Springs 191.
Climax 408.
Clinch Mts. 341.
Clinton (Ia.) 389. 301. 323.
— (Ky.) 320.

Clinton (Wis.) 289.
—, Mt. 132.
Cloudland 341.
Cloud's Rest 457.
Cloverdale 434.
Coahoma 321.
Coahuila 483.
Coal City 400.
Coatesville 232.
Cobleskill 158. 195.
Cochituate, Lake 61.
Cochran 342.
Cocoa 359. 364.
Coeur d'Alène Lake 375.
Coeyman's 149. 151. 195.
Cohasset 86.
Cohoes 143.
Cohuttah 341. 342.
Colebrook 111.
Coleraine 134.
Coles 460.
Colfax (Cal.) 397.
— (Ia.) 390.
Collegiate Peaks 420. 421.
Colma 437.
Colorado (state) 405.
— City 423.
— Desert 422.
— Grand Cañon 413.
— Junction 408.
— Springs 415. 423.
Colton 462. 448.
Columbia (S. C.) 347. 350.
— (Penn.) 319.
—, the 461. 301. 394. etc.
—, District of 252.
— Falls 301.
Columbus (Ga.) 336.
— (Ky.) 324.
— (Neb.) 391.
— (Ohio) 264. 303. 340.
— (Tex.) 467.
— (Wis.) 289.
— Junction 401.
Colvin, Mt. 174.
Comber 271.
Commerce 324.
Como 408. 409.
—, Lake 293.
Compton 446.
Conanicut 71.
Conception 401.
Concord (Mass.) 112. 113.
— (N. H.) 116. 118.
Conemaugh 234.
Conewago 232.
Coney Island 55.
Conger 152.
Connecticut (state) 57.
—, the 59. 62. 134 etc.
— Lakes 111.
— Valley 109. 142.
Connellsville 243. 266.

Convent 325.
Conway 93. 110. 121.
— Junction 121.
Cookshire Junction 111.
Coolidge 413.
Coon Rapids 388.
Cooper 340.
Cooperstown 158.
Coos 111.
Copley 459.
Copple Crown Mt. 118.
Cordoba 494.
Corinne 396.
Corinth 343.
Cornelia 335.
Corning 197. 199.
Cornwall 441.
— Bridge 153.
— Landing 207.
Coronado Beach 449.
Corpus Christi 466.
Corry 231. 243. 278.
Corvallis 460.
Corydon 315.
Coshocton 264.
Coteau 371.
— Junction 145.
— Landing 207.
— Rapid 207.
Cottage City 88. 87.
— Farm 61.
Cottonwood 448.
— Springs 409.
Coulee 375.
Council Bluffs 388. 389. 390. 391.
— Grove 403.
Courtenay 364.
Covington 304. 305.
Cowpens 335.
Cranberry 340.
Cranston's Hotel 148. 152.
Crater Lake 460.
Crawford House 126. 111.
— Notch 126. 111.
Crazy Mts. 373.
Creede 418.
Creedmoor 56. 57.
Creighton 242.
Crescent City 360.
Cresson Springs 284.
Crested Butte 421.
Crestline 263. 306.
Creston (Ia.) 391.
— (Wy.) 392.
Crestview 366.
Crewe 333.
Crookston 300.
Crow's Nest Mt. 148.
Crown Point (Fla.) 362.
— — (Ind.) 264.
— — (N. Y.) 185. 144.
CrystalCity 324.

Cuba 278. 343.
Cuchara 418.
Cullmans 319.
Culpeper 334. 236.
Cumberland (Md.) 266.
— (Me.) 97. 105.
—, the 320.
— Gap 341.
— Mts. 318. 341.
— Valley 236.
Cumbres 419.
Cupertino 437.
Currecanti Needle 422.
Custer 372.

Dade City 364.
Dailey's 380.
Daleville 404.
Dallas 469. 400.
— City (Ill.) 323.
— Divide 419.
Dalles, the 461. 394.
— City 394.
Dalton (Ga.) 341.
— (Mass.) 134.
Damariscotta 99.
Dana Mt. 458.
Danbury 62.
Danielsonville 67.
Dannemora 168.
Danville (Can.) 109.
— (Me.) 105. 108.
— (N. Y.) 197.
— (Va.) 334. 347.
Davenport (Fla.) 361.
— (Ia.) 390. 290.
Davis Jn. 388.
Dayton (Ky.) 318.
— (Ohio) 306. 278. 310.
— (Ore.) 461.
Daytona 359.
Dayton's Bluff 293.
Deal Beach 222.
Dearborn 402.
De Beque 424.
Decatur (Ala.) 343. 319.
— (Ill.) 278. 301. 401.
Deerfield 142. 134.
Deer Isle 100.
— Lodge 373.
— Park Hotel 266.
Defiance 267. 310.
—, Mt. 144.
De Funiak 366.
Deland 360.
Delano 442.
Delaware (state) 244.
— (Ohio) 306.
—, the 211. 244. etc.
— Valley 198.
— Water Gap 196.
Delmar 388.
Del Monte 439.

32*

Del Norte 418.
— Rio 465.
Delta (Cal.) 459.
— (Col.) 422.
De Luz 449.
Deming 464.
Denison (Ia.) 389.
— (Tex.) 400.
Dennison 264.
Denver 406. 290. 414.
Denville 196.
Deposit 199.
De Smet 374.
Des Moines 391. 401. 403.
De Soto 325.
Detour 276.
Detroit (Mich.) 271. 269.
— (Minn.) 371.
Devereux 90.
Devil's Lake 300.
— River 465.
— Thumb 477.
Devon 231.
Dexter 98.
Diablo, Mt. 434.
Dickerson 265.
Dickey 408.
Dickinson 372.
Dickinson's Landing 207.
Dillsborough 345.
Disappointment, Mt. 447.
Discovery Passage 473.
Dismal Swamp 333.
Disputanta 333.
Dixon 388.
Dixville Notch 111.
Dobbs Ferry 150. 147.
Dodge Centre 290.
Dolores 419.
— Hidalgo 483.
Dome Rock 408.
Donaldsonville 325.
Donner Lake 397.
Dorchester 67. 72.
Dotsero 420.
Douglas Island 477.
Dover (Me.) 98. 99.
— (N. H.) 95.
Downington 232.
Drake 400.
Drewry's 346.
— Bluff 330.
Drifton 366.
Driftwood 231.
Dublin 113.
Dubuque 290. 323. 401.
Dudswell 111.
Duluth 295. 276. 300.
Dumas 400.
Duncannon 233.
Dundas Islands 474.
Dunderberg Mt. 148.
Dunkirk 267.

Dunlay 465.
Dunnellon 364.
Dunmore Lake 114.
Dupont 354.
Du Quoin 320.
Durango (Col.) 419.
— (Mex.) 485.
Durant 320.
Durham 335.
Durkee 393.
Duston's Island 116.
Dutch Flat 397.
— Gap Canal 330.
Duxbury 86.
Dwight 302.
Dyersburg 320.
Dyersville 290.

Eads Jetties 326.
Eagle Lake 177.
— Pass 465. 484.
— Peak 457.
Eastatoia Falls 336.
East Buffalo 199. 229.
— Dubuque 323.
Eastham 89.
Eastman 342.
Easton (Pa.) 227. 196.
— (Wash.) 376.
Eastport 107.
East River 3. 23. 66.
— Thompson 62.
Eatontown 225.
Eau Claire 289.
— Gallie 365.
Echo 393.
— Cañon 395.
— Lake (N. Conway) 123.
— — (Profile Ho.) 129.
Eddy 469.
Eden 365.
Edgartown 88.
Edgecumbe, Mt. 479.
Edgefield 319.
Edgemont 250.
Edgertown 415.
Edgewood 460.
Edson 414.
Edwall 301.
Effingham 302. 310. 320.
Egg Harbor 225.
Elberon 222.
El Castillo 487.
El Dorado 403.
Eleven Mile Station 453.
Elgin 388.
Elizabeth (N. J.) 208. 209.
—, the 331.
Elizabethport 209. 222.
Elizabethtown (N.Y.)177.
— (Pa.) 232.
Elk Mts. 421.
— River 300. 371.

Elkhart 270. 269.
Elkhorn 391.
Elko 396.
Ellaville 365.
Ellensburg 376.
Ellis 405.
— Island 3.
Elliston 340.
Ellsworth (Kan.) 405.
— (Me.) 99.
Elmira 197. 199. 228.
Elon College 335.
El Paso 464. 469. 485.
— — del Norte 464.
El Robles 434.
Elroy 289.
El Salto 488.
El Toro 449.
Elwood 444.
Elyria 269. 270.
Embudo 418.
Emigrant Gap 397.
Emmetsburg 238.
Emory Grove 250.
Emporium 231.
Encarnacion 487.
Englewood 278.
Enon 263.
Enterprise 360.
Equinox, Mt. 145.
Erastina 51.
Erie (Pa.) 267. 231. 275.
— Canal 154.
—, Lake 193.
Errol Dam 109. 111.
Escalon 485.
Escondido 449.
Esopus Valley 163.
Española 418.
Esperanza 493.
Esquimault (B. C.) 472.
Essex (Can.) 271.
— (N. Y.) 185.
— Junction 115. 107.
Estabrook 408.
Estes Park 408.
Estrella 463.
Euba Mills 177.
Eugene 460.
Eureka (Cal.) 434.
— (Fla.) 361.
— (Utah) 396.
Eutaw 547.
Evanston 395.
Evansville (Ind.) 315.
— (Wis.) 289.
Everett 301.
—, Mt. 137.
Evergreen 337.
Excelsior Springs 402.
Exeter 95.

Faber's 364.

Fabyan House 127. 111.
Fairfield 57.
Fairhaven (Mass.) 88.
— (Wash.) 301. 471.
Fairmount 266.
Fair Oaks 329. 330.
Fairplay 409.
Fairport 195.
Fairweather Mts. 478.
Fall River 72.
Falls View 204. 271.
— Village 135.
Falmouth 87.
Fargo (Can.) 271.
— (N. D.) 371. 299. 300.
Farmingdale 223. 225.
Farmington 106.
Farmville 333.
Far Rockaway 56.
Fayetteville 335. 346.
Felton 440.
Fenner 414.
Fergus Falls 300.
Fernandina 355.
Fernando 443.
Finlayson Channel 474.
Fire Island 56. 2.
First View 405.
Fisherville 116.
Fishkill Landing 151.
Fitchburg 113.
Fitzhugh Sound 473.
Flagstaff 413.
Flathead Valley 301.
Fleischmann's 165.
Flomaten 337. 366.
Florida 353. 354.
Florilla 342.
Florissant 423.
Florence (Cal.) 446.
— (Col.) 420.
— (S. C.) 346.
— (Tenn.) 343.
Flowing Well 463.
Flume, The 130.
Flushing 57. 66.
Folkston 354.
Fonda 187.
Fond du Lac 291.
Ford City 242.
Fordham 57.
Forest Grove 440.
Forked Lake 179.
— River 224.
Forks Creek 407.
Fort Adams 325.
— Ann 144.
— Assinaboine 300.
— Benton 300.
-- Buford 300.
— Collins 408.
— Crawford 420.
— Dearborn 279.

Fort Douglas 427.
— Edward 144. 276.
— George 183.
— Gratiot 276.
— Hancock 464.
— Keogh 272.
— Logan 408.
— Madison 400. 323.
— McHenry 249.
— Mill 347.
— Monroe 332.
— Montgomery 152.
— Niagara 206.
— Payne 343.
— Pierce 365.
— Pillow 324.
— Pontchartrain 271.
— Riley 405.
— Scott 403.
— Snelling 293.
— Steele 392.
— Sumner 349.
— Ticonderoga 185.
— Tongas 476.
— Totten 300.
— Wayne 270. 263. 310.
— William 298.
— William Henry 183.
— Worth 469. 400.
— Wrangell 476.
Fostoria 270.
Fountain 434.
— City 323.
Fourth Lake 179.
Franconia 130. 119.
— Mts. 128.
— Notch 129.
Frankenstein Cliff 111.
Franklin 116.
—, Mt. 133.
— Road 99.
Franklinville 231. 266.
Frederick 265. 250.
Fredericksburg 326. 236.
Fredericton 98.
Fredonia 241.
Freehold 222. 223. 225.
Fremont 391.
French Broad River 341. 344.
Fresnillo 486.
Fresno 442.
Frontenac 289. 323.
Front Royal 338.
Fryburg 372.
Fryeburg 110.
Fulton (Col.) 434.
— (Ill.) 434.
— (Ky.) 320.
— Chain 178.
— Junction 389.
— Lakes 178.
Fundy, Bay of 107.

Gainesville (Fla.) 363. 365.
— (Ga.) 336.
Galena 291.
Galesburg 390. 402. 400.
Galilee 223.
Galion 306. 310.
Gallatin 373.
Gallejo 485.
Gallitzin 234.
Gallup 413.
Galveston 467. 410.
Gananoque 206.
Gap 232.
Garden City (Kan.) 411.
— (N. Y.) 56. 57.
— of the Gods 416.
Gardiner (Me.) 97.
— (Wy.) 380.
Garos 409.
Garrison 373.
Gate of the Mountain 301.
Gaylord 273.
Genesee (Idaho) 375.
— Falls 193.
— Junction 195.
Geneseo (Ill.) 290.
— (Kan.) 403.
Geneva 190. 228.
George, Lake 182.
Georgetown (Col.) 407.
— (D. C.) 262.
— (Ky.) 317.
— (S. C.) 346.
Georgeville 120.
Georgia (state) 335.
—, Gulf of 472.
Georgiana 365.
Germantown (N. Y.) 149.
— (Pa.) 221. 209.
Gettysburg 250.
Geyser Springs 434.
Geyserville 434.
Giant of the Valley 174
Gibson 459.
— City 301.
Giffords 51.
Gila Bend 463. 302.
Gilman 301.
Gilroy Hot Springs 439.
Girard 243.
Glacier Bay 478.
— Point 455. 456.
Gladstone 372.
Glasgow (Ky.) 339.
— (Va.) 318.
Glen 110.
Glendale 136.
-- (Ore.) 460.
Glendive 372.
Glendora 447.
Glen Echo 262.
— Ellis Falls 124.

Glen House (N. H.) 125.
110. 132.
— Lyn 340.
— Onoko 228.
— Summit 228.
Glenn's Ferry 393.
Glen's Falls 144.
Glenwood Hot Springs
424. 421.
Glorieta Pass 412.
Gloucester (N. J.) 211.
— (Mass.) 92.
Glyndon 371.
Godfrey 302.
Goff's 414.
Gogebic Range 296.
Gold Creek 374.
Golden 407.
— Gate, the 429.
Golden's Bridge 51.
Goldsborough 335. 346.
Gordonsville 304.
Gore's 361.
Gorham 125. 109.
Goshen (Ct.) 198.
— (Cal.) 442.
— (Va.) 304.
Gouldsborough 367.
Governor's Island 3.
Grafton (Ill.) 324.
— (W. Va.) 266.
Grahamville 361.
Grand Bay 338.
— Crossing 270. 302.
— Forks 299. 300.
Grande, Rio 412.
— Ronde Valley 393.
Grand Gorge 165.
— Hotel Station (Catskills) 165.
— Island 391.
— Junction 422. 320. 424.
— Lake 325.
— Manan 108.
— Rapids 273. 270. 274.
— Tower 324.
Granger 392. 395.
Granite 421.
— Cañon 391.
— Gate 423.
Graniteville 350.
Grant City 51.
Grant's 394.
— Pass 460.
— Sulphur Springs 452.
Graymont 408.
Gray's Peak 408.
Great Barrington 137. 136.
— Bend 459.
— Falls (Mont.) 300. 374.
— — (N. H.) 121.
— Salt Lake 427.
— Smoky Mts. 341.

Greeley 410. 408.
Greenbrier White Sulphur Springs 305.
Greenbush 134.
Greencastle (Ind.) 310.
— (Pa.) 233.
Green Cove Springs 359.
Greenfield 134. 142.
Greenland 93.
Green Mts. 117. 114.
— Mt. Fall 423.
— River 392.
Greensboro 335. 346.
Greensburg (Ind.) 303.
— (Pa.) 235. 230.
Greenvale 79.
Greenville (Ala.) 337.
— (Ct.) 67.
— (Fla.) 365.
— (Ill.) 302.
— (Me.) 99. 106.
— (Miss.) 325.
— (S. C.) 335.
— (Tenn.) 341.
Greenwich 57.
Greenwood 317.
— Lake 198.
Gregory 466.
Grenada 320.
Grenville Channel 474.
Gretna 299. 367.
Greylock 141. 134.
Grimsby Park 274.
Grinnell 390.
Grosse Point 273.
Groton 62.
Grottoes 339.
Groveton 109. 119.
Grub Gulch 452.
Guadalajara 482.
Guadalupe 486.
— Hidalgo 492.
Guanajuato 487.
Guilford 63.
Guinea 326.
Gunnison 421. 409.
Gurdon 404.
Guthrie 411.
Guttenberg (Ia.) 323.
— (N. J.) 51.
Gypsum City 403.

Hackberry 414.
Hackensack Valley 152.
Hackettstown 196.
Hadley (Mass.) 142.
— (N. Y.) 176.
Hagerman Pass 424.
Hagerstown 233. 236. 250.
265. 338.
Hagerville 271.
Hague 184.
Hailey 393.

Haines's Falls 164.
Halfway 408.
Halleck 396.
Halstead 411.
Hamburg 324.
Hamilton (Can.) 274. 271.
—, Mt. 437.
— (Ohio) 306.
Hammond 274. 278.
Hampton (Fla.) 363.
— (Mass.) 93.
— (Va.) 332.
— Roads 331.
Hannibal 401. 402.
Hanover (N. H.) 143.
— (Pa.) 232.
— Junction 250.
Hardeeville 359. 364.
Harlem 401.
Haro, Canal de 472.
Harper's Ferry 265.
Harriman 318.
Harrington 301.
Harrisburg (Can.) 274.
— (Ore.) 460.
— (Pa.) 232.
Harrison (Me.) 110.
— (Miss.) 321.
Harrison's Landing 329.
Harrisville 113.
Hartford 59. 66.
Hartland 98.
Hartsel Hot Springs 423.
Harvard 83.
— Junction 289.
— Mt. (Cal.) 447.
— — (Col.) 409.
Harwood 467.
Hastings (Minn.) 289. 322.
— (N. Y.) 147.
Hatfield (Ky.) 340.
— (Mass.) 142.
Hauser Junction 375.
Havana 363.
— Glen 191.
Haverford 231.
Haverhill 95.
Haverstraw 148. 152.
Havre de Grace 244.
Hawk's Nest 305.
Hawleyville 62. 66. 135.
Hawthorne 364.
Hayden Divide 423.
Hayes, Mt. 125.
Haymond 411.
Hays City 405.
Hayt's Corners 228.
Helderberg Mts. 149. 158.
Helena (Ark.) 325.
— (Ga.) 342.
— (Mont.) 373. 301. 392.
Hell Gate 50. 66.
Hell's Half Acre 361.

Henderson Lake 176.
Hendersonville 345.
Hennings 320.
Herkimer 187. 179. 145.
Herndon 442.
Heron 375.
Hetch-Hetchy 458.
Hickman (Ark.) 324.
— (Ky.) 324.
Hickory 344.
Higginsville 401.
High Bridge (Ky.) 317.
Highgate Springs 115.
Highland (Fla.) 363.
Highlands (Hudson) 148.
High Torn 152.
Hilliard 395.
Hillsdale 270.
Hill Top 409.
Hinckley 414.
Hingham 86.
Hinton 305.
Hobart 165.
Hoboken 51. 196.
Hoffmann, Mt. 458.
Hogarth's Landing 359.
Hois'ngton 403.
Holbrook 413.
Holliday 410.
Hollins 250.
Hollister 439.
Holly Springs 320.
Hollywood 222.
Holy Cross Mt. 408.
Holyoke 142.
—, Mt. 142.
Homer 414.
Homestead 242.
Homosassa 364.
Hondo 484.
Honeyville 396.
Hood, Mt. 394. 462.
— River 394.
Hooper 423.
Hoosac Tunnel 134. 141.
Hoosick Falls 135.
— Junction 135.
Hopatcong, Lake 196.
Hope (Ark.) 404.
— (Idaho) 375.
Hopkins 290.
—, Mt. 174.
Horace 403.
Hornbrook 460.
Hornellsville 199. 278.
Hornos 484.
Horse Plains 375.
Horseshoe Curve 234.
Hot Springs (Ark.) 404.
— — (Neb.) 396.
— — (N. C.) 345. 341.
— — (Va.) 304.
— — (Wash.) 376.

Houghton 296. 297.
Housac, Mts. 134.
Housatonic 136.
—, the 134.
— Valley 135.
Houston 467. 466.
Howbert 423.
Howell's 198.
Howe's Cave 158.
Hoxie 404.
Hudson (N. Y.) 151. 149.
— (Ohio) 243.
— (Wis.) 289.
—, the 146. 3.
Hugo 406.
Hulett's Landing 184.
Hull 85.
Humboldt 396.
Hunter 163.
Huntingburg 315.
Huntingdon 233.
Huntington (Ore.) 393.
— (W. Va.) 305.
Huntsville 343.
Hurdland 400.
Huron 299.
—, Lake 276.
Husted 415.
Hutchinson 403. 411.
Hyannis 88.
Hyattsville 251.
Hyde Park (Mass.) 62. 65.
— (N. Y.) 151.

Iceboro 97.
Icy Strait 478. 480.
Idaho (state) 375. 392.
— Springs 407.
Ignacio 419.
Ilion 187.
Illilouette Falls 458.
Illinois 270.
Indiana 269.
Indianapolis 302.
Indian Pass 176.
— Reservations 300. 371.
392. 419. 463. etc.
— River 364.
— Territory 410.
Indio 463.
Ingleside 321.
Inspiration Point 453.
Intervale 110.
Iola 361.
Iowa (state) 290.
— City 390.
Ipswich 93.
Irolo 493.
Iron River 296.
— Springs 411.
Ironton (Col.) 419.
— (Ohio) 305.
Irvington 147. 150.

Ishpeming 296.
Island Pond 109.
Isle au Haut 101.
Isles of Shoals 94.
Isleta 412.
Itasca Lake 322.
Ithaca 190.
— Falls 190. 228.
Ixtacalco 492.
Ixtaccihuatl 492.

Jackson (Ala.) 341.
— (Mich.) 274.
— (Miss.) 320.
— (N. H.) 110. 124.
— (Tenn.) 320.
Jacksonville (Fla.) 354.
— (Ill.) 400. 401.
Jajalpa 484.
Jalapa 496.
Jalisco 487.
James, the 330. etc.
Jamesburg 223.
James Peak 408.
Jamestown (N. D.) 371.
— (N. Y.) 278. 243.
— (R. I.) 71.
— (Va.) 331.
Janesville 289.
Jaral 484.
Jefferson (Mont.) 374.
— (N. H.) 111. 119.
— City 403.
— Hill 130.
—, Mt. 133.
Jeffersonville 316.
Jenkintown 210.
Jennings 301.
Jersey City 51.
Jessup's Landing 176.
Jesup 342. 354.
Jimulco 485.
Jocko 374.
Johnson City 340.
Johnsonville 135.
Johnston (Ga.) 354.
— (N. Y.) 187.
Johnstone Strait 473.
Johnstown 234.
Joliet 290. 302. 399.
Jonesborough 320.
Jordan, the 423.
Juan de Fuca Strait 471.
Juanacatlan, Falls of 487.
Juanita, the 233.
Julesburg 391. 410.
Junction City 317. 405.
Juneau 477.
Juno 365.
Jupiter 365.

Kaaterskill Clove 160.
— Hotel 162.

Kaaterskill Junct. 163.
— Mt. 149.
— Station 164.
Kalamazoo 274. 270.
Kalispell 301.
Kamela 393.
Kanawha Falls 305.
Kane 231.
Kankakee 301. 302.
Kansas City (Kan.) 400.
— — (Mo.) 400.
Katama (Mass.) 88.
— (Wash.) 377.
Kearney 391. 401.
Kearsarge, Mt. (N. Conway, N. H.) 123.
— — (Warner, N. H.) 117.
Keating 230.
Keene Valley 172. 144.
Keeseville 145. 170.
Keithsburg 323.
Kenedy 466.
Kennebec, the 97.
Kennebunk 95.
Kennebunkport 95.
Kenner 321.
Kennet 459.
Kenosha 408.
Kenova 340.
Kent 135.
Kentucky 305.
— River 317.
Keokuk 323.
Ketchum 393.
Keyport 222.
Keyser 266.
Keystone 408.
Keyville 347.
Key West 363.
Kilbourn 289.
Killington Peak 114.
Kimball 270.
Kinderhook 401.
Kineo, Mt. 99.
Kingfield 106.
Kingman 414.
Kingsbury 442.
King's Mt. (Ky.) 317.
— — (S. C.) 335.
Kingston (Can.) 206.
— (Mass.) 86.
— (N. Y.) 153. 163. 249.
— (Pa.) 228.
Kingville 347.
Kinsley 411.
Kirkwood 314.
Kissimmee 362.
Kit Carson 406.
Kittanning Pt. 234.
Knobel 404.
Knoxville 341. 318.
Kootenai 375.
— Falls 301.

Kramer 414.
Ktaadn, Mt. 99.
Kuttawa 320.

Labadie 402.
La Bota 494.
Lachine Rapids 208.
La Cima 484.
Lackawanna, the 197. 198.
La Colorada 486.
Laconia 118.
Lacoochee 362. 364.
La Crosse 289. 291. 323.
La Cruz Mts. 484.
Lafayette (Ind.) 302. 311.
— (La.) 468.
—, Mt. 129.
Lagos 486.
La Grande 393.
— Grange 318.
Laguna 412.
La Jara 418.
— Junta 411. 409.
Laka 393.
Lake Charles 468.
— City (Fla.) 365.
— — (Minn.) 289. 323.
Lakeland 363.
— Park 423.
Laketon 423.
Lakeview (Miss.) 321.
— (Wash.) 377.
— Village 118.
Lakewood 225. 278.
Lama Junction 273.
Lamanda 447.
Lamar 411.
Lamy Junction 412.
Lancaster (Cal.) 442.
— (N. H.) 111. 119.
— (N. Y.) 207.
— (Pa.) 232.
Land's End 93.
Lanesboro 140.
Lanesville (N. Y.) 163.
— (Mass.) 93.
Langhorne 210.
Langtry 464.
Lansing (Iowa) 323.
— (Mich.) 273. 274.
Lapeer 273
La Porte 270.
Laramie City 392.
Laredo 467. 482.
— Nuevo 482.
Larkspur 415.
La Salle (Ill.) 290.
— — (N. Y.) 199.
Las Cruces 412.
— Vegas 411.
Lathrop 441. 398.
Latrobe 235.
Laurel Hill Station 164.

Lawrence (Mass.) 95.
— (Kan.) 410.
Lawrenceburg 303.
Lawrence Junction 243.
Lawrenceville 160.
Lawson 402.
Lawtey 363.
Leadville 423. 420. 409.
Leavenworth 315. 402. 410.
Leavittsburg 278.
Lebanon (Ky.) 318.
— (Mass.) 140.
— (Pa.) 233.
— Springs 140.
Le Claire 323.
Lee 139. 136.
Leechburg 241.
Leeds (Me.) 106. 97.
— (N. D.) 371.
Lehi 423.
Lehigh Water Gap 227.
Leicester Junction 114.
Leland 321.
Lenoir 344.
Lenox 139.
Lenoxville 109. 120.
Leon 486.
Lerdo 485.
Lerma, Rio 484. 487.
Lethbridge 301.
Lewiston (Me.) 105. 97.
— (N. Y.) 206. 195.
— (Pa.) 233.
Lexington (Ky.) 317. 316.
— (Mass.) 113.
— (Mo.) 400. 403.
— (Neb.) 391.
— (Va.) 304.
Leyden 134.
Liberty (Tex.) 468.
— (Va.) 334.
Lick Observatory 437.
Lima 278.
Lime Ridge 112.
Limon 406.
Lincoln, Mt. 409.
Lineville 401.
Lisbon 119. 130.
Litchfield (Ct.) 135.
— (Ill.) 310. 311.
— (Ky.) 320.
— (Wis.) 299.
Little Falls (Minn.) 371.
— — (N. Y.) 187. 195.
— Neck Bay 66.
— Rapids 179.
— Rock 404.
— Rockies (Mts.) 300.
Littleton 119.
Live Oaks 365.
Livermore 106.
Livingston (N. Y.) 50.
— (Mont.) 373. 380.

Lizard Head Pass. 419.
Lloyd's.366.
Lock Haven 230.
Lockport (Ill.) 302.
— (N. Y.) 192.
Logan (Utah) 396.
— (Wash.) 373.
Logansport 264. 303. 311
Lomax 403.
London (Col.) 409.
— (Ohio) 271. 274.
Long Beach (Cal.) 446.
— — (N. Y.) 56.
— Branch 223.
— Island 55. 2.
— — City 55. 66.
— — Sound 66. 55.
— Lake 178.
Longport 226.
Longmeadow 60.
Longmont 403.
Long's Peak 403.
Longview 468.
Lonsdale 65.
Lookout Mt. 342.
Loon Lake 179. 168.
Lorain 270.
Loretto 234.
Lorimer 290.
Los Alamos 439.
— Angeles 445. 443.
— Gatos 440.
— Olivos 439. 444.
Louisiana (state) 338.
— (Mo.) 324.
Loudon 341.
Louisville (Ky.) 315. 318.
— Landing (N. Y.) 207.
Loveland 408.
Lowell 116.
Lowville 188.
Ludlow (Cal.) 414.
— (Ky.) 317.
Lula 321. 336.
Lundy's Lane 204.
Lunenburg 112. 120.
Luray 339.
Luzerne Lake 177.
Lyell, Mt. 458.
Lynchburg 334. 304.
Lyndhurst 147. 150.
Lyndonville 120.
Lynn 90.
— Canal 478.
Lyon Mt. 168.
Lyons (Iowa) 323.
— (N. Y.) 195.

Machias 101.
Mackinac Island 273. 298.
Mackinaw 273. 270. 271.
Macon (Ga.) 342. 365.
— (Mo.) 402.

Madera 442.
Madison (Me.) 106.
— (N. H.) 121.
— (Wis.) 289.
— Mt. 133.
Madrid 383.
Madrone 439.
Magnolia (Fla.) 359. 361.
— (Mass.) 92.
Magog 120.
Mahkeenac Lake 133.
Mahoney.230.
Maine 94. 96.
Malabar 365.
Malone 179. 145.
Malta 421. .
Maltrata 494.
Malvern 404.
Mammoth Cave 318.
Manassa 418.
Manassas 334.
Manchester (Ct.) 62.
— (Mass.) 92.
— (N. H.) 116.
— (N. J.) 225.
— (N. Y.) 229.
— (Va.) 327. 347.
— (Vt.) 145.
Mancos Cañon 419.
Mandan 372.
Mandarin 359.
Manhattan (Kan.) 405.
— (N. Y.) 22.
— Beach 56.
Manitou 417. 423.
— Park 423. 415.
Manlius 189.
Manomet 86.
Mansfield 263. 267. 278.
—, Mt. 117. .
Mantoloking 224.
Manuelito 413.
Manunka Chunk 196.
Maple River Junction 389.
Maplewood 128.
Maravatio 483.
Marblehead 90. 91.·
Marceline 400.
Marcy, Mt. 174.
Mare Island 433.
Marfa 464.
Marfil 486.
Marianna 366.
Maricopa 463.
Marietta 269.
Marion (Ind.) 264. 278. 310.
— (Iowa) 388. 402.
— (Va.) 340.
— Junction 306.
Mariposa Grove 452.
Mark West 434.
Marquette (Kan.) 403.
— (Mich.) 297.

Marshall Junction 375.
— Pass 421.
Marshalltown 401.
Marshfield (Mass.) 86.
— (Vt.) 119.
Martha's Vineyard 88.
Martin 320.
Martinez 441.
Martinsburg 233. 250. 266.
Maryland 244.
Marysville 459.
Maryville 341.
Mascoma, Lake 117.
Mason (Ill.) 400.
— (Wis.) 296.
Mason & Dixon's Line 233. 236.
Massachusetts (state) 60.
— Bay 74.
Massawepie, Lake 179.
Massawippi 120.
Massena Springs 188. 207.
Mast Hope 199.
Matamoras 484.
Matawan 222.
Mattapoisett 88.
Mattawamkeag 98.
Mattoon 301. 310.
Mauch Chunk 227.
Max Meadows 340.
Mayport 356.
Maysville 305.
Mayville 243. 278.
McAdam 98.
McCammon 396.
McClenny 365.
McCloud 459.
McGee's 409.
McGregor 323.
— —, Mt. 182.
McIntyre, Mt. 175.
McKeesport 266.
McKeever 178.
Meacham, Lake 179.
Meadville 278.
Mears Junction 421.
Mechanics Falls 108.
Mechanicsville 329.
Mechanicville 144. 135.
Medford (Mass.) 116.
— (Ore.) 460.·
Medical Lake 375.
Medicine Bow Mts. 392.
Medina 221. 220.
Medora 372.
Megantic, Lake 93. 99.
Melbourne 365.
Melrose 94.
Memphis 320. 325.
— Junction 319.
Memphremagog, Lake 120. 109.
Mendota 390.

Menlo Park (Cal.) 437.
— — (N. J.) 208.
Menomonee 289.
Mentone 448.
Merced 441.
— (Yosemite) 453.
Meredith 118.
Meridian 343.
Merrimac, the 93. 95.
Merritt 364.
Merritton 274.
Metlakatla 474. 476.
Mexico (Mo.) 401.
—, City of (Mex.) 489.
—, Gulf of 326.
Micco 365.
Michelville 319.
Michigamme 296.
Michigan 270.
—, Lake 276.
Middleborough (Mass.) 88.
— (Tenn.) 341.
Middlebury 114.
Middle Park 407.
Middlesex 117.
— Fells 116.
Middletown (Ct.) 62.
— (N. Y.) 198.
— (Pa.) 232.
Mifflin 233.
Milan (N. H.) 109.
— (Tenn.) 320.
Milano 411.
Miles City 372.
— Pond 112.
Millbank Sound 473.
Millboro 304.
Millbræ 437.
Millbury 269.
Millen 351.
Miller's 267.
— Falls 134. 63.
Milltown 315.
Millwood 419.
Milton (Cal.) 398. 451.
— (Fla.) 366.
— (N. H.) 121.
— (Pa.) 230.
— (Tenn.) 320.
Milwaukee 276.
Mineola 65.
Mineral Pt. (Mo.) 403.
— (Pa.) 234.
Mineville 185.
Minot 300.
Minot's Ledge 86.
Minturn 421.
Minneapolis 293.
Minnehaha Falls 293.
Minnesota 289.
Minnetonka, Lake 295.
Minnewaukan 371.
Miser 392.

Mississippi (state) 338.
—, the 322. 292. 293. 321.
324. 325. 463. etc.
Missoula 374.
Missouri (state) 400.
—, the 322. 324. 389. etc.
Mitchell, Mt. 348.
Moat Mt. 124.
Moberley 401.
Mobile 337.
Modesto 441.
Modjeska 449.
Mohawk 195. 186.
— Summit 463.
— Valley 187.
Mohegan 67.
Moingana 389.
Moira 179. 189.
Mojave 414. 442. 448.
Monadnock, Mt. 114.
Monarch 421.
Monclova 484.
Monee 302.
Monmouth 223. 208.
Mono Lake 458.
Monongahela, the 240.
— City 243.
Monroe (N. Y.) 198.
— (Ohio) 269.
—, Mt. 133.
Monrovia 447.
Montague 460.
Montana 372.
Montauk Pt. 54.
Montecito 444. 443.
Monteith 350.
Monterey (Cal.) 439.
— (Mex.) 482.
— (Ohio) 278.
— (Pa.) 250.
Monte Vista 418.
Montezuma 485.
Montgomery (Ala.) 336.
319. 354.
— (Va.) 340.
Monticello (Fla.) 366.
— (N. Y.) 198.
— (Va.) 304.
Montpelier (Idaho) 392.
— (Mich.) 277.
— (Vt.) 117.
Montreal 109. 145. 208. etc.
Montrose (Col.) 422. 409.
— (Iowa) 323.
Monument Beach 87.
— Park 417.
Moorehead 371. 299. 300.
Moors 396.
Moosehead Lake 99. 98.
Mooselucmaguntic, Lake 106.
Moosilaukee Mt. 119.
Moqui Reservation 413.

Morehead 335.
Morgan City 467.
Morgantown 344.
Moriah, Mt. 125.
Morley (Cal.) 459.
— (Col.) 411.
Morrisburg 207.
Morristown (N. Y.) 188.
— (Tenn.) 341.
Morrisville 209.
Mosier 394.
Moundsville 266.
Mountain Ho. Station 160.
— Lake Park 266.
— View 437.
Mount Airy 335.
— Carmel 315.
— Clement 273.
— Desert 101. 99.
— Holly Springs 232.
— Hope (R. I.) 65.
— — (Pa.) 250.
— Hope Bay 71.
— Pleasant (Iowa) 390.
— — (N. H.) 111.
— St. Vincent 147. 150.
— Union 233.
— Vernon (Ala. 342.
— — (Ill.) 315.
— — (Pa.) 233.
— — (Va.) 263. 262.
— Wilson 250.
Muir Glacier 478.
Mullan's Pass 374.
Mulvane 410.
Munesing 298.
Munhall 242.
Murphy's Camp 398.
Murrysville 241.
Muscatine 323. 401.
Muscogee 400.
Mystic, the 86.

Nahant 90.
Nampa 393.
Nanaimo 472.
Nantasket Beach 85.
Nanticoke 228.
Nantucket 87.
Napa 434.
Naples 401.
Napoleon 310.
Narragansett Bay 65. 72.
—, Fort 64.
— Pier 64.
Narrows 365.
Narrowsburg 199.
Nashua (Mont.) 300.
— (N. H.) 116.
—, the 113.
Nashville 319.
Natchez 325.
Nathrop 421.

Natick 61.
National City 450.
Natural Bridge (Va.) 339.
Nancalpan 484.
Naugatuck 340.
Nauvoo City 323.
Navajo Reservation 413.
Navesink Highlands 2.
223.
Navy Yard 251.
Neche 299.
Needles, the 414.
Neelyville 404.
Neenah 291.
Negaunee 296.
Neihart 301.
Neola 388.
Nestoria 296.
Nevada (state) 396.
— Falls (Yosemite) 457.
Nevado de Toluca 483.
New Albany 315. 316.
Newark (Col.) 440.
— (N. J.) 203. 196. 209.
— (Ohio) 267.
New Bedford 89. 72.
— Berne 335.
— Brighton 50.
— Britain 61.
— Brunswick (Can.) 98.
— — (N. J.) 208.
— Buffalo 274.
Newburg 153. 148.
Newbury (N. H.) 116.
— (Vt.) 143.
— (W. Va.) 266.
Newburyport 93. 95.
Newcastle (Cal.) 397.
— (Col.) 421. 424.
— (Me.) 99.
— (N. H.) 95.
New England 57.
Newfield 225.
Newfoundland, Banks of
2. 5.
Newhall 443.
New Hampshire 93.
— Haven 58.
Newington 403.
New London 63.
— Madrid 329.
— Mexico 411. 464.
— Milford 135.
Newnan 336.
New Orleans 366. 243.
Newport (Ark.) 404.
— (Ky.) 307. 309.
— (Me.) 98.
— (Ore.) 462.
— (R. I.) 68.
— (Vt.) 120.
— News 331. 332.
New Richmond 291.

New Rochelle 57.
— Smyrna 359. 360.
Newton (Kan.) 410.
— (Mass.) 61.
— (N. H.) 95.
Newtown 135.
New Westminster 471.
— York (state) 134. 197.
etc.
New York 6.
Amsterdam, Fort 26.
Annexed District 50.
Arsenal 40.
Ascension, Ch. of 33.
Assay Office 26.
Astor Library 31.
— Place 31.
Bankers 19.
Barge Office 25.
Baths 19.
Battery, the 25.
Bellevue Hospital 40.
Bible House 31. 36.
Blind Institution 40.
Bloomingdale Insane
Asylum 48.
Booksellers 18.
Boulevard 33. 26.
Bowery 29.
Bowling Green 25.
British Consul 21.
Broad St. 27.
Broadway 26.
Brooklyn Bridge 30. 11.
Bryant Park 40.
Carnegie Music Hall 40.
Carriages 13.
Castle Garden 25.
Cathedral (Epis.) 48.
— (R. C.) 35.
Central Ave. 50.
— Park 40.
Century Club 34. 18.
Chamber of Commerce
27.
Chemical Nat. Bank 30.
Chickering Hall 34.
Chinatown 29.
Children's Aid Soc. 31.
Churches 19. 32. 34.
35. etc.
City Hall 28.
— Park 28.
Clearing House 27.
Clubs 18. 34. etc.
Collections 21.
College of the City of
New York 38.
Columbia Coll. 39. 43.
Columbus Monum. 33.
Commerce 25.
Concerts 16.
Consulate, British 21.

New York:
Cooper Institute 31.
Cotton Exchange 27.
Court House 28.
Criminal Court 28.
Croton Aqued. 49. 50.
Custom House 26.
Dakota Flats 40.
Deaf Mutes, Institution
for 38.
Delmonico's 9. 32.
Depots 6.
De Vinne Press 31.
Dutch Reformed Ch.
34.
East River Bridge 30.
Eighth Ave. 40.
Elevated Railroads 10.
Ellis Island 3.
Equitable Life Ins. Co.
27.
Exhibitions 16. 21.
Express Service 15.
Ferries 14. 28.
Fifth Ave. 33.
First Ave. 40.
Fire Department 20.
Five Points 29.
Fourteenth St. 32.
Fourth Ave. 36.
Fraunces Tavern 25.
Fulton Market 28.
Governor's Island 3.
Grace Church 31.
Grand Central Depot
37. 34. 6.
— St. 31. 18.
Grant's Tomb 48.
Harbour 23. 2.
Harlem Heights 48.
High Bridge 49.
History 24.
Horse Exchange 33.
Hospitals 35. 38. 39. 40.
Hotels 7.
Industry 25.
Islands (East River) 50.
— (Harbour) 2.
Jefferson Market Po-
lice Court 40.
Judge Building 34.
Leake & Watts Orphan-
age 48.
Lenox Library 36.
Lexington Ave. 38.
Liberty, Statue of 3.
Libraries 19.
Little Church round
the corner 34.
Madison Ave. 38.
— Sq. 32.
— — Garden 16. 37. 39.
Manhattan Club 34.

New York:
Masonic Temple 32.
Mercantile Library 31.
Messenger Service 15.
Methodist Book Con-
cern 34.
Metropolitan Ins. Bldg.
32.
— Museum of Art 12.
— Opera House 33. 15.
Morningside Park 48.
Mt. Morris Sq. 36.
Mulberry St. 29.
Murray Hill 37.
Museums 41. 42.
Mutual Life Ins. Co. 27.
Nat. Acad. of Design 37.
— Hist. Museum 41.
Newsboys' Lodging
House 29.
Newspaper Offices 29.
28. 33.
Newspapers 19.
New York Academy of
Medicine 34.
— Historical Society 40.
— Hospital 34.
— Life Ins. Co. 30.
Ninth Ave. 40.
Normal College 38.
Omnibuses 13.
Panorama 16. 37.
Park Ave. 37.
— Row 29.
Parks 28. 40. 48. 50.
Petroleum Exchange 26.
Picture Galleries 16.
Police Stations 21.
Post Office 28. 14.
Produce Exchange 25.
Prot. Epis. Theol. Sem.
40.
Quarantine Station 2.
Racquet Club 34.
Railway Stations 6. 34.
37.
Reading Rooms 19.
Register Office 29.
Restaurants 9.
Rialto 32.
Riverside Park 48.
Roosevelt Hospital 40.
St. Bartholomew's Ch.
39.
— Francis Xavier 34.
— John the Divine
(Cathedral) 48.
— Luke's Hospital 35.
— Mark's Ch. 40.
— Patrick's (Cathedral)
35.
— Paul's Ch. 28.
— Thomas Ch. 35.

New York:
Second Ave. 40.
Seventh Ave. 40.
— Regt. Armoury 38.
Shops 18.
Sixth Ave. 40.
Slave-Market 32.
Sport 27.
Statue of Columbus 33.
— Farragut 32.
— Franklin 29.
— Garibaldi 33.
— Greeley 29.
— Lafayette 32.
— Lincoln 32.
— Seward 32.
— Washington 32. 48.
26.
Steamers 6.
Stock Exchange 27.
Stores 18.
Streets 20.
Stuyvesant Sq. 40.
Sub-Treasury 26.
Synagogues 34. 36. 38.
Tammany Hall 32.
Telegraph Offices 14.
Telephone — 15.
Temple Emanu-El 34.
Theatres 15. 32.
Third Ave. 40.
Tiffany House 39.
Tiffany's 31.
Tombs 30.
Tramways 11.
Transfiguration, Ch. of
34.
Trinity Church 27.
— — Cemetery 48.
Twenty Third St. 32.
Union League Club 34.
— Square 31.
— Theological Semin-
ary 38.
— Trust Co. 27.
University of the City
of New York 33.
Vanderbilt Houses 35.
Wall St. 26.
Washington Bridge 49.
— Building 26. 25.
— Centennial Arch 33.
— Heights 49.
— Market 28.
— Square 33.
—, Statues of 26. 32. 48.
Water Supply 49.
Western Union Tele-
graph Co. 28. 14.
Worth Monument 32.
Young Men's Christian
Association 37.
New York Mills 371.

Niagara Falls 199. 195.
271.
— Junction 229.
Nicholson 343.
Niles 441.
Nineveh 159.
Niota 400.
Niverville 134.
Noon Mark 174.
Nordhoff 443.
Nordmont 230.
Norfolk 331. 244.
Normal 302.
Norridgewock 106.
Norristown 229.
North Adams 141. 134.
Northampton 142.
North Beach 462.
— Bennington 145.
— Berwick 94. 95.
— Carolina 334.
— Conway 123. 94.
— Creek 177.
— Dakota 371.
— Duxbury 117.
— East 244.
— — Harbor 104. 100.
— Elba 171.
Northfield 117.
North Hero 186.
— Mt. 304.
— Ontario (Cal.) 447. 462.
— Park 392.
— Pepin 323.
— Platte 391.
— River 3. 22.
— Shore (Mass.) 92. 85.
— Stratford 109. 111.
Northville 187.
North Woodstock 119. 129.
Norton Mills 109.
Norumbega 86.
Norwalk (Ct.) 57. 66.
— (Ohio) 269.
Norwich (Ct.) 67. 63.
— (Vt.) 143.
Norwood 189.
Nototuck, Mt. 142.
Nyack 147.

Oakdale 318.
Oakland (Cal.) 399.
— (Fla.) 362.
— (Ill.) 315.
— (Me.) 106.
— (W. Va.) 266.
Oaklawn 365.
Oakley 405.
Oberlin 269.
Obion 320.
Obsidian Cliffs 382.
Ocala 364.
Ocean City 226.

Ocean Grove 222. 223.
Oceanside 449.
Ocean View 437.
Ocklawaha, the 360.
Ocoyoacac 484.
Odenton 251.
Odessa 469.
Odin 320.
Oelwein 290. 401.
Ogden 423.
Ogontz 226.
Ohio 267.
—, the 240. 243. 307. etc.
Oil City 243.
Ojai Valley 443.
Ojo Caliente 418. 485.
Oklahoma 410. 411.
Old Colony House 85. 86.
— Forge 178.
— Orchard Beach 95.
— Point Comfort 332.
Oldtown 98. 99.
Olean 231. 278.
Olympia 377.
Olympic Mts. 470.
Omaha 388.
Oneida (N. Y.) 189.
— (Tenn.) 318.
— Lake 189.
Oneonta (N. Y.) 159.
— (Ore.) 394.
Onondaga, Lake 189.
Onset 89.
Ontario (Can.) 270.
— (Col.) 462.
—, Lake 206. 201.
Ontonagon 297.
Opelika 336.
Oquossoc Lake 106.
Orange (Cal.) 449. 448.
— (N. J.) 196.
— (Tex.) 468.
— (Va.) 304.
— Grove 364.
— Mills 359.
— Park 359.
— Springs 361.
Orangeville 278.
Oregon (state) 460.
— (Ill.) 291.
— City 460.
— National Park 460.
Oriskany 188.
Orizaba 494.
—, Mt. 493.
Orlando 362.
Orleans 89.
Ormond 359.
Ortega 443.
Ortiz 485.
Osage City 403.
Osakis 300.
Osceola 391.

Oshkosh 291.
Ossawattomie 403.
Ossipee 121.
Osterville 89.
Oswego 189. 195.
Osyka 320.
Otis (Ind.) 270.
— (Wash.) 375.
— Junction 198.
Otisville 198.
Otsego Lake 158.
Ottawa (Ill.) 290.
Ottawa (Kan.) 403.
Otter, Peaks of 334.
Ottumwa 391. 402.
Otumba 493.
Ouray 420.
Overlook Mt. 149. 163.
Owasco, Lake 190.
Owego 199. 228.
Owl's Head Mt. 120.
Oxford Junction 388.
Oyster Bay 66.
Ozark Mts. 404.

Pablo Beach 356.
Pacific Congress Springs 439.
— Glacier 479.
— Grove 440.
— Junction 300. 391.
— Ocean 437. 433. 440. etc.
Packerton 227.
Paducah 320.
Paila 484.
Painesville 267.
Painted Cave 464.
Paint Rock 346.
Paisano 464.
Pajaro 439. 441.
Palatine Bridge 187.
Palatka 359. 361. 365.
Palenville 160.
Palisades 146.
Palm Beach 365.
Palmer (Mass.) 63.
— (Wash.) 376.
—, Lake 415.
Palmilla 418.
Palm Springs 463.
— Valley 463.
Palo Alto 437.
Palmyra (Mo.) 402.
— (N. Y.) 190.
Pana 301. 310.
Panasoffkee 364.
Panzacola 493.
Paoli 231.
Parachute 424.
Paradise 375.
Paris (Ky.) 317.
— (Me.) 108. 110.
Parkersburg 306.

Park Rapids 300.
Parlin's 409. 421.
Parma 274.
Parmachenee, Lake 107.
Parryville 227.
Pasadena 446.
— Lake 364.
Pasco 375.
Paso, El 464.
— del Macho 494.
— de Robles 439.
Passaic 196. 198.
Passamaquoddy Bay 107.
Pass Christian 338.
Passumpsic, the 112. 120.
Paterson 196. 198.
Patterson Glacier 477.
Patterson's Creek 338.
Patzcuaro 483.
Paul Smith's 168. 179.
Pawtucket 65.
Paxton 301.
Payne 270.
Peabody (Kan.) 410.
— (Mass.) 91.
Peach Blow 424.
— Springs 414.
Pecos 469.
Pedrito 486.
Peebles 309.
Pee Dee 346.
Peekskill 151. 148.
Pemaquid 99.
Pembroke 340. 346.
Pemigewasset, the 119.
Pend d'Oreille, Lake 301.
Pendleton 393.
Pen-Mar 250.
Pennsylvania 198. 209.
Penobscot, the 98.
Pensacola 366.
Pepin, Lake 289. 323.
Pequonnock, the 58. 135.
Pequop 396.
Percy Peaks 109.
Peril Strait 479.
Perma 374.
Perris 448.
Perryville 244.
Perth Amboy 222.
Peru 311.
Pescadero 437.
Petaluma 434.
Peterboro 113.
Petersburg (Pa.) 234.
— (Va.) 333. 346.
Peterson 395.
PetrifiedForest(Ariz.)413.
— (Cal.) 434.
Peyotes 484.
Philadelphia (N. Y.) 188.
Philadelphia (Pa.) 210.
Academy of Arts 216.

Philadelphia:
Academy of Natur.
Sciences 216.
— of Music 218.
Arch Street 218.
Art Club 218.
Baldwin's Locomotive
Works 217.
Betz Building 213.
Broad St. Station 213.
Bourse 214.
Carpenters' Hall 215.
Chestnut Street 213.
Christ Church 218.
City Hall 212.
College of Physicians
215.
Cooper's Shop 219.
Cramp's Ship-building
Yards 219.
Custom House 214.
Deaf and Dumb Asylum 218.
Drexel Building 214.
— Institute 219.
Eastern Penitentiary
217.
Exhibitions of Art 211.
Fairmount Park 220.
Franklin's Statue 214.
— Tomb 219.
Girard College 217.
Historical Society 215.
Horticultural Hall 220.
Independence Hall 214.
Insane Asylum 220.
Laurel Hill Cem. 220.
League Island 218.
Market Street 218.
Masonic Temple 213.
Memorial Hall 220.
Mercantile Library 213.
Merchants' Exchange
215.
Mint 213.
Naval Asylum 219.
North Broad Street 216.
Penn House 220.
— National Bank 218.
— Treaty Monument
219.
Philad. Library 215.
Philosophical Society
214.
Post Office 213.
Public Buldings 212.
Railway Stations 210.
213. 215. 218.
Ridgeway Library 218.
Rittenhouse Sq. 215.
SS. Peter and Paul 216.
School of Industrial
Art 217.

Philadelphia:
Shackamaxon 219.
South Broad Street 218.
Stock Exchange 214.
Streets 212.
Swedes' Church 219.
Theatres 211.
Union League Club 218.
University 219.
Walnut Street 215.
Wanamaker's 213.
Washington Sq. 215.
West Philadelphia 219.
Wissahickon Drive 220.
Zoological Garden 221.
Phillips 106.
— Beach 90.
Phillipsburg 243.
Phoenicia 163. 164.
Phoenix 463.
Phoenixville 229.
Picolata 359.
Pictured Rocks 297.
Picture Rocks 230.
Piedmont 266.
Pigeon Cove 93.
Pike's Peak 417.
Piketon 340.
Pilot Knob 404.
— Rock 460.
Pine Bluffs 391.
— Forest Inn 362.
— Grove 408.
— Hill 165.
— Knot 439.
Pinkham Notch 124.
Piqua 264.
Piscataqua, the 94.
Pitkin 409.
Pittsburg 240.
Pittsfield (Mass.) 140. 136.
— (Me.) 98.
Pittsford 114.
Pittston 228.
Placer 408.
Placerville 419.
Placid, Lake 171. 144.
Plainfield 209.
Plainville 67.
Plant City 362. 364.
Plaquemine 468.
Platte River 408. 409. 415.
Plattsburg 167. 145. 186.
Pleasant Hill (Ill.) 400.
— — (S. C.) 346.
—, Mt. 110. 133.
— Valley 422.
Pleasantville 225.
Plymouth (Ind.) 264.
— (Mass.) 86.
— (Mich.) 273.
— (N. C.) 346.
— (N. H.) 119.

Plympton 86.
Pocasset 87.
Pocatello 392. 396.
Pocomtuck, Mt. 134.
Point Judith 67.
Point Levi 109. 112.
— of Pines 90.
— Pleasant 222.
— Reyes 433.
— of Rocks (Cal.) 448.
— — — (Md.) 265.
— — — (Wy.) 392.
Poland Springs 108.
Pomona 447.
Poncha 421.
Pontchartrain, Lake 370.
367.
— Junction 338.
Popham Beach 99.
Poplar 300.
— Bluffs 404.
Popocatepetl 492.
Popotla 492.
Porta Costa 399. 441.
Portage City 289.
— (N. Y.) 199.
— Falls 199.
— Lake 297.
Port Allen 468.
— Allegheny 231.
— Chester (Alaska) 476.
— — (N. Y.) 57.
— Dalhousie 271.
— Gibson 321.
— Harford 439.
— Henry 185. 144.
— Huron 271. 273. 276.
— Jackson 186.
— Jervis 198.
— Kent 186. 170. etc.
Portland (Me.) 96.
— (Ore.) 460. 395.
— Inlet 474.
Port Louis 207.
— Moody 471.
— Richmond 50.
— Royal 350.
— Simpson 474.
Portsmouth (N. H.) 92.
— (Ohio) 340.
— (Va.) 331.
Port Stanley 271.
— Tampa 363.
— Townsend 471.
Potomac, the 252.
— Great Falls 262.
Potosi 403.
Potter Place 116.
Pottstown 229.
Pottsville 230.
Poughkeepsie 151. 149.
Powell 414.
Prairie du Chien 291. 323.

Prescott (Ariz.) 414.
— (Can.) 207.
— (Wis.) 322.
Presumpscot, the 108. 110.
Price 422.
Prickly Pear Cañon 301.
— — Junction 373.
Prince of Wales Island 476.
Prince's Bay 51.
Princess Royal Island 474.
Princeton (Ill.) 315.
— (Ky.) 320.
— (Mass.) 113.
— (N. J.) 208.
—, Mt. (Col.) 409.
Prior 341.
Proctor 114.
Profile House 129.
Promontory 376.
Prospect, Mt. (Ct.) 135.
— — (N. H.) 119.
— Rock 159. 161.
Prosser 376.
Providence 64.
— Forge 332.
Provincetown 89. 85.
Provo 423.
Puebla 493.
Pueblo 418.
Puget Sound 470. 301.
Pulaski 340.
Pullman 286.
Punta Gorda 362.
Purcell 411.
Put-in-Bay Islands 271. 273. 275.
Putnam 62. 67.
Puyallup 376.
Pyramid Harbor 478.
— Park 372.

Quaker Street 158.
Quantico 326.
Quebec 109. 120.
— Junction 111.
Queen Charlotte's Sound 473.
Queretaro 488.
Quincy (Ill.) 402. 324.
— (Mass.) 72.
Quinnimont 305.
Quinsigamond, Lake 61.

Race, Cape 5.
Racine 287.
Radford 340.
Rahway 208.
Railroad Pass 464.
Rainbow Lake 179. 168.
Rainier, Mt. 377. 470. etc.
Raleigh 335.
Ramapo 198.

Randall's Island 50.
Randolph (Va.) 347.
— (Vt.) 117.
— Hill 125.
Rangeley 106.
— Lakes 106.
Rapidan 334.
Rappahannock 334.
Raquette Lake 177. 179.
—, the 169. 178.
Rascon 487.
Rathdrum 375.
Raton Mts. 411.
Ravenna 278.
Rawlins 392.
Raymond 442. 451.
— Hotel 446.
Reading 229. 233.
Read's Landing 323.
Reata 484.
Red Bank 222. 224.
— Cliff 421.
Redding (Cal.) 459.
— (Ct.) 135.
Red Hill 118.
Redlands 448.
Red Mts. 386.
— Oak 391.
Redondo Beach 446.
Red River 299. 300. 325.
— — Landing 325.
— — Valley 300.
— Wing 289. 322.
Redwood (Cal.) 437.
— (Miss.) 321.
Relay 250. 251.
Remington Park 359.
Remsen 179. 188.
Reno 396.
Renova 230.
Revere Beach 90.
Rhinebeck 151. 149.
Rhode Island 71. 64.
Richelieu 98. 115.
Richfield Springs 188. 187. etc.
Richford 115. 120.
Richmond (Ind.) 310.
— (Va.) 326. 354.
Richmondville 158.
Rico 419.
Ridgefield 135.
Ridgway 419. 420.
Rifle 424.
Rincon (Cal.) 441. 443.
— (N. M.) 412. 464.
Rio Grande 412. 464. etc.
Ripley 305.
River Junction 366.
Riverside (Cal.) 398. 448.
— (Mass.) 86.
— (Mo.) 403.
— (N. Y.) 177.

Riverton 338.
Roan Mts. (N. C.) 340.
— — (Utah) 422.
Roanoke 334. 340.
Robinson 408.
Rochester (N. H.) 121.
— (N. Y.) 191. 195. etc.
— (Pa.) 197. 243.
Rockaway Beach 56.
Rockbridge Alum Springs 304.
Rock Creek 392.
— Island 290. 232.
— — Rapids 301.
Rockland (Me.) 100. 96.
— (Tex.) 468.
Rockledge 364. 359.
Rockport (Ky.) 320.
— (Mass.) 93.
— (Tex.) 466.
Rockville 233.
Rockwood 419.
Rocky Ford 409.
— Mount 346.
— Mts. 406. 374. 385. etc.
— Point 65.
Rodney 325.
Rogers 464.
Roger's Rock 184.
Rogue River 460.
Rome (Ga.) 341. 342.
— (N. Y.) 188.
Romley 409.
Rondout 153. 149. 163.
Roodhouse 400.
Rosamond 442.
Rosebud 372.
Rosenberg 411. 467.
Roseville 397. 459.
Ross 433.
Rotterdam 135. 195.
Round Island 206.
— Lake 144.
Rouse's Point 145. 115. 189.
Rowe 411.
Rowena 394.
Rowlsburg 266.
Roxbury (Mass.) 65.
— (N. Y.) 165.
— (Va.) 332.
— (Vt.) 117.
Royal Gorge 420.
Ruedi 424.
Rugby (N. D.) 300.
— (Tenn.) 318.
— Junction 291.
Rumford Falls 108.
Rural Retreat 340.
Rutherford 198.
Rutland 114. 145.
Rye (N. Y.) 56.
— Beach (N. H.) 93.

Sabbath Day Point 184.
Sabinas 484.
Sabine Pass 468.
Sabula 323. 388.
Sackett's Harbor 188.
Saco 95.
Sacramento 398. 459.
Saez 485.
Sag Harbor 57.
Saginaw City 273.
Saguache or Sawatch Mts. 409. 424.
Sailors' Snug Harbor 50.
St. Albans 115. 120.
— Andrews 98.
— Anthony's Falls 293. 322.
— Augustine 356.
— Catherine 364.
— Catherine's 274.
— Clair 273.
— —, Lake 276.
— Cloud 300. 371.
— Croix 289.
— Elmo 409.
— George 50.
— Helena, Mt. 434.
— Helens, Mt. 462.
— Hubert's Inn 173.
— Hyacinthe 110.
— Ignace 273. 297.
— John 98.
— John River (Fla.) 359.
— — — (Can.) 98.
— Johnsbury 119.
— Joseph (La.) 325.
— — (Miss.) 401.
— Lambert 110.
— Lawrence River 206.
— Louis 311.
— Lucie 365.
— Malo 111.
— Paul 291.
— Petersburg 362.
— Regis, Lake 168. 179.
— Simon's Island 342.
— Vincent Convent 147.
Ste. Genevieve 324.
Salamanca 199. 278. 488.
Salazar 484.
Salem (Mass.) 91.
— (Ore.) 460.
— (Va.) 340.
Salida 420.
Salina 403. 405.
Salisbury (Mass.) 93.
— (N. C.) 335. 344.
— (Vt.) 114.
Salmon Falls 95. 121.
— River 179.
Salt Lake 427. 396.
— — City 424. 395. 423.
Saltillo 483.

Salton 463.
Saltville 340.
Salvatierra 483.
Samalayuca 485.
San Andres 493.
— Antonio (N. M.) 412.
— — (Tex.) 465.
— —, Mt. 447.
— Bernardino 447.
— — Mts. 442. 447. 462.
— Bruno 437.
— —, Mt. 433.
— Buenaventura 443.
— Clemente 447.
Sanderson 464.
San Diego 449.
Sand Key 363.
— Point 301. 375.
Sandusky 269. 275.
Sandwich 89.
Sandy Hook 2. 223.
Sanford 360.
San Francisco 428. 281.
— — Bay 433. 440.
San Gabriel 462.
Sanger Junction 442.
Sangre de Cristo Mts. 421. 420.
San Gregorio 437.
— Jacinto 448.
— — Mts. 462.
— Joaquin Valley 441.
— José 438.
— Juan 449.
— — del Rio 488.
— — Islands 472.
— — Mts. 409. 419.
— — Teotihuacan 493.
— Lorenzo 440.
— Lucas 439.
— Luis Obispo 439.
— — Park 418.
— — Potosi 483.
— Marcial 412.
— Marcos 466.
— Mateo (Cal.) 437.
— — (Fla.) 359.
— Miguel 439.
— — de Allende 483.
— Pedro 446. 484.
— Rafael 433.
Santa Ana 449.
— Anita 447.
— Barbara 443.
— Catalina 446.
— Clara 438. 440.
— — Valley 437. 440. 443.
— Cruz (Cal.) 441.
— — (N. M.) 418.
— — (island) 444.
— — Mts. 440.
— Fé 412.
— — Springs 448.

Santa Margarita 439.
— Maria 439.
— Monica 446.
— Paula 443.
— Rosa 434.
— — (island) 444.
— Rosalia 485.
— Ynez Mts. 443.
Santo Domingo 412.
Sapinero 422.
Saranac Inn 169. 179.
— Lakes 169.
— Village 169. 179. 181.
Saratoga 179.
— Lake 182.
Sargent 421.
Sargent's 439.
Sarnia 274. 276.
Saticoy 443.
Satsuma 360.
Saugerties 149.
Saugus 442.
Sauk Centre 300.
— Rapids 371.
Sault Ste. Marie 298. 271. etc.
Sausalito 433.
Sauz 485.
Savanna 388. 291. 323.
Savannah 351. 350. 354.
Savoy 300.
Saw-Tooth Mts. 293.
Sawyer's River 110.
Sawyersville 111.
Saxon 296.
Saybrook 63.
Sayre Junction 228.
Scarborough 96.
Schenectady 187.
Schenevus 158.
Schooley's Mt. 196.
Schroon Lake 177.
— River P. O. 185.
Schuylkill, the 209. 211.
— Haven 230.
Schuylersville 182.
Schwanders 409.
Scioto Valley 340.
Scituate 86.
Scott 403.
— Junction 112.
Scranton (Miss.) 338.
— (Pa.) 197. 228.
Sea Bright 223.
— Girt 225.
— Islands 353.
— Isle City 226.
Seal Harbor 104.
— Islands (Alaska) 474.
Seattle 470. 301.
Sebago Lake 110.
Sebastian 365.
Seco 396.

Sedalia (Col.) 415.
— (Mo.) 403.
Sellersville 226.
Selma 342. 346.
Seloy 356.
Seneca (S. C.) 335.
— Falls 190.
— Lake 191. 228.
Sentinel Butte 372.
Sepulveda 443.
Sequoia National Park 442.
Serpent Mound 309.
Seven Lakes 416.
Seymour Narrows 473.
Shakers 158.
Shandaken 165.
Sharon 117.
— Springs 158. 195.
Sharp's 364.
Shasta, Mt. 459.
Shawsville 340.
Sheffield (Ala.) 343.
— (Mass.) 136.
Shelburne 108.
— Falls 134.
Shelby Junction 301.
Sheldon 302.
— Junction 120.
— Springs 115.
Shelter Island 57.
Shelving Rock Mt. 183.
Shenandoah 339.
— Junction 250. 265. 338.
— Valley 338. 263. 265.
Shendun 339.
Sherbrooke 98. 99. 109.
Sheridan 408.
Sherman 391.
Shirley 330.
Shoals, Isles of 94.
Shokan 163.
Shoshone Falls 393.
Shreveport 468.
Shrewsbury River 225.
Shumla 464.
Siasconset 88.
Sidnaw 296.
Sierra Blanca (Col.) 418.
— — (Tex.) 464. 469.
— Madre (Cal.) 447. 446.
— Mojada 485.
— Morena 437. 458.
— Nevada 397. 458.
Silao 487.
Silver City 464.
— Plume 408.
— Springs (Fla.) 361. 364.
— — (N. Y.) 199.
Silverton 419.
Sing Sing 151. 147.
Sioux City 299. 391.
— Falls 299.

Siskiyou Mts. 460.
Sisson 459.
Sitka 479.
Skaneateles, Lake 190.
Skowhegan 98.
Slatington 227.
Sleepy Hollow 50. 47.
Smith's Ferry 142.
—, Paul 168.
Smoky Mts. 341. 344.
Snake River 393.
Snohomish 301.
Snowden 423.
Socorro 412.
Soda Springs 392. 458.
459.
Soldier Summit 422.
Soledad 439. 484.
— Pass 442.
Somerset (Ky.) 317.
— (Mass.) 72.
Somerville (Mass.) 90.
— (S. C.) 112. 116.
— (Tex.) 411.
Somes's Sound 105. 100.
Somesville 105.
Songo, the 110.
Sonoma 434.
Sonora 398.
Soo Junction 297.
Sorrento 99.
Soukhoi Channel 476.
South Acton 113.
— Ashburnham 113. 134.
— Bend 270.
— Berwick 121.
— Boston (Va.) 347.
— Braintree 72. 88.
Southbridge 62.
South Carolina 335.
— Dakota 299.
— Deerfield 142.
— Dome 455.
— Fork 418.
— Framingham 61.
— Gilboa 165.
— Haven 274.
— Lee 136.
— Mt. (Md.) 236.
— — (N. Y.) 161.
— Norwalk 135.
— Paris 108.
— Park 407. 408. 423.
— Schenectady 195.
— Vernon 63. 143.
— West Harbor 104. 100.
— Westminster 301.
Spanish Peaks 418. 411.
Sparrow's Point 246.
Sparta 289.
Spartanburg 335. 345. 347.
Sphinx 380.
Split Rock Mt. 185.

Spinney 423.
Spofford Junction 465.
Spokane 301. 393.
Spottsylvania Court House 326.
Sprague 375.
Spring City 318.
Springdale 373.
Springfield (Ill.) 302. 401.
— (Ky.) 318.
— (Mass.) 60.
— (Ohio) 306. 267.
Spring Park 299.
Springville 422.
Spuyten Duyvil Creek 150. 147.
Squam Lake 118.
Staked Plain, Great 469.
Stamford (Ct.) 57.
— (N. Y.) 165.
Stampede Tunnel 376.
Stanbridge 115.
Stanford University 437.
Stanhope 196.
Stanstead 120.
Stanwoood 471.
Staples 371.
Stapleton 51.
Starr King, Mt. (Cal.) 457.
— — — (N. H.) 130.
State Line (Ala.) 319.
— — (Mass.) 134.
— — (Pa.) 267.
Staten Island 50. 2.
Statesville 344.
Staunton 304.
Steelton 232.
Steep Falls 110.
Stein's Pass 464.
Sterling 389.
Steubenville 264.
Steven's Point 291.
Stillwater 373.
Stockbridge 137. 136.
Stockton (Cal.) 398. 451.
— (Iowa) 290.
Stonington 63. 67.
Stony Clove 163.
— Creek 63.
— Hollow 163.
— Point 148.
Storm King, Mt. 148.
Stoughton 72.
Stowe 117.
Strong 106.
— City 410.
Stroudsburg 197.
Sublette 419.
Sudbury 61.
Suffern 198.
Sugar Hill 130.
— Loaf Mt. 148.

33

Suisun 398. 434. 441.
Sullivan's Island 349.
Sulphur Springs 340.
Summerville (Ga.) 351.
— (S. C.) 347.
Summit (Cal.) 397.
— (Mont.) 301.
— (N. J.) 196.
— (Vt.) 114. 120.
— Hill 199.
— House 131.
Sunapee, Lake 116.
Sunbury 233.
Sunset 408.
Superior 296.
—, Lake 297.
Surfside 88.
Surprise, Mt. 125.
Suspension Bridge 203. 199.
Susquehanna 199.
—, the 228.
Sutherland 362.
Sutro Heights 432.
Sutton Junction 120.
Suwanee (Ga.) 336.
—, the 363.
Swampscott 90.
Swanton 120.
— Junction 115.
— Water Station 266.
Swarthmore 221.
Sweet Springs 305.
— Grass Hills 301.
— Water (Fla.) 356.
— — (Tex.) 469.
Swoope's 304.
Sycamore 290.
Sylvania 270.
Symon 486.
Syracuse 189. 195.

Tacoma 376. 470.
—, Mt. 377.
Tacuba 484.
Tacubaya 492.
Taconic Mts. 134. 136.
Tahawus 176.
Tahoe, Lake 397.
Taku Inlet 477.
Tallahassee 366.
Tallulah Falls 335.
Tama 389.
Tamalpais, Mt. 439.
Tamasopo Cañon 487.
Tampa 362. 354.
Tampico 487. 484.
Tannersville 164.
Taos (pueblo) 418.
Tappan 152.
— Zee 147.
Tarentum 242.
Tarpon Springs 362. 364.

Tarrytown 150. 147.
Taunton 72.
Taurus, Mt. 148.
Tavares 360.
Taylorville 433.
Tecoma 396.
Tehachapi Pass 442.
Tehama 459.
Tejeria 494.
Telluride 419.
Temecula 448.
Temple Junction 411.
Tenaya 455. 458.
Tenino 377.
Tennessee (state) 317.
— Pass 421.
—, the 318. 320.
Tepetongo 483.
Terra Alta 266.
Terrace 396.
Terre Haute 310.
Tetons, the 378. 382. 421.
Texada Island 472.
Texarkana 405. 468.
Texas 464. 411. 468.
Texcoco 492.
—, Lake 489. 493.
Thackerville 411.
Thames 63. 67.
Thenard 446.
Theresa Junction 188.
Thistle 422.
Thomas 271.
Thomaston 296.
Thomasville (Ala.) 342.
— (Ga.) 354.
Thompson's Falls 375.
Thompsonville 60.
Thousand Islands 206.
Three Rivers 109.
Thunderhead Bay 341.
Tiburon 433.
Ticeska 393.
Ticonderoga 184. 114.
—, Fort 185. 144.
Tilton 118.
Tintah Junction 299.
Tinton Falls 225.
Tippecanoe 270.
Tipton 442.
Tiptonville 324.
Titusville (Fla.) 359. 364.
— (Pa.) 243.
Tivoli 149.
Tlalpam 492.
Tlaxcala 493.
Tobyhanna 197.
Tocaloma 433.
Toccoa 335.
Tocoi 359. 361.
Tolchester 249.
Toledo 269. 310.
Toltec Gorge 419.

Toluca 483.
Tom, Mt. 142.
Tomah 289.
Tom's River 224. 225.
Tompkinsville 51.
Tonawanda 195. 199.
Topeka 405. 410.
Topo Chico Springs 482.
Toronto 195. 271. 274.
Torreon 485.
Torrey's Peak 469.
Tottenville 51.
Tower City 371.
Towner (Col.) 403.
— (N. D.) 300.
Toyah 469.
Tracy 441.
Treadwell Mine 477.
Tremont 88.
Trempealeau Island 323.
Trenton (Ohio) 269.
— (N. J.) 209.
— (S. C.) 350.
— Falls 188. 178.
Tres Piños 439.
Treviño 484.
Trimble Springs 419.
Trinidad 411. 418.
Trinway 264.
Tropic 365.
Troy (Idaho) 301.
— (N. H.) 113.
— (N. Y.) 145. 144. 135.
Truckee 397.
Truro 89.
Tsimpsean 474.
Tuckerman's Ravine 132.
Tucson 463.
Tula 488.
Tulare 442.
Tunnel Station 159.
Tunnelton 266.
Tuolumne Cañon 458.
— Meadows 458.
Tupper Lakes 179. 169.
Turner's 198.
— Falls 134.
Tuscaloosa 343.
Tuscarora Gap 233.
Tuscola 301.
Tuscumbia 343.
Tuxedo 198.
Twin Lakes 424. 409.
— Mt. House 127.
Tybee Beach 353.
Tyngsboro 116.
Tyrone 234.

Ukiah 434.
Umatilla 393.
Umbagog, Lake 106. 109.
Uncompaghre Mts. 409. 429. 420.

Union (Ohio) 264. 310.
— (Ore.) 393.
Upper Bartlett 110.
Urbana 264.
Utah 425. 395. 422.
— Hot Springs 396.
Utawana, Lake 177.
Ute Pass 423.
Utica 187. 195.
Uvalde 465.

Valentine 464.
Vallejo 399. 433.
Valley City 371.
— Cottage 152.
— Forge 229.
Valparaiso 264.
Vanceboro 98.
Vancouver 472.
— Island 472.
Vandalia (Ill.) 301.
— (Mo.) 401.
Van Deusenville 136.
— Etten 228.
— Wert 263.
Varina 330.
Vassar 273.
Vera Cruz 494.
Vergennes 114. 185.
Vermillion 270.
Vermont 109.
Vernal Falls 416.
Versailles 310.
Verstovaia, Mt. 479.
Vesuvius 339.
Veta Pass 418.
Vicksburg 321. 325.
Victor 448.
Victoria (B. C.) 471.
Viga Canal 492.
Villa Nova 231.
Vinal Haven 100.
Vineland 225.
Vineyard Haven 88.
Virginia (state) 326.
— Beach 331.
— City 397.
— Valley 338.
Volcano Springs 463.
Volusia 360.
Voorheesville 158. 195.

Wabash 311.
Wabasha 289. 323.
Wachusett 113.
Wadena 371.
Wades 324.
Wagon Mound 411.
— Wheel Gap 418.
Wahpeton 299.
Wahsatch Mts. 395. 422.
Wakefield 94.
Wakulla Springs 366.

Waldo 363.
Walkerville 271.
Wallabout Bay 66. 54.
Wallace (Kan.) 405.
— (N. M.) 412.
Wallface, Mt. 176.
Wallula 376. 393.
Walpole 114.
Waltham 112.
Walton 317.
Wamego 405.
Wanatah 264.
Ward's Island 50.
Wareham 89.
Waretown 224.
Warren (N. H.) 119.
— (Pa.) 231.
— (Wash.) 377.
Warsaw (Ill.) 323.
— (Ind.) 264.
Washburn, Mt. 387.
Washington (state) 375.
Washington (D. C.) 251.
Arlington House 262.
Army Medical Museum 256.
Botanic Gardens 256.
Bureau of Engraving and Printing 258.
Capitol 253.
City Hall 261.
Columbian University 259.
Court House 261.
Department of Agriculture 258.
— of the Interior 260.
— of Justice 259.
Executive Mansion 259.
Corcoran Art Gallery 260.
Fish Commission 256.
Ford's Theatre 261.
Georgetown 262.
Government Printing Office 261.
Howard University 262.
Institute for the Deaf and Dumb 262.
Judiciary Square 260.
Lafayette Square 259.
Lincoln Square 261.
Long Bridge 259.
Marine Barracks 261.
Monuments:
Dupont 262.
Farragut 262.
Franklin 262
Garfield 256.
Greene 262.
Henry 257.
Jackson 259.
Lafayette 259.

Washington:
Lincoln 261.
Luther 262.
McPherson 262.
Marshall 256.
Rawlins 262.
W. Scott 262.
Thomas 262.
Washington 253. 262.
National Cemetery 262.
— Museum 256.
Naval Observatory 261.
Navy Yard 261.
Patent Office 260.
Peace Monument 256.
Pension Building 260.
Post Office 252. 260.
Railway Stations 251.
Smithsonian Institution 257.
Soldiers' Home 262.
State, War, & Navy Department 259.
Treasury 259.
University (R. C.) 262.
Washington Obelisk 258.
Weather Bureau 262.
White House 259.
Zoological Garden 262.
Washington (N. J.) 196.
— Junction 250. 265.
—, Lake 471.
—, Mt. (Mass.) 137.
— — (N. H.) 131.
— — Railway 132.
Washita 411.
Washoe Mts. 393.
Watch Hill 63.
Waterbury (Ct.) 62.
— (Vt.) 117.
Waterford 144. 231.
Watertown (Iowa) 299.
— (N. Y.) 188.
Waterville 98. 106.
Watkins (Col.) 406.
— (N. Y.) 191. 288.
— Glen 191.
—, Mt. 453.
Waveland 365.
Wawbeek Lodge 169.
Wawona 452.
Waycross 354.
Wayland 197.
Wayne Junction 210. 266.
Waynesborough 339.
Waynesville 345.
Way's 354.
Wayzata 299.
Weatherford 469.
Weber Cañon 395.
Webster (Col.) 408.
— (Iowa) 402.

Weedsport 190.
Weehawken 51.
Weirs 118.
Weiser 393.
Welaka 360.
Weldon 331. 346.
Weld Pond 106.
Welland 271.
Wellesley 60. 61.
Wells 396.
— Beach 95.
— River Junction 119. 143.
Wellsville 243. 278.
Wenatchee 301.
Wenham 93.
West Albany 186.
— Baldwin 110.
— Brighton 56.
— Chazy 145.
Westchester 221.
West Chop 88.
— Davenport 165.
— End 222.
— Englewood 152.
Westerly 64.
Western North Carolina 343. 344.
Westfield 134.
West Hartford (Vt.) 117.
— Hurley 163.
— Lebanon 117.
— Liberty 290. 390.
Westmoreland 113.
Westminster 250.
West Nyack 152.
Westonia 359.
West Ossipee 118. 121.
Westover 330.
West Pittsfield 134.
— Point (N. Y.) 152. 148.
— — (Va.) 330.
Westport 170. 144. 185.
West Superior 296.
— Troy 143. 157.
— Virginia 233.
Weverton 233. 250. 265.
Weymouth 86.
Wharton 410.
Whatcom 471.
Wheatland 389.
Wheeling 266. 243. 264.
White Bear Lake 295.
— Beach 63.
Whiteface, Mt. 172.
Whitefield 119.
Whitehall 144.
White Haven 228.

White Mts. 121.
— Mt. House 111.
— — Notch 126. 111.
White Pigeon 270.
— Plains 396.
— River 325. 404.
— — Junction 117. 114.
— — Valley 117.
— Sulphur Springs 305.
— Water 463.
Whiting 225.
Whitley 277.
Whitman 86.
Whitney, Mt. 442.
Wichita 410. 413.
Wickford 64. 71.
Wilcox (Ariz.) 464.
— (Pa.) 231.
Wilderness, the 326.
Wildwood 364.
Wilkesbarré 228. 159.
Wilkeson 377.
Wilkinsburg 235.
Willamette, the 460. 462. 395.
Willard 396.
—, Mt. 127.
Willey House 128. 111.
Williams 414.
Williamsburg 332.
Williamson 221.
Williamstown 141. 135.
Willimantic 62. 63.
Williston (N. D.) 300.
— (Vt.) 117.
Willmar 299. 300.
Willsborough 144.
Wilmington (Del.) 244.
— (N. C.) 346. 335.
Wilna 464.
Wilson 346.
— Peak 447.
Wilson's Point 66.
Wilton (Ct.) 135.
— (Me.) 106.
Winchendon 113.
Winchester 233.
Windermere 359.
Windsor (Can.) 271.
— (Vt.) 143.
Winfield 410.
Wingate 413.
Wing Road 119.
Winnemucca 396.
Winnepesaukee, Lake 118.
Winnipeg 299. 371.
Winona 289. 291. 323.

Winslow (Ariz.) 413.
— (Me.) 98.
— Junction 225.
Winston-Salem 340.
Winter Park 362.
Wissahickon 220. 221.
Wolfeborough 118. 121.
Woodbury 225.
Woodlawn 57.
Wood's Holl 87.
Woodstock (Can.) 274.
— (Vt.) 117.
Woodsville 119.
Woolwich 99.
Woonsocket 65. 62.
Worcester 60. 65.
Worth, Lake 365.
Wrangell Narrows 476.
Wright's 441.
Wyandotte Cave 315.
Wyoming (state) 391.
— Valley 228.
Wytheville 340.
Xenia 303.

Yakima 376.
Yale University 58.
—, Mt. 409. 420.
Yamaska Mts. 110.
Yaquina 460.
Yardley 210.
Yarmouth (Mass.) 89.
— (Me.) 97. 108.
Ybor 364.
Yellowstone Fa'ls 387.
— Grand Cañon 387.
— Lake 385.
— Park 378. 373.
— River 372. 386. 382. etc.
Yemasseé 350.
Yonah, Mt. 335.
Yonkers 150. 147.
York (Pa.) 250.
— Beach 94. 93.
Yorktown 330.
Yosemite 450. 453. 398.
Ypsilanti 274.
Ysleta 464.
Yucca 414.
Yukon 475.
Yuma 463.

Zacatecas 486.
Zanesville 266.
Zealand 128. 119.
Zuni (Ariz.) 413.
— (Tex.) 464.